CPSIA information can be obtained
at www.ICGtesting.com
Printed in the USA
JSHW010820140822
28878JS00002B/51

A COMPANION TO WOMEN IN THE ANCIENT WORLD

BLACKWELL COMPANIONS TO THE ANCIENT WORLD

This series provides sophisticated and authoritative overviews of periods of ancient history, genres of classical literature, and the most important themes in ancient culture. Each volume comprises approximately twenty-five and forty concise essays written by individual scholars within their area of specialization. The essays are written in a clear, provocative, and lively manner, designed for an international audience of scholars, students, and general readers.

ANCIENT HISTORY

Published

A Companion to the Roman Army
Edited by Paul Erdkamp

A Companion to the Roman Republic
Edited by Nathan Rosenstein and Robert Morstein-Marx

A Companion to the Roman Empire
Edited by David S. Potter

A Companion to the Classical Greek World
Edited by Konrad H. Kinzl

A Companion to the Ancient Near East
Edited by Daniel C. Snell

A Companion to the Hellenistic World
Edited by Andrew Erskine

A Companion to Late Antiquity
Edited by Philip Rousseau

A Companion to Ancient History
Edited by Andrew Erskine

A Companion to Archaic Greece
Edited by Kurt A. Raaflaub and Hans van Wees

A Companion to Julius Caesar
Edited by Miriam Griffin

A Companion to Byzantium
Edited by Liz James

A Companion to Ancient Egypt
Edited by Alan B. Lloyd

A Companion to Ancient Macedonia
Edited by Joseph Roisman and Ian Worthington

A Companion to the Punic Wars
Edited by Dexter Hoyos

A Companion to Augustine
Edited by Mark Vessey

A Companion to Marcus Aurelius
Edited by Marcel van Ackeren

A Companion to Ancient Greek Government
Edited by Hans Beck

A Companion to the Neronian Age
Edited by Emma Buckley and Martin T. Dinter

A Companion to Greek Democracy and the Roman Republic
Edited by Dean Hammer

A Companion to Livy
Edited by Bernard Mineo

A Companion to Ancient Thrace
Edited by Julia Valeva, Emil Nankov, and Denver Graninger

LITERATURE AND CULTURE

Published

A Companion to Classical Receptions
Edited by Lorna Hardwick and Christopher Stray

A Companion to Greek and Roman Historiography
Edited by John Marincola

A Companion to Catullus
Edited by Marilyn B. Skinner

A Companion to Roman Religion
Edited by Jörg Rüpke

A Companion to Greek Religion
Edited by Daniel Ogden

A Companion to the Classical Tradition
Edited by Craig W. Kallendorf

A Companion to Roman Rhetoric
Edited by William Dominik and Jon Hall

A Companion to Greek Rhetoric
Edited by Ian Worthington

A Companion to Ancient Epic
Edited by John Miles Foley

A Companion to Greek Tragedy
Edited by Justina Gregory

A Companion to Latin Literature
Edited by Stephen Harrison

A Companion to Greek and Roman Political Thought
Edited by Ryan K. Balot

A Companion to Ovid
Edited by Peter E. Knox

A Companion to the Ancient Greek Language
Edited by Egbert Bakker

A Companion to Hellenistic Literature
Edited by Martine Cuypers and James J. Clauss

A Companion to Vergil's *Aeneid* and its Tradition
Edited by Joseph Farrell and Michael C. J. Putnam

A Companion to Horace
Edited by Gregson Davis

A Companion to Families in the Greek and Roman Worlds
Edited by Beryl Rawson

A Companion to Greek Mythology
Edited by Ken Dowden and Niall Livingstone

A Companion to the Latin Language
Edited by James Clackson

A Companion to Tacitus
Edited by Victoria Emma Pagán

A Companion to Women in the Ancient World
Edited by Sharon L. James and Sheila Dillon

A Companion to Sophocles
Edited by Kirk Ormand

A Companion to the Archaeology of the Ancient Near East
Edited by Daniel Potts

A Companion to Roman Love Elegy
Edited by Barbara K. Gold

A Companion to Greek Art
Edited by Tyler Jo Smith and Dimitris Plantzos

A Companion to Persius and Juvenal
Edited by Susanna Braund and Josiah Osgood

A Companion to the Archaeology of the Roman Republic
Edited by Jane DeRose Evans

A Companion to Terence
Edited by Antony Augoustakis and Ariana Traill

A Companion to Roman Architecture
Edited by Roger B. Ulrich and Caroline K. Quenemoen

A Companion to Sport and Spectacle in Greek and Roman Antiquity
Edited by Paul Christesen and Donald G. Kyle

A Companion to Plutarch
Edited by Mark Beck

A Companion to Greek and Roman Sexualities
Edited by Thomas K. Hubbard

A Companion to the Ancient Novel
Edited by Edmund P. Cueva and Shannon N. Byrne

A Companion to Ethnicity in the Ancient Mediterranean
Edited by Jeremy McInerney

A Companion to Ancient Egyptian Art
Edited by Melinda Hartwig

A Companion to Food in the Ancient World
Edited by John Wilkins and Robin Nadeau

A Companion to Ancient Aesthetics
Edited by Pierre Destrée & Penelope Murray

A COMPANION TO WOMEN IN THE ANCIENT WORLD

Edited by

Sharon L. James
and Sheila Dillon

WILEY Blackwell

Library of Congress Cataloging-in-Publication Data

A companion to women in the ancient world / edited by Sharon L. James and Sheila Dillon.
    p. cm. – (Blackwell companions to the ancient world)
  Includes bibliographical references and index.
  ISBN 978-1-4051-9284-2 (hardback : alk. paper) ISBN 978-1-119-02554-2 (paperback)
1. Women–History–To 500.   2. Civilization, Ancient. I. James, Sharon L. II. Dillon, Sheila.
  HQ1127.C637 2012
  305.4093–dc23

                             2011029133

A catalogue record for this book is available from the British Library.

Set in 10/12pt Galliard by SPi Publisher Services, Pondicherry, India

1 2015

Contents

List of Illustrations

Maps

Figures

Notes on Contributors

Lindsay Allason-Jones was Director of the Centre for Interdisciplinary Artefact Studies and Reader in Roman Material Culture at Newcastle University until she retired in 2011. She was previously Director of Archaeological Museums for the University. An acknowledged authority on Hadrian's Wall, Roman Britain, and Roman and Medieval Sudan, she is the author of thirteen books, including *Women in Roman Britain* (2005) and *Daily Life in Roman Britain* (2008). She is Trustee of many of the Hadrian's Wall museums as well as the Hadrian's Art Trust.

Rhiannon Ash is Fellow and Tutor in Classical Literature at Merton College, Oxford University. She has broad interests in Latin Literature of the Roman Empire, but her particular research is in the sphere of Roman historiography, above all Tacitus. She has published various books and articles on Virgil, Plutarch, Pliny the Elder, Pliny the Younger, and Tacitus, including a commentary on Tacitus' *Histories* 2 (2007). Her next project is a commentary on Tacitus' *Annals* 15.

Elizabeth Bartman is an independent scholar specializing in ancient Roman art and past President of the Archaeological Institute of America. She has written numerous articles and reviews as well as the books *Ancient Sculptural Copies in Miniature* (Brill 1992); *Portraits of Livia: Imaging the Imperial Female in Augustan Rome* (Cambridge 1999); and *The Ince Blundell Collection of Classical Sculpture: The Ideal Sculpture* (forthcoming). This latest project has opened up a range of interests related to the reception of the antique in the eighteenth century, especially Grand Tour collecting and the restoration and fakery of ancient marbles.

Anne Bielman has been Professor of Ancient History at the University of Lausanne (Switzerland) since 2005. She received her doctorate from Lausanne in 1994 with a thesis on the release of prisoners in Ancient Greece. She has been a visiting scholar in Paris, Rome, and Oxford. Since 1998 her work has focused on the epigraphical evidence for female public activities in Hellenistic Greece and Republican Rome.

T. Corey Brennan is Associate Professor of Classics at Rutgers University-New Brunswick; he has also taught at Bryn Mawr College. He was appointed Andrew

W. Mellon Professor in the American Academy in Rome, 2009–2012. His books are *The Praetorship in the Roman Republic* (2000) and *East and West: Papers in Ancient History Presented to Glen W. Bowersock* (co-editor with Harriet I. Flower, 2009). He has written extensively on Roman history and culture.

Elizabeth D. Carney is Professor of History and Carol K. Brown Scholar in the Humanities at Clemson University. She is the author of *Women and Monarchy in Ancient Macedonia* (2000) and *Olympias, Mother of Alexander the Great* (2006), *Arsinoë of Egypt and Macedon: A Royal Life* (Oxford University Press, 2013), and co-editor (with Daniel Ogden) of *Philip II and Alexander the Great: Father and son, lives and afterlives* (2010). She is currently at work on a monograph about Eurydice, mother of Philip II and grandmother of Alexander.

Cheryl A. Cox is Associate Professor of Classics at the University of Memphis. She is the author of *Household Interests* (1998) and several articles on the family and household in ancient Athens.

Eve D'Ambra is the Agnes Rindge Claflin Professor of Art History at Vassar College, where she teaches Greek and Roman art and archaeology. She has published *Roman Art* (1998) and *Roman Women* (2007) as well as articles on the commemorative art of Roman citizens of the lower social orders. Her current research focuses on the sculpted portraits of Roman women and beauty.

Marguerite Deslauriers is Associate Professor in the Department of Philosophy and Director of the Institute for Gender, Sexuality, and Feminist Studies at McGill University. She is the author of *Aristotle on Definition* (2007), in Brill's series *Philosophia Antiqua*.

Sheila Dillon is Professor and Chair of the Department of Art, Art History & Visual Studies at Duke University, with a secondary appointment in the Department of Classical Studies. Her most recent book is *The Female Portrait Statue in the Greek World* (Cambridge University Press, 2010). She has extensive fieldwork experience in both Greece and Turkey, and was a member of New York University Excavations at Aphrodisias from 1992 until 2004. Her current project is a history of portrait statuary in Roman Athens, which explores the impact of Rome and Roman portrait styles on Attic portraiture and honorific practices.

A. A. Donohue is the Rhys Carpenter Professor of Classical and Near Eastern Archaeology at Bryn Mawr College. Among her publications on the history and historiography of classical art are *Xoana and the Origins of Classical Sculpture* (1988), *Greek Sculpture and the Problem of Description* (2005), and a volume co-edited with M. D. Fullerton on *Ancient Art and Its Historiography* (2003).

Cristiana Franco teaches at University for Foreigners in Siena. Her research focuses on the role played by cultural representations of animal species in the process of naturalization of gender ideology in ancient cultures. Besides many articles she has published a study on the connection between the dog and the female in ancient Greek literature and myth (*Senza ritegno: Il cane e la donna nell'immaginario della Grecia antica*, 2003, published in English by the University of California Press as *Shameless. The Canine and the Feminine in Ancient Greece*, 2014), and an essay on the myth of Circe (*Il mito di Circe*, 2010).

Amy R. Gansell is Assistant Professor of Art History at St. John's University in New York City, where she teaches courses on ancient and non-Western art. She received her PhD from Harvard University in 2008 and was a post-doctoral fellow at Emory University's Bill and Carol Fox Center for Humanistic Inquiry. She is currently working on a book about feminine beauty and female imagery at the Neo-Assyrian Northwest Palace at Nimrud and has previously published on the Royal Tombs of Ur, Iron Age Levantine ivory sculptures of women, and ethno-archaeological interpretations of ancient Mesopotamian adornment.

Judith P. Hallett is Professor of Classics at the University of Maryland at College Park, where she has been named a Distinguished Scholar-Teacher. She received her PhD from Harvard University in 1971, and has been a Mellon Fellow at Brandeis University and the Wellesley College Center for Research on Women as well as the Blegen Visiting Scholar at Vassar College. Her major research specializations are Latin language and literature; gender, sexuality, and the family in ancient Greek and Roman society; and the history of classical studies, and the reception of classical Greco-Roman literary texts, in the United States. In 2013 Routledge published *Domina Illustris: Roman Literature, Gender and Reception* (ed. Donald Lateiner, Barbara K. Gold and Judith Perkins), a volume of nineteen essays in her honor.

Emily A. Hemelrijk is Professor of Ancient History at the University of Amsterdam. She has published numerous articles on Roman women. Her book, *Matrona docta: Educated Women in the Roman Élite from Cornelia to Julia Domna*, was published in 1999. She is currently working on a project called *Hidden Lives – Public Personae: Women in the Urban Texture of the Roman Empire*, for which she received a Vidi grant from the Netherlands Organization of Scientific Research (NWO). She is preparing a book on women's public roles in the cities of the Latin West (outside Rome), that is entitled *Hidden Lives – Public Personae: Women and Civic Life in Italy and the Latin West During the Roman Principate*.

Madeleine M. Henry is Professor of Classics and Head of the School of Languages and Cultures at Purdue University. Her main research interests are women's life in ancient Greece, Greek comedy, and the history of encyclopedia literature and of literary criticism. Her recent publications include *The Greek Prostitute in the Ancient Mediterranean* (2011, co-edited with Allison Glazebrook). Current and future projects are *Neaera: Writing a Prostitute's Life* (book), "Orphic themes in J. J. Phillips' *Mojo Hand*," and "Mythic dimensions of the city of dreams: New Orleans as a Hellenistic space" (essays). She teaches Latin, Greek, courses in translation, and sometimes Women's Studies.

Maura K. Heyn is Associate Professor in the Department of Classical Studies at the University of North Carolina at Greensboro. Her research focuses on the funerary sculpture of Palmyra, and she has recently published "Gesture and identity in the funerary art of Palmyra" in the *American Journal of Archaeology*. She has also written several papers on the mural decoration of the Temple of the Palmyrene Gods in Dura-Europos.

Lora L. Holland is Associate Professor of Classics at the University of North Carolina at Asheville, and was recently Blegen Research Fellow at Vassar College and Visiting Scholar in Greek and Roman Religion at the Center for Hellenic Studies in Washington, DC. She is the author of *Religion in the Roman Republic*, forthcoming in Wiley-Blackwell's *Ancient Religions* series, and of various articles on Greek and Roman religion and culture.

Vedia Izzet is Research Fellow in Archaeology at the University of Southampton, UK. She was formerly a fellow of Christ's College, Cambridge, and a Rome Scholar at the British School at Rome. She has directed British excavations at the Sant'Antonio sanctuary in Cerveteri and magnetometry survey at Spina. She is the author of *The Archaeology of Etruscan Society* (2007), and is co-editor of *Greece and Rome*.

Sharon L. James is Associate Professor of Classics at the University of North Carolina at Chapel Hill and has published numerous articles on women and gender in Latin literature, as well as *Learned Girls and Male Persuasion: Gender and Reading in Roman Love Elegy* (2003). She has recently completed a book manuscript on women in *New Comedy*. In 2012, she co-directed the NEH Summer Institute, "Roman Comedy in Performance." Videotaped scenes are on-line at YouTube.

Ioli Kalavrezou earned her PhD at the University of California Berkeley, and is now Dumbarton Oaks Professor of the History of Byzantine Art at Harvard University. She has also taught at the University of California Los Angeles and the University of Munich. Since 1989 she has been on the Board of Senior Fellows of Dumbarton Oaks and the Center for Byzantine Studies in Washington, DC. She has also served on the National Advisory Board on Research and Technology of Greece (2004–2010). Her research covers a range of topics: ivory carving, imperial art, manuscript illumination, the use of symbols and relics in the empire, the cult of the Virgin Mary, and the everyday world of the Byzantines, especially for women.

Alison Keith is Professor and Chair of Classics at the University of Toronto. Her work focuses on Latin epic and elegy, and especially on the intersection of gender and genre in Latin literature. A past editor of *Phoenix*, she has written books on Ovid's *Metamorphoses*, women in Latin epic, and Propertius, and edited volumes on Latin elegy and Hellenistic epigram, the European reception of the *Metamorphoses* (with S. Rupp), and Roman dress and society (with J. Edmondson).

Ross S. Kraemer is Professor Emerita of Religious Studies and Judaic Studies at Brown University. She is the author of numerous studies on gender and women's religions in the Greco-Roman Mediterranean, including *Her Share of the Blessings: Women's Religions among Pagans, Jews and Christians in the Greco-Roman World* (1992) and *Unreliable Witnesses: Religion, Gender and History in the Greco-Roman Mediterranean* (2011). She holds a BA in religion from Smith College, and an MA and a PhD in religion from Princeton University.

Mireille M. Lee is Assistant Professor in the Department of History of Art at Vanderbilt University, with a secondary appointment in Classical Studies; she is also an affiliated faculty member in Women's and Gender Studies. She has published widely on various aspects of Greek dress and gender. Her first book, *Body, Dress, and Identity in Ancient Greece* (2015) uses contemporary dress theory to uncover the social meanings of ancient Greek dress. Her current research focuses on Greek bronze mirrors.

Barbara Levick, Emeritus Fellow and Tutor in Literae Humaniores at St. Hilda's College, Oxford, besides working on Asia Minor in ancient times, is the author of *Tiberius the Politician* (1976), *Claudius* (1990), *Vespasian* (1999), and *Augustus, Image and Substance* (2010). In the field of gender studies she has published *Julia Domna, Syrian Empress* (2007), and with Richard Hawley co-edited the collection *Women in Antiquity: New*

Assessments (1995). She is currently working on a study of the Antonine Empresses: *Imperial Women of the Golden Age: Faustina I and II.*

Laura S. Lieber is Associate Professor of Late Ancient Judaism in the Religion Department at Duke University. She is the author of *Yannai on Genesis: An Invitation to Piyyut* (2010) and *A Vocabulary of Desire: The Song of Songs in the Early Synagogue* (forthcoming). She is also co-editor with Deborah Green of *Scriptural Exegesis: Shapes of the Religious Imagination, a Festschrift in Honour of Michael Fishbane* (2009).

Maria A. Liston is Associate Professor and Chair of the Anthropology Department at the University of Waterloo, and cross-appointed to the Classical Studies Department. She has studied cremation and inhumation burials from various sites in Crete and mainland Greece. In addition to the skeletons from wells in the Athenian Agora and the remains of the Theban Sacred Band from the Battle of Chaironeia (338 BC) she has recently begun working with the early Byzantine burials in the Sanctuary of Ismenion Apollo in Thebes.

Rachel Meyers is Assistant Professor of Classical Studies at Iowa State University in Ames, Iowa. She earned her Ph.D. in Classical Studies at Duke University in 2006. She is currently working on a book on the dynastic commemoration of the Antonine imperial family and has previously published on the topics of female benefactors and Roman numismatics.

Jennifer Sheridan Moss is an Associate Professor of Classics and former Director of Women's Studies at Wayne State University. Her primary research interest is documentary papyrology from the late Antique period. Her work includes studies of taxation, women's legal rights, and women's literacy. She is currently writing an article on the ongoing misuse of Plutarch's description of Cleopatra.

Jenifer Neils is Elsie B. Smith Professor in the Liberal Arts at Case Western Reserve University. She is the author of *The Parthenon Frieze* (2001) and has published two major exhibition catalogues, *Coming of Age in Ancient Greece* (2003) and *Goddess and Polis: The Panathenaic Festival in Ancient Athens* (1992). Her most recent book is entitled *Women in the Ancient World*, published in 2011 by the British Museum and the J. Paul Getty Museum.

Marianna Nikolaïdou is a Research Associate at the Cotsen Institute of Archaeology, UCLA, and has taught archaeology and anthropology at UCLA Extension and the California State University, Los Angeles. Her fieldwork and publications focus on the Neolithic and Bronze Age cultures of the Aegean and the Levant. The co-author of the first book on gender in Aegean prehistory in 1993, she has been publishing extensively on gender archaeology and politics in the Aegean. Other research interests include symbolism and ritual, iconography, ceramics, adornment, and technology, with a co-edited volume on prehistoric shell technologies (2011). Current projects include the ceramic technologies at Tell Mozan, Syria, the prehistoric pottery from Ancient Methone, Northern Greece, and the iconography of religious symbols on Minoan pottery from Crete.

Maryline Parca teaches in the History Department of the University of San Diego. She has edited Latin inscriptions, published Greek literary and documentary papyri, and co-edited a volume of essays on the religious lives of ancient women. She is currently at work on wet nursing contracts and is acting as co-editor of the special issue "Gender, East and West in the Ancient World" for *Classical World.*

Holt Parker received his PhD from Yale and is Professor of Classics at the University of Cincinnati. He has been awarded the Rome Prize, the Women's Classical Caucus Prize for Scholarship (twice), a Loeb Library Foundation Grant, and a Fellowship from the National Endowment for the Humanities. He has published on Sappho, Sulpicia, sexuality, slavery, sadism, and spectacles. His book *Olympia Morata: The Complete Writings of an Italian Heretic* (2003) won the Josephine Roberts Award from the Society for the Study of Early Modern Women. *Censorinus: The Birthday Book* (2007) is the first complete English translation of that curious piece of learning. With William A. Johnson he has edited *Ancient Literacies: The Culture of Reading in Greece and Rome* (2009). His translation of *The Hermaphrodite* by Antonio Beccadelli is part of the I Tatti Renaissance Library.

Werner Riess holds a PhD in Ancient History from the University of Heidelberg, Germany and is currently Professor of Ancient History at the University of Hamburg, Germany. He is the author of *Apuleius und die Räuber: Ein Beitrag zur historischen Kriminalitätsforschung* (2001) and *Performing Interpersonal Violence: Court, Curse, and Comedy in Fourth-Century BCE Athens* (2011).

Christina Riggs is a Senior Lecturer in the School of Art, Media and American Studies at the University of East Anglia in Norwich, UK. Her books include Unwrapping Ancient Egypt (2014), Ancient Egyptian Art: A Very Short Introduction (2014), and The Beautiful Burial in Roman Egypt: Art, Identity and Funerary Religion (2005); she has also edited the Oxford Handbook of Roman Egypt (2012) and published many articles on art, archaeology, and the body in ancient Egypt.

Christina A. Salowey is Professor of Classical Studies at Hollins University in Roanoke, Virginia. She has served twice as the Gertrude Smith Professor at the American School of Classical Studies at Athens. Her interests are burial monuments of the Archaic, Classical, and Hellenistic periods and the cults of Herakles. She has published on Herakles as a cult figure, Archaic funerary korai, and the use of math and science in the teaching of ancient art.

Gillian Shepherd is Director of the A.D. Trendall Research Centre for Ancient Mediterranean Studies and Lecturer in Ancient Mediterranean Studies at La Trobe University, Australia. Her research interests are in the ancient Greek settlement of Sicily and South Italy, especially burial and votive practices, and interaction between different cultural groups, as well as childhood in antiquity. She has published on ancient Greek burial practices and sanctuaries in Sicily and is co-editor of the forthcoming *Oxford Handbook of the Archaeology of Childhood*.

Eva Stehle is Professor Emerita of Classics at the University of Maryland, College Park. She has published in a number of areas, often focusing on the implications of performance for understanding the reception of ancient texts in their original context and on the gendered origin of the speaking voice, whether as performer's voice or as textual voice. Her book *Performance and Gender in Ancient Greece: Nondramatic Poetry in its Context* appeared in 1997. She is completing a book on Greek women's religious ritual and its influence on the development of new religious forms in Classical Greece.

Kasia Szpakowska is Associate Professor of Egyptology at Swansea University, Wales, a Fellow of the Society of Antiquaries, London, and Director of the Ancient Egyptian Demonology Project: Second Millennium BC. She publishes and lectures on Ancient Egyptian private religious practices, dreams, and gender. Her monographs include *Behind Closed Eyes: Dreams and Nightmares in Ancient Egypt* (2003) *and Daily Life in Ancient*

Egypt: Recreating Lahun (2008), which uses the life a young girl as a model for reconstructing a snapshot in time. She is currently researching *Clay Cobras and the Fiery Goddesses of Ancient Egypt*.

Lauren Talalay is Curator Emerita and Research Associate at the Kelsey Museum of Archaeology, University of Michigan. Her research focuses on gender and figurines in Mediterranean prehistory as well as archaeology and popular culture. She has written numerous articles and is the author or co-editor of several books, including *Deities, Dolls, and Devices: Neolithic Figurines from Franchthi Cave, Greece* (1993), *What these Ithakas Mean: Readings in Cavafy* (2002), *Prehistorians Round the Pond: Reflections on Prehistory as a Discipline* (2005), and *In the Field: the Archaeological Expeditions of the Kelsey Museum* (2006).

Kathryn Topper is Associate Professor of Classics at the University of Washington. Her research focuses on Greek painting, gender and ethnicity in antiquity, ancient banquets, and word and image studies. Her publications include *The Imagery of the Athenian Symposium* (Cambridge UP, 2012), as well as articles on a variety of topics in Greek and South Italian vase painting. Her current project is a study of the Hellenistic banquet.

Monika Trümper is Professor of Classical Archaeology at the Freie Universität Berlin. She has written two books and a number of articles on various monuments on Delos (domestic architecture, urban development, clubhouses of associations, shops, synagogues, and Agora of the Italians), and a book on Graeco-Roman slave markets. She is co-editor of the book *Greek Baths and Bathing Culture: New Discoveries and Approaches* (2013) and has published a number of articles on Greek bathing culture, which is the topic of her current fieldwork and research.

Preface and Acknowledgments

Our collaborative work on women in antiquity began ten years ago, when we first started to plan a graduate course on the subject, to be held jointly between our two universities. We had taught the course twice when we were invited to edit this *Companion*, which is shaped by our experience of bringing together and learning to integrate our very different backgrounds and specialties. We hope that the volume's interdisciplinary contents will be useful to readers from all fields.

Naturally, we have incurred debts and obligations, which we gladly acknowledge here. First thanks go to Cecil Wooten, chair of Classics at the University of North Carolina, Chapel Hill, for departmental support of this project, and to Serena Witzke, Anna Haldeman Ruddle, and Hannah Rich for assistance with the bibliography and illustrations. We want to thank also Daria Lanzuolo of the Deutsches Archäologisches Institut (DAI) in Rome, Dr. Joachim Heiden of the DAI in Athens, Anja Slawisch of the DAI in Istanbul, Dr. Michael Kunst of the DAI in Madrid, and Dr. Ulrich Mania at the Rheinische Friedrich-Wilhelms-Universität Bonn for their generosity with illustrations. Special thanks are owed to Corry Arnold and Donald Haggis. We would like particularly to acknowledge Amy Gansell, who stepped in with virtually no notice when the article arranged for women in Mesopotamia fell through very late in the process of our editing. Amy rapidly produced, with great professionalism, the elegant essay found herein, and we are both extremely grateful to her and proud to open the volume with her contribution.

Sharon L. James and Sheila Dillon
Carrboro, North Carolina
April 18, 2011

Abbreviations

List of Abbreviations not in *L'Année Philologique*

ABV	Beazley, J. D. 1956. *Attic Black-Figure Vase-Painters*. Oxford: Clarendon Press.
AfO	*Archiv für Orientforschung*
AJPA	*American Journal of Physical Anthropology*
ARIM	*Annual Review of the Royal Inscriptions of Mesopotamia*
ARV²	Beazely, J. D. 1963. *Attic Red-Figure Vase-Painters*. 2ⁿᵈ edition. Oxford: Clarendon Press.
BA	*Biblical Archaeologist*
BASOR	*Bulletin of the American Schools of Oriental Research*
BCSMS	*Canadian Society for Mesopotamian Studies, Bulletin*
ÉtTrav	*Études et travaux. Studia i prace. Travaux du Centre d'archéologie méditerranéenne de l'Académie polonaise*
CAJ	*Cambridge Archaeological Journal*
DaM	*Damaszener Mitteilungen*
FuB	*Forschungen und Berichte. Staatliche Museen zu Berlin.*
JAOS	*Journal of the American Oriental Society*
JCMNS	*Canadian Society of Mesopotamian Studies Journal*
JESHO	*Journal of the Economic and Social History of the Orient*
JNES	*Journal of Near Eastern Studies*
MDOG	*Mitteilungen der Deutschen Orient-Gesellschaft zu Berlin*
NIN	*Journal of Gender Studies in Antiquity*
SAAB	*State Archives of Assyria Bulletin*
SAAS	*State Archives of Assyria Studies*
WVDOG	*Wissenschaftliche Veröffentlichungen der Deutschen Orient-Gesellschaft*

Abbreviations for Collected Inscriptions

AE	*L'Année épigraphique*, Paris 1888–.
CIL	*Corpus Inscriptionum Latinarum*, Berlin 1863–.
IAM	*Inscriptions antiques du Maroc 2. Inscriptions latines*, Paris 1982.
ICUR	*Inscriptiones Christianae Urbis Romae*, Rome 1922–.
IG	*Inscriptiones Graecae*, Berlin 1873–.
ILAlg	*Inscriptions latines d'Algérie*, Paris 1922–.
ILCV	*Inscriptiones Latinae Christianae Veteres*, Berlin 1924–.
ILLRP	Degrassi, A. *Inscriptiones Latinae Liberae rei publicae*, Florence, 1957–1963.
ILS	*Inscriptiones Latinae Selectae*, ed. H. Dessau, Berlin 1892–1916.
OGIS	Dittenberger, W. (ed.) 1960. *Orientis Graeci inscriptiones selectae*, I (Hildesheim, repr. of 1903 edition).
RIT	Alföldy, G. 1975. *Die römischen Inschriften von Tarraco* [Madrider Forschungen 10]. Berlin.

Abbreviations for Collected Papyri

P. Athen.	Petropoulos, G. A. (ed.) 1939. *Papyri Societatis Archaeologicae Atheniensis. Nos.* 1–70 [*Pragmateiai tês Akademias Athênón* 10]. Athens.
P. Berl.	BGU (*Aegyptische Urkunden aus den Königlichen Museen zu Berlin, Griechische Urkunden*. Volumes 1 and 5. Berlin.)
P. Cairo Zen.	Edgar, C. C. (ed.) 1925 (Vol. I) and 1928 (Vol. 3). *Zenon Papyri, Catalogue général des Antiquités Égyptiennes du Musée du Caire.* Cairo.
P. Col. Zen.	Westermann, W. L. and Hasenoehrl, E. S. (eds.) 1934. *Columbia Papyri III, Zenon Papyri: Business Papers of the Third Century B.C. dealing with Palestine and Egypt* I. New York.
P. Elephantine	Rubensohn, O. (ed.) 1907. *Aegyptische Urkunden aus den Königlichen Museen in Berlin: Griechische Urkunden*, Sonderheft. *Elephantine-Papyri*. Berlin.
P. Giessen	Eger, O., Kornemann, E., and Meyer, P. M. (eds.) 1910. *Griechische Papyri im Museum des Oberhessischen Geschichtsvereins zu Giessen*. Pt. I, nos. 1–35. Leipzig and Berlin.
P. Münch.	Hagedorn, U., Hagedorn, D., Hübner, R., and Shelton, J. C. (eds.) 1986. *Griechische Urkundenpapyri der Bayerischen Staatsbibliothek München*, vol. 3, Part I. Stuttgart.
P. Oxy.	*Oxyrhynchus Papyrus.* 1898–.
P. Tebtunis	Grenfell, B. P., Hunt, A. S., and Smyly, J. G. (eds.) 1902. *The Tebtunis Papyri*, I [University of California Publications, Graeco-Roman Archaeology I; Egypt Exploration Society, Graeco-Roman Memoirs 4]. London.

ETRURIA

Cerveteri

Ithaca   Thebes

Thera

CRETE

LYC

0   200   400   600 Miles
0   300   600   900 Kilometers

N
W   E
S

Ancient World Mappi

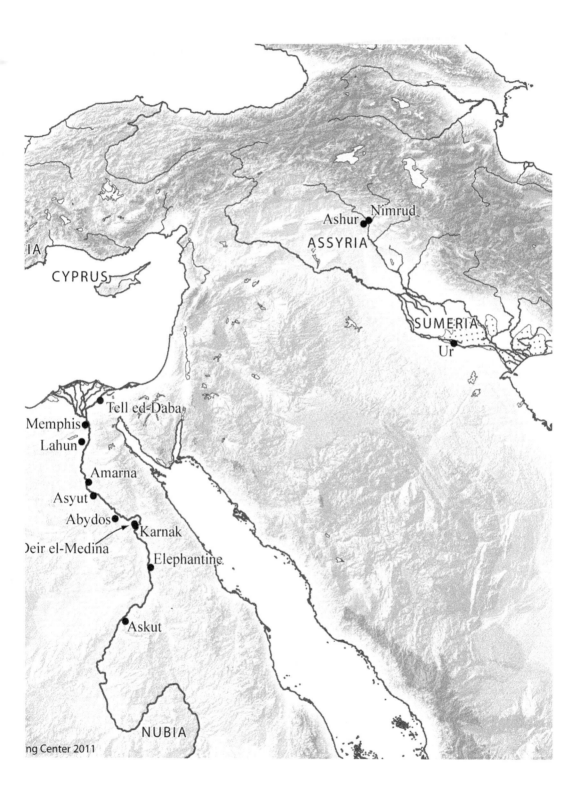

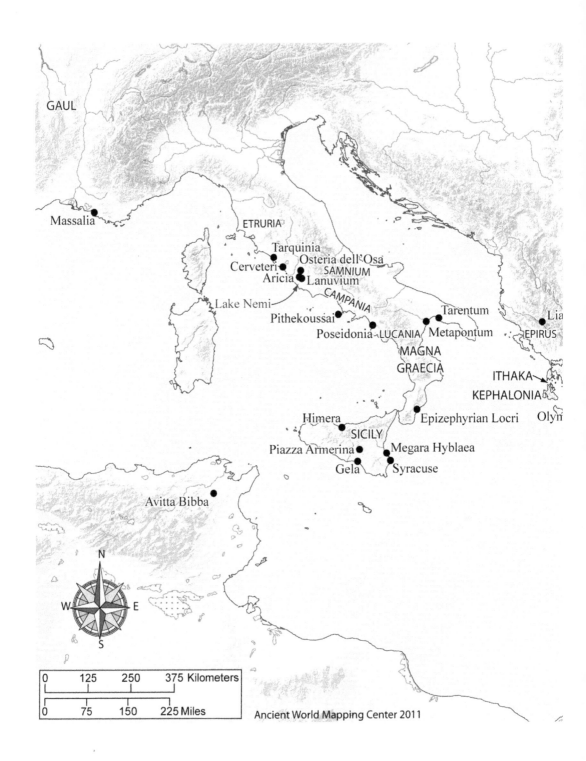

GAUL

Massalia

ETRURIA

Tarquinia
Cerveteri
Aricia
Lanuvium
Osteria dell'Osa
SAMNIUM
Lake Nemi

Pithekoussai
CAMPANIA
Poseidonia LUCANIA
Tarentum
Metapontum
MAGNA
GRAECIA

EPIRUS
Lia

ITHAKA
KEPHALONIA

Himera
SICILY
Piazza Armerina
Gela
Megara Hyblaea
Syracuse
Epizephyrian Locri
Olyn

Avitta Bibba

N
W   E
S

0	125	250	375 Kilometers
0	75	150	225 Miles

Ancient World Mapping Center 2011

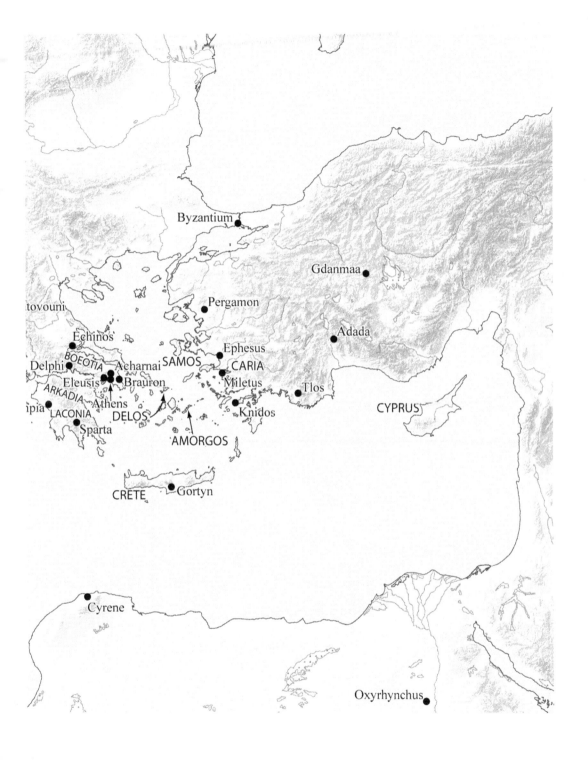

Byzantium

Gdanmaa

Pergamon

Echinos

Delphi

BOEOTIA

Acharnai

SAMOS

Ephesus

CARIA

tovouni

Eleusis

Brauron

Miletus

ARKADIA

Athens

Tlos

ipia

LACONIA

DELOS

Knidos

CYPRUS

Sparta

AMORGOS

Adada

CRETE

Gortyn

Cyrene

Oxyrhynchus

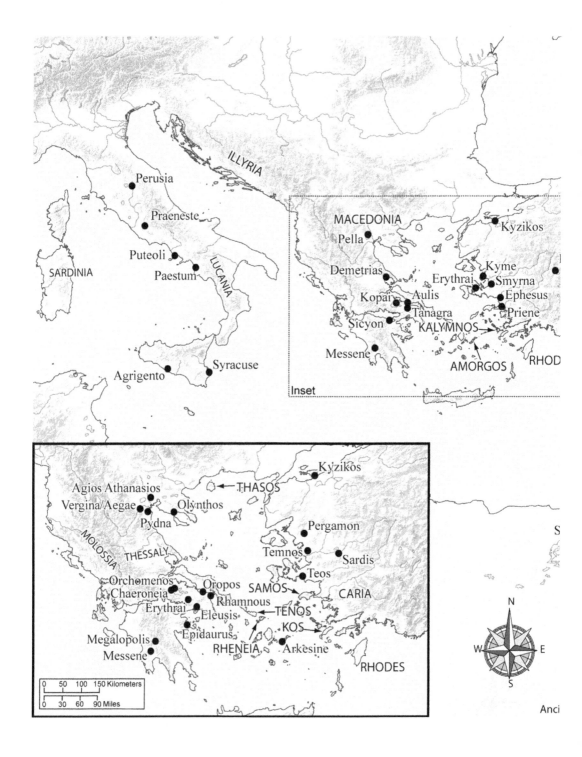

Perusia

Praeneste

Puteoli

SARDINIA

Paestum

LUCANIA

Agrigento

Syracuse

ILLYRIA

MACEDONIA

Pella

Demetrias

Kopai
Aulis

Sicyon
Tanagra

Messene

Kyzikos

Kyme

Erythrai
Smyrna

Ephesus

Priene

KALYMNOS

AMORGOS

RHOD

Inset

Kyzikos

Agios Athanasios

THASOS

Vergina/Aegae

Olynthos

Pydna

Pergamon

MOLOSSIA

THESSALY

Temnos

Sardis

Teos

Orchomenos
Chaeroneia

Oropos

SAMOS

CARIA

Erythrai

Rhamnous

Eleusis

TENOS

Megalopolis
Messene

Epidaurus

KOS

RHENEIA

Arkesine

RHODES

0   50   100   150 Kilometers

0   30   60   90 Miles

N

W   E

S

Anci

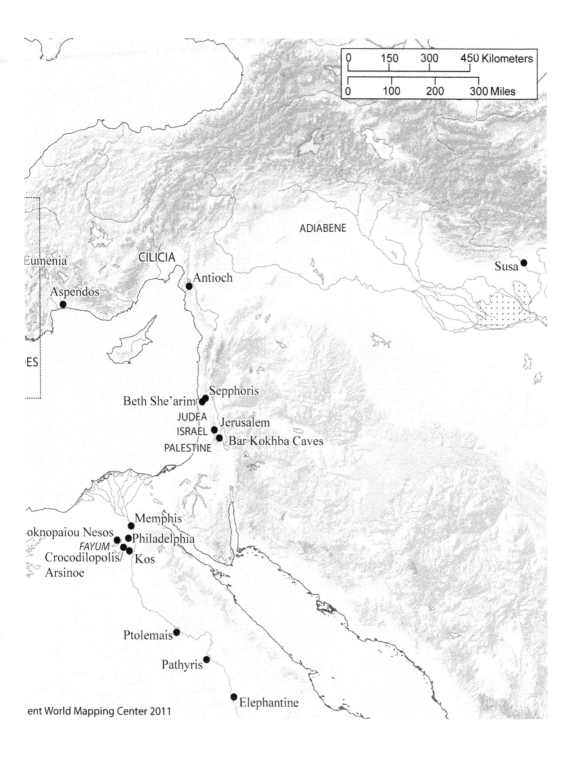

0   150   300   450 Kilometers
0   100   200   300 Miles

ADIABENE

Eumenia   CILICIA   Susa

Aspendos   Antioch

ES

                    Sepphoris
Beth She'arim
            JUDEA
            ISRAEL   Jerusalem
        PALESTINE   Bar Kokhba Caves

                    Memphis
oknopaiou Nesos   Philadelphia
    FAYUM
Crocodilopolis/   Kos
Arsinoe

        Ptolemais

        Pathyris

            Elephantine

ent World Mapping Center 2011

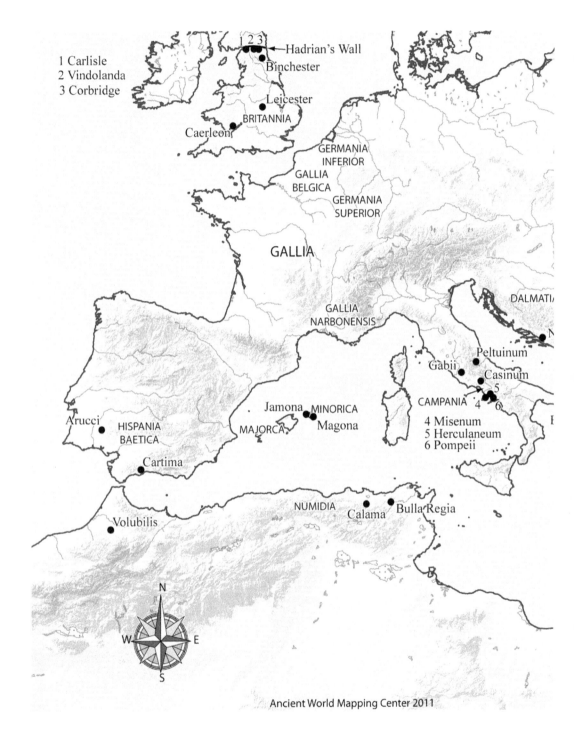

1 Carlisle
2 Vindolanda
3 Corbridge

1 2 3 ← Hadrian's Wall
Binchester

Leicester

BRITANNIA

Caerleon

GERMANIA
INFERIOR
GALLIA
BELGICA
GERMANIA
SUPERIOR

GALLIA

GALLIA
NARBONENSIS

DALMATIA

Peltuinum

Gabii
Casinum
5
CAMPANIA 4 6

Jamona MINORICA
MAJORCA Magona

4 Misenum
5 Herculaneum
6 Pompeii

Arucci HISPANIA
BAETICA

Cartima

Volubilis

NUMIDIA
Calama Bulla Regia

Ancient World Mapping Center 2011

Narona

Philippi

Beroea
Thessaloniki

Antioch
Iconium

Buthrotum

Nysa Aphrodisias
Perge

Palmyra

Corinth

Naukratis

Antinoopolis
Hermopolis Magna
Meir
Coptos
Thebes

0   200   400   600 Kilometers

0   125   250   375 Miles

Introduction

Sharon L. James and Sheila Dillon

Ever since the groundbreaking work of Pomeroy (1975), which brought forth a new era of study in the subject, "Women in Antiquity" has become a standard and expanding field of scholarship in Classics, Ancient History, Archaeology, and Art History, and an increasingly popular course offering in colleges and universities. These fields, however, have historically been split between textual and material evidence, a divide that poses special problems for the study of women. The ancient materials on women pose further interpretive challenges because of unexamined biases in both the sources themselves and in traditional scholarship on the subject, inherited from the nineteenth century.

Methodology thus becomes a primary issue in the study of these materials: inherent biases in the materials mean that what we read and see cannot be taken at face value. For example, how literally should we take sexual invective by the likes of Archilochus and Juvenal? By the same token, how should we read sexualized images of women on Attic vases? Do these sources represent historical or literal truths, as they have sometimes been taken to do? Specialists in a given field know not to treat their evidence naively, but do not necessarily recognize the gender biases in other materials. The ancient sources on women seem so starkly self-evident, and are so visually striking, that they themselves tempt readers and viewers to understand them as unmediated reality.

With this *Companion*, therefore, we have chosen to draw together, in a methodologically self-conscious way, the advances in scholarship since Pomeroy. We hope thereby to have produced a volume that will be of use to a wide range of readers, from advanced undergraduates to established scholars. We present here an integrated, interdisciplinary focus that brings material and visual evidence together with textual evidence, and applies articulated methodologies. We do so in the firm belief that to study women in antiquity on the basis of exclusively or even primarily one form of evidence—textual or material—is more than merely impoverished. It is inadequate. While we would not insist that a literary scholar suddenly include a specialist's examination of the material remains of portraiture (not that we would forbid such a venture, of course), we do insist that textual and material

A Companion to Women in the Ancient World, First Edition. Edited by Sharon L. James and Sheila Dillon.
© 2012 John Wiley & Sons, Ltd. Published 2015 by John Wiley & Sons, Ltd.

scholars benefit from being in conversation with each other, and we hope that this *Companion* offers not only opportunity for, but examples of, such conversation.

We asked our contributors to foreground the problems of interpreting the evidence, and they have done so with a wide range of approaches, demonstrating the diversity of methods available for studying women in antiquity. The essays here that study textual evidence offer treatments theoretical, historical, literary, epigraphical, and papyrological, on a broad scale of subjects. We also asked those contributors who were treating material culture to focus on a limited range of examples, rather than providing a survey of the available evidence. These essays therefore often include focused case studies of selected pieces; we include separate short case studies as well. The purpose of the focused studies is to offer models for examining a broader range of examples from the same period or medium.

Some of the essays here reach skeptical conclusions about whether a given body of evidence can in fact reveal any realities about women in antiquity: thus, for example, A. A. Donohue's essay, "Interpreting Women in Archaic and Classical Greek Sculpture" (Chapter 12), interrogates all its categories—"women," "archaic," "classical," "Greek," and "sculpture"—to conclude that even such familiar terms and concepts, basic to the study of Greek antiquity, are not unproblematic and that they do not offer straightforward evidence about women. More than a few essays undermine received interpretations of very well-known materials. While such conclusions may seem to eliminate what has been considered invaluable and reliable evidence, they instead point forward, as do other essays, to new directions for future research. In this respect, the essays here do more than review the current state of research on women in antiquity: they look ahead in productive ways and they challenge classicists and non-classicists alike not to rely on comfortably familiar notions and interpretations.

Finally, a number of the essays examine the same material—some of the same historical, literary, and visual evidence recurs, as do certain women, throughout. For example, Lucretia and the Etruscan princesses are treated by Vedia Izzet in "Etruscan Women: Towards a Reappraisal" (Chapter 5), Madeleine M. Henry and Sharon L. James in "Woman, City, State: Theories, Ideologies, and Concepts in the Archaic and Classical Periods" (Chapter 6); Judith P. Hallett in "Women in Augustan Rome" (Chapter 27); and Alison Keith in "Women in Augustan Literature" (Chapter 28). Similarly, Eumachia is discussed by Anne Bielman in "Female Patronage in the Greek Hellenistic and Roman Republican Periods" (Chapter 17); Eve D'Ambra in "Women on the Bay of Naples" (Chapter 29); and Elizabeth Bartman in "Early Imperial Female Portraiture" (Chapter 30). Such overlap is inevitable, and is in our view a strength because it exemplifies the diversity of approaches to the ancient materials on women.

No single study, or collection of studies, can accomplish everything. We cannot cover each subject in each historical period, nor for every geographical region. Thus, for example, the study of Greek women's dress and adornment looks at the Archaic and Classical periods only, and there is no twin study on Roman women's dress and adornment. In the brief introductions to the individual parts of the *Companion*, which are ordered chronologically, we provide references to scholarship for subjects not covered in the chapters. In addition, two of the planned essays could not be completed: those on women in classical Attic drama and on women in late antiquity; in the introductions to Parts III and VI, we have provided similar resources.

A further result of our editorial choices is that the focus here on methodology and approach, on problems with the evidence, means that this volume follows the ancient evidence. Since those materials overwhelmingly represent the citizen, even elite, classes and omit the large populations of lower-class citizens, slaves, and foreigners, the contributions here largely also focus on citizens and often on elite women. Even editorial choices involve losses, and this is a loss we feel keenly: our decision to focus on genres of evidence means that we have had, for the most part, to overlook the great majority of women in antiquity, who are little represented in the ancient sources. A growing body of scholarship on slaves, prostitutes, and non-elite citizens is, however, widely available, and in the brief introductions to the parts in this *Companion* we refer readers to those studies. Here we specifically recommend Scheidel (1995, 1996) as covering the widest chronological and geographical range on the subject of rural women in antiquity.

By offering a unified chronological structure with theme-based chapters, this *Companion* seeks to avoid a structure typical of books on the ancient world, in which the Greeks are placed before the Romans. We also hope to avoid a suspect dichotomy inherited from antiquity that locates women in the private sphere and sees them as separate from other aspects of ancient culture. Finally, we aim to avoid a common Atheno-centrism that focuses on the Classical period of Athens to the exclusion of other regions and periods. We have sought to include here aspects of women in antiquity that are normally overlooked, such as Jewish women and women in the near East, and have included essays on women in Egypt throughout the temporal spread of this *Companion*. Our contributors include both established and younger scholars from North America, the UK, Europe, and Australia.

We provide for each chronological part a methodological introduction and one or two brief and focused case studies relevant to the evidence from the period. These short case studies focus on a specific piece of evidence. We do not represent each topic in each chronological part; quite a few of the essays here overflow their temporal boundaries, but had to be located somewhere. That is, for example, the essays studying women's religion, by Eva Stehle ("Women and Religion in Greece," Chapter 14) and Lora L. Holland ("Women and Roman Religion," Chapter 15), are placed in Part III, on the Archaic and Classical periods, but reach forward to later eras as well.

The table of contents lays out our basic organization: Part I surveys women outside Athens and Rome, before the Classical-period polis culture of Greece, and offers a case study of Mother Goddess theory. The broad geographical and chronological scope exemplifies the diversity of evidence and approach that characterizes this *Companion*.

In Part II, we bring together the Archaic and Classical periods in both Greece and Italy. Some chapters are unified between Greek and Roman women (e.g., Barbara Levick's "Women and Law," Chapter 7) while others provide separate treatments for the distinctive and significant bodies of evidence available in this period, such as the visual materials from Athens.

Part III attends to the greater evidence, in the Hellenistic and Late Republican period, for women in the public eye and sphere. As with the previous part, several of these chapters integrate Greek and Roman materials. Because the evidence for this period allows the broadest geographical study, we have included studies here on women in Egypt, and Jewish women.

Part IV considers the short but pivotal period that saw the establishment of the Roman empire (31 BCE–98 CE). Imperial women play a prominent role in the visual and historical evidence of this period, while the literary sources often focus on non-elite women. As elsewhere, we aimed in this part to include women outside the capital city and to chart these women's changing representations.

Part V tracks the changes throughout the developing Roman empire, up to its transition to Christianity. Evidence from this period demonstrates both a re-emergence of local traditions and a new hybridizing of cultures throughout the Roman empire. These essays particularly address the increasing prominence of women in the provinces, and the issues of understanding the conversion of women in early Christianity.

Case Study I

The Mother Goddess in Prehistory: Debates and Perspectives

Lauren Talalay

For over a century, archaeologists, mythographers, poets, psychoanalysts—and many others—have debated the existence and meaning of a so-called Mother Goddess in prehistory. Often contentious, the debate has fallen into two basic camps. On one side are "Goddess movement" proponents who claim that early Mediterranean, Egyptian, and Near Eastern societies worshiped an all-powerful female deity, celebrated nature, and embraced an egalitarian ideal within a matriarchal social structure. Supporting evidence for the worship of the Goddess, it is argued, derives from two sources: the myriad female figurines recovered from archaeological contexts dating from approximately 40,000 years ago to 3500 BCE, and the existence of later Mother Goddess types (e.g., Ishtar, Astarte, Cybele, and the Roman Magna Mater), all of which are thought to represent vestiges of these earlier female divinities. In the opposing camp stand academic archaeologists who discount these "meta-narratives" as an invented past. They argue that such ideas find little support in the archaeological record, cast religion as static despite momentous social changes over the millennia, and are politically driven, most recently by the feminist movement. The academic side is also quick to observe that, even if evidence for a primal Mother Goddess were unassailable, arguments linking the theological realm to the social structures of these early communities are weak. Worship of a nurturing Mother Goddess who oversees cosmological creation, fertility, and death does not necessarily entail or reflect a pacific matriarchy and female power in society.

The debate is complex and sprawling, encompassing issues that extend beyond the topics of religion, prehistoric theology, and the precise roles of such a goddess in prehistory. Over the years, discussions have been shaped by political agendas; discourses of power, sex, and gender in the ancient world; and changing fashions within the academy. Given the larger forces at play, however, the debate provides fertile ground for probing subjects such as the notion of "the feminine" (as opposed to "the masculine") in early theological systems, definitions of "religion" and "goddess" in prehistoric contexts, and relationships between the concept of a female divinity and the social roles of women in antiquity (Talalay 2008).

A Companion to Women in the Ancient World, First Edition. Edited by Sharon L. James and Sheila Dillon.
© 2012 John Wiley & Sons, Ltd. Published 2015 by John Wiley & Sons, Ltd.

It is impossible to do justice to the multiple, thorny layers of the debate in this short introduction (for good summaries, see Goodison and Morris 1998b and Eller 2000: 30–55). Instead, I provide a simplified history of the Great Goddess debate and then extract from that history some general questions and thoughts, many of which have a bearing on the following chapters.

* * *

The genealogy of the Mother Goddess debate is usually traced back to Johann Jacob Bachofen, a Swiss jurist and classicist. In 1861, Bachofen published a landmark book, *Das Mutterrecht*, in which he argued for an evolutionary unfolding of human history. He proposed that society moved from an early stage of sexual promiscuity and communal property through a time when women ruled supreme, and then finally to a patriarchal culture. His thesis was supported by several well-known anthropologists, many of whom also espoused evolutionary paradigms (e.g., Tylor 1871; Morgan 1877). Although a few of these writers discussed the worship of some type of Mother Goddess during the matriarchal stage, many decades ensued before scholars and various specialists fully explored the notion of an all-powerful, divine female archetype. Not until the 1950s and 1960s did books such as *The Great Mother* (Neumann 1955) and *The Cult of the Mother-Goddess* (James 1959), begin to appear. These publications, written by experts from an array of disciplines, contained much speculation on prehistoric goddess worship, mythology, and symbology.

Mother goddess inquiries took a more transparently political turn in the late 1960s and 1970s when feminist writers, usually from outside the academy, entered the scene. Picking up earlier threads that extended back to Bachofen, these authors focused not only on the generative and nurturing powers of an alleged "Mother Creatrix" but also on the transformation of society at the end of the Neolithic Age into a patriarchy (see e.g., Stone 1976). Many of these writers sought academic support in the publications of archaeologist Marija Gimbutas (e.g., 1974, 1989), who wrote extensively about the prevalence of women in the prehistoric iconography of eastern Europe and the Mediter-ranean, and an alleged invasion from the north Black Sea steppes of male, nomadic warriors, who effectively terminated the earlier, pacific, and more egalitarian ways of life.

While the feminist perspective was hardly uniform—some feminists claimed that the Goddess had a darker, more destructive side—most Goddess proponents from the 1960s onward held a common view: there was a time when the nurturing capacities of women, "the feminine," and nature were celebrated, and when authority and power were more evenly distributed between the sexes. The Goddess movement became a "manifesto for change" (Eller 2000: 7), with a desire to reinstitute this lost world.

Although academics largely ignored the popular Goddess movement, several publica-tions surfaced in the late 1960s that challenged its core premise. Most seminal were Peter Ucko's (1968) volume on figurines from prehistoric Egypt and Neolithic Crete, and Andrew Fleming's article "The myth of the mother-goddess," which ended with the statement, "The mother-goddess has detained us for too long, let us disentangle ourselves from her embrace" (Fleming 1969: 259). Both publications stressed the failings of an overarching Mother Goddess theory, pointing out in some detail that it was inadequately supported by the archaeological evidence.

For a while the Great Goddess debate appeared all but dead. Then, beginning in the 1990s, renewed interest in anthropomorphic images, identity, gender, reception theory, and postprocessual paradigms produced a wave of books and articles that re-examined, among other things, the foundations of the debate. These publications, mostly from academic circles, problematized the notion of fertility, explored new ways to analyze figurines, and reconsidered theories of representation and the material expression of divinity (e.g., Talalay 1994; Conkey and Tringham 1995; Meskell 1995, 1998; Goodison and Morris 1998a; Tringham and Conkey 1998; Eller 2000). The resulting scholarship has been both lively and problematic, generating more questions than answers. Some suggest that at certain times in Mediterranean prehistory the divine may not have been personified as an anthropomorphic being (Goodison and Morris 1998a: 119). Others reconsider the political implications of the Mother Goddess debate, arguing that the popular Goddess literature essentializes women by confining their powers to reproductive capabilities. Worse still, these scholars point out, if reproduction has long been viewed cross-culturally as marginal to the processes of larger cultural change, then the Goddess narrative has unwittingly relegated women's status to that of cultural object rather than cultural agent (Talalay 1994, 2008; Tringham and Conkey 1998; Conkey and Tringham 1995; Meskell 1995).

This recent round of debates has produced instructive criticisms, cautions, and questions. Not surprisingly, the overriding message from the academic side is a demand for greater analytic rigor. Academics observe that the apparent abundance of female figurines does not necessarily support the idea of a goddess pantheon, let alone an all-encompassing Mother or Great Goddess. The basic question remains, how do we identify a deity in the prehistoric record? Even if we can, how do we determine the nature of its divine powers? Moreover, it is argued, assigning unitary significance to these depictions is unwarranted; the portrayals vary in form, detail, levels of abstraction, and sexual indicators. Although relatively few are clearly male, many figurines have no sexual features, some are sexually ambiguous, and a handful indicate both sexes. The common belief, therefore, that the prehistoric production of human images was monolithic, confined almost exclusively to forming female images and the occasional male consort, is unfounded. Such variability, however, is instructive. Recent scholarship has explored the fluid and non-binary nature of gender and sex in prehistory (e.g., Hamilton 2000), a particularly challenging topic but one that continues to warrant scrutiny. Just as importantly, academic researchers criticize the tendency to equate possible female authority in divine realms with an elevated status of women in society. Indeed, female authority in the theological sphere of many modern societies often belies the subordinate status of women in socio-political life. At the heart of this observation is the complex issue of how researchers can convincingly move between evidence that might be keyed to ancient theological realms and daily social action.

Archaeological context and figurine production have, until recently, been largely understudied axes of analysis. Academics and non-academics alike have sometimes glossed over contextual data on figurines and failed to pose more penetrating questions, particularly those that are routinely asked of other kinds of data. Were figurines recovered from burials, rubbish pits, or domestic deposits? Do any derive from cultic areas and how are those defined? Were anthropomorphic images deliberately or accidentally deposited or broken? When figurines appear in rubbish deposits, as is common, what kinds of other objects accompany them and what kinds are absent? Can we determine whether figurines took part in any kind of performance, broadly defined? How were figurines formed, with what materials, and how do those differ from other objects? (See Goodison and Morris 1998b: 15; Tringham and Conkey 1998: 28.)

Finally, archaeologists are beginning to deconstruct commonly used terms such as "temple," "shrine," "ritual," "public," "private," "mother," and "goddess." These and other words frequently used in the literature tend to predetermine analytic frameworks, often reflecting modern Western ideas that may not have been valid in the prehistoric world (Tringham and Conkey 1998: 40–3).

The popular literature, conversely, has underscored other significant issues, providing an antidote to overly cautious intellectual constraints. Spirituality and a concept of the divine are central to much of this literature, and are indeed likely to have been part of prehistoric life in the Mediterranean, Egypt, and the Near East. Worship of a Great Goddess may well be a myth, but coping with the vagaries of birth, death, and fertility were, we must imagine, major concerns in prehistoric cultures. How those organizing principles were conceived and expressed in the material record is a vexing and elusive topic for prehistorians. These difficulties notwithstanding, speculation and provocative arguments should be welcomed, provided they are reasonable and informed.

In sum, the Great Goddess debate has produced spirited—sometimes acrimonious—and thoughtful discussions, both within and outside the academy, that raise a host of important questions for the general exploration of women, gender, and female deities in the ancient world. It may be impossible to ever prove one way or the other that a Great Goddess existed in prehistory. As the essays that follow suggest, what is more likely is that interpretations of female deities, their intersection with the roles of women in antiquity, and the place of these debates in modern society will be rewritten many times in the future.

PART I

Women Outside Athens and Rome

This section brings together the earliest evidence for women, across a very wide chrono-logical and geographical range. We begin with an issue that is foundational to the modern study of women in the ancient world, namely the Mother Goddess. As Lauren Talalay demonstrates in Case Study I ("The Mother Goddess in Prehistory: Debates and Perspec-tives"), there was a desire among scholars, particularly in the 1960s and 1970s, to locate a period in the distant past in which women were not secondary, when female power was celebrated, and when an overarching Mother Goddess was the primary divinity. This myth continues to have great appeal, as witnessed in "goddess-tourism" in the Mediterranean even today. While it is no longer an active scholarly theory, the issue of the Mother Goddess continues to be an exemplar for the problems of studying women in antiquity: mysterious images disembodied from their contexts, multiple scholarly biases and motivations, and conflicting interpretations of the scanty and fragmentary evidence.

A common aim of these chapters is to use the mostly, though not exclusively, visual materials to explore the social and political place of women in the earliest periods of the ancient world. Much of the evidence focuses on elite women, as is the case throughout the volume, but the large population of laboring women, both free and enslaved, is broadly perceptible, as Cristiana Franco and Marianna Nikolaïdou demonstrate. In "Hidden Voices: Unveiling Women in Ancient Egypt" (Chapter 2), Kasia Szpakowska analyzes ancient physical evidence, noting throughout that unexamined assumptions and biases in scholarship have led to unsupportable, sometimes illogical, conclusions; she particularly urges us to defamiliarize ourselves from Egyptian artistic evidence, which is easily recognized but not so easily understood. In "Women in Homer" (Chapter 4), Cristiana Franco draws on approaches from anthropology to reader-response literary theory. In "Women in Ancient Mesopotamia" (Chapter 1), Amy R. Gansell studies mortuary evidence from elite funerary contexts to pursue what can be understood from such materials, particularly about the social and public roles of women in this class; she reminds us that much remains to be excavated, and that our understanding will be modified in the future. In "Looking for Minoan and Mycenaean Women: Paths of Feminist Scholarship Towards the Aegean Bronze Age" (Chapter 3), Marianna Nikolaïdou considers how women participated in the continuous technological developments of Minoan and Mycenaean society. In "Etruscan Women: Towards a Reappraisal" (Chapter 5), Vedia

Izzet takes a skeptical look at the evidence for Etruscan women, concluding that many of our conventional beliefs about them are close to baseless and that we must start afresh from these materials, without prejudices and ideas inherited from prior scholarship as well as from biased Greek and Roman sources.

These early periods are those for which it has been most tempting to recreate for women a prominent public role and wider-scale participation in society, rather than strict limitation to the domestic realm. The mysterious and striking visual materials engender unanswerable questions; for example, who are these bare-breasted Minoan women? Were Etruscan women really prominent, as they seem to be in funerary depictions? Without attempting to answer such questions, which may well reflect post-classical rather than ancient categories and issues, the essays here study multiple forms of evidence and thus provide an exemplary opening for this volume's interdisciplinary mission.

1

Women in Ancient Mesopotamia

Amy R. Gansell

Ancient Mesopotamian texts and images carved into sculptures, cliffs, and palace walls monumentalized the primacy of the male ruler. Complementing such large-scale media, thousands of intaglio seals, and their innumerable impressions, legitimated male power through depictions of the ruler in audience with gods and goddesses. Indeed, a patriarchal power structure sustained Mesopotamian civilization. Even so, women played vital roles in all levels of society. In addition to their domestic and reproductive functions as mothers, wives, and daughters, elite women contributed to the male-dominated spheres of the arts, economy, religion, and government.

Information about ancient Mesopotamian women of diverse social classes survives in cuneiform documents (including legal, economic, labor, marriage, adoption, and temple records, as well as personal letters), visual art (especially friezes depicting ritual and votive sculptures), and archaeological contexts (such as intact burials). In drawing upon this pool of evidence, it is easiest to understand elite women because the corpora of complementary textual, visual, and archaeological data are far more extensive for these women.

Ancient Mesopotamian civilization spans more than three millennia, during which time diverse ethno-linguistic entities were politically dominant in different regions of the Tigris-Euphrates Basin, and as a result it is not possible to assemble a comprehensive or linear account of ancient Mesopotamian women's history (a task that has been likened to writing a history of European men from ancient Greece to the present by Bahrani 2001: 2). This essay therefore offers three case studies, each analyzing an elite female burial from a different millennium: Tomb 800 of the Royal Cemetery at Ur represents the third millennium BCE; Tomb 45 at Ashur represents the second millennium BCE; and Tomb II of the Queens' Tombs at Nimrud provides evidence from the first millennium BCE. Additional textual and visual material is incorporated to complement the mortuary record and provide a broader context for these case studies.

1   Evidence from Elite Tombs

Intact elite tombs, which archeologists can analyze layer by layer, provide multidimensional evidence for women's significance within the context of ancient Mesopotamian society. When women, men, and children are interred within shared boundaries (of a cemetery, tomb, or a single sarcophagus), the burials can be compared to one another, and variables such as gender, age, and relative status can be assessed (see also Szpakowska, this volume, Chapter 2; Liston, this volume, Chapter 9; Shepherd, this volume, Chapter 16; and Salowey, this volume, Chapter 18). Elite Mesopotamian tombs are generally associated with privileged sites, such as a temple or palace, indicating an individual's high status and social affiliation. The architectural structure of a tomb and the placement of the body on a bier or in a sarcophagus attest to the special attention and protection given to elite deceased (compared to the common practice of inhumation, or direct burial in the ground). Inscriptions (including curses against those who would disturb the dead) may name the deceased, her spouse or lineage, and office held; they also reiterate membership in a high (literate) social stratum. Intact elite tombs generally contain copious grave goods bearing meaningful iconography and adornments that are sometimes found in place as they were last worn on the body. Finally, when preservation and circumstances permit, scientists can analyze human remains to confirm sex and interpret information such as age, stature, history of physical activity, and cause of death (see also Liston, this volume, Chapter 9).

An intact burial preserves the deceased as she was carefully prepared, deposited in her tomb in relation to a variety of objects, and viewed for the last time by the living. Whether or not a tomb's contents correspond to a woman's possessions and appearance in life, they record how the surviving community constructed her identity for eternity according to established social codes. Archaeologists may interpret the body as both a person with a social presence and an inanimate object at the center of a mortuary tableau (Sofaer 2006; Sørensen 2006). In this manner, the tomb of an elite woman simultaneously presents a portrait of life, indicating her rank, role, and identity, and a portrait of death, indicating how she was recognized, regarded, and idealized within living culture.

The masterfully produced objects of precious materials sealed in elite Mesopotamian tombs may have comprised funerary paraphernalia, offerings from the living, and institutional, familial, and personal assets (Mazzoni 2005). The willingness of the living to part with so much material wealth points to the esteem in which they held the deceased. Ritual and ideological customs may have motivated their disposal of valuable property. A lavish funeral may also have provided an opportunity for the surviving members of the household or community to display their wealth, power, and piety. In addition, at least some tomb "treasures" might have been included in the burial because they were understood as essential aspects of a woman's identity, if not her body. For example, would a queen buried without her crown still be a queen? Would a woman buried without her anklets and earrings be missing essential parts of her self?

Once ornamented and surrounded by a great concentration of wealth, the physically idealized corpse could be vulnerable to tangible and supernatural malice, and therefore required quantities of apotropaic objects in the burial. Ethnographic research shows that, in traditional twentieth century Middle Eastern cultures, the more "beautiful" a bride was on account of her adornments, the more important it was that she wore additional charms to protect herself (Gansell 2007a). If this formula applies to the presentation of ancient

Mesopotamian women in death, the mortuary costume itself might have necessitated another layer of ornamentation.

Overall, elite tombs reveal aspects of an individual's personal, social, and ideological identity, as well as the perspectives of the living toward the dead. The environment of ancient Iraq, the agricultural basis of Mesopotamian civilization, access to natural resources, and relationships with adjacent cultures underlay long-standing values and traditions reflected across all three of the tombs described below. Variations reflect changes in religion, government, and social structures across temporal and geographic distance, as well as differences in the rank, status, and roles of the deceased.

2   Case Studies

Tomb 800 of the Royal Cemetery at Ur, c. 2550–2400 BCE

Perhaps best known as the birthplace of the biblical patriarch Abraham (Genesis 11.31), the site of Ur (modern Tell Muqayyar) is located in southern Iraq about ten miles (sixteen kilometers) from modern Nasiriyah. Excavations at Ur between 1922 and 1934 revealed a prosperous Sumerian city-state dated to the mid third millennium BCE (c. 2550–2400 BCE, the Early Dynastic III period). Near the temple of its patron deity, the moon god Nanna, over 1800 burials were unearthed. These have become known as the "Royal Cemetery at Ur" (Woolley 1934).

In most cases, the deceased were simply inhumed at Ur. But excavators designated sixteen exceptional tombs as "royal" because they consisted of architectural structures containing the bodies of multiple people sacrificed in submission to a primary tomb occupant. Some of the deceased wore seals inscribed with their names and titles, such as LUGAL for "king" and ERESH or NIN for "queen."

In the primary chamber of Royal Tomb 800, the body of ERESH/NIN Puabi was displayed on a bier surrounded by three personal attendants (Figure 1.1). A woman about forty years old and just under five feet tall, Puabi was outfitted in a spectacular array of gold, silver, carnelian, and lapis lazuli adornments. Her headdress entailed gold ribbons, leaves, and flowers (Figure 1.2). This was probably placed upon a bulky wig with gold rings threaded through the hair. She also wore large gold earrings that would have rested on her shoulders, several necklaces, a beaded wrist cuff, ten finger rings, and a circlet over her right knee. A tangle of beads and pendants featuring bulls, goats, male and female date palm branches, and other fruits probably constituted several additional necklaces. Overall, images of nature adorned Puabi and would have evoked agricultural and reproductive fecundity.

The bodies of human sacrifice victims filled the antechamber to her tomb. This "death pit," as scholars call it, also contained banqueting vessels, musical instruments, a cart drawn by two oxen, and a large wooden chest likely used to store organic materials such as food or textiles. Variations in rank are evident among the sacrificed attendants, who might have included high-ranking courtiers, lower-ranking household staff, and/or ritual actors dedicated to the Nanna temple. The attendants do not appear to have been enslaved, because several individuals wore personal seals, which in Mesopotamian culture marked status and implied some degree of official responsibility. In Puabi's Tomb 800, and indeed across the cemetery, almost all of the bodies belonged to adults, indicating that age, and

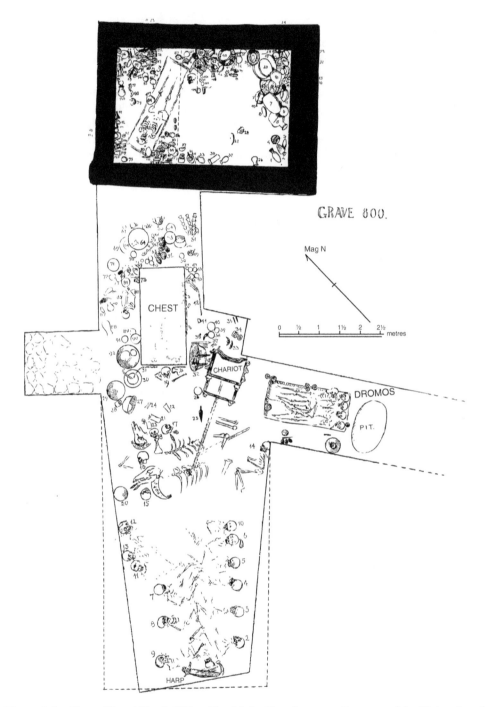

Figure 1.1 Plan of Royal Tomb 800 at Ur, third millennium BCE. Courtesy of the University of Pennsylvania Museum, negative no. S8-56378.

Figure 1.2 Adornment of Queen Puabi, Tomb 800 of the Royal Cemetery at Ur, third millennium BCE. Courtesy of the University of Pennsylvania Museum, negative no. 152100.

perhaps initiation into a group, dictated participation in these death rites, the circumstances of which remain unclear (Baadsgaard et al. 2011).

The sacrificed attendants at Ur included both men and women. For the most part, gender has been assigned according to particular objects or types of adornment that were present in conjunction with inscriptions naming an individual, or with bones well enough preserved to identify sex. In Puabi's burial chamber, at least one male and one female attendant were on hand. In her antechamber, four men, armed with daggers and a spear, accompanied the ox-drawn vehicle, and ten women were associated with musical instruments, including a harp and a lyre. Five additional men equipped with daggers were positioned at the tomb entrance.

An analysis of the deposition of jewelry on bodies across Ur's sixteen Royal Tombs reveals distinct adornment sets based on recurring configurations of standard pieces of jewelry (Gansell 2007b). In addition to signaling collective affiliation across the Royal Tombs, adornment sets illustrate categories that corresponded to gender and sometimes to responsibility. Differences in rank seem to correlate to variations in the material, size, quantity, and design of the standard items in a set. For example, higher-ranking individuals usually wore additional pieces of jewelry that supplemented the basic set, while in the death pits a beaded headband and single earring typically adorned male attendants. Men who demonstrated other forms of privilege, such as having multiple daggers and/or a personal seal, sometimes also wore a string of beads and a garment pin in addition to the standard headband and earring. Most women, some of whom were musicians, were bedecked in a predominantly gold and lapis lazuli adornment set, which entailed a leafy headdress, earrings, a beaded necklace, and garment pins. Puabi's adornment, detailed above, represents an exceptionally elaborate version of this jewelry set since it belonged to a queen. Several unique ornaments supplemented her costume as well.

Puabi and the other primary male and female occupants of the Royal Tombs probably led or belonged to Ur's ruling household—masculine names inscribed on some seals from the tombs correspond to those included in Sumerian king lists (Reade 2001: 17–24). Although men, as kings, held the highest political office, kings and queens received equally extravagant burials at Ur. Their analogous mortuary treatment might reflect the parity of their social or religious, rather than political, status (see also Shepherd, this volume, Chapter 16). Idealized in death, the primary occupants in Ur's Royal Tombs might even have transcended living inequities in emulation of gods and goddesses.

The sixteen Royal Tombs at Ur appear to have been separate burials, prompted by the natural deaths of elite men and women over the course of several decades. Consistency in the adornment of the deceased suggests that the burials belonged to an enduring household or institution, for which the disposal of massive amounts of wealth and human lives must have been an established policy (Pollock 2007). Upon the death of a king or queen, a surviving authority would have had to enforce and coordinate the funeral and the extraordinary requirement of human sacrifice. Whether this power rested with the royal household, temple, or an amalgam of both, the proximity of the cemetery to the Nanna temple suggests the moon god Nanna, who protected the city, would have sanctioned the disposal of riches and human lives.

Since we have yet to find any other burial site comparable in size and lavishness to the Royal Cemetery at Ur, it is difficult to craft a more general history of royal burial of the period. However, a votive object about ten inches (twenty-six centimeters) in diameter, known to scholars as the Disc of Enheduanna, supplements our understanding of elite women in Ur in the third millennium BCE. Created at least a century after the dramatic burials of the Royal Cemetery, the disc was discovered in Ur's sacred precinct. On the obverse, the high priestess Enheduanna is depicted overseeing a ritual; an inscription on the reverse identifies her as the daughter of the usurper Sargon (r. 2300–2245 BCE) and wife of the moon god Nanna (Winter 1987; Zgoll 1997). As princess, priestess, and divine consort, Enheduanna established the legitimacy of her father's rule. She maintained her tenure as high priestess at Ur into the reign of her nephew, Naram-Sin (r. 2200–2184 BCE), who was recognized as a god incarnate during his kingship. The relationship of elite men and women to the divine realm during the Sargonic dynasty may have built upon the precedent of elite proximity to the gods that was established at the Royal Cemetery.

Enheduanna is also credited with composing a corpus of poems to Inanna, the Sumerian goddess of sexuality and fertility. Her prominent position and her literary activities suggest the kinds of opportunities available to elite women in Mesopotamia in the third millennium BCE. In order to function as effective instruments of state ideology, Puabi and Enheduanna would have had to have been publicly recognized at least locally if not regionally. Both women also exemplified conceptions of fecundity that contributed to the coalescence of early Mesopotamian civilization.

Tomb 45 at Ashur, c. 1350–1200 BCE

The site of Ashur (modern Qal'at Sherqat) sits on a plateau overlooking the Tigris River in northern Iraq about sixty miles (110 kilometers) south of modern Mosul and roughly 350 miles (563 kilometers) north of Ur. In 1908, while excavating near the ancient palaces and temples of Ashur's walled inner city, archaeologists discovered a sealed burial chamber associated with a large house (Haller 1954). Tomb 45, as it is known, dates from the fourteenth to thirteenth century BCE (the Middle Assyrian period), when Ashur flourished as the capital of the emerging Assyrian empire. Of all the Middle Assyrian burials unearthed at Ashur and throughout the Mesopotamian heartland, Tomb 45 contained the greatest concentration of riches; it also contained the body of at least one elite woman.

Tomb 45 consisted of an entry shaft leading to a chamber about eight feet (two and a half meters) long and five feet (one and a half meters) wide that contained nine adults and one child. Most of the skeletons were found either collected in a large urn or heaped against a wall as if they had been cleared away to make room for the two most recently deposited bodies, indicating that they had been buried in phases, probably over the course of generations. The two recent burials were positioned flat on their backs, side by side, atop the other remains. Probably influenced by early twentieth-century social conventions, the excavators interpreted the skeletons as a man (on the left) and woman (on the right). They did not scientifically analyze the bones to determine sex, and the bones were discarded after excavation, preventing a modern restudy of the skeletal remains. More recent analyses of the adornment and grave goods associated with the two skeletons strongly suggest that both individuals were in fact female (Wartke 1992; Harper et al. 1995; Feldman 2006a).

Associated with the bodies was an array of jewelry made of gold, lapis lazuli, and carnelian, and banded agate cut into discs with dark centers surrounded by white that closely resembled eyes. The eyestone beads and inlays probably had a protective valence (André-Salvini 1999: 378). Both of the deceased had earrings embellished with "eyes." Loose eyestone beads were associated with the woman on the right, who also wore a necklace or diadem featuring palmette, pomegranate, and floral elements. The skeleton on the left wore pendants in the form of calves.

Vessels, boxes, pins, and combs made of ivory surrounded the two bodies. An ivory jar was found near the skeleton on the right that was embellished with a frieze of plant and animal imagery and contained a pin topped with a female figure holding a tambourine. Also associated with this skeleton was an ivory comb on which women wearing crowns are shown processing among date palms toward a figure (somewhat damaged) that perhaps represents the goddess Ishtar (Figure 1.3). The women carry bunches of dates, a harp, a dish, and what may be wreaths or tambourines. They are probably meant to represent either priestesses or royalty, and the figures are likely engaged in a ritual celebrating the earth's bounty and/or female fecundity. The skeleton on the left was associated with the fragment of a stone ointment jar portraying a winged female figure (perhaps the sexual aspect of the goddess Ishtar, the Assyrian adaptation of Inanna), whose skirt is raised to reveal her pubic area. Also located near the left skeleton was a shallow ivory dish featuring handles in the form of heads of Hathor, the Egyptian goddess of fertility and motherhood.

Some objects and ornaments from Tomb 45 are wholly Mesopotamian, while other items, such as the ivory dish with Hathor-heads, incorporate Mediterranean, Egyptian, and Levantine forms, iconography, and raw materials. The latter category of objects is related to an artistic tradition (often referred to by scholars as the "international style") that the dominant civilizations of the period employed in the production of portable luxury goods that they exchanged as diplomatic gifts (Feldman 2006b). Works such as Tomb 45's ivory jar with a plant and animal frieze and some of the vegetal jewelry designs are also closely related to the international style and would have evoked the cosmopolitan aspirations of their elite owners.

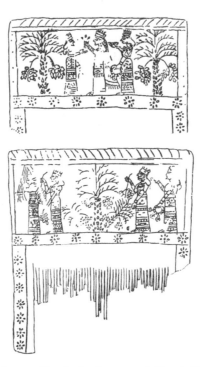

Figure 1.3   Drawing of the front and back of an ivory comb, Tomb 45 at Ashur, second millennium
BCE. H. 4.7 cm. Vorderasiatische Museum, Staatliche Museen zu Berlin, VA Ass 1097 [Ass 14630 ax].
From Haller (1954), Figs. 163a–b. Drawing: Courtesy Deutsche Orient-Gesellschaft.

The archaeological layer immediately above Tomb 45 yielded an archive of cuneiform
tablets that name individuals who probably belonged to the family interred there. Dated
between 1243 and 1207 BCE, the archive includes letters recording the international trade
of raw materials, including ivory, and a shipment of textiles to the Levant. While the
primary participant in these transactions is Babu-aha-iddina, who served as the second-
ranking official in the Assyrian palace, the tablets also mention two of his female relatives,
Marat-ili and Mushallimat-Ishtar. It is impossible to tell whether Marat-ili and Mushallimat-Ishtar were themselves buried in Tomb 45, but they at least are likely to have
received similar burials, reflecting the prosperity and international engagement of their
household.

During the late second millennium BCE, Mesopotamian rulers participated in complex
diplomatic interactions with foreign polities of the eastern Mediterranean, Egypt, the
Levant, and Anatolia. Assyria, with its capital at Ashur, was a latecomer to the world stage,
and letters between the more established powers attest that Assyria was regarded as a
disruptive and immature polity (Moran 1992). Assyrian correspondence, however,
demonstrates that at Ashur the king took international recognition seriously.

The visual and material evidence from Tomb 45 emulates and reiterates the imperial
ambitions of the nascent Assyrian empire (Feldman 2006a). The elite women buried
here participated in Assyrian imperial ideology through their consumption of luxury
goods related to the international style. They may also have engaged in international
trade. Royal women, whose tombs have not been located, would surely have had even

greater stock in international affairs. In fact, princesses themselves were exchanged in marriage between international royal courts to strengthen diplomatic relations (Meier 2000).

The recurrent iconography of fertility on the objects from Tomb 45 highlights women's generative role in sustaining elite bloodlines and perhaps in embodying the vitality of the Assyrian empire. A lapis lazuli seal found loose in the tomb depicts a ewe suckling a lamb by a leafy tree. Above the mother is the cuneiform sign for "god." While it is not certain whether a woman once owned this seal, its imagery (and the impressions it would have proliferated) demonstrate an emphasis among Middle Assyrian elites on the maternal capacity to support life, the fruitfulness of nature, and perhaps the divine protection of their burgeoning empire. Although Ashur's Tomb 45 does not preserve the personal identities and specific roles of the woman or women buried within it, its material culture illuminates the multifaceted significance of elite women in the formation of Assyrian imperial identity.

Tomb II of the Queens' Tombs at Nimrud, c. 750–625 BCE

By the Neo-Assyrian period of the early first millennium BCE, Assyria had become a Near Eastern superpower. Ashur remained the ceremonial center of the empire, but Nimrud (ancient Kalhu, biblical Calah (Genesis 10.8–12)), located roughly forty miles (sixty-four kilometers) to the north on the Tigris River, was rebuilt after almost two millennia of occupation as an administrative and residential capital.

In 1988 and 1989, excavations at Nimrud uncovered four tombs containing several bodies and massive amounts of material wealth mostly dating to the eighth century BCE (Damerji 1999; Hussein and Suleiman 1999; Curtis et al. 2008). Inscriptions naming the deceased and physical remains that were well enough preserved to permit scientific study reveal that the Queens' Tombs, as they are known, contained high-ranking male or eunuch courtiers, children, and generations of elite palace women. The women may have included queen mothers, primary and/or secondary wives, and the sisters and daughters of the king. Biological analysis of their remains indicates that they ate soft foods and led relatively sedentary lives.

Situated beneath the domestic quarters of the palace, where the deceased probably lived, the tombs would have protected the women's bodies and belongings while maintaining their proximity to surviving household members. A vertical five-foot-long pipe concealed beneath the brick pavement of the palace floor rested upon the vault of Tomb II, directly above its sarcophagus. The living would have passed sustenance to the deceased through this channel—an inscription in the tomb refers to offerings of fresh water, beer, wine, and flour. The ritual feeding of the dead, which is archaeologically attested over a thousand years earlier by similar conduits at the third millennium BCE Royal Cemetery at Ur, would have maintained the memory of the deceased and reiterated their status within the palace.

Luckily, ancient robbers left Tomb II undisturbed. Its sarcophagus contained two women, piled one on top of the other, who died when they were between thirty and forty years old. Cuneiform texts and inscribed objects identify the pair as Atalia, wife of King Sargon II (r. 721–705 BCE), and Yaba, wife of King Tiglath-Pileser III (r. 745–727 BCE). Considering their ages at death and the reign dates of their husbands, Atalia would have been interred between twenty and fifty years after Yaba. Because they shared a coffin, it is tempting to speculate that these women were related, but their lineage is not documented.

The names "Atalia" and "Yaba" are of West Semitic origin, suggesting that the women in Tomb II may have been Levantine princesses who entered the Assyrian palace through marriage—Neo-Assyrian rulers regularly gave and received ranking women in diplomatic unions (Dalley 1998). Interestingly, a third name, "Banitu, wife of King Shalmaneser V" (r. 726–722 BCE), is inscribed on objects in the sarcophagus, but it does not refer to a third individual. "Banitu" is an Assyrian translation of "Yaba." At some point, probably when Tiglath-Pileser died and Yaba transitioned into the court of Tiglath-Pileser's son and successor Shalmaneser, Yaba became "Banitu."

Tomb II contained hundreds of grave goods and almost thirty-one pounds (fourteen kilograms) of gold objects and jewelry. Among the luxury items found in the sarcophagus were gold and rock crystal vessels, silver and ivory mirrors, and more jewelry than the women could reasonably have worn—excavators counted nearly ninety necklaces and eighty single earrings. Atalia and Yaba/Banitu wore similar configurations of outsized ornaments made predominantly of gold and agate eyestones. Both women had diadems, earrings, necklaces, bracelets, finger rings, anklets, and, between them, more than 700 tiny gold appliqués that would have decorated their clothing. In addition to funerary gear, the objects in Tomb II may have included offerings or gifts from mourners, riches of the court, dowries, and the women's personal accrued assets—texts record that palace women managed lucrative estates, lent capital, and commissioned large architectural projects (Melville 1999).

Examples of jewelry from Tomb II match those represented on a rare large-scale relief portraying King Ashurbanipal (r. 685–627 BCE) and his primary wife, Libbali-Sharrat, sharing a victory banquet in the royal garden (Figure 1.4). Earrings found in the sarcophagus resemble the type worn by the queen, and the discs etched on her garment probably denote appliqués of the variety found with the bodies. The rosette bracelets depicted on the relief are also analogous to examples recovered archaeologically. Libbali-Sharrat wears a crown of fortified walls, indicating her status as the principal queen (i.e., the mother of the crown prince) and personifying the inviolability of the Assyrian empire (Börker-Klähn 1997; Ornan 2002). No mural crowns, however, have been discovered at Nimrud or elsewhere in Mesopotamia. There are a variety of explanations for this lack; for example, a single state crown may have been passed down from queen to queen, and the women buried at Nimrud would not themselves have had mural crowns if they were not primary wives (at least some of whom texts indicate were buried with the kings at Ashur, but no intact royal tombs have been found there).

In lieu of mural crowns, Tomb II preserved two diadems near the skulls of Atalia and Yaba/Banitu. The first is a rigid circlet comprising three rows of gold flowers. The second consists of a gold mesh headband with a dorsal ribbon inlayed at regular intervals with large eyestones. It also features a large forehead panel embellished with fringes terminating in miniature pomegranates. In Nimrud's Tomb III, yet a third type of crown was found on a child's skull. Sized to fit an adult (perhaps indicating a future privilege assured by birthright), this elaborate headdress incorporates tiers of pomegranates, flowers, winged female figures, and leafy vines from which tiny grape clusters dangle. Juxtaposed with the codified dress of the Neo-Assyrian court, the variety of headdresses in the Queens' Tombs would have differentiated the women, perhaps according to age, ethnicity, status, king's reign, or other variables.

The Tomb II diadem with the forehead panel poses an interesting case. Additional but highly fragmentary examples of this type of headdress were found among the Queens' Tombs, and the forehead ornament also appears on ivory sculptures of women that were

Figure 1.4 Detail of the queen from a relief showing King Ashurbanipal and his queen banqueting in the royal garden, the North Palace at Nineveh, first millennium BCE. British Museum, WA 124920. Photo: © Trustees of The British Museum.

produced in the Levant. Portraying fictive or quasi-divine, idealized, and often nude women, the ivories were imported from Syria or Phoenicia to Nimrud, where they decorated palace furniture and portable objects (Figure 1.5). Atalia or Yaba/Banitu, if of Levantine heritage, might have been buried with her maiden headgear. Alternatively, the diadem might be an Assyrian creation imitating ornaments depicted on the ivory figures. Perhaps the headdress was a diplomatic gift from a foreign court, or a Neo-Assyrian iteration of the second millennium BCE international style (emulated by goods from Tomb 45 at Ashur), which mixed elements of foreign and Mesopotamian artistic traditions.

Regardless of the origin of the headdress, aesthetics may explain why the wife of the Assyrian king would wear the same type of adornment as was depicted on foreign and nude ivory figures decorating objects such as equestrian gear and flywhisks. The full faces and curvaceous bodies of the ivory women would have expressed nourishment, health, and reproductive fertility to both Levantine and Assyrian viewers (Gansell 2009: 156–8). The distinctive forehead ornament may have served as a link between Assyrian queens and the

Figure 1.5 Levantine ivory head of a woman wearing a diadem, the Burnt Palace at Nimrud, first millennium BCE. H. 4.19 cm. The Metropolitan Museum of Art, Rogers Fund, 1954, 54.117.8. Photo: © The Metropolitan Museum of Art.

ideal forms and qualities embodied in the ivory sculptures. Reiterating the significance of the physical appearance of Assyrian queens, the name Yaba/Banitu literally means "attractive" or "well formed," and, in a text carved into palace architecture, King Sennacherib (r. 704–681 BCE) addressed his queen Tashmetum-sharrat as "beloved wife, whose features [the god] Belit-ili has made perfect above all women" (Galter et al. 1986: 32; Reade 1987: 141–2).

In general, the iconography of fruits and flowers on the headdresses from the Queens' Tombs at Nimrud evoke life and fecundity. Images of scorpions, a motif associated with women and reproductive fertility in Assyrian culture, also grace objects from the tombs (Ornan 2002). The prolific use of eyestones, especially on jewelry positioned over the vital sites of the throat and spine, indicates anxiety over women's vulnerability and implies their essential importance. Indeed, elite Neo-Assyrian women played vital reproductive roles in sustaining the royal lineage and, in the case of international marriages, reinforcing diplomatic ties between sovereigns.

Demonstrating their membership in the Assyrian court and implying their ideological inclusion in the affairs of the empire, other elements of the queens' adornment from Tomb II bear official, non-gendered iconography that was also depicted in large scale in the palace. Prominent among this imagery is a stylized tree, understood by scholars to represent the vitality of the empire. Finally, epitomizing the blending of feminine and official imagery, a Neo-Assyrian seal found in the tomb of an unidentified woman at Nimrud depicts a ritual scene of female figures playing pipes on either side of a stylized tree beneath an emblem of the state god (Mallowan 1966: 114). Although no seals were found in Tomb II, additional seals from the Queens' Tombs (Al-Gailani Werr 2008) demonstrate that, with royal and divine sanction, elite women of the palace acted as their own agents, strengthening and sustaining the international primacy of the Neo-Assyrian empire.

3 Summary and Conclusion

Although texts and images represent ancient Mesopotamian women far less frequently than they do men, and although women did not have independent access to political power, elite women nonetheless played crucial roles in the highest levels of society, and many appear to have had some degree of creative, cultic, and economic autonomy. The tombs presented here demonstrate the attention, protection, and wealth dedicated to diverse elite women. In some cases, inscriptions distinguish women by name and office (e.g., Enheduanna's position as high priestess and consort of the moon god Nanna), thus establishing their authority. Meanwhile, adornment illustrates female membership in the dominant elite while communicating rank, responsibility, and other aspects of social, cultural, and personal identity.

The iconography of jewelry and grave goods reflects broad cultural and ideological values. Across the case studies presented here, an abundance of floral and faunal imagery, as well as references to the goddess Inanna/Ishtar, probably evoke the role of women in the cycle of life and regeneration. Women's biological importance may also have been emblematic of agricultural productivity, images of which were ultimately stylized as Neo-Assyrian imperial iconography.

While elite women contributed to state and family lineages by producing heirs, women also legitimated and bonded dynasties through marriage and cultic participation. Texts and images record elite women as patrons of architecture and monuments, managers of personal estates, participants in public rituals, musicians, and priestesses of various ranks. Royal women could serve as regents and in some cases appear to have imparted influence over the politics of their husbands and sons. Less is known about non-elite women, but their lives were not necessarily parallel to those of elite women, whose privileges were most likely politically motivated.

Because a single essay cannot encapsulate three millennia of women's history, this one provides distinctive but complementary windows into the lives of elite women. A focus on tombs maintains consistency across time and geography as Mesopotamian civilization evolved from disparate city-states into a powerful empire. Although elite mortuary evidence presents idealized images of exceptional women, it also offers tangible contexts that were consciously constructed by the living according to established social codes and ideologies.

As demonstrated here, interdisciplinary methodologies are essential as we continue to restore ancient Mesopotamian women into the worlds in which they lived and to which they contributed. Ur, Ashur, and Nimrud remain only partially excavated and will likely yield new evidence, which could resolve many points of speculation (such as whether any Neo-Assyrian queens were buried with mural crowns). Casting a broader net, future initiatives would also benefit from integrating women's histories across social strata, sites, and cultures to build not only a more specific but also a more holistic picture of ancient reality.

RECOMMENDED FURTHER READING

Summaries (Harris 1992; Stol 1995), period surveys (Saporetti 1979; Albenda 1983; Asher-Greve 1985; Kuhrt 1989; Beaulieu 1993), and site-specific studies (Batto 1974; Grosz 1989) of Mesopotamian women are available. Pollock (1999) offers the only history of Mesopotamian civilization emphasizing gender, but its temporal scope is limited to between 5000 and 2100 BCE. Tetlow (2004) covers women's legal history from the third millennium to the first millennium BCE.

A number of studies on marriage, especially texts recording bridewealth and dowry, are available (Dalley 1980; Grosz 1983; Roth 1987, 1989, 1991; Westbrook 1987). Further investigations present the subjects of pregnancy, childbirth, motherhood, and family (Albenda 1987; Scurlock 1991; Roth 1994; Biggs 2000; Harris 2000; Stol 2000). Reflecting available evidence, scholarship on royal Mesopotamian women focuses on the first millennium BCE Neo-Assyrian period (Melville 2004) and the Ur III period of the late third millennium BCE (Weiershäuser 2010).

Outside of the home, women's diverse roles in the economy have been investigated (Veenhof 1972; van de Mieroop 1989; Meier 1991), with the female labor force of the third millennium BCE textile industry being especially well documented (Wright 2008). On prostitution see Assante (2003) and Cooper (2006). Women's participation in religion and in the temple hierarchy is presented in Fleming (1992), van der Toorn (1994), Collon (1999), Westenholz (2006), and Suter (2007). The cloistered second millennium BCE *naditu* priestesses receive specific attention (Stone 1982; Harris 1989), and Abusch (2002) and Sefati and Klein (2002) offer studies on female witches.

Since the 1990s, scholars have theorized Mesopotamian women in terms of gender and sexuality through feminist, psychoanalytic, postcolonial, and historiographic approaches (Asher-Greve 1997; Parpola and Whiting 2002; Bahrani 2003). Orientalism is probed by Bohrer (2003) and Halloway (2006). Asher-Greve (2006) provides a detailed historiography of the legendary Assyrian queen Semiramis, and Solvang (2006) discusses the so-called "harem." Also of contemporary interest, van der Toorn (1995) investigates the practice of female veiling.

For comprehensive bibliographies on Mesopotamian women refer to Asher-Greve and Wogec (2002) and Wilfong (1992), although these are not up to date.

2

Hidden Voices:
Unveiling Women in Ancient Egypt

Kasia Szpakowska

The problems encountered when attempting to reconstruct life in Ancient Egypt in a way that includes all members of society, rather than focusing on the most prominent or obvious actors, are much the same as for other cultures. The loudest voices tend to be heard, while those in the background are muted and stilled. To an extent, when looking to the past, we find what we are looking for, and investigations focusing on previously marginalized groups, such as women, children, the elderly, and foreigners, are allowing hidden lives to be revealed. In all cases, a nuanced view is required—one that avoids hasty generalizations. Work on gender studies emphasizes that there is no monolithic category of "women," a fact that has been well-discussed in relation to Egyptological studies (Meskell 1999). Temporal and geographical contexts must be borne in mind, as well as the status, ethnicity, class, wealth, and age of the individuals under study. There would be little in common between the experiences of an adolescent girl living in a small house in a planned settlement near the Fayum in Egypt of 1800 BCE and those of a royal wife of a Ramesside pharaoh living in the city of Memphis 1200 BCE. In all cases, the interpretations are based on the data that has survived the millennia. It is this evidence, specifically from Ancient Egypt prior to the Ptolemaic period, and the methods of approaching it that are the focus of this essay. The aim is to call attention to some of the specific complications that can be encountered, as well as to highlight some of the recent innovative approaches now underway in current studies on women in Ancient Egypt.

1   Textual Evidence

The range and number of surviving texts remain both helpful and hindering when trying to understand Ancient Egyptian women. They are indispensable for learning about aspects of life that are less visible in the archaeological record, particularly those that pertain to emotions or psychology such as dreams, fears, ambitions, and even love. However, our comprehension of the texts is hampered by their variable survival rate and incomplete state

A Companion to Women in the Ancient World, First Edition. Edited by Sharon L. James and Sheila Dillon.
© 2012 John Wiley & Sons, Ltd. Published 2015 by John Wiley & Sons, Ltd.

of preservation, as well as our limited understanding of the languages and scripts in which they were written. The grammar may be understood, but metaphors, figures of speech, idioms, and humor are always culturally bound, their meaning opaque to the outsider. Monumental texts have a better chance of survival over a wide area, but the bulk of the papyri and ostraka come from a handful of specialized sites that cannot necessarily be considered as typical. These pockets of evidence provide only snapshots of life in a particular place and time. In addition, those with a high level of literacy (able to compose and write) and those responsible for most written record-keeping formed a small segment of society: elite educated males, many of whom were members of the court or in the priesthood. The texts are inherently biased in terms of what they reveal about women of all classes and thus cannot be read at face value.

Textual evidence can be divided into two categories: literary and documentary. Pre-Ptolemaic literary genres include tales; didactic texts; hymns; poems (including love poetry); biographies; and royal, ritual, divinatory, and religious texts, while the documentary genres include decrees; lists; legal texts; spells; labels; correspondence; titles; and scientific, administrative, and medical texts, with of course much overlap. In all cases, the texts are formulaic, and they fit within the decorum of the time. Problems of interpretation are compounded by the fact that there are few known examples of biographies, didactic texts, or literary compositions written by women.

Broadly speaking, the literary texts tend to present a more idealized view of the world—their goal is not to reproduce reality but to present a model of society that is sanctioned by the state. When women are mentioned they conform to the conventional ideals of the time and in a capacity to further the aim of the author. When contemporary documentary texts are examined, however, a very different picture may emerge. For example, Middle Kingdom didactic (teaching) texts present themes that emphasize that the main place of women is in the home, as mothers, wives, and providers of pleasure, and men are advised to keep them from power, as the following text from the *Instructions of Ptahhotep* illustrates: "If you prosper, found your household, love your wife with ardor, fill her belly, clothe her back, ointment soothes her limbs. Gladden her heart as long as you live! She is a field, good for her lord ... keep her from power, restrain her."

But documentary evidence from letters, administrative texts, and scene captions reveals that in reality women held important positions outside the home as priestesses, temple workers, managers, and producers of linen—one of the most important commodities of the time. For example, in a letter from the Middle Kingdom town of Lahun, a woman writes (or dictates a letter) to the lord of the estate about weaving women who refuse to work, and offers an excuse that "there aren't any clothes, because my responsibility is directed to the temple—the threads have been set up, but cannot be woven!" The text here reveals a woman who does hold power, who supervises weaving women (who themselves have the confidence to refuse to work), and who holds a position of responsibility in the local temple. For the study of women, the most useful texts thus may be the administrative texts, titles, and letters. The surviving letters, whether or not they were actually scribed by women, are usually concerned with administrative matters. A number are written from women who are—at least temporarily and perhaps permanently— in charge of managing an estate or an aspect of production. Administrative texts such as attendance rolls and inventories can show where women worked, and in what capacity. New work on textual evidence applying linguistic methodologies is beginning to shed light on the previously hidden voice of women by reading between the lines. Deborah Sweeney, in particular, has been using discourse analysis to uncover the gender of the speaker in mourner's laments, correspondence, love poems, legal texts, and requests (Sweeney 2006).

Titles are important as well, for they are perhaps the most abundant source for the various positions women might have held. They are also found throughout the entire range of textual sources. It is particularly important, however, to keep both the date of the source and where it comes from in mind when analyzing the meaning or historical significance of any title. For example, a study of titles from the New Kingdom based on those found only in Theban tombs should not, without corroborating evidence, be over-generalized as indicative of titles that would have been held in the Delta or elsewhere in the land of Egypt. In addition, the decorated tombs generally belonged to elite men, or at least those employed in skilled crafts and labor. The titles included would be ones that they considered important or advantageous in the afterlife. Titles in general are the subject of debate, and it is often difficult to tell which were held simultaneously, which were held consecutively, which were honorific (ones awarded as a mark of esteem, status, or distinction), and which were earned. Nevertheless, these titles, which have been the subject of a number of careful analyses, have revealed the complexity and range of roles played by women in Ancient Egypt.

2   Representational Evidence

The art of Ancient Egypt has been the subject of so many museum exhibitions, books, and television documentaries, and has been reproduced so frequently, that most people, even young children, can easily recognize it. This recognizability, however, is problematic, for it makes the art of Egypt seem familiar and easily accessible, the images seemingly straightforward to interpret. Geographic, temporal, and social dimensions are often ignored, and Egyptian art is thought of as static and unchanging. Indeed, representations of a very small segment of the Ancient Egyptian populace tend to stand for Egyptian society as a whole. Representations of gender, however, must be interpreted within the larger context of Egyptian art: it is critical to why the art was produced and for whom. Formal Egyptian art was practical and performative—what was represented was believed to be enacted through the process of depiction, and therefore became real, destined to perpetually recur through time. We should understand this imagery as representing an idea rather than reflecting a reality. Created by elite male artists, formal art represents an ideal, a world in which men are tall, active, and powerful while women are slender and passive. Both men and women are generally represented as blemish-free and in their prime; their images conform to contemporary ideals of beauty and represent visually their subject's social status. Age, sickness, and non-conformity are rarely depicted; when they are, they generally mark subjects from the lower levels of society. In their formal, public art, Egyptians, not surprisingly, wanted to be remembered at their best and in a positive light.

Informal art, such as drawings and sketches found on ostraka (Figure 2.1), was not necessarily designed to be seen by anyone other than the artist, and often provides glimpses of Egyptian life that are strikingly at odds with the better-known formal representations. For example, while graphic scenes of sexual intercourse can be found on ostraka, such subject matter is only hinted at in formal art. In the temple of Hatshepsut, there is a scene that shows the god Amun taking Hatshepsut's mother by the hand, followed by a scene in which her pregnancy is discretely indicated by a small stomach bulge, and then finally we

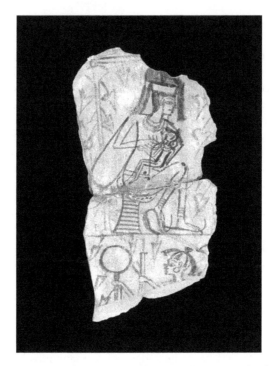

Figure 2.1 Limestone ostrakon of a woman suckling an infant. Note the shelter in which they sit, and the unusual hair and shoes. Below is another female (?) carrying a mirror and cosmetics. Photo: © Trustees of the British Museum.

see Hatshepsut's mother presenting her child to the gods. The mundane human details of sexual intercourse tend not to be represented.

Of course, the bulk of the images that we have to work with come not from informal drawings on ostraka but from stone buildings that have survived through the millennia— the temples and tombs, with the imagery from the latter in particular being used as a key source for gender analyses. Stone architecture, along with its decoration, was built by the Egyptians to last for eternity and to be visible in the world of the divine. The subject matter is therefore related to these aims. In the case of temples, this imagery mainly comprised scenes that depicted the pharaoh as protector of Egypt, administering justice and maintaining the cult of the gods. Women are portrayed as divine: as goddesses in their own right, as consorts of the main gods or the king, or as participants in the service of the cult, mainly as singers or musicians. Even when the main deity is female, however—such as at the New Kingdom temple of Mut in Karnak—the predominant actors in the cult are men. Because males are represented as cultic actors far more frequently and in a greater range of roles than women, women are often thought to have had a less important or more passive role, as background accompaniment to the main male agents in the ritual. However, another viable interpretation is that the music, song, gestures, or movements performed by the women were critical elements of the ritual, and just as necessary to its success as the proper recitation by priests.

Interpreting art from tombs is even more complex. Most tombs consist of a subterranean area reserved for the dead and the gods, and a superstructure or chapel where the living could visit and commemorate the memories of their dead friends and relatives.

Figure 2.2 Menna supervises agricultural work. Mural painting from the vestibule of the Tomb of Menna in Thebes, Egypt. Photo: © DeA Picture Library/Art Resource, NY.

Representations in each area must be analyzed with the intended audience in mind, and with the understanding that in most time periods the owners of decorated tombs were men. Men are thus presented as the main actors, the heroes, in their stories. Again, images of the elite are better known from this context, but closer attention to subsidiary detail in many scenes, especially those placed in the chapel area, reveals the presence of women. In the tomb of Menna (see Figure 2.2), for example, a busy agricultural scene includes a depiction of girls playing (or fighting), another of one girl tending to the foot of another, and a woman carrying a basket. In the background, there is yet another woman seated with her legs out, ankles crossed, and a child on her lap, held tight by a cloth sling. As the woman picks figs from a tree, the child reaches up to play with the woman's earring. The scene is rare, but the fact that it is included means such an image conforms to the Egyptian vision of an ideal world. It is probably not meant to represent a particular woman (she remains unnamed), but it likely represents an event that actually did occur and could regularly be seen. From this image, one could reasonably suggest that women did pick figs, and that this was an activity that could be undertaken even while minding a child. Whether the woman is actually the mother of the child is unclear, and because of the high rate of maternal mortality the care of children would often fall to a host of relatives, nurses, and men. An image such as this belies the stereotype that women worked only indoors in Egypt, and it reveals the presence of children at many activities. Interestingly, this image is not unique, for it also appears a few centuries later in a Late Period tomb.

Finally, it must be remembered that representations are encoded with symbols that are culturally embedded, and not necessarily transferable. Understanding the Ancient Egyptian codes often requires a deeper familiarity that is not possible without material witnesses. Clothing in particular (and the lack thereof) is useful in all cultures to convey specific messages. In Egyptian art, nakedness has been interpreted as representing lower classes, divinity, real practice, youth, or overt sexuality. Here again, interpretations vary and are not necessarily consistent. It has been suggested that women are shown with erect nipples to emphasize their sexuality, but the same interpretation is not applied to contemporary images of bare-chested men. Tattoos, mirrors, hair, mandrakes, lotuses, and monkeys are just a few of the items used in artwork to convey a particular message that was focused and clear to the audience of the time. Decoding that meaning today, however, is difficult, especially for those signs and symbols found repeatedly in Egyptian art but that have yet to be the subject of rigorous and systematic study. Indeed, traditional interpretations of commonly represented objects and symbols are particularly hard to overturn. A case in point is the "cone" that frequently appears on the head of the deceased and other individuals in New Kingdom tomb scenes. For years this object was interpreted as representing perfume or unguent, or a cone of wax or fat. However, a recent systematic study (Padgham 2008), based on the analysis of over 1000 scenes in over 100 New Kingdom tombs, suggests instead that the cone on the head of the male tomb owner was a symbol related to cult offerings. This research could provide a model and a basis for further studies investigating the same symbol on the heads of women. Understanding such ubiquitous icons is an important step to understanding what was being depicted in these highly codified representations.

Clothing, hair, and adornments can also signify a specific role rather than being related to gender. On certain temple walls and columns, Hatshepsut, one of Egypt's female pharaohs, was portrayed wearing a kilt, false beard, and crown—in other words the same clothing that was worn by a male pharaoh. This has led some to describe her as a cross-dresser pretending to be a man. This attire does not symbolize maleness, however: it is royal regalia worn by a pharaoh as the living embodiment of the god Horus. In a similar fashion, when female barristers in the UK wear the same powdered wigs and robes as male barristers, they are not cross-dressing or pretending to be men—rather, they are donning the distinctive garb associated with that specific office, a costume that both masks their individuality and marks them as different from non-barristers.

Finally, conservatism reigns supreme in formal art. Goddesses, for example, are depicted through the millennia wearing the same type of dress they had always worn since the Old Kingdom. Conventions of representation also developed that codified what should and should not be depicted, and these sometimes changed over time. For example, while Old Kingdom figures do show women making pottery, men were more typically involved in crafts such as pottery making in tomb reliefs; indeed, female potters seem to drop out of the artistic record after the Old Kingdom. One should not assume from this that women only engaged in pottery making during the Old Kingdom, but rather that the conventions of representation changed, particularly in scenes of production centers. Women surely continued to make pots, but were simply not shown doing so.

3   Three-Dimensional Finds

For the purposes of this discussion, the archaeological finds will be divided into two categories: objects created and used by humans, and the human remains themselves. The main three interpretive problems that arise when attempting to deal with objects revolve around determining their function, their makers, and their users. Stereotypes abound—kohl (black or green eyeliner) continues to be associated with women, yet all evidence shows that it was used as much by men as women. When jewelry is found, it is assumed to have belonged to a woman, though few studies have actually been done to correlate specific artifacts with a specific gender; and again, such studies would need to be temporally and geographically bound (see also Liston, this volume, Chapter 9).

Anthropoid figurines are notoriously difficult to interpret in any context, and those that have been classified as female are a good example of the problems that can arise through hasty generalizations and oversimplification. This is the case not only for Egyptian figurines but also for prehistoric ones found elsewhere. Gimbutas used objects that she termed "Venus figurines" as evidence of near-universal goddess worship in the prehistoric world (see Talalay, this volume, Case Study I). More recent studies of this material (particularly by Beck 2000) show that no clear criteria were applied by Gimbutas in determining which artifacts would be included in the Venus group. Many of the figures, in fact, are androgynous in appearance, while others are clearly male. The time range was also vast, ranging from 32,000–9000 BP (before the present).

The same situation applies to anthropoid figurines from Ancient Egypt. The assignment of gender has not been based on clearly defined criteria. In general, figures that appear to have breasts or have their pelvic region emphasized are labeled as female, while those that have no breasts or have a phallus are labeled as male. Figures that have no distinguishing gender markers, however, are also labeled as male. Figurines that are large around the belly are variously described as fat, or pregnant, or full-bodied, too often without an explicit reason given. Those labeled female (the male or ambiguous figurines have not yet been the subject of serious investigation) are often lumped together as a cohesive group, regardless of differences in material, features, or context, and associated with sexuality, divinities, or fertility. Only more recently have they been studied as ritual objects (Figure 2.3), as scholars such as Pinch (1993) and Waraksa (2008, 2009) have

Figure 2.3 Wooden female figure, probably Middle Kingdom. Photo: Courtesy of Egypt Centre, Swansea University, Wales.

begun to analyze them more carefully, with rigorous attention to distinguishing characteristics, find-spots, and material. The initial step of establishing a strict typology is tedious, but it must be performed in order to ensure that subsequent analyses, arguments, and interpretations are based on valid premises. We know little about the identity of either the makers or the users of these objects.

New technologies now allow us to explore the surviving finds more thoroughly than in the past, and more attention is being paid to ordinary "things." Smith (2003) has recently demonstrated how analysis of vessel shapes (for storage, service, and cooking), coupled with residue and faunal analysis, can provide insights into the type of cuisine consumed by the residents of an Egyptian fortress at Askut during the Middle and New Kingdom periods. He notes that foodways are often the last bastion for the transmission and retention of ethnicity, identity, and cultural traditions. At Askut, for example, the preliminary scenario that is suggested is that of an increase in the adoption of the local Nubian diet over time, perhaps introduced by servants or women of Nubian origin. Through these mundane pots, the influence of women can thus perhaps be unveiled in ways not previously considered.

Human remains are another resource of information that has been poorly treated, at least until the last few decades (see Liston, this volume, Chapter 9). Few statistics were kept as to the sex and gender of burials uncovered in mortuary sites; more importantly, any distinction that was made seems to have been based on less-than-objective reasoning. For example, once it had been decided that daggers appear more often in male burials, any burial with a dagger was identified as male, without corroboration from the physical remains. Age, as well, can be difficult to assign, a problem exacerbated by the profusion of ill-defined terms that have been used in publications to describe burial contents (e.g., infant, neonate, toddler, child, adolescent, girl, boy, woman, man, adult, old man, old woman). All these terms are relative, and it is only recently that scholars such as Baker et al. (2005) have attempted to ensure consistency in their use, or at least to be clear about what is meant by each term within the context of a specific excavation.

Assumptions related to biology are still cited as fact without having been supported by enough biological data. A case in point is the issue of menstruation. It is still stated that girls in Ancient Egypt would have been married and have begun bearing children by between the young ages of eleven to fourteen. Yet recent research shows that the onset of early menarche depends upon good nutrition, health, and body fat. Even in a single country, the age can be very young in privileged populations (even nine or ten), while menstruation might be staved off until fourteen to seventeen for girls brought up in poorer environments. Recent forensic studies of human remains at sites such as Amarna show a relatively unhealthy population—a finding that should affect our understanding of the maturation of adolescents in Ancient Egypt and in consequence the lives of women. In such areas, we may need to revise the usual scenario in which girls marry and start their child-bearing years early, continue to have children frequently, and produce large families. Higher rates of infant (and maternal) mortality are also associated with poor nutrition, and, again, forensic evidence at some sites has revealed that there may be trends from the Predynastic Period, where women had wider hips, to the New Kingdom, where the pelvic width narrowed, potentially causing further problems in successfully giving birth. Not enough data has been gathered from the mortuary evidence to know whether this was a trend throughout Egypt or whether those sites from which we have data were atypical.

Nevertheless, the often-neglected mortuary data is an important means from which to learn more about women in Ancient Egypt. The types of wear that are found on the bones, as well as muscle and tendon insertions, can, aside from revealing the quality of health and nutrition, reveal the stress of repetitive tasks. These can be matched to the known physical toll of certain activities. Work in cemeteries at Abydos (Baker 1997) reveals that skeletal malformations associated with repeated heavy lifting and physical labor were found in male and female skeletons of all social ranks. This suggests that gender differentiation in terms of work was perhaps not as strict as is suggested by visual representations. Forensic analyses can also be applied together with task analyses, such as that undertaken by Sweeney (2006) on older women in Deir el-Medina, in order to determine the kinds of activities that certain population segments may have been engaged in. These studies focus on analyzing activities according to task stage and try to determine the requirements to complete a task. These requirements comprise things such as knowledge and skill, as well as equipment, fine motor skills, and good eyesight.

4   Architecture and Space

The delineation of space within Egyptian architecture is the final evidence to be considered here. The woman's role within the domestic units in settlements must have been conspicuous. One of the most common titles in all times and places is "Lady of the House," which implies the management of the home and servants, whether it be a small household or a large estate that encompassed business, trade, and personal areas. This role is known through textual evidence but is far less visible in the actual archaeological remains. The question of the function of and areas of activity within dwellings is a subject of some discussion in other ancient cultures, and is beginning to be investigated in relation to Ancient Egypt (see also Trümper, this volume, Chapter 21).

Ethnographic evidence, which can be useful, is often cited in reconstructions. Seeing how other cultures deal with similar environmental conditions, such as heat, lack of rain, and relatively little change of hours of daylight throughout the year, can provide useful models to explore. The use of modern ethnographic analogy can also be risky, particularly when the cultures seem to be markedly different in terms of fundamental religious practices and mores. A case in point is the use of practices in modern-day Egypt to inform us about life in Ancient Egypt. In some respects this comparison can be quite useful, particularly to suggest possible scenarios related to technology, materials, and their production. However, it is clear that the precepts of Islam are fundamentally different from those of the Ancient Egyptian religion, particularly in terms of interpersonal relationships as well as interactions with the divine world and the environment, and therefore extreme care is needed when making such comparisons.

Using modern European traditions can be even more misleading. For example, in many cultures, sleeping quarters are typically located in more private locations within the house and are often situated so that they are sheltered from the wind. This seems to have been the case for Ancient Egyptian houses as well, and in some interior rooms there is sometimes remains of a platform upon which matting could have been placed to be used as a bed. But there is little evidence for specific sleeping arrangements, and we do not know whether women or children had separate rooms, or whether a wife regularly slept with her husband or they slept separately. Despite this lack of evidence, the segregation of women's quarters is often asserted even in studies of modest town dwellings. And, on ground plans of larger houses such as villas, various areas are often identified as "the master's quarters," "the wife's room," and "the harem," without further explanation.

In other types of settlements, the presence of women (as well as children, the elderly, and the sick) within the community has barely begun to be studied. The voices of men and elites resonate in the textual evidence from forts, administrative and military installations, quarries, and trading outposts at Egypt's boundaries. But closer examination of the small finds and architectural features can provide evidence of the domestic life within the residential quarters. At Askut, for example (see Smith 2003), the application of anthropological theory to the archaeology can show how foodways and religious practices provide visible expressions of ethnicity, revealing intermarriage and interaction between the local and temporary inhabitants. Rather than visualizing these areas as inhabited only by Egyptian men, models can be modified to allow for a more inclusive picture of these settlements as organic communities, populated with men, women, and children as well as the healthy, the sick, and the aging.

In religious spaces—whether large temple complexes such as that of Karnak, smaller chapels in forts and settlements, or those demarcated simply by the presence of a sacred cult figurine in a domestic context—the active role of women is indicated, but there is room for further investigation. The few monographs devoted to the study of the clergy in Ancient Egypt focus on the role of male priests in temples, with women only briefly mentioned as singers, dancers, musicians, and observers. This division of roles is based chiefly on the privileging of formal texts, hymns, and the few rituals engraved on temple walls. Temporal studies of religious titles in more fragmentary and administrative evidence show a more complex picture that shifts in terms of religious duties over time. For example, the title "priestess of Hathor" was prominent on statues and stelai during the Old Kingdom, while in the Middle Kingdom the titles are those of the priestess and high priest of a larger number of deities (both male and female), such as Amun, Khonsu, Pakhet, Neith, or Hathor. Unlike the title of ordinary "priest" (*wab*), the title of "high priest" (*hem-netjer*) in Ancient Egyptian was gender-neutral, and did not usually show the feminine ending "t." Thus, the only way to tell the gender of the bearer is by the name of the individual and the pronoun. There is no evidence to suggest that this specific title was honorific in Ancient Egypt, so texts that relate the duties of high priests should not necessarily be treated as speaking about men only, particularly if these texts were composed in a period when female high priests were certainly known.

Representations of female musicians and dancers abound in temples, and female musicians and dancers are mentioned in administrative texts and titles. In New Kingdom Egypt, it is now known that the role of the chantress was central to many ritual acts. These women are depicted in tombs and on temple walls, and are recognizable by their titles or the musical instruments that they carry (the sistrum, an instrument that would be shaken to create a rattling sound, is the most popular). However, their role is often considered passive and secondary. It may be, however, that, along with gestures and words recited by the priest, the sounds the chantresses produced with their voices and instruments were critical for successful fulfillment of the ritual. This is where spatial reconstructions may be particularly valuable. Visualization laboratories (such as those at the University of California, Los Angeles) have been conducting work on virtual reconstructions of sacred spaces in ancient cultures that include not only three-dimensional renderings but also sonification. For rituals in which sound was important, places with specific resonant characteristics such as caves and grottos were selected. Man-made sacred spaces were also designed to enhance these critical ritual elements. The importance of processions in Ancient Egyptian rituals has been acknowledged, but sound has not yet been explored—in part because there are few structures where the roofs have survived.

Nevertheless, churches, temples, chapels, and shrines were clearly designed in such a way as to enhance the source of the important sound in specific areas.

In the case of chapels and votive zones, the gender of the main agents is even less obvious. The structure of smaller chapels was modeled on those of larger temples. Some chapels at Deir el-Medina include benches, a few of which have inscribed names (all male), but interpreting these is difficult. The simplest explanation is that they demarcated areas reserved for the individuals named. But they could also have allocated spaces reserved for the household of the individual named, which would include women, children, and the elderly. Other sacred areas are recognized by the deposits of what has been interpreted as votive figurines. Sacred deposits dedicated to Hathor are prevalent throughout Egypt, and feature a range of objects such as female figurines, phalluses, models of cows, ostraka with sketches, textiles, and faience beads. Women are sometimes assumed to have dedicated these objects, but this is uncertain.

The recent discovery of a trove of over 500 votive stelai and about fifty figurines in a tomb at Asyut, in Middle Egypt (DuQuesne 2007), provides indisputable evidence of the active role of women in a cult of the New Kingdom up to the Third Intermediate Period. These stelai were made of the usual materials, such as limestone, sandstone, and alabaster, but also clay—a material not usually associated with stelai. While many have inscriptions (epithets of the deity they honor, the name of the donor, hymns, prayers, and offering formulae), others are decorated only with images. The stelai are dedicated primarily to the gods Wepwawet and Anubis, whose cult was prominent in that area from the time of the Middle Kingdom. Other gods such as Hathor of Medjed (the consort of Wepwawet), Amun-Re, Osiris-Khentyamentiu, Reshep, Ptah, Taweret, Sobek, Hathor, Harsaphes, and Re-Harakhty also appear. The titles and material reflect a range of class levels from the elite to the lowly. Both men and women are represented. A number of the women seem to have no affiliation with any man, and therefore can be considered to have acted independently.

Some of the clay stelai have holes in the top, so they may have been hung either in the tomb or in a household shrine. The latter were common sacred spaces found in the everyday dwelling places of the Egyptians, and it is here that the presence of women can be attested most firmly. Architectural remains from towns such as Amarna, Deir el-Medina, Elephantine, Lahun, and Tell ed-Daba reveal that religious emplacements, furnishings, libation basins, and altars were a common feature of many houses, and are found in the large estates of the elite as well as the modest houses of workers.

In the New Kingdom, stepped platforms made of stone and mud brick (Figure 2.4), which have been interpreted as altars, were integrated as architectural features into the front room of some of the larger houses in Deir el-Medina (Koltsida 2006). These features are an example of the problems that can arise when attempting to distinguish gender roles in the use of space. When these elevated structures were first discovered, they were called by the excavator "*lit clos*" (closed or elevated bed). This name led to their identification as special beds for conception or as birthing areas. The arguments for associating these platforms with women have also relied on their decoration. A small number of them included preserved pieces of colored plaster featuring the god Bes, a protective deity often found in domestic contexts and sometimes associated with the safekeeping of women and children in particular. Other plaster fragments feature a dancing woman, or a man in a reed boat, or the legs of a woman kneeling. At the bottom of one platform is preserved the feet of a seated woman, behind which are a pair of dark feet. In front of this seated woman are two additional pairs of feet, behind which is a

Figure 2.4 Elevated platform in a house in New Kingdom Deir el-Medina. Photo: Courtesy of Kenneth Griffin.

convolvulus vine. In some ways this scene is similar to two other ostraka that more clearly show a woman breast-feeding an infant (Figure 2.1); this similarity has led to interpretations of the elevated brick structure as the setting for childbirth or sex, or as the main bed (see Koltsida 2006 for more detailed discussion). But such functions are highly unlikely: in nearly all cases, the platforms are located in a very public space, at the very front of the house and close to exterior doors, so that anyone entering the house would have had to pass by them.

Current interpretations now recognize that the Deir el-Medina structures were likely mainly used as altars or cultic spaces. Such a use does not, of course, preclude the presence of women. While the nature of the rituals carried out at these structures is unclear, other evidence suggests that women played an active role in domestic cults. Small shrines or niches have been found embedded in walls or columns in a range of houses. Some of these would have accommodated busts of generic individuals (called "ancestor busts") or stelai dedicated to the dead ("ancestor stelai"). Other shrines and niches were dedicated to deities whose cult is usually associated with larger temples, such as Amun, Ptah, Hathor, Thoth, and Min. Deities whose presence was rare in the temple sphere, such as Bes, Taweret, Meretseger, Shed, and Renenutet, were also accommodated in these domestic installations, as were gods such as Reshep, Qadesh, and Astarte, whose origins lay outside of Egypt. These artifacts have been found in various rooms of the house, including the kitchen; many were likely placed within the niches, shrines, and altars and served as the focus of domestic worship and prayer. It is unusual to find accompanying texts or illustrations depicting both the finds and actual rites, and even more unusual to find the practitioner named, but at Deir el-Medina just such a discovery was made. A small stele was found (Figure 2.5) depicting a woman pouring libations before an ancestor bust. The text

Figure 2.5   After Auguste Mariette (1869–1880). *Abydos: Description des fouilles exécutées sur l'emplacement de cette ville. Ouvrage publié sous les auspices S.A. Ismail-Pacha* (Paris) v. 2, pl. 60.

below the image reads: "Performed by the Lady of the Estate, Irer," and provides incontrovertible evidence for the role women played in the religious life of the community.

RECOMMENDED FURTHER READING

For problems in interpreting gender in material culture in general, see Beck (2000) and Meskell (1999). Robins (1993), Toivari-Viitala (2001), and Szpakowska (2008) provide general overviews. For examples of new scholarship applying a range of methodologies to uncover previously unexplored issues related to women in Ancient Egypt, see Troy (1986), Smith (2003), Asher-Greve and Sweeney (2006), Koltsida (2006), Sweeney (2006), and Graves-Brown (2008). Studies of women and religion in Egypt include Pinch (1993), DuQuesne (2007), Lesko (2008), Waraksa (2008, 2009), Ayad (2009), and Stevens (2009). Baker (1997), Baker et al. (2005), and Richards (2005) examine mortuary evidence. For museum catalogs, see Capel and Markoe (1996) and Wilfong (1997).

3

Looking for Minoan and Mycenaean Women: Paths of Feminist Scholarship Towards the Aegean Bronze Age

Marianna Nikolaïdou

Three distinct but interrelated cultures developed around the Aegean Sea during the Bronze Age, which spanned the third and second millennia BCE: Minoan, centered on the island of Crete; Mycenaean, centered on mainland Greece; and Cycladic, centered on the islands of the Cyclades (Cullen 2001). The geographical landscapes and cultural trajectories of the region were highly diverse, and different ethnic groups interacted and/or coexisted, as indeed was the case all across the eastern Mediterranean and the Near East at the time (see contributions in Laffineur and Greco 2005; Aruz et al. 2008). Settlement patterns and social developments differed over space and time, encompassing rural communities bonded through kinship; chiefdoms; stratified palatial states; towns evolving prior to, alongside, and long after the collapse of palatial systems; and sites with specialized functions (such as ports, sanctuaries, rural farms, dams, fortifications, and industrial installations). The spectrum of cultural accomplishments included prosperous farming economies; thriving trade and seafaring; politics and diplomacy; military skill and warfare; literacy and bureaucratic administration; advanced technologies and crafts; sophisticated art; and elaborate religion and ritual. Long-term occupation of important sites across the region, including the palatial centers themselves, attests to the special power of these places (cf. Haggis 1993; Day and Wilson 2002), as does the use of their cemeteries over many generations. The links of people to their territory would have been felt on economic, social, ritual, and emotional levels alike. In this variegated world a range of roles and related symbolisms—evident in the imagery, paleoenvironment, and material culture of the period—can be inferred for Aegean women (see contributions in Kopaka 2009b).

Starting with the pioneering article of Lucia Nixon (1983), archaeologists working on the Aegean Bronze Age have increasingly developed feminist and gender-sensitive approaches. Scholarly publications and academic courses devoted to the topic (see reviews and collected references in Alexandri 1994, 2009; Kopaka 2009b: xvii–xxviii; Nikolaïdou and Kokkinidou 2007: 44) have proliferated, as have museum exhibits and

A Companion to Women in the Ancient World, First Edition. Edited by Sharon L. James and Sheila Dillon.
© 2012 John Wiley & Sons, Ltd. Published 2015 by John Wiley & Sons, Ltd.

outreach programs. These advances have gone a long way to correct problems of theory and method that had dominated many decades of scholarship: a focus on iconography at the expense of archaeological context, along with simplistic equations of imagery with social reality; anachronistic projections from later periods in Greek antiquity, with exaggerated emphasis on the female roles in religion, myth, and ritual; and outdated notions of matriarchy and matrocentrism, which developed in binary opposition to patriarchal paradigms of the past. Equally important are the scientific and experimental analyses that have shed light on important and hitherto unknown aspects of material and social existence (see especially contributions in Foster and Laffineur 2003, as well as Laffineur and Betancourt 1997).

This essay reviews "gendered" archaeologies of Minoan and Mycenaean women, to demonstrate that a rigorous and theoretically informed focus on women helps us reweave the fabric of ancient societies at large (cf. Barber 1994; Adovasio et al. 2007). Feminist study in Aegean archaeology has been evolving as a three-fold endeavor (discussion and references in Kokkinidou and Nikolaïdou 2009). The first goal is to "resurrect" Aegean women from oblivion and to correct misconceptions caused by a long tradition of androcentric paradigms. The next significant step is to appreciate the varied manifestations of ancient gender, beyond modern stereotypes of "femininity" and "masculinity," age, or ethnicity. Women cannot be studied as a separate segment of society or an afterthought in scholarship. The ultimate aim is to "people" the Aegean Bronze Age societies—to understand them as communities with human faces (cf. Tringham 1991; Nikolaïdou 2002), with individuality and many layers of identity including, but not restricted to, gendered perceptions and behaviors.

In what follows, I will flesh out some of the many roles of women in the prehistoric Aegean. The richness and complexity of the topic far exceed the scope of this essay, however, so my discussion merely touches upon some important areas of analysis, including architecture and spatial organization; subsistence and craft; burial practices; fertility and health; costume and appearance; artistic representation of religious symbolism and of ritual behavior.

It is useful at the outset to place our understanding of women within the wider epistemological context of Aegean scholarship (reviewed in Nikolaïdou and Kokkinidou 1998). Over the course of almost 150 years the discipline has proceeded from an "epic" view of the Bronze Age as the archaeological verification of Homer (and, by extent, as a prelude to Greek antiquity) to a strong interest in historical "objectivity" (to be gained through "scientific" testing of material data instead of reliance on literary testimony) and then to critical reflections that challenge the paradigms of objectivity and of a single archaeological "truth." In the earliest, "heroic," models, women were cast in roles familiar from Greek epic and mythology, along the lines of cross-cultural syncretism: goddesses, queens, mothers of heroes, slaves—with male political supremacy taken for granted.

In its turn, the positivist spirit of New Archaeology and Marxism, from the 1950s onward, opted for "infrastructural" questions of subsistence and productive relations at the expense of "epiphenomena," such as gender, that have social and symbolic ramifications. Again, men were assumed to be the prime motivating forces and agents of cultural process—whether in politics or production—while women were relegated to the sphere of religion, an area of minor research importance at the time. Thus, a polarizing association of women with nature/religion and men with culture/society was uncritically adopted across different schools of thought, and persisted well after feminism had entered other related fields of the humanities, mainly anthropology and classics. It was only with the advance of "postprocessual" archaeologies after the 1980s that archaeologists started to refocus attention on hitherto "invisible" and ignored people and processes (cf. Moore and Scott 1997), including women and gender. The selective, symbolically filtered imagery of the female body, both in its biological and cultural qualities, encodes key concepts about Bronze Age women. And on this embodiment of identities and ideas the following discussion will focus.

1   Ladies, Queens, Leaders: "Gendering Authority"

The early decades of Aegean archaeology were stamped with the larger-than-life person-alities of Heinrich Schliemann and Arthur Evans, and the "mythographies" of their groundbreaking discoveries at Troy and Mycenae and at Knossos (for critical re-evalua-tions, see contributions in Hamilakis 2002, Darcque et al. 2006, and Morris and Laffineur 2007). Schliemann breathed epic life into his findings, among which was the famous "Priam's Treasure," a hoard of gold jewelry that was showcased by the young and beautiful Mrs. Schliemann in the fashion of the splendidly adorned goddesses and queens described by Homer. In reality these artifacts date to the Early Bronze Age (third millennium), about a thousand years earlier than the city that has been identified as Homeric Troy (Korfmann 2006).

For his part, Arthur Evans envisioned an idealized life at Bronze Age Knossos, inhabited by peaceful, art-loving, and reverent people under the leadership of King Minos, the legendary lawgiver and priest-king, under the auspices of the Great Goddess. The voluminous publication of the *Palace of Minos* (Evans 1964), together with extensive concrete restorations at Knossos, crystallized Evans' "ecstatic vision" (Zois 1996) into scholarly dogma as a perfect outlet for the escapist and romantic yearnings of his own European world (Bintliff 1984; MacGillivray 2000; Hamilakis and Momigliano 2006). Evans' Minoan universe was permeated by femininity, elegance, and sophistication, and visualized in the daring reconstructions and evocative labeling of frescoes depicting females (Hitchcock and Koudounaris 2002; Papadopoulos 2005b): "Ladies in Blue," "La Parisienne," and "Court ladies and their beaux" acquired a life as creations of the archaeologist's imagination in the twentieth century (cf. Nikolaïdou and Kokkinidou 2007). Prominently demonstrated in the galleries of the Herakleion Museum, and abundantly reproduced in scholarly publications, mainstream literature, and a thriving industry of tourist paraphernalia and even forgeries, "Minoan ladies" have become "cult" symbols in both the prehistoric past and the present (cf. Lapatin 2002; Simandiraki 2005; Morris 2009).

The perceptive reader today will see through an unsettling discrepancy in this narrative about Aegean femininity: while purporting to acknowledge female authority and celebrate a liberal life of women in the prehistoric past, the narrative subjected women to upper-class European conventions of decorum and social order. For example, Evans postulated a spouse for the King of Knossos and installed her in the "Queen's Megaron" (Evans 1964: III, 354–90), a set of rooms in the East Wing of the palace, identical in plan but less grandiose and more secluded than the complex he recognized as the king's suite (Evans 1964: III, 318–48; see critical discussion in Zois 1996). Evans' identification was based largely on two frescoes from the area. One is a fresco of dolphins, a subject that he deemed elegant and appropriate for the chamber of a lady; this fresco actually belonged to a floor

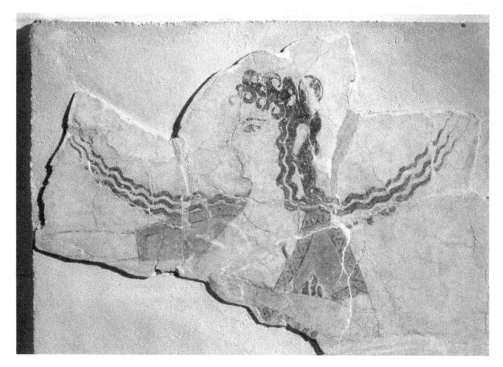

Figure 3.1 "Dancer" fresco from the "Queen's Megaron," Knossos palace. Late Minoan II—Mycenean, fifteenth century BCE. Crete, Herakleion Archaeological Museum. Photo: Nimatallah/Art Resource, NY.

decoration from the upper storey, unrelated to the "Megaron" itself (Niemeier 1987). The other fresco is the fragmentary head and torso of a woman in vivid movement, which Evans interpreted as a "dancer" (Figure 3.1). This image has been persuasively reinterpreted as instead taking the "position of command," a characteristic posture of imposing figures standing or hovering with one hand outstretched. It is an iconographic formula for representing figures in authority, female and male, in a variety of contexts that involve persons of different age and appearance, groups and isolated figures, or transcendental and "real-life" settings (Davis 1995).

Variations in the imagery built around this formula (i.e., the "position of command") indicate that leadership and authority in Aegean societies took complex and nuanced expressions rather than conforming to an explicit and standardized ruler iconography, such as is known from contemporary Egypt and the Near East (Davis 1995). It seems that there existed parallel, complementary authorities worthy of respect and visual celebration (cf. Marinatos 1993; Koehl 1995), not only in Crete but also among the Mycenaeans. The Linear B texts found in Mycenaean palatial archives (fifteenth to the thirteenth centuries BCE) record both a hierarchy of male officials headed by the *wanax* (king), and high-profile women whose role is more difficult to define. It is especially difficult to define the role of the mysterious *Potnia*, a term designating a female personage or personages in high power, who could have been deities, queens, priestesses, or a combination thereof (see especially Kopaka 2001). A recent volume of collected papers devoted to the topic (Laffineur and Hägg 2001) illuminates meaningful ambiguities surrounding the title and the personae associated with it, pointing especially to a confluence between political and spiritual authority—quite different from the Western concept of separation between "church" and "state."

2 Women, Religion, Power: Ritual Experts and Cultural Facilitators

Authority and rank in Aegean societies have too often been uncritically equated with vertical hierarchy and political complexity (Renfrew 1972; Cherry 1984; contributions in Hägg and Marinatos 1987; but see alternative scenarios in Laffineur and Niemeier 1995; Rehak 1995; and Galaty and Parkinson 2007). It is important, however, to keep in mind that power involves not only hierarchical authority—"power over"—but also esoteric power, or "power to" (Miller and Tilley 1984: 5), which is linked to knowledge, values, ritual expertise, and symbolic representation. Cultural aspects of masculinity, femininity, childhood, or "otherness" are integral elements in the web of power relations (e.g., Moore 1988; Conkey 1991; di Leonardo 1991; Kopaka 2009a), which finds complex expressions in religion and symbolism. Far from passively reflecting social reality, spiritual and ritual behaviors can shape cultural attitudes, support or subvert an established order, and interfere with strategies of domination and resistance (cf. Turner 1974; Bell 1992; see contributions in Kyriakidis 2007). This is especially the case in traditional and ancient societies organized around cyclical concepts of life, where rituals punctuate the periodicity of material and social reproduction and the leadership of spiritual "facilitators" is deemed crucial to the welfare of the community (Eliade 1959; Rowlands 1993). It is within this framework that we can best understand the well-documented prominence of Aegean women in the area of religion and ritual.

The worship of a goddess or goddesses with multiple qualities constituted a major aspect of religion throughout the Aegean Bronze Age, variously manifested in elite, urban, domestic, and rural cults/ceremonies of public and private character alike (Goodison and Morris 1998a; Laffineur and Hägg 2001). In these contexts women figure as deities, adorants, officiating priestesses, and ritual performers, in a variety of media (Marinatos 1984, 1993; Verlinden 1984; Goodison 1989; Pilali-Papasteriou 1989; German 2005; Alexandri 2009). Connotations of prestige and authority abound, for example in the scenes of divine females in the "position of command" or seated and receiving adoration.

Linear B documents from the Mycenaean palatial archives indicate that priestesses enjoyed economic and administrative privileges, and performed an important range of civic and spiritual functions (Kopaka 1997). The prestigious, even royal, status of sacerdotal women is most strikingly documented in the lavish female burial from Tholos A in Archanes, where the occupant—splendidly dressed and furnished with luxury items, including several gold signet rings—received an extravagant (and symbolically powerful) sacrifice of horses and bulls. Women performing funerary sacrifices are depicted on the contemporary limestone sarcophagus from Ayia Triada in Crete (Long 1974), while richly attired women involved in ritual acts are depicted on frescoes from the palaces of Mycenae, Tiryns, and Thebes (Kritseli-Providi 1982; Demakopoulou 1988). Notwithstanding the significant evidence on the religious roles of males as well (Marinatos 1984, 1993; Warren 1988; Koehl 1995), the ritual exaltation of women constitutes a long-standing tradition with important cultural implications.

Figure 3.2   "Lady of Phylakopi," terracotta figurine from Melos. Mycenean, fourteenth century BCE. Melos, Archaeological Museum of Plaka. Photo: Erich Lessing/Art Resource, NY.

The so-called Lady of Phylakopi (Figure 3.2) was produced in the context of household and town cults that are best attested archaeologically from the fourteenth century BCE onward (Gesell 1985). This is a large clay idol from the Mycenaean communal sanctuary at Phylakopi in Melos. The Phylakopi "lady" once stood in a niche, a focal point for ritual, in a double shrine that she shared with a male deity (?) represented by a large ithyphallic figure (Renfrew 1985). Her hands, now missing, would have been raised in the characteristic gesture of the "goddess with upraised arms," a widespread iconographic convention for representing female figures of the later Bronze Age that signifies blessing, reverence, or benign authority (Alexiou 1958; Gesell 1985).

Other well-known examples in this tradition include figures from late Minoan shrines at the palace of Knossos and the settlements at Gazi and Karphi, and the long series of the Mycenaen Psi figurines, including the important assemblage from the Lower Akropolis in Tiryns (illustrations in Demakopoulou 1988). The key stylistic features shared, albeit in regional variations, by all these figures are beautifully showcased in the "lady." First, there is differential treatment between the lower and upper part of the body, the former wheel-thrown and schematically rendered as a vessel and the latter plastically modeled with a lesser or greater degree of realism to indicate the female breasts or bust. Second, emphasis is given to the face, sometimes disproportionately large in relation to the body, with vivid and engaging facial expression achieved through large eyes, "smiling" mouth, or face painting. Third, special attention is paid to the rendition of garment, headgear, and ornaments, which are liberally placed on the body, neck, and head of the figure, and which have parallels in both the rich jewelry apparatus (Younger 1992; Nosch and Laffineur 2010) and the representation of textiles on frescoes (Sapouna-Sakellaraki 1971; Tzachili 1986; Barber 1991). Finally, the figures often bear, or are contextually associated with, elements from the natural world, including birds, snakes, or flowers of special sacral significance such as the papyrus and the poppy (Alexiou 1958; Warren 1985; Marinatos 1993).

Breasts and nature associations, gesture, and cultural paraphernalia, including garments and adornment, are focal elements of female imagery across space and time. They can thus be read as materializations of fundamental cultural principles underlying Bronze Age societies. I suggest that women were ritually celebrated in their capacity as nourishers, spiritual experts, keepers of collective memory and tradition, and specialists in important technologies including pottery, weaving, cooking and food management, and possibly also pharmacology and medicine (Kopaka 1997; Nikolaïdou 2002). These technologies played crucial roles in Bronze Age societies, on the levels of household, community, and palace, as sources of sustenance and comfort as well as income and wealth, for display in feasts and ceremonies, as ritual votives or equipment, wedding goods, diplomatic gifts, and coveted trade items. Ceramic and textile manufacture, food preparation, plant gathering, and medicinal processing are the key "maintenance" activities that are still primarily (albeit not exclusively) associated with women worldwide (e.g., Murdock and Provost 1973; Barber 1994; Picazo 1997; González Marcén et al. 2008). Beyond "remedial" task attribution, however, we may best evaluate Minoan crafts in terms of complementary skills (Kopaka 1997; cf. Brumfiel 1991; Bevan 1997), pertaining to gender, age, class, and individual charisma.

3   Crafters, Nourishers, and Providers

Not only workers and consumers but also raw materials, time, knowledge, and products participate in an "engendered universe of activities" (Kopaka 1997: 527–9), where technical expertise condenses and transmits important cultural knowledge and values (Nikolaïdou 2007). Technology also requires the cognitive and social skills for planning, procuring resources, organizing production, learning, applying, and teaching the technical steps, as well as for properly sharing and consuming the finished products (Lemonnier 1992; Pfaffenberger 1992). Crafts hinge on a spectrum of concepts and behaviors, including communication, cooperation, tradition, experimentation, display, hospitality, and performance (cf. Helms 1993; Elster 1997). The Aegean evidence suggests that women's birthing and nourishing capacities were symbolically fused with functions of providing, crafting, and producing.

These associations were visualized very early in a series of anthropomorphic vessels in the shape of a woman holding pots or her breasts and wearing elaborate dress and/or headdress (Fowden 1990; Tenwolde 1992; Goodison 2009). These figures date to the early Middle Minoan period (late third millennium to early second millennium BCE), come

Figure 3.3   Anthropomorphic terracotta vase ("Goddess rhyton") from Mochlos. Early Minoan III, late third millennium BCE. Crete, Herakleion Archaeological Museum. Photo: Nimatallah/Art Resource, NY.

from cemeteries or settlements, and are interpreted as receptacles for libations (rhyta) or even as the first "Goddess" images. An eloquent example is the rhyton from the cemetery of Mochlos in East Crete (Figure 3.3). What immediately attracts attention is the emphasis on the nurturing elements of the female anatomy: the figure is holding her perforated breasts and possesses a full body (denoting pregnancy and/or abundance?). On closer inspection, we also note the rendition of headgear and the rich garment, indicated by painted designs.

References to female physique and technological skill recur, with variations, across the corpus (Goodison 2009): a very similar figure from Mallia bears even richer designs on her body along with a brimmed hat, also seen in votive figurines from contemporary peak sanctuaries (Pilali-Papasteriou 1989). The "Goddess of Myrtos" features a large pubic triangle and phallic-shaped neck, but also has a large jug, a shape characteristic of early Minoan pottery (Betancourt 1985) and an attribute of other rhyta, too; an example from the cemetery at Archanes wears a conical hat and holds a large jar. The occurrence of female-shaped vessels in different parts of Crete, each with distinct and specialized pottery traditions, points to the significance of this imagery as a visual and symbolic thread connecting populations within and across regions. It is important to remember here the strong communal ethos permeating the find-spots of these vessels: the cemeteries, with their collective burials and related rituals (Branigan 1991), or settlements such as Myrtos, with evidence for sharing between households visible in their layout and the organization of activities (Whitelaw 1983; Tenwolde 1992).

What the anthropomorphic rhyta evoke is a range of crafts and skills that thrived through innovative developments from the onset of the Bronze Age and were invested with conceptual and social value. The potters of the third millennium specialized in demanding and sophisticated forms (e.g., Betancourt 1985), many of which (jugs, cups, spouted jars) were intended for the key liquid commodities of the period: oil, wine, and milk, which were the products of new subsistence practices (Renfrew 1972; Sherratt 1981). Above all, water, critical for sustaining crops and life, would have been treasured in the often-arid landscapes of the southern Aegean. The pouring attributes of the "Goddess" vessels—the shape of the figure itself and the pots that she holds—would thus be meaningful references to these profound experiences of production. Such references were further ritualized through the ceremonial consumption of liquids, already a widespread practice from the onset of the Bronze Age (Hitchcock et al. 2008).

The ample archaeological evidence for feasting at both cemeteries and sanctuaries points to contemporary developments (or changes) in diet and culinary skills; these developments involved a broader repertoire of ingredients and social know-how, which may have been connected to expanding trade networks (Wiener 1987). Wool and leather likewise became increasingly important in the diversified subsistence strategies of the times, and there is evidence for technical and formal refinement in clothing and costume, probably accomplished chiefly by women (Colburn 2008). Female votive figurines from the communal sanctuaries of the period are depicted with special emphasis on elaborate dress and hats, while males sometimes wear shoes (Pilali-Papasteriou 1989).

Craft specialization beyond the household, evident in prosperous early Minoan communities (Day et al. 1997; Day and Wilson 2002), evolved along with expanding regional and palatial hierarchies (e.g., Andreadaki-Vlasaki 1997; Knappett 1997) early in the second millennium BCE. Differential access to resources, knowledge, and products (inferable from the archaeological record) imparted a special social position and/or ritual eminence to expert practitioners (discussion in Nikolaïdou 2002). Such a status can be glimpsed in a variety of material categories; for example in the so-called "potters' scenes", schematic representation of humans engaged with pots on a series of protopalatial seals (Goodison 1989: 44–6; Younger 1995: 168–9, pl. LXa–d). Some of these seals may have belonged to enterprising potters, who chose the theme as a mark of professional identification in bureaucratic transactions and/or as a signal of pride and prestige.

Other seals, engraved with motifs recognizable as loom weights and textile patterns and/or with figures involved in weaving (Burke 1997) may have belonged to textile manufacturers or associated entrepreneurs—persons of high status in many ancient societies (cf. Brumfiel 1991; Nordquist 1997). Loom weights and whorls are impressed by seals, and the image of the loom was used as a hieroglyphic ideogram (Barber 1991, 1994, 1997). Good archaeological contexts for textile-related activities have been excavated at important settlements across the island—including the complex industrial-administrative quarter Quartier MU at Mallia (Poursat 1983, 1997), Khamalevri in the west (Andreadaki-Vlasaki 1997), and Pseira in the east—and large concentrations of loom weights have come from the palaces of Knossos and Phaistos.

We may further consider that elaborately dressed female figurines from Early-Middle Minoan peak sanctuaries may depict producers of fine cloth, skilled women who contributed to establishing particular styles in appearance and other material symbolism, by both producing *and* using their works. These figurines are significantly shown in a highly standardized attire of dress and hats, contrary to the more individualized depiction of male votives (Pilali-Papasteriou 1989). Women's highly visible and standardized costume perhaps materialized a strong collective identity of "womanhood" that could have been constructed on many levels: kinship, residence and ethic/cultural affiliation, age, social maturity, and technical expertise. Whether these shared fashions reflect traditional ties of family and homeland independent of the palaces or whether they present a visual canon of femaleness promoted by the palatial authorities as part of their integrative strategies, this widespread imagery highlights women's agency in shaping and preserving identities across a spectrum of social possibilities. Peak sanctuaries and other open-air places of worship were the principal loci of communal worship in the early second millennium (Peatfield 1992) and were therefore prime fields for social display, construction of ideals, and negotiations of power (cf. Conkey 1991).

As the domains where the transformation of nature into culture was achieved through organized and collective effort, productive activities would have promoted cultural identity and a sense of "solidarity" (cf. Bevan 1997), shrouded in the symbolisms of an archetypical "female" order (Goodison 1989; Yiannouli 1992; Kokkinidou and Niko-laïdou 1993). The location of weaving and storage facilities deep in the interior of Minoan and Helladic houses indicates the relative inaccessibility of these activities—a spatial formulation of their material, social, and conceptual importance (Yiannouli 1992). Primary access to the resources and acts that ensured the everyday bread and fabric of the family would have been a means of control for those in charge. It is tempting to see women (perhaps the elders of the family) in this role, as suggested by ethnographic examples worldwide (Murdock and Provost 1973; Moore 1986).

4 Bodies and Personae: Archaeologies of Corporeality and Identity

An area of increasing interest in archaeological research considers ancient perceptions of the human body and the multisensory embodiments of these ideas (Hamilakis et al. 2002). The female body, in particular, found various interpretations in Aegean art, ranging from allusive, metaphorical, or synecdochical reference to abstract and summarized rendering, explicit and naturalistic representation, and selective emphasis on anatomy or cultural traits. These symbolic formulations can thus be fruitfully explored to illuminate underlying concepts and ways of life: that is, how women understood their bodies and how the community perceived them; how the body was nourished and cared for; how it became socialized, ritualized, and celebrated; and how it was incorporated into larger schemata and dynamics of power.

In a broad view of Aegean art, there are two major idioms of expression about the body, each employing a rich and diverse pictorial vocabulary. The first idiom encompasses images of motherhood, fertility, and reproduction, with emphasis on their tangible biological components. The other idiom is woven around cultural aspects and focuses on aesthetics, socialization and social standing, and ritual performance. Far from being mutually exclusive, elements from both expressive styles are often fused in one multivalent image (e.g., as in Figure 3.2 and Figure 3.3). That being said, we may distinguish generally between Minoan and Cycladic body imagery on the one hand and Mycenaean or Mycenaean-influenced body imagery on the other. The former matured mainly along social-cultural connotations, while notions of (physical) mothering and nurturing are more abundant and explicit in the latter (cf. Rutter 2003; Olsen 2009).

5   Growing to Be a Woman: Coming of Age, Fertility, Motherhood

A wide range of images can be considered in the general context of female sexuality, fertility, and reproduction. Some are suggestive references: for example, a series of triangular decorated clay plaques from early Minoan Crete may depict female pubic areas (Goodison 1989). The early Cycladic "frying pans"—shallow circular vessels standing on two feet—have also been interpreted as schematic renditions of the female (pregnant?) body, an idea supported by the explicit depiction of the pubic area on many such vessels. We must note, though, that the most plausible function of these enigmatic vessels is as salt-collecting containers, in which case we may be dealing with "female" connotations of production and technology similar to those embodied in the Minoan anthropomorphic rhyta (Figure 3.3). Both artifact types exemplify the recurrent association of pots with "female-gendered" bodies, as seen also in the "nippled" jugs of the Middle Cycladic period (high-spouted vessels featuring plastic "nipples" accentuated with painted motifs—possibly jewelry—at the base of their necks; see Tzachili 1986, 1997). What these different ceramic shapes particularly evoke are pregnant bodies, representations of which are seen in some marble Cycladic figurines (third millennium BCE) with arms resting over a slightly swollen abdomen (see Rutter 2003, with references).

A few other Cycladic sculptures are groups of adults (female?) and children, early forerunners of the *kourotrophos* imagery that is better known from the late Bronze Age. A few more figurines and ceramic depictions of pregnant and birthing women are known from Early and Middle Minoan Crete, as are also votive effigies of babies in some peak sanctuaries. Human, and especially female, reproduction is important not only on the natural but also on social, demographic, economic, ideological, and ethical levels (cf. Bentley 1996). The wish for large thriving families is especially strong in farming and pastoral societies, where wives are chosen for good health, "productivity," and capacity for parenting and household management. The perforated, pouring breasts and vulvas of Aegean anthropomorphic vessels would have been eloquent visual references not only to the anatomy of birthing and nursing but also to midwifery and nursing skills, crucial areas of female expertise and power.

It was in the Mycenaean period, in particular, that the theme of nurturing woman/ mother gained popularity in the well-known type of *kourotrophos* figurines (clay idols of females cradling, carrying, or nursing babies and small children; see Rutter 2003; Shepherd, this volume, Chapter 16). These charming images celebrate childcare, affection, and bonding. Benevolent symbolisms surrounding the tasks of mothering are indicated by the deposition of many such figurines as grave goods (in children's graves?). The Linear B records of the period provide us with valuable information on family structure in Mycenaean society, in particular the classes of commoner or slave (?) women who, together with their children, were occupied in the palatial textile industries (Olsen 1998, 2009). Such evidence of the everyday existence of "real-life" people provides welcome balance to the generic, idealized imagery of parenthood, childhood, and youth in the artistic repertoire (Rutter 2003). Burials and cemetery sites, many of which have been systematically excavated all over the Aegean from different periods of the Bronze Age, are another potentially rich mine of information on familial ties and the symbolic expressions thereof. Unfortunately, this potential is hampered by the repeated use of many cemeteries for centuries or millennia; the deposition of multiple burials in the same graves, obscuring the reliable identification of individuals; the scarcity of paleoanthropological and paleo-genetic analyses (but see Triantaphyllou 2003; McGeorge 2009); and the biased attributions of sex and age based on "female," "male," and "child" grave goods (see also Liston, this volume, Chapter 9; Shepherd, this volume, Chapter 16, and Allason-Jones, this volume, Chapter 34).

Motherhood has been aptly described as the essential "maintenance" activity that ensures physical and emotional welfare for the individual and the community alike (Olsen 1998; Beausang 2005; Kopaka 2009a). Motherhood weaves together the biological capacities for birth, nursing, and caring and the social skills for rearing, educating, and helping the child towards physical and social growth. These two basic aspects of motherhood do not always coincide in one and the same person; indeed, there are many societies where physical mothers play only a part in the "social" mothering of their children—a complex educational process collectively undertaken by experienced adults, be they senior family members, community mentors, or ritual specialists (Pomadère 2009; Younger 2009).

An ivory trio of two women and a girl from Mycenae (Figure 3.4) can be read as a celebration of exactly this type of "social mothering." A splendid piece of late Minoan craftwork, the group was found in Mycenae and is a luxurious, "exotic" treasure that belonged to a member of the local aristocracy. Traditionally interpreted as a divine triad of two goddesses and a child god (despite the lack of secure contextual information), the group has been fruitfully re-examined with closer attention paid to the gendered and social messages encoded in its rich imagery. The arrangement of the figures conveys an atmosphere of intimacy: the two adult women embrace each other and share a common

Figure 3.4 Ivory female triad from Mycenae. Minoan craftsmanship; Late Minoan I, sixteenth century BCE. Athens, National Archaeological Museum. Photo: Vanni/Art Resource, NY.

cloak, and they gaze attentively at the child, who is placed right in front of them as if under their protective care.

The identification of the small figure as a girl places this composition in the wider context of women-and-girls scenes, an important theme in Aegean iconography and one executed in a variety of precious media, including gold rings and frescoes. Key elements of this imagery, including physique, dress, and activity, encourage interpretation along the lines of female social and ritual education involving mature, skilled mentors and young initiates. The participants are shown in rich attire, consisting of the standardized "Minoan" dress with open bodice and flounced skirt, which identifies the figures as deities or ritual personages. Their bodies are graceful, with slender waists and full breasts that are *not* associated with nursing but rather seem to represent an aesthetic and/or ritualized ideal of feminine physique. The figures engage with each other (as in the Mycenae trio) or act as a group, with the mature females often assuming a guiding or protective role.

On some seals (Rutter 2003: Figures 16 and 17), a mature female figure in ceremonial posture ("goddess"?) is flanked by two young girls in the same stance: are they imitating her? On a gold ring from Mycenae a procession of women and a small girl holding flowers advances respectfully towards a seated goddess, as if the older figures are presenting the child to the divinity, while two other small figures hover in the background (Rutter 2003: Figure 19). A ritual ethos is evident both in the acts represented—offerings, reverence, ceremonial enactment—and in the context and setting of the scenes, notably the frescoes from areas of cultic character, such as Xeste 3 (discussed below). It is not clear whether the women-and-girls iconography represents the actual ceremonies of education and initiation or idealized/divinized perceptions thereof—but perhaps this ambiguity was intentional and all the more powerful. Ritual connotations coupled with the luxurious media of execution (gold, ivory, precious stone, frescoes) bespeak the social importance of women's mentoring and educational skills—and the prestige of the personages actually performing such roles in the community. Artifacts such as the gold ring or the ivory triad are likely to have belonged to women of such elevated status, as is documented by the aforementioned burial of the princess-priestess of Tholos A at Archanes, whose burial gifts included several gold rings decorated with ritual scenes and luxurious pieces of furniture with rich ivory decorations (Sakellarakis and Sapouna-Sakellaraki 1991, 1997).

The richest and most impressive example of this iconography includes the wall decorations of Xeste 3 at Akrotiri, Thera, a Middle Cycladic (seventeenth century BCE) building of luxurious architecture that had a (partly) ritual function focused on the *adyton*, a secluded sunken area perhaps for ablutions (Marinatos 1984; Younger 2009). The elaborate pictorial narrative includes complex rituals of initiation and offering, involving youths and adults (female and male) of varying age, maturity, and rank culminating in the divine status of a centrally seated female. The most unusual scenes dramatically enact the female coming of age, with references to menstruation, fertility, and even healing and obstetrics, probably echoing rites that took place in the building itself. These dramas are visualized through differential body development of the figures, hairstyles denoting different stages of youth, and a constellation of symbols including rich costume, jewelry, and flowers with "female" connotations, notably the crocus, used in antiquity as a remedy for menstrual pains but also as an abortive medium (Rehak 1999, 2002; Younger 2009).

Diverse interpretations have been proposed for the Xeste 3 paintings (reviewed in Younger 2009), but I would like to point out the two key strands that, in my view, link together the different episodes and actors: first, the ritualized vestment of a person's progress to maturity (biological and social), and, second, the offering of gifts as an integral component of the maturity process and one's social persona—the most valuable offering of all being one's body and self, in splendid ceremonial array and adornment (cf. Nikolaïdou 2007; Colburn 2008). Prepubescent and adolescent girls, male youths, and mature women and men are all shown carrying offerings of flowers and crafted goods, presenting themselves in front of altars and the divinity.

6   The Construction of Identities: Ritualization and Performance

A young priestess from the West House at Akrotiri (Figure 3.5) beautifully embodies the same key symbolisms of initiation, maturity, and offering. Her priestly function is most visible in her special garment, a hairy or leathery cloak that envelops her body and is a

Figure 3.5   Young girl (priestess?) with ritual vessel. Wall painting from the West House at Akrotiri, Thera, Late Cycladic I, seventeenth century BCE. Athens, National Archaeological Museum. Photo: Erich Lessing/Art Resource, NY.

well-known attribute of Aegean priestly figures (Marinatos 1993). But other meaningful signifiers surround the figure as well. What one notes first about her are the partially shaved head and the bright red lips and ears. Heads partially shaved and with locks in different stages of growth are a principal iconographic formula for denoting childhood and youth in Aegean art, and apply to both girls and boys; the age of the Thera priestess can accordingly be estimated at prepubescence or early pubescence (Rutter 2003). The color red, well known for its fertility and ritual symbolisms in many ancient cultures (overview in Papaefthymiou-Papanthimou 1979, 1997), signifies the ritual status of the figure and implies her coming of age.

Further references to the girl's femininity and imminent puberty may be found in the items she holds: she carries a peculiar vessel, probably an incense burner, on which she sprinkles strands of a substance that has been interpreted as crocus, the multivalent plant that figures prominently in the Xeste frescoes as well as in the votive faience robes from the Temple Repositories at the Palace of Knossos. The gesture and posture of the figure together with her placement on the jamb of a doorway, leading to a big room where an elaborate offering table was ensconced in a niche, indicates that she was conceived as performing an act of offering herself. Significant contextual support is lent by the depiction, in that very room, of two large male youths each holding sizeable bunches of fish and walking towards the niche with the offering table (reconstruction in Marinatos 1984). In addition, the large earring of the young girl further affirms her position in the fascinating repertoire of idealized, and ritualized, images of youth in Aegean art (see Marinatos 1984; Davis 1986; Doumas 1992; Rutter 2003).

The archaeological and iconographic record of Aegean Bronze Age jewelry is extremely rich in its quantities, repertoire of materials, techniques and typology, modes of application, and contextual and pictorial associations. Similarly prolific, and often sumptuous, was the production and consumption of toiletry articles and cosmetics (Papaefthymiou-Papanthimou 1979, 1997), as well as of ornate textiles (Barber 1992). Together, ornaments, cosmetic treatments, and elaborate dresses illustrate how powerful a symbol the ornate body was in the Bronze Age, on the many levels of its corporeal, social, and ritual existence.

Ornaments and toiletry articles also figure prominently among the burial goods of women, men, and children, as loving gifts to celebrate the memory and persona of the dead (Sakellarakis and Sapouna-Sakellaraki 1997: 254–5). We find quantities of such personal artifacts dedicated in sanctuaries as expressions of piety and thanksgiving, as symbols of status and aspiration, as cult paraphernalia, or as instruments in rites of passage that marked the transition to new stages of maturity, profession, or ritual involvement (Watrous 1996). Figurines of adorants, women and men, from these same cult places are modeled wearing different types of jewelry (Verlinden 1984; Pilali-Papasteriou 1989) as are the persons depicted in a wide range of ceremonial acts: dance, ecstatic worship, offering, sacrifice, funeral rites, lament, initiation, and athletic performance, such as bull-leaping and boxing (Immerwahr 1990; German 2005).

In the "liminal" zone of ritual where such activities took place, boundaries were permeable, as is indicated, for example, by the use of the same types of jewelry for men and women (e.g., Papefthymiou-Papanthimou 1997), the deposition of "female" artifacts (jewelry, loom weights) in male tombs and vice versa, the appearance of male figures in "female" dress (for hieratic "androgyny" see Sapouna-Sakellaraki 1971), and the ambiguous depiction of the "acrobats" in the famous Toreador Fresco at Knossos with male attire but with emphasized breasts and light skin color (Alberti 2002). The Aegean evidence invites more complex readings that do not rely on the customary male-versus-female dichotomy. Gender categories can be fluid, and were variously perceived as functions of age, social affiliation, profession, individual talent, and ritual involvement, as well as in the context of myth and religious belief. Thus the quest for Minoan and Mycenaean women, an endeavor once thought as futile as Penelope's warp, becomes Ariadne's guiding thread through the complex realities of Bronze Age life.

RECOMMENDED FURTHER READING

The pioneering volume of Krzyszkowska and Nixon (1983) is a major reference point of theory and method for "peopling" the past. The contribution of the Linear B texts is illustrated in Shelmerdine and Palaima (1984). On religious sites, a good reference work is Rutkowski (1986). In the area of burial, the publication of Papadopoulos (2005a) brings analyses of artifacts, spatial organization, and paleoanthropological and paleoenviron-mental examination together with a theoretically informed discussion of identity, gender, and status as expressed in funerary rituals. Branigan (1993) offers an engaging narrative based on rigorous fieldwork. A modern female visitor's perspective is found in Hoe (2005). The wall paintings of Akrotiri have been beautifully published in Doumas 1992. Textiles are the focus of some of the most interesting gender-informed work, for example in Anderson and Nosch 2003.

There has also been welcome interest in the historiography of pioneer women archaeologists and contemporary women professionals, in an effort to assess their scholarly and social presence in the wider epistemological context of the discipline (Alsebrook 1992; Bolger 1994; Nikolaïdou and Kokkinidou 1998; Picazo 1998; Cullen 2005; Allen 2009; D'Agata 2009; Kokkinidou and Nikolaïdou 2009; Tsipopoulou 2009).

ACKNOWLEDGMENTS

For valuable input I am grateful to Dimitra Kokkinidou, supportive friend and companion in my archaeological quests for gender.

4

Women in Homer

Cristiana Franco

Women in Homer is a topic that not only involves the vastness of scholarship about women in ancient Greece generally and the issues raised by contemporary literary criticism but also is intertwined with the complexity of the Homeric question. Moreover, scholars' views on "Homeric women" vary not only along with their different assumptions about the genesis, authorship, and narrative cohesion of the texts but also with their own perspectives and interests as readers of the poems. This brief survey can only hint at the richness of the topic and at its inherent difficulties, and discuss a few case studies. Given limits of space, I will consider only the two main poems of the Homeric corpus, the *Iliad* and the *Odyssey*.

1 Homeric Women and Historical Realities

Literary evidence is never a direct source for historical reconstructions, but the Homeric poems, with their unique genesis, are even more unlikely to be successfully used for such a purpose. With the help of archaeological, linguistic, and comparative data, it has been possible to determine the origin of some of the elements accumulated throughout the long oral tradition that passed on the poems to their first written versions. But for the most of the Homeric immaterial world (social values, behavioral patterns, personal relationships) we possess scanty archaeological or linguistic correlates. The actual life of "Homeric women" falls into this category. What we know about women's social roles and lives is mainly what the poems tell us, and overall historical reconstructions of women's social reality based on Homeric poetry turn out to be frustrating enterprises doomed to circularity.

   A debated issue concerns marriage customs. It has been argued that the poems cannot reflect any actual historical context in this respect because they show a puzzling mixture of different practices. In some cases, a bridegroom gives gifts to the bride's father, and the term *hedna* seems to be employed technically to refer to these presents (e.g., *Il.* 22.471–2; *Od.* 6.159, 8.318–19, 15.16–18, 16.390–2, 21.160–2). Yet *hedna* is not a necessary

A Companion to Women in the Ancient World, First Edition. Edited by Sharon L. James and Sheila Dillon.
© 2012 John Wiley & Sons, Ltd. Published 2015 by John Wiley & Sons, Ltd.

practice: a marriage can be celebrated "without *hedna*" (*anaednos* in *Il.* 9.146, 13.366), especially when the groom offers a service to the bride's father (*Il.* 13.366–9), and in some cases the same term (*hedna*) appears instead to refer to gifts from the bride's family to the groom (*Od.* 1.277, 2.53). This opposite case, a bridegroom receiving gifts from the bride's family (e.g., *Il.* 6.191–3, 9.147–56, 22.51; *Od.* 7.311–15), is usually defined by no specialized term, and the "gifts" are rather referred to as *dōra* or *meilia*. Some scholars consider these gifts as a clear instance of dowry, and see in Penelope's and Andromache's epithet *polydōros* a hint at the rich dowry they brought into their husbands' assets (Leduc 1992; Westbrook 2005). Moses Finley held that *hedna* was a general term for all marriage gifts, assuming as a norm the reciprocal exchange of gifts between the two families, but Anthony Snodgrass (1974) and other scholars consider *hedna* and dowry two different practices that cannot coexist in the same system, and thus a clear proof of the fictional nature of the so-called "Homeric society." Some scholars allow for the possibility that both practices were valid in the same social organization (Leduc 1992; van Wees 1999: 20); others point to the "otherness" of the contexts where the bride-price is found and conclude that it functions as a "marked signifier" (Osborne 2004b: 214). It has been claimed that what distinguished the acquisition of a legitimate wife is that she was given by her father to the groom as a gracious gift, whereas concubines were purchased or conquered as part of the war booty. But a wife could also be chosen from among captives (*Il.* 19.298).

To complicate the picture, in the Homeric poems most marriages are virilocal—that is, the bride moves from her father's house to her husband's—but there are also instances of uxorilocal arrangements. Some instances can be ruled out as "marked" cases belonging to foreign traditions: in Troy almost all the king's sons and daughters live at their parents' house with their spouses (*Il.* 6.244ff.); Bellerophon moves to Lycia and marries a local woman (*Il.* 6.191ff.); and Odysseus was expected to stay on Scheria if he accepted Nausikaa as his wife (*Od.* 7.311ff.). This is no doubt a puzzling storehouse of evidence to draw upon, in lack of any external confirmation, for scholars aspiring to a socio-historical reconstruction.

After decades of debate and archaeological discoveries, the majority of scholars have lost hope—still cherished by Sarah Pomeroy in her pioneering 1975 work—of finding in the poems either a direct picture of Mycenaean society or, as Moses Finley argued, the representation of a real archaic world of the Dark Age: the "World of Odysseus" (Finley 1977), the inconsistencies of which could be accounted for as "variants revealing a situation where social relationships are not yet established" (Mossé 1988: 18). Many scholars hold that Homeric society is just as fictional as is Homeric language: it would be a tapestry woven together by an oral tradition over many centuries, a mixture of different elements that no Greek person could have ever experienced *in that form* in real life.

However, some critics insist that the overall picture of Homeric society is consistent and somehow reflects the patterns and expectations of eighth century BCE Greece. There is general agreement on the reasonable assumption that what the bards were singing had to make sense for their audience and that this audience was that of the time when the poems attained their "monumental" form (Morris 2001: 57–91). But there are many ways of "making sense" of a fictional work. In what sense should we understand that figures such as Penelope, Andromache, Arete, or Helen "made sense" to an audience of the eighth century BCE as women? Should we assume that they represent real high-class women of that period, or are they characters of an archaizing fiction, reflecting what the bards (and their audiences) thought a Mycenaean "wife of the *basileus* (king)" ought to have been like? Even admitting that the invention of the heroic past was modeled by the poets on what they knew (and so on pieces of contemporary experience), how should we interpret situations such as women's presence in the main hall where men are entertaining themselves and their guests (*Od.* 4.123ff., 11.335ff., 20.387ff.)? Are they evidence for real upper-class women's participation in male entertainment activities, including perhaps bardic performances, in the eighth century BCE? Or are they part of the "distancing tools" used by the poet—archaization, exaggeration, invention—to conjure the picture of a heroic society in which the wife of a king (*basileus*) is allowed to join the male activities and even to call a male guest "my guest" (*Od.* 11.338)?

2   Epics as Sources for a History of Cultural Conceptions

The archaeological record for Dark Age and archaic Greece tells us about a puzzling variety of different situations, indicating significant regional differences. The Panhellenism of the epics—its remarkable unlocal character and its fiction of a "Panachaian" unity—should not trick us into the illusion of any cultural homogeneity of the real audience, making us forget the social and political diversity within archaic Greek communities. We should always consider that the position of women—aristocratic, lower-class, slaves—could vary a great deal in different contexts. More than reflecting a homogeneous world, epics offered a stable image of the world to audiences who were experiencing different cultural environments and rapid political and social changes. The homogeneity of the "Homeric society" is thus a mystification that needs to be explained in terms of genre and ideology (Scodel 2002: 173ff.).

To take an example, the division of Homeric society into an elite class and an undifferentiated mass of non-elite "dependents" can hardly mirror historical truth. The poor woman at *Il.* 12.433ff., who struggles to make a living for her children, gives us a glance at a world of women workers deliberately elided from the Homeric aristocratic picture. Female slaves are most likely to have had children by male slave partners, but these servile families are never represented in the poems. Slave-mothers conceive with their masters only (e.g., *Od.* 4.11–12). Within the domestic sphere, noble and slave women share more or less the same activities: spinning, weaving, washing clothes, looking after children, bed-making, bathing, preparing meals, feeding animals. Yet occasionally we see female slaves doing harder types of work such as grinding wheat grains and barleycorns (*Od.* 20.105–10) or fetching water (*Il.* 6.457).

Epics ostensibly picture a world that is *not* the world of the poet and his audience. The poems refer to the world of heroes as a world of ancient times, when humankind was different, stronger, and closer to the gods—a "race of demi-gods" (*Il.* 12.23). This generation is thought to have lived between two ages: an older age populated by the strongest men ever (such as Heracles) and by women who could become pregnant by gods (such as Alcmene, Leda, Semele), and current humankind, referred to by the formulaic expression "such as mortals are now" (*oioi nyn brotoi eis*'), one much weaker than the warriors of the Trojan war. Halfway between Heracles' and "our" age, the tremendous kings of epics are possible, though not unproblematic, models for the current generation of men to confront (Clarke 2004: 79–90). The difficult balance of their virility between godlike vigor and beastly savagery has actually been significant not only to aristocrats of the Archaic period but also to many other men (and women) of the following ages. But what can be said about their female counterparts? In what sense could they have been meaningful to different audiences in the late eighth century BCE and throughout the ages, and can they still tell us something about our concept of womanhood and ourselves?

The loss of confidence in using Homer as direct evidence for the social history of real Greek women turns into a gain when we consider that the poems can be seen instead as documents for a history of cultural conceptions: not a passive reflection of historical truths but something that played a crucial role in making history by expressing—more or less intentionally—the ideology of particular groups and cultural traditions. In this perspective, Homeric women are not reproductions of reality but representations of female human beings as they were conceptualized, presented for interested ends or from biased viewpoints, and bound to influence women's real lives owing to the authority of epic poetry even in the later Greek culture and educational system. In this sense it is crucial to consider that texts do not generate meaning *per se* but in a dynamic cooperation with the audience they address.

There are different ways to approach an audience-response-oriented reading of Homeric epics. One approach, still adopting a historicist stance, endeavors to understand how these texts made sense to their original audience; that is, the real social group(s) and individuals that epic poetry addressed at the time it was composed. So, for instance, the Homeric "romanticized" portrait of the marital relationship (Hector and Andromache, Odysseus and Penelope) has been interpreted as the reflection of a new ideological trend prompted by a developing social system based on small individual families (instead of larger clans of the past times) in which male social investment in women would have increased a great deal. The Homeric poems, representing an aristocratic point of view, would naturally, then, stress the positive side rather than the possible failures of this investment, whereas Hesiodic misogyny would reflect instead the anxiety of men striving to ascend the social scale, "for whom the small family was an economic and political necessity" in which wives played a more crucial role (Arthur [Katz] 1984: 25).

A different approach is based on the theoretical concepts of the implied audience (Iser 1978) or the "model reader" (Eco 1979). The "model reader" is by no means a real audience, but a purely semiotic entity. It consists of the strategy by which a text points its audiences towards specific responses. Texts are sense-making devices that demand their audiences' cooperation but exert different degrees of pressure upon them—from very high (very closed texts) to very low (very open texts), with all possible intermediate levels. This pressure can be detected and assessed by analyzing verbal and thematic redundancies, and the distribution of actantial roles and focalizations: it can tell us something about roles played by female characters in orienting an audience's interpretations (Doherty 1995: 9ff.).

3 Female Agency and Male Anxiety

From this point of view one should notice, for instance, that the *Iliad* stresses the role of women as the objects over which men fight each other. Not only was the Trojan War waged on account of (*eineka*) Helen but the very story recounted in the *Iliad* is a strife between Agamemnon and Achilles for the possession of the captive Briseis. More generally, war is something that happens "around" (*amphi* or *peri*) women: it is fought either in defense of (e.g., *Il.* 5.486, 16.833, 24.730) or to conquer (e.g., *Il.* 9.327, 18.265) them. The sack of Troy is represented as revenge extracted from the Trojans through the violation of their marital beds (*Il.* 2.354–5, 3.301). Conversely, defending Troy means to keep safe the women and children within the walls (e.g., 21.586, 24.29f.). Troy itself is compared to a woman whose veils (*krēdemna*) are stripped off by the conquerors (*Il.* 16.100, *Od.* 13.388; see Nagler 1974: 44–60); Andromache's loosing of the *krēdemnon* at the sight of her husband's body being dragged away by Achilles (*Il.* 22.470) is an omen of her imminent destiny.

This perspective naturalizes women's weakness and need for protection and invites the audience to sympathize with them as helpless victims and main witnesses of the effects of war on the defeated (Lefkowitz 2007: 36ff.). In the famous encounter at the city's gates (*Il.* 6.407ff.), Andromache and Hector's dialogue reveals the contradiction inherent in the male heroic condition. Her suggestion of taking a more defensive military strategy is an attempt at reconciling her husband's aspiration to win glory by challenging the enemy with his responsibility as the defender of Troy—that is, Trojan women and children, primarily those of his own family (Arthur [Katz] 1981). Though he loves Andromache and the baby Astyanax, Hector cannot renounce his dignity as a warrior, which entails fighting in the front line to save his social prestige, for otherwise Trojan men *and women* would call him *kakos* ("coward" and thus "base"). He sends Andromache home with the formulaic words used by men to drive women back to "their" sphere of action—"Go into the house and see to your own work, the loom and the distaff" (*Il.* 6.490–3, *Od.* 1.356–9, 21.350–3)—thereby subordinating affective ties to the pursuit of honor and social rewards.

Warfare is men's business. Men and women are separated by the gap resulting from women's exclusion from the the sphere of virile courage (*andreia*) and self-defense (*alkē*) to be displayed on the battlefield. As focalizers in the narrative, women are, with the remarkable exception of Helen, almost always mourners (Martin 1989: 87–8) or predictors of possible defeat. Though potentially subversive in that they reveal how a warrior's *kleos* (fame and glory) is rooted in loss and grief (Murnaghan 1999: 203–217), their voices never express an explicit protest against the system of competition among males, which lies at the very basis of the code of honor and of social hierarchies in general (Thalmann 1998b: 193ff.). No Lysistrata is there to organize the rebellion of women against the masculine way of leading the dispute by violent confrontation. Women in the *Iliad* are represented as the *natural* victims of inescapable events that they can only describe and lament. The captive women in the Achaean camp must keep their sorrow secret from their masters, and even pretend to mourn for the warriors who had reduced them to slavery (*Il.* 19.301–2). Briseis shows no resentment towards Achilles, the one who killed her husband, three of her brothers, and took her away as a captive. She accepts her condition and acts as a surrogate wife, mourning Achilles' best friend as though she was part of his family (*Il.* 19.287ff.). In some cases women even show complicity with men in the heroic values: Meleager's wife gently urges her husband to join the battle (*Il.* 9.590–6); Helen does the same with Paris, and wishes to be married to a better man, one who does not abstain from fighting and is "sensitive to others' blame" (*Il.* 6.337–53; see Andò 2005: 34–6).

Given women's limited agency it is perhaps not surprising that in the *Iliad* we find no outspoken misogynistic statement about women. They are constantly but stereotypically represented—in similes and metaphors—as cowardly and incapable of self-defense (e.g., *Il.* 2.235, 8.163, 11.389), prone to ineffective verbal confrontations, and easily surrendering to sexual temptations (*Il.* 20.252ff., 5.349). But no female character in the plot is ever stigmatized as having evil intents *qua* female, because no anxiety surrounds women as long as they do not take action and let themselves be directed by men's desire. The particular case of Helen is highly revealing. She is significantly represented in a favorable way when considered as the object of Paris' abduction and of the gods' will. In these instances she is seen as someone who cannot decide her own destiny: the gods let her know that she will be "called wife of the one who wins" the duel for her (*Il.* 3.138). When she is endowed with agency and speech, she appears instead surrounded with suspicion on the part of the Trojan women, criticized by her Trojan relatives, prone to self-condemnation, and worried that her behavior will affect her brothers' reputation (*Il.* 3.180ff., 3.410ff., 24.769ff.; see Blondell 2010: 3–24).

In the *Oydssey* women take a more active part in the plot and are also subjects with a certain degree of agency in social institutions such as gift exchange and marriage (Lyons 2003: 100–8). As keeper of the household in Odysseus' absence, Penelope makes decisions of her own, including whether to remarry and whom, and seems able to convey regal prestige on the man who would marry her. Although Penelope's behavior will prove above reproach, textual redundancies in the poem, along with narrative and actantial patterns, insistently warn against the dangers inherent in female agency free from male control. Suspicion surrounding women's nature looms throughout the poem, and much more explicitly than it does in the *Iliad*. The story of Agamemnon is the paradigmatic example of the risks waiting for the hero on his return home, and Clytemnestra is repeatedly evoked to recall how the wife can destroy her husband's *nostos* and affect his final *kleos* (Murnaghan 1986; Nagy 1999: 36f.). In two famous speeches (*Od.* 11.434, 24.201f.) Agamemnon's soul claims that Clytemnestra's crime and treacherous behavior shed shame and mistrust on all women now and forever, "even on her who does what is right." With the same formula, the blame on Eumaios' nurse (who, seduced by a Phoenician man, sold the baby as the price for her freedom) is extended to all women, implying that she is but an instance of the feminine tendency to surrender to sexual temptation, which "beguiles the minds of women, even the one who does what is right" (*Od.* 15.421f.).

Finally, Athena urges Telemachus to go back to Ithaca before Penelope gets remarried, because "women's mind" is such that they easily forget their previous husband and children (*Od.* 15.20ff.). The Hesiodic Pandora, prototype and ancestor of the dangerous wife endowed with a "doggish mind" (*kyneos noos*), is not totally absent from the Homeric picture of women. The dog metaphor as a term of abuse is used four times by Helen against herself, when she admits responsibility for the adultery that led to the war ("me the dog-faced," *Il.* 3.180, *Od.* 4.145; "me, the bitch" *Il.* 6.344, 356); it is often addressed to treacherous women such as Clytemnestra and the unfaithful maids of Odysseus (*Od.* 11.424–7, 18.338, 19.91, 154, 372). The adulteress Aphrodite is also called "dog-faced" (*kynōpis*) by her husband Hephaestus at *Od.* 8.319. This alarming dog imagery, associated with unfaithful women, constitutes the grim background of Penelope's extraordinary virtue as guardian of her husband's house (Franco 2003: 192–263).

4   Women and Other Females

The shift of interest from realities to cultural constructs allows critics to draw upon a wider range of evidence, including female figures such as goddesses, female monsters, and female animals. These characters are conceived in opposition to their masculine counterparts (gods, male monsters, males of the species) and can be evaluated, with suitable caution, as part of the gender ideology embedded in the text. Zeus and Hera's relationship, for instance, might somehow reflect the case of a couple in which the woman has a social status as high as her husband's. Their quarrels may give an idea of what would occur should such a wife claim the right to have a point of view or to support allies different from those of her husband (see for instance *Il.* 8.461ff.). But it should be kept in mind that goddesses are representative of women in a very problematic way (Loraux 1992; Blundell and Williamson 1998: 4–6). Female divinities can represent either crystallized or subversive aspects of human femininity (the eternal virgins such as Athena, Artemis, Hestia; the hypersexual and adulterous Aphrodite) or even possess typically masculine traits (Athena the warrior). Odysseus' encounter with Circe is a good example of how epic narrative plays on the complex intersection between divinity and gender categories. The goddess lives an independent life on her island. Men approaching the place are kindly invited to her house and then neutralized by a metamorphosis into subdued beasts. Only Odysseus, with the help of Hermes, overcomes the magical power of Circe's potion: unbewitched thanks to the antidote *mōly*, he assaults Circe with his sword and "tames" her resistance, whose limits seem to lie in her feminine surrender to the boldness of the male warrior. Therefore, Odysseus becomes the only man ever offered the goddess' bed and the only one ever to win her affection and alliance (*philotēs*) without losing his masculine and human identity. Whereas the first part of the episode focuses on the human-animal-divine categories, the second part stages a confrontation of gender roles, in which Odysseus successfully transforms the goddess into a "bride"—still powerful, as she is divine, but willing to please the hero and fulfill his wishes (Franco 2010).

5   Women's Glory

In epic poems, female identities are almost always defined by their relationship to males (daughter of, wife of, mother of). The list of famous women of the past seen by Odysseus in the Underworld reflects this gender ideology: they are referred to as the "wives and daughters of the best men" (*Od.* 11.227) and are mainly described as mothers of heroes. As Moses Finley pointed out, "Hero has no feminine gender in the age of heroes" (1978: 32). As a matter of fact, the title *hērōs* in the *Iliad* and the *Odyssey* applies only to the warrior.

Yet one Homeric woman at least is said to attain, if not the title of heroine nor a cult, her own *kleos*: Penelope. Her "heroism" rests on the immortalizing effects of her virtue (*aretē*), praised by bards in their songs. Whereas most cult heroines, such as Helen and Eriphyle, attained such a rank thanks to "life stories" (i.e., myths) that have little to do with the "moral" exemplarity of their behavior (Kearns 1998: 99–101), two main epic female characters align with ethical values and earn their fame within different poetic genres: Penelope's virtue will generate a praise song (*Od.* 24.197ff. *aoidē ... chariessa*) whereas Clytemnestra's crime will be matter for blame songs (*stygerē ... aoidē ... chalepēn te phēmin*). When one of the suitors praises Penelope's skills and cleverness, he states that she surpasses all the famous women of the past (*Od.* 2.115–26, transl. Murray-Dimock):

> But if she shall continue for long to vex the sons of the Achaeans, possessing in her mind those advantages with which Athene has endowed her above other women, knowledge of beautiful handiwork, and good sense, and cleverness, such as we have never yet heard that any of the women of old knew, those fairtressed Achaean women who lived long ago, Tyro and Alcmene and Mycene of the fair crown—of whom not one was like Penelope in shrewd device; yet this at least she devised improperly. For so long shall men devour your livelihood and your possessions, as long, that is, as she shall keep the counsel which the gods now put in her heart. Great fame [*mega kleos*] she wins for herself, but for you regret for your abundant substance.

Even the suitors, duped by Penelope's trick of the web, have little doubt that her ability to resist external pressures will gain her a great *kleos* in the future. If, eventually, she is removed from Odysseus' house, this will happen against her desires (as opposed to Clytemnestra's *willing* abduction by Aegisthus, *Od.* 3.272) and only in order to preserve Telemachus' property and comply with Odysseus' parting injunctions (*Od.* 18.269f.). She is stable, "grounded in the earth" (*empedos*), like the wedding bed Odysseus built in their house (Zeitlin 1995). This is what the ideal wife does and what Ithacan people approve of (*Od.* 19.527, 23.150–1): she keeps her husband's household "steadfast" (*Od.* 11.178: "*empeda panta phylassei*").

Penelope's attitude is by no means passive. Not only does she devise the weaving trick but she also manages to control the situation after her ruse has been detected. She keeps the suitors *in limbo* by deceiving them with encouraging messages, a way of "protecting her freedom to choose one of them" (Marquardt 1985: 37). She also solicits gifts from them, pretending to demand the required wooing presents, whereas "her mind has a different desire"; that is, to replenish the household wealth depleted by the suitors.

Yet Penelope's positive agency is undoubtedly exceptional. In order to resist her feminine weakness and fickleness (Peradotto 2002: 9), she had to become mistrustful, "hard," and "strong" like no woman ever, and almost like a man. In fact she is the only female compared in "reverse similes" (i.e., to male beings, such as a just king, a sailor, a lion), as a result of her temporary position as ruler and defender of the household (Foley 1984). Telemachus' reproach to his mother when she refuses to believe that the man in front of her is really Odysseus (*Od.* 23.97–103) is relevant:

> Mother, cruel mother [*dysmēter*] whose heart is unyielding [*apēnea thymon echousa*], why do you thus hold aloof from my father . . .? No other woman would harden her heart as you do [*ou men k'allē g'ōde gynē tetlēoti thymōi*], and stand aloof from her husband, who after many sad toils had come back to her in the twentieth year to his native land: but your heart is always harder than stone [*kradiē stereōterē . . . lithoio*].

Very similar are Odysseus' words to describe Penelope's obstinacy some lines later (*Od.* 23.166ff.): "God-touched lady, to you beyond all women have the dwellers on Olympus given a heart that cannot be softened," and then (addressing the nurse): "the heart in her breast is of iron." Penelope will later explain that her heart had to become mistrustful (*apistos*) because she was afraid that "some mortal man would come and beguile me with his words; for there are many who scheme for their own evil profit (*kaka kerdea*)" (*Od.* 23.216f.). The example she adds makes it clear enough what kind of beguilement she has in mind (*Od.* 218ff.): "No, even Argive Helen, daughter of Zeus, would not have lain in love with a foreigner" had she realized the consequences of her action. But a god led her mind astray: Aphrodite, who beguiled her through Paris' erotic offers. Penelope's mention of Helen's story implies that Aphrodite might have plotted against her too, in order to make her surrender to the charming words of a stranger during Odysseus' absence. She had repeatedly claimed that gods can alter human minds at any time and deceive even the most thoughtful and wise person on earth (*Od.* 23.11–4, 62–82).

Wise and steady though she is, Penelope is kept ignorant of Odysseus' plot against the suitors and even of his identity until after the accomplishment of his plan. Many hypotheses have been formulated (Katz 1991: 77–191), but the overall narrative purpose of this conspiracy of silence may be to cast dramatic irony around Penelope's action (Foley 1995:

103) in order to create suspense and exalt her virtue: the audience, while listening to Penelope's protracted dialogues with the false beggar, is engaged in the torturous pleasure of waiting for the recognition, but the delay also allows the enactment of Penelope's unique *aristeia*. Unsure whether to resist or surrender to the suitors, she eventually decides to set the marriage contest with the bow. She is portrayed as thinking that this will be her final step on the path of remarriage (but does not the fact that the bow is so hard to string raise the suspicion that she hopes to prove her suitors to be unworthy of her hand? See Felson 1994: 33ff.), yet the audience shares Odysseus' point of view and knows that her decision is going to help her husband overcome his rivals. Moreover, the narrator even has her obtain Odysseus' assent to the initiative: she tells the "beggar" about her plan, which he endorses, subsuming it into *his* plot of revenge. In this way Penelope becomes her husband's unaware helper. Her unconscious cooperation with Odysseus' interests depicts her as the perfect match for her husband: she not only shares his intelligence, endurance, and capacity to remember, but cannot, even unintentionally, act in any way but for her partner and for the sake of his bloodline. With the contest of the bow the poet found a highly effective way to mark Penelope's feminine excellence and exemplarity: she wants to help Telemachus against her desires and ends up saving Odysseus' household beyond her intentions.

6   Homeric Complexity and Plurality of Readings

As these examples show, an approach based on the assessment of textual redundancies proves effective in determining how women are by and large conceptualized in the poems. But this method, although devised for analysis of modern literary texts, proves suitable for the Homeric poems, for two further reasons. First, each poem can be treated as a sense-making device, without assuming any authorial intention. The text seems to drive its listeners/readers toward certain readings, whether this is an outcome planned by a bard-editor or merely the unintentional result of an underlying ideology shaping the accumulation and selection of traditional material. A second crucial advantage of this type of analysis is that it leaves room for indeterminacy and plurality of responses. However compelling the pressure exerted by a text may be, no text is ever completely closed and no narration has final control over its audience. This is especially true of the Homeric poems, traditional songs "grown up" through multiple adaptations of heterogeneous material. Moreover, the *Iliad* and *Odyssey* are oral-derived poems, whose poetics differ from those of a written literature. Formulaic repetitions, tyranny of prosody, type-scenes, *ad hoc* inventions, allusions to stories known to their traditional audience, and last but not least the fact that epics were addressed to an audience of spectators/listeners (not readers) and probably involved single episodes (very seldom the whole poem): all these features impose an evaluation of the poetic texture and structure that avoids imposing on epic texts the modern reader's anachronistic desire for coherence.

This applies also to epic characters and their motivations. Some puzzling aspects of Penelope—her divided mind and her decision to remarry after receiving a number of signs that her husband is finally coming back—do not need to be resolved. A certain degree of inconsistency in Penelope's behavior can be the result of the conflation of heterogeneous elements (the cunning queen of the folktale with the faithful wife of the epics; Hölscher 1996: 137), but it is consistent with her critical position in the plot, as long as she finds herself trapped in a sociological *impasse* (a woman in absence of a male tutor; Katz 1991: 193) and involved in a resistance test as other heroines of traditional "return songs" (Foley 1999: 142–57). In a similar way, Helen's ambiguity in both poems is no doubt the unavoidable outcome of the two opposing traditions of blame and praise poetry converging on her semi-divine figure (Austin 1994: 12–68; Graver 1995; Worman 2001: 20–37); but it also functions as a background warning against the problematic effects of women and sexuality on the stability of the household (the "bad-dog wife" motif).

Postmodern theory makes us aware that no reading is ever "innocent." Reading is inevitably compromised by the reader's contextually conditioned opinions, expectations, and interpretive purposes. This observation leads us to the final section of this essay, on the text and its actual audiences. Most of the interpretations referred to so far, based on the presumption of textual determinacy, lay bare the supposedly androcentric view underlying the narrative and aim at resisting its appeals. But this is only one of several possible ways to make sense of the female characters in the Homeric epics. Couples such as Hector and Andromache, Alcinous and Arete, and Penelope and Odysseus show that the Homeric poems champion a certain idea of positive cooperation between husband and wife (the *homophrosyne*, likemindedness) praised by Odysseus at *Od.* 6.183–4) and a form of respect on the husband's part for his wife. From this perspective, it is worth noting the scattered but significant hints at troubles caused by the sexual "double standard." Clearly wives were expected to have intercourse only with their husbands, whereas males were free to have sex at their will and to have children by other women.

Yet the stories of Phoenix and Laertes (*Il.* 9.450–7; *Od.* 1.432–3) reveal that the presence of a concubine in the house could be resented by the wife. Odysseus has sexual intercourse with Calypso and Circe during his wandering, yet they are not women, but goddesses whose will he cannot oppose; remembering his *nostos* and the priority he accords to his wife is as important for the plot as Penelope's celebrated memory of her husband. One might wonder whether Agamemnon's harsh attitude towards women in the *Iliad* is meant to elicit from the audience a recognition of the complex and tragic relationships he had with his female relatives: in mythical tradition Clytemnestra has good reasons to hate a husband who sacrificed their daughter Iphigenia and brought home a Trojan princess as his concubine (on possible reverberation effects of the wider mythological background on the poems, see Slatkin 1991: 100–22 and Dué 2002: 3–20). As Seth Schein puts it, "it would be simplistic to adopt the standard, patriarchal reading . . . without recognizing how the poem partly undoes this reading" (Schein 1995: 25).

Instead of warning against the potential snares of textual determinacy in concealing the androcentric bias underlying the narrative and "seduc[ing] female readers into assuming subordinate subject positions" (Doherty 1995: 104–77), some contemporary critics claim that the *Odyssey* is, rather, an open narrative, and insist on the positive aspects of its indeterminacy. It has been claimed that Penelope's protracted hesitation keeps the plot on the verge of different possible developments, thus enhancing its suspense (Felson 1994: 3ff.). Her character would display an "absence of integrity" consonant with the overall narrative "centered on deferral of truth and refuse of closure" (Katz 1991: 185–90). The fact that the initiative of the contest is attributed to Penelope herself (19.572), then to Athena (21.1f.), and later to Odysseus (24.167f.) by the soul of one of the suitors in the Underworld is but one example of the discrepancies that, being a typical feature of oral-derived poetry, are not to be resolved—as analysts and folklorists try to do by separating different layers in composition or threads in the plot—nor to be ignored, but left "forever open to question" (Katz 1991: 18).

Poems' openings also can be exploited to produce alternative readings that celebrate positive aspects of the female characters in the plot. Penelope is a favorite site for this kind of interpretation. In terms of textual redundancies, her extraordinary fidelity—long celebrated as a form of passive endurance and steadfast "fixation upon Odysseus" (P. Harsh quoted by Doherty 1995: 37), but also recently described as the obsession of a "dizzy housewife" falling asleep every few minutes when a crisis of "dopey narcoleptic trances" occurs (Boer 1992: viii)—hardly offers a subject position suitable for contemporary readers to identify with. But one can choose instead to highlight the textual hints at Penelope's cleverness and intelligence (Marquardt 1985: 32–44), or her ability to keep the suitors at bay and even to "trick the trickster" Odysseus into proving his true identity. It is also possible to read her dream about the pet geese as an unconscious expression of the guilty pleasure she takes in watching the suitors gathered in the palace, who, by wooing Penelope, in effect affirm her freedom of choice (Marquardt 1985: 43; Felson-Rubin 1996: 177). The actual reader can work out a *mise en abîme* of Penelope's skill as a weaver by making it resonate with the poet's own ability as a weaver and unweaver of songs and cunning plots (Bergren 1983; Winkler 1990: 129–61; Clayton 2004: 18–82).

Thus, Penelope surely offers the modern readers more palatable chances for identification and projection. Yet the high degree of sophistication and subtlety employed by many of these interpretations seems to me a clue to the difficulty of resisting the determinacy displayed by the text. After all, while Odysseus is insistently defined by his *poly*-ness (the varied and the multiple implied in epithets such as *polymētis, polytropos, polytlas, polymēchanos, polyphrōn*), Penelope is rather characterized by self-restraint, caution, and firmness (*echephrōn, periphrōn, epiphrōn*) and makes use of her agency to leave everything unchanged rather than make things move (Foley 1984: 62; Heitman 2005: 108–11).

RECOMMENDED FURTHER READING

On the poems as possible sources for historical reconstruction of women's position in real society, see Graham (1995: 3–16). Some of the textual strategies that construct the female agency as inherently dangerous are described by Wohl (1993) and Pedrick (1988). Beth Cohen's (1995) collection of readings focuses on representations of the female in the *Odyssey*. For semiotic and narratological categories, see Doherty (1995). Another important way to detect gender dynamics is speech-act analysis: see Clark (2001). Minchin (2007) gives a thorough survey of gender distribution in speech acts such as rebuke, protest, and storytelling in both poems. On the representation of female slaves in the Homeric society see Prescott (1986), Pedrick (1994), and Thalmann (1998a).

On gender dynamics in divine personae see Larson (1995) and Lyons (1996). The issue seems to apply to Homeric Helen in particular. Besides Worman (2001), see Clader (1976), Suzuki (1989), Austin (1994), Brillante (2002: 76–157), Worman (2001), Elmer (2005), and Roisman (2006). For differing views of Helen, see Loraux (1995) and Edmunds (2003).

On Penelope, begin with Murnaghan (1986), Winkler (1990), Katz (1991), and Felson (1994); see, more recently, Murnaghan (1994), Papadopoulou-Belmehdi (1994), Foley (1995), Fredricksmeyer (1997), Vernant (1997), Andò (2005: 25–58), Heitman (2005), and Mueller (2007).

For other general treatments, see Kakridis (1971: 68–75), Redfield (1975: 119–23), Farron (1979), Cantarella (1981), Woronoff (1983), Blundell (1995: 47–57), and Felson and Slatkin (2004).

ACKNOWLEDGMENTS

I would like to thank Maurizio Bettini and Seth Schein for their precious suggestions and professional advice. Anna Bianca Mazzoni provided me with the illuminating judgment of a sensible "general reader."

5

Etruscan Women: Towards a Reappraisal

Vedia Izzet

It is commonly held that Etruscan women, unlike the women of most ancient societies, were peculiarly privileged. They are supposed to have been independently wealthy and politically powerful. I aim here to reassess this view in the light of recent developments in archaeological and gender theory. A brief examination of current approaches to Etruscan women will be followed by two case studies—one textual, one archaeological—that highlight the methodological problems inherent in the material available for the study of Etruscan women.

1   Current Approaches

In discussions of Etruscan women, it is conventional to start with Athenaeus' description in his *Deipnosophistae*:

> Sharing wives is an established Etruscan custom. Etruscan women take particular care of their bodies and exercise often, sometimes along with the men, and sometimes by themselves. It is not a disgrace for them to be seen naked. They do not share their couches with their husbands but with the other men who happen to be present, and they propose toasts to anyone they choose. They are expert drinkers and very attractive. The Etruscans raise all the children that are born, without knowing who their fathers are. The children live the way their parents live, often attending drinking parties and having sexual relations with all the women. It is no disgrace for them to do anything in the open, or to be seen having it done to them, for they consider it a native custom. They sometimes make love and have intercourse while people are watching them, but most of the time they put screens woven of sticks around the beds, and throw cloths on top of them. . . . they live in luxury and keep their bodies smooth. In fact all the barbarians in the West use pitch to pull out and shave off the hair on their bodies.
> (Athenaeus, *Deipnosophistae* 12.517–8, transl. C. B. Gulick, Loeb Classical Library 1928/1969)

A Companion to Women in the Ancient World, First Edition. Edited by Sharon L. James and Sheila Dillon.
© 2012 John Wiley & Sons, Ltd. Published 2015 by John Wiley & Sons, Ltd.

In this we learn that Etruscan women were sexually licentious, that they were extraordinarily beautiful, that they were decadent and luxurious, and that they exercised and dined alongside men with no shame. Though written in the late second or early third century CE, the *Deipnosophistae* was based to a large extent on the *Histories* of Theopompus, written in the fourth century BCE (Shrimpton 1991; Fowler 1994), and these descriptions set a tone that has characterized many later sources, ancient and modern. The Etruscan princesses of early Roman history, such as Tanaquil, are powerful, determined women who succeed, in the short term at least, in achieving their political goals (for the ancient sources see Sordi 1981 and Rallo 1989a).

Later scholars have been keen to maintain the image of Etruscan women created in the writings of Greek and Latin authors. Archaeological evidence has been added to the textual (notably by Pallottino 1955: 151; see also Heurgon 1964; Gasperini 1989; Nielsen 1989; Amann 2000; Rathje 2000). The early accounts stress the power and public role of Etruscan women—from inscriptions that suggest the use of the matronymic to tomb paintings showing women wearing mantles (outdoor clothing) or dining with men, thus indicating the public visibility of Etruscan women. Because men and women are both present in banqueting scenes, and funerary sculpture gives apparently equal depictions of men and women, these earlier studies argued for male and female equality. They also emphasized the importance of the role of the mother within Etruscan society, as presumed from the many representations of nursing mothers and from the special treatment of females in burial, as seen, for example, in more elaborate carving on funerary beds (Heurgon 1964; Bonfante 1973a, 1973b, 1981, 1986, 1989a, 1989b, 1994). Slightly later accounts have acknowledged the importance of regional and class variation (for the former see Baglione 1989: 115; Nielsen 1989; for the latter see Gasperini 1989: 182; Rallo 1989b; Spivey 1991; Bonfante 1994). The most recent accounts have attempted to draw together the archaeological and textual data, and to set the discussion of Etruscan women in a broader social framework (Amann 2000; Bartoloni 2000; Haynes 2000; Rallo 2000).

2 Evaluating the Evidence: Textual Sources

The evidence for Etruscan women is textual and archaeological. As no significant text in the Etruscan language has survived, the textual material comprises descriptions of Etruscan women by contemporary or later Greek and Roman writers. But Etruscologists, and those studying Etruscan women, have paid insufficient attention to the Greek-ness or Roman-ness of these authors. An early attempt at arguing for caution in using these sources for understanding Etruscan society was made by Dumézil in his study of religion. He warned that Roman authors may have emphasized elements of Etruscan culture that were important to Roman practice (Dumézil 1970: 626) and that the Romans may have been attempting to legitimize their own practices by archaizing them: "The Romans ... were inclined to stamp their practices with the respectable Etruscan label, which gave them the prestige of antiquity and a kind of intellectual warranty" (Dumézil 1970: 661).

Dumézil's words of caution have been noted recently by cultural historians of Greece and Rome. In the sphere of religion, Beard et al. (1998: 20) have shown the specifically Augustan agendas at work in the creation of the texts that deal with Etruscans, and Edwards (1996) has demonstrated the ways in which such works were part of the broader discourse of the construction of the Roman past. In Greek literature, ancient sources containing writing about "other" cultures have received considerable attention, following

Lloyd's analysis of 1966 (Hartog 1988; E. Hall 1989; Cartledge 1993; Henderson 1994; J. M. Hall 1997; Miller 1997; Hölscher (ed.) 2000). For example, the treatment of women (principally Amazons) in these "ethnographic discourses" has been seen as an act of Greek construction of the self by way of comparison with others.

While today such critical approaches seem to be the obvious first step in trying to understand Etruscan women from the writings of Greek and Roman authors, this step has yet to be taken systematically. More recent scholarship has pointed the way to the potential for such an approach in Etruria: see the brief treatment by Spivey and Stoddart (1990: 14–17) of Livy's account of the rape of Lucretia, as well as the interesting discussions of other Italic cultures in Ampolo (1996), Bradley (2000), and Dench (1995). Nonetheless, a comprehensive, critical review of the literature, one that builds on the pioneering work of Rallo (1989a, 1989b) and Sordi (1981), has yet to be undertaken.

The following discussion is intended to give an indication of the complexity of the ancient texts that discuss Etruscan women. The episode is that already touched on by Spivey and Stoddart, the rape of Lucretia from Livy (1.57–9). The translation used is that of B. O. Foster's 1919 Loeb text, selected partly because it is very familiar but also because it highlights many aspects of the treatment of Etruscan women in the ancient texts. This account and others that mention Etruscan women have traditionally been read as accurate and valid descriptions of ancient *realia*, and as passages that can be used to patch together an accurate picture of the lives of Etruscan women. I suggest here, following the example of the approaches towards Roman religion and Amazons mentioned above, that these texts were written for ulterior purposes and that acknowledging this motive means that we must consider their usefulness, as sources for Etruscan women, to be much more ambiguous.

Livy was writing his *History of Rome* at the end of the first century BCE or at the beginning of the first century CE, the time of the Augustan refounding of Rome. It is thus impossible to read the episode of the rape of Lucretia and the role it played in the founding of the Republic without considering the contemporary context for Livy's retelling of the episode (on Livy's Lucretia, see also Hallett, this volume, Chapter 27 and Keith, this volume, Chapter 28). The episode is set during the campaign against Ardea by the Romans, led by their Etruscan king, Tarquin the Proud. In between assaults on the town, the young leaders often meet to dine and drink. At one such party in the quarters of the king's son, Sextus Tarquin, where a Tarquin, Collatinus, is also present, the young men start discussing their wives, and each praises the virtue of his own wife above that of all others. As the discussion and rivalry grows heated, Collatinus suggests that they should resolve the question by returning to their homes to see what their wives are up to in their absence. In the exhilaration of the moment, the princes agree and the party quickly sets off.

They arrive at nightfall, and go to Collatia where they find Lucretia, Collatinus' wife, who "was discovered very differently employed from the daughters-in-law of the king." They had already visited these (Etruscan) princesses and had found them "at a luxurious banquet." This reference by Livy seems to chime with the account of Athenaeus, and would at first glance provide evidence for the *luxuria* of Etruscan women. Further, the Etruscan princesses were dining "with their young friends," another confirmation that Etruscan women dined publically. But Livy did not set out to tell us about Etruscan women, as he himself has already told us: at the beginning of the description of what the men found, Livy explicitly draws a comparison between Lucretia and the Etruscan princesses in order to highlight Lucretia's virtue. In this section of Livy, the Etruscan women are there to act as a foil to the virtue of Lucretia, and it is Lucretia's virtue that was so instrumental in the foundation of the Republic, the theme of Livy's narrative (on this point see also Henry and James, this volume, Chapter 6; Hallett, this volume, Chapter 27; and Keith, this volume, Chapter 28).

This contrast between Etruscan and Roman morals is further developed by Livy: "though it was late at night, Lucretia was busily engaged upon her wool"—that most matronly of occupations. Indeed, Lucretia is not working alone, as her whole household is busily occupied, not frittering time away at a banquet. Livy tells us explicitly that Lucretia's household is "toiling by lamplight," a description that creates a sense of studied activity as they sustain their work late into the night by means of artificial light. We then learn that Lucretia is working "in the atrium of her house"—the central point of the *domus* and symbolic of the domestic realm. This was a suitable location for a Roman woman, unlike the (predominantly) male space of the *triclinium* occupied by the Etruscan princesses. It comes as no surprise to learn that Lucretia carries off the prize for the most virtuous wife: the embodiment of Roman womanly virtue in juxtaposition with Etruscan license and *luxuria*.

The Etruscan princesses' function as a foil to Lucretia is reinforced in subsequent elaborations of the episode. After being acknowledged as the most virtuous of wives, Lucretia welcomes Collatinus and the Tarquins to stay and dine that evening. It was in the house that "Sextus Tarquin was seized with a wicked desire to debauch Lucretia by force; not only her beauty, but her proved chastity as well provoked him." A few days later, Sextus Tarquin leaves the camp secretly and returns to Collatia. He is welcomed civilly by the household of Lucretia: he is given dinner and a guest chamber, where he waits until the household is asleep. Then, "burning with passion" and "with sword drawn," he steals through the house and finds the sleeping Lucretia, whom he rapes. Livy makes much of Lucretia's resistance: threats of death are nothing to her—only the fear of shame overcomes her "resolute modesty." Again, Lucretia's modesty is central in the narrative. Thus, as Tarquin leaves, we read that he is "exulting in his conquest of a woman's honor," emphasizing both Lucretia's modesty and also the dastardly pleasure Tarquin took in overcoming her. The negative light Livy casts on Tarquin is the culmination of disreputable characteristics that Tarquin has displayed so far: his clandestine abuse of the guest-friendship extended to him by Collatinus (and by Lucretia) represents a shocking transgression of the codes of comradeship, hospitality, and virtue. As the Etruscan princesses stand in contrast to Lucretia, so Tarquin stands in contrast to the Roman quality of *virtus*.

Lucretia's response to her rape further underlines her qualities of womanly virtue. In her grief, she calls for the return of her father and husband, the latter bringing Lucius Junius Brutus as companion. On their arrival they find Lucretia "sitting sadly in her chamber" and the sight of her husband makes her weep. When asked whether everything is well, she replies: "Far from it; for what can be well with a woman when she has lost her honor?" The implication of Lucretia's words is that a (Roman) woman's honor is her most important feature. However, Lucretia then goes on to make clear that her "body only has been violated" but that her "heart is guiltless." After exacting a promise for vengeance from her menfolk, she commits suicide. Livy takes pains here to show us the needlessness of this action: her husband and father try to "divert the blame from her who was forced to the doer of the wrong," reiterating that "it is the mind that sins, not the body." Nevertheless, Lucretia, refusing to live on as an example to unchaste women, is adamant that she must be punished. It is Lucretia's own dying words that memorialize her as a model for chastity.

But, if Lucretia is a model of Roman womanly virtue set against the vices of Etruscan women and Tarquin is an anti-model of male behavior, where is the model of male virtue?

It lies, of course, in the friend of Collatinus—the man who will go on to found the Roman Republic: Lucius Junius Brutus. While Collatinus and his family are grieving over Lucretia, Brutus takes the dripping knife from her body and exclaims "by this blood most chaste until a prince wronged it ... I swear ... that I will pursue Lucius Tarquin Superbus and his wicked wife and all his children with sword, with fire, aye with whatsoever violence I may; and that I will suffer neither them, nor any other, to be king in Rome." By removing the sword from Lucretia's body, Brutus reverses the action of its entry. Similarly, Brutus swears to undo the wrong caused by the rape by killing Tarquin. In fact, Brutus swears to kill not just Tarquin but his "wicked" (Etruscan) wife and children. It is not simply a personal act of vengeance, but a political action directed against the institution of monarchy itself, so that there will be no other "king in Rome."

A little later in the story, Brutus urges his compatriots "to take up the sword, as befitted men and Romans," and begins the movement that will lead to the downfall of the Etruscan monarchy in Rome. In his description of Brutus' rallying speech to the crowds in Rome, Livy sums up the justification for the establishment of a new republic in Rome: "He spoke of the violence and lust of Sextus Tarquin, of the shameful defilement of Lucretia and her deplorable death, of the bereavement of Tricipitinus, in whose eyes the death of his daughter was not so outrageous and deplorable as was the cause of her death." The shame felt by Lucretia's father at the circumstances surrounding his daughter's death is now set alongside the wickedness of Tarquin and the virtue of Lucretia and is commended to the crowds of Romans by Brutus.

A second part of his argument concerns the ill-treatment of the commons by the arrogant Etruscan king: "He reminded them, besides, of the pride of the king himself and the wretched state of the commons, who were plunged into ditches and sewers and made to clear them out. The men of Rome, he said, the conquerors of all the nations round about, had been transformed from warriors into artisans and stone-cutters." Brutus here bemoans the fall of the men of Rome from the glory of warriors to the drudgery of artisans and masons.

Brutus then returns to his attack on the monarchy: "he spoke of the shameful murder of King Tullius, and how his daughter [none other than the wife of Tarquin] had driven her accursed chariot over her father's body, and he invoked the gods who punish crimes against parents." Livy then brings to a conclusion the episode that heralds the birth of the new Roman Republic: "With these and, I fancy, even fiercer reproaches, such as occur to a man in the very presence of an outrage, but are far from easy for an historian to reproduce, he inflamed the people, and brought them to abrogate the king's authority and to exile Lucius Tarquinius, together with his wife and children." Tarquin's authority is thus overturned, and, together with his murderous wife, the last king of Rome is sent into exile to the Etruscan city of Caere (modern Cerveteri).

It should be clear from the preceding discussion of the rape of Lucretia that Livy's primary interest did not lie in preserving details of the lives of Etruscan women for later generations of Etruscologists to reconstruct. It was Livy's aim to produce a history of Rome, not a history of Etruscan women. In this section, as we have seen, attention is focused on the creation of a sense of Roman virtue, set against the backdrop of the newly emerging Republic. Etruscan women thus provided Livy with a useful foil for the Roman virtues of chastity and honor. Of course, it could be argued that the foil only works if Etruscan women are known to be licentious and immoral—that there can be no smoke without fire. Certainly, Livy and his audience may actually have believed that Etruscan women were licentious and decadent. However, Livy was writing his history several centuries after the events he describes, and there is simply nothing in his text that can tell us what ancient Etruscan women were really like. It may be disappointing to recognize this point: Livy presents us with a window not onto Etruscan society but onto his own. His history, along with all surviving ancient discussions of Etruscan women, needs to be understood in its specific context, as a product of a particular place and time. This contextualization may not get us any closer to real Etruscan women but it will at least help us to understand the cultural, social, and political agendas that underlie their colorful textual manifestations.

3   Evaluating the Evidence: Archaeological Sources

The archaeological evidence for Etruscan women is much more plentiful and diverse than the textual. Its use, however, has been similarly narrow. This section, incorporating material from Izzet (2007), will take a single object as an illustrative example of the problems and possibilities of using archaeological evidence for understanding the lives of ancient Etruscan women. The object is a bronze hand mirror of the fourth century BCE that shows a depiction of the judgment of Paris (Figure 5.1 and Figure 5.2).

Etruscan hand mirrors, found exclusively in funerary contexts, are an excellent example of the decontextualization of objects that characterizes Etruscology. These objects have been used to illuminate a variety of aspects of Etruscan life, including the clothes Etruscans wore (Bonfante 1975) and what furniture they used (Bonfante 1982), how they conducted ritual (Pfiffig 1975: 117–18), the influence of Greek myth (De Angelis 2001), the details of temple architecture (Bendinelli 1920), and importantly here, the role of women (Bonfante 1977, 1981, 1986). Few of these issues bear any relation to the original use of the mirror in Etruscan society, or to its archaeological context. In many of these studies, the images engraved on the non-reflective side of the mirrors have been taken as straightforward representations of the "real" or "everyday" existence of the Etruscans; there has been little acknowledgment of the culturally constructed nature of these images, or of the problems of interpretation that arise when using funerary material to understand non-funerary spheres of life (see, for instance, Chapman et al. 1981; Parker Pearson 1982; Morris 1987, 1992).

The decontextualization of objects that has resulted from ignoring the funerary origins of most Etruscan material culture has gone hand in hand with an art-historical tradition, as is evident in the frequency of single-object studies in the field. The most extreme version of this is "the catalog," for example the *Corpus Speculorum Etruscorum*. This multivolume catalog of mirrors (still in progress) serves as an invaluable resource for Etruscologists, providing accurate drawings (such as the one in Figure 5.1) and a detailed examination of the objects and the images engraved on them, together with provenance and a comprehensive bibliography. Yet nowhere in the authoritative volumes is the function of a mirror or its funerary significance examined. It is precisely this kind of issue that must be raised if we are to move from description to interpretation, and thus ultimately towards a more meaningful understanding of these objects and their ancient uses, or, as Serra Ridgway puts it, to look at "mirrors as *objects* not just 'pictures'" (Serra Ridgway 1992: 282, emphasis in original).

The mirrors in question are hand mirrors made of cast and beaten bronze, mostly the latter (Swaddling et al. 2000). Roughly 5000 survive. They contain a slightly convex reflective disc, which was highly polished on one side. Experiments carried out at the

Figure 5.1 "The Judgement of Paris." Line drawing of an Etruscan mirror (in Figure 5.2). Fitzwilliam Museum, Cambridge, UK. Drawing: Courtesy of the Syndics of the Fitzwilliam Museum.

British Museum suggest that if the mirrors were kept tarnish-free by buffing they would have stayed reflective indefinitely (J. Swaddling, pers. comm.). On the other side of this disc there was frequently engraved decoration, either abstract or figurative.

As noted above, mirrors have been used extensively in discussions of Etruscan women, partly because they are thought to have been female objects (though see Spivey 1991) and partly because they often show "feminine" scenes such as adornment or bathing. However, more important to their potential for revealing the lives of Etruscan women is their context in burial, and their function. The former is important because of the importance of burial in the creation of social personae. In burial "the deceased is given a set of representations of his or her social identities while alive, which are given material

Figure 5.2   "The Judgement of Paris." Etruscan mirror (fourth century BCE). Fitzwilliam Museum, Cambridge, UK. Photo: Courtesy of the Syndics of the Fitzwilliam Museum.

expression after death" (Parker Pearson 1982: 99). One aspect of this function is the creation, by the buriers, of an ideal "social persona" for the deceased, through "the material expression and objectification of idealized relationships formulated about the dead" (Parker Pearson 1982: 110).

With regard to function: the primary function of a mirror is reflection. It is created in order to throw back an image. In doing so, it creates a very specific image: that of the holder of the mirror. As the viewer perceives it, the image is formed immediately, reflecting him or her as he or she "is." Thus, the holder of the mirror sees an image of himself or herself as he or she is seen by others. By using the mirror the viewer has the opportunity to change his or her appearance according to how he or she wants to be seen. This manipulation of the surface of the body is always carried out within the confines of social and cultural parameters.

Recent archaeological studies have explored the potential of the body itself as a form of material culture (esp. Sørensen 1991, 2000; Marcus 1993), and, while such approaches have been criticized for making the body passive (Meskell 1999: 34), they provide a useful starting point for an inquiry into the manipulation and social reception of the body, particularly in the case of mirrors, which are designed to create images of the body.

The adornment of the body, whether with clothes, coiffure, or cosmetics, involves its socialization. It turns the skin into a "social skin." Alterations to (or decisions not to alter) the appearance of the body are made in the light of an ideal image of how the individual wants to look. This image represents, of course, that individual's culturally specific and socially informed notion of beauty (for female beauty see Perkins 2002; for male beauty see Robb 1997; for the Roman world see Wyke 1994a). For Bourdieu, the principle of beautification "is nothing other than the [principle of the] socially informed body ... which never escape[s] the structuring action of social determinisms" (Bourdieu 1977: 124; see also Bourdieu 1989: 192–3); the same phenomenon is called "social inscription" by Grosz (1995: 104).

That gender is implicated in the creation of personal identity is apparent in the anthropological (Schwarz 1979), sociological (Bourdieu 1989: 200–7; Gottdiener 1995), ethnoarchaeological (Hodder 1982), and archaeological (Gilchrist 1999; Marcus 1993; Meskell 1999; Sørensen 2000) literature. Gendered roles are social constructs, and derive from social and cultural attitudes towards the relative behaviors of men and women. These constructs and attitudes are learned in infancy, as is demonstrated by the diversity of gender roles and distinctions between and within cultures. However, despite the variety in its presentation, gender is nonetheless a regular axis along which societies choose to define and structure individuals.

Although societies construct models of appropriate gendered behavior, these structures are not inextricably binding: they are open to refusal and subversion. Men and women choose to what extent, and when, they will conform to the social expectations of them as gendered individuals. Gender identity, like personal identity, is a malleable construct: the experiences of an individual will change over time, and the changes will both alter, and be reflected in, the individual's evolving gender identity. The active role of the individual in the creation of gendered identity is further explored by Butler (1990: 140, 1993: 12). Echoing Bourdieu's stress on *praxis*, Butler has emphasized the importance of performance in the construction of gender (see also Strathern 1988: ix). Gender roles are created by the active participation of individuals within society; these roles are selected by individuals from a range of behavioral choices open to them within that society, and this selection is done deliberately and with care.

This has been a long preamble to the material under study, but it is important to establish the parameters within which the study of this type of archaeological material must be set. The image on a mirror cannot be seen as a simple representation of actions in the past; the conceptual framework that surrounds (and surrounded) the object must be established in order to interpret outward from the object. When looking, in this case, at each mirror, we must bear several things in mind: (1) the burial context, which affords the mirror a role in the creation of identity, including a gender identity; (2) the function of the mirror, which implicates it in the conscious and elaborate manipulation of the appearance of the body; and (3), importantly, the socially grounded nature of both of these facets.

Many Etruscan mirrors show the process of adornment itself. These are scenes where a figure, male or female, appears to be undergoing the process of adornment, either adorning himself or herself or being adorned by others. Mirrors depicting adornment mostly, though not exclusively, show the female toilette, and the self-reflexivity of such images serves to underline the importance of adornment. Another aspect of the mirrors is their association with marriage. Mirrors were frequently given as wedding gifts (Serra Ridgway 2000: 416), and a common "label" found describing the seated female figure being adorned is "Malavisch," usually translated as "bride" (Bonfante and Bonfante 1983: 148). Thus, the context of female adornment in Etruscan mirrors is set within the broader framework of preparing the female body for being viewed and within the narrower framework of preparing her for viewing by the (male) groom.

The concept of the "male gaze" was first developed by Berger in his study of European post-Renaissance art and was explored further by Mulvey and others (Berger 1972; Mulvey 1989; Bartky 1990). Its premise is that the act of looking at male and female bodies is imbalanced: women refuse to make eye contact with the viewer, while male figures cast an aggressive and objectifying gaze. Authors such as Berger have shown the ways in which the intended viewer of both the image and the female body within it is assumed to be male. If such is the case in Etruscan mirrors, the putative power of Etruscan women, in gender politics at least, is challenged.

In many scenes on Etruscan mirrors, the so-called "male gaze" is elaborated. This has been hinted at above in the brief discussion of the scenes with the adornment of "Malavisch," where the male viewer is the future groom, and it is implied more widely for the use of mirrors in general. There are, however, mirrors in which this male gaze is articulated more explicitly, as in those depicting episodes from the myth of Elina, the Etruscan Helen of Troy (Bonfante 1977; Krauskopf 1988). Elina was reputed to have been the most beautiful woman on earth, and she was the prize given to Alksuntre (Paris) by Turan (Aphrodite) for having chosen her over Uni (Hera) and Menrva (Athena) in the beauty contest of the three goddesses. Various aspects of the story of Elina are depicted in mirrors, and she is often named in captions; the most common element of her story in the mirrors, however, is the one in which she herself does not appear: that of the three goddesses and Alksuntre in the scene of judgment for which Elina is the prize (Bonfante 1977; Martelli 1994; Eriksson 1996; Nagy 1996).

Figure 5.2 shows a fourth century BCE depiction of this scene on a mirror. The mirror is 30.4 centimeters high and so would have been a considerable weight to hold (285.2 grams). The obverse (reflective side, not shown) would have been highly polished, and has minor decoration at the junction of the disc and the handle. On the reverse there is considerable engraved figurative decoration. At the junction of the disc and the handle is engraved a chubby, winged boy, "probably Eros" (Nicholls 1993: 19). He is wearing shoes, but is otherwise naked. In his hands he holds a string or wire that Nicholls (1993: 19) suggests may be a snare for the bird just to the left of him. From behind the figure's head spread two schematic sprigs of foliage, which encircle the central scene and which are "probably intended as laurel" (Nicholls 1993: 19). The choice of a laurel wreath to surround an image of a contest is particularly apposite; the fact that it is a beauty contest that is depicted on the mirror (an object used in beautification) is all the more appropriate.

A double horizontal line and diagonal hatching separate the Eros figure from the main scene (most easily seen in Figure 5.1). The latter shows four figures. To the left a male figure is identified as Elchsuntre (Alcsentre, Alksuntre, Alexander; i.e., Paris) by the label above his right shoulder. He faces the other figures with his weight on his right leg and his left leg crossing it. He wears a chiton and *chlamys*, a Phrygian cap, and leather boots. The hatching on his right arm is an archer's guard, and he carries a club. His left hand is raised as though in indecision, though for anyone familiar with the story the verdict is inevitable. The three goddesses face him in the same pose and with almost the same gestures: their weight on their right leg and their right arms are raised. They have similar, yet individualized, hairstyles and wear similar shoes, bead necklaces, and pendant earrings. They are all named in labels. The left-hand figure is Uni (Hera). The central figure is Turan (Aphrodite), who is shown almost naked with her drapery falling from her body and caught between her legs. She pulls part of it over her head like a veil in a gesture commonly associated with Hera and brides, perhaps alluding to the role of mirrors in Etruscan weddings and to the role of Aphrodite in providing a bride for Paris after he chose Aphrodite in the contest. Turan is a common figure on Etruscan mirrors: she is often shown superintending adornment scenes, and in later mirrors she becomes a stock figure on her own. As goddess of love, her choice on mirrors given as wedding gifts is not surprising, and the overtones of eroticism she brings appear to accord, at least on the surface, with the traditional views of sexual license in Etruscan women. The figure on the right is Menrva (Athena). She holds a spear in her upheld right hand and she wears her aegis with a small gorgoneion and two stylized stars. At the top of the mirror is a small winged female deity who could be a Lasa or an attendant of Aphrodite. The centrality of Turan (and her attendants) as goddess of love and seduction is obvious. The link between the most beautiful goddess and the most beautiful woman on earth is exploited in the mirror, and brings together the themes of beauty and adornment.

But the significance of Turan does not lie only in her association with the sphere of beauty: more important here is her connection with the theme of competition and the judgment of beauty. And, significantly, the judgment of beauty is carried out by a male arbiter, Alksuntre. In the mirror Alksuntre stands casually, leaning on the edge of the frame of the mirror. Thus, he is in a different position from the other figures, distanced slightly from the action. He is on the edge of the scene, looking in on the action, just as we are and just as the Etruscan holder of the mirror would have been. Through this positioning, he includes and implicates us—and the Etruscan viewer—in his own participation in the scene; we are thus encouraged to collude with his judgment. The objects of his male gaze are three female figures, participants in what might be described as the ultimate beauty contest (Berger 1972: 51–2; see also Keuls 1993: 206). In this context it is wholly appropriate that the winner of the contest is the seductive and erotically charged figure of Turan. At the same time, the gift that Turan gives Alcsentre for selecting her is Elina, the most beautiful of women.

The scene on the mirror thus presents a clear message about the importance of female beauty within Etruscan culture, what is at stake in its attainment, and the importance of a male viewer in judging female beauty. The objectified female figures displayed on this mirror are a far cry from recent interpretations of Etruscan women. The notion of the emancipated and powerful Etruscan woman can be derived only superficially from the images engraved on mirrors. Such an interpretation not only fails to take account of the cultural and archaeological contexts of the mirror but also ignores the role of the object and the many webs of meanings in which it is enmeshed. Instead of reading the images on mirrors as snapshots of ancient lives, the data force us to come to terms with a more complex "reality."

4   Conclusion

This discussion has taken two kinds of evidence to explore the shortcomings of current approaches to, and at the same time the potential for the study of, Etruscan women. Both kinds of data are traditionally deployed in a "straightforward" positivist manner, yet the unsustainability of such an approach demands the detailed contextualization of the production of all evidence in order to assess the contribution it can make to our understanding. Sadly, the interpretation presented here suggests that, far from being the emancipated, powerful women of the scholarship of the 1970s and 1980s, Etruscan women were codified by their bodies according to social norms adjudicated by men. In a way, then, the analysis of the mirror here provides a more nuanced feminist reading, a revisionist rebuttal that does not romanticize the seductive visual materials. To say that Etruscan women were just as subject to the male gaze (a demand for female beauty) as other women in antiquity is to stop treating them as exotic "others." If it is to get anywhere near understanding the complexity of ancient Etruscan lives, the study of Etruscan women now needs to move beyond the doctrines of second-wave feminism and harness the theoretical developments in archaeology and gender studies.

RECOMMENDED FURTHER READING

No attempt to engage with Etruscan women should be removed from the wider intellectual framework of gender and feminist writing. This includes the work of philosophers, such as Butler (1993); anthropologists, such as Strathern (1988); and archaeologists, such as Meskell (1999) and Sørensen (2000).

The ancient sources on Etruscan women have been compiled in Sordi (1981) and Rallo (1989a). The earliest significant consideration of archaeological evidence was Heurgon (1964), with systematic working through by Bonfante (1973a, 1973b, 1981, 1986, 1989a, 1989b, 1994). This early work has been developed by Baglione (1989), Gasperini (1989), Nielsen (1989), and Spivey (1991), who have acknowledged regional and class differences. The most recent accounts have attempted a more contextual approach; see Amann (2000), Bartoloni (2000), Haynes (2000), and Rathje (2000).

6

Woman, City, State: Theories, Ideologies, and Concepts in the Archaic and Classical Periods

Madeleine M. Henry and Sharon L. James

This essay briefly considers the attitude of the state—Roman *urbs* or Greek polis—toward women, asking not about women's relation to the state but about the state's relation to women. That is, how did the self-identified state conceptualize woman and integrate her into its population and operations? What were the functions of women in a self-governing state, and what risks did they pose to the state? The legal systems of antiquity suggest that women were a concern in the earliest stages of a state's development, that the issue of managing women was foundational to the state's vision of itself, an issue that remained acute throughout the life of the state. As we shall argue here, in the state's view, "woman" was not a single, unified category. The picture is more complex, as the state required official, well-policed distinctions between the classes of females who may produce legitimate citizen offspring and the classes who may not. Far from being irrelevant to the state, this latter group too was absolutely necessary—particularly the enslaved prostitute, whose captivity and sexual servitude assisted the proper function of the state by enabling peaceable relations among men, as we will discuss below.

Even a minimal acquaintance with Greek culture demonstrates that woman was understood as qualitatively different from man, and as a perennial problem requiring management. In Greek mythic thought, woman was created as the penalty for man's acquisition of fire. She is also the vehicle for procreation (not an unmixed blessing). Thus, as Hesiod inscribes woman, she is a curse on all men and a necessary evil for each individual man, who must support a wife and hope that her children are also his. While a man is a Hesiodic-style private farmer, his wife is chiefly his private problem, though she may certainly expose him to ridicule by his neighbors. She becomes a public problem only by doing something like running away, as Helen of Troy does, but for the most part woman in the Archaic period is governed by an individual man.

It is worth pausing for a moment to note that many women in antiquity would be unlikely to recognize themselves in our analysis. Ideologies that authorize a man's vitriolic expression of Hesiodic misogyny do not necessarily translate into his private life: a man who considered women as a whole inferior creatures might well not only love but also

A Companion to Women in the Ancient World, First Edition. Edited by Sharon L. James and Sheila Dillon.
© 2012 John Wiley & Sons, Ltd. Published 2015 by John Wiley & Sons, Ltd.

respect his wife, mother, sister, daughter, and other relatives. There is good reason to believe that girls could grow up feeling cherished by their fathers and brothers rather than considering themselves a burden. In addition, citizen women felt powerful relationships to their *poleis*, and, if they did not enjoy full participation in its operations, they might well not have sought such participation. But, if citizen women are the only women the state really cares about, they are not the only women the state needs.

The Greek city-state of the Classical period developed slowly from cities in the Archaic period (depicted as allies and friends in Homeric poetry) into *poleis*, city-states that partially identified themselves, and justified their actions, through a collective construction of Hellenic ethnicity (particularly in Athens, which over-dominates the surviving evidence), a program that allowed them to define each other's citizens as foreigners and, eventually, as enemies. The pure and homogeneous ethnic identity of a given polis was one of the markers by which that city-state defined itself against all others, Hellene or non-Hellene. Thus, in Athens, only those who could make a plausible claim to be descendants of the Erechtheids, sprung from the Athenian soil itself, could be citizens. The propagation and continuation of those family lines was a civic priority; hence, within Athens citizen women were a civic necessity (not merely a private necessity for a given citizen man, as in Hesiod). They kept the pure Athenian families alive—a private obligation to their husband's family and a civic obligation to the ethnic homogeneity by which Athens defined itself. After the passage of Pericles' citizenship law, which limited citizenship to people whose parents were both citizens, citizen women were even more important to their city. (Before this law was passed, in 451/50 BCE, citizenship required only a citizen father; see also Levick, this volume, Chapter 7). Women's participation in religion was a necessity for the polis as well. But they had no other officially acknowledged role in the city, as Greek thinking on woman began by excluding her conceptually from man and proceeded to exclude her socially, legally, and culturally from male social/political institutions.

Unlike what we loosely call Greece or Hellas, the Romans were, uniquely, a hybrid people from their very beginning rather than a pure ethnic group native to its own soil. They thus did not need to protect a specific genetic stock. Further, the Romans did not have a story of Roman men before the existence of woman—that Hesiodic dream of a female-free earthly paradise did not plague the male imagination in Rome. Because Rome came into being precisely as a city, a city that would disappear without women to bear children, women were foundational to Rome's origins and early survival—there is literally no Rome otherwise. Thus, woman officially entered Rome very specifically as wife and mother, not merely as a human female. Under the direction of Romulus, Roman men sought not sexual partners but citizen wives, whose presence in the city, as Miles (1995) argues, legitimated the Roman men (previously vagabonds at best and criminals at worst) as peers with the citizen men of the cities around them. Nevertheless, women were not necessarily seen as positive contributors to the *urbs*, let alone as trustworthy members equal to men. As we will discuss here, Rome's early history obsessively rehearsed issues of respectability in citizen females and marked the limitations of woman's activity in the *urbs*.

A final foundational point: Rome came into being not only as a city but also as a city with an active program of imperialist expansion. As a result, the *urbs* needed a constantly growing population. Over the centuries, it supported that goal both by absorbing citizens of other populations (from the beginning, with the Sabines, discussed below) and by encouraging its citizens to produce large families. Where the Greeks typically did not raise more than one daughter per family (preferring to have only one or two sons), the Romans kept every healthy child and encouraged the production of more. In this respect, too, women were crucial to the city: more daughters meant a regular supply of sons for the wars of expansion that Rome pursued almost ceaselessly.

1   The Pre-State Beginnings in Archaic Culture

Rome and Athens inevitably dominate both our sources and their interpretations, with the result that other models of female civic engagement are both a minority and are often presented in stark contrast. So it is crucial to note here that in both Hellas and Italy other, less-attested, states did offer alternate models for the integration of woman into the state. For example, the Etruscans of central Italy, who were later eclipsed by the growth of Roman power, offered gender roles that fascinated both the Greeks and Romans (see Izzet, this volume, Chapter 5). This society, somewhat decentralized and focused on local aristocracies, privileged both male and female parentage, and was viewed by the Greeks as licentious (Theopompus in Athenaeus 517d–518a). Likewise, Sparta, discussed below, was seen as anomalous particularly in its treatment of women (see Neils, this volume, Chapter 11). As we consider the relation of state to woman, we ought to keep in mind that our dominant sources of evidence, particularly Athens, could easily have been seen as the anomalous societies (see e.g., Redfield 2003). We therefore briefly consider a few other *poleis*, below.

Writ large, women's interactions with city and state shared some commonalities in the Greek and Roman worlds: by the Archaic period (that is, the development of urbanization and the notion of heritable property), women's fertility was exploited by men for the purpose of property management. Thus, women's chastity underpinned the stability of the social unit, be it familial or civic—and here it is important to note that chastity means not celibacy but fidelity to one's husband. Because unchaste women were seen as threats to that stability, they were marginalized. Conspicuous consumption and adornment by women, as well as their ability to speak in public, were found threatening and disallowed by law and custom as signifying lack of self-control: if a woman showed physical desires of one kind or another, she would certainly also have excessive sexual desire.

The founding texts of Hellas, the Homeric poems, present a pre-state and emergent-state world that features great status fluidity. Greek warriors leave behind their women and children to recapture Helen, despoil Troy, and enslave women of the enemy. Loot (including women), rather than land, is the primary end of this conflict. The rape and sexual enslavement of women are frequent consequences of war, arguably main points of the Homeric poems (on women in Homer see also Franco, this volume, Chapter 4, including the chapter's bibliographical citations). Masculinity depends on men's dominion over women and children in both war and peace, and the Homeric poems provide a functional or performative definition of masculinity that entails male sex right over all females. (See Herzfeld 1985 on the way that similar performative Greek masculinity persists even in the very recent past.) Feminist scholars such as Gerda Lerner (1986), Carole Pateman (1988), and Catharine MacKinnon (1989) posit that the sexual-social contract of male sex right is in fact the first social contract. While this contract is usually displaced onto marriage, there is an equivalent need for a disposable, prostituted class. This sexual-social contract operates in peacetime and wartime, because warfare is only one stop on the ringroad of state formation, state maintenance, and state destruction.

In rendering imperative the sexual enslavement of females in wartime, the *Iliad* shows us a shadowy, yet consistent, pre-state version of the sexual contract. By making the capture and enslavement of females a defining component of masculinity—one that the gods either support or cannot prevent—the poet centralizes the subordination of females. That the potential fate of all mortal women is capture, rape, and sexual enslavement demonstrates the validity of the sexual contract, as does the *Odyssey*'s "reverse simile," which likens Odysseus' sorrow, in Book 8, to that of a woman on her day of enslavement. The importance of rape and sexual enslavement to masculinity and victory are made programmatic in *Iliad* 1, 9, and 24. The Homeric poet shows sympathy and, often, respect for captive women, but does not imagine another fate for them or even remark upon the injustice of their captivity. If he allows them to speak for themselves, as Briseis does over Patroklos' body, he cannot change the system that has already treated her, repeatedly, as a symbol of male achievement.

The *Iliad* features several individual, pretty female captives, who are referred to by name, identified as a *geras* (prize), and sometimes have patronymics and therefore known fathers. Named females, such as Andromache, will be brought "home" by their captors as concubines and bear them children, yielding later to newer and younger women. Conversely, the *Odyssey* refers frequently to unnamed captive females en masse, and calls them, collectively, *dmōiai*. Although the noun *dmōiai* is usually translated as "slaves," "serving women," and the like, it literally means "captured, tamed ones" (Cole 1984: 97–113).

The ubiquity of female slaves reinforces the sense that archaic Hellas is a raiding culture and underscores what becomes of females who are captured once they have been carried "home." The term *dmōiai* as a collective noun defines these dehumanized tamed beings not as unique individuals but as a group. Additionally, they are not found in the underworld: their non-personhood reaches to the grave. In life, they are owed nothing by their owners and are utterly disposable. Any who dares to act against the interests of the master is brutally punished: the faithless *dmōiai* who worked in Odysseus' household are all executed, and the gods see to it that the Phoenician woman (herself raided from her home and sold into slavery) who stole the baby Eumaios is killed before she can reach home (*Odyssey* 15). The emergence of community justice ends the *Odyssey*, with Athena herself enjoining Odysseus and his allies to find a better way than killing to manage their differences—differences that began precisely with competing, and socially illegitimate, claims to a woman, namely Penelope.

2 The Classical Period: *Polis* and Early *Urbs*

In Greece, the tension between, on the one hand, men's desires to manage their own affairs and to have their own property and, on the other hand, their need to live productively in community, is visible in traditions about marriage, concubinage, and prostitution as the polis developed. Paternally recognized offspring of a concubine became problematic for reasons of property and inheritance, with the eventual exclusion of both bastards (*nothoi*) and concubines (*pallakai*) from civic rights; foreign-born and poor women were increasingly disadvantaged. In Athens, by the time of Pericles' citizenship law (451/450 BCE) the state had become the family (Patterson 1990). Myths of autochthony found in various city-states recapitulate the association of citizenship with place and of woman with earth.

In the emerging polis, woman became a public problem rather than a matter of private household management. The importance of females as transmitters of property is seen in the early appearance of legislation regarding marriage and inheritance. The Athenian lawgiver Solon (fl. 596) is credited with instituting legislation concerning the *epiklēros* (a female whose deceased father left no male heirs; see also Levick, this volume, Chapter 7) and with stipulating a minimum number of times a man must engage in intercourse with his wife each month.

Because urbanization brought men easier access to one another's wives, sisters, and daughters, men's sexual urges also constituted a public danger—hence the many laws also attributed to Solon that regulated female sexuality, including the possible institution of public brothels. The slave prostitute (*pornē*, "purchased female") was a civic necessity for peaceable relations among citizen men. The lowly nature of prostitution made foreign women a likely source for the disposable class in the archaic city-state. Solon's biographical tradition supports the view that he encouraged the prostitution of women (Henry 2011: 31). The alleged connection of one of the seven sages of antiquity, and the legendary lawgiver of Athens, with institutionalized brothel prostitution is not a trivial matter. In addition, because prostituted public slaves would not have been able to serve (or even survive) for very long, the polis would have required an ongoing supply of raided prostitutes. It is worth keeping in mind that many of these enslaved women might well not have known the Greek language: they would have suffered severe linguistic isolation during their short lives of unpleasant prostitution in a foreign country (Marshall 2013).

Various civic officials in late classical Athens may have regulated prostitution. The *astynomoi* (city controllers) established fee caps for performers and settled disputes over their services. There was also a *pornikon telos* (prostitution tax) probably levied on pimps of both sexes as well as on individual service providers. The *hetaira* (companion) was the aristocratic prostitute, though the status of such women was hardly fixed; indeed, it is possible that Solon legislated how a man might prostitute his own female kin (Glazebrook 2005). First seen in the sixth century BCE, the *hetaira* may be an aristocratic reaction-formation, an "invention of the symposium" (Kurke 1999: 181).

The substrate *pornē* is a likely source for the elegant *hetaira*. The *pornē* is first seen in an urban setting, the nascent polis, and there is evidence for *porneia* (brothels) in Athens in the fifth century BCE. Such businesses were not separated, situated in "zones of shame" (McGinn 2011), but were rather interspersed throughout the city; neither were they purpose-built, as found uniquely in Pompeii. Some brothels undoubtedly functioned as places of dual employment, as in the case of Building Z in the Kerameikos near the Sacred Gate, where Thracian slave women worked both in the textile industry and the sex industry (Glazebrook 2011).

The state took its relationship to citizen women very seriously, being dependent on both their fertility and their participation in religious rituals, of which quite a few were conducted by citizen women without male participation. (On women's religion in Greece, see Stehle, this volume, Chapter 14.) The polis of Athens believed that every citizen woman was more or less owed a husband; hence, the death of a man without sons created a civic crisis: his daughter, the *epiklēros*, came under the supervision of the city magistrate. The existence of an office called the *gynaikonomos* (regulator of women), which may have been short-lived in late classical Athens, indicated an interest in limiting consumption and display among citizen women, continuing the tradition, originally ascribed to Solon, of limiting the role of women in mourning as well as women's use of money.

In other archaic societies, women seem to have had some choice of marriage partner. The community of Gortyn on Crete allowed them to inherit; hence, the *epiklēros* (here called *patroiokos*) might buy her way out of the obligation to marry a kinsman. In the literary sources, gender relations in Sparta and, therefore, Spartan women, are represented as the opposite or obverse of "normative" Greek society (see Neils, this volume, Chapter 11). Spartan females, as the future mothers of warriors, were given ample food; there is no evidence of sex-based female infanticide; and females were encouraged to speak and to exercise. They appear to have married relatively late (around the age of 18) and to have been able to mate with a husband and another partner, in what Pomeroy (2002: 40) calls "husband-doubling." The "Constitution of Lycurgus" privileged the nurture of healthy Spartans of both sexes. Nonetheless, religion was the main outlet for authority for Spartan women, as elsewhere in the Hellenic world.

Uniquely, as we have noted, Rome came into being as a city—there was no discernible pre-civic archaic farming period. Rape instantiates the city: Rhea Silvia, violated by Mars, gives birth to Romulus and Remus. The rape of the Sabine women, engineered by Romulus for the purpose of establishing marriage and increasing the population, defines marriage socially, for thereby women are incorporated into their husbands' family and take on their husbands' ethnicity. This mass rape also creates the means for state expansion: Rome could replenish its stock by continued conquest and incorporation.

It is worth noting that the rape of the Sabine women, as Livy tells it, is almost purely utilitarian (though see Joshel 1992a) and is carried out with military order and precision (by contrast, Ovid's version, in *Ars Amatoria* 1, shows a more probable chaos). Even a short meditation on the logistics of the scene, however, reveals problems of basic math. Each Roman man wants a wife, but in a crowd it would not be possible for each man simply to grab the girl of his choice, or even the nearest girl: the daughters of the Sabines (and the other neighboring populations, all subsumed narratively under the Sabines) were accompanied by parents and brothers, who would have required restraint by significant force. Lacking gunpowder, the Romans would have needed probably five to seven men for each girl they stole—and it would not have been possible to keep their neighbors peaceably awaiting the return of each group of Roman men for more daughters. The account of the mass rape or theft literally does not add up, and is likely to be a cover-up for a series of night-time abduction raids on neighboring towns, in which bands of armed men went from Rome to steal daughters not as enslaved sexual loot to be sold but as wives. If so, then the term rape is precise and proper in its modern sense, rather than its ancient sense (derived from Latin) of theft: each girl would have been dragged into an individual man's dwelling and forced by rape to accept marriage—a significant difference from the usual accounts, in which the girls accepted their marriages in a public fashion, in daylight, upon persuasion by Romulus. The marriage of the Sabine women nullifies forcible abduction and rape, converting them into brusque and violent but honorably intended courtship. Whatever the reality was, marriage was used in these foundational myths to legitimate Roman unions with outsiders.

Rape continued to recur throughout Rome's earliest period, to the point of being a structure in the development of the Republic, which spent its first 200-odd years under the rule of kings or ruling cabals. Rape and revolution were inescapably intertwined: the violation of a citizen woman required violent uprising and reprisal by citizen men, with the result that tyrants were overthrown, as in the tales of Lucretia and Verginia, briefly discussed below. Female chastity was seen as so crucial to the survival of the state that sexuality in citizen females was to be strictly controlled: Tarpeia, desiring the enemy leader Titus Tatius, betrays Rome and must be killed; Horatia, weeping at the death of her fiancé, killed by her brother in battle, is killed by her brother as being effectively a traitor. Female political ambition is likewise dangerous, and often linked to illicit sexuality: Tullia, in love with her husband's brother (also named Tarquin), kills her husband and marries her brother-in-law, whom she pushes into murdering her father, King Servius, the last good king of the Roman state (see Hallett, this volume, Chapter 27).

The Roman obsession with female chastity, and perception of it as a necessary element in the safety of state, is so great as to result in a few genuine failures of logic in these tales. For example, Tarpeia, who betrayed Rome for love of its enemy leader (as in the account of Propertius 4.4), is a Vestal Virgin during the Sabine War (and, as we have suggested above, even the account of the rape of the Sabine women fails in plausibility). But the Sabine War is fought over the Sabine women, who were stolen precisely because Rome had no women (at least, no respectable women). If there were no women in Rome, how can Tarpeius have had a daughter who could serve as a Vestal Virgin? He could not have. In addition, Tarpeia's very name betrays Sabine ethnicity; hence the tale is further mystified.

Tarpeia's story exists, then, to explain why Romans traditionally punished traitors by throwing them off the Tarpeian Rock: at some point, Tarpeia herself was invented to explain the practice. The reasoning would have gone something like this: "why do we throw traitors off the Tarpeian Rock? We've always done it, so there must have been a traitor named Tarpeius or Tarpeia in the very beginning. When, in the very beginning, was Rome most at risk? Why, during the Sabine War, when the Sabine men attacked Rome to get their daughters and sisters back. Some woman must have betrayed Rome! Her name must have been Tarpeia. Why do women commit treason? The usual female reasons, of course: sex or desire for finery." Hence the dual tale: Tarpeia sought either Tatius himself (as in Propertius 4.4) or the elaborate armbands worn by the Sabine men (as in Livy's account). In her story, we can see a negative imprint of the value placed on female chastity: if the chastity of the Sabine women proves the respectable status of Roman men, the failure of female chastity puts the entire state at risk.

The theft of female chastity does the same, in Rome's repetitive rape-revolution formula: rape of a respectable woman (Rhea Silvia, Lucretia) leads eventually to overthrow of tyrants, in a step toward Rome's eventual liberation in the Republic (on Lucretia see also Izzet, this volume, Chapter 5; Hallett, this volume, Chapter 27; and Keith, this volume, Chapter 28). The young girl Verginia (Livy 3.44–58) is killed by her father before the tyrannical magistrate Appius Claudius can declare her a slave for the purposes of raping her. The ensuing revolt of the plebs results in the overthrow of the *decemvirs* (ten magistrates ruling the city), the establishment of rights for the plebs, the form of the Twelve Tables, and the widespread publication of those rights in bronze monuments placed around the city. By murdering his daughter to preserve her honor and virginity, Verginius helps to create the Roman Republic. Verginius and his daughter's fiancé Icilius make clear the connection between male civic status and female sexual status, as when Icilius declares to Claudius that the plebs will not tolerate the sexual misuse of their women:

> You have taken from the Roman people the aid and advocacy of the tribunes, the two fortresses of plebeian liberty, but your lust will not be given rule over our wives and children as well. Beat our backs and beat our necks: our women's chastity must at least be safe. If violence is brought to this arena, I will call upon the faith of the Romans here, on behalf of my fiancée; Verginius will call on the faith of the soldiers, on behalf of his only daughter; and all will call upon the faith of the gods and every man. You will not enforce that decree without slaughtering us.
>
> (Livy, *Ab urbe condita* 3.45; transl. S. L. James)

Similarly, Verginius declares to the assembled people of Rome that his own life is not worth living if his daughter cannot be kept chaste—and that the same applies to them:

> His daughter's life was dearer to himself than his own, if daughters were allowed to live free and chaste: but when he saw his daughter seized for violation, like a slave, he thought it was better for her to be set free by death than liberated in outrage, and he had collapsed into grief in contemplation of this cruelty. He had not planned even to survive his daughter, but he hoped for the people's aid in avenging her death. They too had daughters, sisters, and wives .... The record of another man's disaster was given to them as a warning to avoid similar suffering. ...Verginius was ready to defend himself from any other outrage of Appius, with the same spirit he had used to defend his daughter. The rest should look out for themselves and their children. The crowd cried out with Verginius ... and declared that they would fail neither him in his grief nor their own freedom.
>
> (Livy, *Ab urbe condita* 3.50; transl. S. L. James)

In these scenes, the connection between the sexual status (i.e., pure and chaste or despoiled and useless) of the female citizen body and the political status of the Roman citizen male could not be more clear: they are the same thing (for a broad, more global consideration of the relationship between female purity and the state, see Ortner 1978). But of course the citizen female's chastity can be ruined from within, by her own desires, even more easily than from without, by an invading or tyrannical force—and her illicit desires can imperil the state, as in the tales of Tarpeia and Tullia, among others.

In Rome, as at Athens, the prostituted female was a means of preserving the chastity of citizen women and thus of keeping peace between men, as seen in the praise given by Cato the Elder, the notoriously strict censor, to a young man he saw leaving a brothel: "very good, he said! It is right [*aequom*] for young men to come here to relieve their sexual urges rather than interfere with other men's wives" (Horace, *Satire* 1.2.31–5). The same principle would have applied to citizen daughters, of course. For sexual release, Roman citizen men of course always had access to their own slaves (as Horace remarks in the same satire, 116–19), but for more fulfilling sexual engagement they had to go outdoors, to the brothels that were scattered throughout the city. Prostitutes of all levels, from slaves to elite and expensive courtesans, abounded in Rome; and again, as at Athens, were legally regulated chiefly by annual registration fees. (On prostitution in Rome see especially McGinn 1998, 2004).

But for citizen women, *pudicitia* (chastity) was crucial enough to be a matter of social practice, law, and even religion (as in the cult of Pudicitia). Most strikingly, the existence and long tenure of the College of the Vestal Virgins proves how crucial chastity was to the city of Rome. An institution of great antiquity (ascribed to the seventh century BCE), the college of Vestals was overseen by the chief religious magistrate of Rome, the Pontifex Maximus, who controlled the religious boundaries formed by bodies of water. The Vestals tended the sacred perpetual fire. The rape before execution of Sejanus' virgin daughter Junilla (31 CE; see Tacitus *Annals* 5.9) reflects the sacred nature of female virginity, as do the extreme anti-pollutive measures surrounding the punishment of unchaste Vestals, whose virginal bodies represented the health of the state. These punishments included death by burial alive outside the sacred border of the city (Plutarch *Life of Numa*, 10.4–10.7; cf. Beard 1980).

A hallmark of the Republic was its establishment of the rule of law. Within sixty years of the founding of the Roman Republic (509 BCE), the Laws of the Twelve Tables would also define women's roles in the family largely through marriage and reproduction. The Twelve

Tables (451 BCE) made the paterfamilias the head of the family and defined women as property (VI); forbade intermarriage between patricians and plebeians (XI); and served as a precedent for treating women as minors in need of a *tutor* (guardian). But they also granted women the right to own and alienate permanent property (such as land), something never permitted by the Athenians—indeed, the Athenians thought that female ownership of land in Sparta was both peculiar and bad. At least nominally, Roman women needed the permission of their guardians if they wanted to sell property, but their right to ownership was inscribed from the very beginning of published law in Rome. Over the centuries, Roman citizen women gained more rights and exercised more power (see Brennan, this volume, Chapter 26 and Hallett, this volume, Chapter 27). Eventually, by the second century CE, guardianship (*tutela*) was only a name, and it would be gone by the fourth century CE.

Rome, too, depended upon the participation of citizen women in state religion, a role that the women took very seriously. On women and religion in Rome, see Holland, this volume, Chapter 15; here we point to only a few female cults, suggesting the way in which the state both integrated women into its official religion and rewarded them for outstanding achievement. *Fortuna Muliebris*, a cult limited to *univirae* (women who had been married only once), was established after the mother and wife of Coriolanus persuaded him not to lead an enemy attack on Rome. The cult of *Pudicitia Patricia* (Patrician Chastity) was limited to upper-class *univirae*; a rival cult to *Pudicitia Plebeia* (Plebeian Chastity) was established by a woman who had been expelled by the members of *Pudicitia Patricia* because she had married a respected, but lower-class, husband.

These cults demonstrate both that the state was willing to make public acknowledgment of women's achievement and that women understood their *pudicitia* to be their primary contribution to their country—a contribution of which they were proud. The very fact of the *univira*, as a cultural ideal, points to this crucial value for women: a girl might marry very young (as early as twelve years of age), be widowed a year later, and then be honored for the rest of her life because she did not remarry. Rome certainly wanted citizen women to have many children, but even more important was that its citizen women be chaste. And, because Roman parents brought up multiple daughters, there was no shortage of female fertility: indeed, as the cult of the Vestal Virgins demonstrates, female fertility even among the most elite families might be sacrificed to the state's need for chastity in its women.

3 After the Classical Period and Middle Republic

By the late Classical period in Athens, the polis was in decline and the institutions delineated and defended with logic and precision in forensic oratory and other treatises may not have been operative forces. Recent views of the Athenian economy and society (e.g., E. Cohen 2000) suggest that the less-privileged metics (resident aliens), foreigners, and transients (including prostitutes) had a good deal of personal freedom, not to mention some social standing (see also E. Cohen 2006). But when Athens came under Macedonian rule, and ceased to be self-governing, social and legal restrictions upon Athenian citizen women were made even tighter than they had been under Athenian self-rule during the Classical period. As if to enforce their own self-definition, and the definition of Athens as still somehow an independent polis, Athenian men turned in part to stricter control of their women. Thus, again, woman's status was integral to the preservation of the state's identity.

The Roman practice of expanding its territory and citizenry by gradual enfranchisement brought about a gradual expansion of rights for all freed and free persons. In addition, liberalizing developments in the law code made it easier for women to conduct business affairs without the permission of a *tutor* (legal guardian) and to manage some property. Divorce and remarriage became much more common, and, at least among the elite classes, the *univira* became somewhat rarer. Toward the end of the Republic, many elite Roman women became effectively free of all male control (as discussed by Brennan, this volume, Chapter 26). If they practiced sexual freedom, they presented a conceptual paradox to the Roman men who left us all our evidence. Thus, for instance, the notorious Clodia conducted both financial business and adulterous sexual affairs according to her own preferences and judgment; she is described by Cicero as virtually a *matrona-meretrix* (wife-whore), a figure that recurs (as Brennan notes) in the invective leveled against the empress Messalina (on whom see Joshel 1995). More than once does Catullus present Clodia (as his poetic Lesbia) in very similar terms.

The personal and sexual freedom practiced by Clodia is seen in another prominent woman of the late Republic, namely the freedwoman Volumnia Cytheris, a stage mime-actress who was first the fairly public mistress of Mark Antony (even during his marriage to Fulvia) and then the mistress of the politician-poet Cornelius Gallus, who called her Lycoris in his elegies. She attended dinner banquets with very respectable people (e.g., Cicero). Although sexual relations with such a woman were not illegal, as she was not a citizen and thus could not be a wife, they were not the kind of behavior praised, in the *Satire* of Horace cited above. Such an extensive affair caught political attention and eventually came under the scrutiny of law, as we will discuss below.

The rate of procreation among the upper classes declined rapidly in the last 100 years of the Republic, in a way that caught official attention, as in Julius Caesar's programs, in the 40s BCE, that attempted to encourage marriage and reproduction (Suetonius *Div. Jul.* 53). Caesar's grand-nephew and adopted (posthumously) son Augustus took a much more pervasive approach with the Julian Laws (18–17 BCE), the *lex Iulia de adulteriis coercendis* (the Julian law punishing adultery) and the *lex Iulia de maritandis ordinibus* (the Julian law on the social classes that are required to marry). The *princeps* Augustus considered these laws so important to his social program that he named them not in the customary fashion, by the names of the two men who were consuls in the year that a given law was passed, but after his own clan, the Julians. It was certainly an irony of nomenclature, as well as a terrible disappointment to him, when he had to exile his own daughter, Julia the Elder, as well as her daughter, Julia the Younger, for having violated the *lex de adulteriis coercendis*. (On these laws see also Hallett, this volume, Chapter 27.)

The Julian laws, beloved of every Roman emperor thereafter, penalized members, both male and female, of the two upper classes at Rome, the senators and the *equites* (knights), for being unmarried or for not having at least three children (four in the case of freedwomen who were married to *equites*) by levying harsh fines on their inheritances. Rewards for women who produced the requisite number of children included most prominently freedom from *tutela* (guardianship), under the principle of *ius trium liberorum* (rights for having three children). Divorced and widowed women were to remarry quickly—the *lex Iulia de maritandis ordinibus* effectively did away with the long-valued *univira*, the woman who had been married to only one man. Because divorce was so common in the later decades of the Republic, such women were much rarer by the time the

Julian laws were passed, but they still represented a powerful ideal for Roman citizen women. Under the marriage law, an *univira* with fewer than three children who refused to remarry was officially considered anti-social, hostile to her government and nation.

Convicted adulterers were punished with *relegatio*: sent into exile on designated, and unappealing, islands, they were kept separate from each other and from Rome. Financial penalties were levied against them as well. Informants were rewarded for reporting suspected adulterers. A husband who suspected that his wife was cheating on him could be charged with *lenocinium*, a form of pimping, if he did not bring charges against her. Charges under the *lex de adulteriis coercendis* were prosecuted in a new court dedicated to supporting the law. For the first time in Roman history, a wife's adultery was not merely a private concern for her husband but a public crime requiring a public trial and punishment.

From the beginning of the empire, the Julian laws were intended to replenish the population and to restore the *mos maiorum* (custom of the ancestors); they also served, as Judith Hallett (this volume, Chapter 27) points out, to enlarge the populations of the powerful, wealthy elite families that might have posed a challenge to Augustus' authority. These laws contain a perceptible contradiction to each other: the law on marriage actively seeks increased procreation among the upper classes, but the anti-adultery law removes from Rome precisely the women who are supposed to be bearing children under the marriage law. In theory, the two laws are at odds, because an adulterous woman could have been punished with a fine, kept under lock and key until it was evident that she was not pregnant by her illicit lover, and then pressed into having legitimate children by her husband. Such a utilitarian treatment of elite women would have suited the pronatalist attitudes of the marriage law. The apparent contradiction is resolved by recognizing the powerful requirement of chastity underlying both laws. The law on adultery removes *impudicae* (unchaste women) from Rome, and the law on marriage seeks only the children of well-behaved, chaste women. In other words, the government wanted children, but only the right kind of children—those who had the right kind of mothers. And it wanted pure, chaste women.

These laws constituted a massive intrusion into the most private lives of the elite classes at Rome, who were in turn very resentful. They took advantage of every loophole, and even made a public protest to Augustus in 9 CE, twenty-seven years after the passage of the laws (Dio 56.1–10). Augustus responded by rebuking those who had not married and become fathers; in the same year he passed further legislation to strengthen the Julian laws by closing up loopholes (though he did extend the grace period for widows). This law, the *lex Pappia et Poppaea*, contains further irony of nomenclature: it was named in the normal fashion, after the two consuls of the year—both bachelors. The three laws were eventually merged, informally, and designated the *lex Iulia et Pappia*; they remained in effect for centuries.

The woman whose defeat helped set the Roman Republic on the path to empire was the embodiment of many of the forces described above. Cleopatra VII could not be categorized or controlled. She brought to a challenge point the statement by Cato the Censor: "we rule the world but our wives rule us." Consort of two Roman leaders, mother, ruler, foreign, and brilliant, tradition makes Cleopatra a formidable enemy whose defeat cemented Roman *imperium*. Imperial women in Rome would wield power for centuries after, but only in extra-legal, informal fashion: under empire, women gained more legal freedoms than they had previously enjoyed but they failed to gain additional rights to participate in the state.

RECOMMENDED FURTHER READING

The topic of women, city, and state is elusive in part because early treatments of women in Greek and Roman antiquity did not so categorize it (e.g., Pomeroy 1975; Lefkowitz and Fant 2005). The relationship between woman and polity is treated, when it is treated, as a subset of grand theory or through localized examples, examinations of women in a particular role, or study of an influential author's view of women and the state. For grand theory treatments, Lerner (1986), Pateman (1988), and MacKinnon (1989) are very useful. Specialist studies of particular locales include Redfield (2003) on Locri; Pomeroy (1995) on Sparta; and Jed (1989) on Rome. Patterson (1990) examines the state's treatment of *nothoi* (bastards) and thereby the status of their (usually) non-citizen mothers in Athens. For the connection between women, rape, and landscape, see Dougherty (1998). On the Sabine women see Brown (1995). On prostitution see McGinn (1998, 2004); see also the collections edited by Faraone and McClure (2006) and Glazebrook and Henry (2011), which contain studies of female prostitutes and the state.

Levick (this volume, Chapter 7) provides a full survey of women and the law, a topic that can on many points be integrated with the present essay. Treatments of individual ancient authors or works that bear on women and the state include Joshel's (1995) work on the Roman historiographer Tacitus and Lape's (2004) on the Greek comic playwright Menander. The need and merit of all these studies is evident, but all of them together have not yet brought about an integration of the study of women into study of the state in classical antiquity. Women's roles, status, and contributions to ancient Greek and Roman society seem somehow still to be relegated to Women's Studies and Gender Studies courses. Women have not yet entered history, not yet entered theory.

Case Study II

Sex and the Single Girl: The Cologne Fragment of Archilochus

Sharon L. James

The fragmentary Cologne epode of Archilochus, controversial since its publication, records a poetic interchange in which a man seeks to seduce a nervous girl. Interpretation of this unusual poem, which disturbs many readers, is not a goal here: the purpose of this case study is to see what information about women's lives can be gleaned from this text, through the prism of accepted sexual behaviors as opposed to ideological norms. I exclude most of the standard scholarly considerations to focus specifically on sexual ideology, social class, and female reputation.

To begin with, we do not know how much of the poem is missing. Much inference is required even to make sense of the conversation. The extant text begins in mid-speech: a girl first tells a man to constrain his desire and then suggests he take up a specific lovely young woman. The male speaker responds at length, praising by name (Amphimedo) the girl's mother and proceeding to detail, in metaphors both architectural (below the cornice, over the gates) and agricultural (the garden grass), how he plans to have sex with the girl in such a way as to avoid coitus.

In the middle of his speech, he fulminates against Neoboule, a poetic female who plays a complex role in Archilochus' poetry and his biographical reputation in antiquity. Neoboule, says the male speaker, is over-ripe, twice the age of the girl herself, and has lost not only her virginity but her virtue because she has become oversexed. To take her as a wife would subject him to ridicule, and might result in unhealthy children. He prefers the female speaker because she is faithful, and thus more desirable than a woman who is sexually available to many men. Once he has finished speaking, the man places the girl among flowers and wraps her in his cloak. He explores her body, particularly her breasts, and she is startled or shy or fearful, like a fawn. Her youthful beauty is evident, and the male speaker reaches a (non-coital) climax as he touches her bright hair.

Our questions here concern the social class and values of these two people. We may infer that in the lost opening section the male speaker has made a sexual overture to the girl. When she tells him to marry, we know that the two speakers are citizens, for marriage in antiquity was limited to the citizen classes. Further confirmation of citizen status are his

A Companion to Women in the Ancient World, First Edition. Edited by Sharon L. James and Sheila Dillon.
© 2012 John Wiley & Sons, Ltd. Published 2015 by John Wiley & Sons, Ltd.

promise to avoid intercourse, Neoboule's spoiled condition, the risk to his reputation if he should marry Neoboule, the very mention of children, his preference for the virtuous girl, and, finally, his fulfillment of the promise he made her. (His praise of her mother, and the use of her mother's name, may also be considered evidence.)

It is impossible to overstate how peculiar is this poem's representation of premarital sex for a citizen girl. The very idea violates every recorded and accepted sexual ideology for so-called respectable women, even as the poem savagely articulates those very ideologies. (I leave aside the fact that a citizen male could always take recourse to his own slaves and inexpensive, easily available prostitutes, rather than putting citizen women at risk.) The missing part of the girl's speech seems to have included an expression of her anxiety at the prospect of sex, a probability inferable from the male speaker's reassurances that he will avoid coitus.

The girl has much to be anxious about: premarital intercourse puts her at significant risk, as her virginity and her reputation were crucial for her marriage prospects, as is made clear in the male speaker's violent hostility toward Neoboule, discussed below. Pregnancy, of course, would destroy the girl's prospects altogether and render her useless in the social economy of citizen life. (Prostitutes and enslaved women in antiquity also had to fear intercourse, as pregnancy and childbirth were dangerous and would seriously hamper their daily work; however, they did not risk loss of respectability.) So, the representation of premarital sex with a citizen girl, in a poem that makes clear how dangerous and transgressive such sex is, violates our understanding of citizen sexual life— if we are to understand that the girl's reputation will not in fact be damaged by this sexual encounter.

With respect to Neoboule, however, the poem conforms both precisely and vigorously to ancient norms. The tirade against her combines several familiar stereotypes and prejudices—precisely those sexual ideologies that threaten the female speaker. Neoboule is over-ripe, oversexed, too old, he says—even though the female speaker has called her young and lovely. (Here I exclude extra-poetic evidence, although Archilochus' readers, who had far more of his poetry than we have, would not have done so.) Since the girl has effectively offered Neoboule to the male speaker in marriage, he rejects Neoboule on just those grounds, saying that he would be a laughingstock with her as a wife and would prefer to have his female interlocutor instead. As in Hesiod, a wife's sexuality can damage her husband's reputation and standing among men.

When the male speaker says that Neoboule is so oversexed that her children would be born defective, like blind puppies, he invokes the ancient belief that excessive sexual activity in women will produce faulty children. By implication, the female speaker's children would not be defective—but the male speaker's decision not to continue articulating that point may mean that he does not want to remind the girl that sex with him puts her at risk of pregnancy or a damaged reputation (like Neoboule's).

The remainder of the poem is narrative and retrospective, and relates a sexual experience that brought pleasure to the man and indeed did not involve coitus. This fragmentary poem suggests that these two people found a way to engage in extramarital sexual activity without putting the citizen girl's reputation and future at risk—a prospect anomalous in our ancient evidence. The motivating factor is the male speaker's desire; the girl is, at the very least, hesitant. Modern students tend to read this poem, instinctively, as a rape text, and to find it disturbing. It certainly depicts a man pressing himself sexually, for his own gratification, upon a hesitant, worried girl, whose own pleasure is not merely irrelevant but proscribed. His persuasion is disingenuous, from his praise of her mother to the violent rejection of Neoboule, and until the end it is not clear that he will keep his promise of not committing penetration.

Because the poem is part of the ancient iambic tradition, it may have elements of invective that would disgrace the girl simply because she appears in a poem about illicit sex. Scholars have conjectured that the girl is related to Neoboule, but there is no proof either way; if she and Neoboule are kin (perhaps sisters), then the poem depicts an emotionally perverse situation, in which a man praises a girl and her mother (a rather odd detail in itself) while denouncing her sister for the very activity he is trying to coax the girl into. Further, the poem would then be part of what is described in ancient sources as an attack on the entire family of Neoboule, including her father Lycambes. I am inclined to agree with the scholars who do not consider this poetic girl to be related to the equally poetic Neoboule: the extant text does not give us sure evidence on this point. In this iambic tradition, the male speaker too is subject to the effects of insult and satiric moral criticism.

In any case, the poem keeps the reader, both ancient and modern, in suspense until the last line. Thus it plays with standard sexual ideologies while dramatizing a startling violation of standard sexual norms—and it proposes, very surprisingly, that premarital sexual activity might not destroy the reputation and life of a citizen girl. How we are to interpret that suggestion remains a matter of debate, and keeps scholars returning to this disconcerting fragmentary poem.

PART II

The Archaic and Classical Periods

The essays in this section bring together an exceptional spectrum of evidence, from archaic Greek poetry to medical theory to women's religion to funerary and textual evidence for women in Magna Graecia. The authors have scrupulously examined the problems of understanding the ancient evidence, as well as the scholarly biases of the fields of study. The essays peel away layers of scholarship, ancient ideologies, and generic practices to focus precisely on how the ancient evidence can be understood. The evidence for this period, both textual and visual, is largely concentrated on Athens and has dominated scholarship on women in antiquity. Hence, this section has a smaller geographical ambit. Even so, we chose not to seek an exhaustive study of these rich and well-known materials, and as a result we have tolerated some perhaps scandalous absences. Prominent among these are an examination of Archaic korai, representation of women in Attic funerary monuments, Roman women's dress, and women in the early and middle Roman Republic (for whom the textual evidence is mostly much later). In addition, as we were near the end of putting the volume together, the planned essay on women in Attic drama fell through, so we have no chapter on women in Greek tragedy and Aristophanes. Bibliographical references on such subjects are appended at the end of this section's introduction. We are, however, particularly pleased to include Maria Liston's "Reading the Bones: Interpreting the Skeletal Evidence for Women's Lives in Ancient Greece" (Chapter 9), an analysis of osteological evidence that shows what the study of bones can reveal about women's lives.

The section begins with Sharon L. James' "Sex and the Single Girl: The Cologne Fragment of Archilochus" (Case Study II), a case study of the nearly infamous Cologne epode of Archilochus, a mysterious and disturbing episode of apparent extramarital seduction, and proceeds to two essays on concepts, theories, and law concerning women. Madeleine M. Henry and Sharon L. James' "Woman, City, State: Theories, Ideologies, and Concepts in the Archaic and Classical Periods" (Chapter 6) is intended as a "think-piece," and it leads into Barbara Levick's "Women and Law" (Chapter 7). The other chapters examine the ancient and scholarly biases and ideologies that have dominated the treatment and reception of women in this period, a time that is crucial not only for the wealth of evidence that it left behind but also for its astonishing historical, artistic, literary, and political developments. The titles appear to suggest a near-exclusion of women outside Greece, but several essays besides Lora L. Holland's "Women and Roman

Religion" (Chapter 15) and Gillian Shepherd's "Women in Magna Graecia" (Chapter 16) do include Roman women.

This section includes exemplary considerations of the problems in approaching the rich but misleading visual materials on women in Athens: Katherine Topper (in "Approaches to Reading Attic Vases," Chapter 10) and A. A. Donohue (in "Interpreting Women in Archaic and Classical Greek Sculpture," Chapter 12) both interrogate every aspect of their subjects, ranging far beyond the physical objects to draw on theory and analysis of historical scholarship. In "Dress and Adornment in Archaic and Classical Greece" (Chapter 13) Mireille M. Lee brings together textual and material evidence to look at dress and self-presentation by Greek women, a crucial way in which women identified themselves socially. In "Spartan Girls and the Athenian Gaze" (Chapter 11), Jenifer Neils studies the way Athenians looked at young Spartan women, interrogating both literary and visual sources. In "Woman and Medicine" (Chapter 8), Holt Parker provides a wide-ranging survey and analysis of ancient medical theory about women, linking that highly ideological thought sometimes even into the modern era. In "Women in Magna Graecia" (Chapter 16), Gillian Shepherd analyzes evidence from sources historiographical and archaeological and addresses trends in scholarship, which is often influenced (perhaps unconsciously) by its own imperial ideologies. In "Women and Religion in Greece" (Chapter 14), Eva Stehle provides an exemplary study of methodological approaches to women's religion in Greece.

RECOMMENDED FURTHER READING

For female funerary sculpture, see Stears (1995), Karakasi (2003), and Stieber (2004). On women in Attic drama, a good starting-point for Athenian drama (brief but full of information) is the chapter "Gender" in Wiles (2000: 66–88), who approaches the topic as performance rather than literature. Zeitlin (1996: chapter 8), Hall (1997), and the first three essays in Foley (2001) provide overviews of women in this drama. On women's voices in Athenian drama, see McClure (1999) and Mossman (2005). Two essays in Hall (2006) involve a women-centered theme (childbirth) and technique (painted masks). Seminal essays on particular tragedies include Zeitlin (1996: chapter 3), on Aeschylus' *Oresteia*, and essays in Foley (2001) on Sophocles' *Electra* and *Antigone* and Euripides' *Medea, Alcestis*, and *Helen*. For women-centered translations with introductions and notes of four plays by Euripides see Blondell et al. (1999). Other studies to be consulted are those of Powell (1990), Rehm (1994), Wohl (1998), and Ormand (1999). On Aristophanes see Henderson's women-centered translations (with introduction and notes) of *Lysistrata, Women at the Thesmophoria*, and *Assemblywomen*, as well as Zeitlin (1996: chapter 9). On Menander see Lape (2004) and Traill (2008).

Because of the performance conditions in Athens (all-male playwrights, actors, and possibly audiences), questions have been raised as to whether the portrayal of women in this drama has anything to do with real women. For affirmation without criticism of this position see Seidensticker (1995); for a critical view see Rabinowitz (1993).

Women in Roman drama have received less attention to date, but see Dutsch (2008) on comedy, Moore (1998: chapters 8 and 9) on Plautus' *Truculentus* and *Casina*, and Roisman (2005) on women in Seneca. On Roman women's dress and adornment, see most recently Olson (2008a) and the collection edited by Edmondson and Keith (2008; see particularly Fantham, Keith, Olson, and Shumka). See also Richlin (1995), Sebesta (1994, 1997), and Wyke (1994a).

7

Women and Law

Barbara Levick

Eteocles: *O Zeus, what a tribe of women you have given us!*
Chorus of women: *A miserable tribe—like men whose city has been taken.*
(Aeschylus, *Seven against Thebes* 256–7)
It was obvious: the new masters would dictate their law to all the survivors.
(Christa Wolf, *Kassandra*, transl. G. Paul)

This essay faces methodological problems. One is, trivially, the danger of importing modern words that might carry anachronistic ideas into it: "emancipation" has been used, but in connection with women in antiquity it belongs only to a technical act by which a Roman father freed children from his power; like "patronage," it imposes a misleading conception. Another is the question of what is "law" (*nomos* in Greek, *lex* in Latin)? *Nomos* has the wider meaning, and significantly stands for custom as well as enacted law (see Ostwald 1969: 20–54). Among the Romans, too, *mos* (custom) was strong, and established *iura* (rights) were not easily abolished; indeed, they could be affirmed by *lex* (statute), by the edict of a magistrate, or by decree of the Senate (*senatus consultum*). As the Principate advanced, these forms were overshadowed by decisions of the Emperor (*constitutiones*); given by a near-monarch to his people, these decisions held as strong a hold over the people as any law enacted by the public assemblies. To him women had access, as men did. A further source of law, important enough for Lefkowitz and Fant (1992: 98–118) to devote a score of pages to it, was the advice and interpretations provided by authorized jurist-consults for three centuries, starting from the mid first century BCE: we have for example Gaius' mid-second century *Institutes* and the *Digest* published in 533 CE as part of Justinian's codification.

Law and custom offer a system of rules that secure the settlement of disputes without recourse to violence. In an ideal society it need not be written: one remembers Tacitus' pronouncement (*Germania* 19.1) on sexual relations among the Germans: that good practice (*mores*) there was more effective than good laws (*leges*) elsewhere. The close relation between law and custom is exemplified by Athenian marriage as described by

A Companion to Women in the Ancient World, First Edition. Edited by Sharon L. James and Sheila Dillon.
© 2012 John Wiley & Sons, Ltd. Published 2015 by John Wiley & Sons, Ltd.

Patterson (1991: 48): "Although classical … law concerned itself ordinarily with the identification of the wife as bearer of legitimate children and heirs, and secondarily … with prohibiting marital cohabitation of Athenians with non-Athenians, significant aspects … were the domain of social ritual and custom." According to Xenophon (*Memorabilia* 4.4.20) there are "universal laws"—those that deal with honoring parents and preventing incest. Then again it is when established custom begins changing that it becomes enshrined in or displaced by law, and the new rules have to be written down to demonstrate their validity and permanence (though Clark 1993: 9f. offers other occasions for enactment and enjoins caution). Women can be seen as inimical to order and as requiring control. The mythical hero Theseus federalized Attica, and the first threat to the new creation was an invasion of wild Amazons (Just 1989: 250, on Lysias 2, *Funeral Oration* 4–6). The Romans liked to believe that their legendary first king Romulus had enacted a single law that "brought women to prudence and orderly conduct" (see Lefkowitz and Fant 1992: 95, no. 107).

Here, then, no sharp distinction between law and custom will be drawn; still less is it my place to demarcate nature and culture in human society nor to show *how* any ancient society came to organize itself in the way it did. It is legitimate here only to delineate features and to point out what may be family resemblances and differences. Readers will make their own investigations and draw their own conclusions.

Nor is it appropriate to address the question of whether women in general saw themselves as oppressed (Just 1989: 6, 134). It is a vain enquiry in any case: thought-training, including notions of concern for the welfare of women, was part of the very rhetoric of law; concern for the hopelessly weak was natural. Clark (1989: 38–40) has measured pages on this issue, and Blundell (1995: 124) gives a telling quotation from Sophocles on the extent of the training: "And all these things, once a single night has yoked us to our husbands, we are obliged to praise and consider a happy outcome" (Fr. 514 Nauck).

Another problem that is not merely practical is how to order the abundant material that presents itself. To take a chronological view is tempting, and such would have the authority of the seminal work of Pomeroy (1975). But there is no line of development from Greece to Rome, and the cities of Greece were varied in themselves, in spite of the "family" relationships mentioned above. As Lefkowitz and Fant (1992: 82f.) point out, citing texts from Amorgos, elsewhere than at Athens women had more control over their property. The most that Cantarella (1987: 91f.) can claim for her Hellenistic developments—based on papyri from Egypt—is that women could buy and sell, mort-gage, lend and borrow, make wills, be instituted heirs, and inherit. So, in 92 BCE one Philiscus acknowledged to Apollonia, with her guardian (*kyrios*)—that is, her brother Apollonius—that he had received *from her* the dowry he had agreed upon (*PTebt.* 104). On this binding contract, because she owned their property jointly with him, she must obey him as a wife should obey her husband. It seems best to take the material in small chunks divided by category.

1   Public Life and Politics

Although this sphere was closely regulated by law, it must be dealt with cursorily. To do more would be to incorporate too much, as in the patriarchy an all-embracing private world seems to have taken priority (see Thomas 1992). A basic question is that of citizenship. Athenian women were Athenian enough for their origin to be decisive after Pericles' provision of 451/450 BCE for the citizenship of their sons, and for it to become illegal in the fourth century to wed a non-citizen, with a penalty of loss of citizenship and property for any man who passed a woman off as a relative to an Athenian citizen (Apollodorus [Demosthenes], 59 *Against Neaira* 52). But women were hardly citizens proper: the word used of them was *aste* (woman of the city), referring to their participation in civil and economic rights and religious functions, not *politis*, feminine of *polites*, who shared in judicial functions and in office (Aristotle, *Politics* 1276a 20). There was no doubt of the citizenship of Roman women, in spite of their political deprivation: for one thing the word *civis* could be used of either sex, and was available to the comic poets for Athenian women (Terence, *Andria* 859). They were simply unprivileged, something more acceptable in a stratified society like that of Rome than in the developed Athenian democracy.

The Greek and Italian states and Rome were militaristic communities placed in areas of uneven rainfall, often mountainous, and with limited arable land—the source of spats with neighbors. Power in society and political office were accorded to those (men, of course, who were qualified by physical strength) who fought for their *polis* (city-state), the highest going to those who owned most land (*pentakosiomedimnoi* at Athens) or invested the most in defending it, via provision of mounted troops (*hippeis* at Athens; *equites* among the Romans). One Roman assembly, the Comitia Centuriata, which enacted *leges* and elected magistrates with *imperium* (the power of command) at home or over the army, theoretically consisted in the Roman People under arms and was not allowed to meet within the sacred boundary of Rome, the Pomerium; it was presided over by a consul, one of the two annual commanders of the army.

It was unthinkable for a woman to be a member of the Greek Ekklesia or Gerousia, nor certainly the Roman Comitia Centuriata or even the Roman Senate (both "Gerousia" and "senate" are derived from words meaning "old man," and senators are often referred to collectively as *patres*); these were authoritative advisory bodies. Aristophanes' comedy of 392 or 391 BCE, the *Ecclesiazousai* (*Women in Assembly*), relies on the absurdity of the idea it presents. Force openly deployed abroad, and there supported by women (as the anecdote of the Spartan soldiers told to return carrying their shields or on them illustrates), might be implicit at home. But the effective or absolute possession of sometimes enormous properties gave Roman women enormous *de facto* power, expressed in the form of benefactions, and, in some cities of Asia Minor, access to gymnasiarchies and agonothesiae and even to prestigious, if not always potent, magistracies such as the stephanephorate (Clark 1989: 29, with bibliography; Boatwright 1991b). As Clark remarks, "It cannot be shown that such women ever chaired a meeting or addressed an assembly or did more than foot the bills and acknowledge the applause." As far as law is concerned, there does not seem to be much in the idea that women were complicit in the structures of the societies they inhabited.

2   Fathers, Guardians, and Marriage

It is the *kyrios* mentioned in the Philiscus-Apollonia transaction who takes us to the heart of the subject matter: the subjection of women to the head of the house, with its multiplicity of supporting rules. The authority of the *kyrios* went back to classical Athens in very potent form. There a woman was subject to the guardianship of her father or other male kinsman until she was married, at which point she was handed over to that of her husband, who became her new *kyrios*, receiving her dowry from her father on betrothal (*engue*) or marriage. It was the husband's to dispose of, but in the event of divorce, even after his wife's adultery, he had to return the capital to her family, which should have helped to keep it intact, though no more effectively hers. Even *pallakai* (dowerless concubines, who might be taken in addition to the legitimate wife) came under the guardianship of the master of the house, and their inheritance and citizenship rights seem to have been restricted as well. At Rome, by contrast, a man might not have both a concubine and a wife—both were exclusive relationships (Paul, *Opinions* 2.20.1).

All Roman children were in the power of their father (*patria potestas*); as the *Institutes* of Justinian has it (1.9.2f.), "there are no other man who have such control over their children as we have," but women, being scatter-brained, never escaped from male control, for when their father died they passed under the guardianship (*tutela*, on which see Gardner 1986: 14–22) of another male, from which boys emerged at puberty, becoming *sui iuris* (independent; Ulpian, *Rules* 11.1). Alternatively, a woman might pass by marriage (*confarreatio, usus, coemptio*) into the control (*manus*, "hand") of her husband, thus becoming his quasi-child and joint heir with his children. (For forms of marriage and *manus*, see Gaius, *Institutes* 108–13, 136–7a, with Gardner 1986: 11–14; Dixon 1988: 67 n. 7.)

The law and custom that governed marriage was thus very different at Rome, where it was comprehensively defined, from what it was at Athens. Moreover, when the Athenian father handed over his daughter to another man, her consent was not required; in the papyri a woman claims contrariwise that "no law permits taking daughters away from their husbands against their will" (*P. Oxy.* 237 col. 7 l.12), and the Roman bride's consent and *affectio maritalis* were required to validate a marriage (Ulpian, *Digest* 50.17; Justinian, *Codex* 5.1.1). Accordingly, in classical Roman law women had the right to divorce their husbands, though this was brutally limited by the Christian Constantine in 331 CE (*CT* 3.16.1, with Clark 1993: 21–7).

For a woman to pass into the *manus* of a husband depended on continuous "use" (*usucapio*) and that could be avoided, to the advantage of the Roman father's property, if the women absented herself from the marital home for three nights each year: the *trinoctium*, obsolete by Gaius' time (Gaius, *Institutes* 1.111). The *manus* form of marriage declined, and what prevailed was one that did not involve transferring the woman into the power of someone other than her father. Roman practice even came to follow the opinion of Gaius (*Institutes* 1.144f., 190f.) that women were not so scatter-brained, and in his day the institution of *tutela* was merely formal. In a similar sense it is also worth mentioning that the *Institutes of Justinian* (1.11pr.) say that, although women could not adopt because of course they had no power over their own children, "nevertheless by the indulgence of the Emperor they can do so by way of consolation for the children they have lost." The ban on women adopting reinforces Thomas' (1992) conception of *patria potestas* as the institution that embodied women's incapacity to transmit property and power to heirs; he cites *Digest* 50, 16.125.2: "A woman is the beginning and end of her own family." It was this that excluded her from public functions in the community of *gentes* (clans). Dixon (1988: 44) contends, however, that the real affection between a woman and the children of her body encouraged the idea that they were her natural heirs and occasioned change in the law: this idea came to work for intestate succession, allowing for a child to claim improper testation (*querela inofficiosi testamenti*) against the mother.

3 Property

But what of the all-important landownership, already mentioned as conferring rank? At Athens women did not own land: they were *epikleroi*, those who went with the inheritance, through whom property passed from a man to his heirs. That led to their being married to close kin, for preference the paternal uncle, then his son (Harrison 1968: 9–12, 132–8; Just 1989: 83–9, 95–8, on Isaeus 11 *Hagnias* 1f.; Demosthenes, *In Macartatum* 51.54). The enforced marriage of an *epikleros* might entail the previous divorce of either or both parties (Demosthenes 57.41). Sons inherited in equal measure, daughters were excluded, and if a man had only female offspring the property passed through them to males in the next generation; these were the heirs of the father and through them the oikos (house) was continued. The intention of the rule might be frustrated if the husband of the *epikleros*, who might well belong to a generation earlier than that of the bride, was unable or unwilling to perform his marital duties. Two laws ascribed by Plutarch (*Solon* 20.2f.) to the early sixth century BCE lawgiver Solon provided that there must be sexual intercourse between the couple three times a month; if the husband failed the *epikleros* might apply to marry the next of kin. Short of any heirs (a situation to be avoided by individual and state), the property was allocated to a group of close relatives, the *anchisteia* (close kin). If a man adopted a son to preserve his oikos the daughter was married to the newcomer. As Blundell (1995: 118) puts it, women straddled the oikoi, and their original oikos was unlikely to relinquish all control over them. When property was at stake, no matter whether extensive or exiguous—for importance lay in the eye of the beholder—there would be disputes that came to the Athenian jury-court: for example about how the *epikleros* was to be disposed of. Aristophanes (*Wasps* 583–6) suggests that the law was interpreted, even stretched, if a claimant was eloquent in pursuing his claim. Then there was the case of the widow of Diodotus (Lysias, 32 *Against Diogeiton* 11–18, with Lefkowitz and Fant 1992: 62f.), who accused her own father and *kyrios*, the brother of her late husband (killed on campaign in 409 BCE), of cheating her sons of their property—and bringing up in luxury the children he had had by the widow's stepmother.

The rigor of this constraint is surprising. It is one of the jokes of Aristophanes' *Ecclesiazousae* (1024f.) that the women in Parliament note that *kyrioi* should not be permitted to deal in more than the worth of a *medimnus* of barley (like women in real life: Isaeus 10.10; for the value see Just 1989: 29: it might have been seen as feeding a family for up to six days). In practice, and notably when an Athenian *kyrios* was away on campaign, a woman might be charged with great responsibilities in relation to property ([Demosthenes] 50). Law and practice did not always coincide.

At Rome and among all Roman citizens, women could own property disposable (according to the *Twelve Tables*) only by them, with the agreement of their *tutor*. This tutorship was imposed, as in the case of men, if their father had died. Up until then property was in the hands of the *paterfamilias* (father of the family) and any child had only an allowance (*peculium*). This rule applied to *res mancipi* (those that required a formal transfer), not to cash or property outside Italy (see Gardner 1986: 18). But "three centuries after the guardianship of women was formally abolished, both halves of the empire legislated to restrict the rights of clergy to receive legacies from women" (Clark 1989: 33).

4 Adultery and Divorce

Beyond the *pallake* it was illegal for an Athenian to have sex with any woman in *kyrieia*: only slaves and prostitutes were permissible, and if a man caught an adulterer in the act it was lawful under Solon's code for him to kill him out of hand (Demosthenes, 23 *Against Aristokrates* 53)—lawful but not always without penalty; as Lysias' speech (1) *On the Murder of Eratosthenes* shows, such killers might themselves be prosecuted. As to the woman, the husband was constrained by law to divorce her and she was excluded from religious rites. The involvement of the *polis* in the integrity of the oikos is demonstrated by the fact that cases of adultery were public: any male person could prosecute. Blundell (1995: 125) cites Aeschines 1 *Against Timarchus* 183: "The lawgiver seeks to disgrace such a woman and make her life intolerable." This was Athens. According to Xenophon *Constitution of the Lacedaemonians* 1.7–9 and Plutarch *Lycurgus* 15.6, the Spartan lawgiver Lycurgus provided for looser marital relations in the interests of eugenics, but the husband seems to have controlled any polyandrous arrangements. The Athenians' purpose may have been effective with women, but women's recourse to the law did not always prevail against a rich, influential, and bold husband such as the notorious Alcibiades. He would bring prostitutes home, and his wife quit the house (the decisive act in a divorce) and moved to that of her brother Callias (Andocides, 4 *Against Alcibiades*; Plutarch, *Alcibiades* 8). However, divorces had to be registered with the Archon, Athens' chief magistrate, and, when Hipparete appeared before the Archon without her brother, Alcibiades simply carried her off home by main force and got away with it.

A husband had an interest in keeping his wife, for the sake of her dowry. (Plato abolished dowries in his ideal commonwealth to diminish arrogance among women and servility among men: *Laws* 774C.) At Athens, upon the dissolution of the marriage, by death or divorce, the woman returned to her father and his power, taking with her the dowry that had been provided for the use of her husband and that would have raised her standing in the household (oikos) she had joined. A widow might, however, have sons of her own, and then she could opt to stay in the husband's household (oikos), accepting her sons as *kyrioi* or joining them under the guardianship of their *kyrios* (see the succinct statement of Blundell 1995: 114). The mid-fifth century BCE law code of Gortyn in Crete was kinder to women than that of Athens: instead of a dowry, girls had half the inheritance of a son, and when they married they kept their property. In the event of a divorce, they retained this property, instead of it returning to their former *kyrios*, and were also entitled to keep half the cloth they had woven during the marriage (Lefkowitz and Fant 1992: 55 on ii. 45).

At Rome the legislation attributed to Romulus enshrined a man's right to divorce his wife for such reasons as use of magic or drugs without his orders (presumably as abortifacients), counterfeiting keys, and adultery (Lefkowitz and Fant 1992: 9); the adultery was judged by the cognates, and both adultery and drinking wine were punishable by death. The same ancient ordinance forbade a woman to divorce her husband. Custom accordingly approved the stern action of the consul of 166 BCE, C. Sulpicius Gallus, who divorced his wife for appearing outdoors with her head unveiled: "The law [*lex*] prescribes for you my eyes alone to which you may prove your beauty"; Valerius Maximus (6.3.9–12) provides several other such paradigm cases for the edification of his own time, the first century CE. Husbands made their own criteria and guilty behavior was not essential. The first instance of sterility as a cause for divorce came in 235 BCE (A. Gellius 17.21.44).

Valerius Maximus is only one writer to show how much Roman practice had changed, or was seen as having changed, to the moralists' regret. It is interesting to discover that Ulpian, writing *On Adultery* 1, in *Digest* 48.5.24 and noting that earlier jurists had specified that the guilty pair should be caught *in flagrante*, makes reference to what the Greek lawgivers Solon and Dracho (Dracon) had meant by "in the act" (*en ergói*). But at Rome adultery was not a public offense under the Augustan legislation, unless the husband had failed to take action by divorcing his wife (Tacitus, *Annals* 2.85.3).

5 Law-making

The woman had no place in public life, except in religion, and the Athenian *kyrios* represented her in public and legal transactions, notably in those involving marriage and other contracts. The rules of Hellenistic and Roman Egypt may have been more relaxed. In the will of Taarpaesis Isidora of Oxyrhynchus (133 CE, *Sammelbuch* 10, 10,756), one son and two daughters are joint executors. Rowlandson (1998: 155) sketches the developments over centuries that made Egypt a unique case.

But women had no part in passing the legislation that affected them to a great or lesser extent along with the rest of a community; some laws intended to affect them in particular. Either type of legislation may be repressive, or designed for another purpose, which happened to make them repressive. Male politicians would not normally pass laws in women's favor. That ancient protector of the less-well-off, sumptuary legislation— for example that imposed on funerals at Athens (in which women had a role)—was often aimed at women and limited freedom of expression, as the fifth-century BCE law from Ceos, derived from Solon, illustrates (Lefkowitz and Fant 1992: 58f.). Social sanctions, reinforced by law if it became necessary, kept women of rank within the home (oikos, *domus*) more stringently at Athens than at Rome. Women were a danger to the state if uncontrolled, and luxury was a sign that they were out of control, as at Sparta, of all places, where, according to Aristotle (*Politics* 1269b), "women live without restraint, enjoying every license and indulging in every luxury." When Laconia was invaded by the Thebans, the passage continues, women caused more confusion than the enemy.

At a time of war, in 215 BCE—but not to check any excess, as the tribune L. Valerius was to argue—the Lex Oppia was passed, limiting the quantity of gold a woman might possess, the color of her dress, and her use of a carriage, except at religious festivals. Two decades later, long after Hannibal had been defeated, women did the only thing they could to resist legalized oppression (not that male display was not also repeatedly limited by sumptuary legislation): they took to the streets. After a portentous debate the Senate agreed to repeal. The Lex Voconia of 169 BCE was passed in a period of conquest and increasing wealth at Rome: it provided that women of the highest census class could inherit only as agnates within the second degree (i.e., as siblings) and with a ceiling of 200,000 *asses*: the provisions seem to have been relaxed under the empire (Gaius, *Institutes* 1.226ff.). It was in defense of their property again that, under the leadership of Hortensia, daughter of a leading orator, whose own gifts enabled her to write in such a way that one would take her for a man (according to Appian, *Bell. Civ.* 4.32), women once again made themselves felt when the Second Triumvirate pursued its expedient policy of confiscation.

Only if a higher purpose, such as the unity of the citizen body, or the birth rate, claimed priority might a law offer status or even a degree of liberation: the law of 451/450 BCE restricted Athenian citizenship to the children of two citizen parents ([Aristotle],

Constitution of Athens 26.4), and recognized and so to some extent raised the status of the female Athenian— in relation to other women. And that was not its purpose. Augustus' marriage legislation (see Lefkowitz and Fant 1992: 102–4) exempted women with three children (four in the case of freedwomen) who had survived to their first birthday from guardianship (*tutela*); from Egypt we have a petition of 263 CE in which a woman with children applies for exemption (*P. Oxy.* 1467). Augustus' legal restrictions on marriage between orders of society were intended to stabilize the upper classes and preserve the privileges that they valued. Again, Paul, in his *Opinions* (2.21A.1f.) pronounces that a Roman woman, or one of Latin status—that is, at a level just below that of full Roman citizenship—who persists in a liaison with a slave against his master's will may be enslaved herself. This is an enactment of the Emperor Claudius, made in 52 CE. Masters were complaining that free women were cohabiting with their slaves, and, according to the rule that illegitimate children followed the status of the mother, were producing children who were free and so lost to the slaves' masters. Accordingly, the Senate enacted that such children should henceforth be slaves (Tacitus, *Annals* 12.53). This decree was thought up by Pallas, the freedman in charge of imperial finances. The conclusion is obvious: Pallas had an eye for the Emperor's property, the Emperor being the greatest slave-owner of them all. The senators gladly joined in supporting a measure (and rewarding its instigator) in the interests of their own slave property, in spite of the fact that it infringed the rights of free women. In Egypt it is possible to see how the rules that governed the actions of the Idiologus, the official in charge of special Roman revenues, the *Gnomon of the Idios Logos*, were concerned less with the rights of women and men than with extracting the maximum revenue from infringements (*P. Berl.* 1240 with Lefkowitz and Fant 1992: 119f.).

6   Legal Process: Women in Court

Normally, women in law courts appear as mourning dependents—they could not appear on their own behalf—and in Athenian courts possibly only if they were young children or aged (Demosthenes, 25 *Against Aristogeiton* 84, with Just 1989: 112). Women could bear witness, but there were two factors militating against them. First, the convention that a woman should not speak in public, and second, as apparently in Islam, the notion that women's evidence might be taken to be inherently weak: in Athens a woman could testify if she were free and took an oath on the heads of her children (Demosthenes, 55 *Against Kallikles* 27). But there is controversy on this point: according to Just (1989: 34–6, followed by Blundell 1989: 114), her evidence had to be given through her *kyrios*. Lysias *Against Diogeiton* 32.11–18, makes a woman in the presence of her male relatives offer to take oaths on the lives of her children in any temple. A woman might traditionally have authority within the oikos, but she was legally incompetent outside it. Indeed, even as to the Roman empire, in the early third century CE the jurist Paul wrote that women were debarred from appearing as witnesses (*Digest* 5.1.4.2). Thomas (1992) explains this disability persuasively: the word of a woman was not sufficient to underpin public action; it became acceptable only when the role of a *testis* (witness) was weakened into giving factual evidence, which became received practice at Rome. One notorious trial presents us with women appearing as prime witnesses: that of T. Annius Milo, the gang leader accused in 52 BCE of murdering his rival P. Clodius Pulcher; *virgines Albanae*, probably priestesses of the town of Alba; Clodius' wife Fulvia; and his mother-in-law, Sempronia (Asconius, *On Cicero's Speech for Milo* 40C).

7 Advocacy

No actual *lex* forbade women from acting as advocates (it was not thought necessary, any more than Queen Victoria, allegedly, thought it necessary to make female homosexuality illegal), but Ulpian (*Digest* 3.1.1.5, 50.17.2) pronounced that women were banned from bringing suit on behalf of another party or involving themselves in others' cases. The Emperor Constantine was still reiterating the prohibitions in the early part of the fourth century CE (*Theodosian Code* 2.12.21, 9.1.3). In private suits a Roman woman had a right to sue even her husband when, for example, some marital stipulation concerning his behavior had been agreed on and subsequently broken (Papinian, *Digest* 45.1.125.1; cf. Ulpian *Rules* 7.2). It occasionally happened at Rome that women spoke on their own behalf. Hortensia was renowned, and so was her older contemporary Afrania—for her *impudentia* (Valerius Maximus 8.3.2f.). Society frowned, but grudgingly allowed that the phenomenon was permissible when the woman's own property or kinsmen were involved. Egyptian papyri have preserved numerous written applications for justice made by women; in one, Tamuthis, the greengrocer of the village of Bacchias, whose husband (i.e., her *kyrios*) was away, charged a woman called Taosenophis and that woman's husband, Ammonius, before the local Strategos with assault and theft (*P. Berl.* 22, with Lefkowitz and Fant 1992: 126).

8 Women on Trial

Women were naturally subject to the sanctions of the law. Female adultery at Athens was rewarded with a flogging and the treadmill in perpetuity (Lysias, 1 *On the Murder of Eratosthenes* 33, end of the fifth century BCE) and by exclusion from public sacrifices ([Demosthenes], 59 *Against Neaira*). In one famous capital case the wife was charged before a jury-court with poisoning the young prosecutor's father (420s BCE; Antiphon, *Prosecution of a Stepmother*). Women, who were in charge of the kitchen cupboard and its drugs, were particularly vulnerable to such charges, and stepmothers were the worse equivalents of modern mothers-in-law. It is only the facts of social life that mean that we hear of few significant Roman trials involving women before the Principate. Their offenses were too trivial, they were dealt with by their family, or their class was too low for the People or a *quaestio perpetua* to hear them, and so they fail to score in the record. Religious matters allowed an exception: Vestal Virgins were sometimes tried for breaching their vows and some were buried alive. The practice went on into the Principate: there were two trials of Vestals under the conservative emperor Domitian.

Trial by the cognates should have been superseded at Rome when Augustus added adultery to the list of offenses that were tried in the public courts, severely restricting the right of males to kill adulterers caught in the act (A. Gell. 10.23, citing Cato's *On the Dowry*, and passages presented by Lefkowitz and Fant 1992: 104–9), but, as often at Rome, new rules did not entirely replace old practices: in 17 CE the Emperor Tiberius put responsibility for the punishment of the high-born Appuleia Varilla into the hands of her relatives, and four decades later Nero handed Pomponia Graecina over to her husband and family when she was charged with foreign superstition (Tacitus, *Annals* 2.50.3, 13.32.2).

The doubtful capacity of women came into view in the Roman Senate in 21 CE: the debate was over whether provincial governors should be allowed to take their wives with them on overseas service. The practice had been becoming more common and in 19 CE Agrippina, wife of Germanicus Caesar, and Plancina, wife of the governor of Syria, Cn. Piso, had become embroiled in their husbands' disputes. Plancina was charged before the Senate with abetting her husband in the offenses against Rome and the imperial house, but acquitted. The debate concluded without imposing a ban, but husbands were held responsible for their wives' behavior (Tacitus, *Annals* 3.17.1f., 33f., 4.20.4). Even elite Roman women were only partly self-determining individuals.

9 Conclusion

When law unequivocally backs one segment of society, another must use its only weapon: violence or strength of personality. So we learn from Marcianus in the *Digest* (40.9.9), which annuls freedom that a slave had wrung from his master by force. (Readers may recall a celebrated film of 1965, *The Servant*, in which the master became enslaved to his employee.) Athenian law ruled that it was sufficient to invalidate a will that it could be shown to have been drawn up under the influence of a woman (Demosthenes, 46 *On the Crown* 2.14). Respectable women were governed by law; others, prostitutes and the like, according to Just (1989: 214–6), were simply left "to wander in the wilderness of passions which constituted their abode"—reinforcing received opinions about the lawlessness and uncontrollability of women. The clever strategy for the respectable Greek woman, if it were available, might be to take advantage of dissent between one *kyrios* and another (Clark 1989: 37).

One cannot claim that ancient systems of law should be judged by the standards of European and American systems, however much emperors and jurists mitigated the rigor of those ancient systems. The marginal status of women in the category of human was propped up by two notions: the first was that inability to fight, or rather exclusion from the ranks, was accompanied by feebleness of intellect and weakness of will, the *levitas animi* of the mid-fifth century Roman Twelve Tables, which were never abolished; the second was that humans could be bought and sold. The ancients did not make the mistake of equating women with slaves: Aristotle carefully distinguished the two inferior groups (*Politics* 1252a34–69). But the "protective" (i.e., "weakness") argument used by ancient and modern writers as a justification for the treatment of women under ancient and some modern systems was bogus and designed to enshrine the rights of male heads of families and their control of property for themselves and the male descendants who gave them and their house immortality. The systems can be judged in the light of the ancients' own ideals and slogans: *eleutheria, demokratia, isonomia, autonomia, libertas.* There they are found wanting, the more so for the repetitious and contorted efforts the ancients made to defend and maintain them.

RECOMMENDED FURTHER READING

Most works on women in the ancient world touch on the law; for example, that edited by Fantham et al. (1994). For a brief general survey it is good to start with Clark (1989); Cantarella (1987) carries the inquiry into Hellenistic Egypt. All readers will find Lefkowitz and Fant (2005), with its concise but helpful comments, as particularly useful as it has been to the current contributor.

There are separate surveys of Greece and Rome. For Greece, Blundell (1995) must take a prime position. On women's rights and the economy, see Schaps (1979). For Athens a crucial contribution has been made by Just (1989) against the background provided by Harrison (1968). Then came Cohen (1991). Enough is known of Athenian practice to make it worth studying particular aspects, as (very valuably) does Patterson (1991).

For Rome there is a standard work of a stature comparable with that of Just: Gardner (1986). Note too Thomas (1992). As with Athens, enough is known to justify studies of special areas: see Dixon (1984), Marshall (1989), and Bauman (1992). The classic work on Roman marriage is Treggiari (1991); a succinct older book that can still be consulted is Corbett (1931). Motherhood is studied by Dixon (1988).

The long-lasting Roman empire extended over a wide variety of cultures. Hence there is a correspondingly wide range of reading; for the later empire, see Clark (1993). Evans-Grubbs (2002) concentrates on Roman law but has sections on Egypt and on eastern texts. Asia Minor has been a particularly rewarding area of study, as van Bremen's (1996) volume shows; MacMullen (1980) provides a brief survey and for one city there is Boatwright (1991b). The passing of Egypt from Pharaohs to Ptolemies to the rule of Rome makes it a complex area of study: for the earlier two periods see Watterson (1991); for the second period see Pomeroy (1984); and for the last two periods see the invaluable sourcebook of Rowlandson (1998).

8

Women and Medicine

Holt Parker

We begin with a myth, a title, and a question. The myth is that of Pandora. Unlike the Hebrew story, where woman is taken out of man (Genesis 2.21–3), in Hesiod's account (*Op.* 60–71; *Theogony* 570–2) Hephaistos makes woman out of mud. The title is *On the Nature of Woman* (*Peri gunaikeiēs phusios*), perhaps better translated as "On feminine nature," traditionally ascribed to Hippocrates and probably dating to the fourth century BCE. The corresponding title *On the Nature of Man* (*Peri phusios anthrōpou*) is, of course, "On the nature of the human being"; "man," as always, is the unmarked case. The question is from Soranus, a Greek doctor practicing in Rome (c. 100 CE; 3.1): "Are there conditions/diseases [*pathos*] special to women?" He assembles an impressive array of authorities for and against. This tension—whether women are of one substance with men or a separate creation—runs through all of ancient (and modern) thought.

We also begin with a text, one of the most powerful engines of thought ever assembled. It is the Table of Opposites attributed to Pythagoras (c. 530 BCE) and his followers (Aristotle, *Metaphysics* 986a21–6):

Bounded	Unbounded
Odd	Even
One	Many
Right	Left
Male	Female
Resting	Moving
Straight	Crooked
Light	Darkness
Good	Bad
Square	Oblong

So we note, with little surprise, the traditional yin and yang, with female firmly on the wrong side. Male and female are fundamental opposites, irreconcilable. One is bounded,

A Companion to Women in the Ancient World, First Edition. Edited by Sharon L. James and Sheila Dillon.
© 2012 John Wiley & Sons, Ltd. Published 2015 by John Wiley & Sons, Ltd.

self-contained, perfect, complete, unmoving. Female is open, lacking, imperfect, needing to be filled. The dyad is diverse, unbalanced, but can be made stable again (a triangular number) by an addition.

To this set of ideas we can join the associated pairs of

Hot	Cold
Dry	Wet
Solid	Porous
Impermeable	Permeable

(cf. Plato, *Phaedo* 86b; Lloyd 1964). This is all neatly summed up by Aristotle (*PA* 2.2 648a9–18):

> Noblest of all [sanguineous animals] are those whose blood is hot, and at the same time thin and clear. For such are suited alike for the development of courage and of intelligence. Accordingly, the upper parts are superior in these respects to the lower, the male superior to the female, and the right side to the left.

1   Women as Objects of Theory

The philosophers and doctors (and often we should make no sharp distinction between them) needed to account for two intertwined things: the existence of women and the birth of girls; that is, the causes for the physical differences between men and women, and the reasons why half of babies are born male and half female. For the first question, though there are many differences among medical and natural philosophical texts spread over a thousand years and at least two languages (Flemming 2000: 114–16), one can sketch out a common set of beliefs and practices held by men and women, elite and common, educated and not. In particular, the Pythagorean Table of Opposites provided an interconnected system of images for both theory and practice that lasted well into the Early Modern period and has lingering effects today.

Women Are Cold

Already in the Presocratics, heat distinguished men from women. Empedocles (c. 493–c. 433) said that men were naturally hotter than women (fr. A81, B65, B67). There was some early debate on this point. Women were thought to have more blood in them—obviously—and menstruation was thought to be caused by an excess of hot blood (Hp. *Mul.* 1.1). Parmenides agreed (fr. A9). But a consensus soon developed. The full theory is set out most systematically in Aristotle, for whom "destiny is anatomy" (Laqueur 1990: 25). In outline: the primary difference in living things is the amount of heat they contain and that went into their making. The body condenses by a type of cooking (*pepsis*). So nature proceeds down a scale of lessening heat: from men to women to animals to plants (e.g., *HA* 588b4–589a9; *PA* 681a12–28; *GA* 732a12–733a18; *Metaph.* 1058a29). Thus, "women exist by a sort of inability" or weakness (*GA* 728a17, 775a15). The female is a type of mutilated male (737a28), like eunuchs (766a25–30, 784a6–9), incomplete and deformed. But, says Aristotle, nature does nothing without a reason. Therefore, women's incompleteness is a *necessary* deformity, necessary for the continuation of human life (767b7).

Aristotle shows how this necessary deformity works in his theory of reproduction—itself a decoction of previous conceptions (*GA* 721a30–730b31). Men's greater heat cooks the residue of nutrition into sperm (white, foamy, airy, charged with *pneuma* (air/breath)). Women's lesser heat cooks this residue only as far as menstrual blood or milk. Accordingly, there is no female seed. Women contribute to birth but only by providing raw matter, while the male provides the life-giving animation. When Apollo makes his defense of Orestes in the *Eumenides* (658–61), he is drawing on an already very sophisticated science:

> The so-called mother is not the begetter of the begotten,
> but the nurse of the new-sown swelling.
> He who mounts, begets, but she like a stranger to a stranger
> preserves the shoot, if a god does not prevent it.

And so we have reached the master—in the most literal sense—trope that Aristotle announced early on in the *Politics* (1251a5–16, 1254a26–1254b14). In the ladder of hierarchies, male is to female as soul is to body. Male is the spirit, impregnating female matter. Male imparts life and motion (*GA* 716a4–7, 727b31–4, 729b15–21, 765b8–766a36). Thus, the male can usurp the female function of conception and birthing. Here we can see clearly the objectification or reification of woman. Woman is a thing to be animated.

Aristotle's consolidation of the dominant theory shows "a characteristically Greek combination of polarized thinking and inadequate attention to empirical evidence" (Cartledge 2002: 83). Contrary facts are ignored, or else subject to convenient reinterpretation (e.g., *HA* 538a22). Women must be inferior to men. So, three examples:

1. Women must have fewer sutures in their skulls, since men have bigger brains and so need more ventilation (*PA* 653a27–29, 653b1–3).
2. Women must have fewer teeth (*HA* 501b19). That this is not so, Aristotle could have discovered, in Bertrand Russell's memorable phrase, "by the simple device of asking Mrs. Aristotle to keep her mouth open while he counted" (1950: 135).
3. Menstruating woman must turn a mirror dark (*Parv. Nat.* 459b–60a).

We find the last two repeated by Pliny the Elder 400 years later (*HN* 7.71, 38.82).

To this theory, Herophilus (c. 330–260 BCE) and Galen (129–c. 215 CE) added refinements. In essence, males' extra heat causes their sexual organs to pop outside. Galen explains (*UP* 14.6–7 = 2.296–7 H):

> Therefore it is no wonder that the female is more incomplete than the male to the extent that she is colder. Just as the blind mole rat has incomplete eyes ... so too woman is more incomplete than man in the generative parts. For the parts were formed within her when she was still developing in the womb, but they were unable to peep out and emerge on the outside because of a weakness in the heat. This produced a creature more incomplete than one that was complete in every part, but it offered no small advantage to the whole race, for it is necessary that something female exist. For you mustn't think that the creator would deliberately make half of our entire race incomplete and as it were mutilated unless there would be some advantage from this very mutilation.
>
> (cf. Soranus 1.16; [Galen] 14.719; text of De Lacy 1992)

As Galen said, this fact is obvious and known to everyone, and better thus (*UP* 15.1 = 2.337 H).

Women Are Wet

A dry soul is wisest and best.

(Heraclitus fr. B118)

Hippocrates, in the first chapter of *Diseases of Women,* set out his theoretical basis for the treatment of women (1.1):

> I say that a woman is more porous [loosely-textured] in her flesh and softer than a man: since this is so, a woman's body draws up more moisture from the belly and faster than a man's.

There follows a thought experiment (derived in part from tests for moisture in soil): a porous skein of wool, like a woman, will draw up and absorb more water than a tightly woven piece of cloth (i.e., a man). Such analogical thinking drove most of ancient medicine (Lloyd 1966). The Hippocratic *Glands* 16 repeats this basic analogy and gives a fascinating picture of how women's bodies work:

> Women's nature is porous in the glands [here the breasts], as in their entire body, and they change the nourishment which they draw up into themselves into milk. It passes from the womb to the breasts and into the nourishment for the child after birth.

As Dean-Jones (1994: 56) states, "The body of a mature woman was one big gland." *Nature of the Child* 15 states this as a simple fact: "The body of a woman is wetter than a man's, and when the blood is agitated and the veins are full, it comes out, and this is due to her original nature."

Cold and wet are often associated (Lloyd 1964). So one of the *Problems* (4.25, 879a31–5) that stemmed from Aristotle's school ponders this fact, well-known to Hesiod (*Op.* 586), Alcaeus (347a), Hippocrates (*Aer.* 10), Aristotle himself (*HA* 542a32), and Pliny the Elder (*HN* 10.172):

> Why in summer are men less able to have sex but women more so? ... Man is hot and dry but woman is cold and wet. So a man's ability fades but theirs blossoms because it is balanced by its contrary.

The Hippocratic *Diet* agrees on the polarity (1.27 and 34):

> The female is based more on water and grows with things cold and wet and soft, in food or drink or activities. The male is based more on fire and clearly grows with things dry and hot, in food and the other aspects of life-style. Therefore if one wishes to beget a female, one must use a diet based on water; if a male, one must engage in activities based on fire. ... In general, the male is hotter and drier, the female wetter and colder not only because at the beginning each was engendered/grew in their respective conditions, but once they were born the male makes use of a more hard-working life-style, so that he gives off heat and is dried out, but the female uses a wetter and more carefree life-style, and makes her purgation [*katharsis*] of heat from her body every month.

The idea runs through the history of medicine. So, around 100 CE, Rufus of Ephesus takes it as a matter of course: "Everyone would agree that women's bodies are wetter and colder" (in Orib. *inc.* 2.1–2).

Women Are Sinister

The right is naturally better than left.

(Aristotle, *Progression of Animals* 706a20)

In more ways than one. The association of male with right, female with left, is of a venerable antiquity (Parmenides fr. B17; Anaxagoras fr. A107; Pythagoreans generally by Aristotle, *Metaph.* 986a23–b5; Pliny, *NH* 7.37; see Lloyd 1966: 42, 73–4, 1983: 36, 176; Hanson 1990: 44–6; Dean-Jones 1994: 44, 167). Females are generated *from* the left side of the body. So, Hippocrates recommends (*Superf.* 31):

> If one wants to beget a male child: have sex when the periods are tapering off or gone; thrust as vigorously as possible until ejaculation. If one wants a female: when the periods are at their heaviest in the woman or still coming on; tie up the right testicle so it is held up as high as possible. If one wants to beget a male, tie up the left one.

One should presumably therefore take one's time for a female (cf. *Epid.* 6.4.21; *Aph.* 5.38; Aristotle, *GA* 765a11–27; Dsc. 3.126; cf. [Galen] 14.476; Aetius 16.34: quasi-magical).

Females are also generated *on* the left side. There was an unshakeable belief that the womb had two chambers or at least sides (probably influenced by the bicornuate uterus of most mammals). The right pocket produced males; the left, females (Parmenides fr. B17; Hp. *Epid.* 2.6.15, 6.2.15, *Aph.* 5.48 (frequently quoted by Galen) and cf. 5.38, *Prorrh.* 2.24). Or, if not separate compartments, then a literal inclination: male fetuses to the right, female to the left, since (as everyone knows) the right side of the body is hotter than the left (Aristotle, *GA* 4.1.765b2; *PA* 670b17–22). Soranus (1.45) argues against this idea.

Women Are Permeable

Or, as Carson puts it, "women leak" (1990: 153). Unlike the male, who is one/bounded, the female is multiple/unbounded. *Diseases of Women* took as its starting point the idea that women's flesh is more porous. There is an important conceptual difference between the three most important "holes" in the body; two, the mouth and the anus, can be closed voluntarily. But the vagina stays open. Women leak—menstrual blood, sexual lubricant, lochial discharge after giving birth, and yeast infections (leucorrhea).

The principle verb of female physiology is *reó* (I flow). The image of woman as leaky resonates throughout Greek literature. Carrying water in a sieve is the eternal punishment for the husband-murdering Danaids (Carson 1990: 155). Plato uses this myth in *Gorgias* (493b): the soul is a jar (*pithos*) but in the ignorant "the part of the soul where the desires are, the unrestrained and leaky part, he [an unnamed Pythagorean] compared to a perforated jar [sieve], because it cannot be filled." The weak, leaky, ignorant, or feminine soul is like the weak, leaky, feminine body.

This view of the female body led to numerous attempts to "seal" it, or imagine it as sealed. There was no clear understanding of the hymen; instead, various membranes, variously located, were thought to block the womb (Hanson 1990: 324–30; Dean-Jones

1994: 50–4). Here, too, myth sets the pattern in Hesiod's retelling of the ancient Near Eastern story of how Heaven (Ouranos) sealed Earth's vagina with constant intercourse and was castrated by his offspring Kronos from within Earth's vagina (*Theog.* 156–82). The most common therapy for "female complaints" was constant intercourse followed by constant pregnancy (see below).

Thus, a spell to lock a woman's vagina (*Papyri Graecae Magicae* XXXVI.283–94, fourth century CE) meets with numerous medical recipes to dry up and tighten the vagina (e.g., Hp. *Mul.* 10, 17, 18), a state thought to be characteristic of virginity. So, there are recipes to restore that dry appearance ([Gal.] 14.478, 485–6; Aspasia in Aet. 16.66; Metrodora 25). There seem to be no recipes for vaginal lubrication.

Women Are Hollow

It was not Pandora's box; Pandora had a jar, specifically a *pithos* (Hes., *Op.* 94), the wide-mouthed storage pot that Plato made the analogy of the soul and the doctors made the analogy of the womb (Hp. *Mul.* 1.33, *Genit.* 9.3, *Epid.* 6.5.11). Two remarkable images show the way that the womb was visualized as an upside-down jar. Some twenty manuscripts of the Latin translation of Soranus made by Mustio (c. 500 CE?) preserve copies of the late Antique illustrations of the womb as jar. The best is the ninth-century copy in Brussels (Bibliothèque Royale de Belgique, MS 3701–15, fol. 16v). The parts are neatly labeled and the image determined our own medical vocabulary: *fundus*, "bottom" (paradoxically for the top of the uterus); cervix, "neck"; *orificium/os*, "mouth"(cf. Soranus 1.9; Rufus *Onom.* 193–8). The Kelsey Museum (26067) displays an amulet from the third century CE showing the womb as inverted jar, with the god Khnoum approaching with a key to lock the open womb so that the engendering seed will not flow out (Hanson 1990: 325). The author of the Hippocratic *On Ancient Medicine* (22) compared the womb to a suction cup (cf. Soranus 1.9; Galen *Sem.* 4.516.1).

Many sources also show traces of a somewhat inchoate idea that the vagina/womb somehow communicated with a mouth, either diffusely through women's porous flesh or perhaps via a tube or some other kind of direct connection between the upper mouth and lips (*labia*) and the lower mouth and lips (*labia*)—that, in essence, a woman was "an uninterrupted vagina from nostrils to womb" (Manuli 1983: 157). Many of the tests for fertility depend on this idea: something strong-smelling is placed under or in the woman's vagina. The ability to smell it on her breath indicates fertility (Lloyd 1983: 83; Manuli 1983: 157; King 1989: 22–3, 1994: 72–3, 1998: 28–31; Carson 1990: 153–60; Hanson 1990: 317–18, 1992: 239–40; Dean-Jones 1994: 72–3). These tests probably originated in Egypt but are found in Hippocrates (*Aph.* 5.59; *Mul.* 146; *Ster.* 214, 219, 230; *Superf.* 24; cf. *Nat. Mul.* 7), Aristotle (*GA* 747a7–15), Metrodora (33), and Aetius (16.7, said to be from Soranus). Soranus, however, criticizes this idea and its practitioners (1.35).

Fluids leak not only out of women but within them. The permeable nature of the female body allows mucus from the nose to flow directly down to the womb, impeding conception (Hp. *Mul.* 10, 11, 25; Metrodora 20). Fluids can travel up: blood from suppressed menses can appear as a nosebleed or vomit of blood (see below).

Women Are Unstable

Any excuse is sufficient to displace the womb, if it has any weakness.
(Hippocrates, *Diseases of Women* 138)

And so back to the Pythagorean Table of Opposites and resting/moving, women as jars and tubes. But there are two other powerful analogical models for woman and her womb. The most enduring image is the womb as animal. Both men and women, in Plato's account, have a living creature (*zôion*) inside us that drives us to sex (*Tim.* 91a–c). But the one in women is especially troublesome:

> In turn, in women, because of the same things, the womb or what is called the uterus, an animal (living creature) inside that desires making children, when it is without fruit long beyond the best time, gets upset and takes it hard. It wanders everywhere through the body and blocks up the ways out for breath and does not allow her to inhale, and so it throws her into extreme difficulties, and causes all kinds of diseases; until the desire and love of each of the sexes brings them together then.

Men's animal was quickly forgotten but the hysteria caused by the animal-womb, "womb-disease," lived on (for surveys see Simon 1978; Lefkowitz 1981; Manuli 1983: 149–204; Hanson 1990: esp. 319–21; Gilman et al. 1993; Dean-Jones 1994: 69–77; Micale 1995; Föllinger 1996; Gold 1998).

So, we have from Aretaeus of Cappadocia (second century CE; *Causes of Acute Diseases* 2.11):

> Hysterical suffocation. Between the flanks of women lies the womb, a female organ, closely resembling a living animal; for it is moved by itself here and there in the flanks, also into the upper parts vertically to below the cartilage of the thorax [i.e., the floating ribs], to the sides on the right or left, either to the liver or spleen; it also goes straight down to the lower parts, and, to put the matter briefly, it is given to wandering everywhere. It enjoys smells and shoots towards them; and it hates bad smells, and runs away from them; and in sum within a human being the womb is like an animal within an animal.

It is a well-known fact: the womb wanders about in women's hollow bodies and bangs into various organs. Doctors cured it; magicians lured it (Hp. *Mul.* 123–31, 137, 201, 203; *Nat. Mul.* 3, 44, 48, 58, 62; *Loc. hom.* 47; Metrodora 1–3; Aret. 2.11; Aet. 16.67–67bis; Paul. 3.71; for magic, Faraone 2003). The womb is thirsty; it needs moisture, and so will rise to the moister parts above (Hp. *Mul.* 7). It is hungry; it needs sperm. It sucks in seed, absorbs it (Hp. *Mul.* 18, 24, 137, 146, 166; *VM* 22; [Arist.] *HA* 10. 634b33–5, 35a25, 36a5, 37a4, 37a15–30; cf. Aristotle's explicit denial of this idea in *GA* 737b28–32, 39b16–20). Men can actually feel the womb's suction in intercourse (Galen 4.515.18–516.1). It closes on male seed, and digests it (Hp. *Mul.* 1.24, *Genit.* 5; Soranus 1.10). The womb has a mouth: it opens, closes, and conceives the seed; or, if conception fails, the womb "vomits" it out (cf. Soranus' image of the womb as a stomach at 1.36, 1.43, 1.46, 1.47; so, too, Galen, *Sem.* 4.523.10–524.3 and the long comparison at *Nat. Fac.* 3.2–3). There was a widespread belief that women knew almost immediately when they had conceived, a belief shared by women (Hp. *Nat. Puer.* 13.6), that they could actually feel when the mouth of the womb closed (Aristotle, *HA* 582b10–12, 583a35–b3, 584a2–12; Soranus 1.44; Galen, *Nat. Fac.* 3.3, *Sem.* 4.514; Aet. 16.8). If they were dry and nothing flowed out, ideally for seven days, conception had taken place (Hp. *Septim.* 7.448.2–4, *Genit.* 5, *Mul.* 1.10–12, 16, 220; *Carn.* 19; Aristotle, *GA* 758b5–6, *HA* 583a25–7, 83b10–15; Soranus 3.47; Galen 4.542–3, 17A.445, 799).

Hysteria is especially common, says *Diseases of Women* (7), "in those who do not have intercourse with men and with the older more than the younger" (cf. *Mul.* 127, 137; cf. *Nat. Mul.* 3; Metrodora 2; Paul. 3.71.1). The notion that women without men, without regular intercourse and pregnancy, are particularly susceptible to diseases of the womb is fundamental to ancient medicine and philosophy (e.g., Aristotle, *HA* 582b23–5), and still has adherents. The social "fact" is given two primary physiological explanations. First, according to *Diseases of Women* (2, 6–7), the womb is naturally dry, light, and hollow. Unless it is kept moist, preferably by intercourse, or made heavy, preferably by pregnancy, it will tend to rise in the body (cf. *Nat. Mul.* 2, 3). The womb was more likely to move once a woman's internal passages had been opened up (by intercourse, childbirth, lochial discharges) if they were not kept regularly full (by intercourse, childbirth, and lochial discharges) (Dean-Jones 1994: 72; King 1998: 71).

Aristotle disagreed (*GA* 720a12–24 of animals in general; contrast *HA* 10, 582b22–6), as did Galen. Though Galen shows some traces of the view of the womb as an animal, he puts hysteria down to retention of fluids (cf. Paul. 3.71), primarily semen (both male and female) or menstrual blood. Yet, the proximal cause, the cure, and the victims are all the same. The principle cause of hysteria is lack of intercourse. Thus, widows are especially susceptible, "when they previously had healthy menstruation, got pregnant, and had sex with their husbands but now are deprived of these things" (Galen 13.319–20; cf. 8.417, 420, 424, 432, 16.178; cf. Aet. 16.87). As proof, Galen relates a case where a widow suffering from hysteria is treated with warming medications (presumably in tampon form). She feels (as she said) "pleasure similar to that in intercourse," has an orgasm (*sunolkai*, *taseis*), secretes a great deal of thick, retained female semen, and so is cured (*Loc. Aff.* 6.5 = 8.420 K; cf. *Sem.* 4.599 K; [Aristotle] *HA* 10, 636b25–33). Such a story was too good to waste: Aetius repeats its as his personal experience (together with Galen's physiological comments; 16.67; see Debru 1992).

Even Soranus, who dismisses the wandering womb as silly nonsense (3.29), accepts hysteria as a disease, usually preceded by long widowhood (3.26), but he notes other causes, including miscarriage, giving premature birth, retention of the menses, meno-pause, and inflation of the uterus, which are not related to a societal norm of intercourse (in fact, contra-indicated) and pregnancy.

Yet, it seems that, whatever theory is used to explain it, hysteria is the body's revenge on women who fail to fulfill their natural roles (see King 1983; Manuli 1983: 189; Hanson 1990; Dean-Jones 1994: 28, 47–55, 69–77; King 2004): "The womb in its wandering behaves like insane women in myth ... Male attention, therapeutic or punitive, is needed to restore the insane women to society, or the dislocated womb to its normal function" (Lefkowitz 1981: 16–17).

2 The Role of Women in Reproduction

But did they even have a role, beyond that of a passive field for sowing? This analogy was not merely the sophistic reasoning of Anaxagoras and other philosophers (Aristotle, *GA* 763b31–3), the morally bankrupt Creon (Sophocles, *Antigone* 569), and a specious god, but of the Athenian marriage ceremony (Men. *Dys.* 842–3). The role of male seed is obvious, but the ancients were deeply divided on the question of what, if anything, women brought to conception (surveys of opinion at Censorinus 5.4; Aetius [Plutarch], *Plac.* 905d4–f6; Lloyd 1983: 86–94). The various answers are marked by alternations of presupposition, prejudice, and honest attempts to make sense of the fact that babies are born evenly male or female, sometimes resembling one parent, sometimes the other.

Closely tied to the search for female seed was speculation about what fluid in woman corresponded to semen in men, which was tied to a hopeful search for female ejaculation. Aetius [Plutarch] devotes a section to it (5.5, 905b8–c7; cf. Aristotle, *GA* 727b34–28a37, 764a8–12):

5. Do females also emit (προΐημι) seed?

Pythagoras, Epicurus, and Democritus: the female also emits seed, she has spermatic ducts but they are turned in the wrong direction; and so she too has desire for sex.

Aristotle and Zeno: she emits a wet substance, like sweat from exercise; but it is not fully cookable seed.

Hippocrates: females emit seed no less than men, but it does not contribute to procreation, because it falls outside of the womb; and therefore some women often emit seed without men, especially widows. Also bones are from the male, flesh from the female.

Pseudo-Aristotle (*HA* 10, 636a25–37b7), too, in a confused passage imagines that women "emit/ejaculate" not just in the womb but in the vagina, just outside the mouth of the womb (cf. Soranus 1.12, citing a lost "On Seed"). Further:

The path, through which it comes out, is made like this in women. They have a tube (*kaulos*), just as men have genitals, but inside the body. They blow out through this by means of a small opening just above the place where women urinate. Therefore whenever they are ripe to have sex, this place is not the same as it was before they were ripe. From this tube there is an emission.

Here the clitoris makes one of its infrequent appearances (Ruf. *Onom.* 111; Soranus 1.18), with Pseudo-Aristotle remaking it in the image of the penis, while Aristotle himself uses the fact that women emit moisture from a different place (just outside the womb) than the one in which they feel pleasure ("by touch in the same place as in males") as proof that this moisture is *not* seed (*GA* 728a32–34; Dean-Jones 1994: 31, 79, 158). Later authors take "gonorrhea" ("flow of seed") as common to men and women, treating vaginal discharges (yeast infections, etc.) as equivalent to sperm (Gourevitch 1995).

Various combinations of male and female seed were tried, of which Empedocles' theory, glimpsed through Aristotle, is the most intriguing. One seed produces one plant. How then can there be two seeds to make one baby? A sensible objection (especially if we remember that the mammalian ovum was not discovered until 1826 by Karl Ernst von Baer). Empedocles thinks that father and mother each provide a tally, a *symbolon*, two pieces that fit together (frs. 57, 63; Aristotle is opposed: *GA* 722b7–27, 764b4–20).

One of the most thoroughly thought-out of the two-seed theories is that of the Hippocratic *On Seed* (*Genit.* 4–6; cf. 8–9; *Nat. Puer.* 12, 31; *Morb.* 4.32; *Vict.* 27–8, 32):

In women: I say that in intercourse when the genitals are rubbed and the womb is moved, a sort of itching occurs in it and pleasure and heat take hold of the rest of the body. A woman also releases something from her body, sometimes into the womb, which becomes moist, sometimes also outside, if the womb gapes open more than it should. She has pleasure, once she begins to have intercourse, throughout the whole time, until the man also releases something. If she is ripe to have intercourse, she emits before the man, and for the rest of the time the woman does not continue having as much pleasure. But if she is not ripe, then she stops having pleasure at the same time as the man.... The pleasure and the heat flare up when the [female] seed drops into the womb, and then they cease.... This is also the case with women: if they have intercourse with men, they are healthier; if not, less healthy. For two reasons: first, the womb becomes moist during intercourse and not dry; if it is drier than it should be, it clenches together powerfully, and when it clenches together powerfully it causes pain to the body. Secondly, at the same time, intercourse by warming and liquefying the blood makes an easier path for the menstrual fluids, and if the menstrual fluids do not move, women's bodies become prone to illness.

He continues: both male and female emit stronger (male) seed and weaker (female) seed. Strong + strong = boy; weak + weak = female. Lots of strong + little weak = boy; lots of weak + little strong = female. This fairly closely matches Empedocles' view, substituting hot for strong and cold for weak (Cens. 6.6–7), and passes to Lucretius (4.1192–232). What determines when a man or woman emits each kind of seed and in what amounts, the authors do not say.

Hippocrates' *Diseases of Women* 24 agrees: "When women have finished having their periods, they conceive (hold in the belly) especially when they feel desire." This view, that seed in women is proven by their pleasure in sex and the attendant view that female pleasure and orgasm were essential to successful procreation, is seen in [Galen] 19.450 and [Aristotle] *GA* 10 (636b10–39, 637b27–35) (who, indeed, wants the woman to come first, and points to a belief held by women that simultaneous orgasm is best). Even those who did not believe that women had fully functioning seed agreed that female pleasure was necessary for conception (Soranus 1.12, 1.37; Galen 7.127.3–11; *UP* 14.9–11). Aetius said (16.26): "It is a hindrance to conception when a woman is forced or unwilling to have intercourse with her husband, for a woman who is in love (*agapē*) makes the seed fit together and because of this fact intercourse with passion (*erōs*) produces children much faster."

If a woman must eject seed at orgasm into the womb in order to get pregnant, then women's sexual pleasure is important, if only as a matter of pronatalism (Hanson 1990: 315). Even Aristotle says that feminine pleasure plays a subordinate (non-seminal) role (*GA* 739a20–35). This would seem to be a good thing (Rousselle 1988: 27–9), but the theory has profound social consequences. Soranus writes (1.37) that the best time for fruitful intercourse (he does not consider any other kind) is when "the urge and desire for intercourse are present." He makes an analogy:

For just as it is impossible for seed to be ejaculated by males without the urge and appetite, in the same way it cannot be taken up (conceived) by females without the urge and appetite. Just as food swallowed without appetite or with a certain revulsion is not well assimilated and fails its subsequent digestion (*pepsis*), so the seed cannot be taken up or if it is seized cannot be carried to term without the presence of the urge and appetite for intercourse.

He then answers an unspoken objection:

Even if some women have gotten pregnant from being raped, we should rather say in their case that the sensation (*pathos*) of appetite was in fact present in them as well, but it was blocked by mental judgment.

Soranus compares such women to grieving women who are hungry but do not realize it. That is, they enjoyed it even if they didn't know it. Their bodies said "yes," even if their minds said "no."

3   Women as Objects of Practice

The so-called "womanly diseases": The womb is the cause of all these diseases.
(Hippocrates, *Places in Man* 47)

Diseases

Women carry within them the pathogenic organ of the womb (cf. Aret. 4.11.1: "The womb is the source of countless severe diseases"; Cels. 4.27.1). So, nearly all discussion of women and their nature is inherently pathological. It is one of the remarkable features of ancient medicine and society that nowhere does any authority speak directly about what women did during normal menstruation (*Mul.* 11 mentioned rags only as a test; one exception might be the legend about Hypatia disabusing a young man of his infatuation by showing him her "feminine rags" in *Suda* υ 166; perhaps hinted at by Lucr. 4.1174–84).

Numerous failings can affect the womb: it can become "cold, fluid, or haemorrhagic, inflamed, distorted, constricted, lax, inflated or swollen, closed, ulcerated, fistulated, subject to growths or malignancies, indurated, pained, irritated or prolapsed" (Flemming 2000: 173, with examples of each). Any of these states can befall other organs, but the womb is unique in its superabundance of diseased states. The ultimate cause is women's moist, cold nature, what Gourevitch (1984) called "Le mal d'être femme" (the disease of being a woman). Women suffer, in Hanson's phrase (1990: 317), from "drainage problems." There are therefore three principle diseases of women: hysteria, "retention of the menses" (too little liquid purged), and "fluxes" (too much).

Hysteria
Hysteria, the "womb disease," might properly be limited to the attacks that come from the womb's movement in the body (King 1993, 1998: 205–46; Galen makes the same point: 17b. 824–5), but, as the doctors themselves stress, the womb is the source of all female complaints, and hysteria, displacement, and prolapse are not rigorously separated. The womb is metonymy for woman. Women are mobile currency—symbolic counters exchanged by men between households. But they need to be fixed. They are in constant danger of wandering outside, but, when held in their proper place, wet with semen and heavy with child, they are beneficial (Lefkowitz 1981). Accordingly, the best cure is intercourse followed by pregnancy (see, e.g., Hp. *Mul.* 1–7, 119, 121, 127, 137, *Nat. Mul.* 2, 3; Aristotle, *HA* 582b23–5; Galen 13.319–20, cf. 8.417, 420, 424, 432, 16.178; Aet. 16.87; Lefkowitz 1981; Manuli 1983: 189; King 1998: 69, 219–20, 232; Flemming 2000: 117).

In the absence of sexual healing, the womb can be lured back to its proper place by a carrot-and-stick application of sweet and unpleasant smells. Aretaeus (2.11) makes the rationale explicit, as does Soranus in inveighing against it (3.29) while still adapting parts of it. That the Hippocratic corpus seldom explains the underlying rationale does not mean that they had abandoned it (contra Hanson 1998). Thus, for a womb that has ascended to the diaphragm and liver, sweet substances are applied to the vagina (often in the form of wool tampons) while bad-smelling substances are applied to the nostrils. For a womb that has descended, the order is reversed. Fumigations were usually applied by means of a small pot with a pierced lid and attached tube or by a form of sweat bath, where the woman was placed on a stool over the burning materials and then draped with a blanket to keep in the vapor. For descriptions of fumigations and the devices involved, see Hp. *NW* 34, 107; *Mul.* 51, 75, 133, 195, 206, 230; *Superf.* 34; *Loc. Hom.* 47; Soranus 4.14 (citing Straton the follower of Erasistratus); Antyllus in Orib. 10.19; also Pliny *NH* 28.110.

Retention of the Menses

> *When the menses do not flow, women's bodies become sick.*
>
> (Hippocrates, *Seed* 4)

A different form of apoplexy afflicts young women. Everybody knows that virgins are especially subject to a form of hysterical attack, later called *chlorosis* (Shakespeare's "green sickness"), that drives them to hang themselves (Hp. *Virg.*; Plut. *Virt. Mul.* 249b–d). Some blame the gods, others a poisonous atmosphere, but the doctors know the true explanation: after menarche, the menstrual blood pools in the womb, but, since the vagina has not been opened up and straightened out by intercourse, the excess blood flows unnaturally upward towards the heart, lungs, and diaphragm (the *phrenes*, considered the seat of the intellect), causing numbness and eventual insanity. The therapy is to open up the passages so that the blood can flow. In King's memorable phrase, women are "bound to bleed" (1983). Again, the cure is intercourse and pregnancy as quickly as possible (cf. *Mul.* 2, 127; Soranus 1.31; Flemming and Hanson 1998; King 1998: 188–204, 2004).

Menstruation is women's natural way of purging their moist *physis*. The ancient doctors, however, were ignorant about the most basic facts of menstruation, and held varying opinions: menstruation normally occurs every month (Hp. *Mul.* 25, *Oct.* 1, etc.), occurs every three months (Aristotle, *HA* 582b3–4), occurs in all women at the same time as the moon wanes (Aristotle, *HA* 582a34, *GA* 767a2–6, 783a16; Galen 9.903; denied by Soranus 1.21), occurs on the exact same days each month (Hp. *Pror.* 2.24), could occur after conception (*Mul.* 25, *Aphr.* 5.60), consisted of an amount of two Attic *kotylai* (about 544 milliliters; in fact, the mean in healthy women is forty milliliters, with eighty milliliters as the upper normal limit over two to three days) (*Mul.* 6; Soranus 1.20). In short, nearly any form of menstruation could be classed as diseased (Hp. *Aphr.* 5.62, *Mul.* 2, 62).

Retention of the menses, then, is less a symptom than a disease in itself (Dean-Jones 1994: 125–35), and the cause of nearly every other disease (Hp. *Mul.* 1, *Genit.* 4), from headache (Hp. *Mul.* 18, *Epid.* 5.12; Rufus and Aspasia in Aet. 16.50) to gout (Hp. *Aph.* 6.29; Galen 11.165). The later handbooks devote entire sections to the disease (Soranus 3.6–16; Orib. *Ecl.* 146, *Syn.* 2.53; Paul. 3.61; Aet. 16.50).

The blood builds up and tries to escape. It blows out in abscesses (Cels. 2.8.7: "the bloodier, the better"), hemorrhoids (Hp. *Mul.* 2, *Coac.* 511), spitting up blood (*Mul.* 2, Aph. 5.32, *Morb.* 1.7; Aret. 2.2.9), through the breasts (*Mul.* 133), and especially nosebleeds (Hp. *Aph.* 5.33, *Epid.* 7.123; Aristotle, *HA* 587b35–88a2; Soranus 3.7; see King 1989: 24, 1994: 108, 1998: 14–15, 58–60). We are given, by Aspasia, a detailed physiology of how retention of the menses leads to uterine displacement (in Aet. 16.72; see below): the blood that would ordinarily flow into the womb pools in the surrounding arteries, veins, and ligaments of the womb. They become full and sodden, rounder and less long, and so pull the entire womb up, down, left, or right (cf. Galen 8.426).

Dioscorides lists hundreds of plants and other drugs as emmenagogues, and there are numerous recipes (e.g., Hp. *Mul.* 74, *Nat. Mul.* 32; Dsc. *Eupor.* 2.79–80; Orib. *Syn.* 1.22, 2.53). Some scholars have thought that these refer euphemistically to abortifacients (see below). In fact, emmenagogues were thought to serve both conception and contraception (Flemming 2000: 162–3). The best moment for conception was as one's period was waning, and getting one's period was an essential precondition for getting pregnant (Hp. *Mul.* 17, *Nat. Puer.* 15; Aristotle, *GA* 727b10–25, *HA* 582b11–12). So, Soranus (3.9) prescribed things to restart the menstrual flow for women who wanted to conceive. Doctors made a distinction between emmenagogues and abortifacients, but noted that, because of their expulsive properties, the things good for the one will be good for the other (as well as expelling the placenta and moving the lochial discharges; e.g., Hp. *Nat. Mul.* 32; Soranus 3.12; Orib. *Ecl.* 142–43; Paul. 3.61).

The Hippocratics generally were not in favor of bloodletting in cases of retention of the menses (Dean-Jones 1994: 142). But this type of artificial evacuation was eagerly promoted by Galen as a cure-all. He recounts a failure by the followers of Erasistratus in contrast to a case history of his own (11.188–190, 17b.81) where he cured a woman who had not menstruated for eight months. Soranus recommends bloodletting in stubborn cases (3.11).

"Flows"

> *A certain woman, which had an issue of blood twelve years, and had suffered many things of many physicians, and had spent all that she had, and was nothing bettered, but rather grew worse.*
>
> (Mark 5.25–26)

The opposite plumbing problem is too much flow: "If the periods are too much, diseases occur; if they don't happen, diseases occur in the womb" (Hp. *Aphr.* 5.62). The classifications and definitions of the various discharges were a matter of some debate, which can be followed in Soranus (3.43–4; see Archigenes ap. Aet. 16.63–5; Aret. 4.11; Orib. *Syn.* 9.46–7, *Eunap.* 4.111; Paul. 3.63). The unsystematized mass of Hippocratic medicine operated with basically a three-fold division (*Mul.* 110–11) of white (116, 117), red (110, 113), and yellow-red (*pyrros*, 115). Asclepiades (of Bithynia; fl. c. 90–75 BCE in Rome) established the canonical two classes of red and white (Soranus 3.43). Pseudo-Galen (*Def. Med.* 19.429) had four, one for each humor. Galen had five (7.265). Demetrius of Apamaea, the follower of Herophilus (fl. 110–90 BCE), had seven. Soranus rejected the subtle subdivisions of Demetrius, while keeping his broader definition. It is clear that ancient medicine was lumping together the productions of various infections, ulcers, and tumors under the same symptom (see on "gonorrhea" above).

Cancer

Uterine cancer takes up surprisingly little space in ancient gynecology, particularly so in Hippocratic medicine, where it is mentioned only three times, almost certainly because most of the symptoms of a deep, non-observable uterine cancer, such as cessation of menstruation, bleeding, vaginal discharge, etc., are treated under the heading of different diseases, or else as separate diseases in themselves, such as suppression of the menses. For the sources see Hp. *Epid.* 7.116, *Nat. Mul.* 31, *Mul.* 40, 159; Archigenes ap. Aet. 16.106 (cf. 16.119); Galen 17b.854 (retention of menses); Ps.-Gal. *Def. Med.* 305 (19.430); Aret. 4.11.7–8; Orib. *Syn.* 9.51; Paul. 3.67 (cf. 4.26.3). Soranus' treatment is missing (4.7), but cf. Mustio 2.23 and

Cael. Aur. *Gyn.* 2.108–10. Plutarch (*de curios. 7 = Mor.* 518d) mentions cancer of the womb as a disease that causes particular embarrassment to the sufferer.

Breasts

Though there are scattered references, the ancient doctors seem relatively less interested in diseases of the breasts. The Hippocratic corpus has almost nothing (*Mul.* 186). Breasts can become inflamed, hard, and ulcerated, much like other parts of the body (Soranus 2.7–8, 2.28; Aet. 16.35–49; cf. Pliny, *HN* 20.114, 21.132, 27.63, 30.125).

Aetius (16.42–8) considers breast cancer extensively, covering various types of cancers, and surgical and non-surgical treatment (citing Archigenes, Leonidas, Theodorus, and Philoxenos; cf. also Archigenes ap. Paul. 3.35). Leonides (in Aet. 16.44) gives a clinical description of surgery for breast cancer unequaled in horror until Fanny Burney. For Galen's physiology, cf. 11.139–41, 14.786, 15.330–1 (failure of menstruation, esp. to purge black bile), 17b.809, 14.579 (tumors), 11.344, 18a.80 (a case history). Soranus makes no mention of cancer of the breast, and, in general, it seems that the physicians' focus on the womb leaves the breasts as mere adjuncts, bound by sympathy to the womb (Galen, *UP* 14.4, 14.8; Soranus 1.15; cf. Hp. *Aph.* 5.38–9, 50, 52–3 with Galen 17b.827–9, 842–50; *Epid.* 6.5.11, *Nat. Puer.* 15). But this neglect in the literature contrasts with the numerous dedications of model breasts at shrines to Asclepius (Demand 1994: 91–2).

Therapy

If women are cold, they need to be warmed. If women are wet, they need to be dried. If women are empty, they need to be filled. This treatment by opposites stands in contrast to the "like cures like" of sympathetic magic (Hanson 1998: 72). The treatment of women is hydraulics. Any excess heat or moisture needs to be purged/evacuated from their "fluid economy" (Flemming 2000: 17); any insufficiency needs to be made up. Their fluids need careful handling.

Therapy, for men and women, was divided into (1) regimen/dietetics, (2) pharmacology, and (3) surgery. Dietetics plays a surprisingly small role in gynecology, with the exception of restorative foods after a disease or operation (e.g., Hp. *Mul.* 143, cf. *Nat. Mul.* 4, 5). Hippocrates' *Diseases* 1.22 is typical of the way women are passed over. He says that men differ from women and older people differ from younger in speed of recovery; he then ignores women for the rest of the chapter. Women's wet nature requires a generally drier diet (Hp. *Salubr.* 6). Their excessive moisture needs to be controlled (Rufus of Ephesus, *Regimen for Women* in Orib. *inc.* 20; his *Regimen for Girls*, Orib. *inc.* 18, is concerned almost exclusively with ensuring fertility). And yet, "no amount of care over the food she consumed or the life she led could ever relieve a woman from the innate weakness of her body" (Dean-Jones 1994: 124; Flemming 2000: 220–7 for a nuanced overview).

Surgery, too, mercifully played a limited role, in part because of the limitations of pre-anesthesia and pre-antiseptic surgery, and the doctors' knowledge of those limits (Hp. *Aph.* 6.38; Celsus 5.28). Paulus (6.45) says of cancer generally and uterine cancer specifically, "Cancer grows worse when operated on." Surgery is generally recommended only for abscesses in the womb that do not respond to medication (Paul. 3.65, 6.73). Soranus (1.15, 4.39) follows Themision (c. 90–40 BCE) in advocating hysterectomy for a prolapsed uterus that has turned black, but this is a desperate remedy for a desperate condition (his chapter on uterine cancer is missing). We read about Philoxenus of

Alexandria (fl. *c* 75–50 BCE) (Cels. 7 *prooem.* 3; Galen 13.539, 645), who specialized in cancer treatment and wrote extensively on the subject. He recommended surgical removal of cervical cancer.

But one surgical procedure stands out as unique: clitoridectomy. Paulus of Aegina (Book 6) is our most detailed treatment of surgery from antiquity. Chapters are devoted to repairs of pathological conditions of the male genitals (53–8, 1–69: hypospadias, phimosis, hydrocele, hernia, etc.). Castration (69) is against the spirit of medicine. Paulus deprecates the operation to repair an imperfect foreskin or to remove the mark of circumcision (16.53; Cels. 7.25; cf. I Corinthians 7.18): no natural function is impeded and the risks in surgery are too great. The surgical extirpation of the clitoris, on the other hand, is justified if it becomes "overlarge." Paulus is willing to accept hearsay testimony: "Some relate that certain women have an erection in that part similar to men and are roused to intercourse" (6.70), while Philoumenos (in Aet. 16.115) points to the example of the Egyptians (not generally taken as examples for proper conduct) and their "pre-emptive surgical strike" against adolescent girls (Flemming 2000: 218–19; see also [Galen] 14.705–6, Cael. Aur. 2.212, Mustio 2.76, based on Soranus 4.9 [missing]). Female genital mutilation has a distinguished history.

Much of the pharmacology was common to both men and women. The major difference was that the vagina offered one more entrance into the mysteries of the body (Flemming 2000: 219–20). Suppositories (Orib. 8.39; *Syn.* 1.20; Paul. 1.45; Aet. 3.160) are no less popular with the doctors than medicated tampons (e.g., Antyllus in Orib. 10.25; Paul. 7.24, who had three types: softening, tightening, dilating; Hp. *Mul.* 133; Paul. 3.61.4; Archigenes in Aet. 16.86; Cels. 5.21) and both may contain dangerous or repulsive ingredients (von Staden 1992; Hanson 1998: 87–93; Totelin 2007, 2009: 212–14). Yet, there is a tendency to treat what can be treated, and therapy focuses on the reachable womb. The womb is the source of all diseases and so must be treated. The womb can be treated and therefore is the source of all diseases.

Large amounts of ancient therapeutics strike us as grotesque or horrifying, and more so in what was done to women than to men. There is an understandable tendency to focus on the spectacular and horrific: bizarre devices for piping smoke into a vagina; fumigation of eviscerated puppy, stuffed with spices and roasted on the coals (*Mul.* 230); "succussion," where a woman suffering from uterine prolapse is tied upside down to a bed or ladder that is then pounded repeatedly onto the ground (Hp. *Epid.* 5.103 = 7.49 (the patient dies), *Nat. Mul.* 5, *Mul.* 68, 144, *Ster.* 248; see Dean-Jones 1994: 71 n. 98).

The doctors, too, seem to devote extra space to the grisly and the bizarre (Lloyd 1983: 82; cf. King 1995b: 139); for example, excision of a dead fetus (Hp. *Foet. Exsect.*; cf. *Mul.* 70, *Superf.* 7; Cels. 7.29; Soranus 4.9–13; Philoumenos in Aet. 16.23; Paul. 6.74) and uterine prolapse (though this condition may have been more common in antiquity).

Such considerations also raise the question of how often any particular remedy was actually employed. A recipe book is not a guide to what we eat every day. What ancient medicine was like from the patient's point of view is something for which the medical books provide little information (King 1995a, 1995b). If you were a woman complaining of a headache, would the doctor treating you turn first to texts about headache (the unmarked, male, case) or to books about diseases of women, looking for headache as a symptom there? Were you first a sick person or a sick woman?

Manuli went so far as to accuse ancient authors of participating in a "regimen of medical terrorism" ("ragione del terrorismo igienico," Manuli 1983: 161). Other scholars have hoped to find a lost "women's tradition" in the same recipes, focusing almost entirely on drugs said to cause abortion and contraception (see King 1995a, 1995b: 137–8, 1998: 132–56 for detailed criticism). Lloyd (1983: 78) and Flemming (2000: 116) are nearer the mark in pointing out that the doctor in *Diseases of Women* 62 is genuinely concerned for women's wellbeing: he has seen women die because they are being treated no differently than men. Ancient gynecology was strongly focused on the production of healthy babies. In the Hippocratic corpus, health for women means healthy reproduction, with the unfruitful most subject to bodily disorders. Yet it would be wrong to claim that women are seen in the medical works as merely baby factories. There is considerable concern for women in pain, even though diseases in women seem often to be equated with women's diseases. Abortion and contraception (not clearly demarcated until Soranus 1.60; cf. Aet. 16.16) were part of the medical works from the start, however ineffective (e.g., *Mul.* 76; Flemming 2000: 162–3, 167–70). There is no suggestion that doctors considered women less worthy of being cured, or that they received deliberately inferior care (Lloyd 1983: 68).

Yet, of course, every etiology, every diagnosis, every treatment is deeply imbricated in socially approved models. No therapy is recommended more often for women than intercourse and pregnancy. We turn with some relief to the measured and humane approach of Soranus (Temkin 1956; Lloyd 1983: 168–200; Hanson and Green 1994). Soranus rejects the womb-as-animal theory, considering it instead just "very similar" to an animal with its own sense of touch (1.8); he no longer believes in the old etiology of hysteria, but he still keeps faith with the disease and its cure, easily fitting them into his new framework of methodist medicine (3.4; Hanson 1998: 84–6).

4   Women as Healers

Women's roles as tenders of the sick, like most of their activities, are immemorial and invisible, apart from a few glancing references (Xen. *Oec.* 7.37). Though earlier scholars had pointed to their presence as professionals too, this practice was largely invisible until a seminal article by Pomeroy (1978). It has taken a considerable amount of time, but we can say that "It is now a well-established fact that women practiced medicine in the ancient world" (Flemming 2007: 257). There is a lot of work still to be done to reconstruct the intersection of the history of medicine and the history of women.

We have direct evidence of women physicians generally (e.g., Pl. *Republic* 454d2, 455e6–7; Mart. 11.71.7; Apul. *Met.* 5.10) and attestations for more than sixty women who were recognized by their societies as medical practitioners, called by the normal word for physician with a feminine ending (Greek *iatrinē*; Latin *medica*) or cited as authors of medical works or recipes (see Parker 1997; Flemming 2000: 33, 35–7, 359–60, 383–91 for discussion and lists), beginning with Phanostrate (c. 350 BCE from Acharnai in Attica), who is called on her gravestone *maia kai iatros* ("midwife and doctor"), making a clear distinction between the two roles.

We have few details of these women's training or education (true of most male doctors), though we get a glimpse in a few cases. The profession of medicine often descended in families. Antiochis of Tlos (c. 95–55 BCE) was daughter of the physician Diodotus and was honored by a civic statue "for her experience in the doctor's art [*iatrikē tekhnē*]." She was a dedicatee of Heracleides of Tarentum, and in turn cited by Asclepiades Pharmakion (first century CE) as an authority for various diseases. Apollonia's mummy (Egypt, second and third centuries CE) boasted of this type of family training, calling her *iatros iatrou* (doctor and the daughter of a doctor). A similar statue was erected to Aurelia Alexandria Zosime (Adada in Pisidia, date uncertain) by her doctor husband to honor "her medical knowledge." Pantheia (Pergamon, second century CE) was also the wife of a physician (whose father was a physician), as were Naevia Clara (Rome, first century BCE/first century CE), called *medica philologa* ("doctor and scholar"), and Auguste (Gdanmaa in Lycaonia, fourth–sixth centuries CE), who with her husband is called "chief civic doctor" (*arkhi-eiatrēna*). Restituta (Rome, first century CE) was educated by her former owner, Claudius Alcimus, "doctor to Caesar." As a mark of her learning, the funerary relief of Mousa (Istanbul, second/first century BCE) shows her with a scroll in her hand.

It is likely, though we cannot know for certain, that the practice of many women doctors was primarily concerned with women's diseases and childbirth. However, the examples of medieval and Renaissance Europe should warn us against too easy an assumption of a limited practice. There are many indications of a wider sphere. The civic honors accorded to Antiochis, Aurelia Alexandria Zosime, and Auguste all point to a city-wide practice. The epitaph for Domnina (Neoclaudiopolis, second/third century CE) from her husband also points to a extensive practice: "you delivered your fatherland from disease." Likewise, the tribute to Pantheia from her doctor husband, Glycon, also seems to indicate a practice comparable to his (although with classic reservations): "You raised high our common fame in the art of medicine, and even though a woman, you did not fall short of my skill." Geminia (Avitta Bibba, North Africa, c. third century CE) is called the "savior of all through her knowledge of medicine"; Iulia Saturnina is praised as "the best doctor"; and Scantia Redempta is "outstanding in the discipline of medicine."

A number of women are cited as medical authorities (Flemming 2007; Parker forthcoming, for details) by Andromachus the Younger and Asclepiades (both in Galen) and by Pliny the Elder. Aetius takes excerpts from the books of Aspasia (sometime before c. 550 CE; not to be confused with her famous namesake) more often even than Soranus (16.12, 15, 18, 22, 25, 50, 72, 109, 112, 114). Aspasia covers a wide variety of gynecological disorders and treatments including surgery and abortion, and gives greater thought to the care of the patient than Soranus. The cited chapters refer to other places in which she dealt with non-gynecological subjects (109, 112). We also have a full gynecological work preserved in *On Women's Diseases* by Metrodora (probably c. second– fourth centuries CE), whose well-organized treatise covers the whole of gynecology (but not obstetrics). Metrodora takes sides in several medical controversies over symptomatology and etiology (e.g., inflammation of the womb). She makes several unique contributions to theory and etiology. In clinical practice Metrodora employs both digital examination and the vaginal speculum, providing a unique and detailed description of pathology based on its use.

From at least as early as the fifth century BCE in Greece, women doctors have been part of the history of the western world. They called themselves doctors and were recognized as such by their communities. We know little about their training, but then we know very little about the training of their male colleagues. Their practice included gynecology and obstetrics but was not limited to these. Several achieved considerable social standing and high civic honors. Others wrote medical works that were used and cited by their male contemporaries. However, all of these women worked *inside* the great tradition. Metrodora is thoroughly Hippocratic in her understanding and treatment of hysteria (1–2). Aspasia differs little from Rufus or Soranus about the retention of the menses (Aet. 16.50).

What may strike us most forcefully in ancient medicine, especially ancient gynecology, is the triumph of theory over experience, not merely "false consciousness" in the Marxist sense but the alteration of bodily experience. The doctors claimed to have listened to the voice of women (Lloyd 1983: 76–9; Hanson 1990: 309–10; Dean-Jones 1994: 27–31; King 1995b), but what they reported the women to have said often cannot be true: experienced women can *feel* when their wombs close over the seed; feeling dry after intercourse or not seeing the seed fall is proof of conception; Hippocratic doctors can feel the membrane across the vagina blocking the mouth of the womb (*Mul.* 20, 223, *Nat. Mul.* 67; disputed by Soranus 1.17, repeated in Aet. 16.108); men can feel the womb sucking their seed.

RECOMMENDED FURTHER READING

The best introductions are Carson (1990) and Hanson (1990). Lloyd (1983) is indispensable. Dean-Jones (1994) gives full treatment of the Hippocratics; Flemming (2000) traces the story as far as Galen.

9

Reading the Bones: Interpreting the Skeletal Evidence for Women's Lives in Ancient Greece

Maria A. Liston

The study of human skeletons from archaeological sites offers a rich variety of information that informs us about women's lives. Indeed, it is the one field that directly studies the actual women who lived and worked in ancient Greece, and the study of these bones can provide a more robust and accurate understanding of the interactions of biology, environment, and culture that comprised the lives of women in the ancient world. In this essay I will attempt to offer a brief introduction to a number of topics of interest in the biology and pathology of women in ancient Greece. I have included topics that have long concerned anthropologists, as well as subjects that regularly come up in discussions between researchers in the disciplines of classics, archaeology, and anthropology. Because I assume the readers of this *Companion* have no specialized knowledge, I address questions that arise frequently when I give lectures on the study of skeletons from ancient Greece. I also attempt to describe the features and data that are used by biological anthropologists to develop their conclusions. My goal is to encourage archaeologists and historians to use biocultural data, and to be able to evaluate it critically. While I have included a generous selection of the basic bioanthropological literature in the references and the recommended further reading, both are far from complete. The examples of skeletal studies that I have cited are drawn, where possible, from publications on Greek skeletons, and their bibliographies in turn will allow the reader easily to pursue further topics of interest.

1   A Brief History of Skeleton Study

The inclusion of osteological remains in any analysis of mortuary ritual and grave goods is critical for an accurate interpretation of the purpose and significance of burial materials and for a broader understanding of the role of burial in ancient Greek culture. Skeletal studies

A Companion to Women in the Ancient World, First Edition. Edited by Sharon L. James and Sheila Dillon.
© 2012 John Wiley & Sons, Ltd. Published 2015 by John Wiley & Sons, Ltd.

contribute both indirectly, by identifying the recipient of the tomb and grave goods, and directly, by providing information about the growth, lifespan, health, disease, injury, and activities of the people at a site. However, within classical archaeology, skeletal reports, if they are included at all, tend to be added as appendices or separate chapters. This practice isolates information about the primary element of a grave—the deceased—from the associated cultural materials (Roberts et al. 2005: 33–4). For example, Kurtz and Board-man's (1971) landmark study, *Greek Burial Customs*, lacks any entries for "skeleton" or "body" in the index, and gives very few references to them in the text. Although it is now increasingly common to include at least a mention of the age and sex of the deceased with the tomb description, in the past catalogs of grave objects were published with almost no mention of the person for whom the objects were deposited. Yet the careful analysis of skeletal material can add new information to the reinterpretation of burial deposits by clearly identifying the nature and number of the deceased, or contradicting assumptions that were based solely on artifactual evidence (e.g., Bartsiokas 2000; Liston and Papa-dopoulos 2004).

Many studies of objects from mortuary contexts proceed with the assumption that the sex, age, and identity of the deceased can be accurately determined by the nature of the objects or the size and construction of the tomb. Yet there is no universal or fixed relationship between artifacts and gender: that is, the presence of a sword in a burial does not mean the deceased was male. Using artifact types and tomb size to assign age and sex to the deceased frequently results in misidentification. Likewise, the use of grave goods or grave size to identify child and adult burials has been shown to be inaccurate when tested against the osteological evidence (Liston 1993: 133–4), and demographic assumptions based on these data are inevitably skewed (as in Morris 1987: 57–62). In addition, while many graves are initially assumed to have been used for a single burial based on the assemblage of artifacts, when the bones are analyzed, the tombs are found to contain the remains of more than one individual, not infrequently of both sexes. Whether the presence of additional individuals in a grave is the result of deliberate reuse or the accidental incorporation of fill from earlier deposits, the presence of extra bones calls into question the association of the grave goods found within a single burial.

While later historical periods in archaeology provide a rich material and textual record for examining many aspects of antiquity, the skeletal record from historical cemeteries in Greece is extremely limited, particularly when compared to the number of recorded skeletons from prehistoric sites. There are a number of reasons for this disparity. Many Classical and Hellenistic cemeteries, prominently located outside city walls and with obvious monuments of art-historical and epigraphic interest, were excavated quite early in the history of modern archaeology. Since these excavations took place before there was any interest in or appreciation of data derived from human remains, few, if any, skeletons were saved (Angel 1972: 97). Other cemeteries of major Classical and post-Classical sites lie inaccessible under modern constructions, but the smaller towns and cemeteries of the prehistoric period more often remain available for current excavations. Skeletons from the Bronze Age and early Iron Age (Triantaphyllou 1998; Liston and Papadopoulos 2004) have been the subject of considerable attention by bioarchaeologists for several decades. More recently, skeletons from Neolithic and Palaeolithic sites (Papathanasiou et al. 2009; Stravopodi et al. 2009) and from the late antique and medieval periods (Garvie-Lok 2009; Papageorgopoulou and Xirotiris 2009) have begun to be analyzed in Greece; their study presents a wealth of information from a broad time span, through which we can now evaluate daily life in these ancient societies.

2 How Do We Study Skeletons and What Can They Tell Us?

The study of human skeletons begins with an evaluation of basic demographic character-istics: age, sex, stature, geographic/racial group. With those data in hand, further study of pathology, population variation, bone chemistry, and other areas of research may proceed, but it is essential to identify the skeletons as accurately as possible before proceeding to other areas of interpretation.

The human skeleton is not an inert supporting framework but a living malleable organ, which responds to disease, nutrition, activity, and stress, as well as to normal patterns of growth and aging. Reproductive biology necessitates that women's skeletons differ from those of men, in order to accommodate childbirth. Other differences between the skeletons of women and men are the result of variations in the trajectory and rate of growth, and the effect of testosterone on muscle development. In addition to these biological sex differences, cultural variations in gender roles may also result in observable differences in male and female skeletons. Differential access to food resources and medical care, environmental conditions, seclusion or isolation of women, gender-linked activities, and work patterns may all result in distinct physical variation between the sexes.

An important issue in the study of women's skeletons is the distinction between sex and gender. While the terms are often used interchangeably, it is important to recognize the differences between them in the analysis of human remains (Walker and Cook 1998: 255–6). Sex is a biological category, genetically controlled, and determined at conception by the presence of two X chromosomes in the twenty-third pair of chromo-somes (the sex chromosomes). Physiological sex differences include biological develop-ment of size and appearance, response to stresses such as nutritional deprivation, susceptibility to disease and other pathologies as a result of immune activity and physiological response to stress, and of course reproductive activity, including both the production and nursing of children. Gender is a cultural construct that can vary both across time and geography, but also between social classes in a single place and time. Gender differences may include roles and activities within the family, participation in the broader political and economic community, access to food and other resources, and the risk of exposure to disease and trauma. Gender may be reflected not only in grave goods and mortuary practices but also through the impact of cultural practices on health, activity patterns, and nutrition. These gender roles may result in differences in patterns of arthritis, muscle development, dental health, and traumatic injury between high- and low-status women.

Determination of Sex

For too long, the sex of an individual in a grave has routinely been attributed on the basis of grave goods, yet the attribution of those items to male or female burials has been based on our own cultural biases and assumptions. All too often, when these assumptions are tested against the osteological evidence it is found, for example, that weapons—typically associated with male burials—are at times buried with women, and jewelry or spindle whorls, normally presumed to be found in women's graves, may be found in the graves of men as well (Parker Pearson 1999: 97–9). Many graves contain items that, according to our cultural assumptions, could be attributed to either sex. Grave goods are not, therefore, a good way to determine sex (see also Shepherd, this volume, Chapter 16).

The study of women's skeletons first requires the accurate determination of sex from the skeletal remains. While there have been a number of recent attempts to develop methodologies for accurately determining the sex of non-adult skeletons (Weaver 1980; Schutkowski 1993; Fox et al. 2003), only adults can be sexed with confidence through skeletal evidence (White and Folkens 2005: 385–6). Although many skeletal elements show some pattern of sexual dimorphism, in most cases it is simply a matter of size difference or greater muscle development in males. However, two areas of the skeleton, the skull and the pelvis, preserve evidence of reliably distinct sex differences resulting from differing patterns of growth. The biological necessity of giving birth to infants with large human brains has produced strong natural selection in favor of wide pelvises in women. A number of differences in shape and dimension contribute to the wider female pelvis, and these differences can be recognized and evaluated even when the remains are so fragmentary that the complete dimensions of the bone are not preserved (White and Folkens 2005: 386–91).

In women, the earlier onset of puberty and the subsequently shorter growth periods result in size and shape differences that are most noticeable in the skull. In particular, women's faces stop growing several years earlier than men's (Ursi et al. 1993: 47–8), producing differences in shape and size that allow us instantly to identify the sex of a living individual, even in the absence of other cultural clues, such as facial hair, make-up, or hairstyle. These differences in outward appearance are built upon differences in the bone structure of the face and skull, and, like the pelvis, can be evaluated even when only fragments of a skull are preserved (White and Folkens 2005: 392–8).

Previous cultural biases in the determination of sex in skeletal remains have affected the history of skeletal studies. Although the normal sex ratio in any human population is nearly 1:1, except where there are significant cultural practices affecting the survival of one sex, Weiss (1972: 240–1) found consistent bias in favor of identifying males in skeletal populations across the world, including numerous sites in Greece. These skewed sex ratios have been shown to be the direct result of incorrect interpretation, not of actual population structure. In addition, skeletons of women and children are generally smaller and less heavily mineralized, factors that contribute, in some cases, to poorer preservation. The early archaeological practice of saving only the cranium has led to unreliable demographic information from many archaeological sites. Unfortunately the apparent under-representation of women has resulted in an inaccurate view of the population structure and mortuary practices at many sites (see also Shepherd, this volume, Chapter 16).

Skewed ratios with unexpectedly high numbers of males were published in early studies of Greek skeletons, but the dual problems of differential preservation of more robust male skulls and small samples were also noted (Angel 1943: 229–30, 1971: 73; Halstead 1977: 108; Engels 1980: 112). In the study of women in the ancient world, these skewed sex ratios have had a profound influence on the interpretation of women's lives. In particular, Angel's demographic analyses of ancient Greek skeletons (Angel 1969, 1972) and the apparent under-representation of women have shaped others' discussions of women's lives and roles in antiquity (Pomeroy 1975: 68–70; Engels 1980: 112–14), and there is very little representation of women's lives in the exhibits of Greek museums and interpretive literature (Kokkinidou and Nikolaïdou 2000: 42–5; see also Nikolaïdou, this volume, Chapter 3). More recent analyses using more nuanced interpretations of complete skeletal remains have revealed sex ratios closer to the expected pattern of nearly equal male and female numbers, or even greater numbers of females (e.g., Liston 1993: 130; Iezzi 2009: 178–9; Schepartz et al. 2009).

Most securely identified female skeletons are those of adults or adolescents; methods for identifying sex differences in the bones of children (through observation and measurement) are not yet reliable. While the study of ancient DNA offers some hope of identifying the sex of children, the climatic conditions in the Mediterranean result in very poor preservation of DNA. Alternating hot, dry summers and cold, wet winters frequently result in near complete degradation of usable DNA, even in bones and teeth that appear to be well preserved (Evison 2001: 676; Chilvers et al. 2008: 2712–13). In a pilot study of DNA extraction from ten teeth of skeletons from the Athenian agora, only one of the teeth sampled preserved usable DNA fragments (S. C. Fox and A. Papathanasiou, pers. comm.).

Age at Death

Age at death is an important measure of population health. Age in adults is primarily evaluated by examining the surfaces of two major joints in the pelvis: the pubic symphysis, where the two halves of the pelvis meet in the front, and the auricular surface of the ilium, where the sacrum, or base of the spine, articulates with the hip bone (Figure 9.1). These joint surfaces mature and change in patterned ways through adulthood, allowing a fairly accurate estimation of age at death.

The pubic symphysis aging method was first developed in the early twentieth century (Todd 1920, 1921). The Todd method has been found to be somewhat more accurate than subsequent methods of age determination, particularly when corrected for a

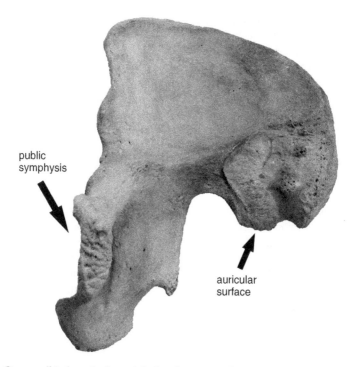

public
symphysis

auricular
surface

Figure 9.1 Os coxa (hip bone) of an adult female, twenty-five to thirty-five years old, showing the auricular surface and pubic symphysis, features used in determining the age of adults. M. H. Wiener Laboratory modern collection, American School of Classical Studies at Athens. Photo: author.

tendency to underage slightly (Meindl et al. 1985: 44; White and Folkens 2005: 375). There are, however, problems with the use of the pubic symphysis for age determination. Most methods tend to under-age older adults, resulting in apparent clusters of mortality around 40–50 years (Jackes 2000: 418–19; White and Folkens 2005: 375). Many methods are less accurate for females, in part because many of the reference collections used to develop the methods were dominated by male skeletons from studies of war casualties and medical school anatomy collections, and also because of differences in the pattern of growth and earlier maturation in females. Remarkably little attention has been paid to the extent to which stresses on the pelvis associated with pregnancy and childbirth affect the age-related characteristics of the pubic symphysis (Stewart 1957). Since Todd's studies (1920, 1921) were based on individuals born in the nineteenth and early twentieth centuries—that is, before the development of modern vaccinations, antibiotics, and other medical interventions—the reference sample may in fact more closely resemble ancient individuals than more recent study collections, and is therefore probably to be preferred for the analysis of Greco-Roman skeletal remains.

In addition, advances in age-determining techniques, and the use of women's skeletons as well as men's to develop age standards, have led to refinements in our use and understanding of skeletal age. A new technique for aging adult skeletons, the analysis of the auricular surface of the ilium, has done a great deal to clarify the actual ages of older adults recovered archaeologically from ancient burials (Lovejoy et al. 1985). With subsequent revisions (Buckberry and Chamberlain 2002; Osborne et al. 2004), this method has proved to be consistent and accurate, expanding the options available for determining age in adults. The auricular surface is more frequently and better preserved in fragmentary skeletons, increasing the importance of this newer method for Greek archaeological studies. This technique, like the one that uses the pubic symphysis, evaluates the gradual development and breakdown of the joint surface. This surface changes in patterned ways that are correlated with the age of the individual. Importantly, these changes continue to be clearly patterned into the fifth and sixth decades of life, extending the range of ages that can accurately be estimated from the skeletal remains. In using demographic data, it is important to note that average age at death and average life expectancy at birth are not at all the same, but too often one statistic is misunderstood for the other. Women in prehistoric societies consistently show elevated mortality rates during childbearing years, but, if they survived the dangers of pregnancy and childbirth, they might ultimately outlive their male counterparts (Armelagos 1998: 3).

The examination of age at death among early Iron Age women from various sites indicates some consistency in mortality patterns. Critical testing of aging techniques (Jackes 2000; Osborne et al. 2004) has shown that the overly precise ages provided in earlier reports are inaccurate and misleading but the general patterns of mortality for women in ancient Greece remain consistent. For example, in early Iron Age cemeteries, there is a peak of deaths in the third and fourth decades, but, if women survive the hazards of childbirth and disease, they may live to a relatively old age, beyond fifty years in some cases.

Beyond basic descriptive characteristics such as sex and age, the bioarchaeological analysis of human skeletons can provide insights into the lives and activities of women in antiquity. Through the careful evaluation of bones, it is possible to perceive patterns in skeletal development, muscularity, and stress that may indicate distinct patterns of activities among women that differ from those of men in the population. Sexually dimorphic patterns of disease and trauma can also offer some understanding of the lived experiences of women in the ancient world.

Pregnancy and Childbirth

An experience that is unquestionably unique to women is pregnancy and childbirth. Ancient medical writers, inscriptions, art, and literature all contribute to our understanding of this important aspect of women's lives. However, the bones themselves may provide less direct data than might be expected. J. L. Angel (1969: 432–3) was one of the first to suggest that parity, or the number of pregnancies a woman completed, could be estimated through the pits and scarring on the pelvic bones. He assigned specific numbers of pregnancies to women using this method and used these data in his demographic analyses of various populations in Greece (Angel 1969: 432–3, 1971: 109–10, 1972: 94–5). Unfortunately, subsequent research has shown that the correlation between pelvic scarring and pregnancy is much weaker than Angel suggested (Kelly 1979; Bergfelder and Herrmann 1980; Andersen 1988; Cox and Scott 1992). It is clear that some pregnancies do cause pelvic scarring, but many do not, so it is impossible to estimate, based on such evidence, the number of pregnancies experienced by a woman. In addition, other traumatic events, such as falls, can result in pelvic scarring, and these scars are occasionally found on male pelvises as well. Finally, there is some indication that such scars can be reduced or eliminated over time as the bone is remodeled during the normal maintenance and aging processes. However, the pattern of mortality among women, with a clear peak during childbearing years, is probably indicative of the stress that childbirth placed on women's skeletons. The occasional discovery of a woman buried with a fetus still within the pelvic cavity gives graphic evidence of the dangers inherent in childbirth for women in ancient Greece (Barnes 2003: 438).

Health in Childhood

Although identifying the sex of children's bones is difficult, the bones of a female adult will preserve indications of health and the stresses that occurred during the woman's childhood. Disturbances in childhood growth can be observed in an adult through the presence of Harris lines in the long bones (Maat 1984; Hummert and van Gerven 1985). These are lines of increased density, visible in radiographs of bones, particularly the tibiae. When growth is slowed or temporarily stopped, a surface of more dense bone is formed at the growth plate, at the junction of the diaphysis (shaft) and epiphysis (joint end) of a long bone. When growth continues, this layer of dense bone remains, marking the point at which the stress occurred. Unfortunately there is no clear correlation of these lines with specific types of disease, nutritional stress, or other growth-inhibiting factors, but they do provide a record of stresses during the life of a child that persists into adulthood, although the lines may eventually be remodeled and disappear.

Growth interruption and stress during childhood can also leave evidence on the adult teeth. If a child is stressed by disease or malnutrition during the period in which the crowns of the teeth are forming in the jaws, horizontal grooves or a series of pits can form in the tooth crown at the point at which growth was disturbed (Figure 9.2; Goodman and Rose 1990: 59–61). These remain visible on the tooth as long as the tooth crown survives. Like Harris lines, these grooves and pits, called linear enamel hypoplasias (LEH), are not specifically connected with particular types of stressors, nor does their size and appearance

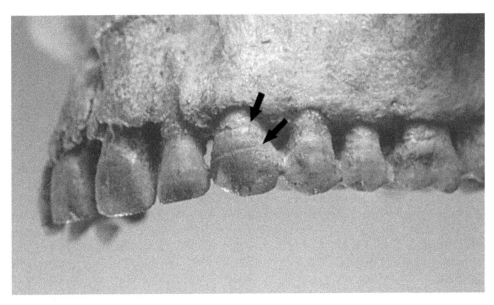

Figure 9.2   Maxilla of an adult female, forty-five to fifty-five years old. Arrows indicate linear enamel hypoplasias (LEH). Athenian Agora, Early Iron Age. Photo: author.

seem to correlate well with the duration of the incidents of stress. However, there does seem to be some consistent connection with their formation at the time of weaning in infants from ancient Greece (Keenleyside 2008: 274–5). Unfortunately, many studies do not provide sex-specific data in their studies, but there are exceptions. At Mycenaean Pylos, for example, females exhibited lower levels of linear enamel hypoplasias than males but they suffered from higher rates of caries (tooth decay) and antemortem tooth loss (Schepartz et al. 2009: 168–9).

   Another indicator of childhood health and nutrition is adult stature. Children who are chronically sickly and undernourished usually will not attain their full growth potential. As a result, stature can be a useful indicator of overall health in a population, or differential growth conditions for males and females (Angel 1984: 52). Stature is most accurately estimated from complete long bone lengths, particularly the major bones of the leg. While the most widely used and accurate calculations come from Trotter (1970), which is out of print and difficult to obtain, the equations have been reproduced in most handbooks and textbooks of human osteology (e.g., White and Folkens 2000: 398–9).

   While it is clear that nutritional and disease stress will reduce adult height, the degree of sexual dimorphism is difficult to interpret. Normally males are taller than females in any given population, but the degree of difference between the sexes can be an important indicator of gendered patterns of health and nutrition. When both males and females are equally stressed, sexual dimorphism should decrease, because females are better adapted to resisting stress during growth than males and therefore should obtain more of their adult height. If males are differentially protected from stress, by having access to better nutrition or protection from disease, sexual dimorphism should be greater than expected for a healthy population. In other words, the less stressed males will obtain most of their potential stature, while the undernourished or more diseased females will reach less of their already potentially shorter height (Goodman et al. 1984: 20–1).

Unfortunately, the destructive taphonomic conditions in Greece make the preservation of complete long bones relatively rare at many sites. Many of the comparative studies of stature and health were done by Angel (1946: 75, 1966: 761, 1972: 98–101). Smith (2000: 110) found significant differences in the statures of males and females from the Bronze Age Athenian agora, with an average difference of 11.8 centimeters, but only 40 skeletons provided long bones sufficiently complete to measure, and the sample was too small to discern status differences.

Reconstructing Diet

One of the more recent advances in skeletal biology has been the development of isotopic and trace element analyses to evaluate diet and migration patterns. While trace element analysis was greeted with great enthusiasm when it was first introduced to bioarchaeology in the 1970s, investigators have struggled to overcome the problems of diagenesis, the postmortem altering of the elemental make-up of bone. Strontium and barium have been shown to be more resistant to postmortem alteration, and have been used to examine regional dietary patterns. In addition, the analysis of lead in the paleopathology of ancient bone has been demonstrated to be a productive use of trace element analysis (Sandford and Weaver 2000: 329–30, 338; Buikstra and Lagia 2009: 27–8).

While trace element analysis has not been as helpful for understanding diet, analysis of stable isotopes of carbon, nitrogen, and strontium has fulfilled some of that early promise for bone chemical analysis (Buikstra and Lagia 2009: 18–19). Stable isotopic analyses have shown changes in the diet of men and women across time and gender-specific patterns in the consumption of animal proteins across time (Garvie-Lok 2001: 467–8; Bourbou and Richards 2007: 69; Keenleyside 2008: 275; Triantaphyllou et al. 2008: 3031), but not all studies have been able to conduct sex-specific analyses because of poor preservation of the bones in some sites, a perennial problem in Greek archaeology (Petrousa and Manolis 2010: 615–16). Surprisingly, many studies of diet in ancient Greece find that marine resources played a very small part in the everyday diet of most individuals, despite the proximity of many sites to the sea and the concomitant accessibility of marine dietary resources (Garvie-Lok 2001: 445; Papathanasiou 2003: 320; Petrousa and Manolis 2010: 619–20).

Another use of stable isotopic analysis that is relevant to the lives of women is the identification of patterns of weaning in children. Nursing infants consuming milk proteins exclusively will have ^{15}N isotope signatures higher than those of their mothers and other adults in the population because of the trophic effect. An infant feeding on proteins produced by the mother's body is feeding at one level above the mother on the food web. The process of breast milk production preferentially filters nitrogen isotopes, resulting in higher ^{15}N values (Fuller et al. 2006: 55–6). The nitrogen isotopic evidence for Bronze Age Greece suggests that many children were weaned between the ages of two and four (Garvie-Lok 2001: 451; Triantaphyllou et al. 2008: 3030), a pattern that appears to continue into the Roman period.

The analysis of oxygen and strontium isotopes is also used to discern migration patterns in ancient populations. The teeth of an individual retain a record of the isotopic profile of the environment during early childhood. The bones of the same individual provide a profile of the person's environment during the last few years of life (Garvie-Lok 2009: 248–50; Richards et al. 2008: 1252–3). When these differ, it is an indication that the individual has migrated during his or her lifetime. Sex differences in isotopic patterns can also be used to detect marital residence patterning, if either males or females relocated over long distances for marriage.

Dental Health

The analysis of dentition can contribute a great deal to our understanding of women's lives. In addition to preserving markers of developmental stress (linear enamel hypoplasias) mentioned above, teeth are useful to the biological anthropologist for a number of reasons. First, teeth are the hardest and most durable portions of the human skeleton, and therefore are the most likely to survive, even in the typical conditions of poor preservation that are found on many archaeological sites in Greece. Teeth are also the one portion of the skeletal system that interacts directly with the environment, and so retain evidence of their use both in chewing and as tools.

Dental pathology is an important and sensitive marker of overall health status. Dental decay and infections can lead to more widespread infections in the body, and have been linked to heart disease. In addition, individuals with poor dental health may become undernourished because they cannot chew available foods. Dental caries, or tooth decay, is strongly related to diet, which in turn is influenced by environment, subsistence patterns, and access to food resources. Meaty diets high in fats and proteins result in fewer caries than plant-based diets high in carbohydrates and sugars. Thus, tooth decay rates can be a marker for both diet and gendered status differentiation. Dental abscesses and antemortem tooth loss are both affected by caries rates, and so may also be indicative of overall health status.

Through chewing and using the teeth as supplemental tools or a "third hand," individuals directly induce wear and breakage on the enamel surfaces, providing a record of that use (White and Folkens 2000: 328). For example, excessive wear on the anterior dentition can be interpreted as an indication of the use of the teeth as tools (Keenleyside 2008: 265). One activity known to have been practiced by most women in ancient Greece is hand spinning (Barber 1991: 42–4, 70, pl. 2.36). Evidence for the use of the teeth in spinning has been documented on women's teeth from Bronze Age and Iron Age sites (M. A. Liston, unpublished data). Shallow grooves are found on the lateral edges of anterior teeth and are consistently seen on the teeth of women but not men (Figure 9.3). Even in very young individuals, with no other visible tooth wear, there may be grooves that have worn completely through the dental enamel on the anterior teeth.

Infectious Disease

An array of pathological conditions can be identified from skeletal remains. Many can provide insight into the lives of women, and how they interacted within their families and within society as a whole. However, the diagnosis of diseases from skeletal evidence is difficult, as few diseases result in damage that is specifically identifiable in bone. It is important to look at patterns, including the predilection of the disease to occur in individuals of a given age and sex, the environmental conditions that can lead to exposure, and the pattern of lesions across the skeleton. Only when all these patterns are visible and distinguishable is it possible to offer a differential diagnosis of the most likely causes of disease or death in a skeleton.

Diet and environment can have a strong influence on the health and pathology of women. Not only the consumption of certain foods but also their preparation and

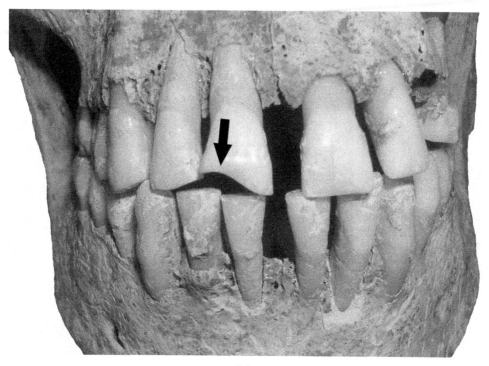

Figure 9.3 Mandible and maxilla of an adult female, thirty to forty years old. Arrow indicates a groove on the maxillary central incisor probably caused by using the teeth in hand spinning. Liatovouni, Epirus, Early Iron Age. Photo: author.

handling can lead to disease. Handling and butchering animals, as well as consuming uncooked meat and milk products, could lead to zoonoses (diseases caught from animals). Two zoonoses that are known to have occurred in ancient Greece are tuberculosis (with a natural disease reservoir in cattle) and brucellosis (which is carried by goats). Both diseases affect the skeletal system only occasionally, so the incidence observed in the bones does not reflect the actual number of cases in a population but it does indicate the presence of the disease at a given place and time. Because women were frequently in close contact with animals and were involved in food preparation, for example handling raw milk and meat products, they may have been particularly susceptible to these infections.

Tuberculosis is one of the pathologies that was identified early on by anthropologists studying human skeletons. Hippocrates and Galen refer to diseases that were probably tuberculosis (Grmek 1989: 190–7). It is primarily known as a respiratory disease, but can also cause skeletal lesions, particularly in the spine, and result in the collapse of one or more vertebral bodies. Despite the ancient literary evidence, skeletal tuberculosis has been identified only rarely in skeletons from ancient Greece (Roberts and Buikstra 2003: 171).

Brucellosis was probably common in the ancient Mediterranean (it remains a problem to this day throughout the Mediterranean; see Geyik et al. 2002: 98), where the infection is also known as Mediterranean Fever or Malta Fever. The undulating daily fever of brucellosis is described in the Hippocratic corpus (*Epidemics* I.XXIV), and the bacterium

Figure 9.4　Sacroiliac joint (top) and thoracic vertebra (bottom) of an adult female, thirty-five to fifty years old. Arrows indicate lesions probably resulting from brucellosis infection. Liatovouni, Epirus, Early Iron Age. Photo: author.

has tentatively been identified in carbonized cheese from Pompeii (Capasso 2002: 126). The primary symptom in goats, spontaneous abortion, is described in Genesis 31.38. A brucellosis infection is acquired by contact with living animals, or handling or eating uncooked meat and milk. Women in the ancient Greek world would have been at high risk for contracting the disease. Symptoms of brucellosis include a characteristic fever that rises and falls on a daily basis, hence the ancient description of the disease—undulant or quotidian fever. The disease is identifiable skeletally through destructive lesions on the vertebrae and sacro-iliac joints (Figure 9.4). Lesions consistent with brucellosis infections have been identified in Greek women's skeletons at Corinth (Barnes 2003: 441) and at Liatovouni in Epirus (M. A. Liston, unpublished data).

　　In addition to the zoonoses, dietary deficiencies were probably not uncommon in ancient Greece. In particular, scurvy, caused by vitamin C deficiency, would have been a problem for women and their children if their diet lacked fresh fruits and vegetables. Since vitamin C is destroyed by cooking, even if the diet included adequate resources, processing may have eliminated the necessary vitamin. Scurvy is manifested on bones through porous lesions and layers of spongy-looking new bone on the mandible, cranium, and other flat bones, as well as on the long bone shafts (Ortner and Erickson 1997: 213–14). Early weaning and differential feeding practices for female infants and children may at times have made girls particularly susceptible to the disease. It has been identified in juvenile skeletons from Stymphalos, and possibly from the Athenian agora burials.

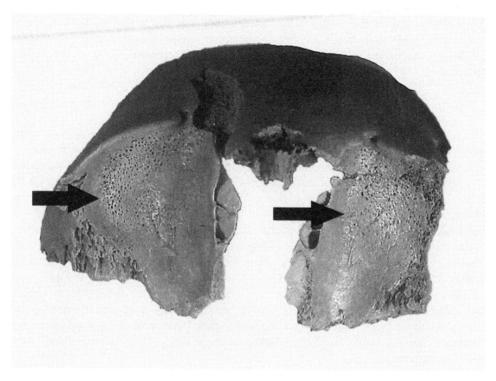

Figure 9.5   Superior surface of the eye orbits of a child, eight to ten years old. Arrows indicate areas of Cribra Orbitalia (CO). Athenian agora, second century BCE. Photo: author.

Anaemias

The interaction of diet and environment has long been debated for other cranial lesions, which provide a good example of the complexity of paleopathological diagnosis and interpretation. Cribra orbitalia (CO) is seen as a spongy, porous area of bone on the superior surface of the eye orbit (Figure 9.5). Porotic hyperosotosis (PH) is caused by an expansion of the marrow-producing spongy bone of the skull into the exterior surface of the cranial vault. The active lesions of both CO and PH are most often seen in children, but traces of healed lesions may persist into late adulthood (Angel 1966: 760–1).

These lesions were first identified in Greece by Angel (1966), who suggested that they may have been symptomatic of thalassemia, a genetic anaemia that is still relatively common in the Mediterranean. While thalassemia was almost certainly present in antiquity, many cases of CO and PH are now known to be caused more often by iron-deficient anaemia, either from diet or intestinal bleeding caused by parasite loads. However, it has recently been shown that there has been insufficient attention given to variations in lesions identified as CO and PH (Lagia et al. 2007: 269–70). Walker et al. (2009: 119–20) have shown that the subperiosteal bleeding associated with dietary deficiencies of both vitamin C and vitamin B_{12} may cause similar pathological bone formation. The increasing use of bone histology in paleopathology is providing more accurate diagnoses of lesions such as these, but this process requires destroying portions of the bone to produce thin sections for microscopic analysis. Destroying bone is always problematic, and should be undertaken only when essential. In Greece, where destructive sampling requires special permits, the application of bone histology in diagnosing pathologies is necessarily limited.

Osteoporosis and Osteopenia

For many women, an almost inevitable consequence of aging is the loss of bone mass, or osteopenia. While the terms osteoporosis and osteopenia are often used interchangeably, in the context of archaeological skeletons, the term osteopenia is preferred. Osteoporosis refers to a specific suite of clinical features, while osteopenia simply denotes loss of bone mass by any cause. While many parts of the skeleton may be affected, osteopenia has its greatest impact on the lives of women when it results in vertebral collapse and catastrophic fractures of the hip (Weaver 1998: 28). In ancient Greece, severe osteopenia was probably less common because of high activity levels for most women, which resulted in greater bone mass in young adulthood, and because of shorter life spans, which meant that most women would have died before severe osteoporosis could develop. However, cases of osteopenia are identifiable in ancient Greek skeletons. For example, a skeleton from the Athenian agora of a woman who died at more than fifty years of age showed she had suffered vertebral collapse and resulting changes to her ribs, which had been warped when the collapse of the spine forced them into contact with one another.

Violence and Trauma

Probably no other category of pathology can reveal as much about the lived experiences and status of women than the rates of traumatic injury, particularly injuries associated with interpersonal violence. Fractures of the facial bones, cranial fractures, and fractures of the forearms and hands can all occur through accidents, but it is clear from both ethnographic and modern emergency room data that these injuries are more likely to occur as a result of violent physical contact between individuals (Walker 1997: 160–1). Fractures of the hands and forearm, particularly the mid-shaft of the ulna, frequently occur as defensive wounds. Outside of the modern world, where the speed of our transportation and of our amusements can lead to high-velocity impacts, fractures of the face and cranial vault are rare except in cases where one person has hit another. When women's skeletons show high rates of these types of injuries, those are likely to be a result of cultural practices that allow or encourage violence towards women. While there is no extensive survey of skeletal trauma from ancient Greece, there is little evidence for consistent violence directed against women (e.g., Angel 1971: 91–2), although, on Kephalonia, Angel found that there were low, nearly equal, numbers of cranio-facial and hand fractures in men and women, a pattern that suggests that interpersonal violence was equally distributed between the sexes (Angel 1943: 247–8). Fractures in women's skeletons do occur, but these appear to have been the result of falls and other accidents. For example, in the early Iron Age burials in the Athenian agora, only two women's skeletons exhibit fractures: one with a fractured wrist and ribs and one with a fractured ankle. The specific characteristics of both clearly suggest that these fractures were the result of falls and not deliberate violence. The woman with the fractured wrist and ribs also suffered from osteopenia, which may have been a contributing factor.

3   Conclusions

Within the field of mortuary analysis, there has been little attempt to reflect critically upon our own attitudes and assumptions toward the material record, especially when attributing objects found in graves to a particular gender or social status. As Charles (2005: 14–15) has observed, our analysis of mortuary behavior suffers from the assumption that there is a clear link between our theoretical and methodological suppositions and the actual behavior of people in the past and the way they responded to death. We should not, for example, assume that a spear or a knife will necessarily be associated with a male burial, or that a spindle whorl or necklace will be buried only with a female (see also Shepherd, this volume, Chapter 16). If we do not examine all the available data, our analysis of mortuary practices will suffer: we will not only miss real cultural diversity but also fail to include the dead themselves in our analysis of their death. The study of skeletal remains has an important contribution to make to the analysis and interpretation of artifacts and the demographic structure of society; by studying the bones we can recover the mundane details, the osteobiographies, of women's lives in a way that is not possible from other kinds of evidence. The inclusion of biological data can challenge our assumptions, clarify our errors, and richly enhance our understanding of what it meant to be a woman in the past.

RECOMMENDED FURTHER READING

There are very few gendered studies of skeletal remains from Ancient Greece; discussion of women's lives, health, and death is usually embedded within general reports of cemeteries. For a recent discussion and extensive bibliography of skeletal studies in Greece, see MacKinnon (2007). Cohen and Bennett (1998) provide a helpful introduction to the analysis of sex and gender in archaeological sites. Methodological reference works rarely address women's bones exclusively, but do include the identification and analysis of women within the broader context.

There are a number of useful works in which the authors address a variety of issues in the interpretation of human remains, including issues specific to the study of women and their roles in society. Ubelaker (1989) provides an introduction, directed toward non-specialists, to the recovery and analysis of human bone. Larsen (1997) provides one of the best comprehensive accounts of the interpretive study of human remains in archaeological contexts. Likewise, Saunders and Katzenberg (1992) assembled a diverse collection of methodological studies by multiple authors evaluating life conditions based on the analysis of skeletal data. İşcan and Kennedy (1989) is also a collection of studies aimed at understanding the lived experience of individuals as determined from the condition of the skeleton—Kennedy's article on activity-induced skeletal markers in this collection is particularly useful in suggesting interpretations of acquired skeletal variations. Hillson (1996) focuses on the wide range of information available from the analysis of the dentition.

The identification and analysis of pathology is critical to understanding the life experience of women in the past. There are a number of general reference manuals on paleopathology; among the most extensive of these are Aufderheide and Rodríguez-Martín (1998) and Ortner (2003). These books introduce a broad range of pathological conditions, including trauma, infection, developmental defects, genetic disease, and dietary diseases.

Finally, the lives of children are inextricably linked to those of women in the ancient world, and juvenile osteology has its own challenges and problems. Hoppa and Fitzgerald (1999) is a collection of studies specifically on the growth of children in the past. Scheuer and Black (2000) provide a comprehensive reference volume on all aspects of fetal and non-adult skeletons, drawing together a vast array of information from sources, many of which are difficult to access directly. Their work is the starting point for all studies of juvenile remains.

10

Approaches to Reading Attic Vases

Kathryn Topper

1   Introduction, or Reading as Metaphor

The painted vases unearthed by the thousands throughout the Mediterranean and neighboring countries are some of our most plentiful, and most problematic, sources for studying ancient Athenian women. Many of these objects lack documented prove-nances, and ancient authors rarely mention them, yet their shapes suggest that they circulated in contexts as varied as the symposium, the gymnasium, women's quarters, religious festivals, and the tomb. They are decorated with a wide range of scenes: in addition to representing familiar goddesses and heroines, the images show hundreds of women adorning themselves, working wool, caring for children, drinking at symposia, dancing, making music, conversing with men, having sex, preparing food, mourning the dead, engaging in religious worship, fetching water, swimming, and interacting with phallus-birds and other animals. These vases have been objects of intense interest during the last few decades, as the study of ancient women has come into its own as a subfield of Classical scholarship, yet there is little consensus about what they can tell us about ancient Athenian women or the principles that should be brought to bear on their interpretation. Because of the continuing debate over almost every aspect of their interpretation, this essay does not attempt to provide a comprehensive survey of women in vase painting, but rather to examine select methodological issues with the aim of defining some ways in which the vases serve as evidence for understanding ancient Athenian women.

Although vases decorated with figural scenes were produced in the Kerameikos as early as the Geometric period, I focus on the sixth and fifth centuries BCE, a period dominated by the black- and red-figure styles. The corpus is by no means homogeneous, but these vases present a sufficiently unified set of questions to merit consideration as a group. Addressing the central question of what the vases tell us about ancient Athenian women involves confronting several related questions: How do we determine what an image represents? What role should an awareness of audience (or audiences) play in interpretation? What was the relationship between the women on the vases and the women of Archaic and Classical

A Companion to Women in the Ancient World, First Edition. Edited by Sharon L. James and Sheila Dillon.
© 2012 John Wiley & Sons, Ltd. Published 2015 by John Wiley & Sons, Ltd.

Athens? Finally, what do the scenes on the vases have in common with other forms of representation—such as poetry, historical texts, or drama—and to what degree should these other representations enter into interpretations of the imagery? My discussion is organized around three case studies, an *epinetron* and two *kylikes*, whose rich but often problematic imagery bring us face to face with these issues.

Before I turn to the images, however, a word on the title of the essay is necessary. The idea that vases are objects to be "read" has dominated the scholarship on vase painting since the 1980s; this tradition is particularly indebted to scholars from the Paris-Lausanne school, who contributed to the *City of Images* project (Bérard et al. 1989), which was itself heavily influenced by the principles of structural linguistics and anthropology. There is no consensus on precisely how the metaphor of "imagery as language" should be applied to the vases, and this is not the place to rehash that debate (recent discussions may be found in Ferrari 2002; Neer 2002; Steiner 2007; Squire 2009). In the interest of clarity, however, I note two assumptions on which I rely throughout this essay: first, images are analogous to language in the sense that both reveal the conceptual frameworks of the societies in which they operate; second, images, like words, bear a constructed relationship to lived experience, and this relationship is not immediately evident to those observing a culture or its artifacts from the outside.[1] The implications of these principles for the study of the vases will become evident in the following sections.

2   Image as Metaphor, or the Taming of the Bride

I begin with an object from the late fifth century, a red-figure *epinetron* attributed to the Eretria Painter (Figure 10.1). This vessel has been an object of much close study, most recently by Rachel Kousser, who has attempted a comprehensive analysis that considers not only the iconographic program but also the interplay between imagery, shape, and circumstances of use (Kousser 2004). I agree with the fundamentals of Kousser's reading, and my purpose in beginning with this piece is not to offer a substantially different interpretation but rather to use this example to establish what is known about the vases before moving to more problematic examples.

Figure 10.1   Red-figure *epinetron*, Eretria Painter. Athens, National Archaeological Museum 1629; *ARV²* 1250.34, 1688; *Paralipomena* 469; *Beazley Addenda²* 354. Photo: Eva-Maria Czakó, DAI-ATH-NM 5126.

The *epinetron* (also called *onos*, although the original name is uncertain) was a semi-cylindrical object that was closed at one end and designed to fit over the thigh to aid in the production of wool. Elaborate examples are embellished with a sculpted female head or bust; on the Eretria Painter's *epinetron*, this takes the form of a nude bust that resembles the votive figurines dedicated in sanctuaries to celebrate girls' successful transitions to maturity (Kousser 2004). The theme of female transitions unites the bust with the painted scenes, which show successive stages of the bride's progress from *parthenos* to married woman. Vignettes from mythological weddings appear on the long sides: one side is decorated with a scene of Harmonia's adornment, while the other shows the *epaulia* (wedding gifts) of Alcestis, who rests against the nuptial bed while receiving visitors (Figure 10.1). The two scenes are connected visually and thematically by a panel that runs behind the sculpted head and shows the abduction of Thetis, who struggles with Peleus amid fleeing Nereids.

This *epinetron* is unusual for the extent to which it combines imagery, form, and function in a manner comprehensible to modern viewers. Frequently the connection between two or more of these elements is unclear. On a black-figure hydria in London (Figure 10.2), for example, it is obvious that the scene of women at a fountain house is connected to the function of the vessel, but it is harder to see how the image of Herakles on the shoulder fits into this scheme (although see Steiner 2004 for Herakles on black-figure hydriae). On the *epinetron*, by contrast, the painted panels are clearly united by the theme of marriage, and they are arranged so that when the vessel is worn on the right leg the sexually charged image of doors opening onto the marriage bed corresponds with the most intimate area of the body. Although this vessel seems to have been a grave gift, its emphasis on female transitions

Figure 10.2 Black-figure hydria, showing women at a fountain house. London, British Museum B 329; *ABV* 334.1, 678; *Paralipomena* 147; *Beazley Addenda*[2] 91. Photo: © Trustees of the British Museum.

would suit any of the uses to which *epinetra* were typically put, including wool working, dedication to a goddess, and deposition in a grave (Kousser 2004).

Our relatively solid understanding of this piece makes it a good starting point for considering what the vases can tell us about ancient women. *Epinetra* were used primarily by women and, while it is far from clear whether or how the decoration was tailored to this audience, its obvious similarity to the large, repetitive corpus of Athenian nuptial imagery suggests that the scenes on the *epinetra* show deeply ingrained clichés that were critical to Athenian constructions of femininity. Particularly prominent is the idea of the maiden as a creature to be tamed. This metaphor, which cast the maiden as dangerously wild but also appealing and potentially productive, is well documented in Greek literature, art, and ritual (Reeder 1995: 299–300; Calame 1997: 238–44; Kousser 2004: 107) and it is a major element in the story of Thetis' marriage to Peleus. The metaphor of domestication is explicit in the Homeric account of their wedding: "me, out of all the other daughters of the sea, *he yoked to a man*, to Peleus son of Aeacus, and I endured a mortal's bed, though resisting greatly" (*Iliad* 18.432–34). The verb δαμάςω can refer to the taming of a woman or of an animal, and on the *epinetron* Thetis is both— as Peleus grabs her human form, a sea creature attacks him from behind. Kousser notes that, when the scenes on the *epinetron* are read in narrative progression from adornment to *epaulia*, the abduction appears in the place of a more traditional wedding procession, with which it shares key features, such as the groom's assertion of dominance over the bride (who is normally grabbed by the wrist or lifted into a chariot) and the presence of the bride's father and companions. The theme of domestication continues in the image of Alcestis' *epaulia*, where the newly tamed bride is juxtaposed with a small bird resting on her companion's hand (Kousser 2004: 108).

In addition to articulating certain ideas about marriage and the sexes, the *epinetron* alerts us to an important point about how images on the vases function within a larger system of representation. The scenes take their meaning not only from their relationship to other images but also from a larger network of associations that extended to literature (or oral performances that have survived as literature) and ritual. Even the most conventional aspects of imagery may participate in this network. For example, the black-figure distinction between white female skin and dark male skin has echoes in the *Ecclesiazousae*, where standing outdoors to darken the skin is critical to the women's cross-dressing strategy (Aristophanes, *Ecclesiazousae* 62–64); in both cases, the message is that women are creatures best suited to the indoors. This point has several implications, but for the present purposes I note only two: first, visual images cannot be adequately understood in isolation from other contemporary forms of representation (and vice versa); second, the relationship between the images and literature (or images and ritual) is more complex than a simple matter of one medium illustrating the other. These observations may seem unproblematic when applied to the *epinetron*, but the following examples will make some of the difficulties clearer.

3 What Kind of Women?

My next example, a kylix by the Ashby Painter from around 500 BCE, is decorated on the exterior with images of men and women at a symposium. Each side shows a young man reclining with a female partner: on one side a reclining woman plays the aulos (Figure 10.3) while on the other a nude woman kneels before her partner and binds her head with a fillet.

Figure 10.3 Red-figure kylix with symposium scene. Attributed to the Ashby Painter. New York, Metropolitan Museum of Art 1993.11.5; *ARV²* 455.8; *Beazley Addenda²* 242. Photo: © The Metropolitan Museum of Art/Art Resource, NY.

How these pictures relate to the one in the tondo, which shows a warrior blowing a trumpet, is unclear. They may be connected by their general association with masculine activities, but we do not know whether an Athenian viewer would see a more precise connection. Because this essay is concerned with ancient women, I limit my discussion to the sympotic scenes, acknowledging that I sacrifice some nuance by not considering the warrior on the interior.

The kylix takes us some distance from the discussion of the *epinetron*, and not only because its shape and imagery both locate it firmly in the masculine world of the symposium. The differences extend to matters of interpretive method, for, while we readily understand both the subject matter and the overall decorative program of the *epinetron*, neither is immediately evident on the kylix, so this piece forces us to consider how we determine what an image on a vase represents. The apparently mundane nature of the sympotic scenes has encouraged their identification as vignettes from contemporary life, and the women are understood as *hetairai* (Peschel 1987), the only women who regularly attended symposia in this period. As courtesans whose activities were discreetly presented as the exchange of favors between companions, *hetairai* were conceptually opposed to *pornai*, common prostitutes (Kurke 1999: 175–219). The indirect quality of many of the literary references has left significant gaps in our understanding of *hetairai*, and scholars have looked to vase painting to fill them in (Keuls 1985: 153–203; Peschel 1987; Kurke 1999: 199–219).

The vases present numerous difficulties, however, particularly because the defining visual characteristics of the *hetaira* have never been well established (Kilmer 1993: 159–67; Lewis 2002: 101–12). Even if we limit ourselves to a consideration of the sympotic scenes—as I will do in order to keep the focus on the example at hand—the women who are classified as *hetairai* are an extremely diverse crowd. They may be nude or clothed, sexually aggressive or modest, sober or rowdy. Some sit quietly at the foot of their *klinai* (couches), while others recline and still others have sex with the men. They recline on couches and on the floor, and their partners are by turns Greek men, foreign men, and women. Apart from their femininity, the only feature that unites these women is their presence at symposia, and it is this that, in modern eyes, earns them their status as courtesans. As François Lissarrague (1990: 33–4) observes, their status "is difficult to define ... the texts reveal that they are never wives, but rather women whose services are hired: *hetairai* (courtesans), musicians, or just companions for the evening who join in the pleasures of the krater." The identification of the female symposiasts as *hetairai*, in other words, is a consequence of expectations that the images will correspond to the texts in a particular way, yet we have seen that literature and vase painting may have a more complex relationship than this formulation implies.

In fact, assuming that all the women in sympotic scenes are the *hetairai* we know from the texts requires us to overlook empirical as well as methodological difficulties. Many images of "*hetairai*" on the vases correspond poorly with our understanding of life in Archaic and Classical Athens. For example, the Ashby Painter's symposiasts recline on the ground, rather than using the more standard couches, and one male symposiast holds a drinking horn (*keras*), a vessel whose associations with the primitive and barbaric (Athenaeus, *Deipnosophistae* 476a) make it an incongruous presence in a scene of contemporary life (Figure 10.3). There are a few ways we might explain these discrepancies: (1) accept the images as evidence that symposiasts in this period sometimes drank on the ground from rustic vessels, (2) understand the incongruous details as symbolic or conventional elements that do not alter the basic identification of the scene, or (3) consider the possibility that the painter has depicted something other than the sort of symposium that was practiced in Athens at the time. I will suggest that the third option holds the most promise.

The first possibility has occasionally been considered, but our only independent evidence for a late Archaic practice of banqueting on the ground relates to religious festivals, and images of symposia without furniture do not seem restricted to scenes of ritual, nor would a ritual context explain such elements as the drinking horn (Topper 2009: 10–12). The second option is the most common explanation for such discrepancies, and it has become a commonplace in iconographic studies to point out that painters were less interested in creating photorealistic depictions of their surroundings than in interpreting them in ways that highlighted their most important elements (Vernant 1989: 7–8; Beard 1991: 19–21; Osborne 2007: 34; Bundrick 2008: 283–4). Mary Beard's comment that a scene on a vase "is not a *picture of*, but a *statement about*" the subject it represents encapsulates this view nicely (Beard 1991: 20). While scholars who favor this approach have shown, often in painstaking detail, the various ways in which images function as constructs, they have been less persuasive in justifying the assumption that contemporary life is the basis for images without obvious mythological content. In fact, it has recently been observed that the category we call "scenes of contemporary life" is defined not by knowledge of what Athenian life looked like but by the modern inability to connect the scenes to myth. A more productive approach, according to the third view, then, is to ask not what Athenian practice or institution a picture illustrates but to what type of discourse—defined as a "collective process of articulating a set of communal values or beliefs" (Hedreen 2009: 125)—it belongs (Ferrari 2002: 11–60, 2003; Peirce 2004).

For the scenes on the Ashby Painter's kylix, then, the question is not whether the image can be attached to a known myth (it cannot) or how closely the scene matches our understanding of Archaic sympotic practices (not closely) but under what circumstances the various elements in the scene came together in the Athenian imagination. The *keras*, it has already been noted, was widely associated with primitive customs, and a variety of evidence from art, literature, and ritual suggests that banquets without furniture were also popularly attributed to primitive or uncivilized societies (Topper 2009; cf. Hedreen 2009). Within this context, the presence of women makes sense not as a statement about Archaic prostitution but as a marker of the symposiasts' distance from civilization, the stability of which depended on the recognition and enforcement of proper gender roles. Societies such as Sparta and Etruria were regularly lampooned for their failure to regulate the behavior of their women, and traces of this tradition have been detected on vases such as Euphronios' psykter, where the female symposiasts speak a Doric dialect (St. Petersburg, State Hermitage Museum B 1650; ARV^2 16.15, 1619), and on the stamnoi of the Perizoma Group, which show women in the traditionally masculine roles of symposiasts, a scenario paralleled in Greek descriptions of the Etruscans (Shapiro 2000; Ferrari 2002: 19–20; see also Neils, this volume, Chapter 11).

Ignorance of proper gender roles also figures in accounts of Athens' own prehistory—stories about the age of Kekrops describe the early polis as an anarchic state where the free and public mingling of the sexes produced disordered lines of inheritance and women abused their political power (Zeitlin 1999). Since the symposium was often envisioned as a microcosm of the polis itself (Levine 1985), the notion of a primitive, disorderly state was effectively conveyed by an image of a symposium in which women participate like men. If this reading is correct, then the images on the Ashby Painter's kylix become valuable not as documents pertaining to Archaic prostitution but as fragments of a popular discourse about how society should manage its women.

Returning to our earlier question of how literary evidence helps us interpret the imagery, we can see that, while the scenes on the kylix are not simple visual counterparts of texts documenting the presence of *hetairai* at symposia, they are related to the texts insofar as both employ similar topoi to describe societies understood to be primitive or barbarian. Like the maiden-as-animal metaphor, the topos of the woman who participates in traditional male activities forged conceptual links between people—in this case, the Spartans, the Etruscans, and the earliest Athenians—who bore no narrative or real-world connection to one another, and, like the maiden-as-animal metaphor, it encoded certain ideas about those whom it described. In fact, both the metaphor of the maiden as an animal and the topos of the uncivilized female symposiast are rooted in ideas about the need to control women's natural wildness, but, while the scenes on the *epinetron* depict the civilizing process in action (Figure 10.1), the images on the kylix show the consequences of leaving that wildness unchecked (Figure 10.3).

4   Trading in Sex?

The problem of how we determine what an image represents remains central to my next example, a red-figure kylix by the Briseis Painter (Figure 10.4), although different circumstances prompt the question. Like many Athenian vases with known provenances, this vase was discovered in Etruria, and the combination of its Etruscan find-spot and sexually explicit imagery places it in a class of vases whose relevance to Athenian culture has recently been questioned (Lewis 2002: 116–28). The scene in question appears in the tondo of the cup and shows a man penetrating a woman from behind, placing his hands on her upper back as she bends forward. Aside from a cushion, a staff, and a cast-off garment, there are no details to establish the setting; the absence of clear sympotic paraphernalia

Figure 10.4   Red-figure kylix, Briseis Painter; tondo with erotic scene. Tarquinia, Museo Nazionale; *ARV²* 408.36; *Beazley Addenda²* 232. Photo: Hermann Wagner, DAI-ATH-Diversa 133.

makes it difficult to be certain that the coupling occurs at a symposium, although the wreaths worn by both figures would be appropriate to such a context. "Erotic" scenes such as this one experienced a surge of popularity in the late Archaic period; the women are most often identified as *hetairai* (Keuls 1985: 174–80), but not everyone has been satisfied with this explanation. In fact, Sian Lewis has proposed that, since approximately seventy percent of erotic scenes with known provenances come from Etruscan tombs, they must have been painted to meet the demands of an Etruscan market. She suggests that in Etruria, where women seem to have enjoyed a decidedly different social status from their Athenian counterparts (see, contra, Izzet, this volume, Chapter 5), women in heterosexual pairings would be understood as wives; more radically, she argues that, since so few of these vases were found in Athenian contexts, they tell us more about the Etruscans than about the Athenians (Lewis 2002: 116–28, *passim*).

  Central to this hypothesis is the belief that the images on the vases were tailored to the preferences of an export market, but finding compelling evidence to support this idea has proven difficult. A major problem is the lack of provenance for so many vases, a consequence of years of illegal excavation and unethical collecting practices; even when we know that a vase was discovered in Etruria, associating it with a particular tomb or tomb group can be difficult. In other words, although we know that the vases were made in Athens, and that many ended up in Etruscan tombs, what happened between production and deposition is largely unclear, and most comments regarding the principles by which vases were selected for export are speculative at best. The limited available information about find-spots, however, does not generally support the hypothesis that painters had foreign markets in mind when they selected themes for their vases (Shapiro 2000: 318;

Steiner 2007: 234–6; Bundrick 2008: 292–4), and one recent trend has been to approach the vases as objects with complex "lives" whose perceptions by both the producing culture and the receiving culture merit consideration (Appadurai 1986; Marconi 2004b; Osborne 2004a; Avramidou 2006; Lyons 2008).

What this means for the Briseis Painter's kylix is that, while Lewis is not wrong to note that the Etruscans would have understood the imagery in a manner consistent with their own culture, erotic images do have something to tell us about the Athenians, and we would do well to ask what the latter would have made of such a scene. Both Lewis and Martin Kilmer have persuasively argued that the identification of women in erotic scenes as *hetairai* depends on an overly simplistic equation between graphic sexuality and prostitution (Kilmer 1993: 159–67; Lewis 2002: 116–28, *passim*), and this equation seems even more problematic when we recognize that sex workers were not the only women whom Athenians represented in an overtly sexualized manner. The remains of Old Comedy attest to a popular stereotype of *all* women as sex-obsessed, and Sarah Stroup has observed some remarkable similarities between the "*hetairai*" of the erotic scenes and the sex-crazed wives of the comic stage (Stroup 2004: 49–56). Although most erotic images predate Aristophanic comedy by several decades, Eva Keuls has noticed considerable overlap between early red-figure and Old Comedy, including a proclivity "towards scatological and genital humor, and [a focus] . . . on aspects of male-female sex relations and sex-role stereotyping" (Keuls 1988: 300). It is thus possible that, instead of presenting us with serious portraits of courtesans, the erotic images portray comic stereotypes about women in general, in the same spirit as a famous skyphos in

Figure 10.5 Attic red-figure skyphos, showing a woman drinking from a skyphos followed by a small maid. Date: 470–460 BCE. J. Paul Getty Museum, inv. no. 86. AE. 265. Photo: The J. Paul Getty Museum, Villa Collection, Malibu California.

Malibu (Figure 10.5) that shows a woman gulping wine from an oversized cup with an urgency that recalls the wine-loving women of Aristophanes (Mitchell 2009: 67, 75–7). Scholars are only beginning to grasp the pervasiveness of humor in vase painting, but recent studies have made clear just how much the painters delighted in comic inversions and other humorous distortions (Walsh 2008; Mitchell 2009), and these considerations will need to be central to future studies of the images.

5   Looking Forward

The vases examined in this essay do not give us anything resembling a straightforward picture of ancient women's lives, but they offer a wealth of information—often paralleled in other realms of representation—in the form of metaphors, artistic conventions, and stereotypes regarding the construction of femininity in ancient Athens. They also provide a sense of the work that remains to be done. Examination of the Eretria Painter's *epinetron* (Figure 10.1), for example, points to the need for more comprehensive investigation into the connection between shape and imagery. At the moment, the principles underlying both the pairing of images and the association of particular themes and shapes are poorly understood, and, until this changes, most attempts to explain the decorative program of individual vessels will have to remain speculative. Along slightly different lines, it has also become apparent that determining what pictures represent remains a pressing matter. The study of painted vases continues to reap tremendous benefits from the principles laid out in *A City of Images*, but an arguably less salutary effect of that project was the devaluing of specific content in the interpretation of pictures. The elevation of what Jean-Pierre Vernant called "major anthropological themes" (Vernant 1989: 7) over specific points of identification was perhaps a necessary step in advancing scholarly understanding of the images—but the suggestion that knowing the protagonists' identities "do[es] not seem indispensable to an understanding of [an] image" (Bérard and Durand 1989: 29) has solidified into a tendency to treat images as ambiguous documents whose precise content is unimportant, since they can represent whatever viewers wish to see (Beard 1991: 20–1; Osborne 2007: 45–6; Bundrick 2008: 297–8). Viewers undoubtedly play a role in the creation of meaning—for example, a bride and a groom are likely to have had different individual responses to the Eretria Painter's mythological scenes (Figure 10.1)—but the fact that an image has no fixed meaning does not imply that a community with a shared visual idiom should be unable to agree about what that image represents. To claim that identities of anonymous figures on the vases are fundamentally ambiguous is most often to conflate modern ignorance with ancient ambiguity, and sidestepping the question of whom or what is represented implicitly denies that the identities of the participants matter to our interpretation of the scene. Yet it makes a difference, as we have seen, whether a symposiast is an Athenian courtesan or an inhabitant of a world whose sexual roles would seem foreign to an Athenian (Figure 10.3), since the latter was a more suitable vehicle for conveying ideas about the need to keep women under control in a civilized society. The images on the vases will be of limited use to the study of ancient women unless we concede that knowledge of specifics *is* indispensable to understanding, even if it by no means exhausts it (Ferrari 2003 discusses this point in detail).

In this vein, another subject on which more detailed work is needed is the study of inscriptions on vases, particularly the "labels" that may accompany individual figures and have traditionally been interpreted as names of ancient Athenians (Peschel (1987: 469) lists names of "*hetairai*"). Recent scholarship has suggested that it is unlikely that labels operate in so simple a manner. It is hard to imagine, for instance, that the Eretria Painter's image of Thetis' abduction would be unidentifiable without the inscriptions, and even the best-understood names sometimes appear in puzzling situations, such as when the name of Leagros, a well-known aristocratic youth, accompanies a woman or satyr (Shapiro 2004). In at least some cases, moreover, names seem to serve a descriptive function, a phenomenon that is familiar from comedy; for example, it has been shown that in images of women at a fountain house (such as the one illustrated in Figure 10.2), names such as Kallipe, Elanthis, Rhodon, and Gluke are more likely meant to evoke pleasing girlish images of horses, flowers, and other sweet things than to identify historical women (Manfrini-Aragno 1992; Ferrari 2003: 45). Yet, although we understand how writing works on individual vases, a comprehensive grasp of the issue still eludes us, and we may hope that further research into the inscriptions will create a more nuanced understanding of how the vases and their images may serve as evidence for ancient women.

It would be possible to continue at length about questions that need further investigation, but, so as not to stray too far from the issues raised in this essay, I will stop here. It should be evident, however, that our ability to make advances in understanding ancient women from the evidence of painted vases will depend on continued openness to engaging with materials and methods that have typically been the province of other areas of the discipline, or of other disciplines altogether. The interpretations offered in this essay rely heavily on analogies between images and literature, and I have proceeded in this way because studies highlighting the relationships between words and images have been among the most rigorous work produced in the field of vase painting in recent years. Literature, however, is not the only field that can contribute to our understanding of this topic, and there are some questions that literary models are not equipped to address (a concern raised most recently by Squire 2009). For example, several studies have attempted to understand vase paintings in light of the contexts in which the vases were used or deposited (Lissarrague 1990; Lewis 2002; Neer 2002; Marconi 2004b; Steiner 2007; Bundrick 2008), and knowing how ancient women interacted with the images is certainly desirable. Yet we do not, on the whole, have a clear sense of which vases women typically used, or how they used them, or under what circumstances, and, while it may seem relatively unproblematic to suggest that women carried white-ground lekythoi to graves, shapes such as kylikes present more difficult questions. Does the fact that a kylix was designed for the symposium mean that it was off-limits to all women but *hetairai*, or does this scenario not sufficiently account for the complexities of ancient domestic life or the individual "lives" of objects (Beard 1991: 19)? Although the latter alternative seems more likely, our inability to answer such questions with certainty results from our limited information regarding the archaeological contexts of so many extant vases. As new material emerges from better-documented contexts, we can hope that some questions will become easier to answer, although an expectation that material will emerge in sufficient quantities to provide definitive answers may be overly optimistic. Advances in the field of domestic archaeology, however, may provide a better understanding of sites that have already been excavated and give us a clearer picture of the spaces that women frequented and the types of objects to which they had access. Finally, continued attention to the studies of gender and sexuality that are being carried out in non-Classical disciplines will be essential as we attempt to gain further insights into familiar material.

RECOMMENDED FURTHER READING

The subject of a number of studies in its own right, the representation of women on Athenian vases has also become a mainstay of more general treatments of women and gender in ancient Greece. Most discussions focus on the sixth and fifth centuries BCE, the heyday of black- and red-figure styles; an important recent exception is Langdon (2008). Although the size of the corpus makes it impossible for any study to offer a comprehensive overview of women in vase painting, representative samples of the extant material (as well as a variety of methodological orientations) may be found in Reeder (1995), Keuls (1985), and Lewis (2002). Two influential studies of the body in ancient art—Bonfante (1989c) and Stewart (1997)—also make extensive use of vase painting.

Issues of interpretive method continue to be actively debated by scholars of vase painting, and images of women frequently assume prominent roles in these discussions. The collection edited by Bérard et al. (1989) played a critical role in shaping current approaches to the evidence; more recently, Ferrari (2002) has critiqued and expanded upon the methods advanced by Bérard and his collaborators. Both studies rely to varying degrees on metaphors of imagery as language, an approach that also informs Sourvinou-Inwood (1991), whose early chapters concern visual constructions of maidenhood. A broader variety of approaches may be found in the collection of Marconi (2004a).

The representation of heterosexual desire is discussed in Kilmer (1993) and Frontisi-Ducroux (1996). Scholars interested in ancient prostitution have often looked to vase paintings, especially sympotic scenes (Peschel 1987), although others urge caution in the interpretation of such images (e.g., Schmitt Pantel 2003). In contrast to scenes of heterosexual love, depictions of female homoeroticism have proven difficult to identify; Rabinowitz (2002) discusses the problems and possible approaches.

Women's ritual is a popular subject in vase painting; several scenes are discussed and illustrated in Kaltsas and Shapiro (2008). The representation of female religious activity is also a major focus of Sourvinou-Inwood (1988) and Connelly (2007). As these studies attest, the interpretation of ritual scenes is frequently hindered by gaps in our knowledge about the rituals themselves. Vases showing female Bacchic activities have proven especially difficult to understand; Hedreen (1994) and Peirce (1998) offer methodologically sensitive treatments of these images and point to larger issues involved in their interpretation.

Women are frequently represented on wedding and funerary vessels; on these objects, see Oakley and Sinos (1993), Oakley (2004), and Reilly (1989).

NOTES

1. The arbitrary connection between signifier and signified is a central principle of structural linguistics; see de Saussure et al. (1959: 67–70). Saussure dealt primarily with linguistic signs; although some argue that visual images are "natural" (as opposed to arbitrary or conventional) signs, this view has proven untenable (Mitchell 1986: 75–94).

11

Spartan Girls and the Athenian Gaze

Jenifer Neils

Let us praise Sparta, where ... the girls, like ponies
Leap along by the Eurotas, raising the dust
With the rapid movements of their feet;
And their hair streams out like that of maenads at play,
Whirling their thyrsoi; and at the head of the chorus
Is the beautiful chaste daughter of Leda.

(Aristophanes, *Lysistrata* 1306–15)

Presented in Athens in 411 BCE, Aristophanes' comedy *Lysistrata* concludes with this encomium on the beauty of Spartan maidens. The Athenian audience had just witnessed a male actor impersonating one of these robust Spartan girls: the character Lampito, who journeys to Athens to join the sex strike. In the era of the Peloponnesian Wars one might expect vilification and abuse but, on the contrary, Lampito, like a latter-day Helen, is roundly admired for her perfect complexion and healthy body, not to mention her buxomness. When Lysistrata exclaims that she looks strong enough to strangle a bull, Lampito replies "Yes, of course, I take exercise and I jump up to my bottom." She may even have executed her notorious *bibasis* or butt-kicking dance, much to the amusement of the audience in the theater of Dionysus. This famous Spartan female perhaps best represents in literary terms the Athenians' perceptions of Spartan girls in the fifth century—healthy, strong, athletic, and beautiful.

As early as the *Odyssey*, references are made to "Sparta of the beautiful women" (*Sparte kalligynaika*, 13.412), but these beauties are seldom seen in the visual arts. Sarah Pomeroy's recent book entitled *Spartan Women* (2002) has a mere ten illustrations of Spartan women, of which three are eighteenth- or nineteenth-century French paintings. Sculpture in Sparta itself is notoriously scanty and women rarely appear in Laconian vase painting (Pipili 1987). With the exception of the legendary Helen and some bronze statuettes (to be discussed *infra*), Greek art has thus far provided us with few images of Sparta's beautiful women.

A Companion to Women in the Ancient World, First Edition. Edited by Sharon L. James and Sheila Dillon
© 2012 John Wiley & Sons, Ltd. Published 2015 by John Wiley & Sons, Ltd.

Figure 11.1   Attic red-figure kylix near the Jena Painter, c. 400 BCE. Boston, Museum of Fine Arts 1900.354. Photograph © Museum of Fine Arts, Boston.

The one definitively identified Spartan female is the personification that appears on an Attic red-figure cup of c. 400 BCE near the Jena Painter (Figure 11.1; Shapiro 1988: pl. 38; *LIMC* 7 1994: s.v. Sparte no. 4). In the tondo a young woman is shown dismounting from a horse as she approaches an altar; her name, Sparte, is inscribed above her. This unique image comes at a time when there was a brief period of Spartan popularity at Athens, between the years 403 and 395 BCE, with the temporary restoration of the Athenian democracy. Because women were not equestrians in ancient Greece, this Spartan female must have appeared quite exotic to Athenian viewers, rather like an Amazon or the moon goddess Selene. The setting, a sanctuary of some sort, as suggested by the altar, gives the scene a religious connotation. Intriguingly, this late fifth-century Attic vase painting of *Sparte* echoes a popular type of votive deposited at Laconian sanctuaries in the later seventh and sixth centuries, namely a terracotta figurine of a woman, probably a goddess, riding side-saddle on a horse (Voyatzis 1992). With over a century separating these representations, it is not possible to establish any continuity, but this nexus of female, horse, and sanctuary is one we will encounter again below.

This investigation of the Spartan female seeks to find in the Attic vase-painting repertoire other images of young Spartan women that have been overlooked or mis-identified. There are at least five contexts in which Laconian women were known to distinguish themselves in contrast to other Greek women: athletics, horsemanship, wine consumption, homoerotic relations, and schooling (Pomeroy 2002). These activities, none of which was associated with Athenian women, offer the best potential for identifying Spartan females on Attic vases, and so we will examine each in turn.

1   Spartan Girl Athletes

In spite of much recent scholarship on athletics in ancient Greece, prompted by the 2004 Olympics in Athens, there remains a major gap in our evidence for the lives of Greek girls, namely their athletic activities (e.g., Miller 2004 devotes a chapter to "Women and Athletics" but it is a mere ten pages long and the illustrations are minimal; see also Arrigoni 1985; Bérard 1986; Bernardini 1986–7; Golden 1998: 123–32; Scanlon 2002). To date, the most complete image of female athletes remains the famous Bikini Girls mosaic from the fourth-century CE Roman villa at Piazza Armerina in central Sicily (Lee 1984). Other than these eight bikini-clad females, there is very little visual evidence for girls' athletic activity, even though there were mythological role models, such as the runner and wrestler from Arkadia, Atalanta (*LIMC* 2 1989: s.v. Atalante [J. Boardman]; Ley 1990; Scanlon 2002: 175–98). The essential challenge is that the bulk of our visual evidence for Greek athletics comes from Athenian vase paintings and most of the literary sources refer to Spartan female athleticism.

With the exception of what appear to be young nude girls, presumably future courtesans, learning to dance (Neils and Oakley 2003: 255–6), most of the physical activities performed by girls as depicted on Attic vases are fairly tame. The repertoire consists of such feats of coordination as playing see-saw, top-spinning contests, balancing a stick, chasing a pet bird with a roller toy, or playing knucklebones. Demanding a little more dexterity was the game of *ephedrismos*, which was played by both girls and boys and involved running towards a target with one's partner carried on one's back (Neils and Oakley 2003: 270–80). But these are more in the realm of play than sport.

Running seems to be the only type of aerobic exercise that young girls in Attika participated in, and perhaps only on religious occasions. The special small-standed kraters, known as krateriskoi, from the rural sanctuary of Artemis at Brauron (and elsewhere) with their slapdash decoration, show young females, some nude and others clothed in short chitons, running in the vicinity of an altar (Reeder 1995: 321–8; Marinatos 2002; Miller 2004: 158–9, Figs. 241–2; see also Lee, this volume, Chapter 13). Whether they are actually racing or being chased by a "bear" is still a matter of considerable debate (Scanlon 2002: 137–74; Faraone 2003; see Stehle, this volume, Chapter 14). Their short tunics, however, suggest a race, for this is the garment found on a few small bronze statuettes of the latter half of the sixth century that clearly depict girls in running poses (Herfort-Koch 1986: 27–9, 93–5 cat. nos. K48–50; Dodona bronze runner: Kaltsas 2006: 166 no. 69). These have been associated with the quadrennial festival at Olympia, not the games in honor of Zeus but those held for Hera, at which girls ran a footrace (Scanlon 2002: 98–120; Miller 2004: 155–6). These female runners were actually allowed to use the Olympic stadium, but the track was shortened by one sixth (Romano 1983: 14). According to Pausanias (5.16.2–6) there were races for three age categories; he goes on to say: "They run in the following manner: their hair hangs loose, a chiton reaches to a little above the knee, and the right shoulder is bared as far as the breast." This description matches the costume of one of these figurines, which in style appears to be Laconian (Swaddling 1999: 42; London, British Museum 208: this figurine has her left foot forward, as runners do in the starting line at Olympia, and looks back). Like their male counterparts the winners received olive wreaths and were allowed to dedicate images of themselves with their names inscribed. None of these *eikones* has survived, unless the Roman marble statue of a bare-breasted girl in the Vatican is a copy of a likeness of one of the victors at the Heraia c. 460 BCE, as some scholars have suggested because of its early Classical or Severe style (Museo Pio-Clementino inv. 2784: Arrigoni 1985: 159–60, pl. 6; Miller 2004: 156, figure 239). An early Hellenistic statue of a female runner, but with both breasts bared (Louvre MA 522), is also a candidate for one of these victor statues (see Arrigoni 1985: 160–1, pl. 7).

Many of the contestants at these "special" Olympics were undoubtedly Spartan girls. In the *Constitution of the Lakedaimonians* the legendary Spartan lawgiver Lykourgos is credited with establishing athletic training for women for the purpose of eugenics:

> Lykourgos, thinking that the first and foremost function of the freeborn woman was to bear children, ordered that the female should do no less bodybuilding than the male. He thus established contests for the women in footraces and strength, just like those for the men, believing that stronger children come from parents who are both strong.

In his *Life of Lykourgos* (14.2) Plutarch states:

> Lykourgos exercised the bodies of the virgins with footraces and wrestling and throwing the discus and the javelin so that their offspring might spring from strong roots in strong bodies.... He removed all softness, daintiness and effeminacy from them and accustomed the girls no less than the boys to parade in the nude and to dance and sing at certain religious festivals in the presence of the young men as spectators.

(For the girls' equivalent of the *agogē* in classical Sparta see Kennell 1995: 45–6.) Authors of illustrated books on Greek athletics at this point usually have to resort to Edgar Degas' 1860 painting in London entitled "Young Spartans," for, in the absence of ancient imagery, it best illustrates Plutarch's description of Spartan female athletes (Salus 1985; Pomeroy 2002: 17, figure 3).

Given this dearth of representations of female athletes in general and Spartans in particular, it is worthwhile reconsidering the late fifth-century images often identified as Atalanta. The Aberdeen Painter, a cup painter around 430 BCE, painted several with similar themes featuring a scantily clad female and nude male athlete in the tondo (*ARV²* 919, nos. 2–5). Because in one instance they are labeled Peleus and Atalanta, all four of the Aberdeen Painter's images have been taken to represent this mythological pair of wrestlers, who are shown in the act of competing on many vases, especially in the latter half of the sixth century (Reeder 1995: 363–71). The example in Boston (Figure 11.2) shows a male athlete with a strigil confronting a female athlete wearing only a pair of trunks known as the *diazoma*. The setting is the palaestra, as indicated by the laver at the far left. However, on three of the Aberdeen Painter's cups the pair are not labeled, and we do know from ancient sources that Spartan boys and girls exercised together. Propertius (3.14) sang the praises of Spartan girls: "I marvel at the many rules of your palaistra, O Sparta, but even more at the blessings of your gymnasium for girls, since a naked girl may take part in the well-known games amid men as they wrestle." While this is a late source, another one contemporary with this cup is Euripides:

> No Spartan girl could ever be restrained even if she wanted to be; they desert their homes to go out with young men with their thighs bare and robes unbelted and they hold races and wrestling contests with them—I would not stand for it! Is it any wonder that you do not raise chaste women? (*Andromache* 595–602)

Figure 11.2   Attic red-figure kylix attributed to the Aberdeen Painter, c. 450–430 BCE. Boston, Museum of Fine Arts 03.820. Photograph © Museum of Fine Arts, Boston.

Even earlier in the sixth century, the writer Ibycus (fr. 339) referred to Spartan girls as "thigh-flashers." The girl on the Aberdeen Painter's cup could be described as a thigh-flasher, and in the exhibit on the ancient Olympics in Boston this cup was tentatively identified as "a scene from Spartan life where young men and women did exercise together" (Herrmann and Kondoleon 2004: 188).

If the literary sources on the nudity of Spartan girl athletes go as far back as the sixth century, does the imagery? A series of Attic early-fifth-century red-figure column kraters seems to show women at their toilette, usually three female nudes standing at a laver washing their bodies. Often a column is present to indicate the setting, probably a courtyard, although one of the earliest shows the laver next to a tree (*CVA* Milan collezione H.A. 2, Italy 51: pl. 2, 1–2). On account of their nudity, which is not the norm for proper Athenian women, such images have usually been identified as *hetairai* or courtesans at their toilette. However, on several of these vases the women are using strigils, and an aryballos and sponge are hanging in the vicinity (e.g., Bari 8693, attributed to the Göttingen Painter: ARV^2 236, 4; Vienna 2166, attributed to the Painter of Tarquinia 707: ARV^2 1111, 1; see Stewart 1997: 123, figure 73; Dresden 321, attributed to the Painter of the Louvre Gigantomachy: ARV^2 1089, 29). These objects are normally found in the context of male athletes and the palaestra, and so the Athenian viewer is clearly meant to read these scenes as female athletes. Since Athenian women did not exercise in the nude, the obvious conclusion is that the scenes represent Spartan girls cleaning up after their rigorous exercise (Arrigoni 1985).

Because these images appear on wine mixing bowls or kraters that formed the centerpiece of the Athenian symposium, they are clearly calculated to attract the attention of the male viewer. *Hetairai* are of course appropriate for this kind of vessel, but how much more alluring to see the well-developed body of what were considered the most beautiful women in Greece, the compatriots of Helen herself? And, while these particular specimens may not be our ideal of Greek beauty, their bared bodies would have been objects of the male gaze, if not the butts of jokes about Spartan women.

Are there other instances of this voyeuristic interest in Spartan female athletes on the part of Athenian vase painters and their clientele? At the end of the sixth century, c. 520 BCE, two unusual amphoras were decorated with scenes of nude women bathing. The first is a technically unique vase painted by the experimental Andokides Painter in which the female figures on both sides are rendered in white-figure (Paris, Musée du Louvre F 203; *ARV²* 1, 4–5, 13; Stewart 1997: 117, Figs. 68–9; Miller 2004: 151, figure 234). On side B the artist has depicted four nude female bathers, one of whom is actually swimming in the fish-filled sea. Like the later red-figure scenes centered around a laver (discussed above), there is a Doric column at the left, and one of the girls is pouring oil from an aryballos, a vase shape usually associated with males, as has been noted. Because there are three Amazons with a horse on side A, the bathers have also been identified as Amazons. As far as we know, Athenian girls did not swim, and we know even less about the bathing activities of Amazons, so there is little to support this suggestion.

The second amphora is even more extraordinary for it depicts seven diminutive nude girls within a landscape setting consisting of two trees, a large diving platform, a grotto with a waterfall, and a body of water in which one of the girls is swimming. Known as the Lerici-Marescotti amphora after the tomb in Cerveteri in which it was discovered, this black-figure vase attributed to the Priam Painter also includes aryballoi hanging from the trees (Rome, Villa Giulia 106463; *Paralipomena* 148, no. 8 ter.). Again, because Dionysus with his retinue of satyrs appears on the other side of the amphora, these girls have routinely been identified as nymphs.

However, there is textual as well as visual evidence for Spartan swimmers. Alcman is credited with a poem called *Kolymbosai*, which translates as "women swimming or diving" (Huxley 1964). It is noteworthy that on both amphoras a girl is depicted in a diving pose. So, might not these nudes be Spartan girls enjoying a skinny-dip in the river Eurotas? In Theocritus' idyll, "Epithalamy of Helen," her former companions recall their girlhood activities: "as age mates, we practiced the same running course and oiled ourselves down like men beside the bathing pools of the Eurotas" (*Idyll* 18: 22–5). As noted, on the Louvre amphora one of the bathers is shown in the act of oiling herself down, while on the other, by the Priam Painter, oil flasks are prominently featured. The visual evidence for Spartan girl swimmers consists of a lost Laconian kylix from Samos attributed to the Hunt Painter of c. 560–550 BCE (Pipili 1987: 37, figure 51; 114, no. 95). In another remarkably naturalistic setting consisting of a river-like body of water, trees, and vines, three nude women are shown bathing. While the cup documents the practice among Spartan women in the first half of the sixth century, the texts were probably the vehicles that brought this practice to the attention of the Athenians such that they commissioned vase painters to portray these exotic and sexy Spartan females on these exceptional amphoras.[1]

2   Spartan Female Horsemanship

Turning to the realm of horsemanship, the first Spartan female who comes to mind is the most famous Spartan horsewoman of all—Kyniska (Kyle 2003). She was the first woman

Figure 11.3 Attic red-figure kylix attributed to the Marlay Group, c. 430–420 BCE. Malibu, J. Paul Getty Museum 86.AE.297. Photo: The J. Paul Getty Museum, Villa Collection, Malibu, California.

to win the chariot race at Olympia—even though she could not be present to see the victory. Encouraged by her brother Agesilaus, the king of Sparta, she entered a *quadriga* or four-horse chariot in 396 and again in 392 and won both times. She earned the right to set up a commemorative statue at the site of Olympia, the inscribed base of which still survives. It reads (*Anth. Pal.* 13.16): "Kings of Sparta were my fathers and brothers, and I, Kyniska, winning the race with my chariot of swift-footed horses, erected this statue. I assert that I am the only woman in all Greece who won this crown." Her wins at Olympia attest to a tradition of female equestrianism at Sparta, as do victories by Spartan women at a later date (Tracy and Habicht 1991: 205, 213–4; Pomeroy 2002: 23–4, 28).

In this context it is worthwhile reconsidering the iconography of an Attic red-figure cup in the Getty Museum in Malibu (Figure 11.3). Formerly in the collection of Molly and Walter Bareiss, it was acquired by the Getty in 1986 and published for the first time by Wendy Raschke in the sports history journal *Nikephoros* in 1994. It has also been published in the *Corpus Vasorum Antiquorum* of the Bareiss collection, where it is attributed to the Marlay Group or roughly contemporary with the Eretria and Codrus Painters, which provides a date of c. 430–420 BCE (*CVA* J. Paul Getty Museum, Malibu 8, USA 33: no. 86). The tondo shows a draped youth playing a kithara confronted by Nike in mid-flight, which we will return to below. On the exterior is a chariot race with nearly identical images on each side: a chariot racing to the left. That we are dealing with a race is indicated by the *terma* or turning post on one side. Both near horses are branded, indicating their value, one with a cross and the other with a *kerykeion* (Braun 1970: 198–269; Kroll 1977).

There are two unusual features about these chariots. First, they are three-horse chariots, or trigas, rather than the more usual four-horse chariot or *quadriga*. In this configuration two horses are attached to the pole and there is one trace horse, better known as the outrigger. The Greek term *dexioseiros* refers to the right-hand trace horse or outrigger, whose position helps to set the pace and make the left-hand turns in the hippodrome. (The term could also be applied metaphorically to an outstanding human individual.) On the Bareiss cup the far horses are the outriggers and are setting the pace for the pole horses. The most common racing chariot is the four-horse *quadriga* and one also finds the *biga* (two-horse cart), as for example on some Panathenaic amphoras (Bentz 1998: 15, 76–8, 217–18). The triga, however, is quite rare, being most common in the late Geometric period, as for instance on the Hirschfeld Painter's krater in New York. Because there is a small tripod there amid the file of trigas, it has been suggested that a chariot race is represented (New York, Metropolitan Museum of Art 14.130.14: *CVA* New York 5, USA 2004: pls. 8–13).

The second and even more unusual feature is the gender of the charioteers. That they are female is evident not only from their long hair, which streams out behind them, but also from their dress, a Doric peplos with overfold rather than the male charioteer's long tunic. Female charioteers are not unknown in Greek art but they tend to be goddesses such as Selene or Athena, who is closely associated with the *apobates* race (P. Schultz 2006). Even rarer are females driving trigas, but Raschke cites one on a calyx-krater from Spina by the Peleus Painter (Ferrara, Museo Nazionale di Spina 2892: *ARV²* 1041, 6). Here the figure is labeled Nike, and so Raschke concludes that the Bareiss cup shows a pair of racing Nikai. Although Nike is often shown driving a chariot, as in scenes of the gigantomachy and the apotheosis of Herakles, in these instances she is equipped with her wings—her most important identifying attribute. Pairs of Nikai in racing chariots are also unprecedented.

So who might these female charioteers be? Another vase attributed to the Marlay Group, a pyxis in New York, also shows two wingless women driving chariots, one of which is again a triga (New York, private collection; *ARV²* 1277, 24). They have been identified as the Danaids because of a fragment of Melanippides that refers to the Danaids "practicing for competition in chariots with seats throughout the sunny groves." This chariot race of the Danaids is otherwise unknown and such races rarely appear in Greek art.

I propose instead that these charioteers are Spartan girls. The first piece of supporting evidence comes from Homer, where the triga is specifically associated with Sparta. In Book IV of the *Odyssey* (4.587ff.), at the end of Telemachus' visit to Menelaus at Sparta, the king offers him a farewell gift of three horses and a chariot to take back to Ithaka. The implication here is that the chariot powered by three horses was a Spartan custom. Second, we have considerable literary evidence indicating that Spartan girls actually drove chariots. In Alcman's sixth-century poem *Partheneion*, the girls compare themselves to horses and comment knowledgeably about the different qualities of various equine breeds. Since they refer to the trace horse and the driver, it is clear that these Spartan girls were familiar with chariot racing. We also know that at their local festival, known as the Hyakinthia, girls raced chariots. Athenaeus (*Deip.* 4.139) describes the festival in some detail and relates that "in the middle of the three-day period there is held a spectacle with many features …. As for the girls, some are carried in wicker carts which are sumptuously ornamented, others parade in chariots yoked to two horses which they race" (Pettersson 1992). While Kyniska's win was about a generation later than the Bareiss cup, she was known to have been a horse breeder and may herself have raced in the Hyakinthia as a girl.

The altar on the Marlay Painter's pyxis lid surely invokes a religious festival, and even more pertinent to the Hyakinthia is the scene in the tondo of the Bareiss cup. With his wreath and long hair, the youth could be Apollo, in whose honor the Hyakinthia was celebrated. But, because Nike is bringing him a victory fillet, it is more likely a musical contestant, a kitharode (Kephalidou 1996). Ancient sources on the Hyakinthia indicate that Spartan boys performed on the kithara at this festival in honor of the god of music. If the tondo and the exterior images are related, as they often are on Attic cups, then two aspects of this festival—the male musical performance and the girls' chariot race—are together illustrated on the Bareiss cup.

The next obvious question is as follows: why would a late-fifth-century Athenian vase painter be so interested in depicting a Spartan festival? And why did he substitute a triga for the two-horse chariots mentioned in the sources? It seems obvious to me that the painter of the Getty cup never actually witnessed a Spartan festival but knew of the Hyakinthia and girls racing chariots. Because of the passage in Homer, the artist associated trigas with Sparta and so naturally represented the Spartan girls with these distinctive and probably difficult-to-drive vehicles. (In Athens women were not even allowed to ride in horse-drawn carriages.) What this cup suggests is that the Athenian male was once again intrigued by Spartan women and their unusual upbringing—such that a vase painter would depict one of their more outlandish rituals on a men's drinking cup.

3 Female Spartan Symposiasts

Another aspect of women's liberation in ancient Sparta was their freedom to drink wine. According to our ancient sources, Spartan women were the only Greek women who consumed wine—at least publicly. Aristophanes alludes to Kleitagora, a Spartan woman poet whose name was associated with a *skolion* or drinking song (Pomeroy 2002: 10). Further, the god of wine, Dionysus, was a god of women in Sparta. Fragments of another early-sixth-century Laconian cup from the sanctuary of Hera at Samos show women reclining at the symposium with men, thus providing visual evidence for Spartan women's presence at wine-drinking events, in the absence of any textual evidence (Samos K 1203, attributed to the Arkesilas Painter; Pipili 1987: 72–3, Figs. 104, 104a). This being the case, could those Attic vase paintings that depict an all-female symposium be identified as Spartan genre scenes?

The most famous example of such a scene appears on the psykter signed by Euphronios as painter in St. Petersburg (Hermitage 664; *ARV²* 16, 15). On first glancing at these massive nudes aligned on their cushions, one would not imagine that they could be anything other than Athenian *hetairai* enjoying their wine and a game of *kottabos*, and in fact this is the usual interpretation. However, it has been noted in terms of the inscriptions on the vase that these women are speaking a Doric dialect. Since Laconian is a Doric dialect, it has been suggested by Gloria Ferrari that these are Spartan women and that the vase is not an actual genre scene but a parody (2002: 20). We shall return to this point but first it is worthwhile examining other images of female imbibers. Like scenes of girls swimming or driving chariots, all-female symposia are relatively rare in Attic vase painting. Contemporary with Euphronios' psykter is a hydria painted by Phintias that features two half-draped female symposiasts on the shoulder (Munich, Antikenmuseum 2421; *ARV²*

Figure 11.4   Laconian bronze mirror handle of a caryatid mirror, c. 530 BCE. New York, Metropolitan Museum of Art, inv. no. 74.51.5680. Cesnola Collection. Photo: © The Metropolitan Museum of Art/Art Resource, NY.

23, 7; see Reinsberg 1993: 113, figure 61). Like the girls on the psykter, the female symposiasts are drinking from deep skyphoi, rather than kylikes. Likewise, one of two nude women on the outside of a cup by Oltos, in Madrid, is holding a skyphos, as well as a kylix, as does the woman labeled Agapa on the psykter (Museo Arqueologico Nacional 11267; *ARV²* 58, 53; *CVA* Madrid 2, Spain 2: pls. 58, 59, 61–62). On all these vases, which are more or less contemporary, the girls are making toasts: to the young Athenian aristocrat Leagros on the psykter; to the vase painter Euthymides on the hydria; and simply "to you" on the cup.[2]

The message of these vases seems ambiguous and enigmatic. The women are toasting Athenians, but in one instance in the Doric dialect. Although female, they have taken up traditionally male activities: reclining on *klinai*, drinking wine, playing *kottabos*, making toasts. They are drinking not from the normal kylix but from extra-large skyphoi. As noted by Venit, the skyphos carries connotations of self-indulgence, lack of control, and even licentiousness. One of the women on the St. Petersburg psykter, in fact the one actually drinking from a large skyphos, is labeled Palaisto, a name known to be Spartan. Might then these carousing females represent the Athenian vase painters' take on those licentious and immodest Spartan women?

It is usually a given in the field of Attic vase-painting that if a woman is shown nude she must be an *hetaira*. While this is quite often the case, it is not incontrovertible and another type of female could be invoked, as we have noted above in the scenes of female athletes at the laver or of female bathers. Female nudity occurs very early in Spartan art in the form of bronze mirror handles produced in the later sixth century (Figure 11.4), as well as four bronze statuettes (listed in Pipili 1987: 119, nos. 216 a–j (caryatid mirrors) and 217–220 (statuettes); see also Stewart 1997: 108–18, 231–4; Pomeroy 2002: 164–5; Scanlon 2002: 127–37; Kaltsas 2006: 170 no. 73, 175 no. 78). Some two dozen of these exist, and of those with a known provenance the majority are from Sparta. Identifications range from the mythological (Atalanta) to the everyday (slave girls), but the cultic is the most persuasive since many of these figures served as votives. Because they were widely exported, these Laconian statuettes of nude girls may have influenced other Greeks' perceptions of Spartan women. The presence of at least two of them on the Acropolis suggests that the Athenians would have been aware of this custom of female nudity—one they normally associated with *hetairai*. From here it is not much of a leap to represent Spartan women, who had a reputation for wine consumption, at their own symposia.

4 Homoerotic Relationships

Because the all-male symposium was often the locus for homosexual liaisons, the Athenian male could possibly view these images of nude women at their own symposium in a similar context (Cantarella 1987: 86–9, 1992). The poetry of Alcman references a homoerotic element in girls' upbringing in Sparta; fragments 1 and 3 of his choral poem *Partheneion* describe an amorous attraction of the Spartan chorus girls for their female chorus leader. A passage in Plutarch (*Lykourgos* 18.4) confirms this implication: "Though this pederastic love was so approved among them that even the maidens found lovers in good and noble women."

 Attempts to uncover depictions of female-to-female relationships on Attic vases have not met with much success (Petersen 1997). One possible example is a skyphos attributed to the Syriskos Painter of c. 460 in Brussels, on which it looks as if the nearly identically posed figures on either side are meant to make a deliberate comparison (Musées Royaux A 11; *ARV²* 266, 86; *CVA* Brussels 2, Belgium 2: pl. 18.2). On one side are two confronted pairs of draped males at a laver: one of each pair is clearly older (bearded) than the other (beardless). On the other side are two pairs of women, also at a laver. One of each pair (wearing snoods) again seems to be distinguished from the other (hair tied back with ends wrapped). There is no doubt that the males are shown in a scene of courtship, the bearded man being the *erastes* and the youth the *eromenos* (Shapiro 1981). Given the deliberate similarity of these couples with those involving women (as well as the similarity in setting), one must make the same assumption for the females—that is, that these are scenes of female courtship. However there is no indication that these women are meant to be identified as Spartans.

 A similar, but equally unusual, scene of female courtship, where older women are paired with younger girls, appears on the outside of a cup in New York discussed in the exhibition *Coming of Age in Ancient Greece: Images of Childhood from the Classical Past* (Metropolitan Museum of Art 06.1021.167; *ARV²* 908, 13; Neils and Oakley 2003: 243, 247–8 no. 46). Attributed to the Painter of Bologna 417 and dating to c. 460 BCE, this kylix features three pairs of draped female figures on each exterior side (Figure 11.5). In each pair one female wears a snood while the other's head is not covered. They all wear chitons with himations, but the four girls at the ends nearest the handles are entirely enveloped in their himations in a manner mostly associated with male *eromenoi*. The women with heads uncovered, whom I would identify as the older women, are making gestures and move toward the others, who stand still. These couplings of distinctly dressed and posed figures

Figure 11.5   Tondo of an Attic red-figure kylix attributed to the Painter of Bologna 417, c. 460 BCE. New York, Metropolitan Museum of Art Rogers Fund 1906.1021.67. Photo: © The Metropolitan Museum of Art/Art Resource, NY.

are often found on the outside of cups by artists such as Douris, and are today commonly identified as male courtship scenes. While female courtship is rarely depicted (I know of only these two examples), the iconography is identical to that of male courtship. In the exhibition catalog we concluded that this was some kind of symposium joke, appearing as it does on a man's drinking cup. Further consideration of this cup's imagery, however, offers a different reading, as I will argue below.

5   Spartan School Girls

Hanging in the background on one side of the New York cup is a wax tablet writing case with a stylus tucked beneath its strings, and the same object is depicted in the cup's tondo. Here it is carried by a girl who is being led by the wrist by a female companion. The girls are dressed exactly like those on the exterior; that is, as another pair. The traditional identification of this unique image is "girls going to school." Since Athenian girls did not go to school, could this be a parody of boys going to school? Another joke like the female courtship scenes on the exterior? Or is this a "real" scene of girls who actually did go to school, namely Spartans?

As Pomeroy has clearly stated (2002: 3–5),

> Only at Sparta did the state prescribe an educational program for both boys and girls beginning in childhood …. The earliest datable evidence for the girls' official program is archaic and continues through the Classical period …. Furthermore, since they were married at eighteen—a substantially later age than their Athenian counterparts—they had as many years as most girls do in modern western societies to devote to their education. They could well have learned reading and writing as well as other aspects of *mousike* (music, dancing, poetry) in such an all-female milieu.

It seems reasonable, therefore, to denominate this unusual scene "girls going to school," with the proviso that the girls are Spartans. The artist of the New York cup clearly intended that the interior with its pair of girls and the exterior with its six female couples should be read together, and thus a single cup illustrates two characteristic aspects of Spartan female life—their relationships with women and their schooling.

6   Conclusions

The question remains of how to interpret these scenes on Athenian vases, which were largely for the consumption of the male citizen. Are they meant to be prescriptive; that is, examples to Athenian women of how *not* to behave? Are they all parodies or humorous takes on girls indulging in male activities? Or do they represent male fantasies about women who can compete with men in their segregated, all-male arenas of the palaestra, the *andron*, and the schoolroom? Can a changing attitude over time toward Spartan women be demonstrated? Is it valid to state that on the earlier vases of c. 520–470 BCE these Spartan girls are generally nude (like the Laconian mirror handles) while on the latest ones, like the Getty and Sparte cups, they are clothed and situated in a religious context? There are many ways to interpret the meaning of these vases in Athenian society, but at a minimum they demonstrate a keen interest in their rival city-state, and in particular in the more exotic female part of it.

Encountering Spartan competitiveness both on the battlefield and in the sports arena, Athenians no doubt always had a love-hate relationship with their fellow Greeks. They both admired and feared—and so sometimes mocked—the lifestyle and culture of the Laconians. Just as they depicted another group of out-of-male-control women, the Amazons, as great warriors and equestrians, so they mythologized Spartan women as school girls, wine drinkers, athletes, and, in the case of the Getty cup, charioteers. The vase painters created stereotypes that in the end may explain more about Athenian attitudes and preconceptions than provide concrete information about the actual lives of Spartan women.

RECOMMENDED FURTHER READING

The basic source for all aspects of Spartan women is Pomeroy (2002). Little has been written about women in sports, with the exception of Arrigoni (1985). Kyniska is studied in depth by Kyle (2003). For a thorough discussion of the roles of female nudity in Greek art see Stewart (1997), and for a new interpretation of Athenian scenes of nude women bathing as citizen women as opposed to *hetairai* see Kreilinger (2007).

NOTES

1. I wonder, too, whether the nude females accompanied by Laconian hounds on the neck of a Nikosthenic-type amphora of c. 525–520 BCE in the Louvre (F 114; *ABV* 226) might also be Spartan athletes. The tripods depicted on the outside of the strap handles perhaps support this identification. For a recent publication see Cohen (2006: 81–3 no. 15).

2. Two further vases with all-female symposia are the unpublished proto-Panaitian cup in a private collection in New York (Centre Island, D. von Bothmer) with six "*hetairai*," four of whom hold skyphoi (see Venit 1998: 127 n. 47), and a cup on the Basel art market by the Curtius Painter in which five female symposiasts encircle the tondo (see Reinsberg 1993: 95, figure 39). Attic vase paintings with scenes of draped women (as opposed to nude *hetairai*) drinking wine are rare.

12

Interpreting Women in Archaic and Classical Greek Sculpture

A.A. Donohue

In the second century CE, the satirist Lucian of Samosata explained his choice of career by recounting a dream in which he was almost literally torn between two women: the attractive and articulate Education and the uncouth and work-dishevelled Sculpture (Lucian, *Somnium*). These rival allegorical figures are striking because in classical antiquity, although Athena was the patron goddess of crafts and was even shown turning her hand to making a statue, women are unattested as sculptors.[1] They commissioned, dedicated, and observed sculpture, but for the modern student women's most prominent link to the medium is their role as subjects for representation (Ridgway 1987). In the sadly fragmentary textual and monumental record of the classical cultures, sculpture constitutes one of the largest bodies of evidence for women in ancient Greece. How this corpus is to be interpreted, of course, is a major question. Our topic invites a series of methodological questions extending from our own basis of interpretation to the very elements of the title of this essay, as even the terms "Greek," "Archaic and Classical," "sculpture," and "women" are not without difficulties here.

1   Interpretive Frameworks

What kind of information about women do we seek from Greek sculpture? Considered simply as an object, a work of sculpture invites questions about how it came into existence at a particular time and place, how and by whom it was used, and how it ultimately became available for study. The forms characteristic of the societies that devoted energy and resources to them (statues and reliefs, architectural and freestanding), the conditions of production (medium and manufacture), and distribution and use (commissioning and placement) can be investigated through technical analyses of artifacts, studies of work-shops and find contexts, and literary and epigraphical texts (Ridgway 1991; Palagia 2006). These aspects are important but tell only part of the story, because, for us, works of sculpture are works of art and therefore have particular qualities with implications

A Companion to Women in the Ancient World, First Edition. Edited by Sharon L. James and Sheila Dillon.
© 2012 John Wiley & Sons, Ltd. Published 2015 by John Wiley & Sons, Ltd.

for their evidentiary value. While antiquity lacked a notion corresponding to the modern "art," recognizing only a broad range of *technai*—the arts of civilization involving mental or physical skill—modern Western culture grants "art" a distinct status. This status is privileged but problematic: it is not agreed whether art is an expression of culture or is autonomous, operating beyond cultural boundaries. Thus, Classical style has been interpreted as an expression of the ideals attributed to mid-fifth-century Athens (Boardman 1996: 13, 23) and as a stage in a universal pattern of formal development (Riegl 1901: 8–9, 101–4, 1985: 9, 61–3). In an extreme view of the latter kind, art would be evidence only for itself. For the most part, however, modern scholars accept that works of art, in both form and iconography, carry information helpful for interpreting culture and society. Sculptural representations are often cited as evidence for costume and other realia, as well as for social practices; how works of art were experienced and understood by contemporaries is also studied, along with the responses of female viewers (Osborne 1994; Stehle and Day 1996).

Although the scholarship on classical art has been criticized for its emphasis on classification at the expense of cultural meanings (e.g., Osborne 1994: 81), in fact, since the Renaissance, its study has been tied to the valorization of classical antiquity as an overall cultural model. Johann Joachim Winckelmann, whose writings in the mid-eighteenth century continue to shape the discipline, advocated the imitation of Greek painting and sculpture as a means of reforming modern society to accord with what he believed to be classical values (Winckelmann 1755). Implicitly or explicitly, the subsequent work of description and classification that opened the extant corpus to meaningful analysis rested on a valorization of Greek art. What characterizes the scholarship of the later twentieth century is not so much a recognition of the social aspects of classical art as a rejection of its cultural assumptions, a rejection that mirrored contemporary critiques of the modern Western context into which they had been absorbed.

Nowhere in classical scholarship has the challenge to the norms of the ancient societies been so clear as in the study of their women. The feminist scholarship that emerged in the 1960s exposed the ideologies of gender operating not only in antiquity but in modern scholarship as well, and arguably set the pattern for exploring a constellation of conditions—age, ethnicity, civil status—that are seen as fundamental in the constitution of society and are increasingly examined within a general category of "identity" studies (Brown 1997; Meyer 2003). Within these studies, the polarities deriving from linguistically based structuralist categories continue to be influential, even as historical anthropology and a variety of poststructuralist approaches have complicated the analyses in which women figure as the paradigmatic "other" in Greek society (Dosse 1998: 223–6; Cohen 2000; Davis 2003: 331–2) and have encouraged the adoption of ostensibly neutral stances (Brown 1997: 13–14).

Interpretations of the representations of women nonetheless continue to reflect two contrasting views, one stressing the exclusion of women from social agency and influence (e.g., Ferrari 2002) and the other stressing women's power within their own, complementary, spheres (e.g., Kosmopoulou 2001: 284–5; Connelly 2007: 2–4), held to extend even to "personal fulfillment" and, further, to socially valued contributions to "civic identity" (Kaltsas and Shapiro 2008: 13). The latter, optimistic, treatments often present themselves as "more balanced" (Ridgway 1987: 399) than negative appraisals or as "a necessary corrective" (Kaltsas and Shapiro 2008: 21) to them. Interestingly, they sometimes claim a value for art as a less biased category of evidence than literature (Ridgway 1987: 399; Kaltsas and Shapiro 2008: 13), although works of art are far from presentations of some absolute reality (Ferrari 2002) and in any case should not be interpreted without reference to other cultural forms. While the iconographic prominence of women has been held to demonstrate that women did not lack importance or even power in Greek society (Osborne 1997; Connelly 2007: 224–7), neither that fact, nor the ethnographic comparanda for sharply gendered spheres of social activity cited to palliate ancient Greek practices (Ridgway 1987: 409; Llewellyn-Jones 2003: 11–14), should cause us to overlook that women themselves often act as enforcers of social norms (e.g., Chinese footbinding: Ko 2005) that require sleight-of-discourse to construe as empowering. The role of ideology in shaping interpretations of Greek art is inevitable and requires recognition (Katz 1995; Donohue 1999).

2   Greek

When we approach the topic of women and Greek sculpture, what do we mean by "Greek"? Herodotus (8.143–4), writing in the late fifth century, has the Athenians rally Greek resistance to the Persians before the battle of Plataea in 479 BCE by invoking ties of blood, language, religion, and way of life—elements on which definitions of Greek identity continue to be founded. In the study of art, the status of Greek art as the unique product of a superior cultural matrix (Winckelmann 1764) has persisted, even as our understanding of its complex ties with other cultures has grown.

While the long history of art made in Greek lands begins early in prehistoric times, well before the arrival of Greek-speakers (Pullen 2008: 38–41), it is not clear whether pieces such as the nude terracotta "Lady of Lerna" and other Neolithic female figurines (Talalay 1993: 53–86; Talalay, this volume, Case Study I) had any bearing on subsequent cultures in the region. From the art produced by the several Aegean cultures of the late Neolithic (c. 4500–3200 BCE) and early Bronze Ages (c. 3100–2700 BCE) linked by complex interconnections, the Cycladic marble "idols"—most of them naked females—are sometimes drawn into the history of Greek art as forerunners of a Greek sense of abstraction and feeling for the material. In the late Bronze Age, the artistic forms and styles of the Greek-speaking Mycenaeans, including their images of women, show the influence of Minoan models; the dissimilarities have been read as expressive of a sharp and gendered cultural difference (Nixon 1994; see also Nikolaïdou, this volume, Chapter 3). The Mycenaean response to Minoan art can be seen as establishing a pattern of Greek receptivity to and transformation of non-Greek traditions. A striking example is furnished by the five nude female ivory statuettes of Geometric date (c. 730–720 BCE) found in a grave in the Athenian Kerameikos, the best preserved of which (Figure 12.1; Kaltsas 2002: 34 no. 1) is frequently reproduced to demonstrate the adaptation by Greek artists of the Near Eastern type of the "naked goddess" in both the style—less rounded than in Near Eastern renderings—and the inclusion of a prototypically Greek meander. What led to the imitations of the Near Eastern type is not clear; we neither know how much original meaning was transferred from their models nor fully understand what significance the figures held in Greek contexts (Bahrani 1996; Böhm 2003).

The same questions surround the repertoire of female types—both naked and clothed—that are prominent through the seventh century, the period conventionally designated as Orientalizing and characterized by strong Near Eastern influence, not only in the visual arts but in literature and other forms of material culture as well (Gunter 2009). While subsequently the nude female all but vanishes from Greek art until the fourth

Figure 12.1 Ivory statuette from the Kerameikos cemetery, Athens, late eighth century BCE. Athens, National Museum 776. Photo: American School of Classical Studies at Athens, Archives, Alison Frantz Photographic Collection.

century, Near Eastern types of clothed females (e.g., Özgen and Öztürk 1996: 26–7), which became hallmarks of the Orientalizing "Daedalic" style (Figure 12.3; Donohue 2005: 131–43), appear to have provided the foundation for the long series so prominent in the Greek production (Ridgway 1993: 152–3). The extent of Near Eastern contribution to Greek art and culture remains a source of vigorous debate.

Another kind of non-Greek involvement in Greek art presents questions of a different kind. Much of what we know of Greek painting and sculpture comes to us through monuments produced in Roman times. Until the advent of extensive exploration and excavation in Greece in the nineteenth century, the great majority of works considered as Greek in fact represented Roman responses to a culture regarded with profound ambivalence. It was recognized in the eighteenth century that many "Greek" statues were not made by Greeks, but until the late twentieth century they were seen as a means to reconstruct the Greek works celebrated in ancient (largely Roman) texts. Only recently has the acceptance of Roman art as a cultural expression in its own right (Brendel 1979) permitted the paradigm of "Greek original, Roman copy" to be challenged from the Greek (Ridgway 1984b) and the Roman (Marvin 1989) perspectives alike. Given the fact that some of the representations of the female body that have been most influential in scholarship are productions of the Roman era, these approaches have implications for interpreting "Greek" sculptural images of women.

Yet another complication arises from the spread of Greek culture to non-Greek regions through trade and colonization. The intensive foundation of settlements overseas beginning in the late ninth century placed the Greeks in varying degrees of contact with local populations (see Shepherd, this volume, Chapter 16), and interpretations of the resulting cultural interactions reflect our attitudes both to the non-Greek civilizations and to colonization as a process (Antonaccio 2007). Especially in the study of sculpture, the art of East Greece has been judged more favorably than that of the Western Greeks, which has only recently been seen as more than colonial and provincial (De Miro 1996; Rizza 1996; Rolley 1996; Barletta 2006). The clear impact on the Greek mainland of types and styles originating in the East, such as the kore, has perhaps also contributed to a perception of the "supposedly more prominent" status enjoyed by women in Asia Minor, although the sculptural evidence in the East provides little evidence for it (Ridgway 1993: 124).[2]

The corpus of sculpture produced in the wider Greek orbit shows an overall similarity in function, types, and style, with a convergence over time toward mainland standards. Images of females sometimes depart from prevailing Greek typologies. For example, the limestone seated woman nursing twins, from the cemetery at Megara Hyblaia (see Figure 16.1) is considered an indigenous production largely by stylistic default (Ridgway 1993: 194), but the theme, all but absent from Greece, is popular in the West (Bonfante 1989c: 567–9; see also Shepherd, this volume, Chapter 16). Specific cult iconography does not seem to account for the popularity in Western Greek votive and funerary contexts of terracotta busts and protomes of females (Uhlenbrock 1988; Barletta 2006: 86–7) but continues to be invoked to explain the Archaic and Classical funerary busts of Cyrene that combine Greek female clothing and hairstyles with featureless pillars in place of faces (Beschi 1996: 439).

Even the presumably mainstream Greekness of the mainland was far from monolithic. The ancient distinction between Dorian and Ionian extends from dialect to social forms; in the course of the nineteenth century, it became a sometimes misapplied conceptual tool (Katz 1995: 22–3; Lee 2003; Donohue 2005: 88–101). The paradigmatic contrast between Ionian Athens and Doric Sparta is intensified by the abundance of evidence for Athenian life and the dearth of it—at least from Spartan sources—for Sparta. One of the signal differences between them is the greater freedom accorded women in Sparta than anywhere else in Greece, which was recognized in antiquity and served as the foundation for much of the modern scholarship on Greek women (Katz 1995: 22–32; see Neils, this volume, Chapter 11). Sparta has yielded little sculpture in stone in any period to compete with the Athenian corpus (Kokkorou-Alevras 2006). It is largely the distinctively Laconian Archaic and early Classical bronze mirror supports in the form of young women, especially those standing naked or running, that furnish visual confirmation of Spartan women's participation in athletic and ritual activities on a footing similar to men's (see Figure 11.4; Pomeroy 2002: 161–70; Kaltsas 2006: 157, 166 no. 69, 175 no. 78). Other areas of mainland Greece, while politically and culturally distinct, offer little to rival the Attic evidence that dominates the scholarship on women.

3 Archaic and Classical

What do we mean by "Archaic" and "Classical"? In the study of art, periodization attempts to define not only the visible features that might constitute "period styles" but also differences and changes that permit an account of historical development. Because the correlation of such internal, relative sequences with chronological frameworks of political and social history is rarely exact, the explanation of artistic features and change remains methodologically challenging, all the more so because classical art offers few monuments that can be dated with precision or security.

It is increasingly clear that cultural phenomena are no respecters of period designations. By one account (Shapiro 2007: 1), the Archaic period began as early as 800 BCE, when characteristic forms of Greek culture such as the Homeric epics were taking shape, and would thus include part of the Geometric as well as the Orientalizing period. In terms of sculpture, the starting point of the Archaic period is usually associated with the appearance of large-scale statuary in marble in the second half of the seventh century BCE (Sturgeon 2006: 32, 43–4), when there is overlap with the Daedalic repertory in limestone and terracotta. The hallmark types of Archaic sculpture are the standing figures of nude youths (kouroi) and clothed females (korai), although they were favored more in some areas than others. While it is possible to discern both stylistic development and regional variation within these types, the fragmentary nature of the corpus and the mobility of sculptors hamper our understanding in more than general terms (Sturgeon 2006: 50). Archaic art in all media is characterized by strongly stylized representations that show a general trend toward naturalism, by which is meant the convincing rendering of organic forms. The end of the Archaic period is conventionally placed at 480 BCE, the date of the Greek victory over the Persians, which appears to coincide loosely with a turn away from stylization in favor of the somewhat heavy naturalism that characterizes the Severe Style of the early Classical period (c. 480–450 BCE). Sculpture in the second half of the fifth century displays a balance of naturalistic rendering and idealized—meaning a preference for typical rather than distinctively individualized—forms. The sculpture of the Periclean age (e.g., Figure 12.3) is often celebrated as a supreme artistic achievement expressing singular cultural values, but, despite the apparent dominance of Athenian models during the period, versions of the Classical style appeared elsewhere in Greece, and work in Athens itself is far from stylistically uniform (Ridgway 1981: 3–14). The Spartan victory in the Peloponnesian War (431–404 BCE) reduced Athenian power and is generally credited with an increase in sculptural activity throughout Greece as well as overseas. Sculpture of the fourth century resists period labels, as its stylistic variety matches the social and political complexity of the time. It can reasonably be seen as a "late Classical" continuation of fifth-century directions or as a foreshadowing of later developments (Ridgway 1997: 3–24), to the extent that "early Hellenistic" is sometimes held to begin c. 350 BCE, considerably earlier than the conventional start of the period (the death of Alexander the Great in 323 BCE).

Stylistic analysis is the basis for our chronology of Archaic and Classical sculpture, which posits increasing naturalism (Donohue 2005: 21–7), a criterion derived from ancient, for the most part Roman, critico-historical formulations and reasonably well confirmed by extant monuments. Representations of women pose a problem because the standard for judging progress along the scale of naturalism is set by the male nude; as the female nude is scarcely present until well into the fourth century, how can we evaluate forms dominated by clothing? The usual solution is to approach such figures as "nudes plus drapery" and measure success in terms of works such as the pedimental sculptures of the Parthenon

Figure 12.2 Marble figures L and M from the east pediment of the Parthenon, Athens, c. 438–432 BCE. London, British Museum 1816,0610.97, Sculpture 303.L and 303.M. Photo: © Trustees of the British Museum.

(Figure 12.2) that show the body through the drapery. By this account, figures such as the Lady of Auxerre (Figure 12.3) and the Archaic korai are failed attempts to attain the goal achieved by the Classical works. It is an approach that badly misunderstands the earlier images. These figures have their own aesthetic and iconographic aims; the costumes are not obstacles to showing the bodies beneath but in some sense constitute the essence of the representations, offering distinct social content relating to status and identity that was clear in their original contexts (Donohue 2005: 155–221; see also Lee, this volume, Chapter 13). Even the Classical figures, in which the transparent drapery is usually taken for the clever circumvention of prudery on the path toward the postulated goal of nudity, are not so easily explained. While the conventions of Classical drapery in sculpture are often treated in terms of their capacity to reveal and emphasize the forms of the body while ostensibly covering it, they too carried social meaning, serving to control and indeed give structure to the female body, which in Greek thought was conceived as formless material lacking the natural articulation of the male (Darling 1998–9).

It is also stylistic chronology that permits us to interpret the types of sculptural monuments and their iconography within the changing social and political circumstances of Archaic and Classical Greece. Thus, the korai, like the kouroi, are viewed as an essentially aristocratic phenomenon, primarily favored in Attica, East Greece, and the islands, that did not survive beyond the social contexts in which they flourished (Hurwit 2007: 269–72, 276–7). It is again the Attic corpus that has been most intensely scrutinized for links between sculpture and its historical and cultural context.

Figure 12.3 Lady of Auxerre, limestone figure probably from Crete, mid-seventh century BCE. Paris, Louvre Ma 3098. Photo: American School of Classical Studies at Athens, Archives, Alison Frantz Photographic Collection.

Yet, even in this comparatively full record, it has proved difficult to reach conclusive interpretations of representations of women. Funerary stelai with figural decoration, known in several areas of Archaic Greece, are a case in point. The Athenian series came to an end around 490 BCE but continued in the other regions where the tradition existed. The Archaic stelai are seen as an aristocratic form, and their cessation has been explained as a consequence of the establishment of the democracy late in the sixth century (e.g., Osborne 1997: 27) and perhaps of sumptuary legislation (e.g., Leader 1997: 684). When they resume, it is with a new iconography that seems to stress not traditionally aristocratic but rather civic or democratic and familial values, and to feature women more prominently than before. Attempts have been made to link the increased emphasis on women with Pericles' decree of 451/450 BCE, which made citizenship contingent on having not only an Athenian father but also an Athenian mother (Stears 1995: 113; Osborne 1997), but the production of figured stelai, dated on stylistic grounds, seems not to resume until considerably later. Their reappearance is generally placed close to 430 BCE and has been linked to a revival and intensification of traditional and religious practices in consequence of the Peloponnesian War and the outbreak of the plague (Pemberton 1989: 46–7; Lawton 2009: 66–7).

Family burial enclosures and the family groups that appear on stelai in the fourth century suggest the possibility of responses to more general social concerns (e.g., the wellbeing of the family; see Closterman 2007). In the context of the overall highlighting of family relationships, stelai showing women in labor (Stewart and Gray 2000) are startling

Figure 12.4 Roman copy of the Aphrodite of Knidos by Praxiteles. Original c. 350–340 BCE; this version comes from the Villa of the Quintilii in Rome. Munich, Glyptothek, Staatliche Antiken-sammlung, inv. no. 258. Photo: Vanni/Art Resource, NY.

demonstrations of the extent of public representation of what strike us as intensely private matters. Conversely, stelai also show women displaying the symbols of their service as priestesses (Connelly 2007: 223–57), and there is even some evidence for the commemoration of women who had occupations (Kosmopoulou 2001). If precise explanations of the stelai and their imagery remain elusive, it is the case that the prominence of women on them is matched in other kinds of sculpture as well as in the iconography of vase painting, in which scenes featuring women conspicuously increase throughout the fifth century (Webster 1972: 226–43). It remains unclear whether this visibility is evidence for women's civic and social power or instead for the use of visual means to reinforce a set of sharply prescribed roles and behaviors (e.g., Reilly 1997).

Similarly resistant to explanation is the abrupt appearance of the unclothed female figure in the mid fourth century in the form of the statue of Aphrodite sold by Praxiteles to the Knidians (Figure 12.4; Havelock 1995: 26; see also Lee, this volume, Chapter 13). In Greek contexts, nudity and partial nudity carried different meanings in representations of males and females (Bonfante 1989c; Cohen 1997). That the Knidia does not represent the final step in a long-postulated progression from fully clothed to partially or quasi-nude figures is clear (Havelock 1995: 141–2); it is rather Aphrodite herself and her roots in and persistent associations with the Near East (Burkert 1985: 152–6; Havelock 1995: 142) that furnish the context for the statue. For the occasion of its creation and responses to it we have only considerably later testimony in texts and images (Havelock 1995: 55); we know its appearance only from Roman replicas, which have their own meanings (Marvin 1989: 36–7; Havelock 1995).

4 Sculpture

How do we define "sculpture," and can it be treated separately in considering representations of women? By "sculpture" we usually mean images carved in stone, either in the round or in relief, but we include—and sometimes value more greatly—statues in bronze as well, which are produced by casting models made in clay (Mattusch 2006), a material with very different properties from stone. In areas such as Western Greece that lack sources of marble, terracotta is used even for large pieces (Barletta 2006: 77–92), although everywhere it is most prominent in smaller formats, both molded and modeled. Despite longstanding theories of the material determination of artistic form (Donohue 2005: 62–88), work in various kinds of stone, metal, wood, ivory, and clay seems to share the general characteristics of chronological, regional, and to a large extent iconographic groupings. Increasing awareness of the extent of polychromy in stone and even bronze works is serving to reinforce similarities across media (Brinkmann and Wünsche 2004). The cost of producing the various categories, while difficult to estimate, will have determined their availability and use.

While much sculptural material is unprovenanced, it seems certain that in Archaic and Classical Greece sculpture was used primarily in funerary and votive contexts and as architectural decoration of religious and civic structures. The choice of imagery is likely to reflect its context, but the connection is clearer in the prevailing iconography of some classes than of others. For example, votive reliefs show women among worshippers bringing offerings to divinities, while in scenes carved on funerary vases and stelai neither the meaning of the actions nor the status of the figures as living or dead is altogether certain. In the large repertory of terracotta statuettes, women are engaged in a variety of activities such as household tasks; such lively figures may have had a place in domestic contexts (Boardman 1996: 178–80), but, like the standing and seated types common in sanctuaries and graves, their iconography may have related to their votive and funerary use (see also Dillon, this volume, Case Study III). Examining the finds in individual sanctuaries (e.g., Demeter and Kore at Corinth: see Merker 2000) and cemeteries (e.g., see Jeammet 2003) contributes to understanding the iconography, but many forms and types are so widespread that it is difficult to interpret the corpus of small-scale sculpture as a whole. Although it was long held that large-scale sculpture set the pattern for small-scale types, the discovery of a late-fourth-century terracotta figure with crossed legs, predating Eutychides' statue of the Tyche of Antioch, which was thought to have introduced the pose, changed our ideas about the sources of sculptural innovation (Rotroff 1990: 27–30) and the connections throughout the sculptural corpus.

Iconographic connections exist as well between sculpture and other media and are often crucial in clarifying subject and meaning. In some cases, the function of the sculpture seems to be reflected in the choice of imagery. For example, women participate in the *dexiosis*, or handshake, that appears in Attic funerary stelai and carved vases, but the motif is absent from related funerary scenes on white-ground lekythoi, even though it occurs in a range of non-funerary scenes on vases and votive and documentary reliefs (Pemberton 1989). It is likewise the social function of architectural sculpture that will have influenced the choice of its themes (Ridgway 1999: 6–10, 143–83). The architectural context, impressive in prominence and often in scale and costliness, heightens whatever meanings are associated with female figures used as supporting elements (caryatids: see Ridgway 1999: 145–50) or shown attacked by centaurs or, in the singular case of the Ionic frieze of the Parthenon, taking part in a procession (Stehle and Day 1996).

Neither Archaic stylization nor the Classical focus on generic forms favors the production of portraiture in our sense, which developed only in Hellenistic times; even then, portraits of women may follow principles different from those for male portraits (Dillon 2007, 2010). Fourth-century images sometimes suggest individualized features (Bergemann 2007), but, as in the case of the stele of the priestess Chairestrate (Piraeus, Archaeological Museum 1031: see Kaltsas and Shapiro 2008: 208–9 no. 86), whose advanced age, mentioned in her epigram, has been thought to be represented by her lined face (Kosmopoulou 2001: 298–9), such renderings seem to be essentially conventional.

5   Women

Whom do we include among "women"? The category presents difficulties. To begin with, the anthropomorphism of the Greek gods means that, in the absence of attributes, decisive narrative contexts, or labels (more common in vase painting than sculpture), images of mortal women are not always easy to distinguish from those of goddesses; the large population of subsidiary figures such as nymphs, Nereids, and Charites; or heroines. The identity of the korai, for example, has not been settled (Karakasi 2003: 11, 28–30, 48–51, 77–8, 89, 135–9). Because divinities reflect the social roles of mortal women—for instance, youthful ones often display behaviors conventional for *parthenoi*, or maidens, such as group activities, bathing, and adornment (Ferrari 2002: 44–52)—we must recognize that their representations in statues, reliefs, and architectural sculpture are likely to have had considerable emotional resonance for their female viewers.

Some mythological figures, such as the Lapith women, do not differ appreciably from mortal women, and their frequent appearance in sculptural centauromachies may reasonably be read as emphasizing their relative lack of agency in the context of marriage and their vulnerability to violence (Stehle and Day 1996). Amazons (Hardwick 1990), in contrast, seem to contradict nearly every Greek social norm for women.

Another problem is posed by mythological characters, whose very form separates them from the mortal realm. Monstrous female creatures are frequently represented in Greek art. In sculpture, they are versatile; in Archaic times, they are often connected with specific contexts—sirens and sphinxes, for example, are associated with funerary monuments (Ridgway 1993: 223–8). The Gorgon Medusa appears on pedimental sculpture, in either a whole form or (especially popular in Western Greece), in her head alone (Barletta 2006: 89–90). To what extent is their being female significant?

6   Conclusion

Perhaps the most difficult question is precisely what sculpture tells us about Greek women. Scenes of "daily life" may be as highly constructed as any mythological representation, and even the evidentiary value of details such as garments is open to question (e.g., Lee 2003; Lee, this volume, Chapter 13). Sculpture is no more obvious in its meanings than other forms of representation, textual or visual, but despite the difficulty of interpretation it yields insights into the experience of women and the world in which they lived.

RECOMMENDED FURTHER READING

The study of women in Greek antiquity has focused more on vase painting than sculpture, with the exception of certain categories such as korai and funerary reliefs. A well-illustrated survey of Greek sculpture is Stewart (1990). The standard reference for the iconography of classical mythology is *LIMC* (1981–); a well-illustrated selection is given in Carpenter (1991). Thematic collections of essays (e.g., Fantham et al. 1994) and exhibition catalogs (e.g., Reeder 1995) remain the best sources for past and current scholarship.

NOTES

1. Athena Ergane models a horse in clay, probably in preparation for casting in bronze, on an oinochoe of c. 470 BCE, Berlin, Staatliche Museen F 2415 (*ARV²* 776.1). Pliny's list of women painters (*Natural History* 35.147–8) is unmatched by one of sculptors; he reports that the potter Butades' invention of terracotta relief was inspired by his unnamed daughter, but her contribution was drawing the outline of her lover's shadow (35.151). The literary evidence for women artists concerns only painters (Kampen 1975; Pomeroy 1977: 53–4). Women do not appear among sculptors' names attested in the literary or epigraphical record (Muller-Dufeu 2002: 1072–9). A damaged relief of the late fifth or early fourth century BCE from the Athenian agora (S 2495) shows Athena with five female figures, perhaps nymphs, involved in working stone, apparently for a building, not sculpture (Lawton 1995: 123–5). The scene on a red-figure kalpis (Leningrad Painter: *ARV²* 571.73) of a woman working in a pottery or metalworking atelier (Kehrberg 1982), much cited as evidence for female artisans, is apparently unique.
2. Such a perception is interesting in light of the influential nineteenth-century attribution of Greek exclusion and seclusion of women to the adoption in Ionia of Near Eastern practices (Katz 1995: 22–3).

13

Dress and Adornment in Archaic and Classical Greece

Mireille M. Lee

Classicists have traditionally dismissed dress and adornment as unworthy of serious study. Projecting modern notions of "fashion" into the past, many scholars viewed dress as a frivolous pursuit. Over the last two decades, influenced by developments in anthropology and sociology, classicists have recognized the important social functions of dress in antiquity (e.g., Llewellyn-Jones 2002; Cleland et al. 2005). In Archaic and Classical Greece, dress was essential to the construction of individual and group identities, in particular gender, age, status, and ethnicity. Because women were primarily responsible for the production of textiles in Greek society (Papadopoulou-Belmehdi 1994; Scheid and Svenbro 1996), dress was especially meaningful for the construction of femininity (Jenkins 1985; Darling 1998–9).

This essay outlines women's dress practices in the Archaic and Classical periods. Following a historiographic overview of the study of Greek dress, we will explore recent theoretical developments that have allowed for a new understanding of the material. The visual, archaeological, and textual evidence for dress will be considered, acknowledging the limitations inherent in each. Although most studies of Greek dress emphasize typologies of garments and accessories, we will consider dress practices broadly defined (to include grooming, for example) and the important social functions of dress at each stage of the female lifecycle. Finally, we will analyze the social meanings of undress, or nudity.

1 Approaches to the Study of Ancient Greek Dress

Most of what we think we know about ancient Greek dress has been inherited from scholarship dating to as early as the Renaissance (Lee 2003: 124–33). As ancient Greek and Roman texts were rediscovered, readers wondered about the appearance of garments named by ancient authors. Most early studies were simply lexica of terms, describing ancient garments relative to current styles of dress. As burgeoning numbers of ancient monuments were recovered, especially in the eighteenth and nineteenth centuries,

A Companion to Women in the Ancient World, First Edition. Edited by Sharon L. James and Sheila Dillon.
© 2012 John Wiley & Sons, Ltd. Published 2015 by John Wiley & Sons, Ltd.

attempts were made to identify the garments depicted in sculpture and vase painting with those mentioned in the texts. "The Learned Father" Bernard de Montfaucon (1721–2: suppl. III, 259) lamented the difficulty of reconciling the visual and textual evidence:

> There is no Part of Antiquities more curious and useful than that which treats of the Habits; and none also more obscure. We are equally at a loss to find out the Shape of a great many Habits mentioned by Greek and Latin Authors, and to discover by what names they called other Habits which Monuments shew us the Form of, without their name.

Subsequent scholars argued over the identification of various garments until the end of the nineteenth century, when the Austrian scholar Franz Studniczka established a basic typology in his *Beiträge zur Geschichte der altgriechischen Tracht* (1886). Although some have quibbled over details, Studniczka's scheme remains fundamental, and has profoundly influenced the way ancient Greek dress has traditionally been studied—namely, in terms of individual types of garments as opposed to dress practices more generally defined (e.g., Abrahams 1908; Johnson 1965; Cleland et al. 2007).

In the early twentieth century, Léon Heuzey (1922) and Margarete Bieber (1928, 1967) investigated the arrangement of ancient garments by draping live models and posing them like ancient statues. Their experiments demonstrated that ancient artists did not necessarily depict garments as they actually appeared, and may have invented details of ancient dress (Bieber 1977). Nevertheless, most assumed that the garments represented in sculpture and vase painting reflected actual dress styles, and that changes in the iconography reflected the vicissitudes of "fashion" (e.g., Boardman 1983: 31; Small 1991: 247). By the middle of the twentieth century, the drapery represented in sculpture and vase painting was studied primarily as a formal indicator of chronology and style, with little consideration of the social significance of dress.

Starting in the 1970s, archaeologists began to investigate the material evidence for textile production, providing important information for our understanding of the fibers, colors, and weaves of ancient garments (Good 2001). E. J. W. Barber's (1991, 1994) synthesis of the archaeological and linguistic evidence for the production of textiles demonstrates the essential role women played in the development of this technology, and the strong ideological associations between women and weaving in ancient Greek society. The proper Greek woman produced textiles, just as she produced children, for the benefit of her husband's oikos.

The meanings attached to dress in ancient Greek society first emerged from critical analysis of garments and textiles as literary tropes. For example, in Aeschylus' *Oresteia*, clothing functions as a metaphor for feminine agency, especially in the famous "carpet scene" (*Agamemnon* 906–74), in which Clytemnestra persuades Agamemnon to tread upon textiles in a prelude to his murder (Morrell 1996–7). Dress serves as an important means of non-verbal communication as early as Homer, as can be seen, for example, in the various disguises of Odysseus (Block 1985).

Recent developments in the interdisciplinary field of dress studies have provided new theoretical models for understanding the social functions of dress in antiquity (Eicher and Roach-Higgins 1992; Entwistle 2001). Instead of a garment-centered approach, dress theorists emphasize the need to understand dress as an embodied social practice. The body, supplements to the body (including garments, but also various accessories), and modifications to the body (both permanent and temporary) all function dynamically in the construction of individual identities, especially gender, status, and ethnicity. As in all cultures, individuals socialized within the ancient Greek "dress code" would have easily understood the social messages of dress. The challenge for modern scholars is to reconstruct the significance of such dress practices from the limited textual, visual, and archaeological evidence.

2   The Evidence for Ancient Greek Dress

No complete garments dating to the Archaic or Classical periods have been recovered archaeologically. A few fragments of textiles give important evidence for fibers and means of production, as well as colors produced by natural dyes (Barber 1991: 126–214; Barber 1999). The appearance of garments must be reconstructed from the visual evidence, namely sculpture and vase painting. Unfortunately, representations of garments are not wholly reliable: artists simplified (or invented) garments, or added details in paint (Brinkmann and Wünsche 2007) or with metal attachments that have not survived. It is also unclear to what degree the garments represented in art reflect those worn in daily life. It is quite likely that most of the garments depicted should be understood as "Sunday best" rather than everyday dress.

Archaeology can provide evidence for other details of dress, especially jewelry (Higgins 1980; Williams and Ogden 1994; Calinescu 1996) and dress fasteners such as pins (Jacobsthal 1956), which are frequent finds in women's graves. When they are found *in situ*, such articles give important evidence for where on the body they were worn. A bronze pin found on the chest was likely a dress fastener rather than a hair ornament, for example. Other funerary objects such as perfume bottles and containers for cosmetics give important evidence for body modification. But the archaeological evidence for dress can be difficult to interpret. For example, we cannot be confident that funerary articles reflect actual dress practices, though dedications of jewelry and dress pins in sanctuary contexts suggest that they held some significance for the living community (see also Shepherd, this volume, Chapter 16). Finally, the value of such objects on the antiquities market means that their provenance is often unknown, so that archaeologists are robbed of important evidence for dress practices in specific contexts.

The textual sources are essential to our understanding of the social meanings of Greek dress. Greek drama, in particular the comedies of Aristophanes, gives important evidence for the gendered connotations of various dress practices, such as the wearing of cloaks (Compton-Engle 2005) or the depilation of pubic and body hair (Bain 1982a, 1982b; Kilmer 1982). Conversely, the literary sources cannot always be taken at face value: ancient authors often had their own purposes for citing such details of dress. Inscriptions give important evidence for dress in ritual contexts, in the form of sartorial regulations (Mills 1984; Culham 1986; Gawlinski 2008), as well as inventories of garment dedications (Linders 1972; Cleland 2005). As with the literary evidence, it is often difficult to reconcile the names of garments listed in the epigraphic sources with the visual and archaeological evidence.

A final problem that must be acknowledged is that much of the evidence for ancient Greek dress reflects the practices and interests of the elite, who controlled the production of the artistic, archaeological, and textual materials on which we base our interpretations. The evidence for non-elite dress practices is either absent or filtered through an elite lens, which reflects stereotypes rather than actual practices. Despite such limitations, it is possible to reconstruct a wide range of women's dress practices in Archaic and Classical

Greece. While in most cases we cannot associate particular behaviors with specific individuals, the patterns of women's dress practices comprise a dress code that both reflected and constructed the feminine ideal. In the sections that follow, we will consider the dynamic relationship between the female body and various types of garments, accessories, and body modifications in order to reveal Greek constructions of feminine gender.

3   Types of Garments

Although dozens of different garments are named in the textual sources, the most common women's types seem to have been the peplos, the chiton, and the himation. The peplos is generally considered to have been an indigenous garment worn by the earliest Greek peoples (Lee 2003, 2005). It is the primary garment worn by female characters in Homer, and is consistently represented in Greek art of the eighth and seventh centuries BCE. Both the literary and the visual sources suggest that it was made of wool, and was often decorated with woven geometric patterns, animals, and human figures. Like most other Greek garments, the peplos was neither cut nor sewn, but simply draped around the body and fastened at the shoulders with pins (Figure 13.1a). Representations of the peplos in early Greek art show it as a heavy, enveloping garment that obscured the contours of the female body under thick layers of wool. Hundreds of dress pins (*peronai*) have been recovered archaeologically from women's graves and from sanctuaries, where they were dedicated as votives (Jacobsthal 1956). Interestingly, these dress fasteners generally disappear from the archaeological record around the same time a new garment appears in the visual sources.

The artistic and archaeological evidence both suggest that the chiton replaced the peplos as the primary women's garment at the end of the seventh century BCE (Ridgway 1984a; Harrison 1991). Originally imported from the East, the chiton was first adopted by men (van Wees 1998), who subsequently rejected it when its use by women became widespread. A voluminous garment of fine linen, the chiton carried with it connotations of luxury and high status (Geddes 1987: 311). It was buttoned or pinned at intervals along the edges of the fabric to create billowing sleeves (Figure 13.1b). Representations of the chiton in sculpture and vase painting often emphasize the fine quality of the fabric, revealing the form of the female body underneath (see also Dillon, this volume, Case Study III).

The himation was a type of overgarment similar to a large shawl (Figure 13.1c). In general, it is depicted as being made of a heavier fabric such as wool, which would have provided warmth as well as a means of concealment for the wearer. As a simple rectangle of cloth that was neither pinned nor sewn, the himation could be arranged in a variety of ways to suit the needs of the wearer in different social contexts. A primary function of the himation seems to have been as a veil: a proper woman would draw her himation over her head as a means of shielding herself from the male gaze (Llewellyn-Jones 2003: 54–6, 189–214). Interestingly, men also wore the himation, though by the fifth century they generally dispensed with the chiton underneath (Geddes 1987: 323–31; van Wees 1998). For both genders, proper draping of the himation indicated elite status.

We should imagine that garments would have communicated a great deal about the social identity of the wearer. Garments are highly visible, and easily imbued with social messages by means of their color and decoration (Guralnick 2008) as well as their arrangement on the body. As discussed above, women were primarily responsible for

Figure 13.1 Diagram of the main types of Greek garments: (a) peplos, (b) chiton, (c) chiton with himation. Drawing by Glynnis Fawkes.

the production of textiles in Archaic and Classical Greece, and it is quite likely that particular colors and decorative motifs were imbued with meaning within local weaving traditions, as was the case for traditional Greek dress in the modern period (Barber 1991: 297–8). Because garments both envelop and reveal the body, they comprise an important social layer between the dressed individual and her community. For example, the kore Phrasikleia (Figure 13.2), identified by her inscription as an unwed maiden, wears a red-sleeved chiton adorned with rosettes and medallions, which has been interpreted as a bridal dress (Stieber 2004: 169). The garment clings softly to her body, emphasizing her undeveloped breasts. The belt, which certainly carried bridal connotations (see below), is highly visible. Other accessories, including the elaborate shoes and jewelry (crown, earrings, necklace, and bracelets), identify her as the daughter of an elite family, and specifically a bride.

4 Accessories

Although the articles we generally classify as "accessories" were not as visible as garments, they were nevertheless important indicators of social identities, especially gender and status. As mentioned above, the peplos, and sometimes also the woman's chiton, was

Figure 13.2   Statue that stood atop the grave of Phrasikleia; Parian marble statue made by Aristion of Chios, c. 550–540 BCE. Found at Merenda (ancient Myrrhinous), Attica. Photo: Vanni/Art Resource, NY.

fastened with pins or buttons, which were often finely wrought of bronze, silver, or gold, even ivory and bone (Jacobsthal 1956). Jewelry is worn almost exclusively by women in Greek art, as seen on Phrasikleia (Figure 13.2), and the many extant rings, earrings, necklaces, and bracelets demonstrate those articles' fine materials and workmanship (Higgins 1980; Williams and Ogden 1994; Calinescu 1996). Certainly such luxury items reflected the wealth of the wearer (or rather, the wealth of her oikos), but they often communicated other ideas as well. The popular pomegranate motif, as seen on Phra-sikleia's necklace, carried notions of fertility, and special carved stones set in rings or strung on cords served as magical amulets to protect the wearer from the "evil eye" (Bonner 1950).

More visible were articles worn on the head, such as diadems and wreaths, as well as various head wraps and hair nets (Jenkins and Williams 1985). Women bound up their long hair with fillets, a *sakkos* (a type of snood), or a *mitra* (a kind of turban). Because a woman's hair was ideologically associated with her sexuality, proper containment of the hair demonstrated submission to social conventions surrounding sex (Myerowitz Levine 1995; such submission was not accomplished exclusively through marriage, as *hetairai* are also depicted wearing such headgear).

Footwear may be less visible than other articles of dress, but it was no less significant, especially in terms of gender and sexuality (Blundell 2006). The erotics of the feet, a common motif in Greek literature, carried over into footwear, which is frequently represented in Greek art. Brides (like Phrasikleia) fasten sandals on their feet as part of wedding preparations; but *hetairai*, too, put on sandals in anticipation of their clients.

Hetairai also wear boots, which are conspicuously removed in the context of the symposium. Footwear was also a luxury import, to judge from the numerous references to Persian slippers in Greek literature.

Hand-held accessories were important indicators of gender and status. Interestingly, although men are frequently represented in Greek art holding various external symbols of their power and status, including money bags and walking sticks, women are more likely to hold an article of jewelry, or, like Phrasikleia, to grasp a garment in one hand, suggesting that their identity stems primarily from their personal adornment. This idea is underscored by the fact that women are frequently represented gazing at their reflections in mirrors, whereas men never are (Frontisi-Ducroux and Vernant 1997). Actual mirrors made of polished bronze are frequent finds in women's graves. Several especially elaborate examples display a finely dressed figurine on the handle, as if to provide a model for the woman performing her toilette.

5   Body Modification

Although permanent modifications to the body such as tattooing were considered barbaric, temporary body modification was common, and reflected Greek constructions of gender and status (Lee 2009). Whereas the masculine ideal was a muscled physique and tanned skin acquired through exercise out of doors, women's bodies were supposed to be pale and soft as a result of leisure time spent indoors. While men washed following exercise in the public context of the gymnasion or palaestra, women generally bathed in private, domestic spaces (see also Trümper, this volume, Chapter 21). Men had their hair cut and beards maintained in barber shops located in the city center, while women attended to their own hair at home, perhaps assisted by a maid. Although both men and women engaged in similar practices of body modification, the repeated performance of which reflected elite status, they did so in different contexts: public for men; private for women.

The evidence for perfumes is complex, but it is clear that they were used by both sexes, with different scents appropriate for men and women (Lee 2009: 170–2). Certainly the expense of perfume meant that it always had luxurious connotations. Perhaps its use was restricted to special occasions such as the symposion, as described by several ancient authors. The evidence for cosmetics is likewise complicated, even contradictory (Lee 2009: 169–70). According to several ancient authors, cosmetics were employed by women with intent to deceive. The most explicit statement against women's use of cosmetics is Xenophon's *Oeconomicus*, in which Ischomachus chastises his young wife for making up her face "with a great deal of white face powder so that she might appear paler than she was, and with plenty of rouge so that she might seem to have a more rosy complexion than she truly had" (10.2; transl. Pomeroy 1994). Conversely, the archaeological evidence for women's use of cosmetics is widespread. Cosmetics boxes called pyxides are frequent finds in women's graves; some have been recovered with their contents intact, confirming the use of white lead carbonate as powder and red alkanet as rouge (Shear 1936). Interestingly, a recent rereading of Xenophon suggests that men also employed powdered pigments in order to darken the tanned effect on their bodies (Hannah 2004).

If men and women shared various means of body modification, it is certainly the case that women were valued for their beauty in a way that men were not. As mentioned above, women are repeatedly shown in both vase painting and relief sculpture gazing at their own reflections in mirrors. The self-referential nature of such images underscores the value of women's beauty as an end to itself.

6   Dress and the Female Lifecycle

Although dress was significant for both genders in Archaic and Classical Greece, it was especially meaningful for women and girls throughout their lives. Certainly the birth of a girl was generally less desirable than that of a boy, but infant girls are celebrated in sculpture and vase painting, albeit with less frequency than infant boys (Neils and Oakley 2003). While baby boys are depicted without garments, in order to display their genitals, baby girls are invariably shown swaddled or wearing miniature versions of women's garments. This fundamental association between the female body and dress is played out at various stages of a girl's development into adulthood.

Representations of girls in Greek art change according to period and medium. In early Archaic sculpture and vase painting, children of both sexes are depicted like miniature adults. By the Classical period, girls are represented with physiognomy and dress to match their age. Younger girls are generally shown with convex bellies and flat breasts, their too-large garments often dragging on the ground, or open to reveal the undeveloped body underneath. Parthenoi, unmarried girls who had achieved menarche, are indicated by their budding breasts and concealing garments (namely, peploi), visibly belted at the waist to reflect their submission to the strictures of society.

Rituals of maturation marked important transitions in the female lifecycle; invariably, such rituals involved special articles of dress. Aristophanes' *Lysistrata* includes the following account of religious roles undertaken by elite girls in Classical Athens:

> As soon as I turned seven I was an Arrephoros
> Then when I was ten I was a Grinder for the Foundress;[1]
> And shedding my saffron robe I was a Bear at the Brauronia
> And once, when I was a fair girl, I carried the Basket
> Wearing a necklace of dried figs. (641–7)

The *arrephoroi* were girls between the ages of seven and eleven who were chosen from among the Athenian elite to live on the Acropolis for one year, helping to weave the sacred peplos dedicated to Athena at the Panathenaia. Between the ages of seven and eleven, girls "acted the she-bear" in the Arkteia, a festival to Artemis celebrated at the rural sanctuary at Brauron. A series of small vases called krateriskoi depicting young girls running naked or wearing special yellow dresses may represent participants in the ritual (Sourvinou-Inwood 1988; see also Stehle, this volume, Chapter 14). Perhaps the most important role played by an Athenian parthenos was as a *kanephoros*, or basket-bearer, in the Panathenaic procession. In addition to the necklace of dried figs described by Aristophanes, *kanephoroi* are depicted wearing special festival mantles pinned over their belted peploi, as seen in the east (Ionic) frieze of the Parthenon (Roccos 1995).

The belt, or *zonē*, was imbued with great significance, and played an important role in the transition from girl to adult (Sabetai 1997: 321–8). As we have seen, Phrasikleia's belt is highly visible, and seems to have been an important element of her dress and therefore her identity. We know that girls ready for marriage dedicated their *zonai* to Artemis.

The loosening of the *zone* on her wedding night symbolized the deflowering of the parthenos. Finally, women in childbirth dedicated their *zonai* to Artemis in order to secure her protection during this dangerous liminal period.

Dress was essential to the ancient Greek wedding at every stage. Many red-figure vases of the Classical period depict the preparations of the bride, including the nuptial bath (see further discussion in "Undress," below) and adornment by female attendants and Eros, the god of sexual desire. The bride is often depicted wearing a diaphanous garment that delineates the contours of her body underneath, emphasizing her sexual desirability as well as her fertility. Black-figure vases of the Archaic period, in contrast, often show the bride dressed in elaborately decorated garments, emphasizing the wealth of her family (and, by extension, her desirability as a marriage partner). The imagery on these early vases generally focuses on the actual transfer of the bride from her father's oikos to that of her new husband. Invariably, the bride performs a special gesture known as the *anakalypsis*, in which she grasps the edge of the mantle veiling her head. A recent reanalysis of the evidence for the *anakalypsis* has demonstrated that the Greek wedding involved multiple veilings and unveilings, in anticipation of the consummation of the marriage (Llewellyn-Jones 2003: 98–110).

A Greek woman did not become a true adult woman, or *gynē*, until she had borne a child, preferably a boy. Interestingly, despite the importance of childbearing, images of pregnant or breastfeeding women are exceedingly rare in Greek art. The scant evidence suggests that special maternity dress was unnecessary, given the draped arrangement of regular Greek garments (Lee forthcoming). Conversely, there is strong evidence that dress played an important role in pregnancy and childbirth. Various literary and epigraphic sources describe the practice of dedicating garments to Artemis following childbirth, and inscribed inventories from the sanctuary at Brauron confirm the social and monetary value of such dedications (Linders 1972; Cleland 2005). A remarkable votive stele from a sanctuary to Artemis at Echinos dating from the fourth century BCE (Figure 13.3) has been interpreted as representing a new mother, completely enveloped in her garment, in a scene of ritual purification following the birth of her daughter, who is held by a female attendant

Figure 13.3 Marble votive relief to Artemis, found at Echinos in Thessaly, c. 300 BCE. Lamia Archaeological Museum, inv. AE 1041. Drawing by Glynnis Fawkes.

(Morizot 2004). Above the figures, various types of garments (including shoes!) are displayed as if hanging from a clothesline, a visual reminder of women's labor—in textile production and in childbirth—as well as their piety.

Dress was likewise important in death, both for the deceased and for the bereaved. Representations of the prothesis, or laying out of the dead, on painted vases and votive plaques show the deceased laid out on a bier covered with a shroud and sometimes wearing a crown or wreath. Actual examples of gold funerary wreaths have been recovered archaeologically, along with various other metal accessories such as jewelry and dress fasteners (Higgins 1980; Williams and Ogden 1994; Calinescu 1996). It seems likely that the deceased would have been dressed for burial in her finest garments and accessories, as a gesture of respect, but also to create an impressive display for those attending the funeral. The potential for ostentatious display at funerals is perhaps reflected in the sumptuary laws attributed to Solon (Plutarch, *Solon*, 21.4) restricting the number of garments that could be worn by female mourners. The visual evidence suggests no such extravagance, but emphasizes the disheveled hair and lacerations to the face that accompanied women's lamentation. Images on Classical white-ground lekythoi show female and male visitors to tombs wearing garments of red, yellow, blue, and black, giving us important evidence for the colors of ancient textiles.

7   Undress

Given the profound relationship between women and dress, feminine undress is likewise significant. Until recently, scholars have emphasized the distinction between nakedness and nudity famously formulated by Kenneth Clark (1956: 3):

> To be naked is to be deprived of our clothes, and the word implies some of the embarrassment most of us feel in that condition. The word "nude," on the other hand, carries, in educated usage, no uncomfortable overtone. The vague image it projects into the mind is not of a huddled and defenseless body, but of a balanced, prosperous, and confident body: the body re-formed.

For Clark and his followers (e.g., Salomon 1997), masculine nudity in Greek art and life carried positive connotations of heroism or idealism, whereas feminine nakedness conveyed the opposite: victimization or the anti-ideal. Certainly, female victims of sexual violence in Greek art are generally represented with their garments rent by their attackers (Cohen 1993, 1997), as, for example, the Lapith women in the west pediment of the temple of Zeus at Olympia (Figure 13.4). Likewise, *hetairai* are generally depicted undressed in vase painting: as non-ideal figures, they do not conform to the same dress code as proper women (Lewis 2002: 98–129). Conversely, brides are represented undressed in the context of the preparations for the wedding, especially the bridal bath (Sabetai 1997). Should such figures be identified as naked or nude?

Clark's false dichotomy has obscured analysis of the social meanings of women's undress, which are specific to social context and role (Barcan 2004). As mentioned above, it has been suggested that girls ran undressed in the Arkteia celebrated at Brauron. Undress is a frequent component of coming-of-age rituals, in which visual confirmation of physical maturity was required (Bonfante 1989c). The undress of a bride preparing for her wedding similarly emphasizes her physical readiness for marriage, the sexual desirability of her body

Figure 13.4 Lapith woman and centaur, west pediment, temple of Zeus at Olympia. Photo: D-DAI-ATH Olympia 3362, Hermann Wagner.

for her husband, and her potential fertility. Likewise, *hetairai* are represented without garments to indicate their role as sex-workers; they are valued for the pleasure they give to the male viewers, and users, of their bodies.

The sexual connotations of the undressed female body are clearly implicated in the famous Knidian Aphrodite, ascribed to the fourth-century sculptor Praxiteles (see Figure 12.4). Famous in antiquity (especially among Roman writers) for the torturous longing the statue inspired in her (male) viewers, the Aphrodite of Knidos is generally acknowledged as the first monumental sculpture of its type, replicated for centuries for the pleasure of the male gaze (Havelock 1995). Although Salomon (1997) has emphasized the shame and humiliation demonstrated by this "naked" female statue, such a reading does not acknowledge the divine sexual powers of the goddess Aphrodite. The key to understanding the significance of her undress is, in fact, the garment she holds in her hand. Unlike the Lapith women in the temple of Zeus (Figure 13.4), whose garments are ripped away by their attackers, the Knidian Aphrodite manipulates her own garment; she is in control of the viewing and obscuring of her body, and, therefore, the desire of her onlookers. Although she is a divinity, not a mortal, the message is one of feminine agency, not humiliation and shame.

Our conception of feminine dress in Archaic and Classical Greece has changed dramatically in recent years. Rather than typologies of garments or formal analysis of drapery styles, scholars now emphasize the social functions of dress and the lived experience of dressed individuals. By resituating our study of dress with the body, we can understand the important messages communicated by dress, even though the garments, and their wearers, no longer survive.

RECOMMENDED FURTHER READING

Although scholarship on Greek dress has burgeoned in recent years, a good general monograph in English is still woefully lacking. Interested readers must make do with short entries in Cleland et al. (2007), or *Brill's New Pauly*. Though outdated, Abrahams (1908, reprinted 1965) contains much useful information. Some recent international conferences have resulted in edited volumes, such as Cleland et al. (2005) and Llewellyn-Jones (2002). Veiling is extensively treated in Llewellyn-Jones (2003). For dress and constructions of femininity see also Darling (1998–9) and Jenkins (1985). Textiles have been the subject of several important studies: for techniques of production see Barber (1991); for social aspects see Barber (1994); for the ideology of textiles and weaving see Scheid and Svenbro (1996). Bonfante (1989c) remains the fundamental study of nudity in ancient Greece.

NOTE

1.   Probably a reference to the grinding of grain for ritual cakes dedicated to Demeter at Eleusis.

14

Women and Religion in Greece

Eva Stehle

Religious activity was the only area of civic life in which women had public roles in ancient Greece, and it created one of their main opportunities to associate with other women in undertaking collective projects apart from men. As important as women's religious practice therefore is to the study of ancient women, it is also difficult, partly because women's activities were relatively ignored by classical authors when not the object of fantasy, but also because appropriate methodologies for studying their rituals have not been sufficiently explored or debated. Since methodology is one of the concerns of this *Companion*, I focus on presenting some different approaches to each of two important women's rituals, the Thesmophoria and the Brauronia, and their implications for our view of women. I include information about other rituals similar to these and end with a brief sketch of individual women's participation in male-dominated rituals.

First, it is helpful to get an overview of some of the methodologies used to study women's ritual. Functionalism is still popular in classicists' work. For functionalists ritual is a mystified projection of the social system that naturalizes social categories and can move groups from one category to another; for example, from child to adult. By these means, ritual not only articulates the social order but also creates a sense of unity among the members of the society. There are numerous variants of functionalism, but for all of them the "meaning" of ritual inheres in its social effects and/or expression of the social order, while the participants' actions and goals in performing the ritual are only a vehicle for the real function. However, many anthropologists (including feminist anthropologists; see Geller and Stockett 2006) have moved toward questions of agency and formation of identity; that is, taking the social system as a contested and polymorphous entity and investigating how groups or individuals are able to create openings for their own interests in, for example, ritual. For these scholars, "meaning" inheres in the interplay between ideology and agency. Yet another trend in anthropology and performance studies focuses on the performing body in ritual as active and communicative, the locus of a degree of agency that exceeds the ability of ideology to define the performer. Ritual therefore implicitly enables alternative constructions of worth and power. For these

A Companion to Women in the Ancient World, First Edition. Edited by Sharon L. James and Sheila Dillon.

scholars, "meaning" inheres in the performers' activity as they experience and interpret it. These three approaches generate very different descriptions of the goals, meanings, and effects of women's rituals. As illustration we can look at three different interpretations of the Thesmophoria.

1   The Thesmophoria

The Thesmophoria at Athens, the best-attested instantiation of a widespread Greek women's ritual, was celebrated in the fall, shortly before plowing and sowing of winter wheat took place. All citizen wives in good standing were eligible to participate. (Whether concubines could is less clear.) A priestess oversaw it, and an inscription (IG II^2 1184) from the deme Cholargos, dated to 334/333 BCE, refers to two *archousai* ("female magistrates") who are to give her provisions. The ritual lasted three days, of which the first was called Anodos ("way up"), the second Nesteia ("fasting"), and the last Kalligeneia ("beautiful birth"). Women gathered at local Demeter sanctuaries and spent the three days there with huts for shelter, two women to a hut.

What the women did on the first day is unknown; plausibly they set up the huts. On the second day they fasted, sitting on the ground (or on mats made of branches of the *agnus castus* tree, whose leaves were thought to suppress sexual desire in men if steeped in a tea and which late authors identify as having anaphrodisiac properties even for women sitting on them). They then broke out in *aischrologia* ("speaking shameful things"), a form of mocking and sexually transgressive speech. The evidence for the names of the days, the huts, and the women's fasting comes from Aristophanes' comedy *Women at the Thesmophoria* and its scholia (marginal notes in the manuscripts). That the women practiced *aischrologia* is first stated by Pseudo-Apollodorus (1.5.1), but there are earlier hints of it. For one, the *Homeric Hymn to Demeter* (197–205) depicts Demeter, in the company of women, smiling and breaking her fast after a woman named Iambe, whose name derives from a term for mocking speech, begins to mock and joke. This section of the *Hymn* has been persuasively taken to reflect the Thesmophoria (Clinton 1992: 28–37) even though the *Hymn* as a whole is about the founding of the Eleusinian Mysteries. For another, Aristophanes' play depicts a male intruder out-mocking the assembled women, a scene that is even funnier if he is outdoing the women at their own practice.

The only activity mentioned by a classical source that can plausibly be assigned to the third day is a banquet, the food for which was provided by the husband of one of the women (Isaios 3.80). There is, however, a scholion in one manuscript of Lucian's *Dialogues of the Courtesans* (at 2.1) that asserts that women at the Thesmophoria brought up the remains of rotten piglets from underground pits, also bailing up *plasmata* ("figurines"?); they later took the figurines back down and threw piglets down into the pits (for the next year's bailing). The piglet remains are said to have been piled on altars, from which farmers could take some to mix with their seed grain to ensure a good harvest. There are difficulties in understanding the scholion; among other things, it switches at one point to describing a different ritual then goes back to the Thesmophoria without marking the latter transition. Because of the confusion, some scholars think that the Thesmophoria involved throwing pine branches and cakes in the shape of snakes and male genitals into the pits along with the piglets; I do not. The larger question is whether to accept this evidence as valid for the Athenian Thesmophoria in the Classical period. There are arguments for doing so, including that piglets were such a common offering to Demeter that one would expect them to be included in the Thesmophoria at Athens. Certainty is out of reach, but all three of the scholars whose interpretations I summarize (and indeed most scholars) accept the scholion's account as describing the Athenian Thesmophoria. The bailing, taking figurines up and down, and throwing piglets in would then plausibly occupy the third day along with the feast.

Robert Parker (2005: 270–83) chooses a functionalist analysis as providing the best account of the meaning of the ritual. He lists three "propositions," or interpretations of the festival (275–6): (1) that it encouraged the fertility of the fields; (2) that it encouraged the fertility of women; and (3) that it defined the participants' status as citizen women. The first is attested in Greek literature as the goal of the ritual. For the second proposition Parker relies mainly on the name of the third day, Kalligeneia ("beautiful birth")—although the epithet, when used in connection with Demeter, can refer to agricultural growth (Cole 1994: 202). The third proposition has no direct ancient support, as Parker notes, but he argues that the self-assertion that the women display in Aristophanes' comedy is a symptom of their status as the wives of citizens.

Parker then comments (276):

> If we attempt to rank these propositions, a paradox emerges. The first proposition has the strongest support in "native" testimony, but is the weakest in explaining the form that the festival actually takes: a handful of women could have conducted the jiggery-pokery with piglets and penis cakes, while the rest remained at home. Proposition two is needed to explain why all the Athenian wives attended, and proposition three to explain why they alone did so.

That is, the essence of the festival is its sorting of women by social role, allowing citizen wives to distinguish themselves from other women while reinforcing their acceptance of their function: giving birth to legitimate children. The expressed intention to foster the crops, in Parker's view, does not tell us anything significant about the ritual, although he does remark that all three of his propositions should be allowed to coexist as explanations, since the bailing cannot be explained as expressing status (276). For Parker the meaning inheres in the messages about social relations created by the status of the attendees and exists at the level of the society as a whole, not in the minds or the activities of the actors.

Barbara Goff also investigates ritual as a manifestation of the social system but focuses on ideology as a pervasive system underpinning it, one that naturalizes the power structure (2004: 4): "Like any other social practice, ritual is an ideologically charged activity, and as such one of its goals in ancient Greece was to produce women who performed successfully within a male-dominated and often explicitly misogynist community." In bringing in ideology she offers a more complex functionalist model than Parker's, one that draws on Anthony Giddens' view that ideology incorporates alternatives to the hegemonic power structure in order to secure the cooperation of subordinated groups. Goff summarizes Giddens on the relationship between ideology and individual agency as showing "that the constraints in social life are actively reproduced by subjects engaging in their own daily routine, and that agency and constraint are thus produced and reproduced in the same gestures" (12). She therefore looks at the dialectic between agency and ideological shaping of identity, in which oppression and creativity may be at work simultaneously (17).

Goff discusses the Thesmophoria from two perspectives: first the way it shapes women's expression of their individual sexual identities and second its relationship as an institution to the city. In the first discussion (125–38) she introduces the Thesmophoria with the comment that "at Athens, the Thesmophoria makes a good claim to be the prime site in which are worked out the contradictory imperatives of female identity." One aspect of the contradictory imperatives is the idea of the "chaste wife"; women enact abstention from sex by sitting on anaphrodisiac mats, while at the same time they engage in "dirty talk" (*aischrologia*). This combination made them agents (speakers) while teaching them management of desire. At the same time speaking about the body identified them with their bodies as their assigned role. However, if *aischrologia* included passing on knowledge about techniques, such as plants with pharmacological powers, for controlling their fertility, then it served women's agency, though without constituting resistance to imposed gender identities.

The myth of Demeter and Persephone stresses the mother–daughter relationship and acknowledges women's power, offering them (132–3) compensation for "the denial of their significance in any other sphere." The "imaginary solution" (133) of Persephone's return was a model for the women's progress from a potentially antisocial condition to the embrace of Kalligeneia, just as it reconciles Demeter to partial loss and renews her commitment to making the earth fertile. Through the myth, the Thesmophoria also allowed women to recapture their earlier identity as virgin daughters and heal the break in their lives caused by marriage. Conversely, its training in proper behavior was a social technique for containing female violence, such as is portrayed in stories of men's invading the women's ritual and suffering at their hands as a consequence (136–7). In sum, "the Thesmophoria signifies at many levels, constructing female identity not only out of the various contradictions produced by patriarchal gender ideology but also out of versions of specifically feminine experience" (135).

In her second discussion (205–11), Goff looks at the Thesmophoria as an imitation of and alternative to the male politically constituted version of the city. Although in some ways—for example, the presence of female magistrates—the Thesmophoria resembled a polity, Demeter sanctuaries were usually located away from civic centers, and at Athens state business was halted during Nesteia. The Thesmophoria was described by Plutarch and other late authors as enacting a "primitive" way of life, which places it in the era before civilization. On balance, therefore, the Thesmophoria enacted women's disqualification from political participation. Meaning for Goff is located in ideological coercion as women perceived it, mitigated by some space for agency.

In Stehle (2007, forthcoming), I emphasize the engagement of the body in ritual and draw on techniques of performance analysis in both anthropology and theater studies (Bell 1998; Shepherd 2006) to analyze the Thesmophoria as women's performance and production of meaning for themselves. From this perspective it is significant that the Thesmophoria, unlike typical sacrificial ritual, was mimetic. By building huts the women set up an all-female community. Then they adopted postures of mourning when they sat on the ground, fasting. By custom, other women lamented together with a bereaved woman, so at the Thesmophoria women constituted themselves as a community of mourners together with Demeter, who was the audience for their action. Moreover, since performers' actions project their ideal audience in a certain location and relationship to themselves, the women constructed Demeter as present among them in the role of a mourner. At the same time, they would bodily pick up and amplify one another's emotional states by a process of "reverberation" (an important phenomenon in theater analysis: Shepherd 2006). The stronger the women's collective investment in sharing Demeter's state, the more powerfully they would feel her through their bodies as "present."

From their state of mourning the women shifted to speaking *aischrologia*. That meant switching from a physical state of emptiness and grief to an energetic ex-pression (a "pushing out") of sexual humor in engagement with one another and required a drastic change of energy and orientation. However it happened (perhaps the priestess initiated it, or perhaps it emerged spontaneously among them), shifting to *aischrologia* was emotional labor. In stimulating each other to open up, they could feel Demeter's mood alter as well. Thus, they enacted a successful rousing of Demeter to initiate a new agricultural cycle. The sexual character of *aischrologia* was an element in the transforma-tion from closed to opened bodies and suggested a human sexual model for agricultural fertility, but a wholly female one, with *aischrologia* as the fertilizing substance that provoked new growth. This stage must have ended with the women breaking their fast, perhaps by drinking a *kykeon*, a mixture of coarse-ground barley, water, and herbs, as Demeter does in the *Hymn to Demeter*. The women's own fertility was not at issue.

The bailing on the third day enacted the same dynamic but now in terms of the earth instead of female bodies. In analogy with drawing *aischrologia* out of depleted bodies, women went down into pits and brought up the fertilizing piglet remains and figurines (?). Bringing up figurines (or the fertilizer itself) plausibly served as a symbolic restoration of Persephone to Demeter and completed the preparation for sowing the seed. Finally, piglets were thrown down, by analogy with breaking the fast, to rot in preparation for next year's bailing.

On this analysis the women intervened as agents in the cosmic order and confirmed their collective power while experiencing an intimate encounter with a goddess. They constructed the female body as potent without male input. Meaning from this perspective is located in women's bodily experience of the ritual as they intervened in the cosmos and interpreted the results, making the Thesmophoria a place where women could revise Hesiodic ideology.

In the preceding discussion I have left aside disagreements about the use of evidence, even though these are not insignificant. All three interpreters are working with the same outline, so the differences in perspective are generated by the different interpretive strategies adopted. Each analysis in order makes a greater effort to privilege women's experience of enacting the ritual. In Parker's account, since meaning lies in women's marking of their status, he treats the specific actions as irrelevant to it. He does not say (though he perhaps implies) that confirming their status and encouraging their fertility were women's own goals in participating, and he does not ask how women perceived the actions. Goff treats the women as aware of the contradictions and constraints in their lives and of ritual's effect of reinforcing them. In her analysis, women enacted their submission to patriarchal marriage, despite their potential anger, and were forced to identify themselves with their bodies even in their speaking. But, because ideology must attribute some agency to subordinated groups in ways that do not counter the hegemonic system (since sheer coercion does not ultimately work), the ritual did give women some room to assert always-already-coopted identities, trade knowledge about controlling their bodies, and reidentify with earlier premarital selves. For Goff, as for Parker, the ritual's function was to impose social norms, but Goff sees conflict and resentment as endemic to the process, which could not foreclose on resistant, even if contained, assertions of agency. In Stehle's analysis the ritual was meaningful for women as a means of interaction with a divinity and intervention in the cosmos. Their agency was thus confirmed, independent of men's view of it, and they could potentially articulate a competing ideology.

Each of these approaches implies a critique of the other two. From Parker's perspective both Goff and Stehle attribute to women a non-acceptance of their subordinate role for which we have little evidence—only Sappho's expressions of resistance, and her elusive poetry must itself be interpreted. From Goff's perspective Stehle's analysis ignores the social subordination of women and overvalues their experience of a (delusory) power, which is one of ritual's techniques for reconciling subordinated groups to their lack of power. From Stehle's perspective, Goff attributes too pervasive a power to a single ideological formation and underestimates women's power to create meaning for themselves through bodily action. In discussing the effects of repetition (123–5), Goff does suggest that the Thesmophoria's insistent reinforcing of ideological demands could lead women to recognize its coercive nature and develop resistant interpretations. Here she envisions the possibility that historical women did employ ritual to "make and remake culture." At the same time Stehle's analysis does not dispute the physical and emotional constraints under which women lived their lives. It should be noted, however, that Parker and Goff must accept the unsupported (as Parker acknowledges) view that the Thesmophoria was primarily about women's own fertility in order to sustain their analyses. In sum, one's choice of analytic strategy depends on what aspect of a complex event one wants to explore and what view one has of individual lives in relation to groups and to society.

The Thesmophoria is the best-attested example of adult women's segregated rituals for Demeter, but there were others. An inscription from a sanctuary of Demeter in the Piraeus (*LSCG* 36 = *IG* II^2 1177) forbids anyone to make use of the sanctuary without the priestess, except when the Thesmophoria, Plerosia, Kalamaia, and Skira occur and on any other day the women gather there according to ancestral custom. About the Skira we are told only that women practiced *aischrologia*, and about the Plerosia and Kalamaia we know essentially nothing. At another Attic festival, the Haloa, magistrates laid out a feast for the women in the sanctuary then departed (schol. Lucian, *dial. meretr.* 7.4). This ritual too seems to have included *aischrologia*, if that is what the scholiast's shocked statement that the priestess whispered recommendations of adultery into the ears of the women reflects.

It is possible that women at Athens gathered to celebrate Dionysus also, although the evidence is tenuous. Several series of Attic vases, the so-called Lenaia vases, show women alone celebrating in front of a mask of Dionysus on a pole. The ritual may be artists' fantasy; if it did reflect, however imaginatively, a civic rite, we do not know what it was. Women gathered informally for Bacchic rites and for celebrations of Pan, of Aphrodite at Kolias, and of Genetyllis (a goddess associated with Aphrodite), or so Lysistrata remarks in deploring women's failure to appear with equal alacrity to her summons (*Lysistrata* 1–2). In all, women seem to have had numerous occasions for gathering together to enjoy ritual performances.

2 The Brauronia

My second example of a women's ritual whose interpretation is disputed is the so-called Arkteia ("Bear-ritual"; this name occurs only in Hesychius) performed by girls before puberty at the Brauronia, a festival of Artemis celebrated at Brauron on the east coast of Attica. I chose it in part because it is the best example we have of an Attic ritual for girls or young women and illustrates a different kind of ritual activity, but also because it presents an analysis with a different set of problems. The problems arise in the first instance because the scattered pieces of evidence offer too few points of contact to allow us even to agree on a basic set of actions. In this case, producing any account of the ritual at all depends on a prior decision about what kind of ritual it was.

The main evidence is as follows. In Aristophanes' *Lysistrata* (642–6) the old women of the chorus claim that they can appropriately advise the city, since it raised them in luxuriance:

> When I turned seven years old straight away I served as an arrhephoros, then I was a grain-grinder at ten for the Leader-Goddess, and then wearing [or "and letting flow down"] my saffron robe I was a Bear at the Brauronia, and I served as a basket-bearer once when I was a beautiful young woman wearing a necklace of figs.

There is a problem with the text in lines 644–5, which can be fixed by reading either "and then wearing" or "and letting pour down." Textual considerations slightly favor the first, but one's choice of reading will inevitably be decided by interpretation of the ritual.

Several scholia comment on the line about being a Bear. One says,

> When females used to perform the secret rite, they imitated a bear. Those playing the bear for the goddess used to don a saffron robe and together perform the sacrifice for Artemis of Brauron and Artemis of Mounichia, young women who were selected [or "were called <Bears>"] and neither older than ten nor younger than five. And the girls also performed the sacrifice, placating the goddess, since the Athenians had once encountered a famine after they had killed a tame bear to the displeasure[?] of the goddess. (Translation from Faraone 2003: 51–2)

Mounichia was the site of another Artemis sanctuary.

Another scholion gives an origin-story for the ritual:

> A bear was given to Artemis' temple and it was tamed. Once a young woman taunted it and her face was scratched by the bear. Her brother got angry and killed the bear. Artemis got angry and commanded that every young woman should imitate the bear before her wedding and take care of the temple while wearing the saffron robe, and this used to be called playing the bear. (Translation from Faraone 2003: 52; the ritual was slightly different at Mounichia)

A third scholion associates Iphigenia with Brauron, claiming that Agamemnon sacrificed her there and that Artemis substituted a bear rather than a deer for her at the last moment, wherefore the people perform a secret ritual for her. This is the only attested connection between Iphigenia and the Arkteia, but Euripides' *Iphigenia at Taurus* ends with Athena's statement that Iphigenia will be a priestess of Artemis at Brauron and be buried there; she will receive dedications of the garments of women who die in childbirth (1462–7).

Several late writers on language usage report that in a speech Lysias (if it was he) used the term "to play the bear" to mean "to be dedicated (to Artemis)." More confusingly, one of them asserts that Lysias said that the verb "to play the bear" meant "to tithe" (dedicate a tenth) and that Lysias said that the verb "to tithe" meant "to play the bear" because ten-year-old girls used to play the bear. It is not possible to extract from this what Lysias actually said or even whether he used the word "to tithe." That word is introduced in a quotation from Demosthenes speaking about a young woman, "not to tithe her nor to initiate her [into the Eleusinian Mysteries]." The point of this grammarian's discussion is to explain Demosthenes' phrase "to tithe her" as a reference to arranging for her to play the bear.

Apart from variants on these explanations of the ritual, this is the extent of the written evidence. There is one other category of evidence. The sanctuaries of Brauron and Mounichia have been excavated, and at both numerous small vases of the type called krateriskos (an open bowl set on a high flared foot), dating to the sixth and fifth centuries, were found. These are the two sanctuaries that are mentioned in connection with playing the bear. Some of these krateriskoi are decorated with simple, crudely painted scenes. Most of the vases from Brauron have not been published, but Lilly Kahil, who studied them, summarizes the images (1977: 86; cf. 1965) as falling into two groups: one shows girls, nude or dressed in a short chiton, running in the vicinity of an altar, often carrying a torch or a wreath in one hand, often with a palm tree in the picture field; the other shows similar figures rhythmically but slowly moving around an altar or approaching an altar, usually with a palm tree in the picture. Ioanna Tsirigoti-Drakotou (2008: 102) says, apropos of the Brauron vases, that the running girls are usually nude while the dancing ones wear a short chiton, often swirling around the knees. The vases were so numerous that it is plausible to link them with a ritual, and some show signs of burning inside the bowl. Although the find-spots and the images of girls engaged in ritual certainly suggest that the krateriskoi are connected with playing the bear, nothing in the images demonstrably connects the girls with bears.

Fragments of two larger, red-figure krateriskoi, of far higher artistic quality, have been published. They are by different artists, and one is more elaborate in its secondary decoration than the other. Their find-spot is unknown, as is their relationship to the small krateriskoi found in the sanctuaries. In a picture field that runs around the body of the vases, girls are shown running, clothed in one case, nude in the other. On the former vase, two older women tend an altar, past which a girl runs, while a third woman interacts with a standing girl. On the latter, the more elaborate vase, the girls run in opposite directions on the two sides. One runner has her hair bound up—unlike the others, whose hair falls down their backs—suggesting that she is older. Positioned somewhere in the picture field, over a handle according to Kahil, was a bear standing in front of a palm tree. Kahil suggests that there was an altar above the opposite handle and that the girls were running from the bear toward the altar rather than the reverse.

The Brauronia was a major Attic festival for Artemis that took place every four years. Aristophanes (*Peace* 873–4) refers to a drunken religious junket to it. One late source (Hesychius) says that rhapsodes sang the *Iliad* at it. The dining rooms in the sanctuary must have been for male officials (for only men reclined), and were surely in use at the sanctuary's major festival. This was the festival at which the chorus women of *Lysistrata* claim to have played the bear, dressed in saffron robes, but we do not know anything about the festival program or how the girls fit into it. Mounichia had a less important yearly festival.

So, we have the following. (1) Girls wearing saffron robes played the bear at the Brauronia before marriage, between the ages of five and ten, appeasing Artemis of Brauron and Artemis of Mounichia by making a sacrifice. (2) Assuming that the krateriskoi depict actual rituals, girls of different ages ran (usually naked) and danced (dressed) at Brauron and Mounichia. The bear on one of the red-figure krateriskoi could just be a means of identifying the sanctuary, or it could mean that the depicted activities were one part of playing the bear, although the saffron robes are missing, and it is not evident how running and dancing represented being a bear. (3) A girl could be "tithed"—that is, dedicated to Artemis—which is said in a confusing passage to mean that she played the bear. (4) Late sources refer to "secret" rituals, which means very little since most unusual rituals are so called in late sources. (5) The Brauronia was a pan-Attic festival in which men participated. No good impression of the character of the Arkteia emerges from these. See Parker (2005: 228–48) for detailed discussion.

In this situation scholars assign a goal to the ritual and then arrange the fragments of evidence in the way that best supports it. The prevailing idea has been that the ritual was an age-class initiation for girls, to move them from childhood to readiness for marriage. (Age-class initiation is known from other cultures but is not well attested in Greece; see Graf 2003 for an account of the rise of "initiation" as an interpretation of numerous Greek rituals.) Expanding on earlier scholars' work, Christiane Sourvinou-Inwood (1988) argues that we can correlate the images on the vases with other evidence to deduce the outline of the initiation ritual. The age at which the girls perform the ritual, between five and ten (i.e., before the tenth birthday), seems young, but Sourvinou-Inwood justifies it by arguing that (1) since the Brauronia was held only every four years some girls had to undergo it early, (2) the process lasted up to a year and had to be finished before the tenth birthday (so one had to begin shortly after turning nine), and (3) ten was the age at which a girl began a long transition to marriageability that ended with menarche (for which twelve is the earliest age mentioned and fourteen the usual age in Greek texts).

Correlatively, the vase paintings use certain conventions to distinguish the approximate ages of the girls: mainly different head-size-to-height ratios and flat chests versus "budding breasts." According to these criteria (in various combinations), the girls depicted are either quite young or else close to ten; that is, at the lower or the upper end of the age range. Because of the fragmentary state and sketchy drawing of the small krateriskoi, these criteria are very difficult to apply to them, so Sourvinou-Inwood relies mainly on the two red-figure krateriskoi for her conclusions. On those two vases she finds that the naked running girls are older than the clothed running girls (without noting that the overall styles of drawing are quite different). In depicting the naked girls as older, she adds, the vase painters show that the moment of nakedness comes at the end of the initiation. Then, adopting the reading "and letting flow down my saffron robe" in *Lysistrata*, she argues that the girls shed their robes near the end of their initiation to signal their transition to the next stage and thus appeared nude in their final ceremony, the public performance at the Brauronia. (She also adduces Aeschylus' *Agamemnon* 239 in which Iphigenia is described, as she is held over the altar to be sacrificed, as "letting her saffron-dyed robe flow down toward the ground," but Iphigenia is not shedding her robe; rather, it is billowing down around her, as Sourvinou-Inwood acknowledges.) Saffron robes were associated with marriage and female sexuality, but, in shedding them, Sourvinou-Inwood argues, the girls reject wild sexuality and submit to patriarchal strictures. Thus, they present themselves to the community as compliant with social mores at the moment when they are about to begin the transition to sexual maturity. Iphigenia is a model for initiatory "death" and new status.

Although the scholion says that all Attic girls played the bear before marriage, the sanctuary at Brauron is far too small for them all to have done so there. Mounichia had a yearly festival, which could have accommodated more (probably not all) girls, but its festival was a lesser event than Brauron's. The scholion's statement is therefore dubious. Moreover, saffron robes were expensive. To account for the less-than-full participation, Sourvinou-Inwood adopts the view that by the Classical period the Arkteia was "representative initiation"; that is, some girls were initiated on behalf of all. (For a more recent study of the Arkteia as initiation see Gentili and Perusino 2002.)

In the context of a conference and published collection of papers questioning the validity of the initiation paradigm as applied to Greek rituals, Christopher Faraone (2003) disputes the premise that "playing the bear" was an age-class initiation. He objects that there is no evidence for girls' change of status as a result of initiation and that "representative initiation" is unparalleled (so also Graf 2003). He rejects the reading "and letting flow down my saffron robe" in *Lysistrata* on the grounds that the marginal notes on *Lysistrata* all clearly reflect the other reading ("and then wearing") and points out that the vases nowhere show a girl letting a garment fall. He does not discuss the vases except to remark that the relationship of the two red-figure vases to the ritual is unknown since their find-spot is not known and they differ very significantly in style from the small krateriskoi.

Faraone emphasizes instead that the origin-story speaks of Artemis' anger at the killing of the bear and that one of the *Lysistrata* scholia says that the ritual was meant to placate Artemis. In the Mounichia version of the origin story, Artemis demands that someone sacrifice his own daughter, but a clever man dresses up a goat as his daughter and sacrifices it instead, which mollifies Artemis. Another late source speaks of "expiation." Faraone argues that in the Aegean area, which includes Athens, Artemis was a plague goddess more prominently than a goddess of the hunt. As such, she had to be assuaged regularly to avert devastating plagues, and young girls were the best positioned to do so, given Artemis' fondness for the young. "Playing the bear" was therefore a ritual of appeasement, such as is known from all over eastern Greece and the Ionian cities of the Aegean.

In his attempt to make sense of the evidence, Faraone distinguishes between a communal appeasement rite performed by selected girls at the Brauronia and a private ritual of dedication to Artemis that each young woman performed individually before her marriage—although both types were called "playing the bear" and involved saffron robes. The latter then constitutes the "tithing" and "dedicating" of individual girls that the grammarians mention. Faraone identifies the origin stories of Brauron and Mounichia as belonging to the private rituals because three of the four versions conclude with the statement that "every young woman," or "girls" in general, played the bear before marriage. These two kinds of ritual, he adds, became confused in later sources.

Parker, probably rightly, rejects Faraone's distinction between two kinds of rituals as going much too far (2005: 238 n. 84). But Parker supports the initiation hypothesis by suggesting (233) that the mismatch between the available space and statements that all girls undertook the ritual arises because initiation was open to all girls but a relatively small number actually participated. Conversely, Sourvinou-Inwood assumes that the girls were secluded for a long period of time even though nothing in the available evidence suggests that, and she gives a strained meaning to the saffron robe, which is connected in the scholia with appeasing Artemis. Parker in fact ends his discussion with the thought that the initiation is really an appeasement, but he keeps the initiatory focus by suggesting that the girls have to appease Artemis' potential anger at them.

The two approaches in fact imply different relationships between the girls and the state. Under the first scenario the city intervenes to direct the girls' development toward marriageability, and in the second the city calls on girls to act for the common good. The first is a clear example of functional analysis, the ritual as a mode of impressing its social role on a group within the society. Age-class ritual is "performative" in that the very act of undergoing the ritual effects the goal—in this case moving the girls into the stage of transition to sexual maturity. The girls' attention, therefore, would be on their future experience of marriage and childbirth in relation to Artemis, since the transition was inevitable. From this perspective Sourvinou-Inwood's analysis is similar to Parker's analysis of the Thesmophoria, for both see concern with social standing and birth-giving as a central focus of ritual, whether consciously or unconsciously on the part of the practitioners.

The second interpretation posits that agency was attributed to the girls in that they could persuade Artemis to show favor to the community. The ritual itself would confirm their agency, for their vigorous activity, as depicted on the vases (the running and dancing), would combine with their attention directed toward the goddess to give them a sense of efficacy. They may simultaneously have felt constrained by Artemis' potential anger and demand for purity, and if they knew the origin-story that has come down to us they may have recognized that they were compelled to atone for male violence, the brother's killing of the bear—potentially a potent lesson about the double-bind within which women lived. Faraone's approach, because it links the ritual to the origin-story and posits orientation toward the goddess, can be aligned with either Goff's or Stehle's analysis of the Thesmophoria.

Unlike in the case of the Thesmophoria, however, both interpretations cannot be correct, though of course both could be wrong. If one had to choose one of these, the best question to ask would concern which analysis is more in keeping with more clearly documented Greek ritual practices. I would opt for placating the goddess, as this was a ritual type often mentioned in ancient literature and paralleled in ritual practice. A ritual of the same type in Attica, cited by Faraone, is the procession of young women to the temple of Apollo Delphinios (and probably Artemis) carrying suppliant branches (Plutarch, *Theseus* 18). The young women may have sung en route and/or danced in a chorus when they arrived, although we are not told that. Similarly, the Athenian Aiora was expiatory. At it, young women swung on swings hung from trees in honor of Erigone, the maiden whose father introduced Attic farmers to wine and then was killed by them because they did not understand its effects. Erigone hanged herself as a result (see Parker 2005: 301–2). For another example, at Thebes young women went in procession to two temples of Apollo, the Ismenion and the Galaxion, carrying suppliant branches. On one occasion they sang a song composed by Pindar (*parth.* II = 94b Snell-Mahler).

3   Other Festivals

Choral singing and dancing was also the one way in which young women in general could participate in civic and aristocratic religious ritual more broadly. At Athens, maidens danced at the *pannychis* ("all-night festival") connected with the Panathenaia, the major festival for Athena and a joyous occasion (Euripides, *Heraclidae* 782–3). Outside of Attica female choruses are better attested. At Sparta, young women performed extensively; for instance, a long fragment of a song for the Dawn Goddess, sung to accompany a gift for her (probably a robe), survives (Alcman, *parth.* 1). On Lesbos Sappho wrote wedding hymns to be sung by choruses of young women (e.g., 30 Voigt; see Stehle 1997: 278–82). Maiden choruses at Delos and Delphi, both shrines of Apollo, were famous. Here too the problem of interpretation arises. Calame and others take this choral activity as evidence of initiation rituals; that is, of religious activity focused directly on the young women. Some, including Stehle, think that the initiation paradigm is being imposed on rituals that had other goals, such as honoring and delighting a deity, and that young women's choral performance was one aspect of the strategy for creating delight. The latter view does not preclude recognition that choral performance was a form of education for young women and presented them to the public as (soon to be) ready for marriage.

Also attested outside Attica are races for young women. At Elis, site of Olympia in the western Peloponnesus, a board called the "Sixteen Women" held races in the stadium at Olympia for three age groups of girls (Pausanias 5.16.2–3; the ages are not given). The winners received a prime piece of the meat from the sacrifice. The Sixteen also arranged choruses of young women to sing and dance for two local heroines (5.16.6–7). These too have been taken as initiatory, but too many questions remain—for example how many girls and young women participated and what the rituals of which these activities were a part aimed to do—for us to pass judgment on their nature.

In addition to the collective activities, of which the Thesmophoria and "playing the bear" are examples, women individually or in small groups engaged in many other kinds of ritual activity. I can only mention some types with references for further reading. Overall, see Kraemer (2004), Dillon (2007), and Kaltsas and Shapiro (2008). Women served as priestesses or priestesses' assistants in numerous cults, usually for a goddess (see Connelly 2007). Usually these were older women. Attached to sanctuaries there were sometimes groups of women, informal probably as well as formal, who assisted the priestess, kept the sanctuary, or participated in weaving a robe for the goddess. The Sixteen Women at Elis also wove a robe for Hera. The women who wove the peplos for Athena on the Acropolis at Athens may have been an informal group of volunteers since we do not hear of any official group. Women dedicated votive offerings to the gods, for themselves or as part of a family (see Day 2010: 187–96, *passim*).

In the demes (towns) of Attica, women had ritual activities that we occasionally glimpse from inscriptions. Households, including women, seem often to have gone to a sanctuary for a private sacrifice and to appeal to a divinity. Votive plaques show such scenes, sometimes with a woman at the front of the procession, holding out a baby to the statue of the god (see van Straten 1995). Birth, marriage, and death were surrounded with rituals in which women had major roles. See, for these, Oakley and Sinos (1993), Demand (1994), and Stears (1998).

At Athens a few girls and young women served Athena on the Acropolis. In the passage from *Lysistrata* quoted above, two groups are mentioned, the Arrhephoroi and the Aletrides. The Arrhephoroi were two (or possibly four) girls between the ages of seven and eleven who lived on the Acropolis for an unknown period, possibly as long as a year. They had two known tasks. One was to help set up the loom for the women who spent nine months or so on the Acropolis weaving a robe for Athena. The other was to take an enclosed basket down from the Acropolis to an underground location near the Ilissus River and bring something else back from there (Pausanias 1.27.3), an action reflecting the founding-legend of Athens, the birth of Erichthonios from the earth. The Aletrides ground grain, presumably for sacred cakes (and possibly for Demeter rather than Athena). Another pair of young women, the Plyntrides, washed either the clothes or the statue of Athena Polias once a year. These positions of sacred service had a domestic character and assimilated the Acropolis to a household and hence a feminine space. Artemis had an extension of the Brauron sanctuary there too. On the Acropolis see Brulé (1987) and Loraux (1993).

Processions conducting animals to sacrifice were often led by a young woman carrying a basket on her head that contained grain and the sacrificial knife. She was beautifully dressed, to judge from vase paintings. Otherwise, apart from priestesses, women had few roles in sacrifice and may often not have been present. Women could, however, perform sacrifices in some cases; see Osborne (1993).

RECOMMENDED FURTHER READING

For other discussions of the Thesmophoria see Brumfield (1981), Zeitlin (1982) (an early feminist discussion), Detienne (1989) (structuralist), Winkler (1990), Versnel (1993) (who combines functionalism with a psychological approach), Demand (1994), and Dillon (2007). For young women's choral performance, see Calame (1997) and Stehle (1997: 71–118).

15

Women and Roman Religion

Lora L. Holland

A famous tale from antiquity relates how the Vestal Virgin Tuccia, when accused of unchastity, snatched up her sieve and made the following prayer: "Vesta, if I have always applied chaste hands to your rites, make it happen that I may draw water from the Tiber with this and carry it into your house" (Valerius Maximus 8.1.5). The goddess granted the prayer, and the "miracle," that is, carrying water in a sieve, was accepted as proof of Tuccia's innocence. Had she been proven guilty, she would have been ritually buried alive, the punishment for Vestals who place the Roman state in danger by attending to the goddess' rites while in an unchaste condition. Tuccia has been extolled as an example of feminine virtue far beyond her Roman setting; for instance, in the Christian writer St. Augustine and in works of art such as the famous painting by the Italian Renaissance artist Andrea Mantegna. Even in the modern era, Queen Elizabeth I commissioned a series of portraits that depict her holding Tuccia's sieve, which are evocative of the virgin's power in matters of state. The imagery of the intact vessel as a metaphor for the female body was also used in one of the first applications of a women's studies approach to the material evidence for women in Roman religion: Amy Richlin's 1997 article "Carrying water in a sieve: Class and the body in Roman women's religion." Here, too, the Vestal Tuccia introduces this overview of the role of women in Roman religion and of the methodologies used by scholars in the modern era to interpret the ancient evidence.

How we understand sex, gender, and the "proper" role of women in society has changed dramatically since the inception of the study of Roman religion in the modern world. It is not an insignificant coincidence that Roman religion emerged as a sub-field of Classical Studies in the early twentieth century at the same time as the social and educational emancipation of women, particularly in North America, first afforded female scholars the opportunity to conduct research on an equal footing with men. There is no space in this study to explore the fascinating contributions of early female scholars, many of whom are already in danger of being forgotten; but their interest in the female role in Roman religion was significant, even if their methodologies and cultural assumptions generally differed little from those of their male counterparts.

A Companion to Women in the Ancient World, First Edition. Edited by Sharon L. James and Sheila Dillon.
© 2012 John Wiley & Sons, Ltd. Published 2015 by John Wiley & Sons, Ltd.

The sexual asymmetry (the term used by Josine Blok 1987) of ancient Roman culture—that is, the imbalance of participation by gender in various societal institutions—was interpreted mostly in terms of the assumptions inherent in nineteenth and early twentieth century Western culture. By positing women as "other" and therefore having a "position" on the fringes of male-dominated societal institutions, scholars in those early years of Classical Studies, Blok argues, set biased parameters for interpretation of the ancient evidence, which, in turn, embeds its own biases. In the study of Roman religion, these biased parameters apply equally to male and female participation in religion: by under-valuing the role of women, the male contribution is overvalued.

Mainstream scholarship on Roman religion is increasingly accepting of new approaches, but the hold the biases have had, and at times still have, on methodologies and on the interpretation of the evidence remains problematic. For instance, the view prevalent in the early twentieth century was that women's religious roles were either completely under male control or concerned primarily or even exclusively with tradi-tional female spheres (e.g., Wissowa 1912). There was also an idea that male gods were primarily concerned with male spheres of interest, and goddesses with female concerns. These and other erroneous assumptions have been slow to disappear from handbooks, reference books, and companion studies, if they are even dealt with at all; far more prevalent has been the assumption that women, apart from the Vestals, mattered little in a definition of Roman religion that focused on and privileged the state public rites over all other forms of worship.

In light of this history, perhaps it is not surprising that the two main camps in modern scholarship today differ substantially in their conclusions about the role of women in Roman religion. On the one hand are scholars who hold the participation of women, with the exception of the Vestals, to be of little importance. John Scheid (1992), in an article entitled "The religious roles of Roman women," concluded that the lack of a constitu-tional role for women in Roman society necessarily meant that their religious role was inconsequential, and, further, that this forced women to seek out exotic and foreign cults and to dabble in magic in order to fulfill the religious urges that their festivals did not satisfy. A similar viewpoint is implicit in a recent companion to Roman religion, edited by Jörg Rüpke (2007), in which consideration of the role of women is largely confined to a few brief references in some of the contributions. In the other camp are a growing number of scholars who argue for a more organic and essential religious role for women at all levels of Roman society than is evident from previous interpretations of the evidence. In other words, the extent to which the biases evident in early work on religion—and in more recent methodological issues—are not taken adequately into account affects not only the study of women but also our understanding of the Roman religious experience as a whole.

The gains possible from new methodologies and approaches are best illustrated in a recent book by Celia Schultz (2006), which looks well beyond the literary evidence to outline a broad base of participation by women in civic rites during the Republic. Activities by females ranged from state supplications and expiations in Rome by *matronae* (freeborn married women); to women at all levels of society, whom the epigraphical evidence confirms held magisterial, ministerial, and sacerdotal posts in various cults in Italy; to dedicating private votives and other gifts in sanctuaries to male and female deities alike. Their participation was regulated not only by their gender but also by their social status, sexual status, and marital status. Rüpke's magisterial collection of the evidence for cultic functionaries in the city of Rome, *Fasti Sacerdotum* (2008), is a gold mine of information waiting to be explored for posts held by women during the empire. Other recent work concentrates on particular cults or festivities, for example Fanny Dolansky's (2011) reassessment of the Matronalia festival, which she argues required both public and private rites, the latter involving the entire household (*domus*), not the *matronae* alone. Other work has tackled gender issues from different perspectives, for example Carin Green's (2007) study of the cult of Diana at Aricia, which demonstrates that it was not a cult primarily for women, as some earlier scholars asserted, but appealed to a wide range of worshippers.

Other approaches require that scholars look to models beyond the familiar bounds of Western culture. For example, one comparative anthropological model is derived from the study of some patriarchal villages in modern Turkey. The Norwegian scholar Jørgen Meyer (2004) proposed the model and applied it to Classical Greece, but it is also being applied to Roman studies. Ingvar Mæhle (2004: 55), in a paper on female religious power during Rome's struggle of the orders, states Meyer's position succinctly: "We should not look for equality, but equilibrium in the gender-based division of labour, social space and power." Just as women were sometimes excluded from the male sphere, men were sometimes excluded from the female sphere; but each had its own important role in the society as a whole. Further exploration of this and similar approaches in Roman studies will no doubt bring additional advances in our understanding of women in Roman religion.

Until recently most of the attention to women in Roman religion in the modern era was concentrated in those aspects that most attracted the attention of the ancient male elite, for which, as a result, we have the most literary evidence. Because the interests of the ancient male writers lay within a narrow framework in which what most women were doing in the religious sphere was of little or no interest to them, the literary picture of women's religious roles is necessarily skewed. New approaches are beginning to loosen the hold that ancient negative attitudes and biases towards women have held in modern scholarship. One of the most important new trends in the scholarship focuses on the evidence for the participation of men and women in religion together rather than in isolation. Looking at as wide a range of evidence as possible and shedding the presumption that the religious roles of men and women were almost always gender-segregated permits us to look at the topic more holistically. Women's participation was one factor in the huge web of religious activities that characterized Roman society, and is best conceived as something inseparable from the whole.

1   Female Priesthoods

Though freeborn married women (*matronae*) did not vote, hold political or military offices, or have legal autonomy in Roman culture, they did have social, economic, and religious power. *Matronae* shared in some married priesthoods, and in public rites that required the participation of both men and women of high status. Unlike the relatively substantial and at times lurid evidence for the Vestals, however, the ancient literary sources offer few clues for understanding these other female priesthoods.

The *flaminicae* (a type of priestess) and the *regina sacrorum* (queen of sacred rites) were elite priestesses that held office in tandem with their husbands, the *flamines* and the *rex sacrorum*. In modern scholarship the female halves have been treated mostly as a less important appendage to, not part and parcel with (the distinction is key), their male marriage partners and fellow priests (e.g., Rüpke 2004: 189). Despite the paucity of evidence, some scholars have attempted focused treatments of these priestesses, for example Dolores Mirón Pérez (1996) and Nicole Boëls-Janssen (1993). In addition, Emily Hemelrijk's (2005a) study has traced important changes in the role of the *flaminica* during the empire, showing that the *flaminica* was no longer always the spouse of a *flamen*. It is not clear whether these priestesses performed these duties together in the same space and time with their husbands or separately. In other words, one question to be asked of these priesthoods is whether or not the rites were considered to be gender-exclusive or inclusive; that is, did the male priest act on behalf of Roman men and his wife on behalf of Roman women, or did they perform the rites together on behalf of the Roman people as a whole?

The flaminate was divided into two categories: the major priests (*flamines maiores*) and the minor priests (*flamines minores*). The major flaminate consisted of the priesthoods named after Jupiter, Mars, and Quirinus; of these, we have specific information in the literary sources only about the *flaminica Dialis*, the wife of the *flamen Dialis* and priestess of Jupiter (*Dialis uxor et Iovis sacerdos*, Festus L 82). Divorce was not allowed, and if one of the pair should die the spouse had to leave office. According to Macrobius (*Sat.* 1.16), the *flaminica Dialis* regularly sacrificed a ram to Jupiter on market days (*nundinae*) in the Regia (the official residence of the Pontifex Maximus), among other tasks assigned to her. The *regina sacrorum* also had public duties that were performed in the Regia. Various ancient sources confirm that she sacrificed to Juno on the special days of the Roman month (Kalends, Nones, Ides), while her husband sacrificed to Jupiter. The *flaminica Dialis*, like her husband, was required to wear special clothing and was subject to various prohibitions that were probably designed to protect her purity; and, just as her husband had a freeborn boy whose parents were still alive as an assistant (*camillus*) at public rites, so she had a freeborn girl whose parents were still alive to serve as her "little priestess" (Festus L 82). In sum, she seems to have been fully vested in her office, rather than positioned in a subsidiary or auxiliary role.

Matronae and Vestals sometimes conducted rites in tandem, as in the worship of the "Good Goddess," Bona Dea. The participation of *matronae* in other cults, however, could be controversial, as in the cult of Bacchus. Bona Dea was believed in antiquity to be the euphemistic name given to Fauna, who is variously identified in the sources as the daughter, sister, and wife of Faunus, a legendary king in Latium. Roman myth records several stories that explain Fauna's deification after her death, including a story that Faunus beat her to death when he caught her drinking wine, and another that he turned himself into a snake so that he could copulate with her, though she was his daughter and had already rejected his incestuous advances. The Fauni were prophetic deities in some accounts, but also seemed to have healing powers. Snakes were housed in the Bona Dea's sanctuaries, which is reminiscent of the use of snakes in the cult of the Greek healing god Asklepios.

It was widely held in modern scholarship that Bona Dea's cult was restricted to women, largely because literary sources say little about the cult apart from recounting a scandalous attempt by Clodius, one of Cicero's enemies, to cross-dress and attend a gender-restricted rite conducted by the Vestals and aristocratic women led by the chief magistrate's wife in her home. Henrik Brouwer's (1989) epigraphically focused study of this goddess, however, conclusively demonstrates that, like most Roman deities, the Bona Dea was worshiped by men and by women alike in cult, though the rite conducted by the Vestals was gender-restricted. In a similar vein, Schultz (2000) uses epigraphical evidence to show that there were female worshipers in cult for Hercules in Rome, though they were excluded from the specific rites at the Ara Maxima that literary sources emphasized.

In other words, how Roman deities were gendered did not universally translate into worship that was likewise gendered on the human plane.

One of the most notorious incidents involving *matronae* was the Bacchanalia scandal in the early second century BCE. The cult of Bacchus, as the Greek god Dionysus was known in Italy, was very popular in Republican Rome, especially with women. Both men and women held sacerdotal and ministerial posts in this cult. Since some of the rites were restricted to women only, the Romans no doubt engaged in some prurient speculation about the nature of its mysteries. The Etruscans, who differed from the Romans in their ideas about gender and sexuality, seemed particularly accepting of the cult, perhaps in part because they also had their own wine god, Fufluns. Despite the cult's long history in Italy, the Roman Senate in 186 BCE felt compelled to issue a decree to its citizens and allies limiting and regulating participation in this cult, especially by freeborn men.

We are fortunate to have both a copy of that original decree written on stone, fortuitously discovered in the twentieth century, and a later literary account of the Senate's action; this permits a comparison of the two sources of information. Celia Schultz (2006: 82–8), building on the work of Staples (1998), points out the historian Livy's gender bias in his account of the affair, written nearly 200 years after the event. Livy cites sexual depravity instigated by women in the cult, and the general instability of the female character as a whole, as important factors in the Senate's decision to restrict the cult in Italy; the epigraphical evidence, however, suggests that the Senate was primarily concerned with the possible political consequences of widespread male participation (both citizens and allies) in the rites. In other words, the Romans wished to prevent the cult from becoming a political force that could challenge their authority. Though the cult may have been distasteful to some Romans because of the reports of its sexual activities, its potential as an agent of political change was the real threat.

As a result of not considering the possibility of ancient gender bias in the ancient texts, classical scholars until recently have largely accepted, and thus perpetuated, Livy's interpretation of the role of the female in the Bacchanalia affair. Since Livy wrote his account long after the fact, it makes more sense to look for contemporary social issues that may have prompted Livy to cast the story the way he (or his historical source) did. Recognizing the embedded gender bias in Livy's account is essential to a fuller understanding of the incident's political and historical implications. Celia Schultz's analysis also provides a cogent example of how challenging the male bias can correct misperceptions about female religious activity as it is portrayed in Latin literature.

Modern scholarship has also reflected bias in the coverage of topics for research, some of which still await detailed attention. For instance, the ritual and religious aspects of the Roman wedding have not been treated adequately in general studies of the Roman family and its institutions; moreover, the Roman wedding itself has not been the subject of any monograph until recently (Hersch 2010). Aspects of the wedding and of marriage in general touch on issues that have long been central to the study of Roman religion (e.g., Linderski 1986). The role and status of the Vestal Virgins is a case in point.

Vestals could be selected as early as age six, and were part of the pontifical college of priests, the only state college that included females. The number of Vestals is generally cited as six, and their term of office was thirty years: the first ten years were spent in learning their duties, the second decade in performing them, and the last in instructing the next generation. During their tenure they were required to remain chaste, but were free to marry, if they wished, later in life. Such peculiarities as the Vestals' matronly dress, their bridal hairstyle (*seni crines*), and their legal relationship to the Pontifex Maximus, posed in terms similar to marriage (*captio*, "the taking," was a religious rite performed by the Pontifex after the selection process of the young girls was completed), suggested to some scholars of the nineteenth and early twentieth centuries an original function as wives. Other scholars held the view that the Vestals were originally daughters of the early kings, as suggested by their virginal status. In subsequent decades the debate raged on, but the initial premise was that the Vestals must have been one or the other, since it was assumed that these were the only roles available for women.

In 1980 Mary Beard argued that the Vestals were perceived both as wives and as daughters, introducing anthropological theory as a key to understanding their status. A desire for assimilation to the dominant male sphere soon became a very popular way to explain various aspects of Roman religion that seem to transgress gender boundaries. The Vestals, like men, made their own wills, and, like male magistrates, they were accompanied by lictors; unlike anyone, however, they were legally free of parental control. In fact, Beard (1995) reconsidered her earlier reading of the Vestals in favor of seeing their sexual status not in isolation but in terms of a cultural system that had its own normative gender categories and its own ways of negotiating them. Beard's student Ariadne Staples (1998) subsequently argued that, because the Vestals stood outside the normative gender categories, they were able to represent the Roman people as a whole.

State rites throughout the year required either the participation of the Vestals or the use of materials provided by them, though their constant duty was to tend the sacred hearth-fire of Rome housed in Vesta's round temple. Several times a year the senior Vestals prepared a grain-and-salt mixture called *mola salsa* that was used to sprinkle sacrificial victims at all state sacrifices, as well as a similar mixture that also contained the blood of a sacrificed horse along with the burnt ashes of an unborn calf whose mother was sacrificed to Tellus (Earth) during the spring festival called the Fordicidia. The Vestals distributed cakes made from *mola salsa* during the Lupercalia festival in February, and sacrificed *mola salsa* cakes to Vesta in June, when they celebrated the Vestalia festival along with the married women of Rome. On the last day of that festival, millers, bakers, and even the draft animals involved in producing grain were given a day of rest. Thus we see that this festival included participation by men and women alike, though modern scholarship tends to regard it solely as a women's festival focused on virginity and fertility.

That the Vestals were primarily concerned with fertility—that is, a role closely associated with women's concerns—was a largely unquestioned assumption in early modern scholarship. Since at that time the role of the Vestals was understood in terms of wives or daughters, this seemed a logical assumption. Emphasis on the participation of women in Vesta's cult, as well as the priestesses' own sexual status, seemed to offer additional support for this view. Sarolta Takács (2008) sees the Vestals as protectors of Rome's prosperity in her larger study of the annual rhythms of women's participation in religious festivals in Rome. Holt Parker (2004) reads their requisite virginity narrowly in terms of the purity required for the scapegoat ritual, by which Vestals were sentenced to being buried alive at times of crisis in Roman history (Livy records the first scapegoat, the Vestal Oppia, in 483 BCE). Robin Lorsch Wildfang's (2006) study, the first monograph in English devoted solely to the Vestals, has put the fertility issue to rest conclusively: the Vestal's primary role was one of purification, namely to keep the grain supply purified. This was vital not only to the health of the individual but also to the Roman state as a whole. We have come a long way from the old question of daughters or wives.

2   Gendered Deities and Domestic Cult

The attention paid to gender in the divine sphere is noteworthy in a number of cults. Early scholars worked on a basic assumption that most gods had a strictly defined sphere of influence, and that these spheres were regularly delineated along the boundary of gender. For instance, the worship of Juno Sospita in Latium was seen as a women's cult concerned with fertility because of a literary description of one of her annual rites at Lanuvium. In this rite, described by the Augustan poet Propertius (poem 4.8), a virgin (probably a priestess of Juno) descends into the goddess' sacred cave to make a food offering to an ancient serpent who is hungry from a long winter's fast. If she returns to the surface unharmed, she is judged to have made the offering chastely and the farmers consider her success a propitious omen for a fruitful year. Celia Schultz (2006: 22–8) points out that the point of this story concerns purity, not fertility. This reminds us of the importance of purity in the conduct of the Vestals, discussed above.

The bulk of our sources about Juno Sospita emphasize her military aspect, which is reinforced by her iconography. Cicero charmingly affirms that the Romans could conceive of this goddess in no other way than with her helmet, shield, and spear, not even in their dreams (*De nat. deor.* 1.77). A number of female deities in Roman religion besides Juno Sospita had "virile" aspects, such as the hunting goddess Diana, often depicted with spear or bow; the war goddess Bellona; and Minerva. Recent scholarship helps us to better understand how both men and women perceived such deities. Eve D'Ambra's study of imperial funerary altars explores how parents memorialized young girls in Latium who died a premature death in the guise of Diana. She concludes that the parents so depicted their young daughters on funerary altars "not only because the goddess' status as chaste maiden reflected the girls' stage of life but also because the huntress could signify the heroic mode of representation or even *virtus*, the premier male virtue of courage and valor" (2007: 248). In other words, the relationship between deity and worshiper was complex, and did not necessarily follow strict gender ideologies.

The activities of ordinary people comprise the bulk of everyday religious activity, to judge from the number of inscriptions and votives dating from the fourth century BCE to the fourth century CE. Of these, inscriptions by women are relatively rare until the end of the Republic. During the Republic, a specialized type of votive was once thought to speak to widespread gender-exclusive cult. Most of these votive offerings were not inscribed, so the sex of the giver is not known. At sanctuaries dedicated to female deities, the presence of anatomical votives of female body parts as well as of women holding children were attributed to a concern for women, even though the gender of the dedicators of such votives were unknown, male body parts and male figurines were also present, and similar votives were known from sanctuaries dedicated to male deities. It is now generally agreed that anatomical votives are a widespread Italic phenomenon in sanctuaries, and speak to a general belief in the healing power of deity (for detailed discussion see C. Schultz 2006: 95–120).

One example illustrates how an initial interpretation of a votive's meaning can mislead. In 1895 the Italian archaeologist Felice Barnabei published a short notice about a votive deposit of mid-Republican date from Diana's sanctuary at Lake Nemi. Among the votives were inscriptions made by men, an inscription by a woman on behalf of her son, a bronze spear point dedicated to Diana by a wet nurse, and a small bronze breast with no inscription. After deciding to pair the spear with the breast, Barnabei then postulated that their meaning together should refer to the worship of Diana as a *kourotrophos* (literally "child-nurse"). Barnabei's idea was accepted without question. Consequently, scholars throughout the twentieth century cited this votive as a prime example of Diana's concern for women. Marja-Leena Hänninen's study of "traces of women's devotion" at the sanctuary thus cites the spear dedication even while it points out that the numerous dedications by men are indications that Diana was not primarily a goddess of women's concerns (2000: 45–50). I myself have argued (Holland 2008) that the spear-point dedication is better understood as a freedwoman's votive. Diana's assimilation to Juno Lucina, the iconic Roman goddess of childbirth, argues for a special relationship to women in one aspect of her cult, but it also points to changes in her cult over time. Beard et al. (1998) are silent on the issue of Diana's nature, but implicitly reject the earlier view by including in their volumes only political, legal, or civic evidence for her cult. During the Roman empire, anatomical votives disappear by the end of the second century CE except in the Gallic provinces (Scheid 2003b: 101).

Domestic cult is the category of religious participation most commonly associated with women. The Roman calendar includes several festivals traditionally associated with the participation of women, for example the Matralia, Matronalia, Vestalia, and the Caprotine Nones. Other festivals certainly included women, for example the Terminalia, a boundary festival that included the entire family, and the Lupercalia, a February purification festival during which women offered their bodies to be struck by men with goatskin whips. Ovid's *Fasti*, or calendar poem, is one of our richest sources of information about these festivals, at least from January through June. Sarolta Takács (2008) usefully examines the festivals in isolation as a way to gain insight into female rhythms of the year, but other recent analyses attempt to integrate the festivals into a more holistic understanding of their significance for men and women together, for example Dolansky's (2011) new study of the Matronalia, mentioned earlier. The festival for deified ancestors (Parentalia) opened with public rites performed by the Vestals, but also included private, familial rites (Beard et al. 1998: 50). Ovid (*Fasti* 2. 537–9) describes sacrifices of garlands, wheat, salt, bread, and violets, which suggests that women were at least involved in the preparation of these offerings, if not in the performance of the rite itself.

The Roman household gods included familial spirits of the living; that is, the *genius* of the male head of household (*pater familias*) and (by the beginning of the empire, at least; see Rives 1992) the *iuno* of the female head of the household (*mater familias*), the Lares, Penates, and Vesta, whose hearth was adorned with offerings on the three special days of the Roman month (C. Schultz 2006: 123). The speech of the household god in *Aulularia* (lines 15–25) is one of the most interesting prologues, in religious terms, in the comedies of Plautus:

> When the man who had entrusted the gold to me died,
> I began watching to see whether his son would worship me
> Any better than his father had. And darned if he didn't
> Spend less and less on the upkeep of my cult,
> And less often adorned me with the honors of sacrifice.
> I rewarded him in the same way, and he died in poverty like his father.
> His son lives here now, but he's just as stingy
> As his father and grandfather were.
> This Euclio has one daughter, and she supplicates me daily
> With incense or wine or whatever she has. She gives me garlands.

In his speech, the god (*lar familiaris*) implies that the care of his cult properly belonged to male and female together, but in his case, only the daughter displays the proper piety. This passage is sometimes interpreted to mean that a daughter did not normally perform ritual for the *lar*, but we can just as easily infer that she did.

Women of child-bearing age also worshipped Juno Lucina, both during the public cult of the Matronalia festival, discussed above, and also in the home, since that is where babies were born and raised. In Roman comedy, for example, women giving birth regularly cry out to Juno Lucina. We get only rare glimpses of these women's rituals for children at home. Helper gods (*indigitamenta*) for babies, such as Cuba, who watched their sleep, and Cunina, who protected them in the cradle, receive brief mention in the sources (e.g., the Christian writers Augustine, *Civ. Dei* 4.10 and Lactantius 1.20, and the scholia on the comedy playwright Terence, *ap. Donat. ad Ter. Phorm.* 1.1.14). Varro informs us that a child's nurse, who was usually a household slave, customarily made a bloodless sacrifice to the deities who protected children, such as Edusa and Potina, respectively the divinities of a child's first food and drink (*Logistorici* fr. 9 Bolisani). In sum, though our information about the details of domestic ritual is limited, we may infer that women played an important role in the upkeep of domestic cult for the family, just as the Vestals were charged with tending the public hearth of Rome on behalf of the Roman people as a whole.

3   Women and the Imperial Cult

The Roman empire brought with it new categories of religious participation, some by women. Much of this was at first centered on the worship of the imperial *genius* and *iuno*, and eventually on the deified dead. Members of the imperial family began to receive worship, especially in the Greek East, from the time of Augustus, but the first woman to be deified was Drusilla, the sister of Caligula, followed by Livia, the wife of Augustus. There is now a huge bibliography on the empress Livia, starting with the first female-authored study of Livia and her role in the imperial cult (Grether 1946). Maureen Flory has a very interesting study of Livia's use of laurel (1995a) and a more general study of the deification of Roman women (1995b). Susan Fischler (1998) argues for a central role for women in the imagery of Roman imperial cult in the Greek East. By the time of Matidia, the emperor Hadrian's mother-in-law, deified women were granted temples, *flamines*, and other accoutrements of public cult (for priestesses of the imperial cult see Hemelrijk 2005a, and for women in power more generally Mirón Pérez 1996).

Inscriptions by women, including slaves and freedwomen, attest to their increasing participation—or at least the increased documentation of their participation—in religion as well (see Hughes 2007 for freedwomen and the use of the veil). For example, two female sacristans (*aedituae*) are known from Rome. The name and offices (*aeditua* and *ministra*) of Lollia Urbana, a freedwoman, are given without mention of a deity (*CIL* 6. 2213), but Rüpke suggests she may have served a private establishment (Rüpke 2008: 774 no. 3). Doris, slave of Asinius Gallus, was caretaker for a temple of Diana (*CIL* 6. 2209). Women also held significant posts in the cult of Isis and other cults, including Christianity, that came to prominence during the early empire. There has been an enormous body of work since the 1990s on provincial cults and other aspects of the religion of the empire, for example Hemelrijk's study (2008b) on women and men together in sacrificial rituals, and British archaeologist Louise Revell's (2009) study of Roman identity in the provinces of the empire, which moves beyond the elite male paradigm to incorporate the wider community (for the empire's religion generally see Rives 2007).

4   What's Next for the Study of Women in Roman Religion?

Finally, lest we assume that overlooking or downplaying the contributions of women is a thing of the past, I will make a brief reference to the modern study of Roman religion. In recent years, the history of scholarship on Roman religion has begun to attract serious attention. C. R. Phillips' article on the subject, though excellent in many respects, pays scant attention to the work of female scholars, notably in the "Recent Developments" section (2007: 24–6; cf. Fear 1997 and Rives 1999). Phillips cites three women in his text: Agnes Lake Michels and Louise Adams Holland, Bryn Mawr scholars of the early to mid twentieth century, and Mary Beard, the British scholar who is perhaps best known for her 1998 watershed collaboration with John North and Simon Price. The feminist scholar Ursula King's critique of the "deeply rooted" androcentrism in the general history of the study of religions is relevant here. She notes that in editor Mircea Eliade's *Encyclopedia of Religion* only four women are named as "scholars of religion," including Jane Harrison for ancient Greek religion (King 1995a: 219). There is no mention of any work done by women for Roman religion, though, as I noted earlier, women were intimately involved in the field from its inception.

In conclusion, there are important gains to be made by re-examining the methodo-logical foundations upon which our basic assumptions about men and women in Roman religion have been based. In looking forward to what may lie ahead in the twenty-first century, one challenge will be to read the ancient literary texts for what they are: the perspective of one gender who was nevertheless in a constant state of negotiation at the boundaries of religious participation. Using new comparative and theoretical models to assess the growing body of material evidence will also present its challenges. The study of women in Roman religion has emerged from its "infancy" (Richlin 1997b: 331), and is growing up quickly. Studies that question the dominant male perspective on religion, ancient and modern, and new approaches to Roman history and historiography, such as Augusto Fraschetti's (2005) anthropological reading of Roman foundational mythology, will also have implications for the study of Roman religion. As a better understanding of men and women together in Roman religion evolves, women are being freed from a marginalized "position" to being "active participants in an intelligible cultural system" (Richlin 1997b: 332).

RECOMMENDED FURTHER READING

As yet there is no history of women's roles in Roman religion in a single monograph. I am sure the following omits many items of interest and importance, but there is room for mention of only a few recent articles in this burgeoning field. Beard et al. (1998) is still the best introduction to Roman religion generally, though coverage of women is spotty. Other introductions, companions, and reference books on Roman religion are less helpful on the topic of women.

For the Republic, Celia Schultz's book (2006) presents arguments for a more integrated, rather than gender-segregated, approach to the evidence as a series of case studies—a must-read for the serious student. A similar approach is taken by Dolansky (2011) on the Matronalia. For the empire, there is some interesting work focused on imperial women in Rome (beginning with Grether 1946), and Roman women in the provinces (Fischler 1998; Hemelrijk 2005a, 2008b), but no overarching study in English. Sawyer (1996) approaches gender and religion in the Roman empire as fluid categories that resist the imposition of modern meaning. For the late empire, Pérez Sánchez and Rodríguez Gervás (2003) offer the view that the functional aspect in women's religious roles continued as before into the Christian era. Wood (2009) argues against earlier views about gender and iconoclasm in the Byzantine period.

Richlin (1997b) is still worth reading on priestesses in Rome. Less methodologically satisfying than Schultz, but still useful, is Takács (2008), on the calendrical rhythms of women's religious participation. Wildfang (2006) on the Vestals is very informative, is well illustrated, and does a good job of assessing both literary and material evidence. Hersch (2010) covers an interesting range of topics in her book on the Roman wedding, including the evidence for same-sex marriage, as well as the various religious aspects of marriage and its ceremonies. A very interesting study by Hughes (2007) on imperial freedwomen and the veil in Italy makes use of modern approaches to Muslim practice.

16

Women in Magna Graecia

Gillian Shepherd

Around the middle of the sixth century BCE, an extraordinary statue was erected at the Greek city of Megara Hyblaea in Sicily (Figure 16.1). Recomposed today from over 900 limestone fragments, the statue depicts a heavy-set seated female suckling two infants (*kourotrophos*) protectively enclosed by her arms and mantle. The statue fragments were found in the North Necropolis of Megara Hyblaea. This cemetery appears to be a small but elite necropolis in use in the second half of the sixth century BCE, composed mainly of the monumental built chamber tombs, known as "hypogeic cellae," which distinguished a minority of wealthy graves among the thousands at the site. The *kourotrophos* statue is likely to have ornamented Tomb I, a grandiose hypogeic cella over two meters long (Gentili 1954: 99–103).

Because it lacks any obvious parallels as a piece of funerary sculpture, the precise significance of the *kourotrophos* is unclear. One interpretation (Holloway 1975: 34, 1991: 82–3) sees the group as Night nursing the twins Sleep and Death, on the basis of Pausanias' description of a similar scene on the Chest of Kypselos at Olympia (5.18.1). While such a subject might be appropriate for a funerary monument, the interpretation is by no means universally accepted (e.g., Wilson 1994: 218). At the very least, such an impressive piece, in an area where funerary statuary seems to have been rare, must have testified to the wealth and status of the occupant(s) of the tomb and their kinship group. The image it projects of the significance of motherhood and female nurturing also readily finds a place in the art of Italy and Sicily, where—unlike mainland Greece—depictions of nursing mothers are common (Ridgway 1993: 194; Bonfante 1997). The motif appears to derive largely from local indigenous culture, but was adopted also in the Greek settlements of Sicily and southern Italy: in the fourth century BCE and later, terracotta votive figures, often stylistically based on Greek models but depicting the distinctively Italic subject of the *kourotrophos*, were deposited in quantities in sanctuaries in Italy and Sicily (Bonfante 1986).

In fact, the *kourotrophos* statue is only one of numerous depictions of women in various roles in the art and material culture of Magna Graecia. Many of these images appear to reflect, to a greater or lesser degree, contact and interaction between Greek settlers and

A Companion to Women in the Ancient World, First Edition. Edited by Sharon L. James and Sheila Dillon.
© 2012 John Wiley & Sons, Ltd. Published 2015 by John Wiley & Sons, Ltd.

Figure 16.1 Limestone statue of a *kourotrophos* from the North Necropolis of Megara Hyblaea, mid-sixth century BCE. Syracuse, Museo Regionale Paolo Orsi. Photo: © Scala/Art Resource, NY.

local populations. Women also appear very prominently in the red-figured vase painting of southern Italy and Sicily of the fifth and especially fourth centuries BCE, often in the form of a motif of a female head (Figure 16.2), but also in ritual, funerary, and domestic scenes, including those of the toilette or bridal preparations. Sometimes details of dress appear to indicate varying ethnic identities. Gisela Schneider-Herrmann's work, for example, studies dress as a way of identifying "Samnite" women on fourth-century Campanian vases. She notes in particular the significance of libation scenes marking the departure or return of a warrior and the depiction of females (and males) in "Samnite" or "Greek" dress together on a single vase (Schneider-Herrmann 1996). Although the correlation between ethnic identity and dress is probably more complex and less direct than Schneider-Herrmann's approach allows, her work highlights the complexities of intercultural interactions in Magna Graecia and the role and significance of women within those interactions.

The tomb paintings of southern Italy are also a valuable source of information. As in vase painting, among the most popular subjects for figured scenes are "returning" warriors greeted by women with libations, and depictions of the prothesis (laying out of the dead body) with related funerary scenes (processions and so on). In the procession scenes, the attendants are usually females, and sometimes male flautists or children are present; the deceased is sometimes also a woman. Such images, together with grave goods (in the absence of skeletal evidence), might provide the best evidence for the sex of the tomb's occupant, since males are not shown explicitly as deceased but instead often appear in "heroized" form as warriors receiving libations from women (Corrigan 1979; Pontrandolfo and Rouveret 1992: esp. 42ff. with figure 45).

Figure 16.2 Red-figure South Italian pelike, attributed to the Darius-Underworld Circle; 340–300 BCE. London, British Museum inv. no. 1756,0101.485. Photo: © Trustees of the British Museum.

Similarly gender-specific imagery is also observable on South Italian *hydriai* (water jugs), where funerary scenes show only female mourners around the *naiskos* (shrine), suggesting that the shape—unsurprisingly—was especially related to deceased women (Trendall 1989: 267). Equally, however, some combinations of scenes might suggest that the gender spheres were not as separate as we often assume: Tomb 53 of the Andriuolo Necropolis has a scene of females mourning a deceased woman on one long side but scenes of chariot racing and armed men dueling (funerary games?) on the other.

1 Who Are the Women of Magna Graecia—Are They Greek or Indigenous?

Women are central to the issue of interaction between the different ethnic groups in Italy and Sicily following the establishment of Greek settlements there in the eighth century BCE. Their prominence in the material culture of southern Italy and Sicily suggests that this evidence should supply important resources for understanding the role and position of women in ancient Magna Graecia, even if literary sources are scarce. Apart from actual images of females, female activities and agency have long been recognized in sacred contexts. For example, at the extra-mural Poseidonian sanctuaries of Aphrodite at Santa Venera and Hera at Foce del Sele, small-scale offerings relating to women's activities (e.g., loom weights and dress items) have been found by the thousands, along with scores of figurines depicting females and goddesses, with new, Italic-derived types (including kourotrophoi) introduced in the "Lucanian" fourth century (Pedley 1990; Ammerman 2002).

Unlike their Athenian counterparts, the women of Magna Graecia have received relatively little attention in their own right. The ethnicity of these women remains a major question: were they born in Greece or were they native to southern Italy and Sicily? In other words, did the Greek colonizing expeditions regularly include women (i.e., wives) or were they composed only of men who then married local women in the regions of their new cities? The main aim of this essay is to address this question, as it is critical to understanding the social identities of women in the Greek West.

This goal involves examining earlier time periods (especially the eighth to sixth centuries BCE) and different forms of evidence. There is some literary evidence relating to the roles of women in Greek settlement overseas, but much of the most important evidence is mortuary in nature. In addition to the *kourotrophos* of Megara Hyblaia (Figure 16.1), the graves and their contents—both artifactual and skeletal—of Greek sites in Magna Graecia are crucial to the investigation of the role and position of women in the settlement of Sicily and southern Italy by the Greeks (see also Liston, this volume, Chapter 9). Although the term "Magna Graecia" in its strictest sense denotes only southern Italy, here the term will be used in its more casual sense to include Sicily also. Before we examine the funerary evidence, however, we must briefly review the limited textual evidence relating to the migration of Greek women and intermarriage with local women, together with the approaches of modern scholars.

The case of the foundation of Cyrene in Libya by the Therans is often central to modern discussions of the participation and roles of women in Greek settlement abroad. Herodotus (4.150–8) provides two versions of the story, one told by the Therans and one by the Cyreneans. In the Theran version, a party was sent to Cyrene under the oikist (colony-founder) Battus, in response to an oracular command and an ensuing drought. In the selection process, brothers from all seven villages of Thera drew lots to determine who should go. Two penteconters (Greek oared ships with fifty rowers) were sent. In the Cyrenean version, unspecified problems and an oracle resulted in Battus and his party likewise setting off for Africa in two penteconters.

The fact that Herodotus here alludes only to males in the settlement stories is not particularly significant: the activities of spouses and relations rarely feature in ancient texts unless they play a particular role in the narrative. Herodotus might have expected his audience to assume that women and other dependents would have accompanied the men selected for the mission. A little later, however, Herodotus (4.186) makes a passing reference to the fact that the women of Cyrene, like the Libyan nomads, did not eat cows' meat, out of respect for Egyptian Isis. This remark has been taken to mean that the settlers were indeed all male and that upon arrival they took indigenous wives, who retained their traditional eating customs. While earlier modern scholarship was often reluctant to accept that Greeks abroad might have intermarried with local populations (see further below), this passage has had great appeal for more recent scholars, who are less influenced by the models of modern imperial practices and are thus open to evidence of intermarriage between Greeks and indigenous populations. It has also been taken to indicate not only that the Greeks did intermarry with locals but also that overseas initiatives were arranged on a very practical basis. Men, ideally young, would be best suited to set up the new foundation, on the basis of the practical work required; women, children, and old people would be hindrances; and the men could find wives and establish a sustainable population for the settlement after the initial ground work had been done.

Nevertheless, the applicability of this evidence to Magna Graecia in particular remains highly problematic. The selection of the settlement party (at least in the Theran version) appears highly organized, and even if this account reflects a reality—as opposed to Theran hindsight of a "fair" approach—there is no evidence to suggest that similar systems were applied in other cases. Indeed, while the foundation of Cyrene has the flavor of a state-organized venture, other Greek states abroad are just as likely to have started off as private enterprises. Their contingents may have been determined on a different basis.

Moreover, there are dangers in assuming that practicality was a ruling factor in deciding who joined. While it might seem obvious to send only those best equipped to found a new settlement, accounts of such ventures in the modern period show that such a principle was not always the case. For example, the history of the early European settlement of North America often displays a staggering lack of practicality: ships from Europe arrived in the middle of the harsh northern American winter, and settler groups did not necessarily include individuals with the requisite practical skills such as hunting or farming or, in the case of Jamestown in Virginia, who were even prepared to do the work necessary for their own survival. Yet such settlements could survive, despite numerous deaths, and women and children were among the first arrivals in the New World. Whether or not the circumstances of Greek settlement abroad encouraged a more pragmatic approach is debatable and cannot be assumed. In any case, even if practicality was important in the first place, women could of course have arrived from Greece at a later stage in the settlement process (as in Murray 1980: 110–11).

Other literary evidence for the roles and identities of women in Greek settlements abroad, including those relating specifically to Magna Graecia, has been used to argue both for and against the participation of Greek women (see Shepherd 1999, with references). Accounts of intermarriage relate to rather isolated or unusual circumstances, such as the case of Demaratus who, escaping Kypselid Corinth, fled to Etruria and married a local Tarquinian (Cicero, *De Republica* 2.19–20). Even if his companions (cf. Strabo 5.2.2) did likewise, they joined an Italian community as asylum seekers, a situation very different from that of independent Greek settlements. So too with the founding of Miletus, where, according to Herodotus (1.146; cf. Pausanias 7.2.6), the Greeks did not take women with them but acquired local Carian women as wives, having first disposed of the women's male relatives—the explanation, Herodotus claims, for the traditionally unsociable behavior of Milesian women towards their husbands.

The evidence for the involvement of Greek women, especially in Magna Graecia, is slightly stronger, but still far from convincing. Polybius (12.5.3–11) claims a remarkable role for the women of Epizephyrian Locri in Italy as bearers of noble bloodlines derived from women of the 100 leading families of Locri in Greece. Equally, as van Compernolle (1976) argues, this tale may be a fabrication of the Classical period designed to serve political ends (see also Pembroke 1970). In other accounts, individual Greek women are named as occupying particular positions: in the foundation story for Taras in Italy

(Pausanias 10.5–8), the wife of the oikist Phalanthos plays a crucial role in the narrative by crying over her despondent husband as she comfortingly de-louses him, thus instantiating the Delphic instruction that he should establish his city where he felt "rain under a cloudless sky [*aethra*]." An oikist's wife might have been an exceptional member of the settler group and should not be taken as indicative of the regular participation of Greek wives. In addition, her name, Aethra, is suspicious here, and suggests a back-formed tale from a later period. At Massalia (modern Marseille), one Aristarcha is named as a priestess, again a specific and prominent role; but equally, as argued by Rougé (1970), she may be a later invention to account for the Temple of Artemis of Ephesus at Massalia.

At its best, the evidence relates to Greek women in particularly high-status roles (see also Graham 1980–1) but tells us nothing about more ordinary women: the activities of prominent women in the creation of Magna Graecia neither indicate nor preclude a broader level of female participation. But, even for these special women, the possibility of later invention to explain particular circumstances cannot be discounted. Most of the situations cited by ancient authors are unusual, and their individuality explains their inclusion in the literary record but provides little to illuminate the wider roles, positions, and identities of the women of Magna Graecia.

The scanty nature of the literary evidence and the differing ways in which it might be interpreted have, unsurprisingly, given rise to varying modern opinion regarding the early women of Magna Graecia. Such views have arguably been influenced as much by shifts in wider approaches to antiquity (and indeed in modern society) as they have by the actual evidence. Thus, as the later twentieth century saw the rise of feminist and multicultural debates and theories, which played a significant role in the development of research themes such as the study of women in antiquity and postcolonialism, so the scholarly community became more amenable to the idea of intermarriage between Greek males and southern Italian or Sicilian women. If today it is fair to say that the general consensus is that intermarriage between Greeks and indigenes did occur, and was a significant factor in the formation of Greek societies in the West—together with wider social implications, such as bilingualism (e.g., Coldstream 1993)—then it is also true to say that scholars thought the opposite until more recent decades.

Early studies of the Greek West devoted little space to the question of women and intermarriage, in part no doubt because of the scarcity of evidence but also perhaps as a reflection of the subsidiary roles of women in modern society. Anglophone scholarship particularly shows the influence of modern-era imperialist views on racial intermixing. While the presence of indigenous women in Greek settlements was entertained as a possibility, it was also dismissed as a rarity or aberration that had little or no impact on Greek culture. Thus, for example, Edward Freeman, in his four-volume work *A History of Sicily from the Earliest Times*, published between 1891 and 1894, postulated that at Megara Hyblaea in Sicily the "mixture of Greek and Sikel blood may have been greater … than in most Sikeliot cities." He based this remark on the grounds that the Megarians had been given their land by the local king Hyblon (Thuc. 6.4). But he immediately undermined the idea with the observation that our sources do not tell us of a marriage between the Greek leader and the daughter of the Sikel "prince"—or indeed of what he tellingly refers to as the "rarer form" of a marriage between the Sikel prince and the daughter of the Greek leader (Freeman 1891–4 vol. I: 389–90).

In any case, since Freeman held the view that the Sikels were so susceptible to Hellenization that they could readily be turned into "artificial Greeks" (1891–4 vol. I: 308), any Sikel women must have been of negligible consequence. Subsequent scholars felt the need to act as apologists for those Greeks who might have intermarried. Aubrey Gwynn (1918: 109), with Cyrene in mind, excused those who did on the grounds of the extenuating circumstances of relative remoteness and the absence of skin-color differences, while Thomas Dunbabin (1948: 160, 186) argued that intermarriage might have occurred in some Greek settlements in Italy with weak mother cities, confused foundation traditions, and "a mixture of men from many states of Greece." For Dunbabin, however, the clinching evidence for his argument that "the citizen bodies of the colonies [of Magna Graecia] were as pure Greek as those of Old Greece" (Dunbabin 1948: 192) came from the archaeological record. The archaeological exploration of Magna Graecia, and especially that of Sicily, progressed rapidly over the late nineteenth and earlier twentieth centuries, with the result that material culture could more readily be deployed by Dunbabin and others. At this point the burial evidence first becomes particularly critical to our understanding of women in Magna Graecia. Despite Dunbabin's concession that "on general grounds some intermarriage is likely enough," he reinforced the argument for the migration of Greek women through his assertion that

> The strongest argument that Sikels and other native peoples were not admitted to the Greek colonies except perhaps as slaves lies in the cemeteries of the colonies … thousands of archaic graves have been excavated … not more than one or two of them contain objects which can be regarded as Sikel or Italian.
>
> (Dunbabin 1948: 46)

This newer evidence certainly chimed well with the approaches of Dunbabin—who outlined his own working model of the British empire in the preface of his work—and others who were not predisposed to view the Greeks as consorting with the natives, but it also raised an important issue regarding the interaction of Greeks with Sikels and Italians, whether female or not. Although the interpretation of some of this material evidence has altered more recently (see below), it was, and remains, extremely difficult to identify objects of Sikel or Italian origin or derivation within Greek settlements in the West. There are some exceptions—notably the metalwork—but Dunbabin's point also raises the methodological problem of the ethnic significance of material culture and the overwhelmingly "Greek" nature of the archaeological evidence for the states of Magna Graecia, especially for earlier periods.

By the late 1960s, scholarly attitudes could be very different: Moses Finley (1968: 18) for example, declared that "it is hardly likely that an adequate number [of women] (if any) were brought from Greece." Subsequent opinions were along similar lines; for example, Sarah Pomeroy's (1975: 33–4) view that "when colonizing expeditions were predominantly or totally male, the colonists were often forced to find wives among the native population" or Carol Dougherty's assertion (1993: 67) that "there is little doubt that intermarriage took place, despite the reticence of the Greeks to mention it" (see also Boardman 1980: 163, 190). Not all of these more recent views supported their assertions with evidence, being perhaps as much at the mercy of wider contemporary thinking about the position of women and inter-cultural relations as their more imperially minded predecessors had been (see Snodgrass 2005). Dougherty's study, which identified metaphorical allusion to intermarriage in ancient literature, was an important exception in this shifting scholarly stance (Dougherty 1993).

2   Case Study: Pithekoussai

The lack of archaeological evidence noted by Dunbabin—the absence of Sicilian or Italian objects at Greek sites in Magna Graecia that might indicate interaction with local women—has on the whole not been addressed, with some notable exceptions. One of the most important of these was Giorgio Buchner's analysis of the funerary evidence at the earliest Greek settlement in Italy, Pithekoussai (Buchner and Ridgway 1992).

Pithekoussai, on the island of Ischia in the Bay of Naples, was founded some time before 750 BCE by the Euboeans, from Greece. One of the better known areas of the site, the San Montano cemetery, has been partially excavated and yielded 501 graves of late Geometric date (c. 750–700 BCE). Owing to the acidity of the soil, its geothermal heat, and the use of cremation as well as inhumation, skeletal material is not well preserved and is as such of limited use. Instead, the method so often applied in separating the genders—the categorization of burials by their "male" as opposed to "female" grave goods—was used here and was often based on metal jewelry items in the graves (see Liston, this volume, Chapter 9).

Among these jewelry items, some of the most important were fibulae of various designs. The pattern of their deposition does suggest some rationale, which is very likely gender-based: on the chest of the deceased there was either a single "serpentine" fibula, which may have bound a cloak or shroud, or there were other types of fibulae (Figure 16.3: *navicella*, leech, bone and amber, etc.), which were found in multiples, often at the shoulders in a manner typical for female dress. The interpretation of these fibulae has altered since Dunbabin wrote, at which time some of the fibula types, notably those with a bone and amber decoration on the bow, were thought to be imports from Greece (see Shepherd 1999). They are now understood to be of Italian make or at least derivation, and in fact the Mezzavia industrial quarter of Pithekoussai has produced evidence for the manufacture of the bone-and-amber type. All this led Buchner to correlate the origin of the fibulae with that of the grave occupants and make the argument that here, at last, was clear evidence for the presence of indigenous women as wives in the Greek settlements of the West: Italian women married Greeks but retained their traditional dress.

Buchner's argument was well received by a scholarly community that was by then much more amenable to concepts of intermarriage and also much more interested in women in antiquity. Yet it is also methodologically problematic: much recent research has highlighted the pitfalls of direct correlations between artifacts and ethnic identities, and as luxury metal items the fibulae carry extra potential for crossing ethnic and cultural boundaries, as is well illustrated by the possibility of Greek "male" use of the serpentine fibula. These fibulae do not occur exclusively, or even mostly, in the graves of adult women: around half of the graves containing fibulae were those of children (some of them very young), among whom gender distinctions are potentially weaker or blurred, and the fibulae appear to have functioned less as actual dress items and more as ostentatious grave offerings designed to advertise family status.

The same is true at other Greek sites where fibulae have been found (although in much fewer numbers), such as Syracuse, Megara Hyblaea, and Gela in Sicily (Shepherd 1999). In addition, as has been pointed out by those who remain unconvinced that significant migration of Greek women did not occur, Greek straight dress pins abound among the grave goods of Greek sites in the West (although they are rare at Pithekoussai) and thus form as much an argument for the presence of Greek women as the fibulae do for the presence of Italians and Sicilians (Graham 1982; see also Holloway 1991: 51–2;

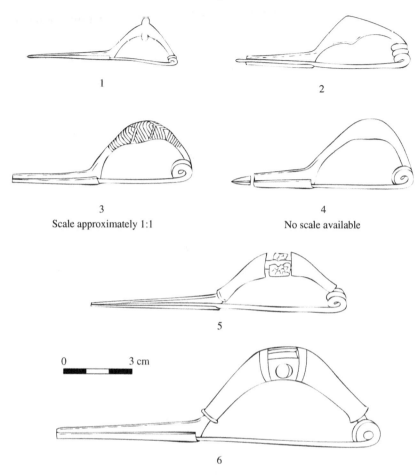

Figure 16.3 Italian fibulae types from Syracuse. Nos. 1–3: Navicella fibulae; No. 4: Leech fibula; Nos. 5–6: Bone-and-amber fibulae. Similar types occur at Pithekoussai and other Greek sites in Italy and Sicily. Drawing by H. Buglass after Orsi (1895).

Hodos 1999). In sum, while the fibulae and other metalwork in the graves of Magna Graecia have given us better evidence for interaction at some level (at the very least trade), they do not help us much more than the literary evidence in terms of illuminating the origins of the women of Magna Graecia. A more persuasive indication of interaction with local populations might be found in the assemblages overall at Pithekoussai, where closer links with Italian practice might be found in the considerable quantities, as much as the types, of metal work deposited, but this situation is harder to detect elsewhere.

Nevertheless, the analysis of grave goods and patterns in their distribution has contributed to the identification of women in the archaeological record of the Greek West, especially when used in conjunction with advances in skeletal analysis. Unfortunately the latter evidence is not always available, especially from the excavations of the late nineteenth and earlier twentieth centuries, and it is also the case that patterns in grave goods that might illustrate gender are not always readily detectable (see also Liston, this volume, Chapter 9).

Yet some patterns are distinctive enough to allow tentative identification of women, such as in the fibulae distribution at Pithekoussai. At Syracuse, for example, some very large and deep archaic *fossa* (trench) graves cut in the bedrock contained very ostentatious bronze nails that may once have adorned (rather than simply held together) wooden coffins or biers—one such grave contained around five kilograms of such nails (Orsi 1893). Dress pins of bronze, iron, or sometimes silver are relatively common finds at Syracuse, but rarely occur in the fossa graves or in conjunction with the nails; rather, they appear in another type of elite grave, the monolithic sarcophagus. The apparent separation of nails and pins into different grave types can be explained in more than one way: wealth might play a role, but gender is certainly another possibility. If the pin distribution and grave types do allow us to identify females, then it also appears to be the case that women in Syracuse at least could be defined, at death, in parallel, rather than hierarchical, gender terms. While their often wealthy burials might still have been designed to denote the status of the wider (male) kinship group, nevertheless they were accorded an equivalent, rather than inferior, treatment in the funerary arena.

3   Case Study: Pantanello

The graves of the Pantanello Necropolis (sixth to third century BCE), a rural necropolis in the chora of Metaponto in southern Italy, have been subject not only to grave-good analysis but also independent analysis of the skeletal data, which has provided some intriguing new insights into the definition of women through funerary systems. As elsewhere, gender distinctions via grave goods are not always easy to detect. Vase shapes do not appear to be related to the gender of the deceased, although a possible exception might be the *lebes gamikos*, which was usually associated with female graves, although it occasionally appeared with males and children. The connections between this shape and marriage and (premature) death proposed for other areas of the Greek world may have operated at Pantanello as well (Carter 1998: 187–8, with references). Equally, some of the gender associations proposed for other sites in the Greek West do not seem to have applied at Pantanello. For example, Luca Cerchiai (1982: 291–2) has proposed that at Epizephyrian Locri between c. 550 and 450 BCE women were clearly identified through personal ornaments, while males were defined through the drinking vessels (skyphoi, kylikes, etc.) that accompanied their burials. At Pantanello, these vase shapes do not appear to have carried gender correlations, as they appear in female graves as well as male (Carter 1998: 586).

Thus, the implication is that females and males could be defined in different ways at different places and times and that such definitions might contribute towards distinguishing the burial systems of individual *poleis* in Italy and Sicily. In death at least, female identity in Magna Graecia may not have been conceived in wholly universal terms, but rather its precise formulation was closely tied to the cultural definition of the wider but immediate community.

The sort of detailed anthropological analysis carried out at Pantanello is unfortunately not typical, and for most cemeteries of Magna Graecia no skeletal analysis has been possible. Thus, much of the identification of women in the funerary record may be based on our own generic notions of how Greek female identity might have been portrayed (cf. Carter 1998: 583). While sex determination on the basis of skeletal evidence is also far from unproblematic, nevertheless, when certain it is obviously critical in assessing any variations in the treatment of the sexes at death. Reassuringly, the Pantanello material does reinforce some of our more traditional associations between grave goods and gender—such as that between mirrors, jewelry, toilet articles, and females (Carter 1998: 584–5)—but it also introduces some more subtle nuances into the picture and raises some intriguing new questions.

One question relates to the use of strigils in graves. These tend to be interpreted as "male" objects when found in graves throughout the Greek world, although females are known to have used them (Carter 1998: 584; Prohá34szka 1998: 801, with references; see also Neils, this volume, Chapter 11). Many strigils are indeed associated with male graves at Pantanello as well. Yet, at least three (and possibly up to five) females were also buried with strigils, and the anthropological evidence not only allows these women to be securely identified but also suggests that smaller, finer strigils were associated with them (a subtlety nicely illustrated by grave T. 189, where a woman was buried with an iron strigil, a bronze mirror, a shell cosmetic container, and two coins: see Carter 1998: 801ff.). The fact that strigils in female graves do not appear before the end of the fifth century BCE is also a reminder that artifacts associated with female (and male) gender could also change over time.

The Pantanello analyses also deliver a timely reminder that gender division through material culture may not have been as concrete a concept in the ancient mind as we would like it to have been. While the correlation of grave goods and sex does seem broadly to confirm our expectations, the gender division is not always expressed in clear or unequivocal terms. In one or two cases it may be positively breached, if we have understood the evidence correctly. Tomb 231 at Pantanello (late fifth to early fourth centuries BCE), for example, contained six fibulae and a bronze mirror. Based on patterns observed elsewhere in the cemetery, the grave goods suggest a female burial, as males usually received only one or two fibulae. Yet the analysis of the relatively well-preserved skeletal material found the occupant to be a male. For Tombs 209 and 292 (respectively later fifth and later sixth centuries BCE) the skeletal evidence was more equivocal, but again both were identified biologically as males and both had "female" goods: in the first case, these included a mirror and two *lebetes gamikoi*, as well as an *alabastron*, a shape more often associated with females than males (Carter 1998: 186, but cf. 760); in the second, the goods included six pins (like fibulae, multiple pins appear to be associated with females), tweezers, a mirror, an alabastron, and a glass bead.

Skeletal analysis of graves, especially at Pantanello, has raised two further issues regarding women in Magna Graecian society. The first relates to the identification of dental characteristics apparently specific to Italian populations, in particular the "Etruscan" upper lateral incisor (see also Liston, this volume, Chapter 9). This feature has not as yet been identified in skeletons in mainland Greece, but is well attested in Italy and appears with some frequency at Pantanello, with the obvious explanation being that there was intermarriage between the Greeks of Metaponto and local populations and a consequent mixing of inherited biological characteristics. The high frequency of the "Etruscan" incisor at Pantanello, a cemetery serving a rural population, might further suggest—perhaps unsurprisingly—that more extensive interaction took place in rural than urban areas, a situation also hinted at through other metric dental distinctions between rural and urban females between the seventh and fifth centuries BCE (Henneberg and Henneberg 1998: 515–17, 2001; Carter 2006: 82–3, with references).

4   Cemetery Demographics

Another resonance of local populations may be detectable through the burials of women: the second intriguing social phenomenon identified in the Pantanello Necropolis (also encountered elsewhere) is the proportion of women to men. Although the ratio of female to male burials should be around 1:1 if the full dying population is represented, at Pantanello women outnumber men by approximately 2:1 for individuals between the ages of fifteen and forty-nine in the period 500–301 BCE (from which the majority of the burials derive). A distinct imbalance is also observable in the urban Crucinia Necropolis of Metaponto, and Saldone, a small rural cemetery. Greek cities are known to have suffered from *oligandria* (shortage of males), yet here the longevity of the problem seems to suggest rather that many males under fifty were buried elsewhere in an as yet undiscovered cemetery—perhaps one related to citizen achievements, rather like the *demosion sema* of Athens—and other areas were reserved predominantly for females (Carter 1998: 147–8, 153–5; Henneberg and Henneberg 1998: 509).

Female prominence in major cemeteries is not a situation we expect to see in a Greek context, even taking into account the limited skeletal analysis available for the Greek world generally, but it has been encountered in other Italic contexts. For example, further north, the Iron Age cemeteries of Osteria dell'Osa and nearby Castiglione (Lazio) display similarly skewed sex ratios, even if for rather different periods (Bietti Sestieri 1992: 99ff.). Back in Magna Graecia, a preponderance of females has also been observed from the (admittedly scanty) skeletal evidence from Pithekoussai, where social interactions between Greeks and local populations may have been similar to those at Metaponto (Becker 1995). Only further analysis of the cemetery populations of Greece as well as Italy will be able to clarify whether or not this was a more widespread phenomenon in the ancient world, but again the women of Magna Graecia seem to have been accorded a different, but arguably parallel, identity at death in relation to the male population, rather than an inferior one, and in this case at least this identity seems to have been derived from Italic custom rather than from Greek practice.

5   Domestic Architecture

While the funerary arena provides some of our best evidence for examining the position of women in Magna Graecia, other contexts may also prove fruitful. In Greece, the arrangement of domestic space and the study of Greek women has received much attention, especially in relation to the possible separation of genders within the house (see Trümper, this volume, Chapter 21). The evidence for domestic architecture in Magna Graecia is to date very limited in quantity and quality, but what does survive suggests that, although there are broad similarities with the houses of mainland Greece, social interaction—including that between the genders—was not reflected in, or regulated by, house design in Magna Graecia. In fifth-century Himera, for example, the position of the courtyard could vary considerably, while at Gela the courtyard seems to have been relatively small, suggesting that here it played a less central role in domestic activities and movement than it seems to have done in Greece. The rarity of single-entrance courtyard houses in the West before the mid-fourth century further suggests that separation between household members—especially females—and outsiders did not require such clear delineation as it did in Greece itself (Nevett 1999). Further work will help to expand this picture; for the present it might be noted that Himera, which provides one of the best assemblages of preserved domestic structures, has also produced a higher amount of indigenous pottery than has thus far been found on other sites in Sicily (Antonaccio 2005, with references).

6   Conclusions

In general, then, certain aspects of Greek culture in the West do not match those of mainland Greece as well as was often thought in the past—temple architecture of the Archaic period presents an obvious example—and in such areas the Greeks of Magna Graecia clearly forged a somewhat different cultural profile that, while recognizably Greek, was also distinctively Western Greek. Interaction with local populations may well have been a contributing factor in the formulation of Western Greek culture, a process in which women may have played a particularly important role. The extent of intermarriage and interaction remains difficult to establish, but it is clear nevertheless that a rather different culture prevailed in Magna Graecia. This difference may mean that the position and role of women in Magna Graecia was also rather different, and that the lives they led were not precisely the same as those of their mainland Greek counterparts.

RECOMMENDED FURTHER READING

While women in Classical Greece—and especially Classical Athens—have received extensive treatment in scholarly literature, there is no similarly extensive bibliography for women in Magna Graecia. Indeed there is little scholarship that addresses the issue of women for this area of the Greek world in any dedicated or systematic manner. Vase and tomb painting studies obviously look at the depiction of women (and especially their dress) and highlight some areas where women appear to have particular roles or the material is female-specific: for south Italian vase painting the numerous and fundamental studies by A. D. Trendall are essential, but a useful introductory summary is provided in his *Red Figure Vases of South Italy and Sicily* (1989). More specific examination of details of women's dress and their ethnic associations can be found in Schneider-Herrmann (1996), although more recent thinking on material culture might see more complex cultural interaction in these images. For tomb paintings, the essential study (with excellent illustrations) is Pontrandolfo and Rouveret (1992), but Corrigan (1979) is also useful. Ideas about women's activities and status are often drawn from Athenian evidence (for which see the recommendations for further reading in relevant essays in this volume).

On intermarriage, a longer account with further reading is provided in Shepherd (1999); on the historiography of Greek settlement overseas, see especially Snodgrass (2005) and Shepherd (2005). The Pantanello Necropolis of Metaponto has been used extensively in this essay: it is superbly published in Carter (1998), with important sections from other contributors, and is an excellent illustration of the value of the application of modern scientific techniques to mortuary evidence. For Pithekoussai, an invaluable introduction and analysis of the site is Ridgway's *The First Western Greeks* (1992), while a full report on the San Montano cemetery is contained in Buchner and Ridgway's *Pithekoussai I* (1992). Accounts of Sicilian Greek cemeteries are often rather indigestible nineteenth-century excavation reports (e.g., Orsi 1893 and 1895), but a summary of the evidence is provided in Shepherd (1999) with further discussion in Shepherd (1995). For a survey of housing in Magna Graecia and its social interpretation, see especially Nevett (1999).

ACKNOWLEDGMENTS

I would like to thank Sheila Dillon and Sharon James for their kind invitation to contribute to this volume and also for their editorial help and patience; thanks are also due to Elizabeth Pemberton, and to Ian McPhee, Director of the Trendall Centre, Latrobe University (Australia), where much for the research for this essay was done.

PART III

Women in a Cosmopolitan World: The Hellenistic and Late Republican Periods

In this section, there is an expansion of evidence well beyond Athens, and thus we return to a broader geographic scope. Although the rich sources of imagery from Attic vase painting effectively disappear in this period, new forms of evidence become available, from inscriptions to papyri to portraits. Named historical women, from a range of social classes, become well-attested in both textual and material evidence. We offer two case studies to begin the section—Sheila Dillon's "Hellenistic Tanagra Figurines" (Case Study III) and Sharon L. James' "Domestic Female Slaves in Roman Comedy" (Case Study IV) —both of which look at the representation of non-elite women in bodies of evidence that have tended to be overlooked in the study of women in antiquity. Other subjects here that have been little examined include female portrait statues, the relation of women to public space in both Greece and Rome, and a generational shift for elite women in the late Republic. Monika Trümper's "Gender and Space, 'Public' and 'Private'" (Chapter 21), Christina A. Salowey's "Woman on Hellenistic Grave Stelai: Reading Images and Texts" (Chapter 18), and Cheryl Cox's "Women and Family in Menander" (Chapter 20) allow us to consider the experience of ancient women on their own terms—that is, not conceptualized according to modern concerns, but understood in ways that ancient women would have recognized. As before, problems of approach and method are highlighted in this section.

A new phenomenon appeared in this period, namely the political and public prominence of specific elite women, who exercised power in a number of ways and left behind a range of evidence about themselves. These women need not have been be royal, as demonstrated by Anne Bielman in "Female Patronage in the Greek Hellenistic and Roman Republican Periods" (Chapter 17) and T. Corey Brennan in "Perceptions of Women's Power in the Late Republic: Terentia, Fulvia, and the Generation of 63 BCE" (Chapter 26), and they perceived themselves as having a right to take an active role in the lives, politics, and even wars of their cities. The Macedonian queens, of course, felt free to conduct war themselves, as Elizabeth D. Carney shows in "Oikos Keeping: Women and Monarchy in the Macedonian Tradition" (Chapter 22). Female public patronage began in this period, on many levels, from helping individual citizens to paying public debts to providing important public buildings. This pattern of female prominence and participation in public life appeared throughout this cosmopolitan period. In "Women, Education, and Philosophy" (Chapter 25), Marguerite Deslauriers traces less obvious social changes for upper-class women, whose education and participation in philosophy were not evidenced before this period. Among the elites in Rome, a new phenomenon began here, as Corey Brennan's essay shows, in which men publicly showcased their maternal ancestry, which helped to shore up their political status.

Our chronological spread here occasionally violates the designations "Hellenistic" and "Late Republican," as both Laura S. Lieber's "Jewish Women: Texts and Contexts" (Chapter 24) and Sheila Dillon's "Female Portraiture in the Hellenistic Period" (Chapter 19) extend further, to both before and after the Hellenistic period, well into the third century CE. Papyrological evidence becomes much more common in this period, and provides us with rich sources of information about women's lives in Egypt, as Maryline Parca's "The Women of Ptolemaic Egypt: The View from Papyrology" (Chapter 23) demonstrates, pointing forward to further papyrological study in the rest of this volume.

Case Study III

Hellenistic Tanagra Figurines

Sheila Dillon

Tanagra figurines (see Figure CS III.1) are the small terracotta ladies that were discovered in large numbers beginning in the late nineteenth century in a cemetery at Tanagra in Boeotia, but that were produced all over the Hellenistic world (Higgins 1986; Jeammet 2003, 2007, 2010). They survive in very large quantities, and have been found in a variety of archaeological contexts, including tombs and sanctuaries. Many preserve a great deal of polychromy, and provide valuable evidence for the range of lovely colors that once enlivened the marble statues of Hellenistic women. The Tanagra figurines are also of clear interest in the exploration and representation of female elegance, beauty, and charm.

Who are the women represented in the Tanagra figurines and what are these figurines meant to represent? These questions are not as easy to answer as one might think. The ladies of Tanagra wear sumptuous clothing, which they manipulate with style, wrapping their bodies tightly in yards of elegant and colorful fabric. They have elaborate fashion hairstyles, sport earrings, and strike poses that are both coquettish and self-possessed. Many wear straw sun hats, and carry fans or floral wreaths. Some are completely muffled in drapery, and wear mantle veils that cover much of the hair and sometimes wrap across the bottom of the face; frequently their hands are completely hidden. A very small number wear a face veil, not covering the face but thrown back over the head. A few do wear the face veil in place, but most of these are the so-called Mantle Dancers, figurines that are thought to represent dancers at religious festivals. In fact, it was suggested long ago by Dorothy Burr Thompson that the elaborate covering of head, hands, and face represented in some of the Tanagra figurines should be associated with religious ritual, and that this covering signified cleanliness before the deity (1963: 50–2). While Lloyd Llewellyn-Jones has recently asserted, based mostly on the evidence of the Tanagra figurines, that women in the Hellenistic period wore the face veil whenever they went out in public (2003, 2007), the face veil would seem, rather, to have had a very specific ritual context.

Indeed, it is clear both from visual and written evidence that in the Hellenistic period women could regularly be seen out and about in the public spaces of Hellenistic cities. Theocritus' Gorgo and Praxinoa (*Idyll* 15), for example, venture out into the crowded

Figure CS III.1 Three terracotta "Tanagra" figurines. Paris, Musée de Louvre. Photo: Réunion des Musées Nationaux/Art Resource, NY.

streets of Alexandria to make their way from Praxinoa's house on the outskirts of the city to the royal palace at the city's center to attend the festival of Adonis. On this journey, the women come into direct physical contact with male strangers, have a run-in with a horse, talk back to strange men, and are so roughed up by the crowd trying to get into the palace that Praxinoa's summer cloak is ripped in two. These two women were also long-distance travelers, originally from Syracuse; their presence in Alexandria shows the cosmopolitan nature of Hellenistic urban populations, particularly in port cities. While Gorgo and Praxinoa are of course fictional characters, the long-distance travel of real women is clearly attested, for example in the grave reliefs from Hellenistic Delos, which document the presence on the island of women from all over the Mediterranean (see Salowey, this volume, Chapter 18).

Like Gorgo and Praxinoa, real women were certainly present at a variety of public festivals. For example, women and children were among the welcoming party that greeted Attalos I when he visited Athens in April of 200 BCE (Chaniotis 1997: 236–7; Polybius 16.25.3–7). Women took part both as costumed role players and as priestesses, and probably also as onlookers, in the Grand Procession of Ptolemy Philadephus in Alexandria. Indeed, Hellenistic decrees concerning festivals encourage everyone—young, old, citizen, foreigner, men *and* women—to participate actively, to dress appropriately, to follow the processions, and to attend the sacrifices (Chaniotis 1995: 154–60, 1997: 246). In fact, in their role as priestesses, women of elite families would have been constantly in the public eye (van Bremen 1996: 142–90). Given, however, the prominent ideology of feminine modesty, especially before unrelated males, how did women negotiate these public appearances? Did they, for example, deploy particular sartorial strategies when presenting themselves for public view?

Here the Tanagra figurines provide particularly compelling vivid evidence for the ways in which women might present themselves in public. Indeed, I would argue that many of the Tanagra figurines represent women in the world of religious rituals and public festivals: the world of women on the public stage. In this world women are imagined as presenting themselves in public elegantly dressed, elaborately coiffed, and self-confidently posed. While female modesty was indeed important, it was much more important for women of elite families to be sumptuously dressed and to show themselves off in public. Elite women aimed not for public invisibility but for quite the opposite—they aimed to be noticed. Drapery played a crucial role in this public performance. The Tanagra figurines and marble statues show us that women wore luxurious and brightly colored clothing, including yellow, blue, pink, green, and red, sometimes edged with gold. Their finely pleated dresses are at times so long that they trail out behind, and they wear beautiful fringed mantles made of fine imported silk so thin as to be nearly transparent, pulled so tightly around the body that the vertical folds of the dress beneath show through. The great care with which the artists reproduced the textiles and their textures underscores the importance of clothing to these representations. These are distinguished women, who could not only afford such obviously expensive garments but knew how to wear them, to control them—as Christiane Vorster has recently pointed out, "perfection in the handling of her clothing was considered a sign of a woman's education and manners and therefore revealed much about the origin and social status of the person so depicted" (Vorster 2007: 120). Managing one's drapery effectively demanded knowledge, care, and exquisite attention to detail.

While it has long been recognized that the Tanagra figurines emulate large-scale sculpture, this influence has typically been explained purely in artistic terms of style, pose, and composition. I believe, though, that there was also a close *functional* relationship between these two genres of artistic production. Both categories of artifact—the Tanagra-style figurines and the portrait statues of women—emerged in Athens at roughly the same time, around the middle of the fourth century BCE, a synchronism that has been overlooked in previous scholarship. Further, both served as votive dedications. Terracotta figurines had been dedicated in sanctuaries since the Bronze Age; and, while there are female figurines from the Archaic and Classical periods, these seem mostly to represent goddesses. What changed with the introduction of the Tanagra figurines was the regular representation of women who are clearly and obviously mortal.

We see a similar trajectory in large-scale sculpture. It is difficult, for example, to be certain whether statues of draped women made in the Archaic and Classical periods represent goddesses or mortals; the age-old controversy surrounding the identity of the Acropolis korai, for example, demonstrates this difficulty well. The first securely identifiable portrait statues of draped women were set up in Athens beginning in the fourth century, in sanctuary contexts, as votive dedications. They frequently represent women who served as priestesses. Sometimes these statues show their subjects performing a ritual act—pouring a libation, like the portrait of Aristonoe (see Figure 17.1), or carrying a ritual object, such as a hydria, as the statue of Nikeso is thought to have done (see Figure 17.3; Dillon, this volume, Chapter 19). Other priestess statues simply stood, perfectly composed, in control of their drapery, with hands and sometimes head covered. The Tanagra figurines represent a miniaturized and more economical version of these life-sized portrait statues, an option that would have been available to many more women and that would have served a similar function—that is, to commemorate in a tangible and longer-lasting form women's participation in ephemeral religious rituals. Because they were much less expensive than a bronze or marble portrait statue, the Tanagras also tend to be less formal and less conservative in their poses and subject matter; they show us women playing, dancing, making music, conversing, and socializing. Their affordability and portability offered positive representations of women's lives to a broad range of women, who could take pleasure in these charming statuettes. They offer us a precious glimpse of the lives of Hellenistic women enjoying the social aspects of public religious festivals.

Case Study IV

Domestic Female Slaves in Roman Comedy

Sharon L. James

Roman comedy shows an array of domestic slaves, most prominently the male clever slave, or trickster. In the background, however, are female slaves of all types: minor or silent characters, elderly nurses, maids-of-all-work, prostitutes of all sorts, and non-commercial sex slaves. The question here is how to approach this group. The first task is to recall that these plays trade in broad social stereotypes and are popular entertainment, so they cater to standard social views. In other words, they offer comically exaggerated depictions of all the social categories—male, female, citizen, non-citizen, free, unfree, foreign, native—that filled daily life in antiquity. With respect to slaves, these depictions sometimes come very close to reality.

The next issue is the category "domestic slave." The term is normally understood to designate a slave who belongs to a citizen family. But the word *domus* (house) is not limited to the citizen home: many private houses were occupied by non-citizens, and the private slave could belong to a business operation that was not concerned with family life. Many of Roman comedy's homes are small private brothels, in which female slaves may be either houseworkers or prostitutes—or both. In a citizen household, a slave woman might well be specifically a sex slave, a woman bought for the purposes of sex (a function also fulfilled by other household slaves). The category "household" must be kept broad.

Finally there is the issue of Roman comedy. These plays were translated from Greek originals and freely adapted by the Roman playwrights. They retain Greek names and settings, presenting a mixture of Greek and Roman laws, customs, and references. I have argued elsewhere (James 1998; 2006) that the Romans received these plays as speaking about Roman social and sexual values rather than depicting Greek customs. (Of course, to a large extent the lives of enslaved women were very similar all over the ancient world.)

In Roman comedy, young women slaves (as well as enslaved boys) are the objects of predatory sexual desire by male owners as well as male fellow slaves. Plautus' *Mercator* offers one example of the calculations by men to gain sexual access to a beautiful young slave. This young woman, probably seventeen or eighteen years old, is the object of sexual fascination and comic competition between the father, Demipho, and his son Chalinus,

A Companion to Women in the Ancient World, First Edition. Edited by Sharon L. James and Sheila Dillon.
© 2012 John Wiley & Sons, Ltd. Published 2015 by John Wiley & Sons, Ltd.

who has brought her home after two years of traveling with her. He does not want to tell his father that she is his concubine, so he says he is bringing her as a gift to his mother. His father objects, articulating a theory about female household slaves:

> She doesn't have the right looks for our house. We don't need a female slave unless she weaves, grinds meal, chops wood, makes wool, sweeps the house, takes a beating, cooks the household's daily food. (395–8)

The Latin verb *vapulo*, "to take a beating," stands out here in this list of constant hard work for the domestic slave. Its casual inclusion as part of the enslaved woman's daily lot tells us much about the unspoken attitudes of the owner classes in antiquity toward their slaves. The hard and varied (i.e., non-specialized) domestic labor would occur constantly throughout the (long) day, punctuated by physical abuse at the owner's whim. (The same applies to old female slaves: see Staphyla of *Aulularia*, Halisca of *Cistellaria*, Scapha of *Mostellaria*; in Menander, see Simiche of *Dyskolos* and Sophrone of *The Arbitrants*.)

In other Roman comedies, women slaves are intimate confidantes of their mistresses, and they know all the secrets of the house. A teenaged girl made pregnant by rape may seek secret assistance from an older slave, as in Plautus' *Aulularia* and *Truculentus*; in Terence's *Eunuchus*, the old nurse is the only person who knows the tokens that identify the girl Pamphila as a long-lost citizen daughter. Mysis of *Andria* and Sophrona of *Phormio* continue to look after their orphaned young mistresses, as does Giddenis of *Poenulus* with her kidnapped young charges. In *Casina*, the wife of the old lecher conspires with her slave Pardalisca and a neighbor in a plot to keep the old man from getting his hands on the young slave.

Slaves owned by courtesans tend to be fully integrated partners in their mistress' business operations (as in *Eunuchus*, *Miles Gloriosus*, *Persa*, and *Truculentus*), but they are not necessarily safe from threats, by those same mistresses, of abuse (*Eunuchus*, *Hecyra*)—even though such owners may well have been slaves themselves once (even recently, as in *Mostellaria*). In *Truculentus*, a maid comes on stage having just suffered torture, precisely for having kept secret the pregnancy by rape of her young mistress. Prostitutes owned by pimps are slave women in houses—Roman comedy does not feature large brothels—and as part of their daily lot they face not only physical abuse by their owners (as in *Pseudolus*) but the prospect of being sold away, usually to go on campaign with an unpleasant soldier. Former prostitutes, even freed former slaves, may find themselves forced back into slavery once they are too old to attract customers (Scapha of *Mostellaria*).

But, for all the grim realities of life for its female slaves, usually shown in quick sidelong glimpses, Roman comedy also allows these women to speak their own minds and show their perspectives on citizen society. As a rule, those perspectives are skeptical, even cynical: Pardalisca of *Casina* mocks the gluttony of her mistress. The witty Acropolistis of *Epidicus* makes fun of the owner class right to their faces. Syra of *Mercator* delivers an extraordinary speech lamenting the sexual double standard: this elderly female slave, loyal to her mistress, voices sentiments not recorded elsewhere in antiquity, in words no citizen woman would be permitted to say:

> Goodness, women live under a hard law—and it's so much more unfair than for men. Because if a man brings a whore home, behind his wife's back, and she learns about it, he can't be punished. But if a wife goes out of the house behind her husband's back, he's got cause for

divorce, and she's dumped. If only the law were the same for a wife as for a husband! See, a good wife is content with a single husband—why should a husband be less content with a single wife? Goodness, if I could fix it, if men were punished the same way, when anybody brought home a whore behind his wife's back, the way women are divorced who bring it on themselves, there'd be a lot more men being dumped than there are women now! (*Mercator* 817–29)

Enslaved women in Roman comedy are visible on a broad spectrum, then, from silent brothel prostitutes to lively, active participants in household affairs. The genre portrays both impossible fantasies, such as the restoration of a brothel slave to her citizen family (still a virgin), and the ugly daily realities of the lives of female domestic slaves in antiquity.

17

Female Patronage in the Greek Hellenistic and Roman Republican Periods

Anne Bielman

The support given to ancient communities by women from the fourth to the first centuries BCE will be analyzed here under the term "female patronage," which one might call "public patronage." "Private patronage" (Dixon 2001: 89–106), namely the support given to one individual by another individual in the context of personal relationships, will not be discussed, and, since the relevance of a comparative approach in terms of women's studies has recently been demonstrated (Cova 2006), I shall consider, in parallel, Greek and Roman/Italian documents.

The comparative method and women's history pose particularly sharp problems of translation in a subject such as ancient female patronage, for two reasons. First, the subject results from the analysis of institutions, yet some seemingly similar concepts overlap different realities in the societies of the Greek Hellenistic and Roman Republican periods. For example, the concept of "patronage" (from Latin *patronus*, "patron")—that is, support given by a person of influence—has no precise equivalent in Greek: the term "euergetism" (from Greek *euergetes*, "benefactor/benefactress") means all acts of good-will on the part of an individual towards his fellow citizens. Further, the terms describing the public role played by an individual are rooted in a male reference system, just as they are in modern Western society. This lexical pattern makes it difficult to apply certain terms to women: the Latin word *patrona* is derived from the masculine form *patronus*, which is itself formed from *pater* and refers to an essentially masculine authority. In addition, the rights and duties of the *patronus* and of the *patrona* were not necessarily the same. (In modern French, for example, the use of the feminine noun *patronne* carries with it a negative connotation that the masculine noun *patron* does not have.)

Second, in order to grasp the meaning of Greek and Roman texts, we must use a translation that establishes a correspondence between ancient and modern concepts—yet ancient and modern concepts evolve along with the social morals of their times. Hence, certain words in ancient documents dealing with "female patronage" do not carry the same

A Companion to Women in the Ancient World, First Edition. Edited by Sharon L. James and Sheila Dillon.
© 2012 John Wiley & Sons, Ltd. Published 2015 by John Wiley & Sons, Ltd.

meanings when brought into modern English, German, or French. Indeed, a great number of concepts relating to contemporary institutions derive their meanings from the nineteenth century, as their original meanings were linked to the history and language of each European country. Thus, the English word "patronage" refers directly to the Latin *patronus* and means primarily the favors accorded by an influential person; yet, the expression "political patronage" has a specific institutional meaning in modern-day Canada. The French word "*patronage*" refers to the protection of a saint, and in the nineteenth century also came to refer to bourgeois charity work; to mean the financial or moral support of a powerful person, the French language opts for the word "*parrainage*."

This study aims to analyze "female patronage" based on practices confirmed by texts engraved in stone and destined from the outset to preserve the memory of a person engaged in the public cause; literary sources, notably those of the Republican period, will also be employed. Two major aspects of "female patronage" emerge from primary sources: (1) donating money to the community and (2) acting personally, to make oneself seen and/or listened to by the community.

1 Donating Money and Public/Civic Buildings

Several documents (Bielman 2002: no. 32) issued by the city of Kyme, around 130–100 BCE, evoke the constructions financed by Archippe: she had the Council building restored (the *bouleuterion*). In this project, she afforded the building plans, the cost of the work, and the salaries of the workmen. Archippe's family situation is only partially known: the daughter of a benefactor from Kyme, she had a brother called Olympios, who may have died prematurely, thereby forcing Archippe to bear the sole responsibility of managing the paternal fortune. Hers is not the sole example: Megakleia, in second-century BCE Megalopolis, financed a guesthouse to lodge the public guests of the city, while at the end of the first century BCE Theodosia restored the agora of her city of Arkesine (Bielman 2002: nos. 31, 33).

These Greek women's architectural works echo that of Eumachia of Pompeii in the Augustan era (Frei-Stolba and Zimmermann 1998: 100). She had a building erected (measuring sixty by forty meters) in the forum and her name and her son's name were inscribed on it (see D'Ambra, this volume, Chapter 29). A descendent of a Campanian *gens* that had gained its wealth from owning vineyards and pottery workshops, Eumachia was the widow of a Pompeian *duumvir*. It was after her husband's death that she launched into this architectural undertaking. She may be compared to the widow Mineia, who commissioned the reconstruction of the forum's basilica in Paestum at the end of the first century BCE; on it she had inscribed the names of her husband, son, brothers, and nephew (Torelli 1996: 154–8).

The similarity between the situations of Archippe, Eumachia, and Mineia is striking: these mature, wealthy women, without husbands, show originality in their choice of architectural projects. To restore the *bouleuterion* or build an edifice in the forum affirmed the power and fortune of a woman in a masculine community. Clearly, these women builders felt sufficiently integrated into their communities, and were esteemed enough, to contribute to the development of their cities, in much the same way as the male members of those communities.

A number of women financed military work as well. In the beginning of the third and second centuries BCE at Aspendos in Pamphylia, two women holding the highest magistracy of the city donated a considerable sum of money for the restoration of the city walls (Bielman 2002: no. 16). The maintenance of the walls drained the city's budget, so the magistrates often had to contribute to the expenditure. Unlike Archippe or Megakleia, the two women of Aspendos did not choose the kind of construction that they financed: the amount of expenditure and its allocation were imposed upon them within their magistracy.

In the same manner, Phile, who held the highest office of Priene during the first century BCE, was encouraged to finance a holding tank and a network of pipelines (Bielman 2002: no. 18). Social pressure and the weight of tradition led the women who were placed at the head of their cities to spend colossal sums of money on public works, just as their male counterparts might do. It is worth noting here that the involvement of women in the field of military construction remained specifically part of the Hellenistic world, and was connected with opportunities available to Greek women who held public office.

Religious buildings in particular attracted the interest of benefactresses. In the first century BCE, Epie, a citizen of Thasos, had several temples restored (Bielman 2002: no. 8). She took these initiatives as *neokoros*, the individual chosen by the city to maintain sanctuaries. Epie bore successively or jointly the responsibility for several sanctuaries, as no other Thasian citizen wanted to be in charge. Hers is not the only example of female activity: indeed, several Greek priestesses were responsible for restoring the sanctuaries of the divinities they served.

In Pompeii in the Augustan period, the priestess Mamia P. F. (daughter of Publius), who was responsible for the cult of Venus Pompeiana, had a temple erected in honor of the Genius coloniae, probably the goddess Venus (Frei-Stolba and Zimmermann 1998: 98). In Paestum, Mineia, who had the basilica of the forum restored, having added a temple of Mater Matuta, saw herself honored in a spectacular fashion: she was named *patrona* of the city's most important religious college and the Senate authorized a *semis* (a low-value coin) to be struck in her image and in her name (Torelli 1996: 153–8). Livia, the wife of Augustus, rebuilt the temple of Fortuna muliebris, which was falling into ruins, as well as that of the Bona Dea. She also had consecrated in the Porticus Liviae a sanctuary in honor of the goddess Concordia, which symbolized the unity of the imperial couple (Frei-Stolba 1998).

The founding of a sanctuary by a woman is extremely rare in Republican Italy. In fact, when Roman women are involved in religious architectural benefactions, these public works seem to be made only on behalf of female deities. Indeed, gendered allocation of religious benefactors appears to have been stricter in Rome than in Greece; by controlling women's initiatives in this way, Rome reduced the gap between the traditional roles assigned to women and their involvement in the public sphere. (I leave aside in this study the frequent intervention of women in the construction of family mausoleums since such projects are not formal public activity.)

In the Greek oikos, if one believes the advice of Xenophon in the Oeconomicus, the woman of the house made sure that everyone in her home was clothed and fed. Studies have shown that, beginning in the Hellenistic period, elite families considered the entire city to be part of their oikos. It is no wonder, then, that the women of these clans were concerned with the welfare of the inhabitants of the city. At Kyme, for example, Archippe twice gave money for a sacrifice and a banquet to the Council members, to the tribes of the city, to the *metoikoi* (resident aliens), and to the freedmen, and offered a collation to the citizens and residents of the city. Archippe's bounties were apparently a spontaneous sign of her gratitude for the honors accorded to her by the city. Later, in other places, the distribution of food during popular banquets seems to have been inscribed in the specifications of the magistrates. Documents show that this was the case; for example, in Syros during the Imperial period, a couple of Syrian magistrates, the male *archon* and his female counterpart the *archis*, marked the beginning of their political mandate by offering a sacrifice to Hestia, accompanied by a public banquet and the distribution of food, wine, and money to their fellow citizens (van Bremen 1996: 63). The *archis* probably had to provide food only for the female population. Another city in Aegia, Tenos, was known from the second century BCE to have had a jointly exercised archonship, and it is very possible that the Tenian *archis* also had to contribute to the provision of food during the banquets (van Bremen 1996: 63).

In Italy, in 216 BCE, the wealthy Busa distributed wheat, clothing, and money to 10,000 Roman soldiers after their defeat at the hands of Hannibal at Cannae. For this she received honors from the Senate at the end of the war (Livy 22, 52.7). This is the only intervention of a woman mentioned in this domain during the Roman Republic; on the contrary, female aid in replenishing supplies and restoring losses multiplied in the Imperial period. For example, Livia supplied dowries for many daughters of Senators who had suffered financial penalties in war (Cassius Dio 58.2.3).

In the Greco-Roman East, the expense of oil distribution to athletes was sometimes borne by women as part of their duties as gymnasiarch. Indeed, the gymnasiarchy—which was strictly a male activity in the Classical period, when the function entailed the active supervision of athletic training—was feminized from the moment it became a financial liability and no longer required the supervision and training of young male citizens. The earliest testimonial of a female gymnasiarch appears in Erythrai, in Asia Minor, and dates to the very end of the first century BCE (Bielman 2002: no. 53).

The funding of athletic games, the *agonothesia*, remained a male bastion. In the Greek East, such expenditures were allocated to women only under the empire. The first known example comes from Thasos in the mid-first century CE, where Hekataia placed two gladiators she owned against a couple of her husband's gladiators in the arena (van Bremen 1996: 115 n.3). Nevertheless, the first woman of ancient times known to have assumed the sponsorship of games alongside her husband was Livia (in 27 BCE), on the occasion of her young son Tiberius assuming the toga of manhood (Frei-Stolba 1998). However, the distinction must be made between funding games and presiding over the events: the funding of games was open to women from the end of the Hellenistic and the Republican periods, but presiding over games remained a male prerogative throughout the Imperial period.

At the beginning of the second century BCE, the city of Kopai in Boeotia concluded an agreement with two women, Kleuedra and Olympicha, so that they might loan money to the city. The city was having difficulty paying its debts, so the two women covered the totality of Kopai's debts in exchange for grazing rights, on the city's land, for their 400 heads of cattle (Bielman 2002: n. 24). Again in Boeotia, in 223 BCE, a woman named Nikareta filed a complaint for non-repayment of some 18,000 drachmas that the city of Orchomenos had borrowed from her (van Bremen 1996: 208–12). After several months of negotiations, an agreement was reached between both parties, and Nikareta was repaid. Other such documents show that wealthy Boeotian women were in no way inferior to their male counterparts in terms of financial power and patriotism in terms of interest-free loans.

While there were certainly sufficiently wealthy women in the Greek world to come to the aid of cities in a financial crisis, these examples remain isolated: of the 118 loans reported in the Hellenistic period, only three relate to creditors. These were probably owed to family circumstances that placed these women at the head of a family fortune (widowhood or death of a brother who had been primary heir). However, the participation of women in public subscriptions through modest financial contributions (e.g., repairing the city wall or supporting the maintenance of a public building) is well documented; one subscription at Kos dating to 205–201 BCE was thus open "to the voluntary citizen men and women" (Bielman 2002: no. 25). Such evidence confirms that civic duty was not only reserved for Greek men.

Wealthy Roman women made decisions themselves concerning the management of their property (Dixon 2001: 92–100). Terentia, Cicero's wife, exploited the land of *ager publicus*, but refused to pay taxes to the fiscal authorities (Cicero, *Letter to Atticus* 2.15.4). The Italian authorities, however, never considered addressing her directly in this business matter. In another example, the extremely wealthy matrons who were taxed by the triumvirs in 42 BCE refused to comply, and justified their refusal by their abstention from Roman public life (Appian, *Civil Wars* 4.32–4). Female patriotism was not conceived of in the same manner in Rome as it was in Greece.

The origins of the fortunes of Greek benefactresses are hardly mentioned. As for men, their wealth most likely came from land ownership. Female gymnasiarchs probably owned olive groves that furnished the necessary oil. Some women, such as Timo of Rhodes in the second century BCE, were active in the production of amphoras and international trade (Bielman 2002: no.38), but no specific acts of benefaction can be attributed to them. The documentation of Italy is better: several women who had a public role at Pompeii at the end of the Republic came from the *gentes*, who had made their fortune owning farms or in the tile-making industries. Literary and archaeological evidence, such as stamps on amphoras and bricks, tell us of the origins and the extent of the wealth of Roman women (Dixon 2001: 89ff.).

2 Acting Personally: Making Oneself Seen and Heard

Having a large fortune put an individual—man or woman—in a position of being able to negotiate with his or her city. This was what Archippe attempted to do: she paid, from her own money, the accumulated sum of Kyme's public debts and asked, in return, to be exempted from liturgical taxes. The liturgies of the Hellenistic period encompassed a range of public services that varied from city to city. The benefit that Archippe requested was not financial: documents allude to her poor state of health, and one might think that she wanted to avoid duties that required her presence. If so, she would have left aside the main motivation of any benefactor, namely occupying a position of prestige and being personally invested in public space. Benefactors did not consider money as an end in itself, but rather as a means to take part in social life and thereby obtain public honor.

Solidarity among Greek citizens constituted the glue of Greek society, especially in the Hellenistic period, when political upheaval made everyone's future uncertain. Trade intensified but travel was made hazardous owing to the increased number of pirates, who captured and sold citizens. Indeed, Demosthenes classified the payment of ransom to free captives from pirates as a citizen's most honorable act. One woman made herself well known in just this way: Timessa from Aigiale on the island of Amorgos (Bielman 2002: no. 29). In the third century BCE, Timessa purchased some inhabitants of Aigiale who had been kidnapped and put up for sale in the local slave market. After purchasing them, Timessa welcomed them into her house and then helped them to return to their own homes. She knew that, particularly in a small town, the loss of a few individuals could be fatal to its economic and social stability. It was thus because of patriotism that Timessa intervened in what was otherwise a man's duty. The decree that thanked her for this intervention used a term rarely applied to a woman, that of *politis* (citizen), and Timessa received an honor generally reserved for men: a place of honor in the *proedria* (theater) (Bielman 2002: no. 29).

Female support of the arts may be briefly considered here. In the Hellenistic world, some women were praised by a city for having given public lectures of their poetry or for having their works produced in a concert in a sanctuary as part of an artistic contest. These female citizens, as far as can be judged, belonged to the middle class (Bielman 2002: nos. 40, 42, 45). In Rome, women of the Republican aristocracy protected and aided some artists by organizing *salons littéraires* in their homes: see, for example, Cornelia, mother of the Gracchi (Plutarch, *Life of Cornelius Gracchus* 19.2–3), and Clodia, sister of Clodius and wife of the consul Metellus Celer, who was the benefactress and mistress of Catullus.

Many women benefited from the offices in which they were invested to fill a public role. This was the case for some Greek priestesses, whose status and privileges are discussed elsewhere in this *Companion*. They will not be discussed further here except to underline the fact that Hellenistic priesthoods—female as well as male—were considered part of the *archai* category of the public offices.

From the third century BCE, some cities of Greece and Asia Minor admitted women as magistrates. We have dozens of testimonials about women archontesses, *demiourgoi*, and *stephanephoroi*. However, the proportion of female magistrates remained very low in comparison to their male counterparts: in Miletus, where we have the most complete list of eponymous *stephanephoroi* since the sixth century BCE, only one woman was listed as having held the stephanephorate (in 3/2 CE) (van Bremen 1996: 63). Unlike the priesthood, a non-religious magistracy was not normally one of the elements a Greek woman had marked on her tombstone—a pattern that further demonstrates that a civic office for women did not hold the same prestige as did a religious office.

In Italy during the Republic, women were not allowed to be magistrates. The accession of women to the head of non-religious colleges in the Republican period has been considered, particularly for Eumachia in Pompeii, on the basis of an inscription and the statue of Eumachia dedicated by the fullers (see D'Ambra, this volume, Chapter 29 and Figure 29.2), but this hypothesis has been strongly contested (Frei-Stolba 1998: 100). We know almost nothing about the public activities required of holders of annual Greek magistracies—either male or female—apart from the fact that they improved the finances of the city through repeated donations and that they filled the function of representation, for example presiding over public banquets. The religious component of these offices was considerable (supply of sacrificial victims, maintenance of altars) but the administrative work was probably limited. Nevertheless, some women obtained, as equal to men, the eponymous magistracy—that is to say, their names were placed on all official documents issued during their year in office.

Menophila, a wealthy young woman citizen of Sardis, who died in the second century BCE after having filled the office of *stephanophoros* in her city, was portrayed on her funerary relief with a crown on her head (Bielman 2002: no. 44). We may deduce that the bearer of this magistracy, just like religious dignitaries, wore an attribute (in this case, a crown) that made the wearer identifiable, highlighting him or her before the eyes of fellow citizens. In addition, we may reasonably assume that the two privileges granted to priests and priestesses must also have been granted to male magistrates as well as to their female counterparts: walking at the head of processions during civic ceremonies and occupying a seat of honor at the theater. Is it possible that at the banquet at Tenos, which was sponsored by a couple of archontes, the female *archis* attended the banquet along with her husband? It is probably more likely that the *archis* offered and presided over the banquet reserved for the women of the city, while her husband did the same for the men.

The Vestal Virgins participated in the banquets for the college of pontiffs, but this was an exception: in the Roman world, at least until the beginning of the Imperial period, there was without doubt a gendered separation on the occasion of official banquets. In 9 BCE and again in 7 BCE, banquets were organized to celebrate Tiberius' military victories: whereas Tiberius received the senators, Livia received the wives of the senators in another place (Cassius Dio 55.2.4; 55.8.1). Likewise, because the organization of games required that a great deal of time be spent in the public eye (being seated in seats of honor, giving the opening speech, presenting the awards, presiding over banquets), both the Greeks and the Romans were reluctant to leave these events in the hands of women.

The existence of direct relations between city authorities and female benefactresses is well documented. Decrees concerning Archippe refer to discussions between the benefactress and her city: Archippe requests that the city make land available for the construction of the *bouleuterion*, transmits her opinion on the most appropriate building project to the inhabitants via the authorities, and negotiates her exemption from liturgies. The action verbs used in the documents make Archippe the interlocutor with the city.

The accession of a man or woman to any public office required the approval of the civic authorities. The sale of the priesthoods, both male and female, was done under the strict control of the city, just as was the allocation of a priesthood outside the sale procedure: Epie, who spent a fortune as *neokoros* in Thasos, was raised to the rank of priestess of Zeus Euboulos by the city in gratitude for her donations. The sacred laws of Kos attest to the fact that the priestesses of Demeter swore an oath when they took office, in the same way that magistrates did (Bielman 2003: 183 n. 39). The authorities also supervised the appointment of Hellenistic men and women to the office of magistrate, although we have little information about this procedure. A document from Capua (Frei-Stolba and Zimmermann 1998: 115) of the Augustan period indicates that the local senate elected the person (probably a woman) who was in charge of the priesthood of the titular deity. The Vestal Virgins were recruited through public proceedings and incorporated into the college of pontiffs.

The annual rendering of accounts connected with a religious office held by a woman is attested in a document of Delos dating from 194 BCE (Bielman 2002: no. 20). This was, however, an unusual situation: the *hieropoios* (overseer of temples) Teleson died during his year in office and it was to his daughter and sole heir that the responsibility of submitting the accounts of the sanctuary to the magistrates on his behalf was assigned. The girl, who was still very young, was represented by her guardians. However, the bent key associated with some Athenian priestesses on their tombstones (Bielman Sánchez 2008: 150–3, 156–8), which signified the responsibility of these women for the treasure of the sanctuary, implies that these priestesses rendered the annual accounts to the city, just as their male colleagues did. We do not know whether these priestesses did so in person or via their guardians as intermediaries.

An example of financial negotiations between a woman and the city is provided by Nikareta, who disposed of a personal bank account and who personally conducted the negotiations with the authorities of Orchomenos. Greek women, who were individually registered in public subscriptions (for which a dozen cases were reported), were obliged to appear in person before the Assembly to register their donations.

Relations between Roman authorities and benefactresses or influential women are mainly reported by literary sources, and often in a biased manner. Thus, Fulvia, the wife of Anthony, reportedly got herself involved in public affairs and imposed her will upon the Senate, was harangued by the soldiers, and was challenged by the senators who were on their way to the Curia. Fulvia is presented by the literary sources (Cicero, Cassius Dio, Appian) as a counter-example of correct Roman women's behavior (see Brennan, this volume, Chapter 26). The Roman matrons' intervention before the senators in 195 BCE (Livy 34.1) in support of the repeal of the Lex Oppia (a law introduced during the Second Punic War in order to regulate the wearing of jewelry and women's clothing) seems to have shocked Cato because of the direct interaction between the women and the authorities. A woman's support of a public cause was more properly done through the mediation of a male relative, particularly her husband. This roundabout way of supporting a public cause was, however, no less effective: thus, the Roman people demanded the help of Caecilia Metella, the wife of Sulla, in persuading the dictator to call back the supporters of the exiled Marius (Plutarch, *Life of Sulla* 6.22).

Nevertheless, two examples of direct intervention of a Roman woman before the authorities are favorably viewed. One example is Turia, who pleaded the cause of her husband before the triumvirs Lepidus after Pharsalia (*Laudatio Turiae* 11; see Riess, this volume, Chapter 36). The other example is Hortensia, the daughter of the orator Hortensius, who defended the case of the 1400 wealthiest matrons of Rome, subjected to tax before the triumvirs in 42 BCE. Hortensia argued that, since the matrons were neither able to fulfill public duties nor obtain public honors, they should not be bled by the state (Appian, *Civil Wars* 4.32–4). The anecdote delineates the public role conceded to the women of the Roman elite and the terms of their connection with the authorities.

Greek priestesses, magistrates, and benefactresses received the same marks of esteem as men, for example the *proedria* (the front rows of the audience at the theater). Likewise, the Vestal Virgins enjoyed seats of honor at the theater that faced the organizer of the show; no other category of Roman women seems to have benefited from this privilege under the Republic. It is unclear, however, how other priestesses in charge of priesthoods were treated in the cities of southern Italy.

The erection of a statue in an individual's likeness during his or her lifetime was a remarkable honor (see Dillon, this volume, Chapter 19). Greek priestesses were awarded this high honor at least as often as priests were. Statues of priestesses were often placed within the precincts of the temples. However, the erection of statues of priestesses was not limited to sacred space alone. At Kyzikos in the first century BCE, for example, a group of women asked the Assembly for permission to set up a statue of the priestess Kleidike on the men's agora beside the monument of her ancestors and the statue of her brother. To be awarded such a prominent memorial at the center of the city, Kleidike's ancestors must have played an important role in the foundation of the city or in the history of Kyzikos, a history that explains the favored location accorded to her statue (van Bremen 1996: 171).

From at least the third century BCE, civic benefactors received public honorific portrait statues in exchange for their benefactions. According to our sources, this great privilege was given to only a single female benefactress: Archippe. A bronze statue of Archippe being crowned by the People was erected in front of the *bouleuterion* of Kyme; next to her statue was placed one of her father. Some time later, Archippe received a golden statue placed within the precinct of the *bouleuterion*; an inscription indicated that the statue had been offered to Archippe by the People "in recognition of her merit." By contrast, one study (Kajava 1990) shows that, from about the time of Sulla, most Roman women who were honored with portrait statues by Greek cities were so not because of their own acts of goodwill but because the cities wished to honor one of their male relatives who had held public office in the region.

In Rome, the granting of a statue of a woman was even more exceptional: in the second century BCE, Cato the Elder strongly protested against the erection of statues of women in the provinces (Pliny, *Naturalis Historia* 34.31). It was not until 35 BCE that the Roman Senate set up statues for Octavia and Livia in public places, and then only under the exceptional situation that had been created by the civil wars (Frei-Stolba 1998). The date of the statue of Cornelia, mother of the Gracchi, set up in Rome itself, is debatable.

Statues of female benefactors were accompanied by an inscription that indicated the name of the portrait subject so that the honorific effect of the monument was doubled. The name reflected the influence of an individual on public space. Even for men, such honor was not easy to attain; for women it was harder. Nevertheless, Greek cities authorized some female builders to inscribe their name on the buildings they had funded. In a game of mirrors, the names of these benefactresses were also mentioned in the decree that granted them the first honor, and such decrees were displayed in a busy place of the city. Similarly, in Augustan Italy, Mamia, who had ordered the construction of the temple of the Genius coloniae in Pompeii, obtained the right to affix a dedication in her name. Eumachia also had her name engraved on the imposing building that she had built on the Forum of Pompeii, and Mineia did the same on the basilica at Paestum. Some prestigious Roman marks of honor, such as the ceremonial chariot or the *lictor*, were accorded to specific women: the Vestal Virgins and Livia. Still, according to one analysis conducted on the status of the empress Livia (Frei-Stolba 1998), she never had powers, in connection with the Roman state, equivalent to those of a Roman magistrate—a situation that applies to all female members of the elite in the Roman Republic.

The prestige attained by members of the elite reached its zenith at the time of their death. Archippe was entitled to a funeral procession in which her body was carried by the ephebes and the gymnasiarch and the procession led to the spot where other benefactors of Kyme were buried. We recognize here the characteristic features of the Greek public funeral, accorded to individuals both male and female whom the city wished to honor and remember. We also have evidence for the erection of statues that were crowned annually on the date of the subject's death. The memory of the funeral ceremony that the city orchestrated was inscribed on the tombstone by means of a crown of leaves bearing the seal of the People. We find such wreaths on the gravestones of several Hellenistic priestesses, including priestesses of Demeter from Smyrna and a priestess of Isis (Bielman Sánchez 2008: 158–60). An identical crown adorns the pediment of the stele of Menophila, who was *stephanophoros* at Sardis in the second century BCE and who died young and unmarried. The Greek authorities thus honored the memory of their deceased magistrates, male and female alike, based on criteria that were unrelated either to gender or to age.

Under the Roman Republic, public funerals were reserved for men, a principle that was respected until the end of the second century BCE. In 102 BCE, however, Quintus Lutatius Catulus delivered the eulogy at the funeral for his mother, which was a clever way of putting his own merits in the forefront, and one that began the fashion for female eulogies. An early example of Roman funeral honors accorded to a woman is those of the priestess Mamia at Pompeii: the decurions granted a place of prestige to her tomb, and, contrary to common use, the tomb was an individual monument and not a family mausoleum. The prestige of this woman, who dared commission the construction of a temple, is reflected in this exceptional honor.

Some documents suggest an affective relationship between cities and their benefactors, particularly towards the women who took on this role. Thus, when Archippe fell seriously ill, the inhabitants of Kyme decided to offer sacrifices for her recovery, and at the news of her recovery they celebrated thanksgivings. This "domestication of public life" (van Bremen 1996: 185) became increasingly common, beginning in the latter part of the first century BCE. Upon their deaths, benefactresses were praised not only for their actions but also for their moral qualities. Feelings of grief were expressed in increasingly strong terms; the grief of close relatives was taken into consideration by the authorities, who addressed decrees of consolation to the family. This phenomenon was echoed in 9 BCE in Rome when the Senate granted Livia a statue in consolation for Drusus' death (Frei-Stolba 1998). Little by little, over the centuries, affective, quasi-familial relationships were established between the women who practiced public patronage and the communities they endowed.

3   Conclusion

It is clear from this overview that the possibilities for public patronage were more numerous and varied for women in the Greek world than in the Roman world. Documents from the Hellenistic period demonstrate that, although the religious realm provided the most opportunities for women as priestesses and benefactresses, it was not the only area in which they might perform a public function. As benefactresses or magistrates, Greek women had a wide range of opportunities to spend their wealth for the public good. With the exception of presiding over the games, no area of public activity was closed to them. In contrast, in southern Italy, religious offices were the main way—if not the only way—for women to act publicly, to finance buildings, and to have their names inscribed in civic space. The city of Rome was even more restrictive.

As a corollary to the above remarks: in the Hellenistic world, wealthy female citizens were treated on an equal footing with their rich male counterparts in that both groups were seen as providers of public services, able to contribute to the good management of the community. In Greece, money had no gender. Conversely, in Italy during the time of the Republic, and especially in Rome, the public and religious activity granted to women was exercised in a manner complementary to the role of men but not in an autonomous fashion (Scheid 2003a: 147). The same was true for public patronage. In the Roman world, considerations of gender outweighed the financial needs of the community. The Hellenistic practices of female patronage were eventually adopted, little by little, in the cities of southern Italy towards the end of the Republican era. Nevertheless, we should stress the pioneering role of Livia in female public patronage, for she provided the model that was then emulated by elite women of the Imperial period.

Beyond the differences of customs and practices, one common objective united the women who engaged in actions of community support in both the Hellenistic and Republican periods: that of inscribing their actions within a family tradition. It is clear in both cases, for example, that female benefactors from prominent families desired to follow ancestral tradition and to promote male relatives through their public benefactions. Similarly, the glory and civic honor obtained in exchange for their donations not only went to the women themselves but also extended to their entire family line. This principle of familial glorification certainly motivated male benefactors, but it was an even greater motive for women, who had only limited independence from their male relatives.

RECOMMENDED FURTHER READING

For Hellenistic Greece, the basic reference is van Bremen (1996), who examines the different forms of female euergetism. Ferrandini Troisi (2000) and Bielman (2002) translate and comment on many Greek epigraphical documents from the fourth to the first century BCE, illustrating several sectors of public activities in which women were admitted. See also the specific studies of Bielman (2003) and Stavrianopoulou (2006) on the public roles of women in the cities of Asia Minor and of the Aegean islands. Funerary monuments sometimes give information about female patronage, as shown in several articles published in Frei-Stolba et al. (2003) and Bertholet et al. (2008).

For Republican Rome, many examples of female patronage are recorded and analyzed by Bauman (1992), Dixon (2001), and Badel (2007). Some well-known women, such as Cornelia, the mother of the Gracchii, or Terentia, Cicero's wife, are studied by Raepsaet-Charlier and Gourevitch (2001), Dixon (2007), and Treggiari (2007), while some works edited by Cébeillac-Gervasoni (1996) record and analyze the data on female patronage in the cities of Republican southern Italy.

18

Women on Hellenistic Grave Stelai: Reading Images and Texts

Christina A. Salowey

Elpenor to Odysseus: Do not go leaving me unwashed and unburied, lest I be a cause for some retribution from the gods for you. But burn me with whatever armor I have, heap up a mound for me along the sea shore, so that others might learn what a wretched man I was.

(Homer, *Odyssey* 11.72–6)

Odysseus: When the corpse and his armor had been burned, we heaped up a mound, marked it with a stele, and at the top fixed the oar that he used to row with.

(Homer, *Odyssey* 12.13–15)

The earliest Greek literature stresses the sacrilege of leaving a corpse unburied. The humblest of persons, even the drunken Elpenor, who fell off a roof, deserve a funerary mound and a stele as a reminder of his death and life. Grave markers, from stone piles to elaborate mausoleums, are ubiquitous in the archaeological record (Boardman and Kurtz 1971: 218–48). Most widely found of all types is the simple stone slab, or stele (stelai in the plural). In form, stelai can be rectangular, square, or cubic and adorned with pediments, akroteria, monumental palmettes, or even small animal figurines. Their surfaces can be left flat and plain, contoured with slight depressions, carved to resemble a small shrine or *naiskos*, or adorned with rosettes, architectural moldings, and chthonic herms. The memorial image for the deceased can be carved, painted, or a combination of the two, with standardized scenes illustrating funerary ritual, mourning, or familial connections.

Many gravestones survive inscribed with a name and quite often a patronymic or, in the case of women, the genitive of a husband's name. In many cases an ethnicity, a city or region of birth, is also recorded. The mere preservation of women's names on grave stelai is a significant contribution. During her lifetime a woman may have been addressed by the possessive form of her father's or husband's name, but the birth names of women were recorded on grave stelai (Demand 1994: 9). In Attika, women's names on grave stelai are feminized versions of male names, abstracted qualities of femininity, or diminutives (Golden 1986). Outside Athens and Attika, where the collection and publication of grave stelai have been more sporadic, a prosopography has yet to be developed.

A Companion to Women in the Ancient World, First Edition. Edited by Sharon L. James and Sheila Dillon.
© 2012 John Wiley & Sons, Ltd. Published 2015 by John Wiley & Sons, Ltd.

On some stelai, the inscribed texts also offer a longer encomium for the deceased woman that can reveal details of her life. The personal biographies or public histories of women generally are not abundant in the decrees and honors preserved in stone or in the military exploits and political stratagems recounted in historians' accounts. Exciting tales of courageous and influential women crowd the mythologies, tragedies, and comedies of ancient Greece, but snapshots of real women are sorely lacking. For these, we can find some evidence in the grave markers to which even poor and outcast women were entitled. Stelai survive for women as often as men, but, in the former case, they remain the only written record of the lives of unremarkable women—the priestess, the cloistered wife, the unmarried daughter, the unfortunate immigrant.

In all four Hellenistic grave stelai discussed here, the combination of an image with a text increases the possibilities for their analysis and broadens the nexus of associations for the deceased (Bielman Sánchez 2008: 148, esp. n. 6). The epitaphs for women often fall into well-established thematic categories such as *mors immatura* or death in childbirth, but expressions of regret, melancholy, or feelings of isolation in death also appear (Pomeroy 1990: 72–3; Bruss 2005: 49–51). In the Archaic and Classical periods, sepulchral epigrams rarely evoked an emotional response from the viewer, and were intended more as permanent records of ritually prescribed performances in honor of the dead (Day 1989, 1994). In contrast, Hellenistic epigrams contain stronger statements of familial loss and personal hardship in death.

The wording of the epitaphs can be reinforced or contradicted by the iconography of the decoration. Close observation of the stone *in situ*, especially in the case of painted stelai, is essential for discovering small artistic choices that guide the experience of the viewer. Slight differences in standardized scenes add meaning to these memorials. In combination with a careful reading of the epitaph, the biography of the deceased woman can be sketched in broad strokes, and, since the stones reliably originate from a cemetery, we know we are becoming acquainted with real women, not the fictional characters of Hellenistic literary epigram.

Stelai, however, are rarely found in conjunction with an undisturbed burial. Despite the heft and solidity of stelai, ranging in height from one to three meters and reaching weights of 75–225 kilograms, they are surprisingly transportable. Their utilitarian shape means that they can be reused in a variety of building projects, and this is often how the archaeologist will encounter them: reused in other tombs, providing a door threshold, fortifying wall foundations. For the most part, we must be resigned to studying grave stelai apart from the physical remains of the honored dead. However, even their transposed resting places can communicate much about the stresses or exigencies forced upon a community that caused that community to plunder a cemetery for building material.

Studies of the display and meaning of funerary commemoration are generally limited to Athens and Attika, where both the physical remains and adequate contextual materials make suppositions about the purposes of epitaphic material easier to prove (Clairmont 1993). In general, grave displays not only commemorated the dead but also recorded the presence of family groups and broadcast those families' fecundity and success (Closterman 2007). In the four examples chosen for this essay, two from Demetrias and two from Delos, both prominent cities from the Hellenistic period, the stelai are divorced from their original context, and, while the design, epitaph, and iconography of the stele present much about the deceased and her family unit, the full context is regrettably lacking.

1   Painted Stelai from Demetrias

Between 1907 and 1925, A. S. Arvanitopoulos excavated over 360 grave stelai from the foundations of the fortification walls in the southern part of the Thessalian city of Demetrias (Arvanitopoulos 1909: 63–93, 1928; Batziou-Efstathiou 2002: 7–9). Demetrias, a Hellenistic city founded by the Macedonian king Demetrios Poliorketes sometime after 294/3 BCE, remained a stronghold of the Macedonian kingdom until the defeat of Perseus at the hands of the Roman general Lucius Aemilius Paulus in 168 BCE, at which time the walls of Demetrias were demolished. The subsequent history of these walls provides the key in determining the date of the painted grave stelai. No significant threat faced Demetrias until 88 BCE, when the fleet of Mithradates, king of Pontos, aimed to capture the cities along the coasts of Euboea and Magnesia. In order to repel this incursion, the inhabitants of Demetrias hastily collected material to rebuild their walls and increase the size of the towers in order to support the new military catapults. The extended foundations of the towers were filled in with grave stelai from the cemeteries and covered with waterproof clay. This casing of clay preserved the paint on the grave monuments until they were uncovered in the early twentieth century (Helly 1992). Arvanitopoulos' excavation of the fill of five towers on the east and south walls of Demetrias unearthed most of the painted stelai on display in the Athanasakeion Museum in Volos today; others were recovered from excavations in the north cemetery of Demetrias. The chronological history of the walls allows the stelai to be dated to the 200 years between the founding of the city and the beginning of the first century BCE (Helly 1992).

The stelai are original works of Hellenistic painting and, as such, are an important source for painting techniques (von Graeve 1979; von Graeve and Preusser 1981; von Graeve and Helly 1987). The stone, after being dressed to its final form by a marble worker and engraver, was painted. The surface was not prepared by polishing or rough dressing before the application of paint. The details of the scene were outlined by a charcoal cartoon. Recent studies by Brecoulaki confirm the use of encaustic methods for the application of pigments rather than egg-tempera paints (von Graeve 1979; Brecoulaki 2006). Stronger colors were layered on top of this lighter wash to create the chiaroscuro observed on several of the stelai. The pigments used have been identified through chemical analysis and recent x-ray fluorescence studies as Egyptian blue; charcoal or burnt ivory for black; calcium carbonate and white lead for white; malachite; copper arsenate; cinnabar; ochre; and a yellowish lead oxide (von Graeve and Helly 1987: 26–7; Brecoulaki 2006).

In general the scenes depicted on this corpus of stelai are derived from Attic funerary iconography: the clasping of the right hands of individuals in farewell (*dexiosis*), the deceased at a funerary banquet (*Totenmahl*), soldiers depicted with weapons, single individuals accompanied by a household servant. Several stelai, however, move away from the Attic tradition and are striking for their depiction of interior domestic space or for vivid vignettes of the deceased in life or in death. More than half of the stelai discovered commemorate women. Two of these stelai, for Hediste and Archidike, through a careful viewing of the painted scene and reading of the longer poetic epitaph, yield individual portraits for women living in this cosmopolitan city in the third/second centuries BCE.

The stele made to commemorate the death and mark the tomb of Hediste (Figure 18.1) has received the most attention in the scholarly literature (Arvanitopoulos 1909: 97–104, 215–19, 1928; Schefold 1967: 229, pl. 245; Pollitt 1986: 4, 194). The two pieces of this remarkable stele were found in excavations years apart. The stele is dated to between 200 and 150 BCE. The upper half, found first, preserves an expressive scene that has as its subject

Figure 18.1 Stele for Hediste. Volos, Athanasakeion Archaeological Museum inv. no. Λ1. Date: 200–150 BCE. Photo: author.

the deathbed of a young woman who has recently given birth, surrounded by family and members of the household. The paint on the lower half has almost completely faded, but a four-line metrical epitaph survives that reveals the name of the deceased, Hediste, and verifies the circumstances of her death, in childbirth. Had either one of the pieces survived without the other, either would have functioned as a clear memorial of a woman's final travails, one by means of an image, the other with a text. However, the combination of the painting and the poetry does more than provide a name for the deceased or illustrate the faces of the dead and the grieving: the image and the text work together to heighten the emotional impact of the public marker and to heroize the deceased.

Arvanitopoulos (1909: 97) calls the form of the stele a *naiskos*, and suggests that this shape indicated that the deceased was honored as a hero. The form is a flat-roofed structure, not pedimental, adorned with antefixes and framed by pilasters. Stewart, in a discussion of Attic stelai with scenes of women dying in childbirth, points out that the shape is not really a *naiskos*, but is generally used to frame scenes of women dying in childbirth (Stewart and Gray 2000: 250–3; on the Attic stelai see also Vedder 1988). This shape is infrequent among the grave stelai from Demetrias and would certainly require more preparatory stonework than a simple slab with a pediment. Of the three other flat-roofed stelai from Demetrias, one for the daughter of Hephaistion (Volos Λ350, unpublished) depicts a scene similar to the one on Hediste's stele, but is unpainted, preserved only in charcoal cartoon. On one of the other two, for Klymene, daughter of Agathokles (Volos Λ286; Arvanitopoulos 1949: 155–6, figure 2), a crude depiction of a snake rampant on the top of an altar may allude to hero cult, confirming Arvanitopoulos' conjecture that the form is reserved for heroized individuals. If the shape of the marker did not immediately evoke the importance of the deceased, then the image and the epitaphic text would.

The stele shows a woman, laid out on a decorative couch and closely observed by a man seated at her feet. In the background, a complex, multidimensional architectural scene is depicted. A partition wall separates the couch from a back hallway in which an older woman, perhaps the midwife, stands, cradling an infant in her arms. The midwife is a prominent element in fourth-century BCE Attic grave stelai that depict a woman struggling or dying in childbirth. In fact, Demand (1994: 123–8) argues that several of these stelai might be grave monuments for the midwife rather than the deceased mother. But the Attic examples are compositionally different from the Hediste example. Hediste is displayed stretched out on a couch, in repose, whereas in the Attic relief, the pregnant woman, barely able to balance on the edge of an upright stool or throne, collapses into the arms of a waiting attendant (Vedder 1988; Stewart and Gray 2000). In Demetrias, the composition used for the stelai of Hediste and the daughter of Hephaistion has as its central element an elaborate couch that stretches across the width of the scene. It is tempting to see this element as derived from the *Totenmahl*, or funerary banqueting scene, found on many of the cemetery's stelai (Volos Λ27; Arvanitopoulos 1909: 183–8, 1928: 160–1; Volos Λ245; Arvanitopoulos 1949: 6–7; Volos Λ356, unpublished).

The compositional change for the scene of a woman dying in childbirth is mostly likely a Hellenistic innovation, although the fourth-century BCE Attic type continued, as seen on an Alexandrian painted stele of the early third century BCE (Brown 1957: 15, pl. II.1). However, a funerary epigram attributed to Perses (*AP* 7.730), so perhaps dated as early as the late fourth century BCE (Gow and Page 1965: II.446, 451) provides an ekphrasis of a grave stele comparable to Hediste's. The deceased couple in the epigram, Mnasylla and Aristoteles, are described as gazing at a γραπτὸς ... τύπος (a painted representation) of their daughter Neotima, who died giving birth: ἅς δή ποκ᾽ ἀπὸ ψυχὰν ἐρύσαντο/ὠδῖνες, κεῖται δ᾽οἵα κατὰ βλεφάρων/ἀχλύι πλημύρουσα φίλας ὑπὸ μητρὸς ἀγοστῷ (whom birth pangs once dragged from her soul, so she lies down by the arm of her dear mother, her eyes drowned in mist, *AP* 7.730. 3–5). The verb κεῖται (she lies down) and the description of her eyes shrouded in mist correspond with details seen in Hediste's portrayal.

Behind the couch, a doorway leads into an area in which a younger individual, gender undefined, stands looking alarmed. Beyond and above the head of this household attendant can be seen the foliage of a tree (maybe a cypress), perhaps to indicate the inner garden of the house. This partition of space and illusion of receding domestic realms is found in at least seven other painted stelai from Demetrias and became a popular motif among the artists of the third century BCE (Gigante 1980: 135). The painting is not only compositionally elegant but also vividly adorned with rich colors and expressive shading: the chestnut hair and golden skin tone of Hediste, the brilliant red color of the elder woman's *sakkos* and baby's swaddling clothes, the flushed cheeks of the husband.

These elements allow the grave monument for Hediste to present a compelling narrative of vigilant husband, startled attendant, and grieving midwife or grandmother. Despite its similarity to the stele for the daughter of Hephaistion, suggesting a copybook scene used frequently for the common circumstance of death in childbirth, this tableau is more than an emblematic display of the deceased surrounded by family and friends. Another distinguishing factor on the stele for Hediste is, in fact, the poetry, which is rife with allusions to the Homeric epics.

The language of the epigram supports the idea of an epic, almost mythological, narrative for the deceased:

Λυπρὸν ἐφ' Ἡδίστηι Μοῖραι τότε νῆμα ἀπ' ἀτράκτων/κλῶσαν, ὅτε ὠδῖνος νύμφη ἀπηντίασεν

The Fates spun out a painful thread from their spindles for Hediste, when she, as a bride, encountered childbirth.

In other poetry, the image of the Fates spinning out a thread is associated with men of glorious exploits. For example, in the *Odyssey*, Alkinoös addresses the still-unnamed wanderer Odysseus with the trope "from thence he will suffer his destiny as much as the heavy Spinners allotted for him with the thread at his birth, when his mother bore him" (Hom. *Od.* 7.197–9). Hellenistic epigrammists of the third century BCE, presumably even those in Thessaly, were well versed in Homeric philology, so literary intertextuality of varying degrees of sophistication is to be expected (Sistakou 2007: 407–8). In this epigram, Hediste's life, and in particular her current travail and its tragic outcome, is described in epic terms by reminiscing on the Fates, who doled out her destiny when she was born. The Fates played an important role in the biographies of several Homeric heroes, and Hediste is equated with them here.

σχετλίη! οὐ γὰρ ἔμελλε τὸ νήπιον ἀνκαλιεῖσθαι,/μαστῶι τε ἀρδεύσειν χεῖλος ἑοῖο βρέφους

Oh enduring is she, not intended to embrace her infant, nor even to water the lip of her own offspring with the breast.

The word σχετλίη means "able to hold out, unwearying, unflinching" (*LSJ, sv.* σχετλίος) and acquired the meaning of "wretched." In Homer, it is used of heroes to express their endurance in battle. For example, in the *Iliad*, Odysseus wakes up Diomedes with the words "You are unflinching, old man [σχετλίος ἐσσι, γεραιέ]; never once have you ceased from the hard work" (*Il.* 10.164). Both these denotations apply to Hediste here and thus create in the reader's mind a vivid representation not only of Hediste's ceaseless efforts to bring this child to birth but also of the wretched conclusion. In the end, she has failed, but not because of cowardice or weakness. Her destiny was premeasured by the Fates and Tyche, or Fortune, led her and her child into a single tomb, as expressed in the last lines:

ἓν γὰρ ἐσεῖδε φάος καὶ ἀπήγαγεν εἰς ἕνα τύμβον/τοὺς δισσούς, ἀκρίτως τοῖσδε μολοῦσα, Τύχη

One light looked upon them both and Tyche led them both into a single tomb, coming upon them indistinguishably.

Tyche, the divine personification of Fortune, was a prominent motif in Hellenistic philosophy, art, and religion. Pollitt (1986: 1–4) outlines the role Tyche was considered to have played in the political vicissitudes of some great male leaders of the Hellenistic period: Demetrios of Phaleron, King Eumenes, and Alexander the Great, among others. Hediste's path is governed by the same force, Tyche, that ruled the great and the mighty.

Death in childbirth was most likely an all-too-common occurrence among women in Thessaly in the third/second century BCE. Childbearing was risky business even among women attended by midwives or Hippocratic doctors (Demand 1994: 70–86; Stewart and Gray 2000: 260–3). Mortality rates are difficult to assess since evidence from grave stelai and epitaphs is sporadic, and attention has only recently been given to skeletal remains. The recent re-evaluation of the Geometric tomb of the "rich Athenian lady" completed by Liston and Papadopoulos (2004) demonstrates how valuable information can be obtained by the analytical methods of physical anthropology (see also Gansell, this volume, Chapter 1; Liston, this volume, Chapter 9; Shepherd, this volume, Chapter 16). Liston and Papadopoulos point out that, unlike the marker for Hediste's tomb, the iconography of the tomb material and marker for the "rich Athenian lady" do not make it obvious that she died while either pregnant or giving birth. However, the grave marker for Hediste does not categorize her indistinguishably as one of many to whom this tragedy has happened. The compositional artistry of her portrait and the lyrical poetry of "one of Demetrias-Pagasai's most distinguished writers" (Arvanitopoulos 1928: 147) elevate her to the status of an epic hero.

The Archidike stele and its metrical inscription are less well known (Figure 18.2; Arvanitopoulos 1909: 155–64). The stone tapers towards the top and is crowned with a pediment topped by three palmettes that are shallowly carved with leaves and volutes. A pomegranate, an appropriate funerary symbol for a woman, is painted in the center of the pediment. The inscription begins below the painted cyma, is carefully spaced out in six lines, and ends before two rosettes. The rosettes are carved as two concentric circles around a central nipple; details of the flowers would have been marked in paint, of which only a trace remains. The painted scene below shows a woman seated on a cushioned stool, facing right. At her left side, a young female attendant stands, her right arm bent up to her chin and her left hand cradling her right elbow. She gazes at the seated woman. The motif of a deceased woman seated and attended by a coeval or younger attendant is taken from the Attic oeuvre (Clairmont 1993), but here, in Thessaly, has a more personal, haunting feeling, conveyed with gazes, gazes averted, and the coloration of the room and clothing.

The inscription is carefully carved, laid out with setting lines, although the letters are somewhat idiosyncratically formed. As with the Hediste stele, the poetry distinguishes the monument. Written in elegiac couplets, the poem is particularly effective in evoking a sense of place, while also elevating the deceased woman by associating her with other Cretan heroic dead:

> εἰ κέκρικας χρηστὴν, Ῥαδάμανθυ, γυναῖκα καὶ ἄλλην
> ἢ Μίνως, καὶ τήνδ "οὖσαν Ἀριστομάχου
> κούρην. εἰς Μακάρων Νήσους ἄγετ'! Εὐσεβίαν γὰρ
> ἤσκει καὶ σύνεδρον τῆσδε δικαιοσύνην.
> Ἣν Τυλισὸς μὲν ἔθρεψε, πόλις Κρῆσσ', ἥδε δὲ γαῖα
> ἀμφέπει ἀθάνατον—μοῖρα σοί, Ἀρχιδίκη!

If you have judged another woman as worthy, O Rhadamanthys or Minos, then judge this woman, daughter of Aristomachos, the same way, and lead her towards the Islands of the Blest! For she has made religious piety her practice and righteousness her own co-counselor. Tylissos, a Cretan city, nurtured her, but this land will surround her for eternity. Fate be with you, Archidike!

Figure 18.2 Stele for Archidike. Volos, Athanasakeion Archaeological Museum inv. no. Λ20. Date: 225–200 BCE. Photo: author.

We do not learn the woman's name, Archidike, until the final line, in fact the final word. She is defined first with respect to her father, but the references to her native city and land are stronger: she hails from Tylissos, Crete. Mythological references to Minos and Rhadamanthys also create a very Cretan feel, for these two judges of the underworld were kings of Crete before their assignment to the land of the dead (Hom. *Od.* 11.568–71; Pl. *Gorg.* 523a), a path Archidike herself is about to tread. The three Cretan brothers who become judges in the underworld, Minos, Rhadamanthys, and Aiakos, are not commonly invoked in funerary poetry or iconography (Bettenworth 2007: 74–6). Rhadamanthys and Aiakos were painted on the façade of the Tomb of Judgment in Lefkadia but this is a unique representation in Macedonian funerary paintings (Brecoulaki 2006: 204–17). So, the evocation of the Cretan judges here is noteworthy.

How does a woman brought up in Tylissos, Crete, end her life interred in a cemetery in Thessaly? The grave stele does not indicate a husband, but other members of her family are recorded on stelai from Demetrias. Her brother, Hygiamenes, and perhaps a cousin, Polytimos, are recorded together (Arvanitopoulos 1909: 157; *IG* IX.2.1181;

Spyridakis 1992: nos. 67, 106) on a single stele that also reports their ethnicity as
Tylissian. A record of her niece, Anthis, Hygiamenes' daughter, survives as well
(Arvanitopoulos 1909: 157, 292–4). The names of eight other Cretans are recorded
on stelai from Demetrias (Th. Arvanitopoulos 1952–3: 55; Spyridakis 1992), and these,
all male, are often interpreted as mercenaries. Cretan soldiers were particularly sought
out as the mercenaries that predominantly filled the ranks as Hellenistic soldiers (Griffith
1935: 245; Spyridakis 1992). The Cretans buried in cemeteries in Demetrias were most
likely paid soldiers in the Macedonian military and may have lived out their lives with
wives, children, and relatives as émigrés to the cities that their employers founded or,
more rarely, on plots of land bestowed on them for military service (Griffith 1935:
313–16). Mercenaries traveling with families are attested (Trundle 2004: 139–41). An
example from nearby Pharsalus in Thessaly specifies that Pelopidas' soldiers left families
behind in the city while they were on campaign (Plut. *Pel.* 27). Archidike's unmarried
status makes it harder to speculate on the reason for her presence in Demetrias. Perhaps
her father was a mercenary who was joined by his wife and children as he decided to settle
in Demetrias, or perhaps she was the sole survivor of her family when her brother left to
serve and she followed him rather than being left alone in Crete. Whatever the
circumstances, the family attained some status and wealth to be able to commission
a finely painted grave stele complete with a poetic epitaph. And the epitaph in its
personification of Crete as Archidike's nurturer betrays a strong sense of loyalty to and
even longing for her *patria*, Crete.

The poet has used well-placed epideitic pronouns to affect Archidike's transference
from the living realm to resting eternally in the ground at Demetrias. In lines two and 4,
the accusative, τήνδ᾽, and the genitive, τῆσδε, of the the epideictic pronoun ἥδε ("this
woman here") refer to Archidike. In line 5, however, ἥδε switches its referent to the land
(γαῖα) in the cemetery, almost as if the poet were stressing, in the grammar, Archdike's final
and permanent placement in the ground in Demetrias instead of in her place of birth,
Tylissos. The poetry conveys the idea that, though this land is Thessaly, one corner of it will
remain forever Cretan with Archidike in it. A similar sentiment is expressed in a much later
ode by the English poet Rupert Brooke: "If I should die, think only this of me:/That
there's some corner of a foreign field/That is forever England" (*The Soldier* 1914).

2   The Delos Stelai

The Cycladic island of Delos is renowned for its mythological pedigree as the birthplace of
Apollo and Artemis and its subsequent importance as a well-known and oft-consulted
Ionian religious center. Pilgrimages led to its rise as a commercial center and brought
international interests. During the course of the sixth and fifth centuries BCE, Athenian
influence over the island increased and by the last quarter of the fifth century the Delians
had literally lost the right to live and die on their island. All graves on the island of Delos
were packed up and moved to the neighboring island of Rheneia in 426/25 BCE, and births
and deaths were forbidden on the sacred island.

A cemetery was developed on the east coast of Rheneia, just across from the ancient site
of Delos. The necropolis extended from Cape Glaropounda in the north to just south of
the bay, Kato Generale. The grave stelai found on the island are mostly stored in the Delos
and Mykonos museums; many more have been identified in museum collections around
the world (Couilloud 1974: 39–49; Bruneau and Ducat 2005: 111–13). Unlike the

Figure 18.3 Stele for Aline. Mykonos Archaeological Museum. Date: end of second century BCE. Photo: EFA/Emile Sérafis.

corpus from Demetrias, the stelai from the cemetery at Rheneia have scenes sculpted in relief, with no traces of paint. The motifs are very much derived from an Attic oeuvre, except for a few noteworthy shipwreck scenes, stark reminders of the dangers of navigation in the Cyclades. The stelai are generally inscribed with a name, patronymic, and occasionally some indication of ethnicity, but longer poetic epitaphs are not a regular feature; in this respect the two stelai discussed below are unusual.

The grave marker for Aline (Figure 18.3), dated to the end of the second century BCE, is a pedimental stele with three akroteria, the one on the right destroyed (Couilloud 1974: 204–5, no. 468). A funerary scene is sculpted in low relief in a square recessed panel. On the right side of the scene, a woman sits in left profile on a backless chair, which is topped with a cushion and draped all around. Her feet rest on a low stool. Her left elbow rests on her lap with the hand supporting her right arm. The right arm is bent up, with the hand cradling her chin. She wears a himation, which is pulled up over her head and swathes much of her body.

The inscription fills the bottom third of the stele, running from edge to edge, in seven lines that match the metrical line divisions. The letters are well carved, with sharp apices. There is a break in the stone running from the right edge diagonally to the middle of the bottom edge of the stone that interferes minimally with a reading of the text.

Ὦ ξῖνε, τόνδε τύμβον ἄγχι σε βλέπων
δάκρυε τὴν τάλαιναν, τὴν ἐπὶ ξένης
ἔκρυψε κευθμὼν ἔγκυον πεπρωμένης
Ἀλίνην ποθὲν Φοίνισσαν, ὡς ἀπ' Ἀσκάλω(ν?),

μόνην πλανῆτιν δημότιν λελει(μ)μένη[ν],
ἐλέου χάριν δάκρυε, τῆι δ' ἐπιστρέφων
ἀπευχαρίστει τωι θάψαντι γνησίως.

Oh stranger, looking at this tomb near you, weep for the wretched woman, whom, while pregnant, a hole has hidden in a foreign land destined for her, Aline, a Phoenician woman, once from Askalon. With pity, weep for her, alone, a wanderer, having left her citizenry. Turning from her, give thanks to the man who fittingly buried her.

Aline's memorial, both in the image and the poetry, stands in stark contrast to the one for Hediste, discussed above. Both women were with child at the time of their deaths. Hediste's epitaph clearly states that she died while giving birth, but it is not indicated whether Aline had brought an infant to term or not. Hediste's epitaph concentrates on the roles that Fate and Fortune had in her tragic death, and the ennobling poetry elevates her travail. The iambic trimeter epitaph for Aline, however, entreats the passing stranger to weep for her circumstances: she is a wretched wanderer, pregnant, bereft of her country-men, and alone. The burial is described as undistinguished, a mere hole in the ground. Although her burial in a foreign land is characterized as destined, there is no accom-plishment in her death. There is no mention of an infant, a husband, or even family. The epitaph ends by urging the passerby not to think once more on Aline but to thank the man who fittingly buried her. The relationship of the man to Aline is not specified and the impression is given not of affection but of a duty fulfilled, for which the donor of the tomb should be thanked.

The memorial is modest and the seated deceased is depicted without any visible symbols of family or domestic provisions. The void on the left side of the scene communicates loudly her isolation. Comparable stelai would have a family member, household attendant, or minor possessions such as a jewelry box or *kalathos* (a wool basket) filling out the tableau. The space beneath her chair is curtained, a feature found in other stelai from Rheneia, but here it heightens the shrouded nature of the scene. The only mourner seems to be the deceased herself, whose pose of tight introspection conveys sadness and grief.

Like the epitaph for Archidike, one whole line of the poem is given over to the identification of Aline's ethnicity: Phoenician. The end of the line ὡς ἀπ' Ἀσκάλω(ν) could also be rendered as ὡς Ἀπᾶς κάλω (thus Peek 1960: no. 235). Apas, a name attested elsewhere, here could be the name of the man who buried Aline. Alternatively the ποθὲν and ὡς could govern the sense and mean that Aline was once Phoenician but more recently hailed from Askalon. In either case, she is foreign. Delian inscriptions attest to thriving communities of foreigners from the Near Eastern populations (Roussel 1916: 72–96; Lacroix 1932; Couilloud 1974: 307–27).

The stone is not a history text, but it adequately documents the dire straits that a woman, cut off from her family and kinsmen, might fall into in a foreign land. Pregnancy makes a woman vunerable to disease (Demand 1994: 71–86). Without adequate shelter and food, death might come quickly. Society did not owe this woman health benefits, prenatal care, or any sort of social services, but it did owe her an adequate burial, which a male of her acquaintance, perhaps a fellow Phoenician, did supply.

The epitaph on the pedimental stele for Isias (Figure 18.4), dated to the second half of the second century BCE, describes a rather bleak setting for the tomb that contrasts with the conventional illustration of domestic industry in the relief scene, highlighting the reality of

Figure 18.4   Stele for Isias. Mykonos Archaeological Museum. Date: second half of second century BCE. Photo: EFA/Emile Sérafis.

the final judgment that death brings (Couilloud 1974: 205 no. 469). The epitaph, arrayed in eight tightly packed lines at the bottom of the stele, reads:

Πέτρης εἰναλίοιο λαχοῦσ' εὐήνεμον ἀκτὴν
κεῖμαι ναυτιλίης πόλλον ὁρῶσα πλόον
Ἰσιὰς ἡ φιλόεργος, ἐρημαίη δ' ἐπὶ χώρηι
ἄψυχος κεῖμαι, δισσὰ λιποῦσα τέκνα
νήπια καὶ συνόμευνον, ἐνὶ ζωοῖσι μεγίσταν
ἐξ ἔργων φήμαν οἴκῳ ἐρεισαμένα.
Χαίρετε, καὶ θείης ὑπὸ φροντίδος οἶκος ἄθραυστος
μείναι ἀεὶ καὶ ἐμῆς εἵνεκεν εὐσεβίης.

Having been allotted this breezy headland of briny rock, I, industrious Isias, lie looking at the long route of ships. I lie in this barren land, soulless, having left behind two young children and a spouse, having fixed a great reputation among the living for domestic accomplishments. Greetings; a spotless house eternally remains both from marvelous care and on account of my pious character.

Isias' epitaph suggests that her tomb was situated on a high, rocky promontory with a view out to the sea and the ships that came and went to Delos, a striking ekphrasis of the cemetery at Rheneia. Her resting place is harsh, lifeless, and empty in contrast to her active life, when she was φιλόεργος (industrious) and surrounded by family. The poetry invites the viewer to contemplate the contrasts of life and death: bustling activity as compared to solitude, the sustenance of children versus soullessness. The only solace the reader might experience is the possibility that Isias' prayer in the last two lines might be fulfilled, that the domestic vibrancy of her former home might go on uninterrupted because of the care she gave it and the pious devotion she showed in life.

The image is more straightforward in its representation than that of Aline. In a recessed panel on the pedimental stele, a seated woman, Isias, is depicted on the left, stretching both her arms out towards a small figure, perhaps a household attendant. Her feet rest on a low stool behind which is a *kalathos*. Isias is wrapped tightly in a himation and holds an unidentified object in her hands, which she has perhaps just withdrawn from the box held by the household attendant. The scene, especially with the attributive wool basket, illustrates Isias' epithet, φιλόεργος, and is a finely carved example of the funerary motif oft-repeated in the Delian collection. However, the image does not communicate the regret and longing found in the epigram. It is not unusual to find that epigrams speak of personal misfortunate, premature loss, and disappointment whereas the relief transmits a more canonical expression of societal norms or ideals (Zanker 1993: 224). The epigram, here in the voice of the deceased, Isias, engages the passerby, but for what purpose?

This is a vexed question, which has been examined elsewhere (Day 2007 with further bibliography). In the examples presented here, a personal narrative, brief and limited in scope, for each deceased woman is related in the inscription and guides the viewer through the schematic visual memorial, imbuing it with emotion and emphasis. The artistry in the poems creates an individual portrait for each woman that preserves aspects of her life that would otherwise be lost. Pathos and tragedy are offered for viewer response, but so are triumph, accomplishment, and remembrance.

RECOMMENDED FURTHER READING

Many surveys on women in the ancient world will mention only one or two Hellenistic grave stelai for women. Brief but good discussions of Hellenistic funerary monuments for women can be found in Pomeroy (1990), Fantham et al. (1994), and Lefkowitz and Fant (2005). Further study of the portrayal of women on Hellenistic grave stelai requires mining the general scholarship for both funerary sculpture and the Hellenistic epigram.

For a comprehensive look at the grave stelai of the Classical period in Greece, Clairmont (1993) is well-organized and comprehensive. No comparable compilation exists for the Hellenistic period, except for the regional study by Pfuhl and Möbius (1977) and (1979). Some archaeological excavations with significant numbers of grave stelai have published study volumes for the grave stelai from the site, for example Delos (Couilloud 1974) and Demetrias (A. S. Arvanitopoulos 1908, 1909, 1928, 1947–8, 1949). For collections of painted grave stelai, not only Arvanitopoulos on the group from Demetrias but also Brown (1957) and Carter and Mack (2003) are useful. Thematic studies of grave stelai that are particularly instructive include Zanker (1993) and Bielman Sánchez (2008), whose article illustrates well the utility of looking at text and image as a unit.

Scholarship on the Hellenistic epigram has exploded in the last decade and there have been many studies looking at the content, formulae, and grammar of both inscriptional and literary funerary epigram. While Bing and Bruss (2007) does not contain a chapter dedicated specifically to funerary epigram, the book provides an excellent introduction to the genre and many entries offer insights into surviving inscribed epigrams, for example Bettenworth (2007) and Sistakou (2007). Bruss (2005) is an important introduction to the literary funerary epigram and traces many mortuary themes from the abundant inscribed epigram tradition.

ACKNOWLEDGMENTS

All translations are mine. I would like to thank G. Frederic Franko of Hollins University and Lisa R. George of Tulane University for their generous review of and comments on the translation of the four funerary epigrams for Hediste, Archidike, Aline, and Isias.

19

Female Portraiture in the Hellenistic Period

Sheila Dillon

Open most books on Greek art of the Hellenistic period and you will find a chapter devoted to portraiture. Indeed, individualized portraiture is widely considered to be one of the signature achievements of Hellenistic sculpture. The bronze portrait statues of the Athenian orator Demosthenes and the New Comedy poet Menander, set up in Athens in the early third century BCE and preserved in multiple marble versions of the Roman period, are well-known and well-studied examples of the genre, recognized as brilliant and penetrating visual analyses of their subjects. The roughly contemporary marble portrait statue of the priestess Aristonoe from Rhamnous (Figure 19.1), on the other hand, is absent from these studies, although it is one of the most fully documented, original portrait statues of the Hellenistic period. We know, for example, where this statue was set up, and we know who dedicated it and why; and the three crucial components of a portrait statue monument—the head, the body, and the inscribed base—are in this case all preserved. The lack of interest, on the part of portrait specialists, in this statue in particular and in Greek female portraiture in general is surely owed to the fact that these images are strongly idealizing constructions, with very little physiognomic individuality. While the inscription on the base of Aristonoe's statue clearly tells us that the image represents a particular woman, the portrait's face seems to contradict these claims to individuality. What the faces of female portraits show us is that physiognomic specificity and differentiation were not requirements of Hellenistic portraiture; the status of an image as a portrait did not necessitate an actual visual correspondence between subject and statue. The imposition on the ancient material of modern expectations that a portrait resemble its subject—and the more faithfully the better—has effectively erased the female portrait from the history of Greek art.

The aim of this essay, then, is to reintegrate the female portrait into the art of the Hellenistic period and to provide an overview of the historical phenomenon of the commemoration of women in portrait statues. I explore how one might identify examples of female portrait statues among the material remains, consider who might have dedicated portrait statues of women and where these statues might have been displayed, and offer

Figure 19.1 Portrait statue of Aristonoe from Rhamnous. Athens, National Museum inv. 232. Statue H. 1.62 meters. Photo: Meletzis, DAI Athens neg. NM 5211.

case studies of four female portrait statues where the subject of the statue, the context of its display, and the approximate date of the dedication are known. My focus is on the portraits of non-royal women. Not only is there little evidence for the portraits of royal women outside of Ptolemaic Egypt, but also the portraits of the local elite do not appear to be dependent on or derive from royal models. Because of the difficulty in dating much of this material with precision, the importance of the earlier fourth century BCE in the history of the genre, and the continuation of the Hellenistic style of female portraiture well into the Roman period in the Greek East, this essay will necessarily stray somewhat beyond the confines of the Hellenistic period at both ends of its chronological boundaries.

1 Finding the Female Portrait in Greek Art

It is clear from both the sculptural and the epigraphic remains that portrait statues of women in both bronze and marble were a major component of Greek sculptural production, particularly in the Hellenistic period. There are, however, a number of methodological problems one faces in dealing with this rich body of material. First and foremost is the identification of female portrait statues among the many, mostly fragmentary, sculptural remains. By this I do not mean identifying the subject of the portrait—that is, the name of the individual who is represented by the statue—but simply being able to tell whether a particular statue or statue fragment *is* from a portrait. For, unlike the portrait statue of Aristonoe, the head, the body, and the inscribed base (on which the portrait statue stood and that named the subject of the image) are only very rarely found together. Instead, we have many marble female statue bodies that survive without their portrait heads, and heads that are found without their statue bodies. Most of these statue fragments tend not to be found anywhere near where they were originally displayed, having been rebuilt into later walls or buildings, so they cannot be associated with particular inscribed statue bases. How then do we know that *this* female body or *that* female head, or even statues that preserve both body *and* head, originally came from a portrait statue monument?

For draped female statue bodies, costume, pose, and the scale of the figure can be helpful in determining whether the subject of a statue is either mortal or divine. Both the Small and Large Herculaneum statue formats, for example, are very modestly draped in thin tunic and thick mantle, standard dress for many mortal women on Greek grave reliefs. Both are posed as if arranging or manipulating their clothing, a mundane gesture with which real women must have been very familiar and through which the signification of an image as that of a mortal woman could have been communicated (Zanker 1993); goddesses, that is, would not fuss with their clothes. Some statues have a more modern, transparent "drapery-through-drapery" style of costume, which was new in the Hellenistic period. These statues wear a thin mantle probably meant to evoke the fashionable silk of Kos (Weber 1969–70) or fine Egyptian linen, wrapped tightly over a long tunic made of thicker fabric. The skill with which the different textures and weights of these fabrics were rendered by Hellenistic sculptors represents a striking technical innovation in Greek sculpture and shows the importance of this new fashion as a symbol of luxury and affluence. A few of these statues, like the Kleopatra from Delos (Figure 19.2), also have a fringed edge along the left side of the silky transparent mantle, a detail that adds richness and visual interest to the clothing, and significant expense to the carving of the statue. Such garments were expensive sartorial status symbols that were clearly worn by elite women in real life; otherwise, the carefully detailed representation of this clothing in these statues would have made little sense.

Statues of mortal women might also wear the same kind of costume one finds worn by images of goddesses. Such divine costume was perhaps meant to identify these women as priestesses, dressed in special clothing for ritual occasions (Connelly 2007). In the Hellenistic period, the peplos probably had special sacred or ritual connotations; by this time it would certainly have appeared decidedly old-fashioned, if not antique. Even the mid-fourth-century marble portrait statue of Queen Eurydice, mother of Philip II, looks very conservative and venerable, dressed in tunic, mantle, and peplos (Schultz 2007). Found in the sanctuary of Eucleia at Vergina, this votive statue was dedicated to the goddess in what was clearly a ritual context. The peplos is also worn by a series of eight marble statues of young women that were set up beginning in the later Hellenistic period in the sanctuary of Artemis in Messene; three of the statues are identified as priestesses of Artemis and five represent young initiates of the goddess (Connelly 2007; Dillon 2010). This divine imitation in dress can of course make it even harder to identify a statue as either

Figure 19.2 Statues of Kleopatra and Dioscurides, from the House of Kleopatra and Dioscurides on Delos. Delos Museum inv. A 7763, A 7799, A 7997a. Statue H. 1.48 meters. Photo: G. Hellner, DAI Athens neg. 1970/886.

a portrait of a priestess or an image of the goddess herself. While the scale of a statue may be suggestive, without additional external evidence, such as provenance or attributes, it is very difficult to determine with certainty whether such an image is mortal or divine.

Heads are even more problematic. A disembodied and fragmentary female head is very difficult to identify as a portrait of a mortal woman, rather than as an image of a goddess, based on appearance alone; women and goddesses in fact looked very much the same in Greek art. This is a problem one rarely encounters when dealing with male heads; statues of gods and men were carefully differentiated from one another and are now easy to tell apart, even in a fragmentary state. As with statue bodies, scale can help in determining whether a female head is mortal or divine. Heads that are well over life-size are more likely to represent a goddess, whereas a head that is life-size is more likely to come from the statue of a mortal woman, although the fact that portraits of Hellenistic queens were sometimes well over life-size adds an additional layer of complexity to the categorization of this material (Stewart 1998; cf. Palagia 2007). Life-size heads that are also veiled can probably be safely categorized as images of mortal women; mature women on Greek grave reliefs are frequently represented as veiled. While female portrait heads of the Hellenistic period have a mostly "ideal" or generic-looking appearance, as do images of goddesses, some heads do incorporate subtly individualizing traits, such as naso-labial lines or a slight double chin, which help to inflect these heads with "portraitness." For the most part, the spectrum of variation in female portrait faces occurs around a narrowly defined set of repeated design elements, similar to the variation that one can see in the heads of women on Attic gravestones (Bergemann 1997). Female hairstyles are also limited, and, unlike Roman fashion hairstyles, they do not change much over time. Mature women tend to wear a simple coiffure; their hair is parted at the middle, arranged in graceful waves on either side of the face, and drawn up into a bun at the back. Younger, perhaps unmarried, women might wear their long hair in a ponytail, or arranged in the so-called "melon" coiffure, named after the wedge-shaped sections into which the hair is divided, which are then gathered together in a bun at the back of the head. A few heads sport a more unusual hairstyle that I have nicknamed the "peak" coiffure, a style in which the hair is drawn up into a tall peak of waves over the middle of the forehead, adding extra height to the face and emphasizing the graceful triangle shape of the forehead. This hairstyle may have been a modified version of the "little torch" coiffure (*lampadion*) worn by courtesans. Both the melon and peak hairstyles are worn by women on Attic grave reliefs from about the middle of the fourth century and by the terracotta Tanagra figurines (Dillon 2010; Jeammet 2010).

Indeed, because women are represented on Classical grave reliefs (beginning in the second half of the fifth century) well before they appear in portrait statues (by about the middle of the fourth century), the principal conventions for the representation of mortal women in sculpture were probably first worked out in funerary art. The basic model for a female portrait statue was therefore not the subject of the portrait but another image, with the precise identity of the subject given by the name inscribed on the statue's base. Inscribed statue bases provide crucial evidence for the historical practice of dedicating portrait statues of women, particularly for the beginning of the practice in the fourth century, from which very little sculptural evidence is preserved. Identifying the bases that once supported portrait statues of women is straightforward as long as the inscriptions use the nominative-accusative honorific formula, which names the dedicator of the statue in the nominative case and the subject of the statue, the person honored, in the accusative case. The nominative-accusative pairing, which was first developed in the early fourth century for the very prestigious public honorific portrait statue, became the canonical form also for privately dedicated votive portrait statues in the Hellenistic period (Ma 2007). So, for example, we have the full public honorific formula used for the statue of Philotera dedicated by the demos of Pergamon, probably in the mid second century BCE (Dillon 2010: 38):

> Ὁ δῆμος ἐτίμησεν
> Φιλωτέραν Λιμναίου διά τε τὰς Λιμναίου
> τοῦ πατρὸς αὐτῆς πρὸς τὸν δῆμον εὐεργεσίας
> καὶ διὰ τὴν Κυνίσκου τοῦ ἀνδρὸς αὐτῆς ἀρετὴν
> καὶ πρὸς τὸν δῆμον εὔνοιαν καὶ διὰ τὴν αὐτῆς
> τῆς Φιλωτέρας πρός τε θεοὺς εὐσέβειαν
> καὶ τὴν πρὸς Κυνίσκον τὸν ἄνδρα καὶ
> πρὸς τὰ τέκνα φιλοστοργίαν.

The demos has honored Philotera, daughter of Limnaios, on account of the benefactions of her father Limnaios towards the demos, and on account of the moral excellence [*aretē*] of her husband Kyniskos and his good will [*eunoia*] towards the demos, and on account of the piety [*eusebeia*] of Philotera herself towards the gods, and her affection towards her husband Kyniskos and towards her children.

Inscriptions on privately dedicated votive portrait statues of women tended to be somewhat less loquacious, while typically also giving priority to the person who set up the statue. The late fourth century inscription on a base from Priene for the statue of Niko is typical in its economy (Dillon 2010: 42):

[Μ]ενέδημος Εὐμένου[ς]
Νικοῦν τὴν θυγατέρα
[ἱ]ερησαμένην Ἀθηνᾶι
Πολιάδι.

Menedemos son of Eumenes
(dedicated) Niko his daughter
having been priestess of Athena
Polias.

Some portrait statues of the Hellenistic period, however, continue to use the more old-fashioned votive formula of "X (name in the nominative) dedicated to Y," well known from the Archaic period; such examples did not explicitly name the subject of the statue. Such nominative name labels were used for some honorific statues in the fourth and early third centuries, particularly in Athens; the statue of Menander that stood in the Theater of Dionysos is a well-known example of this practice (*IG* II^2 3777). The nominative name label, according to John Ma, "allows the subject of the statue to exist in the absolute, as an autonomous actor" (2007: 207). While no one has questioned the portrait status of the statue of Menander, there has been some disagreement about the status of monuments for women that use the nominative name label formula. Ridgway, for example, has questioned whether the statue of Nikeso from Priene (Figure 19.3) represents Nikeso herself or the goddess Demeter (Ridgway 1990: 210–11). The marble statue that stood on this base is preserved, and is discussed in more detail below as one of the case studies. The inscription on Nikeso's monument (*IPriene* no. 173) reads simply:

Νι[κ]ησὼ Ἱπποσθένους
Εὐκρίτου δὲ γυνή,
ἱερῆ Δήμητρος καὶ Κόρης.

Nikeso (daughter of) Hipposthenes
wife of Eukritos,
priestess of Demeter and Kore.

Since we know that nominative name labels were used for portrait statues of men, it seems reasonable to assume that the same formula could also have been used for portrait statues of women. Indeed, a second female portrait statue from Priene for a priestess named Timonassa also uses the nominative name label (*IPriene* no. 172) on its base, which perhaps suggests a local preference for this old-fashioned formula.

The empty footprints on the top of the base show that the statue of Timonassa was made of bronze, the preferred medium for public honorific portrait statues in the Hellenistic period. A good number of bases for female portraits preserve the cuttings for the attachment of a bronze statue. There are also a small number of female portrait statues in bronze actually preserved, for example the spectacular draped bronze woman found recently off the coast of Kalymnos, now on display in the local museum, and the more fragmentary bronze statue known as the Lady of the Sea in Izmir. The vast majority of female portrait statues that are preserved, however, are made of marble. Marble was clearly the material of choice for most

Figure 19.3 Cast of the portrait statue of Nikeso from Priene on its base. Statue H. 1.73 meters. Photo: Akademisches Kunstmuseum Bonn.

funerary statuary and for many votive portraits of women, particularly it would seem in the later Hellenistic and early Imperial periods, to which many of the extant marble statues of draped women have been dated. The use of marble for votive statuary has, of course, a long history—in fact, the earliest surviving monumental votive marble statue was dedicated by a woman sometime in the second half of the seventh century BCE: Nikandre's statue set up in the Sanctuary of Apollo on the island of Delos. Indeed, marble statues of standing draped women were extremely popular as votives in the Archaic period—the korai from the Athenian Acropolis are undoubtedly the best-known examples of this genre.

With the introduction in the fifth century of bronze as the prestige material for large-scale votives, marble seems to have fallen briefly out of favor; it came back into use in the late Classical and Hellenistic periods for large-scale prestige statuary of all kinds, including votive portraits of women. There is, for example, the marble portrait statue of a woman that was set up in the Sanctuary of Apollo at Delphi with the so-called Delphi Philosopher (Dillon 2007: 73). Marble was also used for the many votive portraits of women that crowded the Artemision of Messene (Themelis 2003: 74–6). Marble portraits of priest-esses stood inside the Temple of Artemis at Aulis (Connelly 2007: 157–61), and the marble statue of the priestess Aristonoe was found in the so-called Little Temple at Rhamnous near the statue of the goddess Themis (Petrakos 1991: 20–3).

In such cases, marble may have been chosen because it could impart something of a sacral character to a votive portrait, particularly when the portrait was set up near the marble statue of a divinity. The use of marble for both votive priestess portraits and images of goddesses could express materially the profoundly intimate relationship between the deity and her sacred servants, while imparting a strong visual coherence to the accumulated images, which in most cases would have been assembled over a long period of time. There may also have been something about the qualities of marble that made it especially desirable for female portrait statues. Perhaps it was its whiteness and luminosity, the way in which it could be carved so as to resemble flesh, and its ability to be colored that made it so attractive for statues of women; only with marble could a sculptor realize the full effect of pale flesh against the kind of colorful clothing that elite women were known to have worn and that was such an important part of a woman's public self-presentation. A marble statue would probably also have been less expensive than one of bronze, a factor that may also have played a part in the choice of material. That economics sometimes played a role in statue honors is suggested by an example from Erythrae: when the people of Erythrae honored both Maussollos and Artemisia with statues and crowns, they gave Maussollos a bronze statue set up in the agora and Artemisia a marble one set up in a shrine of Athena. In addition, the crown awarded to Maussollos was worth almost twice as much as the one given to Artemisia (Rhodes and Osborne 2003: 266–7).

In addition to inside temples or shrines, where else might one have found female portrait statues? Sanctuaries, perhaps unsurprisingly, seem to have been the main context for votive portrait statues of women, set up either as single figures or as part of family groups. Statues of women might be found in other locations, such as agorai, theaters, and private houses, but the archaeological and epigraphic evidence for statues in these display contexts comes mainly from the later Hellenistic and early Imperial periods. Female portrait statues were also primarily private family dedications set up by the women's closest male relatives: their husbands, fathers, and sons. Although less frequently attested, women could also dedicate statues to family members: the statue of Archippe, for example, was set up by her mother, who commissioned the great sculptor Praxiteles to make the portrait (Agora I 4568; Dillon 2010: 47), and a woman named Demokrite set up bronze statues of her father and her son in the sanctuary of Amphiarion at Oropos (Petrakos 1997, nos. 424–5; Dillon 2010: 49). Women were only very infrequently honored with statues by public civic bodies such as the demos and/or the boule, particularly before the Imperial period. The extraordinary statue honors given to the female benefactress Archippe of Kyme in the second century BCE, which included a bronze portrait statue set up in the agora and a gilded statue set on a column, while well known and much discussed (van Bremen 1996: 13–19; see also Bielman, this volume, Chapter 17) were not at all typical. Much more usual were the statue honors accorded to Nikeso from Priene, Aristonoe from Rhamnous, Kleopatra from Delos, and Flavia Vibia Sabina from Thasos, which are the focus of the following case studies.

2   Case Studies

The following case studies focus on female portrait statue monuments for which the inscribed base, the statue, and the context of the monument's display are all preserved.

The statues are broadly spaced both geographically and chronologically, come from a range of contexts, and were set up for a variety of reasons. These examples also show us the variety of options available for statue formats and portrait costumes. The four monuments highlighted here are highly representative of the larger phenomenon of female portrait statue honors in Greece and the Greek East from the Hellenistic to the Roman period.

Nikeso from Priene

The marble statue of Nikeso (Figure 19.3) stood in a prominent location near the entrance to the sanctuary of Demeter and Kore at Priene (Eule 2001: 43–4; Connelly 2007: 137–8). The statue, which is usually dated to the first half of the third century and is now in the Pergamon Museum in Berlin, is the earliest surviving female portrait statue found together with its base. The inscription tells us that Nikeso was the daughter of Hipposthenes and the wife of Eukritos, and that she was a priestess of Demeter and Kore. While the dedicator(s) of the monument is not explicitly named, the mention of both her father and husband suggests that these two male relatives may have been responsible for setting up the statue. The figure wears the usual costume of tunic and mantle, but the mantle has been very carefully and finely textured to indicate the special quality of the fabric from which it is made. The finely engraved vertical texture lines, which make the mantle look like a pleated silk Fortuny dress, are combined with horizontal and diagonal fold lines that animate the surface of the statue and give interest to the statue's somewhat static frontal pose. The folded edge at the top of the garment indicates that the entire mantle was doubled, an arrangement reinforced by the double line engraved along the mantle's bottom hem. The unusual texturing of the mantle indicates that it was made of special—indeed exotic—material; the ample amount of cloth, together with the arrangement and rendering of the drapery, imparts a tactile richness and sumptuousness to this portrait statue that make it stand out among preserved examples.

In addition to Nikeso's elaborate costume, the attribute that was held in the statue's now-missing right hand must have communicated information about the subject's sacral status. Some have argued that the statue may have carried a hydria on its head, and terracotta figurines from Priene do depict such hydriaphoroi, who had a special connection to the cult of Demeter and Kore (Mantes 1990: 98–9). Others have suggested that the statue held a large torch, like the images of priestesses of Demeter one finds on Hellenistic grave reliefs as well as in figurines from Priene (Kron 1996: 148). Fragments of large Pentelic marble torches were indeed found during the excavation of the City Eleusinion in the Athenian agora, in which stood portrait statues of women dedicated to Demeter and Kore. If Nikeso held a torch, this might explain the depression in the upper surface on the right side of the base on which the statue of Nikeso stood: to accept the end of this large marble torch.

Nikeso's hairstyle is also unusual among female portrait statues of women. Although the head of the statue is missing, there are preserved three long locks of hair in front of either shoulder, and a long length of hair made up of nine or ten thick locks hanging down the statue's back. Recalling as it does the hairstyles of the Acropolis korai, such an arrangement looks distinctly old-fashioned and indeed archaizing. Such shoulder locks seem not to have been worn by the mortal women depicted on Greek gravestones; neither is long, unbound hair hanging down the back a hairstyle that is typically associated with married women, as we know Nikeso to have been from the inscription on the statue's base. Perhaps Nikeso's unusual coiffure is meant to evoke the hairstyle worn by the goddess she serves, a counterpart to the sartorial strategy of dressing in "divine" costume that we sometimes find employed, for example, by priestesses of Demeter and Isis on Hellenistic grave reliefs. What we may have here is an early example of the adoption of a divine hairstyle—better known from Roman portraiture—in the portrait of a mortal woman, perhaps as part of the special costuming she wore as a priestess.

Aristonoe from Rhamnous

The marble portrait of Aristonoe (Figure 19.1), a private votive statue dedicated by her son Hierokles to the goddesses Nemesis and Themis, stood in the cella of the so-called Little Temple in Rhamnous, near a marble statue of the goddess Themis dedicated by Megakles and made by the local sculptor Chairestratos (Petrakos 1991: 20–3). The costume of Aristonoe's statue clearly shows the continued use of late Classical drapery styles for female portraits into the Hellenistic period. Indeed, although the statue has been dated on the basis of its style to the third century BCE, a recent analysis of the inscription places the monument in the mid-second century (Tracy 1990: 165). The statue of Aristonoe, now in the National Archaeological Museum in Athens, clearly demonstrates the difficulty of dating female portraits based on sculptural style; both the style of the portrait head and the drapery are closely related to representations of women on late Classical Attic grave reliefs. Female portraits in general tend not to change all that much over time; there was, in fact, a great deal of stylistic continuity in female representation from the late Classical to the Hellenistic periods, and in fact even into the Roman period.

The portrait of Aristonoe depicts a mature and dignified female subject. The face of the statue is oval in shape, broader at the chin and narrowing to a point above the middle of the forehead. The forehead is smooth and unlined, forming a graceful triangle framed by center-parted hair. The waved strands of hair form a sort of halo or crown around the face, as if they have been brought up and over and then tucked behind the wide, flat band worn around the head that is clearly visible at the hair's central parting. The forehead swells slightly above the eyebrows, which curve directly into the long nose. There is a subtle break in the profile at the root of the nose. The large eyes have subtle but distinct "bags" beneath and there are shallow naso-labial lines that modulate the soft, smooth flesh of the cheeks; these traits inflect the facial features with some indications of age and "portraitness." The mouth is small, with full lips that are gently parted. Soft creases mark the outer corners of the mouth. The chin is rounded and prominent, which is especially visible in profile, where one can also detect a slight double chin. The neck is long and graceful, the flesh marked by two obvious "Venus" rings. The head, which was worked separately from the body and then inserted into a cavity in the statue's neck, is turned slightly to the right.

The statue stands with the weight on the right leg, the left lightly bent at the knee. Both arms are bent at the elbows and held out in front of the body in a ritual gesture. Originally the statue held a phiale in the right hand; the separately attached right forearm, hand, and phiale are, however, now missing. The more open, active gesture of this statue is characteristic of many priestess portraits and was surely meant to call to mind publicly performed religious duties. Participation in cultic rituals provided one of the few sanctioned opportunities for women to present themselves in public, and, in some circumstances, at least probably gave them a degree of independent agency. Indeed, it is because of their role as priestesses that women first receive votive portrait statue monuments.

Kleopatra from Delos

The statue of Kleopatra from the island of Delos (Figure 19.2) was set up in a very different context and for a very different reason than the statues of Nikeso and Aristonoe. The statue, which stood on a large base next to a portrait of her husband Dioscurides, was set up after 138/7 BCE in the courtyard of their house in the Theater Quarter (Dillon 2010: 49–50). In the inscription on the base (*IDelos* 1987), Kleopatra is named as the dedicator of the statue of her husband, set up in honor of his dedication of two silver tripods in the Temple of Apollo. Interestingly, there is no indication in the inscription that Kleopatra herself is represented, but that is of course self-evident to anyone viewing the monument. Although clearly a private dedication in the fullest sense of the word—the monument was not set up in public space—the inscription itself commemorates a public dedication made by Dioscurides and borrows language from the public sphere in its reference to an Athenian archon for the dedication's date.

The statue of Kleopatra is in the so-called Pudicitia format, which was one of the most popular statue types for female portraits in the Hellenistic and Roman periods. The Pudicitia is characterized by the pose of the arms in front of the body, with the right held tightly across the body at the waist and the left bent at 90 degrees with the hand held close to the face. The gesture is one of restraint and modesty (hence the name), but it also has an air of elegance and charm. The portrait costume favored for statues in this format comprises a very long tunic of thick fabric over which is worn a large mantle made of thin, transparent material. This mantle, which in Kleopatra's statue is augmented by a lovely fringed selvage, is pulled so tightly around the body that the vertical folds of the tunic worn beneath it are clearly visible; this "drapery-through-drapery" effect is a hallmark of the best Hellenistic sculpture. While the body-covering gesture of the arms suggests modest comportment, the silky transparency of the tightly wrapped mantle reveals the softly rounded feminine shape of the body. Indeed, the format's modest pose and enveloping drapery well express the somewhat contradictory desired feminine ideals of restraint and propriety on the one hand and beauty and desirability on the other.

The visual contrast between the statues of Kleopatra and Dioscurides illustrates clearly the standout quality of female portrait statuary. Diocurides' body is almost completely obscured by the thick himation he wears, which falls in a series of straight, simple folds on both the front and back. Kleopatra's statue, conversely, is so tightly wrapped by the mantle that the swelling forms of the body are lovingly revealed; her hourglass shape is particularly visible at the back. The tunic falls in deep pleats around her lower legs, and consists of so much fabric that the hem of the dress piles up on top of the plinth. Add to this richness of detail the lively polychromy of the original statue and the overall effect must have been electric; in order to understand the difference in the visual impact of these two statues, we need to mentally reconstruct for Kleopatra a gown of bright blue, pink, or yellow with gilded edges, as we see in the Tanagra figurines, and imagine Dioscurides dressed perhaps in white or brown. This difference was surely carried over to the now missing portrait heads. Dioscurides' portrait face was undoubtedly quite distinct and individualized, perhaps like the so-called Worried Man, a beautifully detailed bronze portrait head found in the Granite Palaestra and dated to the second half of the second century (Queyrel in Marcadé 1996: no. 100). The portrait face of Kleopatra was surely just as beautifully indistinct; in fact, it probably did not look all that different from the face of Aristonoe. Indeed, female portrait identity seems to have been expressed visually through the individuality and particularity of the draped statue bodies, which show an elaborate and complex variety of poses and drapery patterns. With her beautifully detailed (and colorful) drapery, the portrait statue of Kleopatra is exemplary of this emphasis on the body as the marker of identity in female portraiture.

Flavia Vibia Sabina from Thasos

The statue of Flavia Vibia Sabina (Figure 19.4), now in the Archaeological Museum in Istanbul, clearly demonstrates how little the appearance of female portraits might change over the course of the approximately 350 years that separate this statue from the one, for example, of Aristonoe. Indeed, had this statue not been found directly in front of a base with an inscription of the early third century CE, the statue itself would likely have been dated based on its style to a much earlier period, as in fact it has been by a number of scholars (Eule 2001: 191). The report of the original discovery of the statue, however, makes clear that the statue indeed stood on this base (Dillon 2010: 147–8); while it is of

Figure 19.4 Statue of Flavia Vibia Sabina, from in front of the Arch of Caracalla, Thasos. Istanbul Archaeological Museum inv. 375. Statue H. 2.11 meters. Photo: W. Schiele, DAI Istanbul neg. 78/291.

course possible that the statue was reused in this context, there is no archaeological evidence to suggest that this was the case. The statue of Flavia Vibia Sabina is a version made in local Thasian marble of the well-known and popular "Arm-Sling" format, named after the characteristic way in which the right arm is bent up across the chest and held close to the body, supported by the folds of the mantle. The male equivalent of the format, from which the female version was surely derived, was the most common statue type for male portrait statues in the Hellenistic period (Lewerentz 1993: 18–57), including the statue of Dioscurides discussed above. Developed in the later fourth century BCE, the format continued to be used for both male and female portrait statues into the Roman period; its simplicity and elegance were obviously felt to be an extremely satisfying solution for statuary self-representation (Smith 1998: 65–6). The face of Flavia Vibia Sabina also shows the continued use of the idealized, "non-portrait" style for the portraits of women even after a more distinctly Roman style of portraiture, with its emphasis on individualized physiognomy and fashion hairstyles, became an available option for images of women in the Greek East beginning in the late Hellenistic period.

Both the base and its inscription, however, show what *is* new in female portraiture of this period. The statue and base are each about 2.10 meters in height; the combined height of Flavia Sabina's monument would have been a very impressive 4.2 meters (almost 14 feet), with the statue towering above its viewers. Portrait statues of the Hellenistic period tended to inhabit much the same space as the viewer, with bases averaging around thirty to seventy-five centimeters and statues typically a bit less than two meters in height. The statue of Flavia Sabina also stood in a very prominent public location: in front of the Arch of Caracalla on the side that faced the agora. In the Roman period, female portrait statue monuments could be found inhabiting the same public spaces as male portrait statues. This is a public statue also in the sense that it was dedicated by the Council of Elders or Gerousia, rather than by Flavia's family members. In fact, in the inscription (*IG* XII 8, 389; van Bremen 1996: 115 n. 3, Appendix 3 no. 3, 349) she is praised as "most noteworthy high priestess" (*archiereia*) and is said to share "in the same honors as the *gerousiastai* as first and only." Her family is only referred to in the most general terms—she is Mother of the Gerousia *apo progonon*—so Flavia Sabina was not, as were so many women before her, defined by her relationships to specific named male family members.

What is also distinctly Roman about the statue itself is that it is nearly identical both in appearance and in detail to another portrait statue from Thasos, found in the Sanctuary of Artemis Polo (Dillon 2010: 142–4). Although many Hellenistic female portraits share the same statue format and follow the same basic design, there is usually a wide range of creative variation in the details of the drapery and fold patterns. The strict stereotyping of female statue bodies—that is, the use of a limited number of carefully replicated statue types, as exemplified by these two statues from Thasos—is a phenomenon primarily of the Roman Imperial period. While her portrait statue may look much like the statues of other women, the inscription on the statue's base claims for Flavia Vibia Sabina great distinction and indeed astonishing singularity.

3   The Female Portrait Statue in the Hellenistic Period: A Brief History

A survey of the epigraphic and archaeological evidence for female portrait statues shows that sculpted images of women occupied a prominent place within the population of votive statues on display in Greek sanctuaries. According to the available evidence, the practice of setting up votive portrait statues of women is first attested in Athens in the fourth century BCE; in the Hellenistic period, female portrait statues could be found in sanctuaries throughout the Aegean. The number of women so honored with portraits gradually increased over this long period, so that by the later Hellenistic period female portrait statues were a common type of votive dedication. This increase in the number of portrait statues of women suggests an increased interest on the part of families in commemorating publicly and permanently the roles their female members performed on behalf of the family, whether as priestesses or as mothers, wives, and daughters. The revolution in public honors in the fourth century made the portrait statue the most prestigious award a city could bestow on a civic benefactor. Since only a small number of individuals ever received such prestigious public honors, the increase in the number of privately funded portrait monuments constituted attempts by the families to share in this prestige. The successful completion of religious duties provided one handy occasion for such a dedication; in fact, it had been customary for a priest or priestess to dedicate an *anathema* to the deity at this time (van Bremen 1996: 176–9). The portrait statue became the most prestigious of *anathemata*.

Family group monuments, which also began in the fourth century, also had a dedicatory function. These votives, an ostentatious display of religious piety and familial pride, need not have been associated with the fulfillment of specific religious duties: they were first and foremost gifts to the gods (Löhr 2000). Female portrait statues were often set up as part of these larger family groups, their statues standing together with the images of other family members. The inscriptions show us that even those women who received individual statue monuments were honored as representatives of their families; the statues were usually set up by their closest male relatives, whose own names would typically come first in the text on the statue's base. The inscriptions for those female statues that were part of family groups were also usually much briefer than those for the statues of their male relatives, and there were usually fewer female statues than male. However, even if they might have taken second place in terms of numbers and length of text, female portrait statues must have stood out visually among this forest of male figures in their variety, the richness of their surface details, and—when made in marble—the vivid color of their clothing.

Votive portrait statues were ornaments—beautiful decorations for the sanctuary (van Straten 2000: 211–12). Indeed, physical beauty was an important criterion for the selection of female cult agents, and the statues that represented these women were themselves beautifully crafted objects. Made in both bronze and marble, these expensive ornaments, created by some of the best sculptors of the day, demonstrated a family's wealth and status, as well as their religious accomplishments and civic engagement. This emphasis on collective values is visualized as well in the appearance of female portraiture. During the course of the fourth century, the faces of male portraits become increasingly more differentiated and individualized, giving the impression that they represent the subject's real appearance, whereas female portrait faces are much more uniform in appearance and change little over time. Indeed, the conventions of female portraiture established during the late Classical and Hellenistic periods continued to be used for hundreds of years.

The bodies of these statues, however, present a different story. Whereas the male portrait body is highly standardized and formulaic right from the start, the female portrait body is the site of tremendous artistic creativity. The sophisticated surface treatment of the drapery-through-drapery style of female dress is one of the great sculptural innovations of the Hellenistic period, as distinctive an achievement as physiognomic realism and just as important for the convincing representation of the appearance of the portrait subject. Although some female portrait statues employ costumes that could also have been worn by images of goddesses, many in the Hellenistic period wear this modern style of female dress; this would have set these images sharply apart from those of the divine realm and tied the portrait statue more closely to the contemporary world.

The statue bases name names—they tell us who the statue represents, who set the monument up, and why. The bases also made these portrait statues monuments: by elevating the statues from their immediate surroundings, the bases contributed significantly to the statues' visual impact. The statues themselves depict their female subjects as self-confident, poised, and elegantly dressed in colorful clothing, with beautifully smooth and ageless faces. The subtle variation in these faces was probably more than enough to convey something of the subject's individuality and personal identity, concepts that were never the most important qualities expressed by female portraits in the Greek world. While these portraits may not reveal to us the faces of real women, these statues do show the important and very visible role that women played in the monument landscapes of ancient Greek cities.

RECOMMENDED FURTHER READING

The portrait statues of women in Greece and the Greek East have been the focus of a number of recent studies, including Linfert (1976), Eule (2001), Connelly (2007), and Dillon (2007, 2010); all include extensive bibliographies of earlier sources. Ajootian (2007) is particularly good for the evidence for portraiture in the fourth century BCE. Löhr (2000) gathers the archaeological and epigraphic evidence for family group monuments, an important display context for female portrait statues. Eule (2002) surveys the epigraphic evidence for female portrait statues in Athens. See also the brief sections on women in portrait sculpture in Smith (1991) (Hellenistic period) and Smith (1998) (Roman Imperial period). Studies of individual statue monuments include Kreeb (1985) (on the Kleopatra from Delos) and Vanderpool (2005) (on the portrait of Plancia Magna from Perge, which utilizes the non-portrait face style). Particular statue types are the focus of Filges (1997) (the statue format used for Aristonoe), Daehner (2007), and Trimble (2011) (Large and Small Herculaneum statues). Kron (1996) and van Bremen (1996) are particularly important for the epigraphic evidence of women's civic and religious activity, for which women would have received portrait statue monuments.

20

Women and Family in Menander

Cheryl A. Cox

Before I discuss the information in Menander and the fragments of New Comedy, it would be wise to consider how realistic Menander is. To what extent are his plays reliable sources for social history? In considering Menander as a source, I will look at theatrical space and Menander's use of it, and his reliance on myth and tragedy.

1 Theatrical Space

Menander's plays would have been staged on the theater of Dionysus, which had been rebuilt by Lycurgus by soon after 330 BCE. The theater had a stone stage building with wings projecting fifteen feet from the façade, which was sixty-six feet long (Webster 1956: 20–2, 1962–3: 241–2). The façade was divided by columns into eleven spaces. The third, sixth, and ninth of these spaces were occupied by doors. In comedy, one, two, or three doors were available. This setting was suitable for a play calling for two houses and a shrine. Most, perhaps all, of Menander's plays involve two houses, but the *Dyskolos* and the *Aulularia* have a shrine that requires a third stage door (Webster 1956: 22, 1962–3: 250; Traill 2001: 88–9). Eight intercolumniations were free of doors in the façade and in them were fixed wooden panels (*pinakes*) upon which were painted scenery. The painted scenery in comedy depicts private houses with balconies and windows (Webster 1962–3: 242–5). Although theatrical space is limited, and therefore necessitates a crowding of houses, this crowding could indeed reflect the reality that, certainly for the city, houses were close together.

What do we make of the country setting? As Lowe (1987) maintains, the *Dyskolos* is remarkable for its use of a real location, the Nymphaeum at Phyle in the foothills of the Parnes range. At the rear of the stage are three houses, the central one standing for the Nymphaeum depicted here as a shrine on a village street. Probably to the left of the shrine is the door for Knemon's house, while to the right is Gorgias' house. On the left is probably a *parodos* that runs up into the Parnes foothills. Out of sight up the road lie two plots of land. This appears to have been the normal pattern of settlement in rural demes—the residential community geographically separated from the main agricultural land. The second *parodos*, probably on the right, is the road out of Phyle that passes Kallipides' estate and goes on to Cholargus. Kallipides' farm is close enough to be visited between acts and Gorgias appears to know Kallipides by sight. The Cholargus road brings the crowd that Knemon shuns: Sostratos and his hunting party, Sikon and Getas with the sheep, and finally the whole party under the supervision of Sostratos' mother (Lowe 1987: 126–38).

If, then, there was some realism in the staging of the plays, despite the limitations of space, how do we reconcile studies that emphasize that Menander's plays were heavily influenced by myth and tragedy with attempts to treat the plays as documents for social history?

2 Menander and Tragedy

There is a vast bibliography on Menander's dependence on tragedy (Hurst 1990: 94–5). Although some scholars have minimized the influence of tragedy on Menander (see Katsouris 1975a: 11ff. for a bibliography), the majority of scholars feel that Menander certainly relied on myth and tragedy to develop his plots. Similarities abound in plot structure and character. Besides these similarities in the plots and characters, the characters in Menander can from time to time refer specifically to myth. For instance, Demeas in the *Samia* refers to Danae and Zeus when trying to mollify Nikeratos (Webster 1960: 155; Katsouris 1975b: 165; Gutzwiller 2000: 115).

Besides plot and character, there are similarities in the diction in Menander's comedy with that of tragedy. In some cases in both tragedy and comedy, the first word or phrase of a character's entry is the same word or phrase that was earlier used to refer to that character before his entrance by other characters (Katsouris 1975b: 139).

Menandrian prologues are modeled on Euripidean ones. In Euripides prologues are spoken by powerful gods, while in Menander prologues are spoken by minor deities, personifications, or human characters. Pan in the *Dyskolos* is a prime example. Although a minor deity he speaks as a powerful god of pre-eminent authority. His personality dominates the play like Aphrodite in the *Hippolytus* or Dionysus in the *Bacchae*. Like Aphrodite he desires to vindicate his cult and guarantee its future (Photiades 1958: 111; Gutzwiller 2000: 115).

Given Menander's reliance on tragedy and myth, can we say that he was an indicator of his times? I feel that it would be naive to think that drama cannot reflect attitudes and customs from the society within which it was created. For ancient drama, to take one example, in her book on female discourse in drama McClure discusses briefly the studies of structuralists and anthropologists that focus on dramatic performance as a social institution (1999: 3–8). Attic drama continually engaged in a dialogue with the other facets of polis life, and political and social changes formed the plays. McClure has studied some of the tragedies and some Old Comedy to argue that women's speech disrupted male-governed household activity unless it was suppressed or transmitted into a ritual form. Although tragedy may not be precise documents for family and property law, it can tell us about social attitudes. To take the *Antigone*, for just one example: the eponymous character is the heiress of Oedipus after her brothers' deaths. She does not marry her uncle, Kreon, but is betrothed to his son, her first cousin. The play, moreover, is an informative document on the dichotomy between a young woman's loyalties to her family of origin and her feelings toward her family of marriage (Neuberg 1990: 54–76).

In what follows I will examine the relationships between spouses, between fathers and daughters, and between mothers and daughters. The relationship between brothers and sisters must necessarily be omitted for reasons of space, but I discuss them elsewhere (Cox 2006: 153–6).

3 Husband and Wife

"I betroth my daughter to you for the bearing of legitimate children and I give a dowry of three talents." So says the father Kallipides in Menander's *Dyskolos* (842–4; this formula appears in other fragments both in Menander and outside his corpus: 453 K-A, Menander; 1098 K-A, Anon.). Social historians, basing their statements on political biography and the orations, are used to stating that marriages in ancient Athens were arranged. And, indeed, many marriages in Menander are arranged for both the prospective bride and the groom. The new bride is probably around fifteen years of age, but the groom may at times be in his early twenties. Thus, some examples of arranged marriages in the comedies: Kleostratos in the *Aspis* probably marries his first cousin (father's brother's daughter); Gorgias in the *Dyskolos* has his marriage to Sostratos' sister arranged by Sostratos and the latter's father (813ff.); Pamphile's marriage to Charisios is arranged in the *Epitrepontes*, and in the *Samia* Moschion's marriage to Nikeratos' daughter is arranged by Moschion's adoptive father, Demeas, and Nikeratos (113ff.). The hero in the *Georgos* is betrothed to his patrilineal half-sister by his father (10f.), while marriages are arranged in the *Fabula Incerta*, the *Perinthia*, and the *Plokion*; as Brown (1993: 199) points out, men as well as women could have their marriages arranged without their desires being consulted.

Unlike the speakers in forensic orations, who rarely talk of attraction between prospective spouses, Menander's comedies reveal that young men can become strongly attracted to young girls. For instance, Chaereas in the *Aspis* has grown up with Kleostratos' sister, loves her, and wants to marry her (261ff.). Sostratos' desire is fulfilled in the *Dyskolos* and he ends up marrying the young girl to whom he is strongly attracted. Both Polemon in the *Sikyonios* and Thrasonides in the *Misoumenos* marry the woman with whom they have been cohabiting. Although marriages were arranged and Athenian sources stated that it was in poor taste for men to be sexually attracted to their wives (Is. 3.13–14; Plut. *Cim.* 4.8–9), the sources also reveal true affection between husband and wife (Cox 1998: 72): for instance, spouses show genuine concern when the other is ill (Dem. 30.34, 50.61, 59.56). A fragment of New Comedy explicitly states that a husband loves his wife and his wife loves her husband (*Pap. Antinoopolis* 15 = 1084 K-A, Anon.).

Thus, our views of love and marriage can differ according to the sources. The normative view in the orations is that spouses, although not knowing each other well at first, make the marriage last for the sake of the children. True affection may even develop. For Menander there can be romance leading to marriage, but it is always the romance felt by the young man: the feelings of the young woman or girl towards the young man and towards her marriage are not stated in the comedies. The young woman's emotions are rarely explored, and her character is not developed "beyond the needs of a male-oriented plot" (Rosivach 1998: 1).

In fact, in the comedies men fall in love with women who are poor, or slaves, or prostitutes. Upper-class women were ideally secluded and therefore not as accessible as poor and marginal women. Fathers in New Comedy do allow their sons to marry beneath their class but this is considered remarkable and against society's conventions (Rosivach

1998: 7). Besides men marrying downward in Menander, we are also reminded of Gorgias' marriage in the *Dyskolos*, in which the poorer Gorgias marries the wealthy Kallipides' daughter.

Indeed it is difficult to see from the orations and Davies' register of propertied families (Davies 1971) the frequency of marriages contracted in which there was a great disparity between the wealth of the groom's family and that of the bride. One marriage, that of Mantias to Plangon, seems indeed to have been based on emotion. Plangon's father was a prestigious general who fell into debt. It appears that Plangon may not have brought a dowry into the marriage (Dem. 40. 22). Mantias divorced Plangon, but he maintained a liaison with her throughout his marriage to a woman who brought a substantial dowry. Further, he seems to have remarried Plangon after the death of his second wife (see Cox 1998: 181 and bibliography in nn. 61 and 62).

There seems to be some historical precedent in the orators and propertied families for marriages between spouses of differing wealth. There is even a hint that some marriages were based on love and attraction. But there is another type of marriage that occurs in New Comedy, but is not alluded to in the orations—marriage resulting from rape. Rape was a serious offense to the Athenians. Although many scholars have believed that seduction was a worse crime than rape, the Athenians probably viewed both crimes as equally serious (see Harris 1990: 370 n. 2 for bibliography). Rape was an act of *hybris* (arrogant treatment or violence), and as such the successful prosecutor could suggest and impose a *graphê hubreos* (prosecution for *hybris*). Certainly Gorgias' sentiment in the *Dyskolos* is that rape should be punished with death. (See Arnott 1981: 218; Harris 1990: 372–5; Brown 1991: 533–4; Patterson 1998: 171.) Ogden (1997: 33ff.) argues that rape was punished as severely as adultery but that adultery produced a more visceral reaction in Athenians. Carey (1995: 407–17) argues that rape was viewed as a lesser crime, although he nowhere considers Gorgias' statement in the *Dyskolos*. It is quite likely that lesser punishments such as fines were imposed. In any case it is rare for the comedies to deal with seduction because doing so would have prejudiced the audience against the girl; in rape the victim is blameless (Fantham 1975: 50; Wiles 1989: 21–48). The child from such a union, however, was exposed (Cole 1984: 106).

Menander's plays focus on marriage and the feeling throughout them is that marriage is a necessary institution; what, then, are the relations like between husband and wife in New Comedy? There are many sentiments both for and against marriage in Menander's fragments. Although marriage can be seen as an evil, it is a necessary one (for instance, fr. 59 Sandbach). Wives were good assets because they produced children, nursed sick husbands, and buried them when they died (fr. 276 Sandbach). In the *Hypobolimaios* (374 K-A) the woman lets the man be the guide; any family in which the woman is chief comes to grief.

Despite the passivity of the prospective bride in marital arrangements, the wife seems to have a great deal of influence in New Comedy. Characters in New Comedy do advise the wife to listen to her husband (Philemon 120 K-A), but one non-Menandrian fragment states that a smooth-running household depends on harmony between husband and wife. As the man brings home the fruits of his labors from outside, the woman has been working indoors (Apollodorus 14 K-A). This tendency to admit the influence of the woman supports the view by both historians and social scientists that women could have a great deal of informal influence in the household. This influence can be attributed to the dowry that a woman brings into the marital household and the attention the husband gives to it: the comedies can even depict the husband as enslaved to his dowered wife; for an instance in middle comedy see Alexis (150 K-A). The dowry then seals and stabilizes a marriage (Cox 1998: 69–70 and bibliography n. 5). As in the orations (Cox 1998: 71), spouses in Menander tried to make a marriage work (see also Cohn-Haft 1995: 1–14, who also feels there were few instances of divorce and that divorce was not a casual or frivolous action). Indeed, in the two plays where spouses are separated, Pamphile and Charisios in the *Epitrepontes* and Knemon and his wife in the *Dyskolos*, there is reconciliation between the spouses. In both the *Epitrepontes* and *P. Didot* 1 (1000 K-A, Anon.), wives do not want to follow their father's advice and leave their husbands. In the former play Pamphile defends her loyalty to her husband and he in turn, before he finds out that Pamphile's baby is his own, eventually forgives his wife for having borne a child, a *nothos*. Scholars have interpreted Charisios' behavior in various ways. Fantham (1975: 70) points out that Charisios was at the mercy of *doxa*: he would have shamed himself if it were known that he condoned an unchaste wife. Konstan (1994: 217–25), argues (226ff.) that Charisios was not concerned so much with the issue of lost virginity as with the production of a child.

In the *P. Didot* papyrus the young woman tells her father that a husband should cherish his wife and she do what pleases him. She informs her father that her husband is a good man and has given her happiness but has lost his wealth (10ff.). She does not want to be divorced from her husband only to be married to a wealthier man. And, if his wealth should fail, she does not want to be passed on to a third man (20ff.). This woman is happy in her marriage even though she specifically states that it was arranged (30ff.). Now that she is married she is the one to decide to stay in the marriage.

Husband and wife present a united front to their family and the community. Fragment 592 (Sandbach) states explicitly that the wife's domain lies between the front door and the yard—she should not take her quarrel with her husband out into the street. So, husband and wife in Menander work together in the events surrounding the lives of their children. Nikeratos in the *Samia* is convinced he will have to talk to his wife concerning the marriage of their daughter (200), and his wife is not above nagging him about the wedding preparations (715ff.). Both spouses may be interested in the relationships in which their son is involved (*Pk* 301–318), while in the *Kitharistes* a husband blames not his wife but himself for their son's spending. In the *Sikyonios*, Stratophanes' adoptive mother knows about her husband's finances and saves their son (Stratophanes) from inheriting his adoptive father's debts (135ff.); see Lloyd-Jones (1966: 135). (This case is not unlike the historical case of Kleoboule, Demosthenes' mother, who knew in detail the amount of wealth left by her late husband; see Hunter 1989b: 39–48. For widows who fought to keep their late husbands' estates intact see Hunter 1989a: 300. For the orations see, for example, Lys. 32.10ff.; Aeschin. 1.98–99; Dem. 36.17–18.) In a Menandrian fragment someone is telling a young man, Kreoboulos, to obey his mother and marry his kinswoman (492 K-A). In a fragment outside Menander, two fathers are discussing the prospect of wedding one's daughter to the other's son. The son's mother had invited her future in-law to the discussions (1063 K-A, Anon.). Outside of family matters *per se*, in the *Samia*, Nikeratos' wife knows about events that happen in their neighbor's house and informs her husband so he can act upon those events (410ff., 421).

Perhaps the most telling influence of the wife is seen when she has been married twice and becomes a link between the two households of marriage. The *Aspis* and the *Dyskolos* are relevant here. In the *Aspis* Chaerestratos had been planning to give his niece in marriage to his stepson Chaereas; the latter is the son of Chaerestratos' wife by a former marriage and seems to have accompanied his mother to Chaerestratos' oikos as he grew up in his household. According to MacDowell, the situation in the *Aspis* is similar to the marital strategy in Demosthenes' family: Demosthenes Senior, the orator's father, willed the guardianship of his children to Aphobos, among others, and gave his widow (Kleoboule) to Aphobos in marriage. Based on Demosthenes' case, MacDowell conjectures that, because Chaereas grew up in Chaerestratos' household and his mother was married to Chaerestratos, the mother may have been willed to Chaerestatos by her late husband (MacDowell 1982: 43; on the willing-away of a widow see Cox 1989: 34–46). For similar reasons, we may conjecture that Knemon in the *Dyskolos* received his wife from her first husband. As Gomme and Sandbach have stated, although Chaerestratos' wife had no legal standing in the context of Chaereas' asking to marry Chaerestratos' niece, she obviously had her say in it (Gomme and Sandbach 1973: 87).

The comedies, then, show strong loyalty between husband and wife, even to the point of challenging the paternal authority of the wife's father. But how strong was the paternal authority of a man in his own oikos with his children before they were married? As the first part of this discussion concentrated on husbands and wives, the next part will concentrate on the relationships between generations.

4   Fathers and Daughters

Menander's plays can present deep affection between father and daughter. Knemon's daughter speaks affectionately of her father in the *Dyskolos* and is distraught when he falls down the well (673ff.). After her father's accident the daughter in the play is a caregiver, helping her father to sit up (700–1). Especially poignant are the scenes in which the father is reunited with his daughter after a long separation. In the *Misoumenos*, Demeas is delighted to be reunited with his daughter after his family has been dispersed by war (210ff.). In the *Sikyonios* Kichesias cries and faints, presumably with joy, that his daughter is still alive (Golden 1990: 177). So, too, Pataikos in the *Perikeiromene* is overwhelmed with emotion when reunited with his daughter, Glykera, and embraces her. He gives her in marriage to her partner Polemon only when Glykera assures him she will again be reconciled with Polemon and when the latter promises not to abuse her in the future (1006ff.). These instances match the close affective ties that we find in tragedy between father and daughter (on tragedy see, for instance, Humphreys 1978: 202; Patterson 1985: 120; Golden 1990: 94–7). Along with affective ties we find in the comedies that the father was indeed the *kyrios* of his daughter, and as such had authority over her upbringing and her marriage, including her dowry.

Let us examine upbringing first. It has been argued by scholars that fathers tended to expose female infants more than male infants (the most recent proponent of the exposure of female infants is Pomeroy 1997: 120). One fragment of Poseidippos would certainly suggest this: "even if a man happens to be poor, he brings up a son; even if rich he exposes his daughter" (12 K-A). Girls in general were devalued, and the birth of a girl could be a source of shame for the father. Girls may even have been fed less than boys; though see Golden (1990: 94–5), who emphasizes that men could care for girls once they had decided to raise them. Cynthia Patterson, who does not believe that female infants were exposed any more than males, does, however, believe that there was an unequal sex ratio favoring males, stressing that in general physically defective babies and illegitimate babies were at high risk (Patterson 1985: 113, 115). This ratio may be partially attributed to an unthinking favoring of the male child in terms of its physical care and nourishment (Patterson 1985: 120–1). Most recently, Ingalls (2002) has echoed this view, pointing out that there is evidence that Athenians wanted girls as well as boys. Aristotle in his *Rhetoric* includes among the components of happiness many children, both male and female. This view is mirrored in statistics—in Davies' register (1971), many families had daughters. Further, although the scholars who argue for the prevalence of female infanticide refer to the burden of the dowry, Ingalls argues that fathers wanted to provide dowries. The dowry attracted a suitable husband, contributed property from the woman's family to her marital oikos, and gave her protection in the event of the death of her husband or divorce (Ingalls 2002: 248–50). Certainly in Menander's plays the two instances of actual exposure of children, in the *Epitrepontes* and in the *Perikeiromene*, involve the exposure of a male child in the first instance and a girl and her twin brother in the second. (In fact, in the *Epitrepontes* the baby is exposed not by his father but by his mother, a victim of premarital rape. Patterson (1985: 116) points out that when the mother was young and unmarried the child was in her hands and the hands of her family.) Although our sample is small, there is no hint in the corpus that female infants were at higher risk of exposure. The child of an informal union, whether male or female, was at risk. There seems to be no prejudice against the female infant, specifically in Menander.

One fact that can be stated about a girl's upbringing is that her father was the defender of her virtue (for the orations: Aeschin. 1.182–83, [Dem.] 40.57, 59.65ff.; Cox 1998: 92). The father in Menander's plays can vacillate between being the sober provider and the volatile defender of family interests, including the virtue of the women in his family. So, in the *Dyskolos* Knemon's daughter is afraid that her father will beat her if he catches her outside unescorted (204–6). Sostratos, in the same play, asserts that a daughter should be brought up by a fierce (*agrios*) father who keeps her from the influence of other older women, such as an aunt or nurse, and keeps her lifestyle free from vice (384ff.). In the *Samia*, Nikeratos is violently upset that his daughter has been seduced by Moschion. He first threatens to kill Chrysis, Demeas' *pallake*, for her influence over the women of his household (558ff.) and then considers having Moschion arrested (716ff.). In fact, when he finally agrees to give his daughter in marriage to Moschion, he gives her away without a dowry—the dowry, all his property, will be forthcoming after his death. Some scholars argue that this may be evidence that if a girl is given in marriage to her violator, a *moichos* (either seducer or rapist), she is married without a dowry. In any case, a father is so concerned about his daughter's virtue that, in the *Sikyonios*, Kichesias, although he may faint with joy after discovering his daughter is alive, is still nonetheless concerned as to whether she is still a virgin (370ff.). The *Misoumenos* balances this picture, however, of the father as strict defender. Here Krateia, a girl who is the war captive of Thrasonides, is reunited with her father, Demeas, in a very emotional scene (210ff.). Demeas does not mention Krateia's status as he knows she had been the *pallake* (concubine) of Thrasonides (210ff.). When Krateia explains to her father that she has lived as Thrasonides' concubine because she had to, Demeas reacts with sadness and understanding (250ff.), fully intending to ransom her from Thrasonides (300ff.). He agrees to give his daughter formally in marriage to Thrasonides only after Krateia assures him that she wants the marriage (436ff.).

As the daughter's *kyrios*, the father arranged her marriage, preferably to someone who was like him in outlook and behavior (*Dys.* 336–7) or who was indeed related to him. In the *Georgos* the father arranges a marriage between his daughter and son by two different wives (10ff.). The father made sure to give his daughter away in marriage with a dowry. In the *Aspis* Chaerestratos is thinking of giving his daughter to his nephew in marriage (260ff.): as his *epikleros*, or heiress, she stood to inherit much of his sixty-talent estate. In the

Perikeiromene Pataikos betroths Glykera, his daughter, to Polemon, giving her a three-talent dowry, and warns Polemon to behave himself in the marriage (1010ff.). Knemon in the *Dyskolos* gives his daughter in marriage with a dowry of one talent, half of his estate (730ff.). In the same play Kallipides gives his daughter in marriage with a dowry of three talents (842–4). In the *Epitrepontes* Smikrines has given his daughter in marriage with a dowry of four talents (134), while Demeas in the *Misoumenos* gives a two-talent dowry with his daughter (446). In a non-Menandrian fragment the father of the bride gives his daughter away with a dowry that consists of a field he had inherited from his father (*P. Tebt.* 693 = 1064 K-A, Anon.).

Compared to the sums found in the orators, which averaged around 3000 to 6000 drachmae, the dowries of Menander's comedies are more substantial (see Finley 1985: 79 on the average dowries in the orators; for dowering daughters and sisters see Cox 1998: 118 Table 3). It is not unusual in Menander's comedies for dowries to be as high as three or four talents, and one dowry, given to an *epikleros* in the *Plokion*, is worth ten talents (fr. 333 Sandbach). Although Finley previously argued that these dowries were a product of comic exaggeration, it is now thought that the families of New Comedy were extremely wealthy and that the dowries were in keeping with that wealth. It is apparent that several of these large dowries are given to inheriting daughters, to *epikleroi*. For instance, Krobyle in the *Plokion* (fr. 333 Sandbach) is given a large dowry of ten talents, has married a relative, and rules her household. Her wealth has made her powerful. In fact, it seems that her husband has had a flirtation with a servant girl and Krobyle has dismissed the girl. She dominates her son and daughter. Her husband, Laches, mourns his position, a sentiment expressed quite frequently in tragedy and comedy in relation to wealthy wives (e.g., Eur. *Hipp.* 616ff.; *And.* 147–54; Men. *Dys.* 820ff.; for further references see Schaps 1979: 76, 142–3 nn. 26–7).

Whether the daughter was an *epikleros* or not, it is evident from the plays that the father is interested in her material welfare after her marriage. Kallipides in the *Dyskolos* at first does not want to give his daughter to a poorer man (795–6). Smikrines in the *Epitrepontes* is very concerned about his daughter's dowry after her husband, Charisios, has walked out on her (1065ff.). Charisios, although living apart from his wife, uses her dotal wealth to gamble and hire a *hetaira* (prostitute) (135–7). Smikrines wants to take his daughter, Pamphile, away from Charisios, but she resists his attempts. She is not to be ordered like a slave (Post 1940: 431). Smikrines tries to persuade her to leave by telling her she cannot compete with the prostitutes whom Charisios will bring home (714ff.). We are not told in the play whether Pamphile has siblings. She may be an heiress, but Smikrines' concern for her dowry is the concern of a father towards the material welfare of his daughter and for his own wealth. Such concern is evident in Kallipides' attitude in the *Dyskolos* and in the *P. Didot* fragment, to be discussed directly below.

This situation is not unlike that of *P. Didot* 1 (1000 K-A, Anon.), in which the daughter, whose father arranged her marriage, now does not wish her father to initiate a divorce between her and her husband simply because the latter has lost his fortune. The daughter feels that now that she is married she has the right to make her own decisions. If her father insists on the divorce, however, she will behave as well as possible so as not to disgrace herself.

One observation that can be made from this fragment is that the father had a good deal of authority to initiate a divorce between his daughter and her husband. There has been much discussion as to whether there was an actual law enforcing the father's right (see Wolff 1944: 47 n. 23 for a bibliography on the issue; see also Harrison 1968: 31

and n. 1 for a bibliography). Harrison (1968) and MacDowell (1978: 88) both argue for a legal right but perhaps the father lost his right if the daughter had borne a son. For this latter point see also Gomme and Sandbach (1973: 350). See also Turner (1979: 122), who feels that the force of a daughter's character would be an important element in whether a divorce took place or not. We can safely assert, however, that, although a father could expect to pressure his daughter, who is young and not quite capable of acting independently, the young woman's husband, nevertheless, can discourage the father from persevering in his pressure (*Epit.* 921ff.).

A second observation that can be made from the Didot fragment is that the daughter had an obligation to obey her father if he insisted on the divorce—to disobey her father publicly would have brought shame on herself and her family. Nevertheless, she could be quite devoted to her marriage and be willing to argue with her father on her husband's behalf. The father, moreover, could also be concerned for his daughter's emotional welfare. Chaerestratos is truly depressed by his nephew's death because his daughter cannot now marry the young nephew and because Chaerestratos' older brother, Smikrines, intends to marry Chaerestratos' niece, an heiress (306ff.). Before the fabricated plot of his own death, Chaerestratos is absolutely appalled, to the point of threatening violence, when confronted with the possibility that Smikrines, an elderly man, may claim in marriage Chaerestratos' own daughter, also an heiress (356).

To sum up, fathers were very concerned in the marriages of their daughters and about the material and emotional welfare of the daughter after marriage. Fathers and daughters could be emotionally close, but the daughter could after marriage become quite loyal to her family of marriage, loyalty that could lead her into conflict with her father. In the orations we found that women retained close ties with their family of origin: the dowry, because it belonged to her family of origin, bound the woman to her natal kin. In the comedies we see strong ties between a woman and her family of origin but these ties do not overpower her ties to her family of marriage.

5 Mothers and Daughters

In Menander's comedies, interests for mother and daughter revolved around marriage and children. Mothers and daughters could actively cooperate in the arrangements for the daughter's marriage. In the *Samia* Moschion approaches Plangon's mother, when Plangon's father is absent, to promise the mother that he will marry Plangon, who has borne his son (51ff.). In the same play both mother and daughter (Plangon) conspire with Chrysis, Demeas' concubine, to keep the maternity of Plangon's baby secret, and the mother is consulted by her husband about the arrangements surrounding the impending marriage of their daughter to Moschion (200). In the *Georgos*, a widow is approached by the young hero, who asks for her daughter's hand in marriage (1ff.). The widow in the play must deal with the fact that her daughter is pregnant by the young hero (29ff.; 87). Rosivach (1998: 51) claims that the mother or female guardian always approves of the relationship of the daughter with her lover. But in this play the widow is clearly unhappy with the young hero's behavior. Only in the *Dyskolos* do we find the women taking a passive role in the marriages of their daughters. Myrrhine leaves behind her daughter in Knemon's house and is not part of the negotiations concerning her daughter's dowry and marriage to Sostratos. Nor is Sostratos' mother active in the discussions concerning the marriage of Sostratos' sister to Gorgias.

Essentially, then, a mother's relations with her daughter were close: a mother could be a confidante, particularly when the young girl had been indiscreet or a victim of rape. Ultimately, however, the mother was concerned about her daughter's marriage and could take an active role in its arrangement.

6   Conclusion

To conclude, Menander's world took marriage seriously: both husband and wife strove to make the marriage work. Although women were relegated to the house, they had a large role in the day-to-day conversations about matters concerning the household. This great concern for marriage entered the father–daughter relationship, where the young woman appeared to be very protective of her marriage and husband. Concerns relating to marriage also shaped the mother–daughter relationship, in which the mother could have a good deal to say in the marriage of her daughter. Menander's world gives us an idea of the daily concerns of women within the familial setting, and as such balances the normative view we so often find in the orations. Menander may have depended on stock themes and characters in his plays but the concerns of women and family would have been well understood by his audience.

RECOMMENDED FURTHER READING

The present paper focused on Athenian family practice and attitudes. Hunter (1989a, 1989b) and McClure (1999) discuss practices and attitudes in the fifth century BCE and in the orations. For classical Athens in general, see Ingalls (2002) and Patterson (1985) for views on the exposure of female infants. Scafuro (1997) discusses the orations and New Comedy. On the politics of rape in classical Athens, consult Omitowoju (2002). For a more literary approach to women in Menander, see Traill (2008).

21

Gender and Space, "Public" and "Private"

Monika Trümper

1 Introduction: The Case of the Fountain House

A black-figured Attic hydria from the last quarter of the sixth century BCE (Figure 21.1) shows five women that are elegantly dressed and bedecked with jewelry collecting water in an elaborately rendered fountain house. This topic was very popular in Athens for some thirty to forty years (525–490 BCE) and was represented on seventy-one black-figured and four red-figured vases (mostly *hydriai* and *kalpides*). The popularity of this topic is often linked to the contemporary improvement of public water supply in Athens, possibly initiated by the Peisistratids, which included the construction of fountain houses (Tölle-Kastenbein 1994: 101–3). From these images and the archaeological remains it recently has been concluded that, in Archaic Athens, female citizens, possibly even of aristocratic families, frequented public fountains such as the fountain house in the southeast corner of the agora. Although the agora in this period would already have housed important male-oriented public and civic activities, a fountain house, with its connotation of feminine activities, was built on this very square, albeit at its border. Thus, the fountain house would have constituted "an important statement about the significance and place of women in civic and communal life: certainly included but literally at the edges" (Foxhall 2009: 505). Further, it proves that women in the Archaic period enjoyed much greater freedom and access to public space than their peers in the fifth and fourth centuries BCE, when literary sources describe the task of fetching water as tedious and unpleasant, best left to slaves (Rotroff and Lamberton 2006: 7–8).

While the archaeological evidence of fountain houses is undisputed (Tölle-Kastenbein 1994: 73–87), the publications cited above ignore a major problem: the interpretation of the images on vases is much debated in every aspect, notably the identity and social status of the women, the location of the fountain houses, and the overall meaning of the scenes, especially with a view to the "socio-historical reality." In a critical review of the many different readings of these images, it has most recently been argued, intriguingly, that these images do not depict scenes of real life (*lebenswelt*) at all, but instead present a

A Companion to Women in the Ancient World, First Edition. Edited by Sharon L. James and Sheila Dillon.
© 2012 John Wiley & Sons, Ltd. Published 2015 by John Wiley & Sons, Ltd.

Figure 21.1 Black-figured hydria of the Priam Painter, last quarter of the sixth century BCE. Boston, Museum of Fine Arts inv. 61.195. Photo: Museum of Fine Arts, Boston.

combination of desirable female qualities, notably beauty and social prestige, with a location and activity that allows for a conspicuous public display of precisely these qualities. The solemn, ceremonial, and dignified atmosphere of the fountain-house scenes thus would draw on real situations, such as the public appearances of women at festivals, but would not refer to a concrete event or practices of daily life, let alone the collection of water. The fountain house would have been depicted as a symbolic topos of questionable encounters between the different sexes and potentially transgressive behavior, in order to illustrate the problematic, dangerous aspects of public visibility and accessibility of women (Stähli 2009).

The "fountain-house case" is highly revealing of crucial methodological problems in the study of gender and space. Three different sources, namely texts, archaeological remains, and images, are drawn on for the reconstruction of a potentially gendered use of public space. The critical and nuanced approach of Stähli (2009), argues, however, that the archaeological remains and images present different discourses that cannot be combined in a simple, straightforward manner to reconstruct a clear, homogeneous picture of female life in Archaic Athens. Rather, the discourses must be studied separately with particular focus on their characteristics as well as agents (patrons, authors, audience) and agendas (meaning, message). Only then may careful comparative analysis show whether they complement or inform each other. While the fountain-house case centers on Athens, a more comprehensive study of gender and space in the Greco-Roman world must take chronological and geographical aspects into account, critically asking when and where sources were made and, consequently, for which period and region they are relevant.

Scholarly focus on the "fountain-house case" suggests a lively interest in the study of gender and space, at least in the Greek world. Research on the larger topic is, however, surprisingly spotty. While it has been extensively treated for Greek domestic architecture ("private" space), far less has been written about the much better preserved Roman equivalent and there has been astonishingly little study of the much wider subject of gender and "public" space, for both the Greek and Roman worlds (Schmitt Pantel 2005: 1–4). Recent studies employ very wide definitions of space (*"raum," "espace"*), including social space, conceptual and virtual space, and—rather rarely—physical and built space (Harich-Schwarzbauer and Späth 2005). Such a broad definition is much inspired by approaches to space in the social sciences that analyze space as the product of social action or social structures (Löw 2008). Studies specifically concerned with gender and "public" space in the Greco-Roman world focus on representations of women in "public" space (e.g., family monuments in sanctuaries, honorary statues, Roman state reliefs) or on female euergetism and, more specifically, patronage in building (van Bremen 1996; Woodhull 2003). Research on gender and space in modern periods and cultures provides different socio-historical contexts and a much better corpus of sources (Agrest et al. 1996; Durning and Wrigley 2000; Stratigakos 2008). Further, this research provides sophisticated comprehensive approaches to the engendering of space, notably through studying and observing its real use (Rendell et al. 2000: esp. 101–221).

While a comprehensive examination of gender and the use of built space in the Greco-Roman world is a desideratum, this essay can provide only some preliminary thoughts. After a discussion of methodological issues, I will consider the problem of gender and space, looking at "private" domestic space on the one hand and selected categories of "public" space, notably civic space, on the other. Some important subjects must be omitted here, such as the representation of gender in space (see above) and the gendered use of sacred and funerary space (of the numerous works on women and religion, which rarely specifically discuss the gender-specific use of sacred space, see, for example, Dillon 2002; Cole 2004; Schultz 2006; Kaltsas and Shapiro 2008).

2   Concerns and Strategies of Gender Differentiation

It has long been maintained, in accordance with literary sources, that Greek society was organized along clear dichotomies such as oikos and polis, private and public, female and male, nature and culture—dichotomies that have obvious consequences for the interpretation of gendered space. The organization of society according to this binary logic—commonly along the opposition of female-private-domestic versus male-public—has been reconstructed for many different cultures, even those in the modern western world. But it has also been extensively criticized in recent gender studies, because it would at best reflect ideal concepts and not reality, which is much more complex and varied (Rendell et al. 2000). Although this binary concept has also been challenged for the Greek world, especially with a view to the mobility and presence of women in the "public" sphere (see, most recently, Schmitt Pantel 2005: 2–3), it is still referred to as a principle that would have constituted a metaphoric-symbolic level of historical reality that would have affected women's lives. This view is based primarily on analysis of literary sources and images and on the notion of social space, which is not congruent with built space but constitutes a cultural-specific form of spatial organization of social interactions (Stähli 2005: 84–5; Löw 2008). Though intriguing as a theoretical concept, it impedes an examination of the real use of physical space. Thus, the discussion of gender and space in the Greco-Roman world is still essentially guided by Atheno and Rome-centric ideological male elite views. Since women (and other marginal groups such as children, slaves, and non-citizens) are largely invisible in literary sources—often being mentioned only in the context of extraordinary events and for obviously disturbing, transgressive behavior—a comprehensive picture of the real use of space, especially of "male public" space, can hardly emerge from an analysis of texts alone.

Central in the debate of gender and space are the terms "private" and "public," whose definitions for the study of the Greco-Roman world are much debated. A differentiated approach to investigating the use of physical space suggests either completely avoiding these terms or at least clearly defining them based on criteria such as ownership, access control, and accessibility. For example, houses were commonly privately owned or rented by individuals or families who inhabited them and could fully control access to them. But houses also served as settings of important rituals and activities such as symposia, banquets, and salutations, which included invited and even uninvited out-siders. Thus, houses had a significant "public" function that is always emphasized for the Roman house, but applied also to Greek houses, with increasing importance in the Hellenistic period. Bath buildings that provided bathing facilities for many persons, and are thus commonly identified as "public," were often privately owned and operated as profitable businesses; these buildings were most likely accessible to the general public, albeit for an entrance fee. Buildings owned by the cities, such as gymnasia, *bouleuteria* (councils), and *curiae* (courts), were by no means all publicly accessible: they were reserved for specific persons such as free male citizens and office holders. Even access to open "public" squares, such as the Agora in Athens, whose boundaries were only symbolically marked, with lustral basins and boundary stones, could be restricted, and persons were regularly officially banished from the Agora (Millett 1998: 224–5). Consequently, the different and changing agendas and perspectives of users of space do not allow for a clear-cut distinction of "private" versus "public" space, so it is advisable to use other terms, such as domestic, civic, and sacred space, which all may include widely varying degrees of access control and accessibility.

Such a terminology implies a differentiation by function that is not without problems. Many ancient buildings and spaces seem to have been multifunctional, and functions may have coexisted or changed according to specific times or occasions. Even for buildings with a relatively clearly defined function, we must differentiate between the intended primary regular function, the temporary extraordinary function, and the regular or temporary secondary function. For example, the gymnasium was mainly used for athletic training and intellectual education by certain restricted user groups; occa-sionally, however, cities celebrated large festivals with banquets in them, inviting a much larger audience. The secondary use of gymnasia may have included all kinds of service activities, which were most likely performed by persons who did not belong to the aforementioned user groups. Thus, use and perception of the same building varied enormously depending on the event and the socio-economic status of users. Whereas the first two functions commonly leave traces in the textual and material evidence, secondary uses—and with them a potentially much wider audience including groups at the margins of society, among them women—remain mostly invisible and can be reconstructed only hypothetically, in a rather anecdotal way.

If a differentiated use of space is intended, the differentiation can be based on different socially distinctive criteria, such as age, social status, ethnicity, and gender, and can employ different strategies (Trümper 2010). Focusing on the distinctive criterion at the center of this essay gives four possible models:

- Model 1: Spaces (understood as umbrella term for open spaces, buildings, and rooms) can be reserved for either men or women only.
- Model 2: The same spaces can be used at different times of the day or days of the month by women and men.
- Model 3: Spaces can include independent areas for men and women that use a common single entrance.
- Model 4: Spaces are provided with separate entrances, giving what would be the most successful segregation of genders.

In models 1 and 2, both the exclusive and the temporary gender-specific use of space commonly leave no conclusive traces in the material evidence and thus can be derived only from textual sources. But both models 3 and 4 may well be detectable in the material record. In addition, a gender-specific use of space can be expressed by, and reflected in, numerous other features such as dress, behavior, gestures, gaits and pace, circulation patterns (preference or avoidance of specific spaces), and communication patterns. Lack of sufficient evidence, however, means that we cannot systematically assess these factors for the Greco-Roman world. The following discussion will refer to the four strategies of gender differentiation, and analyze the contexts in which they were used.

3   Gender and Domestic Space

An investigation of the gendered use of domestic space must deal with the problem of how to reconcile the discourses from different sources. Literary sources from Classical Athens suggest that women had to be isolated and secluded in their homes, in which they even inhabited separate areas (*gynaikonitis*). This notion is now commonly recognized as an ideal concept that was based on the views of male elite authors, and that could be practiced at best (if at all) only by the wealthy elite. Therefore, recent research on Greek houses and households has aimed mainly to explore other, less biased, sources, notably archaeological remains of houses (architecture and finds) from the Archaic through Hellenistic periods for the entire Greek world. Inspired by socio-historical, anthropological, and cross-cultural research, scholarship has primarily examined the dialectic relationship between social relations and the spatial organization of the Greek households, and domestic organization as reflecting wider social and political changes. Most approaches, however, continue to be guided by the social norms conveyed in the Athenian texts, so they still operate on the assumption that the head of the household would strictly control women, in particular their contact with male outsiders, in order to guarantee the legitimacy of his offspring. This strategy for gender segregation is sometimes supported with ethnographic parallels, namely the domestic architecture of various Islamic societies. These comparative examples tend to be mentioned only briefly, with little discussion or exploration of their particular socio-historical context (Nevett 1994: figure 5.2, which shows a single plan of an elite house in Tunis).

The necessity of such strict gender segregation would have had a major impact on the design of Greek houses, which according to this school of thought can be recognized in the development of a specific house type: the fully enclosed, inward-looking, single-entrance, single-courtyard house (most prominently Nevett 1999; see also Morris 1999; Westgate 2007a). The development of this house type from the eighth century BCE onwards is closely linked to the emergence of the democratic polis as a male-oriented community that would have upheld the ideal of the citizen household as an autonomous self-sufficient unit, with a more restrictive life for women. This house type is exemplarily represented in Classical Olynthos, for example in House Avii4 (Figure 21.2), which was provided with one single street-entrance in the south and organized around a central courtyard that gave access to all rooms directly or via the distributive "space f." Thus, individual rooms that were not connected by doors would have been private, but movement between rooms would have been relatively public and could have been fully supervised and controlled from the courtyard or one of the surrounding rooms.

When looking for possible gender-specific space within these houses, scholars particularly explored find-assemblages that—in contrast to architecture—seemingly offer insights into the real use of houses. The analysis of find-assemblages is challenging, however, and its heuristic value is questionable for several reasons. Find-assemblages mainly offer information for a single point of time, notably the last instance of use of a house, and are significantly influenced by complex site-formation processes. Thus, they do not reveal complete pictures. Many objects were multifunctional and cannot be assigned to a specific activity and user, so they cannot serve to determine the presumable single or primary function of an architectural space. Finally, the analysis of a large number of finds is the

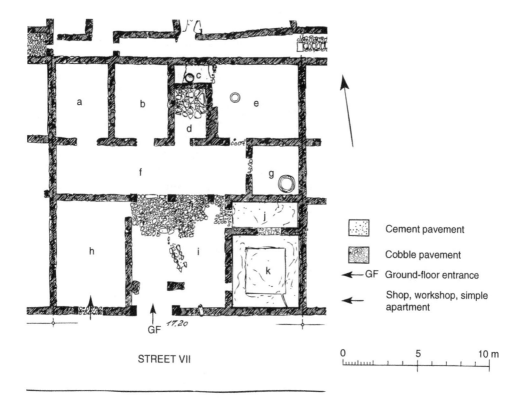

Figure 21.2 Plan of Houses Avii4 at Olynthos. Drawing: M. Trümper after Robinson and Graham (1938: figure 99).

prerequisite for a reconstruction and assessment of general patterns. Analysis requires the use of databases and thus also the labeling and grouping of finds, a process inevitably influenced by individual scholarly judgments (Nevett 2008).

Two different sophisticated studies of find-assemblages from houses in Olynthos, currently the only Greek site with a sizable number of preserved household assemblages, came to the same conclusion (Nevett 1999; Cahill 2002): no spaces in Olynthian houses were obviously strictly reserved for either gender or for gender-specific activities such as cooking and weaving, with the possible exception of *andrones* (rooms for male drinking parties). Andrones yielded almost no finds and thus were mostly identified by architectural features such as a square form, off-center door, raised borders for couches, lavish decoration with mosaics and stucco, and the existence of an anteroom. Although andrones in Olynthos tended to be located adjacent to a street wall, access was often provided from the courtyard—hence, guests of drinking parties had to enter a crucial part of the house.

Thus, important gender relations in Greek households, notably the necessity of male control, should be reflected in the design and architecture of houses. This view, which has recently been challenged for Archaic and above all Classical and Hellenistic houses, can be summarized only briefly here (Foxhall 2009: 498–500; Trümper forthcoming). First of all, if men were mostly absent from the houses during the day, as is commonly assumed, we must ask who would have controlled women in their movements and social interactions.

Further, the archaeological evidence does not support the argument that social control and female seclusion were essential principles of Greek house design. Single street-entrances are the default solution for average-sized houses in many societies, so a higher number of entrances is unusual and requires explanation. For example, a rare multiplication of street-entrances is found in the Late Hellenistic houses of Delos, where they are always clearly ranked as lavish/main versus modest/service entrance. This phenomenon does not betray a lack of control or a more relaxed attitude towards women, as has recently been argued (Nevett 2007b), but is a means of social distinction, which allowed for differentiated access according to social status (guests versus slaves) and activities.

The number of entrances notwithstanding, access to houses could always be controlled by lockable doors. Blocking sightlines from the exterior into the house may have been an important concern in order to minimize contact with the world outside and could be achieved by different means, including screen walls, long vestibules (with a change in direction), and vestibules with two doors. While this latter feature is lacking in many Greek houses, it may also have been used for precisely the opposite effect: in order to dramatize the successive penetration into the house and surprise visitors with sudden views of an impressive interior, as seems to have been particularly the case in Hellenistic houses, with their lavish peristyle courtyards and even axial layouts.

Opening as many rooms as possible onto a central courtyard or space (such as the Roman atrium) was desirable for lighting and airing purposes. This design could not be achieved in many Greek houses, particularly those with rectangular elongated lots (as in Piraeus, Priene, and Agrigento); thus, such houses have interconnected room-suites. In these cases, andrones were even located in the back part of the house, as part of larger room-suites. The courtyard of Greek houses was commonly conceived of and served, weather permitting, as the center of domestic life and activities, but for manifold practical reasons rather than for control purposes. But the courtyard was by no means obligatory, as is obvious from a recent intriguing, comprehensive assessment of Classical and Hellenistic houses in Crete, which is mainly based on access analysis but also explores finds and textual sources. Many Cretan houses had linear circulation patterns, with large hearth-rooms rather than central distributive courtyards. In reference to the single entrance-courtyard houses, these Cretan examples are read as reflecting different social norms and values that are also suggested by textual evidence: households would have been less concerned with privacy, female seclusion, and efficient gender segregation because women would have enjoyed much more freedom and autonomy, and self-sufficiency and authority of male citizens would have been less important than elsewhere in the Greek world (Westgate 2007b).

This brief review of some important gender-related research on the Greek house shows that much current scholarship tends to use the ideal of female seclusion as expressed in Athenian sources as an interpretive frame of reference for understanding houses through-out the rest of the Greek world as well (e.g., Westgate 2007a; 2007b). Indeed, even when the archaeological evidence diverges significantly from the "mainstream" house type, the evidence tends to be interpreted with this Athenian principle in mind. Courtyard houses with many rooms certainly suggest some kind of intended differentiation, but its nature cannot be fully determined from the archaeological evidence alone. Both architecture and domestic assemblages indicate that most rooms were multifunctional, and finds show that architecturally distinct rooms could be used for the same activities in one and the same house as well as across different houses.

Many parameters other than gender may have been crucial in organizing the use of space, such as social status and age of inhabitants; the complex and diverse compositions of households (testified to even in Classical Athens; see Cox 1998: 130–208); climate and weather; and a wide variety of activities, including commercial activities for profit. For example, House Avii4 in Olynthos (Figure 21.2) included a large room with a separate street-entrance and connecting door to the courtyard that was most likely used as a shop or workshop by the inhabitants of the house. Depending on who operated this business—male or female, free or enslaved members of the household—efficient social control may have been either impossible or relatively unimportant. If social differentiation was ever desired, either within households or between its members and outsiders, it could easily have been accomplished even in small, modest houses: in a flexible model of differentiation according to time rather than space. Whenever contact between, for example, outsiders and certain household members should be avoided, the latter could retreat to spaces that were not visible and accessible to visitors. Thus, not an activity itself, but rather its participants, would have determined where the activity took place. All openings could be closed by doors, shutters, or curtains, and space could thus be flexibly negotiated according to individual needs. This model of differentiation according to time is partic-ularly popular in gender-related research, but it cannot be presumed as the primary or only way to organize gender relations in Greek households.

In contrast to their Greek equivalents, Roman houses have barely been investigated for gender relations, most likely because literary sources, written mostly by male elite authors from Rome, do not convey the same concern with female seclusion. While texts generally suggest that women's place was in the domestic sphere, they emphasize at the same time that houses represent the social status and role of the paterfamilias and serve as settings for important events that include outsiders. In the few attempts to engender Roman domestic space, scholars favor literary over archaeological evidence in order to determine to what extent women participated in central male rituals such as salutations and banquets (Wallace-Hadrill 1996; Kunst 2005). By contrast, a recent approach demands a focus on material culture, combining the most suitable offerings from a variety of theoretical frameworks. It is argued, however, that basic assumptions often embraced in feminist theory and gender archaeologies, notably a clear feminine gendering of objects such as perfume bottles and loomweights as well as a simple division of labor (domestic labor being female), cannot be maintained. Thus, the question remains open as to which evidence might be conclusive for reconstructing gender relations in Roman houses and how this question should be explored (Allison 2007).

For both Greek and Roman houses, clearly separated areas for women and men (models 3 and 4) currently cannot be persuasively determined. Thus, gender differentiation, if required at all outside of Athenian elite households, could have been achieved only by negotiating either permanent or temporary exclusive use of space by one of the genders (models 1 and 2).

4   Gender and Civic Space

"Civic" is understood here as an umbrella term for all settlement spaces that were not sacred, funerary, or domestic. It thus includes different categories such as political-administrative, commercial, and entertainment spaces. In reality, the different spaces often physically overlapped, most notably in the central squares of cities, the *agorai* and *fora*. It is particularly challenging to investigate the gendered use of such multifunctional spaces, where several strategies of gender differentiation may have been used simultaneously.

A recent attempt by Millett (1998) to repopulate the Athenian Agora of the fifth and fourth centuries BCE acknowledges the multifunctionality of the city's central square, a place where citizens, non-citizens, and slaves intermingled. Women are not explicitly mentioned in this study, and it is therefore unclear whether they are meant to be subsumed under these three categories. By contrast, a recent groundbreaking study is dedicated specifically to the topic of women in the equally multifunctional Roman Forum from the Late Republican through the mid-Imperial period (Boatwright 2011; see also Köb 2000, although women are considered here as a separate category). Here again, textual sources play a key role. Because the picture emerging from textual sources is necessarily fragmentary and biased, a more comprehensive and nuanced approach to the archaeological evidence may provide additional insights into the organization of gender and civic space. For example, a systematic mapping of the access and circulation patterns might clearly differentiate between fully enclosed buildings and freely accessible open spaces or traffic areas, as shown below.

Gender and Commercial Space

Textual sources confirm that women in the Greco-Roman world participated in commercial-professional activities, such as retail trade and production (Schnurr-Redford 1996: 213–24). While this participation is commonly identified as a dire economic necessity, it certainly applied not only to the lowest echelons of society, namely slaves and non-citizens, but also to (poorer) citizens. Although the number of businesswomen per city cannot be calculated, it is clear that part of a city's female population must have frequented commercial spaces (such as temporary booths, shops, workshops, markets, and warehouses) that were located all over cities, and the traffic areas giving access to them. It has been suggested that at least some commercial spaces such as the *basilicae* in the Roman Forum were reserved "for male business such as diplomacy, high-stake commercial and financial functions, and the administration of justice" (Boatwright 2011: n. 14). Since no law is known that would have forbidden women to enter basilicae, however, access to these buildings must have been regulated by activities or social control—the more so because some basilicae of the Roman world seem to have been fully open to adjacent squares. A gendered hierarchy of commercial activities may well have existed because, for example, women were probably largely excluded from wholesale trade (as opposed to the local petty retail trade). Whether such a hierarchy was also consistently and visibly reflected in the spatial organization of commerce and trade, however, has yet to be explored.

Gender and Political-Administrative Space

A gendered use of space is often postulated for the political-administrative sphere in the Greco-Roman world, where women were excluded from official participation in politics. Fully enclosed structures whose use was primarily or exclusively restricted to men (model 1) offer confirmation of this idea. The *prytaneion*, for example, served meals for male office-holders, honorees, and foreign guests of cities. Documented female presence is confined to entertainment and women past the age of marriage, who took care of the fire on the city's hearth (Miller 1978: 11, 20–1). Whether these women ever came into contact with the male diners or whether these different activities were carefully separated in time or space is unknown: prytaneia are notoriously difficult to identify because they have no fixed building type or standardized plan. Predominant male use can also be reconstructed for *bouleuteria* and *curiae*, which women could enter only in exceptional cases, such as for participation in law courts (Raepsaet-Charlier 2005: 184).

If other, more multifunctional, structures such as theaters were used for political purposes (Moretti 2001: 117–20), however, the spatial exclusion of women was only temporary (model 2). Most difficult to assess is the political use of open, freely accessible spaces: for example, when orators addressed the crowds from *rostrae* or when law courts were held under the open sky in the Roman Forum (Köb 2000: 151–2,155–60). Since ancient authors describe the presence of women during public discussions and assemblies in the Late Republican and early Imperial Forum as "something extraordinary, transgressive, and anomalous" (Boatwright 2011: 119), we must assume that strategies (fences, guards, or social control—screens and curtains are known for partitioning spaces off in basilicae) existed to regulate and control the use of open spaces, if only temporarily (model 2). It is conceivable, however, that female presence during political events could not have been easily prevented and might well have been much more common than elite authors desired and were willing to acknowledge. Alternately, a gendered use of the open space was expressed and reflected in behavior: while men could linger, stand, and listen, women would have primarily been seen moving, passing the square on their way from one destination to another.

Analyzing different phases in the Athenian Agora or the Roman Forum with a view to understanding circulation patterns and accessibility to various structures may yield intriguing changes that could reflect—increased or declining—concerns for a gendered use of space. For example, while in the Classical Agora the political-administrative buildings, concentrated in the southwest corner, were connected by sight, the construction of the Middle Stoa in the second century BCE spatially and visually dissociated the "Heliaia," possibly the meeting-place of civil courts, from this group. Thus, originally male traffic could have prevailed in this area of political-administrative buildings, but the multifunctional nature of the stoa may have attracted women and thus caused an increased mixing of genders in the traditionally male-connoted space.

By contrast, the transformation of the Roman Forum under Augustus may have facilitated gender separation, particularly in the use of open space (Figure 21.3). With the construction of the Temple of Divus Iulius and the adjacent Arch of Augustus, the western part of the Forum gained a new eastern boundary, thereby dissociating both

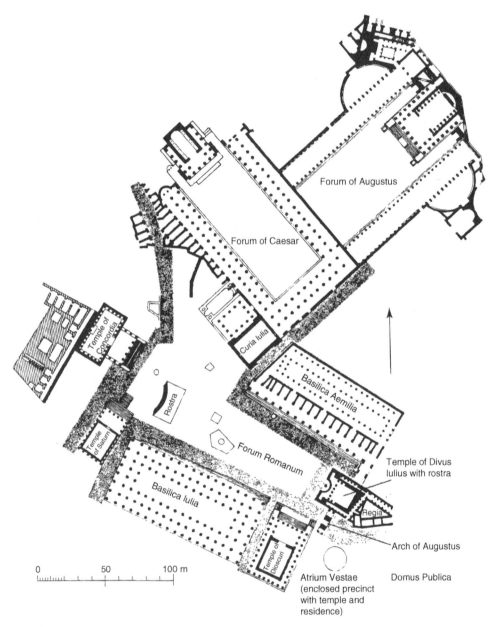

Figure 21.3 Plan of the Roman Forum in the Augustan period. Drawing: M. Trümper after Favro (1996), figure 8.

physically and symbolically the Regia and Atrium Vestae (temple of Vesta, residence of the Vestal Virgins) from the newly defined square. The eastern access to this square—with its two opposing rostrae, two large basilicae, curia, and three state temples, which also served important political-administrative functions (Köb 2000: 40–83)—could probably have been better controlled. The square might have been even more clearly male-connoted, with the exceptions of the single honorary statue of a woman (Cloelia, at the height of the Via Sacra; Boatwright 2011: 120) and the aforementioned seats of important female sacred-ritual activities (Boatwright 2011: 111). It is often stated that women must have frequently appeared in the civic sphere, notably agorai or fora, for religious purposes, although the literary sources tend to overlook such activity (Boatwright 2011: 111). A more detailed study of female movement to sacred areas is required, however, with an attempt to assess which sanctuaries were actually frequented by women for which reasons, and clearly differentiating between regular or extraordinary use (such as festivals and processions). For example, how often did women either individually or in groups visit the temples of the Dioscuri, Saturn, and Concordia in the western part of the Roman Forum?

Finally, even if there was considerable mixing of genders in open spaces and traffic areas of agorai and fora, it must have been clearly noticeable that access to some buildings—permanently or temporarily—was restricted to males. This division would have physically and symbolically reflected and reinforced gendered social roles and privileges.

Gender and Entertainment Buildings

In entertainment buildings, such as gymnasia, baths, and structures for games and spectacles (e.g., theaters, amphitheaters, circuses), all of the models of gender differentiation were employed. A high degree of flexibility in the gendered use of space was necessary for most of these buildings because they were multifunctional, serving also for political and religious purposes (assemblies, festivals, processions).

Textual sources suggest that the use of gymnasia was strictly restricted to men (model 1) (Kobes 2004). While it is unknown how such exclusivity could have been guaranteed in the large park-like extra-urban gymnasia of Archaic and Classical Athens, most of the later examples (fourth to first centuries BCE) had at least fully enclosed palaestra buildings to which access could be easily controlled. This applies equally to gymnasia located at the margins of cities (e.g., Delos "Gymnasium," Priene Lower Gymnasium)—whose remote location may have facilitated gender-segregated urban circulation—as to gymnasia in the very center of cities (e.g., Pergamon, Priene Upper Gymnasium). Although women in Asia Minor of the Roman Imperial period could hold liturgical offices involved with the gymnasium and the organization of athletic games (*gymnasiarchoi, agonothetai*; see van Bremen 1996: 66–76) they were not therefore given access to the gymnasium or required to supervise the (nude) training and education of men or preside over (nude) athletic games.

The presence of women in Greco-Roman entertainment buildings has been much discussed, with arguments primarily based on literary sources and inscriptions. For Classical Athens, the very same sources are cited both to argue against and to argue in favor of the idea that women were present in the theater (Kolb 1989; Henderson 1991; Schnurr-Redford 1996: 225–40; Goldhill 1997; Moretti 2001: 270–5; Moraw 2002). Because Athens' main theater, the theater of Dionysus, was completely remodeled in the second half of the fourth century BCE, archaeology cannot help to solve this problem. From the Hellenistic period onwards, textual sources definitely confirm that women attended theatrical performances and games in both Greek and Roman contexts—albeit with a variety of ways of handling gender segregation. According to seat inscriptions, very few women were granted the extraordinary right to sit among male notables and citizens in the front rows of theaters, usually granted as a reward for particular benefactions to the city (Kolb 1989; van Bremen 1996: 155–6). In other cases, the specific social status of women, notably the Vestal Virgins and members of the imperial family, provided them with the privilege of honorary seats in separate boxes. By contrast, it is commonly assumed that all other women sat somewhere in the back or at the sides of the auditorium (*koilon/cavea*)— in either case marginally placed and most likely entirely segregated from men, in separate sections (*selis/cuneus*, model 3 or possibly even model 4).

But the actual evidence for an entirely segregated seating arrangement is slight. While it is well attested that many different male social groups (citizens organized in *phylai/tribus*, magistrates, priests, senators, knights, associations, boys and their teachers, etc.) had clearly assigned seats in Greco-Roman spectacle buildings (Kolendo 1981; Rawson 1987: 89–91; Kolb 1989), women as a group are referred to in only one or two inscriptions from theaters in Late Republican and Imperial Italy (Rawson 1987: 90, n. 40; Jones 2009: esp. 132–3). A law issued by Augustus (Suet. *Aug.* 44) is much less clear on the seating arrangement for women than is often stated: it says only that, with the exception of the Vestal Virgins, women were not allowed to see gladiators, except from the upper seats (*ex superiore loco*), and that they were strictly excluded from any athletic games. In pre-Augustan Rome, women and men seem to have sat together during some performances, and even in the Roman Imperial period there must have been considerable regional variety and flexibility in seating arrangements at the games.

Most intriguing is the question of gender segregation in the case of public baths (publicly accessible baths that provided facilities for many persons), because bathing in the Greco-Roman world was performed fully naked or only scantily clad. Textual and archaeological sources confirm that both women and men frequented public baths from at least the fourth century BCE onwards, well into late antiquity, and that gender segregation was a considerable concern. All four different models of segregation were employed, albeit with significant chronological and geographical variations. Separate baths built exclusively for one gender (model 1) cannot be identified from the archaeological record, but their existence is suggested by some papyri and inscriptions from the Roman Imperial period (van Bremen 1996: 148, n. 25; Trümper forthcoming: n. 6). That buildings provided different bathing hours for women and men (model 2) is obvious from two inscriptions of the Roman Imperial period from Crete and Portugal (Trümper forthcoming: nn. 9–10). Separate bathing facilities for women and men within the same building that had only one entrance and also other communally usable spaces (model 3; Figure 21.4) can be identified in about a third of all Greek public baths. These buildings most often included two round rooms (*tholoi*) with hip-bathtubs and large niches for storing clothes and bathing utensils. Thus, undressing most likely took place only in the bathing room proper so that men and women did not have to use collective spaces in the nude (Trümper forthcoming: nn. 11–18).

Finally, one single Greek bath from about eighty-five known examples and no more than twenty-nine Roman baths from more than 400 known examples had entirely separate sections for women and men (model 4; Figure 21.4; Trümper forthcoming: n. 7 for numbers). The solution of separate sections was certainly the most efficient way to grant both genders simultaneous access to public baths while keeping them segregated, but it was obviously not very popular. Such a solution is largely confined to baths of the

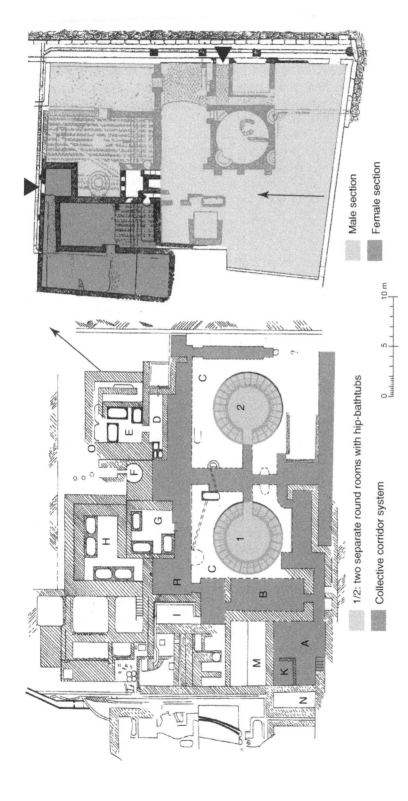

Figure 21.4 Plan of the Greek bath with separate bathing rooms at Krokodilopolis; plan of the Republican bath at Pompeii, with separate bathing sections. Drawing: M. Trümper after El-Khachab (1978) and Maiuri (1950: figure 1).

Late Republican period, when public bathing became common in the Roman world and the typical Roman bath was being developed. While it cannot be determined whether mixed bathing was ever practiced in Greek baths, it is certainly attested in Roman baths in literary sources from the first century CE onwards in baths where single sets of bathing facilities prevailed. To what extent this custom became common, however, is much debated and cannot be securely concluded from any evidence, and a model of "regional, chronological, and even facility-by-facility variation" seems most convincing (Ward 1992; Fagan 1999: 24-9). The analysis of Greek baths has revealed examples with single sets of bathing facilities, but these have two street-entrances and double circulation patterns that may be linked to gender-differentiated use. A detailed exploration of the numerous Roman baths of the Imperial period may yield comparable patterns. The potential significance of the locations of public baths in urban space for their gender-specific use remains to be investigated.

5   Conclusion

Recent studies of modern as well as ancient cities rightly emphasize that space is a social category, constantly produced, changed, and negotiated through human interaction and communication, reflecting, but also shaping, social structure and power relations (Torre 2000: 145; Zimmermann 2009). Thus, the use and perception of physical space and architecture can differ considerably according to users and activities. While textual sources may offer invaluable insights into the use and perception of physical space in societies, Greco-Roman authors often seem to have presented rather ideal or idealized views. Therefore, more attention should be paid to material culture when trying to reconstruct the real use of space, particularly by persons who remain largely invisible in texts. For a comprehensive examination of gender and—especially the much neglected "public"— space, the location and accessibility of buildings and the movements and traffic patterns in urban space, differentiated according to activities and events, should be studied more closely, employing, for example, methods such as access and viewshed analysis. Such studies may result in a much more nuanced picture of how genders would have occupied, appropriated, and negotiated space in Greco-Roman cities. Case studies of single well-preserved cities could be compared in order to assess to what extent the concept of male-connoted "public" space was—particularly beyond Athens and Rome—rather more (literary) fiction than fact.

RECOMMENDED FURTHER READING

There is no comprehensive publication discussing gender and space, notably physical space, in the Greco-Roman world. The state of research is briefly summarized by Schmitt Pantel (2005). For an excellent introduction to the topic in general, extensively discussing approaches and methods, see Rendell et al. (2000). The topic of gender and Greek domestic space has been most intensively and impressively studied by Lisa Nevett in many different works that examine particularly architecture and household assemblages. For the most comprehensive treatment, see Nevett (1999; 2007a). Artifact assemblages and their significance for the reconstruction of gendered space in Greek houses have also been investigated by others, for example Cahill (2002) and Ault (2005). For critical comments particularly on the analysis and interpretation of domestic architecture, see Trümper (2010). The topic of gender and Roman domestic space has most recently been discussed by Allison (2007), who provides a theoretical introduction and a highly critical approach to engendering artifacts and household assemblages.

For the vast topic of gender and "public" space, research mostly focuses on particular spaces or buildings. While "Women and gender in the Forum Romanum" has recently been discussed in an intriguing, comprehensive study by M. T. Boatwright (2011), no equivalent for the Athenian Agora or Greek agorai in general exists. The most popular topic in research seems to be women and spectacle buildings. The presence of women at theatrical performances in Classical Athens has been challenged by Goldhill (1997) but is advocated by many other scholars, for example Henderson (1991) and Schnurr-Redford (1996). The topic seems to have been most comprehensively discussed for the Greek world by F. Kolb, whose German *habilitationsschrift, Theaterpublikum und Gesellschaft in der Griechischen Welt*, from 1975 was never fully published; however, the relevant results are briefly summarized in Kolb (1989).

The seating arrangements in Roman spectacle buildings are much studied, most recently by Jones (2009), who includes a discussion and list of seat inscriptions from the Republican and early Imperial periods and a comprehensive bibliography on the topic, albeit excluding circuses. Central for the inscriptions from the Colosseum are the works by S. Orlandi, particularly that of 2005. For the circus, whose seating arrangements were possibly exceptional, see Polverini (2008). The gendering of Roman public baths was first discussed by Ward (1992), who concludes from an analysis of literary and archaeological sources that mixed bathing was very common in the Imperial period. For a more cautious and nuanced discussion of this question, see Fagan (1999). The possible strategies and archaeological evidence of gender differentiation in Greek public baths have recently been examined by Trümper (forthcoming).

22

Oikos Keeping: Women and Monarchy in the Macedonian Tradition

Elizabeth D. Carney

During the Archaic and most of the Classical periods, city-states (*poleis*) dominated the Hellenic political world while monarchies endured largely on the Hellenic periphery. In most poleis, citizen women played no regular political role; religious activities defined their public role in the life of the city. In the monarchies of northern Greece, however, women in the ruling families participated in the many aspects of public life. The line between public and private, so clearly drawn (at least ideally) in the polis world, was not clear at all in Macedonia: women sometimes did participate in political struggles.

There is a reason for this difference. Everywhere, Greek peoples associated women with the oikos. Oikos can signify both the physical house in which a family lives and the family itself, the household. It can also refer, as does its closest English equivalent, to a dynasty. Initially, at least, these were household monarchies and thus female members of the royal dynasty were part of *basileia* (rule, monarchy, the kingdom), not apart from it. This is not to say that royal women regularly became independent or even partially independent actors on the political stage, but rather that, particularly in certain circumstances, the system made some political actions on their part not only possible, but even likely.

After Philip II established Macedonian hegemony over the Greek peninsula in the second half of the fourth century, monarchy ceased to be a peripheral phenomenon. The conquests of Philip's son, Alexander III or the Great, and the fact that Alexander's early death led to the collapse of his empire and the gradual formation of several monarchies within its former borders, meant that the Hellenistic era (323–31 BCE) was dominated by monarchies in the Macedonian tradition. Each Hellenistic dynasty combined Macedonian with previous regional monarchic tradition and each generation of a dynasty modified this tradition to suit current needs and ambitions. In these Hellenistic monarchies, as in earlier Macedonian monarchy, royal women continued to play a prominent public role, but the extent of their power varied dramatically by dynasty, generation, and individual.

After a discussion of the nature of the available sources and the methodology used in the analysis of the role of royal women in monarchy, this essay will consider royal women associated with Macedonian monarchy in the Archaic period and then focus

A Companion to Women in the Ancient World, First Edition. Edited by Sharon L. James and Sheila Dillon.
© 2012 John Wiley & Sons, Ltd. Published 2015 by John Wiley & Sons, Ltd.

on the late Classical (c. 359–323 BCE) and early Hellenistic (the period of the Successors: 323–271 BCE) periods. It will employ case studies of three women (Eurydice, mother of Philip II; Olympias, mother of Alexander the Great; and Phila, wife of Demetrius Poliorcetes and mother of Antigonus Gonatas), to illuminate the changing role of women in Macedonian monarchy, and will conclude with a glance at the situation of royal women in each of the major Hellenistic dynasties.

Before we turn to these tasks, some general information about Macedonian royal women is necessary. They were not "queens": there was no title until after the end of the Argead (c.700–310 BCE) dynasty, and when a title developed its meaning was apparently broader than the English "queen," encompassing royal daughters and probably royal widows and not being exclusive to a single dynasty (Carney 2000: 225–8). Philip II and his famous son were certainly polygamous, as likely were some earlier kings. There was no titular, institutionalized chief wife, though one woman tended to establish situational dominance; this woman may often have been the king's mother, not any of his wives. Many royal wives were of foreign birth and were apparently allowed to bring their children up with some customs idiosyncratic to their backgrounds. Royal women seem to have had control of some wealth (Carney 2000: 23–31). Royal women were not typical; little, in any case, is known of the lives of ordinary Macedonian women, even of the elite, before the Hellenistic period and even after (Le Bohec-Bouhet 2006: 187–98).

1   Sources and Methodology

Problems with the nature of surviving sources, some distinctive to the analysis of royal women and some common to Macedonian history generally, shape the methodology. Narrative histories prior to Philip II mention Macedonian events only in passing, often by chance, and usually with a non-Macedonian focus, most often Athenian. Even after Philip took the throne in 359 BCE, though the narratives pay more attention to Macedonia, coverage of Macedonian actions is often hostile because of Greek resentment of increasing Macedonian power. After the death of Alexander the Great, Greek narratives once more regard Macedonia as a backwater worthy of only brief mention, making our knowledge of internal events poor for most of the Hellenistic period. Greek historical narrative concentrated on public actions: largely military and political events. The surviving narratives therefore do not really clarify what, if any, method was regular for the determination of succession to the Macedonian throne, doubtless because succession was largely determined through behind-the-scenes maneuvering. Royal women were literally, as we shall see, "powers behind the throne" and thus their actions in terms of succession either went unacknowledged by the sources or were treated in an antagonistic fashion because they were not overt and because the writers (and/or their sources) understood such female action as interference. This stress on public events means that narratives tell us only about royal women who had some kind of independent career, often as widows. In short, the narratives give us detail about the less rather than more typical royal woman.

Speeches given in Athenian courts or the assembly provide contemporary evidence about royal women, but they are frequently explicitly antagonistic to the Macedonians and implicitly antagonistic to royal women. Nonetheless, the speeches give us useful information about royal women not so much because of the intent of the speaker as because of what relevant passages in a speech assume about royal women. For instance, Athenian speechwriters refer to royal women by personal name, often without patronymics (Aeschin. 2.26, 28; Hyp. 4. 20), though Athenians generally avoided referring to respectable women by name (Schaps 1977: 323–30). This distinction in practice suggests that the speakers understood these women as public figures and they assumed that their listeners/readers already knew who, for instance, Olympias was. Though orators and historical writers may mention Olympias without a direct reference to either her husband or son, sometimes they associate her with them, particularly with her son (Hyp. 4. 19); at times the speeches seem to assume that royal women and men were part of the same political entity.

Contemporary documentary material in the form of inscriptions is important and illuminating, but comparatively few inscriptions from Macedonia of any sort survive before the Hellenistic period and only a handful refer to royal women. This means that the information provided could be atypical. For example, four inscriptions involve Philip II's mother, Eurydice (see below). This fact could signify significant growth in the power of royal women or it could be a matter of chance survival. Despite the limitations of inscriptional evidence—inscriptions tend to tell us what an individual did (e.g., dedicate an item at a sanctuary), not why they did it—they can provide an important corrective to the prejudices of narrative sources. An extraordinarily venomous literary tradition pictures Eurydice as a murderous wife and mother (Mortensen 1992: 155–69), yet those four inscriptions make it obvious that her sons honored her and did not consider her murderous; a speech of Aeschines (2.26–9) confirms this. Similarly, the literary tradition about Olympias, dominated by Plutarch's life of Alexander, insists that she had no influence on her son's policy (*Alex.* 39.7) and implies that she had no public position during his reign, whereas inscriptional evidence—records from Cyrene of grain distributions—demonstrates that she (and her daughter Cleopatra) certainly did play a public role (*SEG* IX.2; Laronde 1987: 30–4; Rhodes and Osborne 2003, 2007: 486–93) and implies, if the distributions were politically motivated, that they did indeed have a role in his policy as well. We cannot know whether Olympias and Cleopatra obtained grain on their own initiative and with their own funds or for Alexander and with his funds (Carney 2006: 51).

Currently, archaeological material provides comparatively little help in understanding individual royal women and only somewhat more in understanding the general situation of royal women. No burials can be securely tied to an individual royal woman, though attributions have been made, and none are certainly royal. Macedonian kings of the Argead dynasty (and possibly the Antigonid) were buried at Aegae, the modern Vergina, but so were hundreds of non-royal Macedonians. The only burials generally agreed to be royal—and even here there is no absolute proof—are the three tombs once covered by the Great Tumulus at Vergina, two of which contained the remains of women as well as men. The identity of those buried in these two tombs (I and II) is much disputed (Borza and Palagia 2007: 81–125). A number of other rich burials at Vergina may well be those of royal women (see below) but, as with male burials assumed to be royal, the similarity to Macedonian elite burials (for instance, the various related Derveni tombs (Themelis and Touratsoglou 1997) or those found at Agios Athanasios (Tsimbidou-Avloniti 2004: 149–51)) should make us cautious about assuming that we can always distinguish elite from royal burials. Some burials at Pella from the Antigonid period could also be royal females, but again there is no proof. Nonetheless, the evidence of many female burials, royal or elite, from various Macedonian sites certainly does give us some sense of the material culture available to such women and something about the idealized image those who buried them wanted to create.

Much of the literary evidence about individual royal women appears in the form of anecdote. Many of these anecdotes have an agenda intended to be normative and are obviously stereotypical. For instance, Olympias' elimination of a husband and wife who were rivals for royal power with her grandson leads Diodorus to say that people remembered that Antipater, Alexander's right-hand man, long Olympias' enemy and that of her family, had, on his deathbed, warned against Macedonia ever being ruled by a woman (Diod. 19.11.9). Anecdotal material should always be treated with great caution. Often the anecdote's main thrust is the narrative arc and plot wins out over veracity (Carney 2000: 11). Anecdotes may assume things unlikely to be true or recount incidents unlikely to have had a witness. Conversely, particularly if one looks for material in the anecdote that is not its main point—the moral of the tale—but rather an assumption, an aside of the story, the anecdote may include usable material. Thus, we may doubt Plutarch's assertion (*Alex.* 2.1) that Philip II fell in love with Olympias when both were becoming initiates of the cult at Samothrace—this was clearly a political alliance between two northern dynasties in order to help the rulers cope with the Illyrian menace—but it does seem likely that they were both initiates at Samothrace and met for the first time there. Similarly, the clever remarks the otherwise hostile Plutarch attributes to Olympias may all be spurious (*Mor.* 141b-c; *Alex.* 3.2), but they do signify that he was familiar with a tradition that depicted her as witty and intelligent.

The best way to understand the role of royal women generally, as well as the careers of specific women, entails combining two broad assumptions. First, in terms of extant evidence, documentary and literary sources contemporary with these women's lives deserve the most attention, followed by the parts of surviving narratives that refer to public acts (e.g., the report that a woman appeared in front of an army), and archaeological material (absent evidence demonstrably royal) should still be considered merely suggestive. Least credible is anecdotal material, wherever found. All of this evidence should be read against the grain of the assumptions of the source. Second, this topic should be approached with the presumption that women were not "interfering" in monarchy (a city-state value inappropriately applied to monarchy) but rather were part of it because they were part of the royal oikos.

2   Royal Women in Archaic and Early Classical Macedonia

Few literary references to royal women from this period survive; those that do, whatever their literal historicity, suggest the unsurprising notions that royal women of this period were used in marriage alliances (Herod. 5.21) and that royal women of the period, like Homeric royal women, carried out a number of domestic tasks (Aristid. 45.55; Herod. 8.137.2). This would appear to conform to the general pattern of action for elite women elsewhere in the period.

More information comes from a cluster of nine female burials discovered at Vergina since 1985 (Andronikos 1994: 35–39; Carney 2000: 24–44, 2006: 95; Kottaridi 2002: 75–81), burials likely to be royal because of their richness (gold- or silver-soled sandals, for instance) and location (near the Eucleia sanctuary, with its dedications by Eurydice, and separated by a stream from the rest of the cemetery). Of this group, six date to the sixth and early fifth century. Although all but one has been heavily plundered, the remaining grave goods imply that these women served some ritual function, heavily involving sacrifice (many libation vessels), banqueting, and other more obscure but likely religious functions (one burial included twenty-five terracotta heads, possibly of chthonian deities, and another contained two mysterious golden cones). The only un-robbed grave, the "Lady of Aegae" (c. 500 BCE), presumably suggests the original contents of the rest (Kottaridi 2004: 139–48). A woman of about thirty was laid out in a chiton, peplos, and apron-like garment (some of these dyed purple), all heavily decorated in gold. A collection of golden jewelry completed her outfit, including two huge pins that fastened her clothing together at the shoulders. Among her other grave goods were a bronze hydria, thirteen bowls (twelve bronze and one gilded silver), a tripod, a model cart to which now-decayed wooden draft animals were probably attached, some iron spits decorated with gold, a silver wand, six terracotta busts of a goddess, and a scepter decorated with amber and ivory. Exactly who these women were is unknown; elsewhere in the Greek world female priesthoods were largely held by members of the elite and were sometimes tied to specific families (Connelly 2007: 44–5). It is certainly likely that women of the royal family performed ritual functions, probably as priestesses for a royal cult. A passage supposedly from a letter of Olympias to her son (Ath. 559f–660a) seems to confirm this, if for a later period: Olympias offers to sell to her son a cook experienced in sacrifice, especially Argead and Bacchic. This indicates that there was a royal cult and that Olympias had something to do with it, as these earlier royal women may have (Andronikos 1994: 35–9; Kottaridi 2004; Carney 2000: 24–44, 2006: 95).

3   Eurydice, Wife of Amyntas III and Mother of Philip II

It is with the figure of Eurydice (Mortensen 1992; Carney 2000: 40–6) that we can first learn about the life of an individual royal woman and about the forces that weakened and empowered royal women. After 399 BCE, Macedonia entered a period of instability in which rival Argeads replaced each other on the throne with rapidity, the Illyrians invaded, other foreign powers intervened in Macedonia, and material culture, as evidenced by even elite burials, deteriorated. Amyntas III took the throne in c. 393 BCE but was driven from it at least once, and had to pay off some of his enemies and seek external help against pretenders. Nonetheless, he managed to die of natural causes and all three of his sons by Eurydice, daughter of Sirras, would rule after him, though even the eldest was barely an adult at the time of Amyntas' death.

   Though a tradition that makes Eurydice murderous and adulterous survives (Just. 7.4.7, 5.4–8), it is now clear that this tradition is invalid, likely a consequence of propaganda by Gygaea's faction (Diod. 15.71.1; Ath. 14.629d; Mortensen 1992; Ogden 1999: 11–16), and that the historical Eurydice played a part in securing and maintaining her sons on the throne by her participation in internal and international *philia* networks (Aeschin. 2.29). After her husband's death, her son Alexander II ruled only a short time before he was assassinated by a man named Ptolemy (probably another Argead), who then served as regent for Eurydice's second son, Perdiccas III. Ptolemy may have married Eurydice in this period. The sole evidence for the marriage is the scholiast for Aeschines 2.29. Occasionally regents and/or pretenders married the mothers of minor or very young kings; in this case, it is unclear whether or not Eurydice did marry again. Moreover, the identity of Ptolemy is disputed and Eurydice, in any event, may not have had a choice in the matter or could have believed that the marriage would help her sons (Carney 2006: 43). In any event, it was she, not he, who, when the kingdom was threatened by another pretender, called upon the Athenian admiral Iphicrates to drive this claimant out of Macedonia. Eurydice asked Iphicrates to honor his philia obligations (as an individual and as an Athenian admiral) to her dead husband and sons, and he did so (Aeschin. 2.26–9; Aeschines' story cannot be true in all respects (Ogden 1999: 15) but the broad picture it paints is likely to have been correct and certainly demonstrates the view Philip II apparently preferred). Perdiccas finally managed to kill Ptolemy and rule on his own; when he, in turn, died in battle against the Illyrians, Eurydice's youngest son, Philip II, took the throne, defeated the Illyrians, and eliminated his father's sons by Gygaea (Carney 2000: 46–7).

Four inscriptions connected to Eurydice survive, all dating to the reigns of her sons, likely to the reign of Philip II: one, though its text is corrupt, has long been known because it is part of an essay attributed to Plutarch (Plut. *Mor.* 14c) but the other three have been found since 1985, at Vergina/Aegae and its environs (Saatsoglou-Paliadeli 2000: 387–403). The inscription preserved in the essay refers to Eurydice's late education, when her son was grown, and relates to a dedication she made to or for the sake of citizen women to the Muses (Le Bohec-Bouhet 2006: 190–2). Two of the Vergina inscriptions appear on statue bases found in the sanctuary of Eucleia; Eurydice made these dedications and may have paid for the whole sanctuary, of whose cult she may well have been a priestess. The fourth inscription appears to have been part of a group statue base, most likely for an image of Eurydice, quite possibly part of a dynastic group (Saatsoglou-Paliadeli 2000: 397–400). In addition, we know that Philip II had a circular building (the Philippeum) built at Olympia in commemoration of his great victory at Chaeroneia and that the building contained statues of himself, Alexander, his father, Olympias, and probably his mother, Eurydice (5.17.4, 20.9–10; Eurydice is the usual identification; see Palagia 2010 for the possibility—not one convincing to this author—that the image was actually that of Philip's last wife, who may have been known as Eurydice). An early chamber tomb, with a beautiful throne and stool, has been attributed to Eurydice (Andronikos 1994: 154–61), though this attribution is far from certain.

Eurydice's career seems to mark a change to greater prominence for royal women, probably because of their role as succession advocates but also because of the growing prominence of the Macedonian monarchy. All of Eurydice's sons reached the throne whereas none of Gygaea's did; we have one certain instance in which Eurydice acted publicly for her sons, but there were probably many more. The Vergina inscriptions imply that she and her patronage played a role in establishing and then stabilizing the rule of her sons and also suggest that she, like later royal women, functioned as a kind of patron of the women of the region, particularly as a priestess of Eucleia and of a dynastic cult. Even the hostile tradition about her confirms that she was a public person with a public image, and the inscriptions, the Philippeum, and Aeschines' speech indicate that her son(s), partly to compensate for the slanders of enemies and partly to enhance her image in order to enhance their own, highlighted her role (Carney 2007).

4 Olympias

Olympias, fifth wife of Philip II, mother of Alexander the Great (III), and grandmother of Alexander IV, played a prominent political role, the first woman in the Hellenic world to do so, during three reigns (Carney 2006). Philip treated her son as his apparent heir by the time Alexander had reached his early teens (c. 344 BCE) and the king continued to do so through the battle of Chaeroneia (summer 338 BCE) and its diplomatic aftermath (his only other son—later known as Philip Arrhidaeus—had mental limitations). Olympias, as the heir's mother, had presumably been the dominant woman at court for some years.

This all changed abruptly in about 337 BCE when Philip married for a seventh time, to a young Macedonian noblewoman named Cleopatra. Philip had taken at least one bride since his marriage to Olympias and Alexander was more or less an adult, so the wedding ostensibly should not have changed the succession. However, the bride's guardian, Attalus, proposed a toast that suggested that Alexander was somehow not legitimate and children born of Philip and Cleopatra would be (Plut. *Alex.* 9.4–5; Ath. 13.557d; Just. 9.7.5–7). Alexander and Olympias left Macedonia (she returned to Molossia where her brother was now king); a public reconciliation soon followed (Plut. *Alex.* 9.6, *Mor.* 70b, 179c; Just. 9.7.6), but Olympias and Alexander apparently remained concerned about his succession. When the satrap of Caria offered his daughter in marriage to Philip Arrhidaeus, Alexander, Olympias, and Alexander's friends took his offer as an indication that Philip now intended the throne for Alexander's half-brother, tried to replace him with Alexander as groom, and, instead, precipitated the collapse of the marriage alliance, the exile of some of Alexander's friends, and the renewed wrath of Philip (Plut. *Alex.* 10.1–3). Not surprisingly, when a royal bodyguard assassinated Philip in the midst of the luxurious wedding festivities for his daughter (Plut. *Alex.* 10.4; Diod. 16.93–4; Just. 9.6.4–7.14; Aristotle, *Pol.* 1311b; *P. Oxy.* 1798), people suspected that Olympias and Alexander may have been behind the assassination (Plut. *Alex.* 10.4; Just. 9.8.1–14). Regicide, typically by members of the royal house, was commonplace in Macedonia. Mother and son made plausible suspects, but considerable risk (loss of any chance at the throne) would have been attached to involvement in a conspiracy, so their involvement should not be assumed. Olympias and Alexander did function as a succession unit; she worked for her son's success by diplomatic means, as an advisor and as a proponent of the distinction of her birth and clan and thus those of her son.

Once Alexander was king, Olympias played a more public role than previously. She never worked against her son's interest and sometimes worked in concert with him, but may at times have acted independently, particularly because of his long (334–323 BCE) absence in the East. Olympias almost certainly eliminated Cleopatra and her infant, while Alexander was responsible for the death of Attalus (Just. 9.7.12, 12.6.14; Plut. *Alex.* 10.4; Paus. 7.7.5; Diod. 17.2.3–6, 5.1–2). Olympias and Alexander (and Olympias' daughter, another Cleopatra, now apparently regent of Molossia) probably acted together in terms of patronage in response to a grain shortage to create publicity for the wealth generated by Alexander's conquests (Alexander sent both women plunder (Plut. *Alex.* 25.4) and Olympias made a splendid dedication at Olympia apparently funded by his gift (*SIG* I 252N.5ff.)). They maintained an apparently confidential correspondence (Carney 2006: 53–54). Olympias engaged in political action intended to assert Macedonian presence in Athens (Hyp. *Eux.* 20, 25; Diod. 17.108.7) and, as we have seen, in Macedonia. During this period, Olympias and Antipater, the man generally understood to have acted as regent for Alexander in his absence, became enemies, most likely because Alexander had failed to divide the duties and authorities of each in a clear way. Initially, Olympias seemed to have been the loser in this struggle and she left Macedonia for her homeland, where she and her daughter may have been co-regents for a time. By the end of Alexander's reign, Antipater's power had waned and Olympias (judging by the grain inscriptions that treat her as a head of state and by the clear association of Olympias and Alexander in Athenian speeches) was gaining in strength (Diod. 18.49.4; Plut. *Alex.* 68.3).

Alexander's unexpected death in June 323 BCE changed everything. At first, Olympias stayed at home in Molossia, and kept out of the struggles that broke out almost immediately among the generals (Successors) of Alexander. Nominally, Alexander's half-brother and his posthumous son, Alexander IV, were kings, but in practice the Successors fought for dominance or at least a viable chunk of his former empire. A brisk marriage market, based on the need for new political alliances, developed; again Olympias' interests were pitted against those of Antipater and, again, at first, the latter seemed to win. His daughter married the first regent, Perdiccas, and Olympias' daughter, Cleopatra, was rejected and ultimately lived out her life as the prisoner of one of the Successors (Carney 2000: 123–8). By 319 BCE, however, the situation had altered: the kings were back in Europe, Antipater had finally died, and the current regent, Polyperchon, invited Olympias to return to Macedonia and to take responsibility for her grandson and to assume some public role in the kingdom (Diod. 18.48.4, 57.2). Whatever Polyperchon intended, this seems to have been an unprecedented position. Meanwhile, another royal woman, Adea Eurydice, the wife of Philip Arrhidaeus and herself an Argead (her mother was a granddaughter of Philip II and her father was Philip's nephew), seemed to take charge of the other co-king. There were two kings, neither of whom was competent, and two women who, in effect, acted in their stead. In the past Argeads had fought each other for the throne and this happened again, except that in this case the leadership of both factions was female. Olympias, Polyperchon, Olympias' nephew (Aeacides now king of Molossia), and Alexander IV (and his mother Roxane) accompanied an army into Macedonia. On the western borders, it encountered another army, led by Philip Arrhidaeus and Adea Eurydice. This was the high point of Olympias' career: when the home army saw Olympias, mother of the great Alexander and wife of Philip, they went over to her without a fight and Philip Arrhidaeus and Adea Eurydice were soon captured and executed (Duris *ap.* Ath. 560f; Diod. 19.11.1–9; Just. 14.5.1–4, 9–10).

Olympias' complete failure, however, soon followed. The royal pair she had killed had been allied with Antipater's oldest son, Cassander. He returned to Macedonia with an army that soon eliminated Olympias' military support, besieged in Pydna, and forced her to surrender. Cassander, with some difficulty, arranged the death of Olympias and refused to allow her burial (she was, nonetheless, buried, apparently by surviving kin). He took control of Macedonia at this point (spring 316 BCE), married a half-sister of Alexander, imprisoned Alexander IV and his mother (a few years later he had them killed), and generally began to act like a king, though he did not take the title for many more years (Diod. 19.35.2–3, 36.5–6, 49.1–52.5; Just. 14.6.1–13; Paus. 9.7.2).

Olympias' apparent attempt to safeguard the throne for her grandson by the elimination of rivals ended in failure primarily because Cassander was a good general and Polyperchon was not. Though our sources complain about Olympias' treatment of the royal pair and reprisals against Cassander's faction in her brief moment of success (Diod. 19.11.4–9; Just. 14.6.1), they also admire her brave and, all agree, unwomanly but heroic death, a death they consider worthy of her male kin (Just. 14.6.9–12; Diod. 19.51.2–6). Olympias' career demonstrates how important royal women could be as succession advocates, particularly in periods when adult royal males were scarce, and how compelling they could be as symbols of dynastic power and continuity, but also how central the ability to command armies successfully was to the maintenance of control. All of Alexander's female kin were murdered because they lacked a military base and because their enemies wanted to prevent anyone from using them as symbols of royal power. Any hope of survival of the Argead dynasty died with Olympias.

5   Phila, Daughter of Antipater, Wife of Demetrius Poliorcetes

In the era between the death of Alexander and the establishment of the last of the three great Hellenistic dynasties, the Successors and their heirs gradually established a new kind of monarchy, one based in Macedonian tradition, affected by the monarchic traditions of conquered territories but also shaped by the need, absent any hereditary claim to rule, to establish other paths to dynastic legitimacy. In this transitional period, women played an important role, active and passive, in the process (Carney 2000: 203–33). Phila (Wehrli 1964; Carney 2000: 165–9), daughter of Antipater and, after two earlier marriages, wife of Demetrius Poliorcetes and mother of Antigonus Gonatas, models the rapidly evolving role of women in the emerging dynasties, particularly because her husband Demetrius and her father-in-law Antigonus played such a central role in the formation of Hellenistic kingship. They were the first to employ a royal title and the first to have cults established in their names.

Phila's first marriage ended before Alexander's death (Diod. 18.22.1) and her father, Antipater, next gave her to Craterus (Memnon *FGrH* 434 F 1.4.4; Diod. 18.8.7; Plut. *Demetr.* 14.2), a close associate of Alexander and a general popular with the Macedonian army. Craterus too soon died in battle and in around 320 BCE Antipater arranged yet another marriage, this time to Demetrius, who was supposedly reluctant to marry an older woman, a widow with a son by each of her former husbands, but was persuaded to do so by his father's arguments about political gain (Plut. *Demetr.* 14.2–4, 27.8). Phila had a son, Antigonus Gonatas, and a daughter, Stratonice, by Demetrius (Plut. *Demetr.* 37.4, 31.5). Her husband, apart from his notorious liaisons with various courtesans, married three more times while still married to Phila, and planned a fourth marriage, though it did not transpire until after Phila's death. The Successors, in imitation of the Argeads, practiced polygamy but, like the Argeads, only the males were polygamous.

Soon after (possibly at the same time) Demetrius and Antigonus began to be called *basileus* (king) (Plut. *Demetr.* 18.1–2; Diod. 20.53.2–4), inscriptions term Phila *basilissa* (*SIG* 333.6–7; Robert 1946: 17 nn. 1–2), a female title without Argead precedent whose meaning is not entirely clear; it was used to refer to women married to kings and may have been applied to unmarried daughters of kings and widows as well (Carney 2000: 225–7). Phila was not only the first royal woman attested with a title, but the first with a cult. As with royal men, cult preceded rather than followed the royal title; by 307 BCE Phila had a civic cult in Athens as Phila Aphrodite (Ath. 254a–e) and a private cult as well (Ath. 255c). Equation or assimilation with Aphrodite would be the dominant model for royal women in cult for the rest of the Hellenistic period (Carney 2000: 209–25; Mirón Pérez 1998: 229–33 offers a somewhat different view of the development of female cult). Phila's life was a public one, like that of other royal women of her generation. She had her own bodyguards and probably her own court since her husband was often not with her.

Our sources picture Phila as a dutiful and sensible daughter, wife, and sister as well as a wise patron. Even as a young girl, her father supposedly valued her advice (Diod. 19.59.5) and, of course, she married each groom her father selected. She sent clothes and household goods to Demetrius while he was busy with the siege of Rhodes (Diod. 20.93.4; Plut. *Demetr.* 22.1). Her husband dispatched her to Cassander, her brother, to negotiate an end to their previous hostilities (Plut. *Demetr.* 32.3). She is usually assumed to be long-suffering, grieved by Demetrius' many marriages and amours, but we do not know how she felt about her husband; one could as easily conclude that his other women functioned as something of a relief in dealing with a husband whose colorful personality and predilection for risk were very different from Phila's own cautious and quiet character, one much like that of her father. While no source describes her as witty, Diodorus (19.59.4) does picture her as intelligent and fair, a generous patron of women under her husband's rule, and a just arbiter of cases involving her husband's men.

Like Argead women, Phila also functioned as a symbol of dynastic continuity. After her brother's death and that of their oldest son, Cassander's surviving sons engaged in an internecine struggle that led to the murder of one by Lysimachus and the other by Demetrius. Demetrius then claimed rule of Macedonia, not so much because of his military might or his traditionally murderous ways but more because he was married to the daughter of Antipater and had a nearly grown son by her (Plut. *Demetr.* 37.3). Demetrius, thanks to his self-destructive behavior, did not rule Macedonia long and lost out in around 288 BCE to the more popular Pyrrhus. Demetrius, unfazed by his latest fall from grace, simply married again and lived on in exile. Phila, on the other hand, was humiliated by the latest of her husband's disasters and killed herself (Plut. *Demetr.* 45.1). She did not live to see the day when her son (c. 277 BCE) re-established Antigonid rule in Macedonia, a rule that would endure as long as the kingdom itself. Generally in Greek culture, royal women who committed suicide in circumstances involving honor were considered heroic, or at least tragic, whereas self-inflicted deaths by men received less sympathy. Phila's death, apparently because she could not bear her husband's most recent loss of repute and status, appears to conform to this pattern, just as her husband's endurance follows a kind of male norm (Carney 1993: 50–4).

While we should take the encomium of Phila preserved in Diodorus (19.59.3–6) but doubtless derived from Hieronymus, an adherent of Demetrius and Antigonus Gonatas, with a grain of salt, Phila, like her father but not her brother Cassander, seems to have been less ruthless than many other prominent figures of the period; no act of violence is attributed to her other than her own death. In terms of cult, title, and her role as patron and intercessor, she was a model for the role of women in the Hellenistic dynasties.

6   Women in the Hellenistic Dynasties

By 277 BCE, three great dynasties had emerged, the Ptolemies, based in Egypt; the Seleucids, based in the old heart of the Persian empire; and the Antigonids, in Macedonia. Over time, other monarchies broke away, mostly from Seleucid lands in Asia Minor. These monarchies shared commonalities thanks to their origin in Macedonian monarchy and Alexander's conquest, their exchange of royal women through marriage alliances, their patronage of the same Panhellenic shrines, and their military, diplomatic, and cultural competition. Each dynasty also developed its own signature, though this altered somewhat with every new ruler. For each generalization about Hellenistic monarchy an exception exists. It is even more difficult to speak about "Hellenistic queens." I am less inclined than some others to stress common ground. Once one has said that royal women's public role in the Hellenistic period was more institutionalized than in the previous period—most notably in terms of the female title and statues—saying anything further becomes difficult.

In terms of royal women and monarchy in the Hellenistic period, it might be helpful to think about a line with various points along the way. At one end would be Antigonid monarchy (Carney 2000: 179–202), with its absence (at least in Macedonia itself) of royal cult and the apparent invisibility of its royal women in politics (confirmed by the fact that no one bothered to murder any Antigonid wife). Macedonia was increasingly generically Greek and less distinctive in its culture; there were some Seleucid brides, but also wives from elsewhere in the Greek peninsula. Royal women continued to act as patrons and probably as priestesses, but, partly because of the decline of polygamy, apparently they did not function as succession advocates. Two inscriptions do suggest that the role of the king's wife was to some degree institutionalized as it had not previously been, but not necessarily that this formalization of their role entailed more actual power (Le Bohec 1993: 237–8, 244–5).

In Seleucid realms (Nourse 2002: 223–74; Bielman Sánchez 2003: 41–61) there were cults for kings and for royal women, formal ceremonies connected to marriage to the king and assumption of the diadem, and some important examples of women acting as advocates for their sons and even as regents. Whereas the Antigonids generally followed exogamous marriage patterns, the Seleucids increasingly tended towards endogamy, clearly under Ptolemaic influence.

At the other end of my imaginary line is Ptolemaic monarchy and the role of Ptolemaic royal women. Even early on, Ptolemaic royal women functioned as major patrons and benefactors and engaged in succession disputes. It is certain that even unmarried daughters, not just royal wives, used a royal title; it is not certain that this was true of the other dynasties. From the reign of Ptolemy II onwards, this dynasty increasingly practiced an extreme form of endogamy; the ideal was brother–sister marriage (Ager 2004). By the second century the first Ptolemaic women began to co-rule with their male kin. Of course, the last and most famous of them, Cleopatra VII, came very close to ruling on her own. Ptolemaic women had not only influence but direct public power.

Monarchy involves the rule of a family and thus women as well as men. This need not lead to the acquisition of the power to act independently by any woman, but it virtually always means that this possibility existed in some circumstances. Women were the dynastic reserve troops and could and would come to the fore if adult males were scarce or absent, if factions within a dynasty struggled against each other for the throne, or if continuity needed to be constructed between an old and a new ruling family. As the heroic kingship of Macedonia evolved gradually in the direction of divine monarchy, so too royal women moved from claiming heroic descent to being understood as in some way divine or embodying the divine, like their fathers, husbands, and sons. These assertions strengthened the reputation and claim to rule of their families.

RECOMMENDED FURTHER READING

There is as yet no general study of women in Ptolemaic monarchy. See Pomeroy (1984: 3–40) and Macurdy (1932: 102–223). Ager (2004) is particularly important because of the connections between endogamous marriage and the development of co-rule. On Argead royal women, see Mirón Pérez (2000). For a different view of the career of Olympias see O'Neil (1999); on Hellenistic royal women see Savalli-Lestrade (1994,

2003), who sees more common ground in the role of women cross-dynastically than do I. See also Bringmann (1997). Studies on Hellenistic courts illuminate the role of royal women: see Herman (1997), Schmitt (1989), and Weber (1997). Hazzard (2000) presents a different view of the role of one royal woman in the formation of Ptolemaic monarchy. Many studies consider the use of royal women in the formation of a dynastic image: see Meyer (1992–3), Kosmetatou (2004), and Müller (2009).

23

The Women of Ptolemaic Egypt: The View from Papyrology

Maryline Parca

Greek and Roman literature preserves tenuous glimpses of direct female experience; the images of women that emerge from literary texts belong to discourses variously removed from the original and actual substance of women's lives. Real women, especially non-elite women, are to be found between the lines and in the gaps of the generic, coded records of poetry, historiography, and oratory; they are revealed with greater immediacy and reliability in the objects they touched, the inscriptions they commissioned, and the contracts they signed. Retrieved from the houses, cellars, dumps, and cemeteries of Egyptian towns and villages, papyri provide more direct access to women in the Hellenistic period, from the death of Alexander the Great in 323 BCE to the end of Cleopatra's reign in 30 BCE. There we encounter, to name but a few, administrative memoranda, petitions, contracts, census lists, wills, and private letters; that is, a body of written documentation that reveals the objective reality of women's lives and apprehends women as subjects and agents defined and motivated by social, legal, and cultural norms, expectations, and restrictions.

Women as objects of historical inquiry emerged early among papyrologists. At least two books on the subject appeared in 1939, both written by women (Bringmann and Biezunska-Malowist). Each contrasted the legal status of Greek women in Egypt with that of native women and attempted to explain why the legal status of Greek women in Hellenistic Egypt was different from that enjoyed by women in Classical Athens. One of these scholars lived long enough to offer a critique of her own conclusions. Reflecting on her own work some fifty years later, Biezunska-Malowist (1993) remarked that her insistence on using classical Athenian law as her point of reference had led her to disregard the distinct social structures, legal traditions, customs, and practices of the many other Greek communities that made up the Hellenistic world.

The status of women in the Hellenistic kingdoms and in Egypt in particular was taken up by Claire Préaux in 1959. Préaux pointed out that women's political incapacity did not signify fiscal exemption (as economic agents, women paid the taxes pertaining to the activities they were engaged in, just as men did) but that ethnic affiliation dictated varying

A Companion to Women in the Ancient World, First Edition. Edited by Sharon L. James and Sheila Dillon.
© 2012 John Wiley & Sons, Ltd. Published 2015 by John Wiley & Sons, Ltd.

legal capacity. The tutelage of women continued to be observed in Hellenistic Egypt among the population of Greek stock whereas Egyptian women enjoyed a legal capacity equal to that of men and, therefore, acted independently in matters connected with law and justice. Wholly mindful of the two traditions, Préaux was nonetheless unable to envision the extended legal capacity that Greek women came to possess—over time, in areas with a lesser Greek presence, and in families issued of mixed marriages—as a possible result of the influence of the Egyptian milieu on that of the newcomers. A proponent of what she called cultural "impermeability," she held fast to the view that the evolution had begun in classical Greece.

The publication in 1975 of Sarah Pomeroy's *Goddesses, Whores, Wives, and Slaves* reshaped the way classicists look at Greek and Roman antiquity: it ushered in an explicitly feminist approach to the study of ancient history, one that challenged the established hierarchical valuation of our primary sources (literary versus documentary, Classical versus Archaic and post-Classical, center versus periphery) and established the important place of Egypt in documenting the changing conditions of life for women in the Hellenistic period. What had begun as a single chapter in a volume surveying women's history from Bronze Age Greece to the death of the emperor Constantine led to Pomeroy's *Women in Hellenistic Egypt from Alexander to Cleopatra* (1984; revised in the 1990 paperback edition), a volume devoted to the experiences of women, elite and ordinary, within the particular chronological, geographical, political, and cultural context of Egypt under Ptolemaic rule (305–30 BCE).

This essay will neither rehearse Pomeroy's authoritative treatment of the materials nor presume to replace it. Rather, its goal is to highlight the advances in papyrological research in the last 20 years that update and supplement her influential synthesis. In this contribution, I aim to provide a selected overview of Pomeroy's treatment of women in Hellenistic Egypt, both signaling the topics that scholarly advances now permit a more complete appreciation of and presenting the ways in which new research refines our understanding. The publication in 1998 of *Women and Society in Greek and Roman Egypt*, a richly annotated sourcebook produced by a team of eleven scholars and edited by Jane Rowlandson, paved the way for what is attempted here.

1   Queens

Several Ptolemaic queens enjoyed remarkable prominence (Pomeroy 1990: chapter 1; Rowlandson 1998: 25–41). Early in the dynasty, Berenike I (wife of Ptolemy I Soter, "savior"); her daughter, Arsinoe II (sister and wife of Ptolemy II Philadelphus); and Berenike II (cousin and wife of Ptolemy III Euergetes) were very wealthy women, as was Cleopatra VII, the last and most famous queen of Egypt. They managed their own property, made gifts to gods and sanctuaries, supported the arts, wielded political influence, and even commanded armies. They were also worshipped like goddesses. Alexander the Great had claimed divine ancestry, proclaiming himself son of Zeus, and the Macedonian kings connected him (and themselves) with Heracles and Dionysus, both sons of Zeus by mortal women. The recipient of divine honors in life, Alexander became the object of worship in death as well: Ptolemy I established a cult in his honor in Alexandria. The use of royal cult soon became central to legitimating Ptolemaic rule and enhancing the image of its dynasty, both in Egypt (among Greek settlers and the native population alike) and in its overseas territories (as on the island of Cyprus).

In 272/1 BCE, Ptolemy II instituted a cult of himself and Arsinoe as the "brother-sister gods" (*theoi adelphoi*), and, following Arsinoe's death in 270 BCE, Arsinoe was deified in a Greek cult in Alexandria and served by a priestess called a "basket-bearer" (*kanephoros*). The apotheosized queen was also represented in the Egyptian style on the contemporary Mendes stele (Quaegebeur 1978, cat. no. 7), a monument recording the enthronement of the sacred ram of Mendes in the Nile Delta and promulgating, among other things, that Arsinoe's cult images were to be set up next to divine ones in all temples as "temple-sharing gods," placing the deceased queen on the same level with gods. Ptolemy III further expanded the dynastic cult by adding himself and his wife Berenike II as the "benefactor gods" (*theoi euergetai*) to the pantheon of divine kings, and he extended the ruler cult within the Egyptian temples, as is documented in the famous trilingual Canopus Decree (*OGIS* I 56) of 238 BCE. The text, inscribed in hieroglyphs (the Egyptian sacred script), demotic (the Egyptian administrative and legal script), and Greek, records decisions taken at a national synod of the chief Egyptian priests "to increase the existing honors in the temples to King Ptolemy and Queen Berenike, the benefactor gods, and their forebears, the brother-sister gods, and their grandparents, the savior gods" (lines 21–22) (Bagnall and Derow 1981: no. 136). Additionally, the decree proclaimed the divinity of princess Berenike, Ptolemy III's deceased daughter, along with honors for her in temples across the country. Linking the worship of the living rulers with that of their ancestors thus anchored the Ptolemies in the symbolic realm, and the role granted the indigenous clergy in the royal cult secured the priests' long-term loyalty to the dynasty.

Queen Arsinoe II was particularly popular (Quaegebeur 1988: 42–47). A festival called the Arsinoeia was instituted in her honor, towns (Arsinoe) and villages (Philadelphia) were named after her, the Fayum area was renamed Arsinoite *nome* (or province), and part of a tax levied on orchards and gardens was reserved for the expenses of her cult. Her image was propagated on coins, sculpted portraits, and bas-reliefs in both the Greek and Egyptian styles (Stanwick 2002). She was the recipient of prayers and offerings in Greek shrines and temples consecrated to her, and Egyptian monuments attest to her worship as an individual deity as well as a "resident goddess" alongside native gods across Egypt into the first century BCE. No other Ptolemaic queen was to enjoy such long-lasting veneration.

2   Upper-Class Women

Ptolemy I moved the capital of his kingdom from Memphis to Alexandria, which Alexander had founded on the western edge of the Nile delta. The city was to become the heart of a tightly controlled administrative apparatus and the seat of a court keen to preserve the Greek cultural heritage and secure its continuity in the new land. The first Ptolemies were men of culture and learning. They promoted scientific research and literature through two institutions, built in the vicinity of the royal palace: the Museum or "shrine of the Muses," a residential center of learning for scholars, and the Library, the repository of all works written in Greek and the place where librarian-scholars organized the systematic cataloguing of the collection and undertook painstaking study of the manuscripts with a view to producing reliable editions of earlier authors (Gutzwiller 2007: 16–25). Poets also, as we shall see, were drawn to Alexandria by the promise of royal patronage.

Distinct from the rest of the country both physically and culturally, Alexandria was a cosmopolitan city where Macedonians and Greeks from all parts of the Greek world (La'da

2002b) most probably formed a majority in a population comprised of native Egyptians and various ethnic groups, including a large Jewish community. The Macedonian ruling class was made up of high-ranking army officers and administrators in the service of the king; these men, not surprisingly, were often married to women themselves issued from prominent families. Learning from witnessing the more open arena of activity available to queens, some aristocratic women of the period, as Pomeroy persuasively suggested, put their personal wealth to the service of the community in the form of public works and other acts of civic munificence, winning official and even political recognition for their benefactions (Pomeroy 1995: 125–6). For Ptolemaic Alexandria, evidence for the increased presence of non-royal women in the public arena is not so unconventional: we find inscriptions honoring the wives and daughters of the governing elite that were set up in places where their male relatives held official posts, and the dedications the women themselves put up for members of their family (Pomeroy 1990: 42–5). The Greek social custom according to which the name of a respectable woman ought not to be spoken in public held sway no longer.

3 Priestesses

One of the defining anomalies of the condition of women in ancient societies is their simultaneous general seclusion from public life and broad participation in religious and ritual celebrations. The important role accorded women in the religious life of their communities through their holding priestly offices and performing rites in the course of public ceremonies has been explained as a reflection of women's marginalized political status and alternatively as the acknowledgment of the significance of the presence of women in society (Tzanetou 2007: 6–7). A similar ambivalence lives on in the Hellenistic period. In Ptolemaic Egypt priestesses were found in both Greek and Egyptian temples. The Egyptian clergy was a closed community: priests married within their group, their status and rights were hereditary, and their wives and daughters played a concrete role in the performance of particular rituals (as musicians, singers, prophetesses, and nurses of sacred animals), received the economic profits attached to their function, and could join others in a professional association (Rowlandson 1998: 55–62; Colin 2002). On the Greek side, priestly offices in the ruler cult of the Ptolemies were reserved for men and women issued from prominent Graeco-Macedonian families in Alexandria and in Ptolemais, a Greek city founded by Ptolemy I in the southern part of the country. This priestly personnel was eponymous, which means that the priests' names were part of the dating formula of official documents (papyri and inscriptions), and the term of their office usually lasted one year (Clarysse and van der Veken 1983; Quaegebeur 1988: 41–2; Pomeroy 1990: 55–9). As the dynastic cult spread, queenly priestesses were added to the existing priest of Alexander and of the deified Ptolemies.

Eponymous priestesses bore distinctive titles. Deified Arsinoe II was served by the *kanephoros*, so-called because she carried a basket made of gold in which sacred objects were kept as she led a solemn procession in the capital city, followed by city officials and the young members of the civic body. Berenike II was served by the *athlephoros* ("bearer of the prize of victory"), a priestess appointed to her cult by her son Ptolemy IV Philopator. The *athlephoros*, too, lent her name to the year. These women were mostly of Greek and Macedonian stock (although a few bear Egyptian names) and many were the daughters of military commanders and important officials. That the prestigious appointment often occurred several years after the peak of a father's career (an inference drawn from the fact that a priestess' complete name included her personal name and her patronymic, as in "Kratera daughter of Theodoros") suggests that a daughter's selection for the sacred office was possibly a manifestation of her father's honor. The close association with the father has also been interpreted to mean that the daughter was still young and not yet married (Pomeroy 1990: 57). Whether her virginity was a cultic requirement is not known.

The roles filled by the eponymous priestesses do help to refine the general statement that "religion was the only state-supported activity that reserved an official place for women" (Pomeroy 1990: 59). The worship of the queens of Macedonian origin was naturally closely tied with that of the royal family and, as the object of popular devotion and of official cult, it shared in the active promotion of the Ptolemies' political and religious program among immigrant and native populations. Although it is impossible to document the actual extent of queen Arsinoe II's influence on matters of policy (her title of "king" suggests that she shared the throne with her brother Ptolemy II: Quaegebeur 1988: 45; Pomeroy 1990: 17–20), features of the priesthood consecrated to her reveal a political intention. Created on the model of the *kanephoroi*, who walked the Panathenaic procession in Athens' preeminent civic festival (Neils 1992; Dillon 2002), the Alexandrian priestess served several mutually reciprocal symbolic functions. As a priestess she ministered to the queen-goddess, the guarantor of prosperity for the country and its people, and as the daughter of a prominent man close to the court she simultaneously represented the citizen body in public acts of worship and secured its loyalty for the monarchy. Her physical place in the procession— before city magistrates and priests and ahead of the ephebes, the young men of Alexandria learning their future roles of citizen soldiers through education, military training, and participation in the community's public rituals (Kennell 2006)—inscribes her at the center of the Greek cultural ideology being fashioned.

4   Goddesses

Ptolemaic queens cultivated associations with goddesses, and several favored a particular connection with Aphrodite (Pomeroy 1990: 30–40), perhaps in part because of the goddess' relation with Cyprus, a Ptolemaic possession, but also because of the goddess' embodiment of beauty and love; her power over sky, sea, and earth; and her association with marriage, fertility, and prosperity. Arsinoe II sponsored the Adoneia, a festival celebrating the annual union of Aphrodite and Adonis, a young god of vegetation who dies and whom his divine lover brings back to life yearly. Part of the festival is captured by Theocritus, born in Syracuse and a court poet of the Ptolemies, in a lively account of the visit two Syracusan women settled in Alexandria pay to the royal palace, where they watch the elaborate show put on by the queen. The event concludes with a hymn to Adonis, in which Aphrodite is invoked: "O Kypris [i.e., Aphrodite], daughter of Dione, you have made Berenike immortal from being mortal, so men say, by dripping Ambrosia into her woman's heart. To please you, you of many names and many shrines, the daughter of Berenike, Arsinoe, beautiful as Helen, nurtures Adonis with all good things" (*Idyll* 15, lines 106–111, transl. Rowlandson 1998: 27–8).

Arsinoe II was also venerated as the maritime Aphrodite Euploia ("of the fair sailing") in a shrine that Callicrates of Samos, famous admiral and influential courtier of Ptolemy II, built for her at Cape Zephyrion on the Mediterranean, between Alexandria and Canopus. "This shrine is unique in being the only edifice of the third century BCE commemorated in multiple epigrams by various leading Hellenistic poets" (Bing 2009: 235), and previously unknown poems about Callicrates and his foundation have come up in the recently published papyrus book-roll preserving a collection of short poems (epigrams) by Posidippus of Pella, a contemporary of Ptolemy II and his sister-queen (Gutzwiller 2005; Bing 2009: 235 n. 35). It has been argued that the private founder, through the cult of Arsinoe-Aphrodite-Zephyritis housed in the coastal temple (Zephyritis means "of Cape Zephyrion"), sought to identify the queen with a manifestation of Aphrodite that held special significance to sailors, thus transforming the deified Arsinoe into the patron of the Ptolemaic navy (Hauben 1983: 111 n. 48), and that the shrine itself "served as a conduit through which political/cultural traditions of Greece [e.g., Aphrodite Euploia] could enter into Egypt and from which the Ptolemies could broadcast their own peculiar contributions to that legacy" (Bing 2009: 252).

5 Case Study: Demeter

Alongside Aphrodite, Demeter, Greek goddess of grain and fertility, continued to be worshipped in Egypt, both in the Greek cities (such as Alexandria) and in the towns and villages of the Egyptian countryside. Texts on papyrus and objects of worship afford a glimpse of the place the goddess occupied in the religious lives of women and of the role that her cult enabled her female worshipers to play as agents of cultural assimilation in a mixed society.

The Demeter cult was popular in Alexandria. A district to the east of the capital was named Eleusis, and both a temple of Demeter and a shrine that the goddess shared with her daughter, Kore, are attested in the city (Polybius XV 27.2, 29.9, 33.8). In his sixth hymn, Callimachus, the poet-librarian who lived much of his life in Alexandria, describes a women-only celebration in which a ritual basket (*kalathos*) is carried in procession to a shrine of Demeter. Although the poet is silent about the locale and occasion of the event, the ancient commentator to the hymn situates the procession in Alexandria and ascribes to Ptolemy Philadelphus the founding of the ritual in imitation of an Athenian practice (Parca 2007: 193 n. 12). Outside the capital, we have a demotic letter from the temple archives of Soknopaiou Nesos, a village on the northern end of the Fayum. The letter, dated to 132 BCE, is addressed by the priests of the crocodile god Soknopaios to *Nmpn*, priest of *T3mtr*. The divine name *T3mtr* is that of the goddess Demeter and *Nmpn* is that of Nymphion, who served the goddess in a chapel consecrated to her in the temple of the crocodile god, probably in Crocodilopolis (the district capital before it was re-named after queen Arsinoe). While at times Demeter can be the Greek appellation of the goddess Isis, the fact that in this letter the divine name is in demotic and the priest's name is the Egyptian transcription of the Greek name Nymphion makes it clear that Demeter here is the Greek deity (Quaegebeur 1983: 306), conceived as such, and distinct from her native counterpart.

Mass-produced terracotta figurines used in domestic worship document the goddess' association with, and likely assimilation to, local deities. Since their intended clientele was a population in which ethnic distinction had long ago ceased to be clear, an Egyptian deity was sometimes depicted in Greek guise and at other times could actually be meant to represent the Egyptian equivalent of a Greek god. This explains why numerous figurines are now alternatively labeled Demeter or Isis-Demeter. While Demeter, as discussed above, was worshiped as a Greek deity in Egypt, her personality easily accounts for her becoming "a translation and extension of Isis" (Thompson 1998: 704). The two are Mother Goddesses, both preside over agricultural plenty and human fertility, and each is associated with mystery cults (Dunand 1973: 85–7). What the terracottas document first and foremost is the goddess' ability to stride across ethnic, social, and gender boundaries and unify a diverse population through devotion to her.

Demeter received more than private and individual acts of devotion: we also know of festivals called Demetria or Thesmophoria. In a letter of 258 or 257 BCE (*P. Cairo Zen.* I 59028), the harpist-singer Satyra mentions that an installment of wages reached her for, or at the time of, the festival of Demeter, and complains that she has not received anything since. Although the time of year is not revealed, the fact that Satyra was part of the Alexandrian household of Ptolemy II's finance minister suggests that she may have performed at a festival held in the capital. Another letter, with its reference to the undelivered gift of two jars of wine "for the wife of Amyntas for the Thesmophoria" (*P. Col. Zen.* 19, 2), documents the material support some men extended to their wives' worship of Demeter. And a third letter, dated to 26 November 244 BCE (*P. Cairo Zen.* III 59350.5), mentions the sacrifice of a pig and the theft of the victim fattened "for the fasting of Demeter."

Introduced in Alexandria by the first Ptolemy, the worship of Demeter spread to the countryside with the settlers. The cult offered a space of joint identity for different groups (the newcomers themselves were of mixed origins), and it may have helped to introduce Egyptian wives to the culture of their Greek husbands. Alternatively, immigrant women, who came from cities and regions inhabited by Greeks and Macedonians, introduced the cult into local society through their own mixed marriages (La'da 2002a examines the role of women immigrants as carriers, propagators, and guardians of ethnic and cultural traditions in Hellenistic Egypt). It is tempting to suggest that the active participation of women in her cult in Egypt was a potent factor in the goddess' lasting success (Thompson 1998: 705) and that Egypt, because of the favorable position it accorded to women by custom and in law, guaranteed continued female agency in the religious realm and in society.

6 Wives

Getting married did not require the spouses to draw up a document detailing material aspects of their joint life and outlining the ideal behavior expected of them. Yet such documents are not rare in the corpus of texts of Ptolemaic date, when migrants from widely different parts of the Greek world settled in Egypt. There, in the absence of a uniform legal code and a homogeneous set of norms governing social behavior, they may have wished to protect themselves and their interests by means of a legally binding agreement (Pomeroy 1990: 83–6). A recent comprehensive reassessment (Yiftach-Firanko 2003) of the written instruments documenting marriage and marital arrangements in Egypt draws informative conclusions regarding marriage, dowry, and divorce.

Two acts were enough to create a marriage: the handing over (*ekdosis*) of the bride to her future husband for the purpose of being his lawful wife, and the delivery of a dowry (*phernê*) to the bridegroom. Thus, in Ptolemaic Egypt marriage documents are generally formulated either as *ekdosis* documents, which open with a statement of the handing over of the bride, or as dowry receipts, which begin with the husband acknowledging receipt of the dowry (the supply of which presumed the proper performance of the *ekdosis*); both include provisions regulating the recovery of the dowry in case of divorce. Of the 141 extant marriage documents preserved on papyrus (Yiftach-Firanko 2003: 9–32), twenty-five are of Ptolemaic date; of those, two are *ekdosis* documents (*P. Elephantine* 1 of 311/310 BCE and *P. Giessen* 2 of 173 BCE, both discussed below) and eighteen are *phernê* receipts (a well-preserved example of which is *P. Tebtunis* I 104 of 92 BCE, quoted in Pomeroy 1990: 87–8).

The earliest Greek marriage agreement (which happens also to be the first dated Greek papyrus) from Egypt was recovered in Elephantine (near modern Aswan), where a Greek garrison was stationed. Despite some unique features, the contract bears witness to a society in transition, on the one hand echoing Classical Athenian law and embracing a patriarchal conception of marriage and, on the other, departing from earlier practice and asserting new expectations. The contract involves a man from Temnos (on the coast of Asia Minor) and a woman from Cos (an island south of Temnos), both of whom now find themselves very far from their Mediterranean birthplaces:

> Heracleides takes as his lawful wife Demetria of Cos from her father Leptines of Cos and her mother Philotis (he is a free man, she a free woman), she bringing with her to the marriage clothing and ornaments valued at 1000 drachmas. Heracleides is to supply to Demetria all that is fitting for a freeborn wife. We shall live together wherever it seems best to Leptines and Heracleides deciding in common.

> If Demetria is caught acting fraudulently to the shame of her husband Heracleides, she shall be deprived of all that she brought, but Heracleides shall prove whatever he alleges against Demetria before three men whom they both approve. It shall not be permitted for Heracleides to bring home another wife in insult of Demetria, or to beget children by another woman, or to engage in deception against Demetria on any pretext. If Heracleides is caught doing any of these things and Demetria proves it before three men whom they both approve, Heracleides shall return to Demetria the dowry of 1000 drachmas she brought, and shall in addition forfeit 1000 drachmas of the silver coinage of Alexander. Demetria, and those representing Demetria, shall have the right to exact payment, as if derived from a legally decided action, from Heracleides himself and from all Heracleides' property on both land and sea.

> This contract shall be normative in every respect, wherever Heracleides may produce it against Demetria, or Demetria and those aiding Demetria to exact payment may produce it against Heracleides, as if the agreement had been made in that place.

> Heracleides and Demetria shall have the right to keep the contracts severally in their own custody and to produce them against each other. Witnesses [six names follow]. (*P.Eleph.* 1, lines 2–16, transl. adapted from Rowlandson 1998: 165–6)

Some things have not changed: the important role of the father of the bride (he and the husband decide where the couple will live), the glaring asymmetry between what constitutes reprehensible behavior on the part of the spouses (anything likely to bring shame onto husband versus bigamy, children by another woman, and harmful treatment of lawful wife), and the fact that the woman needs male assistance ("those aiding Demetria" are men) to exercise her right to financial recovery. In other ways, however, the document reveals a changing world: instead of taking place between the bride's father (or another male guardian) and the groom, the giving away of Demetria is performed by her father *and* her mother (in the case of the father's death, the mother alone could carry out the *ekdosis*: Pomeroy 1990: 90; Yiftach-Firanko 2003: 43). Also, should a serious fault threaten the marriage, Heracleides and Demetria can each avail themselves of the same arbitration ("before three men whom they both approve") and, if proven guilty, Heracleides is expected to return the dowry to his wife and additionally pay her a sum of money equivalent to her personal property.

Since marriage contracts are primarily concerned with the material aspects of the relationship, our texts not surprisingly tend to involve well-off people. The second extant Ptolemaic *ekdosis* document (*P. Giessen* 2) introduces us to the propertied class of Greek cavalrymen, military personnel granted very sizable allotments (about ten times what was needed to support a family) for their service to the crown; it also features an exceptionally large dowry, one that could support, as sole source of income, a family for nearly twenty years!

> Olympias daughter of Dionysios son of Maketas, with her own father Dionysios, a Macedonian of the second hipparchy, a one-hundred-aroura holder, as her guardian, has given herself to Antaios, an Athenian of the men under Kineas of the second hipparchy, a one-hundred-aroura holder, so as to be his wedded wife, bringing as dowry reckoned in bronze ninety-five talents and her slave-girl by name of Stolis and her [i.e., Stolis'] nursling child, named [—], worth five bronze talents, making a total of [100] bronze talents. (lines 8–15, transl. from Rowlandson 1998: 168)

In this unique document, the bride performs her own *ekdosis*, with her father as legal representative. Although the contract is in many ways traditional—Olympias acts with her guardian and the contract effects the transfer of her person from one man to another—her passing from the expected position of object to that of subject is remarkable, and her action may very well reflect Egyptian custom. Indeed, by the sixth century BCE, the Egyptian woman's consent to marriage was required, even when the marriage was an arranged one. Similarly, Antaios' provision of (life's) necessities, furniture, and clothing to his wife (lines 16–17) echo the Egyptian "annuity contract," which detailed the husband's responsibility to feed and clothe his wife. Yet the disproportionately high emphasis on the individual rights and duties of each spouse towards the other identifies this document as Greek. The traditional requirement that Olympias "obey" her husband "as is fitting for a wife" (lines 15–16) is in keeping with the social asymmetry defined by gender that was still very much the norm, and following the "do's" come the prohibited behaviors, as is particular to Greek marriage documents. The papyrus is unfortunately damaged, and only one of the actions prohibited to Olympias is preserved—that she may not be absent from the house without her husband's permission. But the list of the injunctions regulating Antaios' behavior is complete, and it includes: no bringing a second wife into the household, no having a concubine or a boy lover, no having children by another woman, no moving in with another woman, and no casting out or otherwise insulting the lawful wife (lines 20–4). Several of the prohibitions already appear in *P. Elephantine* 1 discussed above, but the stipulation that Antaios not have a boy lover is unusual. Why would Olympias, who "gives herself away" as a bride and yet agrees to a rather conservative marriage, request this particular pledge? Here again, it is tempting to invoke the mixed cultural milieu of the Fayum and suggest that Olympias, aware of the advantageous economic and social position that marriage agreements granted Egyptian women, used that knowledge to draft a contract meant best to guarantee and protect her welfare.

The Greek dowry in Egypt usually included cash, clothing, and jewelry; it was meant to support the wife, both in the course of marriage and after its dissolution. The husband could use it to serve the needs of his wife as long as he returned the dowry's original value to her when the marriage ended. It was ultimately the wife's property (Rowlandson 1995: 313). The substantial dowries attested in the Ptolemaic documents suggest that they laid the foundation of the family's fortune alongside the assets of the husband (Yiftach-Firanko 2003: 118–21), and it is likely that a large dowry formed the larger portion of the entire family property. The wife's strong financial position may explain certain provisions in the marriage documents, such as the bride's giving herself away or the woman's right to terminate the marriage and demand her dowry back (in the value originally reported in the marriage document) within a set period of time, without any accusation procedure.

The act of divorce was informal in Ptolemaic Egypt: all it took was the interruption of the joint life by one of the spouses, either "going away" or "sending away." Given that cohabitation and the delivery of a dowry were the constitutive elements of a lawful marriage, the provision that, following the clauses describing the obligations of the spouses, articulates the consequences of their contravention also in effect provides the marriage document with a divorce clause. In *P. Elephantine* 1, for example, the husband who does not fulfill his obligations may be accused by his wife and, if convicted, made to return her dowry (and then some) while the delinquent wife, following an identical accusation procedure, loses her dowry. However, the accusation procedure soon ceased to be required in most of Egypt, and Ptolemaic women could divorce without having to prove their husband's misconduct (Yiftach-Firanko 2003: 197–201).

7 Women and Property

The social environment of the Greek and Macedonian immigrants who made their home in Egypt was not uniform. Whereas the citizen population in the newly founded Greek cities of Alexandria and Ptolemais was and remained solidly Graeco-Macedonian, large numbers of newcomers—reserve troops granted land allotments called *kleroi* by the crown and civilian entrepreneurs looking for opportunities—settled in the countryside (known as *chora*) in the midst of the native Egyptian population. What happened should cause no surprise. By the second century BCE, mixed marriages and social mobility produced a certain blurring in the identification of Greeks and Egyptians; personal names were no longer necessarily reliable markers of ethnic identity but rather reflected a social one, and some individuals employed either a Greek or an Egyptian name, depending on the context (Clarysse 1985: 57–66; Bagnall 1988: 22–4; Thompson 2001: 301–22).

A fascinating case is that of the businesswoman Apollonia (Lewis 1986: 88–103; Pomeroy 1990: 103–26), recently retold with particular attention to the Egyptian side of her story (Vandorpe 2002a). Her papers, in Greek and Demotic, were preserved in the archive kept by her husband Dryton, a cavalry officer from Crete. Posted to the town of Pathyris in Upper Egypt, Dryton met and married Apollonia, a local girl. He was forty-two, she about half his age. Her family, also Greek, had been living in Egypt for several generations and had adopted Egyptian ways and customs. Apollonia ("the one of Apollo") also bore the Egyptian name Senmonthis ("daughter of Montou").

Dryton was an officer and a businessman, and his young wife followed his example. Apollonia has left eight loan contracts dating from the period c. 145–126 BCE; these are loans in wheat, barley, spelt, and money. Three of the contracts are written in Greek, five in Demotic. All five Demotic documents are drawn up by an Egyptian notary and according to Egyptian practice: Apollonia acts without a guardian. In two of the five contracts,

Apollonia presents herself as a Greek woman, bearing a double name, with the Greek one mentioned first. The other three texts are acknowledgments of debt for very small loans, written by the debtor himself. When higher amounts are lent out, as is the case in the three Greek contracts, Apollonia goes to the Greek notary and Dryton is named as her guardian. When doing business, then, Apollonia presents herself as a Greek woman. In private letters and papers, on the other hand, she is known only as Senmonthis. Her case illustrates not only the fluidity of self-representation but also the ingenuity deployed in turning one's mixed cultural heritage to advantage. Apollonia grew up as an Egyptian girl. When she married a Greek officer, she seized the opportunity to reap the benefits of her Greek background and at times opted for social standing over legal independence.

Papyri of the early Ptolemaic period do allow us to apprehend the role of women in the social and economic environment of the *chora* (Rowlandson 1995: 307–15). While large portions of the documentation have been described as "gendered" because they are mostly concerned with masculine activities associated with land management (irrigation, cultivation, taxation), the papyri nonetheless record women's participation in well-established forms of labor and production. We encounter wool workers (working at home, in small weaving businesses, or for large textile concerns), domestic hands, entertainers, beekeepers, and beer sellers, the latter a retail activity in which Egyptian women regularly engaged (Rowlandson 1995: 307–8; Parca 2011).

The role of women in what was essentially an agricultural economy varied according to place and cultural milieu: Egyptian custom did not bar women from working in the fields while Greeks generally held that women's natural physical weakness made them unsuitable for agricultural labor. Productive land in Egypt fell into three categories (temple, royal, and cleruchic), and access to it was generally restricted to men. The temples of Egyptian gods, especially in Upper Egypt, were important production and distribution centers that derived much of their revenue from vast tracts of land. Women of priestly families serving the temples could inherit temple resources, including farmable land, which they could sell or lease, and it seems likely that "only intermarriage (which was probably more common between a Greek man and an Egyptian woman than the other way around) gave the descendants of the Greek immigrants to Egypt access to the status which allowed possession of valuable temple land" (Rowlandson 1995: 309–10). In the Fayum and the Oxyrhynchite district in Middle Egypt, extensive areas belonging to the crown (the second type of productive land) were cultivated by royal farmers, nearly all of whom were male. Similarly, access to the profitable category of cleruchic land was, given the nature of that land, restricted to men, and for most of the Ptolemaic period soldiers could bequeath their *kleroi* to their sons (provided those sons were themselves in a position to serve in a military capacity) but not to their wives or daughters. Cleruchs' testamentary dispositions, however, reveal that women were regularly the recipients of bequests, including houses, slaves, and personal movables (Rowlandson 1995: 312). Property privately owned thus could pass into the hands of women; arable land almost never did, until the descendants of immigrants, through intermarriage, gained access to temple land.

8   Women and Literacy

Letters by women of unexceptional backgrounds have allowed historians to partially rewrite the chapter on women's education in the Hellenistic period (Cribiore 2001: 74–91; Bagnall and Cribiore 2006). Looking beyond the cases of women of high social status and outstanding intellectual accomplishment featured in the literary sources (Pomeroy 1977, 1990: 59–72), Raffaella Cribiore has mined the papyri "to make visible previously unseen aspects of women's participation in the culture of literates" (2001: 75). Not surprisingly, women's access to education in Egypt was dictated by the socio-economic circumstances of their families and, there as elsewhere, even the upper class often felt that daughters were not worth schooling beyond the rudiments of reading and writing. Illiterate women were the norm, and letters sent by women show that those who availed themselves of writing had received primary education and were issued from wealthy, propertied milieus. The letters reveal how, in subtle ways, education enabled women to wield a degree of control over their lives and to some extent shaped the way women thought and apprehended their place in society.

Although papyri emanate from a society circumscribed in time and place, they also reveal the remarkable linguistic, ethnic, and cultural diversity of Hellenistic Egypt. The country's socio-linguistic landscape comprised an indigenous majority speaking Egyptian and large numbers of Greek-speaking soldiers and settlers from all over the eastern Mediterranean who used Greek as their *lingua franca* (Clarysse 1998). The oral use of Greek and Egyptian across ethnic groups is not easy to determine, and Greek and Egyptian written documentation does not neatly correlate with one community or the other. Some individuals operated in both spheres simultaneously, using Greek in some contexts (generally administrative), Egyptian in others (usually dealing with religion), and either language in legal and private dealings (Bagnall and Cribiore 2006: 57–9). By extension, papyri cannot be relied upon to establish how widespread the knowledge of spoken Greek was among women, nor are women's letters in Greek necessarily synonymous with actual fluency in the language or with the ability to write it. Greek overtook Egyptian as a means of communication over the course of the Ptolemaic period, and it continued to be the only available means of written communication for most people during much of the Roman period.

Literate women who sent letters could choose to pen a letter themselves or to dictate it to a scribe or a secretary. An illiterate woman who needed to resort to written documentation had to rely on a scribe, a friend, or a relative, to whom she dictated her letter. Such dictated letters were not necessarily altered and normalized by the scribe, and the lack of smoothness that they often display, rather than signaling a lack of education, may in fact reflect a woman's "train of thought emerging among conventional expressions and may disclose her emotions and her distinctive vocabulary" (Cribiore 2001: 89). Even in dictated letters, the language can get us quite close to the words spoken by the sender. Can we then capture a woman's voice through her letters? The answer is yes if we understand "voice" to refer to a "specific woman's way of expressing herself and her conversational language" (Cribiore 2001: 90; cf. Bagnall and Cribiore 2006: 60), but no if we take "voice" to mean gendered speech. The epistolary corpus does not show that the concerns of propertied men were much different from those of women from the same social and economic strata or that men were less concerned with family matters. And language itself—generic markers such as the forms of address and the epistolary conventions—fails to prove gender specific.

There are about 230 extant Greek letters sent by women from c. 300 BCE to 800 CE (Cribiore 2001: 88), which makes the letters about one-fourteenth as numerous as letters sent by men. Women's letters of the Ptolemaic period form a small part of this corpus. Most are isolated texts and not part of archives, and the stories they tell are like excerpts plucked from books whose titles are lost. The letters reveal women busy with children, family, and home, and they also document women entrepreneurs, women running the household while their husbands (soldiers, businessmen, civil servants) are away, and women traveling to places far from their towns and villages. As the "one genre in which women are definitely expressing themselves on their own behalf and not through a male who controls the representation of their thought," letters allow us "to see the women of Hellenistic and Roman Egypt as agents, faced with disparate circumstances, and prepared to make choices" (Bagnall and Cribiore 2006: 10–11). Letters thus fittingly conclude this essay, allowing us hear the voices of the unexceptional women who once spoke them in short, urgent sentences, bristling with impatience, colored with everyday speech, filled with everyday worries, and brimming with willful energy and confidence.

Brusque request and tentative query alternate in Asklepias' message to Zenon, probably her husband's employer: "Please with regard to the matter Eirenaios instructs you about, give me a travel allowance, in order that I come up country to him and do not appear to neglect him. And he sent me a messenger summoning me. Therefore, what do you bid me? Be well" (*P. Cairo Zen.* III 59408; mid-third century; transl. adapted from Bagnall and Cribiore 2006: 99).

A mother writes, probably in her own hand, "We received the letter from you in which you announce that you have given birth. I kept praying to the gods everyday on your behalf. Now that you have escaped [from danger], I shall pass my days in the greatest joy. I sent you a flask full of oil and ... pounds of dried figs. Please empty the flask and send it back to me safely because I need it here. Don't hesitate to name the little one 'Kleopatra,' so that your little daughter..." (*P. Münch.* 3.57; second century; transl. adapted from Rowlandson 1998: 292 and Bagnall and Cribiore 2006: 109).

Finally, older sisters keep a watchful eye on their younger siblings: "Apollonia and Eupous to their sisters Rasion and Demarion, greeting. If you are well, it is good; we, too, are well. You should light up the light in the shrine and shake the pillows. Devote your attention to learning and do not worry about mother, for she is well already. Wait for us. Farewell. And do not play in the courtyard, but be good and stay inside. Take care of Titoas and Sphairos" (*P. Athen.* 60; first century; transl. adapted from Bagnall and Cribiore 2006: 374).

RECOMMENDED FURTHER READING

An engaging account of the fascinating political, economic, and social history of Egypt under Greek rule is to be found in Bowman (1986), which Manning (2009) supplements with a rigorous analysis of the Ptolemaic state firmly anchored within the context of Egyptian history. Recent books on Cleopatra abound, ranging from "biographies" (Roller 2010; Schiff 2010) to romanticized retellings of her life (Fletcher 2011) to historical monographs that either examine the extant "hard evidence" about the queen's life (Tyldesley 2008), focus on her complicated relationship with Rome (Southern 2007), or apprehend her within her contemporary Egyptian context (Ashton 2008). Ptolemaic Egypt was a land of linguistic, religious, and cultural pluralism: Vandorpe (2002b) offers a detailed treatment of the revealing instance of cultural "bilingualism" found in the archive of Dryton and his wife Apollonia (a.k.a. Senmonthis), and the relationship between "mixed" population and religious practice in the Egyptian capital is briefly described in Dunand (2007). Lastly, looking ahead, Vandorpe and Waebens (2010) discuss the impact of Roman rule on the legal position of women in Egypt as well as the Roman regulation of, and restrictions on, "local" women's social mobility.

24

Jewish Women: Texts and Contexts

Laura S. Lieber

1 Background: The Nature of the Sources

According to a papyrus (*CPJ* 128) from Fayum (Egypt) dated to May 11, 218 BCE, a woman named Helladote, daughter of Philonides, lodged a complaint with King Ptolemy against her husband, Jonathas the *'Ioudaios*. Helladote and Jonathas had wed according to the "civil [*politikon*] law of the Jews," but Jonathas repudiated Helladote and cast her out of the house. While Jonathas' unilateral divorce of his wife appears to have been in accordance with biblical law and norms as articulated by later Jewish (i.e., rabbinic) tradition, Helladote—not necessarily a Jew herself—felt free to seek redress in accordance with Hellenistic norms and by means of the Ptolemaic legal system.

This textual fragment suggests the challenge of studying Jewish women in antiquity. Helladote's background is not specified in the papyrus, but, whatever her religion and ethnic background, she had found the legal treatment of a Jewish wife unacceptable. The term *'Ioudaios*, applied to Jonathas, may describe a religion ("the Jew") or an ethno-nationality ("the Judean")—and, because the same term is not applied to Helladote, its use implicitly introduces the topic of endogamy. The nature of "Jewish civil law," its authority, and its relationship to biblical and later Jewish (i.e., rabbinic) law is unclear, but Helladote's petition indicates that she believed Ptolemaic law might supersede it. Finally, as intriguing as Helladote's case is, we must be careful about drawing any general conclusions from the case of a single (probably wealthy) woman in Hellenistic Egypt. The topic of Jewish women in antiquity spans a tremendous range, geographically, temporally, and economically. To discuss Jewish women in antiquity is, in truth, to discuss women in antiquity as a whole.

We possess a wealth of sources concerning Jewish women in the ancient world: legal documents, including marriage contracts and writs of divorce; inscriptions, particularly from the Diaspora; histories, such as the writings of Philo and Josephus; literary works, including the Hellenistic novellas preserved in the Apocrypha and Pseudepigrapha; and the vast body of rabbinic writings from Roman Palestine. None of these sources is simple,

A Companion to Women in the Ancient World, First Edition. Edited by Sharon L. James and Sheila Dillon.
© 2012 John Wiley & Sons, Ltd. Published 2015 by John Wiley & Sons, Ltd.

however. Inscriptions are often formulaic and difficult to date; histories tend to ignore non-elites and mundane matters; and teasing reality out of novellas is a risky enterprise. Most significantly, while Palestinian rabbinic writings provide the greatest quantity of statements about Jewish women in Roman Palestine, as ideological, often theoretical, works of the nascent rabbinic movement, they are unlikely to reflect the experiences of the majority of women in Palestine, let alone the Diaspora, in any straightforward fashion. The recovery of information about women from non-rabbinic sources thus offers a valuable complement to the rabbinic writings. While in recent years epigraphic sources have been privileged in academic discourse, this essay draws on a range of literary and documentary sources in order to offer a composite picture of Jewish women in the land of Israel and the Greco-Roman Diaspora from the fifth century BCE to the early fourth century CE.

2   Changing Ideals of Femininity

The position of women in Jewish society changed in the wake of its encounter with Hellenism, both in terms of lived realities and societal ideals of femininity. Literary sources, in particular, offer insight into innovations in gender construction in Judaism in antiquity. We can assume that there were disconnects between these literary ideals about woman-hood and the daily experience of women's lives. That said, these literary sources suggest ideas about femininity that Jewish women and men likely internalized and that may have indirectly affected the lives of women.

Broadly speaking, Jews appear to have absorbed general Hellenistic ideas about womanhood. The shift in attitudes both was part of the general process of Hellenization within Levantine Judaism and also may have reflected the increased urbanization of Jewish communities (particularly in the Galilee) and technological advances that affected the domestic economy (Miller 2006; Meyer 2008). Women thus may have been afforded more luxury of time (permitting them to work or socialize more outside of the home) at precisely the time when new cultural norms cast such female initiative and independence in a negative light. The earliest Jewish works to discuss women from this abstract perspective come from the body of work known as Wisdom literature, notably Proverbs 1–9 and 31 (which frame the aphoristic material in Proverbs with descriptions of women), Ecclesiastes, and the deuterocanonical Wisdom of ben Sirach.

Proverbs 31.10–31, which is difficult to date to any time other than the pre-Hellenistic period, is the only extended discussion of an ideal spouse of either sex in the Hebrew Bible. The passage praises the unnamed woman primarily for her industriousness on behalf of her household: she works with wool and flax, feeds her family, engages in business and trading ventures, gives to charity, speaks well, keeps busy, and is wise and pious. Sirach, which reflects a later period than Proverbs but is part of the same Wisdom tradition, suggests a deep absorption of Hellenistic ideas about what one should seek in a wife. In Sirach, a good wife is defined by her modesty, beauty, silence, obedience, and attentiveness to her husband's needs. This perfect wife—a lovely, mute ornament—offers stark contrast to the independent, bustling household manager of Proverbs 31. Other Hellenistic Jewish sources—including Philo, Josephus, and the New Testament—likewise reflect an ideal of marriage in which the wife enjoys her husband's benevolent paternalism. These works suggest a profound assimilation of Hellenistic ideas about marriage within Judaism.

Just as Hellenistic writings offer the earliest descriptions of the ideal spouse in Judaism, they also provide the earliest examples of broad generalizations about women. In general, women are more sexualized, essentialized, and treated with suspicion. Ecclesiastes' statement, "I find woman more bitter than death; she is all traps, her hands are fetters and her heart, snares; he who is pleasing to God escapes her and he who is displeasing is caught" (7.26) stands out as the first truly misogynistic statement in Judaism. Hellenistic Wisdom writers had earlier sources upon which they could draw, notably the depictions of Wisdom and Folly from Proverbs 1–9. Both Wisdom and Folly (the "alien woman") operate through aggressive seduction and deployment of erotic charms; Folly, however, is adultery personified and leads to death, while Wisdom, allied with the legal wife and social order, is life-affirming. Even these starkly erotic stereotypes, however, were transformed under the influence of Hellenism, as we see in the Qumranic wisdom material. Two texts in particular stand out: 4Q184, which amplifies the sexual nature of Folly's behavior and transforms her into a frightening, demonic figure, Chaos-personified; and 4Q185, where Wisdom appears but, rather than actively seeking out young men, is passively "given" by God to men who seek to "possess" her (Crawford 1998). Finally, overtly misogynistic statements litter the Wisdom of ben Sirach, where it is written: "Better is the wickedness of man than the goodness of a woman" (42.14). Sirach also offers the first polemic against Eve (see Genesis 3): "From a woman, sin had its beginning, and because of her we all die" (26.24). While biblical Israel was hardly egalitarian, only after the encounter with Hellenism do we see in Judaism the idea that women are ontologically distinct from, lesser than, and dangerous to men (Frymer-Kensky 1992).

Hellenistic Jewish narratives complement the generic descriptions of women, positive and negative, found in the moralistic writings. A comparison of the Hebrew and Greek versions of Esther provides an example. Both works revel in the exaggerated depictions of absurdly opulent Persian courtly life, which includes lengthy beauty treatments for the potential royal brides. The characterization of Esther reveals how ideals of femininity have changed. In both works, the Jewish queen Esther risks her life when she appears unbidden before her husband, the Persian King. In the Hebrew version of the story (from the Persian or early Hellenistic period), Esther prepares for this dangerous encounter by fasting for three days prior to her appearance, calling for the Jews of Susa to fast with her. When she appears before the king, she wears her royal robes and, immediately, "she won his favor" (5.2). Narrative embellishment concerning Esther's appearance and behavior is minimal, and the text never mentions the deity. The Greek version is much more elaborate. Esther's preparations include a lengthy prayer in which she articulates her piety, and her self-mortification includes not only fasting but also the sacrifice of her vanity: "She utterly humbled her body; every part that she loved to adorn she covered with her tangled hair" (Addition C, 14.2). The Greek version of Esther's approach to the king emphasizes her physical presentation: she leans on her maids, she swoons and faints, and she is, simultaneously, "radiant with perfect beauty" (Addition D, 15.5). Even after the king embraces and comforts her, she faints again. She is the perfect picture of fragile femininity. The Greek version transforms Esther into a Hellenistic-style heroine: beautiful, pious, sheltered, and submissive to her guardian Mordecai (who becomes the hero of the tale).

The biblical text does occasionally remark on a woman's appearance: Rebecca and Rachel are both lovely while Leah is "weak of eyes" (Genesis 29.17); in the Hellenistic texts, however, beauty becomes a dominant trope. Susannah, who is defined primarily by her loveliness and modesty (an ideal wife), represents an extreme example of this trend. Two elders succumb to their lust for Susannah and attempt to rape her while she is bathing in seclusion. When she cries out, the elders claim to have interrupted a tryst between Susannah and a lover. The innocent Susannah, sentenced to death for adultery, prays to

God for help, and God sends Daniel to rescue her. The character of Susannah offers a dramatic contrast to Tamar in Genesis 38. Tamar, whose appearance is never described, posed as a prostitute and seduced her father-in-law, Judah, who had failed to comply with his legal obligation to marry her to his youngest son. Like Susannah, Tamar—visibly pregnant—is charged with adultery, but, rather than being rescued by an external agent, she dramatically saves herself by producing evidence that exculpates her behavior and incriminates her accuser. Susannah had to be rescued from injustice; Tamar acted with cleverness and daring to fulfill the demands of justice.

Women in Hellenistic novellas often blend the resourcefulness valued by the biblical authors with the physical beauty and emphatic piety valued by later writers. For example, Judith (the main character in the apocryphal book bearing her name) uses her beauty to manipulate and murder the enemy general Holophernes. In her actions on behalf of her people, she resembles the biblical Jael (Judges 4–5). The Hellenistic novella, however, emphasizes Judith's beauty and her ascetic piety—features absent from the depiction of Jael, who uses societal norms of hospitality to gain the same lethal access to the enemy general, Sisera. Less dramatically, Sarah, in the book of Tobit, is described as "sensible, brave, and very beautiful" (6.12); on her wedding night, she joins her husband Tobias in a prayer that helps to save him from the demon who killed her previous husbands on their marriage night. In contrast to the sexually available women of the novellas (including the widowed, childless Judith), whose piety complements their beauty, mothers—notably the mother of the seven martyrs in 4 Maccabees 8–18, but also Anna and Edna in the book of Tobit—are not described in terms of physical appearance but rather as bearers and transmitters of moral virtues. Their fortitude, piety, and maternal tenderness are in keeping with the ideals of the Greco-Roman matron.

Rabbinic writings reflect the same ideals of, stereotypes about, and ambivalence towards women found in these earlier Jewish writings. While rabbinic sources are vast and complex and resist easy generalization, by and large the Rabbis valued women's modesty, physical reticence, and beauty as much as their non-Jewish neighbors. As with the Wisdom literature, leisure time ("idleness") is associated with sexual licentiousness (*m. Ket.* 5.5). Rabbinic writings frequently weaken and sexualize strong, positive female characters from the Bible (such as Jael), and, while they at times depict spousal affection and articulate respect for the role of women as mothers and enablers, they are frequently disparaging of women as a category. Assertions of women's inferiority to and ontological difference from men—manifesting physically in menstruation and child-bearing and mentally as their "weak-mindedness," which results in diminished moral and intellectual capacity—were used to justify social, legal, and educational subordination to men.

3   Childhood and Education

Sirach writes, "The birth of a daughter is a loss" (22.3) and, as he goes on to describe, "a daughter is a secret source of anxiety to their fathers ... lest she make [him] a laughingstock to [his] enemies, a byword in the city and notorious among the people, and put [him] to shame before the great multitude" (42.9, 11). In rabbinic literature, as well, the birth of a daughter was a disappointment best remedied by the birth of sons. In contrast to Greco-Roman sources, however, there is no record of female infanticide among Jews; indeed, non-Jewish sources and Jewish sources alike remark upon the Jews' acceptance of all children born to them.

Daughters were frequently named for their grandmothers or mothers, just as sons were often named for grandfathers or fathers, a custom of "familial names" that likely reflects the influence of Hellenism, as we have little evidence of this practice from the pre-Hellenistic period (although the name Tamar may have Davidic associations). Daughters also occasionally received feminized versions of their father's name, reflecting adoption of Roman custom: Alexandra (from Alexander), Johannah (from Johannan), Judith (from Judah), Herodias (from Herod), and so forth. In one known instance, perhaps a case of royal exceptionalism, a son was named after his mother: Berenicianus, son of Berenice, daughter of the Judean king, Agrippa I. Children of either sex might be given names in Hebrew, Aramaic, Greek, Latin, or (rarely) Persian. Double names, often from different languages (e.g., Shelamzion Alexandra), were not uncommon; the earliest example of Jewish double-naming appears in Esther 2.7, where we are told that Hadassah was also known as Esther. In legal texts and funerary inscriptions, women (even when married) are most often identified by patronymics, in the formula "X, daughter of Y," although epitaphs from the late Second Temple period (first century BCE to first century CE) often identify women as "X, wife of Y" (Ilan 1995).

In contrast to the gymnasia and academies that educated elite young men (notably in Sepphoris), there was no institutional system for the education of girls. What education girls received took place at home, from parents or tutors, and for most women presumably focused on domestic matters and skills needed to further the domestic economy. In terms of religious learning, the evidence is ambiguous. Josephus states that, among the Jews, "women and slaves know the Torah" (*Contra Apion* 2.181). "Torah" here is undefined: it could refer to a full Jewish education, a basic knowledge of scripture (acquired orally?), or simply the knowledge needed to run a Jewish house (as a slave would have). Roman period rabbinic sources contain scattered references to women's education and knowledge, but the evidence is conflicting and probably reflects the experiences of a small subset (probably urban and elite) of the population of Jewish Palestine, although in later centuries these writings would become normative. While some passages in rabbinic writings restrict women's access to Torah, others seem to indicate that women could learn both Bible and rabbinic law (*m. Ned.* 4.2–3; *t. Ber.* 2.12), acquire the skills of scribes (*m. Qidd.* 4.13; *m. Gittin* 2.5), and teach their husbands (*t. Ket.* 4.6–7). In some passages, women are permitted to read from sacred texts in the synagogue, which suggests that at least in theory they had the knowledge to do so (*t. Meg.* 3.11–12). In a few rabbinic narratives, the daughters, sisters, and wives of Rabbis are depicted as not only knowing Torah but issuing legal rulings (*t. Kel. BM* 1.6 and *t. Kel. BQ* 4.17). The reality behind these references is difficult to ascertain, but the overall tenor of rabbinic writings suggests that Rabbis believed women to be either too busy with domestic obligations or intellectually unfit for serious Torah study.

Beyond the issue of specifically Jewish education lies the question of general education for girls. The Talmud Yerushalmi (fifth century) records a controversy among Rabbis concerning teaching one's daughters Greek (*y. Shabb.* 6.1, 7d; *y. Peah* 1.1, 15c), wherein Greek is described as an "ornament" for women. At least in the context of this anecdote, it seems that in some circles teaching Greek to girls was less controversial than teaching Greek to boys. Knowledge of Greek—signifying affluence and culture—may have improved a Jewish girl's marriage prospects, whereas boys might have been led to collaborate with the Roman government or tempted by Greek philosophy. Women who joined the Jewish-ascetic Therapeutae community described by Philo (*On the Contemplative Life* 27–9)—a very select population—must have also possessed a substantial education, both religious and general, as they devoted themselves to the study of scripture and its allegorical interpretation.

Overall, the education of a Jewish woman resembled that of non-Jewish women of the same social classes and locations. Josephus mentions letter-writing among royal women, both Jewish and Roman, and recounts a story about a Jewish maidservant of Livia, named Acme, who wrote letters to Antipater and Herod, including a forged letter she attributed to Salome (*War* 1.640, *Ant.* 17.134–41). Epitaphs from the Roman catacombs suggest female education, as well: one woman is referred to as *discipulina bona*, "a good student/ disciple"; another as *eudidakte*, "easily taught"; and other epitaphs use the term *philentolos* (or *filentolia*), "lover of the commandments," for women (e.g., *CIJ* I, nos. 132, 190, 215, and 482). An inscription at Beth She'arim records the name Eumathia ("good learner"), perhaps reflecting parental hopes for a daughter (*BS* II no. 113). However, Babatha (second century CE, Palestine), by all records a wealthy woman with many social connections whose archive of personal papers was found in the Bar Kokhba caves and is discussed below, was illiterate, although she could sign her name (Heszer 2001).

4   Religious Practices and Identity

Where non-rabbinic documentary and epigraphic sources have enriched (and complicated) our understanding of Jewish women's educational opportunities and expectations in antiquity, they have revolutionized our understanding of women's involvement with religious practices and institutions, particularly in the Diaspora.

The most important institution in Greco-Roman Judaism was the Temple in Jerusalem, until its destruction in 70 CE. Although women were not Temple functionaries, they participated in various Temple rituals. Josephus and rabbinic sources both mention an area of the Temple called the Courtyard of Women (*ezrat nashim*); this was not reserved exclusively for women but was the furthest within the Temple precincts that a woman could enter. While rabbinic law regarded women as exempt from the obligation to make pilgrimage to Jerusalem for the Festivals, women did apparently choose to make pilgrimage, particularly for Passover (Luke 2.41–50; John 19.25; Acts 1.14) and the Festival of Tabernacles (*m. Midd.* 2.5; *t. Sukk.* 4.1; *y. Sukk.* 5.2, 51b). Women were also obligated to go to the Temple to offer sacrifices on specific occasions, such as after the birth of a child or, if the obligation was postponed, multiple children (*m. Ker.* 1.7, 2.4; *t. Ker.* 2.21). Women could also take the Nazirite vow—a temporary ascetic state that involved abstention from wine and all grape products, avoidance of corpses, and cessation of haircutting for the duration of the vow. Completion of the vow was marked by Temple sacrifices. Three women are recorded as having taken the Nazirite vow: Mariamne of Palmyra (*m. Ned.* 6.11; *t. Naz.* 4.10) and Queen Helena of Adiabene (*m. Naz.* 3.6) are named by the Rabbis while Josephus mentions Queen Berenice (*Jewish War* 2.313).

The Temple was, for all its importance, not the only locus of Jewish religious observance. The book of Judith paints an intriguing portrait of women's religious practices in Judea. Judith is said to fast every day, except for Fridays and Saturdays (the Sabbath), the day before and day of the new moon (in Hebrew, *Rosh Hodesh*), and the day before and days of the Festivals (Judith 8.4–7). As part of her plan to assassinate Holophernes, she persuades the guards that she goes out nightly to pray—a scenario the foreign guards find plausible. And, in the wake of her victory, Judith leads the women in a procession to Jerusalem, while the men follow behind bearing garlands and singing hymns. While the uncertain date and origin of Judith make it difficult to derive substantial historical information from the text, the practices it describes were apparently credible, if exemplary. Similarly, literary sources suggest that women could take responsibility for ritual acts such as the circumcision of sons (1 Maccabees 1.60–1) and that their domestic practices could have the status of a binding custom (Tobit 1.8; Kraemer 1992).

Women were present in various sectarian communities as well. A small number of wealthy, well-educated women—apparently older virgins—joined the Therapeutae, mentioned by Philo (noted above). Members of this rigorously ascetic community of celibates spent most of their time in solitude, studying Jewish scriptures and allegorical commentaries and engaging in prayer. Members of the group, male and female, would come together only for Sabbath prayers and a common meal as well as festival observances. Women also joined the Qumran community—not simply as spouses of non-celibate male initiates but as members themselves. Women are mentioned incidentally in various legislative texts: one text mentions a female scribe (4Q274); another seems to indicate that a woman could testify as a witness (1Qsa); and another refers to male and female "elders" (4Q502). Qumranic legal texts are particularly focused on rules governing marriage and sexuality as well as ritual purity. One text, 4Q284, contains a purification ritual for women following menstruation, while another (11QTa L, 10–12) describes how to proceed after the death of a fetus (Crawford 2003). Rabbinic law, likewise, devotes a great deal of space to delineating purity regulations with regard to women, particularly in regard to menstruation. Such purity laws are particularly addressed in the mishnaic tractate *Niddah* and its Talmudic commentaries.

Two other sects—the Pharasaic movement and nascent Christianity—likewise seem to have benefited from the support of women—notably wealthy women, often of non-Jewish birth. Josephus applies the term "God-fearer" to Poppaea, the wife of Nero, although outside the synagogue context this may refer to a broader sympathy for Jews rather than participation in Jewish rituals (*Ant.* 20.195). Women could also became proselytes. The most famous female convert is arguably Queen Helena of Adiabene. Josephus offers a biography of Queen Helena (*Ant.* 20.17–96); she is also mentioned in early rabbinic sources (see *m. Yoma* 3.10; *m. Nazir* 3.6; *b. Sukkah* 2b), and an inscription from an ossuary found in Jerusalem in the Tomb of the Kings (*CIJ* II no. 1388) appears to belong to Queen Helena, whose Jewish name was apparently Sarah. Various epitaphs, from both Jerusalem and the Diaspora, suggest that women converted to Judaism more frequently than men.

Inscriptions describing women as converts and God-fearers suggest a particularly close connection between women and communal ritual spaces (particularly synagogues). We see this early on. In 400 BCE, the Jewish community of Elephantine in Egypt participated in fundraising for the construction of its own Temple; one-third of the named contributors are female, and the petition includes women among those who will pray for the government of Yehud (Judea) should the petition be granted. While our evidence concerning this community suggests that it is exceptional, the evidence also indicates that women were prominent in the creation and support of religious infrastructure from an early period.

Epitaphs and inscriptions from Roman and late antiquity make it clear that women were not only present in the early synagogues (notably in the Diaspora, insofar as current evidence suggests) but that they could hold positions of esteem and possibly significant influence (Brooten 1982). Approximately thirty percent of all named synagogue donors from the Roman Diaspora are women. The distribution of women with official titles correlates with geographic regions where pagan and Christian women received such honors. As surprising as the prominence of women in these inscriptions may be to modern readers, they were probably relatively unexceptional in their original context.

Women bore an array of titles, some of which varied by location and time: *archisy-nagogos-archisynagogissa* ("head of a synagogue"), *archegissa* ("leader"), *presbytera* ("elder"), *mater* ("mother") or *pateressa* (the feminine of "father"), and *hierissa* ("priestess"); the Babylonian Talmud mentions a female synagogue treasurer (*gizbarit;* in *b. Shabb.* 62a). The meanings of these titles are largely uncertain, whether applied to men or women (or, occasionally, minor children). In particular, it is not known whether "priestess" reflects familial association (the daughter or wife of a priest) or some form of ritual role. With the possible exception of priestesses, however, the women mentioned in these inscriptions apparently held office themselves (perhaps as a result of financial support) and did not merely share the honor of an office held by a husband. Among the office-holders are converts, such as Veturia Paula, whose epitaph states: "Veturia Paula, laid in her eternal home, who lived for eighty-six years and six months, a convert (*proselyta*) for sixteen years with the name Sara, mother of the synagogues of Campus and Volumnius. May her sleep be in peace" (*JIWE* II no. 577). Whether the titles borne by these women indicate any ritual role in the synagogue remains an open question. The absence of women from public religious rituals would represent a striking departure from the tendency of Jewish women to conform to the roles of women more generally.

Women who donated to the synagogue were not necessarily Jewish. Claudia Capitolina, the wife of a senator, describes herself as "a most illustrious woman and a God-fearer" in a synagogue inscription from Tralles in Caria in the third century CE; the inscription commemorates her gift of a Torah platform and mosaics to a synagogue in fulfillment of a vow (*DF* no. 30). Julia Severa, credited in an inscription with building a synagogue in Phrygia (*DF* no. 33), is known to have been a high priestess (*archieria*) in the local imperial cult and a judge at the festival games (*agōnothetis*). Unlike Claudia Capitolina, who was also from a prominent family, Julia Severa does not seem to have joined the Jewish community in any formal way. Her reasons for supporting the synagogue are left unstated, but presumably were part of general "civil" benefaction. Less is known about Tation, daughter of Straton, who gave a synagogue building and the colonnade of the courtyard "to the Jews" and was, in return, honored with a gold crown and a front seat (*proedria*) in the synagogue (*CIJ* no. 738). The statement that Tation gave this gift "to the Jews" suggests that she was not herself Jewish, yet she was given a permanent seat of honor in the synagogue. The gift of the seat raises the question of whether men and women sat separately in the synagogue. Segregated seating is attested for Roman religious ritual (which separated people by class, ethnicity, or sex, much as was done in the Temple) and Christian worship, which usually separated men and women; we do not have firm evidence of separate seating in the synagogue until sometime after the eighth century, however (Levine 2001).

Even inscriptions that ascribe Jewish identity to the benefactor, such as the epitaph of Rufina *Ioudaia*, *archisynagogos* in Smyrna (*CIJ* no. 741), are less than clear. The term *Ioudaia* may be a geographic specifier ("from Judea"), indicating her place of origin; an ethnic identifier, indicating her nationality ("the Judean"); a religious term ("the Jewess"); or even a proper name. If it is assumed that Rufina used the term *Ioudaia* religiously, then the issue is raised of whether she was born Jewish or whether the self-conscious identification indicates non-Jewish origin. The use of the term "Jew/Judean" in inscriptions is sufficiently complicated that such a possibility cannot be dismissed out of hand (Kraemer 1989). The fact that Judaism was in transition from patrilineal to matrilineal transmission at this time only further complicates such questions (Cohen 1999).

The home-centeredness of Judaism gives women's religious observance particular importance, as the synagogue was hardly the exclusive location of Jewish piety. Rabbinic sources speak to women's practices in a limited way. According to rabbinic writings, three observances were specifically incumbent upon women: the lighting of candles at the onset of the Sabbath, the burning of a small piece of dough prior to baking bread (*challah*), and the observance of the intricate laws of menstrual purity. Beyond these three tasks, the Rabbis expected women to refrain from transgressing the negative commandments (prohibitions) but exempted them from positive commandments (active requirements) that were obligatory upon men, if those commandments had to be performed at a specific time. In some cases, male observance of commandments was enabled or eased by female exemption (*m. Sukk.* 3.15). The increased marginalization of women from the world of Torah study and synagogue—if such was actually the case—would presumably have resulted in increased domestic and economic responsibilities (and authority).

Over time, many observances from which the Rabbis exempted women, such as the wearing of phylacteries (*tefillin*) and reading the scroll of Esther on Purim, became in practice prohibited, either through the force of legislation or the pressure of custom (Hauptman 1998). Despite the restrictions placed upon women's activity, rabbinic sources readily acknowledge the importance of women in the domestic observances of Judaism. In particular, the Rabbis recognized that women might be more expert in certain matters of Jewish practice than Jewish men and that they might be actively involved in implementing laws that pertained to the household. Likewise, while rabbinic law exempted women (and children) from the obligation of statutory prayer, some sources regard such practices as meritorious (*y. Ber.* 41a, 9d; *b. AZ* 38b–39a; *Soferim* 18.6; see, too, Acts 16.13, 17.4).

If one were to rely on rabbinic sources alone, the domestic religiosity of Jewish women would be severely underestimated. While rabbinic sources are generally hostile to much of what we might call folk religion, such practices, often medical in orientation, were undoubtedly part of the lives of Jewish women in antiquity. Women—like men—would have used (and likely made) potions, amulets, prayers, and magical acts to keep themselves and their families healthy, to regulate fertility (overcome barrenness, facilitate safe pregnancy and childbirth, protect newborns, and so forth), to protect the financial resources (crops, business transactions, etc.), and other essential elements of household survival. We also have evidence of erotic magic (e.g., "love potions"), which may have been intended to secure a liaison or marriage or to excuse elopements after the fact by suggesting the absence of free will (Satlow 2001). Amulets and incantations are often rich with syncretistic language, making the identity of the author and purchaser difficult to ascertain (Naveh 1985; Naveh and Shaked 1993). The home-centeredness of Judaism, which included special festival and Sabbath meals (already attested in the biblical period), would have been the responsibility of women. There was increasing recognition of women as "ritual experts" in Judaism, far beyond the responsibilities of the Rabbis' emphasis on *challah* and Sabbath candles (Sered 1992).

5   Women in Community Life

The prominence of women in the synagogue raises the larger question of women in community life. As noted above, the ideal Hellenistic woman was, among other qualities, modest, and in Greco-Roman antiquity modesty was often associated with seclusion. There is evidence that, among some social classes in some periods, Jewish women were secluded. Philo, for example, records that the men of Alexandria were indignant when their houses were searched for weapons by the prefect Flaccus' men (Flaccus was notoriously anti-Jewish): searching the houses meant exposing the women of the house, "who for modesty's sake avoided the sight of men, even of their closest relations," to the eyes of (non-Jewish) strangers (*Against Flaccus* 89). Literary sources suggest that seclusion was perhaps more common among unmarried women. 2 Maccabees 3.19 refers to "the young women who were kept indoors," and in 4 Maccabees 18.7 Hannah (the mother of the seven martyrs) describes herself as "a pure virgin" before her marriage, who "did not go outside my father's house."

At the same time, other sources suggest the seclusion of women was not routine. The New Testament states without fanfare that three women (Mary Magdalene; Joanna, the wife of Chuza, Herod's steward; and Susanna) traveled with Jesus "through cities and villages" (Luke 8.2)—that is, not only when traveling on religious pilgrimage. Women likewise appear regularly in the book of Acts and the letters of Paul. Finally, it is worth noting the ritual described in *m. Taan.* 4.8. In this rite, unmarried women would, twice a year, bedeck themselves in white garments, dance in the vineyards of Jerusalem, and beckon to the young men to look upon them and choose a bride. While the historicity of this ritual is uncertain, it is presented not as something scandalous but as appropriate, and something to be nostalgic for.

Economic and social realities no doubt influenced the feasibility of seclusion, even where it was an ideal. Women contributed to their household economies and communities in diverse and significant ways. Wealthy women—particularly widows—might oversee estates, own land and animals, lend money, and engage in substantial domestic enterprises. The labor of less wealthy women was essential to household survival: not only raising children but also working at tasks such as baking, weaving, and healing, which served both their own families and also their communities. The book of Tobit describes Sarah, the wife of Tobias, as engaging in "women's work" after Tobias loses his sight (2.11), apparently referring to the weaving of cloth that could then be sold. Jewish women were midwives, weavers, apothecaries, domestic servants, wet nurses, and prostitutes; in rural areas, they would have participated, along with the men, in agricultural activities. Many of these occupations, not to mention ancillary tasks such as employing a scribe, would have involved activity in mixed company and out in the community (such as at the communal oven or a neighbor's house), although some could have been conducted by agency. The social networks fostered by women's roles both domestically and communally no doubt resulted in the acquisition by some women of informal (and thus unrecognized) but substantial political power.

In the end, seclusion does not seem to have been a universal ideal, let alone a reality, even among the Jewish elites. It was, in any case, practicable only for wealthy families where slaves and servants (male and female) were sufficient to permit such isolation. And, even in situations where seclusion was preferred, it seems that some occasions—particularly religious observances such as pilgrimage or attendance at religious rituals—provided an opportunity for public display. "Modesty" presumably involved not physical isolation but rather modest dress, not speaking to men, not being alone with unrelated men, and other more practical, less extravagant behavioral restrictions.

While the seclusion of women may have been practiced by some wealthy families, the royal women of Judea possessed great autonomy. Like non-Jewish Hellenistic queens (notably Cleopatra), these royal women were active in politics, achieving as a result both fame and notoriety. The Hasmonean queen, Shelamzion Alexandra, ruled Judea from 76 to 67 BCE after the death of her husband, Alexander Yannai. She features prominently in Josephus' history, and she is remembered fondly in rabbinic sources, probably because she was a well-known partisan of the Pharisees against the Sadducees. She is also named twice in the Dead Sea Scrolls (4Q322 and 4Q324). After Shelamzion's death, civil war broke out between her two sons, which led to the loss of Judean independence and, eventually, the rise of the Herodian dynasty under Roman patronage. Shelamzion Alexandra's granddaughter, Alexandra, clashed repeatedly with Herod, who probably drowned Alexandra's son, Aristobulus III (his rival) and eventually executed her daughter Mariamne (his wife). After Herod executed Mariamne, Alexandra plotted a rebellion, which was discovered, and Alexandra—like every other surviving Hasmonean—was put to death by Herod in 26 BCE.

Among the most famous of the Herodian women is Berenice, the daughter of Agrippa I (Herod's grandson) and his queen, Cyprus; Berenice's name as a Roman citizen was Julia, and she is mentioned not only by Josephus but also in rabbinic literature, the New Testament, and by various Roman authors (including Juvenal, who accused her of committing incest with her brother in *Satire* 6.155–8). She was married three times: first to Marcus, a nephew of Philo of Alexandria; then to two kings (the first, Herod of Chalcis, was her uncle; the second, Polemo of Cilicia, was not born Jewish but was circumcised prior to their marriage). Berenice was present in Jerusalem, apparently fulfilling a religious vow, when the Great Revolt against Rome began. While Josephus—probably for diplomatic reasons—depicts Berenice as actively seeking to make peace between the Jews and Romans (*War* 2.313, 333, 402–5), Tacitus asserts that she sided with the Romans (*Histories* 2.81.2), and he reports that Berenice began an affair with Titus (the general who would destroy the Temple) in 68 CE (*Histories* 2.2.1). According to both Suetonius and Cassius Dio, in 75 CE Berenice moved to Rome as Titus' consort, although public pressure led to her dismissal; when Titus became emperor in 79 CE, Berenice apparently made an unsuccessful bid to return to his favor (Suetonius, *Titus* 7.1; Cassius Dio, *Roman History* 66.15.3–4). Although Berenice failed to regain Titus' favor, Josephus refrained from writing anything negative about her until after Titus' death.

As evidence of how small and interconnected the upper class of Jewish society was, Berenice's granddaughter, Julia Crispina (daughter of Berenice's son, Berenicianus), appears in the Babatha archives—discovered in the Bar Kokhba caves—as a guardian of Babatha's sons.

6 Marriage and Divorce

Berenice's first marriage was contracted when she was approximately thirteen, the average age for a Roman woman to marry. Based on epigraphic evidence, the average age among Jews more generally seems to have been somewhat older, perhaps fifteen, although rabbinic sources assume women were betrothed as children and girls could wed at twelve (Satlow 2001).

Marriage ranked among the single most important transitions in a woman's status in antiquity, and it was encompassed by significant philosophical and legal structures. Most important among these are wedding contracts and bills of divorce. These legal records of actual marriages and divorces help to flesh out the extensive, often conflicting, composite that emerges from rabbinic sources, epitaphs, and narrative literature.

We possess four major "archives" of women's documents from antiquity: two from Elephantine (fifth century BCE) and two from the Judean desert (second century CE). The Elephantine documents pertain to the families of two women: Mibtahiah, the daughter of a wealthy family; and Tamet, a slave, and her free daughter, Jehoishma. The two Judean archives belonged to Babatha and Salome Komaise, both members of the wealthy landed class in southern Judea and probably neighbors. These two sets of archives consist of legal documents and as such deal primarily with the economic aspects of marriage: the distribution of property, bride-price, dowries, and so forth. In particular, the documents reveal strategies by which families sought to protect (and improve) the finances of daughters and to retain paternal-family control of estates. Implicitly, these documents attest to relatively small family size and reveal a great deal of fluidity in terms of contract language and marriage custom. Often property transfers and marriage documents appear to be connected not simply to a wedding but to the anticipation of the birth of a child.

The legal language in these archives is significantly more fluid than a strict reading of rabbinic sources would indicate. Of particular interest in the Elephantine documents is the formula of repudiation included in the "documents of wifehood." According to the documents at Elephantine, either spouse could initiate a divorce by publicly declaring his or her "hate" for the other and paying a financial penalty. This directly contradicts rabbinic law, according to which only the husband may initiate divorce. Many documents from antiquity reveal "non-normative" approaches to the dissolution of a marriage, at least as "normative" came to be defined in later periods. (To complicate the picture further, there is evidence that women could initiate divorce within biblical law, contrary to the usual understanding of Deuteronomy 24.1–4.) Helladote, cited above, appealed to King Ptolemy for redress after her Jewish/Judean husband divorced her in a fashion she found unacceptable. In the second century CE, a woman named Shelamzion issued a bill of divorce to her husband Eleazar (Papyrus *Se'elim* 13) and, in 13 BCE, a Jewish couple, Apollonia (apparently Jewish) and her husband, Hermogenes, agreed to a mutual divorce (*CPJ*, no. 144). Josephus describes how the Herodian women, including Herodias and Salome, acquired certificates of Roman divorce (*repudium*), "which was not in accordance with Jewish law" (*Ant.* 15.259–60; see also *Ant.* 18.109–11; 20.141–7). It is evident that "Jewish law" (however it was understood) was not the final authority on divorce in antiquity. During Hellenistic and Roman times, recourse to non-Jewish law (in divorce or other contexts) appears to have been chosen when it was likely to benefit the appealing party.

In terms of marriage partner, the sources indicate, on the one hand, a strong preference for endogamy but, at the same time, the existence of exogamy ("intermarriage"). Families—specifically fathers—were important agents in arranging marriages for daughters, and certainly in negotiating arrangements once a match had been accepted. That said, women appear to have had the right of refusal. Within sectarian movements, such as the Qumran community and the Pharisees, there were severely restrictive rules on marriage. Rabbinic law, likewise, created a system of "castes" within Judaism that further restricted marital prospects. At the same time, in addition to the evidence of exogamy in the legal documents—which can present problems in terms of identifying the religion/ethnicity of named individuals and do not address subjects such as conversion—after 212 CE, Jews could avail themselves of "civil" marriage with non-Jews under Roman law. The fact that the Church council of Elvira in 306 CE and imperial legislation from the fourth century both prohibit Jewish–Christian marriages suggests that such marriages took place.

It is during antiquity that we see a more clearly articulated monogamous ideal in western Judaism, although polygyny (the taking of multiple wives) remained a legal possibility in Judaism and was actively practiced among Babylonian Jews. A preference for monogamy or polygyny depends largely on the expectations of the majority culture (in situations where multiple wives connote status), relative numbers of men and women (affected by deaths in childbirth and war), and finances. In biblical times, polygyny would have been practiced only by the wealthiest members of society, and the biblical text itself reflects ambivalence towards the practice. Although it was presumably rare, Josephus nevertheless felt the need to excuse polygyny as a Jewish *patrios* (ancestral custom) in several locations (*War* 1.477, *Ant.* 17.14). Jewish polygyny remained a sufficiently valid possibility that it was condemned by the Qumran community (*CD* IV.19–V.2) and, centuries later, had to be prohibited by Theodosius in 393 CE and again by Justinian in 537 CE. Non-first wives were typically widows or divorced women—this was the case with Babatha's second marriage, in which she was a second wife. Jewish epitaphs rarely mention the *univira* (the woman who does not remarry after her husband's death), although the literary character Judith is such a type; it seems likely that most Jewish widows remarried. The ongoing practice of levirate marriage, in which a childless widow marries her husband's brother (see Deuteronomy 25.5–9), relied on the ability of men to take second wives, as childless widows would have been less than ideal first/only wives. Jews also practiced non-marital cohabitation, such as we see with Tamet, whose marriage was contracted after the birth of her first child; and there is some evidence of concubinage, in which women had a status between wife and prostitute (Satlow 2001).

Most of the documentary evidence of marriage that we possess is legal in nature and thus sheds little light on emotion or sentiment. Magical charms designed to compel a man to love a woman offer some evidence of female desire, if not empowerment. Philo, who in some locations writes negatively of marriage (in keeping with Platonism), nonetheless writes sympathetically of the man who declines to divorce his barren wife though her failure to bear children permits or even requires him to do so (*On the Special Laws* 3.35). Similarly, the apocryphal story of Tobit depicts affection and mutual respect between married couples, and the marriage between Sarah and Tobias is a love match. Rabbinic sources also include anecdotes attesting to spousal affection and appreciation. Finally, the Latin metrical epitaph for Regina by her grieving husband offers unusual but extremely eloquent testimony of a husband's love for his wife (*JIWE* II no. 103).

7   Conclusions

The lives of Jewish women in the ancient world generally resembled those of their non-Jewish counterparts. Where women were educated, Jewish women were, and where illiteracy was common, it was common for Jewish women as well. Even in settings where Jewish and non-Jewish law conflicted, such as the unilateral male right to initiate divorce in Judaism, some Jewish women appear to have had the means to acquire the rights their non-Jewish peers expected. Judaism was still very much in formation in the early centuries of the Common Era; rabbinic sources, not yet authoritative and widespread, often reflect an attempt to codify and explicitly Judaize existing practices. The result of this codification was often detrimental to women, who were increasingly restricted from the public realm and, in particular, the valued world of Torah study. That said, the rabbinicization of Judaism in late antiquity and the Middle Ages was itself a dynamic and complicated process, with episodes of improved treatment of women and periods of decline.

RECOMMENDED FURTHER READING

The first challenge confronting scholars who work on the subject of Jewish women in antiquity arises from the complicated nature of the source materials, which include legal documents, inscriptions, literary and historical writings, and sectarian religious works (including the massive body of rabbinic writings as well as the New Testament and the Dead Sea Scrolls). Owing to the quantity and complexity of these sources, most secondary works deal with specific subsets of writings, particularly rabbinic writings and inscriptions. An excellent overview of the issues can be gained by reading the chapters by Kraemer (1991a) and Wegner (1991).

Traditionally, rabbinic writings were regarded as descriptive of Jewish life in antiquity; now, however, they are approached as revealing more a set of complicated ideals and possibilities. Among the most important works that approach the status of women through the lens of rabbinic law (particularly the Mishnah and the two Talmuds) are Wegner (1988), Ilan (1997), Hauptman (1998), and Labovitz (2009). In recent decades, the importance of rabbinic exegetical traditions (*midrash*) has also been recognized. Two works focusing on this non-legal rabbinic material are Peskowitz (1997)and Baskin (2002).

In recent decades, documentary and epigraphic materials have provided a significant complement to rabbinic writings, often seriously complicating the theoretical material in the traditional sources. Of particular significance is the groundbreaking work of Brooten (1982). Ross Shephard Kraemer's writings provide a very helpful synthesis and analysis of the most important inscriptions; see, in particular, Kraemer (1992) and its companion volume, Kraemer (2004). Williams (1998) provides a very convenient and accessible source of the most important epigraphic evidence. For a discussion of some of the most important documentary evidence, including the marriage and divorce documents from the Bar Kokhba caves, see Satlow (2001).

Many of the above works, of course, draw on a variety of sources even if they favor a few, and several works stand out for their nuanced synthesis of various kinds of material; in particular, Ilan (1999) and Satlow (2001) are useful studies in terms of both content and method, and relatively broad in focus. Somewhat more narrowly, Ilan (2006) uses the story of Shelamzion Alexandra as a way of modeling how diverse sources—rabbinic works, the Dead Sea Scrolls, and Josephus (among others)—can be used to construct nuanced history. Meyers (2008), in turn, provides a fine example of how material culture can illuminate readings of literary sources.

25

Women, Education, and Philosophy

Marguerite Deslauriers

1   Introduction: Issues and Evidence

Virtually all the surviving evidence concerning ancient philosophy, and women in ancient philosophy, is literary (rather than visual or epigraphic). In what follows, I will, as a preliminary, discuss some of the issues with the evidence for women's philosophical activity and women's education. I will then provide an overview of women who were called philosophers or engaged in philosophy in some way; but the evidence for such women and their intellectual work is questionable. The most extensive evidence we have about women in ancient philosophy and the issues around women is found in men's philosophical treatises, where we find discussions of women's nature, capacities, and virtues. I survey this in the third section. Finally, I consider what we can know of women's education, and how that education probably reflected contemporary views of women's capacities and appropriate social roles.

There is some visual and epigraphic evidence to suggest that some women were literate and educated (see Section 4). The evidence that women engaged in philosophy is, however, entirely literary, and problematic. The different literary forms are of different value (see Pomeroy 1975: x–xi)—we probably should not trust the representations of women in tragedy, whereas rhetorical and philosophical texts do, at least, tell us what the issues were presumed to be. But evidence for the structure of a debate about the nature and social role of women does not tell us much about the facts: did women engage in philosophical practice? If so, what did they say, and what did they write? If not, why were they absent from philosophical activity?

There are two kinds of difficulty in saying anything about women philosophers in the ancient world. The first is that works are sometimes attributed to women when there is no independent evidence to establish the existence of the women in question, or, where there is evidence that the woman lived, no evidence to corroborate that she was the author of the work in question. Since we know that men sometimes wrote pseudonymously as women, we have to doubt authorship in cases where we do not have good evidence linking a

A Companion to Women in the Ancient World, First Edition. Edited by Sharon L. James and Sheila Dillon.
© 2012 John Wiley & Sons, Ltd. Published 2015 by John Wiley & Sons, Ltd.

particular woman to a particular text. We are obliged, then, to question the authenticity of female authorship in some cases because we know that men sometimes presented themselves as women authors. The reason for this practice, implied by Lefkowitz and Fant (2005: 163), is that many of the surviving texts and fragments of texts associated with the names of women are didactic, urging women to avoid lavishness of dress, to practice chastity, to keep their husbands' interests at heart—in short, to follow the norms of contemporary feminine virtue. Because these texts represent, and advocate, the interests of men, we might doubt that they were written by women.

A second difficulty has to do with the determination of philosophical content. What counts as a philosophical text? Surely one that raises philosophical questions. But which questions are those? Do the sort of texts in which women are exhorted to dress modestly and practice chastity amount to contributions to moral philosophy? I am going to stipulate here that they do not, and that I am treating as philosophical only those texts that center on issues that other ancient philosophers would have considered philosophical (this spans a broad range, including logic, natural philosophy, moral philosophy, and metaphysics). On this basis, work in music theory and in gynecology count as philosophical, but moral platitudes do not.

Among the ancient texts that have been transmitted to us, those attributed to women are scant, and few of them are philosophical (many more, for example, are literary). In almost every case where we have a philosophical text (usually a fragment of a text) said to be authored by a woman, it is unclear which woman is supposed to have written it, and there is often evidence to suggest that it was in fact written by a man but attributed—either by its own author or by later commentators—to a woman. In cases where we have independent historical evidence for the existence of particular women said to have been philosophical, we do not have a text, but only second-person accounts of the work. There are, then, very few philosophical texts attributed to a woman with good evidence that a particular historical woman wrote them.

The reasons are several, and one might suppose that literacy and illiteracy were the most important. That is, one might suppose that literacy would be a requirement for philosophical debate, and since women were less likely to be instructed in reading and writing they would be less likely to meet that requirement. But philosophy in the ancient world was as much an oral practice as a written practice—and possibly more. Socrates, most famously, wrote nothing, and the accounts we have of his philosophical methods and of his views come to us second hand. Both the Academy and the Lyceum took spoken discourse as the primary form of philosophical inquiry. So the most obvious practical constraint on women was not illiteracy, but the prohibition on public speech. A woman's modesty, hence her social standing, would be compromised by her engagement in philosophical discussion. Evidence for this can be found in the rumors of sexual license that attend almost every ancient woman philosopher. An interesting instance of this is the following remark: "Generally speaking, famous intellectual women of antiquity are free and easy in matters of sexual morality, for the mere act of being a philosopher would involve abandoning the traditional pursuits of women and entering into debate with men" (Rist 1965: 220). That entering into debate with men should be considered to be a matter of sexual morality reveals the obstacles to philosophical engagement women encountered in a context where philosophy was, first and foremost, a practice of debate.

Moreover, philosophical discussion as it was practiced in ancient Athens was a social endeavor, inclusion in which depended on acquaintance with someone already admitted to a philosophical circle. So, a woman who wished to practice philosophy had not only to be willing to transgress social boundaries but also to know a man willing to help her do so. Hipparchia (c. 250 BCE), who Diogenes Laertius tells us "fell in love with both Crates' discourses and his way of life" and married him, took to wearing the same clothes he did, going about in public with him, and talking philosophy—but she was able to do this only because Crates allowed it (Diogenes Laertius 6.96–8, Hicks 1925; transl. Lefkowitz and Fant 2005: 167).

With respect to philosophy, as with so much else in the ancient world, what we do not know is what women thought, both about the philosophical questions that occupied their male contemporaries and about the exclusion of women from the practice of philosophy. If we can trust the literary sources, philosophers, then as now, were regarded more with disdain or pity (as bumbling, impractical, and unworldly) than with respect—and this may have softened any disappointment women might have felt at their own exclusion from philosophical schools. It is also possible, of course, that women engaged in philosophical debates among themselves, since the absence of evidence of women doing philosophy might be a question of transmission. This is all to say that we do not know what women thought, if anything, about philosophy or their exclusion from it.

The absence of women in the recorded debates of ancient philosophy raises certain questions for the history of philosophy. Philosophy more than other disciplines has had its subject matter determined by its practitioners. Moral and political questions, in particular, have been set by the interests of those who engaged in philosophy. Would the questions central to the history of philosophy have been different had women been admitted to philosophical practice? It is impossible to know. This much, however, is clear: the absence of women from ancient philosophy has meant that answers to the question of sexual difference—whether, and how, women are different from men—were established, and positions marked off, before women had an opportunity to enter the debate.

Moreover, the exclusion of women from reason begins with the exclusion of women from philosophy, and that has had implications for women beyond philosophy. The ancient debate about women and their differences from men centered on the question of whether the rational faculty of women was the same as that of men. That question has a long history into the early modern and modern periods, and, although most philosophers end up asserting that women, like men, have reason, the qualifications to that claim have been sufficient to mark women off in popular conceptions of gender as unreasoning or unreasonable creatures. Feminist reactions to that characterization of women sometimes emerged as hostility to the very notion of reason as a marker of humanity, since reason had become historically so closely associated with masculinity.

Another feminist reaction to the exclusion of women from philosophy has been the attempt to suggest that women were not excluded as thoroughly as we might suppose (see Wider 1986; Waithe 1987). This is motivated by admirable principles—to demonstrate that women are remarkable for being able to overcome obstacles and social forces intended to prevent them from developing their capacities for intellectual and creative work. But we should be careful not to misrepresent the ease with which women have been able to overcome the structural obstacles of institutions and widespread social practices. And that means taking seriously the possibility that there were no, or very, very few, ancient women who engaged in philosophical activities. Philosophy, then as now, was a social practice, engagement with which was predicated on an education and on certain social freedoms, neither of which women enjoyed.

2   Some Women Philosophers

Although there are no contemporary reports from the sixth century BCE of women engaged in philosophy, later writers mention a tradition associating Pythagoras and Pythagorean philosophy with women. If authentic, these would be the first women philosophers. Pythagoras is said to have taken his ethical doctrines from Themistoclea, the priestess at Delphi, suggesting that the origins of Pythagoreanism lay with a woman (Diogenes Laertius 5.341). Moreover, the women in Pythagoras' immediate family circle are reported to have been philosophers. His student and then wife Theano is quoted by Stobaeus (Wachsmuth and Hense 1884: 1.10.13) (although some of the texts attributed to Theano are attributed by Waithe to a second Theano, "Theano II"). Arignote, the daughter of Pythagoras and Theano, is alleged to be the author of one of the "sacred discourses" (Delatte 1915: 217). Another of their daughters, Myia, is mentioned as the author of a letter to someone called Phyllis (Thesleff 1965: 125).

These Pythagorean texts have a number of themes, some clearly philosophical (whether they were actually written by women connected with Pythagoras is another question). As one might expect, given the Pythagorean interest in mathematics, Arignote, in the fragment we have attributed to her, is concerned with number. And in the text attributed to Theano the author writes that all things come to be "in accordance with number." Theano is also supposed to have held views on the immortality of the soul and on chastity. Myia's letter, by contrast, concerns child-rearing. Waithe asserts that this demonstrates "what it is that Pythagorean women see themselves really doing through their letters and texts ... It is their task as women philosophers to teach to other women that which women need to know if they are to live their lives harmoniously" (1987: 16–17). The textual evidence is too fragmentary to support this kind of generalization. In particular, assuming that the authors of these texts were women, we cannot know that they undertook to write *as* women—that is, we cannot know that they thought they had some special epistemological standing as women.

We have some texts attributed to "late" Pythagorean women, who lived between the fourth and second centuries BCE. Among the texts collected by Thesleff, several are attributed to women: Aesara of Lucania, Phintys of Sparta, Perictione I and II, Theano II. As the names themselves suggest, our knowledge of these women is imperfect, and the reasons for attributing the texts in question to them are problematic. For example, two texts are attributed to an author called Perictione (distinguished by Allen and Waithe as two authors), one in Ionic prose (*On the Harmony of Women*) and one in Doric (a text partly identical to a work by Archytas of the same name, *On Wisdom*). Although Perictione was the name of Plato's mother, and there is evidence for her existence, as Plant points out, "Both the dates of the works and their dialects mean Perictione the mother of Plato could not have written them. We have then two Pythagorean texts, attributed to otherwise unknown women named Perictione who should be dated perhaps one hundred years apart" (2004: 76). Moreover, although Waithe argues that *On the Harmony of Women* is a philosophical work invoking the principle of harmony as a normative rule for women's lives, it is largely an exhortation to follow contemporary conventions of femininity and further the interests of men, as are the work *On Chastity* attributed to Phintys and the letters Waithe attributes to Theano II. It is not that these works are devoid of philosophical claims, but rather that insofar as they involve philosophical claims they do so only to uphold the subject position of women without critical analysis.

Two women mentioned by Plato are sometimes described as ancient women philosophers: Aspasia (*Menexenus* 236d–249e) and Diotima (*Symposium* 201d–203a, using the text of Burnett 1903). Aspasia (fl. 450 BCE) is also mentioned by Aristophanes (*Acharnians* 516–39) and by Plutarch, according to whom she was from Miletus (Plutarch 24.2). She was associated with Pericles (and often described as his concubine), and her reputation was both as an intellectual and, especially later, as a sexual expert. But the only texts we have attributed to her are two poems cited by Athenaeus (5.219c, 220e), written around 125 BCE, and they are unlikely to be genuine, and are at any rate without philosophical merit. Diotima is described by Plato in the *Symposium* as a "priestess"; Socrates reports what she told him, and she herself represents what she says as a message from the god. Dover, expressing the opinion of most scholars, says, "We do not know whether Diotima is real or fictitious, and it does not much matter, considering the extreme improbability ... that even if she really existed she entertained the Platonic theory of ideas in any form" (1980: 137). Waithe, by contrast, argues that, because what Diotima is reported to have said differs in certain ways from what Socrates in other dialogues has said, we should suppose that she was a historical figure with independent views. But Socrates himself says different things in different dialogues, so that seems insufficient evidence to warrant the conclusion that there was a priestess Diotima who developed her own philosophical views.

Two women who deserve special attention as philosophically significant are Ptolemais and Hypatia. Ptolemais, whose dates are uncertain but who may have lived around 250 BCE, is mentioned by Porphyry in his *Commentary on the Harmonics of Ptolemy*. According to him, she came from Cyrene and wrote a work called *The Pythagorean Principles of Music*, which Porphyry quotes. Although Porphyry says that he has made some changes in the passage, and it is unclear where the quotation ends and Porphyry resumes his own remarks, this appears to be a genuine example of philosophical work by an ancient woman. The question Ptolemais addresses is the difference between approaches to harmonics based on theory as contrasted with those based on perception. Ptolemais aligns herself with Aristoxenus, who she says "regarded perception as authoritative, and reason as accompanying it, and for necessity only" (Düring 1980: 22–6; Plant 2004: 88).

Hypatia was born in Alexandria around 370 CE and died there, murdered by a crowd of monks, in 415 (see also Moss, this volume, Chapter 37). Since her father taught mathematics at the Museum in Alexandria, we assume that he educated her; she may also have studied philosophy in Athens. Hypatia's work was mathematical (the Byzantine encyclopedia called the Suda *Lexicon*, which is the source of most of what we know about Hypatia, mentions commentaries on Diophantus' *Arithmeticorum*, on Ptolemy's *Syntaxis Mathematica*, and on the *Conic Sections* of Apollonius Pergaeus) but also philosophical. She lectured to students and held some kind of public position, since she was paid by public funds in Alexandria. Hoche argues that she took on the direction of Plotinus' school (1860: 439); Rist claims that she "accepted, taught, and handed on a conservative Platonism to a mixed pagan and Christian audience" (1965: 224). The Suda asserts that all of Hypatia's works had been lost, and most scholars accept that we have nothing of her writings. Waithe, however, argues that part of the commentary on Ptolemy survived "unquestionably," attributed to her father rather than her, and that we may have the commentary on Diophantus "interpolated into the original text." Hypatia was murdered most probably because she was associated with the prefect Orestes and was believed to have prevented his reconciliation with Cyril the patriarch—that is, murdered for political rather than philosophical reasons.

Ptolemais and Hypatia are important because they have the best claim to have engaged in serious philosophical work that was recognized as such by their contemporaries despite their sex. Because their work concerns technical philosophical matters it is unlikely to have been attributed to women as a way of confirming social norms. Musical theory and mathematics were part of the philosophical canon but not among the accomplishments of many women in the ancient world. It is pertinent to mention here a few other women (some of whom may not have existed) whose work raises interesting philosophical points about the soul, points that have some bearing on the capacities of women for intellectual work.

The first is Aesara, a "late" Pythagorean, to whom a surviving fragment of a work called *On Human Nature* is attributed by Stobaeus (1.49.27). In this fragment, Aesara presents a tripartite soul, similar to the Platonic division into reason, "spiritedness," and desire. The soul constitutes a single thing precisely because the parts are different, but the composite whole they constitute, when the best part rules the others, displays "unanimity and friendship and justice." The division of the soul is Platonic, and the claim that differences between the parts contribute to unity rather than disturbing it can be found in Aristotle's *Politics* (II. 2. 1261b6–15). The interesting feature of the discussion in this fragment is that Aesara draws a parallel between the structure of the soul, the household, and the political community, arguing that friendship in the larger social structures depends on differences in the parts, just as the good order of the soul creates unity. This is a contribution to a contemporary debate about the relation of the structure of the individual to that of the household and the city.

The historicity of Phintys, whom Stobaeus tells us was a Spartan and the daughter of Callicrates, and Iamblichus says was the daughter of Theophrius from Croton, is in doubt, as is the authenticity of the work *On the Chastity of Women* attributed to her; the Doric dialect would date the work to the fifth century BCE, but some oddities suggest it was written in the third century in an earlier style (Stobaeus 4.23.61; Iamblichus; Dillon and Hershbell 1991; see also Plant 2004: 84). Further, the content of *On the Chastity of Women* is largely conventional advice to cultivate chastity as a virtue. But it includes a very rare discussion of women and philosophy, in which the author claims that "courage and justice and intelligence are common to both" men and women, implying that women are capable of philosophy, even if it is less natural to them than to men. The author allows that many people think women should not do philosophy any more than they should ride horses or speak in public, and agrees that some activities should be restricted to men (generalship, political activity, public speaking) and some to women (housekeeping, staying indoors, caring for men). At the same time, the author says that the virtues of the body and the virtues of the soul are suitable for both men and women, where those virtues include courage, justice, and intelligence. So, although chastity is the most important of the virtues for women, intelligence, and hence at least the capacity for rational thought and philosophy, is appropriate for women. One can find in both Plato and Xenophon variations on the claim that women and men have the same virtues, but only in the text by Phintys is that claim connected to the suggestion that women might engage in philosophical activity.

Although we have no texts written by the fourth century CE philosopher Makrina, her brother Gregory of Nyssa wrote her biography in the *Vita Macrinae*, and recorded a conversation he had had with her at the end of her life in the dialogue *De anima et resurrectione* (Migne 1857–66: 46; Maraval 1971). This work is interesting insofar as it represents Makrina asserting that the *pathe* (ways in which the soul might be affected;

e.g., anger, desire, sorrow, joy) are not part of the soul, but "incrustations" of it. The evidence for this is (1) that the soul is made "in God's image" and God does not have *pathe* and (2) that we are able to fight our *pathe*, so they cannot be essential to the soul. This view differs from that of Plato and Aristotle, both of whom attribute to the soul a faculty for desire and assume that the affects, while they need to be controlled by reason, are an essential part of a human soul. Why did Makrina separate affect from the soul? Wolfskeel suggests that in reducing the human soul to its intellectual component Makrina is urging a view of the soul as sexless—since women were held responsible for the evil *pathe* (Wolfskeel 1987: 146). The point needs to be elaborated. Aristotle, as we will see, suggested that the rational faculty of women was somehow without authority. Some later commentators assumed this meant that the intellectual faculty of women could be overwhelmed by affect more easily than could men's. So, arguing for the soul as strictly intellectual might make it possible to counter any claim that women are intrinsically more subject to affect than men.

Much of what is attributed to ancient women as philosophy is advice to women— generally to be chaste and temperate in other ways, to dress modestly and without ostentation, and to devote themselves to their husbands' comfort. In the few texts with themes that are embedded more evidently in philosophical debates of the times— concerned with the soul, virtue, reason, politics, or musical theory—there is no thread that unites the work attributed to women. What we find, then, is that the texts attributed to women about women tend, if anything, to affirm the conventions of femininity and the social roles of women. The texts attributed to women that are not concerned with women do not distinguish themselves from work attributed to men. If I have been ungenerous in counting ancient women philosophers, my concern has been not to underplay the obstacles preventing women from practicing philosophy in the ancient world and the obstacles preventing us from knowing whether they did. Attempts to recuperate ancient philosophy by women, with the aim presumably of demonstrating that women have always been capable of philosophy, often overstate the reliability or usefulness of the evidence authenticating the texts. We are perhaps better off acknowledging how difficult it is to know what women in the ancient world thought about philosophy, or achieved in philosophical terms. Although there is no evidence for ancient feminist philosophy by women, and little evidence even that women conceived of their philosophical contributions as peculiarly "feminine," there was a debate in ancient Greece about the nature and intellectual capacities of women, a debate into which women themselves apparently did not enter.

3   Philosophical Issues Concerning Women

The conception of women and men as significantly and intrinsically different probably has its philosophical origins with Pythagoreans and the list of opposites generated in that circle. The lists distinguish not only male and female but also left and right, hot and cold, odd and even, limit and unlimited, one and plurality, resting and moving, straight and curved, light and darkness, good and bad, square and oblong (Aristotle, *Meta.* I. 5. 986a21–6; see also Parker, this volume, Chapter 8). The female is aligned with left, hot, odd, unlimited, moving, curved, darkness, bad, and oblong—the mathematical, the metaphysical, and the moral aligned in inferiority. So the origin of sexual distinction as a metaphysical claim is also linked with the origin of the conceptual denigration of women, but the texts we have are insufficient to warrant the claim that Pythagorean philosophers were committed to the view that women are by nature inferior to men. Moreover, we have to consider the long-lived, although possibly apocryphal, attribution of some Pythagorean texts to women, and so the tradition within philosophical writing that Pythagoreanism was willing to admit women to the philosophical circle.

Although the metaphysical distinction between the sexes certainly appears early in ancient philosophy, it is also contested, both as to fact and as to nature. The distinction is purposefully blurred by Plato, who suggests that the differences between men and women are more like differences between hairy and smooth men than like the differences between people and, say, hedgehogs (Plato, *Rep.* V 454c–e). That is, Plato questions whether the differences between men and women are natural differences that distinguish what purpose each sex should serve or rather natural differences that may interest us but do not determine different functions for the sexes.

Aristotle, reacting to Plato's suggestion, reasserts sexual difference as a metaphysical and functional difference. He claims that male and female are opposites—the most different of the same kind of thing. So, in any given species, male and female are the most different things. But Aristotle, too, is concerned not to treat sexual difference as the sort of difference in essence that would divide a species into sub-species. And so he argues that sexual difference is not a difference in the essence but a difference in the matter of the genus (*Meta.* X. 9. 1058b21–5). What this means is unclear, but it is certainly intended to preserve the integrity of animal species while indicating that sexual difference is not as incidental as the difference between hirsute and smooth men.

Aristotle also treats sexual difference as a biological phenomenon. In so doing he is entering a discussion, initiated by certain pre-Socratic philosophers (Anaxagoras, Empedocles, and Democritus, according to Aristotle *GA* IV. 1. 764a27–b23), about the determination of sex in the embryo—what is responsible for the production of a male or a female offspring? Most ancient accounts understand the sex of an individual to be a question of the resemblance of an individual to one or other of its parents (so that a female hedgehog resembles its mother with respect to sex, just as it might resemble its mother rather than its father in the shape of its snout or some other feature). They assume that both male and female parents contribute something material to the offspring, and speculate about the mechanism that determines which contribution will prevail in the offspring. Aristotle, while denying that the male parent contributes anything material, does preserve the language of prevailing or mastery, and asserts that the offspring will be female whenever the formal contribution of the male (transmitted through motions, usually in the semen) fails to exercise mastery over the matter provided by the female (*GA* IV. 1. 766a16–23).

At the same time, Aristotle extends the discussion of sexual difference begun by the pre-Socratics by asking not only how females are produced but what, exactly, it means for something to be male or female biologically. His answer is that the male is able to concoct blood up to the point where it is semen that can transmit the form or essence of the kind, whereas the female is able to concoct blood only up to the point where it is matter with the potential to be informed by the species form (conveyed by the semen) (*GA* IV. 1. 765b9–15). So, if Aristotle has a metaphysical account of sexual difference as opposition within an essential sameness, he also has a biological account of sexual difference in functional terms, where the differences in concoction that he attributes to male and female are, in bodily terms, differences in heat.

Plato, by contrast, despite some suggestion otherwise (see *Timaeus* 90e–91d), does not have a biology of sex. Indeed, Aristotle is the only ancient who treats sex as both a biological question and a metaphysical or political question. So, for example, the medical writers take an interest in the question of whether male and female contribute different things to the embryo, and that debate runs from the pre-Socratic authors and the Hippocratic author of *On Generation* through Aristotle and beyond to Galen, who takes up the question to disagree with Aristotle (Galen *de Semine* II 67–74). While Aristotle would not have thought that his biological work was less philosophical than his political work, it is true that the discussion of sexual difference as a political difference, in the work of Plato, Aristotle, and Xenophon, has had the strongest impact on the history of conceptualizations of sex and gender.

Plato, through the character of Socrates, is the first to raise the question of whether the social distinctions instituted in Athenian life between men and women are justified philosophically. If the practical question is whether women and men should be educated and trained in the same skills, and should subsequently be assigned the same tasks in city life, the philosophical question is whether women can have the same virtues as men. That is, if women and men have different souls with different capacities for virtue, there is no point educating them in the same way and it would be pointless or, worse, disastrous to give women the same responsibilities as men.

Plato argues explicitly that the virtues of women are identical to those of men (Plato, *Meno* 71a–73d). That is, the moral and intellectual capacities are no different in men and women. Xenophon, too, implies that the virtue of men and women is the same (*Oeconomicus* 7.14–15). If this is the case, then it makes sense to cultivate those capacities in the same ways. In the *Republic*, extending the argument about virtue to its political corollary, and acknowledging that what he says conflicts with contemporary Athenian practice, Plato's Socrates argues that women ought to be educated as men are, ought to live communally rather than privately, and ought to engage in political and military work alongside men (*Rep.* V 456c–d, 457c–d, 455d, 456a). More than this, Plato suggests that the ideal city, the *kallipolis*, depends on treating sexual difference, at least among those in the guardian class, as incidental to political and moral questions.

Aristotle, by contrast, in his *Politics*, suggests that the virtues of women must be different in kind from those of men, and not only in degree (*Pol.* I 13 1259b38–1260a7). Aristotle's discussion is interesting because he recognizes that the exclusion of women from political life is unjust if women in fact have souls that are identical to those of men, and hence have capacities for virtue just like men. At the same time, he also understands that if one justifies the exclusion of women by arguing that women have souls that are not rational then effectively one is arguing that women do not belong to the human species with men. We have seen above that Aristotle does not think sex can divide a species into sub-species, and so he is left to argue that women have a rational capacity but that that capacity is without authority relative to the rationality of men.

The nature and social role of women was clearly, then, a topic of serious debate among men in ancient philosophy and medicine, although it was not a debate that included women themselves. Nor was it conclusive: we find in the discussions of Plato, Xenophon, and Aristotle disagreement about the capacities of soul women and men possess, and hence disagreement about the kind of education that women should be offered and the sort of employments they should be assigned. Explicitly or implicitly, ancient social practices of education always reflect both an understanding of the capacities of the people to be educated and the expectations of the social roles those people will occupy.

4 Education

There is scant reliable evidence for the education of women in the ancient world, and what evidence there is suggests a great deal of variation from place to place, through time, between social classes, and among individual households. In the Classical period there was no public education for girls anywhere except Sparta, where the laws introduced by Lycurgus prescribed a public education, which included a significant physical component (Fantham et al. 1994: 59). Cole says, "Although the reputation of the Spartans for literacy is not very high, Plato says that both Spartan men and Spartan women took pride in their education" (1981: 228). The suggestion is that, good or bad, the education of the girls and boys was not much different in Sparta. Sparta may also have been unusual in encouraging sexual relationships between older and younger women in order to promote the education of the younger women; Plutarch describes such relationships and draws a parallel between these and the relationships men cultivated with youths (Plutarch, cited in Perrin 1958: 18; see also Neils, this volume, Chapter 11).

In Athens in the Classical period women were not educated publicly. Girls of the citizen class were probably educated privately, in order to allow them eventually to assume the role of a wife in a household. We have little evidence of the content of this education, and have to surmise what it included from various hints and images. Pomeroy says, "Since citizen girls were not to look forward to the public careers that brought status to men, it was sufficient for them to be instructed in domestic arts by their mothers" (1975: 74). Citizen boys, by contrast, received instruction in rhetoric and physical education.

Were citizen women literate? In the absence of prescribed education, it is difficult to know how many girls would have achieved literacy. Cole says, "There is no evidence for regular instruction in reading and writing for girls in the Classical period" (1981: 225). At the same time, she notes that the earliest evidence that women could read comes from vase painting, where women are depicted with book rolls almost as often as men or boys (1981: 223).

Evidence for the schooling of girls appears in the Hellenistic period. Women who became literate were unusual, but perhaps less so—pseudo-Plutarch cites an inscription: "Eurydice of Hierapolis set up this tablet, when she had satisfied her desire to become learned; for she worked hard to learn letters, the repository of speech, because she was a mother of growing sons" (*Moralia* 14b–c, cited in Lefkowitz and Fant 2005: 166). Education that was, if not public, at least subsidized, was set up in many cities and "it is clear from the epigraphical evidence that young girls as well as boys benefitted from these local schools"—for example at Teos and at Pergamon—see Cole (1981: 231). But, while boys were learning not only reading and writing but also mathematics and rhetoric, girls were still excluded from instruction in those subjects.

It is difficult from this evidence to draw more than tentative conclusions. Formal instruction for girls in anything beyond domestic skills, inside or outside the household, was probably quite unusual before the Hellenistic period and outside of Sparta, and less unusual afterward. The absence of systematic education for girls almost certainly reflects both philosophical and social views about the capacities of girls and women, and also the expectation that the labor of citizen women would be confined to the household. The causal links between these views and expectations and the very limited education offered to girls can only be inferred. But we should note that limiting the education of a group of people has only ever made it more difficult for that group to demonstrate their capacities or exceed expectations.

RECOMMENDED FURTHER READING

Two works of general interest are Lefkowitz and Fant (2005), which provides translations of primary sources, and Pomeroy (1975, 1995), a social history of women in Greece and Rome. Pomeroy raises some of the historiographical questions that are important in any consideration of the evidence for women's lives in the ancient world.

Discussions of the sources of our knowledge of ancient women philosophers are collected in Waithe (1987) and Plant (2004). Waithe discusses most figures with any claim to have engaged in philosophy, but the scholarship is mixed (see the Review Symposium in *Hypatia* 14.1 (1989), especially the review by Dancy for some helpful correctives). Plant is more careful to weigh the evidence for authorship. On Hypatia, some useful works are Dzielska (1995) and Rist (1965); Richeson (1940) has an enlightening article on the mathematics attributed to her. On Pythagorean women and their virtues, see Lambropoulou (1995).

The primary sources most important for understanding the ancient Greek philosophical debate about the capacities, virtues, and roles of women are Plato's *Republic*, Book V; the opening pages of Plato's *Meno*; and Aristotle's *Politics* I. 13, II. 1–5. Some contemporary assessments of that debate may be found in Freeland (1998) (for Aristotle), in Okin (1977) (for Plato), and in Bar On (1994) (for both).

26

Perceptions of Women's Power in the Late Republic: Terentia, Fulvia, and the Generation of 63 BCE

T. Corey Brennan

A case can be made, in the instance of an important subgroup of elite women in Republican Rome, for "a generation of 63 BCE"—the year of Cicero's consulship and the Catilinarian conspiracy. If we take our sources at their word, the initiative of a small coterie of priestesses and magistrates' wives set in motion a series of events that would do much to pull some of the last remaining threads out of the seriously frayed social fabric of the late Republic. The full story to be sure has to be significantly more complex. But let us start our analysis—which ultimately aims to illuminate the emergence in Roman life and politics over the next decades of powerful women such as Fulvia, then later Octavia, even Cleopatra—by looking at what we are given.

1 Women's Indirect Influence in Roman Politics: The Case of Terentia

If a single incident, more than any other, sheds light on the social and political dynamics of that earlier generation, it would be one that caught the attention of Plutarch and Dio Cassius. It has to do with the portent of a supernaturally rekindled flame at the Bona Dea ceremony of the night of December 3/4 in 63 BCE. Cicero was then one of Rome's two consuls, and, thanks to his magistracy, by tradition the rite was taking place at his home. Yet it was a ceremony that only women could rightfully attend.

Now, as it happens, Cicero had just arrested some very-high-status members of the Catilinarian conspiracy, and he was spending the night outside the house, weighing advice on what to do. Back at his own home, the Vestal Virgins who were present at the ceremony interpreted the weird flame sign, and advised the consul's wife Terentia to buck up Cicero in regard to state affairs. Terentia then took the lead in inciting her husband against the Catilinarian conspirators.

A Companion to Women in the Ancient World, First Edition. Edited by Sharon L. James and Sheila Dillon.
© 2012 John Wiley & Sons, Ltd. Published 2015 by John Wiley & Sons, Ltd.

So we are told (Plut. *Cic.* 20; Dio 37.35; cf. [Sall.] *Inv. In Tull.* 3). But there seems to be a decent factual basis for the basic outlines of this story. In an autobiographical poem, Cicero recounted a very similar flame portent that Terentia observed while sacrificing the previous year, which was interpreted as a sign that her husband would reach the consulship in the upcoming elections. Another source, the near-contemporary Greek historian Diodorus, recounted how a certain Fulvia (not the famous one discussed below), who learned of the Catilinarians' designs through pillow talk, chose first to approach Terentia with the news of the conspiracy (Diod. 40.5 with Sall. *Cat.* 23, 26, 28; Flor. 2.12.6; Plut. *Cic.* 16).

There are ample parallels in the Republic for women making use of an informal network of women in this way. One thinks of Livy's tale of how allegedly in 186 BCE the consul Postumius learned of a massive Bacchanalian conspiracy only through the grapevine that led to his mother-in-law. More contemporary and to the point, in a letter of December 62 BCE, Cicero tells his friend P. Sestius how effective Sestius' wife had been in lobbying Terentia on the matter of his provincial assignment (Cic. *Fam.* 5.6.1).

Now, Plutarch cites Cicero himself as describing Terentia as a woman "by nature neither at all meek nor timorous but . . . ambitious . . . and, as Cicero himself says, taking a larger role in his political affairs than she shared with him in domestic matters" (Plut. *Cic.* 20). Plutarch had at hand something by Cicero that is now lost, but the remark about domestic matters hints that Cicero had written these remarks after he divorced his wife in 47 BCE. There are a sizable number of ancient passages like this; that is, generalizing statements in our sources on women taking indirect part in public life in the Republic and earlier empire.

Others evidently criticized Terentia more roundly for her prominent role in the events connected with the quashing of the Catilinarian conspiracy. One hostile tradition, which comes to us only in a late source, asserted that Cicero conducted trials in his house, with the aid of Terentia ([Sall.] *In Tull.* 3), after the crisis had passed. That seems too much to swallow, and may be a retrojection of the type of gossip that later swirled around the emperor Claudius, with the type of notorious bedroom trial heard before his wife Messalina. But Plutarch is quite insistent that in 61 BCE Terentia gratuitously inserted herself into the most high-profile legal process of the day. This is the trial that the notorious Publius Clodius faced for sacrilege. Specifically, he had dressed as a woman and slipped into the annual celebration of the Bona Dea ceremony that followed the one with the dramatic flame portent.

One can see why Terentia would not want the first anniversary of her greatest public moment turned into a joke (or worse). However, Plutarch supplies a different, and startling, motive: Terentia was jealous of the defendant's sister, Clodia—to be considered another member of the "generation of 63"—who had romantic designs upon the orator. And so she forced Cicero to testify against Clodius. More than one scholar has dismissed this anecdote as "hardly credible" (Carp 1981: 354 n. 32). Yet the passage is quite detailed and unequivocal. Plutarch says:

> Now, Cicero was a friend of Clodius, and in the affair of Catiline had found him a most eager co-worker and guardian of his person; but when Clodius replied to the charge against him [in the Bona Dea trial] by insisting that he had not even been in Rome at the time, but had been staying in places at the farthest remove from there, Cicero testified against him, declaring that Clodius had come to his house and consulted him on certain matters; which was true. (Plut. *Cic.* 29)

Indeed, the statement that it was Cicero who blew Clodius' alibi finds ample corroboration elsewhere.

Plutarch continues:

> However, it was thought that Cicero did not give his testimony for the truth's sake, but by way of defense against the charges of his own wife Terentia. For there was enmity between her and Clodius on account of his sister Clodia, whom Terentia thought to be desirous of marrying Cicero and to be contriving this with the aid of a certain Tullus [i.e., as a go-between] ... So, being a woman of harsh nature, and having sway over Cicero, she incited him to join in the attack upon Clodius and give testimony against him. (Plut. *Cic.* 29)

If Terentia was indeed involved and the motivation is true, this certainly would explain much about the tone of the *Pro Caelio* of 56 BCE. That speech could almost more accurately be called the *In Clodiam*, for it is in essence a prolonged attack on the woman rather than a defense of Cicero's male client Caelius, who was actually on trial.

Yet the immediate results of the Bona Dea process of 61 BCE were disastrous for Cicero and his family. Clodius bribed the jurors lavishly and escaped condemnation, became (in 59 BCE) a plebeian and a tribune, and immediately used that office to send Cicero into exile (in 58 BCE), ostensibly for his handling of the Catilinarians. Things became pressing for Terentia, who stayed behind in the city to look after her husband's affairs and, of course, to lobby for his return to Rome. Such shared concerns—such as house management and the care of children—were traditional and legitimate. But Clodius used Terentia's presence in Rome to humiliate Cicero in his absence. At one point we hear that she even sought refuge at the Temple of Vesta—evidently seeking aid from her half-sister Fabia, the Vestal Virgin— only to find herself led away to face a hostile Clodius and perhaps also some of his fellow plebeian tribunes.

In seeking out her Vestal half-sister, Terentia must have been desperate. Fabia does not seem to have played a very large role in the lives of either Cicero or Terentia—perhaps because Fabia had been put on trial in 73 BCE on the enormously serious charge of *incestum* (i.e., sexual relations involving a Vestal Virgin), with L. Sergius Catilina as co-defendant. The prosecutor was none other than Clodius. The trial resulted in acquittal for both Fabia and Catiline. P. Clodius later reproached her for it, all the same. It was the type of charge that, once made, tended to stick.

The next time we might have seen the Vestal Virgin Fabia, she is conspicuous by her absence. We have a good antiquarian source (Macrobius, *Sat.* 3.13) on participants in a feast for the inauguration of a priest (in this case, a flamen), apparently on August 22, 70 BCE. Those present included the Vestal Virgins Popilia, Perpennia, Licinia, and Arruntia. The mention of four Vestal Virgins—the full college at this time consisted of six—implies of course that two remained at the Temple of Vesta, one to watch the fire and the other to watch her colleague watch the fire. One of those tending the Temple, perhaps tellingly, must have been Fabia.

2 Fulvia: Clodius' Wife in her Generation, and the Next

Despite his acquittal in that Bona Dea trial of 61 BCE, P. Clodius did not come off completely unscathed. Plutarch tells us that

Lucullus [consul 74 BCE] actually produced female slaves who testified that Clodius had intercourse with his youngest sister when she was living with Lucullus as his wife. There was also a general belief that Clodius had intercourse with his other two sisters, of whom Tertia was the wife of Marcius Rex [consul 68], and Clodia of Metellus Celer [consul 62] . . . it was with regard to this sister in particular that Clodius was in evil repute. (Plut. *Cic.* 29)

Whether the testimony was true or not, Clodius still must rank as one of the most transgressive figures that Republican Rome was to produce. Still that was not enough to put off one Fulvia, who married Clodius and thereby became yet another member of the "generation of 63."

The marriage had taken place by 58 BCE, perhaps even a bit earlier. In any case Cicero later intimates (*Phil.* 2.48) that at that time Mark Antony—whose maternal grandmother happened to be a Fulvia—was already having an affair with her. Now, Fulvia brought a large dowry into the marriage with Clodius, and she could claim noble ancestry on both sides. Fulvia was the daughter of one M. Fulvius Bambalio and Sempronia, daughter of the last Sempronius Tuditanus, the son of the consul of 129 BCE—a rich eccentric who was long remembered for dressing in theater garb and tossing out cash from the *rostra* in the forum.

After Clodius met a violent death at the hands of his political rival Milo in 52 BCE, Fulvia stage-managed his funeral in a manner that would be remembered and revisited in years to come. Fulvia's success at whipping Rome's populace into a frenzy—so much so that they carried her husband's corpse into the Senate house and burned it down as a pyre—was not lost on Mark Antony after Caesar's assassination in 44 BCE.

A brief excursus: I propose that Agrippina the Elder was also conscious of Fulvia's success with Clodius' funeral. When her husband Germanicus died in Antioch in 19 CE, the Syrian governor Cn. Calpurnius Piso was immediately suspected of his murder. Rumor had it that his corpse bore marks of poison: black and blue marks, foaming at the mouth, and, most strikingly, a heart that would not burn on the funeral pyre. Agrippina returned to Rome holding her husband's ashes in an urn early the next year (20 CE). She came home on a painfully slow march from Brundisium accompanied by the two children who were with her, Caligula and the baby Julia Livilla. Though no source explicitly mentions it, Agrippina must have had in that urn a complete human heart, allowing people to peek at it and thus exploiting popular beliefs about the sure signs of poisoning.

But back to the generation under consideration. At some point in the years 51–49 BCE, Fulvia married C. Scribonius Curio, who as a tribune in 49 BCE by crossing to Caesar played a crucial role in tipping Rome toward civil war. But Curio perished as tribune in north Africa in the civil conflict that followed upon Caesar's invasion of Italy. Before 45 BCE Fulvia married again, now for the third time, but still (it is said) in possession of a hefty dowry. This husband was Mark Antony. Two sons emerged from this union: M. Antonius Antyllus, whom Octavian selected to marry Julia and be his son-in-law in 36 BCE (but who was killed in 31 BCE), and Iullus Antonius, who married Marcella, niece of Augustus, and reached the consulship of 10 BCE, but was killed in 2 BCE in connection with the sexual scandals surrounding Augustus' daughter Julia. For a child born in 43 BCE, the choice of the highly unusual *praenomen* "Iullus" is quite remarkable. Romans up to that point in the developed Republic had hardly ever deviated from a traditional roster of a dozen and a half first names, with even fewer being in common use. This original choice would have its own influence in the trend toward historically evocative naming practices in the very late Republic and early empire.

Fulvia's public political role really came into its own after the assassination of Caesar in 44 BCE. She vociferously represented Antony's interests in Rome while he fought in the east (and entered into a romantic liaison with the Egyptian dynast Cleopatra). Our sources have much to say about Fulvia's activities in her husband's absence—her "cruelty" and "greed," her role in the proscriptions (including her shoddy treatment of the women of the proscribed), and, as Appian and Plutarch have it, her mistreatment of the decapitated Cicero's head. According to the contemporary biographer Nepos, she found support only in Cicero's friend Atticus, who stayed aloof from factional politics.

By 43/42 BCE Mark Antony was using Fulvia as the model for the face of "Victory" on the obverse of quinarius issues (i.e., half a denarius) that he had minted in Cisalpine and Transalpine Gaul. This is commonly regarded as the first portrait coin of a historical Roman woman, though of course we have no way to check. The personal nature of the issue does come across strongly; the reverse shows Antony's birth sign (Leo) and age (variously forty or forty-one). Even more significantly, c. 41/40 BCE Antony's supporters renamed the city of Eumenia in Phrygia "Fulviana" in her honor. Such an honor does seem indisputably a first for any Roman woman, but demonstrably a bit of an embarrassment for the inhabitants of that town. Coins from the place (Burnett et al. 1992: 3139, 3140) apparently bearing her image in some cases later have the "Fulviana" scratched off, and have a countermark with the old name "Eumenia" in monogram.

It is a pity that we know very little about Fulvia's activities in the crucial year 42 BCE. But, in 41, Fulvia emerges in our sources as one of the most powerful figures in Rome, for example obtaining permission to triumph for Mark Antony's brother Lucius ("it was Fulvia who in reality had the honor," observes the historian Dio of the actual celebration; see Dio 48.4). Then real trouble started. When he returned to Rome from the east, Octavian broke with L. Antonius and Fulvia, and dissolved by divorce the alliance placed on him by his marriage to Claudia, a daughter of P. Clodius and Fulvia. In the conflict that followed—culminating in the civil warfare around Perusia in 40 BCE—the Livian tradition has Fulvia firmly in charge, and Lucius Antonius (and in some sources his troops) following Fulvia's orders. We have from this precise era a unique source on Fulvia; namely, inscriptions on the sling bullets recovered from the site of the siege of Perusia in 40 BCE. As it happens, two of the sling bullets specify that they are seeking to hit Fulvia in the clitoris (apparently insinuating that she is a tribade; i.e., the stereotyped overmasculine woman capable of penetrating others) and another that it is aiming for a target between her inner buttocks (Hallett 1977 has expertly treated this fascinating material).

At Perusia, however, Lucius Antonius lost the day, and Fulvia chose to flee to south Italy and then Greece, where she eventually met up with her husband Antony, who took her to task for her over-involvement in anti-Octavian politics. Our sources stress that Fulvia was deeply upset at Antony's infidelity. Antony returned to Italy, while Fulvia remained in Greece, ill at Sicyon in the Peloponnesus. It was there she died in the middle of the year 40 BCE, as Antony and Octavian reconciled.

Above I mentioned a scattering of ancient criticisms of Cicero's wife Terentia, oblique and not so oblique. However, our sources, especially Plutarch, make Fulvia practically a case study in how elite women should not behave. Granted, Antony's enemy Octavian will be at least ultimately a source for much of this invective, but the list is instructive, regardless: women should not be avaricious or cruel (especially to other women). They should not even be overly serious. They should not use their young children as political capital. They have no place in a war camp.

3   Military Wives in the Republic

For the Republic we can identify a recognizable category of military wives. Some commanders taking up a new province may have had their wives and families tag behind—I use the expression advisedly—as far as the shores of Italy. Valerius Maximus tells how a certain naval prefect sailing to Asia put in at Tarentum, evidently expecting to meet up with his wife, but found she had died there. He slew himself on her pyre. The other spousal rendezvous were surely less spectacular.

For a departing commander to cross back over the *pomerium*, the sacral boundary of Rome, had decisive consequences for the category of religious/constitutional rules known as the augural law. Cicero is eager to emphasize that Verres, after his formal departure for his province of Sicily in 73 BCE, violated his military auspices by tracking back—repeatedly—to the city of Rome to make nocturnal visits to his mistress. That behavior, in turn (it is clearly implied), vitiated anything he did of worth in his province.

Except in times of civil strife, wives, daughters, and young sons remained behind, though older boys (and their male cousins) commonly joined the commander's cohort. Perhaps the governor brought along small statues of absent family members to serve as models for official portraiture and the like abroad. During his tenure in Cilicia, Cicero discovered in the baggage of one shady Roman itinerant five such busts of women (*imagunculae matronarum*), including the sister of Brutus and also the wife of Aemilius Lepidus (Cic. *Att.* 6.1.25).

Yet I must emphasize that, in their time of separation from their husbands, governors' wives played a crucial role in the economic sphere, managing family finances and the household (often more than one). And they no doubt had an impact in the political sphere far beyond what our sources tell us. To take only one suggestive example from late in the year 62 BCE alluded to earlier: Cicero's friend Publius Sestius had been serving as quaestor in Macedonia and was anxious to return home, to the point of writing to various magistrates in Rome so as to be succeeded. But then Sestius changed his mind. Cicero saw difficulties in convincing the incoming tribunes that the quaestor now wanted to stay in his province, but promised his friend to do what he could, especially "after your wife Cornelia called on my wife Terentia and I myself talked with [your brother-in-law] Q. Cornelius" (Cic. *Fam.* 5.6.1).

Cornelia was daughter of the Marian consul L. Cornelius Scipio Asiagenus—hence her special clout. About a year previously, Cicero as consul had appealed directly to the wife and sister of the commander for Cisalpine Gaul—Metellus Celer, married by chance to the famous Clodia—for help in a domestic political matter. It evidently was natural for such women to represent their absent husbands' interests in Rome. A spectacular parallel of a woman shedding her husband at a delicate moment comes from the year 50 BCE. Caelius writes to Cicero (*Fam.* 8.7.2) of the scandal one Valeria Paula caused by instituting a divorce, without disclosing the basis, on the very day her husband was about to return from his province. What caught folks' imaginations was that she had already made plans to remarry (in this case one of Caesar's ex-prefects).

As one might guess, however, when it came to returning magistrates, women were more often the victims of shoddy treatment. When we do get a substantive allegation in our sources for the "generation of 63 BCE," it is most often infidelity. No doubt there were any number of family members, friends, and staff willing to keep the field commander up to date on his wife's comings and goings. The magistrate, very much at the mercy of his sources, had to exercise his own judgment.

In 77 BCE—a bit earlier than the period under examination—the renegade ex-consul M. Aemilius had established a foothold in Sardinia and from there "planned to starve Italy" into submission. But when he saw a letter revealing an extramarital liaison of his wife, Appuleia, he repudiated her from afar—and soon died of heartbreak, so Plutarch (*Pomp.* 16) alleges. Lepidus was a public enemy, and was not sure when (if ever) he might return to Rome. Those in better standing apparently waited until their term of service was up.

Infidelity is why Lucullus severed his marriage to Clodius' sister (one of three named Clodia) immediately after his seven-year eastern campaign. He apparently was convinced of the charge, too: at the Bona Dea trial in 61 BCE, Lucullus produced evidence of Clodia's incest with her brother. Lucullus' successor, Pompey, divorced his third wife, Mucia, immediately on his return to Italy in late 62 BCE. People talked of adultery. But Pompey did not give his reason, either then or later. After all, there were three children from the marriage, two sons and a daughter, whose paternity might be impugned.

A second brief excursus: the woman most effectively destroyed by such allegations has to be the emperor Claudius' wife, Messalina. We might recall, for instance, the story, which Pliny takes at face value, that she had twenty-five lovers in twenty-four hours, and wonder what source would have been authoritative enough to make such nonsense stick. Here I would venture a guess: the *Memoirs* (Latin *Commentarii*) of the younger Agrippina, who succeeded Messalina as Claudius' wife and had good reason to smear Messalina and her son Britannicus. We know of the existence of these *Memoirs* because Tacitus used them and trusted them in the *Annals*.

But back to the Republic, and abrupt divorces. Julius Caesar is another prominent Roman who, when he divorced Pompeia following the Bona Dea affair, did not cite his reasons. In this case Caesar was in Rome, about to set out for the further Spanish province. But still he chose to break the news by letter. (One thinks of today's celebrity text messages or Twitter posts employed for the same purpose.)

Cicero's daughter Tullia and her second husband must have been divorced right before he went as quaestor to the province of Bithynia in 51 BCE. But there we do not know the grounds. Nor is there a good explanation as to why Tullia then immediately chose a third husband, and a politically difficult one at that, as she followed Terentia's advice but not her father's. Perhaps it was because in 51 Cicero had just set out for a command in Cilicia, and there was no telling how long he would be there. The impact of the long absences that came with official service abroad on elite Roman marriages deserves consideration in general. It also may be that Tullia knew her father would forgive her, whatever decision she made.

Just a decade later our sources confront us with a different world. As Cassius Dio has it, in 41 BCE Fulvia aided the consul Lucius Antonius (brother of Mark Antony) by seizing Praeneste and setting up a large advisory council of senators and equestrians. There she "was accustomed to conduct all her deliberations with their help, even sending orders to whatever points required it." Dio continues, "And why should anyone be surprised at this, when she would gird herself with a sword, give out the watchword to the soldiers, and in many instances harangue them?" (Dio 48.10).

That all this activity was deemed deeply transgressive is self-evident. One notes that, although in her (contemporaneous) relationship with Antony Cleopatra is said by Plutarch to have played dice, drunk, and hunted with him, she was allegedly content merely to watch her new lover as he exercised in arms, and did not try her own hand at swordplay.

4 Servilia: Legitimate *Materna Auctoritas*

In general, for the Republic, it would appear that the political activities of respectable women can be viewed as extensions of traditional domestic roles—responsibility for house management, care of children, or sharing the concerns of a spouse—our sources treat them as legitimate expressions of *materna auctoritas* (respectable women's authority).

In our sources, no single individual for the later Republic better manages to parlay that traditional role into a position of real power than Servilia. Servilia was a more or less exact contemporary of Cicero's wife Terentia: each was born c. 100 BCE. But Servilia managed to shape a dynasty. She was the elder half-sister to Cato Minor; mother (by her first husband, who died 77 BCE before reaching high office) of Brutus the tyrannicide; and again mother (by a consul of 62 BCE, who died soon after) of three daughters (one of whom married the triumvir Lepidus and another who was the wife of the conspirator Cassius). To top it all off, she was allegedly one of Caesar's mistresses.

The early death of members of the elder generation of Servilii left Servilia in an authoritative position, for she was older than her brothers and sisters. She even had a certain power over her inflexible half-brother Cato: we find her exercising control over him as he judged a high-profile provincial extortion case in 54 BCE. But Servilia's real influence was over her son Brutus, after the assassination of Caesar. The context for that advice was in their family councils. Cicero gives us a detailed report of a meeting on June 8, 44, in Antium. The question for debate was whether Brutus or Cassius (as noted, respectively son and son-in-law of Servilia) should remain in Italy. More specifically, Brutus, Cassius, Servilia, her daughter Iunia Tertia, and Brutus' wife Porcia discussed the Senate's offer to the "liberators" of somewhat demeaning grain-commissionerships in Asia. We hear with some surprise that Servilia is confident that she can get the decree of the Senate rescinded, thus relieving Brutus and Cassius of this insignificant appointment. On July 25, 43 BCE, we hear of her leading another family meeting, in parliamentary form, to discuss how to deal with the fact that her son-in-law Lepidus had joined Antony and had been declared a public enemy; Cicero and Casca took part. Long ago, Friedrich Münzer noted how Servilia ran her family meetings like a senate meeting (Münzer 1920: 333). In general, Servilia was *the* representative of Cassius and Brutus in Rome in this turbulent period, and communicated news from Rome to them.

5 Untethered Women

Plutarch, in his *Life of Marius*, offers us the following odd notice for the late second century BCE regarding the great commander:

> [Marius] used solemnly to carry about in a litter a Syrian woman, called Martha, and to do sacrifice by her directions. She had formerly been driven away by the Senate, to whom she addressed herself, offering to foretell future events. After this Martha took herself to the senators' wives, and gave them proofs of her skill, especially Marius' wife [Julia, aunt of the famous Gaius Julius Caesar], at whose feet she sat when she was viewing a contest of gladiators, and correctly foretold which of them should win the contest . . . . Because of these and similar predictions Marius and the army sent for her, where she was very much looked up to . . . this made many question whether Marius really gave any credit to her himself, or only was bluffing, when he showed her publicly, to impose his will on the soldiers. (Plut. *Mar.* 17)

There is every reason to accept the existence of this Martha, which is a perfectly good "Syrian name." An inscription from Puteoli yields the intriguing name Iulia/Martha. A relief from Les Beaux in Gallia Narbonensis that pictures three figures—two female, one male—is generally held to represent C. Marius, his wife Julia, and this prophetess Martha. An accompanying inscription reveals the dedicant to be a "Caldus"—in all likelihood the Marian adherent Coelius Caldus who held the tribunate in 107 BCE, the year of Marius' first consulship.

The chronology of events in Plutarch's tale of Martha is noteworthy. First, the Senate showed her the door. (It is of course a remarkable instance of chutzpah on her part to have started by approaching this body.) After this, Martha, as an alternative, networked with Rome's elite women. As for Marius' use of her in a military context, we may compare the outlaw general Sertorius in the 80s BCE and the white faun he pretended to use as a confidant in Spain, or the Thracian woman, a devotee of Dionysus, who followed Spartacus and his rebel slave followers in the late 70s uttering Delphic prophecies.

But women like Martha, who were deemed influential, consistently caused the greatest anxiety of all, probably because they were wholly "untethered." Courtesans very much fell into this class. Consider Praecia, an influential *hetaira* in Rome, whose activities in the 70s BCE allegedly as head of a political "salon" drew the attention of Plutarch, but also comments by Cicero and Sallust. She grew enormously powerful, in large part because she had in her group the praetorian P. Cornelius Cethegus, a consummate senatorial insider. Plutarch says that in 74 BCE Lucullus needed to bribe and flatter Praecia, to get through to Cethegus, in order to land Cilician command (Plut. *Luc.* 6).

Then there is Chelidon, a plebeian client of the praetor Verres. According to Cicero, she was Verres' mistress. Cicero portrays her as running a legal salon, using language that makes her an archetype for *puella* of Latin love elegy (on whom see Hallett, this volume, Chapter 27; Keith, this volume, Chapter 28). After detailing the transactions of her law studio, Cicero concludes, "her house was packed not with a courtesan's crowd but with a praetor's clientele" (Cic. *Verr.* 2.1.137). The picture here is deliberately hilarious. What does seem certain is that Chelidon was dead by 70 BCE, so Cicero could freely abuse her in the *Verrines*. And there is every reason to believe Asconius' report that, by instituting Verres as her heir, at her death she made him rich.

6   The Nobility of Women: A Major Development of Fulvia's Generation

We have to wait until the high empire, namely the jurist Ulpian, for someone willing to outline succinctly the legal situation of women in Roman public life. "Women are barred from all civil and public office," explains this second-century CE jurist (from a section entitled "Various Rules of Early Law"), "and therefore they cannot be judges, hold a magistracy, bring a suit, intervene for another, or be a representative in a trial" (*Dig.* 50.17.2 pr). Clear enough. Yet Ulpian himself elsewhere in the *Digest* complicates this basic statement, as in his discussion of the quasi-magisterial prerogatives that fell to the wives of ex-consuls (*Dig.* 1.9.8–9).

Paradoxes were even more rife for elite women at Rome in the framework of a Republic, especially in the period before Sulla and then Caesar, when *mos maiorum* (accepted but unwritten custom or precedent) belatedly but rapidly saw itself transmuted into positive law. The story of how so many of the Republic's women, though in essence quasi-citizens, managed to develop public influence and acquire public honors surely was highly complex. I say "surely," since for us it is largely irrecoverable in detail.

To be sure, attempts by elite women at more direct influence in Republican public life mostly receive a rocky reception, depending in severity on the predisposition of the source. For a particularly heavy-handed approach at getting ahead, indeed involving murder, consider Livy's account of the supplementary elections of 180 BCE. He tells how one Quarta Hostilia was condemned for murdering her husband Piso—a consul of the year. Suspiciously, elected in his place was his stepson, Hostilia's natural son, Q. Fulvius Flaccus—who had already failed on three previous occasions in his candidature for the consulship. Evidence was produced that Hostilia had told her son that, despite his setbacks, and the election of her own husband to the top office, she "would manage in less than two months to have him made consul" (Liv. 40.37.6).

Elite women of subsequent generations come off—mostly—as more subtle in their techniques. We have enough information for the "generation of 63 BCE" to disengage a few events or themes that must stand as representative significant trends that were firmly established at Rome even before Augustus' reign. One of the most important of these trends has to do with the concept of nobility at Republican Rome—the elite status that derives from having one of Rome's eponymous chief magistrates as an ancestor—and its extension past the male line to include also the female line. This notion had not yet emerged, or was still emerging, at the time of Terentia's and even Fulvia's birth, but was a development that was quite taken for granted by the time of the early empire, with resonances so deep that it upended the whole tradition of Roman nomenclature.

It probably began with Q. Lutatius Catulus, a protégé of Marius and consul in 102 BCE, who at about that time was the first to pronounce an encomium over his mother at the highly stylized funerals traditional in Rome's nobility. We know nothing of this woman, Popilia—or Catulus' father, for that matter. Catulus was from a distinguished consular family—but one that had not produced any consuls since 242 BCE. Popilia, however, must have been related to the Popilii Laenates, who had produced three consuls in the second century BCE, and dated back to a consul of 359 BCE, one of the very first plebeian consuls.

Then there is the case of Iunia, probably a Brutus, who died in 91 BCE, whose funeral included (like those of noble men) actors role-playing her (male) ancestors with appropriate personal masks (*imagines*). Next attested is Julius Caesar, just starting out in his political career in 69 BCE, who staged a similar display for his aunt Julia, who was married to Marius. The speech he delivered on the occasion was thought memorable enough that it was preserved. Suetonius shows how Caesar counted Julia's nobility through both the male and (provocatively) female lines:

> "Her mother," he said, "was a descendant of kings, namely the Marcii Reges, a family founded by the Roman King Ancus Marcius; and her father of gods—since the Julians (of which we Caesars are a branch) reckon descent from the goddess Venus. Thus Julia's stock can claim both the sanctity of kings, who reign supreme among mortals, and the reverence due to gods, who hold even kings in their power." (Suet. *Div. Jul.* 6)

Caesar seems to have offered a similar speech the next year when his wife Cornelia died— the first (says Plutarch) ever to eulogize a younger woman at a public funeral. Cornelia was the daughter of a three-time consul, unlike Caesar, whose father was only of praetorian rank.

Now, probably at every stage in the developed Republic lesser-born men saw the possibilities that derived from gaining coveted *imagines* (ancestor portraits) through marriage. For instance, Antonia, daughter of the pirate-fighting commander Creticus and the sister of Mark Antony, when marrying C. Vatinius is said to have moved the *imagines* of her father and grandfather to her new home (or, as Cicero terms it in 56 BCE, a *carcer*, "jail").

But a significant development was marked in the mid-first century BCE when assertive male politicians started counting nobility more or less officially in both the male and female lines. Caesar's assassin Marcus Brutus seems early to have set up a family tree in his home library showing descent from the Lucius Brutus (consul 509 BCE) in his father's line and the fifth-century hero Servilius Ahala in his mother's. By c. 54 BCE he was proclaiming this lineage publicly, as can be seen from a coin that he issued with L. Brutus on the obverse and Ahala on the reverse.

After that, there was no turning back. According to Suetonius, the emperor Galba (who reigned in 68 CE) ostentatiously set up a genealogical chart in his atrium on which he traced his father's side of the family to Jupiter and his mother's to Pasiphae. I should think that the phenomenon of polyonomy, which reached its peak not long after Plutarch's day, hints at the content and complexity of such charts. For instance, the full name of Q. Pompeius Sosius Priscus, co-consul in 169 CE, contained thirty-four more names between Pompeius and Sosius (fourteen family names, twenty *cognomina*, and four *praenomina*, drawn from both paternal and maternal sides). Such a name really had to be constructed from an elaborate table.

7   Roman Male Discourse about Female Power

If there is one woman of the Roman Republican era for whom it is possible for us to write a biography, it is Terentia, Cicero's wife. In the early twentieth century, one of the more perceptive students of Roman society and religion, the English historian and ornithologist William Warde Fowler counted Terentia as the best example of the "two or three" women of the first century BCE of whom "we do in fact know a good deal" (1908: 150).

This is thanks to the fact that we have some of Cicero's letters to her (more than twenty in all). And there are allusions to Terentia in many other letters, mostly to Cicero's friend Atticus. Terentia finds mention even in some of Cicero's public speeches. As we have seen, Plutarch's *Life of Cicero* collects some startling items, which at the least reflect contemporary gossip. An assortment of other sources from the earlier empire, both Latin and Greek, manage to both elucidate and confuse.

Accordingly, since 1990 Terentia and her daughter Tullia have found themselves the subject of numerous articles and, as I count them, four separate monograph-length studies. Each places a premium on a nuanced and generally sympathetic rereading of the available sources. But Fowler provides a succinct summary of the facts of Cicero's marriage as we have them:

> [Terentia] lived with her husband for about 30 years, and until towards the end of that period, a long one for the age, we find nothing substantial against her ... there is not a sign in the letters that Cicero disliked or mistrusted her until the year 47 BCE ... then, after his absence during the [civil] war, he seems to believe that she had neglected himself and his interests ... Cicero, after divorcing her, married a young and rich wife [the 15-year-old Publilia, about 45 years his junior, and his legal ward], and does not seem to have behaved very well toward her. (1908: 151)

Most recently, Susan Treggiari uses Terentia's life as a platform for explorations of a more general nature: Terentia's friendships, her hospitality, her economic role as steward of her husband's property, the (significant) wealth that she herself brought into her marriage, her political patronage and mediation. By a careful reading of the sources Treggiari also disengages Terentia's literary interests, or rather the fact that she must have had some. A freedman of Caesar gave her a Phoenician scholar as a present; Terentia freed him, and he went on to found a school at Rome—with perhaps a cut of the tuitions going to Terentia as patron.

But, if one is going to write a biography of someone like Terentia, in this case (rightly) as a vital behind-the-scenes player who was equally shrewd in her patronage and in her business dealings, one needs to be able to take in the world in which she moved as a whole to assess this woman's ambition, achievement, and influence. And there lies a problem. We do have a 1987 prosopography of senatorial women for a later period, by M. Rapsaet-Charlier, which aims to list all known women of senatorial rank in the high empire, including wives, daughters, sisters, and mothers of senators. No equivalent for the Republic has yet appeared, with the result that we simply are not in a position to offer a comprehensive study of the senatorial class as a whole in this (long and crucially important) era. Here there is a felt need, since my impression is that the same narrow ring of Republican women are used as *exempla* in secondary works again and again, often with no source criticism.

But another question must be asked: can Terentia exist for us without Cicero? Put another way, when our ancient sources—including Cicero himself—are talking about Terentia and her activities, is this not just another way to characterize Cicero? The same goes for Fulvia and her various husbands, and basically all of the other women (most admittedly thinly attested) I have mentioned above.

Problems really present themselves at every stage, for the source problem on women and especially politics in the Republic and for that matter the high empire is acute. As Kate Cooper has pointed out for a later period, "Roman male discourse about female power served more often than not as a rhetorical strategy within competition for power among males themselves" (1992: 151). The one thing that is clear is that sources such as Cicero, Plutarch, Tacitus, Suetonius, and Dio preserve ample bits of this discourse. These texts, supplemented by documentary materials, allow us to reconstruct the outlines of how Roman male—and occasionally also female—elites seeking self-aggrandizement in the public sphere exploited powerful women to both positive and negative effect.

But it is indeed difficult, especially given the tendency of the literary sources toward stylization of gender roles, to disengage precisely how actual historical women managed to sidestep the restrictions posed by institutions such as guardianship and function as political agents. Hence, the focus of any study of Roman women, particularly in the Republic, might necessarily have examined "perceptions" as opposed to attempting to reconstruct the practically unreconstructable, namely the development of women's civil rights, economic power, and political influence at Rome.

Much of course becomes topsy-turvy under the Imperial system, when so much of the *res publica* came under the purview of the emperor's personal domain. Here I return to the devastating portrait of Claudius' wife Messalina that is so well-known from sources such as Pliny the Elder, Tacitus, and Suetonius, and my suggestion that it must have its origin in the political autobiography of Agrippina the Younger, a work known from Tacitus.

As I noted, Agrippina had ample reason to impugn the sexuality of Messalina—or, more to the point, the paternity of Messalina's son Britannicus. This is a two-edged sword: bias and misinterpretation of a woman's actions at its worst—ironically, at the hands of a woman. But, the fact that Agrippina wrote a political memoir in the first instance, whether or not it included those exact charges, marks another landmark phase in the effort of Roman elite women to manage perceptions of themselves.

SUGGESTIONS FOR FURTHER READING

For a general historical narrative of the period under consideration, Christopher S. Mackay (2009) deserves special praise. On the networks of elite families in the Republican period, F. Münzer (1920; English translation 1999) remains unsurpassed. For non-elites, the best concise social history for Rome now available is Knapp (2011).

For elite women of the Republic, Treggiari (2007) is a major contribution, which does not merely re-examine the evidence for Terentia's life but also uses Terentia's life as a platform for explorations of a more general nature. The volume is an installment in an important series co-edited by Ronnie Ancona and Sarah B. Pomeroy, originally entitled "Women of the Ancient World" (with Routledge) and now "Women in Antiquity" (with Oxford). Relevant to the Republican period are Dixon (2007), Roller (2010), and Skinner (2010). Forthcoming in the series is a biography of Fulvia by Judith Hallett. Taken together, these volumes offer a superb entry into the massive bibliography of more particular scholarship on women in the period under consideration.

Finally, I should note that this essay owes some debt to the "group biography" approach of Fried (1996), particularly his third and fourth chapters entitled "The Generation of 1863" and "Manet in his Generation" (185–364).

PART IV

The Beginnings of Empire

This short section focuses on the pivotal Julio-Claudian period, the time when Rome came to dominate the ancient Mediterranean. This age saw an explosion not only of Roman empire across most of the known world but also of Roman art, which gives us a wealth of historical, artistic, and literary material on women. There had been a long tradition of publicly displayed female portrait sculpture in the Greek world, but the regular representation of Roman women in public portrait statues began only in this period, with Octavia and Livia, the sister and wife of Augustus; this subject is traced by Elizabeth Bartman in "Early Imperial Female Portraiture" (Chapter 30). As with politically important maternal lineage in the late Republic, the public display of dynastic women in the Julio-Claudian clan began a program that would continue throughout the Roman empire.

In this period, a phenomenon begun in the Hellenistic period really took hold, namely our fuller, and more secure, knowledge about the producers of the evidence being studied. Much of this material is propagandistic in nature and intent. As a result, the problems of studying the evidence shift: no longer are we confronted with mysterious images whose creators are mostly unknown, as with Attic vases, and whose meanings are obscure. Approaches to the evidence for women in this time must be very alert to political aims hidden under what may not seem to be political subjects, as in the case of the *docta puella* of Roman elegy, discussed here by Judith P. Hallett in "Women in Augustan Rome" (Chapter 27) and Alison Keith in "Women in Augustan Literature" (Chapter 28).

The literary materials of this era have much to say about women, as is made evident in the essays of Hallett and Keith. Some of these materials are preoccupied with the pre-Roman past: both Vergil and Livy revisit the earliest periods of Roman foundational myth, participating—one way or another—in an Augustan program of reshaping Rome's future according to its ancient past. This program was much concerned with women. In fact, it is fair to say that the Augustan principate was heavily invested in reorienting women back into the domestic sphere, a program enacted into policy by the Julian laws (also discussed by Levick, this volume, Chapter 7, and Henry and James, this volume, Chapter 6).

At the same time, women continued the patterns of public patronage that were established in the Hellenistic period, as Eve D'Ambra's "Women on the Bay of Naples" (Chapter 29) shows. In this period, female patronage has a specifically Roman model at hand in the public programs of Livia and Octavia. The prominence of the Julian women is visible in the trickle-down effect of hairstyles on female statues (see Bartman essay and Meyers, this volume, Chapter 33), an iconographic program that continued throughout the empire. In Rome itself, monuments and iconography were at least monitored by the Julio-Claudians, but, outside of Rome, locally prominent women were free to conduct programs of public participation and patronage.

The most prominent woman of the Augustan period, of course, is Cleopatra, who remains largely unrepresented in this volume—another loss owed to editorial choice. Accessible modern scholarly resources on Cleopatra are widely available, and we refer readers to them: see Jones (2006a, 2006b), Hamer (2008), Roller (2010), and Schiff (2010), among others. Other Egyptian women are, however, very present here, and are studied in Christina Riggs' essay, "Portraits, Prestige, Piety: Images of Women in Roman Egypt" (Chapter 31), which looks at women in funerary art and points ahead to the period studied in Part V.

27

Women in Augustan Rome

Judith P. Hallett

Rome's Augustan age, long extolled and investigated as its "glory days," lasted a mere four decades: from 27 BCE, when Julius Caesar's great nephew and heir Octavian assumed the title of Augustus, until 14 CE, when Augustus died. The legal, political, and social circumstances of Roman women underwent several important changes during this forty-year period, changes that particularly affected women of elite background who had been accorded public prominence as representatives of their families, and in some instances as representatives of the female gender itself (on such women in the previous forty years see Brennan, this volume, Chapter 26). *ILS* 8393, a much-discussed material artifact from this era—the so-called *Laudatio Turiae*, a funerary inscription from approximately 5 BCE, apparently based on a speech addressed by an aristocratic husband to his deceased wife at her burial ceremonies—illustrates the value of focusing on such women.

Its speaker not only portrays the dead woman as a representative of her privileged family, allied with her sister in having avenged their murdered parents, and thereby recovering their public standing and financial fortunes, but also repeatedly characterizes her as a commendable representative of her gender: sharing praiseworthy traits with other married women of her privileged background but surpassing them in her display of moral excellence. At the same time he foregrounds aspects of her conduct that reflect Augustan-era preoccupations with marital fidelity and female fecundity. For example, he reports that, when she proved unable to bear children, she proposed that her husband divorce her and wed a woman of her own choosing who could provide him with offspring. He asserts, too, that she promised to view these children as hers as well, to refrain from insisting on a share of their jointly held property, and to adopt the duties and devotion of a sister or mother-in-law toward him. (On this inscription see also Riess, this volume, Chapter 36.)

Various other literary texts and material artifacts—not all of them from the Augustan era itself—document the changes that occurred in women's circumstances at this time. They testify to the ideological dimensions of these changes, some when depicting women who lived during these four decades, others when portraying women of earlier, historical and mythical, Roman times. Yet many depictions of women who lived during the Augustan age, and of women from the pre-Augustan—usually distant—past by authors who lived during the Augustan age, frequently blur distinctions between imagination and reality, fictionalizing even when they purportedly furnish facts.

After reviewing some significant changes in women's circumstances during Augustus' principate, I will consider how several literary works, many written in the Augustan era, reflect, elaborate, and contest these changes. My discussion focuses on the relationship between these depictions and Augustan ideological thinking about women. It pays close attention to the complex relationship between lived realities, experienced by actual women, in Augustan Rome, and fictionalizing Augustan Roman literary representations of women. But, inasmuch as nearly all of our sources on women in Augustan Rome were written by men, many in eras far later than the people and events that they portray, we cannot necessarily determine what these realities were.

1   The Changing Social and Cultural Landscape for Women: 27 BCE–14 CE

Augustus' own legislation, along with his transformation of Roman governing structures and practices, can claim major responsibility for the notable changes that occurred in women's legal, political, and social circumstances during his principate. A series of laws generally known as his moral and marital legislation, enacted in the years 18 and 17 BCE and revised in 9 CE, deserve scrutiny first. The "Julian law on repressing adulteries" imposed more severe penalties than there had been previously for extramarital sexual intercourse with and by a respectable free woman. Such illicit conduct, until then regarded as a private family matter, now became a crime, to be tried publicly by a special court. This law, moreover, allowed fathers and husbands to kill adulterous women, and their lovers, under certain circumstances. At the very least it required a husband with clear evidence of his wife's adultery to divorce her or be liable to the charge of sexual procuring, and penalized adulterous men and women by banishment to certain islands as well as by partial confiscation of property and dowry.

These laws also restricted women's range of marital options. They prohibited marriages of Roman senators—and their immediate descendants—with freed slaves, and of freeborn citizens with those belonging to disreputable professions (such as acting on stage); they also made it illegal to wed a woman convicted of adultery. Only women of high moral standing from Rome's highest social classes were, therefore, eligible to marry men of those same, elevated, ranks. In addition, Augustus' laws provided rewards to married women for childbearing by exempting freeborn women who bore three offspring and freed women who bore four offspring from the legal guardianship (*tutela*) that Roman law had since its inception required of all women and minor children.

These laws sent a ringing ideological message to both women and men in Augustan Rome about cultural expectations regarding their sexual, marital, and reproductive conduct. They compelled women of all social stations to place a high premium on sexual chastity if they were not married and on marital fidelity once they had wed, and also pressured them to produce multiple offspring. These laws also placed a certain amount of pressure on elite men to marry, as long as they married women of a social class deemed suitable for their particular rank.

Augustus' motivations for enacting these laws attract a variety of explanations. In 17 BCE he publicly celebrated Rome's fifth *Ludi Saeculares,* performance events honoring a new age, or *saeculum,* for which the poet Horace composed a festival hymn, known as the *Carmen Saeculare.* Owing to the hymn's emphasis on the sexual purity of the boys and girls chosen for its choral performance, as well as its promotion of childbirth and marriage, historians traditionally interpret this group of laws as a vehicle for moral rearmament. They have argued, too, that Augustus was eager to repopulate Rome's highest—senatorial and equestrian—social classes, since these ranks had been sorely depleted by decades of civil wars, the proscriptions of 82 and 43 BCE, and marriage-averse patterns of sexual behavior by males from affluent and powerful families.

But Augustus may have had additional goals in mind. By marrying, and producing several legitimate children, men from Rome's most affluent and powerful families were compelled to divide their financial resources among a larger number of family members than they would have by remaining single. In this way they weakened their and their families' political clout, diminishing the likelihood that they might rival, or challenge, Augustus' supreme control of the Roman state.

Augustus secured that control by transforming Rome from a representative, republican form of government to a hereditary monarchy, although he claimed in his *Res Gestae* to have restored the old Roman Republic in 28–27 BCE. The permanent concentration of political control in the hands of Augustus' ruling family also gave the women of that family more power and more visibility. In dynastic political arrangements of this kind, men's links to and through women, by birth and by marriage, were likely to determine their succession to powerful positions. Indeed, Augustus' own efforts to identify and train a male political heir illustrate the value he himself accorded such links.

Lacking a son, Augustus selected and groomed a series of successors, all related to him through his female family members. He initially looked to Marcellus, the son of his sister Octavia, as his political heir. After Marcellus' untimely death, he then turned to Gaius and Lucius Caesar, the two elder sons of his daughter, Julia. When they, too, lost their lives at early ages, he finally chose Tiberius, the son of his third wife Livia, to take over the Roman state from him. In addition, while Augustus also relied for several years on the political and military strengths of his close friend Marcus Vipsanius Agrippa, to whom he was not related by blood, he strengthened his ties with Agrippa by marrying him to Julia. Earlier he had wed Julia to Marcellus; after Agrippa's death he married Julia to Tiberius, her stepbrother.

Another consequence of the Roman governmental shift under Augustus—to a hereditary monarchy that added to the visibility, as well as the power, of women in the ruling family and beyond—was the public prominence accorded to maternal as well as paternal lineage. It is in this period that we first observe the practice of identifying children related through their mothers to powerful men of earlier generations by naming them after their maternal grandfathers rather than their fathers. Augustus' own household again illustrates this social and cultural development. While Julia's younger daughter and youngest son by Marcus Vipsanius Agrippa were called Vipsania Agrippina and Agrippa Postumus respectively, her two older sons and elder daughters took their names from Julius, the official *nomen gentilicium* (family name) of their maternal grandfather Augustus: Gaius Julius Caesar, Lucius Julius Caesar, and Julia.

In Roman Republican society prior to the Augustan age, a small group of elite families, who vied with one another for political predominance, controlled Rome's governing structures. The women of these households exercised some control of their own in family matters of social and political consequence. They participated, for example, in arranging marriages among younger family members, thereby creating alliances with other powerful families; they also helped to support and finance the political activities of male kin. Among these women was Cornelia, whose father, Publius Cornelius Scipio Africanus, defeated the Carthaginian general Hannibal and won the Second Punic War for Rome in 202 BCE, and whose sons were the radical political reformers Tiberius and Gaius Gracchus. Also in this number were two women from the final years of the Roman Republic in the mid-first century BCE: Servilia, mother of Julius Caesar's assassin Marcus Junius Brutus (and longtime lover of Julius Caesar himself), and Fulvia, wife of Mark Antony (on these two women see Brennan, this volume, Chapter 26).

Ancient Roman sources remember and praise Cornelia for influencing her sons' eloquent speech and for devoting herself to their training for public life in the political milieu that had become their family business. Both Tiberius and Gaius were assassinated by their political enemies while serving as tribunes of the people, in 132 and 121 BCE respectively. A compellingly written letter from Cornelia to Gaius, dated to approximately 124 BCE, urging him to abandon his plans to seek the tribunate, testifies to both her communicative skills and her efforts to influence his political agenda and career. Various authors also detail Cornelia's own enmities with another powerful political figure— Publius Cornelius Scipio Aemilianus, who was not only her first cousin and adoptive brother but also her son-in-law—owing to his opposition to her sons. One author even suggests that Cornelia and her daughter may have had a hand in Aemilianus' mysterious death.

As for Servilia, after Caesar's assassination in 44 BCE she is reported to have worked actively for the Republican political cause, whose leadership her son inherited from Servilia's half-brother Marcus Porcius Cato the Younger and solidified through his marriage to Cato's daughter Porcia. Fulvia, wife of the political demagogue Publius Claudius Pulcher and his friend Gaius Scribonius Curio before wedding Antony, is remembered for leading Antony's soldiers against Octavian at the battle of Perusia in 41 BCE; both literary and inscriptional testimony indicates that she was regarded at that time as a threatening military and political foe. Such women of the Republican period provided precedents and role models for female members of Augustus' family (see also Brennan, this volume, Chapter 26). Nevertheless, with power concentrated in a single, autocratic, and unaccountable family, women's familial involvements acquired far greater political significance.

2 Literary Reflections of Women's Changing Circumstances

Inscriptions, art works, and coins as well as literary sources attest to these legal, political, and social developments affecting women in the Augustan age, and their impact on specific individuals. Several literary representations of other elite women with connections to Augustus' household warrant scrutiny as well. Chief among these historical personages is Augustus' own daughter, and only child, Julia. We have discussed her three successive marriages to her father's chosen political successors, and her offspring resulting from the second union to Agrippa, three identified by names noting their maternal rather than their paternal ancestry.

Sources on Julia's conduct while she was married to but estranged from her third husband Tiberius, before her exile for adultery in 2 BCE, offer a valuable vantage point on the actual impact—as well as the ideological message—of her father's moral and marital legislation. According to the late antique writer Macrobius (*Saturnalia* 2.5.1–10), Julia was notorious for her outspoken remarks about her provocative, often sexually transgressive, behavior, even joking that her children only resembled her much older husband Agrippa because she waited until she was already pregnant to take on lovers. Nevertheless, since Agrippa died ten years before her father sent Julia into exile, it seems likely that her father was aware of her sexual misbehavior and did nothing about it, only punishing her when she took up with Mark Antony's son, Iullus Antonius, and appeared to be involved in a political conspiracy aimed at overthrowing her father himself.

Information furnished by two later authors—the historian Tacitus and biographer Suetonius—about Julia's two daughters by Agrippa, Julia the Younger and Vipsania Agrippina (known to us as Agrippina the Elder), merits mention in this context too. They portray both women as responding to Augustus' moral and marital prescriptions, but in different ways. Tacitus (at *Annales* 3.24.5 and 4.71.8–9) and Suetonius (at *Divus Augustus* 65 and 101.3–4) report that, after falling afoul of her grandfather's authority and legislative edicts, Julia the Younger herself was exiled for adultery less than a decade after her mother.

They depict Agrippina the Elder, conversely, as cultivating the role of devoted, exemplary wife. She was married to Germanicus, grandson of Augustus' wife Livia, and bore him nine children, accompanied him on his military campaigns to the Rhine and the east, and—after his death in 19 CE—forged an alliance with a group of Roman senators opposed to the increasing influence of Sejanus, the emperor Tiberius' right-hand man. At *Annales* 1.41.3, Tacitus hails her for embodying and publicly displaying the outstanding traits of her father Agrippa and maternal grandfather Augustus, including military leadership. According to Suetonius, Tiberius (who had Agrippina arrested and banished in 29 CE on political grounds) had previously been happily married to her half-sister Vipsania, Agrippa's eldest daughter by his first wife Caecilia Attica. After Vipsania had borne him a son and become pregnant with a second child, he was forced against his will to divorce her and enter an unhappy union with Agrippina's own mother Julia, his stepsister. His experiences with his two wives may have contributed to his complicated feelings towards, and harsh treatment of, Agrippina.

A poem by the Augustan elegist Propertius (4.11) commemorates the death, in 16 BCE, of Cornelia, the Elder Julia's half-sister (and Augustus' stepdaughter). It portrays her as personifying and promulgating the moral and marital standards for elite women promoted by Augustus' legislation at this very time. Propertius represents the newly dead Cornelia as justifying the conduct of her life to the divinities who render judgment in the underworld. In enumerating her earthly achievements, she initially cites the military accomplishments of her dead male ancestors, who included the African conquerors Publius Cornelius Scipio Africanus and his adopted grandson Scipio Aemilianus. But she then emphasizes her roles as wife to Lucius Aemilius Paullus, censor in 22 BCE; sister to the consul of 16 BCE; mother of three children (and hence as having earned exemption from legal guardianship); and daughter to Augustus' former wife Scribonia and hence half-sister to Augustus' daughter. She also takes special pride in her moral excellence as a *univira* (wife who has been married only once) and hence an ideal role model to her now motherless daughter.

It warrants attention that one of Cornelia's sons, Lucius Aemilius Paullus, who married his first cousin, Julia the Younger, and obtained the consulship in 1 CE, was executed in 8 CE for conspiring against Augustus. As observed earlier, Lucius Aemilius Paullus' wife—Cornelia's niece—was exiled for adultery shortly thereafter. While individual female members of Augustus' family may have endeavored to exemplify and promote his moral and marital expectations for women, they did not necessarily inspire their own female and male kin to behave in the same, upstanding way. At least, these family members do not receive credit from our Roman sources for behaving in the same way: perhaps because they failed to conduct themselves according to these prescriptions, or perhaps because their political associations and activities made them vulnerable to charges, however accurate, of immoral behavior.

Eleven love elegies about and by Sulpicia, an aristocratic female poet writing in the years immediately preceding Augustus' moral and marital legislation, are of special significance to this discussion, since they furnish an elite woman's perspective on her Augustan social and cultural milieu. Like Propertius' Cornelia, Sulpicia prides herself on her privileged pedigree and the men who provided it: her poems refer to both her late father, the illustrious jurist Servius Sulpicius Rufus, consul in 51 BCE, and her uncle and guardian Marcus Valerius Messalla Corvinus, consul in 31 BCE. Renowned as a general, statesman, and literary patron, Messalla occupied a prominent and powerful place on the Augustan scene, although he—and Sulpicia—did not belong to Augustus' family itself (on Sulpicia see also Keith, this volume, Chapter 28).

It is, however, possible that the young man whom Sulpicia merely identifies by the pseudonym Cerinthus, disguising his true identity (though she broadcasts her own), and with whom she represents herself as engaged in a torrid, illicit affair, was somehow related by blood or marriage to Augustus or his kin. Whatever the actual identity of her lover, these poems, most of them in the first person, portray Sulpicia as happily behaving in ways that Augustus' legislation sought to punish; she even asserts that "it is pleasing to have misbehaved" (*peccasse iuvat*). Presumably the powerful and privileged male legally responsible for her, her kinsman Messalla, tolerated such misconduct, much as Augustus overlooked his own daughter's alleged sexual transgressions for many years.

A verse inscription by Sulpicia (*AE* 1928.73.2) contextualizes and reinforces the messages of her poetry. Commemorating a female slave from her household named Petale, a *lectrix* ("performer of Greek and Latin literary works aloud"), it celebrates artistic talent and endeavor much as her poetry itself does. Sulpicia's writing not only privileges the practice of writing poetry, depicting it as helpful in the successful pursuit of love, but also validates the transgressive erotic agendas of female figures from earlier literary works such as Helen of Troy in Homer's *Iliad*.

But we find the ideological implications of the legal, political, and social developments affecting women in the Augustan era more fully elaborated, affirmed, and contested in Augustan literary texts that portray women from outside the Augustan imperial household. Some of these texts reimagine and rewrite the Roman past, using it as a scenic backdrop for addressing contemporary concerns about women's conduct. The accounts of Rome's formative years by the historian Livy in his *Ab Urbe Condita* are particularly illuminating.

Preoccupied with Rome's moral decline from the early second century BCE onwards, and with women's responsibilities for that decline, Livy extols certain legendary women for what he deems their virtuous behavior: behavior that entails placing a high premium on sexual chastity outside marriage and absolute fidelity within it, and viewing the welfare of the Roman state as taking priority over personal ties and feelings. As Livy's writings on early Rome predate Augustus' moral and marital legislation by several years, they may well have influenced Augustus' decision to make elite Roman morals and marriages the business of Roman government. Further, although Livy draws on accounts of early Roman events by historians of previous generations, fictional elements heavily permeate his narrative.

Livy's first book covers several hundred years of early Roman history, from before the city's founding by its first king Romulus in 753 BCE to the establishment of the Republic in 509 BCE (on women in Livy see also Izzet, this volume, Chapter 5; Henry and James, this volume, Chapter 6; and Keith, this volume, Chapter 28). His narrative casts the Sabine women, who were abducted and raped by the band of male renegades Romulus recruited to his new settlement, in a favorable light. At 1.9ff., he portrays these women as persuaded to accept their abductors as husbands by Romulus himself, who blamed their plight on the arrogance of their own parents for refusing their neighbors the right to intermarry; he depicts them as further mollified by the "sweet talking" (*blanditiae*) of their husbands themselves, who excused "their deed on the grounds of desire and love" (*factum purgantium cupiditate atque amore*; all translations here are my own). Further, Livy claims that a few years after their abduction these women stopped a battle between their Sabine menfolk and Roman husbands by hurling their bodies into the midst of the flying weapons, then beseeching fathers-in-law and sons-in-law "not to stain themselves with unspeakable bloodshed, nor to pollute, through the slaying of male parents, their own offspring, at once grandchildren to their fathers and children to their husbands."

His history similarly glorifies the noblewoman Lucretia, whose rape—by Sextus Tarquinius, the son of Rome's final king—and subsequent suicide caused her husband Collatinus and kinsman Lucius Junius Brutus to overthrow monarchic rule and found a republican form of government (see also Izzet, this volume, Chapter 5 and Keith, this volume, Chapter 28). According to Livy at 1.57–60, Lucretia agreed to submit to Sextus Tarquinius' lust only when he threatened to kill her and then kill a male slave and leave the slave's naked body by her side to foster the rumor that she had had been "put to death in shameful adultery." Livy represents Lucretia as immediately summoning her father and husband, assuring them "that only my body has been violated; my heart is guiltless; death will be my witness," then demanding that they punish the adulterer. Although her menfolk place the blame on the rapist Sextus, telling her that the mind, and not the body, misbehaves (*peccare*), she responds: "Although I absolve myself from misconduct [*peccato*], I will not exempt myself from punishment. No unchaste woman in the future will live following the example of Lucretia."

Yet the first book of Livy's history also features—at 46–49, as a negative moral and political example contrasted to both the Sabine women and Lucretia—an unchaste, disloyal, and bloodthirsty woman from Rome's ruling household: Tullia, the wife of Rome's final king, Tarquin the Proud, who was father of the rapist Sextus Tarquinius (see Izzet, this volume, Chapter 5). Livy blames this king's political and moral failings on this woman, the daughter of Tarquin's royal predecessor Servius Tullius. Indeed, Livy tells us, she had originally been married to Tarquin's brother and he to her sister. But, once she determined that he possessed the desire and boldness his brother lacked, "their similarity to one another quickly brought them together, as generally happens; evil is most suited to evil; but the beginning of disturbing everything rose from the woman."

Livy reports that Tullia constantly disparaged her sister and husband to Tarquin as inferior, cowardly, and unworthy, and finally married him "when, after deaths followed closely upon one another, they had made their respective houses free for a new marriage." Next, Tullia spurred Tarquin to have her own father, the king, assassinated. As soon as her husband had done so, says Livy, Tullia summoned Tarquin publicly from the Senate House and was the first to hail him as king. And, although Tarquin asked her to withdraw from such an uproar and return home, she proceeded to drive her own carriage over her father's corpse. Likening this murderous family scenario to that of a Greek tragedy, Livy remarks that Tullia was "frenzied by the avenging furies of her sister and former husband . . . and carried on the vehicle some of her murdered father's blood to her own and her husband's household gods, owing to whose anger at the evil beginning of this reign a similar conclusion followed before too long."

Livy portrays Tullia as different from the Sabine women and Lucretia in her sexual and political behavior, but at the same time as resembling them through her exercise of independent agency. After all, Livy represents the Sabine woman as autonomously deciding to risk their own lives in an attempt to stop the battle between their fathers and husbands, and Lucretia as having freely chosen to reject the forgiveness proffered by her father and husband by committing suicide. Yet Livy also makes it clear that there are limits to the agency possessed by both the Sabine women and Lucretia, since they cannot control men's access to their bodies.

The Sabine women are forced to engage in sexual relations with males not (yet) their husbands because they are physically powerless to resist abduction and rape. Lucretia submits to Sextus out of physical powerlessness as well. Livy, however, justifies and even prettifies the rape of the Sabine women by having Romulus provide a political explanation, and their Roman husbands voice sentimental excuses, for treating them in this way. He likewise has Lucretia's menfolk try to explain away and excuse her sexual submission to Sextus, and resort to political action in wreaking vengeance on Sextus and his royal household.

By way of contrast, Livy portrays Tullia as totally controlling and uncontrollable where both her own body and the Roman state are concerned: she takes the initiative sexually and politically in stealing her sister's husband, Tarquin, and then pressuring him to overthrow her father; she then insists on authorizing Tarquin's political accession and desecrating his predecessor's remains. Livy may explain Tullia's behavior, but he never excuses it, and eventually indicates its utterly immoral, wholly unacceptable nature by representing it as divinely accursed.

Strikingly, in his first book, and in later episodes of his history, Livy presents his readers with female figures of questionable chastity whose actions prove—like those of the Sabine women and Lucretia, and unlike those of Tullia—of value to the Roman state, but whose moral lapses are not excused by male kinsmen, much less by influential political leaders. The mythic Vestal Virgin Rhea Silvia in 1.4 serves as a case in point. Daughter of Numitor, whose brother Amulius had wrongfully deposed him as king of Alba Longa, she was the mother of Romulus and his twin Remus. After stating at 1.4 that Rhea Silvia was raped, Livy proceeds to remark "when she had given birth to twin sons, whether she actually thought this had happened, or whether because a god was a more honorable agent of misbehavior, she named Mars as the father of her offspring whose paternity was unclear." By so doing, he depicts her as desperate to render her pregnancy respectable, without help from men in her family. At Book 39.8–19 Livy credits Hispala Faecenia, a freedwoman who formerly received payment for her sexual favors, with exposing the threat posed to Rome's welfare by the Bacchanalian conspiracy of 186 BCE in order to help her young lover.

Livy's account of Rhea Silvia's rape and impregnation thus acknowledges that some women, even those from elite families, cannot rely on supportive male kin for exoneration when forced to accede to the sexual demands of physically and socially powerful men.

His narrative about Hispala Faecenia's role in what appears to be an actual Roman historical event—independently documented by an inscription (*ILLRP*511) recording the senatorial decree about this episode—deals with the difficult circumstances faced by women, especially those of disadvantaged backgrounds, who are required to engage in sexual activity with men other than their husbands if they are to survive. To his credit, he recognizes that such women are capable of politically and morally commendable conduct on behalf of other human beings, and of the Roman state itself. With women characters such as these, one briefly sketched, the second characterized at length, Livy undercuts and complicates the narrow definition of Roman female virtue as inseparable from sexual chastity and marital fidelity that he articulates elsewhere in the *Ab Urbe Condita*, and raises questions about Augustan ideological assumptions about female behavior in the process.

Vergil's epic *Aeneid*—still incomplete at the time of its author's death in 19 BCE, also set in the time of Rome's mythic beginnings, and highly fictionalized as well—similarly addresses contemporary Augustan concerns about appropriate female sexual and political conduct (see Keith, this volume, Chapter 28). To be sure, Vergil does not follow Livy's practice of parading before his readers a series of female characters attractively described as dutiful daughters, faithful wives, and fecund mothers. Vergil may have been seeking to avoid comparisons between such women and Aeneas' sexually transgressive, divine mother, the goddess Venus, whom Vergil portrays as unreliable and even deceitful towards her son. In fact, unlike Lucretius and Ovid, Vergil does not mention Venus' renowned adulterous coupling with the god Mars and their humiliation at the hands of her cuckolded husband, Vulcan. Rather, at 8. 370ff., he describes Venus and Vulcan as on such loving nuptial terms that Vulcan and his forge assistants speedily comply with Venus' request to make special armor for Aeneas.

Admittedly, Vergil represents his major female character—Dido, Queen of Carthage—as engaging in sexual activity with Aeneas outside the bounds of lawful Roman wedlock, and divinely compelled to do so. Such behavior seriously transgressed the moral and marital standards already endorsed in Livy's writings and later codified in Augustus' legislation. Yet Vergil portrays such behavior as consequential, and as damaging to Dido: she is emotionally devastated when Aeneas abandons her, fears for her reputation and her city's safety, and ultimately takes her own life.

Significantly, too, Vergil accords sympathetic treatment not only to the distraught Dido but also to other women in the *Aeneid*, whose lack of emotional self-restraint undermines public order: the Latin queen Amata and the Trojan women in Aeneas' entourage, especially the mother of the slain Trojan warrior Euryalus. Even so, Vergil depicts these women as problematic social presences, overcome by *furor* (frenzy) and thereby threatening political and cultural stability. Like Livy's portrait of the depraved Tullia, Vergil offers these depictions to affirm and elaborate a powerful ideological message: that control of women, even mature maternal women, by male kin is a political and cultural desideratum.

Other Augustan Roman literary texts, however, contest the ideological messages about women's proper conduct enshrined in Augustus' moral and marital legislation, endorsed by Livy's history, and validated by Vergil's propagandistic national epic. But they set their works in their own, contemporary Roman surroundings: reimagining, dramatizing, and indeed eroticizing this Roman milieu, with themselves and their female love interests at center stage. These writings by the elegists Tibullus, Propertius, Ovid, and Sulpicia thereby continue a literary tradition launched by the Late Republican poet Catullus that fictionalizes while it purports to depict present-day Roman reality.

Such writers celebrate extramarital sexual liaisons in the elegiac meter and the genre of love elegy as well as in their own urban and urbane Roman environment (although Propertius and Ovid also write about the distant, mythic Roman past). The three male elegists portray the women they love, and Sulpicia portrays herself, as demanding and dominating personalities, utterly uninterested in marriage and children, chastity and fidelity, conventional Roman politics, and patriotic Roman ideals. Their work can be read as a subversive, albeit complex, response to conventional expectations about how Roman women should behave.

In Propertius 2.7, for example, the poet-speaker represents his lover Cynthia as rejoicing at the removal of a law requiring at least one of them to marry and the two of them to part. After asserting that the god Jupiter would not be able to separate a pair of lovers against their will, he relates Cynthia's retort: that the law would have been hard to resist because "Caesar is mighty in arms." Propertius then claims that he himself would not have been able to endure extinguishing the flames of their passion owing to the "custom of a bride" or "a threshold barred by a husband." He states that the sound of a Roman wedding pipe (*tibia*) would be sadder for him to hear than that of a funeral horn (*tuba*); he inquires, rhetorically, "how could I supply children for our country's triumphs"; he proclaims that he could display military might only if he were to follow "the true camp" and military leadership of his girl. These details—especially his references to Augustus Caesar, a pair of Roman musical instruments, and his country's triumphs—impart an unmistakable, and realistic, Roman flavor to Propertius' words, affording the impression that he is reporting on an actual incident in his own life.

Propertius never specifies the legal status of his female *inamorata*. Cynthia, the name by which he identifies her, is a pseudonym, presumably the metrical equivalent of her actual name, and associates her with a site consecrated to Apollo, god of poetry. His elegies in which she appears imply that she is either a freedwoman, and thus of a much lower social class than he; or the wife of another man; or—as in this poem—eligible to marry a man of Propertius' social station but unwed at the moment. What Propertius does make clear is that their passionate and poetic relationship differs sharply from a conventional Roman marital union, and that neither he nor Cynthia wishes to trade their liaison for a socially respectable, legally sanctioned connubial arrangement.

Propertius represents his interactions with Cynthia as occurring in his own urban Roman ambiance. Nevertheless, the details of their relationship that he provides are often difficult to reconcile with one another. Admittedly, both an early poem such as 1.3 and a later poem such as 4.8 depict Propertius and Cynthia as sharing a domicile—to which in the former poem he returns, in an inebriated state, to find her sleeping; and to which she returns in the latter poem, from a dalliance with a wealthy rival, to find him simultaneously dallying with two other women. But in 4.7—which portrays the dead Cynthia as appearing to him in a dream—Propertius has her recall descending on many a night from an upper-storey window in the tawdry Subura district, stealthily, by a rope, and making love with him at the crossroads, an improbable situation for a couple cohabiting in the same residence.

Also in 4.7, the dead Cynthia speaks of several surviving household slaves as her own property. Yet she implies that Propertius himself is in a position to punish and reward them. One of these slaves, described as an aged woman tortured for bringing garlands to Cynthia's grave, shares her unusual name—Petale—with the dead *lectrix* commemorated by the elegist Sulpicia. Another, also portrayed as suffering unjustly, shares her name, Lalage, with a woman the Augustan poet Horace portrays as his beloved. A third, male, slave is called Lygdamus: while several Propertian elegies, including 4.8, feature a man with this name as one of Propertius' household attendants, the name is also used as a pseudonym by another Augustan elegist, whose poems appear along with the Sulpicia elegies in the third book of Tibullus' poems.

A scholarly study therefore speculates that in 4.7 Propertius wittily populates both Cynthia's household, and his own, with figures whose names allude to the writings of various contemporary love poets (Fabre-Serris 2009). Significantly 4.7, about the dead Cynthia, is immediately followed by 4.8, which portrays her as very much alive, physically attacking Propertius when she comes upon him trying to solace himself with two other female sexual partners. Hence it is possible that Cynthia's death in 4.7, like the slaves of her own and Propertius' household, may be a figment of his dramatic, erotic imagination as well.

One explanation for the inclusion of such inconsistent and unlikely details is that Propertius' poems, written in the first person, ostensibly to share key moments from his life and love affair, merely aim at a general impression of verisimilitude, rather than seeking to document a verifiable, coherent, lived reality. He expected his readers, especially those who were acquainted with him personally, to interpret the contemporary Roman settings and trappings as evidence that these poems were in some sense about him, his own amatory experiences, and his dealings with his female beloved and others inhabiting contemporary Roman society. But these poems also depict him as performing in what are obviously fictionalized erotic scenarios, marked by dramatic conflicts and heightened emotions, full of literary and other learned allusions. These fictionalizing elements, moreover, invest Propertius' writing with greater literary authority. The love poems written in the first person by Propertius' fellow Augustan elegists Tibullus, Ovid, and Sulpicia operate in much the same fashion.

As his second book of elegies is generally dated to the mid 20s BCE, Propertius 2.7—like Livy's history and Vergil's *Aeneid*—predates Augustus' moral and marital legislation by several years. Like Livy's history and Vergil's *Aeneid*, Propertius' elegy testifies that the restrictions imposed by this legislation emerged from ideas that had been percolating and circulating in elite Roman circles long before they became formally codified; indeed, Propertius here suggests that Augustus himself may have launched at least one unsuccessful effort to make these restrictions legal and binding. Yet this poem and the work of the Augustan elegists generally also serve as evidence for persistent and popular efforts to challenge Roman ideological assumptions about how women were to conduct themselves sexually and politically.

3   Literary Women: Their Relationship to Augustan Social and Cultural Realities

Studies of Latin love poetry have long pondered the relationship between portrayals of women in these elegiac poems—which are set in contemporary Rome, and frequently make mention of historical individuals such as Propertius' patron Maecenas and Augustus himself—and actual Roman social and cultural realities. Calling attention to the presence of fictional elements in their narratives, like the implausible and inconsistent details we have just observed, can only intensify an already strong skepticism about the value of these texts as historical sources on Augustan Roman women. Noteworthy, too, are resemblances between female figures featured in Augustan elegy and those from Rome's Republican and even legendary past depicted by Vergil—most notably his love-struck Dido—and especially by Livy, all of them fictionalized if not fictitious characters. We have already mentioned the *meretrix* (sex worker), Hispala Faecenia, in Livy's account of the Bacchanalian conspiracy in Book 39; Livy represents her as the lover of a well-born Roman youth named Aebutius, and as exercising control over him in the fashion of an elegiac mistress. At 1.11 Livy relates the story of Tarpeia, who sought to betray Rome's citadel to the invading Sabines, perhaps out of greed for the golden weapons of their commander, Titus Tatius.

Complicating matters further, Propertius and Ovid feature several legendary women depicted in the pages of Livy—Tarpeia, the Sabine women, and Lucretia—in their own elegiac poems, often emphasizing the erotic dimensions of these stories. At 4.4, for instance, Propertius represents Tarpeia as passionately enamored of Titus Tatius. Such similarities between the women of Latin love elegies set in Augustan Rome and the women of legendary times further detract from the credibility of elegiac poetry as a window on the worlds of actual Roman women, and demand explanation from readers today. Some scholarly specialists in the area of Roman erotic poetry even refer to the individual female figures in Augustan elegies as "written women," products of unfettered authorial imagination with no necessary connections to actual living females.

Yet we should recognize that depictions of historical female figures from the Augustan period, such as Augustus' daughter Julia and granddaughter Agrippina, also bear resemblances to portraits of women in Augustan love elegy—portraits replete with unlikely and probably fictional details. Julia's witty words about, and insouciant attitude toward, her marital infidelities have much in common not only with what Sulpicia writes about her own illicit love affair but also with what Propertius portrays his Cynthia as saying about theirs in elegies such as 4.7 and 4.8. Tacitus' representation of the Elder Agrippina in the first book of his *Annals*, exhibiting as it does military leadership in a human environment likened to a conquered city (*victa urbe*), recalls Propertius' description of Cynthia in 4.8: as reclaiming her erotic sway over him like a conquering military hero, and as creating a scene no less memorable than that of a captured city (*spectaculum capta nec minus urbe fuit*).

By describing Cynthia's physical assault on him and his two female partners when she returns unexpectedly from an outing with a male lover in 4.8, Propertius humorously evokes and parodies the conduct of Homer's Odysseus, who dispatches his wife's suitors upon his homecoming; Propertius, though, cleverly reverses the genders of the protagonists and their victims. While Homer's Odysseus displays impressive military prowess in disposing of these men, Propertius uses the language of warfare metaphorically for Cynthia's treatment of him and his slave, though he asserts at lines 65ff. that she bruised his face, bit his neck, and pummeled his eyes before he, her captive, "made a peace treaty with her." Still, Propertius' mere, albeit figurative, association of Cynthia with military leadership is worth noting, since Tacitus employs similar language in describing, altogether seriously, Agrippina's actual ambiance and activities.

Reports by ancient sources about the women of Augustus' family, however, most likely contain fictional elements too. Macrobius did not actually hear, or record verbatim, Julia's remarks about her wayward sexual behavior, uttered centuries before he wrote. Tacitus was not himself present when Agrippina the Elder did her male forebears public credit by supporting Germanicus' military endeavors. Although he indicates at *Annales* 4.53 that he has consulted the memoirs of Agrippina's daughter, these are not eyewitness accounts, since she was only a small child when this episode occurred.

Further, Ovid, at *Tristia* 2. 423ff., and the later Apuleius, at *Apology* 10, attest that some of the pseudonyms used by the Augustan elegists to refer to their mistresses—Tibullus' Delia and Propertius' Cynthia—are the metrical equivalents of their actual names, much as Catullus referred to his beloved Clodia as Lesbia, and Cornelius Gallus his Cytheris as Lycoris. Sulpicia, of course, refers to herself by her own name, reserving a pseudonym for her male lover. If the Augustan elegists are presenting their readers with "written women," so are the historical sources depicting actual female figures such as Augustus' female family members.

In conclusion, it merits emphasis that the definitions of appropriate female behavior represented by Augustan legislation and various ideologically motivated writings were prescriptive in nature: as we have seen from our sources on Augustus' own daughter and granddaughter, and in Sulpicia's love elegies as well, some actual, and vocal, Romans ignored or defied these regulations and expectations. Again, Augustus himself furnishes a memorable example of this phenomenon, as he evidently indulged Julia for many years, overlooking her adulterous conduct until it threatened Rome's government and apparently his own life. Nevertheless, defiance had its consequences. Sulpicia apparently stopped writing her transgressive erotic verse around the time of Augustus' moral and marital legislation. So, too, Livy's supposedly historical narrative about the Bacchanalian scandal, written around the time of this legislation, seems to contain veiled criticism of Sulpicia's poetry and behavior. Its cast of characters includes an elderly aristocratic matron named Sulpicia, presumably her ancestor. The mother-in-law of Rome's consul, she rehabilitates the sexually misbehaving *meretrix* Hispala Faecenia while helping to rescue the Roman state from the Bacchanalian threat and restore Roman morality.

RECOMMENDED FURTHER READING

As a compact, accessible introduction to the topic of women in ancient Rome, D'Ambra (2007) wears its impressive learning lightly. Addressed to a specialist readership, Hemelrijk (1999) examines our ancient sources on such elite, educated women as Cornelia, Sulpicia, Julia, and the elder Agrippina. See Treggiari (1991) for Augustus' moral and marital legislation.

Two books designed for use in the college classroom present and contextualize the important primary sources on women for this period. Lefkowitz and Fant (2005) features Greek as well as Latin sources in English translation. Raia et al. (2005) annotate a number of major texts for Latin students at, or above, the intermediate level of proficiency in their Latin reader. Hallett (2002a, 2002b) are two chapters that furnish a general introduction to the women writers discussed in this essay.

In Hallett (2006), I attempt to elucidate the exile of Augustus' daughter Julia by considering Augustus' complex and conflicted relationship with the mother of the man accused of adultery with her; in Hallett (2009) I analyze the Petale inscription by Sulpicia—unearthed in the 1920s but rediscovered by Jane Stevenson only in 2005 (see Stevenson 2005: 42–4)—and relate it to the concerns voiced in Sulpicia's elegies. For the representation of women in Vergil's *Aeneid*, see Hallett (2002c) and James (2002). Keith (1997) draws significant connections between Sulpicia's self-representation and Vergil's depiction of Dido. The essays in Wyke (2002) include a reprint of Wyke (1987a), a ground-breaking article on the female in Propertius as fictive rather than historical.

Case Study V

Vergil's Dido

Sharon L. James

More ink may have been spilled on Dido than on any other subject in Vergil's *Aeneid*. She is the poem's most compelling character: readers from antiquity onward have been captivated by her, as St. Augustine testifies when he recalls weeping over her death as a schoolboy (*Conf.* 1.13.20–1). What stands out about her story is just what Augustine focuses on: she dies for love. Because her doomed passion for Aeneas dominates Book 4, while Aeneas seems to shrink by comparison, Dido is chiefly recalled as a woman driven tragically mad by love—a sacrificial victim of Aeneas' fated, and enforced, journey toward Rome and its eventual world empire. But the lasting impression of her rage and grief tends to overwhelm Vergil's complex depiction of her. His innovations on Dido's story make her wholly a Vergilian creation, rather than a legacy of the Aeneas myth, and she serves multiple functions in the poem. This case study briefly notes the ways in which Dido offers, in just the period when the Roman Republic finally dissolved into empire (an empire that already ruled the known world), a model of the interaction of woman and empire in Roman thought.

I begin by noting that it may not be possible to pin down this model, for two main reasons: first, Roman thought (a broad and unwieldy category) on the relationship of woman to empire may not have been fully worked out; second, categorical evaluation of any character in the *Aeneid* is impossible, as contradictory, even indeterminable, characterization is one of the ways Vergil keeps the *Aeneid* mysterious.

Dido is no exception to this rule. When she first appears, she is like the goddess Diana among her followers (1.497–504). From her throne, she dispenses justice regally and fairly (1.505–8). When the Trojans ask for assistance, she generously offers them half her kingdom, even before she meets Aeneas (1.571–4). She has protected her people from her malicious brother, and presided over the founding and development of a well-built, impressive city. She is gracious with Aeneas and the Trojans, and with young Ascanius she is motherly and affectionate—to her own destruction, as he, impersonated by Cupid, is the vehicle for her becoming poisoned with a passion she cannot control.

A Companion to Women in the Ancient World, First Edition. Edited by Sharon L. James and Sheila Dillon.
© 2012 John Wiley & Sons, Ltd. Published 2015 by John Wiley & Sons, Ltd.

Control of passion proves impossible throughout the *Aeneid*, but the greatest failure is always seen as Dido's. Her failure sets the pattern for other women's obstructionist behavior: via her female subordinates Iris and Allecto, Juno tricks the Trojan women into burning the fleet (Book 5) and infects Queen Amata, already angry at the transfer of her daughter to Aeneas, with a poisonous rage that wreaks havoc upon her own land (Book 7). Men too are overcome by passion (usually in battle), and Turnus is likewise infected by Allecto at Juno's behest. But Dido's loss of control and her ensuing descent into grief, madness, and destruction are depicted at far greater length, and with remarkable sympathy. She is the victim of Juno, Venus, and Aeneas' fate—not to mention the latter's behavior toward her, which many readers find disturbingly inadequate.

All the sympathy of narrator and readers, however, means neither that Dido's tragedy was avoidable nor that she herself is without blame. The poem's narrator specifies her failing: Dido calls her liaison with Aeneas a marriage, and under that name she hides her fault (*culpa*, 4.172). Here the obvious is worth pointing out: Aeneas engages in extramarital sex with Dido—a widower with a widow—but for him it is not a *culpa*. It is a mistake, as Mercury makes clear to him (4.265–77), but it is not a moral, sexual fault. Thus, Aeneas and Dido exemplify the ancient sexual double standard, and her punishment is not only her death, made more bitter by her consciousness of disgrace, but also the destruction of her city.

Her city, as well as her sex, is what must make Dido's tragedy not preventable. Carthage was Rome's long-standing foe, as the poem repeatedly recalls (see e.g., *inimica in gente*, 4.235)—a reminder the ancient Roman reader hardly needed. The North African queen is simultaneously a hold-up on Aeneas' journey to Italy, a ruler of the Carthaginians (conquered almost 200 years before Vergil began the *Aeneid*), and Cleopatra VII, the recently defeated queen of Egypt, who recurs in Roman poetry of this period as a conceptual enigma that cannot be resolved.

Cleopatra captivated, and bore children to, two of Rome's greatest leaders: Julius Caesar and Mark Antony. Like Dido, she was a queen (*regina*) governed by mad passion (*furor*, Horace, *Ode* 1.37.7, 12) and a woman brave enough to take her own life upon recognizing that all was lost (Hor. *Ode* 1.37.21–32). She ruled a powerful nation and posed a threat to Rome through both military/political means and her sexual attraction. The Roman conceptual confusion about her reached perhaps its apex in the oxymoronic phrase *meretrix regina*—"whore queen" (Propertius 3.11.39)—a marker of instability in the very category of a queen who is sexually active outside of marriage. Although Cleopatra and Antony had three children, the Romans did not consider the couple to be married, as Antony and his wife Octavia were not formally divorced until 32 BCE. (Likewise, when Cleopatra was residing with Julius Caesar in one of his country homes, in 46 BCE, he was still formally married to Calpurnia.)

Dido believes that she and Aeneas are married (4.171–2, 316), but he rejects that designation (4.337–3), as the narrator has already done (noted above). Unlike Cleopatra, Dido does not have children by Aeneas—a further marker of her failure, as the production of a son was the primary obligation of any queen in antiquity. Giving Aeneas a son is precisely the purpose of his future wife Lavinia, who is in every way Dido's opposite, as Vergil presents her: modest, shy, chaste, fearful, virtually invisible—a vehicle for uniting Trojans and Italians.

The sacrifice of its most gripping character is one of the ways the *Aeneid* marks the nature of Rome's imperial future as requiring the subordination of personal passions to greater public causes. The relation of woman to that cause is, in the poem, pervasively obstructionist, as woman—even an intelligent, wise, powerful, generous queen—is always vulnerable to the attack of dangerous emotion. Even after Aeneas has broken off with her, Dido's passions are seen as endangering his mission; hence, Mercury returns to chastise the slow hero. In the god's notorious phrase, *varium et mutabile semper/femina* (woman is always an unpredictable and changeable thing, 4.569–70). Dido's exceptionalism, as a capable female ruler, is a conceptual problem for the Romans simply because she is female. She exerts a powerful attraction emotionally, for the reader, especially in comparison with the reticent Aeneas, but a queen can never be a stable ruler.

As a poet and thinker, Vergil is too subtle and complex to present Dido as merely irrational: like Cleopatra she is powerful, attractive, and dangerous, and her power must be acknowledged. But it is not to be trusted. In Roman thinking, woman and power cannot coexist. However well a woman has ruled her country, she will always fall prey to her passions, especially sexual desire. If historically the Romans loathed rule by a single male monarch—a prospect to which they were having to become accustomed, in the person of Augustus—they could not have conceived of rule by a woman. In the centuries that followed the *Aeneid*, many a male emperor proved vulnerable to personal and physical passions, but no woman had the chance to do better. Private influence by women was common, and commonly lamented, but law and the state never fell into female hands. A Roman *imperatrix* (empress) was beyond imagination.

28

Women in Augustan Literature

Alison Keith

In the aftermath of the wars that ended the Republic, Latin literature exploded across a wide spectrum of genres—satire and lyric, epic and elegy, history and oratory. The poetry of Vergil, Horace, Ovid, and the elegists Propertius and Tibullus, as well as the history of Livy, are conventionally ascribed to an "Augustan" period, which derives its name from the title "Augustus," conferred by the Senate on the first Roman emperor, Caesar's grandnephew and heir Octavian, on January 16, 27 BCE. The literary works of our authors, like their lives, encompassed the end of the Republic and birth of the principate, with the earliest authors— Vergil (70–19 BCE) and Horace (65–8 BCE)—active already in the so-called "triumviral" period, after the Battle of Philippi (42 BCE), but before the Battle of Actium (31 BCE) established Octavian as supreme ruler of the Roman world.

1   Satire and Lyric

Among the earliest collections of verse published after Octavian inherited Julius Caesar's name and ambitions were Horace's two books of *Satires* (c. 35 and 30 BCE) and collection of *Iambi* (c. 30 BCE). Horace's earliest poetry can be characterized as "blame" poetry, whether in the Greek form of iambics or in the Latin form of satire, for both are genres of invective poetry and target representatives of social out-groups to make negative examples of them. The first three satires of Horace's first collection, for example, attack greed (*Sat.* 1.1), sexual folly (1.2), and intolerance (1.3) as exemplary instances of antisocial behavior. *Satire* 1.2 is of particular interest to us, for it illustrates the tight ideological connection between sexual decorum, financial probity, domestic stability, and civil order, and their opposites—sexual indecorum, financial ruin, domestic instability, and civil unrest.

Horace opens *Satire* 1.2 with the suggestion that excessive generosity entails the breakdown of social hierarchies (1.2.1–4): "The college of female flute players, quacks, beggars, mime-actresses, and buffoons—this whole set is sad and upset at the death of the singer Tigellius. Indeed, he was generous" (all translations here are my own). Generosity,

---

A Companion to Women in the Ancient World, First Edition. Edited by Sharon L. James and Sheila Dillon.
© 2012 John Wiley & Sons, Ltd. Published 2015 by John Wiley & Sons, Ltd.

as the hallmark of the freeborn man, was traditionally valued by the Roman upper classes for the preservation of the social status quo rather than for the potential to transform the class-standing of members of such disreputable "companies" as flute players and clowns. Tigellius' inappropriate generosity thus contrasts with the improper avarice excoriated in the previous satire, but only obliquely introduces this satire's theme of sexual folly, perhaps in the reference to flute players and mime actresses. Women of both types were of servile or freed status in Roman society and therefore, by definition, sexually available to freeborn Roman men. Their inclusion in the catalog of Tigellius' hangers-on may therefore be seen, retrospectively, to anticipate Horace's insistence on the close association of sexual misconduct with financial ruin and thereby to hint at the satire's focus on sexual folly as an index of social disorder. By aggregating the members of the lower orders into "companies," or types, moreover, Horace contrasts them pointedly with the singular, wealthy Tigellius. This gendered and hierarchical strategy of interpellation implies the speaker's elite male perspective on Roman society, such as we might expect from the genre's antecedent in the thirty books excoriating political enemies and commending like-minded friends composed by the wealthy aristocrat Lucilius (182–102/1 BCE).

Horace continues by contrasting the generous Tigellius with a man so afraid of earning the reputation of a spendthrift that he behaves like the cheapest miser (4–6). He reiterates the opposition between profligacy and excessive frugality in the opposing examples of a glutton wishing to avoid the reputation of cheapness (1.2.7–11) and the miserly usurer Fufidius, who squeezes youths just come of age but is so tight-fisted that he spends nothing on himself (1.2.12–22). The contrasts point to the moral of the satire (1.2.24): "While fools avoid vices, they run into their opposites." Neither the opening movement of the satire nor the stated moral explicitly announces the sexual focus of the rest of the satire; but the examples that follow repeatedly return to the financial ruin that sexual misconduct apparently inevitably entails and sustain Horace's assertion that "there is no mean" (1.2.28). Thus, the ostensible contrast between "those who would not touch any women but those whose ankles are covered by the flounce on the matron's hem" (1.2.29–30)—that is, a respectable married woman—and "another who would touch none but a woman in a stinking brothel" (1.2.31) vanishes in the inevitable loss of patrimony that attends all adulterers, whatever the class of the women they desire (1.2.59–63):

> Is it abundantly sufficient for you to avoid the person, not the role [of adulterer] that is universally detrimental? To lose one's good reputation, to squander one's father's estate, is an evil in all cases. What's the difference whether your transgression is with a married woman, a slave, or a prostitute?

Horace's emphasis on the causal relationship between adultery and financial ruin obscures the social issue the satire both confronts and occludes—the disruption of traditional patterns of circulation of money, land, and women among elite men during the recent civil wars. Taking as his limit-cases Sallust and Marsaeus, Horace satirizes them for priding themselves on avoiding sexual relations with respectably married matrons only to incur ruinous expenses on freedwomen (1.2.47–59):

> But how much safer is spending on the second class—of freedwomen, I mean: after whom Sallust is no less mad than he who commits adultery. But if he wishes to be good and generous, as far as his estate and reason would urge, and as far as one might be generous with moderation, he would give as much as would be sufficient and not what would be to his ruin and disgrace.

But he hugs himself on this one point, loves it, praises it: "I touch no matron." Just as once Marsaeus, the notorious lover of Origo, who bestowed on a mime actress both his paternal estate and town-house, said: "I've never had anything to do with other men's wives." But you have with mime actresses, you have with courtesans; whence your reputation derives greater harm than your estate.

By emphasizing the dangers posed by all female sexual activity to the Roman elite's monopoly on wealth and political privilege, Horace frames sexual profligacy as a danger to the stability of elite Roman male society. The association of sexual license with societal breakdown thereby displaces anxieties raised by the social upheaval of the contemporary civil wars onto the battle between the sexes and uses women to address men about how they should, or should not, interact with each other (Oliensis 2007).

A similar rhetorical strategy, in which social tensions are displaced onto gendered hierarchies, is visible in *Satire* 1.8. Here Horace yields the speaker's role to a statue of Priapus, the phallic god whose image protected Roman gardens from thieves and birds, set up on the Esquiline hill in Rome. Formerly home to a slave cemetery, an extensive tract of the Esquiline was purchased by Maecenas, who soon after the Battle of Actium began the construction of a palatial mansion and tower within a sprawling suburban complex that eventually included the Roman townhouses of Vergil and Propertius. The unusually genial and pacific Priapus of this satire complains about the lingering unhealthiness of the site, despite Maecenas' efforts, and explains that a pair of witches, Canidia and Sagana, frequent his garden by night to work black magic. They thereby undermine Maecenas' socially salubrious project of cleaning up the Esquiline and, by implication, Octavian's politically salubrious project of restoring Rome to old-fashioned virtue and Horace's literary project of cleaning up Lucilian satire (Anderson 1972). The witches thus function as negative foils to the satirist and his grand friends, whose projects Priapus seems to approve. On this reading, Horace uses the women to address men about pressing socio-political concerns, enlivening his argument by displacing the contest for control of Rome onto the genial statue of Priapus and the abject figures of the two witches, whom Priapus invites us to mock as they flee his garden (and Maecenas') in disarray (1.8.46–50):

> For I, a fig-tree, farted from my cleft buttock, as a burst bladder sounds; and they ran in to the city. You could see, with much laughter and mirth, Canidia's teeth and Sagana's high wig, the herbs and enchanted love-knots drop from their arms.

The comical ending obscures the larger social purpose of the satire, which works to align Roman elite interests with those of Maecenas and, by extension, Octavian.

In his *Iambi*, too, Horace represents the lecherous Canidia as threatening both his poetic projects and his grand friends' political projects. Thus, *Iambi* 5 reports the wicked rites practiced by Canidia and Sagana to prevent adultery and rouse love, including the live burial of a youth (to cut out their victim's marrow and liver for use in a love potion) and visits to graves (as in *Sat.* 1.8) to harvest the ingredients for noxious poisons. The ugliness of the poem's imagery vividly evokes the ugliness of the civil conflicts of the 30s BCE, with the malicious witches symbolizing political foes (whether of Octavian or including Octavian, in the unsettled period of Horace's composition of the *Iambi*) who are so devoted to the dead, destructive past, that they continue to engage in the same fatally dangerous activities (Oliensis 1991; Mankin 1995).

Such allegorical interpretation of the Canidia poems is compelling, but critics have been unwilling to confront the palpable misogyny that animates it. After all, *Satires* 1.8 also deploys a fig-tree Priapus allegorically, but the statue does not elicit such unbridled vitriol from Horace. The question is particularly pressing in *Iambi* 8 and 12, in which the speaker rejects a grotesque old hag, unnamed but often taken to be Canidia, who makes aggressive sexual demands on him. In *Iambi* 8, Horace justifies his impotence with a vivid catalog of her repulsive physical attributes (8.1–10):

> That you, rotting with lengthened age, should ask what weakens my powers? When your tooth is black, and old age furrows your forehead with wrinkles; and your disgusting ass-hole gapes between withered buttocks, like that of a sick cow. But your chest and stinking breasts, like mare's udders, and your soft belly, and skinny thigh added to swelling legs disgust me.

In the lines that follow, he contrasts her disgusting physical features with her apparently high social status, associating her with the attributes of the Roman elite—triumphs, funerary images, expensive jewelry, silk, and book-learning (8.11–16). The woman has therefore been interpreted as a symbolic figure, representing either an old-fashioned poetics (Clayman 1975), or youth's characteristic dread of impotence (Fitzgerald 1988), or even Rome herself, "horribly repulsive, yet still strangely fascinating" to Horace and his readers (Mankin 1995: 153). On any of these interpretations, Horace deploys the women to address men about political, social, or literary issues, while the misogyny of his verse legitimates the continuing necessity of masculine rule.

Horace's rhetorical deployment of female characters in his blame poetry to justify closing elite (male) ranks against an abjected (female) outgroup and, by implication, to support the political, literary, and social projects of Maecenas and his other grand friends, continues in the lyric *Odes*, a genre that traditionally included amatory verse among its varieties of "praise" poetry. Thus, the last of the Roman Odes—to be sure, the most overtly political poems of *Odes* 1–3 (23 BCE)—contrasts the virtuous Sabine women of old, who trained their men-folk for foreign wars of imperial expansion, with Horace's vicious female contemporaries, who openly disdain old-fashioned morality (3.6.17–32):

> Generations fruitful in crime have first stained marriages and then the family line and households. Destruction derived from this source has flooded the country and people. The marriageable maiden delights in being taught Ionic dances and is trained for the seductive arts, and from her earliest youth plans unchaste love affairs. Amidst her husband's wine-cups, she seeks younger adulterers, nor is she choosy upon whom she hastily bestows illicit joys when the lights are removed. But when bidden, she rises openly, not without the knowledge of her husband, whether a shopkeeper calls her or the captain of a Spanish ship, the extravagant purchaser of her disgrace.

Roman men's complicity in their wives' adultery appears to be the central target of Horace's political message here, for he closes the poem, and the sequence, with reflections on the destructive impact of adultery on the patriarchal social fabric of Rome (3.6.45–8): "What has the ruinous passage of time not spoiled? Our fathers' generation, worse than our grandfathers', has brought us, more wicked still and soon destined to produce an even more degraded progeny."

When Horace does address women directly in his lyric poetry, it is to denounce the aging man-eater (e.g., 1.25) or menace the shy beauty, as, for example, in *Odes* 1.23, where Horace urges the adolescent Chloe to recognize that the time has come to accept a lover:

Chloe, you shun me like a fawn seeking its timid mother on pathless mountains, not without groundless fear of breezes and forest. For it trembles in both heart and knees, whether the arrival of spring has rustled amid the quivering leaves or the green lizards have stirred the brambles. And yet I do not pursue you like a savage tiger or a Gaetulian lion, to break you. At last stop following your mother, now that you're ready for a man.

The predatory imagery of a fierce tiger or lion tracking a motherless fawn implies the violence with which the speaker's predatory desire threatens the maiden, even as he explicitly disavows it. Yet, as we have seen, rhetorical violence is a consistent feature of Horace's poetry about women, whether he writes ostensibly amatory or avowedly invective verse.

Horace's lyric poetry typically enmeshes the beloved in the passage of time but exempts the speaker from temporal processes (Ancona 1994), and a related stance, which Horace assumes throughout the *Odes*, is that of ironic detachment from the vicissitudes of erotic fortune (Oliensis 2007). The first amatory poem in the collection illustrates the speaker's characteristically distant, even voyeuristic, perspective on love (1.5):

What graceful youth, on many a rose and perfumed with liquid scent, courts you, Pyrrha, in some pleasant grotto? For whom do you braid your golden hair, restrained in your elegance? Alas, how often will he bewail your broken faith and the altered gods, and unaccustomed, wonder at the seas roughened by dark storms, who now unsuspectingly enjoys you, golden as you are; who, all unaware of the deceptive breeze, hopes that you will always be available, always loving. Wretched are the men whom you dazzle, untried. The temple wall shows on a votive tablet that I have hung up my dripping robes to the god that rules the ocean.

Here the speaker implies that he has left the age of erotic love behind, and in *Odes* 4.1 he similarly represents himself as resisting the summons of Venus to renewed composition of lyric with the argument that he is too old to resume the lover's role. Throughout his lyric verse, however, he shows a recurrent scopophilic interest in other people's love affairs, and a constant sympathy for the male "victims" of women's erotic appeal. Thus, in *Odes* 3.7, he chides his addressee, Asterie, for doubting the constancy of her absent lover Gyges and charges her with secretly admiring Enipeus, who serenades her by night.

Horace associates the chain of unrequited love such as is on display in *Odes* 3.7—where Gyges' Bithynian hostess pursues him while he remains faithful to Asterie, who in turn seems to be smitten with Enipeus—especially closely with a rival genre of contemporary love poetry, *viz.* elegy. In *Odes* 1.33, for example, he addresses an Albius, who has been plausibly identified as the elegist Tibullus, and contrasts the advantages of lyric with the disadvantages of elegiac love:

Albius, do not indulge in excessive sorrow, remembering your harsh Glycera, nor keep on uttering piteous elegies, asking why she has broken her faith and prefers a younger man to you. Love of Cyrus fires Lycoris, beautiful with her low forehead, while Cyrus turns his affections to harsh Pholoe; but she-goats will mate with Apulian wolves before Pholoe will sin with so base an adulterer. Thus it seems good to Venus, who delights in cruel mirth, to subject to her bronze yoke ill-matched figures and minds. When a better love wooed me, the freedwoman Myrtale, more passionate than the Adriatic's straits, which curves Calabrian bays, entangled me with her pleasing fetters.

Albius' mistress bears the speaking name Glycera, "Sweetie," which appears nowhere in extant Latin elegy, but which, in conjunction with the adjective "harsh," sums up the arrogant appeal of the beautiful, but unyielding, elegiac mistress. Both the names Lycoris and Pholoe, moreover, have antecedents in contemporary elegy, the former as the name of the elegiac poet Gallus' mistress (Verg. *Buc.* 10; cf. Gallus fr. 145 Hollis) and the latter as that of the harsh mistress of Tibullus' elegy 1.8, who cruelly disdains the love of the youth Marathus, himself the object of the Tibullan speaker's desire in elegies 1.4 and 1.9.

2 Elegy and Epic

If elegy too traffics in women, as it undoubtedly does, the genre not only explores more personal aspects of women's lives than the clichés of satire and the politics of lyric allow but also offers a more complex and nuanced portrait of women's personal relations with men. Throughout the 20s and 10s BCE, the three Augustan elegists—Tibullus (c. 55—19 BCE), Propertius (c. 50–c. 15 BCE), and Ovid (March 20, 43 BCE—17 CE)—published collections of *amores*, or "love poems," in the model of the slightly earlier love poetry of Catullus (c. 84—c. 54 BCE) and Gallus (70/69–27/6 BCE). Autobiographical in form, this poetry records the speakers' love for beautiful, often unavailable, courtesans (James 2003).

Propertius' first collection (c. 29 BCE) opens by invoking the woman who gives her name to the book and presides over his prostrate form (1.1.1–2): "Cynthia first captured me, wretch that I am, with her eyes; before, I'd been touched by no Desires." The passion and immediacy of the Cynthia elegies have long provoked interest among Propertius' readers in the autobiographical origins of his elegiac poetry and he himself plays on public curiosity about the intimate details of his love affair at the outset of his second book (2.1.1–2): "You [pl.] ask whence my love poems are so often written, whence my soft book comes to recital." Few readers have been able to resist the invitation of these lines to biographical speculation and, indeed, the challenge was taken up in antiquity, as the second century CE orator and philosopher Apuleius illustrates (*Apology* 10): "Propertius ... says Cynthia to conceal Hostia; and Tibullus ... loved Plania in his heart, Delia in his verse." Social historians and literary critics alike, however, have called into question whether the identification of supposed historical girlfriends can provide meaningful access to the historical women and the circumstances of their lives, let alone explain their literary significance (Wyke 2002). Feminist critics have demonstrated that women enter classical literature as "gendered" objects of (mostly) male writing practices and have persuasively argued that such "written" women are further shaped by the literary genre in which their authors inscribe them (Keith 2000; Dixon 2001; Wyke 2002).

Catullus sets the precedent for the naming practices of the Augustan elegists by concealing the identity of his beloved behind a pseudonym, Lesbia, which evokes the Greek poet Sappho. The debt of Propertius and Ovid to Catullus is evident in the former's explicit invocation of Catullan precedent (2.25.1–4, 32.45–6) and representation of Cynthia as a poet herself (1.3.41–4, 2.3.19–22) who rivals comparison with the Greek poets Sappho and Korinna (2.3.19–22), and also in the latter's application to his mistress of a name, Corinna, that not only belonged to a Greek poetess but is also both a Latinized diminutive of the Greek word for "girl" (*korê*) and the metrical equivalent of the Latin synonym regularly used of the elegiac "girlfriend" (*puella*). Significant too is the debt of Propertius and also Tibullus, in his first book of elegies (c. 27/26 BCE), to the example of Gallus, who conceals the name of his mistress Cytheris (itself a stage name of the freedwoman and mime-actress Volumnia: Servius, *ad* Verg. *Buc.* 10.1, 6) beneath the pseudonym Lycoris (a feminized form of the cult-title of Apollo at Delphi), for both Cynthia and Delia are feminized forms of cult titles of the god Apollo, divine patron of poetry (Cynthius: Call. *Hymn* 4.9–10, Verg. *Buc.* 6.4; Delius: Soph. *Aj.* 701, [Tib.] 3.6.8). Moreover, Nemesis, the girlfriend of Tibullus' second book (c. 19 BCE), bears the name of the goddess of retribution, who frequently pursues arrogant lovers in Hellenistic epigram. The elegists thus endow their girlfriends with names that have intensely literary resonances (Randall 1979).

Propertius invites metapoetic interpretation of his Cynthia from the start, for it was conventional in antiquity to identify literary works by their opening word (Wyke 2002). Propertius' first collection of elegies will thus have circulated under the title of "Cynthia." The elegist plays with the double valence of Cynthia as both woman and text when he imagines writing her name on the bark of trees (1.18.21–2), self-consciously foregrounding his role as amatory elegist by inscribing "Cynthia" on the original writing surface (McNamee 1993). Cynthia's textualization is also central to her characterization in Book 2 (c. 25 BCE), where Propertius promises to write epic once his mistress has been "written" (2.10.8) and reflects on the fame the wide circulation of his "Cynthia" among contemporary Roman readers has brought him (2.24.1–2). (On Propertius see also Hallett, this volume, Chapter 27.)

Tibullus, by contrast, wears his learning and literary commitments more lightly in the idealized portrait he offers of his mistress, Delia, in Book 1. In the opening poem, he announces his modest ambition to enjoy a small crop and embrace his girlfriend (1.1.43–6), and contrasts his amatory service, in thrall to Delia, with military service under Messalla's command (1.1.53–6; cf. 1.73–8), which the ancient *vita* suggests he saw (cf. Tib. 1.3, 1.7, 2.6). He longs to die in Delia's company, rather than on military service (as he fears may happen in elegy 1.3), and he repeatedly sketches amatory idylls of life on the farm with his mistress (1.5.21–34, 1.10.39–68; cf. 2.1, 2.5.83–100), in images of rustic domesticity that pay homage to Vergil's *Georgics* at the same time that they elaborate a union similar to the ideal Roman marriage (on which see Treggiari 1991).

Ovid elaborates the settings and themes of Propertian and Tibullan elegy in his *Amores* (a second edition is extant, perhaps published two decades after Ovid first began to compose elegiac poetry c. 25 BCE), which offer the fullest and most coherent narrative of a love affair in extant Roman elegy. The first book introduces his mistress along with the stock scenes (party, locked-out lover's complaint, quarrel) and standard characters (*uir*, door-keeper, bawd, hairdresser, go-between) of an elegiac affair; the second complicates the affair with the introduction of rivals to both Corinna and the speaker, but also with the separation of speaker and mistress while on journeys and in ill health; and the third recounts the waning of the speaker's passion, graphically figured as impotence in 3.7, and his increasing distance from and disillusionment with his promiscuous mistress. Ovid's elegy embodies a carnal physicality alien to that of Tibullus and Propertius, starting with the sexual double entendre in his description of the rhythm of the elegiac couplet in the very first poem (1.1.17–18) and continuing in poems detailing Corinna's naked charms (1.5); the speaker's susceptibility to a variety of women (2.4), including Corinna's hairdresser (2.8); his stamina in bed (2.10, 2.15); and his unexpected impotence (3.7). Ovid's descriptions of elegiac women's beauty, sartorial preferences, and deportment exemplify the stylistic sophistication of his own elegiac verse, transformed through metaphor into the figure of the mistress (Keith 1994).

The textualization of the elegiac mistress, and her concomitant circulation among men, is a central gender dynamic of the genre and can be paralleled throughout Augustan literature. Thus, Propertius' elegy 1.1 describes the poet-lover's passionate love for her, but the poem itself plays a wider function in the collection since it is addressed to his patron Tullus. Cynthia, both the lover's mistress and the poet's book of elegies, is thereby subsumed into the gift presented to Tullus, who, as the addressee of the first poem, is the dedicatee of the collection (Keith 2008: 115–38). Cynthia circulates between Propertius and his patrons Tullus and Maecenas (2.1, 3.9), as well as other friends and rivals, just as Delia and Nemesis circulate between Tibullus and his patron Messalla (1.1, 1.3) and his friend Cornutus (2.3), and Corinna and his other mistresses between Ovid and Atticus (*Am.* 1.9), Graecinus (2.10), and Macer and Sabinus (2.18). The elegiac mistress' general circulation brings literary renown to the poet but leaves her vulnerable to the lover's charges of promiscuity (Fear 2000), for elegiac poetry, like the other genres we have been considering, circulated among the Roman political elites within a culture of institutionalized social relations that consolidated male authority in and through women's bodies. By addressing members of the Roman social and political elite as patrons, friends, and literary rivals, the elegists appeal to and consolidate the homosocial bonds of elite male friendship and implicitly document the social and political entitlements of their own class and gender. Roman elegiac composition and performance was an exercise in masculine cooperation and competition, as Propertius' and Ovid's genealogies of the genre illustrate (Prop. 2.34.85–94; Ov. *Am.* 1.15).

Despite the autobiographical and homosocial frame of the genre, however, Latin elegy is unusual in endowing its female characters with speech. Propertian elegy is especially noteworthy in this regard, for Cynthia utters nine speeches in direct discourse, occupying all or part of 137 lines. While Delia and Nemesis do not speak in Tibullan elegy, Ovid gives each of them voice in his epicedion for the dead Tibullus (*Am.* 3.9), as he also does Corinna elsewhere in the *Amores.* Even more striking, perhaps, is the inclusion in individual elegies of lengthy speeches by the bawds Acanthis and Dipsas (Prop. 4.5; Ov. *Am.* 1.8), who directly oppose the goals of the elegiac speaker. The openness of elegy to female expressions of desire may explain, in part, both the existence and the survival of the *elegidia* of Sulpicia ([Tib.] 3.9, 11, 13–18). The granddaughter or great-granddaughter of S. Sulpicius Rufus (cos. 51 BCE) and Messalla's sister Valeria, Sulpicia is generally agreed to have been born in the mid-40s BCE and her elegies dated to the penultimate decade of the century (Syme 1981; Parker 1994; Keith 1997). Sulpicia's opening poem ponders the impropriety necessarily involved in a Roman woman's avowal of love ([Tib.] 3.13):

> At last love has come; and such a love it is that the rumor of having concealed it would shame me more than baring all. Entreated by my Muses' prayers, Cythera's mistress has brought and placed him in my lap. Venus has fulfilled her promises. Let my joys be told by all of whom it can be said that they have missed their own. I would not choose to entrust my messages to tablets under seal, that none might read them before my lover. Instead my sin delights me, and I am loath to compose a mask for rumor. Let me be said to have been worthy of my worthy beloved.

Sulpicia's emphasis on her daring freedom of speech finds expression in the offer of her tale of love to others, for she invites those who lack their own joys to narrate as their own her private compact with the goddess of love. This oral dissemination constitutes the initial informal publication of her love poetry, but a figure for its formal literary publication follows in the image of the unsealed tablets, which make her elegies available to any reader and contrast strikingly with the conventionally sealed tablets surreptitiously conveyed by a go-between from elegiac poet-lover to beloved. (On Sulpicia see also Hallett, this volume, Chapter 27.)

The openness of elegy to women's voices and the expression of female desire contrasts strikingly with the place of women in the early hexameter poetry of Vergil. Though "cattle" are the ostensible subject of Virgilian pastoral (*Buc.* 1.45), the world of the *Bucolics* (c. 37 BCE) is intensely human and homosocial, focusing on male social bonds and their structural importance in the contexts of friendship, rivalry, mentorship, patronage, love, and sexuality (Oliensis 1997). The sole female singer of Vergilian pastoral goes unnamed and is doubly ventriloquized, for she speaks not directly in her own voice but through the report of a male singer, Alphesiboeus (*Buc.* 8.64–109), while her song adapts a poem by Vergil's admired Greek model Theocritus (*Id.* 2.1–63). Similarly, though "cultivation of fields and flocks" (*Geo.* 4.559) is the ostensible subject of Vergil's *Georgics* (29 BCE), the intimate interconnection of the natural world with gendered human culture occasionally asserts itself. Vergil treats the destructive force of love and sexual passion among cattle (3.209–85) in human terms, referring to the divisive role of the "female" (*femina*, 3.216) in inspiring passion, drawing on the technical vocabulary of prostitution and elegy (3.217–18) and including at the climax of the passage a human *exemplum*, Leander's death for love of Hero (3.258–63).

In the *Aeneid* (19 BCE), however, Vergil explicitly thematizes gender with the focus on the "man," Aeneas (*uirum*, 1.1). He and the surviving Trojans are destined to fulfill Jupiter's divine plan to establish the Roman race in Italy despite Juno's relentless opposition. The opposition between Jupiter and Juno on the cosmogonic level symbolizes the gendered struggle between good and evil, order and chaos, that pervades the poem and reappears in the opposition between Aeneas and Dido on the mythological level (in Books 1, 4, and 6) and Augustus and Cleopatra on the historical level (on the Shield of Aeneas in Book 8). The opening lines of the *Aeneid* announce the goal of Aeneas' journey to Italy as Latium, particularized in the phrase "Lavinian shores" (1.1–2), where tradition located the original Trojan foundation of Lavinium. Vergil derives the name of Lavinium from Lavinia, the daughter of the indigenous Latin king Latinus, and he predicates the political foundation of Lavinium, which lies beyond the narrative scope of the *Aeneid*, on the dynastic marriage of Aeneas with Lavinia. Sex and empire are further linked in the poem through Aeneas' dalliance in North Africa with the Carthaginian queen Dido, which constitutes a divergence from his imperial mission as an indulgence in the "wrong" dynastic marriage (See also James, this volume, Case Study V.).

The Dido episode well illustrates the process by which a story about a woman becomes a story about her sexuality in Augustan literature. As a woman operating in the public sphere, Dido necessarily constitutes and is constituted as a disruptive force in the *Aeneid* and, in accordance with Roman discursive codes about the female, the focus of the narrative "naturally" narrows to Dido's sexuality, so that her deviant political and military ambitions come to be recast as inappropriate erotic desires. The banquet to which Dido hospitably invites Aeneas, after welcoming the shipwrecked Trojans to her city, is the site of her transformation in the narrative from an effective political leader (*dux*) into a politically disabled lovesick woman (*femina*, 1.364). Vergil's descriptions of Dido's richly appointed banquet and the sumptuous luxury of her palace implicate her in Roman moralizing discourses linking excessive wealth with excessive lust (Edwards 1993). In this excessively luxurious setting, Dido is necessarily, (ideo)logically, represented as succumbing to excessive erotic desire (1.748–9): "unfortunate Dido drew out the night in varied conversation and drank down long draughts of love." By the beginning of the fourth book, excessive desire constitutes the whole of her identity (4.1–2): "but the queen, long since struck with a serious passion, nourishes the wound in her veins and is consumed by an unseen flame." Building projects stand unfinished throughout Carthage (4.85–9), reflecting Dido's abandonment of political and military projects in preference for love (4.84). Her political decline is complemented by her abuse of religious ritual to further erotic rather than political goals. Sexual union with Aeneas not only disables Dido politically but leads, seemingly inevitably, to her death (4.169–70): "that day was the beginning of her doom, the first cause of her troubles."

In the depiction of Dido's excessive passion and her resulting political downfall and death, a pattern of protocols valorizing female sexual purity can be discerned that overlaps with Augustan ideology concerning the state regulation of female sexuality. The close temporal conjunction between the promulgation of the marital and moral legislation of 18 and 16 BCE in the name of Augustus and the publication of the *Aeneid* on the authority of Augustus in 17 BCE suggests that Dido's sexual transgression may be related to Augustan suspicion of unregulated female sexuality. Viewed through this androcentric elite Roman perspective, Dido's nationality and gender (ideo)logically combine to construct her as socially disruptive and sexually deviant.

Nor is Dido alone in this regard: the Latin queen Amata, herself driven by love for Turnus, overturns the compact forged between her husband Latinus and the Trojans, and thereby drives two peoples destined for political union into (proto-civil) war. Turnus is protected on the battlefield by his patron goddess Juno, who consistently opposes Aeneas and the Trojan mission, and by his sister, Juturna, who overturns a second compact between Trojans and Latins in the final book of the epic. Mercury famously defines "woman" as "ever changeable" (*mutabile semper/femina*, 4.570), but the women of the *Aeneid* are, in fact, remarkably consistent in their opposition to the Roman mission, despite the dictates of Jupiter and Fate. Thus, Georgia Nugent (1999: 260) has observed that the great female characters of the *Aeneid* "refuse, in various ways, their traditional roles of passivity, domesticity, and subordination; they refuse the mission of Rome; they even refuse to give credence to the pronouncements of the gods." Even the Trojan women reject the authority of Aeneas and his mission, choosing in Book 5 to settle in Sicily rather than continue on the voyage to Latium. We learn in Book 9 that a single intrepid Trojan woman, the (unnamed) mother of Euryalus, has completed the journey to Italy; yet, true to female form, she too opposes masculine authority and (proto-Roman) military values when, in her grief at her son's death, she threatens the Trojans' will to fight.

The *Aeneid* regularly introduces young male warriors on the battlefield only for them to die at the hands of greater heroes; but it also seems to demand the deaths of its female characters: both Dido and Amata kill themselves, while Aeneas' first wife, Creusa, is lost in the aftermath of the Trojan War, the Amazonian Camilla is slain on the battlefield before Latinus' city, and Juturna sinks beneath the Tiber, refusing immortality. If we read the *Aeneid* as a narrative about the hierarchy of gender in Roman society, we can see Aeneas and the Trojans—purged of feminine weakness by the abandonment of Creusa at Troy and the Trojan women in Sicily, as well as the deaths of Dido, Camilla, and Amata—as constituting an all-male proto-Roman society that anticipates the masculine, militarized society of Augustan Rome idealized on the Shield of Aeneas (8.626–730).

3   History and Oratory

A quintessentially Roman and, indeed, Augustan obsession with moral exemplarity emerges as well in Livy's assessment of the use of historical study in the preface to his great work, the first pentad of which is now generally agreed to have been composed in the years 27 to 25 BCE (*pr.* 9):

> What chiefly makes the study of history wholesome and profitable is this, that you behold the lessons [*exempli*] of every kind of experience set forth on a conspicuous monument; from these you may choose for yourself and for your state what to imitate, from these mark for avoidance what is shameful in conception and shameful in the result.

Here Livy (59 BCE–17 CE) emphasizes the utility of historical inquiry, and he expresses this obsession with particular urgency when he comes to narrate the tale of Lucretia (1.57–9), whose death he presents as the cause of the overthrow of the Etruscan kings and establishment of the Roman Republic in 509 BCE (on Livy's women, see also Izzet, this volume, Chapter 5; Henry and James, this volume, Chapter 6; and Hallett, this volume, Chapter 27).

The narrative opens with the protracted Roman siege of Ardea (c. 510 BCE), where the Etruscan princes and Roman officers pass their time in extravagances such as drinking parties, at one of which the subject of wives arises. As the officers compete to praise their wives, Lucretia's husband proposes that they ride to Rome and see for themselves whose wife is the most virtuous. Accordingly, they ride to Rome, where they find the princes' wives enjoying a luxurious dinner party while Lucretia is discovered late at night surrounded by her maidservants, all spinning by lamplight: "which wife had won the contest in womanly virtue was no longer in doubt" (1.57.9). The contest in womanly virtue doubles as a contest in masculine virtue, and vice. Soon after, the Etruscan king Tarquin's son Sextus, fired by lust, returns to debauch Lucretia, thus proving Etruscan monarchal vice (anticipated in the high living of the princes' wives). When the chaste Lucretia rejects his advances, he offers her the "choice" of rape or dishonor, threatening to kill her and lay out the body of a slave beside hers, as if "caught in adultery with a servant [she had] paid the price" (1.58.4). Lucretia submits, but after Sextus' departure she summons her kinsmen to disclose her disgrace and demand not only Sextus' punishment but also her own, vowing "never shall Lucretia provide a precedent [*exemplo*] for unchaste women to escape what they deserve" (1.58.10).

If unchaste women deserve death, Roman men deserve self-rule, and so Brutus seizes the moment to instigate the overthrow of the Etruscan monarchy (1.59.1):

> Brutus drew the bloody knife from Lucretia's body, and holding it before him cried: "By this girl's blood—none more chaste till a tyrant wronged her—and by the gods, I swear that with sword and fire, and whatever else can lend strength to my arm, I will pursue Lucius Tarquin the Proud, his wicked wife, and all his children, and never again will I let them or any other man be king in Rome."

Livy grounds the masculine virtue of Brutus and Lucretia's kinsmen in the dead woman's blood, and he concludes the first book of his history with their exhibition of her prostrate form to the populace. He thereby identifies Lucretia's rape and death as the precipitating cause of both the Tarquins' expulsion and the establishment of the Republic (1.59–60).

The historian thus predicates masculine political rule on the chastity of Roman womanhood.

Livy explicitly links the exemplary death of the aristocratic Lucretia to that of the plebeian Verginia (3.44), who escapes the sexual assault of the tyrannical decemvir Appius only because her father murders her before Appius can debauch her. Verginius then follows the example of Brutus, the "Liberator," in inciting a public outcry against Appius' arrogance, which leads to the overthrow of the decemvirate, the re-establishment of the tribunate, and the resumption of the normal workings of the political institutions of the Republic (3.44–58). The stories of both Lucretia and Verginia found Roman (male) republican government on the chaste bodies of Roman women, and tale after tale in Livy's history illustrates the interdependence of Roman women's chastity and the masculine arenas of Roman politics and warfare (Joshel 1992a).

Barred from participation in the masculine pursuits of war and politics, Roman women earn Livy's praise by putting their chastity, piety, and money at the service of the state. Thus, Livy describes with approval the repeated religious initiatives and financial contributions of Rome's matrons during the Hannibalic war (21.62, 22.1, 22.52, 25.1, 27.37). One such financial subvention, furnished in the aftermath of the Battle of Cannae (216 BCE), arose as a result of the Senate's passage of the Oppian Law, which limited the public display of wealth by Roman *matronae* (34.1.3). The legislation remained in force even after Hannibal's defeat in 202 BCE, and it was not until seven years later that the law was repealed (34.1–8). Livy reports with disapproval the pressure Rome's matrons brought to bear on their husbands and elected magistrates in order to repeal the legislation (34.1.5–6):

> The matrons could not be confined within doors by the advice of their husbands, by respect for their husbands, or by their husbands' command; they beset all the streets of the city and all the approaches to the Forum, and as the men came down to the Forum they besought them, in view of the flourishing state of the commonwealth, at a time when the personal fortunes of all men were daily increasing, to allow the women also the restoration of their former luxuries.

In the ensuing narrative, Livy includes a formal debate between the elder Cato, one of the consuls of 195 BCE and a staunch supporter of the *lex Oppia*, and Valerius, the tribune who proposed its repeal (34.2–7).

Such set-piece rhetorical debates were a conventional feature of Roman political oratory and senatorial historiography, the latter genre often drawing on published versions of the former. Whether or not the speeches of Cato and Valerius were available to Livy when he composed his history, their rhetoric certainly reflects contemporary Augustan clichés about Roman womanhood. Thus, Livy's Cato invokes ancestral custom to emphasize Roman men's long-standing authority over their womenfolk: "our ancestors allowed no woman to transact business, not even privately, without a guardian and wanted women to be under the control of fathers, brothers, husbands" (34.2.11). His formulation vividly documents contemporary male social and financial power over women and reflects Augustus' reinscription of these principles at the heart of his marriage and adultery legislation of 18 and 16 BCE. In support of the law's repeal, Cato's opponent Valerius likewise appeals to feminine stereotypes (34.7.5–9):

> But by Hercules, there is sorrow and indignation among them all, when they see permitted to the wives of our Latin allies the adornment denied to them, when they see those women

bedecked with gold and purple, when they see them carried through the city while they themselves follow on foot, just as if dominion lay in the Latin women's cities and not in their own. This could wound the feelings of men; what do you think it does to foolish little women, whom even small things move? No magistracies, no priesthoods, no triumphs, no marks of power, no gifts, no spoils of war can come to them; elegance, adornment, clothing—these are women's marks of power, in these they rejoice and glory, this is what our ancestors called a "woman's world."

The feminine clichés to which Livy's magistrates appeal in their speeches not only strengthen male social bonds and elite authority over women but also naturalize the hierarchy of the sexes on display in every genre of Augustan literature, including history and oratory. Although no complete examples of Augustan oratory survive (Balbo 2004), the elder Seneca (c. 50 BCE–c. 40 CE) celebrated the rhetorical culture of the early principate (Griffin 1972) in two treatises on Augustan declamation: *Controversiae* (speeches on a disputed point of law) and *Suasoriae* (speeches of empathetic impersonation). Seneca self-consciously cites the elder Cato in the preface to his *Controversiae*, implicitly taking the republican censor as his model in rhetoric: "What then did that famous man [*ille uir*] say? 'An orator, Marcus my son, is a good man [*uir bonus*], skilled in speaking'" (*Contr.* 1 *pr.* 9). The androcentric focus of oratory, rhetoric, and declamation could hardly be more clearly expressed.

Like Livy, the elder Seneca asserts the exemplary value of his work (*Contr.* 1 *pr.* 6):

> But, my young men, you are pursuing an important and useful matter because, not content with the examples [*exemplis*] of your own day, you wish also to know those of an earlier generation. First since the more examples [*exempla*] one examines, the more the benefit to one's own eloquence.

The exemplary declamations Seneca recorded in his treatise on *Controversiae* rehearse conventional themes of law, politics, and warfare in their application to a wide range of stock characters, including women: wives (1.6, 2.2, 2.5, 10.3), stepmothers (4.5, 4.6, 6.7, 7.5, 9.5, 9.6), daughters (1.6, 4.3), and priestesses (1.2), especially Vestal Virgins (1.3, 6.8). Appeals to Roman social codes and conventions pervade this material: "all rich wives demand slavery" of their husbands (1.6.5) and "a wealthy wife is an unchecked evil" (1.6.7). Wives are proverbially avaricious (2.5.7):

> Is she burdensome in her expenditure, does she weigh hard on your income? Certainly that is what the age is like—luxury spreads from bad to worse, and the ambitions of women, competing with each other, bring madness to private households—and harm to the state.

It is a truism of the declamation halls that women's desire for wealth and luxury undermines the stability of the state. Nor is their desire limited to material objects—their lust knows no bounds: "a woman is unchaste if she even desires sex without having it" (6.8) and "even married women have much to teach in the matter of lust" (1.2.20). Female adultery—a major focus of Augustus' social legislation—is the theme of several *controversiae* (1.4, 1.7, 2.1.34–6, 2.7, 4.7, 6.6, 7.3.6, 7.5, 7.6.2, 8.3, 9.1) and even one of the *suasoriae* (*Sua.* 3.1–3). The declamations also bear witness to women's "well-known" garrulity (*Contr.* 2.5.12) and skill in poisoning (6.6, 7.3, 9.5, 9.6), the latter particularly associated with stepmothers (9.5, 9.6).

The elder Seneca's treatises offer us insight into contemporary social relations between elite Roman men and their inferiors (women, slaves, foreigners) and reveal significant alignment in their treatment of female sexuality with Augustus' social legislation on adultery (1.4, 1.7, 2.1.34–6, 2.7, 4.7, 6.6, 7.3.6, 7.5, 7.6.2, 8.3, 9.1; cf. *Sua.* 3.1–3, and fr. 1W), prostitution (1.2, 2.4, 9.2), and rape (2.5, 3.5, 7.6). In this regard, we may see women's rhetorical and historiographical stylization by elite men as reflecting the patriarchal concerns of the state in this period, with the emergence of Roman women's sexuality into the public domain (McGinn 1998; Richlin 1997a).

4   Conclusion

I have argued that the (mostly male) Roman authors of this period deploy female figures in their works to address contemporary social and political concerns from the discussion of which real historical women were (again for the most part) excluded. But there is no question that some of the women on display in Augustan literature were interpreted—by men and women alike, from antiquity to the present—as complex and fully developed characters, capable of achieving real moral stature and eliciting significant sympathy. Thus, when Augustan elegy opens up space for the expression of female desire, a Roman woman seems to have seized the opportunity to explore that space in a feminine register. Moreover Ovid, the youngest of the Augustan poets, repeatedly investigates the nature of women's desire in his poetry, both elegiac (especially in the *Heroides*) and epic (*Metamorphoses*) and, indeed, in *Heroides* 7 and *Metamorphoses* 14 we find our earliest evidence of the lasting impact of Dido on European literature. In *Tristia* 2, Ovid contends that the Dido narrative was the most popular part of the *Aeneid* and this (admittedly biased) discussion is borne out by statements in the work of later authors, such as the early second century CE satirist Juvenal, who implies that women responded to the *Aeneid* most passionately by identifying with Dido (*Sat.* 6.434–7), and the early fourth century CE church father Augustine, who clearly identified strongly with Dido himself (*Conf.* 1.13). These reflections inaugurate a rich and sophisticated tradition of reception and exploration of women in Augustan literature that spans every genre of the European arts.

FURTHER READING

Feminist criticism has spurred interest in gender and sexuality in Latin literature and Roman culture generally, and in the Augustan period in particular. Good points of entry to cultural specifics are: on women and law, especially Augustus' moral legislation, Gardner (1986) and McGinn (1998, 2004); on Roman marriage, Treggiari (1991); on the Roman rhetoric of immorality, Edwards (1993); and on sex and gender in ancient Rome Hallett and Skinner (1997), Wyke (1998), Hemelrijk (1999), Dixon (2001), and Ancona and Greene (2005).

   A great deal of work has been done on the representation of women in Augustan elegy and epic. On elegy, see especially Wyke (2002), which collects her ground-breaking studies of the late 1980s and early 1990s: Wyke (1987a, 1987b, 1989a, 1989b, 1992, 1994a, 1994b). See also, on the names of elegiac mistresses, Randall (1979); on Ovidian elegy, Sharrock (1991, 1994, 2002) and Keith (2009); and on Propertian elegy, McNamee (1993), Greene (1998), James (2003), and Keith (2008a). On Sulpicia in particular, see Santirocco (1979), Lowe (1988), Parker (1994), Keith (1997), Flaschenriem (1999), Milnor (2002), and the studies collected in a 2006 special section in *Classical World* entitled "Engaging with Sulpicia" (Hallett 2006; Keith 2006; Merriam 2006; Parker 2006). On women in Vergil's *Aeneid* see Perkell (1981), Wiltshire (1989), Nugent (1992, 1999), Oliensis (1997), and Keith (2000). On women in Ovid's *Metamorphoses* see Sharrock (1991), Salzman-Mitchell (2005), and Keith (2000, 2009). On women in Horatian satire and lyric, see Manning (1970), Ancona (1994), Anderson (1972), Clayman (1975), Henderson (1989), Oliensis (1991, 2007), Richlin (1992), and Mankin (1995). Livy has received less detailed discussion, but see Joshel (1992a). On the afterlife of Dido, see Desmond (1994).

29

Women on the Bay of Naples

Eve D'Ambra

The bay of Naples offers stark contrasts between vivid impressions of life in bustling farm towns or seaside villas and the devastation caused by the eruption of Mount Vesuvius in 79 CE. Through the startling extent of ruins encompassing city blocks packed with shops, shrines, and offices, along with the more intimate spaces of home and hearth, Pompeii and its environs have long dominated the picture of life in ancient Rome. In particular, the houses have sparked the imaginations of visitors, who have sought out everyday experiences instead of the vaunted spectacles of the civic life of antiquity. The private sphere of the *domus* frames women and the family, but it is not only in domestic interiors that the lives of women come into focus. The archaeological evidence of Pompeii attests to a range of activities of women in the public as well as in the private spheres, in prominent positions as supporters of political candidates and in lowly enterprises making textiles or leather goods.

Historical accounts of the Bay of Naples frequently begin with the end; that is, with the area's blanketing with ash in late August of the year 79 CE. This cataclysmic event buried towns, farms, and the countryside, blotting out the life of these communities but tracing their contours in the form of walls, foundations, and possessions that eventually came to light. The preservation and recovery of Pompeii and Herculaneum occurred in fits and starts from the eighteenth century and continues today with an unprecedented number of international teams of archaeologists working on the sites every summer. The wealth of archaeological evidence is impressive, even though much has been lost, if not to the eruption then to the zeal of earlier generations of excavators and enthusiasts, who ripped paintings out of walls and paid little attention to the physical context of artifacts. Current research aims to restore objects to their rightful places on site, and to consider the functions of spaces and buildings for the imperatives of civic institutions or the routines of daily living. Women, no less than men, spent their days in the shelter of porticoes and marketplaces. They also possessed a full panoply of material goods ranging from instruments of domestic utility to luxurious items of adornment. The evidence of monumental and intimate artifacts creates a more richly textured picture of women's lives.

A Companion to Women in the Ancient World, First Edition. Edited by Sharon L. James and Sheila Dillon.
© 2012 John Wiley & Sons, Ltd. Published 2015 by John Wiley & Sons, Ltd.

This essay begins with the monumental façades lining the streets of Pompeii. It focuses on three women in Pompeii who can be said to have had public profiles because buildings bear their names. The names inscribed on public buildings testify to the system in which the wealth of private donors paid for public amenities, such as temples, bathhouses, or theaters. Civic benefactors garnered the highest prestige in their hometowns, and elite women used their wealth to foster goodwill and create political capital for sons or husbands seeking public offices. In their roles as patrons of architecture, elite women participated in public life by rebuilding their town and shaping its institutions.

1   Eumachia's Building

Eumachia is the foremost example of a Pompeian woman remembered because of the building that she erected (Figure 29.1). Because of its size (about sixty-seven by forty meters) and location, the building of Eumachia stands out: it not only stands open to the Forum of Pompeii but also dominates the view of the Forum from the via Marina and also

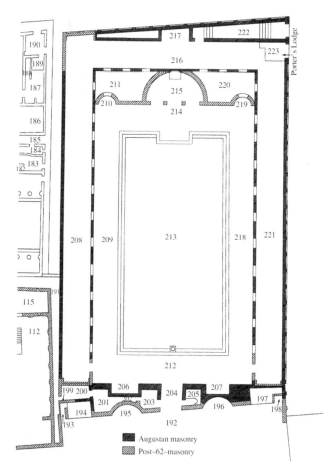

Figure 29.1   Plan of the Building of Eumachia. Drawing: after Dobbins AJA 98: 2008, figure 16.

from the via dell'Abbondanza (Dobbins 2007: 165–7). Its dedicatory inscriptions inform passersby that

> Eumachia, Lucius' daughter, public priestess, built at her own expense in her name and in the name of her son Marcus Numistrius Fronto the porch, the colonnaded courtyard, and corridors and she dedicated them to Concordia Augusta and Pietas. (*CIL* X 810)

Thus the inscriptions (a fragmentary one on the frieze of the forum colonnade, *CIL* X 811, and a marble plaque, translated above, at the southeast entrance) recount that the monumental structure was built by a woman, Eumachia, out of her own funds, on behalf of both herself and her son. Further, the inscriptions refer to the building by listing its parts: *chalcidicum*, *porticus*, and *crypta* (the three sections being respectively a front porch with statue niches, a colonnaded courtyard, and corridors along three sides of the courtyard). The architectural features enumerated on the plaque reflect those of imposing public edifices providing spacious and luxurious settings in the town center. The rectangular colonnade formed a standard type of interior with a covered corridor around the edges and a central open space that allowed for both the circulation and repose of visitors. This plan was appropriate for many of the functions attributed to Eumachia's building: a pocket park or an inviting space next to the Forum, a meeting place for the woolworkers' guild (because textile workers dedicated a statue of Eumachia, see below), or a slave market (by comparison with the *chalcidicum* in nearby Puteoli, which housed such transactions in human bodies). It is more likely that the building sheltered different types of gatherings, from the informal mingling of pedestrians spilling over from the Forum to more organized events (cuttings in the pavement at the entrances indicate that there were doors to secure them; Dobbins 2007: 167), although the evidence of the site does not mandate any of the specific uses mentioned above.

Eumachia's building possesses allusions of grandeur in the decoration of its façade with statues of Aeneas and Romulus in niches, as attested by extant inscriptions (*CIL* X 808, 809). These statues of the founders of empire amount to quotations from the Forum of Augustus in Rome, where the ancestors of the state and its leading men were represented by a series of statues in niches marked by inscriptions. The dedication of the Forum of Augustus in 2 BCE gives us a date after which Eumachia's building was constructed (although Descoeudres 2007: 17 argues for a Tiberian date). Further, a marble molding carved with graceful vegetal motifs imitates another Augustan monument, the Ara Pacis, with its vine scrolls. The Ara Pacis is a monumental marble altar erected in Rome between 13 and 9 BCE representing Augustus, along with his contemporaries and the founders of the empire, Aeneas and Romulus. Eumachia's building evokes the splendid monuments of the capital that align Augustus with the heroes of Rome's deep past and affirm the present state of Rome as a culmination of a long and glorious past.

Eumachia's building participated in a program of patronage at Pompeii that involved the sampling of prestigious metropolitan motifs and the transportation of some of the magnificence of the capital to the bay of Naples (Dobbins 1994: 648–61). Dated to the early first century CE on the basis of its Augustan themes and ornament, the building was a showplace that reflected the connoisseurship of its patron and her high cultural reach (Dobbins 2007). In a pattern that was played out across the empire, Eumachia assumed a key role as a member of the local elite who transmitted the imperial message of Rome's venerable past and gleaming future to her fellow townspeople (Zanker 1998: 93–101).

The rectangular space within the building formed an open courtyard surrounded by a colonnade, the standard multipurpose space of antiquity. As a gathering place or point of congregation, such buildings fit the urban plan as forecourts to temples or as extensions of colonnaded streets. The courtyard retains traces of sculpture erected on bases, although it is less clear whether there were fountains or beds for greenery.

In a niche on one end stood a statue of a female personification representing Augustan Concord and Piety, virtues to whom the building was dedicated, as stated in the building's inscription. Only a fragment of the statue is extant in the form of a gilded cornucopia (a horn of plenty), the attribute held by the marble figure. The statue's head may have borne a likeness to Augustus' wife, Livia. Livia and her son, Tiberius, built a porticus dedicated to Concordia Augusta in 7 BCE in a crowded neighborhood in Rome, and this porticus, described as a community center by one scholar, may have been what Eumachia had in mind for her structure, which she also dedicated with her son (Zanker 1998: 97). Further, the two flanking niches may have been adorned with statues of Livia's sons, Tiberius and Drusus, to make the filial motif complete (Bernstein 2007: 531; although Dobbins 2007: 167, following Richardson (1978), suggests that statues of the personifications of Concordia and Pietas flanked the central figure of Livia). If either of these reconstructions is correct, the statues celebrate the Augustan regime although in a slightly different key than that of the sculptures of Aeneas and Romulus on the façade. Rather than the mythical founders of the Roman empire, the statue within the building may have depicted the first lady of the empire in the guise of a symbol of feminine virtue, her reputation enhanced by her two sons who served the empire. The imagery of the personification extends the emperor's sphere of influence into the households of his subjects.

Further, a fountain at the building's southeast entrance on the via dell'Abbondanza was adorned with a relief depicting the head of the same personification of Concord (Savunen 1997: 53–4). The simple hairstyle of the personification, with locks swept back from a central parting, recalls that of the portraits of Livia, wife of Augustus, and supports the idea that the statue of Concord in Eumachia's building depicted the imperial woman in the guise of the premier domestic virtue promoted by her husband. It is interesting that the motif of the personification is depicted within the building and on the street, and that this overflow of imperial imagery adorns a spigot from which water pours into a basin, a vital resource for a town baked by the sun for much of the year. The message implies that Concord, in her varied manifestations, benefits the public in its basic needs.

Eumachia's presence was also manifest in her portrait statue, erected by the fullers, workers who treated and cleaned wool (Figure 29.2). The base of the statue was inscribed *Eumachiae L[ucii] F[iliae] Sacerd[oti] publ[icae] Fullones* (*CIL* X 812): "To Eumachia, daughter of Lucius, public priestess, [dedicated by] the fullers." That the statue was dedicated by the fullers has spurred speculation about the building's function either as a workshop for dying fabrics (highly unlikely, as fullers required urine for their treatment of wool) or a meeting place for those in the textile industry (possibly, but not exclusively). Further, although Eumachia's family obviously had interests in the wool industry, they were also active in the wine trade (Welch 2007: 558–61). The bases of the many other statues erected in the building would no doubt have had inscriptions attesting to the presence of other professional or civic groups dependent on Eumachia's patronage. Although the statue of the building's patron is significant, its dedicators may not have had sole use of the building—nor did they have to be her primary base of popular support.

Figure 29.2   Statue of Eumachia. Naples, Museo Archeologico Nazionale, inv. no. 6232. Photo: Anger/DAI-Rom 1989.0113.

The location of the statue is telling: it was set up in a rectangular niche in the east wing of the *crypta* directly behind the statue of Concordia-Livia in its niche (the *crypta*, or corridors, were entered from the western ends of the portico and from an entrance by the southeast; windows to the portico lit the *crypta*; Dobbins 2007: 167). The two statues can be seen in relation to one another as an honorary depiction of the emperor's wife, a patron of citizens throughout the empire, and the esteemed benefactor of the building, a patron in her own right in her hometown. Livia, along with the motifs of Romulus and Aeneas favored by her husband Augustus, provides the imperial model.

The statue of Eumachia, however, differs from the statue of Livia in that it does not depict its subject in the guise of an imperial virtue, whether Concordia or Pietas. Nor does it represent her in a manner that allows us to glimpse the personality of the prominent benefactor. Our postmodern cult of celebrity requires the famous to assert their individuality above all. In antiquity, however, portrait statues tended to use statue types that were highly standardized in order to be easily understood; these statues, particularly those of female subjects, were highly formulaic in the styles of both their heads and bodies, and, most importantly, these images were bound up in centuries of tradition (see also Dillon, this volume, Chapter 19). In the Augustan period the statues depicting distinguished and honorable women demonstrated a narrow spectrum of choices among statue types and styles that exhibited more uniformity than creative differences or challenges to the norms. The portraits depicting younger-looking women appear idealized; that is, their symmetrical, regular, and ageless features bear the gloss of earlier Greek sculpture of goddesses or Hellenistic queens (Welch 2007: 558; Dillon 2010).

The face of Eumachia's portrait is stamped by idealization through its oval shape, large almond-shaped eyes under well-defined brows, straight nose with a sharp profile, and full, fleshy lips. There is little to distinguish it as a portrait of a specific woman. Lacking are the kinds of features frequently incorporated into the portraits of middle-aged Roman women such as Eumachia, like lines engraved around the mouth or a sagging jawline, traits that telegraphed gravity or high moral standards and that are seen in other portraits of mature Roman matrons contemporary with Eumachia's statue. Clearly the highly idealized classical style of Eumachia's portrait, which replaces her own facial features with those of the bland, indistinct, and characterless beauty of mythological heroines and goddesses, does so in order to elevate its subject.

Further, the wavy strands of hair arranged off a central parting usually graced statues of Aphrodite and Venus (Welch 2007: 558). The choice of hairstyle complements the classically idealized facial features, but it also may have been significant for Eumachia's role as a public priestess, an office mentioned in the statue's inscription (Welch 2007: 558). In Pompeii, the prominence of the cult of Venus allows us to assume that Eumachia served that cult, an honorary position for women wealthy enough to support and organize the cult activities. Both the inscription and the statue suggest the range of interests and the sphere of influence of elite women in their towns across a spectrum of religious and civic institutions. The Venus locks adorning Eumachia's portrait reiterated the link between the portrait's subject and the goddess, whose attributes signifying beauty and grace were borrowed for effect. In other words, the face of Eumachia's statue expresses no individual features nor personal characteristics but, rather, looks like that of a statue with its formal and remote appearance.

The rest of the sculpture emulates portrait statues of worthy women in a uniform that modestly cloaks their bodies while revealing the contours of the maternal anatomy, such as the breasts and hips. Depiction of the body swathed in garments—from the tunic and mantle over the body to the mantle pulled up as a veil over the back of the head (appropriate for a priestess)—was familiar to Pompeians as a traditional statue type (Welch 2007: 561; Dillon 2010; see also Dillon, this volume, Chapter 19). The statue of a high-profile woman, such as Eumachia, could be produced only in the highly stylized forms borrowed liberally from the classical repertory of statuary. The borrowed statue type endowed her with an esteemed public face and an elegantly draped, full figure. Further, the motifs' association with higher beings and personages from divinities to Hellenistic queens lent Eumachia a monumental stature replete with dignity and honor. For a visitor strolling through the building, the statue was more than the sum of its parts.

2 The Properties of Julia Felix

Pompeian women who were not of the upper social orders also owned and managed property for profit. In the period following the earthquake of 62 CE, when the public baths were not in full operation and much of the town was undergoing restoration, entrepreneurs saw opportunities. Julia Felix advertised the availability of her property for rent (Figure 29.3):

> To rent for the period of five years from the thirteenth day of next August to the thirteenth day of the sixth August, the Venus Bath fitted for the well-to-do, shops with living quarters above, apartments on the second floor located in the building of Julia Felix, daughter of Spurius. At the end of five years, the agreement is terminated. (*CIL* IV 1136)

Figure 29.3   Properties of Julia Felix, view of the garden. Photo: Christopher Parslow.

This advertisement was inscribed on a wall at the building's entrance on the via dell'Abbondanza, a major street that crossed the town and led into the Forum alongside Eumachia's building (Bernstein 2007: 529). Julia Felix's property is located on the other side of Pompeii from Eumachia's building, near the amphitheater, which was a neighborhood that underwent change in the years following the earthquake (Parslow 2007: 218). Homeowners turned their gardens into open-air bars or restaurants to profit from the street traffic drawn to the arena. Julia Felix's complex of house, gardens, baths, and shops is large by the neighborhood's standards, and was formed from the combination of two lots after the earthquake (Nappo 2007: 359). It consisted of the core of a private house with extensive street frontage, grounds, and outbuildings. In today's real estate lingo, the parcel would be termed a multipurpose complex, both residential and commercial with several entertainment concessions (see also Nappo 2007: 359).

Although the complex included a house and apartments, its appeal is evident in the reception and dining rooms, which recreated exotic or luxurious environments. These facilities offered a sumptuous atmosphere with a dining room overlooking a pristine garden that featured a long pool or canal. As the centerpiece of the garden, the canal had a marble border with apses, niches, and a series of diminutive bridges spanning it. The garden was shaded by a pergola on two sides, which included seats fabricated as if to appear roughhewn, inviting strollers to sit as if they were in a seaside grotto. The showroom of the complex was the adjoining dining room with its built-in seating. That is, masonry couches allowed the diners to recline and take in the delightful setting: an artificial waterfall in the form of a water-stair fountain, walls painted blue with scenes of the Nile delta, and a barrel-vaulted ceiling fashioned from stone chips to simulate a rocky cavern (Parslow 2007: 218–19).

This type of ostentatious décor, blurring the boundaries of the indoor and outdoor, the artificial and natural, evoking fabled destinations in particular or landscapes of leisure in general, was not unique in Pompeii: it appears in other houses with elaborately landscaped grounds and dining rooms opening out onto them. The dining pavilions with miniature canals and fake grottoes have been explained as imitations of the more deluxe amenities of the villas of the wealthiest Romans in the surrounding countryside and coastline (Zanker 1998: 154–6). To dismiss these stunning assemblages as merely derivative ignores the imaginative and creative implementation of designs fitted into backyards rather than sprawling villas (some of which had designs and motifs just as eclectic as those of Julia Felix's property—scholarly consensus about taste and social status is changing). While Julia Felix's establishment admitted patrons for the price of a meal, the property itself does not differ substantially from the grand houses of Pompeii. Indeed, without the inscription at the doorway, it would have been impossible to detect its commercial uses (Wallace-Hadrill 1994: 133).

The property also included other public facilities, including fully equipped baths, although on a smaller scale than the public baths; they were the only ones serving this part of town (Parslow 2007: 218; on public baths see also Trümper, this volume, Chapter 21). In the rental notice they are called "the Venus Bath fitted for the well-to-do," suggesting that they were already known in the quarter for the excellence or elegance of their setting, fixtures, and comfort. The upscale clientele no doubt sought out the sauna or sweating chambers and the open-air swimming pool, features not found in smaller, private baths. Bathers could also dine here in the grand pavilion with a view of the garden, or take light refreshment at the tavern flanking the baths. The tavern offered varied seating arrangements: booths with upright masonry seats, and masonry couches around a circular table for reclining (Nappo 2007: 361). Attached to the property was a snack bar that sold drinks and snacks on the street (Nappo 2007: 361). The variety of services and concessions available for different grades of customers or the varying occasions of street life seems to indicate organization and management by a clever entrepreneur trying to cover the market.

There is nothing startling about this business strategy except that a woman controlled it. Unlike Eumachia, Julia Felix did not come from one of Pompeii's influential families—on the contrary, the inscription states that she was low-born, an illegitimate "daughter of Spurius"; alternatively, she may have descended from imperial freedmen—that is, the emperor's ex-slaves (Savunen 1997: 57). One scholar has proposed that Julia Felix came from Rome after the earthquake of 62 CE, specifically to engage in business in Pompeii (Parslow 1988: 37–48). By renting out the house renovated into several commercial venues, Julia Felix stood to make a good income. The grand gestures of public benefaction, along with the office of public priestess, were unattainable for someone like Julia Felix. Further, in the last phase of Pompeii, from 62–79 CE, many large houses in this district were bought up by artisans and merchants and broken up into workshops, inns, and smaller houses or rooms to let (Wallace-Hadrill 1994: 106–7). In the period after the devastation, when recovery and making-do were the norm, the elegant townhouse open for catering and bathing maintained high standards for discriminating patrons.

Both the business savvy of Julia Felix and the public patronage of Eumachia raise the question of women's rights to property in the Roman empire. Roman women owned land and other kinds of property in their own names if they were independent of their fathers and husbands. Most fathers did not live long into their daughters' lives (beyond the early years of their first marriage, if that), and women in the periods of the late Republic and empire did not come into the legal control of their husbands (Treggiari 1996: 118–19).

These women were not, however, completely free to dispose of their property at will. Legal guardians had to approve the transfer of women's property, but Augustus granted special rights, under the Julian laws, to mothers of three children (and to freedwomen who had four children) to waive the requirement of securing a guardian's approval (on the Julian laws see Henry and James, this volume, Chapter 6; and Hallett, this volume, Chapter 27). For almost a century before Augustus, however, elite women could easily bypass the need for the guardian's approval to sell or buy land, to give a dowry to a husband, or to make a will to leave an estate to children. The guardianship requirement became a mere formality.

The legal stipulations indicate that property, although it passed through women's hands, began and ended as a family matter. The sparse evidence for the families of the women in question is not promising. The bare mention of Julia Felix's out-of-wedlock birth in the rental notice suggests an irregular domestic situation. She may have needed a guardian to buy the property on the via dell'Abbondanza, but not to rent out its various units. If she had a husband, he was not involved in her real estate business (or at least as far as we can see from the rental notice). At the upper echelons of the social order, Eumachia's family was well-established, although her husband is not known. He may have been M. Numistrius Fronto, who held high office in 2–3 CE but died during this period (some scholars identify this Numistrius Fronto as Eumachia's son, although if that were the case his office should have been noted in her building's inscription, along with his name: Savunen 1997: 55). It may be likely that Eumachia was a widow (Savunen 1997: 55). As a priestess, she would have been in the public eye through her service and generosity towards the cult. We can imagine that Eumachia received the goodwill of her peers and the respect of the townspeople as a result of her charitable work. No doubt this experience prepared her to undertake the building project on the Forum for the good of the town and her son's career.

It is worth noting that the real estate developed by the two Pompeiian women reflected contemporary standards of high culture: Eumachia's building, decked out in the themes of Augustan Rome, presented this politically correct image to her peers, while Julia Felix's townhouse offered a soothing atmosphere of a green glade refreshed by running water, the setting for leisurely cultivation. The mechanisms by which they realized their objectives differed, and reveal the distance between their positions in the social hierarchy. With her high status and wealth, Eumachia could well afford to be generous to her town; in fact, the prominence of her family obliged her to endow cults and to make civic improvements, both as a return for the political participation of her male kin (including the anticipated career of her son) and for their power in local affairs. Eumachia's building was open without charge to the public for strolling, although on occasion it could have been reserved for meetings of groups, such as fullers or vintners.

Without inherited wealth and friends in high places (so we assume), Julia Felix had to exploit her property to produce an income. It appears as if the complex of commercial facilities was designed so that customers could move from the baths to the tavern or the more formal restaurant with garden seating, paying for the various services or refreshments along the way. Julia Felix wanted to rent out the baths, along with shops and apartments, to a third party, and we may assume that she managed the dining facilities by herself with a staff. Julia Felix may not have been alone in her enterprise, as the name "Julia" often indicates affiliation with the Julio-Claudian imperial dynasty because their freed slaves took the family name. Freedmen and freedwomen with marketable skills occasionally went into business with their ex-owners as silent partners investing in a workshop or market stall. It is tempting to insert this scenario into the account of Julia Felix because her house and décor were expensive, with marble Corinthian pillars in the portico, a bronze tripod, and elaborate wall paintings depicting the Pompeian Forum, among other subjects (Savunen 1997: 57).

In order to attract well-heeled customers, Julia Felix had to maintain a fashionable interior fitted with furnishings of quality, and a garden as carefully manicured as a park. The architectural elements and wall paintings probably were already installed in the house, while Julia Felix may have added some of the other features, such as the outdoor seating and statuary, when she converted the house into a commercial venture. Clearly she must have had the funds to buy the house, which had seen better days as a posh private residence, and to convert it into a banqueting hall. Julia Felix may have possessed significant assets, but her wealth did not bring her the social status that mattered for the political class. Among the artisans and merchants of the amphitheater district, Julia Felix may very well have been distinguished as an accomplished businesswoman. The ancient sources, however, are not usually sensitive to these fleeting impressions.

Without the buildings' inscriptions, there would be no way to tell that the owners of both the public portico and the entertainment complex were women. Julia Felix and Eumachia engaged in activities typically seen to be in the male domain: commerce and public benefactions (Dixon 2001: 89–132; see also Bielman, this volume, Chapter 17). Other women in the Roman empire ran businesses or endowed their cities with porticoes, but their livelihoods more typically depended on market days, and charitable giving involved the women's families (often more emphatically than in the case of Eumachia). We do not know whether Julia Felix and Eumachia acted more boldly in their own interests because they had no living husbands. In a familiar strategy of elites, Eumachia used her family's wealth and influence to introduce her son to society and ease his way into political office (but she was no mere intermediary as the building is dedicated in her own name as well). Julia Felix and Eumachia were not alone among their peers, but they stand out because their names are inscribed on enduring monumental structures of beauty and utility that they built or developed.

3   Final Resting Places

Tombs are another form of monument bearing inscriptions that identify those who erected them and those commemorated by them. Prominently located on access roads outside of the town gates, tombs were public monuments that attested to the private bonds of kinship, obligation, and emotion within families and their extended households. Sepulchers were the primary roadside attraction as one entered Roman towns and cities, and the prominent monuments skirting the roads provided passersby with a roster of great families and influential citizens along with their descendants. Travelers did not have to crane their necks to read the inscribed tomb façades because they were tightly packed side by side, close to the curb like the buildings lining a city street. Since tombs served to preserve the memory of the departed, the architecture often assumed monumental effects, or at least borrowed elements of the designs of civic edifices that commanded attention and evoked grandeur. Memorials took the shape of sacred architecture in the form of small temples, altars, or shrines. Other tomb types presented lavish façades that were articulated with niches for sculpture (or had niches inside for cinerary urns) or with columnar displays; some tombs towered over their neighbors due to their high podia or upper stories.

One type of tomb, the *schola*, merits consideration here because it served to commemorate a few notable women, including Eumachia (although men were honored with *scholae* as well). Unique to Pompeii, the schola tomb features a stone semicircular bench set on a platform. The benches are ample in accommodation and offer a high back, as well as gracefully carved lions' paws or griffin's feet as décor at either end (Cormack 2007: 586–8). Of the eight schola tombs from Pompeii, three commemorate women (Savunen 1997: 153). Benches set up in Hellenistic cities in the eastern empire as honorary dedications may have provided inspiration for the *scholae* of Pompeii, even though the latter served as funerary monuments. Both the Hellenistic and Pompeian benches grace the urban environment by widening the street and allowing pedestrians a place to stop and rest. In a city or along a busy road, the pedestrian seated on the *schola* looks out towards the passing crowds. In the *schola* tomb, the pedestrian also had the opportunity to read the epitaph and consider the career of the individual named on the bench, who would have been recognized because those honored by the benches served in the highest offices in the town as the senior magistrates or public priestesses (Cormack 2007: 586–8).

The location of the *schola* tombs in the highly desired zones immediately outside the gates also reflects the luster of those commemorated. Further, the clustering of the Pompeian *scholae* close to the town wall affirms their utility as urban architecture, curbside seating to watch the passing crowds. The steps of Mamia's tomb have been scuffed by the shoes of many strollers (Zanker 1998: 124; see below). As funerary monuments, the graceful arcs of the *scholae* provide focal points and gathering places for casual strollers as well as those celebrating funerary rites for the deceased. Some of the *scholae* have a central base to support a column or urn to hold the ashes of the deceased (Zanker 1998; 122–4).

One of the largest tombs belongs to Eumachia and was erected both for her family and for herself (according to the epitaph: Savunen 1997: 62). It stands prominently outside the Nuceria Gate on a terrace with altars and seating in front of the semicircular façade adorned with alternating niches and marble reliefs. The reliefs depict a battle with Amazons, a standard theme for Greek temples but relatively rare for a Roman tomb (especially a tomb for a stately and highly visible woman; Beard 2008: 310). This Augustan tomb is a highly elaborate form that incorporates the *schola* in a complex façade. A simpler version of a *schola* tomb commemorates another public priestess, Mamia, daughter of Publius, outside the Herculaneum Gate (on Mamia, see also Bielman, this volume, Chapter 17). The inscription on the tomb states that both the land and the tomb were given to her by the town council, a very high honor and one that shows her great distinction (Bernstein 2007: 533). The *schola* tomb of Mamia is canonical in its design, with a low platform and high back. It is close to the Herculaneum Gate, and its form echoes another nearby *schola*, a larger monument in honor of Aulus Veius. His tomb was also erected by the town, no doubt in recognition of his having served two terms as one of Pompeii's leading magistrates.

In the period of Tiberius or Claudius, N. Herennius Celsus dedicated a *schola* tomb for his young wife, Aesquillia Polla, who died at the tender age of twenty-two. In this case the town council granted the burial plot outside the Nola gate because of the distinguished public career of N. Herennius Celsus, who held the highest offices. In fact, all the *scholae* tombs honor individuals who were granted public funerals by the town council (Savunen 1997: 153). The evocative monument to Aesquillia Polla features a tall Ionic column supporting an urn. The vertical extension of the column on its high pedestal forms the centerpiece of the monument and commands attention, particularly as her epitaph is placed on the side of the column's base facing the street (Figure 29.4). Those who sat on

Figure 29.4 Inscription from the *schola* tomb of Aesquillia Polla, Porta di Nola Necropolis, Pompeii. Photo: Eisner/DAI-Rome 1963.1280.

the low, sweeping curve of the bench looked out onto the street instead of gazing at the inscription. Schola tombs promote congregation and even socialization for those who step off the street and sit in the area formed by the stone seat. We tend to think of cemeteries as lonely, uninhabited places, but in antiquity the street of tombs tended to be a lively and convivial spot—some tombs included dining facilities for the extended family to feast in celebration of the deceased's birthday and on other sacred days of the dead.

As funerary monuments the *scholae* accommodate street life under the auspices of the deceased, whose names decorate the plaques. The public bench is a gift to the town on a smaller scale than the benefaction of Eumachia. An urban phenomena, the benches that gently hug the road not only honor members of the political class but also allow them to develop the town's public spaces and to dominate public life both at the city center and on its periphery. We may imagine street-corner bards and busybodies holding forth at the *scholae* as the traffic passed from the town gates. The crowded tomb may have been a sign of the donor's popularity or prestige, or it may have merely reflected the dedicator's good sense in knowing where travelers needed to rest. The simple beauty of Aesquillia Polla's monument lies in the relationship of its parts: the sole column supporting nothing but a flaring full-bodied urn above the low-slung, rounded bench. The column marks the memorial site, and the bench not only provided seating but also gathered disparate individuals into a group. In this way, the *schola* is more inclined to the life of the street than to the realm of the dead.

Aesquillia Polla, however, is not well served by her tomb. The inscription enumerates her husband's prestigious career, and we learn only that she died prematurely. N. Herennius Celsus, the husband who dutifully and (we assume) lovingly dedicated his wife's funerary monument, was awarded the burial plot for his wife from the town council due to *his* public service (Savunen 1997: 155). The monument's prominence and visibility were determined by Celsus' standing in the community, not by his wife's. Aesquillia Polla seems to have been a mostly silent partner. This submergence of female identity was common in a culture in which honor was derived from political or military accomplishments, spheres of activity from which women were excluded.

4   Conclusions

A few women, however, did have access to the elite channels of civic service and did serve as benefactors, as witnessed by the generous gifts that Eumachia and Mamia made to their town. Women of established families had opportunities to achieve prominence through priesthoods, and used their riches to improve or maintain their city as well as their standing among their peers and townsfolk, just as men did. Other women who were less fortunate in their birth, such as Julia Felix, entered the public sphere through commerce. Julia Felix engaged in business transactions and developed an atrium house into an entertainment complex, which entailed substantial capital, planning, and vision. This, too, is what men did for a living, although such service industries did not gain for their owners or managers the kind of public honor bestowed on individuals like Eumachia. Many more women made or sold goods on the streets or in markets, but their activities, carried out mostly on a subsistence level, were not considered worth mentioning in the written sources. The ancient written sources do not credit these activities as beneficial to civic life, and, if female vendors or craftsworkers are mentioned at all, it is only to castigate their morals or to decry their presence on the streets or in the marketplace.

The distinction between the public and private realm fades when one considers how many women of all ages and social ranks were out and about in public. For example, paintings from the atrium of the House of Julia Felix depict scenes from the Forum in Pompeii in which women and girls are represented bargaining with salesmen, giving alms to beggars, or otherwise taking in the urban scene on their own (Beard 2008: 72–8). Their public appearances did not mean that they were prominent people, nor would their names become part of the historical record—it takes an inscription carved in stone to ensure the latter. Although elites—and elite males—dominated the avenues to distinction, there are exceptions. One is found on an epitaph on a tomb in the form of a small column outside the Porta Nocera: "Clodia Nigella, a freedwoman of Clodia and a public pig herder, the place having been decreed by the town council" (*PN 5 OS*; Bernstein 2007: 533). Why the ex-slave pig herder had her tomb paid for by the town council, an honor also bestowed on Mamia and Aesquillia Polla, is not known. The epitaph does give evidence, though, for remarkable public honors for a woman in a humble role.

RECOMMENDED FURTHER READING

The renewed interest in Pompeii and the Bay of Naples has spurred a continuous stream of publications, in which women and the family receive some attention. Recent surveys of Pompeii that feature sound introductions to the site and good illustrations include Ling (2005), Berry (2007), and Cooley and Cooley (2004). Exhibition catalogs offer discussions of specific artifacts and art works: Borriello et al. (1997), d'Ambrosio et al. (2003), and Mattusch (2008). Aspects of social organization are analyzed in Laurence (2007), while Allison (2004) focuses on the houses' contents and domestic life from an archaeological perspective. Jashemski (1993) considers the Pompeians' use of outdoor space, their landscape, and gardens. Dunbabin (2003) looks more broadly at the ritual of dining in the Roman empire.

30

Early Imperial Female Portraiture

Elizabeth Bartman

Thanks to a rich trove of sources, both literary and visual, we know more about the women of the Julio-Claudian clan than about any other women in Roman history. In the last several decades, inspired by the feminist movement, gender studies, and the *Annales* School of history, scholars have mined these sources to write important studies that have transformed our thinking of Livia and her successors. A number of leading Julio-Claudian females have been the subject of detailed biography (Kokkinos 1992; Barrett 1996, 2002; Fantham 2006), while more general works have discussed how the women of the dynasty, notwithstanding their exclusion from official roles, wielded considerable power in the social, political, and religious life of Rome (Kleiner and Matheson 1996; Rose 1997). In light of these comprehensive works, my essay will concentrate on some new discoveries that deepen our understanding of female representation during this era. Many of its conclusions are valid not only for the ladies of the court but also for members of the senatorial and equestrian elite, whose imagery aped the imperial model. While the imperial women were trendsetters, they also borrowed from those lower down the social ladder. Consequently, in style and iconography, the portraits of the Julio-Claudian women—unlike those of their menfolk—did not differ dramatically from those of their private contemporaries (Smith 1985; Alexandridis 2004). All portraits embody some tension between individual and type, but the Julio-Claudian women who form our subject—and arguably all ancient women—tended to subordinate the former to the latter: hence most of the portraits we will examine emphasized the subject's status as matron or mother or semi-divinity at the expense of her physiognomic individualism (see also Dillon, this volume, Chapter 17).

1 The Historiography of Julio-Claudian Portraiture

Attempts to identify images of Julio-Claudian women began in the Renaissance, when antiquarians such as Andrea Fulvio, Fulvio Orsini, and Enea Vico compiled illustrated

A Companion to Women in the Ancient World, First Edition. Edited by Sharon L. James and Sheila Dillon.
© 2012 John Wiley & Sons, Ltd. Published 2015 by John Wiley & Sons, Ltd.

volumes featuring medallion portraits, reminiscent of—if not actually copied from—surviving examples of ancient coins (Cunnally 1999). At the time, the paucity of finds meant that many of the portraits were modern inventions, but by the late nineteenth century so many Roman portraits had come to light that scholars such as Johann Bernoulli could venture identifications with considerable accuracy. Portrait studies of the period reflected contemporary cultural events: from the natural sciences, scholars borrowed the notion of taxonomies and evolutionary models while the Industrial Revolution provided a model of artifactual production that stressed identicality and multiplication. Hence was born the notion of the official "portrait type," which envisioned typological inventions made at Rome and reproduced throughout the empire with little variation. While there is no doubt of the essential validity of the portrait type as a concept, the scholarly emphasis on identifying types has encouraged a narrow, largely descriptive approach that, at least for women, has fixated on hairstyle.

2   The Hellenistic and Republican Inheritance

Influential as the portraits of the Julio-Claudian women were to be, the idea of depicting real (historical) women did not originate with the dynasty. Rather, portrait artists in the decades around the turn of the millennium (at the start of the Julio-Claudian era, dated from 31 BCE to 68 CE) drew upon established—if divergent—traditions from the Mediterranean. From the Hellenistic world of the Greek East, the Romans derived the notion of honorific portraiture set up in public, although eastern women typically possessed idealized visages that did not distinguish physiognomic individuals (Dillon 2010). An exception is found in the images of Cleopatra VII, although a credible theory argues that her more unflattering rendering on a series of coins represents the Egyptian queen's effort to ingratiate herself with the emerging power of Rome by looking more Roman (Smith 1988). From the local Etruscan and Italic workshops, Romans learned a more veristic representational language, albeit one employed primarily in the funerary realm. During the Republic few living women received public portrait honors—the seated statue of Cornelia, mother of the Gracchi, whose base alone survives, is a rare exception (Coarelli 1978; Flower 2002). As their involvement in Rome's social, political, and religious life grew (Schultz 2006; Treggiari 2007), however, the stage was set for elite women in the imperial circle to have a more public persona and to receive one of its perquisites: public statues.

3   Livia (59 BCE–29 CE)

During her long life and even after, Livia Drusilla occupied a critical dynastic role as wife of Rome's first emperor, Augustus; mother of his successor, Tiberius; great-grandmother of Caligula; grandmother of Claudius; and great-great-grandmother of Nero. A Claudian by marriage to Tiberius' father, her first husband, she grafted the distinguished Claudian line to the Julian when she married Octavian/Augustus. Her prominence and shifting roles within the dynasty necessitated the creation of various images, while her longevity and undoubted popularity—notwithstanding the negative press of certain ancient writers such as Tacitus—meant that more portraits of her survive today than of any other Roman woman.

Without official public roles (other than religious), even elite women such as Livia were not seen as warranting honorific statuary commemoration during the Republic. Her receipt (along with her sister-in-law Octavia) of a public statue in 35 BCE was therefore a rare honor, most likely political in motive. No trace of this portrait commemoration survives, but many imagine that Livia was depicted in the conservative "Marbury Hall" typology, epitomized in the bust now in Liverpool (Bartman 1999: Cat. 37). Although youthful, Livia's face projects a certain severity in its angular jaw and small, set mouth. Her hair is carefully coiffed with a projecting plait over her forehead (*nodus*) and its side waves and bun convey restrained economy. Completing her matronly look is the *stola*, a pinafore-like overgarment whose strap is visible on the bust's right shoulder. Worn by respectable married women, the *stola* underscores Livia's image as modest and matronly, the visual embodiment of the family values promoted by her husband.

Livia's unprecedented rank and status, however, required a portrait image that designated her as special. Thus, during her lifetime—even at Rome itself, where political sensitivities typically restrained non-traditional imagery—she is represented with hints of the divine. On the Ara Pacis of 9 BCE, for example, she wears her hair in a style of loose waves resembling those of contemporary depictions of goddesses and female personifications. On a cameo gem of circa 14 CE in Vienna, she sits enthroned and bears attributes that connect her with Cybele (a turreted crown and tympanum) and with Ceres (wheat) (Kampen 2009: pl. 3). These visual representations find numerous parallels in inscriptions from across the empire, which endow Livia with a divine identity: as Juno/Hera, as Ceres/Demeter, as Isis, as Venus. A recent addition to this corpus, in fact, stems from the redating of an inscription from Rhamnous to Livia as *Thea Livia* (Lozano 2004). If correct, the rededication of Rhamnous' Temple of Nemesis dates to the Augustan period, several decades earlier than previously thought. The redating may find confirmation in the recent identification of a marble replica of the cult statue of Nemesis as the body type used for a portrait of Livia in Buthrotum (Bumke 2008). Its head, missing in the 1990s (Bartman 1999: Cat. 54), is now on display in the Butrint Museum. Previously no such assimilation between the empress and Nemesis was known.

Livia's most popular image, the so-called Fayum type, blended Republican traditionalism (in its retention of the by-then old fashioned *nodus* coiffure) with an idealizing gloss that hinted at the divine. In comparison with her earlier Marbury Hall type, these portraits show Livia with a rounder face and perkier features, most especially a small and curvaceous mouth. Looser waves replace the tightly wound hair she first wore. Stylistically and iconographically akin to the Prima Porta type invented for Augustus about 27 BCE, Livia's Fayum type became an important vehicle for expressing Augustan ideology: its message of calm classicism and idealizing perfection embodied Augustan notions of female beauty and power.

A head of the Fayum type now in Oxford but long associated with Narona has recently been joined to a draped body still in Croatia (Figure 30.1; Marin and Vickers 2004). Dated to the Tiberian era, the statue may have been part of a Julio-Claudian dynastic group erected either in a custom-built temple (Augusteum) or in the Forum. Unusually, Livia is portrayed with a stock body type, a Pudicitia similar to that employed for the statue of Eumachia found at Pompeii (see Figure 29.2; and D'Ambra, this volume, Chapter 29). As the majority of her surviving statues employ body types otherwise attested for divinities, the Narona Livia makes a significant contribution to the corpus. Its somewhat quotidian (and decidedly mortal) implications have inspired the suggestion that Livia was also portrayed in a second statue (now headless); although clad in a *stola*, the woman depicted

Figure 30.1 Livia, composite of head in Oxford (Ashmolean AN 1941.808) and body in Narona. Photo: Hrvoje Manenica, Director of the Archaeological Museum Narona.

here is enobled by a rich costume close in its drapery to the Claudian-date Livia as Ceres from Pozzuoli (Bartman 1999: Cat. 28). The recent excavations at Narona have also augmented the corpus of known Livia portraits by at least one other image—a glass paste imitation of a cameo gem, a stray find from the site, bears a portrait of the empress (similar in its iconography and dimensions to another glass paste now in the British Museum; Bartman 1999: Cat. 100). The Narona find suggests what we would have expected from these mold-made imitation gems: that they were produced in multiples. As such, were both gems gifts to (relatively low-level) Augustan loyalists?

Another recently found portrait of Livia, a silver bust from Herculaneum, is decidedly more upscale (Figure 30.2; Borriello et al., 2008). Ancient literary sources (specifically Ovid, *Pont.* 2.8.61 and 4.9.105–12) mention images of Livia and other members of the imperial family in precious metals, but few survive. The bust's find-spot at the ancient shoreline suggests that, whether looted or safeguarded, it was someone's treasure, lost by someone trying to escape the eruption in 79 CE. The bust is squashed almost beyond recognition, but can be identified as Livia because of her coiffure, large eyes, and small chin; interestingly, a silver bust of the emperor Galba has also been found at Herculaneum.

Figure 30.2 Silver bust of Livia from Herculaneum. Herculaneum deposit inv. 4205/79502. Photo: Soprintendente Archeologo Pompei.

Although not found together, it is tempting to associate them because they share some technical details, and the two personas were linked by household if not blood (Bartman 1999: 138).

Such family relationships, whether real or fictive, were the intended message of many of Livia's portraits: sometimes she displays a physiognomic similarity to her son Tiberius while at other times she gains—or confers—prestige from the company of other Julio-Claudians. Her co-appearance with family members iterated the concept of the *domus Augusta*, a notion that transcended the literal meaning of "household" to promote the more ideologically loaded connotations of dynasty and semi-divine status. Promoted through image and ritual, the *domus Augusta* put many of Livia's less-prominent relations in the public eye (Flory 1996).

4 Antonia Minor (36 BCE–37 CE)

After the death of her husband, Drusus, in 9 BCE, Livia's daughter-in-law Antonia Minor largely withdrew from public life. Nevertheless, her substantial personal wealth and the large client base she inherited from her father Mark Antony precluded the total withdrawal that some of the sources suggest for the grieving widow. In any event, portrait statues—her visual surrogates—ensured her lasting presence in cities throughout the empire.

Her shifting status within the dynastic framework—first as wife of Augustus' stepson Drusus and as such Rome's potential first lady, later as priestess of the deified Augustus and mother of the emperor Claudius—required multiple portraits. As with Livia, posthumous attention by Claudius brought everlasting youth, and so Antonia's portraits embody the paradox of looking increasingly younger as time went on. Comparison of the rather austere bust from Wilton House, with its slightly bloated face and small mouth with the hint of an overbite, with the fragile beauty rendered in the full-length statue at Baiae makes the point. The range of portrait types, not all anchored in coins bearing identifying legends, has led to confusion about whether similar portraits represent Antonia or another Julio-Claudian, or even a private lady. A case in point is the draped statue of a woman from Herculaneum. Although long identified as the daughter of the equestrian Balbus, it was found not only with her putative father and other relatives but also with statues of Augustus, Claudius, and other imperials. In view of the statue's high quality—superior to that of the Balbus group— could the woman herself be a member of the imperial family? The same issue of quality comes up with the celebrated "Clytie" in the British Museum in London. At a time when one would imagine that the imperial family monopolized the finest artists, should this superb bust be interpreted as private (Walker 1993)?

Although initially identified as Antonia, a recently discovered female head from Pantelleria (Tusa et al. 2004) cannot, however, be said with certainty to be part of her portrait corpus. The head is carved for insertion and depicts a strong-featured woman characterized by a square jaw, prominent nose, and large eyes. Her hair is combed into soft waves emanating from a middle parting above her forehead, but diverges from Antonia's standard iconography with the addition of long, coiled ringlets hanging onto the shoulder. Both her features and coiffure, in fact, recall those of a prominent Julio-Claudian of the next generation, Agrippina the Elder. Admittedly, Antonia's portrait iconography varies (see especially the different shapes her mouth assumes), but on the grounds of both appearance and iconography the Pantelleria head is more likely to represent Agrippina the Elder than Antonia. As the widow of Germanicus and a much-respected woman, Agrippina garnered multiple portraits during her lifetime.

5 Agrippina the Younger (16–59 CE)

Of Agrippina the Elder's many daughters, her namesake Agrippina the Younger occupied the highest public standing and as a result had the most extensive portrait history. Promoted by her brother Caligula when he was emperor, she later married his successor Claudius—her uncle—to become Rome's first lady for a brief period of five years. When her son Nero gained the throne she remained in the public limelight, even if her public role was not always appreciated by her son. Because Nero was a mere teenager when he acceded to the throne, Agrippina initially assumed a regent-like role, unprecedented for a woman. Like Livia, her behavior and representation were both innovative and contentious.

Agrippina's appearance on one of the reliefs from the Sebasteion at Aphrodisias (Figure 30.3) embodies this mix. In a scene of unprecedented iconography, Agrippina crowns her grown son Nero. Though the crowning in the scene is figurative, not literal— there is no sign of the Senate!—the relief places the maternal Agrippina, complete with cornucopia to emphasize her fertility, at the heart of the Roman state. While women had long been included in dynastic groups to underscore their role as the bearers of the next generation, the Sebasteion relief is overt in its message of womb as kingmaker.

On the relief, Agrippina wears a *stephane* (crown) to indicate her (unofficial) divine status, as well as her signature early coiffure of ringlets and superimposed rows of tiny snail

Figure 30.3 Relief from the Sebasteion at Aphrodisias depicting Nero and Agrippina. Photo: New York University Excavations at Aphrodisias.

curls. Indeed, this distinctive hairstyle has facilitated the identification of many of her portraits, including a damaged head in dark stone now in Copenhagen (Bartman 2009). Recently Italian restorers determined that the head—an orphan without known provenance but likely to have come from Rome—belongs with a magnificent headless draped female torso from the Capitoline Museums (Figure 30.4). Found on the Celian, the figure may possibly have belonged to a Julio-Claudian dynastic portrait group executed in Egyptian greywacke. With her heavy drapery, downturned head, and veil, Agrippina projects a modest image appropriate for her position of priestess (specifically *flamenica*) of the deified Claudius. Yet the use of a rare, expensive stone and the crown perched on her curls hint at a higher status.

As a direct blood descendant of Augustus, Agrippina had an enviable pedigree that solidified her position and that of her son, Nero. Like Tiberius before him, Nero's dependence upon his mother for legitimacy weakened him politically (Osgood 2011) and inevitably spawned resentment that spilled beyond the family into the public sphere. Nero's several attempts to have his mother killed, while ultimately successful, contributed later to his own downfall. After her death in 59 CE, Agrippina underwent a *damnatio memoriae*; her public statues were removed and mutilated: indeed, the extensive damage suffered by the Montemartini torso may have stemmed from such an attack.

In the first assassination attempt, the plot was foiled because Agrippina had a maid-servant impersonate her. In explaining the empress' narrow escape, Gradel (2007: 24) suggests that people did not know what she looked like, an idea he derives from the notion that her many statues did not look like her (or at least that it was credible to the average

Figure 30.4 Statue of Agrippina in Egyptian greywacke, body from Centrale Montemartini (inv. MC 1882/S) and head from the Ny Carlsberg Glyptotek. Rome, Musei Capitolini, Centrale Montemartini. Photo: Archivio Fotografico dei Musei Capitolini.

person that she was a visual cipher.) To be sure, there was almost certainly a wide gulf between image and reality in the portraits of all the Julio-Claudians, both male and female. On the whole their portraits were idealizing, and as instruments of political propaganda it was more important that they projected a specific message—whether of dynastic bloodlines or of suitability to rule or, in the case of the women, to bear heirs to the throne—than that they depicted individuals accurately. At the same time, however, the gap between image and reality underscores the degree to which the imperial woman was limited in her public operations. As for modern-day royals such as Crown Princess Masako of Japan or Diana, Princess of Wales, Roman court life must have been imprisoning in its protocols and restrictions. In documenting the extraordinary powers and honors bestowed upon the Julio-Claudian women, recent scholars have perhaps unintentionally led us to believe that they functioned as independent women and played large on the public stage. Wealth and a large client base could of course bolster their positions, but even Livia and Agrippina had to negotiate their positions in the *domus Augusta* with care.

6   Reconciling the Visual and the Literary

From Tacitus' *Histories* to Robert Graves' *I, Claudius*, literary accounts contend that the Julio-Claudian women, with a few exceptions such as Augustus' sister Octavia, were power-hungry viragos who used sex and violence to ensure their own success and that of their children. Official portraits of the women from the imperial court paint a different story—of dutiful wives, modest matrons, loving mothers, and pious priestesses. To be sure, their reproduction of standardized images must have—at some level—met with court approval. But, nonetheless, the widespread dissemination of these images and, more importantly, their survival for decades after their creation, attests to the esteem with which their subjects were regarded. At the same time, recent commentators such as Ginsburg (2006) have gone a long way towards dispelling the stereotypes that typically define the Julio-Claudian empress. While their menfolk challenged the norms of government inherited from the Republic, the Julio-Claudian women—notably Livia and Agrippina—posed an unacceptable threat to established ideas of gender relationships and the family.

RECOMMENDED FURTHER READING

Jane Fejfer (2008) provides what is currently the best summary in English of the methods, materials, and aims of Roman portraits; Fejfer addresses some of the conclusions of Alexandridis (2004) here and in Fejfer (2006).

Sheila Dillon (2010) offers the most comprehensive treatment of the Greek precedents, while Sally-Ann Ashton (2008) presents a highly readable history with many illustrations, if not full art historical analysis. Paul Zanker (1988) gives the definitive postwar book on Roman art, viewing a range of artistic monuments—from monumental architecture to miniature gems—through an ideological lens. Many portraits are discussed.

As an outgrowth of Zanker's ideological approach, several scholars have examined the phenomenon of Julio-Claudian portrait groups, a primary means for advertising the political fortunes of members of the dynasty. C. Brian Rose (1997) and Dietrich Boschung (2002), in richly illustrated works, tackle this important subject. For in-depth studies of individual women see Bartman (1999) and Wood (1999).

ACKNOWLEDGMENTS

To RB, who has never underestimated women.

31

Portraits, Prestige, Piety:
Images of Women in Roman Egypt

Christina Riggs

1 Introduction

The land-owning families based in and around the towns of high imperial Egypt occupied a subtly shifting terrain. In terms of social, economic, and cultural stratification, these families and their households slotted in somewhere between the urban elite, who had greater wealth and more potent ties to the civic and provincial Roman administration, and the Egyptian priestly class, which had lost many of its legal privileges but retained influence based on the learned traditions of the temple scriptoria (Frankfurter 1998). The first century of Roman rule saw Egyptian society realigned according to status designations, such as membership of the newly defined, and subsequently hereditary, *metropolite* class (Nelson 1979; van Minnen 2002; Riggs 2005: 14–26). The establishment of this class, based in the provincial capitals (*metropoleis*), fit a pattern of urbanization encouraged by Rome, which furthered the process of Hellenization begun by the third century BCE wave of Greek immigration (Bowman 2000; Bowman and Rathbone 1992). Social relations in the high Imperial period set the stage for the transformations of the third century CE and late antiquity, marked by the concentration of land ownership in large estates, the entrenchment of the urban elite as a group, and the more fluid social negotiations of individuals, especially from second- or third-tier "sub-elites," such as the Egyptian priesthood and the metropolite class of the provincial capitals (Tacoma 2006; van Minnen 2002).

In the complex social milieu of imperial Egypt, the visual arts were an important instrument for the assertion of status and the construction of identity. In particular, the genre of portraiture gained rapidly in popularity from the mid first century CE onwards. Whether for funerary or civic commemoration, portraiture demonstrated a patron's familiarity with imperial art forms and laid claim to elite qualities such as Hellenic dress, demeanor, and education. Moreover, the technical requirements of portrait sculpture and painting, in terms of both skill and materials, ensured that the genre retained some aura of exclusivity. Although forms of portraiture were widely disseminated, and their symbolism

A Companion to Women in the Ancient World, First Edition. Edited by Sharon L. James and Sheila Dillon.
© 2012 John Wiley & Sons, Ltd. Published 2015 by John Wiley & Sons, Ltd.

well understood, there was a range of qualities, exemplified in the corpus of mummy portraits: encaustic examples on fine-grained wood reflect greater skill and expense than tempera painted on coarser woods (Cartwright 1997; compare examples in Walker 2000: 69–87). Portraits in stone and less-well-preserved materials, like bronze, will have displayed a similar range.

A second factor in the negotiation of status was the role of women and girls in social networks, especially in relation to marriage and motherhood. Roman legal statutes applied only to Roman citizens, who were a small minority until 212 CE. But the Roman administration did concern itself with status designations, many of which had an impact on taxation rates, and sets of rules such as the *Gnomon of the Idios Logos* strove to establish clarity where there was potential for confusion, such as a marriage or birth to parents of different standing (Rowlandson 1998: 174–95; Riccobono 1950). As preserved in a second-century papyrus, the *Gnomon* forbade marriage between Roman citizens and Egyptians, the latter term designating anyone who was not a citizen of one of the four Greek poleis of Egypt, namely Alexandria, Naukratis, Ptolemais, and Hadrian's new foundation, Antinoopolis. If such a marriage did take place, by error or ignorance, the children would not inherit Roman status, only Egyptian. Status, age, and motherhood also helped to determine a woman's inheritance rights, and her right to allocate her own property: women who were over the age of fifty, or else childless and unmarried, could not inherit property, but younger women with at least three children could, a structure that replicated the standard of *ius trium liberorum* (special rights for those who have three children) in Roman law.

Women's property and status mattered at many levels of society, and women appear in Greek documentary papyri as owners of land, houses, slaves, and movables, enabling them to carry out financial transactions (e.g., selling, buying, lending) and giving them some degree of economic independence. For metropolite families, or families who lacked this specific status but operated in the Greco-Egyptian sphere of the towns or larger villages, the lifecycles of women and girls were imbricated in a larger social network, helping to create, cement, and sustain both personal and professional ties. Matrilineal descent of seven generations was required to secure metropolite status by the late first century CE, so that a mother's family line was as important as the father's. This requirement encouraged the adoption, for the first time, of matronyms in Greek, a practice previously tied only to Egyptian-language use (Depauw 2010).

The prevalence of images of women and girls in the funerary art of Roman Egypt relates to their roles in this social network as well as the nature of commemoration. Nearly half the corpus of mummy portraits is for women (based on Parlasca 1969, 1977, 1980), and there are nearly as many females as males among other groups of funerary art as well, including coffins, mummy masks, and painted shrouds. Fewer funerary or votive stelae for women have been documented than for men, but stele emplacements may have accommodated women in some other way: some stelae also depict mixed male and female groups, which may represent families (e.g., Abdalla 1992: 101, with examples; Riggs 2005: 89 figure 36). Similarly, decorated tombs represent only one individual, male or female, but the tomb itself may have served for a number of burials, whether of family members, professional or cult associates, or unaffiliated individuals.

Where an inscription in either Greek or Demotic Egyptian is included in a work of funerary art, it often names the father of the deceased woman or girl, following the Greek pattern of patronymic use (e.g., Riggs and Stadler 2003). In a metric Greek epitaph in a tomb at Tuna el-Gebel, the cemetery that served the metropolis of Hermopolis Magna, a father apotheosizes his dead daughter Isidora as a nymph after her early death, possibly by drowning (Rowlandson 1998: 54–5). Premature death may well have been a contributing factor in terms of who—male or female—was memorialized in funerary art and monuments. The adornment of the mummified body or tomb and the performance of attendant rituals bestowed sexual maturity and fertility on prepubescent girls, which in Egyptian thought contributed to the regeneration of the dead. Unmarried girls, or women who died young, perhaps in childbirth, might have been considered especially worthy of the expense that a portrait or other form of artistic commemoration represented, as observed for the representation of young men in mummy portraits as well (Montserrat 1993).

This essay looks in more detail at funerary art made for women and girls in the Roman Period, including portraits and masks made for mummification burials and tomb sculptures based on classical forms. A select number of examples highlight the range of commemorative options in the funerary art of Roman Egypt, which used Egyptian and Greek or Roman imagery in a flexible and distinctive way. The works discussed here also underscore the twin themes of prestige and piety, setting the lives of the women represented in their social context. The examples probably depict women from different social strata, yet together they offer a glimpse of women's roles in privileged local groups, and of the way in which the visual arts created and sustained identity, in life and after death.

2 Portraits

A linen shroud in the Metropolitan Museum of Art was made to wrap the mummified body of a woman, encapsulating the deceased in protective scenes and symbols of Egyptian myth (Figure 31.1). The find-spot of the shroud is unknown, but decorated full-length shrouds are attested at several Nile Valley sites, including Saqqara (the necropolis of Memphis), Asyut (Lykopolis), Akhmim (Panopolis), and Thebes (Diospolis Parva, modern Luxor). On the New York shroud, a gesso ground supports paint in colors dominated by pink, purple, and white, with traces of red and blue as well. When in place, the left and right sides of the shroud covered the sides of the supine body. These are subdivided into registers like the jambs of an Egyptian temple gateway, an architectural association continued in the frieze of cobras (*uraei*) above, and the winged sun disc at the top of the shroud's central section. The registers of each side form symmetrical pairs, from top to bottom: the goddesses Isis and Nephthys shown as red kites; the four mummy-shaped "sons of Horus" associated with the bodily integrity of the corpse; a jackal associated with solar transit and cemetery space; the ibis of the god Thoth (viewer's left) and the falcon of the sun god or the sky god Horus (viewer's right); and at the bottom mirrored scenes of the dead woman taking her place in the afterlife, accompanied by Horus (viewer's left) and Anubis (viewer's right). The central section of the shroud corresponded to the "top"—that is, front—of the mummy, positioning a naturalistic, bust-length portrait over the face and chest, an image of Isis and Nephthys in mourning over the abdomen, and the patterned stripes of a protective collar (the *wesekh*) over the legs.

The portrait (Figure 31.2) depicts the woman wearing a dark purple tunic with a lighter purple *clavus*, and a dark purple tunic draped over her left shoulder. In her left hand she holds a floral wreath on which a trace of red of remains. Surface abrasions obscure the lower half of her face, but her wide-open eyes, long nose, and loop earrings are intact, with white highlights glinting on their pearls. Her dark hair is dressed in the "Nestfrisur" of late Flavian and early Hadrianic times, the coil on top of her head held in place with a white hair

Figure 31.1 Painted linen shroud for a woman, c. 100–125 CE, L 140.0 centimeters. Provenance unknown. New York, Metropolitan Museum of Art 26.5. Photo: © The Metropolitan Museum of Art/Art Resource, NY.

stick (cf. Borg 1996: 32–8). This competently executed portrait is striking in its own right, framed as it is by the Egyptian iconography and hieroglyphic inscriptions. Columns on either side of the woman's head are legible invocations to the god Osiris and appear to have given the subject's name as well, although the relevant hieroglyphs are lost. But the portrait is even more striking because another shroud from the same workshop, but made for a man, chose not to incorporate a naturalistic portrait: instead, an *en face*, Egyptian-style figure of the god Osiris filled the central panel of the male shroud (Riggs 2005: 253 figure 125). The options for representing the dead were not limited to a stark choice between "Egyptian" and "Greek" or "Roman," as Roman Egyptian society defied simplistic categorization, despite the administration's best efforts to separate "Greeks" from "Egyptians" and thus encourage a Hellenized urban elite. As van Minnen (2002: 351) observes, the gymnasium-joining "Greeks" in the villages of the *chora* had in some sense been Egyptian all along. How Egyptian and how Greek was situational.

It is this Greco-Egyptian milieu, concentrated in larger villages or small, non-metropolite towns, that seems likely to have yielded this pair of shrouds, one with its portrait and

Figure 31.2   Portrait detail of the shroud in Figure 31.1, c. 100–125 CE. The Metropolitan Museum of Art, Gift of George D. Pratt, 1926 (26.5). Image © The Metropolitan Museum of Art.

the other with a more conservative depiction of Osiris. The carefully selected imagery and accurate hieroglyphs, together with the use of linen and implied mummification, point to a level of specialized knowledge that fell under the sphere of influence of Egyptian priests and temple scriptoria. At the same time, the willingness to incorporate a naturalistic portrait and the ability to replicate fashionable clothing, jewelry, and hairstyles demonstrate that such imperial styling was both accessible and desirable. The pair of shrouds in New York raise the question of whether the representation of women and girls was in some sense more flexible or open to innovation where "new," non-Egyptian art forms were being used in an otherwise Egyptian context.

If what has survived is at all representative of ancient practice, then historically far fewer females than males received decorated burial ensembles in pharaonic and Ptolemaic Egypt, and hardly any had their own tombs. As a result, when the number of decorated female burials appears to increase in Roman Egypt, there was less of a precedent for crafting funerary art specific to female mummies. Being of lower status or importance than the men of their own social rank, women were also less subject to restrictions of decorum in the mindset of Egyptian art, which tended to confine formal innovations or iconographic experimentation to depictions of subsidiary figures such as servants, or of liminal activities such as mourning. Thus, these twin interests converged in Roman Egypt, first in commemorating women and girls as a factor of social status and identity and second in exploiting the idiom of classical art, especially the novel potential of naturalistic portraiture.

The cultural context of the shrouds and many other portraits was at once Egyptian, through their association with mummification and the expert use of Egyptian imagery, and

Greco-Roman, through their use of self-fashioning to make assertions about Hellenic heritage and identity. An encaustic portrait in Stuttgart bears a Demotic inscription identifying the young woman represented as Eirene, the daughter of a Serapis priest, a reminder of how the Egyptian language co-existed with Greek language use and naming patterns (Walker and Bierbrier 1997: 115–16). In a similar vein, magical rubrics on the feet of some portrait mummies (erroneously identified as "children's drawings" by the excavator Flinders Petrie) link funerary practices in the *chora* to the world of the Greek and Demotic magical papyri, where translation extends beyond language to ritual and knowledge as well (Römer 2000; Dieleman 2005). The privileged minority in villages and small towns were not a true elite in terms of political or economic influence, or their legal and fiscal status under Roman law, but they enjoyed the wherewithal to model themselves as "citizens of an ideal country—Greece" (Cribiore 2001: 9), with images of women and girls central to the evocation of familial and social unity, and cultural prestige.

3   Prestige

Another example of how Egyptian, Greek, and Roman practices informed the commemoration of women is the elaborate mummy of Artemidora (Figure 31.3), which dates to the late first or early second century CE and comes from Meir in Middle Egypt, a cemetery that

Figure 31.3   Mask in place on the mummy of a woman named Artemidora, made of linen cartonnage with added plaster, painted and gilded, and inlaid with glass and stone. From Meir, late first century or early second century CE. L 78.0 centimeters. New York, Metropolitan Museum of Art 11.155.5. Gift of J. Pierpont Morgan, 1911. Photo: © The Metropolitan Museum of Art/Art Resource, NY.

served the metropolis of Cusae and perhaps nearby villages as well. The mummy is wrapped in hundreds of meters of linen and adorned with painted and gilded figures of Egyptian gods and hieroglyphic inscriptions (Walker 2000: 132–5). In addition, a Greek inscription on the foot of the mummy takes the form of a *tabula ansata* and identifies the deceased as "Artemidora, daughter of Harpokrates, [died] untimely, 27 years [old]. Farewell." Other mummies found with this one, or elsewhere in the cemetery, also bear both Greek and Egyptian inscriptions, and two male mummies had both Greek and Egyptian names (Riggs 2005: 119–21).

The mummy of Artemidora has a carefully crafted and richly decorated mummy mask made of plaster-coated linen cartonnage with applied paint and gilding and inlaid glass and stone. Both the mask and the mummy represent a tremendous expense and, like the shrouds discussed above, a deep familiarity with Egyptian forms of knowledge. The hieroglyphic texts are prayers to Osiris; the god Anubis and two mourning goddesses appear at the foot of the mummy; and the sides of the mask show a procession of gods in a format that echoes Egyptian temple decoration. The mask incorporates Greek and Roman modes as well: Artemidora is shown wearing a red tunic with purple *clavi*, and her hair is dressed in a tall frontlet of tiny curls, a style made popular under the Flavians. The corkscrew curls that fall behind and around this frontlet assimilate Artemidora to Egyptian goddesses such as Isis, in a trope that owes much to earlier portraits of Ptolemaic queens (Riggs 2005: 123). Classical and Egyptian art forms could be marshalled together to convey prestige in imperial Egypt, at this stratum of society. The standing of Artemidora as a gendered individual, and as part of a family and social group, must have occasioned her commemoration in this way, and her "untimely" death may have been a factor as well.

In larger metropoleis such as Oxyrhynchus, the urban elite or metropolite class of the high Imperial period used Roman portrait sculpture to a similar end, but without explicit Egyptian references. The cemeteries of Oxyrhynchus have yielded a number of near-life-size portrait sculptures carved in relief in the local nummulitic limestone. The portraits are framed by apsidal niches with slender columns on either side and a scallop shell in the top of the apse (Figure 31.4). Unfortunately, there is little information about the structures from which the reliefs originate: Petrie's cursory exploration in the early 1920s only described a subterranean tomb with fresco paintings and a "burial pit," without recording architectural details or information about the burials themselves (Petrie 1925). Most examples of the Oxyrhynchus reliefs come from unrecorded excavations in the 1960s, with many cut out of the integral niches to facilitate export to the European art market, and others misleadingly restored with modern paint and plaster for the same reason (Schneider 1975, 1982; Severin 1995; von Falck 1996).

The size of the reliefs, and Petrie's mention of an "elaborate" underground structure, call to mind Alexandrian catacombs of the Roman Period, which combine burial places with space for funerary rituals and commemoration (Venit 2002). The urban elite of Oxyrhynchus may have used a similar model, with tomb space shared by families or associates, funerary reliefs that mimed imperial marble sculpture, and both men and women represented by individual statues, as at Kom el-Shugafa in Alexandria (Venit 2002: 129–34). Moreover, burials in such a space were as, if not more, likely to have been inhumations rather than mummifications. A second-century will from Oxyrhynchus refers to an "Egyptian" fashion of burial, suggesting that a range of treatments was available for the corpse, just as a range of artistic forms and styles—some more Roman than Egyptian—presented alternatives for commemorating the dead (Montserrat 1997: 33). Nor was Oxyrhynchus the only site in the Nile Valley where funerary sculpture based closely on

Figure 31.4 Limestone funerary relief of a woman, c. 160 CE. Provenance unknown, possibly Oxyrhynchus. H 68.0 centimeters. Harvard University Art Museums 1977.197. Photo: © The President and Fellows, Harvard College, Harvard University Art Museums.

Roman models was employed, for similar reliefs have been found at Coptos (Duthuit 1931: pl. IID), near Esna (Thomas 2000: figure 72), and elsewhere. Although less visible in the archaeological record than decorated mummies like that of Artemidora, these alternative forms of burial and commemoration practiced by a wealthier, more cosmo-politan elite will have been highly visible in the large and influential towns of imperial Egypt.

An Antonine funerary sculpture in the collection of Harvard University exemplifies the use of a local material—poor-quality limestone—to reproduce Roman models of com-memorative portraits (Figure 31.4; Zayed 1962: 168–9). According to Zayed (1962: Introduction), the relief was part of a group of objects purchased from the dealer Albert Eid in Cairo and subsequently exported by the Egyptian antiquities service. Probably from Oxyrhynchus, based on its similarity to excavated examples (Petrie 1925: pl. XLV.10, now British Museum EA1795), the Harvard relief is at a smaller scale than comparable sculptures, around half life-size. The deceased stands within a niche exactly as wide as her shoulders. The left side of the niche has been restored, but the right side bears the remains of a column capital at the height of the subject's shoulder, and above this, at head height, springs the low arch over the apsidal top of the niche. The front of the arch has traces of a flat molding, and a molding runs around the inside of the niche at the base of the arch. A scallop with seven flutes fills the top of the arch directly over the subject's head, and both the niche and the shell serve to elevate the deceased to a divine or semi-divine state. Both male and female funerary reliefs employ the scallop shell motif, which for images of women and girls might have had the additional association of assimilating the deceased to Aphrodite and to nymphs. The Tuna el-Gebel tomb of Isidora, with its Greek epitaph about the drowned girl becoming a nymph, also incorporated a shell-topped niche with side pillar, probably for an image of a deity or the deceased (Gabra 1941: pl. 32).

The woman commemorated in the Harvard relief wears a tunic and a mantle caught up around her right arm, which is bent across her body so that her open right hand lies flat against her left breast. Her left arm hangs alongside her body, the hand cradling a looped floral wreath like the wreaths seen on painted portraits and mummy masks of the period. The pose and drapery are not exact copies of favored Roman portrait types derived from Hellenistic models, like the "Pudicitia," Ceres-type, or Large and Small Herculaneum women, but the Harvard relief shares their closed stance and binding of the body with clothing, which conveys the virtues of modesty, femininity, and restraint (Alexandridis 2010; Davies 2002, 2008; Trimble 2000; see also Dillon, this volume, Chapter 17; Bartman, this volume, Chapter 30). Here, the subject wears two necklaces of regularly shaped beads at the base of her throat and perhaps a ring on the fourth finger of her right hand, where there is discoloration on the stone surface. The woman's hair is parted in the middle of her low forehead, gathered into symmetrical ridges at the sides of her head that just cover the tops of her ears, and formed into a bun on top of the head, a style associated with the empress Faustina Minor (see Meyers, this volume, Chapter 33).

A plaster undercoat and the painted surface originally finished the sculpture, but only traces of these survive in the crevices of the soft limestone. Hues of pink, red, green, black, brown, yellow, and white would have given the sculpture a startling, bright, lifelike effect, especially when seen in flickering lamplight in the tomb. Although the relief has sustained damage and pigment loss, and its generic posture, hairstyle, and clothing convey no specific information about the subject herself, such as her age or marital status, the formulaic nature of the image is revealing nonetheless, because it is indicative of the familiarity and desirability of Roman portrait sculpture in imperial Egypt. The style of the relief, rather than its material, was the vehicle of prestige, allowing the urbanized, well-to-do families of Oxyrhynchus to assert their status by commemorating individual women alongside men in funerary structures befitting the classical architecture, colonnaded streets, and Hellenizing aspirations of their town (Bailey 1990; Parsons 2007).

4   Piety

Women also had a role to play in religious practice in Roman Egypt, from dedicating offerings and statues to serving as priestesses (Dunand 1978; Rowlandson 1998: 55–70; Colin 2002). Religious functions brought elite women out of the domestic sphere and into a semi-public one. Further, the property rights they had in Egypt gave some women scope to fund cult-related activities, while the appointment and regulation of priestesses, like that of priests, came under Roman administrative control. Both Greek and Egyptian cults incorporated priestesses, and in the Imperial period women are attested serving in a range of cults, including those of goddesses such as Athena-Thoeris—an Egyptian goddess of childbirth—and Demeter, attested in a form modeled on her Eleusinian mystery cult (Rowlandson 1998: 61–2) but elsewhere associated with Isis and the Egyptian agricultural goddess Thermouthis. Like other forms of rank, sacerdotal status became increasingly linked to lineage, inheritance, and a degree of fiscal privilege under Roman rule, encouraging endogamy within delimited social groups (Colin 2002: 117).

Figure 31.5 Limestone funerary relief of a woman holding a pyxis, with traces of paint, late second or early third century CE. H 142.5 centimeters. From Oxyrhynchus. Hannover, Museum August Kestner 1965.29. Photo: Courtesy of the Museum August Kestner.

Women participated in cults in less official ways as well, whether as members of associations based around a deity or through expressions of personal piety such as the making of offerings or having recourse to oracles, prayers, and magical practice.

Several other funerary reliefs from Oxyrhynchus commemorate women in such pious roles. Although the possibility that these women were priestesses cannot be ruled out, the gesture of making an offering was a fitting way to depict both men and women in a funerary context. A relief in the August Kestner Museum, Hannover, is one of the examples cut out of its apsidal niche for export in the 1960s (Figure 31.5). The Hannover relief is 142.5 centimeters high—nearly life-size. Traces of light brown paint adhere to the center-parted hair, and a substrate of red pigment and plaster appears on the face, neck, and drapery folds near the breast. The eyebrows and large irises are black, and a yellow gamma outlined in red adorns the mantle over the woman's left thigh. The mantle is gathered in a "hip bundle" that lies horizontally across the body, and the subject wears a thick yellow-painted necklace at the base of her throat and earrings with three pendant elements; the hairstyle and jewelry

Figure 31.6   Limestone funerary relief of a woman in the dress of an Isis cult initiate or priestess, late second or early third century CE. H 115.0 centimeters. From Oxyrhynchus. Brussels, Musées Royaux d'Art et d'Histoire/Koninklijke Musea voor Kunst en Geschiedenis inv. E.8239. Photo: Courtesy of the Musées Royaux d'Art et d'Histoire/Koninklijke Musea voor Kunst en Geschiedenis.

point to a late second or early third century date. In her left hand, the woman holds a pyxis with a conical lid, and her missing right hand would have held a pellet of incense as if extended towards an altar (cf. examples in Schneider 1982: 42, 44–5). The sculptor worked within the confines of the niche to suggest depth and movement, hollowing the limestone to a greater depth at the hip of the right leg, which does not support the body's weight, and pooling the hem of the tunic in swags over the feet.

   Still other reliefs from Oxyrhynchus depict women dressed as initiates or priestesses of the Isis cult, a visual trope attested on only two mummy portraits (Borg 1996: 112–14). The specific Isis iconography—corkscrew curls of hair falling onto the shoulders, fringed mantle knotted between the breasts, floral bandolier across the torso, and *situla* held in one hand (if shown)—is otherwise better known from monuments outside of Egypt, such as a series of funerary stelae from Attica, dating from the late first century BCE into the third century CE (Walters 1988). As Walters observes (1988: 57), cult initiation in the Greco-Roman manner was costly, further limiting its accessibility and emphasizing the high status of the women thus portrayed, and by association their families. One of the Oxyrhynchus sculptures in Isiac dress is in Brussels (Figure 31.6), and another is in the Museum of Fine Arts, Boston (D'Auria et al. 1988: 212). On the Brussels relief, the molding and arch of the apse are preserved behind the head of the deceased, but the remainder of the niche is evident only in the confined pose of the body and the structural traces along the subject's right arm. The figure is broken off below the knees, and two fragments of stone depicting the lower right arm from elbow to wrist, and the right hand holding a *situla*, are not shown in Figure 31.6 but have been restored since the photograph was taken. Comparison with the Boston piece suggests that the left wrist and hand filled the break midway down the right side of the relief, and would have held or cradled a round pot or a pyxis. No paint and very little plaster survive on the surface of the limestone.

The woman's hair is dressed in a version of the "melon" coiffure close to her head, with one or two long, sausage-like curls at either side of her neck. Like the figure in Hannover, the Brussels figure wears earrings with three hanging elements and a necklace at the base of her throat, here with a circular pendant in the center. The mantle knot is in the center of the chest and takes the form of three regularly shaped tufts of cloth above the knot and a single fall below, weighted at the corner. The floral bandolier follows the parallel lines of a narrow stole that drapes from the left shoulder, across the Isis knot, and around the right side of the waist; the other end of the stole trails from the left shoulder and conceals the left edge of the body. There are three horizontal bands in raised relief at the end of the stole, suggesting a woven pattern in the textile. Deep fold lines are carved with confidence to indicate the tunic and mantle drapery, contrasting with the more subtle carving of the facial features, hairstyle, and "Venus rings" on the neck.

Even in its damaged condition, the Brussels relief and its counterparts are ambitious on many levels: their technical complexity, the concomitant scale of the structure into which they were incorporated, and their construction of gendered social identity. The sculptures exemplify the extent to which Egypt's urban population aligned itself with the cultural norms of the Roman empire, to an even greater degree than the lower-tier elites of the villages and smaller towns, whose Greekness coexisted with more overtly Egyptian practices. Like honorific and funerary statues of women elsewhere in the empire, the Oxyrhynchus reliefs expressed the feminine virtue of piety in visual form and thus commemorated women in a suitably decorous way while exerting the interrelated concerns of social prestige and familial lineage.

5 Conclusion

The funerary art that survives from Roman Egypt—from coffins and mummy masks to mummy portraits and sculpture—represents nearly as many women and girls as men and boys, in contrast to earlier periods, when the commemoration of women and children was less common, and such burials tended to be subsumed in the burials of their husbands or fathers. Changes in burial practice may account for some of the increase in funerary art made for women: for instance, burials made in reused tombs or grouped in pits or chambers meant that more attention was paid to decorating individual mummies rather than the burial space itself.

The commemoration of individual women also cemented social ties and evoked their important role in connection with the status and identity of the land-owning elites and sub-elites, whose position had been redrawn by the legal reforms of the early empire.

In rural areas, gymnasial "Greeks" countered their legal status as "Egyptians" in mummy portraits that emphasized familiarity with Hellenic culture and Roman art, and displayed their power and prestige through elaborate mummifications (like that of Artemidora) that interwove Egyptian and Classical traditions. In the provincial capitals, the wealthy urban elites, or metropolites, were likely responsible for the large, rock-cut structures that have yielded integral reliefs such as the Oxyrhynchus sculptures, which mime imperial styles in local limestone, rather than imported marble. Like Roman women, these women were portrayed in forms derived from Hellenistic sculpture, their bodies concealed by drapery and their postures and gestures emphasizing qualities of modesty, virtue, and piety.

There are a number of similarities between the representation of women in Roman Egypt and images of women elsewhere in the empire, since the copying and adaptation of imperial modes and models was a well-established practice. At the same time, however, there were marked differences based on the Egyptian context. In both Egyptian and Greco-Roman art, the assimilation of women to goddesses offered an array of iconographic options for emphasizing the deceased's status in life as well as her elevation, or apotheosis, in the afterlife. Mummification itself helped to accomplish this goal, and in funerary art the application of gold to mummy portraits functioned similarly, as did inserting a portrait into Egyptian framing devices derived from temple architecture, or merging elements such as fashionable and "divine" hairstyles. In Egypt, unlike Italy or Roman Greece, the rarity of images that represent women in the dress of Isis may single out these women as priestesses, rather than cult affiliates, echoing the similarly rare commemoration of men and boys attired as priests or at least initiates of the Serapis cult (Walker and Bierbrier 1997: 69–70, 118–20; Riggs 2005: 229–32).

Roman Egypt offered a unique set of social circumstances that affected the commemoration of women in funerary art: women retained the rights to own property and to represent themselves in legal matters, which derived from Egyptian law, and Roman status regulations demanded clear articulation of maternal as well as paternal descent, which was novel to Greek, though not Egyptian, practice in Egypt (Depauw 2010). The greater frequency with which women were commemorated, whether in decorated mummification burials or elaborate tomb sculptures, may reflect the increased importance of women—and specifically of motherhood—in establishing the status of their families and, by association, social groups. Thus, in both the villages and the towns of high imperial Egypt, privilege often had a female face.

RECOMMENDED FURTHER READING

For the history and archaeology of Roman Egypt, two books published by the British Museum Press offer excellent introductions: Bowman (1986) and Bagnall and Rathbone (2004). David Frankfurter (1998) offers a thought-provoking study that, while it does not address women specifically, explores the relationship between social change and religious piety on a local level. The experiences of women and girls are brought to life through written evidence by Rowlandson (1998), who uses Greek, Latin, Demotic, and Coptic sources to discuss the social roles, lifecycles, and legal specificities of being female in Roman Egypt, as well as the Hellenistic and Byzantine periods.

There are a number of well-illustrated books on mummy portraits published in English, including Roberts (2008) and Doxiadis (1995); the exhibition catalogs edited by Walker and Bierbrier (1997) and by Walker (2000); and a collection of British Museum conference papers edited by Bierbrier (1997). A concise overview of funerary art in Roman Egypt is given in Corbelli (2006). Two specialized studies of the topic are Riggs (2005) and Venit (2002).

Parsons (2007) is highly readable and provides a succinct overview of the provincial capital of Oxyrhynchus, which is far better documented by its papyrological remains than its archaeology. There is to date no complete study of the Oxyrhynchus reliefs, and most publications about them are in languages other than English. However, there is some discussion of the group in Thomas (2000). The exhibition catalog of D'Auria et al. (1988, repr. 2000) publishes one relief of a woman dressed as a follower of Isis, and Bailey (2008) collects small-scale terracotta images of Isis followers and related subjects, which were used for private devotions, votive offerings, and festival occasions.

32

Women in Imperial Roman Literature

Rhiannon Ash

In the literary texts that survive from the early Imperial period across a whole range of different genres, vibrant and memorable portraits of women abound. While some such representations are undeveloped and undeniably shaped by stereotypical conceptions of archetypal female (as opposed to male) traits, other depictions of women, evolving subtly over extended stretches of narrative, are much more nuanced and multifaceted, allowing scope for complex and divergent reactions from an audience. We can compare here the different ways in which we react to characters preserved in static "snapshots" as opposed to those appearing in complex films. Of course, the process of characterizing *any* individuals in ancient texts, whether men or women, is influenced by various factors. Two of the most important are how an author responds to the preconceived "rules" of a given literary genre (which are often subverted in inventive ways) and the practice (particularly prevalent in Roman texts) of creative allusion, which involves filtering one character or situation through another pre-existing text. It should never be forgotten that ancient readers were highly sophisticated consumers, with the ability to draw on their knowledge of previous Greek and Latin authors and engage in a lively "dialogue" with a new text.

Take, for example, the intriguing opening sequence of Juvenal's sixth *Satire* about women, which shows the impact that generic interplay and allusion can have on an audience:

> credo Pudicitiam Saturno rege moratam
> in terris uisamque diu, cum frigida paruas
> praeberet spelunca domos ignemque laremque
> et pecus et dominos communi clauderet umbra,
> siluestrem montana torum cum sterneret uxor
> frondibus et culmo uicinarumque ferarum
> pellibus, haut similis tibi, Cynthia, nec tibi, cuius
> turbauit nitidos extinctus passer ocellos,
> sed potanda ferens infantibus ubera magnis
> et saepe horridior glandem ructante marito.

A Companion to Women in the Ancient World, First Edition. Edited by Sharon L. James and Sheila Dillon.
© 2012 John Wiley & Sons, Ltd. Published 2015 by John Wiley & Sons, Ltd.

I believe that when Saturn was king, Chastity lingered on earth and could be seen for a long time. This was in the days when a freezing cave provided a tiny home, a hearth-fire and household gods, and enveloped both herd and owners in a communal gloom, in the days when a mountain wife would spread her woodland couch with leaves and straw and skins of neighboring beasts. She wasn't a bit like you, Cynthia, nor you, whose shining little eyes were spoiled by a dead sparrow. Giving her breasts to her huge babies for suckling, she was often more even uncouth than her acorn-belching husband. (Juvenal, *Satire* 6.1–10)

Juvenal begins with (what looks as if it will be) a traditional picture of idealized primitive life, alluding in general terms to the familiar vision of the ages of man (cf. Hesiod, *Works and Days* 109–201), whereby humans lived side-by-side on earth with the divinities (such as Chastity) in a golden-age idyll. Typically, this was an era unregulated by laws (which were not necessary, since people were naturally good), before the invention of the first ship (so people stayed put in their own land and had no engagement with mercantile activities), and at a time before warfare and agriculture, when the earth and trees spontaneously provided simple but nourishing food and sustenance, while the weather was in a state of perpetual spring in a landscape ruled by Saturn (cf. Ovid, *Metamorphoses* 1.89–113). For many authors, such pleasing images of the golden age offer powerful scope for moralizing, and the chance to highlight a sharp contrast between an idyllic "then" and corrupt "now" (cf. Catullus 64.384–408). Indeed, Juvenal himself engages in just such a polarized set of moral comparisons at *Satire* 13.38–59 in his mock *consolatio* to Calvinus for being cheated of ten sestertii.

Yet here the picture is peculiarly mismatched with the usual trope, as Juvenal deftly plays with his audience's expectations, raised by their knowledge of the golden age from other literature, and reverses the traditional idealization of the mythical past through a set of surprising and funny twists. Instead of enjoying a perpetual spring and living in the open air, these golden-age inhabitants have to inhabit chilly caves, a detail that Ovid pointedly associates instead with the silver age (*Metamorphoses* 1.121), and, on top of that, they even have to share the gloomy cave with their herd, another dissonant note for the golden age, when farming was not yet supposed to be part of life.

So, by the time Juvenal zooms in on a particular individual and introduces us to the simple "mountain wife" busily setting up her "woodland couch," we are already primed to expect further inventive twists. Normally, such an image of a hardy golden-age woman would be held up as an object of admiration and as a symbol of standards of behavior (often focused on virtues such as chastity), which contemporary women could no longer match. This is not straightforwardly the case here, however. Juvenal wittily interrupts his own golden-age fantasy and collapses the chronological gulf by directly addressing two famous literary women. First of all, in order to express the kind of woman the mountain wife does *not* resemble, he introduces Propertius' famous elegiac mistress, the elegant and beautiful Cynthia. That picture of the practical mountain wife arranging leaves, straw, and animal skins on a woodland couch may specifically trigger associations for an ancient audience with Propertius 1.3. This is the famous poem in which the drunken Propertius, returning late at night after a party, comes across Cynthia sleeping lightly on a couch in the glimmering moonlight, where she has been awaiting his return. The whole description is mediated through the poet's eroticized gaze.

The obvious incongruity between the two women, the graceful Cynthia and the rugged mountain wife, and the creative interplay between the two genres (satire and love elegy) that results must clearly enhance an audience's enjoyment. So too does the next point of comparison. Juvenal does not bother to name his second addressee, but he clearly alludes to Lesbia, the mistress of Catullus, whose famous pet sparrow is the subject of two poems (Catullus 2, 3). In particular, his depiction of her "shining little eyes … spoiled by a dead sparrow" recalls Catullus 3.17–18, where *tua nunc opera meae puellae/ flendo turgiduli rubent ocelli!* ("Thanks to you, now the darling little eyes of my girl are swollen and red from weeping!"). Juvenal's repetition of the diminutive form *ocelli*, suggestive of delicacy and affection, is meant to accentuate the differences between Lesbia and the mountain wife, with the latter's rough and ready home and "huge babies." What is more, the concept of keeping a bird as a bijou pet purely for entertainment contrasts sharply with the practical sorts of animals that inhabit the cave. And, as a closing touch in returning to the golden-age scene, Juvenal deploys bathos. We could hardly imagine a more pronounced contrast between the pair of elegant mistresses and the lactating mother, who is memorably tagged as often being more uncouth than her acorn-belching husband, powerfully undercutting idealized images of womanhood: the fact that Juvenal does not describe directly what form her coarseness takes is arguably more effective than giving details, as he leaves our imagination to do the work. How *could* she be more coarse than her acorn-belching husband?

What this close reading of the opening of Juvenal's sixth satire is meant to suggest is an important proviso in approaching this whole topic. Images of women in imperial Roman literature are often shot through with sophisticated literary devices, which should prompt us to resist easy categorizations about what ancient male authors "think" about women more generally. Here, for example, at the opening of an infamous satire that has prompted some critics simply to dismiss Juvenal as hopelessly misogynistic, the poet is actually playing a complex series of games. While initially it might seem as if he is holding up a vignette of life in the golden age as a kind of shorthand to indicate a set of moral standards that contemporary women can implicitly no longer maintain, the picture is not necessarily so clear-cut.

Life in the golden age in fact seems unpleasantly grim and hard, and the introduction of the mistresses Cynthia and Lesbia as points of comparison (made more immediate and vivid by Juvenal's direct address) opens up a more attractive world, where sex is pursued by men and women for pleasure rather than procreation, and the obligations of marriage are there to be avoided. Juvenal deftly and astringently appears to deflate the golden-age world for which contemporaries would normally have been made to feel a sense of nostalgia and approval (just as Ovid deploys similar deflationary dynamics in his description of the rough and ready arrangements for ancient theatrical productions at the time of the rape of the Sabine women; *Ars Amatoria* 1.103–8). Indeed, Juvenal's prominent opening allusions to the poetry of Propertius and Catullus add weight to the idea that in this particular satire he is not giving vent to an unreconstructed outpouring of bile against women in general, but instead is offering us a parody of a type of rhetorical set piece, the deliberative speech on the theme of whether or not a man should marry (as Braund 1992 suggests, citing, among other texts, Quintilian 2.4.24–5). In so doing, Juvenal presupposes a well-informed and perceptive contemporary audience, who would have been reading his satires collaboratively. We too should aim to respond to images of women in ancient literature in this way, even if we have to work hard to try to understand the cultural context in which these texts were originally produced.

Other factors too can have an impact on the characterization of women in ancient literature. As well as the genre of a text and the author's deployment of allusion, we have to consider issues such as whether we are dealing with historical women as opposed to literary constructs, how far an individual's class is being used by an author to shape a particular portrait, and whether there is any exaggeration or over-simplification in play as a result of an author's desire to pursue exemplarity or moralizing in constructing a character sketch. In addition, we need to assess how far an author is using either direct speech or (alternately) non-verbal rhetoric as a characterizing device, and how far "foiling" (i.e., sharp contrasts with other characters in the narrative) is in play. How individuals are presented as interacting with other people around them can often have a particularly significant bearing on an audience's response to a character.

1   Granny with a Heart of Gold: Pliny's Ummidia Quadratilla

Keeping these issues in view, let us now consider one of Pliny the Younger's letters, *Epistle* 7.24, dated by Sherwin-White (1966: 38) to c. 107 CE and written to his friend and protégé Geminus Rosianus (cf. *Epistles* 7.1, 8.5, 8.22, 9.11, 9.30, 10.26) about the death of an elderly woman, Ummidia Quadratilla. She happened to be the grandmother of Ummidius Quadratus, an up-and-coming orator and another of Pliny's young friends, who was also supported by him (cf. *Epistles* 6.11, 6.29, 9.13). Thus, the letter is a constituent element in a complex and ongoing network of male patronage, which no doubt has an impact on the way in which Ummidia Quadratilla is portrayed:

Gaius Pliny sends greetings to his friend Geminus:

Ummidia Quadratilla has passed away, having almost reached the age of seventy-nine, although she was the picture of health right up until her very last illness, having a wiry and robust physique beyond the limit of a woman in her prime [*ultra matronalem modum*]. She passed away leaving a most honorable will: she left as her heirs her grandson, with two-thirds of the estate, and her granddaughter, with the other third. I hardly know the granddaughter, but I have the greatest affection for the grandson. He is a remarkable youth, not just for those to whom he is related by blood, and he inspires love among his kinsmen. In the first place, although conspicuous for his good looks, he escaped all gossip of the malicious, both as a boy and as a young man. He was a husband before he was twenty-four and, if god had granted it, he would have been a father. He lived in fellowship with his pleasure-loving grandmother in a most upright fashion, but nevertheless very respectfully [*uixit in contubernio auiae delicatae seuerissime et tamen obsequentissime*]. She used to own some pantomime actors whom she treated with an indulgence more effusive than befits a woman of her high rank. Quadratus did not watch them in the theater, or at home, and she did not insist that he do so. When she was entrusting her grandson's studies to me, I heard her explain that (as a woman in that state of leisure typical of her sex) she was accustomed to relax by playing draughts and that she habitually watched her pantomime actors, but when she was about to do either one of these things, she always instructed her grandson to go off and study. It seems to me that she did this just as much from respect for the boy as from love of him.

You will be amazed at the following, just as I was amazed. At the most recent priestly games, after the pantomime actors had been brought onto stage at the commencement, when Quadratus and I were leaving the theater together, he said to me: "Do you know that today was the first time I had seen my grandmother's freedman dancing?" So said the grandson. Yet, by Hercules, total and utter strangers, in a bid to honor Quadratilla (I am ashamed to have called it honor when it was by way of flattery) used to run into the theater, jump up and down, applaud, marvel and finally used to respond to the individual gestures of their mistress with songs. These are the men who will now receive (as the bounty for their theatrical work) utterly tiny legacies [*exiguissima legata*] from an heir who did not see them. I have told you these things because if any news happens, I know that you are usually keen to hear it, and secondly because it is pleasant for me to relive the pleasure I experienced by writing about events. For I am delighted at the family affection of the dead woman [*pietate defunctae*] and at the honor done towards an excellent young man [*honore optimi iuuenis*]. I am happy too that the former household of Gaius Cassius (the man who was the leading light and founder of the Cassian school) will serve a master no less distinguished. My dear Quadratus will fulfil and adorn it, restoring to it again its former grandeur, fame, and glory by emerging from there having become as great an orator as Cassius was a jurist. Goodbye.

I start from the basic assumption that Pliny's central objective in writing and publishing this letter is not primarily to celebrate the life of a colorful old lady (even if that is what ultimately he achieves) but to help further the career of his young friend, Ummidius Quadratus, as the latter starts to use his rhetorical skills in a very public forum, the lawcourts. In this context, the flamboyant lifestyle and activities of Ummidia Quadratilla could potentially have been a real source of embarrassment to the young man, particularly since Roman orators (well-versed in the ways of invective) had always been adept at mining the private lives of their opponents for damaging material, which could then be used as a weapon to discredit them and undermine their credibility as advocates. Rather than ignoring Quadratilla, a strategy that would have been highly problematic in this context, Pliny goes on the offensive and acknowledges (what he regards as) her eccentricities, which he concedes are not really appropriate for a woman of her rank, but even so he sets them out in the context of a likable and very engaging portrait, which humanizes Quadratilla and suggests that she has got her priorities right. Further, Pliny then sets out to demonstrate to the wider world how Quadratus managed to satisfy the demands of two conflicting pressures, the need on the one hand to show *pietas* to a prominent member of his family and the need on the other hand for a young man who was destined for a legal career to live in a respectable and austere way, so that (in the spirit of Cato the Elder) he could be held to account for his private life as well as his public career.

Pliny begins by accentuating both Quadratilla's longevity and her remarkably fine state of health until her final illness intervened. Since the ancients tended to believe that a person's lifestyle had a direct impact on their health, and that the longer one lived the deeper was the impact of the sort of temptations that could lead to moral degeneration (Plutarch, *Moralia* 611e), this emphatic opening is pointed. It artfully pre-empts any charge that Quadratilla's fondness for pantomime actors was accompanied by any of the more dissolute activities that were often associated with those who kept company with such déclassé members of society. Pliny also uses loaded language here, describing Quadratilla's physical state as being strong and wiry *ultra matronalem modum* ("beyond the limit of a woman in her prime"), thereby suggesting that at least in one respect she outclasses the average *matrona* (respectable married woman).

Quadratilla further demonstrates her moral caliber by her well-judged will, whereby she leaves two thirds of her property to her grandson and a third to her granddaughter. Although by modern standards this arrangement might seem less fair than a fifty-fifty split, the expectation was that the responsibility for supporting the granddaughter financially would lie mainly with her (future) husband. Pliny might also have in mind here Quad-ratilla's admirable sense of independence, whereby she chooses not to leave a sizable legacy to the emperor Trajan. Of course, Trajan was a ruler of whom Pliny approved, but some of his more autocratic predecessors had exerted considerable pressure on aristocrats to leave them a legacy, and many complied, in the hope that this concession would enable the remainder of their property to be handed on to their relatives (cf. Suetonius, *Caligula* 38; Tacitus, *Annals* 14.31.1, 16.11.1). So, Tacitus derides Domitian, named by Agricola as his joint heir together with his own wife and daughter, for regarding this move as a gesture of respect, when in fact he should have known that "no emperor except a bad one is designated an heir by a good father" (*Agricola* 43.4).

Having established Quadratilla's credentials as a specimen of health and as a woman who has a fierce sense of loyalty to her family, Pliny embeds in the letter a laudatory description of Quadratus the grandson, endowed with physical handsomeness, but morally upright (so much so that he has managed to avoid the sort of malicious gossip that tended to associate good looks with loose sexual *mores*; cf. Cicero, *pro Caelio* 6); and, in addition to this, we learn that he is already respectably married (at an early age, too) and that only bad luck has so far prevented him from becoming a father. Only now does Pliny move on to the domestic sphere that Quadratus shared with his hedonistic grandmother (quite possibly an arrangement that had ceased upon his marriage: at least, the verb *uixit*, "he lived," is in the past tense). Pliny's language here is striking. He says that Quadratus lived *in contubernio auiae delicatae seuerissime et tamen obsequentissime* ("in fellowship with his pleasure-loving grandmother in a most upright fashion, but nevertheless very respectfully"). The juxtaposition of *delicata* ("pleasure-loving") and *seuerissime* ("most upright fashion") instantly polarizes in the strongest possible terms the decadent elderly woman (whose tastes cohere with what were seen as the self-indulgent values of the Neronian era) and the decent young man (born into the more austere world of the Flavian dynasty). There may also be a touch of humor in Pliny's use of the word *contubernium* ("fellowship"), which perhaps has a hint of military metaphor about it, if it retains a trace of the original meaning (the state of soldiers sharing the same tent).

Yet, despite their vastly differing outlooks, the pair manage to coexist quite happily, it seems. The grandmother adopts a "do as I say, not as I do" attitude and does not force her grandson to watch the shows put on by her troupe of performers; and, with a deft touch, Pliny postpones naming the young man until he is underscoring the fact that "not in the theater, not at home" did Quadratus watch these *pantomimi* (Lada-Richards 2004: 17 offers a helpful definition of ancient pantomime as an art form: "a ballet-style stage entertainment that integrates bodily, verbal, and musical discourses in the form of a solo masked dancer impersonating mythical characters to the accompaniment of music and a singing chorus"). Instead, the grandmother concerns herself with arranging her grandson's education and selects Pliny to help Quadratus make the transition to the law courts. This arrangement enables Pliny to bring Quadratilla back to life by putting words in her mouth.

In the event, the conversation recalled by Pliny presents us with a rather defensive Quadratilla, who explains her activities as attempts to alleviate the monotony of the life of an aristocratic woman by playing board games and watching her troupe of *pantomimi*. We should perhaps resist seeing this reported statement as a reflection of real embarrassment on Quadratilla's part about her lifestyle, however, and perhaps more as an artful *captatio beneuolentiae* of a potential tutor and patron, as Quadratilla sets out to reassure Pliny that, whatever he may have heard about the household, her grandson is an industrious young man and a good prospect for the future, who had regularly heeded her instructions that he should go off and study whenever she was about to engage in "frivolous" activities (even playing a board game!). The context of the exchange is therefore important. After all, this is a woman who is trying to get Pliny to agree to do something for her family, even if it emerges subsequently (from the conversation between Quadratus and Pliny) that she was actually telling the truth about her grandson's never having seen the troupe of *pantomimi* in action.

Quadratilla herself appears to have taken some pride in the *pantomimi*, as we can see from the fact that she enters them for a public competition and that opportunist flatterers in the theater habitually mimic her own enthusiasm in the hope of winning her favor. This is an interesting incidental detail. The fact that the spectators bother to do this at all suggests that Quadratilla is a woman who has power and status in her own right (even if what these insincere and predatory types are really seeking is financial reward). She is also level-headed, in that the legacies she leaves for these flatterers are described by Pliny as *exiguissima* ("utterly tiny"). This returns us by ring composition to the topic of the will, raised at the start of the letter, and allows Pliny in concluding to associate the grandmother with conspicuously good qualities, as he takes delight in the *pietate defunctae* ("family affection of the dead woman," presumably a comment on her arrangements for Quadratus in her will) and the *honore optimi iuuenis* ("honor done towards an excellent young man"). The true purpose of the letter is now becoming clear, as Quadratilla fades from the scene completely to be trumped by a different role model, and one more appropriate for the young Quadratus, namely the lawyer C. Cassius Longinus, a man who "towered above the rest in his knowledge of the law" (Tacitus, *Annals* 12.12.1), was a byword for strictness (Tacitus, *Annals* 13.48, 14.43–5), and was exiled under Nero (Tacitus, *Annals* 16.7–9).

Although this letter certainly contains some elements suggesting Pliny's disapproval of Quadratilla's lifestyle, the impression given is that these negative traits are ultimately outweighed by her virtues. We are thereby left with a memorable portrait of a powerful and independent woman who brought up her grandchildren in a devoted way, almost certainly after their own parents had died (Syme 1979: 288, 292 suggests that Quadratus was born early in Domitian's principate in 83 or 84, and that his parents could have been dead for many years by the time of the letter). Moreover, after successfully compartmentalizing her colorful life so as not to distract her serious-minded grandson from his studies, Quadratilla tenaciously secures for him a highly respected tutor and thereby equips the young man with the training and patronage required to embark upon a successful legal career. She achieves this goal, at least as far as Pliny's letter implies, without the help and advice of any male relative (perhaps her own husband was dead). We know from subsequent developments that her efforts bore fruit, in that Quadratus reached the consulship in 118 and was a prominent figure during Hadrian's principate, while her great-grandson went on to marry the sister of Marcus Aurelius. Quadratilla can thus be seen to have fulfilled her family obligations as an aristocratic woman and secured a rosy future for her grandson, even if she is represented as doing so while enjoying a rather bohemian personal lifestyle.

While Quadratilla is a real historical woman with her own complex life story (unlike the examples from Juvenal we discussed earlier), that reality is mediated through and subordinated to a system of male values shared by Pliny and his immediate addressee, Geminus (as well as the wider circle of readers being targeted by Pliny). In this instance, as is often the case, our capacity to respond to the portrait we are offered is hampered by a lack of comparative literary evidence, since Quadratilla does not feature elsewhere in surviving Classical literature, despite the subsequent prominence of her grandson. Yet we do have some fascinating inscriptions where she appears, including one celebrating her building projects in her home town of Casinum: "Ummidia Quadratilla, daughter of Gaius, built this amphitheater and temple with her own money for the citizens of Casinum" (*CIL* 10.5813 = *ILS* 5628). In so doing, she appears to be operating in a family tradition, as we know from another lacunose inscription: "Ummidia Quadratilla, daughter of Gaius, restored with her own money her father's theater, worn out from old age, and gave a feast in dedication to the *decuriones*, the people, and the, women" (*AE* 1946: 174, with Fora 1992; see also Hemelrijk, this volume, Chapter 35).

This program of building and civic activity (which explicitly includes women) all begins to sound much more significant than just the idle pastime of an eccentric old lady. On this reading, Quadratilla's cultivation of her pantomime troupe is only one component in a much wider program of cultural patronage, and an activity that Sick (1999) contextualizes as contributing to an efficiently run, profitable business enterprise (hence, the legacies left to the grandson and granddaughter may have been considerable). Indeed, Sick plausibly speculates (1999: 345) that Quadratilla's ownership of such a skillful set of pantomime actors would have meant regular approaches from upper-class friends, anxious to secure their services at various public and private events, and therefore would have given her considerable power and leverage. There may in fact be considerably more to Quadratilla than first meets the eye in Pliny's letter. Although in methodological terms this sort of illuminating comparative evidence from the archaeological sphere is not always available to those seeking to view literary portraits from a different angle, Quadratilla is a good example of how enriching engagement with epigraphic material can be when accidents of survival are on our side.

2 Embarrassing the Men: Tacitus' Epicharis

Finally, we turn to a different sort of woman, this time a freedwoman called Epicharis, who features as a bit player in Tacitus' account of the failed conspiracy that unfolded in 65 CE, when an attempt was made to replace the ruling emperor Nero with a more palatable alternative, Piso. The inter-related literary tropes in play within conspiracy narratives have understandably attracted scholarly attention recently (Pagán 2004), and such events naturally appear to have held a special interest for imperial Roman writers, operating in a society where real power seemed to be located behind closed doors within the imperial *domus*, rather than out in the open, in the senate or the lawcourts (cf. Cassius Dio 53.19 on the difficulties of writing imperial as opposed to republican history in these circumstances).

Indeed, once power was concentrated in the hands of one man, the whole political system became much more volatile and vulnerable to the impact of assassinations: after the murder of Julius Caesar in 44 BCE, potential plotters had before them the necessary proof that the elimination of such men was really possible. The subsequent history of the principate is littered both with traces of unsuccessful plots and with examples of emperors whose conduct resulted in assassination (Caligula, Domitian). The murky, liminal world of such emerging plots (where by definition it was almost impossible to reconstruct what really happened) allowed writers to draw on their powers of imagination to shape a plausible narrative through the technique of *inuentio*. In that context, lower-class women (as well as other marginalized members of society) were the perfect figures to operate and move around in that shifting landscape. Unfortunately for Epicharis, however, her efforts to enlist other people in the plot backfired, and Nero had her arrested. Tacitus outlines what happened after the plot had started to fragment:

> Meanwhile Nero, recalling that on Volusius Proculus' information Epicharis was being detained, and deeming her womanly body [*muliebre corpus*] unequal to pain, ordered her to be mauled by torture. But in her case, neither beatings nor fires nor the torturers' anger (all the fiercer, lest they be spurned by a female [*ne a femina spernerentur*]), prevailed over her denials of the imputations. Thus was the first day of the inquisition passed. On the next, when she was being dragged back to the same rackings by the conveyance of a chair (she was unable to stand on her dislocated limbs), she attached to the canopy of the chair, in the manner of a noose [*in modum laquei*], the banded fastening which she had torn from her bosom, and, inserting her neck and straining with the weight of her body, she expelled her now faint breath—a woman and a freedwoman [*libertina mulier*] defending by her more brilliant example in such an extremity, others whom she scarcely knew, when the freeborn—men and Roman equestrians and senators [*ingenui et uiri et equites Romani senatoresque*], all untouched by torture—were each betraying the dearest of those to whom they were bound.
> (Tacitus, *Annals* 15.57; transl. Woodman 2004)

Here Tacitus uses Epicharis in a vivid death scene to open up a sequence of powerful polarities, all of which work together to underscore the moral bankruptcy of her craven male counterparts. Although she is a freedwoman, who does not have any personal friends among her fellow plotters, she nonetheless endures extraordinary levels of pain in order to protect these people, who are undeserving of her protection, as it happens, since they are denouncing friends and family left, right, and center: just in the previous chapter, for example, we hear that Lucan points the finger at his own mother, Acilia (Tacitus, *Annals* 15.56). This shocking contrast (articulated along gender and class lines) between Epicharis and her fellow plotters naturally casts shame on the historical protagonists within the text in the eyes of posterity. Yet it must also have generated feelings of intense discomfort in the external readership, particularly among those men who fell into the categories laid out at the end of the chapter ("the freeborn—men and Roman equestrians and senators"). It is striking too that Tacitus in his Latin here uses *polysyndeton* (the syntactical device whereby several conjunctions are used in close succession, when some might be omitted), precisely in order to decelerate his account just at the point where the damning moralism is most biting.

In general, Tacitus also goes to some trouble to play up Epicharis' gender at every opportunity (*muliebre corpus; ne a femina spernerentur; libertina mulier*). Even the inventive way in which she kills herself, by improvising a noose from her bra, accentuates her identity as a woman, in that the classic means of suicide for a woman was hanging herself (Loraux 1987); and this detail has the added bonus of aligning Epicharis at the end of her life with a variety of grand female figures from the tragic stage (transcending her lowly status as a freedwoman). When Tacitus first introduced Epicharis to his narrative as a plotter, he made a point of saying that she had not previously shown any concern for honorable deeds (*Annals* 15.51): from such unpromising beginnings, Epicharis has risen hugely in stature and been transformed into a compelling force for moral denunciation. Tacitus depicts her in fairly general terms during her death scene (during which she does not speak, for example, although her death constitutes a powerful piece of non-verbal rhetoric). In so doing, he allows her to evoke other exemplary female heroines, such as Lucretia, whose tragic suicide after being raped led to the overthrow of Tarquin the Proud, the last king of Rome, and then to the establishment of the Republic. So, the Tiberian writer Valerius Maximus calls Lucretia "the leader of Roman chastity, whose manly spirit [*uirilis animus*] by Fortune's malignant spirit was allotted a woman's body [*muliebre corpus*]" (*Memorable Words and Deeds* 6.1.1). This notion of male bravery in a woman's body is very much the essence of Tacitus' Epicharis, but in her case the combination is meant to seem all the more striking because of the fact that class is thrown into the mix as well: unlike Lucretia, Epicharis is a former slave, whose "voice of freedom" (Pagán 2000) is more powerful and memorable than many of those of her male counterparts in the narrative.

3 Conclusion

The images of women in imperial Roman literature are remarkably diverse, so much so that it is difficult and dangerous to generalize about them. For example, one of the pervasive focal points of Augustus' principate is his marriage legislation and active program of moral reform (developments that naturally had a serious impact on the lives of women, particularly those living in the imperial household). Yet beneath this austere public exterior lurk intriguing instances of a spirited lack of compliance in private. So, Macrobius (writing in the fifth century CE) offers us a fascinating reconstruction of an intimate conversation that is described as having taken place between Augustus' daughter Julia and a close friend (unnamed), who expresses surprise that Julia's children look like their father, Agrippa, given Julia's tendency to have affairs (*Saturnalia* 2.5.9). Julia's witty (yet practical) reply is that she "never takes on board a passenger unless the ship is full" (*numquam enim nisi naui plena tollo uectorem*). Of course, what she means is that she only takes a lover when she is already pregnant. Whether or not this scene in the boudoir reflects any kind of historical reality is perhaps less important than the impression it gives of Julia. She emerges as a smooth operator, who has a careful set of rules in place in order not to fall afoul of her father's marriage legislation, but she is not obviously being condemned (at least by Macrobius) for having such affairs. To some extent her ingenuity is being put on display as something impressive, even if in the end her precautions came to nothing when she was banished in 2 BCE by Augustus.

The transition of the Roman state from republic to empire was of course a crucial period of political and historical development, but it heralded many important cultural and social changes as well. We are lucky that the huge geographical scope of the imperial structure and (consequent upon that) the survival of an increasing amount of evidence in different forms (whether inscriptions, monuments, or texts) allow us to engage in revealing comparative analyses. The images of women that emerge from this process are often rich and nuanced. More specifically, the relative stability of the early Imperial period (despite the civil wars of 68–69 CE) provided the circumstances and incentives for writers to produce creative literature across many genres. Roman writers of the early empire developed a highly competitive ethos, apparently keen to surpass not only the distant and daunting literary monuments of Greek culture but also their own more tangible and immediate Roman predecessors in a given genre. In their bid to secure a kind of immortality through their writings (e.g., Ovid, *Metamorphoses* 15.871–9) they have left us a remarkably vibrant body of literature. I hope to have conveyed some sense of this in the detailed readings of individual women from the early empire offered here.

RECOMMENDED FURTHER READING

Milnor (2005) is perhaps the best general survey of women under the empire. There is potentially a vast amount to read on representations of women in Juvenal's *Satires*, but Richlin (1987) is a good starting-point, and Braund (1992) and Gold (1998) are also very useful. Keane (2002) discusses the opening of *Satire* 6 as a programmatic piece of writing. On the nature, problems, and opportunities of using literary and non-literary sources, see Konstan (1991) and Hallett (1992).

A good, up-to-date, and methodologically aware book-length study in English of the women depicted by Pliny the Younger is still needed, but there are a number of helpful articles about individual women (e.g., Shelton 1990 on Pliny's wife; De Pretis 2003 on Calpurnia), and Marchesi (2007) is an excellent introduction to the advantages of applying to Pliny's letters a critically sophisticated mode of reading more usually associated with analysis of poetry. Saller (1984) and Dixon (1992) analyze Roman conceptions of the family (of which Quadratilla's household is an unconventional example), while Boatwright (1991a) offers a good study of imperial women during the principates of Trajan and Hadrian. For women as patrons of the arts during the early Imperial period, see Kleiner (1996).

Good starting points for thinking about women in Tacitus are Baldwin (1972) and Santoro L'hoir (1994), but there are also extensive detailed studies of prominent individuals, such as Barrett (1996) and Ginsburg (2006) on Agrippina the Younger and Purcell (1986) and Barrett (2002) on Livia. In the edited collection by Joshel and Murnaghan (1998), there is a useful article by Parker on stories about loyalty and betrayal by slaves and wives. Epicharis is of course a freedwoman, but the piece is still relevant. The death scene of Epicharis can also be considered in a broader context: Pomeroy (1991) discusses death notices in the ancient historians, while Ash (2003) discusses Pliny the Younger's reason for giving obituaries such an important role in his letters.

PART V

From Empire to Christianity

The essays in this final section look widely around the ancient world, from Britain to Byzantium. Female portraiture is again a focal concern, in Maura K. Heyn's case study of "Female Portraiture in Palmyra" (Case Study VI) and Rachel Meyers' "Female Portraiture and Female Patronage in the High Imperial Period" (Chapter 33). Emily A. Hemelrijk takes the subject of female patronage into the Western Roman provinces in "Public Roles for Women in the Cities of the Latin West" (Chapter 35). Epigraphical evidence is important throughout, particularly in Werner Riess' essay, "*Rari exempli femina*: Female Virtues on Roman Funerary Inscriptions" (Chapter 36), which (like others in this volume) extends past the specific period of this section. The range of visual and literary materials is likewise broad, from painted portraits to carved ivory, from shoes in garbage dumps to grave goods, and from satire to historiography, as seen in Rhiannon Ash's "Women in Imperial Roman Literature" (Chapter 32).

A recurrent theme in this section, as throughout the volume, is the difficulty of reconciling the literary evidence with the visual, and the problem of recovering women's "lived realities" through material evidence that tends toward the stereotypical and the formulaic. As in previous sections, personal adornment and female beauty continue to be overriding concerns in images of women, and the family and familial connections continue to define (and to circumscribe) female power and influence. A major turning point here, of course, is the shift to Christianity. It is just as difficult to assess the actual difference made to the lives of real women in this period by this massive change as it is to gauge the effects of increased mobility in the greatly expanded Hellenistic world.

The women studied here also vary widely: British women resisting Roman imperial forces, priestesses of the imperial cult, empresses, private citizens, prominent provincial women. The record of public female patronage in this period matches the scale of the Hellenistic period. In "Women in Roman Britain" (Chapter 34), Lindsey Allason-Jones provides a cautionary study of the problems for studying women in Roman and pre-Roman Britain. Late antique Egypt is represented in "Women in Late Antique Egypt" (Chapter 37) by Jennifer Sheridan Moss, who looks at the full social spectrum of women in this period, as well as in the essay of Ioli Kalavrezou, who studies the visual evidence for women in this period, extending up to the Byzantine era, in "Representations of Women in Late Antiquity and Early Byzantium" (Chapter 38). The essay on women in late antiquity (outside of Egypt) that was scheduled for this section could not be completed in time, but we offer a bibliography in the Appendix. Finally, Ross S. Kraemer's chapter, "Becoming Christian" (Chapter 39) studies the processes—and the problems of understanding those processes—by which women became Christian. This essay closes the *Companion* by opening up a vista toward the medieval period.

Case Study VI

Female Portraiture in Palmyra

Maura K. Heyn

The Syrian city of Palmyra offers a rich corpus of funerary sculpture dating to the first three centuries CE, when the city was under Roman control. The most common type of sculpture is the portrait bust, carved in high relief on a rectangular limestone plaque and used to seal the burial niche inside the tomb. The deceased is depicted frontally from the waist up, and the name and genealogy (in the local Aramaic dialect) are often included above one shoulder. Palmyrene funerary portraiture has clear affinities to the style that was popular in Rome at the end of the Republic, with interesting local features. The two women featured in this case study (Figure CS VI.1 and Figure CS VI.2) are typical of the female portraits from Palmyra. In contrast to the men, who adopt western styles of dress, the woman wear local dress styles, as indicated, for example, by the turbans underneath their veils (see Balty 1996).

These images of Palmyrene women are famous for their ornate jewelry. A portrait relief of No'om in the Ackland Museum in Chapel Hill provides a good illustration of this elaborate adornment (Figure CS VI.1). Her tunic has embroidered bands running down the front and on both sleeves. In addition, she wears a diadem across her forehead, earrings, a bracelet on each wrist, a ring on her pinkie finger, and multiple necklaces. A leonine fibula attaches the cloak to her tunic. The significance of the L-shaped key that hangs from the fibula is not certain. It may allude to her control of the domestic sphere, or it may have allowed her entrance into the afterlife (Colledge 1976: 70; Drijvers 1982: 720; Parlasca 1988: 216–17; Ploug 1995: 91). The weaving tools of spindle and distaff held in her left hand underscore the connection to domestic responsibilities.

Children often accompany the bust-length figure in Palmyrene funerary portraiture, depicted as full-length, small-scale adults. Although usually depicted behind the shoulder of the adult, children also occasionally appear in the arms of the deceased. For example, the unidentified woman in a relief now in the Fitzwilliam Museum in Cambridge (Figure CS VI.2) cradles a child in her left hand while pulling back her garment to reveal the breast, perhaps to suggest breastfeeding. The child rests its right hand on the bared breast. Although the woman in the Cambridge relief is not as heavily encrusted in jewelry as is the figure of No'om, this lack of adornment is probably not connected to her activity. Rather, the comparative paucity of jewelry may have more to do with the date of the relief,

A Companion to Women in the Ancient World, First Edition. Edited by Sharon L. James and Sheila Dillon.
© 2012 John Wiley & Sons, Ltd. Published 2015 by John Wiley & Sons, Ltd.

Figure CS VI.1 Unknown, Syrian, Roman: Funeral relief of No'om (?) wife of Haira, son of Maliku, c. 150 CE, sandstone, 19 ¾ × 15 ⅝ × 7 ⅝ inches (50.2 × 39.7 × 18.7 centimeters). Ackland Art Museum, University of North Carolina at Chapel Hill. The William A. Whitaker Foundation Art Fund. 79.29.1.

as another Palmyrene portrait that depicts a similar scene shows the woman very elaborately adorned (National Museum of Damascus, inv. no. 6906/5840).

Harald Ingholt (1928) long ago divided the known Palmyrene funerary portraits into three distinct chronological groups by taking the small number of dated examples and gathering around these reliefs that were stylistically similar. While Colledge (1976: 253–64) later refined Ingholt's groupings, the basic rationale has been maintained in most analyses of Palmyrene portraiture. Ingholt's typology revealed some interesting trends. The women in his earliest group (50–150 CE) wore little jewelry and often held a spindle and a distaff in the left hand. In his second group (150–200 CE), women wore more jewelry, including necklaces, bracelets, and rings, rarely held the spindle and distaff, and frequently raised the right hand to hold the veil back from the face. In the latest group (200–273 CE), a few women displayed even more jewelry, and many used their left hand to hold the veil. According to this typology, the relief of No'om would date to c. 150 CE, because her attributes and jewelry put her on the cusp between the first and second groups. The relatively unadorned breastfeeding woman would also belong to the second group.

The correlation between the quantity of jewelry and the date of production is not foolproof. Sadurska (1994: 188) has recently argued that the amount of jewelry is more indicative of the wealth of the subject depicted. This argument then raises the following questions: how realistic is Palmyrene portraiture, and what can these images tell us about

Figure CS VI.2 Palmyrene portrait bust. Fitzwilliam Museum, Cambridge, inv. GR.9.1888. Photo: courtesy Fitzwilliam Museum.

the role of women in ancient Palmyrene society? The spindle and distaff, for example, are interpreted as symbols of domestic virtue and thus appropriate attributes for the ideal wife and mother (Colledge 1976: 70; Ploug 1995: 41; Balty 1996: 438). However, these attributes become much less popular in the reliefs made after 150 CE. Does this mean that women had stopped spinning and weaving, or that the spindle and distaff were no longer considered ideal female attributes? Sadurska (1996: 286) argues that the iconographic shift from spindle and distaff to jewelry reflects the increasing emancipation of women in Palmyrene society, but this is difficult to verify because of the lack of corroborating evidence from the city. The connection between jewelry and wealth is also tricky because the women depicted in these reliefs were probably always among the more affluent members of Palmyrene society (Cussini 2004: 236 n. 7).

Epigraphic evidence from Palmyra adds to our understanding of the role of the women who belonged to these powerful and wealthy families. While Palmyrene society was male-dominated, women did on occasion both receive and make honorific dedications, including statues; they could buy and sell portions of tombs; and they participated in ritual activities in the city's various sanctuaries (Sadurska 1996: 286; Yon 2002: 165–86; Cussini 2005a). Despite this evidence for activities beyond the domestic sphere, the status of a Palmyrene woman was clearly tied to that of her family (Yon 2002: 166–74). The strength of this family was emphasized in the funerary sphere by the representation of women who engaged in appropriate activities, such as spinning, weaving, and taking care of children, and who displayed the wealth of their family through their elaborate jewelry.

33

Female Portraiture and Female Patronage in the High Imperial Period

Rachel Meyers

Although portraiture and patronage may seem like two distinct topics, they are in fact closely connected, especially in the second century CE. That is, with the increase in female-sponsored public munificence came more opportunities for portraits of both imperial and non-imperial women to be displayed in public contexts. Women who donated funds for building projects, public feasts, and games were often rewarded by their cities with a portrait statue set up in a prominent public location. How they were represented is one topic of this essay, but first I will examine some of the techniques and styles of these portraits, and then I will show how portrait statues are connected to civic benefaction.

1   Female Portraiture

Since portraiture has been treated in earlier chapters (see, for example, Dillon, this volume, Chapter 17; Bartman, this volume, Chapter 30; and Riggs, this volume, Chapter 31), it is unnecessary here to repeat the history of the study of Roman portraiture or the methods of production and distribution. Instead I shall turn my attention to the portraits produced in the second and third centuries CE and focus on the styles of portrait heads and statue types popular during this period, and deal with some of the issues that concern female portraiture in the early empire. The sculptural remains from the second century are unusually rich in terms of both quantity and quality. They attest to some conformity to contemporary styles and trends, but they also show us that a great deal of subtle variation was possible, in terms of facial expression, the treatment of the hair, and the arrangement of the drapery.

Recognizability

Since a portrait aims to represent an individual, recognizability is one desirable quality of portraiture. Recognizability should not be confused with representational accuracy,

A Companion to Women in the Ancient World, First Edition. Edited by Sharon L. James and Sheila Dillon.
© 2012 John Wiley & Sons, Ltd. Published 2015 by John Wiley & Sons, Ltd.

however, as portraits did not necessarily reproduce how a person actually looked (Stewart 2008: 89–90; Dillon 2010). For example, one should remember that youthful portraits of Livia continued to be produced throughout her life and after her death, at the age of eighty-six (Bartman 1999; Bartman, this volume, Chapter 30). While some images of Livia incorporated subtle indications of her age, she was never depicted as old. It is also sometimes very difficult to distinguish between the portraits of imperial women and women who followed imperial styles, a difficulty that is found much less frequently in dealing with Imperial period male portraiture. Indeed, when classifying female portraits as either imperial or non-imperial, most scholars have proceeded quite cautiously, acknowledging the difficulties involved, especially when dealing with portraits made outside Rome or with examples that are of lower quality or are less detailed (Fittschen and Zanker 1983; Smith 1985). In her study of Roman portraits, Jane Fejfer examines the imperial and private portraits of women together because she sees an "intentional difficulty in distinguishing visually between the empress and private women" (2008: 331). She argues that the similarity between the images of imperial and private women during the first three centuries CE was a means of expressing visually the close relationship with the empress that private elite women sought to claim in their portraits.

Personal identity can indeed be difficult to discern because the portraits of many women, imperial as well as private, are rendered with an idealized beauty (see also Dillon, this volume, Chapter 17). The portraits of Sabina, for example, depict the empress with softened features and youthful beauty. The same kind of delicate features can also be seen in a portrait statue of an unknown woman from the Antonine period, now in the Dallas Museum of Art (Figure 33.1). Idealized beauty was seen as a virtue (Matheson 1996), although it was not the only mode of female portrait representation. Artists certainly could and did produce portraits with more individualized traits. Sabina's grandmother Marciana is depicted with a strong brow, heavily lidded eyes, and a small, thin mouth. Her matronly and austere facial features contrast with her elaborate hairstyle of tightly wound curls across the forehead (Figure 33.2). Similarly, a portrait of an older woman, who wears a hairstyle similar to that of Matidia, portrays the age of the subject through slightly hollowed cheeks, a strong brow, and tightly drawn lips, all of which combine to present a more non-idealized face (Figure 33.3).

These few examples, which juxtapose the portraits of imperial with non-imperial women, demonstrate the challenge involved in separating imperial from private and in more precisely identifying female portraits. These portraits also demonstrate that various modes of representation—from idealized beauty to more realistic—were available concurrently to women. One can observe a trend in the recognizability of portraits from the early to the later Imperial period. While portraits of imperial and private women of the first and second centuries are more difficult to distinguish, by the mid third century, empresses are shown with more individualized physiognomic traits that make it easier to separate the portraits (Fejfer 2008: 356). The change to greater individuality may reflect a desire to broaden the gap visually between the representations of empresses and those of other women.

Hairstyle

In addition to physiognomic characteristics, the hairstyles worn by women in their portraits are very helpful in creating typologies and in assigning identities. Hairstyles became

Figure 33.1 Statue of a Woman. Roman, second century CE. Marble. H 69 1/4 inches (175.9 cm). Dallas Museum of Art, gift of Mr. and Mrs. Cecil H. Green. Photo: Courtesy, Dallas Museum of Art.

increasingly more elaborate during the first century, culminating in the towering coiffures that are characteristic of female portraits in the Flavian period and under Hadrian. The well-known portrait of a young woman in the Capitoline Museum in Rome wearing an elaborate and beautifully rendered Flavian coiffure is an exquisite example of this fashion hairstyle, which features rows of tight ringlets stacked high above the forehead, with the rest of her hair gathered in tightly constructed braids and wrapped into a large and intricate bun at the back of the head. While this portrait is now thought by many to date to around 120 CE, the hairstyle it sports was popular several decades earlier. The elaborate layering of the curls that make up this distinctive hairstyle was made possible through the virtuoso use of the drill, which had previously been used mostly for speedily cutting away large amounts of stone. In the Hadrianic period, sculptors also begin to use the drill to delicately demarcate the pupils and irises, which greatly enlivened the appearance of second century marble portraiture.

Female hairstyles of the early second century become more elaborate, more varied, and more tightly constructed. Rather than the elaborate pile of soft curls exemplified in the

Figure 33.2   Marciana, Boston, Museum of Fine Arts 1916.286. Photo: Museum of Fine Arts, Boston.

Figure 33.3   Portrait of woman with hairstyle similar to Matidia. Madrid, Museo del Prado inv. 356-E. Photo: DAI Madrid, neg. no. D-DAI-MAD-WIT-R-081-87-06, P. Witte.

Figure 33.4   Idealized portrait of Matidia. Luni marble. Rome, Palazzo dei Conservatori, Musei Capitolini. Photo: Vanni/Art Resource, NY.

Capitoline portrait, female portraits sport stiff bands of hair fanned out above the forehead and across the front of the head. Portraits identified as Matidia, Trajan's niece, for example, wear the hair sectioned into several braids that are then wrapped into a large, slanting nest at the back of the head. At the front, the hair is worn in a tightly crimped fringe across the forehead, above which are a series of stacked of cylindrical curls (Figure 33.4). Another hairstyle of the Trajanic and early Hadrianic periods worn by the portraits of non-imperial women features an elaborate turban-like coiffure, composed of rows of stiff, projecting braids that frame the face and a series of braids wrapped around the head, which are then secured into a low bun at the back (Figure 33.5).

Although Faustina the Elder was alive only during the first three years of her husband's reign, numerous portraits of her were produced posthumously. In her third portrait type, known in twenty-six reproductions, her hair is parted in the center and the wavy tresses are set into braids, usually four on each side. The braids are gathered and wrapped up and around the top of the head, forming a bun, with the ends of the braids disappearing under the mass of coiled hair (Meyers 2006). This intricate architecture of hair was worn by a number of women in the Antonine era.

In the wake of these elaborate and stiffly formed hairstyles there is a noticeable trend towards more simplicity and softness, beginning with Faustina the Younger, which continues into the basic style of the third century. The earliest hairstyles worn by Faustina depart significantly from those of the first half of the second century (Fittschen 1996: 44). In her earliest portraits, Faustina wears the youthful and elegantly simple "melon" coiffure, with a row of softly looping curls across the forehead and a small bun at the

Figure 33.5 Marble portrait of early Trajanic woman (perhaps Marciana). London, British Museum inv. no. 1879.0712.17. Photo: © Trustees of the British Museum.

nape of the neck. Her hairstyle tends to become less complex in her later portraits (Meyers 2006: figures 83, 89, and 99), which show the hair simply parted at the center and wound into a large bun at the nape of the neck; variations do occur among her many portrait types, and include the size of the bun worn at the back, and whether the center-parted hair is wavy or straight.

The hairstyles of the late second century and the early third follow these simpler hairstyles worn by Faustina the Younger in her later portraits. The coiffures become smoother and flatter, with softly undulating locks parted in the center, pulled back to the nape of the neck, and secured in a chignon. The hairstyle depicted in portraits of Julia Domna diverges from this course somewhat; the hair is thicker and the waves have a more modeled and exact appearance with a substantial bun at the back of the head. Overall, female hairstyles in the mid to late Severan period are flat, showing little evidence of the drill. Occasionally there are echoes of hairstyles from the previous century. After the mid third century, sculpted portraits of imperial women decline in number and portraits on coins are also less frequent. While portraits of private women continue to appear, their numbers decline fairly sharply after the mid third century as well, particularly in comparison with the number of female portraits produced in the second century.

While the hairstyles depicted in female portraits, particularly in the late first and early second century, appear so complex as to be unachievable, they probably reproduce styles that were actually worn in real life. Indeed, such complex coiffures were undoubtedly accomplished through the use of wigs and other hair attachments (D'Ambra 1996;

Bartman 2001). In that case "then the hairpiece itself is an artificial adornment, like jewelry or cosmetics, to be put on or taken off when the occasion demanded" (D'Ambra 2000: 110). The artificial, more ostentatious hair conceals the subject's genuine hair below and therefore acts like a veil, maintaining the woman's modesty. Republican matrons covered their heads with a headband or a net cap, and a veiled head remained an ideal for elite women into the Imperial period (Myerowitz Levine 1995: 104). Thus, a public portrait of a woman with an elaborate hairstyle may have actually preserved the modesty of the subject, just as if she were in public with her head veiled. In both situations the woman's real hair was mostly covered or obscured, visible in the portraits at least as wisps or strands delicately carved at the temples or the nape of the neck as if escaping from beneath the elaborate helmet of artificial hair.

Statue Types

The resemblance between imperial and non-imperial portraits can be detected not only in the portrait heads but also in the statue bodies. The portraits of the emperor generally fall into one of four categories: bust, togate statue, cuirassed statue, or heroic nudity (Price 1984: 181–5). Portraits of imperial women, however, are not so easily divided. There are many more variations in both the clothing and the poses of female portrait statue bodies. The Large and Small Herculaneum types seem to have been particularly popular in the first and second centuries, while in the Antonine period twenty-eight different portrait statue types have been identified (Lenaghan 1999; Trimble 2000), mirroring the great expansion in the range of female hairstyles in the second century. Many statue types were used both for the portraits of women in the imperial family and for the portraits of non-imperial women, and some of these were based upon images of goddesses. This crossover between imperial and non-imperial and mortal and divine is particularly well represented in a small number of monuments in the eastern part of the empire.

The monumental Nymphaeum of Herodes Atticus at Olympia, actually dedicated by his wife Regilla in 153 CE, features this intersection of imperial and non-imperial portrait statues. The Nymphaeum displayed an impressive statue gallery along a two-tiered semicircular columnar façade punctuated by eleven niches on each level (Bol 1984). The programmatic statuary display included members of the families of Herodes and Regilla, members of the Antonine imperial family, and two statues of Zeus. The Large Herculaneum statue type was used for the portraits of Sabina, Faustina the Elder, and Regilla. In the early second century at Perge in Asia Minor, Plancia Magna financed the construction of a horseshoe-shaped gateway, courtyard, and triple arch for her home-town, Perge (Boatwright 1991b). The elaborate gateway included two stories of niches filled with statues of gods, legendary city founders, and Plancia's father and brother (Boatwright 1991b: 250–1). The triple arch featured statues of the imperial family, including Augustus, Nerva, Trajan, Hadrian, Plotina, Marciana, Matidia, and Sabina. Two statues of Plancia, one of them in the Large Herculaneum type, were erected in niches in a display wall just south of her renovated gate and visually linked to it (Dillon 2010: 156–9).

Two other statues of the Large Herculaneum type were found in the area of the arch and thus most likely represent two of the imperial women (they are the same scale as the statue of Hadrian), possibly Sabina and Matidia or Marciana. In addition to sharing the same statue type, the representations of Plancia and the two imperial women used the same portrait style as well: an oval-shaped face, idealized features, and hair parted in the center and brushed back in waves, features that were typical of earlier Hellenic statues of women but not particularly associated with the portraits of these empresses (Dillon 2010: 159). The identity of these imperial portrait statues is, in fact, in doubt because they do not adhere to their established portrait types, but seem rather to follow local traditions. Perhaps this was done so that anyone entering the town through Plancia Magna's gate would visually connect her, the wealthy local benefactress, with the women of the imperial family, here represented in such a strikingly similar manner.

It has been suggested that, in contrast to the portrait statues of men, the costumes worn by portrait statues of women did not look like the kind of clothing women would have actually worn in everyday life (Fejfer 2008: 345). For example, the clothing on female statues is often depicted as if made of copious amounts of sheer fabric, while regular clothing would probably have been more practical, less voluminous, and much less revealing. The difference between how a woman looked in real life and how she appeared in her portrait statue was intentional, and meant to make the statue look decidedly artificial. Portrait statues of women, particularly those set up in public places, were constructed in such a way as to distinguish clearly "between the 'real' Roman woman and statuary representations of those few who held outstanding positions in the city" in order to lessen male unease about the presence of women in public. Although female portrait statues were prominently displayed in public spaces, the apparent artificiality of these images helped to maintain female absence (Fejfer 2008: 345).

Portraits and Family Values

Portrait statues of women tend to celebrate the subject's family connections: women are mostly honored for being someone's wife, mother, or daughter. This family cohesion is sometimes expressed visually in imperial female portraiture by assimilating traits of the emperor's physiognomy in the portraits of imperial women. For example, some of the best portraits of Faustina the Younger clearly yet subtly evoke certain physical features of the portraits of Marcus Aurelius, especially the prominent brow and the pronounced, almond-shaped eyes. Since women of the imperial family owed their standing to their relationship to the emperor, it follows that this relationship should be emphasized visually. Further, the assimilation of the emperor's features into the female portraits demonstrates the cohesiveness of the imperial family and the projected continuity of the dynasty (Smith 1985).

The images of Faustina the Younger demonstrate another form of family values. This phenomenon is most evident on coinage produced during the reigns of Antoninus Pius and Marcus Aurelius, which features her portrait on the obverse and a variety of depictions of goddesses and personifications on the reverse, representing ideas that the Antonine family wanted to promote: fertility, motherhood, and abundance (Fittschen 1982). For example, the personification of Fecunditas appears on a *sestertius*, holding a baby in each arm and with a small child on either side of her; these may represent the number of children Faustina and Marcus had at the time the coin was minted (*RIC* 1635). The ideas of motherhood, happiness, and fertility were so significant at this time because for nearly 100 years the Roman emperor had not had a son to appoint as his heir and successor. Marcus and Faustina produced fifteen children, one of whom—Commodus—did succeed his father as emperor. Thus, the Antonines were promoting the fertility of the empress and their success in following the wishes of Augustus, who had tried for many years to appoint a son, natural or adopted.

2 Female Patronage

Although much of the male-authored literature proscribes for women a quiet and obedient nature, a great deal of evidence shows that women actively and publicly contributed to the life of their city by holding office, donating money or resources, funding public entertainment, and funding the construction of buildings (see also Bielman, this volume, Chapter 17 and D'Ambra, this volume, Chapter 29). These women were part of an elite culture of public munificence undertaken by citizens throughout the Roman empire; Asia Minor is particularly well documented and well studied. What follows is a brief overview that tries to answer the following questions about female patronage: Who were these patrons? What did they donate? And why did they make these benefactions?

Definition, Sources, and Geography

In addressing these questions, we must start with a definition of patronage (see also Bielman, this volume, Chapter 17 and Hemelrijk, this volume, Chapter 35). The type of patronage under discussion here is that in which an individual provides, out of his or her own wealth, a benefaction to a town or a smaller group within a town. Boulanger (1923) and Marrou (1948) used the expression "euergetism," based upon the wording of Hellenistic honorific decrees (*euergetein tēn polin*), to refer to this phenomenon of private individuals giving for public benefit (Veyne 1990: 10). Paul Veyne, who wrote the seminal work on euergetism in Greek and Roman societies, points out that, while *euergesia* means "benefaction," there existed no term in Greek or Latin that encompassed the entire concept (1990: 10). *Liberalitas* describes any form of liberality, and *philotimia* emphasizes the motives behind public benefaction, but neither word addresses this remarkable process, in which wealthy citizens responded to their communities' expectations for feasts, spectacles, and the construction of public buildings.

Literary sources occasionally mention substantial benefactions, but inscriptions and architectural remains are the primary material evidence of public munificence. A feast or a staging of games may have been commemorated on a plaque set up in the forum or agora, while monumental benefactions are usually known through building inscriptions. Very few examples of female-sponsored patronage occurred in the Roman Republic (see Bielman, this volume, Chapter 17); many more date to the second and third centuries CE.

Certain forms of patronage are more prevalent in particular geographic areas, while other areas seem to be devoid of any evidence of female benefaction. A number of examples of female-sponsored euergetism are found in Asia Minor, which has made the area a focus of several publications (Zuiderhoek 2009; van Bremen 1996; MacMullen 1980). Zuiderhoek asserts that it is only natural that a large proportion of evidence of patronage comes from Asia Minor because euergetism, the form of patronage discussed here, was an entrenched aspect of Greek culture that had its roots there (2009: 12–13). Because the Latin West and the Republican period are covered elsewhere in this volume (by Hemelrijk and Bielman, respectively), what follows focuses on female benefactors in the Greek East in the high Imperial period.

Case Study—Julia Antonia Eurydice from Nysa

A closer examination of one female benefactor in particular will allow us the chance of answering the questions posed at the outset. In the middle of the second century CE, Julia

Antonia Eurydice left money in her will for the building of a new *gerontikon* in her hometown of Nysa in Asia Minor. While no evidence indicates that she made any public benefactions during her lifetime, she saw fit to bequeath the finances to build a meeting house for the *gerousia*, or council of elders.

This building is partially preserved; from the remains it is clear that Eurydice's building would have made a significant impact on those who used and visited it. The structure, which replaced an older building, was located in a prominent location on the eastern side of Nysa next to the agora. The previous building on the site was described by Strabo (*Geography* 14.1.43). The shape of the new building followed the form of Roman theaters of the Imperial period, just as many council houses in the eastern empire did (von Diest 1913: 36). The back wall of the stage, or *scaenae frons*, was revetted with marble slabs and punctuated by five doorways. There were four large podia set across the stage on either side of these entrances; each podium supported two columns to form *naiskoi* for portrait statues (Balty 1991: 449). Fragments of carbonized wood and iron girders provide evidence for a wooden roof.

In addition to these architectural remains, inscriptions and statues help to provide an idea of the original appearance of the columnar façade. Seven fragmentary statue bases inform us that portrait statues of Antoninus Pius, Marcus Aurelius, Lucius Verus, Faustina the Younger, and Domitia Faustina were displayed in the scaenae frons, along with a statue of Sextus Julius Maior Antoninus Pythodorus, who dedicated all the statues on behalf of his mother, and one of his sister Julia. There is no evidence for a statue of Eurydice herself, although she was probably represented. A nearly complete toga-clad statue that probably portrayed Marcus Aurelius, a fragmentary cuirassed torso possibly belonging to the statue of Antoninus Pius, and the feet of a female statue have been recovered. A possible reconstruction places the portrait statues of Domitia Faustina, Lucius Verus, Marcus Aurelius, and Faustina the Younger in the four niches in the lower storey across the stage. The statue of Antoninus Pius, as reigning emperor the most important figure, could have been placed in a niche above the central doorway, and statues of Pythodorus and his sister stood on top of the pilasters on either side of the orchestra. The display was a snapshot of the imperial family at the time of the building's dedication circa 148–150 CE.

No dedicatory inscription for the building itself remains and we are left with no other evidence as to why a woman would have chosen to use her own money to finance a building that was mostly used by the town's male elders. It is possible that her husband or a male relative was a member of the *gerousia* or that she was trying to secure her son's admission to the council of elders in the future. By Eurydice's time, *gerousiai* were more like social clubs that allowed female members as well. Although only a few female members are known in the Greek East, it is possible that Eurydice was a member of the organization at Nysa. Her motive(s) may not have been simple or straightforward, but what she accomplished was certainly important. By reconstructing the *gerontikon* in lavish form and including an impressive array of imperial statues, Eurydice reinforced and publicized her family's connection with the city and the people of Nysa as well as with the imperial family. Her monument and her motives were therefore similar to those of Plancia Magna of Perge.

Eurydice descended from the royal house of Pontus and a distinguished family of Nysa (*PIR*^{2} I 644). Her ancestor Pythodorus married Antonia, a daughter of the triumvir Marcus Antonius, and their daughter Pythodoris was queen of Pontus in the early Imperial period (Sullivan 1980: 920–1). Strabo records that Pythodoris and her husband, King Polemo, produced two sons and a daughter, Antonia Tryphaena, who went on to a noteworthy career herself (*Geography* 12.3.29.556). Eurydice came from this line, and was the great-granddaughter of Tryphaena. Although nothing is known about her own parents, we know some of the details of the careers of her husband and her son Pythodorus. She was married to Sextus Julius Maior, who served as *legatus Augusti propraetore* in Lower Moesia and Syria, consul suffect, and probably as proconsul of the province of Asia in the 120s and 130s CE (*PIR²* I 397). Her lineage was therefore impeccable: Eurydice came from an extraordinarily well-connected family.

Eurydice left a structure that was used and admired for at least several generations of Nysaeans. Her act of public generosity may have prompted her son Pythodorus to sponsor benefactions at Epidaurus and Pergamum (*IG* IV² 1, 88, 514; *IvP* III no. 23; Paus. 2.27.6). Julia Antonia Eurydice, a wealthy woman from an elite family, perpetuated the legacy of her family by bequeathing the resources necessary to construct a new, splendidly appointed *gerontikon* in her hometown. Her benefaction not only provided a necessary structure for the town but also promoted her family and their connections to the imperial family. Eurydice was part of a small group of women, like Plancia Magna, who legally and financially were able to bestow monumental gifts upon their towns and fellow citizens.

Motivations for Benefaction

Benefactors were often commemorated for their acts of public generosity with an inscription. These honorary inscriptions, however, omit any explanation of why the benefaction was made. Why did these women choose to spend their wealth for the public good? What was the motivation behind these benefactions? Legal changes in the early Imperial period allowed for the accumulation of greater wealth by women (Gardner 1986: 166; van Bremen 1996: 265). They could, however, have chosen to hold on to their money and to pass it on to their children, as many women no doubt did. In order to address the question of what motivated women to carry out public acts of generosity, it is necessary to try to understand what these generous acts provided for the donor herself.

The type of benefaction made affected the return the donor experienced, and the impact of *memoria* should not be underestimated. For the Romans, *memoria* did not mean simply "memory," but rather the act of remembering or a remembrance. A small benefaction, such as financing a public feast or providing oil for the gymnasium, was remembered for a short period of time. Perhaps the donor had the honor of walking at the head of a parade and/or had her name inscribed on a plaque. Financing a public building, on the other hand, allowed the donor's name to be remembered for generations to come. A building was a lasting structure, occupying a visible part of the town. Visitors saw the donor's name inscribed in large letters on the building's façade, and might have been thankful that such a beautiful structure graced their city. Benefactions on a large scale helped both to shape and to reveal the donor's personality to her fellow townspeople (see also D'Ambra, this volume, Chapter 29). As Woolf observes, "the primary function of monuments in the early empire was as devices with which to assert the place of individuals within society" (1996: 29). Acts of civic munificence established and then preserved the benefactor's relationship with other members of her town, both elite and non-elite. Thus, donating on a large scale in particular secured the donor's short-term notoriety as well as lasting remembrance after her death.

Some donors may have been prompted to give because of their innate sense of generosity or because of the satisfaction they derived from making an impact on their town and its people (Veyne 1990: 230, 237, 319). Pliny writes in a letter to a friend that his abhorrence of money turned itself into a fondness for generosity (*Letters* 1.8). In his hometown of Como, Pliny donated a library and a school and established a foundation for poor children. A new building or a generous donation to establish an alimentary fund would have made an impression on citizens and non-citizens alike, and these acts of euergetism may have inspired others to do likewise.

Not only did civic munificence help to assert a donor's position within the society of her town, but it could also demonstrate her relationship with the imperial family, as in the dedications of Plancia Magna and Julia Antonia Eurydice mentioned above. With her generous donation, Plancia Magna provided a grand entryway into her city that was a beacon to travelers and a source of pride for residents. Additionally, through the choice of statuary Plancia firmly established her own status in Perge among its mythical and historical leaders, and asserted her (actual or aspirational) link to the imperial house. The *bouleuterion* at Ephesus provides yet another example of the display of imperial and private portrait statues situated in a lavish architectural setting. In the mid second century CE, Vedius Antoninus and his wife Flavia Papiane financed the construction of the council house, a theater-like building in the heart of the administrative district of Ephesus. The *scaenae frons* of the council house, a two-tiered columnar façade formed by red granite columns, was decorated with statues of Antoninus Pius, Faustina the Elder, Marcus Aurelius, Faustina the Younger, Lucius Verus, Domitia Faustina, as well as statues of the donors themselves (Kalinowski and Taeuber 2001; Kalinowski 2002). These three examples illustrate a trend in the second century of wealthy donors who not only constructed monumental buildings for the public good but also juxtaposed within the columnar façades of these buildings portrait statues of themselves and other family members, and sometimes local heroes, with statues of the imperial family. This sort of composition asserted and reinforced the family's place in the history of its hometown, its status among contemporaries, and its relationship to or support of the imperial house.

Making a permanent donation, such as financing the construction of a building, reflected and helped to create the donor's persona in the eyes of the public (Valone 2001: 317). The type of building, its location, and its design tell something about the person who constructed it. For example, dedicating a temple may show to others that the donor is a pious person who respects traditions, whereas constructing baths or a theater may imply a donor interested in leisure activities. Setting up a structure in a city was a very important activity because "buildings mold both the physical and cultural environment of a given place" (Valone 2001: 317). A building communicated the patron's ideas and beliefs to the town's visitors and residents. The great expense required to complete a building project prohibited most people from ever contemplating this form of benefaction (Woolf 1996: 30). Thus, those donors who did carry out construction projects were rewarded with the prestige associated with having their name on a prominent feature of their city.

Thus, the question originally posed in this section—why did women make benefactions?—should be turned on its head. Why should women *not* have desired the same kind of glory that men received for participating in civic life by holding office and engaging in euergetism? Although women could have spent their wealth quietly by using a male relative as proxy, a small number of elite women chose to step out of the private sphere and into the public realm of the city. Perhaps it was, as van Bremen observes, a breakdown in the division between what was traditionally "private" and "public" that allowed women the opportunity to step into urban affairs in many of the same ways that men did (van Bremen 1983: 236–7).

In fact, the individual acts of euergetism described in this essay contradict the type of behavior elaborated and praised in many ancient literary accounts. Van Bremen notes that the written sources from the Hellenistic and Roman periods show a "remarkable preoccupation" with the topics of women and marriage (1983: 234). Writers and philosophers such as Antipater of Tarsus, Musonius Rufus, Plutarch, and various neo-Pythagoreans wrote extensively on the proper demeanor a woman should exhibit, and the kinds of activities that were and were not acceptable (van Bremen 1983: 234). In his *Advice to The Bride and Groom*, Plutarch recommends that a wife should be subordinate to her husband and remain mostly at home, though he does hint at the notion that marriage is a partnership (33–142E and 30–3 = 142 C–D; cf. Treggiari 1991: 225). While the same sentiments about women pervade much of the literature from the Hellenistic and Roman periods, other evidence—often in the form of an inscription and the remains of large and elaborate buildings—demonstrates that women engaged in office-holding, liturgies, and sumptuous benefaction.

Events and circumstances in the Augustan era may have helped to bring about changes in Roman culture that allowed women more opportunities for stepping out of the private sphere and into the public sphere. In becoming acquainted with the public realm, women may have seen benefaction as an outlet worth their time, effort, and resources. Some scholars point to a dismantling of the boundary between private and public necessitated by the euergetistic system (van Bremen 1983; Veyne 1990). Numerous inscriptions record that prominent citizens were given the honorary titles of "father," "mother," "son," and "daughter of the city." Such titles demonstrate the overlap between the family and the state. Boatwright argues that the women of the imperial families served as role models for elite women in the provinces (1991b: 260). Several women in the Julio-Claudian, Antonine, and Severan families were especially important for their part in continuing their dynastic lines and may have encouraged other women to undertake public roles. In addition to imperial women, the wives and daughters of Roman officials may have inspired provincial women to great deeds. Several women who accompanied their male relatives to the provinces during their time as governor or legate were honored for their own generous donations to towns around the empire (Boatwright 1991b: 261).

3   Conclusion

Investigating female patronage in the Roman empire requires a methodology that considers not only literary sources but also a wide variety of documentary and archaeological evidence. By analyzing inscriptions and the physical remains of buildings and their sculptural decoration, we can begin to understand who these women were and what they actually did. While their numbers are not great, some women did sponsor public works, performances, contests, and feasts just like wealthy men. Donors may have desired to see their names on grand monuments in the center of the city. They may have enjoyed the act of giving itself, or they may have felt pride in securing a place for their family in their city's history. Although the women's exact motivations may not be apparent, it is possible to imagine the prestige they received for "doing good for the city."

One aspect of the prestige accorded benefactors was commemoration through a public portrait statue, and this is one area where the topic of portraiture and patronage intersect. Portraits of Julio-Claudian women were conceived to portray them in certain roles: the dutiful wife or the king-maker (see Bartman, this volume, Chapter 30). The range of statue types employed in the first century was narrow and was generally confined to well-known goddess types. An expansion seems to have occurred in the second century. The large corpus of material that survives from the second century might be attributed to the increased use of marble and the virtuoso skill of sculptors. Imperial women were commemorated by more portraits, and a greater number of private women were honored in this way as well. Women in the second century could chose from a much broader array of statue types—some of the types show only subtle variations in clothing, pose, or attributes, but these differences must have meant something to the subject and the audience. Thus, the second century was remarkable for a number of reasons: the use of marble increased, women were able to be more active members of their communities, and women were honored with a wide range of portrait statues.

RECOMMENDED FURTHER READING

A succinct and up-to-date introduction to subjects pertinent to the study of women in the ancient Roman world is found in D'Ambra (2007). The two *I, Claudia* volumes (Kleiner and Matheson 1996, 2000) present an array of essays that touch on topics such as portrait and statue types, propaganda, and display contexts, as well as the roles of women in Roman society.

While Wood (1999) provides an excellent examination of imperial women in the Julio-Claudian period, no similar study exists for the second or third centuries. Carandini (1969) and Fittschen (1982) focus on the iconography of just one imperial woman in their respective studies. The detailed work of Alexandridis (2004) draws attention to hundreds of marble and coin portraits of imperial women and contains some general trends in the images of women during the first three centuries of the Imperial period.

On imperial and non-imperial images and the mixing of the two in the same display context, see Rose (1997). See also the chapter on Roman material in Dillon (2010). A number of inscriptions recording female-sponsored building projects are mentioned in Rogers (1992). Nicols (1989) also treats the subject of female patrons in the Roman world.

34

Women in Roman Britain

Lindsay Allason-Jones

When studying the women who lived in Britain between the first and fifth centuries CE, it is essential to begin by identifying exactly who is being discussed, as these women did not form a homogeneous group. Britannia had a population made up of the independent tribes who had inhabited the country before the Romans arrived as well as those people who followed the army and made their homes in the province, either temporarily or permanently, over the centuries. The latter could have come from the Mediterranean heartlands of the Roman empire, but could equally have originated in Africa, southern Russia, or Syria. Within both the native population and the groups of incomers, there would have been a wide variety of ideas as to the status of women and how they should conduct their lives. Trying to pick apart these ideas and attitudes from the written sources and the often contradictory archaeological evidence is not as simple as many modern scholars would wish.

It is unwise, for example, to rely on the ancient writers' descriptions of the province of Britannia. Writers such as Julius Caesar and Tacitus did not necessarily gather their information themselves, nor were they trained anthropologists, with sufficient evidence available to allow them to differentiate between hearsay, myth, and actual fact, and it would be unreasonable to expect them to do so. For example, in regard to the Britons, Julius Caesar recorded with some fascination that "groups of ten or twelve men have wives together in common, and particularly brothers along with brothers, and fathers with sons, but the children born of the union are reckoned to belong to the particular house to which the maiden was first conducted" (*De Bello Gallico* V.14). That this image of the sex lives of the women of Roman Britain was still current in Rome several centuries later can be deduced from the empress Julia Domna's query to the unnamed wife of the Caledonian chieftain, Argentocoxus, about "the free intercourse of her sex with men in Britain" (Cassius Dio, *Roman History* 77.16.5). This interchange may suggest that some British tribes were matrilineal. On the other hand, it is possible that in Argentocoxus' tribe there was a system similar to that of the Roman *pater familias*, but rather than becoming the

A Companion to Women in the Ancient World, First Edition. Edited by Sharon L. James and Sheila Dillon.
© 2012 John Wiley & Sons, Ltd. Published 2015 by John Wiley & Sons, Ltd.

technical daughter of a male guardian, as in the Roman system, a widow became his nominal wife.

Alternatively, some of the British tribes may have practiced a system similar to that of the Levirate of the Sudan, where young widows are accepted into the homes of their dead husband's brother in order to protect the family line and keep their children within the kinship group. In cultures beset by warfare, when many men die young, leaving behind a high number of fertile widows, systems such as the Levirate are developed to ensure the continuation of kin groups and tribes. It is not unreasonable to suggest that some British tribes may have had such systems. We must, however, be cautious in presuming that anthropological sources will necessarily provide answers to our questions about the life, rituals, and laws of the indigenous population in pre-Roman and early Roman Britain. It is quite possible that the stories recorded by the ancient writers were nothing more than travelers' tales, based on no real facts and simply repeated as "evidence" of the weirdness of those who lived outside the boundaries of the empire.

Iron Age Britain was made up of many tribes and sub-tribes and, although we cannot be sure exactly where all the tribal boundaries lay (Allason-Jones 2009), we can be confident that the status and legal position of women varied from tribe to tribe (Ehrenberg 1989). Just because all these tribes are usually referred to by ancient and modern writers as "Celtic" does not mean that they shared the same attitudes to women as all other Celtic tribes. Recent research into Iron Age Britain indicates considerable divergence in the lifestyles, religious beliefs, and burial practices of the tribes (Haselgrove and Moore 2007). The careers of two women, Cartimandua and Boudica, as recorded by the Roman writers, indicate that this divergence included the status of women.

According to Tacitus, Cartimandua owed her position as leader of the Brigantes, a large tribe or confederation of tribes centered at Stanwick in Yorkshire, to "the influence which belongs to high birth" (*Histories* III. 45); in other words, Cartimandua was a noble woman suitable for high office. The written texts indicate that Cartimandua, and not her husband Venutius, was the ruler, although it is less clear whether she had inherited the throne or had been installed as ruler by the Roman authorities. The former is the more likely, given the Roman government's dislike of female rulers. As one reads the classical writers on the subject of Cartimandua, however, it becomes evident that they had little interest in her political status but were completely enthralled by what they regarded as her louche lifestyle.

The first record of Cartimandua in the surviving texts is of her betrayal of Caratacus to the Romans after he had sought refuge at her court following his defeat by Ostorius Scapula. "From this," recorded Tacitus, "came her wealth and the wanton spirit which success breeds," and she divorced her husband and took his armor-bearer, Vellocatus, as her lover (*Histories* III. 45). Tacitus offers two versions of the subsequent tale as a warning of what can occur if women do not behave in the approved Roman way. In *Histories* he states that "her house was at once shaken by this scandalous act" (III. 45), and as a result her husband, supported by outraged tribesmen, attempted to oust her from office. In the *Annals*, however, Tacitus records that "her enemies, infuriated and goaded by fears of humiliating feminine rule, invaded her kingdom with a powerful force of picked warriors" (XII. 40). This second version reveals more about Tacitus' Roman attitude to women than it offers an accurate record of a political situation, as Cartimandua had already been accepted as their ruler by the Brigantes. It is possible that she had revealed an intention to invade the lands of neighboring tribes or created some other political uncertainty that offered Venutius the opportunity to stir up rebellion. Whatever the situation, the Roman army appears to have considered the *status quo* as being in the best interests of the province and provided the necessary support to ensure Cartimandua retained her throne. Venutius' coup was defeated, although he made another, more successful, attempt in 69 CE (Casson 1945; Richmond 1954; Mitchell 1978; Braund 1984; Howarth 2008).

The story of Boudica, as recorded by Tacitus and Cassius Dio, also provides an exciting story, designed to confirm in Roman readers' minds that such behavior was only to be expected from barbarians, rather than to archive an unbiased and accurate description of a historical event. Boudica (also referred to as Boadicea or Boudicca) was the wife of Prasutagus, king of the Iceni tribe, who was confirmed as a client king of Rome in 47 CE. We know remarkably little about her, considering the vast number of books and films that have emerged over the years with Boudica as the heroine. According to Cassius Dio, "in stature she was very tall, in appearance most terrifying, in the glance of her eye most fierce and her voice was harsh; a great mass of bright red hair fell to her hips" (LXII. 2.4). Even in the face of this detailed description, however, caution must be used, as female leaders who hampered the Roman advance across the known world are invariably described as large women lacking femininity. For example, Candace of Meroe (modern Sudan) was described by Strabo as "a masculine sort of woman and blind in one eye" (*Geography* XVII). All we can be sure about is that Boudica had two daughters, to whom Prasutagus left his kingdom jointly with the emperor Nero.

Space is too short here to discuss the various versions and details of Boudica's rebellion, but two points can be made. First, despite the limited information about both women, Boudica has, over the years, attracted more interest than Cartimandua, and as a result considerably more has been written about her—perhaps because in the nineteenth century Cartimandua's private life would have limited her appeal as a womanly role model, whereas Boudica's fight for her daughters' rights would have struck all the right notes. Second, each generation creates a new Boudica, depending on the political climate of the time. A quick trawl through Google Images reveals a fascinating development from the well-bred aristocrat of John Opie's painting of 1793, *Boadicea Haranguing the Britons*, to the inspired and courageous Boadicea (also *Haranguing the Britons*) depicted in H. C. Selous' painting of c. 1840, who would have appealed to a Britain that had recently crowned the young queen Victoria. There are also striking contrasts between the motherly Boudica of J. Havard Thomas' 1913–15 sculpture, owned by Cardiff City Council; the feisty, liberated woman portrayed by Alex Kingston in the 2003 film *Boudica*; and the curiously muscular Boudica painted by fantasy artist Jed Dougherty in 2006. These images remind us that, as well being aware of the ancient authors' biases when discussing the women of Roman Britain, we must consider the mindset of more modern writers and artists, who invariably use Boudica to express their own attitudes to women.

This caution in regard to specific women must also be exercised when using ancient texts concerning law, as it pertained to women in general (on women and law see Levick, this volume, Chapter 7). It has become increasingly clear that each province in the Roman empire had a legal code that was developed to amalgamate the existing native law codes with that of Rome. It is also clear that these legal codes changed through time, and that a law passed in the first century CE may not have been on the statute books two centuries later. The surviving law codes reveal that some laws were continually being adapted or even reintroduced, as, for example, the laws requiring women to be under the legal guardianship of *patria potestas* (Allason-Jones forthcoming). In Rome during the first century BCE, Cicero declared that guardianship for women was only reasonable, as "our ancestors established the rule that all women, because of their weakness of intellect, should be under the power of guardians" (*Pro Murena* 27). But in Egypt in the reign of Constantius II, letters in the archive of Flavius Abinnaeus, a cavalry officer in charge of the fort of Dionysias in the Fayum, indicate that women were often left to fend for themselves when their appointed *paterfamilias* failed to carry out his duties (Bell et al. 1962: 116–17). It is unlikely that those British tribes who had been used to a female leader would have seen eye to eye with Cicero about the intellect and legal needs of women, whatever their standing in society.

The extensive quantity of epigraphic evidence available for the study of Roman Britain can also hide from view those women—the majority—who left no written evidence of their existence. Most of the inscriptions found in the province are related to the military; indeed, the practice of epigraphy is invariably referred to as a military habit, and most of the tombstones, altars, and building inscriptions from Roman Britain are certainly to be found in the Military Zone. It has been estimated that only ten percent of the inscriptions surviving from the province refer to women (Allason-Jones 2005) and the content of this ten percent varies from merely a name to potted biographies. For example, most graffiti on pots simply indicate who owned that pot at some stage in its life: Vitia is only known from the letters "VITIA X" scratched on a grey-ware pot from Darenth villa ("Vitia, her mark": Wright and Hassall 1971: 298, no. 54).

The tombstone of Regina, from South Shields, on the other hand, provides not only an image of Regina with her clothing, jewelry, and furniture but also a clear inscription recording that, although she herself was a tribeswoman of the Catuvellauni who died at the age of thirty (*RIB* 1065), she was the freedwoman and wife of Barates, a Palmyrene (see Figure 34.1). The suggestion that her husband, who was clearly wealthy enough to

Figure 34.1   Tombstone of Regina from South Shields (*RIB* 1065). Photo: courtesy CIAS, Newcastle University.

Figure 34.2   The Aemilia finger ring, from Corbridge, is decorated with the letters "Aemilia Zeses" (Amelia may you live) in the *opus interrasile* technique (*RIB* 2422.1). Photo: courtesy CIAS, Newcastle University.

commission an elaborate tombstone in the Palmyrene tradition, was a trader in flags comes from a memorial at Corbridge to a man called Barates who may or may not have been Regina's husband—Barates being a common name in Palmyra (*RIB* 1171). Regina's tombstone offers compelling evidence for mixed marriages in Roman Britain, for the bi- or trilingual abilities of the population, and for clothing and the wearing of jewelry. It also poses the still-unanswerable question of how Regina became enslaved when she appears to have been born a freewoman of the Catuvellauni sometime in the late second century CE. Inscriptions are seized upon by archaeologists as offering reliable data, but their readings can often result in more questions than answers.

The epigraphic record is strongly biased towards the upper- and middle-class Romanized population, especially those with links to the military, for they came from a group with a tradition of publicly recording their lives, achievements, and activities. Further, such people could afford to do so—it is unlikely that Regina, as a British freedwoman, would have considered commissioning such a lavish tombstone for herself. The Palmyrene influence of the carving, as well as the Palmyrene text under the Latin epitaph, confirm that the memorial was to Barates' taste and reflected his funerary traditions. The occasional small finds that provide the names of their owners, such as the Aemilia finger ring from Corbridge (Figure 34.2), which may or may not be the earliest Christian artifact from Roman Britain, may reflect the taste of their wearer but alternatively could indicate the taste of their gift-givers or forebears (Allason-Jones 1991).

Only fifteen percent of the inscriptions that refer to a woman reveal her to be of low status—for example, Armea, the girlfriend of a tile-maker at Binchester (*RIB* 2491.146), and Verecunda, the actress and associate of Lucius the gladiator at Leicester (*CIL* VII 1335. 4), and much of this evidence is from graffiti rather than formal inscriptions. The balance is redressed slightly by the lead curse tablets found at Bath and Uley (Tomlin 1988— referenced as *Tab. Sul.*; Woodward and Leach 1993). The writing tablets from Vindolanda, Carlisle, and elsewhere (Bowman and Thomas 1983, 1994, 2003; Tomlin 1998, 2003) often reveal fascinating details of the concerns and problems of ordinary women, such as Oconea, who had a pan stolen from her at Bath (*Tab. Sul.* 60), or Tretia Maria, who was cursed by an anonymous enemy at London (*RIB* 7). Again, however, it is important not to read too much into the sparse information about individual women. Was Vilbia, for example, who is referred to on a lead tablet from Bath, a slave or a concubine, and was she really the victim of a dastardly kidnapping plot by a group of eight named people (*RIB* 154)?

Relying too heavily on the epigraphic record can also result in an inaccurate picture of the women's day-to-day activities. For example, if the evidence of the artifacts and parallels from other provinces is ignored, it would be easy to fall into the error of presuming that the women of Roman Britain engaged only in domestic work and were not involved in manufacturing or other income generation outside the home. Indeed, from inscriptions we know of only two women who are recorded by their profession. As one is a priestess (*RIB* 1129) and the other, the previously mentioned Verecunda, is an actress (*CIL* VII.1335.4), they are unlikely to be representative of all the women of the province. However, the number of male artisans who have left written evidence of their existence in Roman Britain is hardly more impressive, despite the huge numbers of smiths, potters, miners, etc. who must have existed in the province over time. In this context, having the names of only two women is less significant (Allason-Jones 1996).

The women who are lost to us are not only those who could not afford an inscription, had no reason to compose one, or did not come from a tradition that considered an inscription to be a useful means of communicating with other people or the gods: some women are mentioned on inscriptions but still manage to remain invisible. The struggle to persuade academics that there were women attached to Roman forts, particularly on the northern frontier of Britain, has been long and hard, and somewhat curious given the number of women who are recorded on altars and tombstones (Campbell 1978; Saller and Shaw 1984; Roxan 1991; Allason-Jones 1995, 1998, 1999, 2003a, 2005; van Driel Murray 1995; Phang 2001; Allison 2006a, 2006b, 2008, 2009).

Even today, many academics tend to concentrate on the wives, daughters, and con- cubines of the military. They thus overlook the mothers, mothers-in-law, sisters, and nieces of the soldiers who served in Britain (Allason-Jones 2003a, forthcoming). At Risingham, one of the outpost forts north of Hadrian's Wall, Dionysius Fortunatus buried his mother Aurelia Lupula (*RIB* 1250). A soldier commemorated at Caerleon, who died "on the German expedition" at the age of thirty-seven, had clearly been responsible, even during his absence, for his mother Tadia Vallaunia, who died at the age of sixty-five, and his sister, Tadia Exuperata, who survived to erect their joint tombstone (*RIB* 369). Another sister, Vacia, buried her brother Aelius Mercurialis, a *cornicularius*, at the frontier fort of Great Chesters (*RIB* 1742). There are more examples but these serve to remind us that, despite inscriptional and mortuary evidence indicating that the norm in the province was two children per family, most people in Roman Britain had extended family networks and were not merely members of nuclear families (Allason-Jones 2005: 30–6; see also Allason-Jones 2003a).

A final group of women has remained invisible in the epigraphic record: those who lived in the country from the early third century onwards. The latest consular date for an inscription from Roman Britain is 286 CE, a date that can be deduced from a dedication to Jupiter Dolichenus (*RIB* III.3299). After that, the practice of inscribing names on stone blocks, or even marking one's possessions, died out in the province. As a result, it is not possible to name ordinary individual people after that date or to identify their existence, except through the evidence of their unmarked belongings (Collins and Allason-Jones 2010). These belongings can be notoriously difficult to assign to a male or female owner. Britain does provide a rich quantity of Roman material culture, particularly jewelry found in graves, which can indicate the sort of artifacts being worn and at what date. This jewelry can sometimes indicate where on the body such objects were worn or carried. There are only a few visual depictions of women on tombstones or wall paintings, and it is not clear whether, or how, they can be taken as accurate images of individuals. As Swift has pointed out, the majority of images that show how women wore their hair, clothing, and jewelry come from other Roman provinces and thus may not be relevant to everyone in Britain (2011: 203). Swift further points out that "representation at death may also show an ideal rather than actual version of typical dress." We must, therefore, work with the tools available to us, namely the artifact assemblages.

It is important, however, that we not introduce our twenty-first century baggage into our studies of these artifacts. This principle holds for studies of all periods but is a particular problem in the Roman period, as generations of Britons were educated in the classical tradition. This tradition caused scholars to absorb the Roman mores and attitudes and to presume that, if the Romans did things in a particular way, it must be a sensible way to do things. Such presumptions were followed by the circular argument that, if we do things in this way, therefore, it is only reasonable to expect the Romans to have done things in the same way. This scenario has been discussed in detail by Richard Hingley (2000). If we use modern, or more usually mid-twentieth century, attitudes to identify artifacts as being used solely by men or women, then we endanger our understanding of the data. The Romans were not politically correct people, and there is no point in trying retroactively to make them so.

In the early 1990s researchers were tempted to use the evidence of the finds as a basis for their theories of space allocation within buildings or sites, but it has become clear that attributing gender to individual finds or even groups of finds is not a simple task. Carol van Driel's work on shoes, particularly at Vindolanda, has shown that shoes can be attributed to male, female, and infant wearers, but they are found more often than not in rubbish deposits (van Driel Murray 1995); because they were discarded, we cannot easily assume that women and children were in the forts. Necklaces, earrings, hairpins, and objects made from jet (Allason-Jones 1995, 2003b) were worn mostly by women, and the large crossbow brooches of the fourth century are mostly associated with military and civilian elite men (Collins 2010). Once an artifact type is firmly associated with one sex or the other, however, the discovery of such an object in a context that links it irrefutably with "the wrong sex" requires some tortuous arguments to explain the apparent anomaly (Allason-Jones 1995; Swift 2011; see also Allason-Jones 1988).

Even when an artifact is found within a grave, we must be confident that the body itself has been correctly identified as male or female. The case of a skeleton found at Catterick, for example, is instructive: it was discovered wearing a necklace, two bracelets, and an anklet. This large skeleton was initially presumed, because of this jewelry, to be a woman—but it proved to be that of a male aged between twenty and twenty-five years. It is now postulated that the individual was one of the transvestite priests of Cybele who castrated themselves in her service and tended to wear female dress and adornments (Wilson 2002a: 176–8, 2002b: 109 no. 8, 177 nos. 1–3, 384 no. 952, see also 41–2).

The discovery of "female" artifacts in religious contexts has also led to some interesting discussions. John Clayton, very much a man of his time, worked on the hypothesis that the jewelry found in Coventina's Well on Hadrian's Wall indicated female worshipers, referring to "lovesick damsels" who, he believed, "cast into the Well their spare trinkets in the hope of obtaining the countenance of the Goddess in their views" (Clayton 1880: 310). All the inscriptions from the Well refer to male worshipers, a fact that may not be significant, as the ratio of female dedicators to male in Roman Britain is about one in ten. Coventina herself is clearly female, so a piece of jewelry may have been considered an appropriate offering with which to attract the attention of a female deity. The assemblage found in the Well is very mixed, however, and does not show a preponderance of *ex votos*, hairpins, and bracelets that might suggest a high proportion of female worshipers (Wheeler and Wheeler 1932: 42; Allason-Jones 1995: 29–30).

Several projects (led by the GIS work of Penelope Allison 2006a, 2006b, 2008; see also Becker 2006) have attempted to use artifact assemblages to identify the presence of women in Roman military contexts. This innovative work, however, has been seized upon by young scholars, who have not always grasped the problems inherent in this method- ology—problems that were quite clear to the original researchers. Becker laid out the primary need first to catalog the finds (Becker 2006: 37); but one must then check the assemblage for oneself, rather than rely on the published catalogs. Many site reports published in the nineteenth and twentieth centuries were selective in what they published, as are some twenty-first century reports, and as a result many incomplete or unidentifiable objects were omitted. Objects traditionally identified as being female, such as bracelets or hairpins, may survive as broken fragments, but were excluded for lack of space or importance.

In assessing an artifact assemblage, the importance of what is not there should also be taken into consideration. Such a category may include objects that have been made from recyclable material, such as glass or metal. Mike Bishop (2011: 115) has stated, in reference to Roman military equipment: "In order to understand what Roman military equipment can tell us, we need to feel comfortable about its taphonomy: in other words, how did it get into the archaeological record and what happened to it before, during, and after that event?" The same is equally true of artifacts that might indicate the presence of women.

In 1989, Bishop offered the opinion that there were six reasons that military objects were deposited: concealment, burial rites, dedications, battles, booty, and chance. To Bishop's original list may be added two further considerations: (1) a catastrophic event, such as the eruption of Vesuvius at Pompeii in 79 CE, and (2) abandonment of the object because it was broken or no longer had any value. As a rule, only objects that cannot be recycled or reused for another purpose are thrown onto the rubbish heap and, as Bishop pointed out, in these circumstances, "only items which were susceptible to damage in the first place stood a chance of ending up in the ground" (Bishop 1989: 1). In other words, undamaged objects would be handed on, sold, or stolen; they would thus remain in circulation. In the case of the excavations at Housesteads and Wallsend, one study used the artifacts to suggest that the individual buildings that replaced the traditional barrack blocks at these sites in the late third century were married quarters (Daniels 1980). This conclusion was found to be based on a flawed understanding of the context of the individual finds. A more detailed examination revealed that most of the apparently feminine objects were recovered from redistributed material used in repairs to the rampart backing, so they provided no evidence for who lived in the fort buildings (Rushworth 2009).

It is essential to bring a clear understanding of how Roman forts and towns work before attempting to decide whether an object is or is not out of its gender context. Evidence from artifacts and inscriptions has long confirmed that a number of women lived inside forts. For example, the commanding officers would have had their wives, children, and female servants with them; indeed, two of the earliest and most famous women in the Military Zone are commanding officers' wives: Sulpicia Lepidina, wife of Flavius Cerialis, prefect of the ninth Cohort of Batavians at Vindolanda, and her correspondent, Claudia Severa, the wife of a commanding officer at another, unnamed fort (Bowman and Thomas 1994). Julia Lucilla, a senator's daughter, married to Rufinus, the commander of the outpost fort of High Rochester in Northumberland, is another example of a commanding officer's wife who was in residence in a military establishment along with her retinue of servants (*RIB* 1271, 1288).

Centurions were also among the military who were allowed to marry while serving, prior to the Severan edict of 197 CE, which extended this right to all serving soldiers. The wives of some of these centurions are known from epigraphic evidence; for example, Flavia Baetica, who was married to a centurion serving on the Antonine Wall (*RIB* 2115), and Aurelia Censorina, who buried her centurion husband, Aurelius Super, at York (*RIB* 670). Careful assessment of the distribution pattern of feminine artifacts in forts invariably reveals that they come from within the commanding officers' houses or centurions' quarters.

The second most common context for female artifacts within forts is road surfaces or the drains at the roadsides. In Britain, forts are invariably built with roads passing through them. After the establishment of the Vallum on Hadrian's Wall, if one wished to go from north to south or south to north there was little choice other than to go through a fort. In these circumstances objects could be dropped. Equally, women may have needed to enter a fort to make a complaint to the commanding officer or sort out a tax problem. There is evidence that markets were set up inside the forts of Newcastle and Wallsend in the fourth century; markets would certainly have brought women into the forts on a regular basis (Brickstock 2010: 86). The argument that women were present in forts has long been won; attention now needs to concentrate on exactly where and when they were there, as well as why. Thus, for example, we know from a tombstone from Roman Carvoran, a fort on Hadrian's wall, that Aurelia Aia, wife of Aurelius Marcus, died at Carvoran (Figure 34.3), but we do not know when or where she lived.

To conclude, anyone studying the female population of Roman Britain must be alert to the biases of both classical writers and modern scholars. In particular, students should not presume, relying on modern criteria, that artifacts can be assigned to one gender or the other; they should always check the accuracy of the context in which the objects were found. It is also important to recall that the Roman empire covered a vast geographical area while the province of Britannia lasted from the Claudian invasion of 43 CE to an uncertain date around 410 CE. During this time many women from across the empire will have visited the province, bringing with them material possessions from their homelands as well as their moral, religious, and familial traditions. Such travel provides a rich mix of evidence that needs to be treated with common sense and care.

Figure 34.3   Tombstone for Aurelia Aia, daughter of Titus and wife of Aurelius Marcus, a soldier in the century of Obsequens (*RIB* 1828). Photo: courtesy CIAS, Newcastle University.

RECOMMENDED FURTHER READING

For a general debate about Iron Age Britain, Haselgrove and Moore (2007) provide an excellent start, while Ehrenberg (1989) offers a comprehensive review of our knowledge of the lives of British women up to the first century CE. The many biographies of Boudica vary considerably in scope and quality; most recommended are Dudley and Webster (1962), Webster (1978), Trow (2003), Sealey (2004), Collingridge (2005), Hingley and Unwin (2005), and Waite (2007). On Cartimandua less is written, but see Casson (1945), Richmond (1954), Mitchell (1978), and Braund (1984) for detailed analysis of elements of her life. Howarth (2008) provides a lively and comprehensive discussion of Cartimandua and her political environment.

For an in-depth assessment of the evidence for the women who visited or lived in Roman Britain, from empresses to slaves, see Allason-Jones (2005), *Women in Roman Britain* (first edition 1989). For women from a single British site see Allason-Jones

(1998). For other aspects of women's lives in Britain see Allason-Jones (1996, 1999, 2003a, forthcoming). Phang (2001), Roxan (1991), and Saller and Shaw (1984) refer to the British evidence but take an empire-wide view. Much of the work that has attempted to use artifact assemblages for identifying the presence of women in Roman military contexts has been carried out in Germany (see Allison 2006a, 2006b, 2008; Becker 2006), but this scholarship offers a methodology and puts any future work in Britain in context. Researchers must, however, be clear as to which artifacts were worn or used solely by women; attention is, therefore, drawn to Allason-Jones (1988, 1995, 2003b) and van Driel Murray (1995).

For general introductions to artifacts in Roman Britain, see Allason-Jones (2011) and Collins and Allason-Jones (2010), both of which have lengthy bibliographies. The epigraphic evidence on stone can be found in Collingwood and Wright (1965; referred to as *RIB* I (*The Roman Inscriptions of Britain* I)), which covers all material found before 1955, while Tomlin et al. (2009: *RIB* III) amasses the monumental inscriptions found in the next half-century. Smaller inscribed objects found before 1987, invariably called *instrumentum domesticum* (domestic implement), have been collected in *RIB* II, which has been published in several fascicules by several editors. The hundreds of writing tablets of lead and wood found since 1973 are consolidated in *RIB* IV but can be found individually in volumes of *Britannia* or Bowman and Thomas (1983, 1994, 2003: Vindolanda), Tomlin (1988: Bath), Tomlin (1998: Carlisle), Tomlin (2003), and Woodward and Leach (1993: Uley). Military diplomata have been published by Roxan (1978, 1985).

35

Public Roles for Women in the Cities of the Latin West

Emily A. Hemelrijk

In the mid-third century CE, the local council of Avioccala, a small town in Africa Proconsularis, decided to set up a statue in honor of a distinguished fellow citizen in one of the public areas of the town. The battered inscription on its base, which preserves only part of her polyonymous name, Oscia Modesta Cornelia Patruina Publiana, praises her "conspicuous merits in rendering illustrious her city of origin" (*originis suae patriam*, *CIL* VIII.23832 with Hemelrijk 2004a). As the wife of a consul, Oscia Modesta (as I shall call her) lived most of her life outside her *patria*, accompanying her husband on his tours of duty in the Greek provinces and residing in Rome, where she educated her grandson (*CIL* VI.1478). After a long life, she was buried in Rome leaving a remarkable epitaph in pseudo-Homeric Greek (presumably composed by herself) in which she dwells on her marriage to a consul, her sorrow for the early death of her children, and the consolation she found in the Muses (*IG* XIV.1960). Yet, no word is spent on her North African background nor on the small provincial town that so proudly presented her as its citizen (*civis*) and patroness (*patrona*).

The example of Oscia Modesta shows to what extent Rome and the local cities were worlds apart. Feelings differed depending on the point of view one took: from Rome or from the local cities. Whereas a provincial background might be felt as somewhat embarrassing for members of the senatorial elite in Rome (Champlin 1980: 5–19; Hemelrijk 1999: 142, 199–200; cf. D'Arms 1984 on *viri municipales*), the local cities took great pride in their successful compatriots, both male and female. They honored them with public statues and hoped to profit from their high position and social connections by co-opting them as patrons of their communities. Such tokens of honor were impossible in the capital, where public statues and the construction of public buildings were, from the reign of Augustus onwards, more and more the privilege of the emperor and his family (Alföldy 1991: 296–7; Eck 1984, 1992; Lahusen 1983: 97–107). In imperial Rome, therefore, women such as Oscia Modesta did not receive public statues, nor could they erect public buildings; a co-optation as a patroness of the city was unthinkable. In the capital, non-imperial women of the upper classes have hardly left any trace of a public role; both in the written sources and in the material evidence, they are heavily overshadowed by the women of the imperial family.

Despite their prominence in the local cities, women such as Oscia Modesta fall outside the scope of the ancient authors. Focusing on Rome and the imperial family, the literary sources only rarely pay attention to women in the cities outside Rome. Moreover, most moralizing senatorial authors firmly bind women to their homes and families, allowing them hardly any respectable role outside the domestic domain and severely criticizing those who ventured beyond these boundaries. Yet, this should not lead us to assume that this moralizing attitude towards women was faithfully copied in the local municipalities, despite their reputation for traditional morals and rusticity (Pliny, *Epistulae* 1.14.4, 6; Tacitus, *Annales* 3.55, 16.5; Seneca, *Consolatio ad Helviam* 17.3; Martial, *Epigrammata* 11.16.8; Juvenal, *Saturae* 6.45, 55–7, 66). On the contrary, numerous inscriptions testify to a much higher public profile for women in the local cities. Though this disparity may partly reflect differences of "genre" between the inscriptions and the literary sources (Dixon 2001), the sheer number and consistency of these inscriptions make clear that women could indeed play a prominent role in local civic life and be publicly honored for it. As civic benefactresses, priestesses, patronesses, and "mothers" of cities and of civic associations (*collegia*), they left their mark on the cities of Italy and the Latin-speaking provinces in the first three centuries CE.

The predominance of the literary sources and their Rome-centered approach has led to an under-representation of women from the Italian and provincial municipalities in modern studies. Of course, our knowledge of them is, at best, fragmentary, since it stems from brief and often formulaic inscriptions on statue bases for women, on the public buildings they erected, and on their tombs, all of which present their public *personae* but conceal their individual lives. Moreover, there is great regional diversity in the number of such inscriptions for women, which has to be accounted for. Yet, on closer inspection the inscriptions set up by, and for, these women show us glimpses of the rich variety of women's public opportunities, which are neglected by the literary sources. On the basis of a body of roughly 1400 inscriptions, this essay presents a brief sketch of women's public roles in the local towns, which both counters and complements our evidence from the city of Rome. Because of the differences from the Greek East, which shows a great variety of public roles for women unknown in the Latin West, the Greek-speaking provinces are not taken into account (see van Bremen 1996 on female *gymnasiarchoi, agonothetai, stepha-nephoroi,* etc.).

1 Women of Wealth

In the cities of the Latin West, women are found in a limited number of public roles: as civic benefactresses they financed public buildings; provided feasts, games, and distributions for their fellow citizens; and sometimes bestowed other, less common, donations on their cities, such as *alimenta* (child support schemes). Further, we meet them in priestly functions, first of all as priestesses of the imperial cult but also as priestesses of other, mostly female, deities, such as Ceres and Venus (Drine 1994; Gaspar 2011). Finally, a few women were co-opted as patronesses or "mothers" of cities and of civic associations (Hemelrijk 2004a, 2008a). Numerous women combined these functions by being, for instance, both a patroness and a priestess, or a priestess and a benefactress, and sometimes fulfilling these roles in more than one city. Their social status varied: it ranged from senatorial rank to freedwomen and from women of ancient Roman families to those who had only recently acquired Roman citizenship. Yet, most were of local birth and belonged to the decurial elite or to wealthy families just below or outside it, whose social status I shall refer to as sub-decurial. Moreover, all were women of (some) wealth who were willing to devote money, time, and energy to the benefit of their cities and fellow citizens.

One of their most widely attested public roles is that of priestess of the imperial cult (Hemelrijk 2005a, 2006a, 2006b, 2007). Though fewer in number than male priests of the imperial cult (Fishwick 1987–2005), imperial priestesses were in many respects the male priests' female counterparts, with male priests serving the cult of the emperor and his deified predecessors and female priests that of the living and deified empresses. Their priestly titles (*flaminica* and *sacerdos* (*divae*) *Augustae*) closely correspond to those of their male colleagues (*flamen* and *sacerdos* (*divi*) *Augusti*) and, like them, priestesses were elected by the local council, or for the provincial priesthood, by the provincial assembly (*AE* 1984: 528 = *AE* 1979: 339: *ex decreto splendidissimi ordinis* and *RIT* 327 = *CIL* II. 4246: *consensu concili(i) p(rovinciae)*). Both priests and priestesses usually held their priesthood for one year, after which time some of them received the honorific title *perpetuus/a*, retaining the honor and privileges of their priesthood after their period of office. Though holding complementary priesthoods, priest and priestess of the imperial cult were, as a rule, no married couple, but fulfilled their priesthood in their own right (Hemelrijk 2005a; for priestly couples in the Greek East see van Bremen 1996: 114–41).

Though of different rank and extraction, priestesses of the imperial cult were all Roman citizens and women of wealth. Holding an imperial priesthood was expensive: not only were priestesses expected to pay a considerable sum (*summa honoraria*) when entering office but they probably also contributed to the costs of their priestly duties during their term of office. Being elected to a priesthood without the obligatory sum (*gratuita*) counted as a special honor to be bestowed on a few women from families of special merit to the city (*AE* 1982: 680 = *AE* 2005: 1006). Numerous priestesses, on the other hand, voluntarily augmented the legitimate *summa honoraria* by financing temples, porticoes, or aqueducts in honor of their priesthood; by setting up statues in precious metal; or promising great sums for distributions, banquets, and public entertainment (Hemelrijk 2006a). The magnitude of their gifts suggests that there was strong competition among women desiring to be elected to an imperial priesthood.

Over and above these more or less compulsory costs, priestesses of the imperial cult— like any wealthy (wo)man—were expected to display "spontaneous" generosity, not directly related to their priesthood. Their motives for spending so much money on their cities must have been complex, combining feelings of obligation or a desire to contribute to the amenities of the city with an aspiration for prestige and self-aggrandizement. Yet the effect was the same for all: by holding a prestigious priesthood and spending money on public building, distributions, or entertainment, the women in question acquired great public prestige. Depending on their rank and extraction, this enabled them to maintain or enhance their social status within the city. For a woman of (sub-) decurial rank, a priesthood of the imperial cult must have been attractive as a means of social promotion, bringing public recognition for herself and often leading to upward social mobility among her descendants. For those of recently enfranchised families, it may also have served to display their Roman citizenship and their adjustment to Roman culture and values. Women of senatorial or equestrian rank, however, seem to have been less in need of local recognition. Their motives for holding a civic priesthood and bestowing benefactions on their home towns may at least partly have been influenced by feelings of social or moral obligation. Nevertheless, prestige and the perpetuation of their memory were also important for them: by setting up public statues for them their native towns allowed them to enjoy the public honor and commemoration they lacked in Rome.

Civic priesthoods and benefactions entailed various negotiations with the city council, which decided whether to accept the donations and also decreed the award of public honor (for the role of city councils in civic munificence, see Johnston 1985 and Mackie 1990). An example may illustrate the scope of women's activities and the publicity this brought them by decree of the decurions. In the late first century CE, Iunia Rustica of Cartima in the Spanish province of Baetica bestowed several benefactions on her city and was honored by the local council with a public statue with the following inscription:

> Iunia Rustica, daughter of Decimus, first and perpetual priestess in the *municipium* of Cartima, restored the public porticoes that were ruined by old age, gave land for a bathhouse, reimbursed the public taxes, set up a bronze statue of Mars in the forum, gave at her own cost porticoes next to the bathhouse on her own land with a pool and a statue of Cupid, and dedicated them after having given a feast and public shows. After having remitted the expense, she made and dedicated the statues that were decreed by the council of Cartima for herself and for her son, Gaius Fabius Iunianus, and she likewise made and dedicated at her own cost the statue for Gaius Fabius Fabianus, her husband. (*CIL* II.1956 = *ILS* 5512 with Donahue 2004)

Iunia Rustica's perpetual priesthood, which she was the first to hold since the town had received municipal status under the Flavians, and her benefactions presuppose preliminary dealings with the city council, which both accepted her donations and had her elected to the priesthood. The official dedication of her public buildings, which required the presence of the donor, brought her into the center of public attention; she enhanced the festivities— and, probably, the number of attendants—by giving a feast and public shows. Iunia Rustica's lavish generosity also led to a polite exchange between her and the city council concerning her public honor. In gratitude for her benefactions the council voted public statues to her and her son. Accepting the honor, she remitted the expense, set up the statues herself, and added one for her husband, thus creating a family group. Incidentally, this group of statues (of which only her inscription has survived) warns us not to misunderstand family groups as invariably paying tribute solely to the achievements of its male members. Though stemming from an opulent family (Haley 2003: 166–7; Dardaine 2001: 30; Donahue 2004: 878–84), her husband, as it seems, had no independent claim to a public statue: both he and their son owed their public statues to the generosity and social prominence of Iunia Rustica.

When we turn to the upper end of the social scale, to women of senatorial rank, we find a slightly different pattern. Being a minority (roughly twelve percent) in my corpus of civic benefactresses and priestesses, senatorial women are over-represented among patronesses of cities and—together with women of equestrian status—of *collegia*. Though greatly outnumbered by male patrons, patronesses were expected to convey similar services to the cities and *collegia* they patronized. Most important among these was the protection of the interests of the city or *collegium* with the authorities, both locally and in Rome, by means of their social connections. Most patronesses of cities were women of the highest senatorial families who lived at least part of their lives in Rome; their grand family name and their extended social network in the capital made them attractive as patronesses for their (native) cities. Not only was a senatorial patroness capable of intervening on behalf of the city and of furthering its interests by means of her social connections, but, by officially co-opting such a highly placed woman as its patroness and associating her name with theirs, the city hoped to bask in the sun of her glory. In the eyes of the decurions of a local town, a woman of senatorial rank must have been awe-inspiring, as appears from the deference that speaks from the co-optation decree for Nummia Varia in 242 CE. Having attained her consent, the decurions of Peltuinum Vestinum, a small town in central Italy, offered her a bronze tablet confirming and commemorating her co-optation, in which they summarized the reasons for their choice as follows:

> All expressed the opinion that Nummia Varia, a woman of senatorial rank, priestess of Venus Felix, had started to act with such affection and goodwill towards us in accordance with her custom of benevolence, just as her parents too had always done, that she should rightfully and unanimously be made *patrona* of our *praefectura*, in the hope that by offering this honor, which is highest in our city, to her so illustrious Excellency, we may be more and more renowned by the repute of her benevolence and in all respects be safe and protected ... All members of the council have decided to proffer on Nummia Varia, a woman of senatorial rank, priestess of Venus Felix, in accordance with the splendor of her high rank, the patronage of our *praefectura*, and to ask from her Excellency and extraordinary benevolence, that she may accept this honor we offer to her with willing and favourable inclination and that she deign to take us and our *res publica*, individually and universally, under the protection of her house and that, in whatever matters it may reasonably be required, she may intervene with the authority belonging to her rank and protect us and keep us safe. They decided that a bronze tablet containing the wording of this decree of ours was to be offered her by the chief magistrates, Avidiaccus Restitutus and Blaesius Natalis, and the foremost men of our order, Numisenus Crescens and Flavius Priscus. (*CIL* IX.3429 = *ILS* 6110)

The submissive tone of the decree shows that Nummia Varia, a daughter and sister of consuls, was regarded as ranking high above the decurions of the town, with which she was probably connected by landed property in the neighborhood (Andermahr 1998: 360–1). The local councils honored their illustrious patrons and patronesses, such as Nummia Varia, with public statues and bronze *tabulae patronatus*, praising them for their virtues and their extraordinary "love" or "affection" for the city (Hemelrijk 2004a; Nicols 1980, 1989). The hierarchical relationship between a highly placed patroness and a local town is thus cast in emotional terms, the local city laying claim to the goodwill of a patroness by pointing to the tradition of her family or by emphasizing her local citizenship and extraction (see the example of Oscia Modesta). Though for (wo)men of senatorial rank the new *patria* was Rome, care for their native *patria* was considered praiseworthy: it expressed the persisting emotional ties between (wo)men of the senatorial order and their home towns (Eck 1997; for the notion of *duae patriae*, Cicero, *de Legibus* 2.2.5; Lintott 1993: 163–7; Krieckhaus 2004). Moreover, by accepting the patronage of their city of origin, by bestowing benefactions on it, or by holding a local priesthood, city patronesses showed themselves to be worthy citizens.

     In comparison to patronesses, most "mothers" of cities and *collegia* were of much less elevated rank. *Mater municipii* or *coloniae* was a rare title of honor for meritorious women of (sub-)decurial rank, which seems mainly restricted to cities in central Italy. The somewhat more frequent "mothers" of *collegia* were mostly from families below the elite; they were of the same class as most members and officials of *collegia* (Harland 2007; Hemelrijk 2008a, 2010). All "mothers" of cities and *collegia* were local women, who received the title because of their benefactions or other achievements for the town or association. Most "mothers" of cities were honored with a public statue in their hometown. Because of their modest social status, no such honor fell to the share of "mothers" of *collegia*. Instead, they were honored within the *collegia*: their names received a prominent place in the membership lists, which were carved on large marble plaques in the clubhouse, and they shared in the distributions and privileges of the *collegium*. Moreover, the title was carved on their tombs and dedications, which shows that, in their own eyes and those of their peers, being a *mater collegii* was a reason for pride and an important aspect of their social identity.

2 Public Honor

Various kinds of public honor were bestowed on women, the most important of which was a public statue. Such statues were mainly reserved for members of the (local) elite; only rarely was a public statue decreed for a woman of lower social rank. Not all public statues were set up for women of proved merit. Some statues were erected without any stated reason, perhaps as part of a family group or as a tribute to the high rank and renowned family of the honorand. By setting up an honorific statue for a woman of elevated rank and associating its name with hers in the inscription, the city enhanced its prestige. Moreover, a public statue encouraged the honorand to reciprocate by using her wealth and social connections for the good of the city. Thus, a public statue was set up not only as a reward for past benefactions but also with an eye to future ones. Lavish gifts, city patronage, or the outstanding fulfilment of a public priesthood often led to public honor, sometimes even eliciting the award of more than one statue. For example, Annia Aelia Restituta, *flaminica perpetua Augustarum* of Calama (Africa Proconsularis), was honored with five public statues because of her "conspicuous liberality": she promised 400,000 sesterces for the construction of a theater in her hometown (*ILAlg* I.287 = *CIL* VIII.5366 and *ILAlg* I.286 = *CIL* VIII.5365 = *CIL* VIII.17495). Consequently, in the first centuries CE a small but growing percentage of the portrait statues that decorated the public areas of the local towns were set up in honor of women.

Signaling their esteemed position in their cities, the honorific statues of the foremost women encouraged others to emulate their example, thus leading to a lively competition for public honor among local women. Following "the example of distinguished women" (*exemplo inlustrium feminarum*), Agusia Priscilla, priestess of Spes and Salus Augusta in Gabii (Italy), incurred expenses because of her priesthood and showered benefactions on her city and fellow citizens. In return, she was honored by the city council with a public statue, the costs of which she offered to bear herself (*CIL* XIV.2804 = *ILS* 6218). Women's eagerness for public statues is not only manifested in their frequent willingness to bear the costs: some women actually demanded a public statue as a condition for their benefactions or ordered one in their will. For example, Baebia Crinita, priestess in Arucci (Hispania Baetica), left 200,000 sesterces to her native city for a temple and a public banquet, ordering a public statue to be erected of her from this sum as well (*CIL* II. 964 = *ILS* 5402; see also Fabia Fabiana, *CIL* II.1923).

Though a public statue honoring a priestess or benefactress greatly contributed to the prestige of her family, we should not assume that these women sought public honor only for the sake of their families (Navarro Caballero 2001). Women were not isolated from their social context, and the Roman preoccupation with public recognition and personal commemoration must have affected them as much as their male peers. Inscriptions show

Figure 35.1 Busts of Cassia Victoria and her husband, L. Laecanius Primitivus, on the tympanum of the sacellum of the Augustales at Misenum. Photo: courtesy of Paola Miniero, after figure 4a, *The Sacellum of the augustales at Miseno* (Electa Napoli, 2000).

that the prestige and perpetual remembrance that a public statue guaranteed was coveted also by those to whom it was not awarded and who, therefore, tried to achieve it for themselves. This could be done by means of a funerary foundation for the perpetual remembrance of the deceased (for instance, *CIL* XIV.2827 = *ILS* 6294) but also during their lifetime by setting up a public building that perpetuated the name of the donor. Inside such a building, moreover, portrait statues could be set up for the donor and her (or his) family without the authorization of the city council (Lahusen 1983). In an exceptional case, the donor went beyond these restrictions: embellishing the *sacellum* of the *Augustales* with a monumental *pronaos*, Cassia Victoria, priestess of the *Augustales* in Misenum (Italy), boldly portrayed herself and her husband on its pediment (Figure 35.1; *AE* 1993: 477, with Adamo Muscettola 2000). In their unusual self-presentation on the pediment of a temple devoted to the imperial cult, the couple imitated imperial portraits: the portrait of Cassia Victoria was modeled on that of the younger Faustina while her (probably deceased) husband showed the, at that time old-fashioned, look of Antoninus Pius.

  Among the provincial women whose statue bases have been preserved, quite a few appear to have stemmed from non-Roman families, who had only recently received Roman citizenship. An example is Fabia Bira: her Punic or Libyan *cognomen*—together with the indigenous name of her father (Izelta)—points to a non-Roman background. She was the first priestess of the imperial cult (*flaminica prima*) in Volubilis (Maur. Ting.), which earned her two statues on the local forum (*IAM* II.439–40). The much-debated concept of Romanization seems relevant for women like her, in spite of its controversial nature (for different opinions in this debate see Millet 1990; Whittaker 1997; Woolf 1998; MacMullen 2000; Webster 2001; Mattingly 2002, 2004; Hingley 2005). When the claim of homogeneity of Roman culture with its simplifying dichotomy of "Roman" and "native" is avoided, it is, to my mind, a very useful concept for understanding what was going on in the western provinces. Therefore, I shall use it here as an umbrella term for participation in a way of life, customs, and values that, despite local differences, were recognized as "Roman." In this sense, Romanization is not a static or homogeneous concept but a dynamic process or "discourse" (Revell 2009) that led to locally specific identities and experiences of what it meant to be "Roman."

In the discussion on Romanization, surprisingly little attention has been paid to women and gender. The assumption that because of their domesticity and their exclusion from political office women were less affected by Roman culture than men (Cherry 1998: 156–7; Croom 2000: 124; Fontana 2001: 161–72) needs reconsideration. Though not directly involved in the Roman administration, women were affected by it in varying ways depending, for instance, on their social status and domicile. The influence of Roman rule on women in the frontier regions (Allason-Jones 1999; van Driel Murray 2008, 2009; Allison 2009) must have been of a different nature from that on women in Roman *municipia* and *coloniae* in the Mediterranean areas, and women of the poorer classes were probably affected differently—though not necessarily less—from women of wealthy families. Obviously, the women discussed here are a special group: though predominantly of local descent, most were Roman citizens belonging to families of the political or economic elites of their towns. We know of them because they set up or were honored by inscriptions in Latin and their portrait statues conform to the Greco-Roman tradition of public statuary: they are slightly over life-size standing figures with standardized body types and more or less individualized heads. Let us, for example, have a look at the statue of Minia Procula (Figure 35.2), perpetual priestess of the imperial cult in Bulla Regia in Africa Proconsularis (*CIL* VIII.25530; Hemelrijk 2007). It shows her as an elderly woman, dressed in a *tunica* and a mantle (*palla*). Her raised hand, as in prayer, and her covered head indicate her priestly status or, at least, her piety and female modesty. The heavy and complicated drapery and modest pose of such honorific statues are in accordance with traditional female values, while at the same time showing them to be women of substance. Moreover, the timeless dress, which may have been very different from what women wore in their daily lives, underlines their assimilation to Roman values and customs (Davies 1997, 2002, 2008; Trimble 2000; Hemelrijk 2004a: 227–31).

3 Public Roles for Women: A By-Product of Romanization?

In spite of the differences in rank and extraction, provincial women such as Oscia Modesta, Iunia Rustica, Fabia Bira, and Minia Procula had in common that they were Roman citizens, held priesthoods in cults that were oriented on Rome (such as the imperial cult), and used their wealth for the benefit of their cities in agreement with the Greco-Roman tradition of "euergetism." They were honored with public statues, which portrayed them as chaste and dignified women, dressed in what may be called the uniform of Roman womanhood: a *tunica* and a mantle (*palla*), in some cases showing the *stola*, a symbol of the Roman *matrona*, between these garments (Scholz 1992; Sebesta 1994). Their Roman-style portraits and inscriptions demonstrate their successful adaptation of Roman values and customs. Yet this does not mean that their lives and possibilities were the same as

Figure 35.2   Portrait statue of Minia Procula from Bulla Regia, now in the Bardo Museum in Tunis. Photo: courtesy Joop Derksen.

those of women in Rome. Contrary to what we might expect, their prominence within their cities surpasses that of women of similar rank in the capital and is, to some extent, reminiscent of the public role of the empresses (Hemelrijk 2007). This raises the question as to how far these women were exceptions or representative of a wider group of women in public life. To assess the scope of women's public roles in the cities of Italy and the western provinces I shall look at their spread, focusing especially on civic benefactresses and priestesses of the imperial cult.

Of the 354 inscriptions for benefactresses who alone (or at most with one co-donor) bestowed substantial benefactions, such as public buildings, the majority are found in the cities of Italy (with the exception of Rome, where public building was in the hands of the members of the imperial family), followed by the cities of the North African provinces and those of Spain (Figure 35.3). Apart from a few benefactresses from the cities of Gaul (mainly Narbonensis) and Germania Superior there is hardly any evidence for civic benefactresses in the other western provinces. When we consider the benefactresses' chronological spread, we find inscriptions for them in the cities of Italy from the last

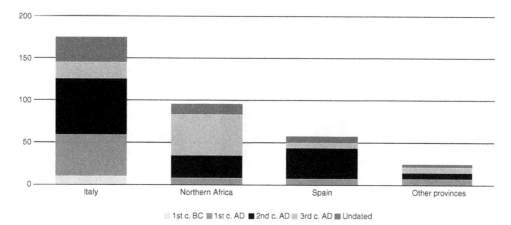

Figure 35.3   Graph of inscriptions of civic benefactresses (total = 354).

decennia of the Republic onwards, with a peak in the first and early second centuries, followed by a steep decline in the third. In the provinces of northern Africa and Spain, the evidence for women's benefactions started later, in the mid-first century; increased in the second; and, for Spain, sharply dropped in the third. In northern Africa, the peak lay in the early third century. A similar pattern is found for priestesses of the imperial cult (Figure 35.4). Here, however, the greatest number of inscriptions is found in the cities of northern Africa, followed by those of Italy (again with the exception of Rome), Spain, and Gaul, mainly Gallia Narbonensis. A few priestesses of the imperial cult are attested in Germania Superior, Dalmatia, and the provinces of the Alps (Hemelrijk 2005a, 2006a, 2007).

When we differentiate within these areas, the picture is striking. Apart from Italy, the provinces that were most densely urbanized and Romanized, such as Africa Proconsularis (with parts of Numidia) and Hispania Baetica, predominate: eighty to ninety percent of the inscriptions recording benefactresses in Spain and northern Africa are found in these provinces. Moreover, they were attested there mainly at the time of the highest prosperity, which was for Spain in the late first and second centuries and for northern Africa in the second and early third. The inscriptions of benefactresses and imperial priestesses that are found outside Italy, Spain, and northern Africa are mainly from the cities of Gallia Narbonensis, which, again, is the most Romanized and urbanized region of Gaul. Virtually no civic benefactresses or imperial priestesses were attested in the more thinly urbanized provinces of the northwestern part of the empire such as Britannia, Gallia Belgica, and Germania Inferior.

The concentration of inscriptions for civic benefactresses and imperial priestesses in the more densely urbanized, and Romanized, Mediterranean regions during periods of peace and prosperity roughly conforms to the spread of the "epigraphic habit" (Mac-Mullen 1982; Meyer 1990; Woolf 1996, 1998: 77–105). Yet, their virtual absence from the area with the highest "epigraphic density," the city of Rome, and from the inscriptions of the militarized frontier zones, shows that their distribution cannot be interpreted as merely reproducing the "epigraphic habit." Like the habit of setting up inscriptions, civic munificence and imperial priesthoods were typically urban phenomena

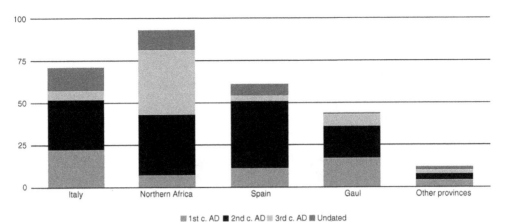

Figure 35.4 Graph of inscriptions of priestesses of the imperial cult (total = 281).

that were closely connected with Romanization and the spread of Roman citizenship (Mackie 1990; Meyer 1990). Possible influence of indigenous traditions notwithstanding, the participation of women in public life in the cities of the Mediterranean regions may be explained by these interconnected factors, especially by the spread of Roman citizenship and Roman civil law. Of special note are the Roman laws of inheritance, the separation of property between husband and wife in Roman marriage without *manus* (the common form of marriage in the Imperial period), and the *ius trium liberorum* (the right of three children), which gave full legal capacity as property-owners to female Roman citizens with three or more children. Together, these rulings made wealthy women *sui iuris* ("not in a man's power"; that is, women married *sine manu*: "without a living (grand)father") unprecedented legal and financial independence (Gardner 1990, 1993: 85–109, 1995; Champlin 1991; Treggiari 1991). Even when still in *tutela*, women in the Imperial period were not much hampered by it; as has been remarked by Jane Gardner (1995: 393), "where property is concerned, the legal capacity of Roman men and Roman women is virtually the same."

The application of Roman law for Roman citizens must have enabled an increasing number of female citizens in the provincial cities to inherit, own, administer, and control vast amounts of property virtually without male interference. According to a recent estimate, the spread of Roman citizenship and the adoption of Roman civil law in provincial cities in the second and early third centuries brought thirty to forty-five percent of the private property of the civic elite into the hands of women (Arjava 1996: 70–1; for a lower percentage see Champlin 1991, criticized by Pölönen 2002). Despite regional variation, this accumulation of wealth in the hands of (some) women and their legal capacity to control it made it hard for their cities to overlook them, especially when those cities faced financial difficulties. Though outnumbered by male benefactors and imperial priests by almost five to one (Hemelrijk 2006b: 187 n. 31), their wealth gave them a public face. By spending their money for the embellishment of their cities, by holding expensive priesthoods, and by using their social connections for the benefit of their towns, they reaped prestige and informal authority both for themselves and for their families. In reward, they received the same signs of public honor as their male colleagues and the statues and inscriptions set up for them betray no prejudice against their public prominence.

4 Epilogue

The literary authors are almost completely silent about the public role of women in the local towns. Apart from possible objections of a moralizing nature, they may simply have regarded such roles as uninteresting. The munificence expected from wealthy women is mentioned in passing by Apuleius, who felt forced to celebrate his marriage to the rich widow Aemilia Pudentilla in her suburban villa in order to avoid the pressure of the city populace flocking together for a distribution of money (Apuleius, *Apologia* 87.10–88.1). Incidentally, his remark reveals that not all donations were bestowed willingly and that social pressure and a feeling of moral obligation must have mingled with other, philanthropic or self-seeking, motives of civic benefactors, both male and female. The disparity between the literary sources and the inscriptions is even more striking in Pliny's letter on the death of Ummidia Quadratilla, a woman of senatorial rank from Casinum. In his lively sketch of the old lady, Pliny dwells on her physique, her character, and her habits, such as her inappropriate predilection for her troupe of pantomimes (*Epist.* 7.24), but pays no attention whatsoever to her importance as a benefactress to her home town. Inscriptions from Casinum, however, show that she built a temple and an amphitheater, and repaired the local theater, giving a public banquet to the decurions, the people, and the women of the town to celebrate the theater's dedication (*CIL* X.5183 = *ILS* 5628 and *AE* 1946: 174 = *AE* 1992: 244). These conspicuous public buildings, which still carry her name, changed the face of her town and perpetuate her memory until this day. When reading solely Pliny's letter this aspect of Ummidia Quadratilla's life is ignored; only the epigraphic evidence illuminates her public role as a prominent local benefactress (see also Ash, this volume, Chapter 32).

As we have seen, the difference between the literary sources and epigraphy is not merely a matter of perspective: it also reflects a real difference between Rome and the local towns. As the capital of the empire and the seat of the imperial administration, Rome differs fundamentally from the other cities of the Roman empire. Moreover, the presence of the senate and the imperial family greatly influenced the social position and the opportunities for public display of (men and) women of the elite within the city of Rome. Therefore, we must be wary of using the more ample evidence for the city of Rome as if it were valid for the other cities of the Roman empire. In imperial Rome, a possible public role for women was both controversial in the light of traditional values and overshadowed by the imperial family, whereas the local cities showed no scruples in acknowledging the public roles of women of wealth. As civic benefactresses, priestesses, patronesses, and "mothers" of cities and *collegia*, women contributed to the beauty and amenities of their towns and to the wellbeing of their fellow citizens, thus enhancing the pleasures of city life. Their honorific statues and the public buildings carrying their names lent them prestige and also reminded later generations of their benefactions or priestly roles. In this, no contradiction seems to have been felt between their private lives and their public roles. Their heavily draped statues, which portray the women in accordance with traditional female values and bear inscriptions extolling their selfless "love" for their cities, their "extraordinary" generosity, and their exemplary moral and civic virtues present them both as virtuous women and as ideal Roman citizens.

RECOMMENDED FURTHER READING

On Roman portrait statues for non-imperial women see Fejfer (2002, 2008) and Hemelrijk (2005a). An in-depth study of honorific statues of non-imperial women addressing (regional) variations within the well-known types remains a *desideratum*. For women's dress see Olson (2008a) and the collections edited by Cleland et al. (2005) and Edmondson and Keith (2008). Schultz (2000, 2006, 2007) and Spickermann (1994a, 1994b) discuss aspects of women's religion, as does Holland, this volume, Chapter 15.

36

Rari exempli femina: Female Virtues on Roman Funerary Inscriptions

Werner Riess

1 Introduction

Inscriptions are an invaluable source for our understanding of Greco-Roman antiquity. When Romans buried their relatives or honored benefactors, when they made vows with their gods or worshipped the emperor, and when they inaugurated a building or issued a decree, they often inscribed their messages in stone or bronze so as to preserve them permanently. Most inscriptions are funereal and date to the Imperial era. Because epigraphic formulae are highly stereotypical and standardized over centuries, Latin epigraphy offers no access to the real women hidden behind its highly formulaic texts. Hence, this contribution offers methodological discussions rather than hard facts. In looking at Latin funerary epigraphy from the city of Rome I will advert more pointedly than has previously been done to the potential pitfalls in the search for women's "lived reality" in inscriptions. I will also address what remains to be done in future research. In addition, this essay seeks to examine the extent to which epigraphy can be opened up to a feminist analysis; that is, to explore the extent to which female virtues in Latin epigraphy were shaped by men and attributed to females.

This undertaking is based on one of the most fundamental tenets of gender studies, the thesis that gender roles are not a natural given but a social and cultural construct. And, in this respect, Latin epigraphy has something to tell us. Especially when we compare Latin to Athenian epigraphy the contrast is striking. Whereas Attic tombstones of the classical era commemorated women, if at all, in short epigrams, the virtues almost always being *arête* and *sôphrosynê*, Roman women were portrayed with more and varied epitheta. Or, to put it in Pomeroy's words, "The reward of the 'good' woman in Rome was likely to be praise in stereotypical phrases; in Athens she won oblivion" (1995: 229). This sideways glance at Athenian epigraphy alone warrants a closer examination of Latin inscriptions. How did Romans verbalize female ideals and express them on stone, and what does this practice tell us about Roman society at large, more so than about the women themselves?

A Companion to Women in the Ancient World, First Edition. Edited by Sharon L. James and Sheila Dillon.
© 2012 John Wiley & Sons, Ltd. Published 2015 by John Wiley & Sons, Ltd.

2   Female Virtues in Latin Literature

In order to gauge epigraphic discourses, a brief look first at the female canon of values as established in Latin literature is necessary. Livy praises Lucretia's *castitas* (chastity), *obstinata pudicitia* (resolute purity), as well as her *decus muliebris* (womanly honor) (Liv. 1.57.6–11, 1.58–60). In order to save her from being abused, Verginius killed his daughter Verginia with his own hands (Livy 3.44–58; Cicero, *De re publica* 2.63, *de finibus bonorum* 2.66, 5.64). Verginia's chastity, her *pudor*, is praised by Livy and Cicero in terms similar to those used for Lucretia. In both cases, the chastity and purity of a Roman woman as well as her sexual inviolability symbolized the invulnerability of Rome itself. The honorable female body stood for the Roman body politic as a whole. The proper relationships between husband and wife, mother and son, father and daughter, with all the mutual duties they entailed, encapsulated by the term *pietas*, were regarded as the pivotal core of Rome's social and political cohesiveness. As in Greek culture, personal and family issues were political in official ideology. The mythological violence inflicted on Lucretia and Verginia can be understood as foundational violence, according to René Girard. Lucretia's suicide triggered the fall of the Tarquins and thus accelerated the dawn of the Roman Republic. The death of Verginia ended the tyrannical decemvirate and led to a new *concordia* between patricians and plebeians during the struggle of the orders. Lucretia and Verginia thus became foundational figures, guiding parameters for ideal female conduct in the Roman imagination as expressed in Roman mythology and moralistic historiography. (On Lucretia see also Izzet, this volume, Chapter 5; Hallett, this volume, Chapter 27; and Keith, this volume, Chapter 28; on Verginia see also Henry and James, this volume, Chapter 6.)

Nearly 400 years after Verginia's death we have more firm evidence for Cornelia, the mother of the Gracchi. Born in the high nobility of Rome (she was the younger daughter of Scipio Africanus Maior), she received a Greek education and lived the most honorable life of a Roman *matrona* (wife), thus embodying female ideals. After the death of her husband Tiberius Sempronius Gracchus in 154 BCE, she decided not to remarry, thus living up to the ideal of the *univira*, the woman who only knew one husband. As a widow she dedicated her life to educating her children. She wrote, entertained a literary salon, and conversed with the leading and most cultured men of the time. In recognition of her outstanding role, the Romans dedicated a bronze statue to her in the Porticus Metelli (*CIL* VI.31610). In its brevity this inscription is typical of many *matrona* inscriptions.

Based on this literary evidence, von Hesberg-Tonn (1983: 103f.) discerns five different types of morally respectable women: (1) the amiable and loving wife who venerates her husband (e.g., Calpurnia, wife of Pliny), (2) the heroine willing to sacrifice her life, especially for her husband and family (e.g., Lucretia, Verginia, Cloelia, Arria the Elder), (3) the stern and austere, morally impeccable *matrona*, (4) the morally impeccable *matrona* who is also social, urban, and educated (e.g., Cornelia and Ulpia Epigone), and (5) the morally impeccable woman who appears in public only to help maintain the existing social and political order (e.g., Hortensia, Turia, Murdia). These types overlap, but they can serve as heuristic categories for exploring women in the epigraphic record.

3   Female Virtues in Latin Funerary Inscriptions

The question now is whether or not we find the same types also represented in Latin epigraphy. The virtues presented so far all relate to upper-class women exclusively, but the majority of grave inscriptions commemorate ordinary women. Epigraphy demonstrates fewer of the types of women and a more restricted vocabulary of praise than Latin literature. When it comes to mourning adult women, we encounter type three, the ideal *matrona*, in the vast majority of cases. In reading inscriptions we are hardly confronted with a display of affection (type one); we do not find many of the heroines of type two (exceptions confirm the rule); representing type four is a risky undertaking, as I will discuss shortly, but some rare examples do exist; and type five occurs very occasionally. A great example for the narrow range of expression in epigraphy is the Augustan inscription for Cornelia, the mother of the Gracchi (*CIL* VI.31610) as noted above: *Cornelia Africani f(ilia) Gracchorum* (Cornelia, daughter of Africanus, mother of the Gracchi). Even if the original, much earlier inscription might have mentioned her sons and father, the terseness of Cornelia's characterization in contrast to the literary portrayals is remarkable (cf. Sehlmeyer 1999: 187ff.).

If we want to find out more about epigraphic *encomia* of female virtues we must have a look at inscriptions that were dedicated to women. We do find female voices in inscriptions in the form of fictive dialogues between husband and wife and women mourning their daughters, mothers, patronesses, and also themselves. But these constitute a decided minority of cases. Mostly men dedicated inscriptions to women. And, even if we read only inscriptions commissioned by women, these used the same epigraphic formulae and conventions as those commissioned by men. A cursory reading of the relevant corpora quickly reveals the adjectives that were used to characterize the five most frequent female roles, which are, in descending order of frequency, daughters, mothers, wives, sisters, and patronesses. The adjectives are *dulcissima* (sweetest), *pia* (dutiful) and its derivates, *bene merens* (well deserving), *sua* (his/her), *carissima* (dearest), *optima* (best), and *sanctissima* (holiest). These seven adjectives characterize most women across all social strata and epochs of Roman history, with minimal variation. Two questions impose themselves: first, what did men and women do in order to give more individuality to their womenfolk, if this was their goal, and second, how was it possible that seven to ten adjectives were capable of representing thousands of women of so many different generations and social classes in a way obviously satisfactory to all?

4   How to Make a Difference: Accumulation and Unusual Formulations

Epigraphic encomia were not meant to be personal but to be applicable beyond the single individual. Many men, however, were eager to emphasize that their female relatives were not merely generic types but individuals, human beings of flesh and blood. People did feel that with rhetorical formulae and topoi alone they could not do justice to their beloved womenfolk. Deviations from the prevalent forms were necessary: only an exceptional tone could reveal the cherished individuality of one's mother, wife, sister, or daughter. The commissioners basically employed two techniques: (1) a list of standard positive traits or (2) inclusion of individuating details.

The easiest way to emphasize the manifold virtues of a woman was to enumerate her outstanding qualities at length. Two examples shall suffice in this context. The freedman C. Plinius Soterichianus praises his wife Plinia Euphrosyne, who originally belonged to the same master as he did. They lived together as slaves and then, after the manumission, as *conliberti.* The previous *contubernium* was legalized and Soterichianus is clearly proud of his Roman marriage and his legitimate *uxor* (*CIL* VI.24294):

> D(is) M(anibus)/Pliniae Euphrosy/nes uxori sanctissi/mae piissimae rarissi/mae sibique karissi/mae et desiderantissi/mae C(aius) Plinius Soteri/chianus maritus pi/us cum qua vixit an/nis XXXV sine ulla/reprensione

To the gods of the underworld; Caius Plinius Soterichianus, dedicated husband to Plinia Euphrosyne, the most holy, dedicated, rarest wife, dearest to him and most beloved, with whom he lived for thirty-five years without any offense.

A Christian father characterizes his daughter thus (*ICUR* II.4568 = *ILCV* 4708):

> [Eximi]ae casti[ta]tis fidei sa[pien]tiae bon[itatis]/[iusti]tiae genero[sita]tis continentiae patentia[e]/[omn]ium bonorum feminae/[Claud]iae Marcellae Christian[ae]/[fid]elissim (a)e sinc<c=F>ritatis puella[e]/[Cl(audius)] Aristobulus virginiae/obsequentissimae ab[sti-nentissimae(?)]/vixit ann(os) XXI

Claudius Aristobulus to the most amenable and most temperate virgin Claudia Marcella Christiana, a woman of extraordinary chastity, faith, wisdom, good-heartedness, justice, generosity, self-control, patience, and of all good things; to a girl of outstanding trustworthiness and honesty. She lived twenty-one years.

The second method used (sometimes along with the accumulation of virtues) was the employment of unusual formulations and metaphors, which give Latin funerary epigraphy its distinctive charm. The most frequent deviations from the epigraphic norm are grave inscriptions, in which husbands emphasize that they lived with their wives for decades without any quarrel (*CIL* VI.7579 = 7581; 16753; 19008; 20580; 37242; cf. von Hesberg-Tonn 1983: 174). A variation of this stereotype is an inscription (*CIL* VI.15696) in which a husband claims to have never exchanged rough words with his wife (*sine ve[rbo s]cabro*). One woman or rather girl is compared to a butterfly killed in the net of a cruel spider (*CIL* VI.26011 (p. 3532) = *CLE* 1063; cf. von Hesberg-Tonn (1983: 197). Women also lived on as flowers (*CIL* VI.18385 = *CLE* 1184) or in the hearts of those who stayed behind and mourned them (*CIL* VI.19049 = *CLE* 545). Highly unusual is the apotheosis of a deceased woman, as in the case of the physician Primilla (*CIL* VI.7581: *deae sanctae meae Primillae medicae* (to my holy goddess Primilla, doctor)) or the freedwoman who is called by her husband *dea et sanctissima* (goddess and most holy one) (*CIL* VI.18358). The most famous inscription in which a wife is closely associated with goddesses is that for the freedwoman Claudia Semne: *Fortunae/Spei Veneri/et/memoriae/Claud(iae) Semnes/sacrum* (To the goddesses of fate, hope, and Venus and to the memory of Claudia Semne, holy) (*CIL* VI.15594). The inscription is only part of a larger grave monument. It consisted of a garden with a summerhouse, a little vineyard, and a well. In some buildings statues of Claudia Semne were put up. The whole precinct was enclosed by a wall (von Hesberg-Tonn 1983: 207).

Most intriguing are inscriptions that do not overlook the domestic qualities of the women, especially their chastity and diligence, but also emphasize, sometimes indirectly, their sexual attractiveness. A famous example is that for Claudia (*CIL* VI.15346 = *CLE* 52 = *ILS* 08403 = *ILLRP* 00973 = *AE* 2001: 11):

Hospes quod deico paullum est asta ac pellege/heic est sepulcrum hau(d) pulcrum pulcrai feminae/nomen parentes nominarunt Claudiam/su<u=O>m mareitum corde deilexit s{o} uo/gnatos duos creavit horunc alterum/in terra linquit alium sub terra locat/sermone lepido tum autem incessu commodo/domum servavit lanam fecit dixi abei.

Friend, I have not much to say; stop and read it. This tomb, which is not fair, is for a fair woman. Her parents gave her the name Claudia. She loved her husband in her heart. She bore two sons, one of whom she left on earth, the other beneath it. She was pleasant to talk with, and she walked with grace. She kept the house and worked in wool. That is all. You may go. (transl. M. Fant in Lefkowitz and Fant 2005: 16)

In this Republican inscription the typically female virtues still predominate, but it is a different matter in the later inscription for the artist Glyconis. Her life revolves around play, singing, and garlands. She even drinks wine. Glyconis is celebrated not for her motherly qualities but for the sweet love she gave to her husband and children (*CIL* VI.19055).

Praising women for their sex appeal meant walking a thin line, for no husband was eager to portray his wife as lascivious. The elaborate praise of Allia Potestas' beauty (*CIL* VI 37965 = *CLE* 1988; von Hesberg-Tonn 1983: 183–6) by her patron Allius—unusual in the mentioning of her nice breasts and thighs as well as her depilation (*pectore et in niveo brevis illi forma papillae/quid crura Atalantes status illi comicus ipse/anxia non mansit sed corpore pulchra benigno/levia membra tulit pilus illi quaesitus ubique*)—is counterbalanced by the usual catalog of domestic virtues. She is the first to get up and the last to go to bed and she is also active in woolwork (*prima toro delapsa fuit eadem ultima lecto/se tulit ad quietem positis ex ordine rebus/lana cui e manibus nuncquam sine causa recessit*). The most piquant detail is that she probably had two lovers, whom she was diplomatic enough to reconcile. To underscore his education, the patron-dedicant compares his relationship, not without irony, to that other man as similar to that between Orestes and Pylades (*ut fierent similes Pyladisque et Orestae/una domus capiebat eos unusque et spiritus illis*).

We encounter a similar play with the tension between matronal rectitude and sex appeal in the famous grave relief of Ulpia Epigone. The inscription does not tell us much, but the visual depiction does. Ulpia is half-nude and reclines on a *klinê* (couch), which links her to Venus and emphasizes her sexuality and fertility. But care is taken to avoid any misunderstandings. The wool basket at her feet points to her traditional role in the household (D'Ambra 1989). Beauty and chastity are praised simultaneously. Maybe the visual allusion to the high moral standard of Ulpia Epigone even aroused more erotic feelings in the ancient spectator of the monument. This deliberately ambiguous funerary relief could be read as a visual commentary on the inscriptions commemorating Glyconis and Allia Potestas.

5   The *Laudatio Turiae*

All inscriptions mentioned so far are exceptional pieces, but one piece that has received much scholarly attention might tell us more about the woman behind it. Before we tackle some parts of the text of the so-called *Laudatio Turiae* and the virtues expressed in it, we should approach the *laudata* as the ancients did, taking into full consideration the monument as a whole. Honorific and memorial statues for women were very rare during the Republic, for women were normally excluded from the public, male culture of Rome. The female statues Romans might have seen at the end of the Republic embodied heroines of old—Gaia Taracia, Gaia Caecilia, Cloelia, Quinta Claudia, and of course Cornelia, the mother of the Gracchi. With the reign of Augustus, female representation—that is, representations of members of the imperial family—changed considerably within the urban space of Rome. Outside Rome, in the Hellenistic East, female statues had been in vogue for a long time and included representations of wives of Roman magistrates, but within the city of Rome Livia and Octavia were the first contemporary women to be honored by public honorific statues, in 35 and 9 BCE respectively (Flory 1993). Statuary representations of women in private contexts had become somewhat more common at Rome during the first century BCE. The dedicants did not seek to enter into competition with the imperial house, but in Turia's case the size of the inscription alone—the slabs must have been each 2.65 meters high and together 1.7 meters wide—testifies to the self-confidence of her senatorial husband. Turia was neither a legendary heroine of Rome's founding generations nor a member of the imperial household, but her monument did reach out to the public even though it was erected right at the grave site.

Whereas the old statues honoring women often came without inscriptions, the one for Cornelia being very terse, Turia was honored in a long eulogy. Her family made massive use of two media at the same time: statuary representation and epigraphic text. This unique eagerness to display female virtues in a very tangible way cannot be overestimated in its historical and cultural importance. Alongside the textual representation we have to envision the sculptural image of the female dedicatee. She may have been represented as a *palliata* in *pudicitia* pose, as Keegan (2008: 2) suggests. Although the statue embodied the ideal of the conservative *matrona* in her pose of self-restraint and modesty, the non-verbal code of the female statue left some room for a partly eroticized depiction that stood in contrast to the text, which was full of the virtues of old, above all chastity and modesty. But even the text transcends the usual expectations: in opposition to Augustan legislation, a marriage full of mutual affection is deemed to be worth more than procreation. When the couple remained childless, Turia suggested that her husband divorce her and marry another woman so as to be blessed by legitimate offspring, a proposal that the senator vehemently rejected.

As for all Latin inscriptions, text and image must be read together. As with the grave relief of Ulpia Epigone and the inscriptions mentioned above, which played with the tension between conventional morality and sex appeal, we find the same kind of toying here—extolling conventional female virtues and at the same time transcending this very catalog of values in image and text. In the extent to which the statuary iconography of *castitas* and *sanctitas* leaves room for erotic imagination, the text plays with gender roles (Hemelrijk 2004b). At least during the absence of her husband, Turia is portrayed as a courageous, self-confident, and daringly independent woman. Masculinity and femininity therefore become ambiguous. Whereas the *laudata*'s boldness is characterized with military vocabulary and metaphors, the husband stylizes himself as weak, if not feminine. The wife is full of manly *virtus* (lines 2.6a and 19), and shows *firmitas animi* (lines 2.8a and 15), *constantia* (line 1.25), and *patientia* (line 2.21) in times of trouble. She is a *speculatrix, propugnatrix* (line 2.61), and a stronghold of defense (line 2.65: *praesidiis*).

In the light of the husband's taking on the female role as weak and defenseless victim of the proscriptions, the conventional gender roles are almost reversed. But are they really?

The husband carefully balances out his gender-game with the explicit evocation of the traditional and stereotypical canon of values. They are taken for granted, but still need to be mentioned so as not to run the risk of portraying the deceased as a furious virago like Fulvia, Mark Antony's wife. In the form of two rhetorical questions, the speaker of the *Laudatio Turiae* hastens to drop the conventional virtues—the asyndeta even accelerate the pace—(Flach 1991: 84 on lines 30–6; on the enumeration of traditional female virtues in these lines cf. von Hesberg-Tonn 1983: 220) and quickly proceeds to point out her *propria* (merits she does not share with other women). Even the wool-work, the arch-symbol for the matron's domesticity, is not missing in the accumulation of traditional female values (line 30). The speaker is aware that the formulaic praise does not do justice to his wife's extraordinary achievements, and that to touch the viewer he must do more than content himself with the usual. Just because the *laudata* at times lived a dangerous and unconventional life in which she had to adopt male qualities, the *laudator* now had to invoke the traditional image. By doing so he was free to play with the concepts of masculinity and femininity without risking permanently undermining traditional roles and values.

This rather historical assessment of the document's importance can be linked to feminist theory. Joy Connolly has suggested that in Greco-Roman culture oratory was a "manly pursuit" (1998: 149). Oratory shaped male identity and affected body posture and language, the gaze, and the whole conduct of a man, which was constructed in stark contrast to female and slave-like behavior. Since oratory could under no circumstances be effeminate and slavish, oratorical theory and practice excluded women and slaves. If we understand funeral inscriptions and especially funeral eulogies for women as a kind of oratory, a funerary oratory, then the language of praise in the *Laudatio Turiae* is, paradoxically, a form of exploitation and marginalization of women, as subtle and innocuous as it may seem. Why? Because however hard her husband tries to individualize Turia, he fails. For the text really does not depict her personal individuality, but rather a type, even in its most detailed *encomium*. The enumeration of collective values reproduces that very codex of norms. All that Turia does ultimately remains within the prevalent scope of norms, circumscribed by *pietas*. The fact that she goes beyond the ordinary has to do with extraordinary circumstances: during the civil war, she tries her best to save the assets of two families and, most of all, save the life of her husband, all of which is nothing more than the duty of any *uxor*.

Thus, Turia fits nicely into von Hesberg-Tonn's type five. With her actions, she does not challenge the existing social order; she only acts freely as long as her husband is absent. As soon as he returns home, she withdraws to the domestic duties of the diligent housewife. Behind the collective ideas of virtues that are brilliantly expressed in the *Laudatio Turiae*, we must not forget that the hyper-positive images of women were also used to increase the reputation of their whole household and especially the men living in it. The male catalog of virtues is inextricably tied to the female canon of values. So, by fulfilling social norms and expectations, women also shaped the male canon of values and enhanced the social standing and symbolic capital of male family members. Turia's actions certainly honored her, but her courage and exemplary conjugal loyalty also put into relief her husband's blessings and thus bolstered his powerful role in society. The honorific text and ostentatious material display of extraordinary female virtues helped to keep Turia's memory alive, but was most of all beneficial for her living husband.

6   Desiderata

What remains to be done in the study of Latin epigraphy in relation to Roman women? The study of the epigraphic texts alone is certainly not enough. Women are characterized differently in accordance with the specific roles they fulfill in family relationships. Daughters, mothers, *et aliae* all deserve studies in their own right. Women's social rank and status is of prime importance, and region and geography play a crucial role. The image of the ideal woman is always culturally specific and so might have differed considerably from Britain to Africa and from Spain to Syria. The age of the woman or girl is also by no means of negligible significance. A three-year-old is praised differently from a fifteen-year-old, who might have been engaged. Although the Latin canon of female values remained extremely stable over the centuries, the chronological development still warrants closer scrutiny, especially in light of the transition from pagan to Christian culture. Above all, these markers of the honoree, the sex, familial role, and status of the dedicant must not be neglected. It is too often forgotten that the surviving dedicant communicated with his living community and wanted to convey to contemporaries in his own social field relevant messages about a deceased woman in his family. All these factors need to be explored in their inter-relationship with one another, so that we may come closer to understanding how and why women were characterized the way they were. It is especially important to embed epigraphy properly in its iconographic, spatial, archaeological, and architectural context. Above all, text and image constitute an inseparable unit, and so the message that the monument's type, size, shape, and artistic adornment convey must be integrated with the epigraphy.

In recent years, Feraudi-Gruénais (2003) has problematized the concept of self-representation for funeral inscriptions within (originally closed) funerary monuments. These hidden inscriptions cannot have been designed for a wide readership. Natalie Kampen has pled time and again for a full consideration of the extent to which art, architecture, typology, iconography, burial forms, and, we might add, epigraphy, were socially determined (e.g., Kampen 1981: 19). Only this heightened awareness of the intricate relationship between social stratification and visual imagery will do justice to the complex category of gender understood as a social and cultural construct. The spectrum available to represent women in the Roman world was huge. Honorific statues and those set up in a private, funeral context—sarcophagi, state reliefs, stelai, funerary altars, gems, clay lamps, figurines, shop decorations (which provide pictorial evidence for working women), frescoes, mosaics, plaques in columbaria, and freedmen's grave reliefs—all convey gender-specific information in different genres and from different social points of view. Often these monuments came with inscriptions, and the form and style of these inscriptions were dependent on the type of the monument and the message that the commissioner intended to convey.

A quick look at inscriptions that mention women at work may be permissible in this context. They make up only one-third of the so-called occupational inscriptions, most of which come from Rome and Ostia. Two-thirds mention men in their professions. Women often worked as physicians (*medicae*), nurses (*nutrices*), hairdressers (*ornatrices*), and midwives (*obstetrices*). Apart from these typically female professional activities, they were also small retailers (saleswomen) and worked in the businesses, shops, and taverns of their husbands. With regard to slaves mentioning their jobs, Joshel (1992b: 165) remarks: "The claim of these slaves to their own labor appears to me to be part of a resistance to depersonalization and desocialization." I propose to expand on this statement and consider its applicability to women. When women strove for dignity within a world full of restrictions, they might have understood their domestic chores or rather their proud expression of them as one way to resist depersonalization and desocialization. To whom could a woman turn? Her family was her cosmos. Being celebrated for her work within the household gave her the only recognition that was possible under seemingly unchangeable circumstances.

7   Conclusion

Let us return to the stereotypical language of Latin epigraphy that seems to have confined women to immobile types, regardless of the length of the praise they received. A feminist analysis could run as follows: men did not have the monopoly of defining what was appropriate for women and what was not. Women were granted only limited agency in this process. Thus, men assigned "female" virtues to women, especially with regards to sexual morals, and in this way kept them under male control. Although this female gender-identity would have been initially shaped predominantly by men, women adopted it and made it an intrinsic part of their self-definition. Women ultimately could not imagine other norms and modes of expression. They would have internalized this canon of values, designed by men, and wholly appropriated it. For that reason women spoke like men in inscriptions, if they spoke. The language of Latin epigraphy is gendered and worked as a subtle instrument to maintain male dominance over women. Can we go that far? Is this theory right, given that men are not characterized with more adjectives than women, and most of the time even with the same adjectives? It is true that Roman law always put women at a disadvantage, notwithstanding some improvements in social life, and that inscriptions ascribe a typical "female" sexual morality to women, but was that so also for men?

These questions notwithstanding, it seems to me that we might come closer to the women of Roman antiquity if we take into consideration the function of Latin inscriptions as a whole. Gender studies elucidate the relationship between women and men, and it might be possible that inscriptions fulfilled similar purposes for women and men. In their connection to the pertinent monument type, inscriptions confirm the historically variable dimension of gender constellations. Gender is a social construct and is conveyed to a community via certain carriers of meaning or symbols. Epigraphic formulaic language is a very symbolic system. It remained stable over centuries, undergoing little or no change, which means that the symbolic reproduction of domesticity and femininity was also partly achieved via inscriptions as carriers of symbolic meanings. Serving as such, epigraphy had to reach out beyond the individual. It could not express individual sentiments. Like the Gregorian chant, epigraphy was concerned not with polyphony but with harmony in the sense of idealizing relationships among individuals and between social classes as appropriate (*pietas*). Inscriptions were media that helped one to express one's social rank and status and one's tasks in society. Exceptions confirm the rule. The uniformity of topoi, to us clichés and stereotypes, was not tedious to the ancient viewer of these inscriptions. In inscriptions and monuments people emphasized their adherence to a precisely defined catalog of values, social norms, and gendered roles. Epigraphy helped people in their self-integration into the prevalent cosmos of norms, social expectations, and exemplary behavior. In spite of increasing social differentiation over time, this normative canon of values remained stable for centuries.

What does this stability suggest? There does *not* seem to have been a striving for individualistic self-realization in a pluralistic society with a multitude of competing role models and social mores. For the history of mentalities, epigraphy is important evidence, not merely as a medium of self-representation, as has been reiterated so often in the scholarship. Yes, within certain boundaries, people were eager to say something about themselves, but most people were not keen on excessive self-display and a kind of self-exhibitionism. From this perspective, it is not surprising that Latin epigraphy accelerated greatly with Augustus, who was a genius in seeing epigraphy's propaganda value in terms of stabilizing his and his successors' reign. Epigraphy was not a medium to challenge the gendered assignments of social norms and roles but one to make them firm, steadfast, even immobile (cf. von Hesberg-Tonn 1983: 216f.). Herein lies the political function of epigraphic uniformity, to which we shall return shortly.

In concluding his magisterial study on the power of images in the age of Augustus, Paul Zanker drew a sober, if not depressing, conclusion on Rome's material culture under the empire:

> At this point we must nevertheless ask at what cost this culture of uniformity and prosperity, in which so many could participate, was achieved. A comparison with the culture of the Early Hellenistic Age suggests itself and reveals in almost every sphere of intellectual activity—philosophy, rhetoric, poetry, scientific research, and technology—the same process of standardization and stagnation as in art and architecture. Intellectual progress, artistic creativity, the evolution of rational thought and technical change came to a virtual standstill during the Empire, and in some areas ground was actually lost. Instead the arts of copying, compilation, and technical virtuosity flourished. (1990: 338f.)

Zanker is influenced here by three powerful strands of the German history of ideas, all dating back to the classical age of German literature and intellectual thought, the eighteenth century, with its philhellenism, the cult of the genius in the wake of the Romantic movement, and the belief in eternal progress derived from Enlightenment ideals. These idealistic assumptions might not do justice to a much more slowly moving pre-modern world. Uniformity is not always a lack of creativity (in relation to the refined and always inventive Greeks) and is not the consequence of a totalitarian state (which Zanker does not claim); in the case of the Roman empire it is a social, cultural, and especially politically desired construct. There was of course change, but at a snail's pace. Subtle changes did not make it into the media that constructed and represented social ideologies. There is an eminently political dimension to the question of why people complied with this system and kept on writing similar inscriptions for hundreds of years, obviously feeling that the inscriptions adequately represented them. The multiethnic Roman empire, with its innumerable centrifugal forces, could not have done without these centripetal expressions of loyalty to this very order.

Epigraphy testifies to this loyalty, this willingness to integrate oneself, this cohesion, which were not only based on Roman military might but also on the exclusion of outsiders and marginal groups such as criminals and also the suppression of women by men: in sum, an overarching social concept and political ideology that assigned precise functions to women and men of all social ranks, ages, and professions. This glue, this cohesive bond, was engendered by Roman men and, dare we say, women, and found widespread acceptance throughout the Roman world because it stabilized the Roman socio-political system. Similarly to the two Herculaneum female statue types, which were replicated for centuries (Trimble 2000), fixed epigraphic formulae articulated, and imparted to different peoples at different times, the highly gendered and hierarchical imperial ideology. Once created, epigraphic conventions helped people to express their and their womenfolk's loyalty and adherence to this system in prefabricated formulae. The few epitheta were semantically broad enough to allow everybody to see one's beloved wife, mother, daughter, or sister well represented in stone. This political usefulness of the stereotypical epigraphic language explains the extraordinary longevity and stability of the epigraphic discourse. The formulaic praise of women (and men) not only subjected women to male rule and dominance but also stabilized Roman social relations and thus Roman power in general by making the gender hierarchy permanent. Investigating femininity, the private and public realm in the Augustan age, Milnor coined the fortunate phrase "women's politicized domesticity" (2005: 93). This term also holds true for the epigraphic evidence, whose purpose it was to represent women in their politicized domesticity.

Epigraphy and visual art remained so conservative for so long and under such diverse circumstances because the old notion of the inseparability of private and public did not wane at Rome. The city and the empire could only thrive if the mutual obligations formulated by *pietas* were fulfilled meticulously. Any deviation from this belief was considered un-Roman in the sense that falling short of *pietas* ultimately endangered Rome and its order, which at least guaranteed stability for most of its inhabitants. Epigraphic language partakes of this discourse and is not more, but also not less, than a powerful agreement with Rome's existing order, which was and always remained male.

RECOMMENDED FURTHER READING

Hesberg-Tonn (1983) is the standard work on female characterization in Latin epigraphy; Joshel (1992b) is indispensable for understanding ancient women at work. Closely related is Kampen (1981), who pleads for integrating inscriptions and their accompanying monuments while at the same time considering the social status of the dedicant and the honoree. More politically oriented is Milnor (2005), who elucidates the public value of ostentatious female domesticity. The standard edition of the *Laudatio Turiae* is Flach (1991). Keegan (2008) contextualizes this unique inscription within Roman epigraphic culture in general, whereas Hemelrijk (2004b) focuses on ideas of masculinity and femininity in this same inscription. (See also see Ramage 1994 and Wistrand 1976.) Trimble (2000) explains why two statue types successfully represented women of diverse social backgrounds over a long period of time, a finding that has considerable bearing on our understanding of the epigraphic record. Forbis (1990) is a prime example of a regional study demonstrating to what considerable extent representations of women vary from region to region according to the respective cultures underlying the specific characterization.

General works on Roman funerary monuments and art include Kleiner (1977) and Kockel (1993); Lattimore (1942) reviews general themes in Greek and Roman epigraphy. For more studies of women in funerary monuments see Wrede (1971), Kleiner (1987a, 1987b), and D'Ambra (1989, 1996). Kleiner and Matheson (1996, 2000) offer images of Roman women in art and life.

37

Women in Late Antique Egypt

Jennifer Sheridan Moss

There was a woman in Alexandria called Hypatia ... She so excelled in her studies that she surpassed the philosophers of her time ... For this reason those wishing to study philosophy flocked from everywhere to her side ... Indeed there was nothing shameful about her presence in a company of men, for they all had the greatest respect and admiration for her because of her outstanding decorum. But hatred was then marshalled against her. Since she visited Orestes [the governor] quite frequently, this stirred up a false accusation among the people of the church ... Some hot-headed men ... plotted together and kept an eye out for the woman to return home from some outing. They threw her out of her carriage, dragged her to the church ... and after stripping off her clothes, killed her by [throwing] broken tiles. When they had torn her limb from limb, they brought the limbs together ... and destroyed them by burning. (Socrates, *History of the Church* VII.I 5)

We know of the legendary philosopher-queen Hypatia (also discussed by Deslauriers, this volume, Chapter 25) largely because of her prominence as a woman who stepped outside traditional boundaries, which led her to be the subject of both curiosity and wrath. But what about ordinary women who passed their lives in the small cities, villages, and countryside of Egypt during late antiquity?

Of course, most women in late antique Egypt lived less colorful, and less dangerous, lives than did Hypatia. They filled traditional female roles, such as mother, wife, and daughter, but also some roles that were less traditional, such as businesswoman or ascetic. The women we can study are the ones who have come to us by chance, principally because they were wealthy enough to produce paperwork, or because they are inadvertently mentioned in the papers of men or women of means. Although we may never have a complete picture of the lives of women in late antique Egypt, our evidence shows women engaging in a wide variety of activities and living interesting lives in the far reaches of the Roman empire.

There has been no extensive study of women in late antique Egypt. Instead, evidence from late antique Egypt has been incorporated into many broader studies of social history, such as those on the subject of women and the law (Arjava 1996; Beaucamp 1990, 1992)

A Companion to Women in the Ancient World, First Edition. Edited by Sharon L. James and Sheila Dillon.

or widows and orphans (Krause 1994–5). There are also many smaller studies on specific corpora of texts or narrow topics (Sheridan 1998; Wilfong 2002b). Other articles and monographs focus on women in Christianity, incorporating or focusing on Egyptian women (Krawiec 2002). In this essay I will focus on women as they appear in the documentary sources. Although this will create a rather uneven portrait of women's lives, it will be a clear indicator of the limits of the sources.

1   Defining the Period

Specifying the parameters of "late antiquity" in Egypt is a challenge in itself. It is generally accepted that the changes brought to Egypt by Diocletian in 284 CE marked a new era for the administration of the province. Christianity's hold on the population, particularly on those upper classes who appear in the documents from the period, was well in place by the beginning of the fourth century CE. The Arab conquest (641 CE) effectively marked the end of the period, although the Islamization of the government and culture of Egypt, like the Christianization that preceded it, happened gradually in some areas. Thus, the texts discussed here will span, roughly, the late third through the eighth centuries, and cover a wide variety of areas within Roman Egypt. Obviously, drawing broad conclusions from material that spans four centuries and a broad swath of land would not be judicious, and it will not be done here except where the evidence so warrants.

2   The Sources

The vast majority of evidence concerning life in late antique Egypt comes to us from the papyri and ostraka (potsherds) used by residents to record the everyday transactions of their lives. While such documentary texts are plentiful, their discovery, editing, and availability have not been systematic. We are thus dealing with evidence acquired fortuitously and randomly. The women depicted in these texts do not represent women of all social classes or all geographic locations, and generalizations made based on the texts are always problematic. In some cases, however, the documentation is extensive enough, particularly in an archaeological context, to allow the scholar to go beyond exposition, to analyze definitions of gender in a particular time and place. In other cases, we are left with tidbits that merit comment but do not allow true analysis.

The study of women through handwritten texts presents a number of challenges. The ephemeral documents recorded in these media are, for the most part, the papers of a man's world. They record business transactions, governmental affairs, and personal finance, none of which are traditionally the domain of women. There are large archives from the period under discussion (e.g., that of Dioskoros of Aphrodito) that mention virtually no women by name. When we do find a woman named in the papyri, it is usually the case that only part of her life is documented. For a number of the women I will discuss, we have, for example, some of their financial papers but no personal letters or marriage contracts.

The papyri are, therefore, both a blessing and a curse: they provide us with interesting insight into the lives of common women of the period, even when we are forced to view them without any context. The literary sources from the period generally address women who would not appear in the papyri, such as Hypatia, or the martyrs of hagiographic literature. As a result, comparison is generally not possible.

Another challenge to our understanding of this period comes from the nature of the texts themselves. Papyri from this period are either in Koine Greek or Coptic (Egyptian), and many are lacunose and difficult to understand even for experts, both because of the lacunae and because people's personal papers often assume knowledge on the part of their readers that modern editors lack (imagine, for example, a letter from a mother to her son that says "Why did you do that to me?" with no further explanation). For many people who wish to study this period, it is difficult even to get access to texts published long ago or in obscure journals. In this essay, therefore, I have tried as much as possible to focus on texts that are available in English translation in readily accessible volumes, such as the sourcebook of Rowlandson (1998) and the collection of women's letters by Bagnall and Cribiore (2006).

3   The Socio-Economic Spectrum: Women of Means and Slaves

The vast majority of women who appear in the papyrological record are affluent. Agreements about property transfers occasioned by marriage, divorce, and death dominate late antique documents concerning women. This fact is not surprising, as wealth, by its nature, generates the paperwork that is the source of our evidence. Slaves, as property or commodities that can be transferred from one party to another, also appear in business transactions.

Many women in late antique Egypt were landholders: scholars estimate that women owned between ten and twenty-five percent of all land. Women could, of course, own more than farmland, and there is evidence of their owning a variety of other items, such as houses, household goods, personal items, livestock, and slaves. The papyrological record provides us with the dossiers of three women—Aurelia Charite, Elizabeth, and Koloje—who, while they lived several centuries apart and in different areas, offer representative case studies for the class of wealthy women.

Aurelia Charite lived in the city of Hermopolis during the first half of the fourth century CE. Like many women of the ruling class (members of the city's boule, or ruling council), Charite was a prosperous landholder whose frequent business dealings left behind an extensive dossier of papers that document her life (her papers are collected as *P. Charite*).[1] She was born toward the end of the third century CE. Her parents, Amazonios and Demetria (also known as Ammonia), came from families belonging to the local political elite. Charite married a man named Adelphios and had at least one child, a son named Asklepiades. She was widowed early, probably in her late twenties or early thirties, and then lived to the age of between fifty and sixty.

Charite was a landowner who had extensive holdings in both her own city and in the countryside surrounding Hermopolis, where she owned some 280 acres of farmland and orchards. Charite acted as a landlord to tenant farmers, and on occasion she lent money to them as well. Given that she owned so much taxable property, her most documented activity is the payment of taxes. Indeed, her paperwork looks very much like that of a wealthy man.

What distinguishes Charite from other wealthy women known from late antique Egypt, and even from many wealthy men, is that we have extensive evidence of her literacy. She was not merely a "knower of letters," as she is described: she actually wrote and signed business documents. Her handwriting is that of an experienced writer who not only writes in a fluid hand but also understands the standard abbreviations and symbols used in financial transactions. Interestingly, she appears to have begun writing and signing documents after she became a widow, a phenomenon that implies that she found her own voice and strength in her independence, and was able to exercise it in her own social milieu.

Because Charite and her family have left behind so many documents (those of her husband and son Asklepiades remain as well), we might expect significant information about her personal life. Unfortunately, the documents we have do not provide this information. Further, we lack an archaeological context in which to place Charite. It would be enlightening, for example, if her home was excavated. The one "personal" letter that we have, written by Demetria to her daughter Charite (*P. Charite* 38), concerns a transfer of money rather than words of maternal affection or disapproval. Charite was a Christian, so we can reasonably assume that some social aspects of her life were markedly different from those of her pagan ancestors. Charite probably had more than one child (her son Asklepiades survived to adulthood and was, like his father, a city magistrate), but may well have lost one or more in infancy.

Our second case study, Elizabeth, daughter of Epiphanios and Maria, was born in Jeme c. 680 CE (see Wilfong 2002b). The dossier of papers that she deposited at a nearby monastery demonstrates that she was a woman of some means. She owned, through inheritance, half of a house (the other half belonged to the daughter of her late sister), land both in town and in the countryside, and household goods. Her assets included enough cash to regularly lend money to family members. We know much more about the personal life of Elizabeth than that of Charite, in part because Elizabeth's family engaged in disputes over property, thereby exposing the family's structure and internal tensions. Her household was multi-generational: she cared for and cohabited with her mother during her widowhood, until Maria died.

Elizabeth had three children during the course of two marriages. Georgios, her son from her first marriage, appears to have been a thorn in her side. Documents reveal that Elizabeth's attempt to encourage Georgios' independence backfired: she paid his taxes and perhaps tried to set him up in a trade, but he continued to seek further financial support. At one point she turned all her possessions over to her second husband in order to protect his and their children's inheritance after her death; later she agreed to give her son various items that he claimed as part of his legacy from his father. Although he had promised to drop the matter, Georgios sued his stepsiblings after Elizabeth's death in order to get his hands on even more property belonging to his mother.

A trove of ostraka from Jeme describes the life of a woman named Koloje, who may have been influential in her community, as she was an entrepreneur whose recorded interactions are with individuals outside her own household. Like her grandmother (and perhaps other female relatives), Koloje ran a bank, from her centrally located home, for Jemeans and those in neighboring villages. She regularly lent money to various people (both men and women), and the texts found in her home document the terms of these loans. In each, repayment is expected either in money or in agricultural products (such as wheat or dates); the timing of the loans corresponds with the agricultural cycle of Egypt (i.e., borrow to buy seed, repay from the harvest). Her rate of interest, sixteen and two-thirds percent, is high but customary. The care and attention to detail shown in Koloje's documents attest to her intimate knowledge of the moneylending business. She sometimes requires collateral, and occasionally takes ownership of it. In other situations, probably with people well known to her, she simply lends money. Her documents are formulaic, and she may have written some of them herself. Being a businesswoman paid off for Koloje. She owned a house at the center of Jeme, not far from the church, and clearly had fine material possessions, such as some Ancient Egyptian faience beads.

While slaves fall at the opposite end of the economic spectrum, they are sometimes mentioned in the papyri of the economic elite. We can assume that slaveholding was universal among this class, as they had large households to maintain in their villages or towns as well as agricultural estates in need of a labor force. The evidence does not depict clear differences in the experiences of slavery for women and men. A few documents do, however, suggest certain gendered conditions that may have applied more to female than to male slaves. Foundlings are a case in point. Female infants were certainly more likely to be abandoned by parents unwilling or unable to raise a daughter. In one example, an unnamed girl, perhaps no older than a toddler, is sold to a buyer to use as he chooses. The girl is a foundling and has been nursed by the woman who is now selling her (*P. Kellis* I.18).

Household work for slaves, as for free persons, was gendered, and weaving was women's work, done by both free women and slaves. Our evidence preserves an agreement in which a woman named Athenodora sends an unnamed female slave to complete an apprenticeship as a weaver (*P. Kellis* 19.a appendix). It appears that the slave woman will be absent from the household for two years, a significant potential economic loss to her owner, Athenodora. She will, however, return with skills that will help within the household, and may also make her valuable as rented labor outside the household. Hence, Athenodora is making a major investment in the skills of this woman. Certainly such a skilled slave would be as an asset within the economy of the home.

4   Monastic Women

By the fourth century there were women in monastic communities all over Egypt. Monastic women indulged in a form of Christianity that required extreme self-sacrifice that went beyond the bounds of personal faith: they took vows to their church, the leadership of the monastery, and to God. Most of these women lived communally, working and praying from dawn to dusk, but there are examples of female monks living in their own homes as well. Maria, a nun, reports in a letter to her anchorite that she has taken an orphan into her home (*O. Brit. Mus. Copt.* add 23 = Bagnall and Cribiore 2006: 200).

Monastic women functioned within gender norms that were circumscribed by both the lay and the religious community. The concerns expressed by nuns are those we would expect from married women: for example, a group of women presumed to be nuns (because their letters contain references to groups of sisters) discuss clothing, food, and money in a pair of preserved letters (*P. Oxy.* 14.1774 and *SB* 8.9746 = Bagnall and Cribiore 2006: 193–7). A monastic woman named Rebecca wants to make an offering to ensure the salvation of her parents (*O. Crum VC* 70 = Bagnall and Cribiore 2006: 202); this was a religious obligation of all Christian women. Like lay women, nuns could own property; Rebecca had surrendered her property to the head of the community when she entered it, but she is still able to draw on her possessions. There may have been some restrictions placed on women's commercial activities once they took their vows, as in the case of a woman who complains that she is not allowed to buy wheat because she is a woman (*P. Neph.* 18 = Bagnall and Cribiore 2006: 207).

5 The Litigants: Pity the Widow and Orphan

It is clear from a variety of documents that, although women did not hold major positions of public authority, such as magistracies, they did wield power in their own sphere, namely the home and family. The exercise of this power, as it appears to us in written sources, falls into familiar categories of female intimidation, such as the maternal guilt trip (for other examples of private letters by women in Egypt see Parca, this volume, Chapter 23):

> To my son Theodoulos from your mother Kophaëna. Your mother . . . is ill, for thirteen months and you have not even tried to write me a letter, because you know that I have treated you better than my other sons. (*BGU* 3.948 = Bagnall and Cribiore 2006: 224–5)

The sisterly guilt trip was known as well:

> To my brother Aphynchios greetings. Putting off everything, at once come to us since our mother died and we need very much your presence . . . We have also sent our brother Martyrios in order that you come to us . . . Do not be neglectful and then repent later on. (*P. Wisc.* 2.74 = Bagnall and Cribiore 2006: 387)

And certainly long-distance gossip and innuendo must have their day:

> Artemis writes to Sarapion also called Isidorus . . . If you want to draw conclusions about the fornications of your daughter, do not question me but the Elders of the church, how the two of them leapt up saying "We want men" and how Loukra was found beside her lover, making herself a courtesan. (*P. Grenf.* 1.52 = Bagnall and Cribiore 2006: 397–8)

When traditional methods of family persuasion failed, it appears that many women did not hesitate to take their relatives to court. The papyri preserve several fairly large family archives from different areas of Egypt from the early fourth century. While the archives center on the activities of men, women both appear in greater numbers than in the general corpus of papyri (according to Bagnall 2004, one quarter of petitions belong to women) and also can be viewed in the context provided by related texts. Women in these extended families appear to have believed that they would get more satisfaction in family disputes from the courts than from counting on the kindness of relatives—indeed, the language used in these disputes suggests their belief that the court would side with them because of their female inherent fragility and vulnerability. We do not know the outcome of any of these lawsuits: in all cases, we have only one side of the story, and of course petitions, by their nature, are self-serving. So the lawsuits are of interest not because of their outcomes but rather because of what they show about the state of mind of the women who brought them.

One group of lawsuits concerns a woman named Artemis, who lived in the Fayum at the end of the third century CE (*P. Sakaon* 31, 36, 37, 59). She was a young widow (her husband, Kaët, was a shepherd) with at least five children. Artemis, the owner of at least two houses, was financially comfortable. She also was legally independent (via the *ius liberorum*, which gave women with children the right to act independently) and acted as the guardian of her children, although such behavior was technically illegal. It appears that she was not forced to remarry.

Artemis sued her husband's business partner, claiming that the man had stolen some of her husband's sheep as he lay dying. She later sued her sister-in-law, Annous, who was not paying her share of the taxes on land that was jointly held by her late husband and his sister; she brought this lawsuit on behalf of her under-aged children, who held the land in partnership with their aunt. In these lawsuits, Artemis casts herself as a downtrodden widow trying to protect herself and her children from various scoundrels. In all her texts, Artemis uses the rhetoric of pity, portraying herself and her children as powerless and desperate. She begs the justice system to recognize her particular vulnerabilities. For example, she refers to the theft of sheep as "an act of violence." She also reminds the court of her status as a widow, and of her children's tender age:

> Conscious of your love of equity, my lord prefect, and your solicitude for all, especially women who are widows, I approach you asking to obtain your help. (*P. Sakaon* 36)

Many widows, like Artemis, stereotype themselves as defenseless, calling themselves "weak" or "helpless." Although an appeal to pity might seem an obvious choice for widows involved in legal wrangles, it is in fact a late antique phenomenon. There are remarkably few occurrences of the word "widow" in the papyri, but almost all of them occur in late antiquity. Further, half of them refer to women who pointedly identify themselves, in the petitions, as widows, although women were not required to identify themselves as such in legal documents. Charite, for example, never calls herself a widow; we assume that status because her husband disappears from the papyri.

The appeal to pity is not unique to widows. We have a set of family lawsuits involving a pair of female orphans, Taësis and Kyrillous, who go to court against their stepmother, aunts, and uncles (*P. Cair. Isid.* 62, 63, 64 = Rowlandson 176). Acting through their maternal uncle, Ammonius, they first ask that their stepmother be forced to produce documents supporting her claims against the father's estate, since at the time of his death she claimed nothing. The girls next settle disputes over property with their father's siblings. In each case, there is agreement for an equitable division of the property among the parties, allowing the sisters to inherit their father's share of his patrimony. As such an arrangement should have been the natural course of events, the need for the agreement indicates both that there was some dispute and that it could not be settled without legal intervention.

The reason for the sisters' litigiousness becomes clear in a later document. Although Taësis has reached majority age and is no longer represented by a guardian, she now presents herself as a helpless orphan, robbed by her paternal uncle, Chairemon, his wife, and their daughters, two of whom are also named Kyrillous and Taësis:

> Bereft of my parents while still an infant, I lived with my mother's brother Ammonius, who reared me, because my paternal inheritance was stolen and appropriated by Chairemon. Under these circumstances, while I was still a minor, I took no action, but when I had become of age, I deemed it necessary to bring suit against Chairemon concerning my paternal inheritance, which he retains in his possession. And once and a second time, when I petitioned, he ordered him to restore whatever he had appropriated, but he did not do so ... Yesterday, his daughters Kyrillous, Tasoucharion, Taësis and their mother Thatres attacked me with blows, dragged me around by the hair, tore my clothing to pieces, and left me prostrate on the ground. (*P. Cair. Isid.* 63)

Soon after, Kyrillous too approached authorities about the allegedly stolen inheritance, which was substantial.

Like the widow Artemis, Taësis and Kyrillous are trying to recover property that is rightly theirs. But how did they lose it in the first place? The documents tell us that Ammonios, their uncle, brought them up and acted as their guardian. But guardianship was onerous, perhaps even more so when combined with foster parenthood, and Ammonios does not seem to have taken his responsibilities as a guardian very seriously. Instead, it appears that Chairemon was not challenged until the girls were grown and took an interest in their own affairs. In fact, the pressure to recover the property may have come from their husbands. It is interesting that, when the girls petition on their own, they turn to the appeal to pity, pointing out as weaknesses not only their almost lifelong status as orphans but also their gender, whereas their earlier petitions did not include such references.

The majority of women who identify themselves as widows in papyri are Christians. Christian attitudes toward widows, known from biblical and other early texts, were somewhat different from those in the pagan world. The Greeks and Romans shared a basic attitude toward the widowed woman: she was a family problem, an unattached female in a world where females were supposed to be attached. If she was young enough, she was usually quickly married off to another family member; if she was too old for reproduction, she joined the household of her married son. The Christian attitude was somewhat different: a widow was viewed as a community problem rather than a private problem. Indeed, under Christianity widows were often not forced to remarry. The Christian community was exhorted to pity widows and orphans, and advocated that believers should extend charity and welfare to them (in the papyri we see this generosity taking the form of handouts of food and wine).

What we are observing in these early fourth-century petitions from women is a change in attitudes that came with Christianity. As before, widows and orphans were no more vulnerable to the maldistribution of property than anyone else—not surprisingly, most papyri concerning property disputes involve men. The very existence of these papyri concerning lawsuits brought by widows and orphans demonstrates that the legal system allowed women to protect themselves. The papyri also show us that women could function with a surprising amount of independence. A new social ethos, however, told them that it might very well help their case to appeal to a religious principle, namely that society should care for widows and orphans, show them pity, and protect them from harm.

Unfortunately, we cannot tell whether the women themselves decided to appeal to pity in their petitions. Such documents were generally written by professional scribes, and part of their duty was to write a petition that was as persuasive as possible. Still, if male scribes believed that they could arouse sympathy by mentioning that female petitioners were widows or orphans, they must have been following cultural trends. The trend itself was short-lived: petitions from women drop in number later in the fourth century (Bagnall 2004).

6 Conclusion: Women *In Situ*

Although I have focused here on textual evidence, our understanding of women in late antique Egypt is more likely to reach fruition if we can combine textual knowledge with the evidence of the tangible realia of women's lives. Recent excavations of sites in Roman Egypt may provide us with an opportunity to view women both through documents and through the physical remains of their living environment.

One site that holds out promise is Kellis (modern Ismant el-Kharab), a city in the Dakhleh Oasis, an area some 300 kilometers southwest of the Nile Valley. It thrived for centuries until it was abandoned toward the end of the fourth century when it filled with sand and became uninhabitable. The area around Kellis has been the subject of extensive excavations since the 1980s. Texts in both Greek and Coptic were discovered among the ruins of houses and other buildings, along with many other types of artifacts.

Kellis preserves what we can consider a fairly typical Roman Egyptian town of this period. Culturally, those who lived in Kellis knew a mixture of traditions. They read Isocrates and decorated their walls with pictures from the *Odyssey*, but named their children after Ancient Egyptian gods. Residents operated in a bilingual world in which they spoke Egyptian but could also function, when necessary but perhaps regularly, in Greek; still, most of them would have been illiterate in both languages. Their religion was a mixture of cultures, including temples to Egyptian gods, Greco-Egyptian gods (e.g., Serapis), and Roman gods (e.g., Castor). By the fourth century, standard Christianity and Manicheanism were celebrated alongside the ancient cults; Kellis did not exist long enough to see the fading of paganism.

One interesting group of documents from Kellis comes from so-called House 3. This dwelling, in a residential district, featured many rooms and a courtyard. Excavations revealed not only the structure of the house but also many objects related to domestic life. Among the documents are a group that connect the house to the family of Makarios. Maria, who is probably the wife of Makarios (or possibly his sister: Egyptians loosely used the terms "brother" and "sister" to refer to non-siblings), lived in her house in Kellis between c. 350 and 380 CE, while her menfolk, Makarios and her sons Matthios and Piene, were living in the Nile Valley. The family was quite mobile: the men visited Kellis now and then, and Maria seems to have visited them during their travels. In their absence, Maria lived with Kyria, probably her sister.

We learn about Maria's life from a series of letters written to her by her kin; that is, the roles of Maria are defined for us by men. Unfortunately, no letters written by Maria are preserved; this loss is particularly unfortunate because there is some evidence that Maria was literate (*P. Kell. Copt.* 26). If we are to believe the menfolk, Maria was often remiss in answering their letters. They complain in each of the letters that they are starved of news from home, need answers to particular questions, and find her letters too pithy. The letters that are preserved represent a cache maintained by Maria herself. Since the letters are not related to business, Maria must have saved the correspondence for emotional reasons.

While the men were away, Maria was expected to maintain the family home as a base of operations. The letters indicate practical, emotional, and spiritual needs: as the men travel, sometimes independently of each other, they expect Maria to preserve a sense of home for them. Because the men seem to have been working from an uncertain economic base, Maria also became the family financial manager. For example, her husband Makarios asks her to sell household goods in order raise traveling money for their sons (*P. Kell. Copt.* 19). She is approached by a certain Ammon, who asks about his wages; a startled Makarios tells her that he tended to the matter (*P. Kell. Copt. 22*) and is surprised that Ammon is bringing this up. All the letters addressed to Maria ask for goods to be sent. Many requests are for clothing, which would traditionally have been the responsibility of women (as is seen time and again in letters addressed to women). She also sends household goods, money, sacred objects, food, and medicine.

Maria worries about her children while they are out of her sight, and in return Matthaios expresses his affection for his mother:

> To my mother, my loved lady, very precious to me, the beloved of my heart: The one whose memory and worthy motherhood are sealed in my heart every hour; the one whose kindnesses and goodness that she performs for me at all times are sealed in my inmost thought. My mother, very precious to me, Maria. (*P. Kell. Copt.* 25)

In one letter, Makarios suspects that Maria is angry because the boys are not with him (*P. Kell. Copt.* 20). He reassures her with the information that their son Piene is being allowed to learn Latin by traveling with a prestigious religious leader, and that Matthaios is being cared for well. In another letter, he assures her that he has had news of Piene, who is living in Alexandria (*P. Kell. Copt.* 24); Matthaios also reassures her of his brother's wellbeing. While Piene is in Alexandria, Matthaios appears to be staying in Hermopolis and its environs.

The letters also make clear that Maria is a devoted Manichaean. It seems likely that her husband and sons are in the Nile Valley for the purpose of evangelizing. An itinerant life such as this would explain the family's uncertain income and constant need for goods from home.

Many questions about the life of Maria remain. For example, how much of House 3 was occupied by Maria and Kyria? Is there evidence of men living in the home? What was Maria doing to maintain a cash flow for the family? Future research, done by textual historians in concert with archaeologists, may be able to connect the physical remains of life in Kellis with the documentary evidence. If so, we might someday have a more comprehensive idea of how women led their lives in late antique Egypt.

RECOMMENDED FURTHER READING

Many texts by and about women from late antiquity can now be found in English translation in Rowlandson (1998) and Bagnall and Cribiore (2006). Both of these sourcebooks also include historical commentary and interpretive essays. On late antique Egypt in general, the standard survey is Bagnall (1993).

A number of comprehensive studies of women's social and legal status include evidence from late antique Egypt, such as that of Arjava (1996) on women and law, and Krause (1994–5) on widows and orphans. The monumental work of Beaucamp (1990, 1992) on the legal status of women in the Byzantine world also includes material from Egypt. Those wishing to use this will find that the review article by Bagnall (1995) is the best place to begin.

There are two studies of women in a particular setting, that of the women in Jeme by Wilfong (2002b) and that of the religious women of the White Monastery by Krawiec (2002). Wilfong (2002a) studied homoerotic behavior among women at the White Monastery as well. Sheridan's study (1998) focuses on women's literacy, and Bagnall (2004) explores petitions by women in late antiquity.

NOTES

1. All papyri are cited by the standard abbreviations established by John F. Oates, Roger S. Bagnall, Sarah J. Clackson, Alexandra A. O'Brien, Joshua D. Sosin, Terry G. Wilfong, and Klaas A. Worp, *Checklist of Greek, Latin, Demotic and Coptic Papyri, Ostraca and Tablets*, http://scriptorium. lib.duke.edu/papyrus/texts/clist.html.

38

Representations of Women in Late Antiquity and Early Byzantium

Ioli Kalavrezou

The near silence on the daily existence and routine activities of women in Byzantine historical texts has created a distorted view of the role and place of women in Byzantine society. Aristocratic women figure most prominently because they are more visible; the other prominent group consists of female saints, whose lives have been studied to a great extent. But both categories constitute the exception, rather than the norm. Only a few women were famous in Byzantium, such as the sixth century CE empress Theodora, the wife of Justinian, who started out as a dancer and performer at the hippodrome and later became wife of a great emperor, or the rich widow Danielis from the Peloponnese, who with her rich gifts and support helped the future emperor Basil I to come to power in the late ninth century.

But there is little textual evidence for average Byzantine women who were involved with everyday domestic activities, such as childrearing, who had more mundane professions, or who were concerned with trying to secure their legal rights. A much greater variety of source material is needed for a better understanding of the place and role of non-elite women in Byzantine society. Hagiographical texts, epigrams, wills, and other legal documents must be brought together with archaeological evidence. Byzantine art is full of images of women, but they too offer very few details of the female perspective on everyday life. Other kinds of material evidence offer such information. The sparsely documented visual record can be complemented with the evidence from more mundane artifacts that surrounded women every day. Indeed, it is the material culture of daily life that enables us to gain a better understanding of women's everyday experience.

The focus of this essay is to present what the visual record can tell us about women in the Late Antique and Byzantine periods. Naturally, any discussion of the representation of females depends on the surviving visual evidence, and must take into consideration the period in which the work of art or object was produced, as traditions evolve and change over time, although not as drastically as in modern society. We must also note from the outset that art in all media was, like the texts, produced by men. In addition, art was costly and thus not affordable for everyone. Hence we have hardly any depictions of women from

A Companion to Women in the Ancient World, First Edition. Edited by Sharon L. James and Sheila Dillon.
© 2012 John Wiley & Sons, Ltd. Published 2015 by John Wiley & Sons, Ltd.

the lower classes of society, and especially not of women in rural populations, which accounted for a large part of society. The other limiting factor of much of the surviving portrayals of women in the early Christian and Byzantine periods is that most of the material has a religious subject matter and thus does not help to establish the historical or contemporary woman of the times. Representations of historically recognizable individuals are in most cases of upper-class women and empresses—and even these are rare.

Portraiture was the most direct way to represent an individual, and female portraits, found mostly in funerary monuments, survive in greater numbers only from the early Byzantine period. These include the painted figures of catacombs and carved images on sarcophagi and other tomb reliefs. In such memorials we see women represented in the context of their families. A woman may be depicted either together with her husband, for example on the front of a sarcophagus, or, as in many simple funerary stelai, with her children or extended family. These images, however, hardly address the place of the woman in society or even within the family. They are generic depictions of heads and faces, and for the large majority of monuments there is no attempt to create a truly individualized portrait of the deceased.

Outside the funerary context in the early centuries (from the fourth to the late sixth centuries), we still have the tradition of private and public portraiture in sculpture. These portraits are mainly of women of the imperial families, who receive visual attention in the public town space, but also show upper-class women in the more private environment of their homes. From these early centuries a number of busts or heads of women have survived, made usually of marble. Portraits of empresses were set up in public spaces. We know, for example, that a statue of Helena, the mother of Constantine, was erected in the *Augustaion*, the large, open public square between the palace and Hagia Sophia in Constantinople.

An example of the kind of statue of an imperial figure that could be seen in public settings is the statuette, now in the Cabinet des Medailles in Paris, of either Aelia Placilia or Pulcheria, both prominent members of the Theodosian dynasty of the late fourth or early fifth century. Although smaller than life-size, she is shown with all the attributes and accoutrements of her imperial status. She wears a diadem made of a double row of pearls and a central large jewel set as a cabochon in the center above her forehead. The diadem is incorporated into the hairstyle. Her hair is drawn back and folded over the top to form a broad roll—the well-known *Scheitelzopf* style worn by empresses in this period. She holds a diptych and wears a long tunic over which is draped a mantle (*palla*) that is pulled diagonally over her body, covering almost her whole left arm. Around the upper part of the tunic, along the neckline and on the sides of the tunic, the marble has been prepared to receive metal attachments of gilded bronze representing the gold embroidered *clavi* or bands of the tunic. Around her neck she would have worn a series of precious collar-like adornments, like those worn by Theodora in the famous mosaic in San Vitale in Ravenna. These collars, as well as earrings, would have been attached to the statue, and thus would have endowed the figure with an air of reality as well as displayed a rich and extravagant appearance. A statue like this would have been quite striking when seen in public.

The concept of portraiture was never lost, but by the seventh century (and after the period of Iconoclasm), three-dimensional sculpture—public and private portraits carved in marble—was no longer produced. Any portraits found from the later centuries are in low relief and in two-dimensional media such as painting, mosaics, and manuscript illustration. A nicely preserved private marble portrait, although not one of an empress, from the later part of the fourth century, is the head of a young woman of rank in the

Figure 38.1   Marble head of a female figure, c. 375–400 CE. New York, Metropolitan Museum of Art, Fletcher Fund 47.100.51. Photo: © The Metropolitan Museum of Art/Art Resource, NY.

Metropolitan Museum in New York (Figure 38.1). The portrait was carved separately from what would have been most likely a bust into which it rested. It was joined at the level of the neck where the garment ended, so that the junction of the two marble pieces was not visible. The woman has an overall appearance of the court style of the Theodosian period: a slender face, almond-shaped eyes with heavy lids and thin eyebrows, and a small mouth. The marble surface of the face has been worked to a high gloss to add radiance to the portrait. In contrast, her turban-like hairstyle is worked much more roughly and has a matte finish. It emphasizes the mass of long hair wrapped in braids around the head, which was seen as a sign of luxury and also seduction. This kind of hair design was popular with empresses of the late fourth century, who also set the fashion for the aristocratic women of the times.

Another portrait bust of a woman of rank most likely of the sixth century, now in the Metropolitan Museum in New York and sometimes identified as Juliana Anicia, is a nice example of a woman not only of high standing but of high education. Although damaged on the left side of the body and at the nose, the subject wears a dress draped around her body and shoulders that is reminiscent of a toga, a garment often seen on men of learning and wisdom in this later period. The figure is also shown with a scroll in her right hand, a symbol of someone who is knowledgeable and well educated. The scroll is an unusual attribute for a woman to hold, as it is more commonly seen in the hands of men in late Roman sarcophagi, as a marker of their educated status. The fact that the woman holds a scroll does not, however, mean that she had an official position or an administrative role.

The majority of Late Antique and Byzantine women exercised authority only within the bounds of their own family. As caretakers of the home they were responsible for the wellbeing of their husband and children. Any references to women's seclusion from public view derive from texts written by men of the church, such as John Chrysostom, who idealized domesticity as the place where Christian values such as modesty and chastity could be brought to bear. This program is, however, more of an ideal than a daily reality. Indeed, evidence suggests quite the opposite: women from both the upper and lower classes were involved in activities outside the home. Spinning and weaving, for example, were tasks of women either at home or as part of the textile business in workshops. Well known are the textile workshops in Constantinople, where women were included in the organized system of guilds. Their guild held an annual fair where the women not only presented and sold their textiles but also celebrated certain days with a festival, where the women also had the opportunity to dance publicly.

There are no sources suggesting that women were assigned any kind of public office, that is, any administrative position. When women are referred to in the sources with extra, adjectival, surnames, these were derived from administrative positions held by their husbands, not to any office that they themselves held. At the palace (i.e., at the empress' court), however, women could hold a number of important positions, such as the *patrikia zoste* or *protovestiaria*, who were responsible for the wardrobe of the empress.

Empresses, of course, were different. Often in the early Christian period they seemed to hold more earthly power than in previous centuries, when they had received a sort of sacred aura but had not necessarily wielded authority. For example, on a gold medallion we see Galla Placidia, Augusta of the western Roman empire (421–50), wearing a cuirass and the *paludamentum* or *chlamys*, a mantel of bright purple usually worn by military emperors and fastened with a golden brooch or fibula on the right shoulder. At the same time, she is shown with the imperial diadem composed of jewels and pearls and a necklace, a diadem such as any imperial female would have worn in this period. What is unusual in her representation is not so much the *paludamentum*, which had been worn some years earlier by Eudoxia in 400–1, but the cuirass that she wears underneath. Its significance as a statement of power is supported on the reverse of the medallion. The simple but forceful inscription SALUS REI PUBLICAE (the wellbeing or health of the state), emphasizes her key role in state affairs, as she is seen here as the one in control of the wellbeing of the empire. With an elaborate diadem and a scepter in her hand, an enthroned female figure, most likely Galla Placidia herself, stresses the kind of image of assertion of power and authority of one who is on the throne.

An impressive enthroned empress is depicted on an ivory panel in Vienna in the Kunsthistorisches Museum, most likely representing the empress Ariadne (Figure 38.2). She was the daughter of Leo I, and sat on the throne with her first husband Zeno from 466 to 491. Maintaining her place as the sole heir to the imperial office, she chose to take Anastasios I as her second husband, and ruled with him until her death in 515. Ariadne was an unusual figure of authority, who dominated and controlled the court. This ivory panel and another in the Bargello Museum in Florence, which represents the same empress in a standing position, prove her unusual dominating role. Ariadne is portrayed in the Florence panel wearing an impressively elaborate diadem with high pinnacles in the front and long *perpendoulia*, or strings of pearls, hanging down on either side of her face. This is the typical imperial female headgear of the late fifth and early sixth centuries. She is dressed, however, in the full regalia of a ruling emperor. She wears the *paludamentum* or *chlamys*, appropriately bejeweled along its long borders with two parallel rows of pearls that have been greatly enlarged in order to be immediately recognizable to the viewer. In both representations she hold the *globus cruciger*, the orb topped with a cross, the symbol of

Figure 38.2   Enthroned empress Ariadne (?), d. 515 CE, ivory. Kunsthistorisches Museum, Vienna, Austria. Photo: Erich Lessing/Art Resource, NY.

Christian rule over the world. The orb is not an attribute held by other empresses; Ariadne is the first to be so depicted, in what is most likely a panel that officially commemorates an imperial consulship. In the Florence panel she also holds a scepter, which completes all the insignia of an emperor's power. In Ariadne's imperial portraits her special position, as mentioned in the sources, is clearly displayed. It is a rare case in which the image and the textual sources complement each other and provide us with the visual language appropriate to express the political situation of the times and the power and authority exercised by this empress.

A near-contemporary woman who has left us a record of her deeds is the princess Anicia Juliana, mentioned above. The daughter of Galla Placidia, she was herself a patroness of the arts, and was known for her philanthropic work. She had several churches built and embellished in Constantinople, where she also resided. Most famous are the churches of St. Euphemia and St. Polyeuktos, from the latter of which two beautifully carved piers are now on display in front of the San Marco cathedral in Venice, brought there by the crusaders. We know of Anicia Juliana's activities and generosity from the sumptuously illustrated and medically significant herbal codex of Dioscurides, *De materia medica*, which was presented to her in 512 in gratitude for her benevolent work (now in the Austrian National Library in Vienna). A dedicatory illustration at the frontispiece of the manuscript shows her enthroned and flanked by two personifications. They represent Magnanimity and Prudence, signifying two of her great qualities. Bending at her feet is a third personification, identified as Gratitude of the Arts, who presents her with the actual codex. The whole scene is framed by an intricate circular rope design that allows for the addition of subsidiary scenes depicting the construction of buildings. It is important to

Figure 38.3   The Projecta Casket, fourth century, gilded silver. London, the British Museum, inv. 1866,1229.1. Photo: © Trustees of the British Museum.

point out that the gift Anicia Juliana is presented with is a medicinal text, given to her by the citizens of a suburb of Constantinople. The codex has lavish illustrations of plants and detailed information concerning their pharmacological use. The choice of gift speaks for the receiver, a well-educated woman who could appreciate such a text.

Besides their healing powers for all kinds of ailments, plants were used to produce creams and other oils and perfumes for cosmetic purposes. Women in the Late Antique period wore cosmetics and jewelry for their own embellishment as well as to attract and secure the affections of men. A well-known representation of a woman preparing her toilette is on the famous fourth-century large silver-gilt box now in the British Museum (Figure 38.3). On one of its long sides Projecta, a Christian woman, is depicted walking with her attendants to the bathhouse. Her servants carry a variety of containers with the oils, soaps, and perfumes she will need and the clean wardrobe she will change into after her bath. On the other side of the box she is seated, applying cream to a strand of hair, while looking at the mirror held by an attendant. Interestingly, Aphrodite is represented on the lid of this large box, in one of her most characteristic gestures, namely fixing her hair (a popular subject on jewelry and other articles of adornment). Thus the box juxtaposes a fourth century woman imitating this famous gesture of Aphrodite—which was well known throughout the ancient world—with Aphrodite herself, doing likewise.

This touch of coquetry is also the motif on an exceptional piece of Byzantine jewelry, a lapis lazuli shell pendant of the sixth century in the Dumbarton Oaks collection. A golden Aphrodite stands naked inside the shell, arranging her hair with playful gestures. In a similar pose, a naked Aphrodite is represented on a sixth-century pyxis in the Walters Art Museum, in the scene of the Judgment of Paris, in which Hermes presents her with the golden apple (Figure 38.4). Images of Aphrodite are appropriate for mirrors or containers such as this pyxis, which was used to store cosmetics and jewelry. In general, female figures

Figure 38.4 Aphrodite receiving the golden apple from Paris, ivory pyxis. Baltimore, The Walters Art Museum, inv. no. 71–64. Photo: Walters Art Museum.

from classical mythology continue to be popular symbols to be depicted on objects of secular use. Because Byzantium's cultural heritage was that of the classical world—a heritage clearly reflected in its visual language—the Greco-Roman repertoire of images and forms persisted, but within a Christian context that continued to develop and transform over the centuries. Later, in the medieval period, other types of women were introduced from the Old and New Testament as examplars for a Christian life.

Representations of women attending to their personal beautification and appearance, such as that of Projecta, are often found on objects from domestic environments. An unusual example of domestic decoration is the painted fourth-century coffered ceiling of the imperial palace located beneath the cathedral in Trier. Two women portrayed there have been identified as members of Constantius Chlorus' imperial family. Whether they are historical figures is not clear, but both are clearly connected with the themes related to female beauty discussed above. One is looking, self-absorbed, at a mirror, while drawing her veil slightly to the side, as if she were checking her hairdo or her earring. The other woman acknowledges the viewer and looks outward, presenting a necklace of pearls, which she is pulling from a rectangular box full of what appear to be coins. She holds the box close to her body as if it were her private treasure. Both women wear garments of precious textiles, most likely silks, and have the overall appearance of women from aristocratic circles. The laurel leaves, as part of the decoration of their veils, is unusual and might have had a specific celebratory meaning. The sumptuous, wide necklace of gold and emeralds worn by the woman who also holds the pearls is of the kind usually found around the necks of empresses.

Personal adornment of the more common woman can be studied from the surviving funerary portraits that have been excavated in the Fayum, which depict women living in Egypt in the late Roman and early Byzantine period. These women belonged to a level of society affluent enough that a woman might own a pair of gold earrings, a gold necklace, or a gold chain with semi-precious stones. Such women also could afford to have their portrait painted to cover the face of their mummified body. These portraits are very valuable for the study of women, as they offer a more private setting of self-presentation. One such funerary portrait at the Arthur M. Sackler Museum at Harvard depicts a rather young woman with a long, oval face, small chin, and large brown eyes (see Doxiadis 1995: 113, pl. 85). She is modest in her appearance, with her hair pulled tightly back, and her only adornment is the pair of small lozenge earrings of gold with a pendant pearl attached. She wears a deep purple garment with a white undergarment. The portrait is of the highest quality and represents the height of naturalism possible for encaustic painting, a technique that mixed pigments with melted hot wax applied to a gesso-primed wooden panel, which enabled the painter to create a very fine modeling of the face, giving the skin its translucency.

Another Fayum portrait in the same museum, depicting a slightly older woman, is in tempera, and hence from a later date, probably the fourth century (Harvard Art Museums/Arthur M. Sackler Museum 1939.111). The woman's head is almost completely frontal and she gazes into the distance instead of at the viewer. Her hair is parted in the center and pulled back in neatly arranged strands highlighted in white—a suggestion that her hair is slowly turning gray. She has a slightly worried expression, marked by a few horizontal lines on her forehead. Her earrings are composed of gold hoops with three small pearls attached. What makes this portrait atypical is her uncharacteristic simplicity. She is dressed in a white tunic, most uncommon for a woman, as women's tunics were colored usually in tones of maroon, deep red, and purple. In a collection illustrating most of the known Fayum portraits, only three women are depicted wearing white (Doxiadis 1995). They are so few that one wonders whether this dress color signified something very specific to the subject's profession. Interestingly, if these women wear jewelry, their only adornment is simple earrings. One, Hermione Grammatike, from the first century, has her name and profession, γραμματική (schoolteacher), written on her white dress (Doxiadis 1995: 50–1, pl. 33). The other, from the second century, is identified by name as Klaudiane, but the second line of the inscription is hard to make out (Doxiadis 1995: 152, figure 94). No jewelry or inscription further distinguishes the third woman in white in this publication, the so-called "Jewish woman," also from the second century (see Doxiadis 1995: 25 pl. 20). It is possible that plain appearance and white dress already in the pre-Byzantine period visually identify a woman as having a profession.

Numerous rings have been excavated from funerary contexts in parts of the Mediterranean. They are of various types and metals, some in gold, others of copper, with precious or semi-precious stones. One category that has depictions of women on the bezel is marriage rings. In these we encounter the bride and the groom engraved as small heads facing each other. In most cases a cross stands between them, designating their Christian identity. Often they have inscriptions with words such as OMONOIA (concord), XAPIC (grace), and ΥΓΙΕΙΑ (health), all wishes and good blessings for the couple's successful marital life together. Here it must be observed that the concepts of ideal conditions of wellbeing, used as blessings on the rings, are all of female gender. Greek language gave the feminine form to almost all abstract ideas and virtues. This pattern created a whole world of personifications of these values, not only as ideas but also as part of the visual language.

Thus, the female element is present in all parts of life in representations of females. Although they are not specific personages, they partake in the human activities and ideas. Such images can be found in domestic contexts, as in the large textile of the sixth century now in the collection of Dumbarton Oaks. This woolen wall hanging represents an enthroned female figure identified by the inscription above her head as ECTIA ΠΟΛΥΟΛΒΟC (Hestia Rich in Blessings). She is flanked by two other females whose names have unfortunately been lost. Small *putti* on either side present her with globes inscribed with the various blessings that can bring happiness and bounty into the home: wealth, mirth, blessing, virtue, joy, and prosperity.

Another example of this kind of imagery, which decorated floors or walls of houses and other buildings, is a floor mosaic from near Antioch with the personification of ΑΠΟΛΑΥCIC (Enjoyment). Although this mosaic now greets visitors to the Dumbarton Oaks Center for Byzantine Studies in Washington DC, in antiquity it decorated the cold-water plunge pool of a bath building. This female personification holds a rose between her fingers, welcoming the women to refresh themselves in the cool waters of the pool. These are only a few examples of the type of female personifications that one might encounter in an urban environment.

Other types of female personifications are those of abstract qualities and virtues, elements that could not otherwise be depicted in a portrait or in a narrative, such as Wisdom, Clemency, Truth, Justice, and Friendship. Because Greek and Latin tended to give a female gender to most human emotions, qualities, sensibilities, and sensations, the female character has a strong visual presence in the Greek and Roman late antique world. Female personifications of abstract notions have a lasting presence in the imperial art of Byzantium and can be seen until the late Middle Ages. In this way both language and art reinforce the connection of abstract qualities and positive characteristics with women, even when these virtues are being ascribed, as they usually are, to men.

Similarly, female mythological figures and the classical past maintain a presence in the Byzantine period. We still see a selection of female mythological figures on an ivory box in the Victoria and Albert Museum, the famous Veroli Casket. Besides a number of goddesses, other famous women are represented, such as Helen, Europa being carried away by the bull, and Iphigenia being prepared for sacrifice. These figures symbolize another aspect of the female not unrelated to women's beauty and appeal: their subordinate place in relation to men, who are either their fathers, husbands, or lovers. These heroines' survival in the art of the Mediterranean world shows a familiarity with mythology and especially with these female characters and their power to express feminine matters in a way that touched the lives of women. In general, however, from the eleventh century onwards, depictions of mythological figures are found less and less frequently in works of art.

The role of mythological characters in visual representations was slowly replaced over time with biblical narratives and characters. In this shift, the illustrations of Old Testament stories provide insight into the daily activities of women, especially of their domestic environment, which is otherwise not portrayed. Most of these images come from Psalters and Octateuchs. Biblical subject matter also provides images of the most important role of a woman, namely motherhood. Motherhood was a woman's most esteemed function, and the rearing of the children her highest priority. Given the high rate of infant mortality, a woman spent many years of her life being pregnant and rearing children who often did not reach adulthood. The most unusual representations are those of women giving birth. Several depictions of childbirth—a very personal moment in a woman's life—appear in a series of Octateuchs of the eleventh and twelfth centuries. One excellent example is in Vatican gr. 747, where Rebecca is giving birth to Jacob. She is shown twice in the scene: on the left she is seated pensive and sad next to her husband, who is praying to God to make them fertile. There she appears dressed in the familiar manner of Old Testament and holy women, with a long gown and a scarf over her hair. On the right side she is shown in a squatting position with her legs parted as she is giving birth. The child is visible, as its head appears between her legs. It is remarkable that this very private moment is actually represented in such manuscripts, implying an openness and freedom in expressing human emotions and representing the intimate relationship between a mother and her child.

Scenes of domesticity and agricultural activities are represented through the arche-typical couple of Adam and Eve, whose encounter with God defined the life of all mankind. Most of these images, carved on small ivory plaques that were then applied to wooden boxes, show the couple toiling to survive after their expulsion from Paradise. Many of the scenes are not part of the biblical narrative. On one, Adam and Eve are shown together gathering the grain and Eve is actually carrying a bundle on her shoulder. She is not shown spinning, the image that became traditional for the West. Eve's role here is to participate in labor, which is usually not considered a woman's domain. She also assists Adam at forging metal by working the bellows (Figure 38.5). While this is an unusual subject, it is a surprisingly common scene on this type of container. These scenes are used to convey the ideal of marital harmony through collaborative labor. Adam and Eve exemplify the hard work of the path to a prosperous life.

Figure 38.5 Ivory plaque of Adam and Eve at the forge, Byzantine eleventh–twelfth century CE. The Metropolitan Museum of Art, gift of J. Pierpont Morgan, 1917; inv. no. 17.190.139. Photo: © The Metropolitan Museum of Art/Art Resource, NY.

Like Eve on the ivory images, women did work in agriculture, although female participation in rural activities is rarely recorded. A unique illustration of women working in the fields is found in the Vatican Octateuch gr. 747. Two women with bare arms, wearing scarves on their heads, are shown bent forward gathering grapes and harvesting grain. This part of rural life is mostly lost to us; we may be able to gain a more complete picture of female participation in rural activities through the excavation of Byzantine farm sites and the study of mundane tools such as loom weights and grinding stones.

Reconstructing the role and place of women in Byzantine society through the historical and visual record is hampered by the scarcity of sources and the fact that almost all information is incidental and elite. This is the case for the textual as well as the visual and physical record. This essay has attempted to present, through selected representations, some aspects of the lives of women of the Late Antique and Byzantine world, aspects that might be otherwise overlooked. Empresses have fared much better than other women, but even in their case we know only those who have left a more extensive record, perhaps through their own ingenuity and political knowhow. For the others, the chance survival of an image or portrait has allowed us to take a peek into their personal existence.

In order to fill in the gaps of this incomplete historical record, more material must be assembled and evaluated. Textual sources are being re-examined with new methodologies and new questions, and greater attention is being paid to statements made about women and their lives. Archaeological evidence continues to be added to the material record, evidence that will help to reconstruct women's domestic as well as public lives. It must be said, however, that even with the information gained from such new evidence the fact remains that literary and visual representations of historical women will always be fewer—and always secondary—to the literary and visual representations of men. Women simply occupied a less prominent place in late Antique and early Byzantine society, so their representation was less important.

RECOMMENDED FURTHER READING

The bibliography on this subject is quite large. A few recent studies with additional bibliographical references will help the reader to gather most of the essential bibliography: the collections edited by Garland (2006) and Kalavrezou (2003, the catalog from the exhibition *Byzantine Women and their World* at the Harvard Art Museums in 2002–2003). The analysis by Laiou (1992) presents the historical record. For early Byzantine empresses, see McClanan (2002). New publications continue to appear, adding further analyses and questions regarding women's place and role in society. See Angelova (2003, 2005), Cassis (2005), Kaldellis (2010), and Neville (2010).

39

Becoming Christian

Ross S. Kraemer

1 Introduction: "Becoming Christian"

The phrase "becoming Christian" seems simple enough, whether applied to women in antiquity or to women and men. In popular discourse, and some scholarly discourse as well, the term "Christian" is often applied to devotees of Jesus from his lifetime on. Yet it occurs in the New Testament exactly three times (Acts 11.26, 26.28; 1 Peter 4.16), and early followers of Jesus seem to have had various terms for themselves: the "Way"; the "assemblies of God"; the "slaves of God," or even just the "brothers," a term that is sometimes clearly gender-inclusive and at other times not so obviously so (Kraemer and Eyl 2011). Similarly, the earliest occurrence of the Greek term "Christianismos" occurs in the letters attributed to Ignatius of Antioch, thought to have died in the early second century, and its precise meaning is much debated. When, precisely, there is a new "religion" (another much contested term, particularly as it applies to ancient devotion to divine beings), centered on devotion to Jesus Christ, and distinct from its Judean beginnings, is also the subject of substantial disagreement (Reed and Becker 2003). The parameters of this essay are generously inclusive, and include Judean women who followed Jesus of Nazareth as Messiah of Israel. This does not mean, though, that such women would have understood themselves to be part of a "new religion" distinct from the one in which they were raised (nor even that they might have thought in terms of such categories, categories that many scholars would argue are modern, etic ones). Such a shift did eventually occur, but for the purposes of this essay when, precisely, is immaterial. At the same time, it seems reasonable that such women, and men, would have understood themselves to have departed in some significant ways from their prior practices and ideas, by thinking, for instance, that Jesus of Nazareth was God's son, was the Messiah of Israel, that the Reign of God was at hand, and that these cosmological shifts entailed some substantial changes in their daily practices and their social interactions.

It is not merely the designation "Christian" that requires explication. The language of "becoming" is similarly problematic. It implies a social process other than of simply being

A Companion to Women in the Ancient World, First Edition. Edited by Sharon L. James and Sheila Dillon.
© 2012 John Wiley & Sons, Ltd. Published 2015 by John Wiley & Sons, Ltd.

raised as a Christian from birth. Obviously, Jesus' earliest followers may all be considered to have "become" his followers, rather than to have grown up as Christian children, in Christian families, and this extends to the earliest Christ-assemblies known from the correspondence of Paul. However, we know very little about the subsequent demographic distribution of groups that venerated Jesus: that is, how many persons were raised in such practices, and how many took up such veneration voluntarily after childhood. This essay focuses only on persons who were not raised in such veneration, of whatever form, and not on the broader formation of "Christians" within existing practicing households.

2 Vignettes

In the New Testament book of the Acts of the Apostles, probably written in the early second century CE, women are regularly among those persuaded by the rhetoric of Jesus' earliest apostles. Paul's speech in the synagogue at Psidian Antioch (Acts 13.50) persuades many "gentiles" to become believers: women who are "(God)-fearing" and men who are "leading." At Thessalonika in Greece (Acts 17.4), Paul's speech again persuades women and men, although this time it is the men who are "(God)-fearing" and the women who are "leading." In the synagogue in Beroea (Acts 17.12), Paul's speech persuades high-standing women, and not a few men (and neither group is said to be "(God)-fearing"). Paul's speech also persuades a woman named Lydia, who trades in costly purple dyes; she is part of a group of women he finds engaged in Sabbath prayer outside the city of Philippi (Acts 16.13). Women are not necessarily included in all such displays of Paul's rhetoric: at Iconium (Acts 14.1ff.), Paul's (and Barnabas') speech in the synagogue in Iconium persuades a great number of Judeans and Greeks, all masculine plurals, with no specific mention of women. Although the author of Acts narrates occasions where people "become Christian" when they witness the signs and wonders performed by Paul and other apostles (e.g., Acts 19, set in Ephesus), in Acts, women are rarely if ever explicitly said to be persuaded by miracles alone.

In these accounts, women (and men) sometimes seem to "become Christian" in a single, defining moment, although at other times they listen to Paul's preaching over a matter of days and weeks. Occasionally, Acts notes that their assent to the preaching of Paul is followed by their baptism (e.g., Lydia and her household), but in most instances such rites are not noted and, even when they are, virtually no detail is provided. Acts is largely silent on the consequences of "becoming" Christian.

By contrast, a series of so-called apocryphal *Acts* of various apostles, composed from perhaps the mid-second century on, recount elaborate, lengthy tales of how women and men "became Christian" in response to the teachings of many apostles, fanned out across the ancient world. One of the longest, the story of an Indian woman named Mygdonia, occurs in the *Acts of Thomas*, composed in Greek and translated into Syriac in perhaps the third century CE. Mygdonia had been married for less than a year to a man named Charisius, himself a relative of the Indian king, Misdaeus, when the apostle Thomas, traveling about India, came to their city. Carried on a litter by her slaves, befitting her high status, Mygdonia goes out to hear the new apostle preaching the new god. Thomas preaches the futility of either wealth or poverty, and the necessity of sexual purity, temperance, and meekness. Hearing him, Mygdonia is transformed. She springs off her litter, throws herself before Thomas, takes hold of his feet, and implores him to care and pray for her. In response, Thomas instructs her to remove her jewelry, explaining that adornments, clothing, worldly power, and "filthy" marital intercourse are of no use to her, then tells her to go in peace.

Things do not go well when Mygdonia returns home. Her husband reproves her for having left her house and gone to hear idle words and see acts of sorcery, unbefitting her status as a free woman. Over the next several days, Mygdonia refuses either to dine with her husband or to have sex with him, going out daily to see Thomas and hear him preach. Her distraught husband tries to dissuade her, pointing out that Thomas speaks deceit and practices sorcery, and that many other women he deceived have since come to their senses. Failing to win back her affection, Charisius enlists Misdaeus to arrest Thomas. But Thomas, like many other apostles from the canonical Acts on, miraculously escapes prison, and soon gives Mygdonia the seal of Jesus Christ.

Mygdonia's transformation appears to be contagious. Hearing a heavenly voice affirm Mygdonia's sealing, her childhood nurse, Marcia, also requests the seal. Misdaeus tells the tale of Mygdonia's bewitchment to his own wife, Tertia, imploring her to try to dissuade Mygdonia from her new allegiance, only to have Tertia herself instantly persuaded by Mygdonia to hear the stranger and worship the God whom he teaches. When Misdaeus and Charisius, now united in their anger at Thomas, send the king's son, Vazan, to interrogate Thomas, he, too, is persuaded instantly by the preaching of the apostle, and soon he and his own wife, Mnesara, receive the seal.

As do many of the apocryphal *Acts*, that of Thomas ends with his martyrdom, at the hands of the outraged Misdaeus. Before his death, Thomas appoints Vazan a deacon. Mygdonia and Tertia are ultimately allowed to live as celibates. Finally, sometime after Thomas' death, one of Misdaeus' sons is afflicted by a demon, and the desperate, distraught king goes to the tomb of Thomas, hoping to cure his son with a bone of the apostle. Although Thomas' body turns out to have been removed by a follower to Mesopotamia, dust that had been in contact with a bone proves sufficient to heal the son, coupled, with Misdaeus' declaration of faith as he, too, becomes a Christian.

A very different account of "becoming Christian" comes from the *Letter of Severus of Minorca on the Conversion of the Jews*, which narrates how the entire Jewish population of the tiny island of Minorca, 540 persons in all, converted to Christianity in the space of a single week, in February 418 (Bradbury 1996). According to the *Letter*, the Christians on Minorca were suddenly seized by a desire to convert the substantial and influential Jewish community there not long after an unnamed priest (perhaps Paul Orosius) brought some relics of the protomartyr, St. Stephen, to a church in Magona (modern Mahon or Mao) on the eastern end of the island. Severus' *Letter* is full of evasive language, not the least because the likely events—Christian destruction of a licit Jewish synagogue—were illegal in the early fifth century, but its outlines are clear enough. Initially, Christians and Jews agree to some sort of public debate, for which, the author says, the Christians prepare by studying the scripture, and the Jews prepare by stockpiling weapons in the local synagogue in Magona. On the appointed day, Christians from Jamona, the western town, miraculously travel the thirty miles overland to Magona in a few hours. Before the debate can take place, Severus accuses the Jews of storing up weapons, and Jews and Christians alike set out to the synagogue to verify whether this is so.

While they are walking, violence breaks out. The instigators are allegedly "certain Jewish women," who throw down stones on the Christians from some higher vantage point. Roused from their thus-far restrained and gentle behavior, the Christians pick up the stones to throw at the Jews. Miraculously, the author claims, no one is hurt, except for one greedy slave. But somehow, after this harmless stone-throwing, the Jews retreat and the Christians gain control of the synagogue, taking care, of course, not to steal or loot anything (which was also illegal). With similar brevity and avoidance of agency, human or otherwise, the author then says that "fire consumed the synagogue itself" and all its ornaments. With the Jews now in shock at the devastation of the synagogue, the Christians retreat to the church and pray for the conversion of the Jews.

Much of the remainder of the *Letter* is devoted to accounts of how various Jews converted over the next several days, many after various small miracles occur, and how lovingly the Christians received them into the church. The author closes with the conversion accounts of three women who held out until the very end (Kraemer 2009, 2011). All their conversions are constructed in terms of female resistance to, and then subordination to, appropriate male authority. One woman, initially distraught at the conversion of her husband, deserts his house and flees, with various female companions, to a remote cave, where she remains implacable and furious at her husband. Only after the water in the wine vats turns to sweetest honey does she return, chastened and docile, a dutiful wife who now submits to her husband's decision and accepts Christ. Another woman, equally resistant, remains confined to her husband's home while her husband and a large crowd of "the brothers" pressure her to convert, using a range of tactics from threats to tears to prayers. According to Severus, it is these non-violent forms—prayer, prostration, and weeping—that ultimately lead her to convert. The third woman flees from Minorca on a ship, a rather desperate move in this part of the Mediterranean in mid-February, only to be blown back to the island. There she throws herself at the feet of Severus himself, and begs Severus to accept her and her two twin daughters into the church.

With this, the conversion of the 540 Jews of Minorca is complete. Severus notes that the Jews are now bearing the expense not only of leveling what remained of their synagogue but also of building a new basilica, whose stones they even carry on their own shoulders (30.2). He closes with an exhortation to his reader(s) to "take up Christ's zeal against the Jews, but do so for the sake of their eternal salvation" (31.2–3).

While these accounts are by no means the only conversion narratives from antiquity, accounts of exactly how people became Christian are less common than we might expect, especially given the considerable numbers of people who are likely to have done so. (Some people, of course, would have become Christian merely by being raised in Christian households, as is the presumption of Christian texts such as the pseudo-Pauline pastoral epistles, 1 and 2 Timothy and Titus). Many narratives about new Christians contain no accounts of their protagonists' conversion, for example the martyrdom of a young Roman matron in North Africa and her co-catachumens in the well-known *Martyrdom of Saints Perpetua and Felicitas*. Justin Martyr tells a particularly intriguing story with marked affinities to that of Mygdonia and other women in the apocryphal *Acts*, about an unnamed Roman matron whose adoption of the discipline of Christian philosophy leads her to renounce sexual and other excess, and ultimately results in the death of her teacher, on charges brought by her aggrieved husband (2 Apology 2). He says nothing, however, about how the matron came to study with her teacher and adopt Christian practices and beliefs.

The accounts offered here are representative of the evidence we have and the difficulties they pose. None claims to have been authored by a woman. No Christian women are even known to have written anything before the fourth century (although some scholars continue to think that the *Martyrdom of Perpetua* contains a first-hand diary). Some scholars have speculated that women may have written one or more of the apocryphal *Acts*, but there is neither a consensus on this issue nor adequate evidence (Davies 1980; MacDonald 1983; Kraemer 1991b, 2011). None of these even purports to be a first-person account of self-transformation, although the author of the *Letter of Severus* does claim to be an active participant in the events it narrates, and the story of Lydia and her companions comes from a portion of Acts written in a first-person-plural voice, seeming to be the report of persons accompanying Paul. The canonical Acts acknowledges that it narrates events that took place some time earlier, an acknowledgment that raises questions for historians about the events' veracity even as their utility for the overall rhetorical interests of its author are palpable. The apocryphal *Acts* are even more transparently fictitious and fantastic, and seem often to be elaborating on elements of the canonical Acts. At best, they may reflect some degree of verisimilitude. The artifice of the *Letter of Severus of Minorca* is similarly demonstrable, so much so that for many years it was thought to be a complete fabrication from the seventh century, although more recent scholarship considers it to be fifth-century, and to contain some useful historical information about contemporaneous events (Bradbury 1996; Kraemer 2009, 2011).

Not long after the canonical Acts was written, and perhaps contemporaneously with the earliest of the apocryphal *Acts*, a harsh critic of emergent Christianity named Celsus claimed that Christian teachers only sought out the ignorant, the stupid, the uneducated, and the young, and were only able to persuade "the foolish, dishonorable and stupid, and only slaves, women and little children" (Origen, *Against Celsus* 3.44). He characterized these teachers as menial men whose sphere of operations was private houses and who endeavored to undermine the authority of fathers and "schoolmasters," inviting women and little children to come to "the wooldresser's shop, or to the cobbler's or the washerwoman's shop, that they may learn perfection." Celsus' rhetoric was not unique to anti-Christian writers. Christian authors could also deploy similar rhetoric in opposition to other Christian teachers, such as the author of 2 Timothy (writing in the name of Paul), who "predicts" that unscrupulous men will worm their way into the houses of *gunaikaria*—"ditsy" women incapable of comprehending truth, and easily swayed.

Celsus' critique survives, ironically, only through its refutation by the third-century Christian biblical scholar and theologian Origen of Caesarea. Origen concedes that Christian teachers attract significant numbers of women, children, and uneducated men. But he responds that it calls such persons to make them better, to "deliver women from licentiousness and from perversion caused by their associates, and from all mania for theaters and dancing, and from superstition" (3.56) and also calls persons "much superior to them" (3.49).

In nineteenth- and twentieth-century historiography, Celsus' characterization was frequently reproduced, if more with the valence of Origen than that of Celsus: many women were drawn to Christianity, not because of their inferior intellect and weakness for charlatans (a characterization to which, it should be noted, many ancient Christian authors assented) but because it enabled them to overcome the inherent defects of their sex.

Perhaps most famously, numerous editions of Adolph Harnack's classic and highly influential *Mission and Expansion of the Christian Church in the First Three Centuries*, drawing on the canonical gospels, Acts, the apocryphal *Acts*, and other ancient accounts, asserted that "Christianity was laid hold of by women in particular, and . . . the percentage of Christian women, especially among the upper classes, was larger than that of Christian men" (1908: 73). Generations of subsequent scholars regularly repeated Harnack's assertion without much further investigation or analysis (Lieu 1998), in service of various arguments. In the late twentieth century, Christian theologians along the ideological spectrum (from Schüssler Fiorenza 1983 to Witherington 1984) touted the apparent demographic prominence of women as evidence not only for the egalitarian nature of the earliest movement(s) around Jesus of Nazareth but of Jesus himself. While dissenting from Origen's view of women as sharing Eve's essential inferiority to men and vulnerability to deceit, many contemporary scholars concurred that becoming Christian was universally good for women (even when it came at substantial cost), and they offered various accounts of the precise benefits. Almost a century after Harnack, a prominent sociologist of religion still presumed the essential accuracy of Celsus' calumny and Harnack's historiography, minus, at least, any apparent theological interest one way or the other (Stark 1996; see also Castelli 1998; Hopkins 1998).

At the same time, other scholars have increasingly critiqued both the demographic claim and the explanations for why women might have adopted Christian practices and beliefs. Observing that many ancient Christian writers characterize practices and beliefs they label "heretical" as being particularly attractive to women, or even the work of women themselves, some have argued that these, and other, accounts reflect not reliable demographics but "a rhetoric which identifies women with non-normative or marginalized religion" (Lieu 1998; see also Kraemer 2011). All those ancient elite male authors writing about women are evidencing not the presence of women but rather women "as a topic of concern." Although scholars disagree over the extent to which such rhetorical anxiety might be rooted in historical reality (Matthews 2001; Osiek and MacDonald 2005), most would agree that mistaking rhetorical women for real women makes for bad history.

3   Social History

Until relatively recently, the analysis of the dynamics and mechanisms of becoming Christian in antiquity were largely studied as though Christianity was unique, an assumption undergirding much of the study of Christianity more generally (Gager 1975; Smith 2004). The classic and much-critiqued work of A. D. Nock (1933) privileged conversion to Christianity (and perhaps more generously, conversion to monotheistic religions) over adherence to other "new" ancient religions (such as the spread of the worship of Isis, Cybele, or Mithras in the Roman period), without any recourse to comparative, cross-cultural analysis. Further, most, if not all, scholars writing about these issues were Christians, if of divers stripes, who presumed that becoming Christian was inevitably good. That Celsus might have been onto something in his association of Christianity particularly with women and with lower-class men was potentially disturbing, while considering the role of social factors, and the possibility of non-religious motivations for becoming Christian, was potentially unnerving. Even less considered was the possibility that persons coerced into becoming Christians might not have found it a particularly beneficial experience, whether enslaved persons or household members otherwise compelled to become Christians before the fourth century or the far greater numbers of Jews, Samaritans, and the majority of those polytheists who were increasingly coerced in various forms from the fourth century on (MacMullen 1997), as the example of Severus in this essay suggests.

More recent scholarship, though, has paid considerable attention to the lessons to be learned from the analysis of new religious movements that draws on contemporary ethnography and sociology as well as on historical instances (Gager 1975; Stark 1996; Beard et al. 1998; Sanders 2002). Such studies have delineated various stages in the process of conversion or transformation, beginning with the larger *context* in which such processes take place and ending with the ultimate *consequences* of change for the persons involved (Rambo 1993; see also Sanders 2002). The intermediate stages include crisis, quest, encounter, interaction, and commitment. These studies rarely seem to pay sufficient attention to gender differences, although gender matters significantly in the assessment of these stages in becoming Christian for women in antiquity.

These studies have shown, for instance, that "conversion" (a term that some scholars contest, preferring the language of "transformation," or even of "commitment") is always a process, not a single event; it is contextual, influencing and influenced by "a matrix of relationships, expectations and situations," and it always has a multiplicity of causes (Rambo 1993: 5), often inter-related and cumulative. Social networks are crucial, for both drawing individuals into new movements and maintaining their new commitments. Stark and Bainbridge, for instance, found that a third of Mormon conversions came from meetings arranged through other Mormons, and half occurred when "contact with missionaries took place in the home of [a] Mormon friend or relative" (1980: 1396). Only a tiny fraction came through cold-calling. Virtually *no* conversions (Mormon or otherwise) occurred apart from such networks. Conversely, defections from such movements are in many instances very high.

These studies have also illuminated the initial dynamics between converts and the persons who facilitate their conversion (sometimes called "advocates"). In the encounter stage, advocates endeavor to meet the prospective converts where they are, as it were: communicating the new practices in an understandable manner, and exhibiting some initial flexibility and negotiation. Prospective converts oscillate between old and new beliefs, gradually eliminate more and more elements of their prior practices, take up new practices to replace those abandoned, and sometimes even revert back to their earlier practices (Sanders 2002: 629).

The immediate applicability of the dynamics of new religious movements (as such new movements are often designated) to early Christianity and the ancient world continues to be contentious. Many modern new religious movements seem to be implicated in concerns about modernity (and American modernity at that), which might make them less applicable to antiquity. Perhaps more importantly, many scholars locate the appeal of new religious movements in their ability to address these contemporary crises, thus invoking a form of deprivation theory that many other scholars find discomfiting precisely because a theory that at least some religion, or religious choice, is prompted by deprivation of any sort threatens, at a minimum, the idea that conversion is about "religious truth."

Nevertheless, the findings of recent studies prove highly relevant to Christian antiquity (Sanders 2002). The ancient Christian examples cited here both conform to the evidence of these studies in some ways and confound them in others. For instance, accounts of instant receptivity to the new teachings of a traveling apostle, such as Mygdonia's response to Thomas (or Thecla's to Paul in the now relatively well-known *Acts of Paul and Thecla*, replicated in numerous other similar stories) conflict with research that suggests conversion is a process, rather than the result of a singular moment. (Such research also recognizes, though, that autobiographical and other narratives written after the fact often conform to paradigms of transformation that do construct conversion as a singular moment.)

Many persons who join modern new religious movements have experienced some kind of crisis that either predisposes or actually triggers them to do so. Some of our texts are consistent with this, while others are not. The *Acts of Thomas* says nothing about what might have made Mygdonia receptive to Thomas' particular form of Christian ascetic teaching, nor her nurse, Marcia. The young prince Vazan is said to have already been devoted to celibacy, but no explanation for this is available from the narrative. In the numerous conversion accounts in the canonical Acts of the Apostles, set after the death and resurrection of Jesus, predisposing triggers such as the illness of a child are generally invisible, in contrast to the canonical gospels, which often narrate such triggers. There, women (and men) are regularly persuaded that Jesus is Messiah after seeing him perform a miracle, usually a healing or an exorcism of a demon (themselves often seen as the causes of various kinds of illnesses), and occasionally bringing back to life someone who has very recently died. Sometimes the sequence is reversed: Jesus performs a miracle for women (and men) who already trust in him.

The Gospel according to Luke (but not the three other canonical gospels) claims that Jesus healed Mary Magdalene of seven demons. It is at best implicit that this healing prompted Mary to follow Jesus, and, as in other stories, readers might be expected to think that Mary's trust in Jesus led him to exorcise those demons. Further, whether or not this story is the author's fabrication, it may be part of a Lukan effort to denigrate the role and authority of Mary (similar to the absence of Mary as a witness to Jesus' resurrection in Luke). Since sinning was often understood to render one vulnerable to demonic possession, it may imply that Mary was once a serious sinner. Thus it may be useless as evidence for the impetus to follow Jesus.

In the canonical gospels, many women who follow Jesus share some striking demographic characteristics. They easily qualify as deprived by a multiplicity of criteria. Most are poor villagers (as is true of most of Jesus' male followers as well). In addition to being marginal simply by being women in a culture that privileged men, they are often marginal within ancient norms for femininity, especially for free women. Variously, they tend to be old enough to be married but are not, married but childless, widowed, or in a long-standing state of ritual impurity. They are women accused of sexual impropriety (although the best-known of these examples, the woman about to be stoned on charges of adultery in John 8, is actually a later insertion). Several stories involve mothers with stricken children (and no apparent husbands) who seek Jesus' healing power. Married women with living husbands and healthy children are conspicuously absent from these narratives. These stories must thus be used with extreme caution as reliable representations of women who first followed Jesus (Kraemer and D'Angelo 1999).

Somewhat better evidence is found, perhaps, in the letters of Paul, whose authorship is undisputed. Written in the two decades or so after the death of Jesus, these letters identify various women as active in efforts to "preach" Christ in non-Judean contexts, but they say nothing about how such women came to be part of these groups. (Paul does acknowledge that some were actually "in Christ" before his own revelatory experience, and indicates that he was personally responsible for baptizing a few persons.) Their names suggest that they (like the men) are not of the elite ranks, and are perhaps a mix of free, freed, and even enslaved women. A few might be Judean (Prisca being the more obvious example), but the majority seem to be non-Judean. None are identified by Paul as married, although some seem to be part of missionary pairs that might (also) be spouses: Prisca and Aquila (whom Acts, but not Paul, explicitly calls married); Andronicus and Junia (Romans 16.7); Philologus and Julia; and Nereus and his "sister" (Romans 16.15). Virtually none are identified as mothers, with the exception of the mother of Rufus, whom Paul calls "my mother as well" (Romans 16.13). Some scholars have suggested that many of these early Christians suffered from a kind of status inconsistency that resulted from being, for instance, "independent women with moderate wealth" or freedpersons with more money than rank and social standing. In this view, itself a moderated form of relative-deprivation theory, Paul's Christ cult would have held particular appeal for such persons, with its emphasis on oneness in Christ; the irrelevance of conventional distinctions of noble birth, ethnicity, and gender; and the refusal of norms of wisdom and foolishness. This view is consistent with what many contemporary studies have found.

In the canonical Acts, many if not most of the women who become Christian, or are portrayed as sympathetic to Christians, are said to be elite women, and there is little indication that they share the extreme marginalization of poor, widowed, childless villagers. As they are represented, at least, it seems harder to explain their interest in Christian preaching within models of relative deprivation and status inconsistency, although some scholars have focused on Luke's seeming description of some of these persons as Gentiles with some prior interest in Judean practices to argue that they, too, may have suffered from some status inconsistency that the new Christian teachings addressed (Zetterholm 2003).

In the apocryphal *Acts*, many of the significant characters are elite, like Mygdonia and Tertia, and Thecla (said to be from the most prominent family in Iconium). Others, however, are of lower status: Mygdonia's nurse, Marcia; the four concubines of Agrippa in the Acts of Peter (33.4); an enslaved Hebrew flute player in another tale in the *Acts of Thomas*; and others. When scrutinized carefully, however, even the elite women turn out to share some elements of gendered marginalization: they are generally childless, for instance, and ill at ease in the roles expected of them.

The dynamics between advocates and potential converts in various early Christian narratives conform in some ways to the findings of contemporary research. The apocryphal Thomas is patient with Mygdonia but unyielding: his teachings are absolute and non-negotiable. Paul, however, could be construed as more accommodating and willing to negotiate, at least on some issues and with some correspondents. He writes to the Christ-group in Corinth, for instance, that while it is preferable to be celibate it is permissible to marry and have licit marital intercourse (1 Corinthians 7). While it is better not to eat meat that has been sacrificed to idols, it is not absolutely unacceptable to do so. Paul might be the ultimate example of the advocate who is willing to "go native" in order to bring his target audience to Christ: "I have become all things to all people, that I might by all means save some" (1 Corinthians 9.22). Women prophesying with their heads uncovered, however, appears to be a practice Paul cannot sanction, even while the Corinthians clearly seem willing to engage in their own experiments on this and other issues.

Prospective converts, for their part, conform somewhat less to contemporary paradigms. Rather than the wavering between old and new beliefs, or the gradual process of relinquishing old practices and the acquisition of new ones, early Christian accounts more typically narrate a trajectory of transformation that is continuous (if not necessarily instantaneous) and permanent. Nevertheless, numerous sources, including Paul's letters, contain evidence that some number of prospective converts do return to their prior practices.

In new religious movements, converts are increasingly "encapsulated" through a combination of new relationships, new rituals, new roles, and the acquisition of a new rhetoric. Here, again, the canonical Acts provides the least representation of such processes, while the letters of Paul, the apocryphal *Acts*, and even the canonical stories of Jesus' encounters with various followers provide fuller representations, often consonant with what we might expect. Mygdonia, for instance, is drawn into a close web of personal relationships, not only with Thomas, who as wandering apostle may be expected to leave soon (and who is, in fact, martyred at the end of the story), but with her own nurse, Marcia; with Vazan; his wife Mnesara; the captain Siphor and his family; and the queen, Tertia. Interestingly, all of these were already within Mygdonia's social orbit, even while the new group crosses some social boundaries, in its inclusion, for instance, of the servant, Marcia (who may even be enslaved), and the captain Siphor and his family (and perhaps others). The *Acts of Thomas* contains rather elaborate descriptions of the transformation rituals that incorporate the new practitioners and mark them off from their former associates, including anointing with oil, baptism, new clothing, and the consumption of a eucharist that seems to use water, not wine. Continuing ritual performances, though, are not mentioned, although Thomas is said to appoint Siphor as presbyter and Vazan as a deacon before his death, establishing a few offices and a form of future governance for the small community. In the Acts, Thomas delivers numerous extensive speeches to Mygdonia and others that, as expected, provide both the characters in the narrative and the readers/hearers of the narrative with a rhetoric with which to "conceptualize and interpret the changes involved" in this particular form of being Christian. Similar instances of this may be found throughout the apocryphal *Acts*, with some particularly lovely examples in the Acts of Andrew (such as Andrew's speech to Stratocles in Acts of Andrew 7).

Ancient narratives focus little on the long-term consequences of conversion. Like classic fairy tales and quest narratives, they often end with the equivalent of "and they lived happily ever after," even when the ending is the martyrdom of the facilitating apostle (Perkins 1995). In the canonical Acts, we know nothing of what happens to the apparently many persons who accept Christ: they vanish from the narrative as quickly as they appear. In the *Acts of Thomas*, Mygdonia and Tertia are simply said to live out their lives as they wished. The *Acts of (Paul and) Thecla* is rather unusual in providing at least some indication of the consequences of Thecla's transformation. Before setting out, with Paul's commissioning, to teach the word of God, Thecla reconciles with her mother, who had earlier opposed her refusal of marriage and her ascetic, Christian renunciation. In what is probably the earliest version, Thecla simply devotes the remainder of a long life to teaching the word; in other accounts, she dies a kind of martyr's death. Interestingly, it is often accounts that are not explicitly about conversion that show us more of the consequences of "becoming Christian." Justin Martyr details how his unnamed matron is enmeshed in a close network of other Christians (while continuing her prior social networks at least to some degree) as well as her protracted efforts to persuade her husband to renounce the dissolute life and adopt Christian philosophical discipline, and the legal wranglings that followed his refusal. But, frustratingly, once those affairs lead to the prosecution of her teacher and his other followers, the matron disappears from the account entirely. Similarly, the *Martyrdom of Saints Perpetua and Felicitas* narrates the consequences of becoming Christian in high relief: the incorporation into new social networks, often configured as family; the conflicts with natal family members who object to the conversion; and some indication of the structure, practices, and teachings of the new group.

The partial consonance and partial dissonance between these ancient accounts of transformation and contemporary studies can be explained in various ways. Where they differ, one might argue that contemporary models do not apply to antiquity or are even wrong in some larger sense. But it is precisely where ancient accounts differ that we can often see rhetorical interests at work, suggesting that ancient authors had many reasons to obscure the actual social processes at work.

This is particularly true in the case of conversion narratives about women. It is particularly telling that the canonical Acts conform the least to what we might expect. Acts tells numerous stories of elite women and men regularly persuaded by effective rhetoric, which they hear in public performances: in synagogues, in the agora, in audiences before various courts. These accounts counter the claims of Celsus rather startlingly. First, elite, educated men are regularly persuaded of the rightness of Christian teachings, countering Celsus' accusation that only women, children, and ignorant, lower-class men find them compelling. Second, Acts counters the charge that the women who do accept Christian teachings lack discernment. Rather, the women who "become" Christian in Acts are elite, respectable persons, persuaded not by foolish teachings or misleading displays of power, which a *magos* like Simon could manage, but by wise teaching. Third, Acts places these elite, discerning women in public but respectable venues, implicitly accompanied appropriately by men, not in the suspect shops of woolworkers, out of the sight and knowledge of husbands and fathers. A similar argument might be made for Justin Martyr's representation of the Roman matron who adopts the rigorous discipline of Christian philosophy, demonstrating her respectability, her elite status (she has close connections to the emperor himself), her education, and her powers of discernment. Although Acts seems to have been composed at least a few decades earlier than Justin's *Apology* and Celsus' *True Doctrine*, both Justin and Acts are responding to the kinds of accusations Celsus makes, if not, probably, to the *True Doctrine* directly.

4   The Countercase of Severus of Minorca

All the accounts considered so far presume that persons who "became" Christian did so voluntarily and not under compulsion. Reading more closely, this may not quite be the case: when male characters such as Siphor in the *Acts of Thomas* bring their whole households with them, or Paul writes that he baptized Stephanus and his household, it is impossible for us to know how to envision the consent of the members of those households—wives, minor children, enslaved persons, and freedpersons. But the example of the *Letter of Severus of Minorca* presents us with a very different case, of Jews in the fifth century who are coerced through diverse strategies into accepting Christ (Kraemer 2009, 2011). Severus and his Christian contemporaries uniformly saw this as the product of divine intervention, and he endeavors to persuade us that, ultimately, the Jews themselves shared this interpretation. Yet it seems fairly clear that Severus went to great lengths to mask whatever historical and social processes underlay his account, both before and even after the events he narrates. His reasons for doing so elude us, although he may have done so at least partly because many of the events that transpire in the narrative were illegal in the fifth century, including the episodes of violence, the burning of the synagogue, the removal of its books and furnishings, and the dismantling of the walls, all of which occur in the text without apparent human agency or intent (except the miraculously harmless stone-throwing scene).

Severus' account, as artfully deceitful as it may be, nevertheless retains elements of the kinds of coercions that could be applied to resistant Jews. Some of these were subtle and social: an associate who has already converted tells the head of the community that, if the latter converts, he will retain his social standing and authority. Two leaders of the community end their speech imploring their fellow Jews to join them in becoming Christian by saying that, even if others do not, they and their households will accept Christ, perhaps implying that they compelled or at least expected members of their households, especially wives and children, but perhaps also servants, to convert as well. Human coercion was applied in various forms to the woman pressured for days by her husband and a band of Christian "brothers," while divine pressure in the form of unfavorable winter storms and winds (cast, in fact, as analogous to the experience of the biblical Jonah) compelled the last holdout to accept Christ. As in the cases of apparently voluntary conversions, households and social networks play a significant role in accomplishing these changes, but here we gain some sense of their potential for coercion.

The account also points to the consequences of such conversions. Not only, of course, is the synagogue destroyed and replaced with a church, but the Jews build the church themselves. Severus would have his readers see this as the Jews' own desire—a colonializing fantasy, perhaps (Jacobs 2004)—but it is equally easy to see it, if it has any historical basis, as another instance of the consequences of coerced conversion. In the narrative, acceptance of Christ, or resistance to such acceptance, temporarily ruptures family relations, and perhaps even did so permanently. The wife of the head of the Jewish community is said to be on the neighboring island of Majorca when all this transpires, and is never herself said to convert: the text itself gives us some grounds to imagine that her husband's conversion ruptured the marriage. The Jews on Minorca appear to have extensive ties to other Jews off the island, and one wonders what the impact of the former's corporate conversion might have been. We can only speculate on how the Jews of Minorca might have come to think about their own transformation, and its impact on their social relations and their family structures (if, again, actual historical events underlie this account). One might be tempted to seek analogies in the better historical data for how other groups coerced into converting responded, such as those for Jews and Muslims forced to become Christians in early modern Europe, but that is beyond the limits of this essay. And last, the *Letter of Severus* allows us to think about these issues with regard to Jews who were pressured into becoming Christian, but many of these may also have applied equally to the multitudes of practitioners of traditional ancient Mediterranean religions who were also pressured to become Christian from the fourth century onward (MacMullen 1997; Frankfurter 1998).

5 Conclusions

It seems clear, then, that there are significant limitations to what we really know about women becoming Christians from the mid-first century through the late fifth century. The claims of Celsus and Harnack alike that Christian teachings and practice appealed disproportionately to women (apparently without further discrimination) cannot be substantiated from the available data. The utility of stories about women for various rhetorical purposes, not to mention, in many instances, their demonstrable fictitious nature, undermines our confidence in any of these as reliable sources for ancient social practices. To answer questions about whether, for instance, becoming Christian was appealing to women for different reasons than for men, or whether the consequences of becoming Christian were different for women from those for men, requires a combination of judicious use of ancient sources and arguments from contemporary analogies and theories. At every turn, these questions must also be carefully parsed for different ancient social categories: elite women, free non-elite women, enslaved women, married women, divorced and widowed women, childless women.

Consistently with many contemporary studies that suggest that gender-related misfortune is often the trigger event for women voluntarily adopting new practices (Sered 1994), many accounts of women becoming Christian involve such instances: impoverished widows with ill children, marital stresses, gynecological disorders, and others. Many narratives revolve around issues of the obedience of wives to husbands. In the apocryphal *Acts*, women's conversion is routinely in opposition to their husbands, partly because in these traditions becoming celibate is a non-negotiable component of becoming Christian. Already in 1 Corinthians, Paul responds to the conflicts caused by marriages where one spouse is "in Christ" and the other is not, without suggesting that the spouse in Christ was more likely to be female than male. But, in actuality, women whose husbands chose new practices were more likely to be expected to follow them (as various references to the conversion of a man and his "household" suggest), while women who chose new practices contrary to the wishes of their husbands could expect considerable resistance and conflict. This is particularly apparent in the account of Severus, both in statements attributed to husbands who seem to presume their wives' acquiescence and in the accounts of women whose husbands pressure them to accept Christ (Kraemer 2009, 2011).

Becoming Christian meant adopting new practices, such as weekly assemblies for prayers, singing, and probably dancing, and for a communal meal. Christians heard, formulated, and repeated "authoritative" traditions about the God of Israel and his son, Jesus. They prophesized and spoke "in tongues" (perhaps meaning speech not immediately recognizable as languages they ordinarily spoke, although this is debated), the former, if not also the latter, a practice that often required interpretation by authorized persons. They engaged in charitable activities, including providing for the poor, widows, and orphans, and caring for the sick. They received ethical instructions from teachers, and held themselves to (new) ethical standards that they saw as more stringent than those of other people, including more stringent sexual ethics and other bodily disciplines. They may have abstained from ordinary activities on one day each week (the Lord's day). Followers of Christ appear to have ceased some or all of their former cultic practices, especially the performance of animal sacrifice. Early martyrdom narratives and other sources portray refusal to sacrifice to traditional Roman gods as the basis for Roman prosecution. For some new Christians, of course, these practices would have been more of a radical change than for others. For Jews who became Christians, much of this would already have been familiar: the engagement with biblical traditions, the emphasis on charitable activities, Sabbath observance, abstinence from sacrifices to deities other than the God of Israel (itself virtually impossible after the destruction of the Jerusalem temple in 70 CE). So, too, for the most part, for Samaritans who became Christians. Yet here, too, becoming Christian entailed significant changes, such as reinterpreting authoritative traditions to demonstrate the claims about Jesus; ceasing to celebrate the Sabbath on Saturday and marking out the Lord's Day, Sunday, instead; and celebrating Easter rather than Passover (or at least a radically reconceived Passover). Many Jews who became Christians probably gave up their distinctive practices of circumcision and kosher laws, as well as the celebration of distinctive festivals and other observances, but some may not have.

Both the adoption of new practices and the rejection of old practices had vastly different implications for women, as a few examples demonstrate. Women prophets in the Corinthian assemblies challenged ancient gender distinctions in ways that male prophets, grounded in an ancient cultural logic of public speech as inherently masculine, did not. Paul insists that Corinthian women should cover their heads while they speak in public while men should not, appealing to everything from the order of creation in Genesis to the laws of nature to the practices of all the other assemblies. Women may be the recipients of instruction, but they are far less frequently represented as teachers, and many texts anathematize women teachers, at least as early as 2 Timothy, one of several epistles forged in Paul's name.

The rejection of animal sacrifice had different implications and consequences for women. Mediterranean sacrificial practices, regardless of whether the deity involved was male or female, seem disproportionately to have been the province of men, including the sacrificial banquets where sacrificed meat was distributed and consumed, although there is some evidence for sacrifices by priestesses (Connelly 2007). At least one highly influential study has argued that gender is often implicated in systems of animal sacrifice, serving to create male genealogies and lineages that obliterate the actual roles of women in procreation and ancestry (Jay 1992). For women to renounce animal sacrifice, then, might have been very different than for men.

It is important to note that many scholars have suggested that becoming Christian improved women's standing both in comparison to being Judean and to being polytheist. Christianity, in this view, was far more egalitarian than Judaism, including women in all Christian practices, where Judean women had been excluded from the priesthood, from study in rabbinic academies, and perhaps from the synagogue. Being Christian is thought to have appealed to women particularly for an ideology of the dissolution of gender expressed in Galatians 3.28: "there is neither Judean nor Hellene, there is neither free nor slave, there is no 'male and female,' for you are all one in Christ Jesus" (my translation). Being Christian afforded at least some women, for some time, opportunities to be free of the gender restrictions of ancient Mediterranean culture broadly (for instance, to travel, to be unmarried and childless, to live without being subordinated to a father or a husband).

These are complex issues. Much of this comparison is invidious, grounded far more in long-standing Christian anti-Jewish rhetoric than in any dispassionate assessment of the available evidence (Kraemer 1999). It combines some accurate observations (women were not Israelite priests, nor ancient rabbis) with many erroneous claims, both about Jews and Christians. Women's presence and participation in ancient synagogues, and the denigration of women in rabbinic sources, are complex subjects, as are, similarly, the exclusion of women from early Christian offices, from the later Christian priesthood, and from "speaking in the assembly" in 1 Corinthians 14.33b–36, and the many ancient Christian teachings that subordinate women to men, children to parents, and enslaved persons to their owners. To determine how much issues of gender and the options for participation in communal life factored into actual women's choices in antiquity requires walking a very fine line, exquisitely attentive to the misuses to which such inquiry can be put.

And last, becoming Christian was a very different experience for those, both women and men, who did not do so out of deliberate and uncoerced choice. Up to the fourth century this may have already been true, to some extent, for persons who had only limited autonomy in the ancient Mediterranean, including women of all social classes, freeborn children, and enslaved persons. After the fourth century, though, it was true to some indeterminate extent for even more persons, including many who already were Christians of various sorts (Arians, miaphysites, and others), as the emergent and newly empowered orthodox church increasingly and effectively pressured residents of the empire to become not simply Christian but their particular sort of Christian.

RECOMMENDED FURTHER READING

English translations of many of the ancient sources surveyed in this essay are collected in Kraemer (2004); additional stories of women adopting ascetic forms of Christianity may be found in Elliott (1993). Sanders (2002) is a fine, relatively concise overview of the sources available in studying becoming Christian in the Roman period, and of many of the methodological and theoretical issues; it also contains an additional bibliography.

Readers wishing to pursue the subject of conversion more broadly might read Robbins (1988) and Rambo (1993). Rodney Stark, sometimes with William Bainbridge, has looked extensively at how new movements grow and survive, and his work on the Mormons is particularly instructive for thinking about early Christian growth (Stark 2001). His *Rise of Christianity: A Sociologist Reconsiders History* (1996) was extensively critiqued by several scholars in a 1998 special issue of the *Journal of Early Christian Studies* (6.2), but remains quite provocative and productive. Readers interested in the history of discussions about religious conversion in antiquity might wish to read Nock (1933), a brief, classic, and much-critiqued treatment (those with more fortitude might venture to tackle Harnack 1908).

Judith Lieu's arguments concerning the utility of ancient accounts of women's conversions to either Judaism or Christianity are incisive and insightful (Lieu 1998). Readers wishing to pursue these issues further might read Matthews (2001) on accounts of elite Roman women adopting either Jewish or Christian practices, especially in Josephus and in Luke-Acts, or Cooper (1996), as well as Kraemer (2011). There is a vast literature on broader issues concerning Christian women in the Roman period: some good places to start are MacDonald (1994), Kraemer and D'Angelo (1999), and Osiek and MacDonald (2005). Unavailable to the author until just before this essay went into production is Lipsett (2011), a literary analysis of eroticism and restraint in several conversion narratives that circulated among Christian readers in antiquity. Last, readers interested in a critical perspective on the effects of becoming Christian might read MacMullen (1997), an account of the pressures brought to bear on pagans in late antiquity.

Women in Late Antiquity
(Apart from Egypt): A Bibliography

General

Arjava, A. 2005. "A bibliography on women and the family in late antiquity and the early middle ages (2nd to 7th century AD)." In Muhlberger, S. (ed.), *The ORB: On-line Reference Book for Medieval Studies*. http://www.nipissingu.ca/department/history/muhlberger/orb/arja-va3.htm. Very comprehensive, including much Classical material as well.

Bitel, L. M. 2002. *Women in Early Medieval Europe, 400–1100*. Cambridge.

Clark, G. 1993. *Women in Late Antiquity: Pagan and Christian Lifestyles*. Oxford. A sensitive and comprehensive overview; this bibliography accordingly concentrates on more recent studies.

Gouma-Peterson, T. 1995. *Bibliography on Women in Byzantium*. Wooster, OH.

Kalavrezou, I. and Laiou, A. E. (eds.) 2003. *Byzantine Women and their World*. Cambridge.

Christian Women, Including the Development of Christian Asceticism for Women

Adkin, N. (ed.) 2003. *Jerome on Virginity: A Commentary on the "Libellus de Virginitate Servanda."* Cambridge.

Beagon, P. M. 1995. "The Cappadocian fathers, women, and ecclesiastical politics." *Vigiliae Christianae* 49: 165–79.

Bremmer, J. N. 1995. "Pauper or patroness: The widow in the early Christian Church." In Bremmer, J. N. and van den Bosch, L. (eds.), *Between Poverty and the Pyre: Moments in the History of Widowhood*. London. 31–57.

Breyfolge, T. 1995. "Magic, women, and heresy in the Late Empire: The case of Priscillianists." In Meyer, M. W. and Mirecki, P. A. (eds.), *Ancient Magic and Ritual Power*. Leiden. 435–54.

A Companion to Women in the Ancient World, First Edition. Edited by Sharon L. James and Sheila Dillon.
© 2012 John Wiley & Sons, Ltd. Published 2015 by John Wiley & Sons, Ltd.

Castelli, E. A. 2004. *Martyrdom and Memory: Early Christian Culture Making.* New York. Focuses include autobiography by Perpetua and the late-antique reception of Thecla.

Clark, E. A. 1998. "Holy women, holy words: Early Christian women and the 'linguistic turn.'" *JECS* 6: 413–30.

Clark, G. 1995. "Women and asceticism in late antiquity: The refusal of gender and status." In Wimbush, V. L. and Valantasis, R. (eds.), *Asceticism.* New York. 33–48.

Cloke, G. 1995. *This Female Man of God: Women and Spiritual Power in the Patristic Age, AD 350–450.* London.

Coon, L. 1997. *Sacred Fictions: Holy Women and Hagiography in Late Antiquity.* Philadelphia.

Dumais, M. 1993. *Les femmes Chrétiennes dans l'Empire Romain des deuxième et troisième siècles: De la quête d'autonomie à la dépendance.* Diss. Université Laval.

Elliot, D. 2008. "Tertullian, the angelic life, and the bride of Christ." In Bitel, L. M. and Lifschitz, F. (eds.), *Gender and Christianity in Medieval Europe: New Perspectives.* Philadelphia. 17–33.

Elm, S. 1994. *"Virgins of God": The Making of Asceticism in Late Antiquity.* Oxford. Rpt. 1996. Focuses in Asia Minor and in Egypt.

Gallego Franco, H. 1993. "La 'Cuestión femenina' en el primitivo cristianismo hispano: A propósito de los cánones V, XXXV y LXXXI del Concilio de Elvira." *Helmantica* 44: 237–45.

Gilchrist, R. 1994. *Gender and Material Culture: The Archaeology of Religious Women.* London.

Hoffman, D. L. 1995. *The Status of Women and Gnosticism in Irenaeus and Tertullian.* Lewiston, NY.

Kraemer, R. S. 2009. "Jewish women's resistance to Christianity in the early fifth century: The account of Severus, bishop of Minorca." *JECS* 17: 625–65.

LeMoine, F. J. 1996. "Jerome's gift to women readers." In Mathisen, R. W. and Sivan, H. S. (eds.), *Shifting Frontiers in Late Antiquity.* Aldershot. 230–41.

Mayer, W. 1999. "Constantinopolitan women in Chrysostom's circle." *Vigiliae Christianae* 53: 265–88.

——, 1999b. "Female participation in the late fourth-century preacher's audience." *Augustinianum* 39: 139–47.

Nolte, C. 1995. *Conversio und Christiantas: Frauen in der Christianisierung vom 5. bis 8. Jahrhundert.* Stuttgart.

Osiek, C. 2002. "Perpetua's husband." *JECS* 10: 287–90.

Power, K. 1995. *Veiled Desire: Augustine's Writing on Women.* London.

Rousseau, P. 1995. "'Learned women' and the development of a Christian culture in late antiquity." *Symbolae Osloenses* 70: 116–47.

Schulenburg, J. T. 1998. *Forgetful of their Sex: Female Sanctity and Society, ca. 500–1100.* Chicago.

Smith, J. A. 2001. *Ordering Women's Lives: Penitentials and Nunnery Rules in the Early Medieval West.* Aldershot.

Vidén, G. 1998. "St. Jerome on female chastity: Subjugating the elements of desire." *Symbolae Osloenses* 73: 139–57.

Vuolanto, V. 2002. "Male female euergetism in late antiquity: A study on Italian and Adriatic church floor mosaics." In Setälä, P., Berg, R., Hälikkaä, R., Keltanen, R. M., Pölönen, J., and Vuolanto, V. (eds.), *Women, Wealth and Power in the Roman World.* Rome. 245–302.

White, C. (Transl.) 2010. *Lives of Roman Christian Women.* London. In addition to the third-century Passion of Perpetua and Felicitas, select fourth- and fifth-century lives of dedicated Christian women and select prescripts of Jerome are included.

Other Religions in Women's Experience

Brooten, B. J. 2000. "Female leadership in the ancient synagogue." In Levine, L. I. and Weiss, Z. (eds.), *From Dura to Sepphoris: Studies in Jewish Art and Society in Late Antiquity*. Portsmouth, RI. 215–23

Spickermann, W. 1994. *"Mulieres ex voto": Untersuchungen zur Gotterverehrung von Frauen im romischen Gallien, Germanien und Raïen (1.-3. Jahrhundert n. Chr.)*. Bochum.

Non-Roman Women

Ausenda, G. 1999. "Kinship and marriage among the Visigoths." In Heather, P. J. (ed.), *The Visigoths from the Migration Period to the Seventh Century*. Woodbridge. 129–68.

Kitchen, J. 1998. *Saints' Lives and the Rhetoric of Gender: Male and Female in Merovingian Hagiography*. New York.

Peyroux, C. R. 2001. "Canonists construct the nun? Church law and women's monastic practice in Merovingian France." In Mathisen, R. W. (ed.), *Law, Society, and Authority in Late Antiquity*. Oxford. 242–55.

Stoneman, R. 1994. *Palmyra and its Empire: Zenobia's Revolt against Rome*. Ann Arbor, MI.

Royal Women

Allen, P. 1992. "Contemporary portrayals of the Byzantine Empress Theodora (A.D. 527–548)." In Garlick, B., Dixon, S., and Allen, P. (eds.), *Stereotypes of Women in Power: Historical Perspectives and Revisionist Views*. New York. 93–103.

Baharal, D. 1992. "The portraits of Julia Domna from the years 193–211 AD and the dynastic propaganda of L. Septimius Severus." *Latomus* 51: 110–18.

Bleckmann, B. 1994. "Constantina, Vetranio und Gallus Caesar." *Chiron* 24: 29–68.

Garland, L. 1999. *Byzantine Empresses: Women and Power in Byzantium, AD 527–1204*. London.

James, L. 2001. *Empresses and Power in Early Byzantium*. London. Covers the fourth to eighth centuries.

Lusnia, S. 1995. "Julia Domna's coinage and Severan dynastic propaganda." *Latomus* 54: 199–40.

Miller, D. A. "Byzantine sovereignty and feminine potencies." In Fradenburg, L. O. A. (ed.), *Women and Sovereignty*. Edinburgh. 250–63.

Pohlsander, H. A. 1995. *Helena: Empress and Saint*. Chicago.

Richlin, A. 1992. "Julia's jokes, Galla Placidia, and the Roman use of women as political icons." In Garlick, B., Dixon, S., and Allen, P. (eds.), *Stereotypes of Women in Power: Historical Perspectives and Revisionist Views*. New York. 65–91.

Family, Including Marriage (see also under Law, below)

Aubin, M. 2000. "More apparent than real? Questioning the difference in marital age between Christian and non-Christian women of Rome during the third and fourth centuries. *Ancient History Bulletin* 14: 1–13.

Dossey, L. 2008. "Wife beating and manliness in late antiquity." *Past and Present* 199: 3–40.

Evans-Grubbs, J. 1994. "'Pagan' and 'Christian' marriage: The state of the question." *JECS* 2: 361–412.

Giardina, A. 2000. "The family in the late Roman world." In Cameron, A., Ward-Perkins, B., and Whitby, M. (eds.), *The Cambridge Ancient History XIV, Late Antiquity: Empire and Successors, A.D. 425–600*. Cambridge. 392–415.

Hillner, J. 2003. "*Domus*, family, and inheritance: The senatorial family house in late antique Rome." *JRS* 93: 129–45.

Hunter, D. G. 2003. "Augustine and the making of marriage in Roman North Africa." *JECS* 11: 63–85.

Laiou, A. (ed.) 1993. *Consent and Coercion to Sex and Marriage in Ancient and Medieval Societies*. Washington, DC.

McGinn, T. A. J. 1999. "Widows, orphans, and social history." *Journal of Roman Archaeology* 12: 617–32.

Nathan, G. S. 2000. *The Family in Late Antiquity: The Rise of Christianity and the Endurance of Tradition*. London.

Phang, S. E. 2001. *The Marriage of Roman Soldiers (13 B.C. – A.D. 235): Law and Family in the Imperial Army*. Leiden.

Reynolds, P. L. 1994. *Marriage in the Western Church: The Christianization of Marriage during the Patristic and Early Medieval Periods*. Leiden.

Sivan, H. "Why not marry a Jew? Jewish-Christian marital frontiers in late antiquity." In Mathisen, R. W. (ed.), *Law, Society, and Authority in Late Antiquity*. Oxford. 208–19.

Vuolanto, V. 2003. "Selling a freeborn child: Rhetoric and social realities in the late Roman world." *Ancient Society* 33: 169–207.

Wood, I. N. 2000. "Family and friendship in the west." In Cameron, A., Ward-Perkins, B., and Whitby, M. (eds.), *The Cambridge Ancient History XIV, Late Antiquity: Empire and Successors, A.D. 425–600*. Cambridge. 416–36.

Gender Studies, Representation, and History of Ideas

Bailey, L. K. 2007. "'These are not men': Sex and drink in the Sermons of Caesarius of Arles." *JECS* 15: 23–43. Rhetoric of masculinity and social control.

Brakke, D. 2005. "The lady appears: Materializations of 'woman' in early monastic literature." In Martin, D. B. and Miller, P. C. (eds.), *The Cultural Turn in Late Ancient Studies: Gender, Asceticism, and Historiography*. Durham, NC. 25–39.

Brooten, B. J. 1996. *Love Between Women: Early Christian Responses to Female Homoeroticism*. Chicago.

Brundage, J. A. 1996. "The paradox of sexual equality in the Early Middle Ages." In Mathisen, R. W. and Sivan, H. S. (eds.), *Shifting Frontiers in Late Antiquity*. Aldershot. 256–64.

Cameron, A. 1998. "Love (and marriage) between women." *GRBS* 39: 137–56.

Cartlidge, D. 2004. "Thecla: The apostle who defied women's destiny." *Bible Review* 20: 24–33.

Castelli, E. 1991. "'I will make Mary male': Pieties of the body and gender transformation of Christian women in late antiquity." In Epstein, J. and Straub, K. (eds.), *Body Guards: The Cultural Politics of Gender Ambiguity*. New York. 29–49.

Clark, E. A. 1994. "Ideology, history, and the construction of women in late antique Christianity (ideological representation of the self according to the church fathers)." *JECS* 2: 155–84.

——, 2000. "Women, gender, and the study of Christian history." *Church History* 70: 395–426.

Clark, G. 1998. "Bodies and blood: Late antique debate on martyrdom, virginity and resurrection." In Montserrat, D. (ed.), *Changing Bodies, Changing Meanings: Studies on the Human Body in Antiquity*. London. 99–115.

Clarke, J. R. 2003. *Roman Sex: 100 BC to 250 AD*. New York.

Cooper, K. 1996. *The Virgin and the Bride: Idealized Womanhood in Late Antiquity*. Cambridge, MA.

Dickie, M. W. 2000. "Who practiced love-magic in classical antiquity and in the late Roman world?" *Classical Quarterly* 50: 563–83.

Dunn, G. D. 2005. "Rhetoric and Tertullian's *De Virginibus Velandis*." *Vigiliae Christianae* 59: 1–30.

Frankfurter, D. 2009. "Martyrology and the prurient gaze." *JECS* 17: 215–45.

French, D. R. 1998. "Maintaining boundaries: The status of actresses in early Christian society." *Vigiliae Christianae* 52: 293–318.

Grimm, V. 1995. "Fasting women in Judaism and Christianity in late antiquity." In Wilkins, J., Harvery, F. D., and Dobson, M. J. (eds.), *Food in Antiquity*. Exeter. 225–40.

Harvey, S. A. 2001. "Spoken words, voiced silence: Biblical women in Syriac tradition." *JECS* 9: 105–31.

Hemelrijk, E. A. 1999. *Matrona Docta: Educated Women in the Roman Elite from Cornelia to Julia Domna*. London.

Holden, A. 2008. "The abduction of the Sabine women in context: The iconography of late antique contorniate medallions." *American Journal of Archaeology* 112: 121–42.

James, L. (ed.) 1997. *Women, Men and Eunuchs: Gender in Byzantium*. London. The contributions address fourth-century and later topics.

——, (ed.) 1999. *Desire and Denial in Byzantium*. Aldershot.

Laiou, A. E. 1992. *Gender, Society, and Economic Life in Byzantium*. Aldershot.

Lateiner, D. 1997. "Abduction marriage in Heliodorus' *Aethiopica*." *GRBS* 38: 409–39.

McDonough, C. M. 2004. "Women at the Ara Maxima in the fourth century AD?" *CQ* 54: 655–8.

Miller, P. C. 2005. "Is there a harlot in this text? Hagiography and the grotesque." In Martin, D. B. and Miller, P. C. (eds.), *The Cultural Turn in Late Ancient Studies: Gender, Asceticism, and Historiography*. Durham, NC. 87–102.

Nathan, G. S. 1993. "Medicine and sexual practices in late antiquity." *Epoche* 18: 20–32.

Oppel, J. 1993. "Saint Jerome and the history of sex." *Viator* 24: 1–22.

Schade, K. 2003. *Frauen in der Spätantike: Status und Repräsentation, eine Untersuchung zur römischen und frühbyzantinen Bildniskunst*. Mainz.

Schlatter, S. J. F. W. 1995. "The two women in the mosaic of Santa Pudenziana." *JECS* 3: 1–24.

Stirling, L. M. 1997. "Late-Antique goddesses and other statuary at the Villa of La-Garenne-de-Nerac (Lot-en-Garonne)." *EMC/CV* 16: 149–75.

Usher, M. D. 1998. *Homeric Stitchings: The Homeric Centos of the Empress Eudocia*. Lanham.

Webb, R. 2002. "Female entertainers in late antiquity." In Easterling, P. and Hall, E. (eds.), *Greek and Roman Actors: Aspects of an Ancient Profession*. Cambridge. 282–303.

Law

Arjava, A. 2001. *Women and Law in Late Antiquity*. Oxford.

Beaucamp, J. 1998. "Les femmes et l'espace public à Byzance: Le cas des tribunaux." *Dumbarton Oaks Papers* 52: 129–43.

——, 2000. "Donne, patrimonio, chiesa." In Lanata, G. (ed.), *Il tardoantico alle soglie del Duemila: Diritto, religione, società*. Pisa. 249–65.

de Bonfils, G. 2000. "La 'terminologia matrimoniale' nelle costituzioni di Costanzo II: Uso consapevole della lingua e adattamento politico." In Bianco, O. and Tafaro, S. (eds.), *Il linguaggio dei giuristi romani: Atti del Convegno internazionale di studi, Lecce, 5–6 dicembre 1994*. Galatina. 9–22.

Evans Grubbs, J. 1993. "Marriage more shameful than adultery: Slave-mistress relationships, 'mixed marriages,' and late Roman law." *Phoenix* 47: 125–54.

——, 1995. *Law and Family in Late Antiquity: The Emperor Constantine's Marriage Legislation*. Oxford. Second edition 2010. Bristol.

——, 2000. "The slave who avenged her master's death: Codex Justinianus 1.19.1 and 7.13.1." *Ancient History Bulletin* 14: 81–8.

——, 2001. "Virgins and widows, show-girls and whores: Late Roman legislation on women and christianity." In Mathisen, R. W. (ed.), *Law, Society, and Authority in Late Antiquity*. Oxford. 220–41.

——, 2002. *Women and the Law in the Roman Empire: A Sourcebook on Marriage, Divorce, and Widowhood*. London.

Haase, R. 1994. "Justinian I. und der Frauenraub (raptus)." *Zeitschrift der Savigny-Stiftung für Rechtsgeschichte (Roman. Abt.)* 111: 113–21.

Kennell, S. H. 1991. "Women's hair and the law: Two case studies from late antiquity." *Klio* 73: 526–36.

Kueffler, M. 2007. "The marriage revolution in late antiquity: The Theodosian Code and later Roman marriage law." *Journal of Family History* 32: 343–70.

McGinn, T. A. J. 1997. "The legal definition of prostitute in late antiquity." *Memoirs of the American Academy in Rome* 42: 73–116.

Pölönen, J. 2002. "The division of wealth between men and women in Roman succession (ca. 50 BC–AD 250)." In Setälä, P., Berg, R., Hälikkaä, R., Keltanen, R. M., Pölönen, J., and Vuolanto, V. (eds.), *Women, Wealth and Power in the Roman World*. Rome. 147–79.

References

Abdalla, A. 1992. *Graeco-Roman Funerary Stelae from Upper Egypt*. Liverpool.

Abrahams, E. B. 1908. *Greek Dress: A Study of the Costumes Worn in Ancient Greece, From Pre-Hellenic Times to the Hellenistic Age*. London.

Abusch, T. 2002. *Mesopotamian Witchcraft: Toward a History and Understanding of Babylonian Witchcraft Beliefs and Literature*. Leiden.

Adamo Muscettola, S. 2000. "The sculptural evidence." In Miniero, P. (ed.), *The Archaeological Museum of the Phlegrean Fields in the Castle of Baia: The Sacellum of the Augustales at Miseno*. Naples. 29–45.

Adovasio, J. M., Soffer, O., and Page, J. 2007. *The Invisible Sex: Uncovering the True Roles of Women in Prehistory*. Walnut Creek, CA.

Ager, S. L. 2004. "Familiarity breeds: Incest and the Ptolemaic dynasty." *JHS* 125: 1–34.

Agrest, D., Conway, P., and Weisman, L. K. (eds.) 1996. *The Sex of Architecture*. New York.

Ajootian, A. 2007. "Praxiteles and fourth-century Athenian portraiture." In Schultz and von den Hoff (eds.): 13–33.

Albenda, P. 1983 "Western Asiatic women in the Iron Age: Their image revealed." Biblical Archaeologist 46: 82–8.

—— 1987. "Woman, child and family: Their imagery in Assyrian art." In Durand (ed.): 17–22.

Alberti, B. 2002. "Gender and the figurative art of Late Bronze Age Knossos." In Hamilakis (ed.): 98–117.

Alcock, S. and Osborne, R. (eds.) 1994. *Placing the Gods: Sanctuaries and Sacred Space in Ancient Greece*. Oxford.

Alexandri, A. 1994. *Gender Symbolism in Late Bronze Age Aegean Glyptic Art*. Diss., University of Cambridge.

—— 2009. "Envisioning gender in Aegean prehistory." In Kopaka (ed.): 19–24.

Alexandridis, A. 2004. *Die Frauen des Römischen Kaiserhauses. Eine Untersuchung ihrer bildlichen Darstellung von Livia bis Julia Domna*. Mainz.

A Companion to Women in the Ancient World, First Edition. Edited by Sharon L. James and Sheila Dillon.
© 2012 John Wiley & Sons, Ltd. Published 2015 by John Wiley & Sons, Ltd.

—— 2010. "Neutral bodies? Female portrait statue types from the late Republic to the second century CE." In Hales, S. and Hodos, T. (eds.), *Material Culture and Social Identities in the Ancient World*. Cambridge. 252–79.

Alexiou, S. 1958. "Η μινωική θεά μεθ' υψωμένων χειρών." *Κρητικά Χρονικά* 12: 179–299.

Alföldy, G. 1991. "Augustus und die inschriften: Tradition und innovation. Die geburt der imperialen epigraphik." *Gymnasium* 98: 289–324.

Al-Gailani Werr, L. 2008. "Nimrud seals." in Curtis et al. (eds.): 155–62.

Allason-Jones, L. 1988. "Small finds from the turrets on Hadrian's Wall." In Coulston, J. C. (ed.), *Military Equipment and the Identity of Roman Soldiers*. Oxford. 197–233.

—— 1991. "The Aemilia finger-ring." *Review (National Art Collections Fund)* 87: 126–9.

—— 1995. "'Sexing' small finds." In Rush (ed.): 22–32.

—— 1996. "The actress and the bishop: Evidence for working women in Roman Britain." In Devonshire, A. and Wood, B. (eds.), *Women in Industry and Technology from Prehistory to the Present Day*. London. 67–75.

—— 1998. "The women of Roman Maryport." In Wilson, R. J. A. (ed.), *Roman Maryport and its Setting: Essays in Memory of Michael G. Jarrett*. Penrith. 105–11.

—— 1999. "Women and the Roman Army in Britain." In Galsworthy, A. and Haynes, I. (eds.), *The Roman Army as a Community*. Portsmouth, RI. 41–51.

—— 2003a. "The family in Roman Britain." In Todd, M. (ed.), *A Companion to Roman Britain*. Oxford. 273–87.

—— 2003b. "The jet industry and allied trades in Roman Britain." In Wilson, P. and Price, J. (eds.), *Aspects of Industry in Roman Yorkshire and the North*. Oxford. 12–32.

—— 2005. *Women in Roman Britain*. Second edition. London.

—— 2009. "Some problems of the Roman Iron Age in North England." In Hanson, W. S. (ed.), *The Army and Frontiers of Rome*. Portsmouth, RI. 217–24.

—— (ed.) 2011. *Artefacts in Roman Britain: Their Purpose and Use*. Cambridge.

—— Forthcoming. "Women, the military and *patria potestas* in Roman Britain." In Bidwell, P. T. (ed.), *Roman Frontier Studies: Proceedings of the XX International Congress on Roman Frontier Studies*. Newcastle upon Tyne.

Allen, S. H. 2009. "Excavating women: Female pairings in early Aegean archaeology (1871–1918)." In Kopaka (ed.): 254–261.

Allison, P. E. 2006a. "Artefact distribution within the auxiliary fort at Ellingen: Evidence for building use and the presence of women and children." *BRGK* 87: 387–452.

—— 2006b. "Mapping for gender: Interpreting artefact distribution in Roman military forts in Germany." *Archaeological Dialogues* 13.1: 1–4.

—— 2007. "Engendering Roman domestic space." In Westgate et al. (eds.): 343–50.

—— 2008. "The women and children inside 1st- and 2nd-century forts: Comparing the archaeological evidence." In Brandl, U. (ed.), *Frauen und römisches Militär: Beiträge eines Runden Tisches in Xanten rom 7, bis 9, Juli 2005*: 120–39. British Archaeological Reports Int. Ser. 1759. Oxford.

—— 2009. "The women in the early forts: GIS and artefact distribution analyses in 1st and 2nd Germany." In Morillo, A., Hanel, N., and Martín, E. (eds.), *Limes XX. Roman Frontier Studies*. Madrid. 1193–201.

Allison, P. M. 2004. *Pompeian Households: An Analysis of the Material Culture*. Los Angeles, CA.

Alsebrook, M. A. 1992. *Born to Rebel: The Life of Harriet Boyd Hawes*. Oxford.

Amann, P. 2000. Die Etruskerin: Geschlechterverhältnis und stellung der frau im frühen etrurien (9.–5. Jh. V. Chr.). *Archäologische Forschungen* 5. Vienna.

Ammerman, R. M. 2002. *The Sanctuary of Santa Venera at Paestum II. The Votive Terracottas*. Ann Arbor, MI.

Ampolo, C. 1996. "Livio I,44,3: La casa di Servio Tullio, l'Esquilino e Mecenate." *Parola del Passato* 286: 27–32.

Ancona, R. 1994. *Time and the Erotic in Horace's Odes.* Durham, NC.

Ancona, R. and Greene, E. (eds.) 2005. *Gendered Dynamics in Latin Love Poetry.* Baltimore, MD.

Andermahr, A. M. 1998. *Totus in Praediis: Senatorischer Grundbesitz in Italien in der Frühen und Hohen Kaiserzeit.* Bonn. (*Antiquitas* 3, *vol 37.*)

Andersen, B. C. 1988. "Pelvic scarring analysis: Parturition or excess motion." *AJPA* 75: 181.

Anderson, E. and Nosch, M. L. 2003. "With a little help from my friends: Investigating Mycenaean textiles with help from Scandinavian experimental archaeology." In Foster and Laffineur (eds.): 197–206.

Anderson, W. S. 1972. "The form, purpose, and position of Horace's *Satire* I, 8." *AJP* 93: 4–13.

Anderson, W. S. and Quartarone, L. R. (eds.) 1992. *Approaches to Teaching Vergil's* Aeneid. New York.

Andò, V. 2005. *L'ape che tesse.* Roma.

Andreadaki-Vlasaki, M. 1997. "Craftsmanship at MM Khamalevri in Rethymnon." In Laffineur and Betancourt (eds.): 37–43.

André-Salvini, B. 1999. "L'idéologie des pierres en Mésopotamie." In Caubet, A. (ed.), *Cornaline et Pierres Précieuses: La Méditerranée, de l'Antiquité à l'Islam.* Paris. 373–400.

Andronikos, M. 1994. "The tombs of Vergina." In Ginouvès, R. (ed.), *Macedonia from Philip II to the Roman Conquest.* Princeton. 35–9.

Angel, J. L. 1943. "Ancient Cephallenians: The population of a Mediterranean island." *AJPA* 1: 229–60.

—— 1946. "Skeletal change in ancient Greece." *AJPA* 4: 69–97.

—— 1966. "Porotic hyperostosis, anemias, malarias, and marshes in the prehistoric eastern Mediterranean." *Science* 153: 670–3.

—— 1969. "The bases of paleodemography." *AJPA* 30: 427–37.

—— 1971. *The People of Lerna.* Athens.

—— 1972. "Ecology and population in the eastern Mediterranean." *World Archaeology* 4: 88–105.

—— 1984. "Health as a crucial factor in the changes from hunting to developed farming in the eastern Mediterranean." In Cohen and Armelagos (eds.): 51–73.

Angelova, A. 2005. *Gender and Imperial Authority in Rome and early Byzantium, 1st to 6th century.* Diss., Harvard University.

Antonaccio, C. 2005. "Excavating colonization." In Hurst and Owen (eds): 97–113.

—— 2007. "Colonization: Greece on the move, 900–480." In Shapiro (ed.): 201–24.

Appadurai, A. (ed.) 1986. *The Social Life of Things: Commodities in Cultural Perspective.* Cambridge.

Archer, L. J., Fischler, S., and Wyke, M. (eds.) 1994. *Women in Ancient Societies: An Illusion of the Night.* New York.

Arjava, A. 1996. *Women and Law in Late Antiquity.* Oxford.

Armelagos, G. J. 1998. "Introduction: Sex, gender and health status in prehistoric and contemporary population." In Grauer and Stuart-Macadam: 1–10.

Arnott, W. G. 1981. "Moral values in Menander." *Philologus* 125: 215–27.

Arrigoni, G. 1985. "Donne e sport nel mondo greco." In Arrigoni, G. (ed.), *Le donne in Grecia.* Roma-Bari. 55–201.

Arthur [Katz], M. B. 1981. "The divided world of Iliad VI." In Foley (ed.): 19–44.

—— 1984. "Early Greece: The origins of the western attitude toward women." In Peradotto and Sullivan (eds.): 7–57.

Aruz, J., Benzel, K., and Evans, J. M. (eds.) 2008. *Beyond Babylon: Art, Trade and Diplomacy in the Second Millennium B.C.* New York.

Arvanitopoulos, A. S. 1908. "'Η σημασία τῶν γραπτῶν στηλῶν τῶν Παγασῶν." *ArchEph*: 1–60.

—— 1909. Θεσσαλικὰ Μνημεῖα Ι. Ἀθανασάκειον Μουσεῖον ἐν Βολῷ. Athens.

—— 1928. *Graptai Stelai Demetriados-Pagason*. Athens.

—— 1947–8. "Θεσσαλικὰ Μνημεῖα II and III." *Polemon* III: 1–16, 41–45.

—— 1949. "Θεσσαλικὰ Μνημεῖα IV, V, and VI." *Polemon* IV: 1–9, 81–92, 153–68.

—— 1952–3. "Θεσσαλικὰ Μνημεῖα VII." *Polemon* V: 5–18.

Arvanitopoulos, Th. 1952–3. "Θεσσαλικὰ Μνημεῖα addendum." *Polemon* V: 33–58.

Ash, R. E. 2003. "Aliud est enim epistulam, aliud . . . historiam scribere (Epistles 6.16.22): Pliny the Historian?" *Arethusa* 36: 211–25.

Asher-Greve, J. M. 1985. *Frauen in Altsumerischer Zeit. Bibliotheca Mesopotamica* 18. Malibu.

—— 1997. "Feminist research and Ancient Mesopotamia: Problems and prospects." In Brenner, A. and Fontaine, C. (eds.), *A Feminist Companion to Reading the Bible: Approaches, Methods and Strategies*. Sheffield. 218–37.

—— 2006. "From "Semiramis of Babylon" to "Semiramis of Hammersmith." In Holloway, S. W. (ed.), *Orientalism, Assyriology and the Bible*. Sheffield, 322–73.

Asher-Greve, J. M. and Sweeney, D. 2006. "On nakedness, nudity, and gender in Egyptian and Mesopotamian art." In Schroer, S. (ed.), *Images and Gender: Contributions to the Hermeneutics of Reading Ancient Art*. Fribourg. 125–76.

Asher-Greve, J. M. and Wogec, M. F. 2002. "Women and gender in Ancient Near Eastern cultures: Bibliography 1885 to 2001 AD." *NIN: Journal of Gender Studies in Antiquity* 3: 33–114.

Ashton, S.-A. 2008. *Cleopatra and Egypt*. Malden, MA.

Assante, J. 2003. "From whores to Hierodules: The historiographic invention of Mesopotamian female sex professionals." In Donohue, A. A. and Fullerton, M. D. (eds.), *Ancient Art and its Historiography*. Cambridge. 13–47.

Aufderheide, A. C. and Rodríguez-Martín, C. 1998. *The Cambridge Encyclopedia of Human Paleopathology*. Cambridge.

Ault, B. 2005. *The Excavation at Ancient Halieis, vol 2. The Houses. The Organization and Use of Domestic Space*. Bloomington, IN.

Austin, N. 1994. *Helen of Troy and her Shameless Phantom*. Ithaca, NY.

Avramidou, A. 2006. "Attic vases in Etruria: Another view on the divine banquet cup by the Codrus Painter." *AJA* 110: 565–79.

Ayad, M. 2009. *God's Wife, God's Servant: The God's Wife of Amun*. New York.

Baadsgaard, A., Monge, J., Cox, S., and Zettler, R. L. 2011. "Human sacrifice and intentional corpse preservation in the Royal Cemetery of Ur." *Antiquity* 85: 27–42.

Bachofen, J. J. 1861. *Das Mutterrecht*. Stuttgart.

Baglione, M. P. 1989. "Considerazioni sul 'ruolo' femminile nell'arcaismo e nel tardo-archaismo." In Rallo (ed.): 107–19.

Bagnall, R. S. 1988. "Greeks and Egyptians: Ethnicity, status, and culture." In Bianchi (ed.): 21–5.

—— 1993. *Egypt in Late Antiquity*. Princeton.

—— 1995. "Women, law, and social realities in late antiquity." *BASP* 32: 65–86.

—— 2004. "Women's petitions in late antique Egypt." In Feissel, D. and Gascou, J. (eds.), *La pétition à Byzance. Centre de Recherche d'Histoire et Civilisation de Byzance, Monographies* 14. Paris. 53–60.

Bagnall, R. S. and Cribiore, R. (eds.) 2006. *Women's Letters from Ancient Egypt, 300 BC–AD 800*. Ann Arbor, MI.

Bagnall, R. S. and Derow, P. (eds.) 1981. *Greek Historical Documents: The Hellenistic Period*. Chico.

Bagnall, R. S. and Rathbone, D. (eds.) 2004. *Egypt from Alexander to the Early Christians: An Archaeological and Historical Guide*. London.

Bahrani, Z. 1996. "The Hellenization of Ishtar: Nudity, fetishism, and the production of cultural differentiation in ancient art." *Oxford Art Journal* 19.2: 3–16.

—— 2001. *Women of Babylon: Gender and Representation in Mesopotamia*. New York.

—— 2003. *The Graven Image: Representation in Babylonia and Assyria*. Philadelphia, PA.

Bailey, D. M. 1990. "Classical architecture in Roman Egypt." In Henig, M. (ed.), *Architecture and Architectural Sculpture in the Roman Empire*. Oxford. 121–37.

—— 2008. *Catalogue of the Terracottas in the British Museum, vol. IV: Ptolemaic and Roman Terracottas from Egypt*. London.

Bain, D. M. 1982a. "Katonáke ton choiron apotetilménas (Aristophanes, Ekklesiazousai 724)." *LCM* 7.1: 7–10.

—— 1982b. "Addenda, corrigenda, retractanda." *LCM* 7.8: 111.

Baker, B. J. 1997. "Contributions of biological anthropology to the understanding of ancient Egyptian and Nubian societies." In Lustig, J. (ed.), *Anthropology and Egyptology: A Developing Dialogue*. Sheffield. 106–116.

Baker, B. J., Dupras, T. L., and Tocheri, M. W. (eds.) 2005. *The Osteology of Infants and Children*. College Station, TX.

Balbo, A. 2004. *I frammenti degli oratori Romani dell'età Augustea e Tiberiana. Parte prima: Età Augustea*. Alessandria.

Baldwin, B. 1972. "Women in Tacitus." *Prudentia* 4: 83–101.

Balty, J.-C. 1991. *Curia Ordinis. Recherches d'architecture et d'urbanisme antiques sur les curies provincials du monde romain*. Brussels.

—— 1996. "Palmyre entre Orient et Occident: Acculturation et résistances." In *Palmyra and the Silk Road. Annales Archéologiques Arabes Syriennes* 42: 437–41.

Bar On, B.-A. 1994. *Engendering Origins: Critical Feminist Readings in Plato and Aristotle*. Albany.

Barber, E. J. W. 1991. *Prehistoric Textiles: The Development of Cloth in the Neolithic and Bronze Ages with Special Reference to the Aegean*. Princeton.

—— 1994. *Women's Work: The First 20,000 Years: Women, Cloth, and Society in Early Times*. New York.

—— 1997. "Minoan women and the challenges of weaving for home, trade, and shrine." In Laffineur and Betancourt (eds.): 515–19.

—— 1999. "Colour in early cloth and clothing." *CAJ* 9: 117–20.

Barcan, R. 2004. *Nudity: A Cultural Anatomy*. Oxford.

Barletta, B. 2006. "Archaic and Classical Magna Graecia." In Palagia (2006): 77–118.

Barnabei, F. 1895. "Di una nuova iscrizione arcaica votiva a Diana." *Notizie degli Scavi* 3.2: 435–6.

Barnes, E. 2003. "The dead do tell tales." In Williams, C. K. and Bookidis, N. (eds.), *Corinth, the Centenary: 1896–1996*. Princeton. 435–43.

Barrett, A. A. 1996. *Agrippina: Mother of Nero*. London.

—— 2002. *Livia: First Lady of Imperial Rome*. New Haven, CT.

Bartky, S. L. 1990. *Femininity and Domination: Studies in the Phenomenology of Oppression*. London.

Bartman, E. 1999. *Portraits of Livia: Imaging the Imperial Woman in Augustan Rome*. Cambridge.

—— 2009. "The 'dark lady' of Rome/Copenhagen." *JRA* 22: 546–8.

Bartoloni, G. 2000. "La donna del principe." In Dore, A., Marchesi, M., and Minarini, L. (eds.), *Principi Etruschi: Tra mediterraneo ed Europa*. Venice. 308–26.

Bartsiokas, A. 2000. "The eye injury of King Phillip II and the skeletal evidence from the Royal Tomb II at Vergina." *Science* 288: 511–14.

Baskin, J. (ed.) 1991. *Jewish Women in Historical Perspective*. Detroit.

Baskin, J. 2002. *Midrashic Women: Formations of the Feminine in Rabbinic Literature*. Boston, MA.

Batto, B. F. 1974. *Studies on Women at Mari*. Baltimore, MD.

Batziou-Efstathiou, A. 2002. *Demetrias*. Athens.

Bauman, R. 1992. *Women and Politics in Ancient Rome*. London.

Beard, M. 1980. "The sexual status of Vestal Virgins." *JRS* 70: 12–27.

—— 1991. "Adopting an approach II." In Rasmussen, T. and Spivey, N. (eds.), *Looking at Greek Vases*. Cambridge. 12–35.

—— 1995. "Re-reading (Vestal) virginity." In Hawley and Levick (eds.): 166–77.

—— 2008. *The Fires of Vesuvius*. Cambridge, MA.

Beard, M., North, J., Price, S. (eds.) 1998. *Religions of Rome. Volume I*. Cambridge.

Beaucamp, J. 1990. *La Statut de la Femme à Byzance (4e-7e Siècle) I: Le Droit Impérial*. Paris.

—— 1992. *La Statut de la Femme à Byzance(4e-7e siècle) II: Les Pratiques Sociales*. Paris.

Beaulieu, P.-A. 1993. "Women in Neo-Babylonian Society." *Canadian Society for Mesopotamian Studies, Bulletin* 26: 7–14.

Beausang, E. 2005. *Childbirth and Mothering in Archaeology: Gotarc Serie B 37*. Gothenburg.

Beck, M. 2000. "Female figurines in the European Upper Paleolithic." In Rautman, A. E. (ed.), *Reading the Body: Representations and Remains in the Archaeological Record*. Philadelphia. 202–14.

Becker, M. J. 1995. "Human skeletal remains from the pre-colonial Greek emporium of Pithekoussai on Ischia (NA). Culture contact in Italy from the early VIII to the II century BC." In Christie, N. (ed.), *Settlement and Economy in Italy 1500 BC to AD 1500*. Oxford.

Becker, T. 2006. "Women in Roman forts—Lack of knowledge or a social claim?" *Archaeological Dialogues* 13.1: 36–8.

Bell, C. 1992. *Ritual Theory, Ritual Practice*. Oxford and New York.

—— 1998. "Performance." In Taylor, M. C. (ed.), *Critical Terms for Religious Studies*. Chicago. 205–24.

Bell, H. I., Martin, V., Turner, E. G., and van Berchem, D. (eds.) 1962. *The Abinnaeus Archive: Papers of a Roman Officer in the Reign of Constantius II*. Oxford.

Bendinelli, G. 1920. "Il tempio etrusco figurato sopra specchi graffitti." *Bullettino della Commissione Archeologica Comunale di Roma* 46: 229–45.

Bentley, L. 1996. "How did prehistoric women bear 'man the hunter'? Reconstructing fertility from the archaeological record." In Wright, R. (ed.), *Gender and Archaeology*. Philadelphia. 23–51.

Bentz, M. 1998. *Panathenäische preisamphoren. Eine athenische Vasengattung und ihre Funktion vom 6.-4. Jahrhundert v. Chr. Antike Kunst* Suppl. 18. Basel.

Bérard, C. 1986. "L'impossible femme athlete." *Annali del Seminario di studi del mondo classico: Sezione di archeologia e storia antica* 8: 195–202.

Bérard, C., Bron, C., Durand, J.-L., Frontisi-Ducroux, F., Lissarrague, F., Schnapp, A., and Vernant, J.-P. (eds.) 1989. *A City of Images: Iconography and Society in Ancient Greece*. Transl. D. Lyons. Princeton.

Bérard, C. and Durand, J.-L. 1989. "Entering the imagery." In Bérard et al. (eds.): 23–37.

Bergemann, J. 1997. *Demos und Thanatos: Untersuchungen zum Wertsystem der Polis im Spiegel der attischen Grabreliefs des 4. Jahrhunderts v. Chr. und zur Funktion der gleighzeitigen Grabbauten*. Munich.

—— 2007. "Attic grave reliefs and portrait sculpture in fourth-century Athens." In Schultz and von den Hoff (eds.): 34–46.

Berger, J. 1972. *Ways of Seeing*. Harmondsworth.

Bergfelder, T. and Herrmann, B. 1980. "Estimating fertility on the basis of birth traumatic changes in the pubic bone." *Journal of Human Evolution* 9: 611–13.

Bergren, A. 1983. "Language and the female in early Greek thought." *Arethusa* 16: 69–95.

Bernardini, P. A. 1986-7. "Aspects ludiques, rituals et sportifs de la course féminine dans la Grèce antique." *Stadion* 12–13: 17–26.

Bernstein, F. 2007. "Pompeian women." In Dobbins and Foss (eds.): 526–37.

Berry, J. 2007. *The Complete Pompeii*. London and New York.

Bertholet, F., Bielman Sánchez, A., and Frei-Stolba, R. (eds.) 2008. *Egypte-Grèce-Rome. Les différents visages des femmes antiques. ECHO 7*. Bern.

Beschi, L. 1996. "Sculpture in Greek Cyrenaica." In Pugliese Carratelli (ed.): 437–42.

Betancourt, P. P. 1985. *The History of Minoan Pottery*. Princeton.

Bevan, L. 1997. "Skin scrapers and pottery makers? 'Invisible' women in prehistory." In Moore and Scott (eds.): 81–7.

Bieber, M. 1928. *Griechische Kleidung*. Berlin and Leipzig.

—— 1967. *Entwicklungsgeschichte der griechischen Tracht*. Second edition. Berlin.

—— 1977. *Ancient Copies: Contributions to the History of Greek and Roman Art*. New York.

Bielman, A. 2002. *Femmes en public dans le monde hellénistique*. Paris.

—— 2003. "Citoyennes hellénistiques. Les femmes et leur cité en Asie mineure." In Le Dinahet, M.-Th. (ed.), *L'Orient méditerranéen de la mort d'Alexandre au 1er siècle avant notre ère*. Paris. 176–96.

Bielman Sánchez, A. 2003. "Régner au feminine: Réflexions sur les reines attalides et séleucides." In Prost, F. (ed.), *L'Orient Mediterréen de la mort d'Alexandre aux compagnes de Pompée: Cités et royaumes à la époque hellénistique*. Rennes. 41–61.

—— 2008. "L'éternité des femmes actives: Réflexions sur quelques monuments funéraires féminins de la Grèce hellénistique et impériale." In Bertholet et al. (eds.): 147–94.

Bierbrier, M. L. (ed.) 1997. *Portraits and Masks: Burial Customs in Roman Egypt*. London.

Bietti Sestieri, A. M. 1992. *The Iron Age community of Osteria dell'Osa*. Cambridge.

Biezunska-Malowist, I. 1939. *Etudes sur la condition juridique et sociale de la femme grecque en Égypte gréco-romaine*. Lwow.

—— 1993. "Les recherches sur la condition de la femme grecque en Égypte grecque et romaine, hier et aujourd'hui.'" *Antiquitas* 18: 15–21.

Biggs, R. D. 2000. "Conception, contraception, and abortion in Ancient Mesopotamia." In George, A. R. and Finkel, I. L. (eds.), *Wisdom, Gods, and Literature*. Winona Lake, IN. 1–13.

Bing, P. 2009. *The Scroll and the Marble. Studies in Reading and Reception in Hellenistic Poetry*. Ann Arbor, MI.

Bing, P. and Bruss, J. (eds.) 2007. *Brill's Companion to Hellenistic Epigram*. Leiden.

Bintliff, J. L. 1984. "Structuralism and myth in Minoan studies." *Antiquity* 58: 33–8.

Bishop, M. C. 1989. "O Fortuna: A sideways look at the archaeological record and Roman military equipment." In van Driel Murray (ed.): 1–11.

—— 2011. "Weaponry and military equipment." In Allason-Jones (ed.): 114–32.

Block, E. 1985. "Clothing makes the man: A pattern in the Odyssey." *TAPA* 115: 1–11.

Blok, J. 1987. "Sexual asymmetry: A historiographical essay." In Blok, J. and Mason, P. (eds.), *Sexual Asymmetry: Studies in Ancient Society*. Amsterdam. 1–57.

Blondell, R. 2010. "'Bitch that I am': Self-blame and self-assertion in the *Iliad*." *TAPA* 140: 1–32.

Blondell, R., Gamel, M.-K., Rabinowitz, N. S., and Zweig, B. 1999. *Women on the Edge: Four Plays by Euripides*. New York.

Blundell, S. 1995. *Women in Ancient Greece*. London.

—— 2006. "Beneath their shining feet: Shoes and sandals in Classical Greece." In Riello, G. and McNeil, P. (eds.), *Shoes: A History From Sandals to Sneakers*. Oxford. 30–49.

Blundell, S. and Williamson, M. (eds.) 1998. *The Sacred and the Feminine in Ancient Greece*. London.

Boardman, J. 1980. *The Greeks Overseas*. Second edition. London.

—— 1983. "Symbol and story in geometric art." In Moon, W. (ed.), *Ancient Greek Art and Iconography*. Madison. 15–36.

—— 1996. *Greek Art*. Fourth edition. London.

Boardman, J. and Kurtz, D. 1971. *Greek Burial Customs*. London.

Boatwright, M. T. 1991a. "The imperial women of the early second century A.C." *AJP* 112: 513–40.

—— 1991b. "Plancia Magna of Perge: Women's roles and status in Roman Asia Minor." In Pomeroy (ed.): 249–72.

—— 2011. "Women and gender in the Forum Romanum." *TAPA* 141: 107–43.

Boëls-Janssen, N. 1993. *La vie religieuse des matrones dans la Rome archaïque*. *CEFR(A)* 176. Rome.

Boer, C. 1992. "The classicist and the psychopath." Foreword to Stanford, W. B., *The Ulysses Theme: A Study in the Adaptability of a Traditional Hero*. Dallas. iii–xix.

Böhm, S. 2003. "The 'naked goddess' in early Greek art: An Orientalizing theme par excellence." In Stampolidis and Karageorghis (eds.): 363–70.

Bohrer, F. N. 2003. *Orientalism and Visual Culture: Imagining Mesopotamia in Nineteenth-Century Europe*. Cambridge.

Bol, R. 1984. *Das Statuenprogramm des Herodes-Atticus-Nymphäums*. Berlin.

Bolger, D. L. 1994. "Ladies of the expedition: Harriet Boyd Hawes and Edith Hall at work in Mediterranean archaeology." In Claassen, C. (ed.), *Women in Archaeology*. Philadelphia. 41–50.

Bonfante, G. and Bonfante, L. 1983. *The Etruscan Language: An Introduction*. Manchester.

Bonfante, L. 1973a. "Etruscan women: A question of interpretation." *Archaeology* 26.4: 242–9.

—— 1973b. "The women of Etruria." *Arethusa* 6.1: 91–101.

—— 1975. *Etruscan Dress*. Baltimore.

—— 1977. "The judgement of Paris, the toilette of Malavish and a mirror from the Indiana University Art Museum." *Studi Etruschi* 45: 149–67.

—— 1981. "Etruscan couples and their aristocratic society." In Foley (ed.): 323–42.

—— 1982. "Daily life." In de Grummond, N. T. (ed.), *A Guide to Etruscan Mirrors*. Tallahassee. 79–88.

—— 1986. "Daily life and afterlife." In Bonfante, L. (ed.), *Etruscan Life and Afterlife: A Handbook of Etruscan Studies*. Warminster. 232–78.

—— 1986. "Votive terracotta figurines of mothers and children." In Swaddling, J. (ed.), *Italian Iron Age Artefacts in the British Museum. Papers of the Sixth British Museum Classical Colloquium*. London. 195–203.

—— 1989a. "Iconografia delle madri: Etruria e Italia antica." In Rallo (ed.) 1989b: 85–106.

—— 1989b. "La moda femminile etrusca." In Rallo (ed.) 1989b: 157–71.

—— 1989c. "Nudity as a costume in classical art." *AJA* 93: 543–70.

—— 1994. "Etruscan women." In Fantham et al. (eds.): 243–59.

—— 1997. "Nursing mothers in Classical art." In Koloski-Ostrow and Lyons (eds.): 174–96.

Bonner, C. 1950. *Studies in Magical Amulets*. Ann Arbor, MI.

Borg, B. 1996. *Mumienporträts: Chronologie und Kultureller Kontext*. Mainz.

Börker-Klähn, J. 1997. "Mauerkronenträgerinnen." In Waetzoldt, H. and Hauptmann, H. (eds.), *Assyrien im Wandel der Zeiten, XXXIXe Rencontre Assyiologique Internationale, Heidelberg 6.-10. Juli 1992*. Heidelberg. 227–34.

Borriello, M., d'Ambrosio, Z., de Caro, S., and Guzzo, P. G. (eds.) 1997. *Pompei: Abitare sotto il Vesuvio*. Ferrara.

Borriello, M., Guidobaldi, M., and Guzzo, P. 2008. *Ercolano: Tre Secoli di Scoperte*. Milan.

Borza, E. N. and Palagia, O. 2007. "The chronology of the Macedonian royal tombs at Vergina." *Jahrbuch des Deutschen Archäologischen Instituts* 122: 81–130.

Boschung, D. 2002. *Gens Augusta: Untersuchungen zu Aufstellung, Wirkung und Bedeutung der Statuengruppen des Julisch-Claudischen Kaiserhauses*. Mainz.

Boulanger, A. 1923. *Aelius Aristide et la sophistique dans la province d'Asie au IIe siècle de notre ère*. Paris.

Bourbou, C. and Richards, M. P. 2007. "The Middle Byzantine menu: Paleodietary information from isotopic analysis of humans and fauna from Kastella, Crete." *International Journal of Osteoarchaeology* 17: 63–72.

Bourdieu, P. 1977. *Outline of a Theory of Practice*. Cambridge.

—— 1989. *Distinction: A Social Critique of the Judgement of Taste*. London.

Bowman, A. K. 1986. *Egypt after the Pharaohs*. London.

—— 2000. "Urbanization in Roman Egypt." In Fentress, E. (ed.), *Romanization and the City: Creation, Transformations, and Failures: Papers of a Conference held at the American Academy in Rome, 14–16 May 1998*. Portsmouth, RI. 173–87.

Bowman, A. K. and Rathbone, D. 1992. "Cities and administration in Roman Egypt." *JRS* 82: 107–27.

Bowman, A. K. and Thomas, J. D. 1983. *Vindolanda: The Latin Writing Tablets*. London.

—— 1994. *The Vindolanda Writing Tablets: Tabulae Vindolandenses II*. London.

—— 2003. *The Vindolanda Writing Tablets: Tabulae Vindolandenses III*. London.

Bradbury, S. 1996. *Severus of Minorca: Letter on the Conversion of the Jews*. Oxford.

Bradley, G. J. 2000. *Ancient Umbria: State, Culture, and Identity in Central Italy from the Iron Age to the Augustan Era*. Oxford.

Branigan, K. 1991. "Funerary ritual and social cohesion in Early Bronze Age Crete." *Journal of Mediterranean Studies* 1: 183–92.

—— 1993. *Dancing with Death: Life and Death in Southern Crete, c. 3000–2000 BC*. Amsterdam.

Braun, K. 1970. "Der Dipylon-Brunnen B_1: Die funde." *AM* 85: 129–269.

Braund, D. 1984. "Observations on Cartimandua." *Britannia* 15: 1–6.

Braund, S. H. 1992. "Juvenal: Misogynist or misogamist?" *JRS* 82: 71–86.

Brecoulaki, H. 2006. *Le Peinture Funéraire de Macédoine*. Meletemata 48. Paris.

Brendel, O. J. 1979. *Prolegomena to the Study of Roman Art*. New Haven, CT.

Brickstock, R. J. 2010. "Coins and frontier troops in the 4th century." In Collins and Allason-Jones (eds.): 86–91.

Brillante, C. 2002. "Il mito di Elena." In Bettini, M. and Brillante, C. (eds.), *Il Mito di Elena*. Torino. 39–232.

Bringmann, K. 1997. "Die rolle der königinnen, prinzen und vermittler." In *Actes du Xe Congrès International d'Épigraphie Grecque et Latine, Nîmes, 4–9 Octobre 1992*. Paris. 169–73.

Bringmann, L. 1939. *Die Frau im Ptolemäisch-Kaiserlichen Ägypten*. Bonn.

Brinkmann, V. and Wünsche, R. (eds.) 2004. *Bunte Götter: Die Farbigkeit antiker Skulptur*. Munich.

—— 2007. *Gods in Color: Painted Sculpture of Classical Antiquity*. Cambridge, MA.

Brooten, B. 1982. *Women Leaders in the Ancient Synagogue: Inscriptional Evidence and Background Issues*. Brown Judaic Studies 36. Atlanta, GA.

Brouwer, H. H. J. 1989. *Bona Dea: The Sources and a Description of The Cult*. Leiden.

Brown, B. R. 1957. *Ptolemaic Paintings and the Alexandrian Style*. Cambridge, MA.

Brown, P. G. McC. 1991. "Athenian attitudes to rape and seduction: The evidence of Menander Dyskolos 289–293." *CQ* 41: 533–34.

—— 1993. "Love and marriage in Greek New Comedy." *CQ* 43: 189–205.

Brown, R. 1995. "Livy's Sabine women and the ideal of *concordia*." *TAPA* 125: 291–319.

Brown, S. 1997. "'Ways of seeing' women in antiquity: An introduction to feminism in Classical archaeology and ancient art history." In Koloski-Ostrow and Lyons (eds.): 12–42.

Brulé, P. 1987. *La fille d'Athènes: La religion des filles à Athènes à l'époque classique: Mythes, cultes et société*. Paris.

Brumfiel, E. M. 1991. "Weaving and cooking: Women's production in Aztec Mexico." In Conkey and Gero (eds.): 224–51. Brumfield, A. 1981. *The Attic Festivals of Demeter and their Relation to the Agricultural Year*. New York.

Bruneau, P. and Ducat, J. 2005. *Guide de Délos*. Fourth edition. Paris.

Bruss, J. S. 2005. *Hidden Presences. Monuments, Gravesites, and Corpses on Greek Funerary Epigram*. Leuven.

Buchner, G. and Ridgway, D. 1992. *Pithekoussai I*. Rome.

Buckberry, J. L. and Chamberlain, A. T. 2002. "Age estimation from the auricular surface of the ilium: A revised method." *AJPA* 119: 231–9.

Buikstra, J. and Lagia, A. 2009. "Bioarchaeological approaches to Aegean archaeology." In Schepartz et al. (eds.): 7–30.

Bumke, H. 2008. "Vom verhältnis der Römer zu den kultbildern der Griechen." In Junker, K. and Stähli, A. (eds.), *Original und Kopie: Formen und Konzepte der Nachahmung in der antiken Kunst.* Wiesbaden. 109–33.

Bundrick, S. D. 2008. "The fabric of the city: Imaging textile production in Classical Athens." *Hesperia* 77: 283–334.

Burke, B. 1997. "The organisation of textile production in Bronze Age Crete." In Laffineur and Betancourt (eds.): 413–22.

Burkert, W. 1985. *Greek Religion.* Cambridge, MA.

Burnett, A., Amandry, M., and Ripollès, P. P. (eds.) 1992. *Roman Provincial Coinage I: From the Death of Caesar to the Death of Vitellius (44 BC–AD 69).* Paris and London.

Burnett, J. (ed.) 1903. *Platonis Opera, Vols. III and IV.* Oxford.

Butler, J. 1990. *Gender Trouble: Feminism and the Subversion of Identity.* London.

—— 1993. *Bodies that Matter: On the Discursive Limits of "Sex."* New York.

Cahill, N. 2002. *Household and City Organization at Olynthus.* New Haven, CT.

Calame, C. 1997. *Choruses of Young Women in Ancient Greece: Their Morphology, Religious Role, and Social Function.* Transl. D. Collins, and J. Orion. Lanham, MD.

Calinescu, A. (ed.) 1996. *Ancient Jewelry and Archaeology.* Bloomington.

Cameron, A. (ed.) 1989. *History as Text.* London.

Cameron, A. and Kuhrt, A. (eds.) 1993. *Images of Women in Antiquity.* London.

Campbell, B. 1978. "The marriage of soldiers under the Empire." *JRS* 61: 153–66.

Cantarella, E. 1981. *L'ambiguo malanno.* Roma. [Translated as *Pandora's Daughters.*]

—— 1987. *Pandora's Daughters. The Role and Status of Women in Greek and Roman Antiquity.* Transl. M. B. Fant. Baltimore.

—— 1992. *Bisexuality in the Ancient World.* New Haven, CT.

Capasso, L. 2002. "Bacteria in two-millennia-old cheese, and related epizoonoses in Roman populations." *Journal of Infection* 45: 122–7.

Capel, A. K. and Markoe, G. E. (eds.) 1996. *Mistress of the House, Mistress of Heaven: Women in Ancient Egypt.* New York.

Carandini, A. 1969. *Vibia Sabina: Funzione politica, iconografica e il problema del classicism adrianeo.* Florence.

Carey, C. 1995. "Rape and adultery in Athenian law." *CQ* 45: 407–17.

Carney, E. D. 1993. "Olympias and the image of the royal virago." *Phoenix* 47: 29–56.

—— 2000. *Women and Monarchy in Macedonia.* Norman, OK.

—— 2006. *Olympias, Mother of Alexander the Great.* London.

—— 2007. "The Philippeum, women, and the formation of dynastic image." In Heckel, W., Tritle, L., and Wheatley, P. (eds.), Alexander's Empire: Formulation to Decay. Claremont, CA. 27–60.

Carp, T. 1981. "Two matrons of the late Republic." In Foley (ed.): 343–54.

Carpenter, T. H. 1991. *Art and Myth in Ancient Greece.* London.

Carson, A. 1990. "Putting her in her place: Women, dirt, and desire." In Halperin et al. (eds.): 135–69.

Carter, J. C. (ed.) 1998. *The Chora of Metaponto. The Necropoleis.* Austin, TX.

—— 2006. *Discovering the Greek Countryside at Metaponto.* Ann Arbor, MI.

Carter, J. C. and Mack, G. R. (eds.) 2003. *Crimean Chersonesos: City, Chora, Museum and Environs.* Austin, TX.

Cartledge, P. 1993. *The Greeks: A Portrait of Self and Others.* Oxford.

—— 2002. *The Greeks: A Portrait of Self and Others.* Second edition. Oxford.

Cartwright, C. R. 1997. "Egyptian mummy portraits: Examining the woodworkers' craft." In Bierbrier (ed.): 106–11.

Cassis, M. 2008. "A restless silence: Women in the Byzantine archaeological record." In *The World of Women in the Ancient and Classical Near East*. Newcastle. 138–54.

Casson, T. E. 1945. "Cartimandua in history, legend and romance." *Transactions of the Cumberland and Westmorland Antiquarian and Archaeological Society* 44: 68–80.

Castelli, E. 1998. "Gender, theory, and the rise of Christianity: A response to Rodney Stark." *JECS* 6: 227–57.

Cébeillac-Gervasoni, M. (ed.) 1996. *Les élites municipales de l'Italie péninsulaire des Gracques à Néron*. Rome.

Cerchiai, L. 1982. "Sesso e classi di età nelle necropolis greche di Locri Epizefiri." In Gnoli, G. and Vernant, J.-P. (eds.), *La Mort, les Morts dans les Sociétés Anciennes*. Cambridge and Paris. 289–98.

Champlin, E. 1980. *Fronto and Antonine Rome*. Cambridge, MA.

—— 1991. *Final Judgments: Duty and Emotion in Roman Wills, 200 B.C. – A.D. 250*. Berkeley, CA.

Chaniotis, A. 1995. "Sich selbst feiern? Die städtischen feste des hellenismus im spannungsfeld zwischen religion und politik." In Wörrle, M. and Zanker, P. (eds.), *Stadtbilder und Bürgerbild im Hellenismus*. *Vestigia* 47. Munich. 147–72.

—— 1997. "Theatricality beyond the theater: Staging public life in the Hellenistic world." In Le Guen, B. (ed.), *De la scène aux gradins, Pallas* 47: 219–59.

Chapman, R., Kinnes, I., and Randsborg, K. (eds.) 1981. *The Archaeology of Death*. Cambridge.

Charles, D. K. 2005. "The archaeology of death as anthropology." In Rakita, G. F. M., Buikstra, J. E., Beck, L. A., and Williams, S. R. (eds.), *Interacting with the Dead: Perspectives on Mortuary Archaeology for the New Millennium*. Gainesville, FL. 15–24.

Cherry, D. 1998. *Frontier and Society in Roman North Africa*. Oxford.

Cherry, J. F. 1984. "The emergence of the state in the prehistoric Aegean." *PCPhS* 210: 18–48.

Chilvers, E. R., Bouwmana, A. S., Brown, K. A., Arnot, R. G., Prag, J. N. W., and Brown, T. A. 2008. "Ancient DNA in human bones from Neolithic and Bronze Age sites in Greece and Crete." *Journal of Archaeological Science* 35: 2707–14.

Churchill, L. J., Brown, P. R., and Jeffrey, J. E. (eds.), *Women Writing Latin in Roman Antiquity, Late Antiquity, and the Early Christian Era*. New York.

Clader, L. L. 1976. *Helen: The Evolution from Divine to Heroic in Greek Epic Tradition*. Leiden.

Clairmont, C. 1993. *Classical Attic Tombstones*. Kilchberg.

Clark, G. 1989. *Women in the Ancient World*. New Surveys in the Classics 21. Oxford.

—— 1993. *Women in Late Antiquity: Pagan and Christian Lifestyles*. Oxford.

Clark, K. 1956. *The Nude: A Study in Ideal Form*. New York.

Clark, M. 2001. "Was Telemachus rude to his mother? *Odyssey* 1.356–59." *CP* 96: 335–54.

Clarke, M. 2004. "Manhood and heroism." In Fowler (ed.): 74–90.

Clarysse, W. 1985. "Greeks and Egyptians in the Ptolemaic army and administration." *Aegyptus* 65: 57–66.

—— 1998. "Ethnic diversity and dialect among the Greeks of Hellenistic Egypt." In Verhoogt, A. M. and Vleeming, S. P. (eds.), *The Two Faces of Graeco-Roman Egypt: Greek and Demotic and Greek-Demotic Text and Studies Presented to P. W. Pestman by Alumni of the Papyrological Institute*. Leiden. 1–13.

Clarysse, W. and van der Veken, G. 1983. *The Eponymous Priests of Ptolemaic Egypt (PLBat XXIV)*. Leiden.

Clayman, D. L. 1975. "Horace's *Epodes* VIII and XII: More than clever obscenity?" *CW* 69.2: 55–61.

Clayton, B. 2004. *A Penelopean Poetics: Reweaving the Feminine in Homer's Odyssey*. Lanham.

Clayton, J. 1880. "Description of Roman remains discovered near to Procolitia, a station on the Wall of Hadrian." *Archaeologia Aeliana* second series 8: 1–39.

Cleland, L. 2005. *The Brauron Clothing Catalogues: Text, Analysis, Glossary, and Translation*. Oxford.

Cleland, L., Davies, G., and Llewellyn-Jones, L. (eds.) 2007. *Greek and Roman Dress from A to Z.* London.

Clinton, K. 1992. *Myth and Cult: The Iconography of the Eleusinian Mysteries.* Stockholm.

Closterman, W. E. 2007. "Family ideology and family history: The function of funerary markers in Classical Attic peribolos tombs." *AJA* 111.4: 633–52.

Coarelli, F. 1978. "La statue de Cornelie, mère des Gracques, et la crise politique a Rome au temps de Saturninus." In *Le dernier siècle de la République romaine et l'epoque augustéenne.* Strasbourg. 13–28 [Reprinted in *Revixit Ars.* Rome. 280–99.]

Cohen, B. 1993. "The anatomy of Kassandra's rape: Female nudity comes of age in Greek art." *Notes in the History of Art* 12: 37–46.

—— (ed.) 1995. *The Distaff Side: Representing the Female in Homer's Odyssey.* New York.

—— 1997. "Divesting the female breast of clothes in Classical sculpture." In Koloski-Ostrow and Lyons (eds.): 66–92.

—— (ed.) 2000. *Not the Classical Ideal: Athens and the Construction of the Other in Greek Art.* Boston, MA.

—— 2006. *The Colors of Clay: Special Techniques of Athenian Vases.* Malibu.

Cohen, D. 1991. *Law, Sexuality, and Society: The Enforcement of Morals in Classical Athens.* Cambridge.

Cohen, E. 2000. *The Athenian Nation.* Princeton.

—— 2006. "Free and unfree sexual work: An economic analysis of Athenian prostitution." In Faraone and McClure (ed.): 95–124.

Cohen, M. N. and Armelagos, G. J. (eds.) 1984. *Paleopathology at the Origins of Agriculture.* Orlando.

Cohen, M. N. and Bennett, S. 1998. "Skeletal evidence for sex roles and gender hierarchies in prehistory." In Hays-Gilpin, K. and Whitley, D. S. (eds.), *Reader in Gender Archaeology.* London. 297–317.

Cohen, S. 1999. *The Beginnings of Jewishness: Boundaries, Varieties, Uncertainties. Hellenistic Culture and Society* 31. Berkley, CA.

Cohn-Haft, L. 1995. "Divorce in Classical Athens." *JHS* 115: 1–14.

Colburn, C. S. 2008. "Exotica and the Early Minoan elite: Eastern imports in Prepalatial Crete." *AJA* 112: 203–24.

Coldstream, J. N. 1993. "Mixed marriages at the frontiers of the early Greek world." *Oxford Journal of Archaeology* 12(1): 89–107.

Cole, S. G. 1981. "Could Greek women read and write?" In Foley (ed.): 219–45.

—— 1984. "Greek sanctions against sexual assault." *CP* 79: 97–113.

—— 1994. "Demeter in the ancient Greek city and its countryside." In Alcock and Osborne (eds.): 199–216.

—— 2004. *Landscape, Gender, and Ritual Space: The Ancient Greek Experience.* Berkeley, CA.

Colin, F. 2002. "Les prêtresses indigenes dans l'Égypte hellénistique et romaine: Une question à la croisée des sources grecques et égyptiennes." In Melaerts and Morens (eds.): 41–122.

Colledge, M. 1976. *The Art of Palmyra.* London.

Collingridge, V. 2005. *Boudica.* London.

Collingwood, R. G. and Wright, R. P. 1965. *The Roman Inscriptions of Britain. vol. I. Inscriptions on Stone.* Oxford.

Collins, R. 2010. "Brooch use in the 4th- to 5th-century frontier." In Collins and Allason-Jones (eds.): 64–77.

Collins, R. and Allason-Jones, L. (eds.) 2010. *Finds from the Frontier. Council for British Archaeology Research Report 162.* York.

Collon, D. 1999. "Depictions of priests and priestesses in the Ancient Near East." In Watanabe, K. (ed.), *Priests and Officials in the Ancient Near East. Papers of the Second Colloquium on the Ancient*

Near East *"The City of Life,"* held at the Middle Eastern Culture Center in Japan (Mitaka, Tokyo). March 22–24, 1996. Heidelberg. 17–46.

Compton-Engle, G. 2005. "Stolen cloaks in Aristophanes' Ecclesiazusae." *TAPA* 135: 163–76.

Conkey, M. W. 1991. "Contexts of action, contexts for power: Material culture and gender in the Magdalenian." In Conkey and Gero (eds.): 57–92.

Conkey, M. W. and Gero, J. M. (eds.) 1991. *Engendering Archaeology: Women and Prehistory.* Oxford.

Conkey, M. W. and Tringham, R. E. 1995. "Archaeology and the goddess: Exploring the contours of feminist archaeology." In Stanton, D. C. and Stewart, A. J. (eds.), *Feminisms in the Academy: Rethinking the Discipline.* Ann Arbor, MI. 199–247.

Connolly, J. 1998. "Mastering corruption: Constructions of identity in Roman oratory." In Joshel and Murnaghan (eds.): 130–51.

Connelly, J. B. 2007. *Portrait of a Priestess. Women and Ritual in Ancient Greece.* Princeton, NJ.

Cooley, A. E. and Cooley, M. G. L. 2004. *Pompeii: A Sourcebook.* London and New York.

Cooper, J. 2006. "Prostitution." *Reallexikon der Assyriologie*, 11. Berlin. 12–21.

Cooper, K. 1992. "Insinuations of womanly influence: An aspect of the Christianization of the Roman Aristocracy." *JRS* 82: 150–64.

—— 1996. *The Virgin and the Bride: Idealized Womanhood in Late Antiquity.* Cambridge, MA.

Corbelli, J. 2006. *The Art of Death in Graeco-Roman Egypt.* Aylesbury.

Corbett, P. 1931. *The Roman Law of Marriage.* Oxford.

Cormack, S. 2007. "The tombs at Pompeii." In Dobbins and Foss (eds.): 585–606.

Corrigan, E. 1979. *Lucanian Tomb Paintings Excavated at Paestum 1969–1972: An Iconographic Study.* Ann Arbor, MI.

Couilloud, M.-T. 1974. *Les monuments funéraires de Rhénée: Exploration archéologique de Délos 30.* Paris.

Cova, A. (ed.) 2006. *Comparative Women's History: New Approaches.* New York. [French edition revised, 2009. Lyon.]

Cox, C. A. 1989. "Incest, inheritance and the political forum in fifth-century Athens." *CJ* 85: 34–46.

—— 1998. *Household Interests: Property, Marriage Strategies, and Family Dynamics in Ancient Athens.* Princeton, NJ.

—— 2006. "Sibling relationships in Menander." In Bresson, A., Masson, M.-P., Perentidis, S., and Wilgaux, J. (eds.), *Parenté et Société dans le Monde Grec de l'Antiquité a l'Âge Moderne. Ausonius Éditions Études* 12. Bordeaux. 153–8.

Cox, M. and Scott, A. 1992. "Evaluation of the obstetric significance of some pelvic characters in an 18th century British sample of known parity status." *AJPA* 89: 431–40.

Crawford, S. W. 1998. "Lady Wisdom and Dame Folly at Qumran." *Dead Sea Discoveries* 5.3: 355–66.

—— 2003. "Not according to rule: Women, the Dead Sea Scrolls and Qumran." In Paul, S. M. (ed.), *Emanuel: Studies in Hebrew Bible Septuagint and Dead Sea in Honour of Emanuel Tov.* Boston. 127–50.

Cribiore, R. 2001. *Gymnastics of the Mind: Greek Education in Hellenistic and Roman Egypt.* Princeton.

Croom, A. T. 2000. *Roman Clothing and Fashion.* Stroud.

Culham, P. 1986. "Again, what meaning lies in colour!" *ZPE* 64: 235–45.

Cullen, T. (ed.) 2001. *Aegean Prehistory: A Review. AJA* Suppl. 1. Boston.

—— 2005. "A profile of Aegean prehistorians." In *Prehistorians Round the Pond: Reflections on Aegean Prehistory as a Discipline. Kelsey Museum Publications* 2. 43–72.

Cunnally, J. 1999. *Images of the Illustrious. The Numismatic Presence in the Renaissance.* Princeton.

Curtis, J. E., McCall, H., Collon, D., and al-Gailani Werr, L. (eds.) 2008. *New Light on Nimrud: Proceedings of the Nimrud Conference 11th-13th March 2002.* London.

Cussini, E. 2004. "Regina, Martay and the others: Stories of Palmyrene women." *Orientalia* 73: 1–10.

—— 2005a. "Beyond the spindle: Investigating the role of Palmyrene women." In Cussini (ed.): 26–43.

—— (ed.) 2005b. *A Journey to Palmyra. Collected Essays to Remember Delbert R. Hillers.* Leiden and Boston.

Daehner, J. (ed.) 2007. *The Herculaneum Women: History, Context, Identities.* Los Angeles, CA.

D'Agata, A. L. 2009. "Women archaeologists and non-palatial Greece: A case-study from Crete 'of the hundred cities.'" In Kopaka (ed.): 263–71.

Dalley, S. 1980. "Old Babylonian dowries." *Iraq* 42: 53–74.

—— 1998. "Yabâ, Atalyā and the foreign policy of Late Assyrian Kings." *State Archives of Assyria Bulletin* 12: 83–98.

D'Ambrosio, A., Guzzo, P. G., and Mastroberto, M. (eds.) 2003. *Storie da un'eruzione: Pompei, Ercolano, Oplontis.* Naples.

D'Ambra, E. 1989. "The cult of virtues and the funerary relief of Ulpia Epigone." *Latomus* 48: 392–400.

—— 1996. "The Calculus of Venus: Nude portraits of Roman matrons." In Kampen (ed.): 219–32.

—— 2000. "Nudity and adornment in female portrait sculpture of the 2nd century AD." In Kleiner and Matheson (eds.): 101–14.

—— 2007. "Maidens and manhood in the worship of Diana at Nemi." In Parca and Tzanetou (eds.): 228–51.

Damerji, M. S. B. 1999. *Gräber Assyrischer Königinnen aus Nimrud.* Mainz.

Daniels, C. M. 1980. "Excavations at Wallsend and the fourth-century barracks on Hadrian's Wall." In Hanson, W. S. and Keppie, L. J. (eds.), *Roman Frontier Studies, 1979.* BAR International Seriers 71. Oxford. 173–93.

Darcque, P., Fotiadis, M., and Polychronopoulou, O. (eds.) 2006. *Mythos: La préhistoire égéenne du XIXe au XXe siècle après J.-C. BCH* Suppl. 25. Paris and Athens.

Dardaine, S. 2001. "La naissance des élites hispano-romaines en Bétique." In Navarro Caballero, M. and Demougin, S. (eds.), *Élites Hispaniques.* Paris. 23–44.

Darling, J. K. 1998–9. "Form and ideology: Rethinking Greek drapery." *Hephaistos* 16/17: 47–69.

D'Arms, J. H. 1984. "Upper-class attitudes towards viri municipales and their towns in the early Roman Empire." *Athenaeum* 62: 440–67.

D'Auria, S., Lacovara, P., and Roehrig, C. (eds.) 1988. *Mummies and Magic: The Funerary Arts of Ancient Egypt.* Boston.

Davies, G. 1997. "Gender and body language in Roman art." In Cornell, T. and Lomas, K. (eds.), *Gender and Ethnicity in Ancient Italy.* London. 97–107.

—— 2002. "Clothes as sign: The case of the large and small Herculaneum women." In Llewellyn-Jones (ed.): 227–41.

—— 2008. "Portrait statues as models for gender roles in Roman society." In Bell, S. and Hansen I. L. (eds.), *Role Models in the Roman World: Identity and Assimilation.* Ann Arbor, MI. 207–20.

Davies, J. K. 1971. *Athenian Propertied Families 600–300 B.C.* Oxford.

Davies, S. L. 1980. *The Revolt of the Widows: The Social World of the Apocryphal Acts.* Carbondale, IL.

Davis, E. N. 1986. "Youth and age in the Thera frescoes." *AJA* 90: 399–406.

—— 1995. "Art and politics in the Aegean: The missing ruler." In Rehak (ed.): 11–20.

Davis, W. 2003. "Gender." In Nelson and Shiff (eds.): 330–44.

Day, J. 1989. "Rituals in stone: Early Greek grave epigrams and monuments." *JHS* 109: 16–28.

—— 1994. "Interactive offerings: Early Greek dedicatory epigrams and ritual." *Harvard Studies in Classical Philology* 96: 37–74.

—— 2007. "Poems on stone." In Bing and Bruss (eds.): 29–47.

Day, P. M. and Wilson, D. E. 2002. "Landscapes of memory, craft, and power in Prepalatial and Protopalatial Knossos." In Hamilakis (ed.): 143–66.

Day, P. M., Wilson, D. E., Kiriatzi, E. 1997. "Reassessing specialization in Prepalatial Cretan ceramic production." In Laffineur and Betancourt (eds.): 277–90.

De Angelis, F. 2001. "Specchi e miti: Sulla ricezione della mitologia greca in Etruria." *Ostraka* 11: 37–73.

Dean-Jones, L. 1994. *Women's Bodies in Classical Greek Science*. Oxford.

Debru, A. 1992. "La suffocation hystérique chez Galien et Aetius: Réécriture et emprunt de 'jel.'" In Garzya, A. (ed.), *Tradizione e ecdotica dei testi medici tardoantichi e bizantini (Atti del Convegno Internazionale Anacapre 29–31 ottobre 1990)*. Naples. 79–89.

De Lacy, P. (ed.) 1992. *Galen, de Semine*. Berlin.

Delatte, A. 1915. *Études sur la Literature Pythagoricienne*. Paris.

Demakopoulou, K. (ed.) 1988. *The Mycenean World: Five Centuries of Early Greek Culture, 1600–110 B.C.* Athens.

Demand, N. 1994. *Birth, Death, and Motherhood in Classical Greece*. Baltimore, MD.

De Miro, E. 1996. "Greek sculpture in Sicily in the Classical period." In Pugliese Carratelli (ed.): 413–42.

De Montfaucon, B. 1721–2. *Antiquity Explained, and Represented in, Sculptures*. Transl. D. Humphreys. London.

Dench, E. 2005. *From Barbarians to New Men: Greek, Roman, and Modern Perceptions of Peoples from the Central Apennines*. Oxford.

Depauw, M. 2010. "Do mothers matter? The emergence of matronymics in Early Roman Egypt." In Evans, T. V. and Obbink, D. D. (eds.), *The Language of the Papyri*. Oxford. 120–39.

De Pretis, A. 2003. "'Insincerity,' 'facts,' and 'epistolarity': Approaches to Pliny's *Epistles* to Calpurnia." *Arethusa* 36: 127–46.

De Saussure, F., Bally, C., and Sechehaye, A. (eds.), in collaboration with Riedlinger, A. 1959. *Course in General Linguistics*. Transl. W. Baskin. New York.

Descoeudres, J.-P. 2007. "History and historical sources." In Dobbins and Foss (eds.): 9–27.Desmond, M. 1994. *Reading Dido: Gender, Textuality and the Medieval Aeneid*. Minneapolis, MN.

Detienne, M. 1989. "The violence of wellborn ladies: Women in the Thesmophoria." In Detienne, M. and Vernant, J.-P. (eds.), *The Cuisine of Sacrifice among the Greeks*. Transl. P. Wissing. Chicago, IL.

Dieleman, J. 2005. *Priests, Tongues, and Rites: The London-Leiden Magical Manuscripts and Translation in Egyptian Ritual (100–300 CE)*. Boston, MA.

di Leonardo, M. (ed.) 1991. *Gender at the Crossroads of Knowledge: Feminist Anthropology in the Postmodern Era*. Berkeley, CA and Los Angeles, CA.

Dillon, J. M. and Hershbell, J. P. 1991. *Iamblichus, De Vita Pythagorica*. Atlanta, GA.

Dillon, M. 2002. *Girls and Women in Classical Greek Religion*. London.

Dillon, S. 2007. "Portraits of women in the Early Hellenistic period." In Schultz and von den Hoff (eds.): 63–83.

—— 2010. *The Female Portrait Statue in the Greek World*. Cambridge.

Dixon, S. 1984. "'*Infirmitas sexus*': Womanly weakness in Roman law." *Tijdschrift voór Rechtsgeschiedenis* 52: 343–71.

—— 1988. *The Roman Mother*. London.

—— 1992. *The Roman Family*. Baltimore, MD.

—— 2001. *Reading Roman Women. Sources, Genres and Real Life*. London.

—— 2007. *Cornelia, Mother of the Gracchi*. London.

Dobbins, J. J. 1994. "Problems of chronology, decoration, and urban design in the Forum at Pompeii." *AJA* 98: 629–94.

—— 2007. "The forum and its dependencies." In Dobbins and Foss (eds.): 150–83.

Dobbins, J. J. and Foss, P. W. (eds.) 2007. *The World of Pompeii*. London and New York.

Docter, R. F. and Moorman. E. M. (eds.) 1999. *Proceedings of the XVth International Congress of Classical Archaeology*. Amsterdam.

Dodd, D. B. and Faraone, C. A. (eds.) 2003. *Initiation in Ancient Greek Rituals and Narratives*. New York.

Doherty, L. E. 1995. *Siren Songs: Gender, Audiences, and Narrators in the Odyssey*. Ann Arbor, MI.

Dolansky, F. 2011. "Reconsidering the Matronalia and women's rites." *CW* 104: 191–209.

Donald, M. and Hurcombe, L. (eds.) 2000. *Gender and Material Culture in Archaeological Perspective*. New York.

Donohue, A. A. 1999. "Ideology and historiography in the study of Classical art." In Docter and Moorman (eds.): 155–8.

—— 2005. *Greek Sculpture and the Problem of Description*. New York.

Donahue, J. F. 2004. "Iunia Rustica of Cartima: Female munificence in the Roman West." *Latomus* 63: 873–91.

Dosse, F. 1998. *History of Structuralism 2: The Sign Sets, 1967–Present*. Minneapolis, MN.

Dougherty, C. 1993. *The Poetics of Colonization: From City to Text in Archaic Greece*. New York.

—— 1998. "Sowing the seeds of violence: Rape, women, and the land." In Wyke (ed.): 267–84.

Doumas, C. 1992. *The Wall Paintings of Thera*. Athens.

Dover, K. (ed.) 1980. *Plato: Symposium*. Cambridge.

Doxiadis, E. 1995. *The Mysterious Fayum Portraits: Faces from Ancient Egypt*. London.

Drijvers, H. J. W. 1982. "Afterlife and funerary symbolism in Palmyrene religion." In Bianchi, U. and Vermaseren, M. J. (eds.), *La soteriologia dei culti oriental nell'Impero Romano*. Leiden. 709–33.

Drine, A. 1994. "Cérès, les Cereres et les sacerdotes magnae en Afrique: Quelques témoignages épigraphiques et littéraires (Tertullien)." In Le Bohec, Y. (ed.), *L'Afrique, la Gaule, la Religion à l'Époque Romaine. Mélangesa la Mémoire de Marcel le Glay. Coll. Latomus* 226. Brussels. 174–84.

Dudley, D. R. and Webster, G. 1962. *The Rebellion of Boudicca*. London.

Dué, C. 2002. *Homeric Variations on a Lament by Briseis*. New York.

Dumézil, G. 1970. *Archaic Roman Religion*. Chicago.

Dunand, F. 1973. *Le culte d'Isis dans le bassin oriental de la Méditerranée, I*. Leiden.

—— 1978. "Le statut des 'hiereiai' en Égypte romaine." In de Boer, M. B. and Edridge, T. A. (eds.), *Hommages à Maarten J. Vermaseren, vol 1*. Leiden. 352–74.

—— 2007. "The religious system in Alexandria." In Ogden, D. (ed.), *A Companion to Greek Religion*. Malden, MA. 253–63.

Dunbabin, K. M. D. 2003. *The Roman Banquet: Images of Conviviality*. Cambridge.

Dunbabin, T. J. 1948. *The Western Greeks, the History of Sicily and South Italy from the Foundation of the Greek Colonies to 480 B.C.* Oxford.

DuQuesne, T. 2007. "Private devotion and public practice: Aspects of Egyptian art and religion as revealed by the Salakhana Stelae." In Schneider, T. and Szpakowska, K. (eds.), *Egyptian Stories: A British Egyptological Tribute to Alan B. Lloyd on the Occasion of his Retirement*. Münster. 55–73.

Durand, J.-M. (ed.) 1987. *La femme dans le Proche-Orient: Compte Rendu de la XXXIIIe Rencontre Assyriologique Internationale (Paris, 7–10 Juillet 1986)*. Paris.

Düring, I. 1980. *Ptolemaios und Porphyrios über die Musik*. New York.

Durning, L. and Wrigley, R. (eds.) 2000. *Gender and Architecture*. Chichester.

Duthuit, G. 1931. *La Sculpture Copte: Statues, Bas-reliefs, Masques*. Paris.

Dutsch, D. 2008. *Feminine Discourse in Roman Comedy: On Echoes and Voices*. Oxford.

Dzielska, M. 1995. *Hypatia of Alexandria*. Transl. F. Lyra. Cambridge.

Easterling, P. E. (ed.) 1997. *The Cambridge Companion to Greek Tragedy*. Cambridge.

Eck, W. 1984. "Senatorial self-representation: Developments in the Augustan period." In Millar, F. and Segal, E. (eds.), *Caesar Augustus: Seven Aspects*. Oxford. 129–67.

—— 1992. "Ehrungen für Personen hohen soziopolitischen Ranges im öffentlichen und privaten Bereich." In Schalles, H.-J., von Hesberg, H., and Zanker, P. (eds.), *Die römische Stadt im 2. Jahrhundert n. Chr. Der Funktionswandel des öffentlichen Raumes. Kolloquium in Xanten vom 2. bis 4. Mai 1990*. Köln. 359–76.

—— 1997. "Rome and the outside world: Senatorial families and the world they lived in." In Rawson, B. and Weaver, P. (eds.), *The Roman Family in Italy: Status, Sentiment, Space*. Oxford. 73–99.

Eco, U. 1979. *Lector in fabula*. Milano. [English transl. *The Role of the Reader*. Bloomington, IN.]

Edmunds, L. 2003. "The abduction of the beautiful wife: The basic story of the Trojan War." *Studia Philologica Valentina* 6.3: 1–36.

Edmondson, J. and Keith, A. (eds.) 2008. *Roman Dress and the Fabrics of Roman Culture*. Toronto, ON.Edwards, C. 1993. *The Politics of Immorality in Ancient Rome*. Cambridge.

—— 1996. *Writing Rome: Textual Approaches to the City*. Cambridge.

Ehrenberg, M. 1989. *Women in Prehistory*. London.

Eicher, J. B. and Roach-Higgins, M. E. 1992. "Definition and classification of dress: Implication for analysis of gender roles." In Barnes, R. and Eicher, J. B. (eds.), *Dress and Gender: Making and Meaning in Cultural Contexts*. Oxford. 8–28.

Eliade, M. 1959. *The Sacred and the Profane: The Nature of Religion*. New York.

Eller, C. 2000. *The Myth of Matriarchal Prehistory*. Boston.

Elliott, J. K. 1993. *The Apocryphal New Testament: A Collection of Apocryphal Christian Literature in an English Translation*. Oxford.

Elmer, D. F. 2005. "Helen *epigrammatopoios*." *CA* 24: 1–39.

Elster, E. S. 1997. "Construction and use of the Early Bronze Age Burnt House at Sitagroi: Craft and technology." In Laffineur and Betancourt (eds.): 19–35.

Engels, D. 1980. "The problem of female infanticide in the Greco-Roman world." *CP* 75: 112–20.

Entwistle, J. 2001. "The dressed body." In Entwistle, J. and Wilson, E. (eds.), *Body Dressing*. Oxford. 33–58.

Eriksson, M. C. 1996. "Two engraved mirrors from the Thordvaldsen Museum, Copenhagen." *Opuscula Romana* 20: 21–36.

Eule, J. C. 2001. *Hellenistische Bürgerinnen aus Kleinasien: Weibliche Gewandstatuenin ihrem antiken Kontext*. Istanbul.

—— 2002. "Die statuarische Darstelllung von Frauen in Athen im 4. und frühen 3. Jh. v. Chr." In Blum, H. (ed.), *Brückenland Anatolien? Ursachen, Extensität und Modi des Kulturaustausches zwischen Anatolien und seinen Nachbarn*. Tübingen. 205–29.

Evans, A. J. 1964. *The Palace of Minos: A Comparative Account of the Successive Stages of the Early Cretan Civilisation as Illustrated by the Discoveries at Knossos, Vols. I-IV*. New York.

Evans-Grubbs, J. 2002. *Women and the Law in the Roman Empire: A Sourcebook on Marriage, Divorce and Widowhood*. London.

Evison, M. P. 2001. "Ancient DNA in Greece: Problems and prospects." *Journal of Radioanalytical and Nuclear Chemistry* 24: 673–8.

Fabre-Serris, J. 2009. "Explorations génériques au livre 4 de Properce. Des voix nouvelles dans l'élégie: Quelques réflexions sur les poèmes 7 et 9." In van Mal-Maeder, D., Burnier, A., and Núñez L. (eds.), *Jeux de voix: Enonciation, intertextualité et intentionnalité dans la littérature antique*. Bern. 157–73.

Fagan, G. G. 1999. *Bathing in Public in the Roman World*. Ann Arbor, MI.

Fantham, E. 1975. "Sex, status, and survival in Hellenistic Athens: A study of women in New Comedy." *Phoenix* 29: 44–74.

—— 2006. *Julia Augusti: The Emperor's Daughter*. New York.

—— 2008. "Covering the head at Rome: Ritual and gender." In Edmondson and Keith (eds.): 158–72.

Fantham, E., Foley, H. P., Kampen, N. B., Pomeroy, S. B., and Shapiro, A. (eds.) 1994. *Women in the Classical World: Image and Text*. Oxford.

Faraone, C. A. 2003. "Playing the bear and the fawn for Artemis: Female initiation or substitute sacrifice?" In Dodd and Faraone (eds.): 43–68.

Faraone, C. and McClure, L. (eds.) 2006. *Prostitutes and Courtesans in the Ancient World*. Madison, WI.

Farron, S. 1979. "The portrayal of women in the Iliad." *Acta Classica* 22: 15–31.

Favro, D. 1996. *The Urban Image of Augustan Rome*. Cambridge.

Fear, A. T. 1997. "Women in Roman religion." [Review of Montero Herrero, S. 1994. *Diosas y adivinas: Mujer y adivinación en la Roma antigue*. Madrid.] *CR* 47: 326–7.

Fear, T. 2000. "The poet as pimp: Elegiac seduction in the time of Augustus." *Arethusa* 33: 217–40.

Fejfer, J. 2002. "Ancestral aspects of the Roman honorary statue." In Højte (ed.): 247–56.

—— 2006. "Interpreting images of Roman Imperial women." [Review of Alexandridis, A. 2004.] *JRA* 19: 465–72.

—— 2008. *Roman Portraits in Context*. Berlin.

Feldman, M. H. 2006a. "Assur Tomb 45 and the Birth of Assyrian Empire." *Bulletin of the American Schools of Oriental Research* 343: 21–43.

—— 2006b. *Diplomacy by Design: Luxury Arts and an "International Style" in the Ancient Near East, 1400–1200 BCE*. Chicago, IL.

Felson, N. 1994. *Regarding Penelope. From Character to Poetics*. London.

Felson, N. and Slatkin, L. 2004. "Gender and Homeric epic." In Fowler (ed.): 91–114.

Felson-Rubin, N. 1996. "Penelope's perspective: Character from plot." In Schein (ed.): 163–83.

Feraudi-Gruénais, F. 2003. *Inschriften und Selbstdarstellung in stadtrömischen Grabbauten*. Rome.

Ferrandini Troisi, F. 2000. *La donna nella società ellenistica: Testimonianze epigrafiche*. Bari.

Ferrari, G. 2002. *Figures of Speech: Men and Maidens in Ancient Greece*. Chicago, IL.

—— 2003. "Myth and genre on Athenian vases." *CA* 22: 37–54.

Filges, A. 1997. *Standbilder jugendlicher Göttinnen. Klassische und frühhellenistische Gewandstatuen mit Brustwulst und ihre kaiserzeitliche Rezeption*. Köln.

Finley, M. I. 1968. *Ancient Sicily to the Arab Conquest*. London.

—— 1977. *The World of Odysseus*. London.

—— 1978. *The World of Odysseus*. Second edition. New York.

—— 1985. *Studies in Land and Credit in Ancient Athens, 500–200 B.C.* Revised edition. Oxford.

Fischler, S. 1998. "Imperial cult: Engendering the cosmos." In L. Foxhall and J. Salmon (eds.), *When Men Were Men: Masculinity, Power and Identity in Classical Antiquity*. New York. 165–83.

Fishwick, D. 1987–2005. *The Imperial Cult in the Latin West. Studies in the Ruler Cult of the Western Provinces of the Roman Empire, vols I-III*. Leiden.

Fittschen, K. 1982. *Die Bildnistypen der Faustina minor und die Fecunditas Augustae*. Gottingen.

—— 1996. "Courtly portraits of women in the era of the adoptive emperors (98–180) and their reception in Roman society." In Kleiner and Matheson (eds.): 42–51.

Fittschen, K. and Zanker, P. 1983. *Katalog der römischen Porträts in den Capitolinischen Museen und den anderen kommunalen Sammlungen der Stadt Rom, volume III*. Mainz am Rhein.

Fitzgerald, W. 1988. "Power and impotence in Horace's *Epodes*." *Arethusa* 17, 176–91.

Flach, D. 1991. *Die sogenannte Laudatio Turiae: Einleitung, Text, Übersetzung, und Kommentar*. Darmstadt.

Flaschenreim, B. L. 1999. "Sulpicia and the rhetoric of disclosure." *CP* 94: 36–54.

Fleming, A. 1969. "The myth of the mother-goddess." *World Archaeology* 1: 247–61.

Fleming, D. E. 1992. *The Installation of Baal's High Priestess at Emar*. Atlanta, GA.

Flemming, R. 2000. *Medicine and the Making of Roman Women: Gender, Nature, and Authority from Celsus to Galen*. Oxford.

—— 2007. "Women, writing, and medicine in the classical world." *CQ* 57: 257–79.

Flemming, R. and Hanson, A. E. 1998. "Hippocrates' *Peri Parthenión* (*Diseases of Young Girls*): Text and Translation." *Early Science and Medicine* 3: 241–52.

Fletcher, J. 2011. *Cleopatra the Great: The Woman Behind the Legend.* London.

Flory, M. B. 1993. "Livia and the history of public honorific statues for women in Rome." *TAPA* 123: 287–308.

—— 1995a. "The symbolism of laurel in cameo portraits of Livia." *Memoirs of the American Academy in Rome* 40: 43–68.

—— 1995b. "The deification of Roman women." *Ancient History Bulletin* 9: 127–34.

—— 1996. "Dynastic ideology, the Domus Augusta, and imperial women: A lost statuary group in the Circus Flaminius." *TAPA* 126: 287–306.

Flower, H. 2002. "Were women ever 'ancestors' in Republican Rome?" In Højte (ed.): 159–84.

Foley, H. P. (ed.) 1981. *Reflections of Women in Antiquity.* New York.

—— 1984. "'Reverse similes' and sex roles in the Odyssey." In Peradotto and Sullivan (eds.): 59–78.

—— 1995. "Penelope as moral agent." In Cohen (ed.) 1995: 93–115.

—— 2001. *Female Acts in Greek Tragedy.* Princeton, NJ.

Foley, J. M. 1999. *Homer's Traditional Art.* University Park, PA.

Föllinger, S. 1996. "Σχέτλια ⬛ρῶσι. 'Hysterie' in den hippokratischen Schriften." In Wittern, R. and Pellegrin, P. (eds.), *Hippokratische Medizin und antike Philosophie. Medizin der Antike* 1. Zürich. 437–50.

Fontana, S. 2001. "Leptis Magna: The Romanization of a major African city through burial evidence." In Keay, S. and Terrenato, N. (eds.), *Italy and the West: Comparative Issues in Romanization.* Oxford. 161–72.

Fora, M. 1992. "Ummidia Quadratilla ed il restauro del teatro di Cassino (per una nuova lettura di AE 1946, 174." *ZPE* 94: 269–73.

Forbis, E. 1990. "Women's public image in Italian honorary inscriptions." *AJP* 111: 493–512.

Foster, K. P. and Laffineur, R. (eds.) 2003. *Metron: Measuring the Aegean Bronze Age. Aegaeum* 24. Liège.

Fowden, E. 1990. "The Early Minoan Goddess: Images of provision." *JRS* III-IV: 15–18.

Fowler, M. A. 1994. *Theopompus of Chios: History and Rhetoric in the Fourth Century BC.* Oxford.

Fowler, R. (ed.) 2004. *The Cambridge Companion to Homer.* Cambridge.

Fowler, W. W. 1908. *Social Life at Rome in the Age of Cicero.* New York.

Fox, S. C., Eliopoulos, C., Lagia, A., and Manolis, S. 2003. "Sexing the Sella Turcica: A question of English vs. Turkish saddles?" 72nd Annual Meeting of the American Association of Physical Anthropologists. Tempe, Arizona. Abstract, *AJPA* 120 (Suppl. 36): 96.

Foxhall, L. 2009. "Gender." In Raaflaub, K. A. and van Wees, H. (eds.), *A Companion to Archaic Greece.* Chichester. 483–507.

Franco, C. 2003. *Senza ritegno: Il cane e la donna nell'immaginario della Grecia antica.* Bologna.

—— 2010. "Il mito di Circe." In Bettini, M. and Franco, C. (eds.), *Il mito di Circe.* Torino. 25–380.

Frankfurter, D. 1998. *Religion in Roman Egypt: Assimilation and Resistance.* Princeton, NJ.

Fraschetti, A. 2005. *The Foundation of Rome.* Transl. M. Hill and K. Windle. Edinburgh.

Fredricksmeyer, H. C. 1997. "Penelope *polutropos*: The crux at *Odyssey* 23.218–24." *AJP* 118: 487–97.

Freeland, C. (ed.) 1998. *Re-reading the Canon: A Series devoted to Feminist Interpretations of Major Philosophers, Volume on Aristotle.* University Park, PA.

Freeman, E. 1891–4. *A History of Sicily from the Earliest Times.* Oxford

Frei-Stolba, R. 1998. "Recherches sur la position juridique et sociale de Livie, l'épouse d'Auguste." *Etudes de Lettres. Revue de l'Université de Lausanne*: 65–89.

Frei-Stolba, R. and Zimmermann, T. 1998. "Les prêtresses campaniennes sous l'Empire romain." *Etudes de Lettres. Revue de l'Université de Lausanne*: 91–116.

Frei-Stolba, R., Bielman, A., and Bianchi, O. (eds.) 2003. *Les Femmes Antiques entre Sphère Antique et Sphère Publique*. Bern.

Fried, M. 1996. *Manet's Modernism or, The Face of Painting in the 1860s*. Chicago, IL.

Frontisi-Ducroux, F. 1996. "Eros, desire, and the gaze." Transl. N. Kline. In Kampen (ed.): 81–100.

Frontisi-Ducroux, F. and Vernant, J.-P. 1997. *Dans l'œil du miroir*. Paris.

Frymer-Kensky, T. 1992. *In the Wake of the Goddesses: Women, Culture and the Biblical Transformation of Pagan Myth*. New York.

Fuller, B. T., Molleson, T. I., Harris, D. A., Gilmour, L. T., and Hedges, R. E. M. 2006. "Isotopic evidence for breastfeeding and possible adult dietary differences from Late/Sub-Roman Britain." *AJPA* 129: 45–54.

Gabra, S. 1941. *Rapport sur les fouilles d'Hermoupolis Ouest (Touna el-Gebel)*. Cairo.

Gager, J. G. 1975. *Kingdom and Community: The Social World of Early Christianity*. Englewood, NJ.

Galaty, M. L. and Parkinson, W. A. (eds.) 2007. *Rethinking Mycenean Palaces II*. Los Angeles, CA.

Galter, H. D., Levine, L. D., and Reade, J. E. 1986. "The Colossi of Sennacherib's Palace and their inscriptions." *Annual Review of the Royal Inscriptions of Mesopotamia* 4: 27–32.

Gansell, A. R. 2007a. "From Mesopotamia to modern Syria: Ethnoarchaeological perspectives on female adornment during rites of passage." In Cheng and Feldman (eds.): 449–83.

—— 2007b. "Identity and adornment in the third-millennium BC 'Royal Tombs' at Ur." *Cambridge Archaeological Journal* 17: 29–46.

—— 2009. "Measuring beauty: An anthropometric methodology for the assessment of ideal feminine beauty as embodied in first millennium BCE ivory carvings." In Cecchini, S. M., Mazzoni, S., and Scigliuzzo, E. (eds.), *Syrian and Phoenician Ivories of the First Millennium BCE*. Pisa. 155–70.

Gardner, J. F. 1986. *Women in Roman Law and Society*. London.

—— 1990. *Women in Roman Law and Society*. Third edition. London.

—— 1993. *Being a Roman Citizen*. London.

—— 1995. "Gender-role assumptions in Roman law." *EMC/CV* 39, n.s. 14: 377–400.

Garland, L. (ed.) 2006. *Byzantine Women: Varieties of Experience 800–1200*. Aldershot, UK and Burlington, VT.

Garvie-Lok, S. 2001. *Loaves and Fishes: A Stable Isotope Reconstruction of Diet in Medieval Greece*. Diss., University of Calgary.

—— 2008. "Weaning pains: assessing juvenile scurvy in a Late Roman Greek population." Abstract, Annual meeting of the Archaeological Institute of America. http://aia.archaeological.org/webinfo.php?page=10248&searchtype=abstract&ytable=2008&sessionid=5F&paperid=1490

—— 2009. "Population mobility at Frankish Corinth: Evidence from stable oxygen isotope ratios of tooth enamel." In Schepartz et al. (eds.): 245–56.

Gaspar, V. 2011. "Status and gender in the priesthood of Ceres in Roman North Africa." In Richardson, J. H. and Santangelo, F. (eds.), *Priests and State in the Roman World. Potsdamer Altertumswissenschaftliche Beiträge* 33. Stuttgart.

Gasperini, L. 1989. "La dignità della donna nel mondo etrusco e il suo lontano riflesso nell' onomastica personale romana." In Rallo (ed.) 1989b: 181–211.

Gawlinski, L. 2008. "'Fashioning' initiates: Dress at the mysteries." In Colburn and Heyn (eds.): 146–69.

Geddes, A. G. 1987. "Rags and riches: The costume of Athenian men in the fifth century." *CQ* 37: 307–31.

Geller, P. and Stockett, M. 2006. *Feminist Anthropology: Past, Present, and Future*. Philadelphia, PA.

Gentili, B. and Perusino, F. 2002. *Le Orse di Brauron: Un rituale di iniziazione femminile nel santuario di Artemide*. Pisa.

Gentili, G. V. 1954. "Megara Hyblaea – Tombe arcaiche e reperti sporadici nellaproprietà della 'Raisom' e tomba arcaica in predio Vinci." *NSc.* 80–113.

German, S. 2005. *Performance, Power and Art in the Aegean Bronze Age.* Oxford.

Gesell, G. C. 1985. *Town, Palace and House Cult in Minoan Crete.* Göteborg.

Geyika, M. F., Gürb, A., Nasb, K., Çevikb, R., Saraçb, J., Dikicic, B., and Ayaza, A. 2002. "Musculoskeletal involvement in brucellosis in different age groups: A study of 195 cases." *Swiss Medical Weekly* 132: 98–105.

Gigante, L. M. 1980. *A Study of Perspective from the Representations of Architectural Forms in Greek Classical and Hellenistic Painting.* Diss., University of North Carolina, Chapel Hill.

Gilchrist, R. 1999. *Gender and Archaeology: Contesting the Past.* London.

Gilman, S. L., King, H., Porter, R., Rousseau, G. S., and Showalter, E. 1993. *Hysteria Beyond Freud.* Berkeley, CA.

Gimbutas, M. 1974. *The Gods and Goddesses of Old Europe, 7000–3500 BC.* Berkeley, CA.

—— 1989. *The Language of the Goddess: Unearthing the Hidden Symbols.* San Francisco, CA.

Ginsburg, J. 2006. *Representing Agrippina. Constructions of Female Power in the Early Roman Empire.* Oxford.

Glazebrook, A. 2005. "Prostituting female kin." *Dike* 8: 34–53.

—— 2011. "Porneion: Prostitution in Athenian civic space." In Glazebrook and Henry (eds.): 34–59.

Glazebrook, A. and Henry, M. M. (eds.) 2011. *Greek Prostitutes in the Ancient Mediterranean, 800 BCE – 200 CE.* Madison, WI.

Goff, B. 2004. *Citizen Bacchae: Women's Ritual Practice in Ancient Greece.* Berkeley, CA.

Gold, B. K. 1998. "'The house I live in is not my own': Women's bodies in Juvenal's *Satires.*" *Arethusa* 31: 368–86.

Golden, M. 1986. "Names and naming at Athens: Three studies." *EMC* 30: 245–69.

—— 1990. *Children and Childhood in Classical Athens.* Baltimore, MD.

—— 1998. *Sport and Society in Ancient Greece.* Cambridge.

Goldhill, S. 1997. "The audience of Athenian tragedy." In Easterling (ed.): 54–68.

Gomme, A. W. and Sandbach, F. H. 1973. *Menander: A Commentary.* Oxford.

González Marcén, P., Montón, S., Picazo M., and Sánchez Romero, M. (eds.) 2008. *Engendering Social Dynamics. The Archaeology of Maintenance Activities. BAR* International Series.

Good, I. 2001. "Archaeological textiles: A review of current research." *Annual Review of Anthropology* 30: 209–26.

Goodison, L. 1989. *Death, Women and the Sun. Symbolism of Regeneration in Early Aegean Religion.* University of London, Institute of Classical Studies, Bulletin Supplement 53.

—— 2009. "Gender, body and the Minoans: Contemporary and prehistoric perceptions." In Kopaka (ed.): 233–42.

Goodison, L. and Morris, C. (eds.) 1998a. *Ancient Goddesses: The Myths and the Evidence.* Madison, WI.

—— 1998b. "Introduction: Exploring female divinity, from modern myths to ancient evidence." In Goodison and Morris (eds.): 6–21.

Goodman, A. H., Martin, D. L., and Armelagos, G. J. 1984. "Indications of stress from bone and teeth." In Cohen and Armelagos (eds.): 13–49.

Goodman, A. H. and Rose, J. C. 1990. "Assessment of systemic physiological perturbations from dental enamel hypoplasias and associated histological structure." *Yearbook of Physical Anthropology* 33: 59–110.

Gottdiener, M. 1995. *Postmodern Semiotics: Material Culture and the Forms of Postmodern Life.* Oxford.

Gourevitch, D. 1984. *Le mal d'être femme: La femme et la médecine dans la Rome antique.* Paris.

—— 1995. "Women who suffer from a man's disease: The example of Satyriasis and the debate on affections specific to the sexes." In Hawley and Levick (eds.): 149–65.

Gow, A. S. F. and Page, D. L. (eds.) 1965. *The Greek Anthology. Hellenistic Epigrams.* Cambridge.

—— 1995. "Women who suffer from a man's disease: The example of satyriasis and the debate on affections specific to the sexes." In Hawley and Levick (eds.): 149–65.

Gradel, I. 2007. "Agrippina: Life and legend." In Moltesen and Nielsen (eds.): 13–25.

Graf, F. 2003. "Initiation: A concept with a troubled history." In Dodd and Faraone (eds.): 3–24.

Graham, A. J. 1982. "The colonial expansion of Greece." In Boardman, J. and Hammond, N. G. L. (eds.), *Cambridge Ancient History, vol. III, part 3.* Cambridge. 83–162.

—— 1980–1. "Religion, women and Greek colonisation. *Atti di Centro di Ricerche e Documentazione sull. Antichità Classica* 11: 293–314.

—— 1995. "The Odyssey, history, and women." In Cohen (ed.) 1995: 3–16.

Graver, M. 1995. "Dog-Helen and the Homeric insult." *CA* 14: 41–61.

Graves-Brown, C. (ed.) 2008. *Sex and Gender in Ancient Egypt: "Don Your Wig for a Joyful Hour."* Swansea.

Green, C. M. C. 2007. *Roman Religion and the Cult of Diana at Aricia.* Cambridge.

Greene, E. 1998. *The Erotics of Domination.* Baltimore, MD.

Grether, G. 1946. "Livia and the Roman imperial cult." *AJP* 67: 222–52.

Griffith, G. T. 1935. *The Mercenaries of the Hellenistic World.* Cambridge.

Grmek, M. D. 1989. *Diseases in the Ancient Greek World.* Transl. M. Muellner and L. Muellner. Baltimore, MD.

Grosz, E. 1995. *Space, Time and Perversion: Essays on the Politics of Bodies.* London.

Grosz, K. 1983. "Bridewealth and dowry in Nuzi." In Cameron and Kuhrt (eds.): 193–206.

—— 1989. "Some aspects of the position of women in Nuzi." In Lesko (ed.): 167–80.

Gulick, C. B. (ed.) 1928. *Athenaeus, vol. II.* Cambridge, MA.

Gunter, A. 2009. *Greek Art and the Orient.* Cambridge.

Guralnick, E. 2008. "Fabric patterns as symbols of status in the near east and early Greece." In Colburn and Heyn (eds.): 84–114.

Gutzwiller, K. J. 2000. "The tragic mask of comedy: Metatheatricality in Menander." *CA* 19: 122–37.

—— 2007. *A Guide to Hellenistic Literature.* Malden, MA.

Gutzwiller, K. J. (ed.) 2005. *The New Posidippus: A Hellenistic Poetry Book.* New York.

Gwynn, A. 1918. "The character of Greek colonisation." *Journal of Hellenic Studies* 38: 88–123.

Haggis, D. C. 1993. "Intensive survey, traditional settlement patterns, and Dark Age Crete: The case of Early Iron Age Kavousi." *Journal of Mediterranean Archaeology* 6: 131–74.

Hänninen, M.-L. 2000. "Traces of women's devotion in the sanctuary of Diana at Nemi." In Brandt, J. R., Touati, A.-M., and Zahle, J. (eds.), *Nemi–Status Quo: Recent Research at Nemi and the Sanctuary of Diana.* Rome. 45–50.

Haley, E. W. 2003. *Baetica Felix: People and Prosperity in Southern Spain from Caesar to Septimius Severus.* Austin, TX.

Hall, E. 1989. *Inventing the Barbarian: Greek Self-Definition through Tragedy.* Oxford.

—— 1997. "The sociology of Greek tragedy." In Easterling (ed.): 93–126.

—— 2006. *The Theatrical Cast of Athens: Interactions between Ancient Greek Drama and Society.* Oxford.

Hall, J. M. 1997. *Ethnic Identity in Ancient Greece.* Cambridge.

Haller, A. 1954. *Die Gräber und Grüfte von Assur. Wissenschaftliche Veröffentlichungen der Deutschen Orient-Gesellschaft* 65. Berlin.

Hallett, J. P. 1977. "*Perusinae glandes* and the changing image of Augustus." *AJAH* 2: 151–71.

—— 1992. "Heeding our native informants: The uses of Latin literary texts in recovering elite Roman attitudes toward age, gender and social status." *EMC/CV* 11: 333–55.

—— 2002a. "Women writing in Rome and Cornelia, Mother of the Gracchi." In Churchill et al. (eds.): 18–29.

—— 2002b. "The eleven elegies of the Augustan elegist Sulpicia." In Churchill et al. (eds.): 45–65.

—— 2002c. "*Feminae furentes:* The frenzy of noble women in Vergil's *Aeneid* and the Letter of Cornelia, Mother of the Gracchi." In Anderson and Quartarone (eds.): 159–67.

—— 2006. "Fulvia, mother of Iullus Antonius: New approaches to the sources on Julia's adultery at Rome." *Helios* 33: 149–64.

—— 2009. "*AE* 1928.73 (epitaph of Petale Sulpicia) and Ovid, *Tristia* 3.7: Gender, class and Roman women's poetry." *Paper delivered at International Federation of the Societies of Classical Studies.* Berlin.

Hallett, J. P. and Skinner, M. B. (eds.) 1997. *Roman Sexualities.* Princeton, NJ.

Halloway, S. W. (ed.) 2006. *Orientalism, Assyriology and the Bible.* Sheffield.

Halperin, D., Winkler, J., and Zeitlin, F. (eds.) 1990. *Before Sexuality: The Construction of Erotic Experience in the Greek World.* Princeton, NJ.

Halstead, P. 1977. "The Bronze Age demography of Crete and Greece: A note." *ABSA* 72: 107–11.

Hamer, M. 2008. *Signs of Cleopatra: Reading an Icon Historically.* Second Edition. Exeter.

Hamilakis, Y. and Momigliano, N. (eds.) 2006. *Archaeology and European Modernity. Producing and Consuming the "Minoans." Creta Antica* 7. Padova.

Hamilakis, Y., Pluciennik, M., and Tarlow, S. (ed.) 2002. *Labyrinth Revisited: Rethinking "Minoan" Archaeology.* Oxford.

Hamilton, N. 2000. "Ungendering archaeology: Concepts of sex and gender in figurine studies in prehistory." In Donald and Hurcombe (eds.): 17–30.

Handley, E. and Hurst, A. (eds.) 1990. *Relire Ménandre: Recherches and Rencontres.* 2. Geneva.

Hannah, P. 2004. "The cosmetic use of red ochre (miltos)." In Cleland, L. Stears, K., and Davies, G. (eds.), *Colour in the Ancient Mediterranean World.* Oxford. 100–5.

Hanson, A. E. 1990. "The medical writers' woman." In Halperin et al. (eds.): 309–38.

—— 1992. "The logic of the gynecological prescriptions." In López Férez, J. A. (ed.), *Actas del VIIe colloque international hippocratique.* Madrid. 235–50.

—— 1998. "Talking recipes in the gynaecological texts of the Hippocratic corpus." In Wyke (ed.): 71–94.

Hanson, A. E. and Green, M. H. 1994. "Soranus of Ephesus: Methodicorum princeps." *ANRW* 37.2: 968–1075.

Hardwick, L. 1990. "Ancient Amazons—heroes, outsiders or women?" *G&R* 37: 14–36.

Harich-Schwarzbauer, H. and Späth, Th. (eds.) 2005. *Gender Studies in den Altertumswissenschaften: Räume und Geschlechter in der Antike.* Trier.

Harland, P. A. 2007. "Familial dimensions of group identity (II): 'mothers' and 'fathers' in associations and synagogues of the Greek world." *Journal for the Study of Judaism* 38: 57–79.

Harnack, A. 1908. *The Mission and Expansion of Christianity in the First Three Centuries.* Transl. J. Moffatt. Second Edition. New York.

Harper, P. O., Klengel-Brandt, E., Aruz, J., and Benzel, K. (eds.) 1995. *Discoveries at Ashur on the Tigris.* New York.

Harris, E. 1990. "Did the Athenians regard seduction as a worse crime than rape?" *CQ* 40: 370–7.

—— 1989. "Independent women in ancient Mesopotamia?" In Lesko (ed.): 145–65.

—— 1992. "Women in Mesopotamia." In Freedman, D. N. (ed.), *Anchor Bible Dictionary, vol 6.* New York. 947–51.

—— 2000. *Gender and Aging in Mesopotamia.* Norman, OK.

Harrison, A. R. W. 1968–71. *The Law of Athens.* 2 vols. Oxford.

Harrison, E. B. 1991. "The dress of the Archaic Greek korai." In Buitron-Oliver, D. (ed.), *New Perspectives in Early Greek Art. CASVA Symposium Papers* 16. Washington, DC. 217–39.

Hartog, F. 1988. The Mirror of Herodotus: *The Representations of the Other in the Writing of History*. Berkeley, CA.

Haselgrove, C. and Moore, T. 2007. *The Later Iron Age in Britain and Beyond*. Oxford.

Hauben, H. 1983. "Arsinoé II et la politique extérieure de l'Égypte." In van't Dack et al. (eds.): 99–127.

Hauptman, J. 1998. *Rereading the Rabbis: A Woman's Voice*. Boulder, CA.

Havelock, C. M. 1995. *The Aphrodite of Knidos and Her Successors: A Historical Review of the Female Nude in Greek Art*. Ann Arbor, MI.

Haynes, S. 2000. *Etruscan Civilization: A Cultural History*. London.

Hazzard, R. A. 2000. *Imagination of a Monarchy: Studies in Ptolemaic Propaganda*. Toronto, ON.

Hedreen, G. 1994. "Silens, nymphs, and maenads." *JHS* 114: 47–69.

—— 2009. "Ambivalence, Athenian Dionysiac vase-imagery and the discourse on human social evolution." In Oakley and Schmidt (eds.): 125–33.

Heitman, R. 2005. *Taking Her Seriously: Penelope and the Plot of Homer's Odyssey*. Ann Arbor, MI.

Helly, B. 1992. "Stèle funéraires de Démétrias: Recherches sur la chronologie des remparts et des nécropoles méridionales de la ville." Πρακτικά Διεθνούς Συνεδρίου για την αρχαία Θεσσαλία στη μνήμη Δ.Π. Θεοχάρη. 349–65.

Helms, M. 1993. *Craft and the Kingly Ideal: Art, Trade and Power*. Austin, TX.

Hemelrijk, E. A. 1999. *Matrona Docta: Educated Women in the Roman Elite from Cornelia to Julia Domna*. London.

—— 2004a. "City patronesses in the Roman Empire." *Historia* 53.2: 209–45.

—— 2004b. "Masculinity and femininity in the *Laudatio Turiae*." *Classical Quarterly* 54: 185–97.

—— 2005a. "Priestesses of the imperial cult in the Latin West: Titles and function." *Antiquité Classique* 74: 137–70.

—— 2005b. "Octavian and the introduction of public statues for women in Rome." *Athenaeum* 93.1: 309–17.

—— 2006a. "Priestesses of the imperial cult in the Latin West: Benefactions and public honour." *Antiquité Classique* 75: 85–117.

—— 2006b. "Imperial priestesses: A preliminary survey." In De Blois, L., Funke, P., and Hahn, J. (eds.), *The Impact of Imperial Rome on Religions, Ritual and Religious Life in the Roman Empire*. Leiden. 179–93.

—— 2007. "Local empresses: Priestesses of the imperial cult in the cities of the Latin West." *Phoenix* 61: 318–49.

—— 2008a. "Patronesses and 'mothers' of Roman collegia." *CA* 27: 115–62.

—— 2008b. "Women and sacrifice in the Roman Empire." In Hekster, O., Schmidt-Hofner, S., and Witschel, C. (eds.), *Ritual Dynamics and Religious Change in the Roman Empire*. Leiden. 253–67.

—— 2010. "Fictive kinship as a metaphor for women's civic roles." *Hermes* 138: 455–69.

Henderson, J. 1991. "Women and the Athenian dramatic festivals." *TAPA* 121: 133–47.

—— 1994. "*Timeo Danaos*: Amazons in early Greek art and pottery." In Goldhill, S. J. and Osborne O. (eds.), *Art and Text in Ancient Greek Culture*. Cambridge. 85–137.

—— 2010. *Three Plays by Aristophanes: Staging Women*. Second edition. New York.

Henderson, J. G. W. 1989. "Not 'women in Roman Satire' but 'when Satire writes "Woman."'" In S. Braund (ed.), *Satire and Society in Ancient Rome*. Exeter. 89–125.

Henneberg, M. and Henneberg, R. J. 1998. "Biological characteristics of the population based on the analysis of skeletal remains." In Carter (ed.): 503–62.

—— 2001. "Analysis of human skeletal and dental remains from Metaponto (7th-2nd c. BC)." In *Problemi della Chora Coloniale dall' Occidente al Mar Nero. Atti del Quarantesimo Convegno di Studi sulla Magna Grecia*. Taranto. 461–74.

Henry, M. 2011. "The traffic in women: From Homer to Hipponax, from war to commerce." In Glazebrook and Henry (eds.): 14–33.

Herfort-Koch, M. 1986. *Archaïsche Bronzeplastik laconiens (Boreas suppl. 4)*. Münster.

Herman, G. 1997. "The court society of the Hellenistic age." In Cartledge, P., Garnsey, P., and Gruen, E. (eds.), *Hellenistic Constructs: Essays in Culture, History, and Historiography*. Berkeley, CA. 199–224.

Herrmann, J. J., Jr. and Kondoleon, C. 2004. *Games for the Gods: The Greek Athlete and the Olympic Spirit*. Boston.

Hersch, K. 2010. *The Roman Wedding: Ritual and Meaning in Antiquity*. Cambridge.

Herzfeld, M. 1985. *The Poetics of Manhood: Contest and Identity in a Cretan Mountain Village*. Princeton, NJ.

Heszer, C. 2001. *Jewish Literacy in Roman Palestine*. Tübingen.

Heuzey, L. 1922. *Histoire du costume antique, d'après des études sur le modèle vivant*. Paris.

Heurgon, J. 1964. *Daily Life of the Etruscans*. London.

Higgins, R. A. 1980. *Greek and Roman Jewelry*. Second Edition. Berkeley, CA.

—— 1986. *Tanagra and the Figurines*. Princeton, NJ.

Hicks, R. D. (ed.) 1925. *Diogenes Laertius: Lives of Eminent Philosophers*. Cambridge, MA.

Hillson, S. 1996. *Dental Anthropology*. Cambridge.

Hingley, R. 2000. *Roman Officers and English Gentlemen: The Imperial Origins of Roman Archaeology*. London.

Hingley, R. 2005. *Globalizing Roman Culture: Unity, Diversity and Empire*. London.

Hingley, R. and Unwin, C. 2005. *Boudica: Iron Age Warrior Queen*. London.

Hitchcock, L. A. and Koudounaris, P. 2002. "Virtual discourse: Arthur Evans and the reconstructions of the Minoan palace at Knossos." In Hamilakis (ed.): 40–58.

Hitchcock, L. A., Laffineur, R., and Crowley, J. (eds.) 2008. *Dais: The Aegean Feast*. Aegaeum 29. Leuven.

Hoche, R. 1860. "Hypatia, die Tochter Theons." *Philologus* 17: 435–74.

Hodder, I. 1982. *Symbols in Action: Ethnoarchaeological Studies in Material Culture*. Cambridge.

Hodos, T. 1999. "Intermarriage in the western Greek colonies." *Oxford Journal of Archaeology* 18(1): 61–78.

Hoe, S. 2005. *Crete: Women, History, Books and Places*. Oxford.

Højte, J. M. (ed.) 2002. *Images of Ancestors. Aarhus Studies in Mediterranean Antiquity 5*. Aarhus.

Holland, L. L. 2008. "Diana feminarum tutela? The case of noutrix Paperia." In Deroux, C. (ed.), *Studies in Latin Literature and Roman History, vol 14. Collection Latomus* 315. Brussels. 95–115.

Hollis, A. S. (ed.) 2007. *Fragments of Roman Poetry: C. 60 BC–AD 20*. Oxford.

Holloway, R. R. 1975. *Influences and Styles in the Late Archaic and Early Classical Greek Sculpture of Sicily and Magna Graecia*. Louvain.

—— 1991. *The Archaeology of Sicily*. London and New York.

Hölscher, T. (ed.) 2000. *Gegenwelten zu den Kulturen Griechenlands und Roms in der Antike*. Munich.

Hölscher, U. 1996. "Penelope and the suitors." In Schein (ed.): 133–40.

Hopkins, K. 1998. "Christian number and its implications." *JECS* 6: 185–226.

Hoppa, R. D. and Fitzgerald, C. M. (eds.) 1999. *Human Growth in the Past: Studies from Bones and Teeth*. Cambridge.

Howarth, N. 2008. *Cartimandua: Queen of the Brigantes*. Stroud.

Hughes, L. 2007. "Unveiling the veil: Cultic, status, and ethnic representations of early imperial freedwomen." *Material Religion: The Journal of Objects, Art and Belief* 3: 218–41.

Hummert, J. P. and van Gerven, D. P. 1985. "Observations on the formation and persistence of radiopaque transverse lines." *AJPA* 66: 297–306.

Humphreys, S. 1978. *Anthropology and the Greeks*. London.

Hunter, V. 1989a. "The Athenian widow and her kin." *Journal of Family History* 14: 291–311.

—— 1989b. "Women's authority in Classical Athens." *Classical Views* 33: 39–48.

Hurst, A. 1990. "Ménandre et la tragédie." In Handley and Hurst (eds.): 93–122.

Hurst, H. and Owen, S. (eds.) 2005. *Ancient Colonizations: Analogy, Similarity and Difference*. London.

Hurwit, J. M. 2007. "The human figure in Early Greek sculpture and vase painting." In Shapiro (ed.): 265–86.

Hussein, M. M. and Suleiman, A. 1999. *Nimrud: A City of Golden Treasures*. Baghdad.

Huxley, G. 1964. "Alcman's Κολυμβῶσαι." *GRBS* 5: 26–8.

Iezzi, C. 2009. "Regional differences in the health status of the Mycenaean women of East Lokris." In Schepartz et al. (eds.): 175–92.

Ilan, T. 1995. *Jewish Women in Greco-Roman Palestine: An Inquiry into Image and Status. Texts and Studies in Ancient Judaism* 44. Tübingen.

—— 1997. *Mine and Yours are Hers: Retrieving Women's History from Rabbinic Literature*. Leiden.

—— 1999. *Integrating Women into Second Temple History*. Tübingen.

—— 2006. *Silencing the Queen: The Literary Histories of Shelamzion and Other Jewish Women*. Tübingen.

Immerwahr, S. 1990. *Aegean Painting in the Bronze Age*. University Park, PA.

Ingalls, W. 2002. "Demography and dowries: Perspectives on female infanticide in classical Greece." *Phoenix* 56: 246–54.

Ingholt, H. 1928. *Studier over Palmyrensk Skulptur*. Copenhagen.

İşcan, M. Y. and Kennedy, K. A. R. (eds.) 1989. *Reconstruction of Life from the Skeleton*. New York.

Iser, W. 1978. *The Act of Reading: A Theory of Aesthetic Response*. Baltimore, MD.

Izzet, V. 2007. *The Archaeology of Etruscan Society*. Cambridge.

Jackes, M. 2000. "Building the bases of paleodemographic analysis: Adult age determination." In Katzenberg and Saunders (eds.): 417–66.

Jacobs, A. 2004. *Remains of the Jews: The Holy Land and Christian Empire in Late Antiquity*. Stanford, CA.

Jacobsthal, P. 1956. *Greek Pins and their Connections with Europe and Asia*. Oxford.

James. E. O. 1959. *The Cult of the Mother Goddess*. New York.

James, S. L. 1998. "Introduction: Constructions of gender and genre in Roman comedy and elegy." *Helios* 25: 3–16.

—— 2002. "Future perfect feminine: Women past and future in the *Aeneid*." In Anderson and Quartarone (eds.): 138–46.

—— 2003. *Learned Girls and Male Persuasion*. Berkeley, CA.

Jashemski, W. F. 1993. *The Gardens of Pompeii, Herculaneum, and the Villas Destroyed by Vesuvius*. New York.

Jay, N. 1992. *For All Your Generations Forever: Sacrifice, Religion and Paternity*. Chicago, IL.

Jeammet, V. (ed.) 2003. *Tanagra: Mythe et archéologie*. Paris.

—— (ed.) 2007. *Tanagras: De l'object de collection à l'objet archéologique*. Paris.

—— (ed.) 2010. *Tanagras: Figurines for Life and Eternity. The Musée du Louvre's Collection of Greek Figurines*. Valencia.

Jed, S. 1989. *Chaste Thinking: The Rape of Lucretia and the Birth of Humanism*. Bloomington, IN.

Jenkins, I. 1985. "The ambiguity of Greek textiles." *Arethusa* 18: 109–32.

Jenkins, I. and Williams, D. 1985. "Sprang hair nets: Their manufacture and use in ancient Greece." *AJA* 89: 411–18.

Johnson, M. (ed.) 1965. *Ancient Greek Dress*. Chicago, IL.

Johnston, D. 1985. "Munificence and municipia: Bequests to towns in classical Roman law." *JRS* 75: 105–25.

Jones, P. 2006a. *Cleopatra: The Last Pharoah*. London.

—— 2006b. *Cleopatra: A Sourcebook*. Norman, OK.

Jones, T. 2009. "Pre-Augustan seating in Italy and the west." In Wilmott, T. (ed.), *Roman Amphitheatres and Spectacula: A 21st-Century Perspective*. Oxford. 127–39.

Joshel, S. R. 1992a. "The body female and the body politic: Livy's Lucretia and Verginia." In Richlin, A. (ed.), *Pornography and Representation in Greece and Rome*. Oxford. 112–30.

—— 1992b. *Work, Identity, and Legal Status at Rome: A Study of the Occupational Inscriptions*. Norman, OK.

—— 1995. "Female desire and the discourse of empire: Tacitus's Messalina." *Signs* 21: 50–82.

Joshel, S. and Murnaghan, S. (eds.) 1998. *Women and Slaves in Greco-Roman Culture: Differential Equations*. London.

Just, R. 1989. *Women in Athenian Law and Life*. New York.

Kajava, M. 1990. "Roman senatorial women and the Greek East: Epigraphic evidence from the Republican and Augustan Period." In Solin, H. and Kajava, M. (ed.), *Roman Eastern Policy and Other Studies in Roman History*. Helsinki. 59–124.

Kahil, L. 1965. "Autour de l'Artèmis attique." *Antike Kunst* 8: 20–33.

—— 1977. "L'Artémis de Brauron: Rites et mystère." *Antike Kunst* 20: 86–98.

Kakridis, J. T. 1971. "The role of the woman in the Iliad." In Kakridis, J. T. 1971. *Homer Revisited*. Lund. 68–75. [Reprint of *Eranos* 54: 21–27 (1956).]

Kalavrezou, I. (ed.) 2003. *Byzantine Women and their World*. Cambridge, MA and New Haven, CT.

Kaldellis, A. 2010. "The study of women and children: Methodological challenges and new directions. In Stephenson, P. (ed.), *The Byzantine World*. London. 211–22.

Kalinowski, A. 2002. "The Vedii Antonini: Aspects of patronage and benefaction in second-century Ephesos." *Phoenix* 56: 109–49.

Kalinowski, A. and Taeuber, H. 2001. "A new Antonine inscription and a new imperial statue-group from the Bouleuterion at Ephesos." *JRA* 14: 351–7.

Kaltsas, N. 2002. *Sculpture in the National Archaeological Museum, Athens*. Athens.

Kaltsas, N. (ed.) 2006. *Athens-Sparta: Contributions to the Research on the History and Archaeology of the Two City-States: Proceedings of the International Conference in Conjunction with the Exhibition "Athens-Sparta" Organized in Collaboration with the Hellenic Ministry of Culture and the National Archaeological Museum, Athens, Saturday, April 21, 2007, Onassis Cultural Center, New York*. New York.

Kaltsas, N. and Shapiro, H. (eds.) 2008. *Worshiping Women: Ritual and Reality in Classical Athens*. New York.

Kampen, N. B. 1975. "Hellenistic artists: Female." *Archeologia Classica* 27: 9–17.

—— 1981. *Image and Status: Roman Working Women in Ostia*. Berlin.

—— (ed.) 1996. *Sexuality in Ancient Art: Near East, Egypt, Greece, and Italy*. New York.

—— 2009. *Family Fictions in Roman Art*. Cambridge.

Karakasi, K. 2003. *Archaic Korai*. Los Angeles, CA.

Kassel R. and Austin, C. (eds.) 1983. *Poetae Comici Graeci*. Berlin and New York.

Katsouris, A. 1975a. *Tragic Patterns in Menander*. Athens.

—— 1975b. *Linguistic and Stylistic Characterization: Tragedy and Menander*. Ioannina.

Katz, M. A. 1991. *Penelope's Renown: Meaning and Indeterminacy in the Odyssey*. Princeton, NJ.

—— 1995. "Ideology and 'the status of women' in Ancient Greece." In Hawley and Levick (eds.): 21–43.

Katzenberg, M. A. and Saunders, S. R. (eds.) 2000. *Bioarchaeology of the Human Skeleton*. New York.

Keane, C. 2002. "Juvenal's cave-woman and the programmatics of satire." *CB* 78: 5–20.

Kearns, E. 1998. "The nature of heroines." In Blundell and Williamson (eds.) 1998: 96–110.

Keegan, P. 2008. "Turia, Lepidus, and Rome's epigraphic environment." *Studia Humaniora Tartuensia* 9: 1–7.

Keenleyside, A. 2008. "Dental pathology and diet at Apollonia, a Greek colony on the Black Sea." *International Journal of Osteoarchaeology* 18: 262–79.

Kehrberg, I. 1982. "The potter-painter's wife: Some additional thoughts on the Caputi hydria." *Hephaistos* 4: 25–35.

Keith, A. M. 1994. "Corpus eroticum: Elegiac poetics and elegiac *Puellae* in Ovid's *Amores*." *CW* 88: 27–40.

—— 1997. "Tandem venit amor: A Roman woman speaks of love." In Hallett and Skinner (eds.): 295–310.

—— 2000. *Engendering Rome: Women in Latin Epic*. Cambridge.

—— 2008. *Propertius, Poet of Love and Leisure*. London.

—— 2009. "Sexuality and gender." In Knox, P. (ed.), *A Companion to Ovid*. Malden. 355–69.

Kelly, M. A. 1979. "Parturition and pelvic changes." *AJPA* 51: 541–6.

Kennell, N. M. 1995. *The Gymnasium of Virtue: Education and Culture in Ancient Sparta*. Chapel Hill, NC.

—— 2006. Ephebeia: A Register of Greek Cities with Citizen Training Systems in the Hellenistic and Roman Periods. Hildersheim.

Kephalidou, E. 1996. *Niketes*. Thessaloniki.

Keuls, E. C. 1985. *The Reign of the Phallus: Sexual Politics in Ancient Athens*. Berkeley, CA.

—— 1988. "The social position of Attic vase painters and the birth of caricature." In Christiansen, J. and Melander, T. (eds.), *Proceedings of the Third Symposium on Ancient Greek and Related Pottery*. Copenhagen. 300–13.

—— 1993. *The Reign of the Phallus: Sexual Politics in Ancient Athens*. Second edition. Berkeley, CA.

El-Khachab, A. el-Mohsen. 1978. *Ta Sarapeia à Sakha et au Fayoum ou les bains thérapeutiques*. Cairo.

Kilmer, M. 1982. "Genital phobia and depilation." *JHS* 102: 104–12.

—— 1993. *Greek Erotica on Attic Red-Figure Vases*. London.

King, H. 1983. "Bound to bleed: Artemis and Greek women." In Cameron and Kuhrt (eds.): 109–27.

—— 1989. "The daughter of Leonides: Reading the Hippocratic corpus." In Cameron (ed.): 11–32.

—— 1993. "Once upon a text: Hysteria from Hippocrates." In Gilman, S., King, H., Porter, R., Rousseau, R. S., and Showalter, E. (eds.), *Hysteria Beyond Freud*. Berkeley, CA. 1–90.

—— 1994. "Producing woman: Hippocratic gynecology." In Archer et al. (eds.): 102–14.

—— 1995a. "Medical texts as a source for women's history." In Powell, A. (ed.), *The Greek World*. London. 199–218.

—— 1995b. "Self-help, self-knowledge: In search of the patient in Hippocratic gynaecology." In Hawley and Levick (eds.): 135–48.

—— 1998. *Hippocrates' Woman: Reading the Female Body in Ancient Greece*. London.

—— 2004. *The Disease of Virgins: Green Sickness, Chlorosis, and the Problems of Puberty*. New York.

King, U. 1995. "A question of identity: Women scholars and the study of religion." In King, U. (ed.), *Religion and Gender*. Oxford. 219–44.

Kleiner, D. 1987a. *Roman Imperial Funerary Altars with Portraits*. Rome.

—— 1987b. "Women and family life on Roman imperial funerary altars." *Latomus* 46: 545–54.

—— 1977. *Roman Group Portraiture: The Funerary Reliefs of the Late Republic and Early Empire*. New York.

—— 1996. "Imperial women as patrons of the arts in the early empire." In Kleiner and Matheson (eds.): 28–41.

Kleiner, D. and Matheson, S. (eds.) 1996. *I, Claudia. Women in Ancient Rome.* New Haven, CT.

—— 2000. *I, Claudia II: Women in Roman Art and Society.* Austin, TX.

Knappett, C. 1997. "Ceramic production in the protopalatial Mallia 'state': Evidence from Quartier Mu and Myrtos Pyrgos." In Laffineur and Betancourt (eds.): 305–11.

Knapp, R. 2011. *Invisible Romans: Self-Identity, Imposed Identity, and Power in the Roman World.* London.

Ko, D. 2005. *Cinderella's Sisters: A Revisionist History of Footbinding.* Berkeley, CA.

Köb, I. 2000. *Rom—ein Stadtzentrum im Wandel. Untersuchungen zur Funktion und Nutzung des Forum Romanum und der Kaiserfora in der Kaiserzeit.* Hamburg.

Kobes, J. 2004. "Teilnahmeklauseln beim Zugang zum Gymnasion." In Kah, D. and Scholz, P. (eds.), *Das Hellenistische Gymnasion.* Berlin. 237–45.

Kockel, V. 1993. *Porträtsreliefs stadtrömischer Grabbauten. Zur Geschichte und zum Verständnis des spätrepublikanisch-frühkaiserzeitlichen Privatporträts.* Mainz.

Koehl, R. 1995. "The nature of Minoan kingship." In Rehak (ed.): 23–36.

Kokkinidou, D. and Nikolaïdou, M. 1993. *Η αρχαιολογία και η κοινωνική ταυτότητα του φύλου. Προσεγγίσεις στην αιγαιακή προϊστορία.* Thessalonike.

—— 2000. "A sexist present, a human-less past: Museum archaeology in Greece." In Donald and Hurcombe (eds.): 33–55.

—— 2009. "Feminism and Greek archaeology: An encounter long over-due." In Kopaka (ed.): 25–37.

Kokkinos, N. 1992. *Antonia Augusta: Portrait of a Great Roman Lady.* New York.

Kokkorou-Alevras, G. 2006. "Laconian stone sculpture from the eighth century B.C. until the outbreak of the Peloponnesian War." In Kaltsas, N. (ed.), *Athens—Sparta. Alexander S. Onassis Public Benefit Foundation Exhibition Catalog.* New York. 89–94.

Kolb, F. 1989. "Theaterpublikum, volksversammlung und gesellschaft in der Griechischen welt." *Dioniso* 2: 345–51.

Kolendo, J. 1981. "La répartition des places aux spectacles et la stratifications sociale dans l'Empire romain." *Ktema* 6: 301–15.

Koloski-Ostrow, A. O. and Lyons, C. L. (eds.) 1997. *Naked Truths: Women, Sexuality and Gender in Classical Art and Archaeology.* New York.

Koltsida, A. 2006. "Birth-bed, sitting place, erotic corner or domestic altar? A study of the so-called elevated bed in Deir el-Medina houses." *Studien zur Altägyptische Kultur* 35: 165–74.

Konstan, D. 1991. "Introduction: Documenting gender: Women and men in non-literary classical sources." *Helios* 19: 5–6.

—— 1994. "Premarital sex, illegitimacy and male anxiety in Menander and Athens." In Boegehold, A. and Scafuro, A. (eds.), *Athenian Identity and Civic Ideology.* Baltimore. 217–35.

Kopaka, K. 1997. "Women's arts—men's crafts? Towards a framework for approaching gender skills in the prehistoric Aegean." In Laffineur and Betancourt (eds.): 521–31.

—— 2001. "A day in Potnia's life: Aspects of Potnia and reflected 'mistress' activities in the Aegean Bronze Age." In Laffineur and Hägg (eds.): 15–26.

—— 2009a. "Mothers in Aegean stratigraphies? The dawn of ever-continuing engendered life cycles." In Kopaka (ed.): 183–96.

—— (ed.) 2009b. *Fylo: Engendering Prehistoric "Stratigraphies" in the Aegean and the Mediterranean. Aegaeum* 30. Leuven.

Korfmann, M. (ed.) 2006. *Troia: Archäologie eines Siedlungshügels und seiner Landschaft.* Mainz am Rhein.

Kosmetatou, E. 2004. "Constructing legitimacy: The Ptolemaic *Familiengruppe* as a means of self-definition in Posidippus' *Hippika*." In Acosta-Hughes, B., Kosmetatou, E., and Baumbach, M. (eds.), *Labored in Papyrus Leaves: Perspectives on an Epigram Collection Attributed to Posidippus (P. Mil. Vogl. VIII 309)*. Washington, DC. 225–46.

Kosmopoulou, A. 2001. "'Working women': Female professionals on Classical Attic gravestones." *Annual of the British School at Athens* 96: 281–319.

Kottaridi, A. 2002. "Discovering Aegae, the old Macedonian capital." In Stamatopoulou, M. and Yeroulanou, M. (eds.), *Excavating Classical Culture: Recent Archaeological Discoveries in Greece*. Oxford. 75–81.

—— 2004. "The lady of Aigai." In Pandermalis (ed.): 139–48.

Kousser, R. 2004. "The world of Aphrodite in the late fifth-century B.C." In Marconi (ed.): 97–112.

Kraemer, R. 1989. "On the meaning of the term 'Jew' in Greco-Roman inscriptions." *Harvard Theological Review* 82: 35–53.

—— 1991a. "Jewish women in the diaspora world of late antiquity." In Baskin (ed.): 46–72.

—— 1991b. "Women's authorship of Jewish and Christian Literature in the Greco-Roman period." In Levine, A.-J. (ed.), *"Women Like This": New Perspectives on Jewish Women in the Greco-Roman Period. Early Judaism and its Literature I*. Atlanta. 221–42.

—— 1992. *Her Share of the Blessings: Women's Religions Among Pagans, Jews, and Christians in the Greco-Roman World*. Oxford.

—— 1999. "Jewish women and Christian origins: some caveats." In Kraemer, R. S. and D'Angelo, M. R. (eds.), *Women and Christian Origins*. Oxford. 35–49.

—— (ed.) 2004. *Women's Religions in the Greco-Roman World: A Sourcebook*. Oxford.

—— 2009. "Jewish women's resistance to Christianity in the early 5th Century: The account of Severus, Bishop of Minorca." *JECS* 17: 635–65.

—— 2011. *Unreliable Witnesses: Religion, Gender and History in the Greco-Roman Mediterranean*. Oxford.

Kraemer, R. S. and D'Angelo, M. R. (eds.) 1999. *Women and Christian Origins*. Oxford.

Kraemer, R. and Eyl, J. 2011. "Translating women: The perils of gender-inclusive translation of the New Testament." In Carter, C. (ed.), *Celebrate Her for the Fruit of Her Hands: Studies in Honor of Carol L. Meyers*. Winona Lake, IN.

Krause, J.-U. 1994–5. *Witwen und Waisen im römischen Reich*. Stuttgart.

Krauskopf, I. 1988. "Helene-Elina." *Lexicon Iconographicum Mythologiae Classicae* 4: 563–72.

Krawiec, R. 2002. *Shenoute and the Women of the White Monastery: Egyptian Monasticism in Late Antiquity*. Oxford.

Kreeb, M. 1985. "Zur basis der Kleopatra auf Delos." *Horos* 3: 41–61.

Kreilinger, U. 2007. *Anständige Nacktheit: Körperpflege, Reinigungsriten und das Phänomen weiblicher Nacktheit im archaisch-klassischen Athen*. Rahden/Westf.

Krieckhaus, A. 2004. "Duae patriae? C. Plinius Caecilius Secundus zwischen Germana patria and urbs." In de Ligt, L., Hemelrijk, E. A., and Singor, H. S. (eds.), *Roman Rule and Civic Life: Local and Regional Perspectives*. Amsterdam. 299–314.

Kritsei-Providi, I. 1982. *Τοιχογραφίες του Θρησκευτικού Κέντρου των Μυκηνών*. Athens.

Kroll, J. 1977. "An archive of the Athenian cavalry." *Hesperia* 46: 83–140.

Kron, U. 1996. "Priesthoods, dedications and euergetism: What part did religion play in the political and social status of Greek women?" In Hellström, P. and Alroth, B. (eds.), *Religion and Power in the Ancient Greek World*. Uppsala. 139–82.

Krzyszkowska, O. and Nixon, L. (eds.) 1983. *Minoan Society*. Bristol.

Kuhrt, A. 1989. "Non-royal women in the late Babylonian period: A survey." In Lesko (ed.): 215–39.

Kunst, Chr. 2005. "Frauenzimmer in der römischen domus." In Harich-Schwarzbauer and Späth (eds.): 111–32.

Kurke, L. 1999. *Coins, Bodies, Games, and Gold: The Politics of Meaning in Archaic Greece.* Princeton, NJ.

Kurtz, D. C. and Boardman, J. 1971. *Greek Burial Customs.* New York.

Kyle, D. G. 2003. "'The only woman in all Greece': Kyniska, Agesilaus, Alcibiades and Olympia." *Journal of Sport History* 30: 183–203.

Kyriakidis, E. (ed.) 2007. *The Archaeology of Ritual.* Los Angeles, CA.

Labovitz, G. 2009. *Marriage and Metaphor: Constructions of Gender in Rabbinic Literature.* Lanham.

Lacroix, M. 1932. "Les étrangers a Délos pendant la période de l'indépendance." In *Mélanges Gustave Glotz.* Paris. 501–25.

La'da, C. A. 2002a. "Immigrant women in Hellenistic Egypt: The evidence of ethnic designations." In Melaerts and Mooren (eds.): 167–92.

—— 2002b. *Foreign Ethnics in Hellenistic Egypt.* Leuven.

Lada-Richards, I. 2004. "Μύθων εἰκών: Pantomime dancing and the figurative arts in imperial and late antiquity." *Arion* 12: 17–46.

Laffineur, R. and Betancourt, P. P. (eds.) 1997. *Technē: Craftsmen, Craftswomen and Craftsmanship in the Aegean Bronze Age.* Leuven.

Laffineur, R. and Greco, E. (eds.) 2005. *Emporia: Aegeans in the Central and Eastern Mediterranean. Aegaeum 25.* Leuven.

Laffineur, R. and Hägg, R. (eds.) 2001. *Potnia. Deities and Religion in the Aegean Bronze Age. Aegaeum 22.* Université de Liège: Histoire de la' art et archéologie de la Grèce antique, and University of Texas at Austin: Program in Aegean Scripts and Prehistory

Laffineur, R. and Niemeier, W.-D. (eds.) 1995. *Politeia: Society and State in the Aegean Bronze Age. Aegaeum 12.* Leuven.

Lagia, A., Eliopoulos, C., and Manolis, S. 1997. "Thalassemia: Macroscopic and radiological study of a case." *International Journal of Osteoarchaeology* 17: 269–85.

Lahusen, G. 1983. *Untersuchungen zur Ehrenstatue in Rom. Literarische und epigraphische Zeugnisse. Archaeologica 35.* Rome.

Laiou, A. E. 1992. *Mariage, amour et parenté à Byzance aux XIe–XIIIe siècles.* Paris.

Lambropoulou, V. 1995. "Some Pythagorean female virtues." In Hawley and Levick (eds.): 124–31.

Langdon, S. 2008. *Art and Identity in Dark Age Greece, 1100–700 B.C.E.* Cambridge.

Lapatin, K. 2002. *Mysteries of the Snake Goddess: Art, Desire and the Forging of History.* Boston, MA.

Lape, S. 2004. *Reproducing Athens: Menander's Comedy, Democratic Culture, and the Hellenistic City.* Princeton, NJ.

Laqueur, T. 1990. *Making Sex: Body and Gender from the Greeks to Freud.* Cambridge, MA.

Lardinois, A. and McClure, L. (eds.) 2001. *Making Silence Speak: Women's Voices in Greek Literature and Society.* Princeton, NJ.

Laronde, A. 1987. *Cyrène et la Libye hellénistique. Libykai historiai de l'époque républicaine au principat d'Auguste.* Paris.

Larsen, C. S. 1997. *Bioarchaeology: Interpreting Behaviour from the Human Skeleton.* Cambridge.

Larson, J. 1995. *Greek Heroine Cults.* Madison, WI.

Lattimore, R. 1942. *Themes in Greek and Latin Epitaphs.* Urbana, IL.

Laurence, R. 2007. *Roman Pompeii: Space and Society.* London and New York.

Lawton, C. L. 1995. "Four document reliefs from the Athenian agora." *Hesperia* 64.1: 121–30.

—— 2009. "Attic votive reliefs and the Peloponnesian war." In Palagia, O. (ed.), *Art in Athens during the Peloponnesian War.* Cambridge. 66–93.

Leader, R. E. 1997. "In death not divided: Gender, family, and state on Classical Athenian grave stelae." *AJA* 101: 683–99.

Le Bohec, S. 1993. "Les reines de Macédoine de la mort d'Alexandre à celle de Persée." *Cahiers du Centre G. Glotz* 4: 229–45.

Le Bohec-Bouhet, S. 2006. "Réflexions sur la place de la femme dans la Macédoine antique." In Guimier-Sorbets, A-M., Hatzopoulos, M. B., and Morizot, Y. (eds.), *Rois, Cites, Necropoles: Institutions, Rites et Monuments en Macédoine*. Athens. 187–98.

Leduc, C. 1992. "Marriage in ancient Greece." In Schmitt Pantel (ed.): 233–95.

Lee, H. 1984. "Athletics and the bikini girls from Piazza Armerina." *Stadion* 10: 45–76.

Lee, M. M. 2003. "The ancient Greek peplos and the 'Dorian question.'" In Donohue, A. A. and Fullerton, M. D. (eds.), *Ancient Art and its Historiography*. New York. 118–47.

—— 2005. "Constru(ct)ing gender in the feminine Greek peplos." In Cleland, L., Harlow, M., and Llewellyn-Jones, L. (eds.), *The Clothed Body in the Ancient World*. Oxford. 55–64.

—— 2009. "Body-modification in classical Greece." In Fögen, T. and Lee, M.M. (eds.), *Bodies and Boundaries in Graeco-Roman Antiquity*. Berlin. 155–80.

—— Forthcoming. "Maternity and miasma: Dress and the transition from *parthenos* to *gyne*." In Petersen, L.H. and Salzman-Mitchell, P. (eds.), *Mothering and Motherhood in Ancient Greece and Rome*. Austin, TX.

Lefkowitz, M.R. 1981. *Heroines and Hysterics*. London.

—— 2007. *Women in Greek Myth*. Second edition. London.

Lefkowitz, M. R. and Fant, M. B. (eds.) 1992. *Women's Life in Greece and Rome: A Source Book in Translation*. Baltimore, MD.

—— 2005. *Women's Life in Greece and Rome: A Source Book in Translation*. Third edition. Baltimore, MD.

Lemonnier, P. (ed.) 1992. *Technological Choices: Transformations in Material Culture since the Neolithic*. London.

Lenaghan, J. 1999. *Portrait Statues of Women in the Roman World*. Diss., New York University.

Lerner, G. 1986. *The Creation of Patriarchy*. Oxford.

Lesko, B. S. 2008. "Household and domestic religion in ancient Egypt." In Bodel, J. and Olyan, S. (eds.), *Household and Family Religion in Antiquity*. Oxford. 197–209.

Levine, D. B. 1985. "Symposium and the polis." In Figueira, T. J. and Nagy, G. (eds.), *Theognis of Megara: Poetry and the Polis*. Baltimore, MD. 176–96.

Levine, L. 2001. *The Synagogue: The First Thousand Years*. Second edition. New Haven, CT.

Lewerentz, A. 1993. *Stehende männliche Gewandstatuen im Hellenismus. Ein Beitrag zur Stilgeschichte und Ikonologie hellenistischer Plastik*. *Antiquates* 5. Hamburg.

Lewis, N. 1986. *The Greeks in Ptolemaic Egypt. American Society of Papyrologists Classics in Papyrology* 2. Oxford.

Lewis, S. 2002. *The Athenian Woman: An Iconographic Handbook*. London.

Ley, A. 1990. "Atalante—von der Athletin zur Liebhaberin: Ein Beitrag zum Rezeptionswandel eines mythologischen Themas auf Vasen des 6.-4. Jhrs. V. Chr." *Nikephoros* 3: 31–72.

Lieu, J. 1998. "The 'attraction of women' in/to early Judaism and Christianity: Gender and the politics of conversion." *Journal for the Study of New Testament* 72: 5–22.

Linders, T. 1972. *Studies in the Treasure Records of Artemis Brauronia Found in Athens*. Stockholm.

Linderski, J. 1986. "Religious aspects of the conflict of the orders: The case of *confarreatio*." In Raaflaub, K. and Cornell, T. J. (eds.), *Social Struggles in Archaic Rome: New Perspectives on the Conflict of the Orders*. Berkeley, CA. 244–61. Reprinted with emendations in Linderski, J. 2007. *Roman Questions II: Selected Papers*. Stuttgart. 542–59.

Linfert, A. 1976. *Kunstzentren hellenistischer Zeit: Studien an weiblichen Gewandstatuen*. Wiesbaden.

Ling, R. 2005. *Pompeii: History, Life and Afterlife*. Stroud.

Lintott, A. 1993. *Imperium Romanum: Politics and Administration*. London.

Lipsett, B. D. 2011. *Desiring Conversion: Hermas, Thecla, Aseneth*. Oxford.

Lissarrague, F. 1990. *The Aesthetics of the Greek Banquet: Images of Wine and Ritual*. Transl. A. Szegedy-Maszak. Princeton, NJ.

Liston, M. A. 1993. *Human Skeletal Remains from Kavousi, Crete: A Bioarchaeological Analysis*. Diss., University of Tennessee.

Liston, M. A. and Papadopoulos, J. K. 2004. "The 'rich Athenian lady' was pregnant: The anthropology of a Geometric tomb reconsidered." *Hesperia* 73: 7–38.

Llewellyn-Jones, L. (ed.) 2002. *Women's Dress in the Ancient Greek World*. London and Swansea.

—— 2003. *Aphrodite's Tortoise: The Veiled Woman of Ancient Greece*. London and Swansea.

—— 2007. "House and veil in ancient Greece." In Westgate et al. (eds.): 251–8.

Lloyd, G. E. R. 1964. "The hot and the cold, the dry and the wet in Greek philosophy." *JHS* 84: 92–106.

—— 1966. *Polarity and Analogy: Two Types of Argumentation in Early Greek Thought*. Cambridge.

—— 1983. *Science, Folklore, and Ideology: Studies in the Life Sciences in Ancient Greece*. Cambridge.

Lloyd-Jones, H. 1966. "Menander's *Sikyonios*." *GRBS* 7: 131–57.

Löhr, C. 2000. *Griechische Familienweihungen: Untersuchungen einer Repräsentationsform von ihren Anfängen bis zum Ende des 4. Jhs. v. Chr.* Rahden.

Long, C. R. 1974. *The Ayia Triadha Sarcophagus: A Study of Late Minoan and Mycenean Funerary Practices and Beliefs*. Göteborg.

Loraux, N. 1987. *Tragic Ways of Killing a Woman*. Transl. A. Forster. Cambridge, MA.

—— 1992. "What is a goddess?" In Schmitt Pantel (ed.): 11–44.

—— 1993. *The Children of Athena: Athenian Ideas about Citizenship and the Division between the Sexes*. Transl. C. Levine. Princeton, NJ.

—— 1995. *The Experiences of Tiresias*. Princeton, NJ.

Lovejoy, C. O., Meindl, R. S., Pryzbek, T. R., and Mensforth, R. P. 1985. "Chronological metamorphosis of the auricular surface of the ilium: A new method for the determination of adult skeletal age at death." *AJPA* 68: 15–28.

Löw, M. 2008. "The constitution of space: The structuration of spaces through the simultaneity of effect and perception." *European Journal of Social Theory* 11: 25–49.

Lowe, N. J. 1987. "Tragic space and comic timing in Menander's *Dyskolos*." *BICS* 34: 126–38.

—— 1988. "Sulpicia's syntax." *CQ* 38: 193–205.

Lozano, F. 2004. "*Thea Livia* in Athens: Redating *IG* II2 3242." *ZPE* 148: 177–80.

Lyons, C. L. 2008. "Objects of affection: Genre and gender on some Athenian vases." In Lapatin (ed.): 73–84.

Lyons, D. 1996. *Gender and Immortality*. Princeton, NJ.

—— 2003. "Dangerous gifts: Ideology of marriage and exchange in ancient Greece." *CA* 22.1: 93–134.

Ma, J. 2007. "Hellenistic honorific statues and their inscriptions." In Newby, Z. and Leader-Newby, R. (eds.), *Art and Inscriptions in the Ancient World*. Cambridge. 203–20.

Maat, G. J. R. 1984. "Dating and rating of Harris' lines." *AJPA* 63: 291–9.

MacDonald, D. R. 1983. *The Legend and the Apostle: The Battle for Paul in Story and Canon*. Philadelphia, PA.

MacDonald, M. Y. 1994. *Early Christian Women and Pagan Opinion*. Cambridge.

MacDowell, D. M. 1978. *The Law in Classical Athens*. Ithaca, NY.

—— 1982. "Love versus the law: An essay on Menander's *Aspis*." *G&R* 29: 42–52.

MacGillivray, J. A. 2000. *Minotaur: Sir Arthur Evans and the Archaeology of the Minoan Myth*. New York.

Mackay, C. 2009. *The Breakdown of the Roman Republic: From Oligarchy to Empire*. Oxford.

Mackie, N. 1990. "Urban munificence and the growth of urban consciousness in Roman Spain." In Blagg, Th. and Millett, M. (eds.), *The Early Roman Empire in the West*. Oxford. 179–92.

MacKinnon, C. 1989. *Toward a Feminist Theory of the State*. Cambridge, MA.

MacKinnon, M. 2007. "Osteological research in Classical archaeology." *AJA* 111: 473–504.

MacMullen, R. 1980. "Women in public in the Roman Empire." *Historia* 29: 208–18.

—— 1982. "The epigraphic habit in the Roman empire." *AJPh* 103: 233–46.

—— 1997. *Christianity and Paganism in the Fourth to Eighth Centuries*. New Haven, CT.

—— 2000. *Romanization in the Time of Augustus*, London.

Macurdy, G. H. 1932. *Hellenistic Queens*. Baltimore, MD.

Mæhle, I. B. 2004. "Female cult in the struggle of the orders." In Mæhle and Okkenhaug (eds.): 69–84.

Mæhle, I. and Okkenhaug, I. (eds.) 2004. *Women and Religion in the Middle East and the Mediterranean*. Oslo.

Maiuri, A. 1950. "Pompei: Scoperta di un edifico termale nella Regio VIII, Insula 5, nr. 36." *Notizie degli scavi di antichità, Series 8.IV*: 116–36.

Mallowan, M. E. L. 1966. *Nimrud and its Remains*. London.

Mankin, D. 1995. *Horace: Epodes*. Cambridge.

Manfrini-Aragno, I. 1992. "Femmes à la fontaine: Réalité et imaginaire." In Bron, C. and Kassaplogou, E. (eds.), *L'image en Jeu: De l'Antiquité a Paul Klee*. Yens-sur-Morges. 127–48.

Manning, C.E. 1970. "Canidia in the Epodes of Horace," *Mnemosyne* 23: 393–401.

Manning, J. G. 2009. *The Last Pharaohs. Egypt under the Ptolemies*. Princeton, NJ.

Mantes, A. G. 1990. Προβλήματα της εικονογραφίας των ιερειών και των ιερέων στην αρχαία ελληνική τέχνη. Athens.

Manuli, P. 1983. "Donne mascoline, femmine sterili, vergini perpetue: La ginecologia greca tra Ippocrate e Sorano." In Campese, S., Manuli, P., and Sissa, G., (eds.), *Madre Materia: Sociologia e Biologia della Donna Greca*. Turin. 149–92.

Maraval, P. (ed.) 1971. *Grégoire de Nysee, Vie de Sainte Macrine*. Paris.

Marcadé, J. 1996. *Sculptures Déliennes. Sites et Monuments* 17. Paris.

Marchesi, I. 2007. *The Art of Pliny's Letters: A Poetics of Allusion in the Private Correspondence*. Cambridge.

Marconi, C. (ed.) 2004a. *Greek Vases: Images, Contexts and Controversies*. Leiden.

—— 2004b. "Images for a warrior: On a group of Athenian vases and their public." In Marconi (ed.): 27–40.

Marcus, M. I. 1993. "Incorporating the body: Adornment, gender, and social identity in ancient Iran." *Cambridge Archaeological Journal* 3.2: 158–78.

Marin, E. and Vickers, M. 2004. *The Rise and Fall of an Imperial Shrine: Roman Sculpture from the Augusteum at Narona*. Split.

Marinatos, N. 1984. *Art and Religion in Thera: Reconstructing a Bronze Age Society*. Athens.

—— 1993. *Minoan Religion: Ritual, Image and Symbol*. Columbia, SC.

—— 2002. "The *Arkteia* and the gradual transformation of the maiden into the woman." In Gentili, B. and Perusino, F. (eds.), *Le orse di Brauron: Un rituale di iniziazione femminile nel santuario di Artemide*. Pisa. 29–42.

Marquardt, P. 1985. "Penelope ΠΟΛΥΤΡΟΠΟΣ." *AJP* 106: 32–48.

Marrou, H.-I. 1948. *Histoire de l'education dans l'Antiquité*. Paris.

Marshall, A. J. 1989. "Ladies and law: The role of women in the Roman civil courts." In Deroux, C. (ed.), *Studies in Latin Literature and Roman History. Coll. Latomus* 207. Brussels. 35–54.

Marshall, C. W. 2013. "Sex slaves in new comedy." In Akrigg, B. and Tordoff, R. L. S. (eds.), *Slaves and Slavery in Ancient Greek Comic Drama*. Cambridge. 173–196.

Martelli, M. 1994. "Sul nome etrusco di Alexandros." *Studi Etruschi* 60: 165–78.

Martin, R. 1989. *The Language of Heroes*. Ithaca, NY.

Marvin, M. 1989. "Copying in Roman sculpture: The replica series." In *Retaining the Original. Multiple Originals, Copies, and Reproductions: Studies in the History of Art* 20. Washington, DC. 29–45.

Matheson, S. 1996. 'The divine Claudia: Women as goddesses in Roman art." In Kleiner and Matheson (eds.): 182–93.

Matthews, S. 2001. *First Converts: Rich Pagan Women and the Rhetoric of Mission in Early Judaism and Christianity.* Stanford, CA.

Mattingly, D. J. 2002. "Vulgar and weak 'Romanization,' or time for a paradigm shift?" *JRA* 15: 536–40.

—— 2004. "Being Roman: Expressing identity in a provincial setting." *JRA* 17: 5–25.

Mazzoni, S. 2005. "Having and showing: Women's possessions in the afterlife in Iron Age Syria and Mesopotamia." In Lyons, D. and Westbrook, R. (eds.), *Women and Property in Ancient Near Eastern and Mediterranean Societies,* Washington, DC. http://www.chs.harvard.edu/wa/pageR?tn=ArticleWrapper&bdc=12&mn=1219.

Mattusch, C. C. 2006. "Archaic and Classical bronzes." In Palagia (ed.): 208–42.

—— 2008. *Pompeii and the Roman Villa: Art and Culture around the Bay of Naples.* Washington, DC.

McClanan, A. 2002. *Representations of Early Byzantine Empresses: Image and Empire.* New York.

McClure, L. 1999. *Spoken like a Woman: Speech and Gender in Athenian Drama.* Princeton, NJ.

McGinn, T. A. J. 1998. *Prostitution, Sexuality, and the Law in Ancient Rome.* Oxford.

—— 2004. *The Economy of Prostitution in the Roman World: A Study of Social History and the Brothel.* Ann Arbor, MI.

—— 2011. "Greek brothels and more." In Glazebrook and Henry (eds.): 256–68.

McGeorge P. J.-P. 2009. "Gender meta-analysis of Late Bronze Age skeletal remains: The case of Tomb 2 in the Pylona cemetery on Rhodes." In Kopaka (ed.): 103–14.

McNamee, K. 1993. "Propertius, poetry, and love." In DeForest, M. (ed.), *Woman's Power, Man's Game: Essays on Classical Antiquity in Honor of Joy K. King.* Wauconda. 215–48.

Meier, S. A. 1991. "Women and communication in the Ancient Near East." *Journal of the American Oriental Society* 111: 540–7.

—— 2000. "Diplomacy and international marriages." In Cohen, R. and Westbrook, R. (eds.), *Amarna Diplomacy: The Beginnings of International Relations.* Baltimore, MD. 154–73.

Meindl, R. S., Lovejoy, C. O., Mensforth, R. P., and Walker, R. A. 1985. "A revised method of age determination using the os pubis, with a review and tests of accuracy of other current methods of pubic symphyseal aging." *AJPA* 68: 29–45.

Melaerts, H. and Mooren, L. (eds.) 2002. *Le rôle et le statut de la femme en Égypte hellenistique, Romaine et Byzantine: Actes du colloque international, Bruxelles—Leuven 27–29 novembre 1997.* Paris.

Melville, S. C. 1999. *The Role of Naqia/Zakutu in Sargonid Politics. State Archives of Assyria Studies* 9. Helsinki.

—— 2004. "Neo-Assyrian royal women and male identity: Status as a social tool." *Journal of the American Oriental Society* 124: 37–57.

Merker, G. S. 2000. *The Sanctuary of Demeter and Kore: Terracotta Figurines of the Classical, Hellenistic, and Roman Periods. Corinth* 18.4. Princeton, NJ.

Meskell, L. 1995. "Goddesses, Gimbutas, and "New Age "archaeology." *Antiquity* 69: 74–86.

—— 1998. "Oh my goddess!" *Archaeological Dialogues* 5: 126–42.

—— 1999. *Archaeologies of Social Life: Age, Sex, Class, et cetera in Ancient Egypt.* Oxford.

Meyer, E. A. 1990. "Explaining the epigraphic habit in the Roman empire: The evidence of epitaphs." *JRS* 80: 74–96.

Meyer, J. 2004. "Women in Classical Athens: In the shadow of north-west Europe or in the light from Istanbul." In Mæhle and Okkenhaug (eds.): 19–48.

Meyer, M. 1992–3. "Mutter, Ehefrau und Herrscherin: Darstellungen der Königin auf seleukidischen Münzen." *Hephaistos* 11–12: 107–32.

Meyer, R. 2003. "Identity." In Nelson and Shiff (eds.): 345–57.

Meyers, R. L. 2006. *Visual Representations of the Antonine Empresses*. Diss., Duke University.

Meyers, C. 2008. "Grinding to a halt: Gender and the changing technology of flour production in Roman Galilee." In Berg, I. (ed.), *Breaking the Mould: Challenging the Past through Pottery*. Oxford. 65–74.

Micale, M.S. 1995. *Approaching Hysteria: Disease and its Interpretations*. Princeton, NJ.

Migne, J.-P. (ed.) 1857–66. *Patrologia Graeca*. Paris.

Miles, G. B. 1992. "The first Roman marriage and the theft of the Sabine women." In Hexter, R. and Selden, D. (eds.), *Innovations of Antiquity*. London. 161–96.

Miller, D. and Tilley, C. (eds.) 1984. *Ideology, Power and Prehistory*. Cambridge.

Miller, M. C. 1997. *Athens and Persia in the Fifth Century BC: A Study in Cultural Receptivity*. Cambridge.

Miller, S. G. 1978. *The Prytaneion: Its Function and Architectural Form*. Berkeley, CA.

—— 2004. *Ancient Greek Athletics*. New Haven, CT.

Miller, S. S. 2006. *Sages and Commoners in Late Antique Erez Israel. Texts and Studies in Ancient Judaism* 111. Tübingen.

Millett, M. 1990. "Romanization: Historical issues and archaeological interpretations." In Blagg, T. F. C. and Millett, M. (eds.), *The Early Roman Empire in the West*. Oxford. 35–41.

Millett, P. 1998. "Encounters in the agora." In Cartledge, P., Millett, P., and von Reden, S. (eds.), *Kosmos: Essays in Order, Conflict and Community in Classical Athens*. Cambridge. 203–28.

Mills, H. 1984. "Greek clothing regulations: Sacred and profane?" *ZPE* 55: 255–65.

Milnor, K. 2002. "Sulpicia's (corpo)reality: Elegy, authorship and the body in [Tibullus] 3.13." *ClAnt* 21: 259–82.

—— 2005. *Gender, Domesticity, and the Age of Augustus: Inventing Private Life*. Oxford.

Minchin, E. 2007. *Homeric Voices: Discourse, Memory, Gender*. Oxford.

Mirón Pérez, M. D. 1996. *Mujeres, Religión y Poder: El Culto Imperial en el Occidente Mediterráneo*. Granada.

—— 1998. "Olimpia, Euryidice y el origen del culto dinastico en la Grecia helenistica." *FlorIlib* 9: 215–35.

—— 2000. "Transmitters and representatives of power: Royal women in ancient Macedonia." *Ancient Society* 30: 35–52.

Mitchell, A. G. 2009. *Greek Vase-Painting and the Origins of Visual Humour*. Cambridge.

Mitchell, S. 1978. "Venutius and Cartimandua." *Liverpool Classical Monthly* 3: 215–19.

Mitchell, W. J. T. 1986. *Iconology: Image, Text, Ideology*. Chicago, IL.

Montserrat, D. 1993. "The representation of young males in 'Fayum portraits.'" *Journal of Egyptian Archaeology* 79: 215–25.

—— 1997. "Death and funerals in the Roman Fayum." In Bierbrier (ed.): 33–44.

Moore, H. 1986. *Space, Text and Gender: An Anthropological Study of the Marakwet of Kenya*. Cambridge.

—— 1988. *Feminism and Anthropology*. Cambridge.

Moore, T. J. 1998. *The Theater of Plautus: Playing to the Audience*. Austin, TX.

Moore, J. and Scott, E. (eds.) 1997. *Invisible People and Processes: Writing Gender and Childhood into European Archaeology*. London.

Moran, W. L. 1992. *The Amarna Letters*. Baltimore, MD.

Moraw, S. 2002. "Das publikum—Der mündige Bürger als Ideal." In Moraw, S. and Nölle, E. (eds.), *Die Geburt des Theaters in der Griechischen Antike*. Mainz. 146–53.

Moretti, J.-Ch. 2001. *Théâtre et Société dans la Grèce Antique*. Paris.

Morgan, L. H. 1877. *Ancient Society or Researches in the Lines of Human Progress from Savagery through Barbarism to Civilization*. Cleveland, OH.

Morizot, Y. 2004. "Offrandes à Artémis pour une naissance autour du relief d'Achinos." In Dasen, V. (ed.), *Naissance et Petite Enfance dans l'Antiquité*. Göttingen. 159–70.

Morrell, K. S. 1996–7. "The fabric of persuasion: Clytaemnestra, Agamemnon, and the sea of garments." *CJ* 92: 141–65.

Morris, C. 2009. "The iconography of the bared breast in Aegean Bronze Age art." In Kopaka (ed.): 243–52.

Morris, I. 1987. *Burial and Ancient Society: The Rise of the Greek City-State*. Cambridge.

—— 1992. *Death-Ritual and Social Structure in Classical Antiquity*. Cambridge.

—— 1999. "Archaeology and gender ideologies in early Archaic Greece." *TAPA* 129: 305–17.

—— 2001. "The use and abuse of Homer." In Cairns, D. L. (ed.), *Oxford Readings in Homer's Iliad*. Oxford. 57–91. [Revised version of the original article in *CA* 5: 81–138 (1986).]

Morris, S. P. and R. Laffineur (eds.) 2007. *Epos: Reconsidering Greek Epic and Aegaean Bronze Age Archaeology. Aegaeum* 28. Leuven.

Mortensen, C. 1992. "Eurydice: Demonic or devoted mother?" *AHB* 6: 155–69.

Mossé, C. 1988. *La vita quotidiana della donna nella Grecia antica*. Milan.

Mossman, J. 2005. "Women's voices." In Gregory, J. (ed.), *A Companion to Greek Tragedy*. Malden. 352–65.

Mueller, M. 2007. "Penelope and the poetics of remembering." *Arethusa* 40: 337–62.

Müller, S. 2009. *Das Hellenistische Königspaar in der Medialen Repräsentation—Ptolemaios II und Arsinoë II, Beiträge zur Altertumskunde* 263. Berlin.

Muller-Dufeu, M. (ed.) 2002. *La Sculpture Grecque: Sources Littéraires et Épigraphiques*. Paris.

Mulvey, L. 1989. "Visual pleasure and narrative cinema." In Mulvey, L. (ed.), *Visual and Other Pleasures*. Basingstoke. 14–34.

Münzer, F. 1920. *Römische Adelsparteien und Adelsfamilien*. Stuttgart. Transl. T. Ridley, 1999. *Roman Aristocratic Parties and Families*. Baltimore, MD.

Murdock, G. P. and Provost, C. 1973. "Factors in the division of labor by sex: A cross-cultural analysis." *Ethnology* 12: 203–25.

Murnaghan, S. 1986. "Penelope's *agnoia*: Knowledge, power and gender in the *Odyssey*." *Helios* 13: 103–115. [Reprinted in Doherty (ed.): 231–46.]

—— 1994. "Reading Penelope." In Oberhelman et al. (eds.): 76–96.

—— 1999. "The poetics of loss in Greek epic." In Beissinger, M., Tylus, J., and Wofford, S. (eds.), *Epic Traditions in the Contemporary World*. Berkeley, CA. 203–20.

Murray, O. 1980. *Early Greece*. Glasgow.

Myerowitz Levine, M. 1995. "The gendered grammar of ancient mediterranean hair." In Eilberg-Schwartz, H. and Doniger, D. (eds.), *Off with her Head! The Denial of Women's Identity in Myth, Religion, and Culture*. Berkeley, CA. 76–130.

Nagler, M. N. 1974. *Spontaneity and Tradition: A Study in the Oral Art of Homer*. Berkeley, CA.

Nagy, G. 1999. *The Best of the Achaeans: Concepts of the Hero in Archaic Greek Poetry*. Second edition. Baltimore, MD.

Nagy, H. 1996. "The judgment of Paris? An Etruscan mirror in Seattle." In Hall, J. (ed.), *Etruscan Italy: Etruscan Influences on the Civilizations of Italy from Antiquity to the Modern Era*. Provo. 44–63.

Nappo, S. C. 2007. "Houses of regions I and II." In Dobbins and Foss (eds.): 347–72.

Navarro Caballero, M. 2001. "Les femmes de l'élite Hispano-Romaine, entre la famille et la vie publique." In Navarro Caballero, M. and Demougin, S. (eds.), *Élites Hispaniques*. Paris. 191–201.

Naveh, J. 1985. *Amulets and Magic Bowls: Aramaic Incantations of Late Antiquity*. Jerusalem.

Naveh, J. and Shaked, S. 1993. *Magical Spells and Formulae: Aramaic Incantations of Late Antiquity.* Jerusalem.

Neer, R. T. 2002. *Style and Politics in Athenian Vase-Painting: The Craft of Democracy, ca. 530–460 B. C.E.* Cambridge.

Nelson, C. A. 1979. *Status Declarations in Roman Egypt.* Amsterdam.

Nelson, R. S. and Shiff, R. (eds.) 2003. *Critical Terms for Art History.* Second edition. Chicago, IL.

Neils, J. (ed.) 1992. *Goddess and Polis: The Panathenaic Festival in Ancient Athens.* Hanover, NH.

Neils, J. and Oakley, J. (eds.) 2003. *Coming of Age in Ancient Greece: Images of Childhood from the Classical Past.* Hanover, NH.

Neuberg, M. 1990. "How like a woman: Antigone's inconsistency." *CQ* 49: 54–76.

Neumann, E. 1955. *The Great Mother.* New York.

Nevett, L.C. 1994. "Separation or seclusion? Towards an archaeological approach to investigating women in the Greek household in the fifth to third centuries BC." In Pearson Parker, M. and Richards, C. (eds.), *Architecture and Order: Approaches to Social Space.* London. 98–112.

—— 1999. *Houses and Society in the Ancient Greek World.* Cambridge.

—— 2007a. "Housing and households: The Greek world." In Alcock, S. E. and Osborne, R. (eds.), *Classical Archaeology.* Oxford. 205–23.

—— 2007b. "Greek houses as a source of evidence for social relations." In Westgate et al. (eds.): 5–10.

—— 2008. "Artifact assemblages and activity area analysis: Comparison from Greek domestic contexts." In Vanhaverbeke, H., Poblome, J., Vermeulen, F., and Waelkens, M. (eds.), *Thinking about Space: The Potential of Surface Survey and Contextual Analysis in the Analysis of Space in Roman Times. Studies in Eastern Mediterranean Archaeology* 8. Turnhout. 153–60.

Neville, L. 2010. "Strong women and their husbands in Byzantine historiography." In Stephenson, P. (ed.), *The Byzantine World.* London. 61–71.

Nicholls, R. V. 1993. *Corpus Speculorum Etruscorum, Great Britain 2.* Cambridge.

Nicols, J. 1980. "*Tabulae Patronatus*: A study of the agreement between patron and client-community." *ANRW* II 13: 535–61.

—— 1989. "*Patrona civitatis*: Gender and civic patronage." In Deroux, C. (ed.), *Studies in Latin Literature and Roman History V. Collection Latomus* 206. Brussels. 117–42.

Nielsen, M. 1989. "La donna e la famiglia nella tarda società etrusca." In Rallo (ed.): 121–45.

Niemeier, W.-D. 1987. "Das Stuckrelief des 'Prinzen mit der Federkrone' aus Knossos und minoische Götterdarstellungen." *Athenische Mitteilungen* 102: 65–98.

Nikolaïdou, M. 2002. "Palaces with faces in Minoan Crete: Looking for the people in the first Minoan states." In Hamilakis (ed.): 73–97.

—— 2007. "Ritualized technologies in the Aegean Neolithic? The crafts of adornment." In Kyriakidis (ed.): 183–208.

Nikolaïdou, M. and Kokkinidou, D. 1998. "Epos, history, meta-history in Aegaean Bronze Age studies." In Díaz-Andreu, M. and Sorensen, M. L. L. (eds.), *Excavating Women: A History of Women in European Archaeology.* London and New York. 235–65.

Nixon, L. 1983. "Changing views of Minoan society." In Krzyszkowska and Nixon (eds.): 237–43.

—— 1994. "Gender bias in archaeology." In Archer et al. (eds.): 1–23.

Nock, A. D. 1933. *Conversion: The Old and the New in Religion from Alexander the Great to Augustine of Hippo.* Oxford.

Nordquist, G. 1997. "Male craft and female industry: Two types of production in the Aegean Bronze Age." In Laffineur and Betancourt (ed.): 533–37.

Nosch, M.-L. and Laffineur, R. (eds.) 2010. *Kosmos: Jewellery, Adornment and Textiles in the Aegean Bronze Age.*

Nourse, K. 2002. *Women and the Early Development of Royal Power in the Hellenistic East.* Diss., University of Pennsylvania.

Nugent, S. G. 1992. "Vergil's 'voice of the women' in *Aeneid* V." *Arethusa* 25: 255–92.

—— 1999. "The women of the *Aeneid*: Vanishing bodies, lingering voices." In Perkell, C. (ed.), *Reading Vergil's* Aeneid. Norman, OK. 251–70.

Oakley, J. H. 2004. *Picturing Death in Classical Athens: The Evidence of the White Lekythoi*. Cambridge.

Oakley, J. H. and Schmidt, S. (eds.) 2009. *Hermeneutik der Bilder: Beiträge zur Ikonographie und Interpretation griechischer Vasenmalerei*. Munich.

Oakley, J. H. and Sinos, R. 1993. *The Wedding in Ancient Athens*. Madison.

Oberhelman, S. M., Kelly, V., and Goslan, R. J. (eds.) 1994. *Epic and Epoch: Essays on the Interpretation and History of a Genre*. Lubbock, TX.

Ogden, D. 1997. "Rape, adultery and the protection of bloodlines in classical Athens." In Deacy, S. and Pierce, K. F. (eds.), *Rape in Antiquity*. London. 25–41.

—— 1999. *Polygamy, Prostitutes and Death*. London.

Okin, S. M. 1977. "Philosopher queens and private wives: Plato on women and the family." *Philosophy and Public Affairs* 6: 345–69.

Oliensis, E. 1991. "Canidia, Canicula, and the decorum of Horace's *Epodes*." *Arethusa* 24, 107–38.

—— 1997. "Sons and lovers: Sexuality and gender in Vergil's poetry." In Martindale, C. (ed.), *The Cambridge Companion to Virgil*. Cambridge. 294–311.

—— 2007. "Erotics and gender." In Harrison, S. (ed.), *The Cambridge Companion to Horace*. Cambridge. 221–34.

Olsen, B. 1998. "Women, children and family in the Late Bronze Age: Differences in Minoan and Mycenean constructions of gender." *World Archaeology* 29: 380–92.

—— 2009. "Was there unity in Mycenean gender practices? The women of Pylos and Knossos in the Linear B tablets." In Kopaka (ed.): 115–24.

Olson, K. 2008a. *Dress and the Roman Woman. Self-Presentation and Society*. London.

—— 2008b. "The appearance of the young Roman girl." In Edmondson and Keith (eds.): 139–57.

Omitowoju, R. 2002. *Rape and the Politics of Consent in Ancient Athens*. Cambridge.

O'Neil, J. L. 1999. "Olympias: 'The Macedonians will never let themselves be ruled by a woman.'" *Prudentia* 31: 1–14.

Orlandi, S. 2005. *Epigrafia anfiteatrale dell'occidente Romano. VI. Roma. Anfiteatri e strutture annesse con una nuova edizione e commento delle iscrizioni del Colosseo*. Rome.

Ormand, K. 1999. *Exchange and the Maiden: Marriage in Sophoclean Tragedy*. Austin, TX.

Ornan, T. 2002. "The queen in public: Royal women in Neo-Assyrian art." In Parpola and Whiting (eds.), 461–77.

Orsi, P. 1893. "Siracusa." *Notizie degli Scavi di Antichità*. 445–86.

—— 1895. "Siracusa. Gli scavi nella necropoli del Fusco a Siracusa nel giungo, novembre e dicembre del 1893." *Notizie degli Scavi di Antichità*. 109–92.

Ortner, D. and Ericksen, M. 1997. "Bone changes in the human skull probably resulting from scurvy in infancy and childhood." *International Journal of Osteoarchaeology* 7: 212–20.

Ortner, D. J. 2003. *Identification of Pathological Conditions in Human Skeletal Remains*. Second edition. Amsterdam.

Ortner, S. B. 1978. "The virgin and the state." *Feminist Studies* 4: 19–35.

Osborne, D. L., Simmons, T. L., and Nawrocki, S. P. 2004. "Reconsidering the auricular surface as an indicator of age at death." *Journal of Forensic Science* 49: 905–11.

Osborne, R. 1993. "Women and sacrifice in classical Greece." *CQ* 43: 392–405.

—— 1994. "Looking on—Greek style. Does the sculpted girl speak to women too?" In Morris, I. (ed.), *Classical Greece: Ancient Histories and Modern Methodologies*. Cambridge. 81–96.

—— 1997. "Law, the democratic citizen and the representation of women in classical Athens." *Past and Present* 155: 3–33.

—— 2004a. "Images of a warrior: On a group of Athenian vases and their public." In Marconi (ed.): 41–54.

—— 2004b. "Homeric society." In Fowler (ed.): 206–19.

—— 2007. "Projecting identities in the Greek symposion." In Sofaer, J. (ed.), *Material Identities.* Malden, MA. 31–52.

Osgood, J. 2011. *Claudius Caesar: Image and Power in the Early Roman Empire.* Cambridge.

Osiek, C. and MacDonald, M.Y. 2005. *A Woman's Place: House Churches in Earliest Christianity.* Minneapolis, MN.

Ostwald, M. 1969. *Nomos and the Beginnings of Athenian Democracy.* Oxford.

Özgen, I. and Öztürk, J. 1996. *Heritage Recovered. The Lydian Treasure.* Istanbul.

Padgham, J. 2008. *Interpretation of the Cone on the Head of the Deceased Tomb Owner in New Kingdom Mortuary Art.* Diss., Swansea University.

Pagán, V. 2000. "Distant voices of freedom in the *Annales* of Tacitus." In Deroux, C. (ed.), *Studies in Latin Literature and Roman History X. Collection Latomus* 254. Brussels. 358–69.

—— 2004. *Conspiracy Narratives in Roman History.* Austin, TX.

Palagia, O. (ed.) 2006. *Greek Sculpture: Function, Materials, and Techniques in the Archaic and Classical Periods.* New York.

—— 2007. "Berenike II in Athens." In Schultz and von den Hoff (eds.): 237–45.

—— 2010. "Philip's Eurydice in the Philippeum at Olympia." In Carney, E. D. and Ogden, D. (eds.), *Philip II and Alexander the Great: Father and Son, Lives and Afterlives.* Oxford: 33–42.

Pallottino, M. 1955. *The Etruscans.* Harmondsworth.

Pandermalis, D. (ed.) 2004. *Alexander the Great: Treasures from an Epic Era of Hellenism.* New York.

Papadopoulou-Belmehdi, I. 1994. *Le Chant de Pénélope: Poétique du Tissage Féminin dans l'Odyssée.* Paris.

Papadopoulos, J. K. 2005a. *The Early Iron Age Cemetery at Torone. Monumenta Archaeologica* 24. Los Angeles, CA.

—— 2005b. "Inventing the Minoans: Archaeology, modernity and the quest for European identity." *Journal of Mediterranean Archaeology* 18: 87–149.

Papaefthymiou-Papanthimou, A. 1979. *Σκεύη και σύνεργα καλλωπισμού στον κρητομυκηναϊκό χώρο.* Thessaloniki.

—— 1997. *Τελετουργικός καλλωπισμός στο προϊστορικό Αιγαίο.* Thessaloniki.

Papageorgopoulou, C. and Xirotiris, N. I. 2009. "Anthropological research on a Byzantine population from Korytiani, West Greece." In Schepartz et al. (eds.): 193–222.

Papathanasiou, A. 2003. "Stable isotope analysis in Neolithic Greece and possible implications on human health." *International Journal of Osteoarchaeology* 13: 314–24.

Papathanasiou, A., Zachou, E., and Richards, M. P. 2009. "Bioarchaeological analysis of the human osteological material from Porskynas, Lokris." In Schepartz et al. (eds.): 223–36.

Parca, M. 2007. "Worshipping Demeter in Ptolemaic and Roman Egypt." In Parca and Tzanetou (eds.): 189–208.

—— 2011. "The archive of Zenon: where have the women gone?" In *Proceedings of the 26th International Congress of Papyrology.* Geneva.

Parca, M. and Tzanetou, A. (eds.) 2007. *Finding Persephone. Women's Rituals in the Ancient Mediterranean.* Bloomington, IN.

Parker H. N. 1994. "Sulpicia, the *auctor de Sulpicia,* and the authorship of 3.9 and 3.11 of the *Corpus Tibullianum*." *Helios* 21: 39–62.

—— 1997. "Women physicians in Greece, Rome, and the Byzantine Empire." In Furst, L. R., (ed.), *Women Physicians and Healers: Climbing a Long Hill.* Lexington, KY. 131–50.

—— 2004. "Why were the Vestals virgins? Or the chastity of women and the safety of the Roman state." *AJP* 125: 563–601.

—— Forthcoming. "Galen and the girls: Sources for women medical writers revisited."

Parker, R. 2005. *Polytheism and Society at Athens.* Oxford.

Parker Pearson, M. 1982. "Mortuary practices, society and ideology: An ethnoarchaeological study." In Hodder, I. (ed.), *Symbolic and Structural Archaeology*. Cambridge. 99–113.

—— 1999. *The Archaeology of Death and Burial*. College Station, TX.

Parlasca, K. 1969. *Ritratti Di Mummie, I (Nos. 1–246)*. In A. Adriani (ed.), *Repertorio D'arte Dell'egitto Greco-Romano*, B I. Rome.

—— 1977. *Ritratti Di Mummie, II (Nos. 246–496)*. In A. Adriani (ed.), *Repertorio D'arte Dell'egitto Greco-Romano*, B I. Rome.

—— 1980. *Ritratti Di Mummie, III (Nos. 497–674)*. In A. Adriani (ed.), *Repertorio D'arte Dell'egitto Greco-Romano*, B I. Rome.

—— 1988. "Ikonographische Probleme palmyrenischer Grabreliefs." *DaM* 3: 215–21.

Parpola, S. and Whiting, R. M. 2002. *Sex and Gender in the Ancient Near East: Proceedings of the 47th Rencontre Assyriologique Internationale, Helsinki, July 2–6, 2001*. Helsinki.

Parslow, C. 1988. "Documents illustrating the excavations of the Praedia of Julia Felix in Pompeii." *RStPomp* 2: 37–48.

—— 2007. "Entertainment in Pompeii." In Dobbins and Foss (eds.): 212–23.

Parsons, P. 2007. *City of the Sharp-Nosed Fish: Greek Lives in Roman Egypt*. London.

Pateman, C. 1988. *The Sexual Contract*. Stanford, CA.

Patterson, C. 1985. "'Not worth the rearing': The causes of infant exposure in Ancient Greece." *TAPA* 115: 103–23.

—— 1990. "Those Athenian bastards" *CA* 9: 40–73.

—— 1991. "Marriage and the married woman in Athenian law." In Pomeroy (ed.): 48–72.

—— 1998. *The Family in Greek History*. Cambridge, MA.

Peatfield, A. 1992. "Rural ritual in Bronze Age Crete: The peak sanctuary at Atsipadhes." *Cambridge Archaeological Journal* 2: 59–87.

Pedley, J. G. 1990. *Paestum. Greeks and Romans in Southern Italy*. London.

Pedrick, V. 1988. "The hospitality of noble women in the *Odyssey*." *Helios* 15.2: 85–101.

—— 1994. "Eurycleia and Eurynome as Penelope's confidantes." In Oberhelman et al. (eds.): 97–116.

Peek, W. 1960. *Griechische Grabgedichte*. Berlin.

Peirce, S. 1998. "Visual language and concepts of cult on the "Lenaia Vases.'" *ClAnt* 17: 59–95.

—— 2004. "Myth and reality on Greek vases." In Warden (ed.): 46–60.

Pemberton, E. G. 1989. "The *dexiosis* on Attic gravestones." *Mediterranean Archaeology* 2: 45–50.

Pembroke, S. 1970. "Locres et Tarente: Le rôle des femmes dans la fondation de deux colonies Grecques." *Annales. Histoire, Sciences Sociales* 25(5): 1240–70.

Peradotto, J. 2002. "Prophecy and persons: Reading character in the *Odyssey*." *Arethusa* 35.1: 3–15.

Peradotto, J. and Sullivan, J. P. (eds.) 1984. *Women in the Ancient World. The* Arethusa *Papers*. Albany, NY.

Pérez Sánchez, D. and Rodríguez Gervás, M. 2003. "Religion, women and politics in imperial Rome (4th–5th century A.D.)." In Cimdina, A. (ed.), *Religion and Political Change in Europe: Past and Present*. Pisa. 11–19.

Perkell, C. 1981. "On Dido and Creusa and the quality of victory in Virgil's *Aeneid*." In Foley (ed.): 335–77.

Perkins, P. 1995. *The Suffering Self: Pain and Narrative Representation in the Early Christian Era*. London.

Perkins, W. (ed.) 2002. *Fashioning the Body Politic: Dress, Gender, Citizenship*. Oxford.

Perrin, B. Transl. 1958. *Plutarch: Lives*, Vols. 1 and 3. Cambridge, MA.

Peschel, I. 1987. *Die Hetäre bei Symposion und Komos*. Frankfurt am Main.

Peskowitz, M. 1997. *Spinning Fantasies: Rabbis, Gender, and History*. Berkeley, CA.

Petersen, L. H. 1997. "Divided consciousness and female companionship: Reconstructing female subjectivity on Greek vases." *Arethusa* 30: 35–74.

Petrakos, B. 1991. *Rhamnous*. Transl. W. M. Phelps. Athens.

—— 1997. Οι επιγραφές του Ωρωπού. Athens.

Petrie, W. M. F. 1925. *Tombs of the Courtiers and Oxyrhynchus*. London.

Petrousa, E. I. and Manolis, S. K. 2010. "Reconstructing Late Bronze Age diet in mainland Greece using stable isotope analysis." *Journal of Archaeological Science* 37: 614–20.

Pettersson, M. 1992. *Cults of Apollo at Sparta: The Hyakinthia, the Gymnopaidiai, and the Karneia*. Stockholm.

Pfaffenberger, B. 1992. "Social anthropology of technology." *Annual Review of Archaeology* 21: 491–516.

Pfiffig, A. J. 1975. *Religio Etrusca*. Graz.

Pfuhl, E. and Möbius, H. 1977. *Die Ostgriechischen Grabreliefs, vol 1*. Mainz am Rhein.

—— 1979. *Die Ostgriechischen Grabreliefs, vol 2*. Mainz am Rhein.

Phang, S. E. 2001. *The Marriage of Roman Soldiers (13 B.C.–A.D. 235)*. Boston.

Phillips, C. R. 2007. "Approaching Roman religion: The case for *Wissenschaftsgeschichte*." In Rüpke (2007): 10–28.

Photiades, P. 1958. "Pan's prologue to the *Dyskolos* of Menander." *G&R* 5: 108–22.

Picazo, M. 1997. "Hearth and home: The timing of maintenance activities." In Moore and Scott (eds.): 56–97.

—— 1998. "Fieldwork is not the proper preserve of a lady: The first women archaeologists in Crete." In Díaz-Andreu and Sorensen (ed.): 198–213.

Pilali-Papasteriou, A. 1989. "Social evidence from the interpretation of Middle Minoan figurines." In Hodder, I. (ed.), *The Meanings of Things: Material Culture and Symbolic Expression*. London. 97–102.

Pinch, G. 1993. *Votive Offerings to Hathor*. Oxford.

Pipili, M. 1987. *Laconian Iconography of the Sixth Century B.C.* Oxford.

Plant, I. M. 2004. *Women Writers of Ancient Greece and Rome*. Norman, OK.

Ploug, G. 1995. *Catalogue of the Palmyrene Sculptures, Ny Carlsberg Glyptotek*. Copenhagen.

Pölönen, J. 2002. "The division of wealth between men and women in Roman succession (c.a. 50 BC–AD 250)." In Setälä Päivi, Berg, R., Hälikkaä, R., Keltanen, R. M., Pölönen, J., and Vuolanto, V. (eds.), *Women, Wealth and Power in the Roman World*. Rome. 147–79.

Pollitt, J. J. 1986. *Art in the Hellenistic Age*. Cambridge.

Pollock, S. 1999. *Ancient Mesopotamia: The Eden that Never Was*. Cambridge.

—— 2007. "The Royal Cemetery of Ur: Ritual, tradition, and the creation of subjects." In Heinz, M. and Feldman, M. H. (eds.), *Representations of Political Power: Case Histories from Times of Change and Dissolving Order in the Ancient Near East*. Winona Lake, IN. 89–110.

Polverini, L. 2008. "Donne al circo." In Nelis-Clément, J. and Roddaz, J.-M. (eds.), *Le Cirque Romain et son Image*. Bordeaux. 469–74.

Pontrandolfo, A. and Rouveret, A. 1992. *Le tombe dipinte di Paestum*. Modena.

Pomadère, M. 2009. "Où sont les mères? Représentations et réalités de maternité dans le monde égéen protohistorique." In Kopaka (ed.): 197–206.

Pomeroy, A. 1991. *The Appropriate Comment: Death Notices in the Ancient Historians*. Meisenheim am Glan.

Pomeroy, S. B. 1975. *Goddesses, Whores, Wives, and Slaves: Women in Classical Antiquity*. New York.

—— 1977. "*Technikai kai Mousikai*: the education of women in the fourth century and in the Hellenistic period." *AJAH* 2: 51–68.

—— 1978. "Plato and the female physician." *AJP* 99: 486–500.

—— 1984. *Women in Hellenistic Egypt from Alexander to Cleopatra*. New York.

—— 1990. *Women in Hellenistic Egypt from Alexander to Cleopatra*. Second edition. Detroit, MI.

—— (ed.) 1991. *Women's History and Ancient History*. Chapel Hill, NC.

—— 1994. *Xenophon, Oeconomicus: A Social and Historical Commentary*. Oxford.

—— 1995. *Goddesses, Whores, Wives, and Slaves: Women in Classical Antiquity*. Second edition. New York.

—— 1997. *Families in Classical and Hellenistic Greece*. Oxford.

—— 2002. *Spartan Women*. Oxford.

Post, L. A. 1940. "Woman's place in Menander's Athens." *TAPA* 71: 420–59.

Poursat, J.-Cl. 1983. "Ateliers et sanctuaires à Malia: Nouvelles données sur l'organisation sociale à l'époque des premiers palais." In Krzyszkowska and Nixon (eds.): 277–81.

—— 1997. "Potiers et peintres à Malia (Quartier Mu), Crète: Le Camares provincial entre tradition et innovation." In Laffineur and Betancourt (eds.): 301–4.

Powell, A. 1990. *Euripides, Women, and Sexuality*. London.

Powell, A. (ed.) 1995. *The Greek World*. London.

Préaux, C. 1959. "Le statut de la femme à l'époque hellénistique, principalement en Égypte." In *Recueils de la Société Jean Bodin XI: La femme*. 127–75. Brussels.

Prescott, S. 1986. "Women in Homeric society." *Pegasus* 29: 19–32.

Price, S. R. F. 1984. *Rituals and Power: The Roman Imperial Cult in Asia Minor*. Cambridge.

Prohászka, M. 1998. "Metal objects and coins." In Carter (ed.): 787–834.

Pugliese Carratelli, G. (ed.) 1996. *The Western Greeks*. Milan.

Pullen, D. 2008. "The early Bronze Age in Greece." In Shelmerdine, C. W. (ed.), *The Cambridge Companion to the Aegean Bronze Age*. New York. 19–46.

Purcell, N. 1986. "Livia and the womanhood of Rome." *PCPhS* 32: 78–105.

Quaegebeur, J. 1978. "Reines ptolémaïques et traditions égyptiennes." In Maehler, H. and Strocka, V. M. (eds.), *Das Ptolemäische Ägypten. Akten des Internationalen Symposions, 27–29. September 1976 in Berlin*. Mainz. 245–62.

—— 1983. "Cultes Égyptiens Et Grecs en Égypte hellénistique: L'exploitation des sources." In van't Dack et al. (eds.): 303–24.

—— 1988. "Cleopatra VII and the cults of the Ptolemaic queens." In Bianchi (ed.): 41–54.

Rabinowitz, N. S. 1993. *Anxiety Veiled: Euripides and the Traffic in Women*. Ithaca.

—— 2002. "Excavating women's homoeroticism in ancient Greece: The evidence from Attic vase painting." In Rabinowitz and Auanger (eds.): 106–66.

Rabinowitz, N. S. and Auanger, L. (eds.) 2002. *Among Women: From the Homosocial to the Homoerotic in the Ancient World*. Austin, TX.

Raepsaet-Charlier, M.-T. 2005. "Les activités publiques des femmes sénatoriales et équestres sous le Haut-Empire romain." In Eck, W. and Heil, M. (eds.), *Senatores Populi Romani: Realität und Mediale Präsentation einer Führungsschicht. Kolloquium der Prosopographia Imperii Romani vom 11. – 13. Juni 2004*. Stuttgart. 169–212.

Raepsaet-Charlier M.-T. and Gourevitch D. 2001. *La Femme dans la Rome Antique*. Paris.

Raia, A., Luschnig, C., and Sebesta, J. L. 2005. *The Worlds of Roman Women: A Latin Reader*. Newburyport, MA.

Rallo, A. 1989a. "I fonti." In Rallo (ed.): 15–33.

—— (ed.) 1989b. *Le donne in Etruria*. Rome.

—— 2000. "The woman's role." In Torelli, M. (ed.), *The Etruscans*. London. 131–40.

Ramage, E. 1994. "The so-called *Laudatio Turiae* as panegyric." *Athenaeum* 82: 341–70.

Rambo, L. R. 1993. *Understanding Religious Conversion*. New Haven, CT.

Randall, J. G. 1979. "Mistresses' pseudonyms in Latin elegy." *LCM* 4: 27–35.

Raschke, W. J. 1994. "A red-figure kylix in Malibu: The iconography of female charioteers." *Nikephoros* 7: 157–79.

Rathje, A. 2000. "'Princesses' in Etruria and Latium Vetus?" In Ridgway et al. (eds.): 295–300.

Rawson, E. 1987. "*Discrimina ordinum*: The *lex Julia theatralis*." *PBSR* 55: 83–114.

Rea, R. 1988. "Le antiche raffigurazioni dell'anfiteatro." In Conforto, M. L. and Reggiani, M. L. (eds.), *Anfiteatro Flavio: Immagine, Testimonianze, Spettacoli*. Rome. 23–46.

Reade, J. E. 1987. "Was Sennacherib a feminist?" In Durand (ed.): 139–45.

—— 2001. "Assyrian king-lists, the Royal Tombs of Ur, and Indus origins." *Journal of Near Eastern Studies* 60: 1–29.

Redfield, J. 1975. *Nature and Culture in the Iliad*. Second edition 1994. London.

—— 2003. *The Locrian Maidens: Love and Death in Greek Italy*. Princeton, NJ.

Reed, A. and Becker, A. (eds.) 2003. *The Ways That Never Parted: Jews and Christians in Late Antiquity and the Early Middle Ages*. Mohr Siebeck.

Reeder, E. D. (ed.) 1995. *Pandora: Women in Classical Greece*. Princeton, NJ.

Rehak, P. (ed.) 1995. *The Role of the Ruler in the Prehistoric Aegean*. Aegaeum 11. Leuven.

—— 1999. "The Aegean landscape and the body: A new interpretation of the Thera frescoes." In Wicker, N. L. and Arnold, B. (eds.), *From the Ground Up: Beyond Gender Theory in Archaeology*. Oxford. 11–22.

—— 2002. "Imag(in)ing a women's world in prehistoric Greece: The frescoes from Xeste 3 at Akrotiri." In Rabinowitz and Auanger (eds.): 34–59.

Rehm, R. 1994. *Marriage to Death: The Conflation of Wedding and Funeral Rituals in Greek Tragedy*. Princeton, NJ.

Reilly, J. 1989. "Many brides: 'Mistress and maid' on Athenian lekythoi." *Hesperia* 58: 411–44.

—— 1997. "Naked and limbless: Learning about the feminine body in ancient Athens." In Koloski-Ostrow and Lyons (eds.): 154–73.

Reinsberg, C. 1993. *Ehe, Hetärentum und Knabenliebe im antiken Griechenland*. Munich.

Rendell, J., Penner, B., and Borden, I. (eds.) 2000. *Gender Space Architecture: An Interdisciplinary Introduction*. London.

Renfrew, C. 1972. *The Emergence of Civilisation: The Cyclades and the Aegean in the Third Millennium B.C.* London.

—— 1985. *The Archaeology of Cult: The Sanctuary at Phylakopi*. London.

Revell, L. 2009. *Roman Imperialism and Local Identities*. Cambridge.

Rhodes, P. J. and Osborne, R. (eds.) 2003. *Greek Historical Inscriptions, 404–323 B.C.* Oxford.

Riccobono, S. 1950. *Il Gnomon dell'Idios Logos*. Palermo.

Richards, J. E. 2005. *Society and Death in Ancient Egypt: Mortuary Landscapes of the Middle Kingdom*. Cambridge.

Richards, M., Harvati, K., Grimes, V., Smith, C., Smith, T., Hublin, J-J., Karkanas, P., and Panagopoulou, E. 2008. "Strontium isotope evidence of Neanderthal mobility at the site of Lakonis, Greece using laser-ablation PIMMS." *Journal of Archaeological Science* 35: 1251–6.

Richardson, L., Jr. 1978. "*Concordia* and *concordia augusta*: Rome and Pompeii." *PP* 33: 260–72.

Richeson, A.W. 1940. "Hypatia of Alexandria." *National Mathematics Magazine* 15: 74–82.

Richlin, A. 1987. "Invective against women in Roman satire." *Arethusa* 17: 67–80.

—— 1992. *The Garden of Priapus*. Second edition. Oxford.

—— 1995. "Making up a woman: The face of Roman gender." In Eilberg-Schwartz and Doniger (eds.): 185–214.

—— 1997a. "Gender and rhetoric: Producing manhood in the schools." In W. J. Dominik (ed.), *Roman Eloquence: Rhetoric in Society and Literature*. New York. 74–90.

—— 1997b. "Carrying water in a sieve: Class and the body in Roman women's religion." In King, K. (ed.), *Women and Goddess Traditions in Antiquity and Today*. Minneapolis. 330–74.

Richmond, I. A. 1954. "Queen Cartimandua." *JRS* 44: 43–52.

Ridgway, B. S. 1981. *Fifth Century Styles in Greek Sculpture*. Princeton, NJ.

—— 1984a. "The fashion of the Elgin Kore." *GettyMusJ* 12: 29–58.

—— 1984b. *Roman Copies of Greek Sculpture: The Problem of the Originals. Jerome Lectures* 15. Ann Arbor, MI.

—— 1987. "Ancient Greek woman and art: The material evidence." *AJA* 91: 399–409.

—— 1990. *Hellenistic Sculpture I: The Styles of ca. 331–200 B.C.* Madison, WI.

—— 1991. "Greek sculpture as archaeological avidence." *The Reverend Edward W. Bodnar, S.J. Inaugural Lecture.* Washington, DC.

—— 1993. *The Archaic Style in Greek Sculpture.* Second edition. Chicago, IL.

—— 1997. *Fourth-Century Styles in Greek Sculpture.* Madison, WI.

—— 1999. *Prayers in Stone: Greek Architectural Sculpture Ca. 600–100 B.C.E. Sather Lectures* 63. Berkeley, CA.

Ridgway, D. 1992. *The First Western Greeks.* Cambridge.

Ridgway, D., Serra Ridgway, F., Pearce, M., Herring, E., Whitehouse, R., and Wilkins, J. (eds.) 2000. *Ancient Italy in its Mediterranean Setting: Studies in Honour of Ellen Macnamara.* London.

Riegl, A. 1901. *Die spätrömische Kunstindustrie.* Vienna.

—— 1985. *Late Roman Art Industry.* Transl. R. Winkes. Rome.

Riggs, C. 2005. *The Beautiful Burial in Roman Egypt: Art, Identity, and Funerary Religion.* Oxford.

Riggs, C. and Stadler, M. A. 2003. "The burial of Ta-sheret-hor-udja: A shroud and its Demotic inscriptions in the Museum of Fine Arts, Boston (MFA 54.993)." *Journal of the American Research Center in Egypt* 40: 69–87.

Rist, J. M. 1965. "Hypatia." *Phoenix* 19.3: 214–25.

Rives, J. B. 1992. "The *Iuno Feminae* in Roman society." *EMC* 36 n.s. 11: 33–49.

—— 1999. "Women in Roman religion." [Review of Staples 1998.] *CR* 49: 131–2.

—— 2007. *Religion in the Roman Empire.* Oxford.

Rizza, G. 1996. "Siceliot sculpture in the Archaic period." In Pugliese Carratelli (ed.): 399–412.

Robb, J. 1997. "Female beauty and male violence in early Italian society." In Koloski-Ostrow and Lyons (eds.): 43–65.

Robbins, T. 1988. *Cults, Converts and Charisma. The Sociology of New Religious Movements.* Newbury Park, CA.

Robert, L. 1946. "Adeimantos et la ligue de Corinthe: Sur une inscription de Delphes." *Hellenica* 2: 15–33.

Roberts, C., Bourbou, C., Lagia, A., Triantaphyllou, S., and Tsaliki, A. 2005. "Health and disease in ancient Greece: Past, present and future." In King, H. (ed.), *Health in Antiquity.* London. 32–58.

Roberts, C. A. and Buikstra, J. E. 2003. *The Bioarchaeology of Tuberculosis: A Global View on a Reemerging Disease.* Gainesville, FL.

Roberts, P. 2008. *Mummy Portraits from Roman Egypt.* London.

Robins, G. 1993. *Women in Ancient Egypt.* Cambridge.

Robinson, D. M. and Graham, J. W. 1938. *Excavations at Olynthus, part VIII: The Hellenic House.* Baltimore, MD.

Roccos, L. J. 1995. "The kanephoros and her festival mantle in Greek art." *AJA* 99: 641–66.

Roisman, H. M. 2005. "Women in Senecan tragedy." *Scholia* n.s. 14: 72–88.

—— 2006. "Helen in the Iliad: *Causa belli* and victim of war: From silent weaver to public speaker." *AJP* 127: 1–36.

Roller, D. W. 2010. *Cleopatra: A Biography.* Oxford.

Rolley, C. 1996. "Sculpture in Magna Graecia." In Pugliese Carratelli (ed.): 369–98.

Romano, D. G. 1983. "The ancient stadium: Athletics and *arête*." *AncW* 7: 9–15.

Römer, C. 2000. "Das Werden zu Osiris im römischen Ägypten." *Archiv für Religionsgeschichte* 2/2: 141–61.

Rose, C. B. 1997. *Dynastic Commemoration and Imperial Portraiture in the Julio-Claudian Period.* Cambridge.

Rosivach, V. J. 1998. *When a Young Man Falls in Love: The Sexual Exploitation of Women in New Comedy*. London.

Roth, M. T. 1987. "Age at marriage and the household: A study of Neo-Babylonian and Neo-Assyrian forms." *Comparative Studies in Society and History* 29: 715–47.

—— 1989. *Babylonian Marriage Agreements: 7th–3rd Centuries*. Neukirchen-Vluyn.

—— 1991. "The dowries of the women of the Itti-Marduk-Balātu Family." *Journal of the American Oriental Society* 111: 19–37.

—— 1994. "The Neo-Babylonian family and household." *Canadian Society for Mesopotamian Studies, Bulletin* 28: 19–29.

Rotroff, S. I. 1990. "Building a Hellenistic chronology." In Uhlenbrock, J. (ed.), *The Coroplast's Art: Greek Terracottas of the Hellenistic World*. New Rochelle. 22–30.

Rotroff, S. I. and Lamberton, R. D. 2006. *Women in the Athenian Agora*. Athens.

Rougé, J. 1970. "La colonisation Grecque et les femmes." *Cahiers d'Histoire* 15: 307–17.

Rousselle, A. 1988. *Porneia: On Desire and the Body in Antiquity*. Transl. F. Pheasant. Oxford.

Roussel, P. 1916. *Délos Colonie Athénienne*. Paris.

Rowlands, M. 1993. "The role of memory in the transmission of culture." *World Archaeology* 25(2): 141–51.

Rowlandson, J. 1995. "Beyond the *polis*: Women and economic opportunity in early Ptolemaic Egypt." In Powell (ed.): 301–22.

—— (ed.) 1998. *Women and Society in Greek and Roman Egypt: A Sourcebook*. Cambridge.

Roxan, M.M. 1978. *Roman Military Diplomas, 1954–77*. London.

—— 1985. *Roman Military Diplomas, 1978–1984*. London.

—— 1991. "Women on the Frontiers." In Maxfield, V. A. and Dobson, M. J. (eds.), *Roman Frontier Studies 1989*. Exeter. 462–7.

Rüpke, J. 2004. "Roman religion." In Flower, H. (ed.), *The Cambridge Companion to the Roman Republic*. Cambridge. 177–94.

—— (ed.) 2007. *A Companion to Roman Religion*. Malden, MA.

—— 2008. *Fasti Sacerdotum: A Prosopography of Pagan, Jewish, and Christian Religious Officials in the City of Rome, 300 BC to AD 499*. Transl. D. W. Richardson. Oxford.

Rush, P. (ed.) 1995. *Theoretical Roman Archaeology: Second Conference Proceedings*. Aldershot.

Rushworth, A. 2009. *Housesteads Roman Fort – The Grandest Station. Excavation and Survey at Housesteads, 1954–95, by Charles Daniels, John Gillam, James Crow and others*. London.

Russell, B. 1950. *Unpopular Essays*. New York.

Rutkowski, B. 1986. *Cult Places of the Aegean*. New Haven, CT.

Rutter, J. 2003. "Children in Aegaean prehistory." In Neils and Oakley (eds.): 31–57.

Saatsoglou-Paliadeli, C. 2000. "Queenly appearances at Vergina-Aegae: Old and new epigraphic and literary evidence." *AA* 3: 387–403.

Sabetai, V. 1997. "Aspects of nuptial and genre imagery in fifth-century Athens: Issues of interpretation and methodology." In Oakley, J. H., Coulson, W. D. E., and Palagia, O. (eds.), *Athenian Potters and Painters*. Oxford. 319–35.

Sadurska, A. 1994. "Recherches sur les sculptures." In Sadurska, A. and Bounni, A. (eds.), *Les Sculptures Funéraires de Palmyre*. Rome. 181–95.

—— 1996. "L'art et la société: Recherches iconologiques sur la sculpture funéraire de Palmyre." In *Palmyra and the Silk Road. Les Annales archaeologiques Arabs Syriennes: Revue d'Archaeologie et d'Histoire* 42. 285–8.

Sakellarakis, Y. and Sapouna-Sakellaraki, E. 1991. Αρχάνες. Athens.

—— 1997. *Archanes: Minoan Crete in a New Light. Vols I-II*. Athens.

Saller, R. P. 1984. "*Familia, domus*, and the Roman conception of the Family." *Phoenix* 38: 336–55.

Saller, R. P. and Shaw, B. D. 1984. "Tombstones and Roman family relations in the Principate: Civilians, soldiers and slaves." *JRS* 74: 124–55.

Salomon, N. 1997. "Making a world of difference: Gender, asymmetry, and the Greek nude." In Koloski-Ostrow and Lyons (eds.): 197–219.

Salus, C. 1985. "Degas' young Spartans exercising." *ArtB* 67: 501–6.

Salzman-Mitchell, P. B. 2005. *A Web of Fantasies.* Columbus, OH.

Sanders, J. T. 2002. "Conversion in early Christianity." In Blasi, A., Duhaime, J., and Turcotte, P.-A. (eds.), *Handbook of Early Christianity: Social Science Approaches.* Walnut Creek, CA. 619–41.

Sandford, M. K. and Weaver, D. S. 2000. "Trace element research in anthropology: New perspectives and challenges." In Katzenberg and Saunders (eds.): 329–50.

Santirocco, M. 1979. "Sulpicia reconsidered." *CJ* 74: 229–39.

Santoro L'Hoir, F. S. 1994. "Tacitus and women's usurpation of power." *CW* 88: 5–25.

Saporetti, C. 1979. *The Status of Women in the Middle Assyrian Period. Monographs on the Ancient Near East* 2. Malibu.

Sapouna-Sakellaraki, E. 1971. Μινωικόν ζώμα. Βιβλιοθήκη της εν Αθήναις Ερχαιολογικής Εταιρείας 71. Athens.

Satlow, M. 2001. *Jewish Marriage in Antiquity.* Princeton, NJ.

Saunders, S. R. and Katzeberg, M. A. 1992. *Skeletal Biology of Past Peoples: Research Methods.* New York.

Savalli-Lestrade, I. 1994. "Il ruolo pubblico delle regine ellenistiche." In Allessandrì, S. (ed.), *Historie: Studie Offerti Dagli Allievi A Giuseppe Nenci In Occasione Del Suo Settantesimo Compleanno.* Galatina. 415–32.

—— 2003. "La place des reines à la cour et dans le royaume à l'époque hellénistique." In Frei-Stolba et al. (eds.): 59–76.

Savunen, L. 1998. *Women in the Urban Texture of Pompeii.* Helsinki.

Sawyer, D. 1996. *Women and Religion in the First Christian Centuries.* New York.

Scafuro, A. 1997. *The Forensic Stage: Settling Disputes in Graeco-Roman Comedy.* Cambridge.

Scanlon, T. F. 2002. *Eros and Greek Athletics.* Oxford.

Schaps, D. M. 1977. "The woman least mentioned: Etiquette and women's names." *CQ* 27: 323–30.

—— 1979. *Economic Rights of Women in Ancient Greece.* Edinburgh.

Schefold, K. 1967. *Die Griechen und ihre Nachbarn.* Berlin.

Scheid, J. 1992. The religious roles of Roman women." In Schmitt Pantel (ed.): 377–408.

—— 2003a. "Le rôle religieux des femmes à Rome: Un complement." In Frei-Stolba et al. (eds.): 137–51.

——2003b. *An Introduction to Roman Religion.* Bloomington, IN.

Scheid, J. and Svenbro, J. 1996. *The Craft of Zeus: Myths of Weaving and Fabric.* Transl. C. Volk. Cambridge.

Scheidel, W. 1995. "The most silent women of Greece and Rome: Rural labour and women's life in the ancient world. Pt I." *G&R* 42.2: 202–17.

—— 1996. "The most silent women of Greece and Rome: Rural labour and women's life in the ancient world. Pt II." *G&R* 43.1: 1–10.

Schneider-Herrmann, G. 1996. *The Samnites of the Fourth Century BC as Depicted on Campanian Vases and in Other Sources* (Herring, E. ed.). *Bulletin Suppl. 61 Institute of Classical Studies, University of London; Specialist Studies on Italy* 2. London.

Schein, S. L. 1995. "Female representation and interpreting the *Odyssey.*" In Cohen (ed.) 1995: 17–27.

—— (ed.) 1996. *Reading the Odyssey.* Princeton, NJ.

Schepartz, L. A., Fox, S. C., and Bourbou, C. (eds.) 2009. *New Directions in the Skeletal Biology of Greece.* Princeton, NJ.

Scheuer, L. and Black, S. 2000. *Developmental Juvenile Osteology.* San Diego, CA.

Schiff, S. 2010. *Cleopatra: A Life.* New York.

Schmitt, H. H. 1989. "Zur Inszenierung des Privatlebens des Hellenistischen Herrschers." In Seibert, J. (ed.), *Hellenistische Studien: Gedenkschrift für H. Bengston, Münchener Arbeiten zur Alten Geschichte* 5. Munich. 77–86.

Schmitt Pantel, P. (ed.) 1992. *A History of Women in the West I: From Ancient Goddesses to Christian Saints*. Cambridge, MA.

—— 2003. "Le banquet et le 'genre' sur les images grecques, propos sur les compagnes et les compagnons." *Pallas* 61: 83–95.

—— 2005. "Du *symposion* au sanctuaire: Les espaces des cités grecque entre *gender* et identité politique." In Harich-Schwarzbauer and Späth (eds.): 1–14.

Schneider, H. D. 1975. "Four Romano-Egyptian tomb reliefs from El Behnasa, Egypt." *Bulletin Antike Beschaving* 50/1: 9–11.

—— 1982. *Beelden van Behnasa*. Zutphen.

Schnurr-Redford, C. 1996. *Frauen im Klassischen Athen: Sozialer Raum und Reale Bewegungsfreiheit*. Berlin.

Scholz, B. I. 1992. *Untersuchungen zur Tracht der römischen Matrona*. Köln.

Schüssler Fiorenza, E. 1983. *In Memory of Her: A Feminist Theological Reconstruction of Christian Origins*. New York.

Schultz, C. E. 2000. "Modern prejudice and ancient praxis: Female worship of Hercules at Rome." *ZPE* 133: 291–7.

—— 2006. *Women's Religious Activity in the Roman Republic*. Chapel Hill, NC.

—— 2007. "*Sanctissima femina*: Gesellschaftliche Klassifizierung und religiöse Praxis von Frauen in der Römischen Republik." In Rüpke, J. (ed.), *Gruppenreligionen im römischen Reich. Sozialformen, Grenzziehungen und Leistungen*. Tübingen. 7–29.

Schultz, P. 2006. "The iconography of the Athenian *apobates* race: Origins, meanings, transformation." In Palagia, O. and Choremi-Spetsieri, A. (eds.), *T. Panathenaic Games*. Athens. 59–72.

—— 2007. "Leochares' Argead portraits in the Philippeion." In Schultz and von den Hoff (eds.): 205–33.

Schultz, P. and von den Hoff, R. (eds.) 2007. *Early Hellenistic Portraiture: Image, Style, Context*. Cambridge.

Schutkowski, H. 1993. "Sex determination of infant and juvenile skeletons: I. Morphognostic features." *AJPA* 90: 199–205.

Schwarz, R. A. 1979. "Uncovering the secret vice: Towards an anthropology of clothing and adornment." In Cordwell, J. M. and Schwarz, R. A. (eds.), *The Fabrics of Culture: The Anthropology of Clothing and Adornment*. The Hague. 23–45.

Scodel, R. 2002. *Listening to Homer: Tradition, Narrative, and Audience*. Ann Arbor, MI.

Scurlock, J. A. 1991. "Baby-snatching demons, restless souls and the dangers of childbirth." *Incognita* 2: 135–83.

Sealey, P. R. 2004. *The Boudican Revolt against Rome*. Aylesbury.

Sebesta, J. L. 1994. "Symbolism in the costume of the Roman woman." In Sebesta, J. L. and Bonfante, L. (eds.), *The World of Roman Costume*. London. 46–53.

—— 1997. "Women's costume and feminine civic morality in Augustan Rome." *Gender & History* 9.3: 529–41.

Sefati, Y. and Klein, J. 2002. "The role of women in Mesopotamian witchcraft." In Parpola and Whiting (eds.): 569–87.

Sehlmeyer, M. 1999. *Stadtrömische Ehrenstatuen der Republikanischen Zeit*. Stuttgart.

Seidensticker, B. 1995. "Women on the tragic stage." In Goff, B. (ed.), *History/Tragedy/Theory: Dialogues on Athenian Drama*. Austin. 151–73.

Sered, S. 1992. *Women as Ritual Experts: The Religious Lives of Elderly Jewish Women in Jerusalem*. Oxford.

—— 1994. *Priestess, Mother, Sacred Sister: Religions Dominated by Women.* Oxford.

Serra Ridgway, F. R. 1992. "Etruscan mirrors in the Louvre and the Corpus." *JRA* 5: 278–83.

—— 2000. "Etruscan mirrors and archaeological context." *JRA* 13: 407–18.

Severin, H.-G. 1995. "Pseudoprotokoptika." In Fluck, C., Langener, L., Richter, S., Schaten, S., and Wurst, G. (eds.), *Divitiae Aegypti: Koptologische und verwandte Studien zu Ehren von Martin Krause.* Wiesbaden. 289–99.

Shapiro, H. A. 1981. "Courtship scenes in Attic vase-painting." *AJA* 85: 133–43.

—— 1988. "Local personifications in Greek vase-painting." *Praktika, 12th International Congress of Classical Archaeology.* Athens. 205–8.

—— 2000. "Modest athletes and liberated women: Etruscans on Attic black-figure vases." In Cohen (ed.): 315–37.

—— 2004. "Leagros the satyr." In Marconi (ed.): 1–11.

—— (ed.) 2007. *The Cambridge Companion to Archaic Greece.* New York.

Sharrock, A. R. 1991. "Womanufacture." *JRS* 81: 36–49.

—— 1994. *Seduction and Repetition in Ovid's* Ars Amatoria *II.* Oxford.

—— 2002. "Gender and sexuality." In Hardie, P. (ed.), *Cambridge Companion to Ovid.* Cambridge. 95–107.

Shear, T. L. 1936. "Psimythion." In *Classical Studies Presented to Edward Capps on his Seventieth Birthday.* Princeton, NJ. 314–17.

Shelmerdine, C. and Palaima, T. (eds.) 1984. *Pylos comes alive: Industry and administration in a Mycenaean palace: Papers of a symposium.* New York.

Shelton, J. 1990. "Pliny the Younger and the Ideal Wife." *Classica et Mediaevalia* 41: 163–86.

Shepherd, G. 1995. "The pride of most colonials: Burial and religion in the Sicilian colonies." *Acta Hyperborea* 6: 51–82.

—— 1999. "Fibulae and females: Intermarriage in the western Greek colonies and the evidence from the cemeteries." In Tstetskhladze, G. R. (ed.), *Ancient Greeks West and East.* Leiden. 267–300.

—— 2005. "The advance of the Greek: Greece, Great Britain and archaeological empires." In Hurst and Owen (eds.): 23–44.

Shepherd, S. 2006. *Theatre, Body and Pleasure.* London.

Sheridan, J. A. 1998. "Not at a loss for words: The economic power of literate women in late Antique Egypt." *TAPA* 128: 189–203.

Sherratt, A. 1981. "Plough and pastoralism: Aspects of the secondary products revolution." In Hodder, I., Isaac, G., and Hammond, N. (eds.), *Pattern of the Past: Studies in Honour of David Clarke.* Cambridge. 261–305.

Sherwin-White, A. N. 1966. *The Letters of Pliny: A Historical and Social Commentary.* Oxford.

Shrimpton, G. S. 1991. *Theopompus the Historian.* Montreal, QC.

Shumka, L. 2008. "Designing women: The representation of women's toiletries on funerary monuments in Roman Italy." In Edmondson and Keith (eds.): 172–91.

Sick, D. H. 1999. "Ummidia Qudratilla: Cagey businesswoman or lazy pantomime watcher?" *ClAnt* 18: 330–48.

Simandiraki, A. 2005. "Minoan archaeology in the Athens 2004 Olympic Games." *European Journal of Archaeology* 8(2): 157–81.

Simon, B. 1978. *Mind and Madness in Ancient Greece: The Classical Roots of Modern Psychiatry.* Ithaca, NY.

Sistakou, E. 2007. "Glossing Homer." In Bing and Bruss (eds.): 391–408.

Skinner, M. B. 2010. *Clodia Metelli: The Tribune's Sister.* Oxford.

Slatkin, L. 1991. *The Power of Thetis: Allusion and Interpretation in the* Iliad. Berkeley, CA.

Small, J. P. 1991. "The Tarquins and Servius Tullius at banquet." *MÉFRA* 103: 247–64.

Smith, J. Z. 2004. *Relating Religion: Essays in the Study of Religion.* Chicago, IL.

Smith, R. R. R. 1985. "Honours, empresses, and late emperors." *JRS* 75: 209–21.

—— 1988. *Hellenistic Royal Portraits*. Oxford.

—— 1991. *Hellenistic Sculpture. A Handbook*. London.

—— 1998. "Cultural choice and political identity in honorific portrait statues in the Greek East in the second century A.D." *JRS* 88: 59–93.

Smith, S. K. 2000. "Skeletal and dental evidence for social status in Late Bronze Age Athens." In Vaughn, S. J. and Coulson, W. D. E. (eds.), *Paleodiet in the Aegean. Wiener Laboratory Monograph* 1. Oxford. 105–14.

Smith, S. T. 2003. *Wretched Kush: Ethnic Identities and Boundaries in Egypt's Nubian Empire*. New York.

Snodgrass, A. M. 1974. "An historical Homeric society?" *JHS* 94: 114–25.

—— 2005. "'Lesser breeds': The history of a false analogy." In Hurst and Owen (eds.): 45–58.

Sofaer, J. 2006. *The Body as Material Culture: A Theoretical Osteoarchaeology*. Cambridge.

Solvang, E. K. 2006. "Another look 'inside': Harems and the interpretation of women." In Holloway (ed.): 374–98.

Sordi, M. 1981. "La donna etrusca." In *Misoginia e Maschilismo in Grecia e in Roma*. Genoa. 49–67.

Sørensen, M. L. S. 1991. "The construction of gender through appearance." In Walde, D. and Willows, N. D. (eds.), *The Archaeology of Gender: Proceedings of the 22nd Annual Chacmool Conference*. Calgary. 121–9.

—— 2000. *Gender Archaeology*. Cambridge.

—— 2006. "Gender, things, and material culture." In Nelson, S. M. (ed.), *Handbook of Gender in Archaeology*. Lanham, MD. 105–35.

Sourvinou-Inwood, C. 1988. *Studies in Girls' Transitions: Aspects of the Arkteia and Age Representation in Attic Iconography*. Athens.

—— 1991. *Reading Greek Culture: Texts and Images, Rituals and Myths*. Oxford.

Southern, P. 2007. *Antony and Cleopatra*. Stroud.

Spickermann, W. 1994a. "Priesterinnen im Römischen Gallien, Germanien und den Alpenprovinzen (1.-3. Jahrhundert n. Chr.)." *Historia* 43: 189–240.

—— 1994b. *"Mulieres ex voto." Untersuchungen zur Götterverehrung von Frauen im Römischen Gallien, Germanien und Rätien (1.-3. Jahrhundert n. Chr.)*. Bochum.

Spivey, N. J. 1991. "The power of women in Etruscan society." *Accordia Research Papers* 2: 55–67.

Spivey, N. J. and Stoddart, S. K. F. 1990. *Etruscan Italy*. London.

Spyridakis, S. 1992. "Cretan soldiers overseas: A prosopography." In Spyridakis, S. (ed.), *Cretica. Studies on Ancient Crete*. New Rochelle, NY. 55–82.

Squire, M. 2009. *Image and Text in Graeco-Roman Antiquity*. Cambridge.

Stähli, A. 2005. "Die Konstruktion sozialer Räume von Frauen und Männern in Bildern." In Harich-Schwarzbrauer and Späth (eds.): 83–99.

—— 2009. "Nackte Frauen." In Schmidt, S. and Oakley, J. H. (eds.), *Hermeneutik der Bilder. Beiträge zur Ikonographie und Interpretation griechischer Vasenmalerei*. Munich. 43–51.

Stanford, W. B. 1963. *The Ulysses Theme: A Study in the Adaptability of a Traditional Hero*. Second edition. Oxford.

Stanwick, P. E. 2002. *Portraits of the Ptolemies: Greek Kings as Egyptian Pharaohs*. Austin, TX.

Staples, A. 1998. *From Good Goddess to Vestal Virgins: Sex and Category in Roman Religion*. London.

Stark, R. A. 1996. "The role of women in Christian growth." In Stark, R. (ed.), The *Rise of Christianity: A Sociologist Reconsiders History*. Princeton, NJ. 95–128.

—— 2001. "The basis of Mormon success: A theoretical application." In Eliason, E. A. (ed.), *Mormons and Mormonism: An Introduction to an American World Religion*. Urbana, IL. 207–42.

Stark, R. A. and Bainbridge, W. S. 1980. "Networks of faith: Interpersonal bonds and recruitment to cults and sects." *American Journal of Sociology* 85: 1376–95.

Stavrianopoulou, E. 2006. *Gruppenbild mit Dame. Untersuchungen zur rechtilichen und sozialen Stellung der Frau auf den Kykladen im Hellenismus und in der römischen Kaiserzeit. HABES* 42. Stuttgart.

Stears, K. 1995. "Dead women's society: Constructing female gender in Classical Athenian funerary sculpture." In Spencer, N. (ed.), *Time, Tradition and Society in Greek Archaeology: Bridging the "Great Divide."* New York. 109–31.

—— 1998. "Death becomes her: Gender and Athenian death ritual." In Blundell, S. and Williamson, M. (eds.), *The Sacred and the Feminine in Ancient Greece.* London.

Stehle, E. 1997. *Performance and Gender in Ancient Greece: Nondramatic Poetry in its Setting.* Princeton, NJ.

—— 2007. "Thesmophoria and Eleusinian Mysteries: The fascination of women's secret ritual." In Parca and Tzanetou (eds.): 165–85.

—— Forthcoming. *Sacrifice, Demeter, Dionysus: Women's Rituals and Religious Innovation.*

Stehle, E. and Day, A. 1996. "Women looking at women: Women's ritual and temple sculpture." In Kampen: 101–16.

Steiner, A. 2004. "The Alkmene hydrias and vase painting in late-sixth-century Athens." *Hesperia* 73: 427–63.

—— 2007. *Reading Greek Vases.* Cambridge.

Stevens, A. 2009. "Domestic religious practices." In *UCLA Encyclopedia of Egyptology.* http://www.escholarship.org/uc/item/7s07628w.

Stevenson, J. 2005. *Women Latin Poets: Language, Gender and Authority from Antiquity through the Eighteenth Century.* Oxford.

Stewart, A. 1997. *Art, Desire, and the Body in Ancient Greece.* Cambridge.

—— 1998. "Goddess or queen?" In Palagia, O. and Coulsen, W. (eds.), *Regional Schools in Hellenistic Sculpture.* Oxford. 83–91.

Stewart, A. and Gray, C. 2000. "Confronting the Other: Childbirth, aging, and death on an Attic tombstone at Harvard." In Cohen (ed.) 2000: 248–74.

Stewart, P. 2008. *Social History of Roman Art.* Cambridge.

Stewart, T. D. 1957. "Distortion of the pubic symphyseal surface in females and its effect on age determination." *AJPA* 15: 9–18.

—— (ed.) 1970. *Personal Identification in Mass Disasters.* Washington, DC.

Stieber, M. 2004. *The Poetics of Appearance in the Attic Korai.* Austin, TX.

Stol, M. 1995. "Women in Mesopotamia." *Journal of the Economic and Social History of the Orient* 38, 125–43.

—— 2000. *Birth in Babylonia and the Bible.* Groningen.

Stone, E. 1982. "The social role of the Naditu women in Old Babylonian Nippur." *Journal of the Economic and Social History of the Orient* 25: 50–70.

Stone, M. 1976. *When God Was a Woman.* New York.

Strathern, M. 1988. *The Gender of the Gift: Problems with Women and Problems with Society in Melanesia.* Berkeley, CA.

Stratigakos, D. 2008. *A Women's Berlin: Building the Modern City.* Minneapolis, MN.

Stravopodi, E., Manolis, S. K., Kousoulakos, S., Aleporou, V., and Schultz, M. P. 2009. "Porotic hyperostosis in Neolithic Greece: New evidence and further implications." In Schepartz et al. (eds.): 257–70.

Stroup, S. C. 2004. "Designing women: Aristophanes' *Lysistrata* and the "hetairization" of the Greek wife." *Arethusa* 37: 37–73.

Studniczka, F. 1886. *Beiträge zur Geschichte der Altgriechischen Tracht.* Vienna.

Sturgeon, M. C. 2006. "Archaic Athens and the Cyclades." In Palagia (2006): 32–76.

Suter, C. 2007. "Between human and divine: High priestesses in images from the Akkad to the Isin-Larsa period." In Cheng and Feldman (eds.): 317–62.

Suzuki, M. 1989. *Metamorphoses of Helen: Authority, Difference, and the Epic.* Ithaca, NY.

Swaddling, J. 1999. *The Ancient Olympic Games.* Second edition. London.

Swaddling, J., Craddock, P. T., La Niece, S., and Hockey, M. 2000. "Breaking the mould: The overwrought mirrors of Etruria." In Ridgway et al. (eds.): 117–40.

—— 2006. "Women growing older in Deir el-Medina." In Dorn, A. and Hofman, T. (eds.), *Living and Writing in Deir el-Medina: Socio-Historical Embodiment of Deir el-Medine Texts.* Basel. 135–53.

Swift, E. 2011. "Personal appearance." In Allason-Jones (ed.): 194–218.

Syme, R. 1979. "Ummidius Quadratus: *Capax Imperii.*" 83: 287–310.

—— 1981. "A great orator mislaid." *CQ* 31: 421–7.

Szpakowska, K. 2008. *Daily Life in Ancient Egypt: Recreating Lahun.* Oxford.

Tacoma, L. E. 2006. *Fragile Hierarchies: The Urban Elites of Third-Century Roman Egypt.* Leiden.

Takács, S. 2008. *Vestal Virgins, Sibyls, and Matrons: Women in Roman Religion.* Austin, TX.

Talalay, L. E. 1993. *Deities, Dolls, and Devices: Neolithic Figurines from Franchthi Cave, Greece.* Bloomington, IN.

—— 1994. "A feminist boomerang: The Great Goddess of Greek prehistory." *Gender and History* 6: 165–83.

—— 2008. "Deities," In *The Oxford Encyclopedia of Women in World History.* E-reference edition. http://www.oxford-womenworldhistory.com.

Temkin, O. Transl. 1956. *Soranus: Gynecology.* Baltimore, MD.

Tenwolde, C. 1992. "Myrtos revisited: The role of relative function ceramic typologies in Bronze Age settlement analysis." *Oxford Journal of Archaeology* 11: 1–24.

Tetlow, E. M. 2004. *Women, Crime, and Punishment in Ancient Law and Society, vol 1: The Ancient Near East.* New York.

Thalmann, W. G. 1998a. "Female slaves in the *Odyssey.*" In Joshel and Murnaghan (eds.) 1998: 22–34.

—— 1998b. *The Swineherd and the Bow: Representations of Class in the* Odyssey. Ithaca, NY.

Themelis, P. G. 2003. *Ancient Messene.* Athens.

Themelis, P. G. and Touratsoglou, J. 1997. *Oi Taphoi tou Derveniou.* Athens.

Thesleff, H. (ed.) 1965. *The Pythagorean Texts of the Hellenistic Period. Acta Academiae Aboensis, Humaniora,* series A 30: 1.

Thomas, T. K. 2000. *Late Antique Egyptian Funerary Sculpture: Images for This World and the Next.* Princeton, NJ.

Thomas, Y. 1992. "The division of the sexes in Roman law." In Schmitt Pantel (ed.): 93–138.

Thompson, D. B. 1963. *Troy, the Terracotta Figurines of the Hellenistic Period. Troy: Supplementary Monograph* 3. Princeton, NJ.

—— 1998. "Demeter in Graeco-Roman Egypt." In Clarysse et al. (eds.): 699–707.

—— 2001. "Hellenistic Hellenes: The case of Ptolemaic Egypt." In Malkin, I. (ed.), *Ancient Perceptions of Greek Ethnicity.* Cambridge, MA. 301–22.

Todd, T. W. 1920. "Age changes in the pubic bone I: The male white pubis." *AJPA* 3: 285–334.

—— 1921. "Age changes in the pubic bone." *AJPA* 4: 1–70.

Toivari-Viitala, J. 2001. *Women at Deir el-Medina: A Study of the Status and Roles of the Female Inhabitants in the Workmen's Community During the Ramesside Period, Egyptologische Uitgaven* 15. Leiden.

Tölle-Kastenbein, R. 1994. *Das Archaische Wasserleitungsnetz für Athen und Seine Späteren Bauphasen.* Mainz.

Tomlin, R. S. O. 1988. Tabellae Sulis: *Roman Inscribed Tablets of Tin and Lead from the Sacred Spring at Bath.* [Also published as "Part 4 (The Curse Tablets)." In Cunliffe, B. 1988. *The Temple of Sulis Minerva at Bath, vol 2: The Finds from the Sacred Spring.* Oxford. 59–270.]

—— 1998. "Roman manuscripts from Carlisle: The Ink-Written Tablets." *Britannia* 29: 31–84.

—— 2003. "'The girl in question': A new text from Roman London." *Britannia* 34: 41–57.

Tomlin, R. S. O., Wright, R. P., and Hassall, M. W. C. 2009. *The Roman Inscriptions of Britain vol. III. Inscriptions on Stone.* Oxford.

Topper, K. 2009. "Primitive life and the construction of the sympotic past in Athenian vase painting." *AJA* 113: 3–26.

Torelli, M. 1996. "Les Femmes à Paestum." In Cébeillac-Gervasoni (ed.): 153–78.

Torre, S. 2000. "Claiming the public space: The mothers of Plaza de Mayo." In Rendell, J., Penner, B., and Borden, I. (eds.), *Gender Space Architecture: An Interdisciplinary Introduction.* London. 140–5.

Totelin, L. 2007. "Sex and vegetables in the Hippocratic gynaecological treatises." *Studies in History and Philosophy of Biological and Biomedical Sciences* 38: 531–40.

—— 2009. *Hippocratic Recipes: Oral and Written Transmission of Pharmacological Knowledge in Fifth- and Fourth-Century Greece.* Leiden.

Tracy, S. V. 1990. *Attic Letter-cutters of 229 to 86 B.C.* Berkeley and Los Angeles, CA.

Tracy, S. V. and Habicht, C. 1991. "New and old Panathenaic victor lists." *Hesperia* 60: 186–236.

Traill, A. 2001. "Knocking on Knemon's door: Stagecraft and symbolism in the *Dyskolos.*" *TAPA* 131: 87–108.

—— 2008. *Women and the Comic Plot in Menander.* Cambridge.

Treggiari, S. 1991. *Roman Marriage: Iusti Coniuges from the Time of Cicero to the Time of Ulpian.* Oxford.

—— 1996. "Women in Roman society." In Kleiner and Matheson (eds.): 116–25.

—— 2007. *Terentia, Tullia and Publilia: The Women of Cicero's Family.* New York.

Trendall, A. D. 1989. *Red Figure Vases of South Italy and Sicily.* London.

Triantaphyllou, S. 1998. "Prehistoric cemetery populations from Northern Greece: A breath of life for the skeletal remains." In Brannigan, K. (ed.), *Cemetery and Society in the Aegean Bronze Age. Sheffield Studies in Aegean Archaeology* 1: 150–64. Sheffield.

—— 2003. "A bioarchaeological approach to Bronze Age cemetery populations from Western and Central Greek Macedonia." In Foster and Laffineur (eds.): 217–22.

Triantaphyllou, S., Richards, M. P., Zerner, C., Voutsaki, S. 2008. "Isotopic dietary reconstruction of humans from Middle Bronze Age Lerna, Argolid, Greece." *Journal of Archaeological Science* 35: 3028–34.

Trimble, J. 2000. "Replicating the body politic: The Herculaneum women statue types in Early Imperial Italy." *JRA* 13: 41–68.

—— 2011. *Women and Visual Replication in Roman Imperial Art and Culture: Visual Replication and Urban Elites.* Cambridge.

Tringham, R. E. 1991. "Households with faces: The challenge of gender in prehistoric architectural remains." In Conkey and Gero (eds.): 93–131.

Tringham, R. and Conkey, M. 1998. "Rethinking figurines." In Goodison and Morris 1998a: 22–45.

Trotter, M. H. 1970. "Estimation of stature from intact long bones." In Stewart, T. D. (ed.), *Personal Identification in Mass Disasters.* Washington, DC. 71–83.

Trow, M. J. 2003. *Boudicca.* Stroud.

Troy, L. 1986. *Patterns of Queenship in Ancient Egyptian Myth and History. Acta Universitatis Upsaliensis, Boreas* 14. Uppsala.

Trümper, M. 2010. "Space and social relations in the Greek *oikos* of the Classical and Hellenistic periods." In Rawson, B. (ed.), *A Companion to Families in the Greek and Roman Worlds.* Oxford. 32–52.

—— Forthcoming. "Gender differentiation in Greek public baths." In *Internationales Frontinus Symposium zur Technik- und Kulturgeschichte der antiken Thermen.*

Trundle, M. 2004. *Greek Mercenaries from the Late Archaic Period to Alexander.* London.

Tsimbidou-Avloniti, M. 2004. "The Macedonian tomb at Aghios Athanasios, Thessaloniki." In Pandermalis (ed.): 149–51.

Tsipopoulou, M. 2009. Harriet Boyd's 'granddaughters': Women directors of excavations and surveys in Crete at the end of the 20th and the beginnings of the 21st century." In Kopaka (ed.): 273–83.

Tsirigoti-Drakotou, I. 2008. "Black-figure krateriskos." Cat. no. 45. In Kaltsas and Shapiro (eds.): 102.

Turner, E. G. 1979. "Menander and the new society of his time." *Chronique d'Égypte* 54: 106–26.

Turner, V. 1974. *Dramas, Fields and Metaphors: Symbolic Action in Human Society.* Ithaca, NY.

Tusa, S., Baldassari, R., Fragonara, M., Bennett, C., and Modica, E. (eds.) 2004. *Pantelleria e l'Archeologia.* Alcamo.

Tyldesley, J. A. 2008. *Cleopatra, Last Queen of Egypt.* London.

Tylor, E. B. 1871. *Primitive Culture: Researches into the Development of Mythology, Philosophy, Religion, Language, Art, and Custom.* London.

Tzachili, I. 1986. "Of earrings, swallows, and Theran ladies." In Bonnano, A. (ed.), *Archaeology and Fertility Cult in the Ancient Mediterranean.* Malta. 97–104.

—— 1997. *Υφαντική και υφάντρες στο προϊστορικό Αιγαίο, 2000-1000 π. X.* Herakleio.

Tzanetou, A. 2007. "Ritual and gender: Critical perspectives." In Parca and Tzanetou (eds.): 3–26.

Ubelaker, D. H. 1989. *Human Skeletal Remains: Excavation, Analysis, Interpretation.* Third edition. Washington, DC.

Ucko, P. J. 1968. *Anthropomorphic Figurines in Predynastic Egypt and Neolithic Greece with Comparative Material from the Prehistoric Near East and Mainland Greece.* London.

Uhlenbrock, J. P. 1988. *The Terracotta Protomai from Gela: A Discussion of Local Style in Archaic Sicily.* Rome.

Ursi, W. J. S., Trotman, C.-A., McNamara, J. A., and Behrents, R. G. 1993. "Sexual dimorphism in normal craniofacial growth." *The Angle Orthodontist* 63: 47–56.

Valone, C. 2001. "Matrons and motives: Why women built in Early Modern Rome." In Reiss, S. and Wilkins, D. (eds.), *Beyond Isabella: Secular Women Patrons of Art in Renaissance Italy.* Kirksville, MO. 317–35.

Van Bremen, R. 1983. "Women and wealth." In Cameron and Kuhrt (eds.): 233–43.

—— 1996. *The Limits of Participation: Women and Civic Life in the Greek East in the Hellenistic and Roman Periods.* Amsterdam.

Van Compernolle, R. 1976. "Le tradizioni sulla fondazione e sulla storia arcaica di Locri Epizefiori e la propaganda politica alla fine del V e IV secolo avanti Cristo." *ASNP serie III* 4(1): 329–400.

Van de Mieroop, M. 1989. "Women in the economy of Sumer." In Lesko (ed.): 53–66.

Van der Toorn, K. 1994. *From her Cradle to her Grave: The Role of Religion in the Life of the Israelite and the Babylonian Woman.* Sheffield.

—— 1995. "The significance of the veil in the Ancient Near East." In Wright, D. P., Freedman, D. N., and Hurvitz, A. (eds.), *Pomegranates and Golden Bells: Studies in Biblical, Jewish, and Near Eastern Ritual, Law and Literature in Honor of Jacob Milgrom.* Winona Lake, IN. 327–39.

Van Driel Murray, C. 1995. "Gender in question." In Rush (ed.): 22–32.

Van Minnen, P. 2002. "*ΑΙ ΑΠΟ ΓΥΜΝΑΣΙΟΥ*: 'Greek' women and the Greek 'elite' in the metropoleis of Roman Egypt." In Melaerts and Mooren (eds.): 337–53.

Van Straten, F. 1995. Hiera Kala: *Images of Animal Sacrifice in Archaic and Classical Greece.* Leiden.

—— 2000. "Votives and votaries in Greek sanctuaries." In Buxton, R. (ed.), *Oxford Readings in Greek Religion.* Oxford. 191–223.

Vandorpe, K. 2002a. "Apollonia, a businesswoman in a multicultural society (Pathyris, 2nd-1st centuries B.C)." In Melaerts and Mooren (eds.): 325–36.

—— 2002b. *The Bilingual Family Archive of Dryton, his Wife Apollonia and their Daughter Senmouthis (P. Dryton)*. *Collectanea Hellenistica* 4. Brussels.

Vandorpe, K. and Waebens, S. 2010. "Women and gender in Roman Egypt: The impact of Roman rule." In Lembke, K., Minas-Nerpel, M., and Pfeiffer, S. (eds.), *Tradition and Transformation: Egypt under Roman Rule*. Boston. 415–35.

Vanderpool, C. de Grazia. 2005. "Fashioning Plancia Magna: Memory and revival in the Greek East during the second century AD." In Pollini, J. (ed.), *Terra Marique: Studies in Art History and Marine Archaeology in Honor of Anna Marguerite McCann on the Receipt of the Gold Medal of the Archaeological Institute of America*. Oxford. 12–29.

Van Wees, H. J. 1998. "Greeks bearing arms: The state, the leisure class, and the display of weapons in archaic Greece." In Fisher, N. and van Wees, H. (eds.), *Archaic Greece: New Approaches and New Evidence*. London. 333–78.

—— 1999. "Introduction: Homer and Early Greece." In de Jong, I. J. F. (ed.), *Homer: Critical Assessments*, vol II. New York. 1–32.

Vedder, U. 1988. "Frauentod-Kriegertod im Spiegel der attischen Grabkunst den 4.Jhr.v.Chr." *MDAI(A)* 103: 161–91.

Veenhof, K. R. 1972. *Aspects of Old Assyrian Trade and its Terminology*. Leiden.

Venit, M. S. 1998. "Women in their cups." *CW* 92: 117–30.

—— 2002. *Monumental Tombs of Ancient Alexandria: The Theatre of the Dead*. Cambridge.

Verlinden, C. 1984. *Les Statuettes Anthropomorphes Crétoises en Bronze et en Plomb du IIIe Millénaire au VIIe Siècle av. J.-C.* Providence.

Vernant, J.-P. 1989. "Preface." In Bérard, C. and Bron, C. *A City of Images: Iconography and Society in Ancient Greece*. Transl. D. Lyons. Princeton, NJ. 7–8.

—— 1997. "Au miroir de Pénélope." In Frontisi-Ducroux and Vernant: 253–85.

Versnel, H. 1993. *Inconsistencies in Greek and Roman Religion II: Transition and Reversal in Myth and Ritual*. Leiden.

Veyne, P. 1990. *Bread and Circuses: Historical Sociology and Political Pluralism*. London.

Von Diest, W. 1913. *Nysa ad Maeandrum. Nach Forschungen und Aufnahmen in den Jahren 1907 und 1909*. Berlin.

Von Falck, M. 1996. "Vorüberlegungen zur Datierung einer spätkaiserzeitlichen Denkmalgruppe aus Ägypten: Die Grabreliefs von Behnasa." *Bulletin de la Societé d'Archéologie Copte* 35: 29–35.

Von Graeve, V. 1979. Zum Zeugniswert der bemalten Grabstelen von Demetrias für die griechische Malerei. In *La Thessalie. Actes de la Table-Ronde. 21–24 Juliet 1975*. Lyon. 111–38.

Von Graeve, V. and Helly, B. 1987. "Recherches récentes sur la peinture grecque." *PACT* 17(1.2): 17–33.

Von Graeve, V. and Preusser, F. 1981. "Zur Technik Griechischer Malerei auf Marmor." *Jahrbuch des Deutschen Archäolgischen Instituts* 96: 120–56.

Von Hesberg-Tonn, B. 1983. *Coniunx carissima: Untersuchungen zum Normcharakter im Erscheinungsbild der römischen Frau*. Diss., Stuttgart.

Von Staden, H. 1992. "Women and dirt." *Helios* 19: 7–30.

Vorster, C. 2007. "Greek origins: The Herculaneum women in the pre-Roman world." In Daehner (ed.): 113–39.

Voyatzis, M. 1992. "Votive riders seated side-saddle at Early Greek sanctuaries." *BSA* 87: 259–79.

Wachsmuth, C. and Hense, O. 1884. *Stobaeus, Anthologium*, vol 1. Berlin.

Waite, J. 2007. *Boudica's Last Stand: Britain's Revolt against Rome AD 48–58*. London.

Waithe, M. E. (ed.) 1987. *A History of Women Philosophers 600 B.C.–500 A.D.* Dordrecht.

Walker, P. L. 1997. "Wife beating, boxing, and broken noses: Skeletal evidence for the cultural patterning of violence." In Martin, D. L. and Frayer, D. W. (eds.), *Troubled Times: Violence and Warfare in the Past. War and Society*, vol. 3. Amsterdam. 145–80.

Walker, P. L. and Cook, D. C. 1998. "Gender and sex: Vive la différence." *AJPA* 106: 255–9.

Walker, P. L., Bathurst, R. R., Richman, R., Gjerdrum, T., and Andrushko, V. A. 2009. "The causes of porotic hyperostosis and cribra orbitalia: A reappraisal of the iron-deficiency-anemia hypothesis." *AJPA* 139: 109–25.

Walker, S. 1993. "Clytie—a false woman?" In Jones, M. (ed.), *Why Fakes Matter*. London. 32–40.

—— (ed.) 2000. *Ancient Faces: Mummy Portraits from Roman Egypt*. New York.

Walker, S. and Bierbrier, M. 1997. *Ancient Faces: Mummy Portraits from Roman Egypt*. London.

—— 1994. *Houses and Society in Pompeii and Herculaneum*. Princeton, NJ.

—— 1996. "Engendering the Roman house." In Kleiner and Matheson (eds.): 104–15.

Walsh, D. 2008. *Distorted Ideals in Greek Vase Painting: The World of Mythological Burlesque*. Cambridge.

Walters, E. 1988. *Attic Grave Reliefs that Represent Women in the Dress of Isis. Hesperia Supplement* 22. Princeton, NJ.

Waraksa, E. A. 2008. "Female figurines (Pharaonic period)." In *UCLA Encyclopedia of Egyptology*. http://escholarship.org/uc/item/4dg0d57b.

—— 2009. *Female Figurines from the Mut Precinct: Context and Ritual Function, Orbis Biblicus et Orientalis* 240. Fribourg.

Ward, R. B. 1992. "Women in Roman baths." *HTR* 85: 125–47.

Warren, P. 1985. "The fresco of the garlands from Knossos." In Darcque, P. and Poursat, J.-Cl. (eds.), *L'Iconographie Minoenne*. London. 185–208.

—— 1988. *Minoan Religion as Ritual Action*. Göteborg.

—— 1992. "Die Backsteingruft 45 in Assur. Entdeckung, Fundzusammensetzung und Präsentation im Berliner vorderasiatischen Museum." *Mitteilungen der Deutschen Orient-Gesellschaft zu Berlin* 124. Berlin. 97–130.

Watrous, L. V. 1996. *The Cave Sanctuary of Zeus at Psychro: A Study of Extra-Urban Sanctuaries in Minoan and Early Iron Age Crete. Aegaeum* 15. Leuven.

Watterson, B. 1991. *Women in Ancient Egypt*. New York.

Weaver, D. S. 1980. "Sex differences in the ilia of a known sex and age sample of fetal and infant skeletons." *AJPA* 52: 191–5.

—— 1998. "Osteoporosis in the bioarchaeology of women." In Grauer and Stuart-Macadam: 27–44.

Weber, G. 1997. "Interaktion, Repräsentation und Herrschaft: Der Königshof im Hellenismus." In Winterling, A. (ed.), *Zwischen "Haus" und "Staat": Antike Höfe im Vergleich, Historische Zeitschrift* 23. Munich. 27–71.

Weber, H. 1969–70. "*Coae vestes.*" *Istanbuler Mitteilungen* 19/20: 249–53.

Webster, G. 1978. *Boudica: The British Revolt against Rome AD 60*. London.

Webster, J. 2001. "Creolizing the Roman provinces." *AJA* 105: 209–25.

Webster, T. B. L. 1956. *Greek Theatre Production*. London.

—— 1960. *Studies in Menander*. Manchester.

—— 1962–3. "Menander: Production and imagination." *Bulletin of the John Rylands Library* 45: 235–72.

—— 1972. *Potter and Patron in Classical Athens*. London.

Wegner, J. R. 1988. *Chattel or Person? The Status of Women in the Mishnah*. Oxford.

—— 1991. "The image and status of women in classical rabbinic Judaism." In Baskin (ed.): 73–100.

Wehrli, C. 1964. "Phila, fille d'Antipater et épouse de Démétrios, roi des Macédoniens." *Historia* 13: 140–6.

Weiershäuser, F. 2010. *Die königlichen Frauen der III. Dynastie von Ur*. Göttingen.

Weiss, K. M. 1972. "On the systematic bias in skeletal sexing." *AJPA* 37: 239–50.

Welch, K. E. 2007. "Pompeian men and women in portrait sculpture." In Dobbins and Foss (eds.): 550–84.

Westbrook, R. 1987. *Old Babylonian Marriage Law. Archiv für Orientforschung* 23. Horn.

—— 2005. "Penelope's dowry and Odysseus' kinship." In Wallace, R. W. and Gagarin, M. (eds.), *Symposion 2001: Papers on Greek and Hellenistic Legal History*. Vienna. 3–32.

Westenholz, J. G. 2006. "Women of religion in Mesopotamia: The high priestess in the temple." *Canadian Society of Mesopotamian Studies Journal* 1: 31–44.

Westgate, R. 2007a. "The Greek houses and the ideology of citizenship." *World Archaeology* 39: 229–45.

—— 2007b. "House and society in Classical and Hellenistic Crete: A case study in regional variation." *AJA* 111: 423–57.

Westgate, R., Fisher, N., and Whitley, J. (eds.) 2007. *Building Communities. House, Settlement and Society in the Aegean and Beyond. The Annual of the British School at Athens* Suppl. 15.

Wheeler, R. E. M. and Wheeler, T. V. 1932. *Report on the Excavations of the Prehistoric, Roman and Post Roman Site in Lydney Park, Gloucestershire*. Oxford.

White, T. D. and Folkens, P. A. 2005. *The Human Bone Manual*. Amsterdam.

Whitelaw, T. M. 1983. "The settlement at Phournou Korifi, Myrtos, and aspects of Early Minoan social organization." In Krzyszkowska and Nixon (eds.): 323–45.

Whittaker, C. R. 1997. "Imperialism and culture: The Roman initiative." In Mattingly, D. J. (ed.), *Dialogues in Roman Imperialism: Power, Discourse, and Discrepant Experience in the Roman Empire. JRA* Suppl. 23. Portsmouth. 143–63.

Wider, K. 1986. "Women philosophers in the ancient Greek world: Donning the mantle." *Hypatia* 1: 21–62.

Wiener, M. H. 1987. "Trade and rule in Palatial Crete." In Hägg, R. and Marinatos, N. (eds.), *The Function of Minoan Palaces*. Stockholm. 261–6.

Wildfang, R. L. 2006. *Rome's Vestal Virgins: A Study of Rome's Vestal Priestesses in the Late Republic and Early Empire*. London.

Wiles, D. 1989. "Marriage and prostitution in classical New Comedy." *Themes in Drama* 11: 31–48.

Wiles, D. 2000. *Greek Theatre Performance*. Cambridge.

Wilfong, T. G. 1992. *Women in the Ancient Near East: A Select Bibliography of Recent Sources in The Oriental Institute Research Archives*. http://oi.uchicago.edu/OI/DEPT/RA/WOMEN. HTML.

—— 1997. *Women and Gender in Ancient Egypt: From Prehistory to Late Antiquity*. Ann Arbor, MI.

—— 2002a. "'Friendship and physical desire': The discourse of female homoeroticism in fifth-century Egypt." In Rabinowitz and Auanger (eds.): 304–29.

—— 2002b. *Women of Jeme: Lives in a Coptic Town in Late Antique Egypt*. Ann Arbor, MI.

Williams, D. and Ogden, J. 1994. *Greek Gold: Jewelry of the Classical World*. New York.

Williams, M. 1998. *The Jews among the Greeks and Romans: A Diasporan Sourcebook*. Baltimore, MD.

Wilson, P. R. 2002a. *Cataractonium: Roman Catterick and its Hinterland. Excavations and Research, 1958–1997. Part I. CBA Res. Rep.* 128. York.

—— 2002b. *Cataractonium: Roman Catterick and its Hinterland. Excavations and Research, 1958–1997. Part II. CBA Res. Rep.* 128. York.

Wilson, R. J. A. 1994. [Review of Holloway 1991.] *JHS* 114: 217–18.

Wiltshire, S. F. 1989. *Public and Private in Vergil's Aeneid*. Amherst.

Winckelmann, J. J. 1755. *Gedancken über die Nachahmung der Griechischen Wercke in der Mahlerey und Bildhauer-Kunst*. Dresden. Rehm, W. (ed.), 1968. *Kleine Schriften, Vorreden, Entwürfe*. Berlin. 27–59.

—— 1764. *Geschichte der Kunst des Alterthums*. Borbein, A., Hofter, M. R., and Rügler, A. (ed.) 2002–2007. *Johann Joachim Winckelmann. Schriften und Nachlass* 4.1–3. Mainz am Rhein.

Winkler, J. 1990. *The Constraints of Desire: The Anthropology of Sex and Gender in Ancient Greece*. New York.

Winter, I. J. 1987. "Women in public: The Disc of Enheduanna, the beginning of the office of *EN*-priestess and the weight of visual evidence." In Durand (ed.), 189–201.

Wissowa, G. 1912. *Religion und Kultus der Römer.* Second edition. Leipzig.

Wistrand, E. 1976. *The So-called* Laudatio Turiae*: Introduction, Text, Translation, Commentary.* Göteborg.

Witherington, B. 1984. *Women in the Ministry of Jesus: A Study of Jesus' Attitudes to Women and Their Roles as Reflected in his Earthly Life.* Cambridge.

Wohl, V. J. 1993. "Standing by the stathmos: The creation of sexual ideology in the *Odyssey.*" *Arethusa* 26: 19–50.

—— 1998. *Intimate Commerce: Exchange, Gender, and Subjectivity in Greek Tragedy.* Austin.

Wolff, H. J. 1944. "Marriage law and family organization in ancient Athens." *Traditio* 2: 43–95.

Wolfskeel, C. 1987. "Makrina." In Waithe, M. E. (ed.), *A History of Women Philosophers 600 B.C. – 500 A.D.* Dordrecht. 139–68.

Wood, H. 2009. "Byzantine women: Religion and gender construction." *Rosetta* 7: 19–32.

Wood, S. 1999. *Imperial Women. A Study in Public Images, 40 B.C.–A.D. 68.* Leiden.

Woodhull, M. 2003. "Engendering space: Octavia's portico in Rome." *Aurora: The Journal of the History of Art* 4: 13–33.

Woodman, A. J. 2004. *Tacitus: The Annals.* Indianapolis, IN and Cambridge.

Woodward, A. and Leach, P. 1993. *The Uley Shrines. Excavation of a ritual complex on West Hill, Uley, Gloucestershire 1977–9. English Heritage Archaeology Report* 17. London.

Woolf, G. 1996. "Monumental writing and the expansion of Roman society in the early empire." *JRS* 86: 22–39.

—— 1998. *Becoming Roman: The Origins of Provincial Civilization in Gaul.* Cambridge.

Woolley, C. L. 1934. *Ur Excavations II: The Royal Cemetery.* London.

Worman, N. 2001. "This voice which is not one: Helen's verbal guises in Homeric epic." In Lardinois and McClure (eds.): 19–37.

Woronoff, M. 1983. "La femme dans l'universe epique (*Iliade*)." In Lévy, E. (ed.), *La Femme dans le Sociétés Antiques: Actes des Colloques de Strasbourg (Mai 1980 et Mars 1981).* Strasbourg. 33–44.

Wrede, H. 1971. "Das Mausoleum der Claudia Semne und die bürgerliche Plastik der Kaiserzeit." *Römische Mitteilungen* 78: 125–66.

Wright, R. P. 2008. "Gendered relations and the Ur III dynasty: Kinship, property, and labor." In Bolger, D. (ed.), *Gender through Time in the Ancient Near East.* Lanham, MD. 247–79.

Wright, R. P. and Hassall, M. W. C. 1971. "Inscriptions." *Britannia* 2: 289–304.

Wyke, M. 1987a. "Written women: Propertius' *scripta puella.*" *JRS* 77: 47–61.

—— 1987b. "The elegiac woman at Rome." *PCPS* 213 (n.s. 33): 153–78.

—— 1989a. "Mistress and metaphor in Augustan elegy." *Helios* 16: 25–47.

—— 1989b. "Reading Female Flesh: *Amores* 3.1." In Cameron (ed.): 111–43.

—— 1992. "Augustan Cleopatras: female power and poetic authority." In Powell, A. (ed.), *Roman Poetry and Propaganda in the Age of Augustus.* London. 98–140.

—— 1994a. "Woman in the mirror: The rhetoric of adornment in the Roman world." In Archer et al. (eds.): 134–51.

—— 1994b. "Taking the woman's part: Engendering Roman love elegy." *Ramus* 23: 110–28.

—— (ed.) 1998. *Parchments of Gender: Deciphering the Bodies of Antiquity.* Oxford.

—— 2002. *The Roman Mistress.* Oxford.

Yiannouli, E. 1992. *Reason in Architecture: The Component of Space. A Study of Domestic and Palatial Buildings in Bronze Age Greece.* Diss., Cambridge University.

Yiftach-Firanko, U. 2003. *Marriage and Marital Arrangements: A History of the Greek Marriage Document in Egypt, 4th century BCE–4th century CE.* Munich.

Yon, J.-B. 2002. *Les Notables de Palmyre.* Beirut.

Younger, J. G. 1992. "Bronze Age representations of Minoan-Mycenean jewelry." In Laffineur, R. and Crowley, J. (eds.), *Eikon: Aegean Bronze Age Archaeology, Shaping a Methodology*. Liège. 257–93.

—— 1995. "Interactions between Aegean seals and other Minoan-Mycenaean art forms." In Pini, I. and Poursat, J.-Cl. (eds.), *Sceaux Minoens et Mycéniens. Corpus der Minoischen und Mykenischen Siegel*, Beiheft 5. Berlin. 331–48.

—— 2009. "'We are woman': Girl, maid, matron in Aegean art." In Kopaka (ed.): 207–12.

Zanker, P. 1988. *The Power of Images in the Age of Augustus*. Transl. A. Shapiro. Ann Arbor, MI.

—— 1993. "The Hellenistic grave *stelai* from Smyrna." In Bulloch, A., Gruen, E. S., Long, A. A., and Stewart, A. (eds.), *Images and Ideologies: Self-definition in the Hellenistic World*. Berkeley, CA. 212–30.

—— 1998. *Pompeii: Public and Private Life*. Cambridge, MA.

Zayed, A. H. 1962. *Egyptian Antiquities*. Cairo.

Zeitlin, F. I. 1982. "Cultic models of the female: Rites of Dionysus and Demeter." *Arethusa* 15: 129–57.

—— 1995. "Figuring fidelity in Homer's *Odyssey*." In Cohen (ed.): 117–52.

—— 1996. *Playing the Other: Gender and Society in Classical Greek Literature*. Chicago, IL.

—— 1999. "Utopia and myth in Aristophanes' *Ecclesiazousae*." In Falkner, T. M., Felson, N., and Konstan, D. (eds.), *Contextualizing Classics: Ideology, Performance, Dialogue*. Lanham. 69–87.

Zetterholm, M. 2003. *The Formation of Christianity in Antioch: A Social-Scientific Approach to the Separation between Judaism and Christianity*. London.

Zgoll, A. 1997. *Der Rechsfall der En-hedu-Ana im Lied nin-me-šara*. Münster.

Zimmermann, M. 2009. "Stadtraum, Architektur und öffentliches Leben in der hellenistischen Stadt." In Matthaei, A. and Zimmermann, M. (eds.), *Stadtbilder im Hellenismus. Die Hellenistische Polis als Lebensform* 1. Berlin. 23–40.

Zois, A. 1996. *Κνωσσός: Το εκστατικό όραμα. Σημειωτική και ψυχολογία μιας αρχαιολογίας*. Herakleion.

Zuiderhoek, A. 2009. *The Politics of Munificence in the Roman Empire: Citizens, Elites, and Benefactors in Asia Minor*. Cambridge.

Index of Women

Biblical Women and Women of the Apocrypha

Goddesses and Women of Myth and Legend

A Companion to Women in the Ancient World, First Edition. Edited by Sharon L. James and Sheila Dillon.
© 2012 John Wiley & Sons, Ltd. Published 2015 by John Wiley & Sons, Ltd.

Historical Women and Women Called Historical

Acilia, mother of Lucan   450
Acme, *ancilla* of Livia   334
Adea Eurydice   311
Aelia Placilia   514
Aemilia Pudentilla, wife of Apuleius   489
Aesara of Lucania   346, 348
Aesquillia Polla, wife of N. Herennius
   Celsus   411–12
Afrania   104
Agrippina the Elder   105, 357, 376, 383, 384,
   419
Agrippina the Younger   360, 365, 366, 419, 420,
   420, 421, 452
Agusia Priscilla of Gabii   483
Aline   258–9, 261, 262
Allia Potestas   495
Annia Aelia Restituta of Calama   483
Annous, sister of Kaët of the Fayum   508
Anthis   257
Antiochis of Tlos   122
Antonia Minor, daughter of Mark Antony   418,
   419
Antonia, sister of Mark Antony   364
Antonia Tryphaena, daughter of
   Pythodoris   462–3
Apollonia (*medica*)   122
Apollonia, sister of Eupous   328
Apollonia (aka Senmonthis), wife of
   Dryton   325–6, 328
Apollonia, wife of Hermogenes   340
Apollonia, wife of Philiscus   97, 98
Appuleia, wife of M. Aemilius   360
Appuleia Varilla   104
Archidike   251, 255, 256, 257, 259, 262
Archippe of Kyme   239, 240, 242, 244, 245, 246,
   247, 270
Ariadne, Empress   516–17
Arignote   346
Aristonoe of Rhamnous   233, 263, 264, 265,
   270, 272, 273, 274, 277
Armea of Binchester   471
Arria the Elder   492
Arruntia (Vestal Virgin)   356
Arsinoe II, sister/wife of Ptolemy II
   Philadelphus   317, 318, 320, 321
Artemidora, daughter of Harpokrates, mummy
   of   428–9, 430, 435
Artemis, wife of Kaët of the Fayum   507–8
Artemisia, wife of Maussolos of
   Halicarnassus   270
Asklepias   328
Aspasia (*medica*)   112, 118, 123
Aspasia of Miletus   347
Auguste of Gdanmaa   122, 123

Aurelia Aia   475, 476
Aurelia Alexandria Zosime   122, 123
Aurelia Censorina   475
Aurelia Charite of Hermopolis   504–5, 508
Aurelia Lupula   472

Babatha   334, 339, 340, 341
Baebia Crinita of Arucci   483
Banitu, wife of King Shalmaneser V   20
Berenice, daughter of King Agrippa I   332, 334,
   339
Berenike I, wife of Ptolemy I Soter   317
Berenike II, wife of Ptolemy III Euergetes   317,
   318, 319, 320
Boudica   468, 469, 476
Burney, Fanny   120
Busa   214

Caecilia Attica, first wife of Agrippa   376
Caecilia Metella, fifth wife of Sulla   245
Calpurnia, wife of Pliny   492
Candace of Meroe   469
Cartimandua, leader of the Brigantes   468–9, 476
Cassia Victoria, wife of Laecanius Primitivus   484
Charite *see* Aurelia Charite of Hermopolis
Chelidon, mistress of Verres   362
Claudia (*CIL* VI 15346)   494–5
Claudia Capitolina   336
Claudia, first wife of Octavian/Augustus   358
Claudia Severa   475
Claudia Marcella Christiana   494
Claudia Semne   494
Cleopatra, daughter of Olympias   306,
   310, 311
Cleopatra I, wife of Philip II   310
Cleopatra VII   94, 314, 316, 317, 328, 339, 354,
   358, 360, 368, 370, 371, 393, 415
Cleopatra, sixth wife of Philip II   310
Clodia Luculli, sister of Clodius   357, 360
Clodia Metelli, sister of Clodius   93, 243, 355,
   356, 357, 359, 360, 384
Clodia Nigella   412
Clodia (Tertia) Marci, sister of Clodius   357
Cloelia   299, 492, 496
Cornelia, daughter of Scribonia   376
Cornelia, mother of the Gracchi   243, 246, 248,
   375, 376, 377, 415, 492, 493, 496
Cornelia, wife of Sestius   358, 359

Danielis of the Peloponnese   513
Demarion   328
Demetria of Cos   323–4
Demetria (Ammonia) of Hermopolis   504, 505
Demokrite   270

Timonassa of Priene 269
Tretia Maria of London 472
Tuccia (Vestal Virgin) 204
Tullia, daughter of Cicero 360, 364
Turia 245, 372, 492, 495–7, 501

Ulpia Epigone 492, 495, 496
Ummidia Quadratilla 445–9, 489

Vacia, sister of Aelius Mercurarius 472
Valeria Paula 358
Verecunda (actress of Leicester) 472

Verginia 89–91, 396, 492
Veturia Paula 336
Victoria, Queen of England 104, 469
Vibia Sabina, wife of Hadrian 454, 459
Vilbia of Bath 472
Vipsania Agrippa 375
Vitia 470
Volumnia Cytheris 93, 384, 390, 391
  see also Lycoris (Gallus) in LITERARY/FICTIONAL WOMEN

Yaba, Queen of Nimbrud 19, 20, 21

Literary/Fictional Women

Acropolistis (Plautus, *Epidicus*) 236

Camilla (Vergil, *Aeneid*) 394
Canidia (Horace, *Epodes*) 387, 388
Chloe (Horace, *Odes*) 388–9
Chrysis (Menander, *Dyskolos*) 285, 286
Corinna (Ovid, *Amores*) 390, 391, 392
Cynthia (Propertius) 381–2, 383, 384, 390

Delia (Tibullus) 384, 390, 391, 392

Giddenis (Plautus, *Poenulus*) 236
Glycera (Horace, *Ode* 1.33) 390, 391, 392, 442, 443, 444
Glykera (Menander, *Perikeiromene*) 283, 285

Halisca (Plautus, *Cistellaria*) 236

Krateia (Menander, *Misoumenos*) 284
Krobyle (Menander, *Plokion*) 285

Lampito (Aristophanes, *Lysistrata*) 153
Lesbia (Catullus) 93, 384, 390, 444

  see also Clodia in HISTORICAL WOMEN AND WOMEN CALLED HISTORICAL
Lycoris (Gallus) 93, 384, 390, 391
Lysistrata (Aristophanes) 58

Mysis (Terence, *Andria*) 236

Nemesis (Tibullus) 391, 392

Pamphile (Menander, *Epitrepontes*) 280, 282, 285
Pardalisca (Plautus, *Casina*) 236
Pholoe (Horace, *Odes*) 389, 390
Pholoe (Tibullus) 390
Plangon (Menander, *Dyskolos*) 286
Pyrra (Horace, *Odes*) 389

Sagana (Horace, *Epodes*) 387
Scapha (Plautus, *Mostellaria*) 236
Simiche (Menander, *Dyskolos*) 236
Sophrone (Menander, *Epitrepontes*) 236
Sophrona (Terence, *Phormio*) 236
Staphyla (Plautus, *Aulularia*) 236
Syra (Plautus, *Mercator*) 236–7

Subject Index

abortion 121–3, 135–6
adornment, female 52–3, 73, 143–4, 177,
    179–89, 396–7, 400, 425, 437, 439–40, 474,
    498, 518–20, 525–6
    cosmetics *see* cosmetics
    jewelry 473, 514, 518, 525
    hair *see* hair, hairstyles, female
adultery 59, 101–2, 104, 196, 281, 331–2, 360,
    373, 376–8, 386–8, 395–8, 531
    adultery law *see* laws, Julian
agonothetai, female 299, 479
aischrologia, female 192–6
aletrides 202
archaeological context *see* context, archaeological
Arkteia 186, 188, 196–201
arrhephoroi 202
athletes, female 155–61
athletic competitions, women and 171,
    299–300
Attic vases, interpretation of women on 141–52,
    154–65, 180–8, 196, 198–202, 288–9
authority, female 337, 361, 478–90, 515–17,
    531

Bacchanalia 208, 355, 379, 383–4
Bachofen, Johann Jacob 8
baths, public, women at 300–2
benefactresses, public 238–48, 270, 460,
    478–90
Bikini girls 155
birth *see* childbirth
Bona Dea 207, 240
    ritual, scandal of 354, 355, 356, 360
bones *see* skeletons
Brauronia 186, 191, 196–201
breastfeeding 187, 439–40
brides 12, 54–6, 75–6, 98–100, 142–4, 184–5,
    187–8, 254, 280–5, 310, 322–5
brothels 88, 91, 235–7

buildings, built by women 194, 239–42, 244–7,
    290, 336, 401–9, 448–9, 461–5, 478–89,
    517
burial, royal 11–23, 306, 309, 335
businesswomen 325–6, 405–9
    in Egypt 502, 504–6

Catilinarian conspiracy 354–6
chastity, female 69–70, 86, 89–92, 94, 204, 344,
    346, 348, 373, 377, 379–81, 396, 443, 451,
    492, 494–6, 516
childbearing 130, 187, 255, 373
childbirth 32, 36, 44, 48–9, 82, 102–3, 108–14,
    123, 127–31, 186–8, 193, 197, 200–2,
    210–12, 249–57, 283, 328, 332, 334, 337,
    340–1, 374, 424–5, 521–2
    death in 130, 250, 252–3, 255, 259, 341
chiton, female 155, 163, 182–4, 198, 308
Christianity, women and 3, 212, 335, 437, 503,
    506, 509–10, 528–30, 537–8
citizenship, women and 85, 98, 99, 102
clothing
    color in 102, 180–3, 188, 231, 233, 270, 274,
    276–7, 520
    female 20, 29, 46, 67, 171–2, 180, 207, 231,
    233, 241, 245, 255, 265, 270, 276–7, 308,
    323–4, 397, 427, 431, 459–460, 466, 470–1,
    473, 506, 508, 511, 526, 533
    see also footwear, female
colonization, women and 171
    scholarly attitudes toward 217–27
concubines (pallakai) 55, 63, 87, 99, 192, 236,
    284, 286, 324, 347, 472, 532
context
    archaeological 7, 9, 11, 18–20, 25, 30, 33,
    39, 43, 46, 52, 72, 76, 139, 151, 231, 498,
    503, 505
    mortuary 11, 126
contraception 118, 121–2

A Companion to Women in the Ancient World, First Edition. Edited by Sharon L. James and Sheila Dillon.
© 2012 John Wiley & Sons, Ltd. Published 2015 by John Wiley & Sons, Ltd.

Greek art
  female identity in   141–52, 153–66, 167–78,
    179–90, 231–4, 249–62, 263–77
  interpretations of women in   1, 141–78,
    184–90, 198–9, 215–18, 230, 231–4, 245,
    246, 263–77, 288–9
Greek dress, evidence for   42, 43, 46–7, 50, 52,
  144, 160, 163–4, 179–89, 198–200, 202,
  216, 222, 224, 227, 231–4, 265–6, 271–5,
  276–7, 288–9, 344, 349
Greek sculpture, women in   167–78, 179–90,
  215–16, 231–4, 249–62, 263–77, 404
guardianship, of women   92–3, 98–103,
  282–3, 316–17, 365, 373, 408, 469–70,
  488, 509
gymnasiarch, female   98, 241–2, 246, 479
gynaikonitis (women's quarters)   141, 292–6

hair, hairstyles, female   13, 29, 50, 75, 80, 128,
  155, 160, 163, 171, 184–5, 188, 198, 208–9,
  231, 253, 266–7, 271–5, 331, 403–5, 415–16,
  419–20, 425–7, 429, 431–5, 453–60, 469,
  473, 514–15, 518–20, 522
  see also hairdressers
hairdressers   391, 498
Haloa   196
health, women's   21, 32–3, 34, 39, 48, 86, 89, 91,
  107–24, 127–39, 153, 209, 242, 337, 391,
  445–7, 520, 531
hedna vs. dowry   54–6
heiress *see epikleros* (heiress)
Herculaneum statue type, Large and Small   265,
  431, 459–60
himation, female   163, 182–3, 258, 261, 273
Homeric poetry, women in   5, 40, 54–65,
  86–7, 144, 182, 192, 253–4, 307, 308, 377,
  383
homophrosyne   63
homosexuality   104, 163–4
horses, women and   151, 154, 158–61, 209, 232,
  348
house, household   12, 13, 16, 18, 19, 26, 33–6,
  43–7, 48, 55, 58–9, 61–4, 69, 87, 98–105,
  176, 202, 211–12, 226–7, 235–7, 240,
  242–3, 251–3, 260–1, 279, 281–5, 287,
  292–6, 304, 322, 324–5, 326–8, 330, 333,
  337–8, 348, 352, 356, 359, 361, 374–5,
  377–9, 381–2, 405–9, 417–18, 447–8, 451,
  475, 495–7, 504–6, 510–11, 525–8, 529,
  534–5, 536
husband–wife relationship   26, 33, 58–9, 60–2,
  63, 82, 84, 86, 89–90, 94 97, 99, 101, 102,
  104, 114–16, 148, 149, 186, 187, 188,
  218–21, 236–7, 245, 253–4, 280–7, 312–13,
  322–5, 330–2, 349, 354–60, 376, 378–81,
  395, 397, 465, 492–3, 494–7, 510–11, 522,
  525–6, 527, 536

illness *see* disease
immigrant women   255–7, 258–9, 322,
  325–6
inheritance   87–8, 93, 99, 100, 101, 147, 424,
  431, 488, 505–9
inscriptions, funerary   12, 15, 19, 23, 67,
  183, 249–62, 333, 335–6, 372, 409–12,
  424–5, 428–9, 470–2, 475, 478, 491–501,
  520
  dedications, public   238–48, 300, 336–7, 402,
    449, 461–5, 479, 481–90
  dedications, votive   16, 35, 210, 267–76, 306,
    309, 319, 336, 362, 403, 416, 473–4, 478
  legal   181
  religious   192, 196, 202, 212
  vase   150–1, 161
intermarriage practices, colonial   217–27, 326

jewelry *see* adornment, female, jewelry
Judgment of Paris   71–6, 518–19
Julian marriage laws *see* laws, Julian

Knossos   40–1, 43, 46, 52
kourotrophos   48, 210–11, 215–16, 218

law
  citizenship (of Pericles)   85, 87, 98, 102, 103,
    480, 482, 484
  Greek   85, 88, 96–105, 188, 244, 279, 285–6,
    323–5, 352
  Rabbinic   329, 333, 334–5, 340–1, 536–7
  Roman   91–3, 96–105, 245, 300, 362–3, 424,
    428, 469–70, 488, 499
Law and women
  individual women's engagements with   242,
    244–5, 296–7, 329, 340, 355, 362, 376, 377,
    396, 494
  legal courtrooms, women in   94, 103–5, 373,
    396, 435, 507–11
  legal treatment of   84–9, 91–4, 96–106, 156,
    188, 209, 134, 283, 285–6, 300, 316–17, 322,
    332, 339, 340, 367, 372, 373–4, 396, 398,
    407–8, 424, 463, 469, 470, 488, 502
laws, Julian   93–4, 373–4, 396, 408
legal rights, of women in Egypt   317, 322, 323–6,
  424, 428, 434–5, 507–9
letters, women's   26, 308, 321–2, 326–8, 334,
  346, 375, 504–11
Lex Iulia de adulteriis coercendis see laws, Julian
Lex Iulia de maritandis ordinibus see laws, Julian
Lex Oppia   102, 245, 396
Lex Pappia et Poppaea   94
Lex Voconia   102
literacy, of women   326–8, 344, 352, 504–11
luxury   17, 18, 20, 42, 49, 50, 66–7, 68–9, 100,
  102, 182, 184–5, 222, 233, 265, 330, 393,
  395–7, 515

CPSIA information can be obtained
at www.ICGtesting.com
Printed in the USA
JSHW010820140822
28878JS00002B/51